THE OXFORD HANDBOOK OF

HEGEL

THE OXFORD HANDBOOK OF

HEGEL

Edited by

DEAN MOYAR

OXFORD
UNIVERSITY PRESS

OXFORD
UNIVERSITY PRESS

Oxford University Press is a department of the University of Oxford. It furthers
the University's objective of excellence in research, scholarship, and education
by publishing worldwide. Oxford is a registered trade mark of Oxford University
Press in the UK and certain other countries.

Published in the United States of America by Oxford University Press
198 Madison Avenue, New York, NY 10016, United States of America.

CIP data is on file at the Library of Congress
ISBN 978-0-19-935522-8

3 5 7 9 8 6 4
Printed by Sheridan Books, Inc., United States of America

CONTENTS

PART III. *THE SCIENCE OF LOGIC*

PART IV. THE *ENCYCLOPEDIA* PROJECT, *PHILOSOPHY OF NATURE*, AND SUBJECTIVE SPIRIT

PART V. OBJECTIVE SPIRIT

PART VI. ABSOLUTE SPIRIT

PART VII. HEGEL'S LEGACY

ACKNOWLEDGMENTS

I would first of all like to thank the contributors to this volume for their innovative work on Hegel's philosophy and legacy. Thank you also to Peter Ohlin and to the team at Oxford University Press for seeing the project through to print. The project would not have gotten off the ground without the efforts of Terry Pinkard, whose generous guidance along the way has been pivotal. Some of my initial work on the project was done in Germany with the support of several institutions. I began the project while I was the Dirk Ippen Fellow at the American Academy in Berlin, and completed the initial proposal phase while a Humboldt Foundation Fellow in Münster. My thinking about Hegel has benefited enormously over the years from interactions with the graduate students at Johns Hopkins, whom I would like to thank for their willingness to work through Hegel's texts with me. Thanks go also to my colleagues in the Philosophy Department at Hopkins, who have fostered an ideal environment for research on the history of philosophy. My parents have continued to be a constant source of support, and my children, Lois and Dylan, have kept me grounded. My deepest gratitude is to Sharlyn Moon Rhee, for faith and encouragement throughout.

Note on Citations and Abbreviations

Wherever possible, citations to Hegel's work are given first with the volume number and page number of the *Gesammelte Werke*, edited by the Academy of Sciences of Rhineland-Westphalia, in cooperation with the Deutsche Forschungsgemeinschaft. Hamburg: Meiner, 1968–. While the edition of the *Werke* in 20 volumes by Suhrkamp remains the most accessible German edition, it is time for *GW* to come into regular use as the authoritative edition. The recent release of a more compact edition of the major works will hopefully accelerate this move.

Following are the abbreviations that are used throughout the text for Hegel's four major works. If the German edition referred to is not in the *Gesammelte Werke*, then the edition is listed in the Works Cited section of the chapter. There are multiple translations for all of Hegel's major works. In the cases of *The Science of Logic* and the *Philosophy of Right*, all contributors to the *Handbook* used the same translations, which are listed here. In other cases, such as the *Phenomenology of Spirit* and the *Encyclopedia*, there are multiple translations, and the translation chosen is listed in the chapter's Works Cited section. Also note that the *Encyclopedia* has three parts—Logic, Nature, and Spirit—that are typically cited separately in translation. Since they were part of a single bound volume and have section numbers shared by all editions (of the 1830 text), they all are referred to with a simple 'E'. This means that in the individual bibliographies more than one translation can have the abbreviation 'E'.

Another idiosncrasy of citing Hegel's *Encyclopedia* and *Philosophy of Right* is the use of R (for remark) and A (for addition based on student lecture notes) to distinguish the passage cited from the main text.

In general, the authors do not indicate when they have altered the translation of Hegel's texts.

E   *Enzyklopädie der philosophischen Wissenschaften (1830). Encyclopedia of the Philosophical Sciences in Basic Outline (1830).*

PR *Grundlinien der Philosophie des Rechts. Elements of the Philosophy of Right*, translated by H. B. Nisbet and edited by Allen Wood. Cambridge: Cambridge University Press, 1991.

PS *Phänomenologie des Geistes/Phenomenology of Spirit.*

SL *Wissenschaft der Logik. The Science of Logic*, edited and translated by George di Giovanni. Cambridge: Cambridge University Press, 2010.

Contributors

Mark Alznauer is Associate Professor in the Department of Philosophy at Northwestern University. He has a PhD From the John U. Nef Committee on Social Thought at the University of Chicago (2008). He is the author of *Hegel's Theory of Responsibility* (Cambridge University Press, 2015).

Brady Bowman is Associate Professor of Philosophy at the Pennsylvania State University. He earned his PhD at the Freie Universität Berlin (2000) and held a position as *wissenschaftlicher Mitarbeiter* at the Friedrich Schiller Universität Jena from 2000 to 2007. He is the author of numerous articles and two monographs on classical German philosophy, most recently *Hegel and the Metaphysics of Absolute Negativity* (Cambridge University Press, 2013).

William F. Bristow is Associate Professor of Philosophy at University of Wisconsin–Milwaukee. He is the author of *Hegel and the Transformation of Philosophical Critique* (Oxford University Press, 2007) and of various journal articles and book chapters on German philosophy of the eighteenth and nineteenth centuries

Thom Brooks is Professor of Law and Government at Durham University's Law School. He has held visiting appointments at the universities of Oxford, St Andrews, Uppsala, and Yale. His books include *Punishment* (Routledge, 2012); *Hegel's Political Philosophy: A Systematic Reading of the Philosophy of Right* (University of Edinburgh Press, 2nd ed., 2013); (ed.) *Hegel's Philosophy of Right* (Blackwell, 2012); and (co-edited with Martha Nussbaum) *Rawls's Political Liberalism* (Columbia University Press, 2015). His most recent book is *Becoming British* (Biteback, 2016).

Sybol Cook Anderson is Associate Professor of Philosophy at St. Mary's College of Maryland. She is the author of *Hegel's Theory of Recognition: From Oppression to Ethical Liberal Modernity* (Continuum, 2009), and is co-editor (with Robert Bernasconi) of *Race and Racism in Continental Philosophy* (Indiana University Press, 2003) and (with Ellen K. Feder and Karmen MacKendrick) of *A Passion for Wisdom: Readings in Western Philosophy on Love and Desire* (Pearson, 2004). Her current projects focus upon race and institutional violence.

Karin de Boer is Professor of Philosophy at the University of Leuven. She is the author of *Thinking in the Light of Time: Heidegger's Encounter with Hegel* (State University of New York Press, 2000) and *On Hegel: The Sway of the Negative* (Palgrave Macmillan, 2010), as well as of numerous articles on Kant, Hegel, and contemporary continental philosophy. She also co-edited (with Ruth Sonderegger) *Conceptions of Critique in Modern and Contemporary Philosophy* (Palgrave, 2011). Her current research concerns Kant's *Critique of Pure Reason* in view of his intended reform of Wolffian metaphysics.

Katerina Deligiorgi is Reader in Philosophy at the University of Sussex. She is the author of *The Scope of Autonomy: Kant and the Morality of Freedom* (Oxford University Press, 2012); *Kant and the Culture of Enlightenment* (State University of New York Press, 2005); and editor of *Hegel: New Directions* (Acumen, 2006) and of the *Hegel Bulletin* (2005–2015).

Willem A. deVries earned his BA at Haverford College, working mostly with Richard J. Bernstein. His graduate degrees are from the University of Pittsburgh, with a year at the Hegel Archive in Bochum. He has taught at Amherst College, Harvard University, Tufts University, the University of Vienna, and the University of New Hampshire. He has published books and articles on Hegel (*Hegel's Theory of Mental Activity*, Cornell University Press, 1988) and on Wilfrid Sellars, (*Wilfrid Sellars*, Acumen, 2005; *Knowledge, Mind, and the Given* [with Timm Triplett], Hackett 2000), as well as a smattering of other topics. He is very grateful for the support he has received from his friends, colleagues, employers, and grant-givers such as the Fulbright Program, the National Endowment for the Humanities, and the Mellon Foundation.

Dina Emundts is Professor of Philosophy at the Freie Universität Berlin. She is the author of *Kant's Übergangskonzeption im Opus postumum* (de Gruyter, 2004) and of *Erfahren und Erkennen. Hegels Theorie der Wirklichkeit* (Klostermann, 2012). She edited *Self, World, Art: Metaphysical Topics in Kant and Hegel* (de Gruyter, 2013) and is the co-editor (together with Sally Sedgwick) of the *International Yearbook of German Idealism* (de Gruyter).

James Gordon Finlayson did his doctorate on Hegel's *Critique of Kant* at the University of Essex. He taught philosophy at the University of York and now teaches philosophy at the University of Sussex, where he is currently the Director of the Centre for Social and Political Thought.

Heikki Ikäheimo is Senior Lecturer at the University of New South Wales (UNSW) Australia in Sydney. His research interests include Hegel, personhood, recognition, social ontology, critical social philosophy, and philosophical anthropology. Among his publications are *Anerkennung* (de Gruyter, 2014); *Self-Consciousness and Intersubjectivity* (University of Jyväskylä, 2000); the edited collections *The Ambivalence of Recognition* (with Kristina Lepold and Titus Stahl; Columbia University Press, 2017) and *Recognition and Social Ontology* (with Arto Laitinen; Brill, 2011), and a number of articles. See https://unsw.academia.edu/HeikkiIkaheimo.

Scott Jenkins is Associate Professor of Philosophy at the University of Kansas. He is the author of numerous articles on Hegel, Nietzsche, and other figures in late modern European philosophy.

Kipton E. Jensen is Associate Professor of Philosophy at Morehouse College in Atlanta, Georgia. Jensen published *Parallel Discourses: Religious Identity and HIV Prevention in Botswana* (Cambridge Scholars, 2012) and *Hegel: Hovering* (Cambridge Scholars, 2012). Jensen taught at the University of Botswana from 2004 to 2008.

John Kaag is Professor of Philosophy at the University of Massachusetts Lowell. He is author, most recently, of *American Philosophy: A Love Story* (Farrar, Straus, and Giroux, 2016).

James Kreines is Professor of Philosophy at Claremont McKenna College, in Claremont, California. He is the author of *Reason in the World: Hegel's Metaphysics and Its Philosophical Appeal* (Oxford University Press, 2015), and numerous articles on Kant and Hegel. He is also the co-editor of *Hegel on Philosophy in History* (Cambridge University Press, 2017). He teaches and writes about the history of metaphysics. Future research topics include metaphilosophy and Kant's things in themselves.

Thomas A. Lewis is Professor of Religious Studies at Brown University. He has taught previously at the University of Iowa and at Harvard University. He specializes in religious ethics and philosophy of religion in the modern West and has strong interests in methodology in the study of religion. His publications include *Freedom and Tradition in Hegel: Reconsidering Anthropology, Ethics, and Religion* (University of Notre Dame Press, 2005); *Religion, Modernity, and Politics in Hegel* (Oxford University Press, 2011); *Why Philosophy Matters for the Study of Religion—and Vice Versa* (Oxford University Press, 2015); and articles on religion and politics, liberation theology, communitarianism, and comparative ethics.

Lydia L. Moland is Associate Professor of Philosophy at Colby College in Waterville, Maine. She is the author of *Hegel on Political Identity: Patriotism, Nationality, Cosmopolitanism* (Northwestern University Press, 2011) and of numerous articles on Hegel's political philosophy and philosophy of art, including "'And Why Not?' Hegel, Comedy, and the End of Art" (*Verifiche*, forthcoming); "A Hegelian Approach to Global Poverty" (*Hegel and Global Justice*, Springer, 2012); "An Unrelieved Heart: Hegel, Tragedy, and Schiller's *Wallenstein*" (*New German Critique*, 2011); and "History and Patriotism in Hegel's *Rechtsphilosophie*" (*History of Political Thought*, 2007). She is currently working on a comprehensive interpretation of Hegel's aesthetics. In 2015, she was the recipient of a grant from the *Deutscher Akademischer Austauschdienst* to fund research at the *Freie Universität* in Berlin on a new project entitled *The Prosaic Divine: Humor in the German Age of Aesthetics*.

Dean Moyar is Associate Professor of Philosophy, Johns Hopkins University, where has taught since 2002. He is the author of *Hegel's Conscience*, and the editor of *The Routledge Companion to Nineteenth Century Philosophy*. His work focuses on the development of post-Kantian idealism, especially in Fichte and Hegel, and on contemporary debates about practical reason and the foundations of the liberal political order.

Michael Nance is Assistant Professor of Philosophy at the University of Maryland, Baltimore County. His research focuses on social, political, and legal philosophy in Kant and post-Kantian Idealism. He has published on Kant, Fichte, and Hegel. Recent works include "Recognition, Freedom, and the Self in Fichte's *Foundations of Natural Right*" (*European Journal of Philosophy*, 2015); and "Freedom, Coercion, and the Relation of Right," in *Fichte's Foundations of Natural Right: A Critical Guide*, Gabriel Gottlieb, ed. (Cambridge University Press, 2016).

Karen Ng is Assistant Professor of Philosophy at Vanderbilt University. She specializes in Hegel, German Idealism, and Frankfurt School Critical Theory. Her work has appeared in journals such as *Review of Metaphysics* and *Constellations*. She is currently working on a book on the concept of life in Hegel's *Science of Logic*.

Andreja Novakovic is Assistant Professor of Philosophy at University of California, Riverside. She received her PhD in Philosophy from Columbia University in 2012 and taught at the College of William & Mary for two years before joining the UCR Philosophy Department in 2014. She is in the process of completing a book entitled *Hegel on Second Nature in Ethical Life*, which is under contract with Cambridge University Press and forthcoming in 2017.

Angelica Nuzzo is Professor of Philosophy at the Graduate Center and Brooklyn College (City University of New York). Among her books are *History, Memory, Justice in Hegel* (Macmillan, 2012); *Hegel on Religion and Politics* (ed., State University of New York Press, 2013); *Hegel and the Analytic Tradition* (ed., Continuum, 2009); *Ideal Embodiment: Kant's Theory of Sensibility* (Indiana University Press, 2008).

Terry Pinkard teaches philosophy at Georgetown University. Among his books are *Hegel's Phenomenology: The Sociality of Reason* (Cambridge University Press, 1994); *Hegel: A Biography* (Cambridge University Press, 2000); *German Philosophy: 1760–1860: The Legacy of Idealism* (Cambridge University Press, 2002); *Hegel's Naturalism* (Oxford University Press, 2012); and *Does History Make Sense?* (Harvard University Press, 2017).

Robert B. Pippin is the Evelyn Stefansson Nef Distinguished Service Professor in the Committee on Social Thought, the Department of Philosophy, and the College at the University of Chicago. He is the author of several books on modern German philosophy, including *Kant's Theory of Form* (Yale University Press, 1982); *Hegel's Idealism: The Satisfactions of Self-Consciousness* (Cambridge University Press, 1989); *Modernism as a Philosophical Problem* (Basil Blackwell, 1991), a book on philosophy and literature; *Henry James and Modern Moral Life* (Cambridge University Press, 2000); and two books on film. His most recent two books are *After the Beautiful: Hegel and the Philosophy of Pictorial Modernism* (University of Chicago Press, 2013); and *Interanimations: Receiving Modern German Philosophy* (University of Chicago Press, 2015). He is a past winner of the Mellon Distinguished Achievement Award in the Humanities, and is a fellow of the American Academy of Arts and Sciences, and of the American Philosophical Society.

Michael Quante is Full Professor of Practical Philosophy in the Department of Philosophy at the Westfälische Wilhelms-University. He is Speaker of the Centrum für Bioethik and co-editor of *Hegel-Studien*. His areas of specialization include German idealism, theory of action, personal identity, ethics, and biomedical ethics. His books in English are *Hegel's Concept of Action* (Cambridge University Press, 2004, pbk., 2007); *Enabling Social Europe* (Springer, 2005; co-authored with Bernd V. Maydell et al.); *Discovering, Reflecting and Balancing Values: Ethical Management in Vocational Education Training* (Hampp, 2014; co-authored with Martin Büscher); *Interdisciplinary Research and Trans-disciplinary Validity Claims* (Springer, 2014; co-authored with Carl F. Gethmann et al.); *Hegel's Phenomenology of Spirit* (Cambridge University Press, 2008; co-edited with Dean Moyar); *Moral Realism* (Helsinki, 2004 [= Acta Filosofica Fennica Vol. 76]; co-edited with Jussi Kotkavirta); and *Pragmatic Idealism* (Rodopi, 1998; co-edited with Axel Wüstehube).

Sebastian Rand is Associate Professor of Philosophy at Georgia State University (Atlanta). His primary research focus is in German Idealism; he is currently working on a book about mathematics and the philosophy of nature in Kant, Fichte, Schelling, and Hegel. He has a further research interest in twentieth-century Continental philosophy, particularly regarding the perspective it offers on recent debates about normativity and conceptual form.

Paul Redding is Emeritus Professor of Philosophy at the University of Sydney. His books dealing with Hegel and Hegelianism include *Hegel's Hermeneutics* (Cornell University Press, 1996) and *Analytic Philosophy and the Return of Hegelian Thought* (Cambridge University Press, 2007).

Birgit Sandkaulen is Professor of Philosophy and director of the Center for the Study of Classical German Philosophy/Hegel-Archive at Ruhr-Universität Bochum, co-editor of the journal *Hegel-Studien*, and member of the North Rhine Westphalian Academy of Arts and Sciences. Selected publications: *Gestalten des Bewußtseins. Genealogisches Denken im Kontext Hegels* (ed. with Volker Gerhard and Walter Jaeschke, Felix Meiner, 2009); "Fürwahrhalten ohne Gründe. Eine Provokation philosophischen Denkens," *Deutsche Zeitschrift für Philosophie* 57 (2009): 259–272; "Die Ontologie der Substanz, der Begriff der Subjektivität und die Faktizität des Einzelnen. Hegels reflexionslogische 'Widerlegung' der Spinozanischen Metaphysik," *Internationales Jahrbuch des Deutschen Idealismus/International Yearbook of German Idealism* 5 (2008): 235–275; *System und Systemkritik. Beiträge zu einem Grundproblem der klassischen deutschen Philosophie* (Königshausen und Neuman, 2006); *Friedrich Heinrich Jacobi. Ein Wendepunkt der geistigen Bildung der Zeit* (ed. with Walter Jaeschke, Felix Meiner, 2004); *Grund und Ursache. Die Vernunftkritik Jacobis* (Wilhelm Fink, 2000); *Ausgang vom Unbedingten. Über den Anfang in der Philosophie Schellings* (Vandenhoeck und Ruprecht, 1990).

Ludwig Siep has taught philosophy at various German universities; from 1986 until his retirement in 2011 he taught at the University of Münster, Germany. At present he is Senior Professor in two research groups at the University of Münster (Religion and Politics,

Foundations of Medical Ethics and Biopolitics). Among his books: *Hegels Fichtekritik und die Wissenschaftslehre von 1804* (Alber, 1970); *Anerkennung als Prinzip der praktischen Philosophie* (Alber, 1979; new edition, Meiner, 2014); *Praktische Philosophie im Deutschen Idealismus* (Suhrkamp, 1992); *Der Weg der Phänomenologie des Geistes* (2000; English translation, Cambridge University Press, 2014); *Konkrete Ethik* (Suhrkamp, 2004); *Aktualität und Grenzen der praktischen Philosophie Hegels* (Fink, 2010); *Moral und Gottesbild* (Mentis, 2013); *Der Staat als irdischer Gott. Genese und Relevanz einer Hegelschen Idee* (Mohr Siebeck, 2015); (ed.) *Hegels Grundlinien der Philosophie des Rechts* (Akademie Verlag, 2014); *John Locke, Zweite Abhandlung über die Regierung* (Introduction and Commentary, Suhrkamp, 2013).

Allen Speight is Associate Professor of Philosophy and Chair of the Department of Philosophy at Boston University. A recipient of Fulbright, DAAD, and Berlin Prize Fellowships, he is the author of *Hegel, Literature and the Problem of Agency* (Cambridge University Press, 2001); *The Philosophy of Hegel* (McGill-Queen's University Press/Acumen, 2008); and of numeroius articles on aesthetics and ethics in German idealism; he is also co-editor/translator (with Brady Bowman) of *Hegel's Heidelberg Writings* (Cambridge University Press, 2009) and editor of *Philosophy, Narrative and Life* (Boston Studies in Philosophy, Religion and Public Life, 2015).

Robert Stern is a Professor in the Department of Philosophy at the University of Sheffield, UK. His publications include *Hegel and the Phenomenology of Spirit* (2nd ed., Routledge, 2013); *Hegelian Metaphysics* (Oxford University Press, 2009); *Understanding Moral Obligation* (Cambridge University Press, 2012) and *Kantian Ethics* (Oxford University Press, 2015).

Alison Stone is Professor of European Philosophy at Lancaster University, UK. She is the author of *Petrified Intelligence: Nature in Hegel's Philosophy* (State University of New York Press, 2004); *Luce Irigaray and the Philosophy of Sexual Difference* (Cambridge University Press, 2006); *An Introduction to Feminist Philosophy* (Polity, 2007); and *Feminism, Psychoanalysis and Maternal Subjectivity* (Routledge, 2011); and edited the *Edinburgh Critical History of Nineteenth Century Philosophy* (Edinburgh, 2011).

Christopher Yeomans is Professor of Philosophy at Purdue University, and the author of *Freedom and Reflection: Hegel and the Logic of Agency* and *The Expansion of Autonomy: Hegel's Pluralistic Philosophy of Action* (both from Oxford University Press, 2012 and 2015). He works on German philosophy, philosophy of action, and critical theory.

Rocío Zambrana is Assistant Professor of Philosophy at the University of Oregon. Her work examines conceptions of critique in Kant and German Idealism (especially Hegel), and Marx and Frankfurt School Critical Theory. She is the author of *Hegel's Theory of Intelligibility* (University of Chicago Press, 2015), as well as articles on Hegel, Kant, and Critical Theory.

Shuangli Zhang is Professor of Philosophy, Fudan University, China, and has published extensively on Marx, Lukács, Bloch, and critical theory. Her most recent publication is the monograph on Ernst Bloch, *Darkness and Hope: On Ernst Bloch's Utopian Thought* (Renming Press, Beijing, 2014). She is the second author of the book entitled *The Western Marxist Philosophy in the 20th Century* (Renming Press, Beijing, 2012). She published a series of articles on Marx, Lukács, and Adorno in Chinese academic journals including *Philosophical Researches, Academic Monthly*, and *Fudan Journal*. In addition to these publications in Chinese, she also has published two articles in English and French: "Why Should One Be Interested in the Theological Dimension Within the Project of Modern Politics? On the Chinese Acceptance of Carl Schmitt's Political Theology," *Critical Research on Religion* 2, no. 1 (2014): 9–22; "Les courants anticapitalistes en Chine. Le point de vue d'une philosophe," *Actuel Marx* 52 (2012): 180–196.

CHRONOLOGY OF HEGEL'S LIFE

BY TERRY PINKARD

Year	Town	Important Events in Hegel's Life
	STUTTGART	
1770		August 27: Hegel is born in Stuttgart. Parents: *Rentkammersekretär* Georg Ludwig Hegel and Maria Magdalena Louisa Hegel (born Fromm).
1773		April: His sister, Christiane, is born (dies 1832). Hegel goes to the *deutsche Schule*.
1776		Probable entrance into *Untergymnasium*. May: Birth of brother Georg Ludwig (dies 1812).
1780		Hegel takes the *Landexamen* for the first time.
1783		September 20: Hegel's mother dies from "*Gallenfieber*"; Hegel also is seriously ill from it.
1784		Beginning in the autumn, Hegel is a student at the *Obergymnasium*.
1786		100-year celebration of the Stuttgarter *Gymnasium*.
1788		September: Hegel leaves the *Gymnasium*; he gives the *Abiturrede*.
	TÜBINGEN	
1788		October: Reception in the *Stift* at the same time as Hölderlin. Hegel begins his study with the philosophical faculty.
1790		September: *Magister-Exam* Registration in the theological faculty. He shares a room in the *Stift* with Hölderlin and Schelling.
1793		June: Theological disputation; Starting in July, Hegel is on leave from the Seminary and stays in Stuttgart. September 19–20: *Konsistorialexam*.

Year	Town	Important Events in Hegel's Life
	BERNE	
1793		October: Begins his activity as house tutor with K. F. von Steiger.
1795		May: Trip to Geneva.
1796		July: Hike through the Bernese Alps; End of the year: Return from Berne to Stuttgart.
	FRANKFURT	
1797		January: Hegel begins the *Hofmeister* position that Hölderlin found for him with the wine merchant, Gogel.
1798		First publication: *Vertrauliche Briefe über das vormalige staatsrechtliche Verhältnis des Waatlandes zur Stadt Bern*.
1799		January: Death of Hegel's father in Stuttgart. March: Hegel makes the trip back to Stuttgart.
1800		September: Hegel makes a trip to Mainz, which since 1798 has belonged to the French Republic.
	JENA	
1801		January: Hegel moves to Jena. September: First philosophical book published, *Difference Between Fichte's and Schelling's Systems of Philosophy*. August 27: Habilitation with a Latin treatise on the orbits of the planets; Hegel becomes a *Privatdozent* without *Besoldung* (remuneration).
1802/ 1803		Together with Schelling, he edits the *Critical Journal of Philosophy*.
1805		Named to *außerordentliche Professor*, without remuneration.
1806		October: Completion of the *Phenomenology of Spirit*.
1807		February: Birth of his illegitimate son, Ludwig Fischer (dies 1831 in Jakarta).
	BAMBERG	
1807		March: Moves to Bamberg; editor and *Redakteur* of the *Bamberger Zeitung*. April: Publication of the *Phenomenology of Spirit*.

Year	Town	Important Events in Hegel's Life
	NUREMBERG	
1808		November: Rector of the *Gymnasium* in Nuremberg until 1815: he gives the official year-end speeches.
1811		September: Marries Marie von Tucher.
1812		First volume of the *Science of Logic* published.
1813		Named to *Lokalschulrat*. Second volume of the *Science of Logic* published. Birth of son, Karl (dies 1901).
1814		Birth of son, Immanuel (dies 1891).
1816		Third volume of the *Science of Logic* published.
	HEIDELBERG	
1816		University Professor in Heidelberg.
1817		Publication of the *Encyclopedia of the Philosophical Sciences*. Co-editor of the *Heidelberger Jahrbücher*. Hegel publishes in the *Heidelberger Jahrbücher*, "Proceedings of the Estates Assembly in the Kingdom of Württemberg 1815–1816."
	BERLIN	
1818		October 5: Moves to Berlin. October 22: Inaugural lecture. November 28: Hegel becomes a member of the "*Gesetzlose Gesellschaft*."
1819		June 17: Hegel turns over guardianship of his sister, Christiane, to his cousin, Ludwig Friedrich Göriz. July 27: Hegel writes to the authorities about Asversus.
1820		October: Publication of *Philosophy of Right*. Hegel travels in the fall to Dresden.
1821		Hegel travels again in the fall to Dresden. Hegel becomes Dean of the Philosophical Faculty for a one-year term.

Year	Town	Important Events in Hegel's Life
1822		Hegel writes the preface to Hinrichs's book on the philosophy of religion. *Hallesche A. L. Zeitung* publishes an attack on Hegel, and Hegel fails in his attempt to get the government to intercede for him. October 1822: trip to the Netherlands. Hegel writes a memorandum on the teaching of philosophy and other subjects in the *Gymnasium*.
1823		Redeems the bond he put up for Asversus.
1824		September/October: Trips to Prague and Vienna. September 21–October 5: Hegel's stay in Vienna. November 4, 1824: Hegel writes to the Prussian police on behalf of Victor Cousin.
1825		
1826		Hegel writes, "On a Complaint on Account of a Public Slander of the Catholic Religion." Hegel writes, "Über die Bekehrten," ("On the Converted"), *Berliner Schnellpost*. July 23, 1826: Founding of the *Jahrbücher für wissenschaftliche Kritik*. Ludwig Fisher Hegel leaves the family.
1827		Publication begins of the *Jahrbücher für wissenschaftliche Kritik*. New edition of *Encyclopedia of the Philosophical Sciences*. August–October: Trip to Paris. Return through Brussels, Hegel visits his former student, van Ghert, and discusses Ludwig Fisher. Hegel stops off in Weimar, visits with Goethe. Hegel publishes "On the Episode of the Mahabharata known as the Bhagavad-Gita by Wilhelm von Humboldt" in the *Jahrbücher für wissenschaftliche Kritik*.
1828		"Hamann's Writings" in the *Jahrbücher für wissenschaftliche Kritik*. Review of Solger in the *Jahrbücher für wissenschaftliche Kritik*.

Year	Town	Important Events in Hegel's Life
1829		September: Trip to Prague; visit to the spa in Karlsbad where he accidentally meets Schelling; on the return trip, he visits Goethe. 1829–1830: Hegel is elected Rector of the University. Hegel publishes his review of Goeschel's "Aphorisms on Ignorance and Absolute Knowing" in the *Jahrbücher für wissenschaftliche Kritik*. Hegel publishes his review of "On the Hegelian Doctrine or absolute knowing and modern pantheism—On Philosophy in General and Hegel's Encyclopedia of the Philosophical Sciences in Particular" in the *Jahrbücher für wissenschaftliche Kritik*.
1830		September: Trip to Prague; visit to the spa in Karlsbad where he accidentally meets Schelling; on the return trip, he visits Goethe. 1829–1830: Hegel is elected Rector of the University. Hegel publishes his review of Goeschel's "Aphorisms on Ignorance and Absolute Knowing" in the *Jahrbücher für wissenschaftliche Kritik*. Hegel publishes his review of "On the Hegelian Doctrine or absolute knowing and modern pantheism—On Philosophy in General and Hegel's Encyclopedia of the Philosophical Sciences in Particular" in the *Jahrbücher für wissenschaftliche Kritik*.
1831		New reworking of the *Science of Logic*, vol. 1 (appears 1832). Hegel publishes his review of "Ideal-realism" in the *Jahrbücher für wissenschaftliche Kritik*. "On the English Reform Bill." November 14: Hegel dies in Berlin.

INTRODUCTION

DEAN MOYAR

The mere 'ought' by itself, the subjective concept without objectivity, is devoid of spirit, just as mere *being without the concept*, without its own 'ought' to which it must conform, is an empty illusion. (J 15.17–18/18)

It is notoriously difficult to identify in clear propositional style Hegel's view on familiar philosophical topics and debates. As Hegel scholars, we are supposed to know these views and to be able to express them clearly and succinctly, yet we often have to take a deep breath and launch into an extended framing presentation, the point of which is to show that the traditional formulations of the problem are one-sided and that Hegel's position is motivated by the need to get over certain dichotomies in the previous approaches. The trouble with these extended framings (apart from the limited attention span of one's audience) is that they too often turn into incomplete disjunctive syllogisms: his view is not X, not Y, not Z, all of which gets one *closer* to the position without actually arriving at a satisfying specification. I thematize this difficulty up front because in a *Handbook* one might expect to find a rundown of Hegel's views on various topics. One has some right to expect the table of contents or index of a handbook to direct one to Hegel's positions on the free will debate, on the existence of God, on private property, and so on. The trouble with that kind of topic-oriented handbook in Hegel's case is that it would run a serious risk of obscuring what remains the most distinctive characteristic of his philosophy, namely its rigorously dialectical character. Hegel's motive for philosophizing dialectically is to avoid dogmatism, to avoid merely assuming premises rather than developing them from earlier stages in the argument. In planning this *Handbook* I aimed to respect the method by largely keeping to Hegel's own divisions of the subject matter as presented in his major writings. While these divisions and the dialectical method itself can make a straightforward presentation of Hegel's view very challenging, there is no royal road above the method that would take us straight to our goal. His own philosophy is an exemplary case of his thesis that the purpose of action is constituted by the process and struggle of realizing it.

In this Introduction I will neither offer a detailed interpretation of Hegel's thought nor summarize the chapters. Instead, I will briefly discuss the layout of the *Handbook*, sketch the most important debates within the current scholarship, and fill in some of the more glaring omissions from the *Handbook*. These omissions include, first of all, Hegel's early biography and development. I will lay out the biography up to the point at which he arrived in Jena and then connect his early preoccupations to the concerns of his mature philosophy. In the concluding section I give the outlines of two essential episodes in the story of Hegel's reception—the 'young Hegelians' and 'British Idealism'. Though the movements are strikingly different from each other, both saw the promise of Hegel's philosophy as lying in its *comprehensive* character. The early left Hegelian movement ended in Marxism, a movement opposed to the liberal regime of individual rights that since Hegel's own day has had an increasingly difficult time arguing for any political norms outside the framework of rights. British Idealism, on the other hand, was laid low by the rise of analytic philosophy, which in style if not substance is still the dominant school of philosophy today, and which is increasingly specialized and generally wary of propounding a comprehensive view of the world. By recovering the core of the earlier Hegelian movements, we may thereby also recover an alternative path for philosophy, a different idea of what it is and what it is for.

I.1. THE INTERPRETIVE LANDSCAPE

The *Handbook* largely follows the order in which Hegel's major works were published. Hegel did not reach his mature position until his thirty-fifth year, and much has been written about the fragmentary unpublished writings of his twenties (the 1790s) and the published and unpublished texts of his early thirties (1801–1805). The two chapters in the *Handbook* on his development cover only the latter period, those crucial early Jena years in which he came to terms with the legacy of Kantian and Fichtean philosophy under the influence of Schelling. The mature position is only fully worked out, and fully *expressed*, in the two published works of articulated dialectical philosophy, the *Phenomenology of Spirit* of 1807 and the *Science of Logic* of 1812–1816 (with a revised edition of the first part published in 1832, right after Hegel's death). The *Handbook* devotes six chapters each to these two works, mainly because they are the touchstone for interpreting everything else that Hegel wrote—they are the most difficult but also the most rewarding. The *Encyclopedia*, published first in 1817 and revised in 1827 and 1830, includes all the main elements of the system, but the *Encyclopedia*, because it was written as an outline for students attending Hegel's lectures, itself often reads like a summary; he often announces positions without giving the kind of intricate arguments that we find in the *Phenomenology* and *The Science of Logic*.

The chapters devoted to the *Encyclopedia* focus on the introduction and overall structure, as well as on those crucial parts—nature, anthropology, and what he calls 'psychology'—that are neither covered in other texts nor supplanted by multiple lecture series. The main text for what Hegel calls Objective Spirit is the *Philosophy of Right*, an expanded version of the middle section of the *Encyclopedia*, augmented by student notes from the Berlin lectures. The *Philosophy of Right* continues to provoke lively debates in the literature about Hegel's views on action and morality, and about his relation to the modern liberal tradition. The essay on the philosophy of history (technically part of 'Objective Spirit') and the four essays on 'Absolute Spirit' are engaged mainly with Hegel's lectures in Berlin from the 1820s. Hegel published almost nothing completely new during the last decade of his life, rewriting the *Encyclopedia* and the first part of the *Science of Logic*, but not publishing in strictly dialectical form the vast amounts of material on art, religion, and philosophy that he systematized for his lecture presentations.

While this volume cannot promise an easy summary of Hegel's complex views, it does exhibit the tremendous progress in understanding Hegel's project that has been made over the past decades.[1] Building on the work of the first wave of postwar Hegel scholarship (led by Dieter Henrich), a number of groundbreaking studies appeared in German in the late 1970s and early 1980s, such as Ludwig Siep's *Anerkennung als Prinzip der praktische Philosophie* (*Recognition as the Principle of Practical Philosophy*) and Rolf-Peter Horstmann's *Ontologie und Relationen* (*Ontology and Relations*).[2] English-language scholarship received a decisive impetus from Charles Taylor's 1975 *Hegel*. The publication of other important works in English (by H. S. Harris and Shlomo Avineri, among others), and the renewed attention in Anglo-American philosophy to Kant by philosophers such as Sellars, Strawson, and Bennett, set the stage for the English second wave of postwar scholarship.[3] The most important publication in this second wave is Robert Pippin's *Hegel's Idealism* in 1989, which, together with Allen Wood's *Hegel's Ethical Thought* in 1990 and Terry Pinkard's *Hegel's Phenomenology* in 1994, set the terms for many of the debates over the past two decades.

In selecting the contributors to this volume, I aimed to include eminent scholars in the field and especially to include the work of a 'third wave' of early to mid-career scholars (a group that includes myself). In most cases I invited these younger scholars to write on the text or issues to which they have devoted their early research, and many of them develop here new presentations of work that they have carried out in more detail in just published or soon to be published monographs. The picture of current scholarship

[1] Two other excellent recent collections attest to his progress: Baur and Houlgate (eds.), *A Companion to Hegel*, and De Laurentiis and Jeffrey (eds.), *The Bloomsbury Companion to Hegel*.

[2] For a relatively accessible statement in English of Henrich's groundbreaking work on the period, see the lectures published as *Between Kant and Hegel*.

[3] The most outrageous recent editorial assertion about the field has to be Frederick Beiser's 2008 claim that "[t]he apex of the Anglophone Hegel revival was the publication in 1975 of Charles Taylor's *Hegel*" (Beiser, *Hegel and Nineteenth-Century Philosophy*, 2). Beiser's hostility to readings that depart from the traditional metaphysical line has fortunately not prevented the Anglophone Hegel revival from continuing its upward trajectory.

that arises from the essays in the *Handbook* is of a vibrant field, plumbing the depths of Hegel's thought and confident in setting his arguments into conversation with philosophers working in a non-historical mode. With the exception of the chapters in Part VII on Hegel's legacy, the essays are all marked by a close engagement with Hegel's actual texts. Before one extracts a clear position or relates Hegel's thought to the preoccupations that shape today's philosophical landscape, one must simply *learn how to read him*. It is in this reading that one *does* philosophy with Hegel. If we do this reading carefully, then we need not apologize for discussing Hegel's thought in relation to contemporary philosophical debates.

A distinctive feature of interpretive disagreements about Hegel's philosophy is the way the options are set by the influence of his predecessors on his thought, and especially by the relative importance that one ascribes to these predecessors. So the most prominent line of interpretation in current scholarship is the reading championed by Pippin, which focuses on what in Kant influenced Hegel, especially the Kantian critique of modern ('dogmatic') substantialist metaphysics. On this reading, Hegel's bold speculative theory in the *Phenomenology* and *The Science of Logic* should be read as continuing the project initiated by Kant in the *Critique of Pure Reason*, especially the project of determining the fundamental categories for our thinking about the world. The position that Pippin lays out in *Hegel's Idealism* has in the literature come to be associated with the 'non-metaphysical' label. This label was self-applied by Klaus Hartmann to his own reading of Hegel as a category theorist, but the label is rather misleading even in Hartmann's case, for he also called his account an 'ontology of thought'.[4] While Pippin stressed that Hegel was not committed to anything that would have been subject to Kant's devastating critique of rationalist metaphysics, that is not equivalent to saying that Hegel's theory is in no respect metaphysical. Pippin's interpretation does have a strong negative component—Hegel's Concept, idea, spirit, and so on, are *not* claims about a cosmic spirit, neo-Platonic divinity, and so on—yet Pippin also aimed to show what the constructive account in the *Science of Logic* amounts to. The constructive project consists in showing how Hegel aims to establish the objective validity of the categories of thought without the remainder of a thing-in-itself beyond our cognitive limitations. Pippin's account leans very hard on Hegel's discussions of Kant's transcendental unity of self-consciousness, especially in the introduction to the 'Logic of the Concept' (SL 12.11–28/508–525). The basic idea is to interpret Hegel's claims about the self-relation of the Concept as claims about the unity of objects through the self-relation of thought. It is a tall order, as Pippin is quite well aware (and which leads him in *Hegel's Idealism* to be rather doubtful of Hegel's ultimate claims), to establish in an a priori logic that just these conditions of thought *are* the conditions that constitute objects themselves and not merely objects for us. It is quite difficult to see how Hegel can avoid various forms of subjective idealism in claiming that the determinations of thought really do constitute objectivity without remainder. Hegel's own early attacks on Kant and Fichte as subjective idealists are well known, so the burden of any interpretation that aligns Hegel

---

[4] Hartmann, "Hegel: A Non-Metaphysical View," 111.

closely with transcendental idealism is to show how he can avoid these charges while claiming to establish through thought the categorial structure of reality itself.

On the other side of the interpretive dialectic, some commentators have pushed back against the Kantian reading in the name of reviving a Spinozist, substance-first interpretation.[5] The Spinozist readings of Hegel connect thought and objectivity by asserting an original identity that would unite thought and object from the outset. There are certainly passages that can be cited to support this Spinozist reading, for Hegel does think that Spinoza's philosophy is an extremely important stage on the way to absolute idealism. But Hegel also frequently argues against Spinoza and reinterprets his idea of a self-causing substance through the conception of absolute negativity.[6] Because Hegel identifies this negativity with thinking, there is a plausible interpretation of these claims that remains in a post-Kantian register: absolute negativity is the self-determination of our thinking of substance. Those who resist the Kantian interpretation can, however, note that Hegel thought of the content of his logic as "the exposition of God as he is in his eternal essence before the creation of nature and of a finite spirit" (SL 21.34/29), and it is hard to see how one gets more metaphysical than that. It may be that thought determines reality, but Hegel's claim only seems plausible if the emphasis is put on reality being known *through us* rather than on the determination of reality *by us* through thought. Some scholars also defend a kind of 'no priority' view, where one takes Hegel at his word that thought and being are identical, and one refuses the question of whether the categories are either our activity or the workings of substance. Such an approach has been carried out most successfully by Stephen Houlgate, the author of many detailed readings of Hegel's texts and of one of the best introductions to Hegel's philosophy as a whole.[7]

Alongside Hegel's distinctive conception of self-relating negativity, another key concept clearly distinguishing him from Spinoza is his stress on *purposiveness*. Here, too, scholars have linked Hegel's theory to a historical predecessor, in this case Aristotle. This interpretive route received an early impetus from Robert Stern's 1990 *Hegel and the Structure of the Object*, in which Stern contrasted the atomism of Kant's conception of the manifold with Hegel's attraction to the Aristotelian idea of substance universals. In a similar direction, James Kreines in *Reason in the World* has developed a conception of 'immanent concepts' as the basis of an interpretation of Hegel's argument for superiority of teleology over mechanism (though drawing more on Kant's dialectic than on Aristotelian ideas). The consequences of this turn to Aristotelean purposiveness for an overall interpretation of Hegel remain an issue of lively discussion.[8] The fact that Terry Pinkard (in *Hegel's Naturalism*) and Pippin himself have also embraced Aristotelian readings of Hegel is an indication that one can acknowledge this inheritance in a number of different ways.

---

[5] See Bowman, *Hegel and the Metaphysics of Absolute Negativity*, and Beiser, *Hegel*.
[6] See the essays in Förster and Melamed, *Spinoza and German Idealism*.
[7] Houlgate, *An Introduction to Hegel*.
[8] See also Ferrarin, *Hegel and Aristotle*, for a detailed account of the lines of influence.

Related to the Aristotelian trend is a renewed attention to the concept of *life* that Hegel employs in many contexts. Readers of the *Phenomenology of Spirit* will know that the book's most striking turn at the opening of Chapter IV, "Self-Consciousness," involves a complex appeal to life that prepares the ground for mutual recognition and the master-servant dialectic. The many further appeals to life in that text, along with the surprising introduction of life as the first stage in 'The Idea' within *The Science of Logic*, demonstrate the concept's importance for his philosophy as a whole. The relation of self-consciousness and life presents itself as a key to unlocking what is distinctive about Hegel's philosophy, and has been explored recently by Pinkard and by Karen Ng,[9] among others. Life brings into relief the two sides of Hegelian philosophy: he is, on the one hand, a logician, arguing that thought is the basis of reality and that the thought-determinations can be developed from 'being' to the concept and finally to life and the absolute idea. On the other hand, one expects from a concept of life something that transcends mere concepts, something that will take us from the categories of thought to explanations of the physical world and our activity within it, and Hegel does not disappoint in theorizing mind and ethics through life.

The other set of concepts that bridges Hegel's logic and his practical philosophy comprises those that fall under his philosophy of action. Once again, it is Taylor's early work on this topic that is the first point of entry into Hegel's thinking.[10] The topic was given new clarity and depth in Quante's *Hegel's Concept of Action* (published in German in 1992 and in English in 2004). Focusing on a close reading of the *Philosophy of Right* discussion of action, Quante uncovered the logical underpinnings of the attribution of intention, and set Hegel's speculative theory in relation to the Anscombean and Davidsonian themes that have dominated analytic philosophy of action. Whereas Quante attributes to the agent a distinctive knowledge of her own intention, Pippin has staked out a position that is more socially mediated, and that sees Hegel as attempting to undermine the traditional problems of free will and responsibility by showing them to be misguided.[11] Hegel is indeed some kind of compatibilist, but specifying just how he engaged the issue has proven quite challenging: Is Hegel's a therapeutic approach of overcoming the problem of anxiety about free will, or is it a constructive answer to the question in its own terms? In his important *Freedom and Reflection*, Christopher Yeomans has argued that Hegel does address the issue in his treatment of modality and teleology in the *Science of Logic*, challenging the coherence of explanations of action in terms of mechanistic necessity in favor of explanations in terms of ends. Hegel focuses insistently on *individual* actions. The intuitive point stressed by Yeomans is that general causal laws are poorly suited for explaining individual actions, which are better explained through the complex interplay of intentional activity and context.

A major reason for thinking that Hegel bypasses the traditional free will debate stems from his reinterpretation of freedom in terms of mutual recognition. Recognition has

---

[9] See Ng, "Life, Self-consciousness, Negativity."
[10] Taylor, "Hegel and the Philosophy of Action."
[11] See Pippin, *Hegel's Practical Philosophy.*

been central to the twentieth-century reception of Hegel, and it continues to play an important role in debates over Hegel's political philosophy. There is great intuitive appeal to the notion that one is free in one's action insofar as one is recognized as free by another free agent. Freedom becomes explicit, public, and self-standing through recognition, for a social understanding of freedom need not rely on the metaphysics of the will or on natural scientific debates about causality. Central to the interpretations of the practical philosophy by Siep, Pippin, and Pinkard, among others, recognition is also central for two of the most prominent attempts to 'reactualize' Hegel for a contemporary audience, namely those by Axel Honneth and Robert Brandom. The *promise* of recognition for practical philosophy in general is that it can ground norms that are formal and norms that are substantive, and thus serve equally as the basis of both legal rights (in recognized personhood) and the thick claims of membership. As a theory of social interaction, recognition further melds nicely with the pragmatic dimension of both ethical and linguistic norms. The *problem* with mutual recognition is that it can easily overshadow the rich structure of Hegel's theory, giving the impression that his rationalism is secondary to the social mediation present in spirit.[12] One can seem forced to choose between a theory that is at heart rationalist metaphysics and only secondarily a matter of social realization, on the one hand, and a theory in which all rationality is worked out through the pragmatic dynamics of social processes, on the other. There is enough 'elasticity' in Hegel's Concept to accommodate such differing interpretations, and adapting Hegel's thought to our own time and place is certainly a Hegelian thought, yet we also have to take seriously his claims to the truth and comprehensiveness of the logic of thought.

I conclude this section with a few reflections on the issue of *normativity* in Hegel's philosophy. When the normative is opposed to the merely descriptive, few would disagree that Hegel's philosophy has a strongly normative cast. Yet the normative can also be contrasted with the way things *are*, and normativity is therefore sometimes entangled with the debate over Hegel's metaphysics. Some scholars worry about the line of interpretation that stresses normativity because they think that it implies a kind of pragmatism that inevitably leads to subjective idealism. Hegel was indeed worried that an overly practical conception of philosophy, such as Fichte's, might end up in a one-sided attempt to impose our attitudes on the world and would thus lack a theoretically satisfying conception of reality. This is what he criticizes as "[t]he mere 'ought' by itself . . . devoid of spirit" in the passage I placed at the head of this Introduction. But notice how Hegel then turns the point around to criticize the theoretical posture toward the world: "mere *being without the concept*, without its own 'ought' to which it must conform, is an empty illusion" (J 15.17–18/18). Hegel's frequent critiques of the 'mere ought' might lead one to think that the logic of being and substance render the construction of ideals futile or superfluous. Yet his willingness to describe his own claims about the Concept as themselves implying an ought shows that in both domains, practical *and* theoretical, the ideal is defined in such a way that there is a *standard* set through thinking. He wants to show that abstract norm and its realization or actuality are inseparable, but also to stress that

---

[12] See my discussion in Moyar, *Hegel's Conscience*, Chapter 5.

the actuality is the realization of a norm, and that mere being without the norm is itself unreal.

I.2. HEGEL'S EDUCATION
AND DEVELOPMENT

Hegel grew up the son of an ambitious civil servant in Stuttgart, which at the time was the capital of the small duchy of Württemberg. Hegel's early love of learning came from his mother, Maria Magdelena Louisa Hegel (Fromm). She was a descendant of a line of Protestant reformers and extremely well educated for a woman of her day. It was his mother who began his Latin instruction before he turned five, and whose wish that her eldest son would be educated for the Protestant ministry seems to have won out even after her death when 'Wilhelm', as our philosopher was known to friends and family, was twelve.[13] While his younger brother would attend the *Karlsschule* military academy and become a soldier (eventually being made captain and ennobled before falling in Napoleon's 1812 Russia campaign), Hegel attended the *Gymnasium Illustre*, where he would both be prepared for a theological career and be exposed to the German Enlightenment. Among his favorite authors was Gotthold Ephraim Lessing, whose 'Nathan the Wise' made a deep impression that would be evident in Hegel's early unpublished writings. He grew up in a general aura of new universalist Enlightenment ideas and with a strong sense of the particular Württemberg traditions, a combination that Pinkard has credited with fostering the driving tension between particular and universal in Hegel's mature social and political thought.

Hegel would live through the French Revolution and its immediate aftermath as a rather disgruntled theology student at the Protestant Seminary in Tübingen. He was accepted at the Seminary under the condition that he must become a pastor if there was a position available for him. While he may have thought that vocation was acceptable when he entered the seminary, his experience there and the sentiments sparked by the Revolution soon made that prospect intolerable. In his alienation from his theological studies he was joined by Friedrich Hölderlin, who entered the same year as him and would be one of his best friends for over a decade, well into the time when Hölderlin was writing the work that would make him one of the great German poets. The two of them were joined in 1790 by Friedrich Schelling, who had been given special permission to enter the seminary at age fifteen. The three friends would share a room and an enthusiasm for the French Revolution. Their friendship would lead to one of the more interesting authorship debates in scholarship about the period, namely the question of who wrote the fragment that has come to be known as "The Oldest System

---

[13] I am drawing heavily in this paragraph and the next on Pinkard, *Hegel*. For a shorter version of Hegel's biography by Pinkard, see his "Hegel: A Life."

Program of German Idealism," written in Hegel's hand in 1796/1797, often attributed to Schelling, but most probably composed by Hölderlin.[14] In their years at the seminary they were engaged with the philosophy of Spinoza (through Jacobi and the Pantheism Controversy) and Kant (through the orthodox Kantian Gottlob Storr and the radical Carl Immanuel Diez). The import of these philosophers for Hegel's mature thought is clear, but Hegel himself did not see right away the need to think through the depths of their methods and metaphysics.

In the 1790s Hegel's writings focus almost entirely on practical philosophy, and the lack of systematic method shows. There are nonetheless traces of his mature system throughout, and the youthful enthusiasm on display does much to humanize Hegel, who was not as stern or forbidding a personality as his mature system might lead one to think.

We have a snapshot of Hegel's thinking at the time of his completion of his theological degree from a manuscript that has come to be known as "The Tübingen Essay." This essay represents the first phase of his early engagement with Kant's practical philosophy (the second coincides with his time as a house tutor in Berne and the third with his time as a tutor in Frankfurt). In this essay he takes Kant's practical philosophy as a basic framework for thinking through the issue of how a newly interpreted religious domain can awaken in each individual a sense of virtue. He is concerned less with Kant's Categorical Imperative than with Kant's understanding of the Highest Good and the postulates of God and immortality. Suspicious of Kant's formalism in ethics, Hegel latches onto the Highest Good as a way to theorize a moral religion, and in particular to give an account of moral *motivation*. Hegel is already doubtful that we can find religion and motivation in the form of the law alone, so he seeks to find other ways of interpreting the idea of *providence*. He looks to the ancients for inspiration, mainly for the idea of a public religion, but also for the idea of an objective justice that could mitigate the arbitrariness and guilty conscience of individual subjectivity.[15] Against the deficient Christian conception of providence, he cites the Greeks in a representative passage that runs Kantian reason together with Greek religion:

> On the one hand they [the Greeks] had the basic faith that the Gods are gracious to the good man and subject the evil-doer to the terror of Nemesis—built upon the deep moral need of Reason, and enlivened with love through the warm breath of their feelings—not on the cold conviction, deduced from particular cases, that everything will turn out for the best—[a conviction] which can never be brought into real life; on the other hand misfortune for them was misfortune—sorrow was sorrow—something that had happened and could not be altered—. (*TE* 1.106/501)

---

[14] For a summary of the debate and an argument for Hölderlin's authorship, see Förster, "To Lend Wings to Physics Once Again."

[15] I discuss some of these texts further in Moyar, "Rethinking Autonomy in Hegel's Earliest Writings." See also Harris, *Hegel's Development*, and Lukács, *The Young Hegel*.

Because the suffering was objective, the Greek agent did not experience the "anger, sullenness, [and] discontent" (TE 1.106/501) of the modern individual. This text shows that the young Hegel longs for a world in which modern subjectivity would not be plagued by the alienation required in order to create that subjectivity. He recognizes that suffering and meaningfulness go together, and that the modern use of religion to write off suffering is shallow and self-defeating. In trying to make sense of Greek religion, he writes that Greek sacrifice was not intended to persuade Nemesis to "suspend its laws by which moral equilibrium was maintained—" (TE 1.108/504). This idea of moral equilibrium remains with Hegel throughout his career, but he had a long way to go before he came to the idea of 'Objective Spirit' as a system of right. He would retain the idea of holistic equilibrium, but he would come to better appreciate modern subjective freedom and legal institutions.

In his Berne period, Hegel becomes much more of a devoted Kantian, even writing a "Life of Jesus" that interprets Jesus as the prophet of pure practical reason.[16] The major work of the period is "The Positivity of the Christian Religion," in which Hegel develops his diagnosis of the failings of modern Christianity. His analysis of 'positivity' is an interesting precursor to his mature conception of alienation, for positivity is that which prevents an individual from freely identifying with her actions. A religion is positive when it sets up an unbridgeable gulf between divine authority and the human will. As a measure of his Kantianism in this phase, Hegel apologizes on Jesus' behalf for not appealing to pure practical reason, citing the ignorance of Jesus' audience: "To propose to appeal to reason alone would have meant the same thing as preaching to fish. . . . But if the moral sense has entirely taken the direction of the ecclesiastical faith . . . then the teacher has no alternative save to oppose to it an equal authority, a divine one" (P 1.289/ 91). Because of the context in which Jesus taught, he had to place the authority in God rather than in the law-giving powers of the rational will. Hegel is already thinking of the divine as immanent within the human community, and he thinks that community is compatible with Kantian practical reason. The obstacle to both is the positivity of church dogma and law. In discussing the communal dimension of religion in this period, Hegel thematizes the important issue of *trust*, highlighting the tension between the felt bonds of friendship and the positive laws of a church or a state. He opposes the early Christian model of trusting friendship to the church's institution of a public confessor wielding the judgment of eternal damnation. It is the image of two consciences, two distinct authorities, that he criticizes in the Catholic Church throughout his career.[17]

The great majority of Hegel's work up to 1797 is rather flat-footed, but the quality of his thinking improved dramatically under the influence of Hölderlin when he moved to Frankfurt that year. The tremendous impact of this move is evident in the unpublished "The Spirit of Christianity and Its Fate." His preoccupation with religion remains, but he now develops the concept of life as a basic category through which both religion and

---

[16] On this period see Bondeli, *Hegel in Bern.*
[17] See Pinkard, *Hegel*, 529–530, for an account of Hegel's confrontation with Catholicism in his Berlin years. On the issue of the two consciences, see Moyar, *Hegel's Conscience*, 24–25.

|

Kantian morality can be judged. It is in this period that he turns against Kantian morality and the primacy of lawfulness. Rather than trying to fit Jesus' teaching into a Kantian
model, he now opposes Jesus' teaching of forgiveness to the severity of the Kantian law
and Kantian conscience (as expressed in Kant's *Metaphysics of Morals*, which Hegel read
closely at the time and on which he wrote a long monograph that has long since been
lost). Hegel now views the voice of the Kantian moral law as an inner tyrant, domineering
over (the rest of) the agent and standing in the way of a non-alienated life. He still affirms
the core of Jesus' teaching, but he now thinks of that teaching as primarily a teaching of
love and forgiveness, rather than of Kantian morality. Once again, Hegel focuses on the
issue of transgression and the internal and external response to that transgression. In a
representative passage, he writes,

> Before the law the criminal is nothing but a criminal; if the law were a whole, an
> absolute, then the criminal *would* be only a criminal. Even in the hostility of fate a
> man has a sense of just punishment; but since this hostility is not grounded in an
> alien law superior to the man, since on the contrary it is from him that the law and
> right of fate first arise, a return is possible to the original situation, to wholeness. For
> the sinner is more than a sin existent, a trespass possessed of personality; he is a man,
> trespass and fate are in him. He can return to himself again, and, if he does so, then
> trespass and fate are under him. The elements of actuality are dissolved [*sich auflöst*];
> spirit and body have parted ways; the deed still subsists, but only as something past,
> as a fragment, as a corpse. That part of it which was bad conscience has disappeared,
> and the remembrance of the deed is no longer that conscience's intuition of itself; in
> love, life has found life once more. Between sin and its forgiveness there is as little
> place for an alien thing as there is between sin and punishment. Life has severed itself
> from itself and united itself again. (SC [*Werke* 1, 353–354]/238–239)[18]

Hegel's initial point is that the law does not constitute human agency; the will does not
count as a will solely through conformity to the law. He identifies an 'absolute' with a
'whole', citing the partiality of the law in contrast to the wholeness of life. Hegel introduces fate as a disenchanted version of Nemesis, blind necessity as the pushback of a
world against a will that has acted against it. The true medium of action is 'life', a rather
vague concept at this point in his development, but one defined nonetheless through
its openness to love and through its superiority to law and fate. Hegel is not under any
illusions that Christian love could support a complete ethics or politics, for he notes
explicitly that the true teaching of Jesus runs into the modern institution of property
rights, and in general into the element of 'reflection' that permeates modern life. But the
seeds of Hegel's mature position are certainly there, especially when one notices that he
is thinking already of life and *self-consciousness* as close cousins, taking over the main
methodological principle of Kantian, and especially of Fichtean, idealism, and attempting to rethink it on more naturalistic and holistic lines. Part of his eventual turn to his

---

[18] *W* 1, 353–354; *ETW*, 238–239.

mature ethical position will be a shift (though not quite a reversal) toward favoring the form of the law and a suspicion of attempts to place subjectivity above the law.

The manuscript from 1799–1802 known as "The German Constitution" is Hegel's first real foray into political theory, and it remained unpublished in his lifetime. But it is not a work of pure theory, for Hegel is addressing himself to current events, and the text is largely of interest for its early record of Hegel's doctrine that political theory and political actuality should not be separated (the doctrine most famously expressed by "What is actual is rational, and what is rational is actual" in the Preface to the 1820 *Philosophy of Right*). Hegel is reacting to the state of affairs in German-speaking areas following the French conflict with the Holy Roman Empire and the attempted resolution at the Congress of Rastatt (1797–1799), an inconclusive set of negotiations attended by Hegel's close friends Isaac von Sinclair and Hölderlin.[19] Hegel is eager to point out the gap between the rhetoric of German political theory and political reality. In a passage that might seem to echo complaints often lodged against Hegel himself, he writes of the resentment of those who see in the world only chance and who thus maintain the truth of their empty ideals:

> It is no doubt recent developments above all which have afflicted the Germans with this vice. In the perpetual contradiction between what they demand and what happens contrary to their demand, they appear not only censorious but, when they talk only of their concepts, untruthful and dishonest; for they attribute necessity to their concepts of right [*Recht*] and duties, whereas nothing happens in accordance with this necessity, and they are themselves all too accustomed on the one hand to a constant contradiction between their words and the deeds [of others], and on the other to trying to make of the events something quite different from what they really are, and to twisting their explanation of them to fit certain concepts. (GC [*Werke* 1, 464]/8–9)

Once again, Hegel's aims are mainly diagnostic, as he attempts to show that there actually is no German state or German constitution. In light of his mature conception it is especially interesting to see him arguing that it is the very "drive for freedom" (GC [*Werke* 1, 465]/10) of the Germans (incidentally the same attribute that Machiavelli cites as so praiseworthy in the German city-states in *The Prince*) that has prevented them from forming a single common authority. The result of hundreds of years of stubbornness is that there is no "system of rights, but a collection without principle, whose inconsistencies and confusion required the most acute perception to rescue it as far as possible from its contradictions whenever a collision occurred" (GC [*Werke* 1, 467]/11). Thus, "German constitutional law is not a science based on principles but a register of the most varied constitutional rights acquired in the manner of civil law [*Privatrecht*]" (GC [*Werke* 1, 468]/12). It is in this light that we should read Hegel's qualified support for the Napoleonic code and later his siding with the Württemberg king against the estates in 1816. Hegel always argues for differentiation and local control, but he also worries that prioritizing the local and particular threatens

---

[19] Pinkard, *Hegel*, 81.

to make self-interest the foundation of society, and he insists that it is too shallow a foundation for a robust ethical life.

Hegel moved to Jena in 1801 to join Schelling, who had been appointed at the record-setting age of 23 at a university that had undergone a remarkable transformation in the 1790s. Initially spurred by Goethe and Schiller, the university had become the center of the German philosophical world during Fichte's tumultuous five-year tenure. Fichte was dismissed in 1799 following what is known as the Atheism Controversy, a result of trumped-up charges of atheism stemming from an essay ("On the Basis of Our Belief in a Divine Governance of the World") in which Fichte developed the Kantian idea of a moral religion. In their brief years together (Schelling would leave in 1803) Hegel published a manifesto championing Schelling's system of philosophy over Fichte's, and the two friends co-edited the *Critical Journal*. There remains some dispute over just how much Hegel took over from Schelling's systematic works at this time, but what is not in dispute is how dramatically Hegel shifted toward thinking that only a rigorous, systematic form of philosophy was worth pursuing. He is still concerned with the social and historical conditions of philosophy and religion (his introduction to the "Difference Essay" on the need for philosophy is a testament to this), but he devotes himself to rigorously thinking through the basic justification of philosophical claims. In his 1803 "Skepticism" essay he unpacks the ancient skeptical tradition and compares it favorably with modern skepticism.[20] His many system drafts in these years show him struggling to find the right way to think through a new form of idealism that is not mere subjective idealism, but also not dogmatic metaphysics. The *Phenomenology of Spirit*, in which Hegel finds his mature voice and (more or less) his mature philosophical position, is itself a work that aimed to defeat skepticism by enacting a "self-completing skepticism" (PS 9.56/¶78) with a secure result (absolute knowledge). His departure from his youthful enthusiasm for popular philosophy is evident in his claim in the Preface to the *Phenomenology* that "philosophy must keep up its guard against the desire to be edifying" (PS 9.13/¶9). Later he criticizes modern talk of virtue as exemplary of words that "edify but erect nothing [*erbauen, aber nichts aufbauen*]" (PS 9.212/¶390). Hegel did not give up entirely on his earlier project, but he came to think he needed a phenomenological introduction, a logic and a philosophy of nature, before he could give an account of the spiritual domain of action, ethics, and religion.

What was, then, the insight that allowed Hegel to break through to his mature position? The basic move (examined in various ways in this *Handbook*) involved rethinking the function of *negation* and *self-relation* in the construction of a philosophical system. The challenge that had been set by Schelling's system and by Spinozism generally is to build a system on the basis of a whole, a substance, that must somehow contain both thought and nature. Transcendental idealism (Kant and Fichte) had put systematic philosophy on a sound footing with the appeal to self-consciousness and free activity as the self-starting (and hence epistemically secure) ground of philosophical thought, but they could not in the end account for the coincidence of thought and the world. Hegel

---

[20] See Forster, *Hegel and Skepticism*.

felt keenly both the demand for justified systematicity and the demand to incorporate nature. After flirting with a Schellingean view, he soon discovered problems with any *assumption* of substance or preconceptual unity out of which mind and nature would flow. But he also thought that the idealism of Kant and Fichte was too subjective, too oriented by a posture of thought *against* the world, in a word too *reflective*, to ever satisfy the demands of reason to find itself *in the world*. Hegel's full solution to the mind-world problem is exceedingly complex, but it is grounded in his basic answer to the question of the relation of the subject (the active power of unification) and substance (the bearer of the objective unity). He came to think that substance could only be a *result* of a process of the subject's progressive failure at knowing its object. By tying together the *negations* of knowledge, including the subject's self-negation, in a process of greater self-consciousness, including greater awareness of the social conditions of that knowledge, we eventually arrive at the conceptual comprehension of substance. The Logic of the Concept turns on arguments for the superiority of inference to judgment, of teleology to mechanism, and of the good to the merely true. In the end, Hegel describes the Absolute Idea, or the method of philosophy, in terms of a 'drive', thereby advocating a conception of philosophy *as action*, as ethical, and as an ongoing process of rendering ourselves and the world intelligible.

I.3. Young Hegelians, British Idealists, and the Ends of Philosophy

In his mature system Hegel held together a number of disparate elements in an equilibrium that proved fragile in the decades following his death. These elements include not only a speculative logic and a philosophy of nature, but also within his philosophy of spirit an account of normativity rooted in the natural relation of the individual to the human species, the State as the objective realization of that relation, and a defense of religion as humanism properly conceived. In the following I briefly recount the most important initial unraveling of Hegel's synthesis, the writings of the young Hegelians in the 1830s and 1840s that culminated in Marx's philosophy. I then sketch the migration of Hegel's Spirit to Britain, where for over fifty years British idealism succeeded in productively re-engaging Hegel's logic, his social philosophy, and his philosophy of religion (it is especially unfortunate that the essay commissioned on British Idealism did not come through, given that Oxford University was the original home and focal point of this movement). I have included notes in the following that point to some of the important recent work in this area. There are a number of other important national Hegel literatures that are not included in Part VII, including especially the Italian reception, which in the work of Benedetto Croce in particular has enriched our understanding of the possibilities of

Hegel's thought.[21] Out of the two movements I consider in this section, I will draw in conclusion some lessons for reorienting our own philosophical culture.

The main 'young Hegelians', or 'left Hegelians' as they are sometimes called, are an eclectic group who took up Hegel's philosophy with an emphasis on its critical potential. After his death, Hegel's philosophy declined in influence fairly quickly within the realm of professional German philosophy under the increasing pressure of the success of the natural sciences and natural scientific method. The positive program of an all-inclusive idealism proved hard to defend, and after twenty to thirty years 'back to Kant' became the slogan of thinkers who were interested in giving a systematic account compatible with natural science.[22] But for a group of young intellectuals inspired by Hegel's critical claims and alienated from their economic, political, and religious institutions, Hegel's dialectical method offered a powerful tool for instigating social change.[23] This group included Eduard Gans, Arnold Ruge, David Friedrich Strauss, Ludwig Feuerbach, Bruno Bauer, Moses Hess, and the young Karl Marx, among others. They were distinguished from more orthodox Hegelians by taking his thought in a more practical, less metaphysical direction. They include not only the founder of communism, but also in Moses Hess the earliest proponent of Zionism.[24]

A decisive text in the development of left Hegelianism, which also signaled the beginning of the end of the Hegelian school, is Strauss's 1835 *The Life of Jesus Critically Examined*. It is somewhat ironic, given Hegel's own early attempts to rewrite the life of Jesus from a philosophical perspective, that just such a text—but one with a much more critical edge, based in part on Hegel's own mature method—would expose the fault lines in his mature philosophy. Hegel's mature philosophy of religion walked a very fine line,[25] arguing for a trajectory of the 'demythologization' of religion and interpreting Christianity as just such a process. He thought of Protestant Christianity as the 'absolute religion' and held that it has the same 'content' as speculative philosophy, a thesis that seems to establish a truce between the competing authorities of revelation and rational thought. But Hegel did argue for a certain superiority of philosophical justification, and in Hegel's system the 'representational' mode of religion is clearly deficient in comparison with philosophy, so there is a suspicion that even Christian religion is only a watered-down philosophy for the masses. Strauss takes up Hegel's program but is much less concerned to unify the divinity of the Bible with the divinity of the philosophical Idea, and in particular he places Jesus' humanity front and center. Strauss writes,

---

[21] See the essays in Herzog, *Hegel's Thought in Europe*.

[22] See Schnädelbach, *Philosophy in Germany*, for an illuminating survey of developments in professional philosophy in Germany in the hundred years after Hegel's death.

[23] The most original writer of this period, Søren Kierkegaard, does not stand in the same trajectory as the 'young Hegelians' I discuss here, though the influence of Hegel's philosophy on him is strong. Both the young Hegelians and Kierkegaard were influenced by Schelling's late critique of Hegel that he delivered in lectures in Berlin in the early 1840s. For an account of the influence of Hegel on Kierkegaard, see Westphal, "Kierkegaard and German Idealism," and Stewart, *Kierkegaard's Relation to Hegel Reconsidered*.

[24] See Quante, "After Hegel," for a concise review of Hess's work in the 1840s.

[25] See Lewis, *Religion, Modernity, and Politics in Hegel*.

he commits no sacrilege to the Holy, but rather effects a good and necessary work, if he clears away everything which, though well-intended and perhaps even initially beneficial, is ultimately harmful and a downright pernicious delusion—that is, everything in virtue of which Jesus is said to be a super-human being—and recovers as far as possible the image of the historical Jesus in his ultimately human form.[26]

Despite the sincerity of his belief in the moral community centered on Jesus' teachings, such pronouncements were too much for the reactionary climate of the 1830s, and his conflict with traditional theology kept Strauss from pursuing an academic career. A similar argument was developed by Ludwig Feuerbach, who took the Hegelian reading of religion in an atheistic direction. Feuerbach had studied with Hegel himself in Berlin, and had remained a committed Hegelian for nearly a decade thereafter. But his 1841 *The Essence of Christianity* went further than Strauss in arguing, in what we would now call an anthropological vein, that Christianity can be explained without resort to the spiritual. He saw religion as basically a projection of our own human essence into an otherworldly domain. Late in his life, Friedrich Engels talked about the importance of this book for him and for Marx, and identified its publication as the ending of the era of classical German philosophy that began in 1781 with Kant's *Critique of Pure Reason*.

Bruno Bauer studied with Hegel in the last years of Hegel's life, and in the early to mid-1830s he was a rather conservative defender of the Hegelian system. He even was recruited to respond to Strauss's book in a manner that would distance the Hegelian school from the charges of atheism provoked by Strauss's work. But Bauer himself had a crisis of faith in the stability of the reason-religion alliance in Hegel, and he would become an atheist Hegelian who championed republicanism. In 1841–1842 he published anonymously two works in the voice of a conservative religious thinker criticizing Hegel's philosophy as tantamount to atheism. Michael Quante describes the effect of this as follows:

> Moderate Hegelians were confronted with a dilemma: it seemed either they were not in the position to accurately interpret Hegel; or, conscious of the truth, they were suppressing their knowledge for either political or personal reasons. With this dilemma Bauer sought to dissolve the mediating position in the Hegelian school, insofar as he pressed Hegelians either to embrace atheism or to do that which critics of Hegel by and large demanded: namely, to abandon Hegel's philosophy altogether.[27]

Bauer himself adopted a socially progressive reading of Hegel that emphasized the theme of emancipatory *activity*. In a contrast that still resonates (see section I.1), Bauer argued that interpretation of Hegel splits along Fichtean and Spinozist lines. Bauer read him as a Fichtean, "stressing the active, self-transforming individual, who attains autonomy through the conscious, *personal* enactment of universal interests," while according

---

[26] Strauss, *The Life of Jesus*, cited in Quante, "After Hegel," 201. In this discussion I am leaning heavily on Quante's essay.

[27] Quante, "After Hegel," 202.

to Bauer, Strauss and Feuerbach read Hegel as a Spinozist for whom universality was "an essentially passive and distributive property."[28] For Bauer there was a progressive emancipation that would lead to a republican political order. Unfortunately, alongside this progressive tendency in Bauer's thought, there is also a pronounced streak of anti-Semitism. Bauer's "The Jewish Question" of 1843 prompted the much more famous essay "On the Jewish Question" by Marx. Thirty years later, Bauer would encourage Friedrich Nietzsche to write his "untimely meditation" on Strauss, an interesting bridge from Hegel to Nietzsche that is unfortunately also marred by Bauer's (and to some extent, Nietzsche's) anti-Semitism.[29]

The breakup of the young Hegelian group in the years before the failed 1848 revolutions sheds much light on the revolutionary potential of Hegel's system and on the reactions that his system can provoke. One final jolt to the movement is worth mentioning, namely the radically individualist attack by Max Stirner in *The Ego and Its Own*. The distinguishing mark of Stirner's critique is his rejection of sociality in favor of the unique individual ego ('ego' is not the best translation of *das Einzige*, but it is used in almost all translations), who is not essentially constituted by any connection to humanity (thus the view is sometimes described as an anti-humanism).[30] Stirner's aggressive individualism is interesting less in its own right than in the effect that it had on Marx and in its affinities with certain strains of existentialism. Whereas Marx could have developed his program in the humanist direction of Bauer or Hess, he seems to have accepted the anti-idealism of Stirner, for he joined Stirner in rejecting claims about the rational essence of human beings as illusory. While also rejecting Stirner's individualism, Marx's disturbing contempt for all talk of rights and all variants of mere socialism were shaped by Stirner's critique. The social relations that Marx continued to advocate as determinative for human beings would henceforth have to be interpreted in a historical and material register, and not with the idealization of the consciousness or self-consciousness of freedom. So, many of Marx's critics have alleged, the trouble with that turn is that it goes beyond just criticizing 'false consciousness' and ends up criticizing consciousness itself as an illusion, and that in ethics, and especially in politics, this leads either to anti-rationalism or to a rationality of the system invoked from outside of the subjective perspective of its members.

The pivotal works on Christianity by Strauss and Feuerbach were soon translated into English by Mary Ann Evans—before she began publishing novels under the name of George Eliot. Yet they did not have the effect of convincing British readers—who only were exposed to Hegel in a serious way in the 1850s and 1860s[31]—that the logical conclusion of Hegelianism was a rejection of Christianity. Indeed, the embrace of Hegelianism in the 1860s and 1870s that led to 'British Idealism' was in large part driven by the hope

---

[28] See Moggach and De Ridder, "Hegelianism in Restoration Prussia," 80–81.
[29] See Holub, *Nietzsche's Jewish Problem*.
[30] See Moggach and De Ridder, "Hegelianism in Restoration Prussia."
[31] The earlier transmission of German thought to England by Thomas Carlyle was important in many respects, but it did not contain a serious philosophical engagement with Hegel's thought.

that through absolute idealism Christianity and philosophy could be reconciled. One of the founders of the movement, T. H. Green, even considered translating a major work on Christianity by F. C. Baur, leader of the Tübingen school of theology and teacher of Strauss. A long-standing evangelical movement in Britain, alongside the mounting pressure from science and historical criticism on traditional belief, together go a long way toward explaining how the long British tradition of empiricism gave way for some fifty years to Hegel-inspired idealism. The movement began in Oxford and came to include philosophers at many important British universities. When one considers the centuries-long prominence of Aristotle at Oxford, it is not hard to see how Hegel's Aristotelianism would have had broad appeal. When one recalls that an Oxford education was at the beginning of the century an education for the clergy, we can see British Hegelianism at Oxford as a key part of its transition from a theological school to a modern university. In this narrative the (temporary) embrace of Hegel would be the final stage on the way to the self-secularization of Christianity.

Major thinkers in British Idealism include Green, John and Edward Caird, F. H. Bradley, Bernard Bosanquet, J. M. E. McTaggart, and A. S. Pringle-Pattison.[32] These thinkers for the most part read Hegel's philosophy of religion in tandem with his *Logic*. They were oriented by the *Encyclopedia* and *The Science of Logic*, unlike the young Hegelians in Germany, who were more oriented by the *Phenomenology of Spirit*. While there was certainly a Kantian strain in the thinking of Green and others,[33] they were clearly most inspired by Hegel, and especially by Hegel's thesis of the role of relations in constituting reality.[34] They were holists, espousing a version of an identity-in-difference and arguing for the concrete, rather than the abstract, universal.[35] Much of this work is directly derived from Hegel, though Bradley, McTaggart, and others made their own novel contributions to metaphysics.

While the movement placed a high value on metaphysics and theology, we are more likely to find in the social and political philosophy of British Idealism a living resource for thinking through the relationship of philosophical theory and ethical practice. The most well-known text in practical philosophy from the period—Bradley's *Ethical Studies*—is very Hegelian and yet not entirely representative of the way that the British Idealists molded Hegel's practical philosophy to their specific situation. The most famous chapter of that work, "My Station and Its Duties," lays out how the social conception of the individual answers the emptiness problem with the Kantian 'duty for duty's sake' thesis. Unfortunately, this view—that one simply should take over from social roles the duties through which one realizes oneself—is too often associated with Bradley and with Hegel, when the actual views of both are much more complex. For T. H. Green, the moral question of self-realization also ended in a social register, but in Green's case

[32] See Mander, *British Idealism*, for a comprehensive history.

[33] See Candlish, "British Idealism: Theoretical Philosophy," for an argument that Green took over the central role of the proposition from Kant.

[34] For a concise overview, see Mander, "Hegel and British Idealism."

[35] See Stern, *Hegelian Metaphysics*, Chapter 5, on the 'concrete universal' in British Idealism and a comparison with Hegel's understanding of the universal in *The Science of Logic*.

it was an emphatically political conception. His work *Political Obligation* defines the purpose of the state unabashedly in terms of the realization of the good, and of a positive conception of freedom that "consisted of the right of every individual to make the most of those powers admitted to be worth realizing by the moral consensus of the community."[36] While this may sound too perfectionist or paternalist for modern liberalism, it actually represents a salutary counterweight within liberalism to the doctrine of negative freedom that was being employed at Green's time (and is still being employed today) to restrain government from instituting policies designed to render society more egalitarian. With the seriousness of his moral purpose, Green was able through his teaching at Oxford and his writings to inspire a generation of British leaders who helped transform British society.[37]

The downfall of British Idealism is usually portrayed as the triumph of Bertrand Russell and G. E. Moore, identified with both realism and 'analysis', over an idealist school that no longer inspired in the new century. But there was no single moment of victory, and the actual history of the metaphysical dispute—and in particular the Russell-Bradley dispute over relations—is much more complex and interesting than the standard narrative.[38] One has the impression that the Great War itself had much to do with the dying out of German-inspired philosophy in Britain. A renewed appreciation for clarity and precision in philosophical discourse was certainly part of it, though that appreciation came at a definite cost in the ability of philosophy to inspire social and political reform. There remained initiates into British Idealism well after its supposed defeat in the first decades of the new century. Boucher refers to one such late incarnation, R. G. Collingwood (1889–1943), writing,

> The generation of students brought up on T. H. Green's idealism had been taught that clear philosophical thinking is essential to informing and improving conduct, whereas those exposed to Realism were told that philosophical thinking is a disinterested activity with no contribution to make to practical conduct. It was, then, the separation between theory and practice to which Collingwood objected, and not least of which because it denied the role of the committed intellectual, and absolved philosophy of social responsibility.[39]

What is striking about this downfall from today's perspective is that while the style of analytic philosophy is certainly triumphant, many of Russell's actual positions, and to

---

[36] Richter, *The Politics of Conscience*, 225.

[37] Boucher writes that the idealists "agitated for legislation; assisted government commissions by giving evidence and serving on them; held offices on school boards; actively extended university education to women; and enthusiastically supported extra mural, or university extension schemes and the Workers' Educational Association by organising and delivering lectures" (Boucher, "British Idealism: Practical Philosophy," 692).

[38] See Candlish, "British Idealism: Theoretical Philosophy."

[39] Boucher, "British Idealism: Practical Philosophy," 689–690. Another idealist who lived to resist the triumph of realism and analysis was G. R. G. Mure, whose 1958 *Retreat from Truth* is still well worth reading.

a lesser extent those of Moore, seem rather idiosyncratic and unattractive. While the idealists could be accused of entertaining rather extravagant metaphysical views, their ethical theories and aesthetics were far more substantial than the rather arid positions that replaced them.[40]

It is thus not surprising that scholarly interest in Hegel has picked up again in Anglo-German philosophy over the last 40 years, alongside the resurrection of normatively charged ethical and political theories. There have been calls for a return to moral religion, for thinking through the divinity of moral value or moral community as a substitute for traditional revealed religion.[41] Most such attempts have a decidedly Kantian or Fichtean aura, for they assert the primacy of practical reason over the theoretical concerns of natural science, even going so far as to resuscitate the fact-value distinction in the name of an autonomous sphere of value. Hegel is objecting to such a one-sided appeal to practice in the first part of the sentence I have placed at the front of this introduction.

The lingering question, which I believe we still have not satisfactorily answered, is what Hegel thought the theoretical complement to the practical would have to be in order to accomplish the unification of the two domains. His account of the development of nature into spirit is a key part of this story, and the recent work on Hegel's naturalism would seem to point us in a promising direction. But what is it exactly in nature, or in our grasp of ourselves as natural, that would allow us to say that the practical ought and the theoretical ought coincide? This question mark goes together with a puzzle in deciphering Hegel's relationship to common sense. He is at times quite hostile to common sense, and often in those places—such as when he distinguishes *the* concept from ordinary concepts—where he is celebrating his unique philosophical insight. But he is also committed to thinking that the infinite, or the concept, is already operative in ordinary practice, and that the philosopher is only drawing out what is already conceived and acted upon by ordinary agents. For Hegel there can be no esoteric concept that we would have to know in order to participate in the common life of ethical spirit. Yet the value of our life together does depend on the fact that we are *thinking* creatures, and Hegel's system remains the most comprehensive attempt to think through that fact, and that value.

WORKS CITED

Primary Texts

Hegel, G. W. F. "The German Constitution" [GC], in *Political Writings*, edited by Laurence Dickey and H. B. Nisbet. Cambridge: Cambridge University Press, 1999, 6–101.

Hegel, G. W. F. *Phenomenology of Spirit* [PS], translated by Terry Pinkard. Cambridge: Cambridge University Press, 2017

---

[40] See Mander, *Idealist Ethics*, for a more detailed account of the practical philosophy of the period.
[41] For example, Dworkin, *Religion without God*.

Hegel, G. W. F. "Review, *Friedrich Heinrich Jacobi's Works, Volume III*" [J], in *Heidelberg Writings: Journal Publications*, edited and translated by Brady Bowman and Allen Speight. Cambridge: Cambridge University Press, 2009, 3–31.

Hegel, G. W. F. "The Positivity of the Christian Religion" [P], in *Early Theological Writings*, translated by T. M. Knox. Philadelphia: University of Pennsylvania Press, 1971, 67–181.

Hegel, G. W. F. "The Spirit of Christianity and Its Fate" [SC], in *Early Theological Writings*, translated by T. M. Knox. Philadelphia: University of Pennsylvania Press, 1971, 182–301.

Hegel, G. W. F. "The Tübingen Essay" [TE], in *Three Essays, 1793–1795*, edited and Translated by Peter Fuss and John Dobbins. Notre Dame, IN: Notre Dame University Press, 1984, 30–58.

Secondary Literature

Baur, Michael, and Stephen Houlgate. *A Companion to Hegel*. Chichester, UK: Wiley Blackwell, 2011.

Beiser, Frederick. *Hegel*. New York: Routledge, 2005.

Beiser, Frederick. *Hegel and Nineteenth Century Philosophy*. Cambridge: Cambridge University Press, 2008.

Bondeli, Martin. *Hegel in Bern*. Bonn: Bouvier Verlag, 1990.

Boucher, David. "British Idealism: Practical Philosophy," in *The Routledge Companion to Nineteenth Century Philosophy*, edited by Dean Moyar. London: Routledge, 2010, 689–710.

Bowman, Brady. *Hegel and the Metaphysics of Absolute Negativity*. Cambridge: Cambridge University Press, 2013.

Candlish, Stewart. "British Idealism: Theoretical Philosophy," in *The Routledge Companion to Nineteenth Century Philosophy*, edited by Dean Moyar. London: Routledge, 2010, 658–688.

De Laurentiis, Allegra, and Jeffrey Edwards (eds.), *The Bloomsbury Companion to Hegel*. London: Bloomsbury, 2013.

Dworkin, Ronald. *Religion without God*. Cambridge, MA: Harvard University Press, 2013.

Ferrarin, Alfredo. *Hegel and Aristotle*. Cambridge: Cambridge University Press, 2007.

Forster, Michael, *Hegel and Skepticism*. Cambridge, MA: Harvard University Press, 1989.

Förster, Eckart. "To Lend Wings to Physics Once Again: Hölderlin and 'The Oldest System-Programme of German Idealism.'" *European Journal of Philosophy* 3, no. 2, (August 1995): 174–198.

Förster, Eckart, and Melamed, Yitzhak. *Spinoza and German Idealism*. Cambridge: Cambridge University Press, 2012.

Harris, H. S. *Hegel's Development: Towards the Sunlight, 1770–1801*. Oxford: Oxford University Press, 1972.

Hartmann, Klaus, "Hegel: A Non-Metaphysical View," in *Hegel: A Collection of Critical Essays*, edited by A. MacIntyre. South Bend, IN: University of Notre Dame Press, 1972, 103.

Henrich, Dieter. *Between Kant and Hegel: Lectures on German Idealism*, edited by David S. Pacini. Cambridge, MA: Harvard University Press, 2003.

Herzog, Lisa. *Hegel's Thought in Europe: Currents, Crosscurrents and Undercurrents*. Palgrave Macmillan, 2013.

Holub, Robert C. *Nietzsche's Jewish Problem: Between Anti-Semitism and Anti-Judaism*. Princeton, NJ: Princeton University Press, 2015.

Horstmann, Rolf-Peter. *Ontologie und Relationen: Hegel, Bradley, Russell und die Kontroverse über interne und externe Beziehungen*. Königstein: Athenäum, 1984.

Houlgate, Stephen. *An Introduction to Hegel: Freedom, Truth and History*, second edition. Oxford: Blackwell, 2005.

Kreines, James. *Reason in the World: Hegel's Metaphysics and Its Philosophical Appeal*. Oxford: Oxford University Press, 2015.

Lewis, Thomas. *Religion, Modernity, and Politics in Hegel*. Oxford: Oxford University Press, 2011.

Lukács, Georg. *The Young Hegel*, translated by R. Livingstone. London: Merlin Press, 1975.

Mander, W. J. *British Idealism: A History*. Oxford: Oxford University Press, 2011.

Mander, W. J. "Hegel and British Idealism," in *Hegel's Thought in Europe: Currents, Crosscurrents and Undercurrents*, edited by Lisa Herzog. Basingstoke, UK: Palgrave Macmillan, 2013, 165–176.

Mander, W. J. *Idealist Ethics*. Oxford: Oxford University Press, 2016.

Moggach, Douglas, and de Ridder, Widukind. "Hegelianism in Restoration Prussia, 1841–1848: Freedom, Humanism and 'Anti-Humanism' in Young Hegelian Thought," in *Hegel's Thought in Europe: Currents, Crosscurrents and Undercurrents*, edited by Lisa Herzog. Basingstoke, UK: Palgrave Macmillan, 2013, 71–92.

Moyar, Dean. "Rethinking Autonomy in Hegel's Earliest Writings." *The Owl of Minerva* 42, nos. 1–2 (2010–2011), 63–88.

Moyar, Dean. *Hegel's Conscience*. Oxford: Oxford University Press, 2011.

Mure, G. R. G. *Retreat from Truth*. Oxford: Basil Blackwell, 1958.

Ng, Karen. "Life, Self-consciousness, Negativity: Understanding Hegel's Speculative Identity Thesis," in *The Freedom of Life: Hegelian Perspectives*, edited by Thomas Khurana. Berlin: August Verlag, 2013, 33–68.

Pinkard, Terry. *Hegel: A Biography*. Cambridge: Cambridge University Press, 2000.

Pinkard, Terry. "Hegel: A Life," in *The Cambridge Companion to Hegel and Nineteenth-Century Philosophy*, edited by Frederick Beiser. Cambridge: Cambridge University Press, 2008, 15–51.

Pinkard, Terry. *Hegel's Naturalism: Mind, Nature, and the Final Ends of Life*. Oxford: Oxford University Press, 2012.

Pinkard, Terry. *Hegel's Phenomenology: The Sociality of Reason*. Cambridge: Cambridge University Press, 1994.

Pippin, Robert. *Hegel's Idealism: The Satisfactions of Self-consciousness*. Cambridge: Cambridge University Press, 1989.

Pippin, Robert. *Hegel's Practical Philosophy: Rational Agency as Ethical Life*. Cambridge: Cambridge University Press, 2008.

Quante, Michael. "After Hegel: The Actualization of Philosophy in Practice," in *The Routledge Companion to Nineteenth Century Philosophy*, edited by Dean Moyar. London: Routledge, 2010, 197–237.

Quante, Michael. *Hegel's Concept of Action*, translated by Dean Moyar. Cambridge: Cambridge University Press, 2004.

Richter, Melvin. *The Politics of Conscience: T. H. Green and his Age*. Cambridge, MA: Harvard University Press, 1964.

Schnädelbach, Herbert. *Philosophy in Germany, 1831–1933*. Cambridge: Cambridge University Press, 1984.

Siep, Ludwig. *Anerkennung als Prinzip der praktischen Philosophie*. Freiburg: Alber, 1979.

Stern, Robert. *Hegel, Kant and the Structure of the Object*. London: Routledge, 1990.

Stern, Robert. *Hegelian Metaphysics*. Oxford: Oxford University Press, 2009.

Stewart, Jon. *Kierkegaard's Relation to Hegel Reconsidered*. Cambridge: Cambridge University Press, 2003.

Taylor, Charles. "Hegel and the Philosophy of Action," in *Hegel's Philosophy of Action*, edited by L. S. Stepelevish and D. Lamb. Atlantic Highlands, NJ: Humanities Press, 1–18.

Westphal, Merold. "Kirekegaard and German Idealism," in *The Routledge Companion to Nineteenth Century Philosophy*, edited by Dean Moyar. London: Routledge, 2010, 347–376.

Wood, Allen. *Hegel's Ethical Thought*. Cambridge: Cambridge University Press, 1990.

Yeomans, Christoper. *Freedom and Reflection*. Oxford: Oxford University Press, 2012.

PART I

HEGEL'S DEVELOPMENT IN JENA

CHAPTER 1

HEGEL'S FIRST SYSTEM PROGRAM AND THE TASK OF PHILOSOPHY

BIRGIT SANDKAULEN
TRANSLATED BY BRADY BOWMAN

1.1. INTRODUCTION

THE turn of the nineteenth century brought with it a new turn in the development of post-Kantian thought. The year 1801 saw Hegel's philosophical debut, a publication whose very title sent an unequivocal signal: *The Difference between Fichte's and Schelling's System of Philosophy*. Substantive differences of opinion had been noticeable in Fichte's and Schelling's writings from the beginning, and they grew still more explicit once Schelling embarked on his project of *Naturphilosophie*, but it was not until after Fichte's departure from Jena that they began frankly to address their differences. Initially they did so in private correspondence, and occasional veiled references are to be found in Schelling's 1801 work *On the True Concept of Naturphilosophie*. It was left to Hegel, though, to force the actual rupture. Neither the wider public, he notes at the outset, nor the authors themselves have understood the actual nature of their difference. In his eyes, clearly, Fichte and Schelling had been talking past the real issue in debating whether or not philosophy should begin with the 'I' or with its emergence from nature.

As the friendship between Fichte and Schelling unravels, Schelling and Hegel make common cause. The message they send as joint founders and sole contributors to their *Critical Journal of Philosophy* is a clear one: henceforth they are the arbiters over post-Kantian philosophy; starting now, they are the face of 'true philosophy'. Hegel once again is the one to bring things to a head, staking the journal's claim in strident, even polemical tones. In *Faith and Knowledge or the Reflective Philosophy of Subjectivity in the Complete Range of Its Forms as Kantian, Jacobian, and Fichtean Philosophy*, published in

1802 in the *Journal*'s debut issue, he broadens the critical target to include all the leading philosophers of the day.

The collaboration between Schelling and Hegel was itself but short-lived, however. Though Schelling had already left for Würzburg in 1803, their friendship effectively terminates with the publication of the *Phenomenology of Spirit* in 1807. In the work's Preface, Hegel lashes out at a conception that, despite the omission of Schelling's actual name, seems to implicate him. Schelling's request that Hegel counter this impression goes unanswered. It is Hegel once again who forces the rupture. From that day forward, 'Schellingians' and 'Hegelians' have, as a rule, been at loggerheads. And the histories of philosophy written since unfailingly repeat the same sequence of steps laid down by Hegel at the turn of the nineteenth century from Kant to Jacobi, Jacobi to Fichte, Fichte to Schelling, Schelling to Hegel.

Thus the narrative that has come to frame our understanding of the period: the line of great figures in classical German philosophy apparently ends with Hegel. That is to say, rather than merely continuing the line, Hegel staked out his position by deliberately instigating debates with his contemporaries and deliberately one-upping their positions. When Hegel enters the scene, he does so *as a critic* poised to take the depth of contemporary thought. In assuming the task of critique, Hegel is not engaging in a mere sideline to philosophy, he is setting into motion a mode of philosophizing whose native form is that of critique and which he will go on to develop into a comprehensive history of the shapes of consciousness in his first major work, the *Phenomenology of Spirit*. But what is it, exactly, that Hegel means to critique? What is at issue in Hegel's critical writings?

These questions seldom have been raised in Anglophone studies of Hegel. Taylor hardly touches on the early Jena writings.[1] While no one seems to share Taylor's view of Hegel as propounding a 'cosmic' metaphysics of spirit, the same cannot be said of his marginal interest in Hegel's critical writings. As Hegel's debut, of course, the *Difference* essay receives regular mention, but rarely much detailed attention.[2] Whatever the reasons for this neglect, scholars of Hegel would do well to address it. To overlook Hegel's critical writings is not to skip over some inconsequential episode; it is to miss the crucial link connecting Hegel's Frankfurt manuscripts to the work of his maturity, the

---

[1] Taylor, *Hegel*.

[2] To some extent Harris (*Night Thoughts*) is an exception, though he focuses mainly on Hegel's Jena System Drafts. However, because he mistakenly takes Hegel to be referring to Schelling's *Presentation of My System of Philosophy* rather than the *True Concept* essay, the introduction to his 1977 English translation of the *Difference* essay misconstrues the true line of argument and is therefore unsuited as a guide to the text. Bondeli's survey of Hegel's time in Jena ("The Jena Years") is severely abridged. Siep (*Einführender Kommentar*) and Förster (*Twenty-Five Years*), the latter containing only a short discussion of the *Difference* essay, are both available in English translation. Along with Hegel's other critical writings, the *Difference* essay has been widely discussed in German-language scholarship. Among others, see Bubner, *Deutscher Idealismus*; Düsing, "Spekulation und Reflexion," "Idealistische Substanzmetaphysik," and "Die Entstehung des spekulativen Idealismus"; Henrich/Düsing, *Hegel in Jena*; Horstmann, "Hegels Auseinandersetzung mit Kant"; Jaeschke, *Hegel-Handbuch*; Schäfer, *Dialektik*; Siep, *Einführender Kommentar*; and Vieweg, *Das Kritische Journal*.

Phenomenology. This link is fundamentally important for understanding Hegel's philosophical program, both systematically and in terms of his development as a thinker. It represents a turning point in his own thought, as well as the new foundation he seeks to establish for the philosophy of his time—even as early as 1801, Hegel was never content simply to adopt the position established by Schelling. Looking closely, we can tell that Hegel is operating on a terrain he has yet to secure, one that confronts him with an interesting set of problems that will shape everything he writes thereafter. In short, the *Difference* essay documents the genesis of the philosophy we now recognize as distinctively Hegelian.

Here we cannot begin to address the full scope of Hegel's new beginning in Jena. Hegel weighed into public philosophical discourse at a point in time when the state of debate was already far advanced, embracing numerous, distinct strands of discussion, and Hegel adds his own complexities into the mix; whole books could be written on the debates that Hegel initiated regarding Kant, Jacobi, Fichte, and Schelling, each on its own. In the interest of a clear and lucid presentation of the essentials, the following account will focus mainly on the *Difference* essay's first chapter, which prefaces Hegel's more detailed comparison of Fichte and Schelling. The text is especially suited as the starting point for a problem-oriented discussion because it shows us Hegel as he himself struggles to achieve clarity about his own philosophical program.

1.2. THE PHILOSOPHY OF PHILOSOPHY: THE *DIFFERENCE* ESSAY AND ITS RELATION TO THE *PHENOMENOLOGY*

Of the import of what is at stake, the chapter's odd and somewhat awkward title—*Mancherlei Formen, die bei dem jetzigen Philosophieren vorkommen* (Various Forms to Be Found in Current Philosophizing)—gives barely a hint. It seems to announce a few casual observations that might as easily be skipped. Indeed, the fact that Hegel himself considers it to be a 'defect' that his work begins with 'general reflections' (GW 4.8/DE 83) is not apt to dispel that doubt. And it could well be the case that Hegel really is uncertain about the way he has chosen to begin. On second glance, however, we can recognize in these peculiar opening remarks the earliest instance of a characteristically Hegelian trope. Time and again, he will later assure us that there is no philosophy outside direct engagement in the activity of thinking and that a 'general introduction' to philosophy is therefore misguided in its very idea. And yet time and again, the very same Hegel will nonetheless go on to author prefaces and introductions that are integral to our understanding of his thought.

One of the best known such texts is also one of Hegel's most important, the famous Preface to the *Phenomenology of Spirit.* As soon as we view that Preface next to the opening chapter of the *Difference* essay, we immediately also recognize that the opening of the *Difference* essay constitutes the *prototype* of a Hegelian *groundwork text*. Both are groundwork texts in the sense that they do not focus on the more technical questions that Hegel reserves for treatment within the confines of the system itself—a system that was at the time already under construction, as documented in the manuscripts now known as the Jena System Drafts. Interestingly, what Hegel offers in the way of a preface to the actual execution of the system itself, with its particular divisions and their particular subject-matter (logic, philosophy of nature, philosophy of spirit), is a reflection neither on the system's 'matter' nor on its 'form', but on these fundamental questions: What is the nature of philosophy, what are its tasks, and what are the available means to accomplishing them? At the programmatic core of these prefaces lies the definition of philosophy itself, a 'philosophy of philosophy' that we may describe as a *metaphilosophical reflection* inasmuch as it both precedes and guides philosophy's concrete, material exposition.

However, the *Difference* essay does more than merely establish the prototype for this kind of reflection. A comparison with the Preface to the *Phenomenology* highlights both the underlying continuity in content and the often very substantive modifications it was later to undergo. In respect to both elements of continuity and of change, the two texts are so close as to suggest that the *Difference* essay lay open in front of Hegel while he was writing the later Preface. The same is true of the much later Introduction to the *Encyclopedia of Philosophical Sciences*, which appears to adopt formulations *verbatim* from the *Difference* essay. Like the two earlier texts, this later Introduction also serves as a groundwork, forgoing more technical questions in order to focus directly on the concept of philosophy itself, and here too we find significant parallels to the Preface of the *Phenomenology* and significant changes compared to the *Difference* essay.

These observations suffice to show that the opening of the *Difference* essay is an important source for understanding the conception of philosophy that underlies the entirety of Hegel's material propositions—including especially the problems he would soon be forced to address. Numerous passages could be adduced that further testify to the abiding presence and importance of this text in the genesis and development of Hegel's philosophic program, and as far as space allows, we will point them out as we go along. There is, however, one very striking difference between the opening of the *Difference* essay and the other texts just mentioned, distinct from the later changes in content, but nonetheless related to them. It has to do with *readability*.

To be sure, none of Hegel's writings is light reading, and it should not surprise us if his groundwork texts are even more demanding, situated as they are at a higher level of abstraction. Yet, though the complexity and difficulty of the *Difference* essay's opening chapter far surpasses even that of Hegel's later writings, there is no other pathway to understanding Hegel's Jena beginnings. We have before us a sketch that is compact and opaque, shot through with tacit borrowings and allusions, and hence virtually indecipherable as a linear argument or without the help of additional background. That makes for difficult reading, and it also tells us something about the circumstances of the work's composition.

When he arrives in Jena, Hegel is no beginner in philosophy, but he is an *outsider*. For one thing, he had until recently been employed as a private tutor in wealthy households, so now, at the threshold of an academic career, he is faced with the pressure of public scrutiny and the desire to prove himself in the eyes of his younger—and far more successful—classmate Schelling. Hence, he is forced to catch up in short time on a philosophical discourse the others have been carrying on for years at the highest level of sophistication, to learn its language, and to unlock its potential. This challenge is all the greater for the fact that, until recently leaving Frankfurt for Jena, he had regarded *religion* as higher than philosophy. Now we see him embracing a radical change in view, abandoning his former conviction in favor of the primacy of philosophy.

All that hardly makes for a poised and conceptually satisfying control of his new circumstances. Whatever uncertainty Hegel must have experienced, his grand entrance seems calculated to conceal it, a prime instance being his readiness to adjudicate the difference between Fichte's and Schelling's systems without having established even the barest outlines of a system of his own. At the same time, however, it is clear that he is in the process of discovering the prototype that will guide him in laying the groundwork for such a system. As long as he lacked a programmatic groundwork, Hegel would have no criteria by which to compare the systems of Fichte and Schelling and hence no way of positioning himself within contemporary discourse. Above all, until he had such a groundwork, he would lack the clarity required to orient himself in a completely new terrain. That shows in the text.

1.3. The Plunge into Philosophy and the Need of Philosophy

Hegel's attempt to clarify (for himself as much as for others) the 'task of philosophy' centers on three key concepts, around which further concepts cluster: the *absolute, speculation*, and the *system*. In 1801, all three concepts appear for the first time in his work, henceforth to constitute his core conception of philosophy. At the programmatic level, these concepts remain firmly linked to his intention of providing (1) a universally valid definition of philosophy. From the beginning, this intention goes hand in hand with his claim to provide (2) an *immanent* criticism of the philosophical positions held by historical and contemporaneous philosophers (later to be refined into his controversial procedure of 'sublation'). Further, Hegel ascribes (3) a common basis to these various positions, which he formulates in terms of his own perspective. From 1801 on, this typical interference between the universal scope and highly specific focus of Hegel's claim will be the rule. The *Difference* essay is, however, also marked by (4) the difficulty that Hegel is himself still tacitly struggling to articulate the program that will form the basis of his philosophy.

For the reader, this concatenation of objectives results in difficulties of which the following passage is a prime example. As a way of 'setting the tone', I quote the passage in full:

> The essence of philosophy is a bottomless abyss for personal idiosyncrasies. If the body be the sum of one's idiosyncrasies, then to reach philosophy it is necessary to plunge oneself into it *à corps perdu*. For reason, finding consciousness entangled in particularities, can become philosophical speculation only by raising itself to itself, entrusting itself only to itself and to the absolute which at that moment becomes its object. Reason has nothing to lose thereby but the finitudes of consciousness, and to overcome these finitudes and construct the absolute in consciousness, reason rises to speculation, and in the groundlessness of limitations and personal idiosyncrasies it grasps its own grounding within itself. (GW 4, 11 f./DE 88)[3]

Had Hegel been asked for an abstract of the *Difference* essay, one almost fears that he would have submitted this passage: the call to an unselfsparing plunge into the abysmal depth of a philosophy that is at the same time also the pinnacle of 'reason' where 'speculation' attains to the 'absolute' as its 'object' so as to 'construct it in consciousness'. If that all comes across as completely incomprehensible, it is not the reader's fault, but Hegel's. And that is a sign that something deeper is going on here.

To all appearances, *Hegel took his own plunge into philosophy* when he moved from Frankfurt to Jena. That he is in need of some kind of meta-philosophical clarification is clear to him, but he still has *no idea how to get into philosophy* from the outside. He still has no idea how to frame an *introduction* to philosophy. Hegel will spend all of his remaining time in Jena working on precisely this project. The result will be the *Phenomenology of Spirit*, whose 'task' it is to "lead the individual from his uneducated standpoint to knowledge" (PS 9.24/¶28). Looking back from the standpoint of the *Phenomenology*, then, we can also see that the opening of the *Difference* essay is every bit as vulnerable to the criticism he will launch at Schelling in the Preface to that later work (i.e., his polemical rejection of the "rapturous enthusiasm which, like a shot from a pistol, begins straightaway with absolute knowledge"; PS 9.24/¶27).

Hegel must already have had at least an inkling of this problem in 1801: we can tell so from the ensuing chapter on the "Need of Philosophy" (GW 4.12 ff./DE 89). Here he amplifies the notion of a plunge by appealing to a corresponding 'need' that awakens in highly specific historical and cultural conditions, giving rise to philosophy and defining its task. Hegel's twofold derivation of the 'task of philosophy'—one deductive (GW 4.11/DE 88), the other inductive (GW 4.13; 63/DE 90 f.; 155)—is closely related.[4] Unfortunately, however, this chapter is equally unsuited as an entry point into Hegel's train of thought. It is simply too complex and laden with assumptions—not least because

---

[3] Translations have been tacitly modified for accuracy and consistency with the main text.

[4] This twofold derivation is also bound up with the basic problem of the relation between reason and history—one that will continue to occupy Hegel's thought for the rest of his career; he addresses it repeatedly in the course of the essay without ever getting a firm grip on it.

of the traces it bears of Hegel's time in Frankfurt. Thus our only hope is to reverse direction and, starting from the essay's intended goal, to reconstruct the logical space determined by the three key concepts introduced at the top of this section.

1.4. THE PHILOSOPHY OF THE SYSTEM

The Hegelian program centers on the idea of a 'philosophy of the system' (GW 4.31/DE 114). Now, 'philosophy as such' (GW 4.30/DE 112) does not coincide *eo ipso* with the interest in erecting a system. The fact that philosophy as such is distinct from systematic philosophy is notable, and Hegel will later address it explicitly (cp. E §12). Indeed, he even seems to hold that 'philosophizing as such' promises a kind of 'satisfaction' all on its own, provided one adopts the appropriate frame of mind. However, he is equally convinced that philosophizing inevitably gives rise to a "need to produce a totality of knowing, a system of science" (GW 4.30/DE 113). The idea of a 'philosophy of the system' thereby comes to function in two complementary directions as the criterion by which philosophical positions must be critically assessed.

In the one direction, Hegel opposes "philosophizing that cannot achieve systematic form," criticizing such positions as so much "mystical enthusiasm" (GW 4.63/DE 156). As he will later write in the Preface to the *Phenomenology*: "Philosophy must beware of the wish to be edifying" (PS 9.14/¶9). In the other direction, though, there are systematic philosophers like Fichte and Schelling, who can hardly be faulted as "mystical enthusiasts." In such cases, Hegel's criterion assumes a different meaning, referring to the extent to which "the philosophy of the system and the system itself" coincide (GW 4.31/DE 114). This is what is behind his contention that Fichte's and Schelling's respective principles are not really what makes the difference between their systems. Indeed, Hegel is prepared to acknowledge both systems, at least in principle, as forms of "authentic speculation" (GW 4.32/DE 114)—a point he also extends to Kant, provided we distinguish between the 'spirit' and the 'letter' (GW 4.5 f./DE 79 f.). On this level, the fact that Fichte grounds the *Wissenschaftslehre* on the 'I', while Schelling insists on the primacy of nature, is of no ultimate importance. In Hegel's eyes, Fichte fails because, as a system, the *Wissenschaftslehre* does not attain to a complete, self-contained realization of the program it is based on. In the final analysis, Fichte's focus on the 'I' is merely a symptom of this failure, not its cause.

Hegel's critique stands Fichte's own understanding of his *Wissenschaftslehre* on its head. More than that, though, it represents a completely new form of critique for the period.[5] Accordingly, it is all the more important to recognize that Hegel's program

---

[5] As late as 1801, in the *True Concept of Naturphilosophie*, Schelling still considers Fichte's philosophy to be a perfect, self-contained, methodology of philosophical science, on the basis of which he himself intends to erect a material system of philosophy. We will return to Jacobi's Fichte-critique later, as it anticipates an essential point of Hegel's argumentation.

elevates the *idea of the system* to the status of a *structurally decisive argument*.[6] Among his contemporaries, Hegel was certainly not the first to popularize the idea of a philosophic system, but he embraced it in a way that added disproportionately to its weight: his *Difference* essay would go by a more fitting name were it known as the "system essay." The centrality of the system will remain a fixture of Hegelian thought: "The true shape in which truth exists can only be the scientific system of such truth" (PS 9.11/ ¶5). Hegel's claim to have constructed an all-encompassing system attracted critics from the beginning; even today, it is for many the least palatable aspect of his thought. Be that as it may, from the moment of his arrival in Jena, Hegelian philosophy and the idea of the system remain joined forever more. Note, however, that the *structural* significance of Hegel's idea of a system goes beyond any merely *formal* features—hence Hegel's talk of 'truth' in the passage just cited.

Taken in isolation, Hegel's definition of a system reads like a formal description. A system is said to be

> . . . a whole of knowledge, an organization of cognitions. Within this organization, every part is at the same time the whole [. . .]. As a part that has other parts outside of it, it is something limited, and is only through the others. Isolated in its limitation, the part is defective; it has meaning and significance solely through its coherence with the whole. Hence single concepts by themselves and singular cognitions must not be called knowledge. (GW 4.19/DE 98)

Those lines could have been taken directly from Kant's chapter on the "Architectonic of Pure Reason."[7] For Hegel as for Kant, the fact that knowledge constitutes an interconnected whole, a systematic organization of cognitions, is not the effect of an extrinsically imposed order, but is grounded in the nature of reason as such. However, Hegel's 'philosophy of the system' adds a further key premise: if the system is rightly deemed the 'self-production of Reason', Hegel is equally committed to the thesis that what "shapes itself into an objective totality, a whole in itself held fast and complete, having no ground outside itself, but founded by itself in its beginning, middle and end" (GW 4.30 f./DE 113) is nothing less than *the absolute itself*.

1.5. THE ABSOLUTE

The master concept in Hegel's sketch of a 'philosophy of the system' is the concept of *the absolute*. The meaning we assign to this concept determines how we understand the

---

[6] Cp. Jaeschke, *Hegel Handbuch*.

[7] "By a system I understand the unity of the manifold modes of knowledge under one idea. This idea is the concept provided by reason of the form of a whole in so far as the concept determines a priori not only the scope of its manifold content, but also the positions which the parts occupy relatively to one another" (A 832/B 860).

cognitive goal of 'speculation' and the function the system is to fulfill. It clearly also has implications in gauging the extent to which any given historical system has successfully realized the system program. Despite its obvious importance, however, Hegel plunges into the text without the least explanation of the term. He must have felt the resulting lack of cogency, for he quickly follows up by designating the absolute as a 'presupposition' no philosophy can do without. The absolute is "the goal that is being sought; it is already present—how otherwise could it be sought?" (GW 4.15/DE 93). That does not help much, though. Hegel is plainly borrowing the idea that we can only seek what we already know from Jacobi (cp. GW 4.84 f., note/DE 183); but since, unlike Jacobi, he cannot at this point adequately account for such a presupposition, he disguises its character as a mere *posit* by packaging it in a rhetorical question. This is a problem of elementary importance and we will return to it at the end of this chapter. It belongs among the problems we alluded to earlier—problems that Hegel will subsequently work to resolve.

For the time being, we must follow Hegel in 'presupposing' the absolute and try to come to an understanding of this key concept and what it means "to construct the absolute for consciousness" (GW 4.16/DE 94), since that is the definitive task of Hegel's 'philosophy of the system'. As a first step, we must get our bearings. Unlike the idea of systematicity, 'the absolute' was not commonly used in the nominative case when Hegel wrote the *Difference* essay. So it is not merely novel in the context of his writings; it is a term that first begins to gain general currency in the period after 1801. Only then, for instance, does Fichte begin to adopt it.[8] Far from mere verbal trifling, the rise of the term signals a decisive shift in content.

Instead of 'the absolute,' Kant and Jacobi prefer to speak of 'the unconditioned'. When Kant employs the predicate 'absolute', he does so in order to characterize the 'absolute totality' of conditions as the defining objective of reason, immediately glossing the term as "what is unconditioned without qualification [*schlechthin*], that is, in all relations" (CPR, A 326/B 382). Throughout the 1790s, Fichte too makes exclusively attributive use of the word 'absolute' and does so only in reference to the 'absolute I' as the principle of the *Wissenschaftslehre*. The attributive use of the term is thus essentially contrastive and makes at least implicit negative reference to what is not absolute.

Only Schelling uses 'the absolute' as a substantive, and he does so as early as 1795 in the *Philosophical Letters on Dogmatismus and Criticism*. There the term refers to an 'absolute unity' (SW I, 296) that he portrays as the common basis of two mutually exclusive systems, dogmatism (meaning Spinoza) and criticism (meaning Schelling's own system), which define it respectively as an 'absolute object' or an 'absolute subject' (SW I, 298). 'The absolute' then disappears from view, not to resurface until 1800 in Schelling's *System of Transcendental Idealism*. At a point quite late in the text, he suddenly brings it in to replace the work's original principle, the subject: the absolute, he tells us, is 'something higher' constituting the "ground of identity between the absolutely subjective and the absolutely objective, the conscious and the unconscious." Accordingly, the absolute itself can be "neither subject nor object and also not both at once, but only the *absolute*

---

[8] Jaeschke/Arndt, *Klassische Deutsche Philosophie*, 338–339; Rohs, *Fichte*.

identity in which there is no duplicity at all" (SW III, 600). If we follow Schelling, then, the shift from the attributive to the nominative use of 'the absolute' would appear to be motivated by the idea that there must be an underlying dimension of reality whose very definition is *to stand outside all relations whatsoever*. As a result, it is beyond the grasp of discursive knowledge, accessible only through an intuitive mode of cognition, 'intellectual intuition'. The absolute in this sense soon comes to figure as the master concept in Schelling's *Identitätsphilosophie* or 'philosophy of identity', the first outline of which he published in 1801: *Presentation of My System of Philosophy*.

Here we can do no more than point to Schelling's conception of the absolute and the complications introduced by the repeated shifts in position he later tried to smooth over, implausibly asserting that he had been pursuing a philosophy of identity from the outset (SW IV, 108 ff.).[9] Nor can we go into the question of whether Hegel was already familiar with Schelling's *Presentation* when he wrote the *Difference* essay in 1801. Whatever the case, it is striking that his discussion of Schelling and his judgment of Schelling's superiority over Fichte are based almost exclusively on material from the *System of Transcendental Idealism*, a work belonging to a phase Schelling had seemingly already left behind. *De facto*, however, that effectively means that Hegel is *projecting* the shape of Schelling's current philosophy of identity back onto the position he had held the previous year, in 1800. When we consider that the two men shared an apartment in Jena, conversing with each other on a daily basis, there is even reason to suspect that Schelling's rapid shift from transcendental idealism to the system of identity philosophy was precipitated by Hegel.[10] Conversely—and this is more than mere conjecture—we can infer that Hegel was most certainly not Schelling's 'disciple' in Jena. But that being the case, what can we infer about Hegel's conception of the absolute?

The nominative use of 'the absolute' may very well have originated with Schelling, from whom Hegel could then have adopted the *expression*. What counts, though, is the fact that Hegel gives the term a meaning that deviates significantly from Schelling's definition of it. Hegel may seem to be agreeing with Schelling when he occasionally refers to the absolute as 'absolute identity'. But if his consistent characterization of the latter as the 'identity of subject and object' (GW 4.18/DE 97) already suggests a different conception, then the passage from Schelling's *System of Transcendental Idealism*, quoted earlier, puts the matter beyond doubt. There Schelling defines the absolute as an identity that *stands outside all relations whatsoever*; but the view that Hegel attributes to him is that "the absolute itself is the *identity of identity and non-identity; being opposed and being one are together in it*" (GW 4.64/DE 156, emphasis added).

Word for word, this formula contradicts Schelling's definition and reveals what is unique to the approach Hegel brought with him from Frankfurt: a dialectical mode of thought for which the absolute is neither relative nor beyond all relationality, but rather an overarching and internally differentiated unity embracing within it both identity and difference. In other words, *the absolute is the whole*; relations are not external to it but

---

[9] Cp. Sandkaulen, *Ausgang*, and Sandkaulen, "Was heißt Idealismus?"
[10] Cp. Düsing, "Idealistische Substanzmetaphysik."

belong instead to the internal structure of the absolute. Hegel's concept of 'the system' is the precise counterpart of the absolute, thus constituted. The concomitant of this, Hegel's original conception of *the dialectic*, is the holism distinctive of Hegel's understanding of philosophy: "The true is the whole" (PS 9.19/¶20). One further point of contrast with Schelling follows directly: if, according to Hegel, the absolute is the internally differentiated whole, and if the task of philosophy is "to construct the absolute for consciousness," then philosophy cannot forgo the resources of discursive thought. Here is the root of Hegel's notion of *speculation*, which "must be conceived as the identity of reflection and intuition" (GW 4.29/DE 111)—a notion to which we will soon return.

For the moment, however, our main concern must be to counter the impression that Hegel's structural formula for the absolute is really a *mere formula*, composed in equal parts of abstraction and philosophic bombast. Can the formula be brought to life? Despite the essay's frequently wooden prose and its long arid stretches, which Hegel seems to traverse as if buckled onto conceptual stilts, he would have conceded the force of the question. Or rather, he would have replied that it answers itself, *since the formula itself is the formula of life* as an internally self-differentiating unity, as the whole of reality, binding finite and infinite, nature and spirit (GW 4.14/DE 91).

1.6. THE JACOBI-SPINOZA CONSTELLATION

Hegel's holism bears traces of its origins in the philosophy of life: "I would have to express this by saying, life is the connection of connection and non-connection" (GW 2.343 f.), he notes in one of the latest Frankfurt manuscripts, written shortly before his departure for Jena.[11] That he replaces 'life' with 'the absolute' should not lead us to conclude that he has given up on the philosophy of life. The *Difference* essay itself gives a key role to the concept of life (GW 4.12 ff./DE 89 ff.), demonstrating the continuity in Hegel's interests. However, the seachange in Hegel's thought is visible in the way his system program recasts those interests. In a letter to Schelling, written around the same time, Hegel himself addresses this change: "In my scientific education, which began with the subordinate interests of men, I was inevitably driven to science, and the ideal of my youth had to change into the form of reflection and so too become a system."[12] Hegel greatly exaggerates in suggesting that he already has such a 'system', but his description of the shift in his thinking is accurate: it is less a change in the content of specific philosophical views than a wholesale realignment of his thought *from religion to the systematic form of reflection.*

'Religion' does not here refer to the doctrines of 'positive religion' that Hegel criticizes in his early manuscripts on the philosophy of religion. When, at the very end of his time

---

[11] Hegel's Frankfurt manuscripts have now been made available in a completely new critical edition as volume 2 of the *Gesammelte Werke*, thereby replacing Hermann Nohl's bastardized edition.

[12] Letter to Schelling, 2.11.1800, in Hoffmeister, *Briefe von und an Hegel*, 1.59.

in Frankfurt, Hegel writes, "Philosophy must end in religion precisely because the true infinite is beyond its reach" (GW 2.344), he is pointing to a *lived experience* that discloses life's inner nexus in a way that philosophy never can. For the Frankurt Hegel, philosophy is limited to *reflection*, an operation that is exhausted entirely by the making and fixation of distinctions. In its internally differentiated unity, life cannot be grasped this way: it is a "being beyond reflection" (GW 2.344). At its best, therefore, philosophy can merely point the way to the "elevation of man—not from the finite to the infinite, for these are only products of mere reflection and as such their separation is absolute,—but from a life that is finite to a life that is infinite" (GW 2.343). This experience, through which alone an authentic understanding of living union (*lebendige Vereinigung*) is possible, is beyond the reach of philosophy.

It is important to recognize the extent to which this background is present in the program of philosophy laid out in the *Difference* essay. Let us begin by articulating what, to many, will already have become obvious: Hegel's philosophy of life and hence also its transformation into a philosophy of 'the absolute' are clearly inspired by Spinoza and his metaphysical vision of a single, unitary substance that comprehends within itself, as its own immanent expression, the difference between thought and matter, mind and body, as well as the difference between the infinite and the finite. Like others of his generation, Hegel too fell under the spell of the Spinoza renaissance initiated by Jacobi's seminal work, *On the Doctrine of Spinoza, in Letters to Moses Mendelssohn* (1785/expanded edition 1789). Scholars agree that next to Kant's *Critique of Pure Reason*, Jacobi's *Spinoza Letters* is the other basic book of classical German philosophy. What is surprising, then, is not the fact that Hegel was influenced by it, but rather the way he interprets Lessing's shibboleth of Spinozist unity and totality, *hen kai pan*, preserved and transmitted by Jacobi (JW 1,1, 16; Jacobi 2009, 187).[13]

Hegel first encountered Jacobi's *Spinoza Letters* in a context remote from the philosophical controversies inspired by Kant, and his interest in them was not primarily oriented toward questions of metaphysics and epistemology. Like his brother in arms, Hölderlin, and true to their common commitment to *Vereinigungsphilosophie* ('philosophy of unification'), Hegel was animated chiefly by a practical concern for the life-world, namely, his hope for reconciliation in the midst of the alienating 'divisions' of the modern world. In marked contrast to Fichte and Schelling, Hegel did not feel challenged by Jacobi's alternative either to embrace Spinoza's philosophy as the paradigm of philosophical rigor, thereby accepting the equally rigorous fatalism that goes with it, or to accede to the existential interest in human freedom and altogether to reject the very notion of systematic philosophy with its pretentions to universal explanation. Throughout the 1790s, Fichte and Schelling had sought to evade the alternative of Jacobi's 'Spinoza and Anti-Spinoza' (JW 1,1, 274) by establishing a third option: either a system of freedom that could vie with Spinoza's in terms of rigor or, in Schelling's variation, a pair of complementary sciences, one corresponding to Spinoza's *natura naturans*

---

[13] Cp. Hindrichs, "Spinozismus, Antispinozismus."

(i.e., *Naturphilosophie*), the other committed to a doctrine of freedom (i.e., transcendental idealism). All that lay quite beyond Hegel's Frankfurt purview.

The result is an idiosyncratic amalgamation of practical Spinozism and Jacobi's critique of rationality. In basing his critique of reflection on Jacobi's 'Anti-Spinoza', Hegel falls prey to a confusion with serious ramifications. In the pivotal Supplement VII to his *Spinoza Letters*, Jacobi writes, "We appropriate the universe by tearing it apart, and creating a world of *pictures*, ideas, and words, which is proportionate to our powers, but quite unlike the real one." He continues: "We understand perfectly what we thus create, to the extent that it is our creation. And whatever does not allow of being created in this way, we do not understand. Our philosophical understanding does not reach beyond its own creation. All understanding comes about, however, by the fact that we *posit* distinctions, and then *negate* them" (JW 1,1, 249/Jacobi 2009, 370). Jacobi here diagnoses a constructivism that is inherent to human knowledge and its drive to reduce qualitative features to calculable quantities in the interest of rational uniformity. Spinoza's substance monism is the inevitable result.[14]

Hegel's reading of this passage (like Hölderlin's) completely inverts its meaning. He misunderstands Jacobi's diagnosis of rationality as a criticism of the understanding, which, in judging (*urteilen*), tears apart (*ur-teilen*) what originally belonged together in the world "as it is in actual reality." Instead of recognizing Jacobi's commitment to a view of reality as shot through with qualitative differences, Hegel fixes his gaze on unity. Consequently, he also mistakenly believes himself to be agreeing with Jacobi when he appeals to 'religion' as an alternative to reflection. Even without going more fully into the complexities of the background here, this much ought to be clear: as a would-be disciple of Jacobi's rationality-critique, Hegel is nonetheless committed to a basically Spinozist conception of reality.

With this background in mind, let us return to the *Difference* essay. We should now be able to recognize how important it is to distinguish between the constellation's *epistemological* aspect and its *ontological* aspect—a distinction that Hegel's mature thought will later collapse. From an ontological point of view, Hegel's system program is committed to Spinoza's holism. Hegel's concept of *the absolute* corresponds to Spinoza's concept of *substance*, whose two known attributes he reinterprets as answering to the Kantian distinction between 'subject' and 'object'. In contrast to Fichte and Schelling, Hegel's engagement with Spinoza had never centered on the alleged 'dogmatism' of his metaphysics and epistemology. This difference in orientation is what allows him to become the *first philosopher* in post-Kantian Germany to embrace the Spinozist orientation as a paradigm without alternative, and once he is in Jena, he unilaterally declares that paradigm to be the sole and universal basis of all philosophy.

That Hegel does not explicitly say as much in the *Difference* essay, or that he criticizes Spinoza in the handful of places he even mentions him, is besides the point. The issue here does not concern a particular *theoretical model* with its particular strengths and weakness, but a *basic stance toward reality*. So when Hegel criticizes Spinoza, it is not to

---

[14] On Jacobi's philosophy as a whole, cf. Sandkaulen, *Grund und Ursache*.

question this basic stance, but to demonstrate what he sees as Spinoza's failure to have grasped the actual underpinnings of his own ontology (GW 4.24/DE 105 f.). Yet it is indicative of problems with *Hegel's position*, in turn, that he falls prey to a confusion about Spinoza whose ramifications are as grave as those of his confusion about Jacobi. Things get even more interesting when we observe that Hegel's misunderstanding of Spinoza is nowhere more evident than when he polemicizes against Jacobi's presentation of Spinoza in *Faith and Knowledge*. This nest of problems is the ultimate root of Hegel's famous dictum in the Preface to the *Phenomenology* that everything depends on "grasping and expressing the truth, not as substance, but equally as subject" (PS 9.18/ ¶17). To this point, too, we will soon return.

Three points remain to be noted. First, as we have just seen, Hegel is committed to a specific form of monism (*Identitätsphilosophie*) that is directly related to the Spinozistic element in his thought and which, moreover, he assumes as the standard of comparison for philosophical conceptions generally. In judging philosophies by their degree of success in generating a representation of 'the absolute' (i.e., the inner nexus of reality in the totality of its manifestations [*hen kai pan*]), as he does in both the *Difference* essay and *Faith and Knowledge*, he assumes without argument that this criterion is immanent to the systems themselves.

Furthermore, Hegel apparently recognized the potential for a 'philosophy of identity' (in the holistic, Hegelian sense) in Schelling's thought before Schelling himself did. In any case, he is not relying on Schelling's own profession of Spinozism in the 1801 *Presentation* when he likens Schelling's earlier pairing of transcendental philosophy and the philosophy of nature (in the *System of Transcendental Idealism*) to what "an older philosopher" expressed by saying "the order and coherence of ideas (the subjective) is the same as the coherence and order of things (the objective)" (GW 4.71/DE 166). In projecting Spinoza's parallelism of thought and extension onto Schelling's two sciences, he also asserts their 'inner identity' as representations of the 'absolute' and its 'totality' (GW 4.71/DE 166). The contours of Hegel's own later system, with its division into a philosophy of nature and a philosophy of spirit, are also clearly visible here.

Finally, the resulting relation to Fichte is especially interesting: the Spinozist element in Hegel's own thought allows him to see the potential contained in Jacobi's *Letter to Fichte* (1799), where Jacobi, pairing the same diagnosis and critique of philosophical system-building we saw with Spinoza, lauds the *Wissenschaftslehre* as a "philosophy of *one* piece, a veritable *system* of reason" (JW 2,1, 200/Jacobi 2009, 507). For Jacobi, the success of the *Wissenschaftslehre* rests on the fact that it is an "inverted Spinozism": Fichte's absolute I, as the "absolute identity of subject and object," structurally recapitulates Spinoza's substance, "which underlies extended and thinking being, equally and inseparably bind[ing] them together" (JW 2,1, 195/Jacobi 2009, 502); however, Fichte's principle wholly absorbs Spinoza's substance into the element of knowledge as such.

Though Hegel does not acknowledge Jacobi's *Letter to Fichte* as an eminent source of inspiration for the argument mounted in the *Difference* essay, he clearly was aware of Jacobi's analysis (GW 4.71; 84 f./DE 166; 183). Hegel can appropriate everything Jacobi says about the all-encompassing, Spinozistic logic of Fichte's system almost verbatim, down to his assessment of Fichte's principle as an authentically speculative expression of the "identity of subject and object" (GW 4.34/DE 119)—everything, that is, except for Jacobi's provocative thesis that, on its own terms, Fichte's system, the main target of Hegel's criticisms, is a success. In *Faith and Knowledge*, Hegel finally reveals his source: "Nothing could be plainer than the fact that Jacobi has misunderstood this system, when he says in his *Letter to Fichte*, that he believes that the Fichtean way produced a philosophy which is *all of one* piece, a genuine system of reason, and indeed that the Fichtean way is the only way it can be done" (GW 4.397/FK 167).[15]

Jacobi is the target of Hegel's harshest, most polemical criticism in *Faith and Knowledge*. Yet nothing could be more mistaken than to conclude that Jacobi must therefore be a figure of marginal importance. The opposite is the case, as we have just had further occasion to observe. The genesis of Hegel's thought in Frankfurt and its transformation in Jena is far more intimately indebted to Jacobi than to Kant, and the same can be shown of Hegel's later works as well.[16] The truth is that Hegel's polemical objections to Jacobi's alleged 'philosophy of reflection' in *Faith and Knowledge* reflect Hegel's own quandaries. As late as 1800, the Frankfurt Hegel had still (mistakenly) thought he agreed with Jacobi in setting religious experience above philosophical reflection. The Jena Hegel obviously requires a *different epistemology* if his system program is to entitle him, long before setting forth a system of his own, to pass judgment on the systems of others or, for that matter, on what he has now come to reject as unsystematic 'enthusiasm'.

1.7. REFLECTION AND SPECULATION

Of the three key concepts introduced in section 1.3, the absolute comes first in order of priority: its specific *ontological signature* determines what a 'philosophy of the system' must capture in order to succeed. However, a mediating link is required between the absolute and the system in which it finds expression. This *epistemological* role falls to speculation: it determines whether and how philosophy as such can *establish cognitive reference to the absolute*. The concept of speculation is therefore equally fundamental. Unsurprisingly, though, it is this epistemological aspect of Hegel's system program that proves to be the most complicated. The formal criteria defining a 'system' had already been formulated by Kant and Jacobi and were there for the taking; as for the 'absolute', Jacobi had long since shown how to reformat Spinoza's holism to fit the Kantian and post-Kantian language of subject and object. Stilted though Hegel's appropriation

---

[15] Jacobi's ironic reply to this objection is also a cogent one: "If that is so, then all the better for me. If I already regarded Fichte's system [sc. as an identity philosophy] two years before Schelling published his, that makes me its inventor" (JW 2,1, 365).

[16] Cp. Sandkaulen, "Das Nichtige"; Sandkaulen, "Ontologie der Substanz"; Sandkaulen, "Dritte Stellung."

of this—for him still quite foreign—language often is, that in itself is not the biggest problem.

The decisive challenge facing Hegel is to reorient his thought, hitherto centered on practical questions of the life-world, toward the *theoretical groundwork* required for a 'philosophy of the system'. That is not to say that Hegel must relinquish his worldly, practical concerns. Hegel never placed much store in academic scholasticism and its culture of specialization, but the same disdain for the ivory-tower conception of philosophy is common to all the classical German philosophers. Whatever differences may otherwise divide them, they agreed that insight into the actual world must be the goal of philosophy. However, while the movement's other major figures had for years been devoting their energy to the question how, and by what means, *philosophy* could attain to such insight, Hegel, in faraway Frankfurt, had assigned the task to *religion*. Now it was his turn to face the question, and the term 'speculation' stands for his struggle to come to grips with it. On the one hand, it is hardly more than a placeholder for the stipulative answer to that question; on the other hand, though, it thinly veils a veritable thicket of tangled concepts. The work of clarifying and modifying their interrelations will occupy Hegel throughout the ensuing years—not without significant ramifications to his overall program, as we will see at the end.

What is the meaning of 'speculation'? It clearly has nothing to do with hypothesis or conjecture, nor should we allow misleading associations of the 'absolute' with an other-worldly 'divine being' to suggest anything like spiritual knowledge of transcendent mysteries. But what does it mean instead? As soon as we pose the question, we find that it is hard even to talk about the expression, much less define it. The *Difference* essay is an epistemological field comprising an entire network of mutually interrelated concepts. On the one hand, the expression is informed by Kant's distinction between *reason and the understanding*. Whereas the understanding is limited to the finite, reason surpasses the understanding by virtue of its orientation toward absolute unity. It this *vision of unity* that interests Hegel; he neglects to mention that, for Kant, it has the status of a mere 'idea' rather than objective knowledge, later remarking that "postulating ideas is out of the question" (GW 4.29/DE 111). The same point had already been made by Jacobi, who in contrast to Kant had credited reason with an immediate certainty of the unconditioned. Hegel is thus implicitly taking recourse to Jacobi's conception of reason, which he sees as expressing the same *direct* relation of reason to the absolute that he himself insists on. Hegel's talk of reason thus represents an uneasy blend of Kant and Jacobi. That is important to see, but it does not take us all the way to a positive understanding of Hegel's epistemological project.

A clearer view begins to emerge when we consider how Hegel combines the distinction we have just considered between *reason and the understanding*, on the one hand, with that between *speculation and reflection*, on the other. Here, too, though, we have to be careful. The concepts are not simply interchangeable, as though 'speculation' stood in the same clear-cut relation of superiority to 'reflection' in which 'reason' stands to 'the understanding'.[17] The term 'speculation' is indeed related to the vision of rational unity

---

[17] Cp. Bondeli, "The Jena Years."

and reason's orientation toward the absolute, the identity of subject and object. Hence Hegel's praise of Fichte's philosophy as "authentically speculative." It would nonetheless be misleading to view 'reflection' as doing no work beyond providing a point of contrast to 'speculation' and thus as wholly assimilable to Hegel's critique of the 'philosophy of reflection'. Indeed, the defining feature of Hegel's epistemology is the *multifunctional use* he makes of reflection, and it will impact the entire further development of his philosophy. The concept of reflection marks the very core of Hegel's epistemology; its origins lie in his Frankfurt period, and the term retains its negative connotations. Division and separation belong to reflection essentially, a fact that would seem to render it philosophically useless if speculation is geared toward certainty of an absolute unity. But things are not that simple.

Whether reflection acts as an obstacle to or rather as the "instrument of philosophizing" (GW 4.16/DE 94) depends entirely on context, as does the extent to which the instrument's purely instrumental function can become explicit to thought. In other words, we can begin to untangle the thicket of the text by distinguishing among three different ways reflection can come into play:

1. Insofar as it is identical to the understanding, Hegel speaks of 'fixed reflection' (GW 4.14/DE 91) and subjects it to the same critique.

2. As an 'instrument of philosophizing', in turn, reflection coincides with reason (GW 4.16/DE 94) and shares its constructive relation to the absolute. In this latter case, speculation and reflection are in principle identical, but reflection is still liable to separate off from speculation and 'isolate' itself as an independent mode of cognition (GW 4.16/DE 94). This is the source of the deficits Hegel criticizes in the various forms of the 'philosophy of reflection'.

3. In the contrasting case of 'speculative knowledge', finally, Hegel sees a successful integration of the two moments in what he describes as the 'identity of reflection and intuition' (GW 4.29/DE 111). As we hinted earlier, this conception of 'speculative knowledge' marks both Hegel's proximity to Schelling and his distance; in committing himself to it, Hegel undertakes full responsibility for it as his own. These three varieties of reflection therefore offer a convenient vantage point for surveying the difficulties to which Hegel's first system program is exposed and which Hegel will subsequently work to resolve.

(1) *The culture of the understanding.* "Division is the source of the need of philosophy" (GW 4.12/DE 89). This is a key proposition, and in the passage containing it Hegel imports his Frankfurt critique of reflection directly into the new framework of the *Difference* essay. In doing so, however, he also significantly redefines the target of criticism. Hegel expands his previous criticism of the deficits of *philosophy* when it is fixated on reflection, to encompass the entire *modern paradigm of rationality* and the culture to which it belongs as fundamentally hostile to life. Similarly, what he had until recently still conceived as a *religious need* to experience the inner nexus of life, he now reconceives as the *need of philosophy*. Hegel's account of the genesis of philosophy and

its task is shaped by the fact that he now assigns to philosophy the function he previously understood to be fulfilled by religion. The whole passage is incomprehensible, unless we read it as an implicit reversal of Hegel's own earlier view on the relation of religion and philosophy in favor of his new position. Hegel's explicit account, by contrast, presents the view as though it were a universally applicable account of philosophy, at least to the extent that philosophy's task is determined by 'the culture of the era' (GW 4.12/DE 89).

Hegel's assessment of the cultural state of his times is damning. In its 'fixated reflection', the understanding represents a life-destroying 'power of division' (GW 4.14/ DE 92) that signals the thoroughgoing loss of the absolute.

> With the progress of culture, the antitheses that once displayed their might in the form of spirit and matter, soul and body, faith and intellect, freedom and necessity, etc., and a variety of other forms in more restricted spheres, attracting the whole weight of human interests, have passed over into such forms as the antithesis of reason and sensibility, intelligence and nature and, with respect to the universal concept, of absolute subjectivity and absolute objectivity. (GW 4.13/DE 90)

In the modern world, the paradigm of rationality is a dualistic paradigm: as 'fixated reflection', the understanding sunders what, in the 'world of actual reality' (GW 4.14/DE 91), is originally unified, separating it into artificial pairs of opposites. The consequence of this diagnosis is to place philosophy in the service of *reason*, whose interest and responsibility is to *reclaim the world as it really is*—from the Spinozist point of view. The task of philosophy is thus to overcome division. This same conception underlies Hegel's distinction between the cultural phenomenon of 'absolute division' (GW 4.14/DE 91), on the one hand, and the 'necessary division', on the other, that is one of the 'factors of life' (GW 4.13/DE 91) that philosophy must take into account. Hegel's interest cannot be to eliminate all differences whatsoever in favor of a pure, relationless identity—his holism would not allow it.

However, here we can already begin to see the problems that Hegel faces in transforming his Frankfurt position to fit the requirements of the *Difference* essay's system program. To begin with, Hegel is trying to secure a philosophical terrain completely new to him, where the literally *vital* task of the philosophical enterprise is also its foundation and its source of legitimacy. Yet by pitting philosophy in a 'struggle' (GW 4.15/ DE 93) against the broader culture, reason against the understanding, Hegel effectively isolates philosophy from the very culture it is meant to transform. Philosophy comes to occupy a space that is exclusive and thus at odds with its practical task. The alleged isolation of modern culture from the life-nexus of the absolute provokes a further question: Granted that the understanding constitutes a sphere of its own as 'fixated reflection', from what source does it derive its 'power'? In place of explanation, Hegel merely asserts the "detachment [*Herausgetretensein*] of consciousness from the totality" as a 'presupposition' (GW 4.15/DE 93). It is part and parcel with this aporia that the 'absolute', too, can only be asserted as a 'presupposition'. The ontological difference within the absolute has the character of necessity and is something quite distinct from the division within culture—but then it no longer seems plausible to assume a 'need' for the absolute as the overcoming of division, unless, that is, we have already assumed the totality of the absolute from the outset. Hegel will later make one of the most important changes to his epistemology in direct response to this set of problems. Instead of pitting philosophy against the understanding, he will later seek to integrate the understanding, with major consequences for his attitude to modernity: "The activity of separation is the power and work of the *understanding*, the most astonishing and mightiest of powers, or rather the absolute power" (GW 9, 27/§32).

(2) *The philosophy of reflection.* Contrary to Hegel's intention, the 'need of philosophy' is not the only element he is unable to derive on the basis of his cultural critique. It is equally unclear who or what is supposed to represent the scandal of dualism endemic to the culture of the understanding. The Introduction to the *Critical Journal*, "On the Essence of Philosophical Critique," points to 'Cartesian philosophy' (GW 4.126), while *Faith and Knowledge* presents us with a blanket criticism of Enlightenment thinking, eudaimonism, and empiricism (GW 4.318 ff./FK 58 ff.). At this stage, then, Hegel's theory of culture is hardly more than rudimentary. From later remarks, however, we can glean at least this much: the 'culture of the understanding' cannot be synonymous with the 'philosophy of reflection', despite the fact that Hegel sometimes describes them in virtually identical terms. We must therefore take care in making our way through the thicket of 'reflection': to assimilate the culture of the understanding to what Hegel calls the 'philosophy of reflection' would entail banning Kant, Jacobi, and Fichte from the realm of philosophy altogether and identifying the 'need of philosophy' exclusively with the particular motivations that drive Hegel (and Schelling).[18] But that is precisely what Hegel most needs to avoid. The *Difference* essay's very premise is that the need to overcome the dualism of 'absolute subjectivity and absolute objectivity' cuts across all the contemporary positions addressed there.[19] Since it is this need that motivates the transition away from the understanding and toward a consciousness of reason and its interests, Hegel accordingly acknowledges those positions as sharing in reason's orientation toward the absolute. So the problem Hegel identifies in the philosophy of reflection is distinct from that associated with the culture of the understanding.

The problem is related to philosophy's second task, complementary to that of overcoming of division: "to construct the absolute for consciousness" (GW 4.16/DE 94). Conversely, to overcome the division of subject and object, spirit and nature, requires that the absolute be rendered intelligible to consciousness as the internally differentiated whole of reality, to which the seeming division is fully integral, being the way in which that whole becomes manifest (GW 4.16 /DE 94). Reflection thereby comes into play as an 'instrument of philosophizing' whose systemic function it is to articulate

---

[18] Cp. Siep, *Einführender Kommentar*, 33.

[19] Hegel's own focus on 'division' (*Entzweiung*) leads to a considerable distortion of the actual situation. Kant, Jacobi, Fichte, and Schelling do not approach 'the absolute' on the basis of a presupposed *separation* of subject and object, but on the assumption that knowledge is grounded in their agreement. This agreement is what calls for philosophical explanation.

differences. As we have seen, some philosophers simply refuse to take on this task of reflection; they are the ones Hegel later calls mystical 'enthusiasts'. However, in all other cases the question is whether in carrying on its indispensable work, reflection maintains its orientation toward the fundamental unity of the absolute, or whether in emphasizing the 'positing of opposites' (GW 4.16/DE 94), it becomes isolated from that unity.

In contrast to the 'fixated reflection' associated with the understanding, reason's 'isolated reflection' is still directed toward the absolute, only in a way that distorts and conceals it by granting independent reality to reflection's own posits, instead of recognizing their essentially negative character in relation to the totality. The false employment of reflection takes a variety of forms, which Hegel surveys. It is a mistake to try to overcome the opposition between subject and object by abstracting from just one of them; that makes the absolute identity out to be a one-sided 'abstract identity' (GW 4.19/DE 97).

Attempts to express the absolute as a 'first principle' are equally misguided. Every proposition is determined by virtue of its distinction from an opposing proposition; hence no single proposition can give expression to the whole (GW 4.23 ff./DE 103 ff.). Hegel's critique of a system based on some 'first principle' is directed against Reinhold, but it also bears on Fichte. It foreshadows Hegel's later conception of the 'speculative proposition' (PS 9.45/¶61). Spinoza, too, finds a place among the varieties of isolated reflection: Hegel finds his attempt to express the absolute in the form of a proposition notable for leading to the antinomic conception of the *causa sui*. As a 'contradiction that cancels itself', the antinomy points to reflection's *essentially negative* character, and Hegel accordingly hails it as "the highest formal expression of knowledge and truth" (GW 4.26/DE 108), noting at the same time that it still requires a *positive* grounding. We will return to this point in step (3).

Thus we arrive at the critical framework that Hegel applies to the particular case of Fichte in the second part of the *Difference* essay. In *Faith and Knowledge* he will broaden his focus to include Kant and Jacobi in addition to Fichte. Before moving on, let us briefly consider this more comprehensive critique of the 'philosophy of reflection'. We would be missing Hegel's point were we mistakenly to identify the 'philosophy of reflection' with a mere philosophy of the understanding. While dualism is common to both, the philosophy of reflection succumbs to it because of an *internal conflict between speculation and reflection*. Insight into speculative identity is present and situated at the level of reason, but it is inadvertently distorted by reflection and its work of separation. Accordingly, Hegel focuses his criticism of Fichte on the following charge: though what Fichte is addressing is, essentially, not actually an 'I' in the sense of a one-sided subjective entity, an erroneous use of reflection misleads him to recast it as a one-sided subjective 'I' over against an equally one-sided 'non-I'. The result is that the system as Fichte actually presents it compromises the very unity it claims for the 'absolute I' by converting it into a perennially recurring, but unfulfillable 'ought' (GW 4. 45/DE 132). Thus, rather than concluding with a developed insight into the 'absolute I' with which it began and thereby constituting a complete and self-contained system, the *Wissenschaftslehre* veers off into an unfulfillable and in that sense 'bad' infinity.

In *Faith and Knowledge*, Hegel applies the same critical framework to Kant and Jacobi as well as to Fichte, but goes significantly beyond the analysis in the *Difference* essay. To a certain degree he is forced to do so: the dual perspective of Jacobi's 'Spinoza and Anti-Spinoza' does not fit into Hegel's existing framework, and besides, it would be pointless to reproach a critic of systematicity for failing to present a self-contained system. Hegel therefore intensifies his critique of dualism, focusing now on the overarching dualism of 'faith' and 'knowledge'. He recognizes a speculative potential in all the positions he considers, seeking to articulate it in terms of his brand of holism. However, the positions also all block this potential by allowing reflection to restrict *knowledge* to the knowledge of finite states of affairs and to posit a basic duality between the finite and the absolute, so that the latter has to be relegated to the sphere of 'rational *faith*'. For Hegel, this reflective opposition between faith and knowledge is the form in which the 'metaphysics of subjectivity' (GW 4.412/FK 189) betrays its focus on the finite. He finds the case of Jacobi to be especially egregious in that Jacobi even goes so far as to insist on the importance of the very finitude Hegel regards as a metaphysical 'nullity' (GW 4.377/FK 139). This same view is behind Hegel's unusually polemical assertion that Jacobi's interpretation of Spinoza is based on a complete misunderstanding. This is a point we will return to at the end of this chapter.

(3) *Speculative philosophy*. Schelling opens the 1801 *Presentation of My System of Philosophy* with the thesis that the "system of absolute identity [. . .] completely removes itself from the standpoint of reflection since the latter presupposes nothing but oppositions and rests on oppositions" (SW IV, 113). That is Schelling's thesis, *but it is not Hegel's*. How they were able to work together despite such differences is a fair question. For Hegel, there can be no such thing as completely removing oneself from the 'standpoint of reflection'. Reflection is an indispensable 'instrument' for a system whose goal is to construct the internally differentiated absolute 'for consciousness', because reflection is the means of positing such differences. At the same time, however, Hegel also insists on the *negativity* of reflection, even when it is carried out within the sphere of reason. Every act by which reflection posits some determination must at the same time also reflect the fact that its positing of determinations is not itself absolute; it must show its relation to the absolute totality by pointing to its own negation or 'sublation'. It is this idea that will eventually lead Hegel to discover the concept that forms the core of the dialectic—the concept of *determinate negation*. Hegel will come to be convinced that this progressive reflection of reflection is sufficient in order for knowledge to arrive at a positive result. This process will constitute the distinguishing character of what Hegel later understands by speculative knowledge.

However, the program of the *Difference* essay rests on a different conception, one that couples the 'negative side' of knowledge (i.e., the construction of antinomies), with its "positive side, namely intuition" (GW 4.27/DE 109). We might think of this as the Schellingian aspect in Hegel's thought; he refers to it as 'transcendental intuition' (GW 4.27/DE 109), an unusual term that he himself will later drop. Hegel departs from Schelling, however, in combining the two sides: "Transcendental knowledge unites both reflection and intuition. It is at once concept and being" (GW 4.27/DE 110). There is an implicit reference here to Kant's conception of knowledge as combining concepts and intuitions, though by 'intuition' Hegel clearly does not mean empirical intuition. For whereas in empirical intuition the subjective and objective are separated, in transcendental intuition we are supposed to become aware of their identity. However, the terms seem to shift reference in passing from Kant to Hegel. On the one hand, the identity of *concept and being* seemingly corresponds to the identity of subject and object, spirit and nature, in which case intuition, as the positive moment of knowledge, would refer only to the objective side.

From the standpoint of *Identitätsphilosophie*, on the other hand, that interpretation remains implausible even when we treat the objective side of nature as a 'subject-object' in its own right. A strict 'identity philosophy' demands that the subject-object identity be present on both sides. The being that is present in Hegel's 'transcendental intuition' can therefore be no other than the absolute identity itself, that is, the identity that unites the subjective subject-object with the objective subject-object (cp. GW 4.77/DE 173 f.). For otherwise neither Hegel's distinction between a 'positive' and a 'negative' side of knowledge nor his idea that intuition is able to "complement the one-sidedness of the work of reflection" (GW 4.29/DE 112) would make any sense. If it is really to be a path to *knowledge*, the *via negationis* of reflection clearly has to have some positive point of reference; in aiming at absolute identity, the role of intuition is to keep that positive referent in view. In other words, despite the centrality of reflection for Hegel's epistemology, his concept of speculation remains dependent on intuition in crucial respects. For it is intuition alone that secures speculation's *ontological* relation to the absolute that "lies at the basis of reflection" (GW 4.23/DE 103). But with this, Hegel has landed himself once and for all in an untenable position.

1.8. FROM THE ABSOLUTE AS PRESUPPOSITION TO THE ABSOLUTE AS RESULT: PRODUCTIVE PROBLEMS IN HEGEL'S FIRST SYSTEM PROGRAM

In Hegel's very first system program we can already identify numerous problems that he will never be able fully to put to rest. Not least among them is his representation of other philosophical positions; here, as in future works, Hegel's treatment of them is less a source of 'objective' information than a source of insight into Hegel's own position, provided, that is, we consider the surrounding debates that inform it. In moving on now to consider one final cluster of problems, we are about to see a further case in point: it has to do with the *immanent* problem that, all else aside, Hegel's first system program *fails to live up to its own standard*—hence his later reworking of it.

Hegel is convinced of two things. First, philosophy has to take the form of a system; second, by virtue of this form it has to represent the structure of actual reality as a whole and render it intelligible. That philosophy has a vital interest in reality is beyond question for Hegel, and neither does he doubt that such interest is best promoted by philosophy in the form of a system. Indeed, the two points are intimately connected: the holism of the system corresponds directly to Hegel's holistic conception of reality. His conception of philosophy is based on this assumption, which as such is naturally open to debate. But Hegel has immunized himself against debate from the very outset. It is, so to speak, a 'natural' feature of his holistic conception that it integrates objections or alternative viewpoints by showing them to rely on a false or inadequate understanding of reality, which, in the best of cases, is susceptible to therapy. From this perspective, the *Phenomenology of Spirit* represents a particularly elaborate case of mass therapy.

This prospective glance toward the *Phenomenology* also brings us closer to what is at issue here: the epistemic tools Hegel presents in the *Difference* essay cannot bear out the holism that is a basic, unrevisable assumption of his philosophical position. We are confronted from the outset with the basic problem that the absolute is no more than an opaque presupposition, be it as the demand for an unselfsparing 'plunge' into philosophy, be it as the complementary notion of a 'need for philosophy'. Given his commitment to Spinozism-cum-*Lebensphilosophie*, perhaps Hegel himself saw no particular problem here, as his 'absolute' is nothing other than reality itself, that is, a 'representation' with no determinate reference whatsoever, and most especially no reference to a transcendent being. However he saw it, that changes nothing in the fact that it is an unexamined and to that extent dogmatic posit. This difficulty gives rise to a further one: Hegel fails to render the entrance or transition to philosophy plausible in the form of either a demand or a need. He will later try to remedy the situation by exploring a variety of different types of introduction (e.g., in the *Phenomenology* and the *Science of Logic*), but the real problem lies elsewhere, in Hegel's concept of speculative knowledge.

As the identity of intuition and reflection, this type of knowledge is supposed to mediate between the absolute and its exposition in the system. In point of fact, however, Hegel once again has recourse to a mere assertion. He asserts an identity comprising two wholly distinct sides of knowledge. Bold and simple: reflection is negatively geared toward difference, intuition is positively geared toward unity. Even if the construct of their identity were sound, it would still not map onto what Hegel means by 'the absolute', namely the 'identity of identity and non-identity'. Ever since Hegel coined it in Frankfurt, this phrase never meant simply the piecing together of two opposing sides, but the unifying nexus of an internally self-differentiating whole.

Hegel's failure, in the *Difference* essay, to develop an epistemology equal to the task of representing this unifying nexus has far-reaching consequences. To begin with, the negativism of reflection and the need for a compensating intuition result in a situation in which intuition is able to capture only 'one-half' of the absolute: intuition covers as it were the *hen*-part of the *hen-kai-pan* formula. Otherwise it would be impossible to understand Hegel's initially jarring suggestion of an alliance between speculation and the 'common sense of mankind' which, in the guise of 'faith' (GW 4, 21/DE

100), he apparently wants to link with Jacobi and whose resistance to speculation he is trying here to overcome. If the 'common sense of mankind' were able to grasp the negativity of speculation in its "full scope", writes Hegel, "it would not believe it to be its enemy; for speculation, in its highest synthesis of the conscious and unconscious, also demands the annihilation of consciousness itself, and reason thereby drowns its reflection and knowledge of the absolute identity and indeed itself in its own abyss, and in this night of mere reflection and the calculating understanding, in this night that is the noonday of life, the two can meet" (GW 4.23/DE 103). Quite apart from the question of whether such a prospect is likely to win over the 'common under-standing', here again the absolute is only presupposed, and what is more, its pres-ence extinguishes every difference whatsoever, including that of consciousness itself. Structurally, this finding mirrors the 'satisfaction' Hegel later mentions and which is supposedly to be found "in the principle of absolute identity" (GW 4.30/DE 112). He seems to concede that this position is situated at the threshold of 'enthusiasm', but when he later comes to distance himself from it, it is not in the form of self-criticism, but as an implicit criticism of Schelling: "to pass off its absolute as the night in which, as the saying goes, all cows are black, that is the very naïveté of emptiness of knowl-edge" (PS 9.17/¶16).

Conversely, the negativism of reflection also frustrates hopes of achieving system-atic disclosure of the *pan*-part of the *hen-kai-pan* formula. Here we see the collision of two very different motives within Hegel's system program. As to his concern with actual reality in the totality of its phenomena, there can be no doubt. At the same time, how-ever, reflection must not allow the differences it posits to crystalize into rigid, 'positive' determinations. Accordingly, its operations are to be tolerated only insofar as they also promise their own 'annihilation'. As a consequence, Hegel is led to engage in strident polemics against philosophical engagement with the 'finite'. As we have already men-tioned in passing, in *Faith and Knowledge* Hegel even goes so far as to reject Jacobi's perfectly cogent analysis of finitude in Spinoza's system as a falsification, baselessly asserting that Spinoza held the finite world to be a mere product of the 'imagination' (GW 4.352 ff./FK 104 ff.).

Interestingly, Hegel will stick to this 'acosmist' misreading of Spinoza until the end, making it a permanent feature of his official account of Spinoza's philosophy.[20] Given everything we have said, it is impossible to believe that he himself was committed to the adequacy of such an account.[21] What is really at issue in the charge of acosmism is Hegel's response to weaknesses in his own earlier epistemology, whose reworking will ultimately bear fruit in the Preface to the *Phenomenology*. While retaining the motives of his first system program, Hegel will seek to resolve all its immanent problems by

[20] Morfino, "Spinoza in 'Glauben und Wissen.'"
[21] Hegel's use of Spinoza's concept of substance in the transition from the Logic of Essence to the Logic of the Concept reveals a more sophisticated and robust view of Spinoza's philosophy that belies the simplicity of Hegel's official version: cp. Sandkaulen, "Ontologie der Substanz."

reinterpreting his holism. Instead of basing his system on the presupposition of a substantial absolute, the absolute must be understood as a *result* (PS 9.19/¶20): namely, as the result of a cognitive process that consists in no more than an explication of the whole in its 'becoming' and which develops all the resources it requires through successive applications of determinate negation. In the name of the understanding, the 'tremendous power of the negative' (GW 9.27/¶32) now comes to function as the internal engine of the dialectical progression. The content of 'the absolute' thereby coincides with the progressively richer determinations generated by the system over the course of the exposition. Ontology and epistemology are one. The merging of these two dimensions is what Hegel means when he talks of grasping substance as subject.

Viewing the program of the *Phenomenology* and its continuation in the *Science of Logic* from the vantage point of Hegel's prelude to the *Difference* essay opens the way to a proper assessment of Hegelian philosophy. The background in Kant is not a sufficient basis for understanding his philosophical project. Hegel's holism in particular remains permanently indebted to the Jacobi-Spinoza constellation. Yet we need not fear a metaphysics haunted by a 'cosmic spirit'. Such was never the meaning of 'the absolute'. The decisive innovation in Hegel's later thought is that he ceases to locate the absolute at the beginning of philosophy, as its origin or principle: the failure of his first system program demonstrated the impossibility of giving an epistemologically satisfying account of the absolute thus conceived. Hegel's response was to eradicate, as far as he was able, every trace of such a conception, replacing it with the innovative conception of the absolute as result. What we want to know about the world as a whole under the conditions of modernity can only be disclosed in the progressive unfolding of knowledge itself. The sum of such knowledge is 'the absolute'. Whether this absolute really comprehends everything or whether it only comprehends what is compatible with holism is a question we may well still pose, despite now knowing Hegel's answer to it, or rather precisely because we do know it.

Works Cited

Primary Texts

Fichte, Johann Gottlieb. *Grundlage der gesamten Wissenschaftslehre*. In *Fichtes Werke*, edited by Immanuel Hermann Fichte, vol. 1, 83–328. Berlin: De Gruyter, 1971.

Hegel, Georg Wilhelm Friedrich. *Differenz des Fichte'schen und Schelling'schen Systems der Philosophie* [DE]. In *GW*, vol. 4, 1–92; *The Difference between Fichte's and Schelling's System of Philosophy*, translated by Henry S. Harris and Walter Cerf. Albany: State University of New York Press, 1977.

Hegel, Georg Wilhelm Friedrich. *Enzyklopädie der philosophischen Wissenschaften (1830)*. In GW, vol. 11; *Encyclopedia of the Philosophical Sciences in Basic Outline, Part 1, Science of Logic*, translated by Klaus Brinkmann and Daniel Dahlstrom. Cambridge University Press, 2010.

Hegel, Georg Wilhelm Friedrich. *Frühe Schriften II*. GW, vol. 2, edited by Walter von Jaeschke, 2014.

Hegel, Georg Wilhelm Friedrich. *Gesammelte Werke* [GW], edited by the Academy of Sciences of Rhineland-Westphalia, in cooperation with the Deutsche Forschungsgemeinschaft. Hamburg: Meiner, 1968–.

Hegel, Georg Wilhelm Friedrich. *Glauben und Wissen*. In GW, vol. 4, 313–414; *Faith and Knowledge* [FK], translated by Henry S. Harris and Walter Cerf. Albany: State University of New York Press, 1977.

Hegel, Georg Wilhelm Friedrich. *Phänomenologie des Geistes*. In *GW*, vol. 9; *Phenomenology of Spirit* [PS], translated by A. V. Miller. Oxford: Oxford University Press, 1977.

Hoffmeister, Johannes, ed. *Briefe von und an Hegel*. 4 vols. Hamburg: Meiner, 1952–1981.

Jacobi, Friedrich Heinrich. *Werke. Gesamtausgabe* [JW], edited by Klaus Hammacher and Walter Jaeschke. Hamburg: Meiner, 1998–.

Jacobi, Friedrich Heinrich. *Schriften zum Spinozastreit*. In JW, vol. 1,1; *Main Philosophical Writings and the Novel Allwill*. Paperback edition with new preface, translated and edited by George di Giovanni. Montréal; Kingston: McGill-Queen's University Press, 2009.

Jacobi, Friedrich Heinrich. *Schriften zum transzendentalen Idealismus*. In JW, vol. 2,1; *Main Philosophical Writings and the Novel Allwill*, translated and edited by George di Giovanni. Montréal; Kingston: McGill-Queen's University Press, 2009.

Kant, Immanuel. *Critique of Pure Reason*, translated by Norman Kemp Smith, 2nd ed. New York: Palgrave MacMillan, 2003.

Schelling, Friedrich Wilhelm Joseph. *Darstellung meines Systems der Philosophie*. In SW, vol. 4, 105–212. Stuttgart, Augsburg: Cotta, 1856–1861.

Schelling, Friedrich Wilhelm Joseph. *Philosophische Briefe über Dogmatismus und Kritizismus*. In SW, vol. 1, 281–341. Stuttgart, Augsburg: Cotta, 1856–1861.

Schelling, Friedrich Wilhelm Joseph. *Sämmtliche Werke* [SW], edited by Karl Friedrich August Schelling. Stuttgart, Augsburg: Cotta, 1856–1861.

Schelling, Friedrich Wilhelm Joseph. *System des transzendentalen Idealismus*. In SW, vol. 3, 329–634. Stuttgart, Augsburg: Cotta, 1856–1861.

Schelling, Friedrich Wilhelm Joseph. *Über den wahren Begriff der Naturphilosophie*. In SW, vol. 4, 79–103. Stuttgart, Augsburg: Cotta, 1856–1861.

Spinoza, Baruch de. *Collected Works*, edited and translated by Edwin Curley. Vol. 1. Princeton, NJ: Princeton University Press, 1988.

Secondary Literature

Bondeli, Martin. "The Jena Years: 1801–6," in *Bloomsbury Companion to Hegel*, edited by Allegra de Laurentiis and Jeffrey Edwards. London: Bloomsbury, 2013, 21–38.

Bubner, Rüdiger, ed. *Deutscher Idealismus*. Geschichte der Philosophie in Text und Darstellung 6. Stuttgart: Reclam, 1983.

Düsing, Klaus. "Die Entstehung des spekulativen Idealismus. Schellings und Hegels Wandlungen zwischen 1800 und 1801," in *Transzendentalphilosophie und Spekulation. Der Streit um die Gestalt einer ersten Philosophie (1799–1807)*, edited by Walter Jaeschke. Hamburg: Meiner, 1993, 144–163.

Düsing, Klaus. "Idealistische Substanzmetaphysik. Probleme der Systementwicklung bei Schelling und Hegel in Jena," in *Hegel in Jena*, edited by Dieter Henrich and Klaus Düsing. Bonn: Bouvier, 1980, 25–44.

Düsing, Klaus. "Spekulation und Reflexion. Zur Zusammenarbeit Schellings und Hegels in Jena." *Hegel-Studien* 5 (1969): 95–128.

Förster, Eckhart. *The Twenty-Five Years of Philosophy: A Systematic Reconstruction*, translated by Brady Bowman. Cambridge, MA: Harvard University Press, 2012.

Harris, Henry S. *Hegel's Development: Night Thoughts (Jena 1801–1806)*. Oxford: Clarendon, 1983.

Harris, Henry S. "Introduction to the Difference Essay," in *The Difference between Fichte's and Schelling's System of Philosophy*, edited by Henry S. Harris. Albany: State University of New York Press, 1977, 1–75.

Henrich, Dieter, and Klaus Düsing, eds. *Hegel in Jena*. Bonn: Bouvier, 1980.

Hindrichs, Gunnar. "Spinozismus, Antispinozismus und die Entstehung der Hegelschen Dialektik," in *Kontexte—Spinoza und die Geschichte der Philosophie*, edited by Henryk Pisarek und Manfred Walther. Acta Universitatis Wratislaviensis 2279. Wroclaw: Wydawnictwo Uniwersytetu Wroclawskiego, 2001, 173–202.

Horstmann, Rolf-Peter. "Den Verstand zur Vernunft bringen? Hegels Auseinandersetzung mit Kant in der Differenzschrift," in *Das Interesse des Denkens. Hegel aus heutiger Sicht*, edited by Wolfgang Welsch and Klaus Vieweg. München: Fink, 2003, 89–108.

Jaeschke, Walter. *Hegel-Handbuch. Leben—Werk—Schule*. Stuttgart: Metzler, 2003.

Jaeschke, Walter, and Andreas Arndt. *Die Klassische Deutsche Philosophie nach Kant. Systeme der reinen Vernunft und ihre Kritik 1785–1845*. München: Beck, 2012.

Morfino, Vittorio. "Spinoza in 'Glauben und Wissen,'" in *Glauben und Wissen. Dritter Teil*, edited by Andreas Arndt, Karol Bal, and Henning Ottmann. Hegel-Jahrbuch 2005. Berlin: Akademie Verlag, 2005, 140–145.

Rohs, Peter. *Johann Gottlieb Fichte*. München: Beck, 1991.

Sandkaulen, Birgit. *Ausgang vom Unbedingten. Über den Anfang in der Philosophie Schellings*. Göttingen: Vandenhoeck & Ruprecht, 1990.

Sandkaulen, Birgit. "Das Nichtige in seiner ganzen Länge und Breite. Hegels Kritik der Reflexionsphilosophie," in *Glauben und Wissen. Zweiter Teil*, edited by Andreas Arndt, Karol Bal, and Henning Ottmann. Hegel-Jahrbuch 2004. Berlin: Akademie-Verlag, 2004, 165–173.

Sandkaulen, Birgit. "Die Ontologie der Substanz, der Begriff der Subjektivität und die Faktizität des Einzelnen. Hegels reflexionslogische 'Widerlegung' der Spinozanischen Metaphysik." *Internationales Jahrbuch des Deutschen Idealismus/International Yearbook of German Idealism* 5 (2008), 235–275.

Sandkaulen, Birgit. "Dritte Stellung des Gedankens zur Objektivität: Das unmittelbare Wissen," in *G. W. F. Hegel, Der "Vorbegriff" zur Wissenschaft der Logik in der Enzyklopädie von 1830*, edited by Alfred Denker, Annette Sell, and Holger Zaborowski. Freiburg: Alber, 2010, 166–191.

Sandkaulen, Birgit. *Grund und Ursache. Die Vernunftkritik Jacobis*. München: Fink, 2000.

Sandkaulen, Birgit. "Was heißt Idealismus? Natur- und Transzendentalphilosophie im Übergang zur Identitätsphilosophie: Schellings Systemskizze vom 19.11.1800," in *Grundlegung und Kritik. Der Briefwechsel zwischen Schelling und Fichte 1794–1802*, edited by Jörg Jantzen, Thomas Kisser, and Hartmut Traub. Fichte-Studien 25. Leiden: Brill, 2005, 57–69.

Schäfer, Rainer. *Die Dialektik und ihre besonderen Formen in Hegels Logik— Entwicklungsgeschichte und systematische Untersuchung*. Hegel-Studien Beiheft 45. Hamburg: Meiner, 2001.

Siep, Ludwig. *Der Weg der Phänomenologie des Geistes. Ein einführender Kommentar zu Hegels "Differenzschrift" und "Phänomenologie des Geistes."* Frankfurt am Main: Suhrkamp, 2000. Translated by Daniel Smyth as *Hegel's Phenomenology of Spirit.* Cambridge: Cambridge University Press, 2014.

Taylor, Charles. *Hegel.* Cambridge: Cambridge University Press, 1975.

Vieweg, Klaus, and Brady Bowman, eds. *Gegen das "Unphilosophische Unwesen." Das Kritische Journal der Philosophie von Schelling und Hegel.* Würzburg: Königshausen & Neumann, 2002.

CHAPTER 2

HEGEL'S JENA PRACTICAL PHILOSOPHY

MICHAEL NANCE

2.1. INTRODUCTION

DURING the years between Hegel's arrival at the University of Jena in 1801 and the publication of his *Phenomenology of Spirit* in 1807, Hegel developed a distinctive conception of the central problem that must be addressed by modern social and political philosophy.[1] According to Hegel's conception, modern social and political philosophy must unify two seemingly disparate ideals: first, the classical Greek ideal of a tightly connected political community, the polis, grounded in a robust and widely shared public ethos; and second, the modern liberal ideal of society as composed of autonomous, reflective individuals with subjective rights and freedoms that are exercised in a protected private sphere. The classical Greek and modern liberal ideals appear to be incompatible, for on Hegel's picture, ancient Greek societies were able to achieve their ideal of social unity only at the cost of the free expression of individuality that is so central to modern liberal societies. Modern liberal individualism, by contrast, leads to 'atomism' (i.e., the detachment of individuals from their communities, and the concomitant privatization of public life). Hegel's project in his mature social and political philosophy is the ambitious one of showing that the classical ideal of community and the modern ideal of individual rights and freedoms can be synthesized into a coherent picture of a stable, just society that prevents atomism and alienation while promoting both the subjective freedom and the communal solidarity of its members.

[1] For helpful feedback on earlier drafts of this paper, I am grateful to Dean Moyar, Paul Franks, Steve Yalowitz, and Reed Winegar. For general discussion of Hegel's Jena thought, I thank the students in my upper-level courses at UMBC during Fall 2014 and Fall 2015, from whom I learned a great deal. For funding and research support, I thank the Dresher Center for the Humanities and the CAHSS Dean's Office at UMBC.

Hegel worked out this conception of the proper task of social and political philosophy only gradually during his formative years at Jena. During these years, he also developed a number of strikingly original concepts that would prove crucial to his eventual synthesis of the two ideals. Hegel developed these conceptual tools primarily in highly schematic drafts and lecture manuscripts that he did not publish during his lifetime.[2] These manuscripts present an enormous challenge to scholars of Hegel's Jena philosophy, who must attempt to piece together a coherent view out of fragmentary and frequently cryptic materials. Yet despite this difficulty, Hegel's Jena practical philosophy has been an important influence on twentieth- and twenty-first-century social and political philosophy in the continental European tradition. The two most significant contemporary figures to draw on Hegel's Jena practical philosophy are Axel Honneth and Ludwig Siep.[3] For Honneth, Siep, and a subsequent generation of scholars influenced by their work, it is the young Hegel's use of the concept of *recognition* (*Anerkennung*) that provides the key to his Jena practical philosophy and its continuing relevance.

My primary aim, which occupies most of this chapter, is to present an overview of the development of Hegel's social and political philosophy during the Jena period prior to the publication of the *Phenomenology*. I do so by discussing the evolution of Hegel's views across four texts: the 1802 essay "On the Scientific Ways of Treating Natural Law" (henceforth *NL*); the unpublished manuscript that has come to be known as the "System of Ethical Life" (*SEL*) (1802/1803); and the first (1803/1804) and third (1805/1806) of the three unpublished manuscripts collectively referred to by scholars as the Jena System Drafts (*Jena I* and *Jena III*).[4] In discussing the development of Hegel's views, I focus on Hegel's evolving attitude toward J. G. Fichte's practical philosophy, which Hegel takes as an exemplar of the modern liberal focus on individual rights and freedoms. I distinguish three roles played by Fichtean positions in Hegel's Jena practical philosophy. In *NL*, Fichtean practical philosophy plays no positive role at all in Hegel's presentation of his own views; rather, Fichte provides a case study in how *not* to do practical philosophy. In the subsequent Jena texts, though, Fichtean positions take on one or both of two positive functions: first, Fichtean views serve as stages in a genetic history of human

---

[2] On the Jena System Drafts, see Horstmann, "Probleme der Wandlung in Hegels Jenaer Systemkonzeption," and Harris, *Hegel's Development*.

[3] Honneth, *The Struggle for Recognition* (henceforth *SR*); and, Siep, *Anerkennung als Prinzip der Praktischen Philosophie* (henceforth *AaP*).

[4] I use the following conventions in citing Hegel and Fichte. Citations of Hegel's *NL* include first a page reference to the Suhrkamp German edition, abbreviated "*NR*," and then a page reference to Nisbet's translation, abbreviated "*NL*." For Hegel's *Differenzschrift* I use the abbreviation "*DS*" and then cite first the German Suhrkamp edition and then Harris and Cerf's translation. Citations of Hegel's *Faith and Knowledge* refer first to the German Suhrkamp edition, abbreviated *GW*, and then to Harris and Cerf's translation, abbreviated *FK*. Citations of Hegel's *SEL* refer first to Meist's German edition, abbreviated "*SdS*," and then to Harris and Knox's translation, abbreviated "*SEL*." Citations of the first Jena System Draft refer first to the volume and page number of Hegel's *Gesammelte Werke* (*GW*) and then to Harris and Knox's translation (*Jena I*). Citations of the third Jena System Draft refer first to the volume and page number of Hegel's *Gesammelte Werke* (*GW*) and then to Rauch's translation (*Jena III*), which I modify at several points. Citations of Fichte refer first to the volume and page number of the German edition of Fichte's *Werke* edited by I.H. Fichte, and then to the relevant English translation.

consciousness that ultimately leads to Hegel's own view of the highest form of human community, which he calls ethical life (*Sittlichkeit*); second, Fichtean views are incorporated into the structure of ethical life itself, especially in Hegel's account of *spirit* (*Geist*).

The discussion will be divided up as follows. Section 2.2 lays the groundwork for the rest of the chapter by providing some systematic background and distinguishing between two Statements of Hegel's synthetic project in practical philosophy. The two Statements describe Hegel's culminating understanding of his project in practical philosophy in his final years in Jena, as expressed in *Jena III*. I use these two Statements in connection with Hegel's engagement with Fichte to structure my analysis of each Jena text. Section 2.3 discusses *NL*, section 2.4 discusses *SEL*, and section 2.5 discusses the two Jena System Drafts. I argue for a progressive narrative: each text improves upon the previous one, where 'improvement' is evaluated in terms of Hegel's ability to formulate and carry out the project described by the two Statements.[5] Section 2.6 briefly discusses the legacy of Hegel's Jena practical philosophy for contemporary debates.

2.2. PRELIMINARIES: TWO STATEMENTS OF HEGEL'S PROJECT

Consider the following two formulations of Hegel's central project in practical philosophy:

> *Practical Statement*: Hegel's central project in practical philosophy is to synthesize classical communitarian and modern individualistic conceptions of freedom into a coherent social ideal of ethical life (*Sittlichkeit*).
> *Metaphysical Statement*: Hegel's central project in practical philosophy is to show that ethical life exemplifies the structure of the absolute by integrating individuality, the standpoint of *reflection*, into the social whole, which is known via *speculation*.

To reiterate, these Statements describe Hegel's conception of his project at the *end* of the Jena period. In the earlier Jena texts (especially *NL* and *SEL*), Hegel is less concerned with integrating the reflective standpoint of modern individualism into ethical life. Instead, Hegel *rejects* modern individualistic ideals in favor of a return to classical communitarianism. However, as a result of both practical and metaphysical pressures described in the following, by the later Jena years Hegel arrives at the synthetic conception of his project described by the two Statements.

I call the first Statement 'Practical' because the project is to synthesize two different historical forms of social life, which involve two different conceptions of freedom. The second Statement is 'Metaphysical' because (1) it states a problem of social ontology, and

---

[5] For a contrasting narrative that emphasizes the continuity of Hegel's project across these texts, see Siep, *AaP*, 210–212.

(2) it relies centrally on Hegel's metaphysical idea of the 'absolute'. Ultimately, for Hegel, these Statements are two expressions of one underlying project that can be viewed practically or metaphysically. In the rest of this section, I explain the relation between the two Statements.

First, though, I need briefly to explain Hegel's idea of 'ethical life' (*Sittlichkeit*), which is referred to in both Statements. 'Ethical life' refers to the constellation of institutions, values, customs, and norms that make up a society. In Hegel's *PR* (1820), the term 'ethical life' is reserved for the most developed form of modern human society—Hegel's social ideal. But in the Jena texts, Hegel distinguishes between what I will call 'natural' and 'absolute' ethical life, where only the latter term refers to Hegel's social ideal.[6] Natural ethical life corresponds to what social contract theorists call the 'state of nature' (i.e., the pre-political [but not pre-social] condition of human beings). Natural ethical life is quite different from absolute ethical life, which Hegel associates during the Jena period with classical Greek society. Absolute ethical life refers to the social life of a people within the polis that displays the structure of the absolute. To understand Hegel's idea of absolute ethical life, we thus need to understand Hegel's idea of the absolute, to which I now turn.

The Metaphysical Statement refers to two difficult Hegelian ideas: first, the idea of the 'absolute'; and second, the distinction between 'reflection' and 'speculation'. The 'absolute' in early nineteenth-century German philosophy is a generic term for the metaphysically fundamental and self-sufficient whole (think here of Spinoza's conception of God)—the absolute is that upon which all things depend, but the absolute depends upon nothing outside of itself.[7] Furthermore, a theory of the absolute is supposed to overcome the various dualisms of Kant's philosophy—freedom versus nature, subject versus object, and so on—by providing these dualisms with a unitary metaphysical ground.[8] Now, the German Idealists are acutely aware that a metaphysical system centered on the absolute threatens a specific form of *nihilism*: the annihilation of finite, free subjectivity. For if the absolute is metaphysically fundamental, then the apparent independent existence of metaphysically substantial finite objects and subjects—the common-sense world of human life—may come to seem merely illusory.[9] The fundamentality of the absolute threatens individuality with unreality and insignificance. In response to this

---

[6]   I am stipulating definitions of 'natural' and 'absolute' ethical life. Hegel's terminology across the Jena texts is inconsistent.

[7]   Cf. Sandkaulen, Chapter 1 of this volume. See also Beiser, *Hegel*, pp. 57–61; Chapter 2 of P. Franks, *All or Nothing*; D. Nassar, *The Romantic Absolute*. Hegel's *Differenz des Fichteschen und Schellingschen Systems der Philosophie* (henceforth *DS*) is replete with discussions of the absolute.

[8]   See Hegel, *DS* 47–48/115. Cf. P. Guyer, "Absolute Idealism and the Rejection of Kantian Dualism."

[9]   Thanks to Paul Franks for pushing me to clarify this point. The historical source for the nihilism problem is F. H. Jacobi, who associates the kind of nihilism I just described with Spinoza. See, e.g., Jacobi, *Concerning the Doctrine of Spinoza*, pp. 189–190, in Jacobi, *The Main Philosophical Writings*. See Franks, *All or Nothing*, pp. 194–195, for discussion. Also relevant is Schelling's discussion of Spinoza and the threat of nihilism in his 1795 *Philosophical Letters on Dogmatism and Criticism*, in *The Unconditional in Human Knowledge: Four Early Essays 1794–6*, translation and commentary by F. Marti (Lewisburg: Bucknell University Press, 1980).

threat, by the end of the Jena period Hegel seeks to find a way to *incorporate* finite objects and finite subjects into the absolute as positive 'moments'.

The epistemological distinction between the standpoints of 'reflection' and 'speculation' is closely related to the metaphysical distinction between finite things and the absolute.[10] The standpoint of reflection is the standpoint of our ordinary conceptual engagement with finite objects. We make determinate judgments about objects by using concepts to distinguish and relate items within the manifold of experience. Reflection, which Hegel associates with Kant's conception of the 'understanding' (*Verstand*) and Fichte's account of the 'self-positing I', thus relies on *differentiation* or *negation* as its chief cognitive tool. 'Speculation', by contrast, is the properly *philosophical* standpoint, from which the absolute is 'intuited' as a self-sufficient whole.[11]

For Hegel, modern liberalism is a philosophy of reflection because of its emphasis on differences between, and conflicts among, individual subjects. On the modern approach, exemplified by the social contract tradition and Adam Smith, the interests of independent individual agents are regarded as metaphysically and methodologically fundamental. This feature of modern social and political theory reflects what Hegel regarded as the modern tendency towards *atomism*, the breakdown of community attachments in favor of the pursuit of private interests. By contrast, Hegel approved of what he regarded as the methodological holism of classical political philosophy, which, as we will see in section 2.3, started from the standpoint of speculation with an 'intuition' of the 'people' as 'absolute'.[12] Hegel holds that this feature of classical political thought reflects the metaphysical nature of ancient Greek political community. On Hegel's view, the ancient polis exemplified the structure of the absolute because it possessed a kind of organic self-sufficiency that made it the 'substance' upon which individual citizens depended. The polis instantiates the asymmetrical metaphysical dependence relations characteristic of the absolute—specific individuals depend on the polis, but the polis does not depend upon specific individuals (cf. *GW* 7, 264/*Jena III* 161). For the polis possesses the capacity to reproduce itself by creating new citizens with the ethos necessary for the community's survival. Thus the polis is more self-sufficient and metaphysically 'substantial' than its individual members. Such an account reverses the order of explanation in comparison with the individualist social theories of Hobbes and Smith.

Although Hegel has great admiration for classical ethical life, he comes to realize during the Jena years that the practical result of the classical prioritization of the collective life of the polis is the nullification of individuality, a particular manifestation of the general threat of nihilism. The attempt to appeal to classical ideals to avoid modern atomism

---

[10] *DS* 25–35/94–103. Cf. Sandkaulen, Chapter 1 of this volume.

[11] See Schelling's discussion of 'intellectual intuition' in *Further Presentations*, pp. 209–213; and *DS* 41–43/109–111 and *DS* 114–115/173–174.

[12] Cf. my discussion of Hegel and Aristotle in §2.3. Hegel's earliest motivation for his systematic philosophy was his *practical* concern with freedom as the overcoming of alienation, which makes it more intelligible why Hegel would regard an ideal social and political community as a paradigm of his metaphysics of the absolute. For discussion, see Sandkaulen, Chapter 1 of this volume, and D. Henrich, "Hegels Grundoperation," pp. 208–211.

thus seems to lead directly to nihilism. Hegel's project, captured in the two Statements, is to argue for a form of community strong enough to avoid modern atomism without succumbing to the nihilism latent in classical ethical life. For Hegel, the practical project of unifying modern and ancient political ideals (see the Practical Statement) thus turns out to be an instance of his more general metaphysical project of incorporating the world of finite objects cognized through reflection into the speculatively understood, metaphysically fundamental absolute (see the Metaphysical Statement). As Hegel gradually comes to understand his project in these terms, he develops novel conceptual tools for carrying out the project. In the rest of this chapter, I describe this development.

2.3. NATURAL LAW ESSAY

Hegel's primary aim in his 1802 *NL* is polemical: he criticizes 'empirical' (Hobbes and Locke) and 'formal' (Kant and Fichte) approaches to natural law (*Naturrecht*).[13] Hegel argues that both empirical and formal theories of natural law are mere philosophies of the understanding, which use reflection to set up false conceptions of the absolute.[14] For Hegel, Kant and Fichte mistakenly posit an absolute division between the natural world we inhabit and the requirements of practical reason with respect to achieving moral ends.[15] In their theories, agents strive endlessly to realize their freedom in the empirical world, but no matter how much progress is made, the complete realization of freedom always remains a merely regulative ideal.[16] From the standpoint of Hegel's speculative conception of the absolute, such a dualism of reflection that separates the natural and the normative must be rejected.

The positive view that Hegel sketches at the end of *NL* holds that the realization of freedom should be regarded not as something projected indefinitely into the future, but rather as fully present in the concrete shape of the classical polis, which as we have seen represents the true structure of the absolute. To understand this conception of freedom, it will be helpful first to consider a conception of freedom that Hegel *rejects*. Hegel writes, "That view of freedom which regards it as a choice between opposite determinacies (so that if +A and –A are given, freedom consists in determining oneself *either* as +A *or* as –A, and is completely tied to this *either-or*) must be utterly rejected" (*NR* 476–477/*NL* 136).[17] It is clear that Hegel is rejecting our ordinary understanding of political freedom as the freedom to choose for oneself from among several possible options. True

---

[13] *NL* was published in Schelling and Hegel's *Kritisches Journal* in 1802. On the *Journal*, see "Skepticism, Dogmatism and Speculation in the Critical Journal" by Harris, esp. pp. 252–253.

[14] *NR* 455–458/*NL* 119–121.

[15] *NR* 468–469/*NL* 130. Cf. Kant's "Introduction" to *Critique of the Power of Judgment*.

[16] Cf. Fichte's discussion at IV: 130–131, *SE* 125.

[17] Cf. Pippin, *Hegel's Practical Philosophy*, pp. 38–39; and Clarke, "Hegel's Critique of Fichte in the 1802/03 Essay on Natural Right," pp. 217–221.

freedom, for Hegel, "is the direct opposite of this [empirical freedom]: nothing is external to it, so that no coercion is possible for it" (*NR* 477/*NL* 137).[18]

The clue to understanding Hegel's claim lies in conceiving of his project in *NL* as essentially neo-Aristotelian. Hegel thinks that Kant and Fichte set up a one-sided definition of freedom as a subject's right to assert her individuality in contrast to the social whole. Their theories of right must then resort to coercive force to realign recalcitrant individual wills with the general or universal will, which wills the common good.[19] Hegel's solution to the problem of externality that characterizes Kant's and Fichte's theories of right is simply to 'nullify' their starting point, the modern conception of the free subject.[20] Hegel's thesis about the nullity of the individual subject is his interpretation of Aristotle's claim that "the state is by nature clearly prior to the family and to the individual, since the whole is of necessity prior to the part."[21] According to Hegel, the individual's 'soul' is supposed to be identical with the "pure spirit of a people."[22] This explains why, in a rather Spartan image, Hegel claims in *NL* that freedom shows itself as 'courage', or the willingness to face death on behalf of one's country.[23] Death on behalf of the social whole is the most extreme outward manifestation of the nullification of individuality.

Hegel is not so naïve as to hold that modern individualism can be entirely suppressed. Yet in *NL* he is unable to conceive of the pursuit of private interests, protected by individual rights, that characterizes modern subjectivity as a form of freedom worth preserving. Thus, in his remarks on modern market society, which Hegel associates with the formal conception of private rights advocated by Kant and Fichte (*NR* 482–495/*NL* 141–151), Hegel grudgingly acknowledges its necessity. But he follows Plato in relegating market society to an 'unfree estate' that must be regarded 'negatively' by ethical life (*NR* 491–492, 487/*NL* 148–149, 145). As Hegel himself later comes to realize, this rejection of modern individualism threatens to produce nihilism. Relatedly, the bifurcation of ethical life into negatively related estates threatens to undermine the metaphysical holism that Hegel advocates in his doctrine of the absolute. Hegel has thus clearly not yet arrived at the understanding of his project captured by the two Statements. Practically, there is no *positive* place for modern subjectivity in the social ideal of *NL*. Metaphysically, *NL* embraces precisely the kind of annihilation of finite subjectivity that Hegel later makes it his project to avoid.

---

[18] See also *NR* 476/*NL* 136: "a freedom for which something is genuinely external and alien is not freedom at all."

[19] *NR* 471–472/*NL* 132.

[20] Cf. Hegel, *GW* 382/*FK* 141.

[21] Aristotle, *Politics* I.2, 1253a19–20. Hegel discusses this passage at *NR* 505/*NL* 159–160.

[22] See Ilting, "Hegels Auseinandersetzung mit der Aristotelischen Politik"; Manfred Riedel, *Between Tradition and Revolution*, p. 85; and Wildt, *Autonomie und Anerkennung*, pp. 312–313.

[23] Hegel explicitly contrasts the 'objective' and 'holy' aspects of the 'country, people, and laws' of the Spartans with 'petty subjectivity' in his Jacobi-critique in *Faith and Knowledge*. See *GW* 386/*FK* 145–146.

2.4. SYSTEM OF ETHICAL LIFE

Hegel was evidently dissatisfied with *NL*, for he almost immediately set about rethinking the foundations of his practical philosophy in a manuscript that has come to be known as the "System of Ethical Life."[24] Hegel's work on *SEL* overlapped with his work on *NL*, and the two texts argue for a similar neo-Aristotelian view of absolute ethical life. But the argumentative method of *SEL* is quite different from that of *NL*. In *SEL*, Hegel aims to show that his conception of ethical life can be seen as the *outcome* of a social-developmental process. I will argue that descriptions of different forms of Fichtean practical subjectivity feature prominently as developmental stages in parts one and two of the manuscript. Thus, already in the 1802/1803 *SEL*, Hegel envisions a new, positive role for Fichte's practical philosophy: Fichte provides Hegel with the stages of a genetic account leading to absolute ethical life.[25] After explaining the stages in Hegel's genetic account (sections 2.4.1 and 2.4.2), I relate *SEL* back to the two Statements of Hegel's mature Jena project (2.4.3).

2.4.1. The Theory of Drives

In Part I of the text, Hegel describes '*natural* ethical life', which begins with an account of practical subjects' 'drive' to satisfy basic needs in their interactions with their natural environment (*SdS* 4/*SEL* 102).[26] These needs are divided into two kinds: first, needs for the physical objects required for continued biological existence (food, water, etc.); and second, needs in relation to other subjects, especially the sexual drive. The drive to satisfy each kind of need generates its own set of social relations. The subsistence drive ultimately gives rise to property relations, while the sexual drive ultimately gives rise to family relations.[27]

Hegel first characterizes the subsistence drive and the practical activities to which it gives rise. Hegel divides his analysis into several elements or 'moments'. These moments include the subject's initial desire, which presents itself as a feeling of 'separation' from the desired object; the process of 'effort and *labor*' directed toward the satisfaction of need; and finally the "nullification of the object . . . i.e., *enjoyment* [*Genuss*]" (*SdS* 6/*SEL* 104). The labor process mediates between the first and last moments, as natural objects

---

[24] The title was given to the manuscript by Karl Rosenkranz, Hegel's early biographer. K. R. Meist has argued that *SEL* should in fact be entitled *Critique of Fichte's Naturrecht*, and should be interpreted accordingly. See Meist's "Einleitung" to *System der Sittlichkeit*. My interpretation follows up on Meist's suggestion.

[25] For a contrasting view, cf. Riedel, *Between Tradition and Revolution*, pp. 88–92.

[26] For discussion of the difficult formal structure of the text, which I cannot address here, see Harris, *Hegel's Development*, 106–107; and Chapter 3 of Steffen Schmidt, *Hegels System der Sittlichkeit*.

[27] The terms 'subsistence drive' and 'sexual drive' are mine, not Hegel's, but I take this terminology to capture an important distinction in Hegel's text. See also *GW* 8, 202–213/*Jena III* 99–109.

are reshaped through human activity—"determined by desire," as Hegel puts it—and "enjoyment is obstructed and deferred; it becomes ideal . . ." (106). In laboring to transform nature, subjects learn to defer gratification, and they develop a new form of practical 'intelligence', namely the capacity to reason instrumentally about how to bring about certain effects in nature through, for example, agriculture (109). Hegel uses the term *Bildung*—'formative education'—to describe these effects of need and labor on human agency (109).[28]

Hegel's source for the description of this shape of consciousness is very likely Fichte's *System of Ethics* (*SE*). In *SE*, Fichte presents a similar analysis of human drives, including the division of the natural drive into an initial feeling that "something—we know not what—is missing" (IV: 125/*SE* 119), and the claim that the satisfaction of the natural drive is 'enjoyment' (*Genuss*) (IV: 128/*SE* 122). And the idea that mastering nature is a central task for practical reason, a task to which we are spurred by the drive for independence and self-determination, is extremely prominent in *SE*.[29] Hegel's innovation is that he *historicizes* Fichte's view by presenting it as an account of the state of nature, from which subsequent shapes of consciousness develop in a genetic social history.

Hegel concludes his discussion of the natural subsistence drive with an account of the *tool* and technological change. For Hegel, the tool is the external embodiment of the rationality of the labor process as a form of subject/object mediation. Regarding the tool, Hegel writes:

> In one aspect the tool is subjective in the power of the subject who is working; by him it is entirely determined, manufactured, and fashioned; from the other point of view it is objectively directed on the object worked. By means of this middle term the subject cancels the immediacy of annihilation. . . . In the tool the subject makes a middle term between himself and the object, and this middle term is the real rationality of labor. . . . (*SdS* 15/*SEL* 112–113)

It is obvious from this passage that Hegel sees the tool as a symbol of the new link between subjectivity and objectivity that has been created by human labor.[30] When Hegel says that the tool is the "real rationality of labor," I take him to mean that the tool is a permanent monument to the achievements of laboring subjects in achieving a degree of independence and control over nature. Generations come and go, but tools, which embody rules and methods of labor, are passed down from one generation to the next as a collective achievement of human practical reason.[31]

---

[28] Compare Fichte's discussion of the *Bildungstrieb* ('formative drive') at IV, 121/*SE* 116.

[29] Cf. Michelle Kosch's "Agency and Self-Sufficiency in Fichte's Ethics."

[30] Schmidt-am-Busch emphasizes that the development of the tool is at the same time the development of a form of self-knowledge on the part of the worker, who makes herself 'objective' in the tool. Schmidt-am-Busch, *Hegels Begriff der Arbeit*, pp. 47–58.

[31] Compare *SdS* 16/*SEL* 113: "This is why all peoples living on the natural level have honored the tool, and we find respect for the tool, and consciousness of this, expressed in the finest way by Homer."

Hegel next considers the gradual rationalization of labor due to technological change. In this discussion, Hegel seeks to integrate classical political economy into his speculative philosophical anthropology.[32] Through the development of new productive technologies—new tools for mastering nature—and the corresponding division of labor, economic production becomes more abstract.[33] Individuals now produce for 'need in general', as opposed to production for immediate personal consumption (*SdS* 21/*SEL* 118; see also *GW* 6, 321–323/*Jena I* 247–248). This form of economic production in turn requires the institutionalization of market exchange, for individuals are no longer able to meet all of their needs with what they themselves produce (*SdS* 24/ *SEL* 121). And because some desirable market exchanges require that "the two sides of the bargain are fulfilled separately at different times," we arrive finally at the institutionalization of legal contracts (*SdS* 25–27/*SEL* 122–123). Hegel's analysis has thus moved from the basic natural drive for subsistence, via the tool and technological development, to the social division of labor and ultimately to a regime of property and contract.[34]

Hegel views the development of the most basic forms of human community out of the natural sexual drive as a process that evolves in parallel with the development of labor and property from the subsistence drive. Hegel treats the sexual drive separately because, in satisfying sexual needs, subjects find that the objects of their desire are qualitatively distinct from other objects in their environment: they are objects *that are also subjects*. For this reason, the satisfaction of sexual desire gives rise to a different kind of social structure than the satisfaction of subsistence needs. In the state of nature, when subjects satisfy the sexual drive, "each intuits him/herself in the other, though as a stranger, and this is *love*" (*SdS* 12/*SEL* 110).[35] This initial, brutely natural relationship gives rise to a new relation in which "the union of nature is . . . superseded: This is the relation of *parents and children*" (*SdS* 13/*SEL* 111). The abstract, fleeting feeling of natural love becomes concrete and more permanent in the form of the child as a mediating term between desiring subjects and the objects of their desire.[36] Like labor, family relationships reshape the subjectivity of family members by transforming and rationalizing natural drives, continuing the process of *Bildung*.

---

[32] Hegel's first explicit mention of Adam Smith comes at *GW* 6, 323/*Jena I* 248, but he seems to have Smith in mind in *SEL* as well. For discussion, see Henderson, "Adam Smith's Influence on Hegel's Philosophical Writings"; and Herzog, *Inventing the Market: Hegel, Smith, and Political Theory*.

[33] Compare *GW* 6, 322/*Jena I* 247, *GW* 8, 224–225/*Jena III* 121, and *GW* 8, 243–244/*Jena III* 138–140. On the 'machine' and 'concrete' vs 'abstract' labor, see Schmidt-am-Busch, *Hegels Begriff der Arbeit*, pp. 50–57 and 63–77, respectively.

[34] There are striking anticipations of Marx's views in these arguments. Influential Marxian interpretations of Hegel's Jena practical philosophy include especially Lukács's *The Young Hegel*; and Avineri, *Hegel's Theory of the Modern State*, pp. 87–98. Habermas's "Labor and Interaction: Remarks on Hegel's Jena *Philosophy of Mind*" is also relevant and highly interesting.

[35] At *GW* 8, 213/*Jena III* 109–110, Hegel distinguishes between 'natural' and 'self-conscious' love. What he describes here is 'natural' love. For discussion, see Siep, *AaP* 99.

[36] Cf. Siep, *AaP* 102–104.

2.4.2. Crime and Individualism

Part II of *SEL*, entitled "The Negative or Freedom or Crime," starts from the family and the basic legal institutions of property and contract that emerged in Part I and describes the reassertion of 'the Negative' against these newly emergent forms of 'universality'. The 'Negative' that Hegel refers to in the section title has at least two meanings. First, Hegel uses the term in a metaphysical sense to refer to the determinate individual, who posits herself as an individual by asserting her *non-identity* in relation to other individuals.[37] Second, Hegel uses the term in an *ethical* sense to refer to the social 'negativity' or harmfulness of individuals' assertion of their individual interests in criminal behavior. These two senses of 'the Negative' are connected, for Hegel interprets the reassertion of individuality in Part II of *SEL* as 'crime' (*Verbrechen*), which refers to the intentional violation of social or legal norms.

Within Part II, Hegel's analysis of 'theft' is especially relevant to the thread of argument I have sketched so far. The thief sets out *intentionally* to violate the new property norms that emerged at the end of Part I of the text.[38] Although Hegel's text is somewhat opaque regarding the thief's motivation, Honneth suggests, plausibly, that Hegel's thief is motivated by a sense of social invisibility—non-recognition—within the new system of property rights.[39] The new regime of property rights purports to take into account the interests of all, but it in fact institutionalizes relations of unequal wealth and power. Those whose needs and interests are unrecognized within this scheme of social institutions steal from property owners, igniting a process of social struggle in which thieves try to force the rest of society to recognize their personhood.

Hegel's discussion of crime and social conflict again draws on Fichte's practical philosophy, this time Fichte's *Foundations of Natural Right* (*FNR*). In *FNR*, Fichte first describes an original set of social relations he characterizes as rightful, reciprocal recognition, which is then shattered by individual violations of rights at a subsequent moment Fichte describes as a loss of "honesty and trust."[40] These moments of Fichte's *FNR* correspond, respectively, to the emergence of norms for the recognition of property and legal personhood at the end of Part I of *SEL*, and the subsequent collapse of these norms through 'Crime' in Part II of the text. Hegel draws on Fichte's emphasis on the self-assertion of individuality to portray a stage in the historical development of human practical life.

---

[37] Cf. Fichte's discussion of the 'law of reflective opposition,' *Foundations of Transcendental Philosophy*, pp. 121–125.

[38] These legal norms are probably at this level regarded by Hegel as evolved common-law norms—i.e., as customs.

[39] Honneth, *SR*, p. 20.

[40] Fichte, III, 139/*FNR* 125.

2.4.3. Absolute Ethical Life in *SEL*

Part II of *SEL* describes a period of social conflict and instability, which is closely connected with unequal social status. This stage of conflict mediates between natural ethical life (Part I) and absolute ethical life (Part III). Hegel's basic thought seems clear: he now sees absolute ethical life, which he still conceives along the same lines as in *NL*, as a social innovation that emerges in response to specific social problems, namely those described in 'Crime.' According to Hegel's account of crime, the criminal values her *individuality*, which she finds insufficiently acknowledged by her society. One possible solution to the problem of criminality is to lean on a strong communitarian social ethos that would make individuals identify much more strongly with the interests of the social whole. People would therefore be less insistent on having their particularity acknowledged. It is precisely this kind of ethos that Hegel associates with classical ethical life, and which he presents in the third section of *SEL* as the solution to crime.

This move leaves Hegel's view with the same problem as in *NL*, a problem that he has not yet come to appreciate fully in *SEL*: the threat of nihilism, the annihilation of independent subjectivity. Absolute ethical life in *SEL* suppresses modern individuality in favor of the values and interests of the social whole characteristic of the classical polis. Hegel has thus not yet arrived at the conception of his project captured in the Practical and Metaphysical Statements. But the significance of *SEL* does not lie in its account of absolute ethical life. The originality of *SEL* consists rather in Hegel's methodological repurposing of modern political economy and Fichte's practical philosophy to provide a conceptual framework for a historical/anthropological account of the development of human consciousness and society via social struggles for recognition. As we will see in section 2.5, this methodology in principle allows for a more positive role for modern subjectivity in Hegel's social and political philosophy, even if *SEL* does not capitalize on this promise.

2.5. JENA SYSTEM DRAFTS

Hegel's Jena System Drafts cover much of the same territory as *SEL*. Like *SEL*, *Jena I* and *Jena III* provide phenomenological accounts of labor and the tool, love and the family, and social conflict as a mediating stage leading to the establishment of absolute ethical life. Given this overlap, rather than recapitulating all of this material, in this section I emphasize the important ways in which the System Drafts diverge from *SEL*.

Certainly the most significant innovation in *Jena I* is Hegel's introduction of his idea of *spirit* (*Geist*) as a central ontological, normative, and social-theoretic category. In this section, I first introduce the idea of spirit that Hegel discusses at the beginning of the manuscript (section 2.5.1). Then I discuss Hegel's analysis of the *struggle for recognition*, which in the System Drafts replaces 'Crime' as the transitional stage between the state of nature and absolute ethical life (2.5.2). I conclude by showing how, in *Jena III*, the ideas of *spirit* and *recognition* allow Hegel at last to formulate and address the project described in the two Statements (2.5.3).

2.5.1. Spirit in *Jena I*

The parts of *Jena I* that deal with social and political themes focus on what Hegel will later call *objective spirit*. Contemporary commentators standardly gloss 'objective spirit' as Hegel's term for the sphere of institutions, norms, and social practices that embody human rationality.[41] Hegel regards these norms and institutions, within which human beings live and move, as a matter of 'second nature', as outward expressions of human practical reason—human spirit (or 'mind') made objective. In my view, this standard way of understanding objective spirit is basically correct. Yet such an analysis does little to illuminate Hegel's actual descriptions of spirit in *Jena I*, which rely on highly abstract language that often does not seem to be about social practices at all. I will therefore approach Hegel's initial remarks about spirit in *Jena I* from a different angle. Hegel's remarks, I argue, become more intelligible if we read Hegel as critically transforming Fichte's theory of self-consciousness. I then show how such a reading connects with the standard reading's emphasis on social norms and practices as constituting objective spirit.

On the basis of his engagement with Fichte between *SEL* and *Jena I*, Hegel develops three key ideas that inform his new account of spirit. First, Hegel comes to regard what Fichte calls the 'self-positing I' as providing a model of the absolute that Hegel seeks to replicate in his account of spirit. Second, Hegel adopts a version of the Fichtean claim that self-conscious rational agency is socially mediated. And third, he uses Fichte's concept of reciprocal recognition (*Anerkennung*) to analyze the constitution of the social fabric of spirit that mediates individual agency.

Regarding the first idea, Hegel begins his discussion of spirit by claiming that the 'concept of spirit is what is called *consciousness*' (*GW* 6, 266/*Jena I* 206). Consciousness, according to Hegel,

> is likewise the immediate simple opposite of itself, on the one hand it opposes itself to the one of which it is conscious, by sundering itself into active and passive; and on the other hand [it is] the opposite of this sundering, the absolute union of the distinction, the union of the distinction both in being and superseded. (*GW* 6, 266–267/ *Jena I* 207)[42]

---

[41] For discussion, see Alznauer, "Rival Versions of Objective Spirit"; Thompson, "Hegel's Institutionalism"; Pippin, *Hegel's Practical Philosophy*, pp. 112, 127.

[42] Cf. *GW* 8, 196–199/*Jena III* 95–97.

This passage becomes intelligible when we consider it in relation to Fichte's doctrine of the self-positing, or self-conscious, I. In Fichte's system, there are (at least) two kinds of self-positing I: the 'absolute I' and the 'finite' or 'empirical' I.[43] The self-positing activity of the absolute I is the transcendental condition of the possibility of finite epistemic and practical agency. According to Fichte, the I has the following structural features. In thinking itself, the I (1) posits itself as an actively thinking subject, and (2) posits itself as a passive object of thought. In self-positing, the I is at once agent and patient.[44] These two moments correspond to Hegel's claim that consciousness "sunders itself into active [the positing subject] and passive [the I posited as object]." At the same time, for Fichte, the self-conscious I is (3) itself the whole relation between the I that subjectively posits and the I that is objectively posited.[45] This is the sense of Hegel's claim that consciousness is "the absolute union of the distinction" between active subject and passive object. Hegel says that (self-) consciousness is the "immediate simple opposite of itself," because self-consciousness posits a distinction within itself that is at the same time no distinction at all.[46]

In *Jena I*, the activity of spirit takes the place of the activity of Fichte's absolute I. Just as for Fichte the finite I depends on the activity of the absolute I, for Hegel finite human agency depends on the activity of spirit. Hegel makes this dependence relation clear when he insists that spirit is the 'substance' of individual persons.[47] But Hegel transforms Fichte's account of the absolute I by reconceiving it in *historical* terms as the development of human spirit. Hegel's phenomenological account of the development of spirit recapitulates the moments of Fichte's analysis of the self-positing I in the following way. Spirit (1) initially posits itself as active subject, as the 'negation' of the world of natural objects that it sets out to master through, for example, labor.[48] Then, through its practical activity, spirit gradually transforms the objective world such that (2) spirit comes

---

[43]   See, e.g., I, 97/*Foundations*. 98. Cf. Zöller, *Fichte's Transcendental Philosophy*, Chapter 3; and Breazeale, "The Spirit of the Early *Wissenschaftslehre*," pp. 122–123.

[44]   I, 96/*Foundations*, 97: "The *self posits itself*. . . . It is at once the agent and the product of action."

[45]   I, 110/*Foundations* 110: "*In the self I oppose a divisible not-self to the divisible self.*"

[46]   GW 6, 276/*Jena I* 214: "[consciousness] exists in as much as it is that wherein both terms, the self-conscious being, and that of which he is self-conscious, are posited as one, and also oppose themselves to it [their unity]."

[47]   E.g., GW 6, 315/*Jena I* 242. There is a debate about how to interpret Hegel's claim that spirit is a 'substance'. Literal interpretations take seriously the idea that according to Hegel, spirit provides a metaphysical foundation for individual agents, who are 'accidents' of the spiritual substance. See, e.g., Taylor, *Hegel and Modern Society*, pp. 8–11, 28, 47–48. Metaphorical interpretations hold that individual agency depends on the social fabric of objective spirit, but the dependence is something more like a transcendental condition than a relation of metaphysical inherence. Cf. T. Pinkard, *Hegel's Phenomenology*, pp. 122–124; and Pippin, *Hegel's Practical Philosophy*. The literal/metaphorical debate is closely tied to a second question regarding the unit of agency that drives the developmental process in the System Drafts. For Habermas and Honneth, *SEL* and the System Drafts are the only Hegelian texts in which the social development of spirit is a genuinely intersubjective process, as opposed to a 'monological' process carried out by a substantial spirit. Habermas, "Labor and Interaction" and Honneth, *SR* pp. 61–63.

[48]   See, e.g., GW 6, 274–275/*Jena I* 214–215; and Testa, "How Does Recognition Emerge from Nature?"

to posit itself in the objects of its practical activity. Spirit comes to 'be with' itself in the objective 'media' (e.g., tools and objects of labor) it has created.[49] Finally, (3) within *actual* and *absolute* spirit, the initially posited subject/object dichotomy, the subject's alienation from the objective world, is overcome (*aufgehoben*), yet without nullifying the distinction between subject and object, which remains part of the spiritual relation considered as a whole (*GW* 6, 271–272/*Jena I* 209–210).[50]

The second key idea Hegel takes from Fichte is that self-conscious practical agency is *socially mediated*: standing in certain kinds of practical relations to other agents is a necessary condition for being a practical agent oneself.[51] This is where my interpretation reconnects with the standard reading's emphasis on social practices: the norms and practices that constitute objective spirit function as the social conditions of individual agency. The System Drafts attempt to substantiate the latter claim by providing a genealogy of spirit that shows how individuals come to constitute themselves as free agents in various senses by standing in particular relations, first to other individual agents, and ultimately to the spiritual 'substance' of a people as a whole within ethical life.

The third key concept that Hegel takes from Fichte, the idea of *recognition*, ties together the two ideas just discussed. First, the model of reciprocal recognition illustrates Hegel's Fichtean conception of spirit by explaining how spirit can contain within itself the differentiation between subject and object, while at the same time uniting both. In such relations the subjects reciprocally recognize each other as identical, as members of a genus—as equal legal persons, for example. In the other's expressed recognition, each finds its own identity made objective in its social world, and thus finds itself united with another outside of it. But at the same time, in reciprocal recognition, the subjects distinguish themselves from one another, as recognizer and recognized, subject and object, with different concrete desires and interests that have become socially 'real' through the recognition of the other. Thus a relation of reciprocal recognition embodies the spiritual structure of identity-in-difference that Hegel takes from Fichte's model of self-consciousness. The latter point bears emphasizing, for it gives Hegel a model for how a unified social whole, exemplified by a common will expressed in a relation of reciprocal recognition, can incorporate individuality into itself. Second, reciprocal recognition is related to the sociality of agency because Hegel analyzes the social conditions of individual agency as institutionally mediated recognition relations. Recognition from others as, say, a legal person is a necessary condition for *being* a legal person with a certain kind of practical agency. I discuss these points in more depth in section 2.5.3.

---

[49] *GW* 6, 276/*Jena I* 216–217.

[50] Cf. p. 146 of Habermas's "Labor and Interaction."

[51] See the First Main Division of Fichte's *FNR*. I reconstruct Fichte's argument in Michael Nance, "Recognition, Freedom, and the Self in Fichte's *Foundations of Natural Right*."

2.5.2. The Struggle for Recognition in the Jena System Drafts

With this picture of Hegelian spirit in mind, I turn to consider Hegel's idea that spirit is formed by a *struggle for recognition*. Adapting Fichte's thesis that finite human agency is socially mediated, Hegel argues that absolute ethical life as a shape of spirit (1) emerges historically out of social conflict, and (2) makes possible new forms of individual practical agency.

In his account of the recognition struggle in *Jena I* and *III* (but not in the *Phenomenology*), Hegel again appeals to the idea of the state of nature.[52] Prior to his analysis of the recognition struggle in *Jena I*, Hegel has discussed the emergence of the family and the relations of recognition and economic production that take place within the family structure. At this stage, each individual conceives of its family group as the sole unit of practical agency and concern in the world—as a "singular totality," in Hegel's language. For this reason, family units in Hegel's state of nature initially function as what I will call *naïve egoists*. By 'naïve egoist' I mean a person who conceives of herself as a practical agent entitled to do as she pleases, but who does not recognize the existence of any other agents with such a self-conception.[53] A *sophisticated egoist*, by contrast, understands that other agents like her exist, and that these other agents believe themselves to be normatively entitled to equal recognition. But the sophisticated egoist denies that these other agents *in fact* have equal normative standing. The distinction, then, is that whereas the naïve egoist does not yet have the concept of other agents with equal normative standing, the sophisticated egoist has that concept but denies that it is morally binding. The struggle for recognition is the process by which individuals shed their egoism and come to recognize others as equal persons.

In Hegel's texts, naively egoistic family groups face off against each other in the state of nature. Hegel imagines one family unit unilaterally seizing a piece of land in the state of nature, thereby inadvertently excluding a second family unit from that land.[54] Call these parties the 'excluder' and the 'excluded'.[55] Before the excluder took possession of the land, the excluded party had access to it if she wanted; but now the excluder denies her the possibility of using it. The excluded party thus recognizes the excluder as an agent like herself in a fairly minimal sense: both agents want to be able to possess and use external things. But recognizing the other as a being with desires like her own does not entail recognition of the other as having normative entitlements. And the excluder does

---

[52] The role of the recognition struggle in the *Phenomenology* is quite different from its role in the Jena manuscripts. In the manuscripts, the recognition struggle is explicitly an account of the state of nature and the emergence of political society, whereas in the *Phenomenology* the struggle between master and bondsman takes place in the context of a specifically *epistemological* argument. Cf. Jenkins, Chapter 4 of this volume.

[53] Cf. Harris, "The Concept of Recognition in Hegel's Jena Manuscripts," p. 243.

[54] This is clearer at *GW* 8, 216/*Jena III* 112, and *GW* 8, 218–219/*Jena III* 115.

[55] *GW* 8, 216/*Jena III* 112.

not yet recognize the excluded at all; she is still unaware of the existence of other family groups.

To make the excluder aware of her existence, the excluded must assert herself against the excluder. She does so by 'spoiling' the excluder's possession—ruining the excluder's agricultural fields, for example.[56] Now the two parties are aware of each other, and the conflict escalates. Hegel describes the emergence of this new stage of conflict in the following terms:

> . . . as each affirms his totality as a single [consciousness] in this single [point of offense] strictly, it becomes apparent *that each negates the totality of the other* . . . each [must] posit himself as totality in the consciousness of the other, in such a way that he puts his whole apparent totality, his life, at stake for the preservation of any single detail, and each likewise must go for the death of the other. I can only recognize [myself] as this singular totality in the consciousness of the other, so far as I posit myself in his consciousness as of such a kind that in my exclusiveness [I] am a totality of excluding, [i.e., so far as] I go for his death; when I go for his death, I expose myself to death, I risk my own life. . . . (*GW* 6, 309–310/*Jena I* 239)

This passage requires unpacking. First, each family group is now aware of itself as 'negated' or threatened by the other group. Second, in order to maintain its self-conception as a singular totality, each group must force the other to acknowledge its (purportedly) unique normative standing so that it can "recognize [itself] as this singular totality in the consciousness of the other." Third, in the process of trying to force the other to recognize it *qua* singular totality, each group 'exposes' itself to death. The groups thus find themselves locked in a life-and-death struggle.

Hegel holds that the only successful, stable resolution of this struggle consists in the opposed groups leaving behind their naïve egoism. There are other possible outcomes—one party might enslave or kill the other, or one or both groups might lose their nerve and flee the conflict. But Hegel regards these other outcomes as in some sense contradictory, given the commitments and aims of the families in the struggle.[57] The contradiction is that the victor aims to extract recognition of her supremacy from the other in the struggle. Yet if one party succeeds in absolutely asserting itself in the consciousness of the other, the other is destroyed or totally dominated and therefore cannot recognize the victor as a totality in any meaningful sense, since genuine recognition cannot be forced.

Now, this argument presupposes that the families have a very specific aim in their interaction: to get recognition of their standing as singular totalities from the other. But why does Hegel hold that *this* must be the aim of the parties in the struggle? To assume that the parties want or need recognition from others at the outset of the interaction is question-begging, for at the outset of the interaction the parties do not yet have the *concept* of other agents who could recognize them. They only come to recognize the existence and normative standing of other subjects in subsequent stages of the recognition

[56] *GW* 8, 219/*Jena III* 115.
[57] *GW* 6, 312/*Jena I* 240.

struggle. Another possible answer is that individuals need external confirmation of their subjective self-conception, and that only recognition can provide such external confirmation.[58] This answer points in the right direction. Yet there must be more to Hegel's position than this, for if I think of my group as a 'singular totality' and I manage to subjugate, through death or domination, other groups with whom my group comes into contact, then my self-conception as member of a singular totality would seem to be richly confirmed within such interactions. So if the parties' aim is simply to achieve objective confirmation of their subjective self-conception, it is not clear why cases of subjugation of the other would be in any way deficient or contradictory. Again, the question arises: Why does Hegel hold that *recognition*, as opposed to subjugation, is required to end the social struggle?

Here is a sketch of a more adequate answer, the outlines of which can be discerned in Hegel's texts. Rather than assume from the outset of the interaction that the parties want or need recognition from the other, Hegel starts from the more minimal assumption that each party aims to make its subjectivity—its intentions, goals, desires, and so on—objective.[59] Making one's subjectivity objective requires practically reshaping the objective world to correspond to one's desires, so that one finds one's subjectivity mirrored by the world. As we have seen, subjects in the state of nature routinely achieve this goal by reshaping natural objects in their own image. This is the generic aim of the naively egoistic family units with which the recognition struggle begins. They do not yet seek recognition from other family groups; indeed, they do not yet know of such groups. They seek merely to make themselves objective *qua* singular totalities by practically restructuring the world around them so that the subordinate status of other objects, which are regarded as merely instrumentally valuable, is made explicit.

At the beginning of the struggle, the groups do not regard each other as importantly different from other animals in their natural environment.[60] The groups thus initially interpret their attempts to subjugate each other as continuous with their attempts to master other aspects of nature. However, in the course of their interaction, the groups repeatedly *refuse* to allow the other to make them into or treat them as mere things: rather than submit to the domination of the other, thereby allowing themselves to be reified into mere tools (the extreme case here is slavery), each is willing to 'go to the death' for the sake of their own 'singular totality'.

This experience teaches the parties something new about each other. Each group discovers that the other is, like it, an object who is also a subject, driven not merely by

---

[58] In *SR*, Honneth inteprets the need for recognition along various dimensions as a basic psychological need. Such a psychologizing interpretation in my view does not capture the kind of conceptual necessity that Hegel's argument is supposed to establish.

[59] This assumption, that in action agents seek to overcome the gap between 'inner' and 'outer' and thereby overcome their alienation from the objective world, is central to Hegel's entire theory of action, but I cannot delve into Hegel's arguments in defense of the assumption here. Cf. Schmidt am Busch, "What Does It Mean to 'Make Oneself into an Object'?" See also *GW* 8, 205, 227/*Jena III* 103, 123.

[60] At *GW* 8, 233–234/*Jena III* 129 Hegel distinguishes clearly between subjects' understanding of each other in the state of nature and their understanding of each other in civil society.

natural desires for survival and security, but by a conception of itself as *honorable* or *worthy* of respect. In making this discovery, the groups become *sophisticated egoists* who are aware of the existence of other like-minded agents. It is specifically the willingness of each group to sacrifice its biological existence for the sake of its honor that plays a key role in expressing one's self-conception to the other. As Hegel explains, in the struggle for recognition, "each can only know of the other whether he is [a] totality in as much as he drives him to the point of death, and each proves himself as totality for himself likewise only in that he goes to the point of death with himself" (*GW* 6, 311/*Jena I* 240; cf. *GW* 8, 220/*Jena III* 117). Now, after learning these new facts about each other, each group still has the same aim in interacting with the other: to make its subjectivity objective. But the attempt to accomplish this aim through reifying the other—treating the other purely as an object upon which one imposes one's agency—has failed, for the other refused to allow herself to be reified. Accordingly, the groups' tactics for meeting this goal change with their new understanding of the other with whom they are interacting. The question now is this: How can one make one's self-conception objective in relation to an object that, unlike other objects in one's environment, insists on being treated as a subject?

Hegel's answer is that one can get this other to *recognize* one, as one conceives of oneself.[61] In this kind of interaction, two desiderata are satisfied. First, the recognized subject receives objective, external confirmation of its self-conception through the other's expression of recognition; the recognized subject thereby successfully finds its subjectivity mirrored in the objective world. And second, the other who bestows recognition, by expressing an evaluative judgment, acts *as a subject*, avoiding reification. The desire for recognition from the other can thus be conceived, not as a presupposition of the entire interaction, but as the solution to a specific problem that arises midway through their interaction, which was initiated by the basic practical drive to make subjectivity objective.

Yet merely desiring recognition from the other in the interaction is not sufficient to arrive at a successful resolution of the recognition struggle. For that, the groups in the interaction must also change their self-conceptions. For it is impossible for both groups to achieve recognition *qua* singular totality in the interaction. If one group recognizes the other as singular totality, it thereby must, on pain of incoherence, give up its own conception of itself as singular totality. Recognition, within this conceptual scheme, can therefore only be asymmetrical or non-reciprocal. But, as we have seen, the parties to the interaction are not content with such an asymmetrical relation; instead, they struggle against this form of domination. This shape of consciousness thus proves unable to resolve the social conflict of the recognition struggle.

---

[61] For Hegel's argument to be sound, he needs recognition to be the *unique* solution to this problem. Although I find it plausible, I make no attempt here to defend the necessity claim; rather, I focus on showing why Hegel regards recognition as a sufficient solution to the question just posed.

2.5.3. Absolute Ethical Life in *Jena III*

As in *NL* and *SEL*, Hegel's solution to the social conflict of the recognition struggle in *Jena I* is to transition directly to a strongly communitarian account of ethical life in which individuals give up their conception of themselves as singular totalities in favor of a whole-hearted commitment to the common good. However, in *Jena III*, Hegel introduces the institutions of property, contractual exchange, and private law as the initial resolution of the recognition struggle. These institutions function as intermediaries between the recognition struggle in the state of nature and the thick social attachments of absolute ethical life.[62]

In *Jena III*, the institutions of property, contract, and private law resolve the social conflict that characterized the recognition struggle by introducing the category of *legal personhood* (*GW* 8, 231/*Jena III* 127–128). The concept of legal personhood provides a new way for subjects to conceive of themselves and others, which in turn makes possible genuinely reciprocal recognition relations. A legal person possesses rights to property, freedom of contract, and bodily integrity, rights that are equally possessed by all other legal persons. Thus if I think of myself as a legal person, there is no contradiction in my recognizing other persons under the same description. In fact, where egoism conceptually precludes the recognition of others as equals, legal personhood conceptually demands it. Because the adoption of legal personhood as a practical self-conception allows for and encourages reciprocal recognition, it is a first step in resolving the instability and social conflict of the state of nature.

But this initial resolution of the recognition struggle soon proves itself to be unstable. To see why, consider first that Hegel regards contractual exchange as the central case of legal personhood. In agreeing to a contract, legal persons reciprocally recognize each other as possessing the right to dispose of their property, and the will to engage in a specific, mutually beneficial transaction. I will refer to this form of recognition as 'I-Thou' recognition. The problem, in Hegel's view, is that I-Thou contractual recognition allows for stable social cooperation only if there is a third-party guarantor with the power to enforce contracts between persons. For without the possibility of legal recourse to a third-party guarantor, it is irrational for the contracting parties to trust each other. This is why Hegel says that coercive law is the 'universal' will that is the "substance of the [legal] person" and the "*substance* of the contract" (*GW* 8, 236–237/*Jena III* 132–133).[63] But in Hegel's phenomenological account, the requirement of a third-party guarantor is initially experienced by the parties as a new form of disrespect, for it seems to each party to signal (1) that the other does not regard it as *honorable* (*GW* 8, 232–233/*Jena*

---

[62] The structure of the argument in *Jena III* thus foreshadows Hegel's analysis of ethical life in *PR* as progressing from the family ('natural ethical life' in the Jena texts), to civil society (the sphere of market exchange), and culminating in the state ('absolute ethical life'). Cf. Siep, *AaP* 205.

[63] The universal will of the state acts as the 'substance' of contracts by regulating the marketplace and using state coercion to enforce contracts (*GW* 8, 244–246/*Jena III* 139–142). Hegel also holds that the universal will is the 'substance' of marriage and the family (*GW* 8, 238–243/*Jena III* 134–138).

III 128–129), and (2) that its own recognized will in the contract—its word—is being replaced with the alien will of a third party (*GW* 8, 234/*Jena III* 129).[64] The new normative status of legal personhood initially seemed to offer a socially recognized basis for each person's self-respect as independent and honorable. Yet the institution of a third-party guarantor immediately undermines this newfound independence and honor by exposing it as illusory—I will be forced to fulfill my contractual obligation even if I am dishonorable.[65]

This experience of disrespect initiates a new round of social conflict, which Hegel describes, as in *SEL*, as 'crime' (*GW* 8, 234–236/*Jena III* 130–131). As before, Hegel appeals to the 'substantiality' of the state, conceived along classical lines as a form of collective life based on the "spirit of a people," as the solution to the problem of crime (*GW* 8, 253–254/*Jena III* 151). Hegel's thought is that only solidarity with the 'universal' will of the state, which we can think of as a form of 'I-We' recognition, can legitimize the exercise of legal force by the state that is necessary for the stability of I-Thou contractual recognition.[66] If I identify with the will of the state as an expression of 'our' collective will, then when the state acts as guarantor in my contractual relation to you, I am not thereby subjecting myself to an alien authority. The state's coercive will does not replace my own will in the contract, for the state's will is an *expression* of my own will (cf. *GW* 8, 254/*Jena III* 153).

The problem with this move is the threat of nihilism—the worry that individuals' sense of themselves as independent and 'substantial', which was supposed to be secured by their recognition as legal persons, will be lost in their strong identification with the will of the state. But this is where Hegel's argument in *Jena III* breaks new ground.[67] Consider this passage, in which Hegel clearly acknowledges the nihilism implied by the kind of view he advocated in *NL* and *SEL*:

> In ancient times, the morality of all (*die Sitte aller*) consisted of the beautiful public life—beauty [as the] immediate unity of the universal and the individual.... Yet individuality's knowledge of itself as absolute ... was not present. The Platonic Republic is, like Sparta, this disappearance of the self-knowing individuality. (*GW* 8, 263/*Jena III* 160)[68]

Hegel's new argument attempts to preserve 'self-knowing individuality' by conceiving of the integration of individual wills into the collective will of the state as a spiritual relation in which individuality is both positively recognized and transformed. If the

---

[64] Cf. Honneth, *SR* 54–55 for a different reading. Siep, *AaP* 124–125 is closer to the reading offered here.

[65] I take this argument to be a critique of Fichte, who in *FNR* appeals to the institution of coercive law to stabilize relations of I-Thou recognition. Hegel's critique holds that the Fichtean *Rechtstaat* must be embedded in Hegel's own conception of ethical life, for a thicker set of social attachments—the 'life of a people'—is necessary to stabilize and legitimize coercive law.

[66] Siep introduces the distinction between I-Thou and I-We recognition on p. 97 of *AaP*.

[67] Siep agrees; cf. *AaP* 209–210.

[68] I lightly modify Rauch's translations of *Jena III* throughout this section.

argument can be made to work, individuality need not be swallowed up within absolute ethical life.

Here is what Hegel writes about spirit at the beginning of his discussion of absolute ethical life:[69]

> As force it is only the individual who is the end [of Spirit] . . . Spirit's self-preservation, however, is the *organization* of its life, the spirit of a people, which intends itself. The concept of Spirit: universality in the complete freedom and independence of the individual. (*GW* 8, 254/*Jena III* 151)

Two aspects of this passage stand out. First, Hegel clearly states that 'universality' and the "freedom and independence of the individual" are compatible according to the "concept of Spirit." Second, Hegel provides a clue as to how these two ideals can be synthesized. He writes that spirit has two 'ends' whose 'preservation' it intends: the individual, and itself. Similarly, Hegel states that individuals within ethical life have two ends:

> This unity of individuality and the universal is now present in a twofold way . . . the same individual who provides for himself and his family, who works, enters into contracts, etc., likewise works for the universal as well, and has it as his end. In the former sense he is called *bourgeois*, in the latter he is *citoyen*. (*GW* 8, 261/*Jena III* 158)

Individuals will both the common good of the state and their own individual ends. In identifying with the will of the state for the common good, individuals 'surrender' themselves to the universal: "individuals have to make themselves into the universal [will] through the negation of their own [will], [in] externalization and formation (*Bildung*)" (*GW* 8, 257/*Jena III* 154). But in 'surrendering' themselves, they receive back their own recognized individuality, for they know that the universal will with which they identify is the substance of the social relations that constitute them as individuals—their activities in the family, the market, and the state. Both the state and the individual are now conceived as having dual ends: each wills its own flourishing as well as the flourishing of the other. And each knows that the other has recognized its end, just as it has recognized the end of the other. Thus, although Hegel does not explicitly use this language, these passages suggest that Hegel has come to conceive of the relation of the individual to the universal will of the people embodied in the state as a relation of reciprocal recognition.[70] The recognition model of identity-in-difference gives Hegel a way of conceiving

---

[69]   What I have been calling absolute ethical life is discussed in *Jena III* under the heading "Constitution."

[70]   After introducing this conceptual framework, Hegel describes, very schematically, a process of *Bildung* by which individuals come to know themselves in the universal will of the state. He then transitions to discuss his doctrine of 'classes' or 'estates'. The latter doctrine complicates matters somewhat, since one's relation to the universal will depends on one's estate, but I cannot discuss this complication here. But unlike in *NL*, in *Jena III* every estate is positively recognized and incorporated into the universal.

of ethical life as a substantial unity while avoiding the annihilation of finite subjectivity, which is recognized by both individuals and the universal will.

There are, then, at least two kinds of recognition at play in *Jena III*: contractual recognition, a 'horizontal' relation in which individuals recognize each other as legal persons (*bourgeois*, as Hegel puts it in the preceding passage); and solidarity recognition with the universal will, a 'vertical' relation between individuals conceived as citizens (*citoyens*) and the collective will of the state.[71] The latter kind of recognition is directly a relation between the state and the individual, but indirectly an institutionally mediated solidarity relation with all other individual members of the state who identify with the universal will. The 'vertical' relation to the state thus mediates a second kind of 'horizontal' relation—this time, not between individuals conceived as legal persons (*bourgeois*), but rather between individuals *qua* citizens (*citoyens*). The state thus comes to represent an 'I that is We' (cf. *Phenomenology* §177). I have argued that there is, for Hegel, a deep connection between these two forms of recognition: I-We solidarity recognition between citizens, which is mediated by the state, is necessary to stabilize I-Thou recognition between private legal persons. Corresponding to these two forms of recognition are two distinct kinds of freedom, each of which has a recognized place in Hegel's outline of ethical life in *Jena III*. Stable I-Thou recognition allows individuals the modern individualist freedom to pursue their private good within the market, protected by the rights of legal personhood. In I-We solidarity recognition, individuals "know the universal will as their particular will," which makes possible a kind of communitarian freedom as social autonomy along the lines of Rousseau's doctrine of the general will. Because citizens identify with the common good expressed in the universal will of the state, when they submit to the state's authority, they remain subject only to their own wills. Thus, although Hegel's text is sketchy on the institutional details, *Jena III* for the first time offers a conceptual framework for conceiving of ethical life as uniting modern individualist and classical communitarian conceptions of freedom.[72]

Hegel has finally arrived at the conceptual resources for coping with his mature project in his Jena practical philosophy, captured in the two Statements. Practically, Hegel's framework in *Jena III* allows for members of ethical life to be both *bourgeois* (modern individuals) and *citoyens* (ancient citizens). Metaphysically, Hegel's view allows individuality a positively recognized place within the 'substantial' whole that comprises absolute ethical life. Just as the conscious subject is an essential part of the whole set of relations that constitutes self-consciousness, so the recognized individual is an essential part of the whole set of recognition relations that constitutes absolute ethical life. Hegel's theory of ethical life at the end of the Jena period thus gives him the conceptual resources to avoid both modern atomism and classical nihilism.

---

[71] On the horizontal/vertical distinction, which was first emphasized by Siep, see Siep, *AaP* 33; and Ikäheimo, *Anerkennung*, 70–71.

[72] Cf. *PR* §185Z and 206Z.

2.6. Conclusion

I conclude with a brief remark on the continuing relevance of Hegel's Jena practical philosophy. Although aspects of his metaphysical project may seem quite foreign to contemporary readers, the deep issues Hegel raises regarding modernity, atomism, freedom, and nihilism continue to resonate with present-day concerns. And some of Hegel's conceptual innovations in response to this nest of problems have continued to bear fruit for subsequent generations of philosophers. Certainly the most influential idea from these texts is Hegel's account of the struggle for recognition.[73] Hegel's conceptual framework for explaining how recognition shapes individual agency, how institutions mediate different forms of recognition, and how the systematic denial of recognition can provoke social conflict that leads to social progress has proven to be tremendously fruitful for contemporary political philosophy and critical social theory.[74] And Hegel's idea that there is a special kind of freedom that is closely tied to recognition and social solidarity continues to be influential in these discussions.[75] For these reasons, Hegel's Jena project continues to merit our attention today.

Works Cited

Primary Texts

Aristotle. *Politics*, in *The Complete Works of Aristotle*, edited by Jonathan Barnes, Vol. II. Princeton, NJ: Princeton University Press, 1984.

Fichte, J. G. *Grundlage der gesammten Wissenschaftslehre*, in *Fichtes Werke*, edited by I. H. Fichte, Vol. I, Berlin: Walter de Gruyter, 1971, 83–328. Edited and translated by P. Heath and J. Lachs as *Foundations of the Entire Science of Knowledge*. Cambridge: Cambridge University Press, 1982.

Fichte, J. G. *Grundlage des Naturrechts*, in *Fichtes Werke*, edited by I. H. Fichte, Vol. III, Berlin: Walter de Gruyter, 1971, 1–386. Translated by M. Baur as *Foundations of Natural Right*, edited by F. Neuhouser. Cambridge: Cambridge University Press, 2000.

Fichte, J. G. *System der Sittenlehre*, in *Fichtes Werke*, edited by I.H. Fichte, Vol. IV, Berlin: Walter de Gruyter, 1971, 1–366. Edited and translated by D. Breazeale and G. Zöller as *System of Ethics*, Cambridge: Cambridge University Press, 2005.

Fichte, J. G. *Wissenschaftslehre nova methodo*, edited by Erich Fuchs, Berlin: Felix Meiner Verlag, 1994. Edited and translated by D. Breazeale as *Foundations of Transcendental Philosophy*, Ithaca, NY: Cornell University Press, 1992.

---

[73] On the reception of this idea in twentieth-century French philosophy, see Alison Stone, Chapter 31 in this volume.

[74] In addition to Honneth's *SR*, see S. Anderson's discussion of Honneth in "Liberalism and Recognition," Chapter 34 of this volume.

[75] Cf. the discussions of 'social freedom' in Neuhouser, *Foundations of Hegel's Social Theory*, and Honneth, *Freedom's Right*.

Hegel, G. W. F. *Differenz des Fichteschen und Schellingschen Systems der Philosophie*, in Vol. 2 of Hegel's *Werke: Jenaer Schriften 1801–1807*. Frankfurt: Suhrkamp, 1970. Translated by H. S. Harris and W. Cerf as *The Difference between Fichte's and Schelling's System of Philosophy*. Albany: State University of New York Press, 1977.

Hegel, G. W. F. *Elements of the Philosophy of Right* [PR], translated by H. B. Nisbet and edited by Allen Wood. Cambridge: Cambridge University Press, 1991.

Hegel, G. W. F. "Glauben und Wissen," in Vol. 2 of Hegel's *Werke: Jenaer Schriften 1801–1807*. Frankfurt: Suhrkamp, 1970. Translated as *Faith and Knowledge*, edited and translated by W. Cerf and H. S. Harris. Albany: State University of New York Press, 1988.

Hegel, G. W. F. *Jenaer Systementwürfe I*, in Vol. 6 of Hegel's *Gesammetle Werke*, edited by K. Dusing and H. Kimmerle, Hamburg: Meiner, 1975. Translated in *System of Ethical Life and First Philosophy of Spirit*, edited and translated by H. S. Harris and T. M. Knox. Albany: State University of New York Press, 1979.

Hegel, G. W. F. *Jenaer Systementwürfe III*, in Vol. 8 of Hegel's *Gesammetle Werke*, edited by R.-P. Horstmann and J. H. Trede, Hamburg: Meiner, 1976. Translated by L. Rauch as *Hegel and the Human Spirit*. Detroit: Wayne State University Press, 1983.

Hegel, G. W. F. *Phenomenology of Spirit*, translated by A. V. Miller. Oxford: Oxford University Press, 1977.

Hegel, G. W. F. *System der Sittlichkeit* [*Critik des Fichteschen Naturrechts*], edited by Horst D. Brandt. Hamburg: Meiner, 2002. Translated in Hegel, *System of Ethical Life and First Philosophy of Spirit*, edited and translated by H. S. Harris and T. M. Knox. Albany: State University of New York Press, 1979.

Hegel, G. W. F. "Über die wissenschaftliche Behandlungsarten des Naturrechts," in Vol. 2 of Hegel's *Werke: Jenaer Schriften 1801–1807*. Frankfurt: Suhrkamp, 1970. Translated as "On the Scientific Ways of Treating Natural Law," in L. Dickey and H. B. Nisbet, eds., *Hegel: Political Writings*. Cambridge: Cambridge University Press, 1999.

Jacobi, F. H. *Concerning the Doctrine of Spinoza*, in Jacobi, *The Main Philosophical Writings and the Novel Allwill*, edited and translated by George di Giovanni. Montreal: McGill-Queens University Press, 1994.

Kant, Immanuel. *Critique of the Power of Judgment*, edited by Paul Guyer and translated by Paul Guyer and Eric Matthews. Cambridge: Cambridge University Press, 2001.

Schelling, F. W. J. *Further Presentations from the System of Philosophy*, in *The Philosophical Rupture between Fichte and Schelling*, edited by M. Vater and D. Wood. Albany: State University of New York Press, 2012.

Schelling, F. W. J. *Philosophical Letters on Dogmatism and Criticism*, in *The Unconditional in Human Knowledge: Four Early Essays 1794–6*, edited by F. Marti. Lewisburg, PA: Bucknell University Press, 1980.

Secondary Literature

Alznauer, Mark. "Rival Versions of Objective Spirit." *Hegel Bulletin* 37, no. 2 (2016): 209–231.

Avineri, Shlomo. *Hegel's Theory of the Modern State*. Cambridge: Cambridge University Press, 1972.

Beiser, Frederick. *Hegel*. New York: Routledge, 2005.

Breazeale, Daniel. "The Spirit of the Early *Wissenschaftslehre*," in Breazeale, *Thinking through the Wissenschaftslehre*; Oxford: Oxford University Press, 2013, 96–123.

Clarke, James. "Hegel's Critique of Fichte in the 1802/03 Essay on Natural Right." *Inquiry* 54, no. 3 (2011): 207–225.

Franks, Paul. *All or Nothing.* Cambridge, MA: Harvard University Press, 2005.

Guyer, Paul. "Absolute Idealism and the Rejection of Kantian Dualism," in *The Cambridge Companion to German Idealism*, edited by K. Ameriks. Cambridge: Cambrdige University Press, 2000, 37–56.

Habermas, Jürgen. "Labor and Interaction: Remarks on Hegel's Jena *Philosophy of Mind*," in Jürgen Habermas, *Theory and Practice*. London: Heinemann, 1974, 142–169.

Harris, H. S. *Hegel's Development: Night Thoughts (Jena 1801–1806).* Oxford: Oxford University Press, 1984.

Harris, H. S. "Skepticism, Dogmatism and Speculation in the Critical Journal," in *Between Kant and Hegel: Texts in the Development of Post-Kantian Idealism*, edited by H. S. Harris and G. di Giovanni. Indianapolis: Hackett, 2000, 252–271

Harris, H. S. "The Concept of Recognition in Hegel's Jena Manuscripts," in *Hegel's Dialectic of Desire and Recognition: Texts and Commentary*, edited by John O'Neill. Albany: State University of New York Press, 1996, 233–252.

Henderson, James P. "Adam Smith's Influence on Hegel's Philosophical Writings." *Journal of the History of Economic Thought* 13, no. 2 (1991): 184–204.

Henrich, Dieter. "Hegels Grundoperation," in *Der Idealismus und seine Gegenwart*, edited by U. Guzzoni, B. Rang, and L. Siep. Hamburg: Felix Meiner, 1976, 208–230.

Herzog, Lisa. *Inventing the Market: Hegel, Smith, and Political Theory.* Oxford: Oxford University Press, 2013.

Honneth, Axel. *Freedom's Right.* New York: Columbia University Press, 2014.

Honneth, Axel. *The Struggle for Recognition.* Cambridge, MA: MIT Press, 1995.

Horstmann, Rolf-Peter. "Probleme der Wandlung in Hegels Jenaer Systemkonzeption." *Philosophische Rundschau* 19 (1972): 87–118.

Horstmann, Rolf-Peter. "The Role of Civil Society in Hegel's Political Philosophy," in *Hegel on Ethics and Politics*, edited by Robert B. Pippin and Otfried Höffe. Cambridge: Cambridge University Press, 208–240.

Ikäheimo, Heikki. *Anerkennung.* Berlin: de Gruyter, 2014.

Ilting, Karl-Heinz. "Hegels Auseinandersetzung mit der Aristotelischen Politik." *Philosophisches Jahrbuch* 71 (1963–1964): 38–58.

Kosch, Michelle. "Agency and Self-Sufficiency in Fichte's Ethics." *Philosophy and Phenomenological Research* XCI, no. 2 (2015): 348–380.

Lukács, Georg. *The Young Hegel.* Cambridge, MA: MIT Press, 1975.

Meist, Kurt Rainer. "Einleitung" to *System der Sittlichkeit [Critik des Fichteschen Naturrechts]*, edited by Horst D. Brandt. Hamburg: Meiner, 2002, 177–219.

Nance, Michael. 'Recognition, Freedom, and the Self in Fichte's *Foundations of Natural Right.*' *European Journal of Philosophy* 23, no. 3 (2015): 608–632.

Nassar, Dalia. *The Romantic Absolute.* Chicago: University of Chicago Press, 2013.

Neuhouser, Frederick. *Foundations of Hegel's Social Theory: Actualizing Freedom.* Cambridge, MA: Harvard University Press, 2000.

Pinkard, Terry. *Hegel's Phenomenology.* Cambridge: Cambridge University Press, 1996

Pippin, Robert. *Hegel's Practical Philosophy.* Cambridge: Cambridge University Press, 2008.

Riedel, Manfred. *Between Tradition and Revolution.* Cambridge: Cambridge University Press, 1984.

Schmidt, Steffen. *Hegels System der Sittlichkeit.* Berlin: Akademie Verlag, 2007.

Schmidt am Busch, Hans-Christoph. *Hegels Begriff der Arbeit*. Berlin: Akademie Verlag, 2002.

Schmidt am Busch, Hans-Christoph. "What Does It Mean to 'Make Oneself into an Object'? In Defense of a Key Notion of Hegel's Theory of Action," in *Hegel on Action*, edited by Arto Laitinen and Constantine Sandis. Palgrave Macmillan, 2010, 189–211.

Siep, Ludwig. *Anerkennung als Prinzip der Praktischen Philosophie*, originally published Freiburg: Alber Verlag, 1978; cited from reissued edition, Felix Meiner, 2014.

Taylor, Charles. *Hegel and Modern Society*. Cambridge: Cambridge University Press, 1979.

Testa, Italo. "How Does Recognition Emerge from Nature? The Genesis of Consciousness in Hegel's Jena Writings." *Critical Horizons* 13, no. 2 (2012): 176–196.

Thompson, Kevin. "Hegel's Institutionalism: Social Ontology, Objective Spirit, and Institutional Agency." *Hegel Jahrbuch*. Berlin/München/Bost: Walter de Gruyter, 2014, 321–326.

Wildt, Andreas. *Autonomie und Anerkennung*. Stuttgart: Klett-Cotta, 1982.

Zöller, Günter. *Fichte's Transcendental Philosophy*. Cambridge: Cambridge University Press, 1998.

PART II

PHENOMENOLOGY OF SPIRIT

CHAPTER 3

....

CONSCIOUSNESS AND THE CRITERION OF KNOWLEDGE IN THE *PHENOMENOLOGY OF SPIRIT*

....

DINA EMUNDTS

THE first part of this chapter discusses the aim of the *Phenomenology* as presented by Hegel in his Introduction. The second part of the chapter offers an overview of the first three chapters of the *Phenomenology*. The third part then presents some of Hegel's arguments from the third chapter, "Force and the Understanding"; this is the most complicated chapter of the work, and there is a relative lack of literature on it compared to the first two chapters. The fourth part summarizes the results of the entire section on Consciousness. In the last part I refer to some alternative readings of this section.

3.1. THE PHILOSOPHICAL PROBLEM RAISED IN THE INTRODUCTION

The *Phenomenology of Spirit* begins with a long Preface that outlines a general idea of Hegel's overall philosophical project. The much shorter Introduction, however, is meant to present the idea of the *Phenomenology of Spirit* itself. Three main topics are found in the Introduction:

1. It begins with remarks about the programs of other philosophers. These remarks lead to the claim that it is better to begin immediately with knowledge or the act of acknowledgment and not with prior questions about whether knowledge is possible in the first place.

2. It presents the *Phenomenology* as an introduction to the system of philosophy and characterizes it in this context as "phenomenal knowledge" (*erscheinendes Wissen*), in contrast to absolute knowledge (PS 9.55 ff./¶¶76 ff.).[1]

3. It introduces the specific program of the *Phenomenology* by explaining the structure of consciousness and formulating a task with respect to this structure. Consciousness is defined as a relation of consciousness to an object, and this raises the question of how this relation can be said to produce knowledge. Finding the right interpretation of the structure of consciousness will be the main task of the *Phenomenology*.

All three of these topics are important for an understanding of the *Phenomenology*, and the passages in which they are discussed are far from clear.[2] However, I will focus on the concept of consciousness and will give my view on the leading philosophical problem that Hegel aims to address.

Hegel describes his project[3] as an attempt to determine when knowing (*Wissen*) corresponds to truth (*Wahrheit*). In order to correctly understand what Hegel is up to, one must understand 'knowing' (*Wissen*) as 'holding-to-be-true' (*Fürwahrhalten*), whereas 'truth' (*Wahrheit*) means that something is in fact the case. Therefore, knowledge proper (*Erkenntnis*) is only present when something that is held to be true is also the case. Something is as one's claim to truth asserts that it is, independent of the fact that one (knowingly) refers to it. However, for Hegel the condition of knowledge (*Erkenntnis*) implies more than just this. The nature of knowledge is such that the person who claims to know something also states the grounds on which her knowledge claim is based. The person whom we say knows something is—at least in principle—able to give reasons for her claim that something really is the case. Knowledge is thus linked to *justification*. If this were not the case, the test for knowledge that Hegel has in mind would not be possible, for his test consists in the attempt to justify particular assertions. It is quite obvious that for Hegel 'knowing' (*Wissen*) does not mean the same as 'knowledge' (*Erkenntnis*). *Knowing* rather represents a necessary condition for knowledge, meaning that an individual holds something to be true. This can be learned from his remarks on *Wissen*. He claims that consciousness distinguishes something from itself, "and at the same time it *relates* itself to it" (*worauf es sich zugleich bezieht*) and that this means "[t]here is something *for* [*consciousness*]; and the determinate aspect of this *relating* [...] is *knowledge*" (es ist etwas *für dasselbe*; und die bestimmte Seite dieses *Beziehens* [...] ist das *Wissen*) (PS 9.58/¶82). When Hegel says here that "consciousness distinguishes

---

[1] I will take all translations of the *Phenomenology* (PS) from Pinkard, *Phenomenology of Spirit*. I refer to passages with the volume and page of G. W. F. Hegel, *Gesammelte Werke*, and with the number of the paragraphs (¶) (so that they can be found easily in Miller as well as in Pinkard).

[2] For the role of the *Phenomenology* within Hegel's system, see esp. Fulda, *Das Problem einer Einleitung in Hegels Wissenschaft der Logik*, and Theunissen, *Hegels Phänomenologie als metaphilosophische Theorie*.

[3] In the following section, I am adopting text from an unpublished paper that Amber Griffioen translated. Some considerations go back to the second chapter of Emundts, *Erfahren und Erkennen*.

something from itself," he means that one "holds something to be true." Similarly, "to which it at the same time refers" means "to which it is related in the mode of holding-to-be-true." Furthermore, Hegel claims here that consciousness realizes or appropriates that to which it is related—it is something *for consciousness*—and that this relationship of consciousness to its object, in which something is presented as being *for the subject*, is *Wissen*. Thus, a necessary condition for knowledge in the sense of *Erkenntnis* is that one holds it to be true.

With such a background to start us off, we can consider the problem Hegel wants to solve. When a person claims to know something, she represents it as being true.[4] As has already been clarified, this demand is not met by her state of *holding* something to be true. Additionally, there has to be something so distinct from merely holding something to be true that it can provide independent confirmation of that which is held to be true. Here, however, a problem emerges. If one wants to check whether or not a knowledge claim is true, one needs something objective, something independent, by means of which one can test proposed knowledge (as we have already seen, Hegel uses 'Wissen' to designate proposed knowledge). We need a standard or criterion of measurement for truth. This criterion cannot itself be a mere case of proposed knowledge or of 'holding-to-be-true'. Ideally, one would simply take the object and hold it up to the assertion. But that a given object can function as a criterion is itself a claim that must be tested. If one wants to know if knowledge proper is present, one must answer the question of whether the claim implicit in the assumption of that particular criterion is true or false. Similarly, it is not enough to say that truth consists of mere correspondence; rather, one must also provide a criterion by which it can be determined when there actually is a correspondence between what is held to be true and what is true, such that one's claim can be said to be substantial. In other words, when one defines truth as correspondence, the question becomes how to discern when this correspondence is present. After all, we can, with Hegel, say that a 'contradiction' arises at one point or another in the project of finding a 'standard' for knowledge (PS 9.58/¶¶81–82).

One could simply name the right criterion. For example, one could suggest a set of conceptual principles, as Hegel claims Kant did. Kant wants to find these principles a priori by looking at our ways of judging. But then one cannot convince those who have another conception of the criterion. One simply presupposes one's own ideas and does not solve the criterion problem. Thus, Hegel wants to find an alternative. He looks for the criterion by more closely observing the various suggestions for ascertaining when knowledge is present. He examines already existing opinions regarding the knowledge criterion and attempts in this way to locate the correct one without presupposing his own standard. By determining which criterion is the correct one, we can then determine when we do and do not have knowledge.

---

[4] Maybe we can also say that this is already the case when she *claims* something (and not when she claims to know something). However, for reasons not to be spelled out here, I prefer to speak explicitly of the claim to know something.

Yet, we have not explicitly discussed the fact that Hegel also regards knowledge as a relationship of correspondence between concept and object. According to Hegel, knowledge is present if and only if concept and object correspond.[5] However, Hegel does not simply identify the object (in the sense of an intentional object) with truth and thereby maintain that knowledge is present when the concept and truth correspond. Hegel presents the relationship of concepts and objects in such a way that 'object' means something that exists. For this reason, Hegel says "the existing thing [das Seiende] or the object" (PS 9.59/¶84). However, this leads to another question, or even problem: it seems that Hegel himself suggests here the picture according to which one can hold the assertion (or the concept) up to the object in order to see if it is true. Namely, if by 'object' one understands something that exists (*etwas Seiendes*) and by 'concept' one understands what we say about this thing that exists, then one ends up identifying the concept with knowing and the object with truth. But Hegel cannot claim that this is the only possibility (or the correct one) for characterizing the structure of knowledge and truth. However, there is a solution for this problem: Hegel takes this interpretation only as one possibility among others. Theories that use concepts or laws as a criterion can also be brought under the umbrella of the knowledge-as-correspondence formula. In order to see this, we have to take into account that Hegel explains the relationship of correspondence as moving in two possible directions:

> If we designate *knowledge* as the *concept*, but designate the essence, that is, the *truth*, as what exists, that is, the *object*, then the examination consists in seeing whether the concept corresponds to the object. But if we take *the essence*, that is, the in-itself *of the object*, and designate it *as the concept*, and then in contrast understand by *object* the concept as *object*, which is to say, the concept as it is *for an other*, then the examination consists in our seeing whether the object corresponds to its concept. (PS 9.59/¶84)[6]

According to this passage, both the existing object and concept can be viewed as the in-itself (*das Ansich*), that is, as truth. Correspondingly, both the concept and the object can be understood as the basis for holding something to be true (i.e., for that which is for Consciousness). This means that the concept as well as the object can function as the criterion in this relationship. In his exposition of the concept of knowledge proper in the Introduction to the *Phenomenology* Hegel leaves this open. Thus, Hegel can make use

---

[5] "However, to knowledge, the *goal* is as necessarily fixed as is the series of the progression. The goal lies at that point where [. . .] the concept corresponds to the object and the object to the concept" (PS 9.57/¶80).

[6] "Nennen wir das *Wissen* den *Begriff*, das Wesen oder das Wahre aber, das Seyende oder den *Gegenstand*, so besteht die Prüfung darin, zuzusehen, ob der Begriff dem Gegenstande entspricht. Nennen wir aber *das Wesen* oder das an sich *des Gegenstands den Begriff*, und verstehen dagegen unter dem *Gegenstande*, ihn als *Gegenstand*, nemlich wie er *für ein anderes* ist, so besteht die Prüfung darin, daß wir zusehen, ob der Gegenstand seinem Begriff entspricht" (PS 9.59/¶84).

of the idea of the relationship of correspondence of concept and object without committing himself to the claim that the object, in time and space, must be affirmed as the criterion for true knowing.

This claim about two possible interpretations of the correspondence-relation can initially be read as a historical-philosophical thesis. But it is at the same time the thesis that Hegel develops and discusses in the first chapters of the *Phenomenology*. Some philosophers have entertained the position that the object functions as the criterion, according to which the truth of a judgment is measured. Thus, truth is present when the existing object is as it is judged to be. This general stance sets up the first tests of the *Phenomenology* that are carried out in the chapters on Sense-Certainty and Perception. Other philosophers have put forward the opposite thesis. According to them, an existing object is not the kind of thing that can decide truth or falsehood, but is rather only an appearance. Instead, something conceptual must serve as the criterion for truth. This stance is represented, for example, by Kant and Fichte. These positions are put to the test in the chapters "Force and Understanding" and "The Truth of Self-Certainty."

Hegel proceeds toward the 'criterion test' in the following manner: first, he sets out to clarify what has to be the case in order for us to be able to speak meaningfully of knowledge in the first place, and then he begins with the test of various positions. He begins with the simplest position we can think of and then goes on to more sophisticated ones. The test itself is subsequently implemented in the main sections of the *Phenomenology*. The Introduction to the *Phenomenology*, however, contains the clarification of the concept of knowledge. Here he gives the fundamental conditions that must be accommodated by any particular position regarding knowledge in order for it to even count as a position regarding knowledge. They are as follows:

1. The concept of knowledge has to be able to account for the difference between *holding-to-be-true* and *being-true* (or as Hegel also often puts it, simply 'truth'), while, at the same time, making sense of the fact that, in the cases of knowledge, that which is held to be true *is* true. One should also be able to express the latter as a kind of correspondence between holding-to-be-true and truth. The person who claims to know something must be able to claim that what she is claiming is not only how things *appear* to her, but how things really are. In other words, one has to be able to indicate why that which is claimed to be known represents more than a merely subjective impression. Following my reading, this is the very basic necessary condition for even calling an utterance or a belief *knowledge*. To know something means to say that something is the case, and that means it is not merely dependent on *my* seeing or thinking it. This is what Hegel means when he says that there is something *for consciousness* that *also* has to be thought of as being *in itself*. For Hegel, it is essential that the distinction between how things merely appear to one and how things really are can be made by the person who claims to know something. This point can explain why Hegel thinks that the evaluation of the various positions regarding knowledge is somehow a self-evaluation of the positions.

If we agree that we need to fulfill the criterion and it turns out that we cannot really fulfill it, then the position has to be given up, and this does not require any criticism from outside.

2. It is constitutive for knowledge that one refers to an object. The object has to be something existing (*etwas Seiendes*). With this, Hegel claims, first, that what is known must *be* (i.e., that it really *is*). Second, he claims that that which *is* must be something that can be given by the senses or instantiated by something given by the senses. This second requirement arises already from the fact that Hegel says that the relationship between knowing and truth can be formulated as a correspondence-relation between concept and object.

In light of my interpretation, however, it must be conceded that the relevant remarks in the Introduction to the *Phenomenology* are also associated with certain ambiguities. They might be such that they put my interpretation into question and therefore I want to discuss three problems that one can see here. The first two of them concern Hegel's formulations. First, in presenting what I have called 'fundamental conditions', Hegel employs a vocabulary that usually indicates his desire to distance himself from the description at issue. For example, he calls the determinations of the structure of consciousness 'abstract'. This could lead to the idea that Hegel's description is the description of a structure that Hegel assigns to consciousness but from which he himself wishes to depart.[7] However, this assumption would cost the project of the *Phenomenology* dearly. For in the course of Hegel's examinations, he makes the case that the failure of the particular positions he is discussing is due to the fact that they do not meet the fundamental conditions laid out in the Introduction. The claim that the determinations are abstract does not mean that they must be given up. Instead, it means that it must still be shown whether the given determinations can be realized. The concrete idea of knowledge that is supposed to emerge by the end of the *Phenomenology* is a realization of the initially abstract determination of knowledge from the beginning. In the Preface to the *Phenomenology*, Hegel characterizes that which has not yet been experienced (*das Unerfahrene*) as 'the Abstract' (PS 9.29/¶36). The concretization of the determination of knowledge by experience occurs via the various 'determination experiments' that make up the *Phenomenology*.

A second ambiguity of the text consists in the fact that in a few places Hegel employs a vocabulary that appears to fit his philosophical project, but not those of other philosophers who attempt to provide a theory of how knowledge is possible. For example, he says that he is talking about that "with which one takes possession

---

[7] Cf. Cramer, "Bemerkungen zu Hegels Begriff vom Bewußstein"; Marx, *Hegels Phänomenologie des Geistes*, 69 ff.; Longuenesse, *Hegel's Critique of Metaphysics*, 11f. In my view, there is in fact one specific interpretation of this structure that Hegel wants to hold. He wishes, however, to get past all understanding that takes the two *relata* as being independent of one another, or as being opposite to one another (like the opposite between conceptual and sensible or stable and changeable).

of the absolute" (*wodurch man des Absoluten sich bemächtige*, PS 9.53/¶73). Should we assume that from the very beginning 'knowledge' means something different for Hegel than for other philosophers, and that he is starting with certain ideas about how real knowledge has to be understood?[8] A consequence would be that someone like Kant would no longer be addressed—why should he concern himself with a project that is in fact about knowledge of the Absolute, where the Absolute is construed in the sense of God? Because the *Phenomenology* responds to Kant (among many others), the assumption that Hegel is from the very outset focusing on the knowledge of particular objects creates difficulties for this project. I read these passages alternatively as fitting within the project of figuring out the general conditions of knowledge that are supposed to apply to everyone. To say "we know the absolute" would mean something like "we know something in such a way that we also somehow know, along with this knowledge or through the act of knowing itself (i.e., not by any external observation or operation), that it is."

It could be argued that there is a further difficulty with my interpretation of the Introduction. It concerns the question of whether Hegel is allowed to make presuppositions in his own project of finding the right concept of knowledge.[9] One might say that if Hegel is claiming that the resulting concept of knowledge is able to cover *all* possible accounts of knowledge, his own project must avoid excluding certain types of knowledge before the fact. Thus, it has to emerge without any presuppositions at all. However, knowledge, according to Hegel, is only present when particular conditions (as set out in the Introduction) are fulfilled. Thus, since Hegel provides a fundamental structure of knowledge, it appears that his project is no longer without presupposition. In my view, however, it is not problematic for the project to suggest minimal conditions under which talk of knowledge is meaningful in the first place. In fact, Hegel has to specify certain conditions. Otherwise, a project aimed at testing whether the respective positions are defensible could not be realized at all, since there needs to be some respect in which they can fail. Hegel thus assumes a sophisticated yet vulnerable concept of knowledge. We should be able to distinguish knowledge from mere knowledge-*claims*, in the sense that truth should emerge as distinct from mere holding-to-be-true. Moreover, we should be able to distinguish knowledge from purely conceptual operations. These prerequisites must be met in order to speak meaningfully of knowledge in the first place. Apart from them, Hegel assumes nothing further as the basis for his test. But what is to be said with respect to positions that do not meet these minimal conditions? Concerning those positions, Hegel has nothing left to say in response, other than that those positions cannot in the first place make sense of the term 'knowledge'. Hegel has no interest in further considering such a view because the person who holds this view is satisfied that we can only ever pronounce mere opinions.

---

[8] Bowman, *Sinnliche Gewißheit*, 89.
[9] Cf. Horstmann, "Hegels Ordnung der Dinge."

3.2. THE SECTION ON *CONSCIOUSNESS*

On my interpretation of the *Phenomenology*, the entire first part of the book, including the section on *Reason*, can be understood as an answer to the question, What is the right understanding of knowledge? that unfolds by analyzing different possible positions to see whether they fulfill the criterion (i.e., whether they are able to account with their own resources for a distinction between how things appear and how things really are). What is actually supposed to serve as a criterion—what truth and knowledge are actually supposed to be—is not fully determined by what is said in the Introduction. Thus, in order to provide us with any sort of interesting account, the question of what knowledge actually is must be determined by the particular theories under discussion. And this determination of the criterion is what the rest of the *Phenomenology* is supposed to put to the test. The various positions that Hegel discusses in the *Phenomenology* should thus interpret, in their own respective ways, the general structure of knowledge laid out in the *Introduction* as concerning knowledge and truth. The positions are introduced and examined, and in this process the person who holds such a position can learn not only that she cannot hold the position, but also what must be modified. The modifications are always present in the next position, and if there emerges one position that fulfills the criterion, that position will—at least partially—be the result of the failure of the others.

The section on *Consciousness* is the first section in the *Phenomenology*. It consists of three chapters: "Sense-Certainty," "Perception," and "Force and Understanding."[10] With respect to all three chapters, it is far from clear which philosophers are addressed. It is even not clear whether Hegel indeed always has special philosophers in mind, or whether he is developing a possible position that simply shares similarities with real positions. As a consequence, other questions are still under dispute, for example whether Hegel is following a chronological order. Another question concerns the beginning: Why does Hegel begin with sense-certainty? Concerning this question, one can, however, simply say that Hegel begins with the simplest, most passive position, with the position that reflects least on its possible problems (for instance, that we can be deceived). According to such a position, we know something simply because it is present to us; thus it is the position of sense-certainty. We might think of Jacobi here, who can be seen as someone who tried to establish such a 'naïve' position.[11]

The person in "Sense-Certainty" is claiming to know something and, in accordance with the general criterion of knowledge from the *Introduction*, she (or, speaking in her place, we) must show that she is able to make a distinction between being right and not being right. In the case of sense-certainty, this seems to be difficult because 'certainty' implies that the person has no room for possible error. The person states that she knows something because it is present, and she does not reflect at all on the possibility on being

---

[10] I gave a detailed interpretation of all three chapters in my *Erfahren und Erkennen*.
[11] Siep, *Hegel's Phenomenology of Spirit*, 73.

deceived. However, even she must be able to make the distinction between what only appears to her and what is really the case (for that is what the criterion of knowledge says in its simplest form). Thus, she has to give a reason for why the content of her claim is not totally dependent on *her* being aware of it. In Hegel's scenario the person first gives the following reason: that which she is claiming to be the case has to be true *because* she simply passively learns it from the object. As Hegel says, "The object is indifferent as to whether it is known or not" (PS 9.64/¶93). The person then realizes, however, that she has not formulated the claim in a way that shows how it can be true independently of her taking it to be true. If she reports on something that exists without understanding that thing as a determinate particular with universal determinations like *temporal* and *spatial* determinations,[12] then the presence of the object cannot be grasped in a way that would allow it to count as a criterion for the truth of what she holds to be true. Thus her idea that she can be certain based on the pure awareness of the object fails. This is not the end of the discussion of this position, for there are two possible variations of her position. In a second step, she goes on to claim, in a second try at a defense, that she herself is present in a way that can guarantee the certainty of her claims, and then she claims, thirdly, that the immediate relation between her and the object can itself be used as basis for justification. Thus, she would say things like "I cannot doubt it because I am indeed at this moment standing in relation to this thing." However, it turns out that if she wants to rely on this relation, she already has to understand it as something that is lasting, and this again requires something universal (i.e., determinations of space and time). The resulting claim of this chapter is that we need universals (i.e., temporal and spatial determinations) in order to rely on claims about the object, the subject, and their interrelation. The particular thing, the subject, and the relation have to be determined by something that is universal. The particular somehow has to be mediated by something universal. With this result, the first position itself must, however, be relinquished because it claimed the immediacy of the relation.

With the failure of sense-certainty, Hegel must now put forth a new position that answers the question of how knowledge is possible. This position is called 'perception' and is spelled out in the second chapter. Hegel addresses here surely (though maybe not only) the empiricists (i.e., Hume and Locke). Because the new position builds on the result from the last chapter, the defender of the position knows that, if she wants to take the object as that which makes a claim about it true, she must think of the object as determined by universals, and she must think about her relation to the thing as mediated by the universal. In order to claim to know something about the object, it has to be understood as something that persists over time, and for this it requires universal determinations. One implication of this result is that a person who wants to claim that she knows something has to go on to determine the particular thing as having properties of some sort. If the object (as well as ourselves and our relation to it) has universal

---

[12] Some interpreters tend to already talk here in general about concepts (cf. Taylor, *Hegel*, 197; Pippin, *Hegel's Idealism*, 117), but I think that Hegel wants to introduce the means for conceptual determination step by step, and the first step consists of temporal and spatial determinations.

determinations, it can be understood as a standard according to which the truth of the claim made by the person perceiving the object is measured. Thus, the person chooses the self-identity of the object as the criterion for truth. In this chapter we are supposed to learn that we can only take the thing to be something lasting when we understand it as standing in a dynamic relation to other things. Or, to put it another way, the conception of universals, with which this chapter began, develops in the ongoing investigation into a conception of universals as forces (one can think here not only of Locke but also of Newton). However, this result is only found at the end of the chapter because the dynamic conception already abandons the main idea of perception and self-identity. The next idea that takes forces into account is developed in the chapter "Force and Understanding."

This chapter deals mainly with the Kantian suggestion that natural laws provide the guidelines for what really is the case, and that they can thus function as the standard for knowledge claims. Hegel then discovers (or tries to discover) the problem of a specific understanding of laws which does not recognize that laws must build a complex nexus and must be understood holistically. The problems as well as the solution to this understanding of laws are introduced by Hegel's ideas of inversion and 'inverted worlds'. Hegel presents the notion of an inverted world in order to suggest that there are good and bad ways to understand the inversion of our conceptual determinations. The bad way to invert our conceptual determinations is to posit a supersensible world that is opposed to ours, for this leads to a problematic ontological opposition of appearances and things in themselves. However, we can obtain a positive conception of inversion if we see inversion as a description for the complex and holistic structure of unity and diversity that has to be the structure of the conceptual—that structure is the structure of infinity.

3.3. INTERPRETATION OF "FORCE AND UNDERSTANDING"

The chapter "Force and Understanding" begins with a position according to which one thinks of things as constituted by forces. In the evaluation of this position in the first part of the chapter, it turns out that one must understand forces as something conceptual and not as something given.[13] For this reason, we then have a position that suggests that what there is can be determined only by forces (i.e., by entities that have only this basic conceptual character). This implies that it is only because entities are determined

---

[13] This first part contains §§ 132–142 (GW 9, 82–88). In my view, Hegel refers here mainly to Newton and to Kant's theory of forces in the *Dynamic* of his *Metaphysical Foundations of Natural Science*. We can thus read this first part in two ways: we can read it as the development of the understanding of things before Kant, and we can read it as the content of Kant's theory of matter. The Kantian insight that leads to the Kantian position is that "[t]he truth of force remains therefore merely the *thought* of force" (GW 9, 87; § 141). I will not deal with this part of the chapter here.

by concepts that we can know them. The determination of something by its concepts can be seen as an operation of the 'understanding'. Here it becomes clear that Hegel is addressing Kant (among others) who has defined the understanding as the capacity of concepts and judgments.

In holding this position, one attempts to use concepts of force to determine what things are. Thus one has to specify what particular forces, understood in their conceptual nature, are at work. One does this by determining the laws of the forces in question.[14] Thus, we can now say that we acknowledge things when we determine them as standing in relations of laws to other things. This position will be criticized in the main paragraphs of the chapter. Here, Hegel discusses the position that takes physical laws to be conceptual essences that tell us what is objectively true about things.

The problems that Hegel sees in such a position can be summarized in three steps.

(a) The first problem concerns a quite simple understanding of laws according to which they are as such necessary and tell us what (objectively) is the case.

Hegel uses two main formulations to express the deficiency of this first understanding of laws. He says that there is an *indifference between force and law*, and he says that there is an *indifference between concept and being*.[15] I understand the word 'indifference' (*Gleichgültigkeit*) to mean, in this context, the opposite of 'standing in a necessary relation'[16]. According to Hegel, the basic structure of laws consists of a single concept on the left side, the equals sign, and the connection of different elements on the right side. Concerning the thesis of indifference, we have to identify 'force' and 'concept' with the left side of the law, 'law' and the 'being' with the right side. One might wonder why Hegel identifies the left side with the *concept* of the law. I would suggest this means that we can understand the left side as saying by means of one simple concept what there is; if we do so, we think of the right side as directly referring to what is given, while the left side is meant to be the adequate concept for this. According to Hegel, we can also put it the other way around. In this case, we understand the left side as making a direct reference to what exists, and the right side as giving the law (i.e., the explanation of what exists). This latter case is expressed in the opposition of force and law.

But be this as it may, what is important to realize is that Hegel thinks that there is no necessary connection between the left and the right side of the equation (i.e., between the left side marking the object of the law and the right side explicating the law). However, laws (as the entire equation) can still contain a necessary relation on their right side. For example, it is true that whenever there is a positive charge there also

---

[14] The way in which Hegel introduces the conception of laws is not easy to understand. I take it that he is referring to the idea of the unity of experience when he claims that "the *true* is the simple inner" (PS 9.90/¶148). In ¶149 f. (PS 9.91 f.), Hegel then argues that this conceptual inner must be explicated by laws.

[15] Hegel says, for example, "The indifference of law and force, that is, of concept and being, is present in yet another way than that already indicated" (PS 9.94/¶153).

[16] This is confirmed by Hegel's expression "just as much indifferent to one another and without any necessity for each other" (PS 9.99/¶161).

is a negative one, but this does not mean that there is a necessary connection between the two sides of the law. This means that we can only claim that if there is a positive charge there is also a negative one, but not that we know why and when there is a positive charge. It has to be realized that the concept of laws given so far is such that "its necessity is external" (PS 9.93/§152)—in order to have knowledge, we would need other laws that would tell us when there is a positive charge or knowledge about the fulfillment of further conditions for the existence of a positive charge. One might say that the force has the *property* of expressing itself in the way the law describes, or that the law is a *definition* of the force.[17] But this offers no real explanation, and an explanation is what we are looking for, according to Hegel. Thus, we cannot understand the law as such as explaining what there is necessarily. In this case, laws cannot be taken as guidelines for objective judgment or as criteria for what really is the case, independent of my observing it that way. As a result, this suggestion with respect to the understanding of laws fails.

(b) A variant of the law-based position has a more sophisticated concept of laws. Hegel says that "the law is thereby available in a doubled manner" (PS 9.93/§152). The reaction to the problem of necessity might consist in an understanding of laws as regularities that are, on the one hand, observed and, on the other hand, given the form of laws by the understanding. However, it seems that this conception leads to the problem that the content of laws is only grasped by observation and not given a priori. However, this seems to be now assumed by the position. Thus the position claims that only the form is given a priori and that the understanding serves to establish the necessity that lawful relations imply. But this leads to the problem that laws are solely conceptual operations, analytic truths, or definitions.

For Hegel, there resides in this understanding of necessity a deep subjectivism:

> It is thus merely its *own* necessity that the understanding expresses. It makes this distinction in such a way that it expresses at the same time that the distinction is to be no distinction in the item at stake. (*kein Unterschied der Sache selbst*) (PS 9.94/§154)

(c) This leads to a third position that makes these two aspects—namely the observed facts and the a priori form of laws—more explicit within its understanding of laws by articulating necessary meta-laws and special laws that stand under these laws but are not taken to be necessary in the strict sense. Here, Hegel seems to have in mind a very general law like the principle of the *Second Analogy* or the law in the *Metaphysical Foundation of Natural Sciences*,[18] on the one hand, and all more specific laws, like the law of gravity, on the other hand.

---

[17] PS 9.93/§152.

[18] One of the things he does in the chapter "Force and Understanding" is, as far as I understand, to attack the role that Kant reserved for the *Metaphysical Foundation of Natural Sciences*. Hegel's objection can be summarized as follows: the Kantian principles of the understanding are not specified by the laws

One could tell this whole story about sufficient and insufficient conceptions of laws in terms of an attempt to achieve a correct understanding of Kant's *Analogies*. Hegel thinks rightly that Kant's understanding of laws is grounded in the *Analogies of Experience*, and his thesis is that Kant's understanding of the *Analogies* leads to a deficient understanding of the necessity of laws. However, Hegel wants to prove this mainly in his *Logic*. Instead, in the *Phenomenology* he tells the story of how this understanding of meta-laws is negated by experience. This is what he tries to do with his conception of the inverted world, which I discuss in more detail later in the chapter. However, the structure of law, with its two sides and their relation, actually goes back to the idea of the analogies, and therefore it might be helpful to refer briefly to this here. As mentioned earlier, for Hegel, the basic structure of laws consists of a single concept on the left side, the equals sign, and the connection of different elements on the right side. In order to determine something according to laws, we must presuppose a simple substance. This is due to the *First Analogy* and is expressed by the left side of the law. At the same time, we must also express in a differentiated way what we want to determine, because to determine means to attribute something to something in comparison to other things. This is done on the right side of the law. The way we do this is accounted for by the *Second Analogy*. This explanation of the form of laws can, at least according to Hegel, be attributed to Kant as well as to himself. The crucial question is how to understand the relation between the left side and the right side. They are supposed to be at the same time different and the same. According to Hegel, it is his own philosophy and not Kant's that is able to explain such a structure. We can say that a law expresses, by means of the equals sign, an identity between a simple unity (on the left side) and a distinction (on the right side). If we read the equals sign as expressing two bi-conditional sentences, the law reads: we must understand a simple substance as determined by causal relations; and the different elements of causal relations must be understood as a simple unity. If the form of the law is meant to guarantee the unity of experience, this must be expressed by the simple principle on the left side. But then one must ask how we can confirm that the distinction made on the right side of the law is the same as the unity expressed on the left side. This is not explained by the first two *Analogies* as Kant, according to Hegel, states them. In order to fulfill the demand of the unity of experiences, we must say within a Kantian frame that the distinction expressed by the right side is *simply the same* as the unity on the left side in the sense that "it is *nothing other than the right side*." The claim here is thus that the different elements and the one principle are identical without restriction. As I have noted, in the progression of "Force and Understanding" this turns out to be false. Hegel, on the contrary, will present an idea of unity according to which unity is the product of negating the claimed identities in laws by means of other laws, whereas the entirety of laws provides the basis for necessity. This is the structure of infinity that Hegel wants to reach by describing the 'inversions' of laws.

of the *Metaphysical Foundation*, but rather only repeated. "The unification of all laws into *universal attraction* expresses no further content than precisely that of the *mere concept of law itself*" (PS 9.92/¶150).

The inversion of the world has different meanings within Hegel's framework. It means *first* that laws can have different meanings depending on the context. Laws that seem to say the same thing can have different meanings. An example of this might be the relation between punishment and revenge: it is the 'same' rule, but in one instance it is an official punishment, and in the other instance it is pure revenge. Moreover, various laws can say very different or even contradictory things about the same object. The living being is, for example, determined by physical laws as well as by biological ones. This sort of inversion is deeply problematic for a conception like Kant's because his idea is that the objects are simply determined to be the way they are according to causal laws. Because this is so, Kant cannot really accept laws other than the physical laws, be they biological or practical in nature. This leads to the idea that there are several worlds that stand in a relation of inversion to one another because they make opposite claims that are both supposed to be true. This is the *second* meaning of 'inversion'. Here we cannot only talk of an inversion, but of an inverted world (*verkehrte Welt*) because we think of different worlds that are at certain points incompatible. The world of physical objects is totally different from that of biological objects. This idea of inverted worlds leads to a lot of problems. If we do not want to say that the different worlds are pure fictions, we have to assume that our understanding is deficient. This, however, makes the situation even worse. It could be that what we explain by means of physical laws can, in fact, only be explained by teleological laws. We do not know how the world really is at all. But if this is true, we lose the idea that we acknowledge anything at all. It could be that the world as we conceive it is actually the inversion of the real world.

So far the inversion can mean, first, that laws are dependent on the context, but it can also mean that one can think of two worlds that are inversions of one another. The second meaning is the product of a false understanding of the first. Or, to put it more accurately, the second one is what one makes of the first when one is operating within a Kantian framework.

Third, the inversion of laws plays a crucial role in Hegel's own conception. Namely, we can talk of inversion when we refer explicitly in one law to another law in a way that negates the relation that is stated by the first law. Thus, the inversion of laws really does take place in the determinations of things. According to Hegel, this is what in the end will produce a system of laws in which the laws are genuinely mediated by one another. For example, we have to refer in an 'inverted way' to physical laws within biological laws. To put it simply, we can say that we explain some aspects of the organism with physical laws, but at the same time these laws are negated insofar as they are not the laws that explain the organism. What we learn by the inversion is thus additionally that the meta-law or the meta-laws that are meant to structure reality are themselves not static, but rather have to change in relation to the development of other special laws; for example, the significance of the concept of physical causal relations changes when put in the context of a concept of biological functions. Thus, even very general and basic laws result from our determinations of things and are not simply given a priori. Hegel's idea is that we can connect all 'areas' of knowledge with these kinds of relationships between various realms of laws, and we have to do this not only in order to obtain a unity of laws, but also because only then is it possible to uphold the claim that laws are necessary: a law as such claims its validity without restriction. However, laws are only necessary in specific contexts. We can reflect this restriction *within* laws if we treat them not in isolation, but rather in terms of their explicit links to other contexts in which their absolute validity is explicitly negated. Negation here has a very special role (as it often does for Hegel): we do not negate the necessity of a particular law in general, but we negate it in another context in which it is not valid, and by doing so we can even affirm that it is valid in the previous context. This is meant to establish the status of laws without accepting their absolute validity.

This third meaning of the inversion is the structure that Hegel calls *infinity*. Think again of the basic structure of laws that consists of a single concept on the left side, the equals sign, and the connection of different elements on the right side. This structure tells us that we have one simple principle (on the left side of the law) and that we differentiate it in a way that gives the impression of independent elements (this is the right side of the law). However, the equals sign tells us that the differentiation is nothing other than the unity. To understand how this is possible, we have to understand the procedure of negating the connections described in one law so as to determine things by new laws. This is the structure of infinity. This is the structure that physical laws ought to have and according to which they ought to be understood as laws. However, it is also the structure that brings us to living beings and human beings. The moments of determination in the physical law seem to be self-sufficient, independent elements. However, the elements are only moments in the procedure of determination and have no real independence. Hegel describes this the following way:

> It is not merely that the mere unity on hand is such that *no distinction* would be *posited*; rather, it is this *movement* that *undeniably makes a distinction. However*, because the distinction is no distinction at all, it is *once again sublated*. (PS 9.95/¶155)

Independent objects are only arrived at if we have other principles of determinations than just physical principles. The notion of an independent object goes beyond just physical determination. But this is what the subsequent chapters flesh out. With this insight, we reach the end of the chapter "Force and Understanding."

Thus, this procedure in which a specific law is negated allows us first to produce a unity of all laws, and second, it contains an adequate understanding of their necessity. Third, we can, according to Hegel, gain an adequate understanding of the determination of *objects*. As we have seen, we often refer with different kinds of laws to one and the same object. However, in this procedure the object that we refer to with different kinds of laws—for example, physical and biological laws—shows itself not only to be constituted by physical laws, but as something that remains the same in different conceptual frameworks.

At this point, we have to take into account the fact that we are only talking about the end of the chapter "Force and Understanding." We reach here the structure of infinity, and, according to my reading, this structure is adequate for an understanding of physical laws and physical objects.

3.4. THE RESULTS OF THE SECTION *CONSCIOUSNESS*

Although the aim of the *Phenomenology* is to answer the question of how we obtain knowledge, the results of the book and even of the first section are difficult to pin down. This has to do with Hegel's thesis that there is no simple answer to this question and that, to begin with, it depends on the right understanding of the subject and object. The answer is furthermore only eventually possible if we consider not only the principles of knowledge of physical actuality, but also those of other areas as, for example, the principles of the social world. Taking this into account, we can summarize at least some of the results of the first section on *Consciousness* as follows:

1. It has become clear that we need a holistic understanding of laws and principles in order to establish physical laws and to claim that we know anything about the physical world. This is implied by the structure of infinitude that is reached at the end of this section.

2. It has become clear that physical objects are not self-sufficient entities or substances as such, but rather that self-sufficient substances are products of the acts of conceptual determination accomplished by a subject. This does not apply to living beings, but that is not the topic of the first section.

3. Together with (2) it became clear that the things we can objectively refer to and rely on in our justification of knowledge claims are *conceptually determined things*. Considering the question of the standard for truth, this also means that there are no objects in contrast to concepts and no concepts that exist separate from things and that can be taken alone to be the standard for truth. Instead, following the section on *Consciousness*, it has to be a nexus of principles and laws that are gained through experiences (and not a priori) that can act as a standard.

4. Because it also turned out at the end of the section on *Consciousness* that the determination is accomplished by a subject, we can also say that the structure of objectivity is grounded in a subject and has the structure of the activity of a subject. With this result we reach the topic of self-consciousness. More precisely, we can say that if knowledge has the conditions that are discovered thus far in the *Phenomenology*, then it is also clear that, in order to answer the question of how knowledge is possible, the subject must have an understanding of her own subjecthood. Moreover, we already have some results with respect to the question of what a subject is. Namely, the basic structure of infinitude turned out to be the true structure of the object and of the subject. Thus in the next chapter we need to spell

out what the subject, as having such a structure, really is. This is the starting point of the next chapter.

3.5. A Non-Reductive Reading of Hegel's Account of Consciousness

It is important to be aware of the fact that in the chapters on *Consciousness* different positions are presented that suggest a specific criterion of knowledge (i.e., a standard by which one can know that things really are the way one thinks they are). I understand this investigation as a kind of experiment intended to determine whether the criterion given by the person who maintains her position can be defended. She usually fails, but in her failing, at the same time, it becomes obvious what was missing or what she can learn. This is, however, not to be understood as if it (thereby) becomes entirely clear what the criterion is. Rather, something becomes apparent that is in need of further interpretation if it is to count as a new criterion. For example, in the first chapter it becomes apparent that we need something that is a universal. In the "Perception" chapter, the universal is still thought to be sensual. Only in the end does it become clear that this universal has to be a holistic nexus of concepts or judgments. But this becomes clear only after the structure of the infinite is understood, and even this structure has to be developed further.

According to the reading I have sketched here, the reason that a position fails (i.e., why it has to be changed and, in the end, relinquished) is that the necessary condition for knowledge cannot be established within this position. The subject maintaining the positions fails to support the claim that what she knows is not only and entirely dependent on her. This means that the position provides no standard for knowledge and thus it is not suited to answer the question of how knowledge is possible. However, in most interpretations of Hegel's text, this procedure is described in a slightly different way, and this difference has important consequences. Most interpreters say that Hegel shows that the positions discussed are shown to have *as such* contradictions or incongruences.[19] According to this interpretation, the position of sense-certainty wants to refer immediately to particulars, but it turns out that this is only possible by means of mediating concepts. If interpreters put it that way, I would like to distance my interpretation from theirs with respect to at least two points.

First, in talking about contradictions within the positions and in taking the reference to things as the genuine aim of the position, their description of the procedure by which the position fails is different from mine. Namely, mine simply relies on the criterion question. The positions only get into problems if they try to justify their knowledge claim. For

---

[19] Horstmann, "Hegels Ordnung der Dinge."

example, the position of Sense-Certainty wants to take the immediate object as a standard for truth, and it turns out that this is impossible. The way of relying on the object that is claimed with this position is not suited to take the object as a standard because the object is nothing that lasts when the knowing-subject turns away from it. This is a contradiction in a special sense. It is not simply a conceptual contradiction or a contradiction within the position (i.e., a contradiction of claims the subject makes or has to make for even maintaining what she stated at the beginning). Instead, the problem arises because the immediate relation to things is taken to be the basis for justifying knowledge claims. What is obviously needed in the situation of justification stands in contradiction to what the position maintains. This might sound like a minor difference in description. However, I think it is important because of the consequence one can draw from it.[20]

Second, the consequence they draw from their alternative reading is that it thus turns out that we cannot relate immediately to things. According to my interpretation, this is not a consequence of the *Consciousness* section. The contradictions should *only* be read as relevant to the criterion problem, which has to be separated from the problem of immediate reference or relating to things in general. The universal that turns out to be required is not a condition for relating to things in general, but rather only for relying on claims about things that are meant to justify knowledge claims. According to my reading, one can, for example, even without physical laws, have opinions about things, and one can even make claims about things. Only the possibility of full justification and therefore of knowledge is missing. In my view, the question concerning justification and the relation to particulars as particulars are two different issues, and I would say that Hegel, in the *Phenomenology*, tackles only the first.[21] This must also be the case because Hegel does not simply want to claim that the position of Sense-Certainty is false. He also wants to claim that there has been a rational development in the history of philosophy in which the criterion is only at the end fully established. In my view, it would be much less convincing to say that only at the end of the development of philosophy were people first able to relate to particulars. Furthermore, it appears to me that Hegel would not deny that we can simply be *conscious* of things without being self-conscious. It is only that in this state we cannot really justify our claims. This is why I call my reading a 'non-reductive' reading of consciousness.[22] This also leads to another thesis concerning

---

[20]   I also think that this reading leads to a new understanding of the role of experiences in the *Phenomenology*. For this thesis see Emundts, *Erfahren und Erkennen*.

[21]   This is why I would not say that Hegel and Sellars are arguing for the same thesis concerning concepts. This is an important difference from the interpretations of Brandom, "A Spirit of Trust"; Horstmann, "Hegels Ordnung der Dinge"; Pippin, "Brandom's Hegel"; Pinkard, *Hegel's Phenomenology*; Stekeler-Weithofer, *Hegels Phänomenologie des Geistes*; Moyar, "The Inferential Object"; and many others.

[22]   Note that I do not claim that the other readings have to be reductive in every sense. There could be readings that are non-reductive in denying that for Hegel *only* concepts are real. A non-reductive reading in this sense is provided, for example, by Moyar, "The Inferential Object." What I mean by a non-reductive reading is also the claim that the conceptual does *only* play the crucial role when it comes to the criterion-question, but not for relying on things or referring to them. As I said, we can, for example, refer to things without understanding them as standing in a lawful connection to one another.

the relation between consciousness and self-consciousness. According to my reading, there is consciousness without self-consciousness, although for the real justification of knowledge we indeed require self-consciousness. The alternative reading, in contrast, claims that self-consciousness is the condition for consciousness.[23]

WORKS CITED

Primary Texts

Hegel, G. W. F. *Gesammelte Werke* [GW]. Nordrhein-Westfälische Akademie der Wissenschaften und der Künste in Verbindung mit der Deutschen Forschungsgemeinschaft (ed.). Hamburg: Felix Meiner, 1968ff.
Hegel, G. W. F. *Hegel's Philosophy of Mind* [E], translated by W. Wallace and A. V. Miller; edited by M. Inwood. Oxford: Oxford University Press 2007.
Hegel, G. W. F. *Phenomenology of Spirit* [PS], translated by T. Pinkard. Accessed September 12, 2015. http://terrypinkard.weebly.com/phenomenology-of-spirit-page.html.

Secondary Literature

Bowman, Brady. *Sinnliche Gewißheit. Zur systematischen Vorgeschichte eines Problems des deutschen Idealismus.* Berlin: Akademie Verlag, 2003.
Brandom, Robert. "A Spirit of Trust. A Semantic Reading of Hegel's Phenomenology." Accessed September 12, 2015. http://www.pitt.edu/~brandom/spirit_of_trust_2014.html.
Cramer, Konrad. "Bemerkungen zu Hegels Begriff vom Bewußtsein in der Einleitung zur Phänomenologie des Geistes," in *Seminar Dialektik in der Philosophie Hegels*, edited by Rolf-Peter Horstmann. Frankfurt am Main: Suhrkamp, 1978, 360–393.
Emundts, Dina. *Erfahren und Erkennen. Hegels Theorie der Wirklichkeit.* Frankfurt am Main: Klostermann, 2012.
Fulda, Hans Friedrich. *Das Problem einer Einleitung in Hegels Wissenschaft der Logik.* Frankfurt am Main: Klostermann, 1965.
Horstmann, Rolf-Peter. "Hegels Ordnung der Dinge. Die 'Phänomenologie des Geistes' als 'transzendentalistisches' Argument für eine monistische Ontologie und seine erkenntnistheoretischen Implikationen." *Hegel-Studien* 41 (2006): 9–50.
Longuenesse, Béatrice. *Hegel's Critique of Metaphysics.* Cambridge: Cambridge University Press, 2007.
Marx, Werner. *Hegels Phänomenologie des Geistes. Die Bestimmung ihrer Idee in "Vorrede" und "Einleitung."* Frankfurt am Main: Klostermann, 1986.
Moyar, Dean. "The Inferential Object: Hegel's Deduction and Reduction of Consciousness," in *Internationales Jahrbuch des Deutschen Idealismus/International Yearbook of German Idealism* 11, edited by Dina Emundts and Sally Sedgwick. Berlin: De Gruyter, 2016, 119–143.

---

[23] I would like to thank Rolf Horstmann for our discussions. Many thanks are due to Amber Griffioen and Marcus Lampert for their careful reading and comments on this text or earlier versions of it. Many thanks are also due to Dean Moyar for his helpful comments and suggestions.

Pinkard, Terry. *Hegel's Phenomenology: The Sociality of Reason*. Cambridge: Cambridge University Press, 1994.

Pippin, Robert. "Brandom's Hegel." *European Journal of Philosophy* 13, no. 3 (2005): 381–408.

Pippin, Robert. *Hegel's Idealism: The Satisfaction of Self-Consciousness*. Cambridge: Cambridge University Press, 1989.

Siep, Ludwig. *Hegel's Phenomenology of Spirit*, translated by D. Smyth. Cambridge: Cambridge University Press, 2014.

Stekeler-Weithofer, Pirmin. *Hegels Phänomenologie des Geistes. Ein dialogischer Kommentar*, 2 vols. Hamburg: Felix Meiner Verlag, 2014.

Taylor, Charles. *Hegel*. Frankfurt am Main: Suhrkamp, 1983.

Theunissen, Brendan. *Hegels "Phänomenologie" als metaphilosophische Theorie. Hegel und das Problem der Vielfalt philosophischer Theorien. Eine Studie zur systemexternen Rechtfertigungsfunktion der "Phänomenologie des Geistes."* Hamburg: Felix Meiner Verlag, 2014.

CHAPTER 4

....

SELF-CONSCIOUSNESS
IN THE *PHENOMENOLOGY*

....

SCOTT JENKINS

THE fourth chapter of the *Phenomenology of Spirit* is perhaps the most famous part of the book, and arguably the most essential to its task. "Self-Consciousness" is famous due to the many readings that have been offered of Hegel's dialectic of lordship and bondage. And it is essential to the *Phenomenology* because it is not until "Self-Consciousness" that *spirit* (*Geist*) finally appears:

> It is in self-consciousness, in the concept of Spirit, that consciousness first finds its turning point, where it leaves behind it the colourful show of the sensuous here-and-now and the nightlike void of the supersensible beyond, and steps out into the spiritual daylight of the present. (PS 9.108–109/¶177)[1]

Spirit thus appears as a necessary element in the work's progression from naïve realism to Hegel's own idealism, which again indicates the importance of "Self-Consciousness" for the *Phenomenology* as a whole. The chapter is to begin the process of explaining how the objective world could be grasped by a subject as "only the 'I' itself" (PS 9.103/¶166), or equivalently, how it could be that "self-consciousness alone is the truth of those shapes" that exist outside of it in the world (PS 9.102/¶164). This is actually a twofold task. In connection with the objects of consciousness, Hegel must elucidate the central result of 'Consciousness'—that the sensible world that *appears* to be irreducibly other is, *in truth*, a determination of consciousness. And in connection with consciousness itself, Hegel must provide some account of the subject for which such a relation to an object is possible. As Hegel presents this twofold task in ¶167, the chapter is to illuminate the

---

[1] Citations of the *Phenomenology* provide the volume and page number in the *Gesammelte Werke*, followed by the paragraph number in Miller's translation. I have modified this translation by replacing 'Notion' (Miller's translation of '*Begriff*') with 'concept'.

sublation (*Aufhebung*) of the sensible world by providing an account of a self-conscious subject for which the world could be both *canceled* (as an independently real entity) and *preserved* (as a 'moment of self-consciousness').

But the further we read in "Self-Consciousness," the harder it is to see exactly how the chapter might bear on these idealist themes. Hegel's talk of desire and life, his discussion of mutual recognition and a fight to the death, and the famous relation of lord to bondsman clearly mark some kind of turn to 'the practical' in general. But what sort of turn? And how could it be relevant to the idealist concern with self-consciousness that originates in Kant's claim that "it must be possible for the 'I think' to accompany all my representations"?[2] The thought that one is the subject of a particular representational state would seem to be far removed from any relation to self that could be illuminated through considering desire, or interpersonal relations. And all of this is further complicated by the appearance of spirit, Hegel's notion of (let us say, provisionally) the social context in which self-conscious subjects exist. This step into spirit eventually leads to Hegel's examination of Stoicism, Skepticism, and Judeo-Christian 'unhappy consciousness' as forms of a developing, historical 'World-Spirit'. And again, it is hard to see how any discussion of the structure of history could bear on the task of comprehending a self-relation in relation to an object.

The difficulties involved in integrating "Self-Consciousness" into the fabric of the *Phenomenology* have led some readers to focus on the chapter's significance as an examination of intersubjectivity or social-political themes, but the last 25 years have seen an increased interest in understanding the chapter as a novel account of self-consciousness intended to underwrite Hegel's own idealism.[3] On this reading, Hegel turns to central themes of practical philosophy because he believes that it is only by rethinking in a radical manner what it is to be a self-conscious subject that we can appreciate the unlimited domain of our cognitive faculties. In this chapter I present a reading of "Self-Consciousness" that builds on this recent interpretive trend by showing how Hegel's remarks on death, desire, recognition, and history can be read as essential elements of his account of self-consciousness and knowledge generally. I argue that it is only by understanding Hegel's figure of the bondsman as the paradigmatic self-conscious subject that the unity of "Self-Consciousness" comes into view. On this approach, Hegel takes self-consciousness to be, in the first place, an essentially social relation to one's own bodily desire. This understanding of the figure of the bondsman shapes my approach to other parts of "Self-Consciousness," most notably the struggle to the death, which will end up playing a surprisingly small role in Hegel's account of self-consciousness and knowledge.

---

[2] Kant, *Critique of Pure Reason*, B131. Citations of Kant's *Critique* will employ the standard A/B pagination to designate page numbers in the first and second editions, respectively.
[3] This approach begins with Pippin's *Hegel's Idealism*.

4.1. SELF-CONSCIOUSNESS AND DESIRE

The task of understanding exactly what Hegel means to say about self-conscious subjects and their knowledge of objects is complicated by the fact that it is not obvious what Hegel *means* by the central term 'self-consciousness'. In fact, the term has a number of different senses in the chapter. Hegel first presents self-consciousness as a "new shape of knowing," which is distinguished from the conception of knowing employed in 'Consciousness' by the fact that objects of knowledge "are no longer essences, but are moments of self-consciousness" (PS 9.104/¶167). In this context, 'self-consciousness' picks out a *philosophical position* on the being of objects (not independently real, not 'essences') and knowledge of those objects. This position is an instance of what Hegel, in the Introduction to the *Phenomenology*, terms consciousness's concept (*Begriff*) of itself—its conception of what objects are, and what it is to know such objects (PS 9.57/ ¶80). Self-consciousness, in this sense, is the still-developing conception of knowing that emerges from the first four chapters of the *Phenomenology*. It takes knowledge to be 'infinite' insofar as it is not limited by an unknowable thing in itself. In knowing, the subject "overarches [*greift . . . über*]" what appears to be irreducibly other, ensuring that our knowledge of objects through concepts is not limited to "this side" of the object (i.e., to Kantian appearances) (PS 9.103/¶166).

Hegel also uses the term 'self-consciousness' in a more familiar manner to pick out the relation of a conscious being to itself. Self-consciousness in this second sense can be understood in a number of ways, and all of the following are present in the text. It might pick out the awareness we have of ourselves as being in some particular state. This could be as abstract as a first-personal thought that one is in a particular representational state, for example, "I think representation x and I also think representation y" (to use Kantian terminology), or it could be a matter of understanding oneself in some more concrete manner, for example as having a particular social status. Self-consciousness would then be a form of self-knowledge, or perhaps a more general sense of who or what one is. Hegel is also concerned with the more basic relation to self, or reflexivity of consciousness generally, that underlies any particular instance of self-knowledge. This is what Hegel refers to as a subject's 'pure being-for-self', and it recalls Kant's notion of 'pure apperception' as that which underlies and generates any thought of the form "I think x."[4] Finally, and in connection with self-knowledge and apperception, Hegel sometimes uses the term to pick out the distinctive experience of a subject that is conscious of itself in either of these ways. This is self-consciousness as lived by a particular subject.

A third sense of 'self-consciousness' is perhaps the most common in the chapter. Hegel sometimes speaks of 'a self-consciousness', or of self-consciousness in the abstract, when he has in mind a subject that possesses at least some qualities essential to self-consciousness in the second sense. Used in this manner, 'self-consciousness'

---

[4] Kant, *CPR*, B132.

draws our attention to ways in which a particular subject, or particular instance of the observed consciousness in the *Phenomenology*, might satisfy or fall short of the standard of being a self-conscious subject. This diversity of senses can be confusing, but Hegel's reasons for using the term 'self-consciousness' in these ways—and for failing to provide the reader with any guide to his usage—are grounded in his methodology more generally. As a presuppositionless investigation into the scope of knowledge and the nature of subjects capable of knowing, the *Phenomenology* cannot simply assume any particular understanding of a conscious being's relation to itself and must instead develop its own conception of subjectivity. This means that when Hegel describes to us what 'a self-consciousness' does, is, or aims at, he is often exhibiting for us the gradual development of his own account of a self-conscious subject. That is, he is telling us how self-consciousness (in the second sense) must be understood if we are to realize the 'new shape of knowing' that emerges from the opening chapters (i.e., self-consciousness in the first sense). And this means that it would be a mistake to regard any particular claim about self-consciousness or 'a self-consciousness' in this chapter as articulating a Hegelian *theory* of self-consciousness. Such a claim might be only a stage on the way to Hegel's preferred account of the capacities and experiences that distinguish us from other merely conscious beings.[5]

Hegel's project of rethinking what it is to be a self-conscious subject begins with one of the more striking transitions in the entire *Phenomenology*:

> With that first moment, self-consciousness is in the form of consciousness, and the whole expanse of the sensuous world is preserved for it, but at the same time only as connected with the second moment, the unity of self-consciousness with itself; and hence the sensuous world is for it an enduring existence which, however, is only appearance, or a difference which, *in itself*, is no difference. This antithesis of its appearance and its truth has, however, for its essence only the truth, viz. the unity of self-consciousness with itself; this unity must become essential to self-consciousness, i.e. self-consciousness is *Desire* in general. (PS 9.104/¶167)

This passage presents the idealist position that our consciousness of sensible objects always involves some determinate relation to oneself, what Hegel here terms "the unity of self-consciousness with itself." These sorts of self-relations should be familiar from 'Consciousness', where determinations of an object that are first regarded as simply given to the knowing subject are continually revealed to be, in truth, just some way in which the object is determined *by* and exists *for* the sensing, perceiving, or thinking subject. This idealist position dates back to Kant's groundbreaking thesis, in his transcendental deduction of the categories in the *Critique of Pure Reason*, that consciousness of an object always involves the unity of apperception. By this, Kant means both

---

[5] For example, in describing a mere desiring subject as engaging in 'self-deception,' Honneth ("Desire to Recognition," 84) appears to reify as a self-conscious subject a form of consciousness that is an unreal stage in the development of the observed consciousness. For a related charge, see Pippin (*Hegel on Self-Consciousness*, 73–74).

that the unity of various properties in a single object derives from the unity of thought itself, and that awareness of that object is always, at least implicitly, a matter of being conscious of how the object has been unified or 'synthesized' in thought.[6] Later in the *Phenomenology*, Hegel will attack Kant's claim that the nature of this synthesis can be derived from the forms of judgment, with their associated a priori concepts (PS 9.134–135/¶235), but at this point Hegel means only to emphasize the common idealist view that a sensible object is essentially an object *for* consciousness. As Hegel puts the point in the preceding passage, the object is 'only appearance', and the difference between consciousness and its object is *in itself* 'no difference' (or translated more literally, 'has no being'). "Self-Consciousness" aims to explain how an object can be both phenomenally other than consciousness and, at the same time, nothing beyond how it is cognizable by consciousness.

But Hegel is even more concerned with self-consciousness itself, and the 'unity with itself' that he will understand as complete self-determination—the 'independence' of consciousness generally. The chapter takes a decisive turn when Hegel states that taking such unity to be essential to self-consciousness is equivalent to identifying self-consciousness with '*desire* in general' (*Begierde überhaupt*). *Desire* is evidently Hegel's answer to the question of "how the shape of self-consciousness first makes its appearance" (PS 9.103/¶167), but this answer is both unanticipated and obscure.

There are (at least) four ways we might understand this appearance of desire at the beginning of "Self-Consciousness." First, it could provide an expression of the task facing the observed consciousness. Now in the form of self-consciousness, the observed consciousness is committed to regarding independent, external objects as being, in truth, mere determinations of this unity of self-consciousness. Thus we might see the observed consciousness as taking on the task of *incorporating* what appears to be external to it. Hegel's remark that self-consciousness is desire in general would then serve as useful shorthand for a commitment to this task. This first sense of 'desire' accords with the first sense of 'self-consciousness' outlined earlier.

A second reading of the identification of self-consciousness and desire takes it to be making a very general claim about how self-consciousness must be understood if it is to ground the determinations of an object and thus be (in Hegel's terminology) 'the truth' of those determinations. Since knowledge of an object in general must be understood as something *done* by the subject, its own action, now that the various accounts of knowledge as receptivity have collapsed, Hegel's talk of desire suggests a capacity for *activity* on the part of consciousness generally—what Kant terms the 'spontaneity' of thought, and what Fichte designates, in various contexts, as 'self-activity', 'agility', or 'striving'. Against this background, Hegel's introduction of desire presents the self-determining activity that underlies knowledge as originally a matter of *wanting* something. And since '*Begierde*' connotes a basic, corporeal desire, we can read Hegel as maintaining that it is a fundamental fact about self-conscious beings that they pursue the unity that

---

[6] Kant, *CPR*, A108/B137; B131–133.

arises from incorporating given representations into a previous organization of material within consciousness generally.

A third approach to the identification of self-consciousness and desire understands the latter notion quite literally as animal desire, which appears already in Hegel's remarks in the chapter "Sense-Certainty" on how things stand "in the practical sphere." He states that in contrast to consciousness's realist stance in "Sense-Certainty," mere animals are idealists insofar as they "do not just stand idly in front of sensuous things as if these possessed intrinsic being, but, despairing of their reality, and completely assured of their nothingness, they fall to without ceremony and eat them up" (PS 9.69/¶109). This somewhat amusing talk of animals' despair and idealistic assurance links animal desire with the metaphysical themes of "Self-Consciousness" insofar as animal desire is a kind of needing or wanting that both underlies an animal's activity and determines objects as being of particular kinds (e.g., food, poison, or mere obstacle). This idealist construal of desire also appears in Fichte's account of our relation to objects in praxis: "I do not feel hunger because there is food for me; instead, something becomes food for me because I am hungry."[7] Desire is thus a self-relation in relation to an object *that is what it is* only in relation to that particular desire.[8]

A fourth approach involves some grasp of the previous readings, and perhaps expresses the most general point that Hegel wishes to make about self-consciousness at the beginning of the chapter. If a certain kind of unity 'becoming essential' to self-consciousness is equivalent to self-consciousness being understood as desire in general, we can grasp this as a matter of a being's existence *mattering* to it in some determinate manner, and its thereby wanting something from its environment, and from its future. This accords with the general turn to the practical in this chapter for the simple reason that all mattering—or as Kant would put it, all 'interest'—is ultimately practical. This fourth approach might be understood as cutting across the distinction between theoretical and practical aspects of subjectivity by insisting that *any* self-conscious theorizing or acting is to be understood as a pursuit of unity with oneself. This would anticipate Heidegger's central claim, in *Being and Time*, that our existence is 'an issue' for us as beings who are always 'beyond' themselves or 'ahead' of themselves in their attempts to realize some particular way of existing. On this reading, Hegel's concept of desire would resemble Heidegger's notion of 'care', which is more fundamental than theory or practice and which underlies these activities as the most basic character of our being.[9] If we were to press the question of what, exactly, a subject needs to *be* in order for it to be fundamentally oriented toward achieving a kind of unity with itself, Hegel might simply

---

[7] Fichte, *System of Ethics*, 118.

[8] This structure of desire might suggest a naturalistic approach to Hegel's views on self-consciousness. See Brandom ("Structure," 132–134) and Pinkard (*Naturalism*, 57–58) for articulations of such an approach.

[9] Pippin pursues this reading of Hegel's identification of self-consciousness and desire and notes the affinity between his approach and Heidegger's notion of care (*Hegel on Self-Consciousness*, 36). See especially Pippin's account of desire as 'projection' (55) and self-relations as dependent upon such projection (65).

reject the question as ill-formed and insist that *being* anything at all is to be understood as a matter of achieving some sort of unity with oneself.[10] Or he might instead insist that a self-relation of this general sort is characteristic of any desiring, living thing. This issue will turn on how we understand the notions of desire and life as we proceed in "Self-Consciousness."

4.2. SELF-CONSCIOUSNESS AS GENUS

Following his identification of self-consciousness and desire, Hegel embarks on an extended examination of the object of desire, which he now describes as a living thing. The point seems to be that rethinking self-consciousness requires that we also rethink its objects. I will not discuss many details of the rather obscure remarks in ¶¶168–172 and will focus instead on the account of life itself as a 'reflected unity' that emerges from Hegel's discussion of how we comprehend a natural, living being:

> Contrasted with that immediate unity, or that unity expressed as a [mere] *being*, this second is the universal unity which contains all these moments as superseded [*aufgehoben*] within itself. It is the simple genus which, in the movement of Life itself, does not exist *for itself* qua this *simple* determination; on the contrary, in this *result*, Life points to something other than itself, viz. to consciousness, for which Life exists as this unity, or as genus. (PS 9.107/¶172)

Life exists for us as a unity, or genus, insofar as our understanding of an individual living being as object of desire has led us to conceive of that being as essentially part of life as a whole. The individual living being has been superseded—done away with *as a self-sufficient being*, but at the same time preserved *as a moment of life*. A living being is an instance of life, and its coming into being, self-maintenance, or passing away is now grasped through the activity of life itself, a "self-developing whole which dissolves its development and in this movement simply preserves itself" (PS 9.107/¶171). Understanding life as a reflected unity involves taking the relations and interactions between living things that constitute the development of life to be essential to those living things. We grasp living beings through life.

Hegel takes us through this unfolding of life at least in part for the sake of presenting us with a model for his account of self-consciousness and spirit. The individual self-conscious subject will bear the same kind of relation to its social context that an individual living being bears to life. The main differences between the two cases are found in the distinctive independence of an individual self-consciousness—which is realized in, and in no way threatened by, its existence within spirit—and in self-consciousness's

---

[10] This would parallel Heidegger's insistence that the care structure is not grounded in a self. See Heidegger, *Being and Time*, 236–238.

relation to the genus. Hegel will argue that a self-consciousness is essentially *"for itself* a genus" insofar as an individual subject, considered merely as such, takes itself to be one instance of a kind (PS 9.108/¶176). This self-conception may be more or less explicit, but the essential point is that self-consciousness involves the ability to grasp one's own existence *in the abstract.* This Hegelian position, which emerges with greater clarity in his discussion of lordship and bondage, strongly influenced a wide range of philosophers. Feuerbach, for example, begins his investigation into religion with the claim that "consciousness in the strictest sense is present only in a being to whom his species, his essential nature, is an object of thought."[11] And Marx later describes a self-conscious human being as a "species being" due to its ability to "adopt the species as its object" and "treat itself as the actual, living species"—a view that grounds his early account of the possibility of estranged labor and alienated existence.[12] This notion of self-conscious existence as essentially shared with others (to put the point most generally) finds its most striking expression in Hegel's transition from life to spirit in the *Phenomenology.*

This transition takes place through an examination of the shortcomings (relative to the still-developing standard of being self-conscious) of any subject considered as desire alone. As we have seen, self-consciousness is (in part) a matter of overcoming the independent being of an object by taking that object to exist only for oneself as subject. Hegel now expresses this point by saying that self-consciousness is "certain of itself only by superseding this other that presents itself to self-consciousness as an independent life" (PS 9.107/¶174). For a desiring subject, this supersession is a matter of consuming, incorporating, and thereby destroying the independent object, but Hegel immediately points out that this activity is conditioned by the presence of an object, which means that "it is in fact something other than self-consciousness that is the essence of desire" (PS 9.107/¶175). Hegel's point can be illustrated using the example of a living being that consumes objects it takes to be food and regards other objects only as means or impediments to such consumption. While the determinations of objects derive solely from this being's desire, those objects at the same time determine the state and activity of a desiring being that is dependent on its environment for sustenance and behaves in a manner determined by the layout of its environment. In order for a subject to satisfy the notion of self-consciousness presented in ¶167, this dependence on merely given features of an object (which recalls the realist position of 'Consciousness') must fall away. The object must make possible a 'return from otherness' despite the fact that it is nothing beyond how it is *determined* by the subject—in Hegel's terms, the object "must carry out this negation of itself in itself, for it is *in itself* the negative, and must be *for* the other what it *is*" (PS 9.108/¶175). But how are we to conceive of such an object?

Hegel provides an answer in his famous declaration that "self-consciousness achieves its satisfaction only in another self-consciousness" (PS 9.108/¶175). It is only by relating to another self-conscious subject that a self-relation in relation to an object is possible. This assertion of the essentially intersubjective nature of self-consciousness sets

---

[11] Feuerbach, *The Essence of Christianity*, 1.
[12] Marx, "Economic and Philosophic Manuscripts of 1844," 75.

the stage for Hegel's more complete account of self-consciousness in "Lordship and Bondage" by providing a snapshot of self-consciousness as genus (i.e., as spirit):

> A self-consciousness, in being an object [for another], is just as much 'I' as 'object'. With this, we already have before us the concept of *Spirit*. What still lies ahead for consciousness is the experience of what Spirit is—this absolute substance which is the unity of the different independent self-consciousnesses which, in their opposition, enjoy perfect freedom and independence: 'I' that is 'We', and 'We' that is 'I'. (PS 9.108/¶177)

This passage moves quickly from the bare idea of regarding some object as another subject to the concept of spirit as that *within which* such a relation is possible. Two claims are significant here. First, an 'I' is a 'We' insofar as a self-conscious subject is for itself genus. It regards itself as one among many subjects that share a way of life, and ideally identifies with that way of life as a condition of its own freedom. Second, spirit is a 'We' that is 'I' insofar as the social standards that constitute some way of life develop in a self-sufficient manner, analogous to the self-determination of a free subject (a point that recalls Hegel's earlier account of life as itself a living thing [¶171]). Spirit is 'absolute substance' because its determinations develop internally and in this way depend upon nothing else for their existence. The latter claim concerning the independence of spirit points forward to Hegel's account of the unboundedness of human knowing, while the former underlies his views on the nature of self-consciousness.

Hegel uses the term 'recognition' ('*Anerkennung*') to designate the relation between subjects that is constitutive of spirit: "Self-consciousness exists in and for itself when, and by the fact that, it so exists for another; that is, it exists only in being recognized [*als ein Anerkanntes*]" (PS 9.109/¶178). Recognition is not simply a matter of re-identifying something already known (e.g., an old acquaintance). The recognition that interests Hegel resembles the acknowledgment, or legitimation, that emerges when one country recognizes another—a parallel that Hegel later explores in his *Philosophy of Right* (PR §331). Hegel borrows the term 'recognition'—along with significant parts of the theory itself—from Fichte, who introduces the notion of recognition as part of the deduction of the concept of right that opens his *Foundations of Natural Right*. Since Fichte claims that "the concept of right is itself a condition of self-consciousness," the reciprocal recognition that he takes to be constitutive of this concept is likewise, for Fichte, a condition of self-consciousness.[13] As we will see, Hegel's position is Fichtean in its insistence that recognition is constitutive of self-consciousness, though it jettisons Fichte's attempt to provide transcendental deductions of the norms of ethics and right.

The elaborate process of recognition described in ¶¶178–184 is meant to illuminate the notion of recognition itself (i.e., what is involved in taking another to have the same status as oneself). The distinctive nature of this 'duplication' of subjects comes into focus once we appreciate that it cannot be a matter of a self-conscious subject confronting a

---

[13] Fichte, *Foundations of Natural Right*, 49.

world of mere objects and inferring, on the basis of its observations, that some of those objects are self-conscious subjects.[14] Such an argument from analogy would assume that the subject making this inference is already self-conscious *independent of its relation to others*, and this is just what Hegel aims to deny. So in opposition to the Kantian idea that we relate to others by 'lending' them our own first-personal point of view (Kant maintains that "if I wish to represent to myself a thinking being, I must put myself in his place, and thus substitute, as it were, my own subject for the object I am seeking to consider"), Hegel begins with two subjects and asks us to consider what is involved in their regarding each other as instances of the same kind.[15] He concludes that they would ideally "*recognize* themselves as *mutually recognizing* one another," with each taking the other to bear all of the attitudes toward it that it bears to the other, *including* this very attitude of regarding all attitudes as shared (PS 9.110/§184). These acts establish the complete equality of the two. Each regards the other as a subject, and each accords to the other any particular status that it accords to itself. In this manner there arises an explicit like-mindedness between two independent subjects that are, therefore, dependent upon each other in this distinctive way. The same explicit like-mindedness appears in Fichte's account of two subjects who limit their own freedom on the condition that the other limit its freedom in the same manner. This reciprocal self-limitation in Fichte generates a chain of conditions that continues ad infinitum, and is also, crucially, posited by both subjects as determined in this way.[16] This ideal of reciprocal recognition, which generates an equality of two subjects independent of their merely natural determinations, is the endpoint of Hegel's transition from life to the infinite, absolute substance of spirit.

At this point we should step back from Hegel's discussions of desire, life, spirit, and recognition to ask what he has really accomplished in connection with the project of rethinking self-consciousness. While it is clear that Hegel is committed to the idea that self-consciousness is essentially social and intersubjective, it must also be admitted that the grounds of this commitment are rather obscure. Some commentators have read these sections of the *Phenomenology* as a derivation of Hegel's central notions of desire and recognition, but attempts to derive these notions from the identification of self-consciousness and desire typically depend upon readings of that identification that go far beyond what Hegel gives us in the opening paragraphs of "Self-Consciousness."[17] The formal relation between Hegel's idealist notion of an object (§167) and his account of a recognized subject as both *other than* and *the same as* the recognizing subject (§184) is

[14] This is not to deny that Hegel is interested in the question of how one might establish that another being is completely self-determining. Clarke ("Struggle") reads the life-and-death struggle that follows Hegel's account of recognition as engaging with this question for the sake of producing an immanent critique of Fichte's theory of recognition.

[15] Kant, *CPR*, A353.

[16] Fichte, *Foundations of Natural Right*, 42.

[17] See Brandom ("Structure") and Pippin (*Hegel on Self-Consciousness*) for Hegelian accounts of self-consciousness as necessarily involving desire and recognition. Neuhouser ("Deducing Desire") and Honneth ("Desire to Recognition") provide deductions of desire and recognition more closely related to the text of the *Phenomenology*.

one point of contact between these discussions, but it does little to demonstrate the relevance of practical considerations for an account of self-consciousness generally. In what follows, I aim to show how Hegel's later examination of rudimentary forms of recognition both demonstrates the relevance of the practical for self-consciousness and reveals that perfectly reciprocal recognition is not, for Hegel, a condition of self-consciousness.

4.3. The Life-and-Death Struggle

Having established complete reciprocity as the ideal of recognition, Hegel maintains that when we consider how this duplication of subjects first "appears to self-consciousness," we find instead the complete *inequality* of "one being only *recognized*, the other only *recognizing*" (PS 9.110/¶185). These two figures, later identified as the lord and bondsman, respectively, are the main focus of this part of the *Phenomenology*, so it is essential to determine why Hegel takes the duplication of subjects to begin with complete inequality. His path toward an unequal recognitive relation starts from the merely natural equality of existing as instances of a single species; each being takes its own desire to determine all objects and regards the other living being as just another part of life to be utilized or ignored, depending on the contingent state of its own desire. Since each shows up for the other as a mere living being, each is maximally far away from being recognized by the other. Hegel then maintains that the only way for a living being to overcome this appearance of itself in the eyes of the other is to differentiate itself from other parts of life though presenting itself as "not attached to life" (PS 9.111/¶187) (i.e., as willing to risk harm or even death for the sake of recognition). It does this by putting itself in harm's way in the context of the other's desiring activity. But if this activity succeeds in presenting the one that risks its life as a self-determining subject free from the determinations of life, the other will see this presentation as a threat to its own status as the authoritative point of view on its environment. Thus the other is now 'outside of itself' insofar as another subject seems to usurp the status it claims as its own (PS 9.111/¶187). As a result—and this is the essential point of this part of the chapter—there emerges a need on the part of the other to engage in a more extreme form of the same activity, and we see a steady escalation of what counts as risking oneself. Each attempt at demonstrating superiority serves only to elicit a more extreme act on the part of the other, which in turn undermines the success of the previous act. This escalation cannot continue ad infinitum; it can only result in the death of a living being. Thus, unlike the case of reciprocal recognition, in which two living beings supersede their existence as mere life, but at the same time preserve themselves as living beings within the infinite realm of spirit, the struggle for recognition does away with the life that serves as its condition (PS 9.112/¶188).

The failure of the life and death struggle yields two important results. First, "self-consciousness learns that life is as essential to it as pure self-consciousness" (PS 9.112/¶189)—the observed consciousness is now, for itself, a living being. By this Hegel means not only that it takes itself to be a part of life, but also that its life matters to it.[18] This stance toward life anticipates the emergence, in the figure of the bondsman, of a true self-consciousness for which things can matter. But this new value of life will also create tension in such a subject's self-understanding. The apparent incompatibility involved in regarding oneself as a spontaneous, self-determining 'I' that is *also* determined by its location in the whole of life underlies developments through the end of this chapter, where there is at best an incomplete reconciliation between the independent 'I' and life.[19] The second important result is that the route forward in this chapter, following the failure of the life-and-death struggle, begins with the completely unequal recognitive relation between lord and bondsman. Hegel presents this claim as related to the first insofar as we might see in the relation of lord to bondsman the relation of the self-determining 'I' to its own living determinations, but his strongest reasons for presenting just this relation between desiring subjects as the next step in the dialectic do not involve the life-and-death struggle per se. That is, Hegel is not presenting the relation of lord to bondsman as a superior resolution of the struggle *that might emerge within the struggle as described*. While *we* might see the capitulation of one subject as the only possible resolution (since this would cease the escalation of threats by giving one subject what it wants), the whole point of describing this as a struggle to the death is to show that death is the only possible outcome when two desiring subjects seek recognition in this context. (It is significant that Hegel does not describe a process through which one subject backs down and commits itself to serving the other. This development would be completely inexplicable since there could be no reason that one would back down while the other does not; the two are indistinguishable.) Thus the self-consciousness that learns that life is "essential to it" is not a participant in the struggle, but rather a new form of the observed consciousness present to us, the readers of the *Phenomenology*. So while Hegel's discussion of the struggle might appear to be a genetic account of the emergence of self-consciousness from mere life—one that takes conflict to be essential to self-consciousness—we ought to regard it as showing only that the natural equality of desiring subjects does not contain within it the resources necessary for generating a stable relation of self-consciousness to self-consciousness.[20]

[18] Here I agree with Pippin (*Hegel on Self-Consciousness*, 74–79) that the need to regard life as a value, and not as a 'species imperative', is the main result of the struggle. But Pippin's route to this conclusion, which postulates the 'inescapable conflict' (79) between living beings satisfying their desires in conditions of 'scarcity' (74 n. 21), goes well beyond what is present in Hegel's account of the struggle.

[19] McDowell ("Apperceptive I") reads the entirety of "Self-Consciousness" as concerned with the relation *in a single consciousness* between lordlike abstract thought and the bondage of the given determinations of sensibility or life. While there are certainly elements of this reading in Hegel's text, it must *also* be a story about opposed subjects. See Jenkins ("Concept of Desire," 124–125 n. 58) and Pippin (*Hegel on Self-Consciousness*, 39–51) for two critical accounts of McDowell's "heterodox" reading.

[20] Hegel might be read as offering less than a genetic account of self-consciousness, yet more than an account of its basic structures (the position I outline in what follows). Honneth, for example, maintains that in ¶¶166–176 Hegel "seeks to do no less than explain the transition from a natural to a spiritual being, from the human animal to the rational subject" ("Desire to Recognition," 77). Honneth's explanation, like Neuhouser's 'deduction' of desire and recognition, aims to show the necessity of these notions for any account of self-consciousness, while at the same time avoiding any genetic account (though see note 5,

Hegel is focused, instead, on grasping the most basic form of like-mindedness that might be found in a relation between living subjects. He means to ask, "What recognitive relation is 'closest' to mere life?"—or equivalently, "Which form of spirit presupposes the least on the part of the subjects involved?" While the complete inequality that he puts forward as an answer does emerge from our observation of the life-and-death struggle, it is simply a lesser form of the reciprocal recognition described earlier in the chapter. The unequal figures are in agreement concerning the terms of their relationship, in that there is no disagreement concerning their rights and responsibilities. The bondsman ought to serve the lord by ensuring that the lord's environment conforms to its desires, while the lord has a right to be served in just this way. But despite this agreement concerning the nature of their situation, lord and bondsman obviously do not share the same authority, and they furthermore lack a common grasp of the grounds of their relationship. Unlike two subjects that recognize themselves *as mutually recognizing one another*, the lord and bondsman are sunk in a social world that is simply given to them and is not transparent, or legitimate, for them.

What matters for Hegel's account of self-consciousness is not so much the ideal of recognition sketched in ¶¶178–184, but rather this bare notion of a recognitive relation between subjects who are in agreement concerning the terms of their interaction. So while it is certainly correct to regard the lord and bondsman as falling short of the ideal of recognition, the more important point is that the relation of lord to bondsman and the ideal of mutual recognition are two different forms of the same, fundamental like-mindedness that Hegel terms 'spirit'. This emphasis on spirit itself as a condition of self-consciousness—and not some complex shape of spirit, such as Fichte's relation of right—makes plausible Hegel's claim that these relations to other self-conscious subjects are universal conditions of self-consciousness itself. But this is not at all to suggest that Hegel lacks an account of the authority of norms of ethics and right for a self-conscious subject considered merely as such. His remark that the "pure concept of recognition" will "at first [...] exhibit the inequality of the two" (PS 9.110/¶185) hints that the relation of lord to bondsman is just the starting point in a development of spirit, and that this unequal relation contains within itself the resources necessary for progressing toward the equality of reciprocal recognition present in a social order that is understood by its inhabitants as governed by norms of ethics and right. The relation of right is not a transcendental condition of self-conscious agency, as it is for Fichte, but rather a historical achievement of self-conscious agents who find themselves as such agents within a particular shape of spirit. This gradual self-development of spirit first appears for us in the final section of "Self-Consciousness" and continues through much of the remainder of the *Phenomenology*. What remains for "Lordship and Bondage" is only the presentation of the self-conscious subjects that participate in that progression.

---

as well as Honneth's discussion of infant consciousness [85–86]). I discuss the difference between Hegel's method and a Fichtean deduction in Jenkins, "Concept of Desire," 121–123.

4.4. Lordship and Bondage, Death and Work

Hegel's account of lord and bondsman circumscribes their roles in this primitive social setting, which is viewed first from the point of view of the lord and then from that of the bondsman. The position of the lord at first looks rather enviable. It enjoys recognition by the bondsman, and that recognition is continually manifest to it through the bondsman's faithful service. The bondsman's service also liberates the lord from the contingencies of life by ensuring that the lord's environment is always suited to its desire. This mediated relation of desire to its object means that the lord's desiring activity is no longer "conditioned by the object," as was the case for the simple desiring consciousness in ¶175. Thus the lord seems to have become a true self-consciousness by achieving the complete independence, or being-for-self, characteristic of self-consciousness. But Hegel stresses that the lord's situation in fact falls short of what it aimed to achieve. While recognition by another certainly appears to be present, the bondsman's unconditional service has no value *qua recognition* for the simple reason that the lord does not recognize the bondsman. In the eyes of the lord, the bondsman is "quite different from an independent consciousness" (PS 9.114/¶192), and this means that even its most faithful service is incapable of legitimating the lord's status as an independent consciousness.

Another obvious shortcoming of the lord, considered as a potential instance of self-consciousness, is that neither the thing it consumes nor the subject that facilitates this consumption exists *for the lord* as something independent and other. Recall that self-consciousness, as a "new shape of knowing," preserves within it the standpoint of 'Consciousness' by taking self-consciousness to be a "return from otherness" (PS 9.104/¶167). Yet there is no otherness to be found in the bondsman (which does whatever the lord demands) or in things the lord consumes (which do not put up the least resistance to consumption). The lord thus falls short of being a self-relation in relation to an object (*Gegenstand*) because nothing *stands against* its desiring activity by constraining or guiding that activity. The satisfaction of the lord's desire thus lacks what Hegel terms an 'objective aspect' (*die gegenständliche Seite*) (PS 9.115/¶195). Hegel's articulation of this shortcoming recalls Kant's transcendental notion of objectivity in the *Critique of Pure Reason*: an object of representation is that which prevents our cognitions from being determined in a haphazard or arbitrary manner.[21] For Kant, to know an object *just is* to regard one's experiences as determined independent of one's own arbitrary acts of thought. Here Hegel is maintaining that because objectivity requires this check on the free exercise of a subject's powers, the unmitigated success of the lord's project of freeing itself from any limitation on its activity ensures its failure as an instance of self-consciousness.

---

[21] Kant, *CPR*, A104.

Hegel's account of the bondsman as it is 'in and for itself', that is, not just as it appears from the standpoint of the lord, explains how the bondsman surpasses the lord and satisfies the concept of self-consciousness. While the otherness of objectivity is completely lacking in the things the lord encounters, the bondsman recognizes the lord and thus has before it (what it takes to be) a "pure being-for-self [that] exists for it as its *object* [*Gegenstand*]" (PS 9.114/¶194). As a living being that values its own life over recognition by another, the bondsman also relates to every other part of life as an "alien being before which it has trembled" (PS 9.115/¶196). The entire world that confronts it thus takes the form of objectivity.[22] Hegel will also present the bondsman's work within this world of objects as a relation to self in which the bondsman is at least implicitly aware that it alone determines these objects as the things they are. The bondsman thus satisfies the concept of self-consciousness by relating to independent objects that it can recognize as instances of its 'unity with itself' (PS 9.104/¶167). This development completes the surprising reversal of lord and bondsman, and the challenge confronting readers of Hegel is to comprehend exactly why it is in the bondsman's work "wherein he seemed to have only an alienated existence [*fremder Sinn*] that he acquires a mind of his own [*eigner Sinn*]" (PS 9.115/¶196).

Hegel begins his examination of the bondsman by announcing yet another paradoxical aspect of the lord-bondsman relation, namely that the bondsman raises itself out of the sphere of mere life through a *concern with life* found in its fear of death. This development arises in part through the surprising failure of the lord's attempt at complete independence. While the bondsman's service appeared to liberate the lord from the sphere of life, the lord in fact remained sunk in life insofar as its activity of consuming objects formed by the bondsman remained completely determined by the lord's merely natural tendencies as member of a biological species. Unimpeded enjoyment arising from the satisfaction of desire is still just a satisfaction of the demands of life. We find a similar reversal in the case of the bondsman, which appears to be tied to natural existence insofar as it values its own life over recognition by an other. But the fear of death that grounds the bondsman's service is now put forward as an instance of the "pure negativity and being-for-self" that is the "essential nature of self-consciousness" (PS 9.114/¶194). The significance of fear is one of the more perplexing aspects of Hegel's account of the bondsman, and one that is rarely discussed in any detail. The point at first seems to be that fear of death, through which the bondsman "has trembled in every fiber of its being, and everything solid and stable has been melted away" (PS 9.114/¶194), resembles the activity of thought in general, or imagination in particular, insofar as it relates the bondsman not simply to what is actually given, but to what might exist. This recalls an earlier claim about consciousness in general—unlike something "confined within the limits of a natural life," consciousness always "goes beyond itself" through the negative

---

[22] My earlier focus on the role of desire in Hegel's account of self-consciousness led me to downplay the importance of objectivity in the bondsman's experience (Jenkins, "Concept of Desire," 129). That objectivity, like self-consciousness, is never merely cognitive is one important lesson of this chapter. On this point see Neuhouser, "Deducing Desire," 250.

activity of positing something beyond what is given, such as a region in space beyond what appears in spatial intuition (PS 9.57/¶80). While Hegel clearly has in mind this point concerning thinking, or negativity in general, the significance of fear for self-consciousness becomes clearer when we consider the difference between the bondsman's fear of death and the merely natural concern for self found within the desire of any living being. The bondman's fear of death and orientation toward life are not to be found *within* its desires, but in the separation *from* desire involved in its commitment to forgoing its own satisfaction for the sake of serving the lord. No desire is a "solid and stable" ground of the bondsman's action once it regards the non-natural standard of faithful service as the condition of its own continued existence. Thus the dispositions that characterize the bondsman as an instance of a biological species are no longer sufficient to explain its activity, and the fear of death that underlies the bondsman's commitment to serve actually liberates it from the domain of mere life.

Hegel further maintains that the separation from life found in the bondsman's fear of death is an instance of self-consciousness only if the bondsman is *for itself* this negative relation to desire, and this requires that it engage in the activity of work. Hegel describes work, the activity that "corresponds to desire in the lord's consciousness," as follows: "Work, on the other hand, is desire held in check [*gehemmte Begierde*], fleetingness staved off; in other words, work forms and shapes [*bildet*] the thing" (PS 9.115/¶195). Such formative activity is necessary for self-consciousness, he claims, because without it fear remains 'formal', 'inward', and 'mute' (PS 9.115/¶196). Here it is important not to misread Hegel as making a very simple mistake. One might agree that fear is an instance of self-consciousness only if it is not 'mute' but rather given voice through a first-personal thought such as "I am currently afraid," but one might also worry that this simply presupposes the reflexivity of self-consciousness. Happily, Hegel is not making this simple mistake. The point is, rather, that in work motivated by fear, objects are at least implicitly grasped by the bondsman as determined by its own activity. Here everything turns on understanding just what Hegel understands by desire 'held in check'. Most obviously, the bondsman's desire is held in check by the oppressive context of its labor. It cannot simply consume objects in its environment since it finds itself in the service of a lord that has threatened its very existence as a living being. The constraints on the bondsman's desire appear to be imposed from without by the oppressive situation in which it finds itself. But Hegel wants us to consider more closely the ground of the bondsman's servitude (i.e., how the bondsman comes to find itself in this particular context). And he is suggesting that when we consider the bondsman as it is *for itself*, we see that the only thing holding the bondsman's desire in check is the self-determining activity of the bondsman itself. What appears to be determination by another is, in truth, complete self-determination. It is only *as recognized* that the lord determines what is permissible for the bondsman, and it is only *as feared* that the possibility of its own death rules the bondsman's life.

Work is central to self-consciousness because it involves the possibility of grasping that these constraints on desire, which appear to lie outside the bondsman, are really instances of the bondsman's own self-determination. Hegel first notes that the bondsman's relation to these constraints determines the form it gives to objects in work: "the negative relation to the object becomes its form and something permanent, because it is precisely for the worker that the object has independence" (PS: 9.115/¶195). Since objects are determined by their relation to the constraints of service, these constraints are manifest to the bondsman in the form of the world it confronts. Hegel then maintains that work involves the possibility of grasping that this form derives from the bondsman's own commitment to serve: "The form does not become something other than himself through being made external to him; for it is precisely this form that is his pure being-for-self, which in this externality is seen by him to be the truth" (PS 9.115/ ¶196).[23] In this experience of grasping one's own desire and practical commitments as 'the truth' of objects—a practical analogue of Kant's notion of 'consciousness of synthesis'—we finally have an instance of the experience put forward by Hegel as definitive of self-consciousness. The object of work shows up for the bondsman as an instance of its own unity with itself, and the idealist position of "Self-Consciousness" is realized once the bondsman sees in the object 'only itself as itself'. Thus the activity of work, which appeared to ensure the lord's independence, is the central element in Hegel's account of how the bondsman is *for itself* liberated from the realm of mere life. This is the point of Hegel's remark that "through his service he rids himself of [*hebt . . . auf*] his attachment to natural existence in every single detail, and gets rid of it by working on it" (PS 9.114/ ¶194). The bondsman's existence as a living thing is both preserved and canceled (i.e., *aufgehoben*, sublated) insofar as the bondsman is a desiring, living being that also transcends the realm of mere life by determining its activity in relation to the non-natural standard of service.

4.5. SELF-CONSCIOUSNESS AND SPIRIT

Stepping back now from the details of "Lordship and Bondage," we must consider just how Hegel has illuminated *what it is* for a subject to be self-conscious, and whether he has done so in a manner that demonstrates the relevance of death, desire, spirit, and the like for idealist questions concerning the scope of knowledge generally. To begin with, it should be clear by now that Hegel's surprising identification of self-consciousness and desire is intended to shed light on the apperceptive nature of consciousness generally. "Self-Consciousness" does not attempt to explain the emergence of apperception from mere animality, let alone from mere matter, though it does present an account of the nature of self-conscious subjects and the structure of their conscious experience.[24]

---

[23] Translation modified. Translating 'Form' as 'form', and not as 'shape', creates a closer link between the form of the object and the bondsman's 'formative activity', or *Bilden*.

[24] Pippin (*Hegel on Self-Consciousness*, 14–19) reads "Self-Consciousness" as aiming to grasp all forms of self-consciousness as dependent upon a more fundamental desiring relation to the future, and to others (77). This is not a genetic account of self-consciousness, though it is an explanation of apperception in more basic terms. Whatever the merits of this Heideggerian approach to

Hegel understands self-consciousness as self-limiting activity, a matter of relating to a non-natural standard that is, in truth, one's own. In its most basic form, this is the self-determination of a *desiring* subject that finds itself in relation to a social standard with manifest authority.[25] Self-consciousness is thus grounded in the self-awareness of a living, desiring being, which is always in the background relative to any particular self-conscious state.[26] But self-consciousness is never just this awareness, or just the "unalloyed feeling of self" of lordlike or animal consumption (PS 9.115/§195). By relating to a social standard with manifest authority, a living being bears a negative relation to its own desires, and this is just what is involved in being the subject of those desires, committed to negotiating any conflicts between them and the non-natural standards that govern their satisfaction—standards that are themselves susceptible to internal conflicts. In Hegel's idealized social context, there is just one standard of conduct, and the absolute authority of that standard simplifies the bondsman's task of reflecting on what is called for by a situation. But Hegel is maintaining that recognizing the authority of even this simple social standard provides the distance from life necessary for self-consciousness, a view that he summarizes through an allusion to the Book of Proverbs: "the fear of the lord is indeed the beginning of wisdom" (PS 9.114/§195).[27] The absolute authority of a divine will serves as a model for the authority found in the figure of the lord—and (perhaps equivalently) in the bondsman's imagined death, which it fears as "the absolute lord" (PS 9.114/§194). Of course, *we* can see that these standards arise only through the bondsman's own commitment to serve, or to preserve its life, but this in no way undermines their reality or authority *for the bondsman*. That all limitations on a self-conscious subject's activity are self-limitations, all constraints are self-constraints, and all normativity is *in some sense* internal to subjectivity, is both a central result of 'Consciousness' and an idealist commitment found throughout Hegel's predecessors.

One of Hegel's principal innovations in "Self-Consciousness" is to locate these norms within a living subject *as part of spirit*, that is, as a social being that is for itself genus. To be sure, the individual recognized lord does constrain the bondsman's desire satisfaction, but we can also see this constraint as a matter of the bondsman's being able to step outside its desires by (so to speak) asking itself "What should one do in this context?" That considering how to act in response to a felt desire—taking up a negative relation to

self-consciousness (which Pippin actually takes to be the core of German Idealism [55–60]), its connection to the text of "Self-Consciousness" is somewhat tenuous.

[25] I argue elsewhere that Hegel was influenced by Fichte's claim that "I find myself as myself only as willing" (*System of Ethics*, 24). See Jenkins, "Concept of Desire," 118–123.

[26] Honneth ("Desire to Recognition," 83) maintains that the satisfaction of human desire involves an "unmediated certainty of self" that underlies self-consciousness generally. While I agree with Honneth on this point, I would emphasize that this role for desire becomes clear only once it is "held in check" in the activity of work. Kojève (*Introduction*, 39–42) was among the first commentators to emphasize the importance of work for self-consciousness.

[27] Honneth ("Desire to Recognition," 88) tentatively ascribes to Hegel the view that "the observed subject can attain self-consciousness only with the aid of an experience that already possesses moral content in an elementary sense." This experience of authority is perhaps better termed proto-moral, but it clearly anticipates Hegel's engagement with practical philosophy in the *Phenomenology*.

it—involves a capacity to consider one's situation in the abstract, and in relation to the standards of one's place and time, is a large part of Hegel's emphasis on the sociality of self-consciousness and reason. Hegel's earlier discussions of the move from life to spirit that occurs through recognition of another can thus be read, in retrospect, as concerned in part with this negative relation to one's natural determinations. Spirit, considered as the evolving standards of conduct and social interaction, thereby serves as a condition of self-consciousness and as the ground of the determinations of objects of consciousness.

As the common ground of subject and object, spirit is intended to overcome the epistemic limitation of the Kantian thing-in-itself by introducing a new position on what it is for a norm to belong to, or be authoritative for, a self-conscious subject. As Hegel complains in the Introduction to the *Phenomenology*, Kant's assumption that cognition employs subjective forms of representation located in a transcendental subject inevitably generates an insurmountable gulf between our knowledge of objects and determinations of things in themselves. This issue reappears immediately following "Lordship and Bondage" in Hegel's discussion of the freedom of self-consciousness. There he contrasts a Kantian account of cognition as *representation* with the approach to cognition suggested by the bondsman's grasp of objects, now described as a free determination of them through a *concept* (*Begriff*): "In thinking, I am *free*, because I am not in an *other*, but remain simply and solely in communion with myself" (PS 9.117/¶197). Here Hegel is concerned with a freedom more fundamental than any yearning to be liberated from oppressive circumstances. Since the bondsman's behavior is in truth determined neither by a foreign authority (a 'lord' in general) nor by the inner compulsion of its own desire, a space has opened in which the bondsman must consider how its behavior *ought* to be determined. Its predicament thus suggests situations in which we are forced to step back from the commitments we possess as agents, or as thinkers, to evaluate their authority. For Hegel, this is activity within the realm of concepts, what he now calls *thinking*, and he is suggesting that all such activity is guided by the norms of thought and action that exist at a given point in history (which are themselves open to revision and subject to development through the activity of thinking). This move from Kant's transcendental subject to Hegel's notion of spirit obviously raises a number of questions concerning exactly what this step into the "spiritual daylight of the present" involves. As an 'I' that is 'We' and 'We' that is 'I', spirit must somehow contain all of the norms involved in a subject's relation to itself and to objects, while also possessing a capacity for development analogous to the rational self-determination of an individual subject. But what forms must spirit take? And why think that any set of socially-instituted norms contains an internal, non-empirical principle of development? Hegel must address these questions if he is to substantiate the claim that cognition is grounded in the 'infinite' realm of non-empirical, self-determining concepts. But at this point in the *Phenomenology*, Hegel is suggesting only that abandoning the Kantian model of cognition has the potential to overcome the epistemic limitation of the thing-in-itself. If we could reassure ourselves that our standards of knowing are not merely ours, but rather the standards toward which any particular form of knowing ought to develop, we would have no grounds for worrying that the world is in itself radically different from our cognition of it.

Our progression toward this position on knowledge begins with Hegel's examination of three stages in the actual historical development of spirit: Stoicism, Skepticism, and the 'unhappy consciousness'. These positions on self-conscious subjects, their objects, and the relation between them can all be understood as manifesting a limited grasp of the truth of self-consciousness that stands fast for us, the phenomenological observers—*in thinking, I am free*. They can also be seen as developments of the bondsman's initially limited grasp of its own freedom. First, it maintains that it is completely self-determining despite its actual subjection to the lord. This is the stage of Stoicism, in which a person withdraws from the actual conditions of existence (regardless of whether it finds itself "on the throne or in chains") and understands itself as a "pure universality of thought" that ought to be unaffected by these conditions (PS 9.117–118/¶199). Hegel maintains that Stoicism necessarily gives way to Scepticism—"Scepticism is the realization of that of which Stoicism was only the concept"—and does so when a person renounces all commitments to the existence of anything beyond the contents of thought (PS 9.119/¶202). The historical development of freedom reaches its third stage when the skeptic discovers that Scepticism is internally inconsistent insofar as it cannot express the content of its thinking, or explain the course of its actions, without relying on what appears to be true or good. As a result, consciousness takes itself to be an internally contradictory being, both free in thought and tethered to an alien world that transcends it—a situation that Hegel describes as repeating in a single subject the earlier relation of lord to bondsman (PS 9.121/¶206).[28] Hegel terms this the 'unhappy consciousness' and describes the various forms that this stage of world spirit can take, beginning with Judaism and progressing to the Christianity of his time. This is just the beginning of Hegel's path toward overcoming this transcendence and the associated division within a self-determining subject that is aware of its determinations as an animal, person, or citizen. But following the developments of "Self-Consciousness," that path is now, for us, that of a living, desiring subject that finds itself as such only within a particular form of world spirit.

WORKS CITED

Primary Texts

Feuerbach, Ludwig. *The Essence of Christianity*, translated by George Eliot. New York: Prometheus Books, 1989.

Fichte, J. G. *The System of Ethics*, edited and translated by Daniel Breazeale and Günter Zöller. Cambridge: Cambridge University Press, 2005.

Fichte, J. G. *Foundations of Natural Right*, edited by Frederick Neuhouser and translated by Michael Baur. Cambridge: Cambridge University Press, 2000.

---

[28] Passages such as this demonstrate the value of McDowell's reading of "Lordship and Bondage." But at the same time, they show that Hegel must take lord and bondsman to be distinct subjects earlier in "Self-Consciousness."

Hegel, G. W. F. *Elements of the Philosophy of Right*, translated by H. B. Nisbet and edited by Allen Wood. Cambridge: Cambridge University Press, 1991.

Hegel, G. W. F. *Gesammelte Werke*, Vol. 9, edited by Wolfgang Bonsiepen and Reinhard Heede. Hamburg: Felix Meiner Verlag, 1980.

Hegel, G. W. F. *The Phenomenology of Spirit* [PS], translated by A. V. Miller. Oxford: Oxford University Press, 1977.

Heidegger, Martin. *Being and Time*, translated by John Macquarrie and Edward Robinson. New York: Harper & Row, 1962.

Kant, Immanuel. *Critique of Pure Reason* [CPR], translated by Norman Kemp Smith. New York: St. Martin's Press, 1965.

Marx, Karl. "Economic and Philosophic Manuscripts of 1844," in *The Marx-Engels Reader*, edited by Robert C. Tucker. New York: W. W. Norton, 1978, 66–125.

Secondary Literature

Brandom, Robert. "The Structure of Desire and Recognition." *Philosophy and Social Criticism* 33, no. 1 (2007): 127–150.

Clarke, James. "Fichte, Hegel, and the Life and Death Struggle." *British Journal for the History of Philosophy* 22, no. 1 (2014): 81–103.

Honneth, Axel. "From Desire to Recognition: Hegel's Account of Human Sociality," in *Hegel's Phenomenology of Spirit*, edited by Dean Moyar and Michael Quante. Cambridge: Cambridge University Press, 2008, 76–90.

Jenkins, Scott. "Hegel's Concept of Desire." *Journal of the History of Philosophy* 47, no. 1 (2009): 103–130.

Kojève, Alexandre. *Introduction to the Reading of Hegel*, edited by Allen Bloom and translated by James H. Nichols, Jr. Ithaca, NY: Cornell University Press, 1980.

McDowell, John. "The Apperceptive I and the Empirical Self: Towards a Heterodox Reading of 'Lordship and Bondage,'" in *Having the World in View* by John McDowell. Cambridge, MA: Harvard University Press, 2009, 147–165.

Neuhouser, Frederick. "Deducing Desire and Recognition in the *Phenomenology of Spirit*." *Journal of the History of Philosophy* 24, no. 2 (1986): 243–262.

Pinkard, Terry. *Hegel's Naturalism: Mind, Nature, and the Final Ends of Life*. Oxford: Oxford University Press, 2012.

Pippin, Robert. *Hegel on Self-Consciousness: Desire and Death in the Phenomenology of Spirit*. Princeton, NJ: Princeton University Press, 2011.

Pippin, Robert. *Hegel's Idealism: The Satisfactions of Self-Consciousness*. Cambridge: Cambridge University Press, 1989.

CHAPTER 5

....

REASON, SELF-TRANSCENDENCE, AND MODERNITY IN HEGEL'S *PHENOMENOLOGY*

....

WILLIAM F. BRISTOW

THE "Reason" chapter (Chapter V) of Hegel's *Phenomenology of Spirit* is only one of eight, but it occupies a central position in Hegel's project. In the transition to reason, the protagonist ('consciousness') arrives for the first time at the principle of the true philosophy, the identity of subject and object. In Chapters I–III (collected under "A. Consciousness"), consciousness conceives of the object as 'the true' and of its knowledge as conforming to the self-standing object. The transition to "B. Self-Consciousness" (Chapter IV) reverses this orientation: consciousness conceives itself as 'the true,' as self-standing, and of objects as being *for it*. This conception also proves to be one-sided; in the transition to the third and final part (labeled only "C"), consciousness learns that 'the true' is neither the self-standing object, nor the self-standing subject, but rather the identity of one with the other. In this transition to reason, consciousness attains, apparently, the standpoint of Hegel's own rationalist system of philosophy.[1] All that remains, it would seem, is for consciousness to learn what exactly reason is, that is, what the principle of the identity of subject and object amounts to, exactly.

Would that it were that simple! The "Reason" chapter (labeled "AA. Reason") is but the first of four subdivisions of "C" (along with "BB. Spirit," "CC. Religion," and "DD. Absolute Knowing"). Moreover, the parade of shapes that consciousness as reason (henceforth: 'reason') takes in its itinerary through the "Reason" chapter constitutes a

---

[1] The phenomenology of spirit included in Hegel's later *Encyclopedia of the Philosophical Sciences* ends summarily with the transition to the standpoint of reason, the "essential and actual truth" which "lies in the simple identity of the subjectivity of the concept with its objectivity and universality" (E §438, 433–434).

truly bewildering variety: first empirical natural science, next organic nature, now logic, now the skull bone, now an individual's hedonistic pursuit, now madness, now virtue, now something called 'the spiritual animal kingdom', now the *giving*, now the *testing*, of unconditioned practical laws. Can we discern in this colorful parade a clear and coherent picture of reason in the *Phenomenology*?

In the compressed retelling of the dialectic that follows, the main story is the emergence and development of reason as 'purposive activity'.[2] By seeing how reason becomes, and takes successive forms as, purposive activity, the narrative unity is visible. Reason's development is driven by a fundamental tension in reason's principle from the beginning. Reason comes on the scene as the certainty of our protagonist consciousness that it, an individual, is all reality. In its attempts to show this certainty true, the I's particularity, determinacy, and existence, on the one hand, conflict with its universality on the other (its being, not only real, but *all reality*). Reason's overarching challenge is to make good on its self-assertion both as being *this individual*, the existence of which it is immediately certain, *and* as being *all reality*. In this project, consciousness finds itself repeatedly 'going beyond itself', since the limits through which it is determined as an existing individual are negated by the universality of its consciousness. If consciousness then asserts itself as universal or pure consciousness, it is undone by the resulting *emptiness* and *unreality* of its stance.

After presenting this tension in reason's principle (section 5.1), I show how reason in its first shape ('observing reason') finds itself as organic nature, the essence of which is the concept of purpose or end (*der Zweckbegriff*) (section 5.2). I then show how reason transitions from an observing to a practical stance by recognizing itself as its *own end*, realized through its own activity (section 5.3). The internalization of the end or purpose within reason's activity takes another turn in the transition from self-actualizing reason to intrinsically real individuality, as consciousness reconceives its agency from aiming at an end to being its own end (section 5.4). Finally, I show how reason can only realize itself through the transition to spirit, conceived as an existing social world with which the individual rational agent is immediately identified (section 5.5). On the one hand, this transition is the realization of reason, since the conflict between reason's moments is resolved in social action, in the ethical life of a free nation. On the other hand, this transition occurs through a *repudiation* of reason as the individual's stance of critically questioning existing norms, demanding insight into their rationality as a condition of recognizing their authority—a repudiation that is at the same time a *return* to a *premodern* stance in relation to norms. Finally, I highlight the tension and irresolution at the end of reason (section 5.6).

---

[2] I take as a clue to the unity and coherence of the dialectic in the "Reason" chapter Hegel's claim in the Preface that "reason is *purposive activity* [*das zweckmäßige Tun*]" (PS 9.20/¶22). (NB. I cite Hegel's *Phenomenology* in the body of the text, using the page number of Volume 9 of Hegel's *Gesammelte Werke*, followed by the paragraph number provided in the Miller translation. I follow Miller's translation, with some emendations.)

5.1. REASON'S PRINCIPLE

The representation of reason that arises for consciousness in its transition is "the certainty that, in its particular individuality [*Einzelheit*], it has being absolutely *in itself*, or is
all reality" (PS 9.131/¶230). "The certainty of consciousness that it is all reality" becomes
reason's formula or principle. This conception arises through a reversal of consciousness as self-consciousness. In the "Self-Consciousness" chapter, consciousness attempts
to prove its certainty of itself as 'the true' by negating the apparently independent reality that confronts it. Consciousness as self-consciousness has "a negative relationship to
otherness" (PS 9.132/¶232). The standpoint of reason arises through turning this around
again into a positive relation:

> Up till now it [consciousness] has been concerned only with its independence and
> freedom, concerned to save and maintain itself for itself at the expense of the *world*,
> or of its own actuality, both of which appeared to it as the negative of its essence.
> But as Reason, assured of itself, it is at peace with them and can endure them. (PS
> 9.132/¶232)

Reason emerges as consciousness's *assurance* that that which appears other to itself as
essential being is fundamentally one with itself. This reversal implies a fundamental
change in consciousness's orientation to the world:

> Apprehending itself in this way, it is as if the world had for it [for consciousness]
> only now come into being; previously it did not understand the world; it desired
> and worked on it, withdrew from it into itself and abolished it as an existence on
> its own account.... In thus apprehending itself ... it discovers the world as *its*
> new world, which in its permanence holds an interest for it which previously lay
> only in it transiency; for the *existence* of the world becomes for self-consciousness
> its own *truth* and *presence*; it is certain of experiencing only itself therein. (PS
> 9.132–133/¶232)

Consciousness's newfound interest in *this* world, in contrast to the other-worldly orientation of consciousness in the Christian middle ages, marks (for Hegel) the turn to
modernity.

Consciousness's certainty that *it is all reality* (or, *de dicto*: "*I am* all reality") is hard to
interpret charitably; in fact, it appears mad or deranged. Hegel implies that the *comprehension* of reason's certainty consists in tracing the dialectical path that has produced it.
This certainty, Hegel tells us, just *is* the reduction of the consciousness for which *being*
is the true and of the opposite consciousness in which being is only *for consciousness*
to a single truth, namely, "that what *is*, or the in-itself, only *is* insofar as it is *for* consciousness, and what is *for* consciousness is also in itself or has intrinsic being." Hegel
continues:

The consciousness which is this truth has this path behind it and has forgotten it, and comes on the scene *immediately* as Reason; in other words, this Reason which comes immediately on the scene appears as the *certainty* of that truth. Thus it merely *asserts* [*versichert*] that it is all reality, but does not itself comprehend this; for it is along that forgotten path that this immediately expressed assertion is comprehended. (PS 9.133/¶233)

When it first comes on the scene, reason is merely *certain* that it is all reality—merely asserts this, but does not comprehend it. This certainty is comprehended along the same path through which it is demonstrated; and this path, Hegel says here, lies forgotten behind reason when it first appears. The forgetfulness of reason alludes to the ahistoricism of modern rationalism. The newness of its world for this consciousness, when it first appears, is founded on its forgetfulness. But Hegel implies also that the path *ahead* of consciousness at this point is the path through which it demonstrates and comprehends its principle or certainty; the task ahead is to convert its certainty into truth through the demonstration and comprehension of it. It follows that the path *ahead* of consciousness at this point remembers or recovers (in some sense) the path that lies forgotten behind it.

We achieve a preliminary grasp of reason's principle, and of the fundamental tension that it harbors, by seeing how it combines, in a sense, Kant's principle of pure apperception and Descartes' meditator's immediate self-certainty. Being certain that it is all reality, consciousness is certain that the essential nature of reality is its own essential nature, the nature of its 'I'. Hegel explicitly relates this stance to idealism. In terms of Kant's idealism, the key thought is that the necessary unity of apperception (Kant's principle according to which 'I think' must be able to accompany all my representations) is the same unity that constitutes the object of knowledge or experience. In the wake of Kant's transcendental deduction of the categories, of which pure apperception is the principle, Hegel calls this identity here the *pure category*: "the category means this, that self-consciousness and being are the same essence" (PS 9.134/¶235). In the same breath that Hegel acknowledges (implicitly) reason's Kantian provenance, he complains against that "one-sided, bad idealism that lets this unity again come on the scene as consciousness on one side, confronted by an *in-itself*, on the other" (PS 9.134/¶235). Kant's own principle of pure apperception is, Hegel thinks, a simple unity that fails to produce manifoldness and difference out of itself; in Kant's presentation, this unity is set over against a noumenal realm of things in themselves as source of the sensible manifold. In contrast, Hegel claims here that this pure category should be understood to contain difference *in itself*. Hegel affirms reason's stance as idealism only insofar as the latter is distinguished from the subjectivism, dualism, and formalism of Kant's stance. Acknowledging this departure from Kant, we are free to understand reason's certainty in light of Kant's pure apperception: I am certain of being all reality, in the sense that the necessary unity of my self-consciousness is the same necessary unity that constitutes the object, *qua* object of knowledge; hence, subject and object, thinking and being, are identical.

Consciousness's certainty of being all reality here also invokes modern philosophy's beginning in the immediate, indubitable certainty of Descartes' meditator that he exists, as thinking. Hegel's emphasis on consciousness's *self-certainty*, on the *immediacy* of this certainty, on the break with the past and the new philosophical beginning that this self-discovery implies, all invoke Descartes' cogito. Also, consciousness, in the transition to reason, is certain "that, *in its particular individuality* [*in seiner Einzelheit*], it has being absolutely *in itself*, or is all reality" (PS 9.131/¶230, first emphasis mine). Descartes' meditator's certainty is that "I exist, thinking," as *this individual*. Consciousness's insistence on itself, as an individual, runs through the whole "Reason" chapter. But reason's certainty of its being *as an individual* distances it from Kant's pure apperception, since the latter is *universal* self-consciousness, a mere form embracing necessarily all content of thought.

Reason's certainty thus contains a marked tension: on the one hand, it is *universal self-consciousness*, the certainty of being *all reality*, and, on the other hand, it is the certainty of *existing as this particular individual*, on its own account, as it were. This tension (how reason can be both at once) is a main motor of the dialectic in the "Reason" chapter, generating and negating its successive forms, a tension allegedly resolved only through the transition to spirit.

I am guided in my interpretation of the basic tension in the standpoint of reason by the following passage from the Introduction to the *Phenomenology* in which Hegel comments helpfully on the fundamental motor and goal of the dialectic:

> But the *goal* [*Ziel*] is as necessarily fixed for knowledge as the serial progression: it is the point where knowledge no longer needs to go beyond itself, where knowledge finds itself, where concept [*Begriff*] corresponds to object [*Gegenstand*] and object to concept. Hence the progress towards this goal is also unhalting, and short of it no satisfaction [*Befriedigung*] is to be found at any of the stations on the way. Whatever is confined within the limits of a natural life cannot by its own efforts go beyond its immediate existence; but it is driven beyond it by something else, and this uprooting entails its death. Consciousness, however, is explicitly the *concept* of itself [*Das Bewußtsein ist für sich selbst sein* Begriff]. Hence it is something that goes beyond limits, and since these limits are its own, it is something that goes beyond itself. With the positing of a single particular [*mit dem Einzelnen gesetzt*] is the beyond also established for consciousness. . . . Thus consciousness suffers this violence at its own hands: it spoils its own limited satisfaction. (PS 9.57/¶80)

The tendency of consciousness to "go beyond itself," to "destroy its own limited satisfaction," is grounded in the nature of consciousness as such. Self-transcendence derives from the fact that consciousness, unlike natural life, "is for itself its concept." We human beings, unlike mere natural life, are *for ourselves* in the sense that we exist in relation to our own conception of *what we are*. This implies our finding the limitations through which we are defined in our "immediate existence" too confining (our consciousness is as such universal, and hence transcends these limits), and we ourselves spoil the "limited satisfaction" of our immediate existence in the quest to express the universality of our consciousness. We can only be satisfied through positing ourselves as *unlimited*. This passage diagnoses our condition as that of exasperated, restless spirits running through various forms of life and self-conceptions, unable to find satisfaction. We see this condition exemplified in the forms of distinctively modern consciousness presented successively in the "Reason" chapter. But, at the same time, the passage points to the place where consciousness "no longer needs to go beyond itself," where it "finds itself," where its concept corresponds to its object and object to concept. This is allegedly attained, and the basic tension of reason's principle is allegedly resolved in the transition from reason to spirit at the end of the "Reason" chapter.

Consciousness appears as what Hegel calls 'actual reason' (as distinguished from reason's 'abstract concept') by its awareness that, "*qua certainty*, qua 'I', it is not yet in truth reality, and it is impelled to raise its certainty to truth and to give filling to the empty 'mine'" (PS 9.137/¶239). In contrast to the stance that would rest with the mere assertion that I am all reality, actual reason is aware that, as mere assurance, its certainty sets it the task of *showing that* it is all reality. While, on the one hand, reason recognizes being only insofar as it recognizes itself in it, on the other hand, it is aware that it remains mere assurance that it is all reality apart from the process of actually comprehending reality as rational, hence as one with itself.

5.2. OBSERVING REASON AND "THE CONCEPT OF END [DER ZWECKBEGRIFF]"

Consciousness's conviction in this stance that it is all reality [*Wirklichkeit*] expresses itself initially in the fact that it *observes*: "i.e. Reason wants to find and have itself as existent object, as an object that is actually and sensuously present" (PS 9.138/¶242). At the same time, though, consciousness's activity of comprehension transforms sensibly given things into concepts, which have the universal form of self-consciousness. Hegel writes of reason's first configuration ('observing reason'):

> [I]n its observational activity, [it] approaches things in the belief that it truly apprehends them as sensuous things opposite to the 'I'; but what it actually does contradicts this belief, for it *cognizes* [*erkennt*] things, it transforms their sensuous being into *concepts* [*Begriffe*], i.e., into just that kind of being which is at the same time 'I'.... (PS 9.138/¶242)

Thus emerges the conflict in observing reason between its commitment to universality, in the form of concepts or of self-consciousness, as required by comprehension, and its commitment to particularity and existence, as expressed in its demand that it encounter itself in the senses.

Initially, observing reason attempts to comprehend reality by means of categorizing nature into a system of genera and species. Observing reason, in accord with its assumption that nature itself is rational, assumes that the characteristics [*Merkmale*] by which it distinguishes things into kinds "not merely have an essential relation to cognition, but also are the essential determinations of things" (PS 9.140/¶246). However, consciousness's process of differentiating and categorizing nature proves endless; and, on reflection, the endlessness of this process expresses *reason's own demand*. Because reason at this stage comprehends nature through finding differences, thereby upsetting its previously established categories, it is, Hegel writes, a "restless, insatiable instinct" that "can never run out of material" (PS 9.139/¶245). The essential characteristics on the basis of which observing reason cognizes things are supposed to be passive and fixed determinations through which these things are defined; but, observing reason's process of destabilizing established categorizations on the basis of newfound characteristics shows them instead to be "vanishing moments of a movement which returns back into itself" (PS 9.142/¶248). Observing reason becomes conscious that the allegedly essential characteristics of things necessarily dissolve and flow into each other under further observation. Comprehending nature becomes the process, not anymore of categorizing into genera and species, but rather of articulating a system of laws of nature. Laws of nature capture or encapsulate the fluidity in relations among things that proves the downfall of knowing through categorization.

Laws of nature have, in accordance with reason's demands, the 'form of the concept' in the respect that they are, as such, universal and necessary. However, in accord with observing reason's will "to find and to have itself as existent object, as an object that is actually and sensuously present," "to the observing consciousness, the *truth of the law* is found in *experience*" (PS 9.142/¶249). Hegel tries to show over several paragraphs how "the concept of end [*der Zweckbegriff*]" reconciles this tension between *concept* (universality and necessity) and *actuality*, insofar as it is both "a *concept* of which [consciousness as reason] is *aware*; but it is also no less present as something *actual*. . . ." (PS 9.147/¶257).

Hegel introduces the organism, obscurely, as that "object, in which the process is present in the *simplicity* of the concept." He elaborates:

> It is this absolute fluidity in which the determinateness, through which it would be only *for an other*, is dissolved. The inorganic thing has determinateness for its essential nature, and for that reason constitutes the moments of the concept in their completeness only together with another thing, and therefore is lost when it enters into the process; in the organic being, on the contrary, every determinateness through which it is open to another is controlled by the organic simple unity. (PS 9.145/¶254)

Reason has learned that the *process* of knowing being as an organization of genera and species through comparison, abstraction, and reflection is intrinsically unsatisfying, since it must upset its provisionally established organizations through new discoveries. This, I think, is what Hegel means when he says that the inorganic thing "is lost when it enters into the process." 'The process' here is that of determining being (that is, identifying the essential characteristics of things) through *reason's own* acts of comparing and reflecting. Though these characteristics are supposed to be, as essential, *intrinsic*, they prove instead, as determined through acts of comparison, relational and contrastive. The diverse characteristics of a thing are unified in the simple unity of its concept. But the dialectic has shown that this simple unity of the concept *lies outside* of the objects *in observing reason* itself. Accordingly, observing reason transforms the conception of its object. In the organism, observing reason finds, Hegel says, a sensuously present object in which "the process is present in the simplicity of the concept." The organism is characterized, not through its determinateness, but rather through its own life-process, an organic unity that controls "every determinateness through which it is open to another." That is, the organism's particular forms and features are determined by the development of its own life-process. The main move in the transition to organism as reason's object is the move to a sensuously present object which itself manifests the determining and organizing process that observing reason has learned is both essential to nature, and yet proves external to nature, when the latter is conceived as a system of genera and species.

In the next step, the concept of the end emerges as the essence of organic nature through observing reason's dissatisfaction with its attempt to comprehend organic nature through its relation to inorganic nature. Observing reason attempts initially to explain living things by laws expressing how they are shaped through their interaction with their inorganic natural environment, laws such as "animals belonging to the air have the nature of birds, . . . animals in northern latitudes have thick, hairy pelts, and so on" (PS 9.145/¶255). But such 'laws' lack the necessity that reason requires. Because the relations expressed therein are not conceptual (e.g., "the concept of north does not imply the concept of a thick, hairy pelt"), the laws allow exceptions (e.g., "land animals which have the essential characteristics of a bird, of a fish, and so on"). *A fortiori*:

> The necessity, just because it cannot be grasped as an inner necessity of the creature, ceases to have a sensuous existence, and can no longer be observed in the world of reality, but has withdrawn from it. Finding thus no place in the actual creature, it is what is called a teleological relation, a relation that is *external* to the related terms, and therefore really the antithesis of a law. It is a conception completely freed from necessary nature, a conception which leaves nature behind and operates spontaneously above it. (PS 9.146/¶255)

That is, this approach implies that the reasons that living things are as they are ultimately lie *beyond the natural world itself* in a supernatural designing intelligence, who has, according to this conception, placed things in their relations in nature for purposes of its own. This conception appeals to an *external teleological relation* and loses the necessity *of nature* altogether, by appealing (at least implicitly) to the activity that "operates spontaneously above it." This is an unacceptable consequence to observing reason, given its quest "to find and to have itself as an existent object, as an object that is actually and sensuously present."

Consequently, observing reason transitions to the organism as "in fact, the real End [*Zweck*] itself":

> [F]or since it preserves *itself* in the relation to an other, it is just that kind of natural existence in which Nature reflects itself into the concept, and the two moments of cause and effect, of active and passive moments, which were the result of a necessary separating-out, are brought together into a unity, so that here something does not appear merely as a *result* of necessity. But, because it has returned into itself, the last, or the result, is just as much the *first* which initiated the movement, and is to itself the realized *End*. The organism does not produce something but only preserves itself; or, what is produced, is as much already present as produced. (PS 9.146/¶256)

That the natural organism is "just that kind of natural existence in which Nature reflects itself into the concept" means that the organism, as a naturally existing thing, *itself articulates and organizes itself into its characteristics*, constituting itself as the unity of these diverse characteristics. This process of "reflecting into a concept" previously fell to observing reason. The 'end' (*Zweck*) is the organism's *own* in the sense that the organism's development and articulation into its features *are just* the realization of its own nature, its own self-becoming, self-preserving, and self-articulating activity. We can put this by saying that the organism's life-activity and determinations are nothing but the realization of *the concept of itself*. Thus, Hegel writes that "the concept of End . . . to which Reason in its role of observer rises, is a *concept* of which it is *aware*; but it is also no less present as something *actual*, and is not an *external relation of the latter*, but its *essence*" (PS 9.147/¶257). The organism is "present as something *actual*" in being sensuously present; but it is also *a concept* in being the "simple unity" of diverse characteristics. In the case both of inorganic nature and of the relation of organic to inorganic nature, the simple unity proves external to nature. Once the "concept of end" emerges for observing consciousness, however, it has before it such a concept, as something sensible, objective, existing, actual; and this is only because this sensible thing is *self-organizing*.[3]

---

[3] The transition in Hegel's dialectic from the organism in relation to inorganic nature to the organism as "in fact, the real End itself" recalls Kant's move in his *Critique of the Power of Judgment* from (in Kant's terms) 'external' to 'internal' purposiveness (a distinction Hegel describes in his *Science of Logic* as "one of Kant's great services to philosophy"; SL 12.157/737). Already in the *Critique of Pure Reason*, Kant teaches that it is *reason*'s demand that our cognition of nature have systematic unity. Moreover, Kant teaches that this systematic unity, "the unity of reason," "always presupposes an idea, namely, that form of a whole of knowledge—a whole which is prior to the determinate knowledge of the parts and which contains the conditions that determine *a priori* for every part its position and relation to other parts" (A645 = B673). In the *Critique of the Power of Judgment*, then, Kant presents the living organism, as a particular, empirical natural object, as exhibiting this very unity that reason demands in our cognition of nature as a whole. Kant's conception of the organism as a 'natural end' (*Naturzweck*) is the conception of it as *internally* purposive (§64).—Clearly the initial moves in the dialectic of observing reason play on Kantian themes. The crucial difference is that, whereas Hegel's observing reason struggles to prove true its certainty that *nature itself* is rational, Kant assumes as already established in the *Critique of the Power of Judgment* that we cannot legitimately claim that the unity of reason belongs to nature itself.

This new object crucially incorporates movement or development within itself. Hegel distinguishes mechanical causation in nature from the sort of causation exhibited in natural organisms, when he contrasts here things of nature that are a mere "*result* of necessity" and "the necessity . . . [that] shows itself only in the End [*das Ende*],[4] but in such a way that this very End [*das Ende*] shows that the necessity has been there from the beginning" (PS 9.147/¶257). The change of the purposively organized thing is governed by its end or purpose (*Zweck*), but in such a way that this purpose shows itself only *in the end* [*das Ende*] *of the process*; however, though the purpose *shows itself at the end*, it has *been there, implicitly, from the beginning*. Thus the movement has the form of a "return to self": "in the outcome of its action, [it] returns only to itself; . . . therefore what it arrives at through the process of its action is *itself*" (PS 9.147/¶257). Observing reason's discovery that reason is a process of self-becoming and self-return is never abandoned. Conceiving the movement of self-becoming as self-return implies that the organism, in a sense, "goes outside itself." Hegel refers to this stage when he writes at the end of ¶257: "we have here, it is true, the distinction between what it *is* and what it *seeks*. . . ." That is, before it is fully realized, the organism *is not (yet) what it truly is*. But from the standpoint achieved at the end of the process, this self-difference proves to be illusory (Hegel continues the above quotation: "but this is merely the show of a distinction"). The organism must *achieve* the self-identity or self-unity that it *is* through a process in which it *appears* for a stretch to be other or in opposition to itself. In this process, present in an observed thing, observing reason finds *itself*.

Observing reason finds *itself* in the organism as concept of end because "this is just how *self-consciousness* is constituted; it likewise distinguishes itself from itself without producing any distinction" (PS 9.147/¶258). This recalls the beginning of the "Self-Consciousness" chapter, where self-consciousness is determined as "essentially return from *otherness* . . . it is movement" (PS 9.104/¶167). Self-consciousness is the movement of self-realization through positing a self-difference and then "overarch[ing] this other which, for the 'I', is equally only the 'I' itself" (PS 9.103/¶166). Self-consciousness is constituted the same as the organism or end, *except that the living organism is not, as such, self-conscious*. The living organism's lack of self-consciousness reflects *observing reason's* lack of self-consciousness, exemplified in its failure to recognize itself in its object. Hegel emphasizes that, in *finding itself* in the concept of end, observing reason "finds itself as a thing, *as a life*, but makes a distinction between what it is itself and what it has found, a distinction, however, which is none" (PS 9.147/¶258). Observing reason is reason *in the form of consciousness*, in the sense that, like consciousness in general, it considers its object as other to itself. Hegel compares observing reason's activity to the instinctual activity of a non-rational animal: "Just as the instinct of the animal seeks and consumes food, but thereby brings forth nothing other than itself, so too the instinct of reason in its quest finds only reason itself" (PS 9.147/¶258). But, whereas the instinct-driven (non-self-conscious) animal can be satisfied in this process, Hegel suggests, the rational (i.e., self-conscious) being cannot:

---

[4] Miller translates both *der Zweck* and *das Ende* as 'End', thus obscuring the distinction between them.

The instinct of Reason, on the other hand, is at the same time self-consciousness; but because it is only instinct it is put on one side over against consciousness, in which it has its antithesis. Its satisfaction is, therefore, shattered by this antithesis; it does indeed find itself, viz, the End [*Zweck*], and likewise the End as *thing*. But firstly, the End is for that instinct *outside* of the thing presenting itself as *End*. Secondly, this End, *qua* End, is also *objective*, and therefore does not fall within observing consciousness itself, but in another intelligence. (PS 9.247/§258)

At the beginning of the following section, I draw out of this passage the explanation for the transition from observing to self-actualizing reason, that is, the explanation for reason's inability to be satisfied in the attempt to *find* itself in the form of being, and its need rather to seek its satisfaction as the practical activity of realizing itself as *its own end*.

5.3. From Organism to Rational Action

Reason's satisfaction in the organism is marred insofar as it does not recognize itself in this object, as *purpose or end*. The objectivity of the end implies that it falls outside of the observing consciousness itself. As observing reason, the end that is its object is not its own. The end that is its object is also not wholly identified with that object, insofar as the living organism implicitly refers beyond itself to *some understanding or rational being* who posits or conceives it. Although the organism is its own end *in the sense* that its activity aims at its *own* preservation, and its characteristics manifest its own life-process, at the same time it is not its own end (or concept) in the sense that the unity of the end (or concept) implies some intelligence or rational being to think it.[5] At the end of Observing Reason, Hegel writes, "the organic process is only free *in itself*, but not *for itself*; in the end [*im Zwecke*] emerges the being-for-self of its freedom, but it *exists* only as another being, as a wisdom that is conscious of itself and is outside of this process" (PS 9.189/§341). Accordingly, reason can only be satisfied when the end is not an observed object standing over against it, but is rather itself, which it realizes. Reason becomes "*itself* the End [*Zweck*] at which its action aims . . ." (PS 9.191/§344).

This self-recognition transforms reason's standpoint from theoretical (observational) to practical. Consciousness as reason becomes "for itself its concept" (to recall the characterization in the Introduction, PS 9.57/§80). Unlike 'animal life', rational being is *its own project*; it has itself the problem of defining and achieving its end. In this sense, it is free. The process of self-defining and self-determining just is what reason is, according to this new conception. Reason moves in this transition from a naturalistic stance to a Kantian/Fichtean stance. In the systems of Kant and Fichte, human self-consciousness

---

[5] Kant, in the *Critique of the Power of Judgment* writes that "the unity of the end" "throughout implies relation to a *cause* that has understanding" (§73). Hegel expresses this point at the beginning of the "Self-Consciousness" chapter: "Life points to something other than itself, viz, to consciousness, for which life exists as this unity, or as genus" (PS 9.107/§172).

implies a break with nature, on which our claim to freedom is founded. As self-consciousness, we are *self-positing*; we are what we are only through our own activity, and not through nature. Kant and Fichte both argue that reason cannot be satisfied, cannot attain to the unconditioned, cannot find itself, in cognizing the world from a theoretical point of view. It is only as a principle of *practical* reason that reason attains to the unconditioned. This implies, for both thinkers, that the world *is not*, but rather is *to be made*, rational, and through our own activity. In Hegel's text, self-actualizing reason appears "as the Positive in contrast to something which certainly *is*, but which has for it the significance of something without intrinsic being"; and so it realizes itself by negating the world as given and positing itself as its own end in its place (PS 9.197–198/¶359).

Given that this transition is also to reason as *self-conscious*, that its activity of "negating the world as given" exhibits a dialectic like that of desire at the beginning of the "Self-Consciousness" chapter is unsurprising (cf. PS 9.107–108/¶¶174–175). Just as desiring self-consciousness loses itself in achieving itself, since the negating activity through which it proves its independence presupposes the object it negates, so here, likewise, self-actualizing reason loses itself in attaining its end, since the realization of its end implies the cessation of the purposive activity that it is. Its end or goal is always beyond what it is at present. Self-actualizing reason is *on its way* to actualization, but cannot attain it. By virtue of having itself as its own end, rational being fails to correspond to the concept of itself in any limited, determinate existence. It itself destroys its own limited satisfaction. The realization of reason appears as a problem.

The solution to this problem is attained only in the transition from reason to spirit at the end of the chapter, that is, in the transition to reason embodied in social norms, practices, and customs. Hegel previews this solution in the introduction to self-actualizing reason through introducing the concept of 'ethical life' ('*Sittlichkeit*'). Since self-actualizing reason is *self-conscious* reason, it is already spirit, "which," Hegel writes, "in the duplication of its self-consciousness and in the independence of both, has the certainty of its unity with itself" (PS 9.193/¶347). But this "inner certainty," Hegel writes, must be raised to truth. This happens in the later transition to ethical life, which he characterizes here as "the absolute spiritual *unity* of the essence of individuals in their independent *actual existence*" (PS 9.194/¶349). In the ethical life of a people, Hegel writes here, "reason is in truth realized" (PS 9.195/¶352). In the ethical life of a people, reason's conflict between individual existence and universal consciousness is resolved. In the ethical life of its people, the individual, as individual, has a consciously universal existence: "The single individual consciousness . . . is only this existent unit insofar as it is aware of the universal consciousness in its individuality as its own being, since what it is and does is the universal custom" (PS 9.194/¶349).

Hegel's claim that reason only realizes itself in ethical life points to the end of reason's dialectical path. But Hegel also insists here that rational consciousness can realize itself only by *withdrawing* from ethical life. Hegel notes that the 'discovery' that reason is realized in the ethical life of a people confirms the saying of the ancient sages that "wisdom and virtue consist in living in accord with the customs of one's people" (PS 9.195/¶352). But finding happiness and fulfillment through living in accord with the customs of one's people clashes with reason's individualism. Hegel describes the rational self-consciousness as "the *practical* consciousness, which steps into its world which it finds already *given*, with the aim of duplicating itself in the distinct form of something separate and individual, of producing itself as *this* individual, as this existent counterpart of itself, and of becoming conscious of this unity of its own actuality with the objective being of the world" (PS 9.196/¶356). And "since this unity means happiness," he continues, "the individual is sent out into the world by his own spirit to seek his happiness." The dialectic of self-actualizing reason tracks consciousness's trajectory as it sets out on this path as an individual, "isolated and alone," leaving behind the ethical life of its people as an environment hostile to the cultivation of its individual being, freedom, and happiness. Consciousness as reason leaves ethical life behind, both in the sense that the rational individual cultivates its individuality, of which it is immediately certain, "in opposition to the laws and customs" of ethical life, and in the more general sense that this new world that reason discovers is built in part upon the ruins of the ancient world, the beautiful harmony of ancient Greek ethical life, to which Hegel alludes here.

How ethical life can be both a condition from which reason must withdraw and the realization of reason is a question to which I return in the final section of this chapter.

5.4. From Action Toward an End to Action as End in Itself

Self-conscious reason conceives of itself, as an individual spirit, as essential being, and "its end, therefore, is to give itself as a particular individual [*als einzelnes*] an actual existence and to enjoy itself as an individual in it" (PS 9.197/¶358). This implies that "consciousness appears split into this given actuality and its *end*"; the latter is realized only through negating the former (PS 9.197–198/¶359). Self-conscious reason exists only through being acknowledged, and thus the 'first end' (*der erste Zweck*) of self-conscious reason consists in "seeing itself as *this particular individual* [*dieses Einzelne*] in another, or seeing another self-consciousness as itself" (PS 9.198/¶359). Accordingly, reason's self-realizing activity initially (in "Pleasure and Necessity") consists in seeking union with another. However, in achieving this union, self-conscious reason loses its truth as 'this particular individual', insofar as it becomes, through that action, a plural subject, a 'we', not the realized particular 'I' it aimed at. It becomes an object to itself, not as an individual, Hegel writes, but as a universal (PS 9.199/¶362).

Self-conscious reason next conceives of itself as universal through conceiving its end as a *law*; however, in conceiving of the law as the law of *its own* heart, with which it immediately identifies, it remains true to its self-conception as 'the essence' as an individual 'I'. Prior to carrying it out, its law is something *inner*, and this individual finds itself confronted with 'the real world', the outer, public world-order that, as opposite to the inner truth of its heart, is (to it) an unjust, oppressive, violent world-order. Again, self-conscious reason fails in its very success in realizing its end. Once the individual makes the law part of the world-order, Hegel writes, "the law has in fact escaped the individual; it directly becomes merely the relation which was supposed to be got rid of. The law of the heart, through its very realization, ceases to be a law of the *heart*" (PS 9.203/¶372); it becomes the common possession of all, the public reality in which self-conscious reason at this stage fails to recognize itself.

Through this experience, self-consciousness comes to recognize the reality of that world order, but as opposed to its own inner truth. Self-consciousness then comes to recognize itself as "in its own self a contradiction," as "distraught [*zerrüttet*] in its inmost being" (PS 9.205/¶375).[6] This contradiction is just that between its own individual truth (the law of its own heart) and its being, for itself, at the same time, all reality. By virtue of its consciousness of this inward contradiction, reason is revealed to be 'madness in general' ('*der Wahnsinn im allgemeinen*') (PS 9.205/¶376).

Self-actualizing reason saves its truth by identifying with the universal moment in its divided consciousness and regarding individuality as "the [moment] to be nullified" (PS 9.208/¶381). Self-actualizing reason assumes its third shape, as virtuous consciousness, when consciousness knows itself, as inner law, as what is "*intrinsically* true and good," over against "the way of the world [*Weltlauf*]," characterized as "the single individual which seeks its own pleasure and enjoyment" (PS 9.208/¶382). Virtuous consciousness aims to make actual the universal (or the good), which it conceives as the inner essence of the world, through the nullification or sacrifice of individuality.

The project of the virtuous consciousness fails because it can realize the good only through employing "what are called gifts, capacities, powers" of individuals that belong to the world already. At some level, the knight of virtue, standing over against the vice-ridden way of the world, "knows that his true strength lies in the fact that the good exists absolutely in its own right, i.e., brings itself to fulfillment" (PS 9.210/¶386). Hegel heatedly denounces the vanity, self-conceit, and emptiness of the virtuous consciousness, which would, through its own actions, make the corrupt world rational and good. Virtuous conscious ends in the realization that the good (the rational) is already actual: "What virtue learns from experience can only be this, that its End is already attained in principle, that happiness is found directly in action itself, and that action is itself the good" (PS 9.198/¶359). Consciousness achieves thereby the third and final shape of reason, namely, "individuality which takes itself to be real in and for itself" (PS 9.214–237/¶¶394–437).

Consciousness transitions from a stance in which it aims to *make itself real* to a stance in which it conceives of itself, as an individual, as *already real*. The former project presupposes the "split into this *given* actuality and the *end* [*Zweck*]." Now, "self-consciousness knows itself to be reality in the form of an individuality that directly expresses *itself*, an

---

[6] "The law of *this* particular heart is alone that in which self-consciousness recognizes itself; but this universally valid order has, through the realizing of that law, equally become for self-consciousness its own essential being and its own reality" (PS 9.205/¶375).

individuality which no longer encounters resistance from an actual world opposed to it, and whose end and object are only this expressing of itself" (PS 9.198/¶359). Whereas, in self-actualizing reason, action has its end outside of itself, now action has its purpose within itself, or is its own end.

This transition intensifies the internalization of the end within purposive activity that occurs progressively in the "Reason" chapter. Recall that the organism appears as purposive activity, in a sense, but that reason cannot achieve satisfaction in the organism insofar as the end is revealed to be "*outside* the thing presenting itself as *end*" (PS 9.147/¶258). Consciousness becomes 'self-actualizing reason' in the recognition that the end or purpose is *its own* to realize. However, whereas in self-actualizing reason, the end is beyond what consciousness as reason *is*, and its task is to make that purpose actual through negating the world as present to consciousness, in this new configuration, the end is no longer beyond action or the individual, but is present in action itself. "Since individuality is in its own self actuality," Hegel writes, "the material of its efforts and the end of action lie in the action itself" (PS 9.215/¶396). Hegel describes action here in a way that recalls his earlier characterizations of the organism: "Action has, therefore, the appearance of the movement of a circle which moves within itself in a void, which, unimpeded, now expands, now contracts, and is perfectly content [*zufrieden*] to operate in and with its own self." Action is not directed toward making the world rational, in this third stage of reason, but rather "action alters nothing and opposes nothing"; it is, Hegel says here, "the pure form of a transition from a state of not being seen to one of being seen."

5.5. THE REALIZATION OF REASON AS SPIRIT

Relating the structure of action here to the earlier account of organic nature helps explain this puzzling label Hegel gives to the first moment of the final shape of reason: 'spiritual animal kingdom'. At first, intrinsically real individuality appears as a simple *in-itself*, 'an original determinate nature' (PS 9.216/¶398). The individual's determinacy implies limitation, which would contradict its self-conception as *all reality*. This contradiction is avoided through the individual's identification with its *action*, the process by which it becomes itself. Action, Hegel writes, "is a relation purely of itself to itself: relation to an *other*, which would be a limitation of it, has been eliminated" (PS 9.216/¶398). Hegel means to call to mind the living organism as that "in which the process [of its determination] is present in the *simplicity* of the concept"; or, again, as "the absolute fluidity in which the determinateness, through which it would be only *for an other*, is dissolved" (PS 9.145/¶254). Just as the organism is determinate through its relation to another, but this determinacy is 'controlled' by 'the organic simple unity', so here the determinacy of this individuality is but an expression of its own simple self-identity expressed in action. Hegel makes explicit the analogy with 'animal life':

The original determinateness of the nature is, therefore, only a simple principle . . . ; just as in the case of indeterminate animal life, which breathes the breath of life, let us say, into the element of water, or air or earth, . . . steeping its entire nature into them, and yet keeping that nature under its own control, and preserving itself as a unity, in spite of the limitations imposed by the element, and remaining in the form of this particular [*besondere*] organization the same universal animal life. (PS 9.216/¶398)

The *particular* organization of the universal animal life maintains and preserves *itself*, its own identity, despite the relation to others required for its being determinate. Similarly, the intrinsically real individual *makes itself* and maintains its self-identity in the process of its action, despite its necessary relation to others. The process of action has three parts: first as an object or end, opposed to the given reality; second, as the *movement* of the end, which Hegel also characterizes as 'the *means*': "[a]nd thirdly, as the object again, not anymore as *end*, . . . but as something produced by him, something existing *for him* now as an *other*" [what gets called 'the work'] (PS 9.217/¶400). Hegel earlier wrote of the organism that "it arrives at through the process of action [] *itself*" (PS 9.148/¶257). Here he writes, "action simply translates an initially implicit being [*das Ansichsein*] into a being that is made explicit" (PS 9.217/¶401).

However, the rational individual, unlike the organism, acts *self-consciously*. Hence, "he must have the action in front of him beforehand as *entirely his own*, i.e., as an end" (PS 9.218/¶401). By virtue of this, reason at this stage is (implicitly) *universal consciousness*, and its problem is to find itself within the limits of its individual determinate existence. Criterial for reason here is that "the entire action . . . does not go outside of itself" (PS 9.219/¶401), but, as both universal and allegedly determinately existing, it fails ultimately to meet this criterion. The process of its failure is the derivation of the concept of '*die Sache selbst*', in which is inscribed "the coming to be of Spirit."[7]

The configuration of intrinsically real individuality breaks down initially through the 'fundamental contradiction' inherent in its work (PS 9.222/¶407). The work produced, "the reality which consciousness gives itself" (PS 9.220/¶405), is determinate. But consciousness is universal. "[Consciousness] thus goes beyond itself in the work, and is itself the quality-less void which is left unfilled by its work" (ibid.). Consciousness "preserve[s] its universality" by, in effect, idealizing its work (ibid.). The 'making real' of the individual through action is at the same time its becoming *for others*. But the work 'vanishes' in this process, insofar as its work is, for others, "an alien reality, which they must replace by their own in order to obtain through *their* action the consciousness of *their* unity with reality" (PS 9.221/¶405). Consciousness seems at first to lose its truth in the passing away of its work, but then consciousness bethinks itself: the 'passing away' of the empirical work just shows that it is not 'the true work'. What vanishes, Hegel notes, is the objective reality, but "objective reality . . . is a moment which no longer possesses any truth on its own account in this consciousness" (PS 9.222/¶409). What has truth, for

---

[7] Miller translates *die Sache selbst* as 'the heart of the matter' and 'the matter in hand'. He also occasionally translates *Sache* as 'affair'. I leave the phrase untranslated (mostly) and explain Hegel's meaning in context.

this consciousness, is the *unity of doing and being*, not the empirical reality it produces. The true work is that reality "whose universality is one with action," the essential thing [*die Sache selbst*], or "that which *endures*, independently of what is merely the *contingent* result of an individual action" (PS 9.223/¶409).

Consciousness learns that, in the process of its action, its *own affair* [*seine eigne Sache*] becomes *for others* as well: "actualization is . . . a display of what is one's own in the element of universality whereby it becomes, and should become, the affair [*Sache*] of everyone" (PS 9.227/¶417). The *Sache* is supposed to be *both the individual's own and universal* at the same time. Consciousness learns that the nature of *die Sache selbst* is that "its being is the *action* of the single individual and of all individuals, and whose action is immediately *for others*, or is a *Sache* and only is a *Sache* as action of *each and everyone*: the essence, which is the essence of all beings [*aller Wesen*], viz., *spiritual essence*" (PS 9.227/¶418). *Die Sache selbst*, the true work, is revealed to be the action which is both one's own and everyone's at the same time, *an intrinsically universal* action in which all rational beings are united into one. As such, reason is expressed as *universal ethical law*.

In this transition, consciousness assumes a universal standpoint, or becomes "a *self* in the form of a universal self" (PS 9.228/¶419). Consciousness is both a particular individual and *pure*, and, as the latter especially, *ethical* consciousness, consciousness of *die Sache selbst* that is now *ethical substance* (PS 9.228–229/¶420). Reason is now something that "is and is *authoritative* [*es ist und gilt*]": an *actual* normative demand governing behavior. Consciousness's object here "has the value of the *absolute*, for self-consciousness cannot and does not want anymore to go beyond this object, for in it, it is in communion with itself" (PS 9.229/¶420). Reason has attained to its absoluteness as an unconditionally valid and present universal practical demand. Thus, the shape of reason as authoritative universal practical demand combines absoluteness, objectivity, and immediate identity with the 'I' of individual self-consciousness.

The problem becomes how to marry the commitment to absoluteness and unconditionality, on the one hand, with determinacy and existence, on the other. At first, the ethical substance presents itself as a multiplicity of *determinate laws*, because, Hegel says, "it contains within itself the distinction characteristic of consciousness" (PS 9.229/¶420). The particular determinate ethical laws are recognized as valid *immediately*, as befitting their status as absolutely valid: "we cannot ask for their origin or justification, nor can we look for any other warrant . . ." (PS 9.229/¶421). The testing of this stance (which, as 'immediate ethical certainty', recalls that of sense-certainty) consists in adducing examples of that which is supposedly immediately known. Hegel argues that the *determinacy* of the immediately given ethical laws that he adduces as examples clashes with their status as *universal* and *absolute*. When we press on the determinate laws, we can retain their authority for us only by qualifying and adding conditions to them.

Echoing Kant's derivation of the moral law, consciousness tries to save the unconditioned status of its practical law by abstracting from all determinate content. "Since, then, all idea of an absolute content is given up, it can only claim a formal universality" (PS 9.231/¶426). "All that is left then for making a law is the mere form of universality" (PS 9.231–232/¶427). Reason becomes, then, a criterion (*Maßstab*) for testing "whether a content is capable of being a law or not. Reason as the giver of laws is reduced to a reason which merely *critically examines* them" (PS 9.232/¶428). Reason now occupies the standpoint of Kantian morality, according to which the principle of pure practical reason commands us unconditionally to act only on maxims that we can at the same time will as universal laws. However, in the context of the dialectic of the "Reason" chapter, this maneuver is not promising. Hegel includes an argument, discussing the case of property, for the claim that the criterion that reason has become for testing "whether a content is capable of being a law or not," cannot function as a criterion at all, because it "fits every case equally well" (PS 9.234/¶431). Hegel presumably satisfies himself with a brief, allusive, and elliptical argument because, given reason's commitment from the outset to determinacy and existence, reason's attempt to save the unconditionality of its principle by abstracting from determinate content seems doomed.

Hegel claims that both of these moments (law-giving and law-testing) have proven to be "merely unstable moments of the ethical consciousness" (PS 9.234/¶432). Each undercuts the absoluteness of the ethical law. Both exhibit insolence, Hegel writes (PS 9.235/¶434), and "a negative relation to substance or real spiritual being, or we may say that in them substance does not yet possess reality" (PS 9.235/¶435). That is, in these stances, consciousness denies the being of the laws, as existing in themselves and thus is "still in fact distinct from substance" (PS 9.238/¶438). Through this lesson, reason becomes spirit.

Spirit is the *actuality* of the ethical substance that emerged for consciousness in the transition to law-giving Reason (PS 9.238/¶439). Consciousness comes to recognize the law as having intrinsic being, as *existing in itself*, and this is the way in which spiritual being exists for consciousness:

> The law is . . . an eternal law which is grounded not in the will of the particular individual but is valid in and for itself; it is the absolute *pure will of all* which has the form of immediate being. Also, it is not a *commandment*, which only ought to be; it *is* and is valid. It is the universal 'I' of the category, the 'I' which is immediately a reality, and the world *is* only this reality. (PS 9.235/¶436)

Spirit is the actuality of the ethical substance insofar as it is the social world to which the individual belongs and which is present to the individual as the realized customs in that world.

This recalls the paragraphs at the beginning of self-actualizing reason in which Hegel introduces the concept of *Sittlichkeit* as that in which reason is actualized (PS 9.194–197/¶¶349–358). As Hegel puts the progression at the beginning of the "Spirit" chapter: "Reason is spirit when its certainty of being all reality has been raised to truth, and it is consciousness of itself as its own world, and of the world as itself" (PS 9.238/¶438). The certainty of the 'I' that it, as an individual, is all reality has become truth in its recognition of unity with its social whole through its relation to the ethical life of its people. At every stage of the development of consciousness as reason, its moment of universality goes beyond its particularity as a determinately existing individual. But, in the transition to spirit, the individual's universal consciousness is the existing social whole, expressed concretely for the individual in the intrinsically real laws and customs of its people, through which it has its own action and being:

> [T]his existent unchangeable essence is the expression of the very individuality which seems opposed to it; the laws proclaim what each individual is and does; the individual knows this not only as his own universal objective thinghood, but equally knows himself in them, and in each of his fellow citizens. In the universal spirit, therefore, each has only the certainty of himself, of finding in the actual world nothing but himself. (PS 9.195/¶351)

Not only is the 'I' an (actually existing) 'we', but the 'we' is also an 'I'. "There is nothing here which would not be reciprocal" (PS 9.195/¶351). Just as the individual is conscious of having its being in the life of the whole ("for which he sacrifices himself and in so doing receives back from it his own self"), the social whole exists only through the labor and sacrifice of its individual members, a process through which the social whole "is not a dead essence, but is *actual* and *alive*" (PS 9.239/¶439).

This self-articulating, self-organizing social whole is the direct descendant of observing reason's organism. The purposive activity of the latter failed to satisfy reason, since the organism's end had to lie in some other understanding. Through reason's recognition that it is its own end, which transforms observing into active reason, the attempt to prove that it is unconditional and absolute is made anew. But, with this new configuration, since the given reality and the end to be realized stand in opposition to each other, action and end prove external to each other, and rational purposive action is revealed to be perpetual self-transcendence. Rational self-consciousness then conceives the end as the action itself. Reason's quest to prove its certainty of being, as an individual, all reality takes finally the form of action in and for itself. But the distinct moments of individuality (determinacy, existence) and universality cannot be reconciled in this configuration either, except insofar as the transition is made to *spirit*, which Hegel characterizes as follows:

> Spirit is the *actuality* of [ethical] substance. It is the *self* of actual consciousness to which it stands opposed, or rather which it opposes to itself as an objective, actual *world*, but a world which has completely lost the meaning for the self of something alien to it, just as the self has completely lost the meaning of a being-for-self separated from the world, whether dependent on it or not. Spirit, being the *substance* and the universal, self-identical and abiding essence, is the unmoved solid *ground* and *starting point* for the action of all, and it is their purpose and goal [*Zweck und Ziel*], the in-itself of every consciousness expressed in thought. (PS 9.238–239/¶439)

Spirit, which exists for the individual as its social world, is both what the individual's action proceeds from and what it aims at, its end. Moreover, as social, the action is both the individual's own and everyone's. As social action, as the life of the social whole, consciousness as reason need no longer go beyond itself, or, rather, its going beyond itself is recognized as a return to itself.

5.6. THE APORIA AT THE END OF REASON

This transition to spirit seems the happy end of consciousness's journey. We seem to have arrived at the goal, the point where concept corresponds to object and object to concept, where "knowledge no longer needs to go beyond itself" (PS 9.57/¶80). But this transition is as much the *repudiation* of reason as its realization, and it is not clear how our protagonist consciousness is supposed to be satisfied.

The criticism of law-testing reason is, as befits its place at the end of the "Reason" chapter, the criticism of the stance of reason as a whole. Consciousness learns, through the discovery of the emptiness of its criterion, that its attitude of demanding justification of, or insight into, ethical substance (present as the laws and customs of the social whole to which it belongs) is not only unjustified, but unethical:

> If I inquire into [the] origin [of the laws] and confine them to the point where they arose, then I have transcended them; for now it is *I* who am universal, and *they* are the conditioned and limited. If they are supposed to be validated by *my* insight, then I have already denied their unshakeable, intrinsic being, and regard them as something which, for me, is perhaps true, but is also perhaps not true. Ethical disposition consists just in sticking to what is right and abstracting from all attempts to move or shake it, or derive it. (PS 9.236/¶437)

If I demand insight into the ethical substance that confronts me, then I fail to "acknowledge the *absoluteness* of right," and I am *outside* ethical substance.[8] Consciousness has, accordingly, been outside of ethical substance throughout the "Reason" chapter, insofar as it has been about the business of *proving* its certainty that it is, as an individual, all reality. While this project puts its own stance to the test, it also implicitly demands of substance that it show itself as one with the immediately self-certain individual as a condition of the individual's acknowledgment of it as authoritative or real. The repudiation of this attitude or stance at the end as self-conceit, as the illegitimate self-assertion of the individual in the face of the ethical substance, reaffirms the repudiation of reason's stance at several points earlier in the dialectic: the law of the heart became "the frenzy of self-conceit"; the virtuous consciousness was "inflated with his own conceit" (PS 9.212/¶390); in the spiritual animal kingdom, consciousness's formation breaks down in the discovery that *die Sache selbst* is not only one's own, but everyone's (PS 226–227/

---

[8] "By acknowledging the *absoluteness* of the right, I am within the ethical substance" (PS 9.237/¶437).

¶¶417–418). The affirmed attitude, in which one acknowledges the *absoluteness* of right, without insight or justification, and, in general, without condition, is exemplified famously for Hegel in the following lines from Sophocles' *Antigone*:

> They [the laws] are not of yesterday or today, but everlasting,
>   Though where they come from, none of us can tell. (PS 9.236/¶437)

In deriving this attitude, in which one acknowledges that the laws are valid, without questioning, without inquiring why or wherefore, consciousness as reason is not so much realized as repudiated.

Moreover, though Hegel does not note this, the repudiation of the stance of critical reason at the end of the "Reason" chapter amounts to a repudiation of the standpoint to which the argument of the *Phenomenology* as a whole is addressed. In the Preface, Hegel explains why the *Phenomenology* is necessary by appealing to the right of the individual to demand that the principle of metaphysics or 'Science' ("pure self-recognition in absolute otherness"—the identity of subject and object) be demonstrated to him, starting with his own standard for justification, according to which metaphysics' standpoint is "the inverse of the truth" (PS 9.23/¶26). Hegel, not taking the legitimacy of this right for granted, finds it to be based on the individual's "absolute independence, which he is conscious of possessing in every phase of his knowledge, for in each one, whether recognized by Science or not and whatever the content may be, the individual is the absolute form, i.e., he is the *immediate certainty* of himself and, if this expression be preferred, he is therefore unconditioned being" (PS 9.23/¶26). That is, Hegel appeals in justification of the individual's right to make the demand for rational insight (to which the *Phenomenology* as a whole responds) to the immediate self-certainty of the individual consciousness; he appeals to the same cogito-like self-certainty of modern consciousness that underwrites consciousness as reason. How are we to understand reason's end in the recognition that the individual has no right to demand rational justification or insight, but that its proper attitude is to acknowledge the absoluteness of the right as it presents itself immediately within its social world, without grounds or comprehension? Is *our own appetite* for justification supposed to be sated through seeing *why* this demand for justification is *itself unjustified*?

That question aside (which concerns *our own satisfaction*), the satisfaction of the protagonist consciousness at the end of the "Reason" chapter is doubtful as well. We are told (both at the beginning of the "Reason" chapter, and then periodically throughout) that consciousness as reason, in order to move from certainty to truth, must remember or recover the path that lies forgotten behind it when reason first emerges. This happens, in a sense, in the transition to spirit. The repudiation of the critical stance of consciousness as reason is at the same time explicitly the affirmation of the *premodern* relation of consciousness to law. Reason is realized in *ancient* ethical life, according to the dialectic in the *Phenomenology*. Consciousness as reason comes to realize that reason is realized in that past world. But that world is lost as much to our protagonist consciousness as to us. Reason *had to* withdraw, Hegel tells us, "from this happy state of having realized its essential character and of living in it" (PS 9.195–196/¶¶353–354). It has come to the recognition that reason is realized in that world, but such a recognition hardly reproduces that world. Reason has come to see why Antigone's relation to the laws and customs of her people, an attitude Hegel describes as "a solid and unshaken trust" (PS 9.196/¶355), is the attitude in which its certainty has truth; but insofar as this insight is attained through a process of reflection that emerges through the loss of that very trust, which it does not restore, it is hard to see how there is any satisfaction for consciousness in the realization of reason in ethical life.

Given that the "Reason" chapter ends both in the realization and the repudiation of reason, and given that reconciling these is a problem, the "Reason" chapter ends in aporia. Of course, the dialectic does not end here. The development in the "Spirit" chapter shows why spirit has to "leave behind the beauty of [ancient] ethical life" (PS 9.240/¶441), that harmony of individual and social whole invoked at the end of the "Reason" chapter, and progress to the world of the Enlightenment, characterized by the very sorts of demands for justification and insight that are repudiated here. There may yet be satisfaction along the way.[9] I note, though, that the problem implicitly posed at the end of the "Reason" chapter is central to Hegel's system of philosophy as a whole. For Hegel, philosophy is the cognition of the self-developing whole, within which the individual becomes determined as a mere moment. How, then, does philosophy accommodate the individual's claim to be self-standing, to exist through itself, on its own account, a claim expressed in particular in the individual's demand for intelligible insight or justification, as a condition of recognizing validity or authority? This is one of the most persistent and prominent questions raised about Hegel's system of philosophy. Hegel clearly *aims* to accommodate or recognize the legitimate claims on behalf of the individual, the levying of which he understands to be characteristic of modern culture; and critics question whether his system of philosophy succeeds in this respect. In the "Reason" chapter in the *Phenomenology*, the claim on behalf of the individual consciousness fuels the dialectic that produces the rich parade of forms of modern consciousness that pass before us there. Since the chapter ends with a summary repudiation of the individual's claim, it ends on a note of tension, rather than resolution, referring us to the ensuing dialectic of spirit.[10]

---

[9] But, since Hegel tells us that the future shapes of spirit are not shapes of consciousness, but rather 'shapes of a world', whatever satisfaction may lie ahead, it won't be, it seems, the satisfaction of the protagonist consciousness (see PS 9.240/¶441).

[10] I have been informed, in writing this chapter, by the works on Hegel's *Phenomenology of Spirit* listed in the bibliography. Because of space considerations, I have omitted notes explaining how my account agrees with or differs from those in these works, none of which has quite the same focus and task as I have in this chapter.

Works Cited

Primary Texts

Hegel, G. W. F. *Encyclopädie der philosophischen Wissenschaften im Grundrisse (1830)*, edited by Wolfgang Bonsiepen and Hans-Christian Lucas. Vol. 20 of Hegel's *Gesammelte Werke*. Hamburg: Felix Meiner Verlag, 1992. In English: *Hegel's Philosophy of Mind: Part Three of the Encyclopedia of the Philosophical Sciences (1830)*, edited by William Wallace, translated by A. V. Miller, Oxford: Clarendon Press, 1971.

Hegel, G. W. F. *Phänomenologie des Geistes*, edited by Wolfgang Bonsiepen and Reinhard Heede. Vol. 9 of Hegel's *Gesammelte Werke* (Bd. 9). Hamburg: Felix Meiner Verlag, 1980. In English: *Phenomenology of Spirit* [PS], translated by A. V. Miller, with analysis of the text and forward by J. N. Findlay. Oxford: Clarendon Press, 1977.

Hegel, G. W. F. *Wissenschaft der Logik. Zweiter Band. Die subjektive Logik (1816)*, edited by Friedrich Hogemann and Walter Jaeschke. Vol. 12 of Hegel's *Gesammelte Werke*. Hamburg: Felix Meiner Verlag, 2010. In English: *Hegel's Science of Logic*, translated by A.V. Miller, New York: Humanity Books, 1999.

Kant, Immanuel. *Critique of Pure Reason*, translated by Norman Kemp Smith. New York: Palgrave Macmillan, 2003.

Kant, Immanuel. *Critique of the Power of Judgment*, edited by Paul Guyer, translated by Paul Guyer and Eric Matthews. Cambridge: Cambridge University Press, 2000.

Secondary Literature

Forster, Michael. *Hegel's Idea of a* Phenomenology of Spirit. Chicago: University of Chicago Press, 1998.

Harris, H. S. *Hegel: Phenomenology and System*. Indianapolis, IN: Hackett, 1995.

Hyppolite, Jean. *Genesis and Structure of Hegel's* Phenomenology of Spirit, translated by Samuel Cherniak and John Heckman. Evanston, IL: Northwestern University Press, 1974.

Kreines, James. "The Logic of Life: Hegel's Philosophical Defense of Teleological Explanation in Biology," in *The Cambridge Companion to Hegel and Nineteenth-Century Philosophy*, edited by F. Beiser. Cambridge: Cambridge University Press, 2008, 344–77.

Lauer, Quentin. *A Reading of Hegel's* Phenomenology of Spirit. New York: Fordham University Press, 1993.

McDowell, John. "Towards a Reading of Hegel on Action in the 'Reason' Chapter of the *Phenomenology*," in John McDowell, *Having the World in View*. Cambridge, MA: Harvard University Press, 2009, 166–184.

Moyar, Dean, and Michael Quante, eds. *Hegel's* Phenomenology of Spirit: *A Critical Guide*. Cambridge: Cambridge University Press, 2008.

Pippin, Robert. "Recognition and Reconciliation: Actualized Agency in Hegel's Jena *Phenomenology*," in *Recognition and Power: Axel Honneth and the Tradition of Critical Social Theory*, edited by Bert van den Brink and David Owen. Cambridge: Cambridge University Press, 2007, 57–78.

Pöggeler, Otto. *Hegels Idee einer Phänomenologie des Geistes.* Freiburg; Munich: Verlag Karl Alber, 1973.

Stern, Robert. *Routledge Philosophy Guidebook to Hegel and the* Phenomenology of Spirit. London: Routledge, 2001.

Stewart, Jon. *The Unity of Hegel's* Phenomenology of Spirit: *A Systematic Interpretation.* Evanston, IL: Northwestern University Press, 2000.

CHAPTER 6

....

SPIRIT IN THE
PHENOMENOLOGY OF SPIRIT

....

MARK ALZNAUER

THE task of the *Phenomenology of Spirit* is so ambitious, and the means it takes so unprecedented, that it is not surprising that even careful readers have often disagreed about how a given stretch of text is supposed to contribute to the overall argument. But going on the evidence of the title alone, one might have expected that there would be a universal consensus about the importance of the chapter on spirit (the sixth chapter, according to at least one of the puzzlingly numerous ways of dividing up the book). But, alas, there is no such consensus—and when one turns to the book, it is not hard to see why. Theodor Haering's once influential claim that Hegel changed his mind as he wrote the *Phenomenology*, and that "Spirit" in particular makes no contribution to the project he set out to accomplish, is certainly hyperbolic, but it points us to the central interpretive puzzle facing any attempt to offer a unified reading of the *Phenomenology*. How could an argument ostensibly about epistemological issues, about how we can know the world, be served by what we actually find in this chapter: an extensive and seemingly idiosyncratic survey of Western history that covers Greek tragedy, Roman law, early modern court culture, the paradoxes of the Enlightenment, the problem of the aftermath of the French Revolution, and the dilemmas of the 'beautiful soul'? It would appear that by the time we have gotten here, the train has definitely jumped the tracks.

Of course, that might be for the best. For those less interested in the main argument of the *Phenomenology*, the problem of determining how the "Spirit" chapter could possibly contribute to that argument has been easy to ignore, for the apparent detour into history has plenty of interest on its own. Indeed, Hegel's treatment of Sophocles' *Antigone* in the beginning of the chapter, to choose one salient example, has been profitably analyzed from a staggeringly disparate number of directions: as a treatment of the social basis of gender roles, as a theory of tragedy, as a politics of recognition, and so on. For readers like these, the primary value of the "Spirit" chapter is in its provocative deployment of the dialectical method to treat various issues in political and cultural history—and it would have this value even if these discussions added nothing to the central argument of the book.

It would take a long time and a great deal of interpretive ingenuity to show that all of the twists and turns we find in the "Spirit" chapter are necessitated by the overarching argument of the *Phenomenology*.[1] My ambitions here will be more modest. I hope to show how and why Hegel's general project in *Phenomenology* leads him to develop the kind of social theory we find in "Spirit." It is the basic structure of this theory, not the specific details of its historical application, that I will be focusing on.[2] Hegel's theory of spirit has certainly had an enormous influence on subsequent thought on the human sciences—but its influence was mostly felt in those currents of thought, like Marxism and German historicism, that emphatically and explicitly rejected central elements of Hegelianism as mystificatory or speculative in the bad sense. So although Hegel's theory has always been viewed as an important precursor to genuinely scientific, empirical approaches to human history, the value of that theory has long been thought to be hopelessly compromised by the philosophic commitments that frame it. I will be arguing, however, that it is precisely its philosophic underpinnings that give Hegel's theory most of its interest to us today, for what it seems to offer is a social theory that can simultaneously explain and justify our quintessentially modern commitment to freedom. My account will focus on two key philosophic claims Hegel makes: first, that guidance by practical reason is only possible if we belong to a certain kind of social life, one characteristic of free nations; and, second, that history can be reconstructed as the progressive resolution of the necessary internal contradictions that afflict free nations. It will take the rest of this chapter to see exactly what all this amounts to, and how the "Spirit" chapter argues for it.

6.1. THE PRIMACY OF SPIRIT

The first thing we need to understand is how Hegel's theory of spirit is supposed to fit into the argument of the *Phenomenology of Spirit* as a whole. In his later *Logic*, he gives a brief characterization of what the *Phenomenology* attempts to achieve:

> In the *Phenomenology of Spirit* I have presented consciousness as it progresses from the first immediate opposition of itself and the subject matter to absolute knowledge. This path traverses all the forms *of the relation of consciousness to the object* and its result is the concept of science. (SL 21.32/28)

---

[1] For a recent attempt to do this, see Collins, *Hegel's Phenomenology*.

[2] On the problem of the relation between Hegel's narrative framework and the specific historical episodes that he attempts to interpret with it, see Pippin, "Hegel on Historical Meaning."

As this passage indicates, the *Phenomenology* is supposed to include and examine all possible oppositions between consciousness and its object. And, as is well known, it is supposed to lead us to absolute knowledge *via negativa*: by showing that any assumption that consciousness is distinct from its object breaks down.

This basic characterization of the *Phenomenology* certainly fits the five chapters preceding "Spirit." In these chapters, Hegel addresses various 'shapes of consciousness', each representing one possible way to oppose consciousness and its object, and tries to show that they are all internally contradictory: what they take consciousness to be is incompatible with what they take the object of consciousness to be. Do we see the same kind of argument in "Spirit"? To be sure, Hegel claims that in the "Spirit" chapter we are no longer dealing with 'shapes of consciousness', and this might be thought to indicate a real shift in the program. He says,

[The shapes in Spirit] are distinguished from the previous ones by the fact that they are real Spirits, actualities in the strict meaning of the world, and instead of being merely shapes of consciousness, are shapes of a world. (PS 9.240/¶441)

But although the target of the argument is changing in certain ways, it is easy to see that this change does not imply that we are no longer dealing with various possible oppositions between consciousness and its object. In making the transition to spirit, we have only abandoned certain individualistic or psychological forms of this opposition in order to examine more social forms that this opposition can take. In spirit, the opposition we are interested in is between the social norms that regulate and reproduce social organisms (the object) and the kind of awareness that a given community has of those social norms (consciousness).

For example, in Hegel's analysis of the kind of social order that characterized the Greek polis, we have, on the one hand, certain social norms that are supposed to guide and justify the actions of its citizens, thus enabling the reproduction of the polis. These are, in Hegel's terminology, the 'substance' or 'essence' of Greek society. This is paired with a certain 'consciousness of substance' that is supposed to be characteristic of individuals in this social order: Antigone, for example, is supposed to immediately perceive what she should do according to the norms of the polis as these norms pertain to her case (being a sister, she is supposed to bury her brother). What Hegel wants to argue is that this is an unstable combination of consciousness and its object; our knowledge of social norms cannot be both determinately authoritative and simply a matter of immediate, ethical perception.

At the very least, then, we can say that insofar as there are social forms that the opposition between consciousness and the object takes, spirit is a necessary part of Hegel's project. But spirit is not included just for the sake of completeness, it also has a certain kind of primacy in Hegel's account; and this is, though not the central thesis of the *Phenomenology*, its most historically influential claim. Although the argument of the *Phenomenology* does not start with spirit, but rather retreats back into it, Hegel intends his notion of spirit to take over the foundational role played by consciousness or subjectivity in previous modern thinkers. He wants to show that all human cognition is somehow rooted in a collective, historical subject. In a key passage at the beginning of the "Spirit" chapter, he puts the point this way:

> Spirit is thus self-supporting, absolute, real being. All previous shapes of consciousness are abstract forms of it. They result from Spirit analyzing itself, distinguishing its moments, and dwelling for a while with each. The isolating of those moments *presupposes* Spirit itself and subsists therein; in other words, the isolation exists only in Spirit which is a concrete existence. In this isolation they have the appearance of really existing as such; but that they are only moments or vanishing qualities is shown by their advance and retreat into their ground and essence; and this essence is just this movement and resolution of these moments. (PS 9.239/¶440)

What does it mean to say that the 'shapes of consciousness' analyzed in the previous chapters of the *Phenomenology* presuppose spirit? This passage provides three alternative ways of formulating this dependency relation. Forms of consciousness can be said to presuppose spirit (1) in the way that an abstraction depends on something concrete from which it abstracts, (2) in the way that something which is merely apparently independent depends on something else for its existence, and (3) in the way that a claim about something depends on something else that would ground or justify it.

The failure of the last shape of consciousness treated prior to spirit, "Reason as testing laws," illustrates this dependency very clearly. The shape of consciousness being examined here is a recognizably Kantian model of practical reasoning. According to it, we determine what we ought to do by finding out whether whatever we happen to want to do can survive a universalization test. Hegel argues that such a test is too formal to do what it is supposed to; insofar as it is a mere consistency test, it cannot really rule anything out. To figure out whether we should respect the property of others, for example, Hegel claims that we would need to know and accept some actually existing institution of property. Insofar as this argument succeeds, it shows (1) that the laws of practical reason are abstract and insufficient unless they are considered in conjunction with concrete normative content we derive from our ethical world; (2) that no norms can exist as binding and valid independently of some existing ethical order; and (3) that the attempt to provide a justification of the deliverances of pure practical reason will bottom out in certain social norms.

Although this gives us a fairly clear picture of how pure practical reason in particular might depend on spirit, interpreters have disagreed about the right way to generalize this to all the other shapes of consciousness that precede spirit. To get an overview of the relevant ways of interpreting the primacy of spirit, it is useful to distinguish between transcendental or developmental approaches to Hegel's argument. The reader should bear in mind, though, that most interpretations make use of both strategies.[3]

---

[3] See, for comparison, Charles Taylor's similar discussion of the two forms the dialectic takes in the *Phenomenology* (Taylor, *Hegel*, 131 ff.).

On more transcendental readings, transitions in the *Phenomenology* are supposed to move us from one shape of consciousness to a second that has proved to be the necessary condition for the possibility of the first. When Hegel says that a new shape of consciousness is "the truth of" the old one, as he frequently does, he means to say that the former would be impossible if the latter were not already in place. The opening of the *Phenomenology* has been given a particularly influential treatment along these lines; Charles Taylor argued that the ability to use general terms is a necessary condition for the possibility of determinate cognition of sense-particulars.[4] This has suggested that the entire *Phenomenology* might be read as a series of transcendental arguments.[5] The "Spirit" chapter, though, presents an obvious problem for this kind of reading because it seems to consist of some kind of idealized philosophy of Western history—and it certainly strains credulity to think that the French Revolution, say, is a transcendental presupposition for our capacity to simply pick out sense-particulars.

There are a variety of ways to address this obvious problem while still insisting on the fundamentally transcendental nature of Hegel's argument. One could argue that although spirit as such is a necessary condition for the possibility of consciousness, self-consciousness, and so on—perhaps because all cognition presupposes language and hence the induction into some linguistic community—no particular form of spirit is necessary. Or one could argue that our capacity to make simple empirical claims is differentially realizable: although it is only fully present in modern societies, individuals in premodern societies are not utterly incapable of making such claims, they just do it less well. What is characteristic of the transcendental approach, whatever particular form it takes, is that it reads spirit as revealing an essential dimension of all cognitive activity. On any such reading (although in "Spirit" Hegel appears to be concerned only with one kind of cognition, knowledge of social norms), this has implications for all concept use, for all cognitive claims depend on social norms for their determinacy, or validity, or what have you.

The main alternative to a transcendental reading is a developmental reading. On a developmental reading, the progress of the dialectic does not involve the discovery of conditions that must 'always already' be in place in order for cognition of anything to be possible, but rather the creation or development of richer cognitive frameworks to solve the problems that arise in more abstract and simpler frameworks. This kind of approach is particularly suited to the "Spirit" chapter, which seems to depict just such

---

[4] Charles Taylor, "Opening Arguments." Michael Forster has offered two related reasons for thinking that Hegel's arguments in the *Phenomenology* cannot be transcendental in the strict sense (Forster, *Hegel's Idea*, 162–163). First, such arguments presuppose the indubitability of some experience, and yet Hegel insists his approach is presuppositionless. Second, such arguments are deductive: they move from a true premise to a conclusion (contrary to Hegel's stated methodology, which is a "retreat into the ground"). Although both of these points need to be conceded, Rolf-Peter Horstmann has shown that this can be done without abandoning the idea that Hegel's method is transcendental in the sense of aiming at the "necessary condition(s) for the possibility of knowledge of objects" (Horstmann, "The *Phenomenology of Spirit* as a 'Transcendentalistic' Argument," 52). In light of these differences, though, Horstmann designates Hegel's method not as "transcendental" but "transcendentalistic."

[5] Stewart, *The Unity of Hegel's Phenomenology of Spirit*.

a learning process: one that starts with inadequate Greek conceptions of the authority of social norms and ends with modern forms of mutual accountability. On such readings, the primacy of spirit takes on a different cast. Rather than reading "Spirit" in light of the supposedly transcendental argument that takes place in the early chapters, we are encouraged to interpret everything that precedes "Spirit" in the light of the historical process depicted in "Spirit." When we do this, the *Phenomenology* thus reveals itself as something like a *Bildungsroman*: a narratival account of how the European community has come to understand itself and its relation to the world.[6]

But although "Spirit" is well suited to an exclusively historical and developmental reading, the attempt to read a historical development back into the rest of the *Phenomenology* faces certain obstacles. To carry this project out, we need to connect the shapes of consciousness that we examined in the earlier chapters, shapes that appeared to be independent of history, to their corresponding shapes of spirit. The first problem with this is technical: it is not clear at all how to line up the various shapes of consciousness explored prior to "Spirit" with the shapes of a world that are treated in "Spirit." According to Georg Lukács, who was a pioneer of this kind of reading, there is supposed to be a one-to-one correspondence between the shapes of consciousness and the shapes of a world in "Spirit."[7] To be sure, Hegel himself clearly points to some links between "Spirit" and the shapes of consciousness: suggesting, for example, that Stoicism in the "Self-Consciousness" chapter corresponds to Legal Personhood in "Spirit" (PS 9.261–262/¶¶479–480). This one-to-one model, however, seems to fail at some points in the text and seems forced at many, and this has led to multiple incompatible variations of the developmental approach, often accompanied with elaborate charts that lay out the subtle lines of filiation between the various sections of the *Phenomenology*.

The second problem with a purely developmental approach is more pressing: it is that any merely narratival account would seem to jeopardize Hegel's claims for the necessity of the progression from one shape of consciousness to the next.[8] If the *Phenomenology* as a whole is just an account of how our own community happened to come into being, to tell the kind of the stories we have told ourselves, then its repeated claims to have provided a scientific deduction of absolute knowledge will hardly seem credible. Again, there are a variety of ways to address this problem. One is to just embrace Hegel's narrative and reject the philosophic pretensions of his argument.[9] Another is to articulate a specifically developmental sense of necessity—one modeled, for example, on the necessity of a line of argument going in a certain direction.[10]

---

[6] Hyppolite, *Genesis and Structure*.

[7] In fact, Lukács argues that the *Phenomenology* is composed of *three* retellings of the whole course of human history, so the problem is even more complicated than I am indicating. For a recent defense and elaboration of the three-cycle view, see Forster, *Hegel's Idea*.

[8] PS 9.56–57/¶¶79–80.

[9] See Butler, *Subjects of Desire*, 17; and Cutrofello, *The Owl at Dawn*, 34.

[10] This comes in stronger (Forster, *Hegel's Idea*) and weaker versions (Stern, *Routledge Guidebook to Hegel*).

Most interpretations of the *Phenomenology* do not restrict themselves to an exclusively transcendental or developmental approach, but incorporate elements of both. I will be pursing a similarly mixed strategy in addressing Hegel's argument in "Spirit" in the following. I will assume that Hegel's basic claim about the primacy of spirit—his claim that is the 'essence and ground' of all the previous shapes of spirit—indicates something like a transcendental claim that some shape of spirit is a necessary condition for the truth of all other forms of human cognition. But I will be treating "Spirit" itself as mounting an exclusively developmental argument, one that must display a distinct sort of necessity. In the following, I hope to show how these two philosophic commitments lead Hegel to develop a unique and unprecedented kind of normative social theory.

6.2. THE CONCEPT OF SPIRIT

In order for spirit to serve as the transcendental ground of the other forms of cognition, however that is to be understood, the shapes of a world treated in the "Spirit" chapter must be conceived as independent of the shapes of consciousness explored in the earlier chapters. To say that spirit must be independent of what comes before it is, of course, not to say that a shape of the world—some historically actual form of collective mindedness—could exist apart from consciousness of the world, or of the self, or of reason. Hegel clearly denies this is possible, insisting to the contrary that "consciousness, self-consciousness, reason, and spirit, just because they are moments, have no existence in separation from one another" (PS 9.365/¶679). Rather, it is to say that the authority of the social norms we are under cannot be justified by reference to the world, or the self, or abstract reason, since these forms of cognition have shown themselves to presuppose consciousness of some collectively binding social norms. Their authority needs to be *sui generis*. If it were not, if it turned out that spirit did depend on these other forms of cognition for its justification, then Hegel's account would be viciously circular.

And so it has seemed to many that Hegel's thesis of the primacy of spirit leads us into a blind alley: it traces everything to the social norms we find ourselves with and then offers us no way of rationally assessing those social norms themselves (since any abstract standard would itself require contextualization). At one point, Hegel himself seems to confirm that he thinks the authority of social norms is simply unchallengeable:

> They *are*, and nothing more. . . . If they are supposed to be validated by *my* insight, then I have I have already denied their unshakeable, intrinsic being and regard them as something which, for me, is perhaps true, but also is perhaps not true. Ethical disposition consists just in sticking steadfastly to what is right, and abstaining from all attempts to move it, or shake it, or derive it. (PS 9.236/¶437)

Here Hegel appears to be saying that the question of what I ought to do simply reaches bedrock in given social laws and customs—there is no way to go beneath that. This has been found worrisome for a variety of reasons, but I will be focusing on two of the most common objections. The first is that it seems to involve a category mistake: the dissolution of normative questions—questions about what we should think or do—into sociological ones—questions about what people in fact think and do. A second, related concern with Hegel's approach is that it seems to leave us with a kind of relativism: forms of cognition are only justified relative to their place and time and never as such.

Although Hegel's argument does imply a certain kind of ethical historicism, his account of spirit can, I think, be exonerated from both of these accusations.[11] In this section, I will try to address the first worry—that of sociologism—and at the end of the next section I will be able to say something about the second. In order to meet the first objection, we will need to better understand the concept of spirit that he is deploying in this chapter, clearly distinguishing it from the kinds of concepts that are characteristic of more purely empirical approaches to human society.

In the "Spirit" chapter, we get a clear statement of the kind of community we are concerned with. Hegel says,

> Spirit is the ethical life of a nation in so far as it is the immediate truth—the individual that is a world. (PS 9.240/¶441)

The union between individuals that we are interested in, then, is one that we find exemplified in nations or peoples. It is a unity that is expressed in shared customs and laws. Hegel is quite explicit, though, that it is not every people that has the right sort of unity to count as a shape of spirit: in describing the transition from reason to spirit, for example, he insists that reason is only truly actualized "in a free nation [*in einem freien Volke*]" (PS 9.195/¶352). A *free* nation provides individuals with a context that resolves the impasses of struggle for recognition between the lord and the bondsman, for it allows certain individuals (whomever meets the criteria of citizenship) to understand themselves as united with other similar individuals in a way that preserves the freedom of all.[12] It is only in obeying the laws of a free nation that citizens experience that "perfect freedom and independence" that are the *sine qua non* of spiritual existence.

But what exactly does it mean for a nation to be free? The best way to see what this amounts to concretely is to look at the first example of a shape of spirit that we are given in the *Phenomenology*. In the literature, different answers have been given to the question of why Hegel starts his account of spirit with the Greeks of the Classical Age. Some have suggested that there are merely historical reasons for this: Hegel's contemporaries had idealized the Greek polis as an alternative to modern social life, and Hegel was concerned to show that this idealized picture of social life was incoherent in some way. Another suggestion is that the Greeks represent the best-known example of the simplest

---

[11] On the nature of Hegel's ethical historicism, see Beiser "Hegel's Historicism" and Alznauer, "Ethics and History."

[12] This kind of freedom is entirely compatible with the continued existence of slavery. In the Greek city-states of the fifth century—which Hegel considers the first free nations in history—native-born Greek males recognized each other as free while at the same time treating non-Greeks as property.

and most natural form that consensus-based social orders take in history: a society where social norms are simply taken as authoritative just because that is the way things are done.

Neither of these adequately explains Hegel's choice. To suggest merely historical reasons for starting with the Greeks would undermine the rest of the argument Hegel makes in "Spirit." Any demonstration that Greek society was unstable in a way that cannot ultimately be resolved until we arrive at a specifically modern self-understanding of the authority of social norms only shows the necessity of the latter if there are no real alternative starting places. But to suggest that Hegel started with the Greeks because they are a good example of a traditional social order is highly unlikely; the Greek polis was not a traditional society at all, nor did Hegel think it was. A certain idealization of Greek society is common in the German philosophic tradition, but it would be hard to find another thinker who placed a greater emphasis on the world-historical uniqueness of Greek civilization than Hegel.[13]

The truth is that Hegel starts with the Greeks precisely because he thinks they represent a breakthrough case: on Hegel's account, the Greek polis represents the first form of social order in which the laws are taken as authoritative because they establish the freedom of the individuals they govern. Hegel thinks the creation of this kind of social order, what he calls 'true spirit', presupposes individuals who are incapable of being enslaved precisely because they take freedom to be their essential being, something of infinite worth.[14] These are individuals who, like Hektor in the *Iliad*, are willing to die for their city rather than risk enslavement to a foreign people. In such a cases, individuals can be said to enjoy 'perfect freedom and independence' that is characteristic of spirit precisely because the laws that they obey represent their own will, not the will of another.

So although the "Spirit" chapter offers us a kind of social theory, we can now see that it is not a general account of the origins and nature of social order, but an account that is focused exclusively on a specific kind of normative order: one whose authority over individuals rests not on deference to tradition or to a charismatic leader, but on their own consciousness of the infinite value of freedom (in the very literal sense of non-enslavement). This offers us a clear way to respond to the first of the two worries I identified at the beginning of this section: the concern that Hegel's account makes the mistake of thinking that normative questions about how we should think or act can be answered by reference to empirical or sociological accounts of how we in fact do think or act. We have now seen that Hegel's concept of spirit is quite unlike the pure descriptive notions typically used to analyze society in empirical sociology. A shape of spirit is a social order that is not only taken to be legitimate by the individuals within it, but one that individuals rightly recognize as legitimate because it establishes their own freedom. To ground

---

[13] This feature of Hegel's thought is emphasized in Heidegger, "Hegel und der Griechen," and Shklar, *Freedom and Independence*. Heidegger, of course, shares a similar preoccupation with the Greeks, though he is interested less in the uniqueness of the Greek political experience than he is in their more original experience of Being.

[14] See Hegel's *Lectures on the History of Philosophy*, 230–231; *Vorlesungen*, vol. xi, 194–195.

other forms of cognition in a shape of spirit is thus to ground them in genuinely norma-tive considerations, not in a mere social consensus.

6.3. SPIRIT IN ACTION

But even if we grant that Hegel is innocent of this kind of sociologism, at least in princi-ple, it might appear that the social theory we actually get in the "Spirit" chapter offers us a strange mélange of normative and non-normative issues. The "Spirit" chapter certainly suggests that there is some important connection between the rationality of norms and their historical viability: Hegel seems to want to say, for example, that the Greek polis dissolved *because* its norms were insufficiently rational in some sense. But why should we think that norms must be viable to be valid: that the vicissitudes of the Greek polis have anything to do with rational justification of Greek laws and customs? Throughout the "Spirit" chapter, it looks like Hegel is confusing the normative tasks that are proper to practical philosophy and the explanatory and interpretive tasks that are rightly addressed by the social and historical sciences. To paraphrase Rudolf Haym's famous criticism of Hegel, it looks like we have a practical philosophy brought to confusion and disorder by irrelevant sociological considerations, and a proto-sociological account of history that is ruined by the inexplicable belief that practical rationality is the engine of all significant social change.

Behind these worries is a familiar understanding of the proper division of labor between practical philosophy and the social sciences, one that has led, in our own time, to the development of two separate and largely unrelated literatures on the nature of human action. We have, on the one hand, a philosophic literature that is tailored to the problems of practical reasoning, to the question of what justifies an action. On the other hand, we have a sociological literature that is oriented to the problem of explaining the relations between agents and social structures, of determining how agency contrib-utes to the formation and maintenance of social institutions. Hegel's approach is hard to categorize because he thinks there is a necessary connection between these ques-tions: between the justification of actions and the development of social institutions. This leads him to develop the first intrinsically social theory of rational action.

But what does it mean to think of action as intrinsically social? As we saw in the first section, Hegel's arguments at the end of "Reason" are aimed at undermining a common view of the relation between action and social context, according to which our social context provides us with certain potential reasons to act, which are then validated through some kind of reflective endorsement test. On this more individualistic model of action, we need not be concerned with assessing the substantive rationality of the social inputs of practical reasoning because it is the subjective process of deliberation alone that determines whether some possible action is right or wrong. We also do not need to be concerned with the output or the result of action, with the role that action plays in re-creating social institutions, for what matters for the assessment of the action is just the maxim or intention we had in acting, not how others respond to it or how it reinforces certain social expectations.

In "Spirit," Hegel provides us with the following alternative picture of the relation between action and its social context:

> Spirit, being the *substance* and the universal, self-identical, and abiding essence, is the unmoved solid *ground* and *starting-point* for the action of all, and it is their purpose and goal, the in-itself of every self-consciousness expressed in thought. This substance is equally the *work* produced by the action of all and each as their unity and identity, for it is being-for-self, the self, action. (PS 9.239/¶439; also see 9.240–241/¶444)

Hegel's use of italics in this passage directs us to the point that spirit or ethical substance is playing two distinct roles in this revised theory of moral agency: it is the 'ground and starting-point' of every action, and it is also the 'work' produced by the action of all. We have already seen what Hegel means by the first of these: for an action to be grounded or justified, he thinks the agent must be guided by the ethical norms of her nation—norms which she rightly takes to be legitimate and authoritative because they are the conditions of her freedom. This is what we are supposed to have learned at the conclusion of the preceding chapter. The further point being made in the passage is that insofar as these are real, historical social norms, they must in a certain sense depend on human action just as much as they guide it; for social norms only exist insofar as they are acknowledged, complied with, and enforced. Spirit is thus both the ground of rational action (the input) and the result or product of rational action (the output). These two aspects of spirit, the 'ought' and the 'is', are intrinsically connected and mutually reinforcing: for social norms to be authoritative, they must have social existence; and for them to perdure, they must continue to attract acknowledgment as authoritative. Hegel thus conceptualizes spirit as involving a feedback loop: by acting on certain norms, I reproduce them, and this reinforces their authority over future action. He tends to characterize this process in biological terms: "Just because [spirit] is a being that is resolved in the self, it is not a dead essence, but is *actual* and *alive*" (PS 9.239/¶439). Hegel is saying spirit is 'alive' because, like a biological organism, it can be said to be the result of itself: a form that determines its own continued existence through characteristic kinds of activity.[15] This is what it means to have an intrinsically social theory of action.

In emphasizing this connection between action and social structure, Hegel's characterization of spirit strikingly anticipates some of the basic theoretical commitments of the classical sociological tradition. It is particularly illuminating, I think, to compare Hegel's theory of spirit to the approach to social order Talcott Parsons defends in *The Structure of Social Action*. In that work, Parsons argues that the founding figures of

---

[15]   As we will see, although all forms of spirit are living in the sense of being self-reproducing, Hegel thinks only certain forms of spirit are living in the sense of being organic wholes (see the discussion of 'lifeless spirit' in PS 9.260–261/¶477).

sociology all converged on a single insight: the thought that the stability of the social order could only be explained by the internalization of shared, social values by individuals. The reproduction of normative patterns, Parsons claims, is the most important functional requirement for a social system to maintain itself in homeostasis—indeed, the establishment of social order cannot be fully explained any other way. Hegel's theory of spirit clearly shares this commitment of Parsons's normativist functionalism.[16]

We have already noted one difference, though, between this kind of project and Hegel's, which is that Hegel is not interested in the origins and nature of social order as such, but only in a very specific kind of society, one he thinks the Greeks were the first to realize. So although he might agree that any social order requires a basis in common values and norms, what is crucial about the kind of society Hegel treats in the "Spirit" chapter is that they involve agents who are complying with certain social norms, not just because they have internalized these norms as valid ultimate ends, but because they know these norms are conditions for their own freedom. For most purely sociologically approaches, this would only count as a sub-case of social order.[17]

The differences between Hegel's project and standard sociological approaches become clearest, though, in their respective treatments of social change. It has long been noted that Hegel, at least in the *Phenomenology*, is more interested in what Auguste Comte called "social dynamics" than he is in social statics.[18] Although Hegel does describe the Greek polis, which he takes to be the simplest shape of spirit, as a 'whole' that is a "stable equilibrium of all the parts," his interest in this case does not come from any belief that societies that are based on this sort of normative insight were more capable of maintaining homeostasis than societies based on fear or on merely traditional authority (PS 9.249–250/¶462). In fact, Hegel thought the organic unity of the Greek polis was much less stable over the long term than the unity characteristic of non-Greek traditional and authoritarian societies. Hegel shared a common belief of his age, which is that one crucial difference between the East and the West is that the East never changes; real historical change, for Hegel, takes place exclusively in the West. By forming the first society whose own reproduction depended on its citizens believing it to be a condition of their own freedom, he thought the Greeks created a novel kind of society that, although it was able to temporarily generate an unprecedentedly strong form of solidarity (hence the Greek victory over the Persians), also necessarily included the seeds of its own destruction (hence the dissolution of the polis into the Roman Empire). It is the presence of internal contradictions in free nations that makes true historical progress possible, since a more rational society is just one that has resolved the contradictions of previous societies into some higher unity. Just as Hegel is not interested in social order as such, but only a certain kind of order, he is also not interested in social change as such, but only

---

[16] This has been noted by Knapp, "Hegel's Universal," 587. 'Normativist functionalism' is a term drawn from the account of Parsons in Joas and Knöbl, *Social Theory*.

[17] It should be noted, though, that Parsons himself agreed that the Greek case represented a breakthrough to a new form of social organization (though one that he thinks ran parallel to similar breakthroughs in Israel, China, and India). See Parsons, *On Institutions and Social Evolution*, 294–295.

[18] See, e.g., Adorno and Kaal, " 'Static' and 'Dynamic.' "

in fundamental shifts in the organization of normative authority in Western history—shifts that correspond to a deepening appreciation of human freedom.

By restricting his evaluation of various shapes of spirit to the diagnosis of internal contradictions, Hegel inaugurates what has come to be known as immanent critique. This is perhaps the most well-known and influential aspect of Hegelian social theory, especially as it has been transformed in the hand of various Marxist and post-Marxist thinkers.[19] But there are as many forms of immanent critique as there are kinds of internal contradiction. It is often taken for granted that Hegel's form of immanent critique involves the attempt to measure a society's laws and practices against a norm that that society officially professes to accept; on this model, a society is internally contradictory if it doesn't live up to its own ideals.[20] Opposed to this idealistic form of immanent critique is the more materialistic form often associated with Marx. Here contradictions are not forms of hypocrisy or bad faith, but rather are understood as functional instabilities. The canonical example of this is the contradiction between existing social relations and forces of production that Marx uses to explain historical revolutions. But Hegel's version doesn't fit neatly in either of these categories since, as Rahel Jaeggi rightly notes, it involves an "entanglement of the functional and normative shortcomings of a form of life."[21]

In this respect, Hegelian immanent critique might be thought akin to the kind of criticism we see in Daniel Bell's *The Cultural Contradictions of Capitalism*. Bell attempted to identify contradictions between the various spheres of modern society (the economic structure, the polity, and the culture), like the clash between radical individualism in economics and modernism in culture, which manifest themselves in various social conflicts. But even this is a merely empirical proxy for the kind of necessary contradiction Hegel is after. For Bell, there is no necessity that links any particular economic structure (like modern capitalism) with any particular polity (like democracy), so any contradiction that arises between them is historically contingent.[22] But, for Hegel, the central aim of all philosophy, including the philosophy of history, is to show that things that appear contingent are not. So although it is of course true that we only know of the decline of the Greek polis through historical evidence, a philosophic treatment of this must show that such a decline was not due to some peculiarity of the Greek case, but was inevitable given the kind of social structure that the Greek polis exemplified. For good or ill, Hegel is not guilty of committing a social science.[23]

---

[19] Herbert Marcuse's emphasis on this negative and dialectical aspect of Hegel's thought in *Reason and Revolution* was crucial in displacing the then prevalent Popperian caricature of Hegel as an apologist for Prussian authoritarianism.

[20] This is also the form of immanent critique favored by Michael Walzer in *Interpretation and Social Criticism*, 87, 89.

[21] Jaeggi, "Realizing Freedom."

[22] Bell explicitly rejects the idea, which he rightly attributes both to the Hegelian-Marxist tradition and to Parsonian functionalism, that society must be understood as a 'totality' or as a 'structurally unified system,' in favor of an approach which views the various spheres of society as analytically independent (see Bell, *Cultural Contradictions*, 8–10).

[23] For a contrary view, see Neuhouser, "The Idea of a Hegelian 'Science' of Society." Neuhouser argues that Hegel's science of society is like Adam Smith's political economy in its heavy reliance on

As we saw in section 6.1, the kind of internal contradiction Hegel is interested in diagnosing in "Spirit" is supposed to be the strict social analogue of the problems that afflict the shapes of consciousness examined earlier in the *Phenomenology*: like the impossibility of saying what you mean in 'sense-certainty'. Throughout the *Phenomenology*, Hegel has been showing that various shapes of consciousness necessarily reveal their own self-understanding as inadequate and contradictory in the process of attempting to express themselves. In "Spirit," the relevant contradiction emerges when individuals attempt to act on their own conception of what is required of them according to the social norms they are subject to. Speaking of the first shape of spirit, for example, he says,

> [Self-consciousness] learns through its own act the contradiction of those powers into which the substance divided itself and their mutual downfall, as well as the contradiction between its knowledge of the ethical character of its action, and what is in its own proper nature ethical, and thus finds its own downfall. (PS 9.241/¶445)

Hegel here speaks of two contradictions that are related to each other as the implicit is related to the explicit. The first is the contradiction that exists in the 'substance' latently; in the Greek case, this is the potential conflict between human and divine laws. So long as individuals are not aware that their identification with these laws does not preclude conflict between them, they can continue to reproduce the social order by complying with these norms in the manner prescribed. This implicit contradiction becomes manifest, though, when we come across a second contradiction: a case where an agent who was guided by these social norms (by "knowledge of the ethical character of [her] action") finds out that she has nevertheless acted in a way that does not in fact accord with other norms that can be publicly applied to her action (violating "what is in its own proper nature ethical"). This is the contradiction between what I intended to do and what I did. Hegel thinks Sophocles' *Antigone* shows us how the Greeks themselves came to grips with just such a contradiction. In the play, Antigone is not trying to flout the social norms that pertain to her; in fact, she is trying to adhere to a certain subset of them with a fanatical single-mindedness, but this just reveals to the audience that her full and immediate identification with her role as determined by the norms of Greek society (the divine law) was not enough prevent her from acting in a way that violates other norms (the human law) that have the same warrant. This conflict in action brings to light a conflict that was already latent in ethical substance.

"empirical knowledge of contemporary social reality," only differing from it in being systematic—and he is quite emphatic that "it is important not to confuse 'systematic' with 'a priori.'" But Hegel himself shows no reluctance in characterizing his own methodology as *a prioristic*. Philosophy, he says, "owes its development to the empirical science" but "in return it gives their contents what is so vital to them, the freedom of thought—gives them, in short, an a priori character. These contents are now warranted necessary, and no longer depend on the evidence of facts merely, that they were so found and so experienced. The fact as experienced thus becomes an illustration and a copy of the original and *completely self-supporting* activity of thought" (E §12, *my italics*).

Hegel claims that the recognition of this fact leads to the downfall of *both* the ethical individual and the existing social order, thus giving rise to a new shape of spirit that is the determinate negation of the last. It leads to the downfall of the individual, because when Antigone finds out that she is guilty of something she did not intentionally do, she can no longer think that her previous orientation to the social norms (immediate ethical perception) was capable of securing the rightfulness of her action. She has to adopt a new self-conception of ethical agency. It leads to the downfall of the existing social order, because that order was predicated on the idea that the divine and human laws were in natural harmony, and that has proved not to be the case. On Hegel's reading, Sophocles' *Antigone* dramatizes the experience of the breakdown of a certain shared idea of what social norms are and what it is to be guided by them. The next shape of spirit Hegel analyzes is one that has learned this lesson, and which is built on a different conception of the nature of social norms and of our access to them.

The details of Hegel's account of the demise of the Greek polis are quite complicated and open to contesting interpretations, but we have seen enough to respond to the accusation that Hegel's emphasis on the primacy of spirit is ultimately relativistic. In some sense, this is right: if you want to know whether you should keep a deposit I have left with you despite my untimely demise, Hegel thinks you should consult the existing laws and norms concerning property in your nation (see PS 9.195/¶352). These are authoritative for you because your freedom depends entirely on your being a recognized member of your particular state. There is thus no abstractly universal answer to the question "What ought I to do?" that is not at the same time unhelpfully indeterminate. But Hegel is very far from thinking that all ways of settling this question are equal. He thinks there are more and less rational societies, and that the imperfect rationality of a given society, its latent internal contradictions, will inevitably become manifest in an increasing awareness of the impossibility of acting in accordance with shared norms. Given the nature of spirit, this necessarily leads to the dissolution of that society—its inability to be able to reproduce itself through action—and the rise of new forms of social life that are predicated on a new and improved conception of the nature of social normativity.

6.4. THE ARGUMENT OF SPIRIT

In the previous sections, we have established what spirit is (a free nation) and how Hegel intends to go about analyzing it (an internal critique of its ability to reproduce itself by guiding the actions of individuals). In this final section, I will attempt to summarize the substance of Hegel's argument in the "Spirit" chapter. It is important to recognize at the outset that Hegel's account of spirit in the *Phenomenology* labors under a double burden. First, it is supposed to offer us a complete normative typology of spiritual worlds: one that identifies the various possible forms that a normative social order can take and specifies the form that is most rational. Second, it is supposed to offer us an account of the necessity of the historical genesis of our own, specifically modern world.

Hegel eventually came to think that these two tasks could be, and perhaps needed to be, disaggregated. In his later *Elements of the Philosophy of Right* (1820), he would attempt to provide an analysis of the structure of rational social order that does not follow the 'temporal sequence' in which the various necessary aspects of this social order first appeared (PR §32 R & A). The developmental part of the story was relegated to his *Lectures on the Philosophy of World History* (which were delivered four times between 1821 and 1831 but were never published during his lifetime), and it was expanded to include an extensive treatment of those civilizations that preceded the Greeks and which are not properly considered shapes of spirit. But in the "Spirit" chapter of *Phenomenology*, Hegel attempts to do both of these things at once. He tries to show that the historical development of social order from the Greek polis to the post-Revolutionary modern state passes through various logically necessary stages in the realization of a fully rational social order. This has real consequences for the resulting picture of institutional or social rationality; unlike the account we get in the later *Philosophy of Right*, in the *Phenomenology* the superior rationality of the final shape is depicted as inherently tied to the developmental story. Modern ethical life is more rational than what went before not because it satisfies some independent rational standard but simply because it resolves the internal contradictions of all of the previous shapes of spirit.[24]

Though it is easy to lose sight of it in the welter of historical details, the basic plot of Hegel's story is quite straightforward: it involves increasing collective self-consciousness about the nature of spiritual activity:

> [Spirit] must advance to a consciousness of what it immediately is, must sublate that beautiful ethical life, and, by passing through a series of shapes, attain a knowledge of itself. (PS 240/¶441)

As we have already seen, a social order only counts as a shape of spirit when the norms and laws that constitute that order are reproduced because they are taken to be constitutive of the freedom of individuals in that order. This is what spirit is 'in itself'. In Spirit, the various possible shapes of spirit are arranged from the most 'immediate' (the one that is least conscious of what it means to be free) to the most 'mediated' (the one that is fully conscious of what it means to be free).[25] Hegel identifies three basic stages

---

[24] It would be a gross exaggeration to claim that Hegel's earlier and later approaches to the issue of institutional rationality are flatly incompatible; in both, such rationality consists of the unity of objective and subjective freedom. But the difference between these two ways of justifying Hegel's standard for institutional rationality is worth emphasizing because it has given rise to two very different ideas as to what is of continuing value in Hegelian practical philosophy. Neuhouser, *Foundations of Hegel's Social Theory*; Honneth, *Pathologies*; and Honneth, *Das Recht der Freiheit*, hew closely to the structural rationality outlined in *Philosophy of Right*. Pippin, *Hegel's Idealism*; Brandom, "Some Pragmatist Themes"; and, more recently, Jaeggi, *Kritik von Lebensformen*, have relied more heavily on the intrinsically developmental approach taken in the *Phenomenology*.

[25] From the point of view of the overarching argument of the *Phenomenology*, which aims at providing a ladder to the absolute standpoint, even this last shape of spirit is not the end of the line. Spirit is only truly self-conscious of itself as spirit in religion, which of course is the topic of the chapter

in this process: true spirit (which is immediate and unalienated), self-alienated spirit (which is mediated but alienated), and spirit that is certain of itself (which is mediated and unalienated).[26]

The fundamental contradiction that he sees as working itself out in history is thus the contradiction between what spirit is and what it takes itself to be. The Greek polis counts as a shape of spirit because the Greeks knew themselves to be free: subject only to those laws that could be universally justified to each citizen. But the Greek polis counts as a deficient shape of spirit, one with an inadequate self-consciousness, because the Greeks believed that the content of the laws and norms that they imposed upon themselves was provided by nature (like Creon) or the gods (like Antigone). They did not realize, as we do, that these laws and norms must themselves be derived from the concept of freedom—they must reflect and honor the subjective rights of the individual, chief among these being the right of conscience. The burden of the "Spirit" chapter is to show why it was necessary for spirit to "attain knowledge of itself": for the Greeks, who wholly identified with the laws of their cities, to become us, who recognize only what can be rationally justified to each person. To establish the necessity of this developmental process, Hegel must show that any form of spirit that lacks full self-consciousness of the nature of spirit will run into internal contradictions in reproducing itself. He must also show that these contradictions are only resolved by the development of new forms of social order that are predicated on a greater degree of self-consciousness about the origins of the authority of social norms in the free assent of the individuals who are subject to those norms. Finally, and most controversially, he must show that this process has reached its culmination or fulfillment in modern life (although, as we will see, there is some real ambiguity about whether Hegel thinks spirit has in fact already achieved its proper institutional embodiment or not).

The first shape of spirit, 'true spirit', represents a kind of baseline case in Hegel's account: it is the least self-conscious form of spirit possible. In 'true spirit', the authority of social norms is understood to be rooted in the nature of things (PS 9.260/¶476). What makes a given law right is a substantive rationality that individuals have immediate access to. We have already seen how Hegel's reading of *Antigone* is supposed to reveal the inherent contradiction in such a social order: its inability to resolve conflicts between individuals who are opposed to each other, but have the same warrant for their actions. The upshot of this is the dawning awareness that the authority of social norms cannot be rooted in the substantive rationality of their content. The alternative is that

---

following "Spirit" (PS 9.364/¶677). The subsequent chapters, however, add little to Hegel's social theory (besides a hint, which he develops in more detail in his later work, that it is transformations in religious consciousness which are the most important factor in explaining the kind of historical change he is interested in).

[26] The fourth conceptual possibility, a social order that is experienced both as immediate and alien, would not count as a shape of spirit at all. With that possibility removed or bracketed, it can be seen that Hegel's account of the development of spirit is typologically complete. (In Hegel's mature philosophy of history, he becomes much more interested in this fourth possibility, which he thinks characterizes the pre-Greek 'Oriental World'.)

what makes a given norm right is not its content at all—this is now seen to be a contingent and changeable—but the "formal universality of legality or law" (PS 9.240/¶442).

This insight into the contingency of social norms gives rise to second shape of spirit, 'self-alienated spirit'. Self-alienated spirit recognizes that the specific norms and laws we impose on ourselves are not rooted in nature but are "the *work* of self-consciousness," but it nonetheless experiences this order as alien: "the world has the character of being something external, the negative of self-consciousness" (PS 9.264/¶484). One might wonder how these things are connected: Why does increasing self-consciousness about the nature of spirit lead to alienation? With the loss of the belief in the substantive rationality of norms, Hegel claims that the social order comes to be seen as authoritative simply because it is a universally recognized power above individuals, who are now considered not as parts of a whole, but as a mere aggregate of atomized persons (PS 9.263/¶482). Such an order is experienced as alien because the authority of the law now has nothing to do with its content: the law is authoritative regardless of what it requires of us. Even clearly horrible laws can thus be fully legitimate. Hegel argues that this new 'shape of a world' gives rise to a flight from the realm world and the creation of a realm of 'pure consciousness' or 'faith [*Glaube*]', where we find a higher, but politically unactualizable, form of normative authority: an ought-to-be which floats free of the harsh necessities of political reality. Stoicism, feudal honor codes, and Christianity are all versions of this ideology of flight: they represent privatized normative codes that can coexist with the authority of merely positive law. An alienated individual is one who is split between these two, supposedly non-overlapping magisteria.[27]

Interestingly, although Hegel clearly depicts alienation as a form of individual suffering, he does not think alienation represents a structural defect in this new form of social life. Although it is true that the Greek polis could not survive the development of the reflective, alienated individual, 'self-alienated spirit' is a type of normative order in which alienation, far from being pathological, is in fact a functional necessity. In describing this new order, Hegel says,

> Nothing has a spirit that is grounded within itself and indwells it, but each has its being in something outside of and alien to it. The equilibrium of the whole is not the unity which remains with itself, nor the contentment that comes from having returned into itself, but rests on the alienation of oppositions. (PS 9.265/¶486)

Since self-reproduction of this shape of spirit "rests on the alienation of oppositions," not on a harmony between them, it is described as a mechanical rather than an organic or living unity.

---

[27] Dean Moyar gives a remarkably lucid and helpful explanation of how this argument works in Moyar, "Self-completing Aleination." But I think Moyar's account does not fully differentiate the sort of alienation that is definitive of 'self-alienated spirit' from the kind of failure to identify with your deeds that is a general problem throughout "Spirit" (from Antigone all the way to the beautiful soul). Moyar's definition of alienation fits the latter problem; but here I am concerned with alienation in the narrower sense, the sense that only applies to the second stage of spirit.

The structural defect in this new, more mechanical form of social life is thus not that it gives rise to alienation but that it cannot stay alienated. The reproduction of this social order rests on the continued acceptance of the fact that there is a fundamental opposition between the real world (the political or legal order) and the spiritual world (the ideologies of flight). What Hegel tries to show is that when individuals attempt to act on their alienated, spiritual ideologies, they fail, and in failing realize that they must reformulate these ideologies (just as with Antigone, this is depicted as a failure to have one's deed express the meaning one intended it to have). The process of working through the contradictions involved in this fundamental opposition necessarily culminates in the formulation of an Enlightenment ideology that rejects the very split between the real world and the spiritual world. And so, Hegel says, "[t]he Enlightenment completes the alienation of spirit in this realm" (PS 9.266/¶486). This completing or overcoming of alienation leads to an attempt to overthrow the existing social order: the attempt to realize the demands of the spirit in the medium of the real world. Indeed, Hegel sees exactly this dynamic playing itself out in the French Revolution.

The third and final section of spirit, 'spirit that is certain of itself', treats the form of social normativity that results from this necessary transformation. Like 'self-alienated spirit', this third shape is characterized by absolute mediation: by a recognition that the norms we impose on ourselves are up to us. But unlike 'self-alienated spirit', this is accompanied by a realization that in order for these norms to be freely self-imposed, they must accord with the conscience of the individual. This double-insight is supposed to enable a return to certain features of 'true spirit', a full identification with the content of the social norms, but now on the grounds that those norms are determined by freedom, not by their accordance with nature or the will of God.

This is all, of course, terrifically abstract and programmatic; and that abstractness is precisely the problem Hegel has to work through in this last section. Although in the previous two sections, Hegel has a clear picture of what kind of social order he is dealing with, since they are historically given, here he is looking to the future. The very real question he must answer concerns whether the specifically modern, post-Revolutionary demand that the social order correspond to the dictates of the individual conscience can ever find a stable institutional embodiment. Hegel does not deny that there are forms of this demand that are incompatible with any form of law at all—he even agrees with Edmund Burke that the notion of freedom that motivated the French Revolution was among these—but he approaches this problem through an immanent critique of these positions. He attempts to show that any appeal to subjective certainty about what is morally required will break down, will be impossible to act upon, until we come to understand that our subjective convictions only secure their validity by proving that they can be recognized by others (PS 9.361/¶670). With this insight into the nature of social normativity—that it is constituted by reciprocal recognition—spirit achieves full self-knowledge: it finally realizes what it means to be free.

But although the *Phenomenology of Spirit* argues that only a society that has achieved this self-knowledge will be immune to the kinds of immanent problems we have been concerned with, it does not say anything about what a social order that is built on this foundation will actually look like. The significance of this omission has been interpreted in a variety of ways. Marxist and post-Marxist commentators have viewed the lack of any discussion of actual social institutions in this last section as evidence that Hegel proved unable to resolve the problem bequeathed to him by the French Revolution. Lukács, for example, claims that

> [o]nce he had provided a profound and central analysis of the movement of history, in terms of contradictions which continuously reproduce themselves, once he had given an account of the Enlightenment, of the economy of the capitalist society and of the French Revolution, Hegel was not able to go further and propose a definite social form in which to clothe his 'reconciliation'.[28]

For these readers, Hegel's concluding section is of primarily symptomatic value: it serves as an ideological mask for the unresolved contradictions that still afflict modern life. Others, however, have seen just this indefiniteness as a strength of Hegel's account in the *Phenomenology*: by refusing to identify any specific institutional form as appropriate to modern self-consciousness, Hegel enabled us to view modernity as a unending project to live up to the ideals of modernity, rather than as a something we have fully accomplished and put behind us. On this reading, we should not expect to be done with the contradictions of modernity, and this is exactly the lesson of the *Phenomenology*. A third possible response to this lacuna is to insist that the *Phenomenology*'s account of the genesis of the basic modern commitment to reciprocal recognition needs to be supplemented with the richer and more detailed account of a rational social order that is provided in his later *Philosophy of Right*. All of these options have their contemporary partisans and detractors—and this is a clear sign of the continuing relevance of Hegel's theory of spirit for current philosophic and social thought about the normative foundations of modernity.

WORKS CITED

Primary Texts

Adorno, T., and H. Kaal. "'Static' and 'Dynamic' as Sociological Categories." *Diogenes* 9, no. 33 (1961): 28–49.

Hegel, G. W. F. *Elements of the Philosophy of Right* [PR], translated by H. B. Nisbet, edited by Allen Wood. Cambridge: Cambridge University Press, 1991.

Hegel, G. W. F. *Encyclopaedia Logic* [E], translated by T. F. Gereats, W. A. Suchting, and H. S. Harris. Indianapolis: Hackett, 1991.

Hegel, G. W. F. *Gesammelte Werke* [GW], Deutsche Forshungsgemainschaft. Hamburg; Meiner, 1968–; cited by volume.

Hegel, G. W. F. *G. W. F. Hegel: Vorlesungen: Ausgewählte Nachschriften und Manuskripte* [V], edited by P. Garniron and W. Jaeschke, Hamburg: Felix Meiner Verlag, 1994.

---

[28] Lukács, *The Young Hegel*, 506.

Hegel, G. W. F. *Lectures on the History of Philosophy 1825–6* [LHP]: *Volume 1: Introduction and Oriental Philosophy*, translated and edited by Robert F. Brown. New York: Oxford University Press, 2009.

Hegel, G. W. F. *Phenomenology of Spirit* [PS], translated by A. V. Miller. Oxford: Oxford University Press, 1987.

Hegel, G. W. F. *The Science of Logic* [SL], translated by George di Giovanni. Cambridge: Cambridge University Press, 2010.

Heidegger, M. "Hegel und die Griechen" in *Wegmarken*. Frankfurt: V. Klostermann, 1st ed., 1967, 255–272.

Weber, M. *Economy and Society: An Outline of Interpretive Sociology*, edited by G. Roth and C. Wittich. Berkeley: University of California Press, 1978.

Secondary Literature

Alznauer, M. "Ethics and History in Hegel's Practical Philosophy." *Review of Metaphysics* 65, no. 3 (2012): 581–611.

Bell, D. *The Cultural Contradictions of Capitalism: Twentieth Anniversary Edition.* New York: Basic Books, 1996.

Beiser, F. "Hegel's Historicism," in *The Cambridge Companion to Hegel*, edited by F. Beiser. Cambridge: Cambridge University Press, 1993, 270–300.

Brandom, R. "Some Pragmatist Themes in Hegel's Idealism: Negotiation and Administration in Hegel's Account of the Structure and Content of Conceptual Norms." *European Journal of Philosophy* 7, no. 2 (1999): 164–169.

Butler, J. *Subjects of Desire.* New York: Columbia University Press, 1987.

Collins, A. *Hegel's Phenomenology: The Dialectical Justification of Philosophy's First Principles.* Montreal: McGill-Queens University Press, 2013.

Cutrofello, A. *The Owl at Dawn: A Sequel to Hegel's Phenomenology of Spirit.* Albany: State University of New York Press, 1995.

Dudley, W. "Ethical Life, Morality, and the Role of Spirit in the *Phenomenology of Spirit*," in *Hegel's Phenomenology of Spirit: A Critical Guide*, edited by D. Moyar and M. Quante. Cambridge: Cambridge University Press, 2008, 130–149.

Eisenstadt, S. (Ed.) *The Origins and Diversity of Axial Age Civilizations.* Albany: State University of New York Press, 1986.

Forster, M. *Hegel's Idea of a Phenomenology of Spirit.* Chicago; London: University of Chicago Press, 1998.

Haering, T. "Die Entstehungsgeschichte der Phänomenologie des Geistes," in *Verhandlungen des III. Internationalen Hegel Kongresses 1933.* Tübingen: J. C. B. Mohr, 1934, 118–136.

Honneth, A. *The Pathologies of Individual Freedom: Hegel's Social Theory*, translated by L. Löb. Princeton, NJ: Princeton University Press, 2010.

Honneth, A. *Das Recht der Freiheit: Grundriß einer demokratischen Sittlichkeit.* Berlin: Suhrkamp Verlag, 2011.

Horstmann, R. "The *Phenomenology of Spirit* as a 'Transcendentalistic' Argument for a Monistic Ontology," in *Hegel's Phenomenology of Spirit: A Critical Guide*, edited by D. Moyar and M. Quante. Cambridge: Cambridge University Press, 2008, 43–62.

Hypollite, J. *Genesis and Structure of Hegel's Phenomenology of Spirit*, translated by S. Cherniak and J. Heckman. Evanston, IL: Northwestern University Press, 1974.

Jaspers, K. *The Origin and Goal of History.* London: Routledge, 1953.

Jaeggi, R. "Realizing Freedom: Normativity in History" (unpublished manuscript)

Jaeggi, R. *Kritik von Lebensformen*. Berlin: Suhrkamp Verlag, 2013.

Joas, H., and W. Knöbl. *Social Theory: Twenty Introductory Lectures*. Cambridge: Cambridge University Press, 2009.

Knapp, P. "Hegel's Universal in Marx, Durkheim and Weber: The Role of Hegelian Ideas in the Origins of Sociology." *Sociological Forum* 1, no. 4. (Autumn 1986), 586–609.

Lukács, G. *The Young Hegel: Studies in the Relations between Dialectics and Economics*, translated by R. Livingstone. Cambridge, MA: MIT Press, 1975.

Marcuse, H. *Reason and Revolution: Hegel and the Rise of Social Theory*. London: Routledge, 1986.

Moyar, D., and M. Quante (Eds.). *Hegel's Phenomenology of Spirit: A Critical Guide*. Cambridge: Cambridge University Press, 2008.

Moyar, D. "Self-Completing Alienation: Hegel's Argument for Transparent Conditions of Free Agency," in *Hegel's Phenomenology of Spirit: A Critical Guide*, edited by D. Moyar and M. Quante. Cambridge: Cambridge University Press, 2008, 150–172.

Neuhouser, F. *Foundations of Hegel's Social Theory: Actualizing Freedom*. Cambridge, MA: Harvard University Press, 2000.

Neuhouser, F. "The Idea of a Hegelian 'Science' of Society," in *A Companion to Hegel*, edited by S. Houlgate and M. Baur. Chichester, UK: Blackwell Publishing, 2011, 281–296.

Parsons, T. *The Structure of Social Action: A Study in Social Theory with Special Reference to a Group of Recent European Writers*. Glencoe, IL: The Free Press, 1949.

Parsons, T. "Evolutionary Universals in Society." *American Sociological Review* 29, no. 3 (June 1964): 339–357.

Parsons, T. *On Institutions and Social Evolution: Selected Writings*. Chicago: University of Chicago Press, 1982.

Pippin, R. "Hegel on Historical Meaning: For Example, The Enlightenment." *Bulletin of the Hegel Society of Great Britain* 35 (Spring–Summer 1997): 1–17.

Pippin, R. *Hegel's Practical Philosophy: Rational Agency as Ethical Life*. Cambridge: Cambridge University Press, 2008.

Rose, G. *Hegel Contra Sociology*. London; New York: Verso, 1981.

Shklar, J. *Freedom and Independence: A Study of the Political Ideas of Hegel's 'Phenomenology of Mind.'* Cambridge: Cambridge University Press, 1976.

Solomon, R. C. "Hegel's Concept of 'Geist.'" *The Review of Metaphysics* 23, no. 4 (June 1970): 642–661.

Steinberger, P. "Hegel as a Social Scientist." *The American Political Science Review* 71, no. 1 (March 1977): 95–110.

Stern, R. *Routledge Philosophy Guidebook to Hegel and the Phenomenology of Spirit*. Abingdon, UK: Routledge, 2002.

Stewart, J. *The Unity of Hegel's Phenomenology of Spirit: A Systematic Interpretation*. Evanston, IL: Northwestern University Press, 2000.

Taylor, C. "The Opening Arguments of the *Phenomenology*," in *Hegel: A Collection of Critical Essays*, edited by A. MacIntyre. Notre Dame, IN: University of Notre Dame Press, 1972, 157–187.

Taylor, C. *Hegel*. Cambridge: Cambridge University Press, 1975.

Walzer, M. *Interpretation and Social Criticism*. Cambridge, MA: Harvard University Press, 1993.

CHAPTER 7

RELIGION, ART, AND THE EMERGENCE OF ABSOLUTE SPIRIT IN THE *PHENOMENOLOGY*

ALLEN SPEIGHT

THE chapter entitled "Religion" has a singular place within the *Phenomenology of Spirit*—and, indeed, within Hegel's writings more broadly. Although Hegel, as a theological student and young professor, wrote in the years before 1807 about many of the issues that come up within the chapter—in broadest terms, the set of relationships among religion, art, philosophy, and *Sittlichkeit*, as well as the relationships between nature and spirit, pre- and post-classical culture, revealed and rational religion, and the philosophy and history of religion—it is only in this hastily expanded late section of the *Phenomenology* that he begins to offer anything like a systematic attempt to give order to these relationships. Perhaps because of the apparent confusion and compression of these issues in this late chapter and the unclear relations it bears both within the *Phenomenology* project and to Hegel's later system more broadly, it has often been taken as a problematic bit of text. Scholars have questioned some of the riddlingly obscure details in its internal structure, as well as the seemingly muddled function or functions it serves within the larger narrative arc of the *Phenomenology*, inserted as it is between the otherwise closely linked sections on either side ("Self-Certain Spirit" and "Absolute Knowing").[1] At the same time, in comparison with the high level of scholarly attention that has been devoted to the differing versions of Hegel's Berlin lectures on religion and art, the "Religion" chapter has in general tended over the years to be given shorter shrift.[2]

---

[1] Jaeschke, *Die Religionsphilosophie Hegels*, 61–63.
[2] But see, among others, Jaeschke, *Religion in Reason*, 186–207; Gethmann-Siefert, *Einführung in Hegels Ästhetik*, 204–222; Jamros, *The Human Shape of God*; Lewis, "Religion and Demythologization in Hegel's *Phenomenology of Spirit*"; and Häussler, *Der Religionsbegriff*. The importance of the chapter

Among the issues that particularly repay a closer look at this section is the insight it offers into Hegel's developing account of the three modes of Absolute Spirit that his mature system comes to articulate: art, religion and philosophy. Hegel's ultimate sketch of the relation of these three modes in the Berlin versions of the *Encyclopedia* traces a progression from art, whose content splits into many shapes or *Gestalten*; to revealed religion (*die geoffenbarte Religion*), which brings the shapes into a form of totality, albeit one in the form of *Vorstellung* or picture-thought; and finally to philosophy, which Hegel says is the *conceptual* unity of both (*Dies Wissen ist damit der denkend erkannte Begriff der Kunst und Religion*) (E §572). The consideration of these modes within the "Religion" chapter of the *Phenomenology*, by contrast, has a somewhat different shape: it frames the treatment of art not as a separate mode which then gives rise to religion, but rather (so it would seem) as a moment within a longer story of religion's development between "Spirit" and "Absolute Knowing." While the *Phenomenology* account still functions to sort out the critical separations of the moments of Absolute Spirit required by Hegel's later system, the different contextual and genealogical context of those separations is worth exploring.[3]

In what follows, I will argue that many of the strangest aspects of the chapter—as well as many of the reasons that the account it gives of the separations ultimately required within the realm of Absolute Spirit—can be connected to one issue in particular: how Hegel's emerging thought about the *origins of art as a human activity* provides a key of sorts to understanding the progression of his own understanding of the relation between the human and the divine. As I will make clear in what follows, Hegel's concern here is not primarily one with the particular subset of artworks that can be referred to under the heading of 'religious art,' but rather with what he calls 'art-religion [*Die Kunst-Religion*]'—a term that may sound odd at first, but which recalls the well-known remark in the *Lectures on Aesthetics* where art is said to be a way of "bringing to our minds and expressing the *Divine*," which Hegel glosses in that context as "the deepest interests of mankind, and the most comprehensive truths of the spirit."[4] The central section of the chapter focuses on the emergence of this claim about 'art religion' in what Hegel took to be its strongest historical form: the revelatory experience of the gods in ancient Greek works of art. This claim about Greek art was, of course, strikingly made by the Greeks themselves, as indicated by Hegel's later citation of Herodotus's remark that Homer and Hesiod gave the Greeks their gods.[5] But Hegel's engagement with the significance of the Greek 'art religion' is importantly refracted through a contemporary perspective, as well, in the re-construal of Greek art that took place in the Romantic era. Hegel's

---

strictly for the development of Hegel's philosophy of art has also not been sufficiently appreciated, but see Martin Donougho's essay "The Pragmatics of Tragedy."

[3] The separations not only of the three modes of absolute spirit but also between ethical and absolute spirit are among the tendencies that Jaeschke cites as evidence that the *Phenomenology* Religion chapter "completes the development of the philosophy of religion in Jena"—not just chronologically but also conceptually (Jaeschke, *Religion in Reason*, 186).

[4] *LFA* I.7.

[5] *LFA* II.1047–1048.

linking of art and religion in this context has (as he himself explicitly uses sections of the *Phenomenology* to make clear) both deep resonances and clear differences from the bold claims made by many contemporary figures within the Romantic movement about why art matters.[6]

Ultimately, as I will argue, a central purpose of the whole "Religion" chapter is to connect as well as differentiate religion and art as modes of Absolute Spirit as the narrative of the *Phenomenology* moves toward Hegel's account of the philosophically critical moment of "Absolute Knowing." In this chapter, I will begin (section 7.1) with an account of the genealogical and conceptual tasks that Hegel takes up in this chapter and why Hegel's turn to the religious practice of pre-classical civilizations is important for the ultimate systematic account he will give of art, religion, and philosophy and the relation they bear to each other; then turn (in sections 7.2–7.4) to showing how Hegel's emerging perspective on art's importance offers us a key to the three main sections of the chapter: the development of 'natural religion', the three distinctive phases of the 'art religion' itself ('abstract', 'living', and 'spiritual' works of art, respectively) and the fundamentally altered stance that Hegel comes to take toward Christianity and his overall view of the relation between religion and philosophy more generally. A final section (7.5) takes up some remaining questions raised by this chapter.

7.1. THE TASKS OF THE RELIGION CHAPTER: GENEALOGICAL AND CONCEPTUAL ISSUES

It is interesting to ask where religion can be said first to emerge within the structure of the *Phenomenology of Spirit* as a whole. Hegel in fact begins the "Religion" chapter with a rehearsal of many of the previous moments in the *Phenomenology* where religion in some form has already been in play (PS 9.363–364/¶¶672–676): in the Understanding's consciousness of the supersensible that was nonetheless devoid of self, in the pain of the Unhappy Consciousness' failure to reach objectivity, and in the contrast between the lack of religion within Reason and the decisive appeal within the Ethical World to a religious notion of the underworld. (Interestingly enough, Hegel's account here actually underplays the *Phenomenology*'s prior appeals to religion: he gives no explicit mention, for example, of his introduction of the Lord/Bondsman relationship, which he had

---

[6] The Romantic pull on Hegel at Jena is to be distinguished from the later influence his reading of Georg Friedrich Creuzer's *Symbolik und Mythologie der alten Völker, besonders der Griechen* may have had on the shape of the *Lectures on the Philosophy of Religion*. For discussion of this, see the "Editorial Introduction" to the *Lectures on the Philosophy of Religion*, [LPR] II.10–11; and Pöggeler, "Die Entstehung von Hegels Ästhetik in Jena."

shaped on the basis of an earlier Frankfurt account of the 'fear of the Lord' as the beginning of wisdom in Abrahamic religion.)

But Hegel makes clear at the "Religion" chapter's start that the treatment of religion it must take up is explicitly different from the earlier moments: religion's earlier appearances have been "only from the *standpoint of the consciousness* that is conscious of absolute Being; but absolute Being in and for itself, the self-consciousness of Spirit, has not appeared in those 'shapes'" (PS 9.363/¶672). The treatment of religion as 'self-consciousness of Spirit' will involve two central Hegelian moves—one genealogical and one conceptual—that together give this chapter its distinctive character.

The genealogical point is one that has puzzled many readers of the *Phenomenology*. One might have expected, for example, that the starting point for an account of the self-consciousness of the Spirit whose trajectory began with a rich engagement with ancient Greek sources of ethical spirit might also be an investigation of relevant elements of Greek religion. Instead, Hegel makes a historical appeal to even earlier pre-classical religious and artistic traditions that have previously played no explicit role in the *Phenomenology* (although the exact points of reference have been disputed by scholars, Hegel appears, at least, to be drawing on imagery that connects with his later accounts of Persian, Hindu, and Egyptian religions).[7]

The conceptual issue is that Hegel is undertaking in the last sections of the *Phenomenology* an exploration of how he wants to think through the emergence of Absolute Spirit and the relation of its modes (religion, art, and philosophy); the chapter is in fact structured in a way to offer an account of what religion, art, and philosophy have in common and how they differ. At the time of the writing of the *Phenomenology of Spirit*, however, this is not yet a settled Hegelian doctrine—in fact, as we will see, the triad of modes so familiar to Hegel's Berlin *Encyclopedia* has not yet been explicitly developed, and instead art plays a role (although, as we will also see, hardly a subordinate one) within an overarching account of religion as a moment preceding absolute knowing.

The importance of these genealogical and conceptual points cannot be overstated. By beginning his account with a religious understanding that is prior to Greek religious experience, Hegel sets up a new triadic historical framework that will structure both his mature accounts of art and religion. On the religious side, this will be important for the relation that 'finite' religion will have to some account of 'consummate' or manifest religion; on the artistic side, as Pöggeler has argued, Hegel offers a perspective on art's historical shape that goes beyond the dialectical dualities of classical/romantic that had been characteristic of Schiller and Schlegel (this latter point is especially relevant for seeing that the origins of Hegel's well-known triadic division of the particular forms of art into the symbolic, classical, and romantic is something that emerges in the context of

---

[7] The "Religion of Light" is taken by many scholars to be a reference to Persian religion, although Jaeschke takes it to refer to Judaism. See the discussion in Jaeschke, *Religion in Reason*, 198–204; and Jamros, *The Human Shape of God*, 172–173, fn. 26.

Hegel's developing aesthetics at Jena and not—as Gadamer and others have claimed—the later influence of Creuzer and Heidelberg romanticism).[8]

But more broadly, these new triadic structures that Hegel is developing here *within* his emerging historical and conceptual accounts of art and religion need to be seen against the still *non-triadic* relationship that pertains, as we have mentioned, among the moments of Absolute Spirit as a group—that is, that art in the *Phenomenology* is still the 'art-religion' and not yet an independently structured mode of Absolute Spirit with its own self-standing historical account.

The first point to make about art's relation to religion here is that it is not simply a unique feature of the *Phenomenology of Spirit*'s account of these issues. Many commentators have, for example, remarked upon the fusion (or perhaps confusion) of art and religion within the chapter and have taken this to be part of the chapter's exceptional status within Hegel's account of Absolute Spirit—one that he presumably outgrew. For, it is argued, unlike Hegel's mature system, where art and religion are given their own separate realms, the *Phenomenology* chapter appears to subordinate its treatment of art to a moment within the development of religion. Yet, although the relation between art and religion in the *Phenomenology* is different from that of the Berlin system, it is not exceptional, since in Hegel's first (1817) version of the *Encyclopedia* at Heidelberg, his treatment of art also lacks independence. In the Heidelberg *Encyclopedia*, art is not a separate moment of Absolute Spirit but is still treated as one part of religion, namely the 'Religion of Art', as distinguished from 'Revealed Religion [*Die Geoffenbarte Religion*]'.[9] The *Phenomenology*'s account of art in the context of religion is, then, not a one-off, but seems rather to be representative of a larger approach to the issues raised by the two forms of Absolute Spirit for more than a decade of his philosophical development. I would claim, beyond that, however, that, although Hegel's systematic philosophical account of Absolute Spirit depends on critically understanding both the independence and connection of its three moments, these Jena and Heidelberg accounts of art and religion nonetheless offer crucial insights that can help us construe elements of Hegel's mature thought on these issues that retain their importance through all of the revisionary work that Hegel undertakes on these topics in Berlin.

One of the central insights that the *Phenomenology* account can direct us toward can be neatly framed in the terms of a remark in the standard edition of the Berlin lectures on the philosophy of art: that "*the first interpreter of religious ideas . . . is art alone*" (LFA I.316). Whether one considers the relation of art and religion in the Jena of 1807 (still in the shadow of the ferment of romantic claims linking the two notions) or in the context of our own contemporary views of these issues (where the institutional practices of art and religion may seem to have little to do with one another), this is a remarkable and

---

[8]   Otto Pöggeler, "Die Entstehung von Hegels Ästhetik in Jena," 249.

[9]   Gethmann-Siefert, *Einführung in Hegels Ästhetik*, 227ff. On the shifts in Hegel's thinking about art and religion during this crucial period (and the possibility that in Nuremberg Hegel was already pondering some grounds for the later separation of the two), see also Gethmann-Siefert, *Lectures on the Philosophy of Art*, p. 20, fn. 21.

provocative claim—but one that is, for all that, no less central in the end to Hegel's over-all approach to Absolute Spirit. It is therefore worth looking quickly at what he might mean by it, so I will briefly examine the context of the remark within the *Lectures on Fine Art* before turning back to the *Phenomenology*'s larger argument for this claim.

The comment in the *Lectures* occurs in the introduction to Hegel's treatment of 'symbolic' art (the section that compares directly with Hegel's account of 'natural religion' in the *Phenomenology*, concerned as it also is with the development of Persian, Hindu, and Egyptian views of the divine). At the beginning of that section, Hegel makes a comparison to Aristotle's account in the opening pages of the *Metaphysics* of the emergence of philosophy in wonder—an account, like Hegel's, which stresses some initial commonalities in the origins of art, religion, and philosophy. As Hegel points out, Aristotle had argued that if it is "owing to their wonder that men both now begin and at first began to philosophize," then "even the lover of myth is in a sense a lover of wisdom, for the myth is composed of wonders" (*Metaphysics* 982b12, 18). Aristotle's account is part of a longer story he is offering about the emergence of philosophy as a 'free' pursuit—arising only when human beings already have certain necessities in hand and are therefore unmotivated by practical concerns. Hegel finds this attitude of wonder likewise reflective of what he considers a certain kind of spiritual freedom:

> [W]onder only occurs when man, torn free from his most immediate first connection with nature and from his most elementary, purely practical relation to it, that of desire, stands back spiritually from nature and his own singularity and now seeks and sees in things a universal, implicit, and permanent element. In that case for the first time natural objects strike him; they are an 'other' which yet is meant to be for his apprehension and in which he strives to find himself over again as well as thoughts and reason. (LFA I.315)

The experience of wonder, Hegel says, is crucial for what he calls "the *subjective* aspect of the first origin of symbolic art"—what we might take to be the dispositional stance involved for those experiencing it—but Hegel goes on to talk about the 'objective' side of artistic production of mythological symbols. Art did not come on the scene merely when human beings immediately saw "the Absolute directly in the objects actually present," but "only when the mind produces from its own resources both the apprehension of its Absolute in the form of what is external in itself and also the objectivity of this more or less adequate connection" of spirit with nature (LFA I.316). Art is in fact a sort of middle stance, on his view: one that exists between an (initial, thoughtless) "purely spiritless immersion in nature" and a later (what Hegel likes to call 'prosaic', as opposed to the speculatively-engaged 'poetic') attitude of detachment that is 'altogether freed' from nature as something external to it.[10]

---

[10] There is much to notice about Hegel's view of the origin of art here—including, among other things, his remarkable claim that poetry (historically and speculatively) is prior to prose, and hence more deeply connected with philosophy's speculative interests (LFA II. 973): "Poetry began when the human being undertook to express *herself*; for poetry, what is spoken, is there only to be an expression. When once, in the midst of his practical activity and need, the human being proceeds to collect her thoughts

One can see in this discussion a number of distinctive elements of Hegel's philosophy of art that are worth keeping in mind as we trace its function and relation with respect to religion, philosophy, and the emergence of Absolute Spirit more generally. Perhaps most important is the insight it offers into Hegel's remarkable claim about the very notion of 'art-religion' mentioned earlier (i.e., that art is directly concerned with the divine in the sense of "the deepest interests of mankind, and the most comprehensive truths of the spirit"). This broad claim distinguishes Hegel's approach to art from that of much eighteenth-century aesthetics—in that art, on Hegel's view, is not something which should be best approached simply in terms of notions like aesthetic receptivity or sensibility, but rather must be seen to "proceed from a higher impulse and to satisfy higher needs—at times the highest and absolute needs since it is bound up with the most universal views of life and the religious interests of whole epochs and peoples" (LFA I.30). In turn, this large (non-immediately-practical) aim of art links directly to philosophy and human thoughtfulness in general; as Hegel puts it in a much-quoted passage:

> The universal and absolute need from which art (on its formal side) springs has its origin in the fact that the human being is a *thinking* consciousness, i.e., that the human being draws out of herself and puts *before herself* what she is and whatever else is. Things in nature are only *immediate* and *single*, while the human being as spirit *duplicates* herself, in that (i) she *is* as things in nature are, but (ii) she is just as much *for* herself; she sees herself, represents herself to herself, thinks, and only on the strength of this active placing herself before herself is she spirit. (LFA I.30–31; Knox translation emended)

With these two large connections linking art, religion, and philosophy in mind—we can perhaps call them broadly the 'social' and the 'speculative' interests of Absolute Spirit, respectively—we can now look back directly to the details of the *Phenomenology* chapter. Using Hegel's notion of art as the 'first interpreter' of religious ideas as a sort of key, we can see that the central section of this chapter devoted to 'art-religion' is one that takes up not just one more moment among others, but rather one that in fact plays a key role in the development of religion from start to end. In the next sections, I will examine the importance of this notion of art across the development of the three main sections of the chapter.

7.2. Interpreting Hegel's Account of Natural Religion

We can put Hegel's claim that art is the 'first interpreter' of religious ideas to an initial test by examining the first major section of the "Religion" chapter, Natural Religion.

and communicate herself to others, then she immediately produces a coined expression [*ein gebildeter Ausdruck*], a touch [*Anklang*] of poetry" (*LFA* II.974; Knox translation emended).

This section divides into three subparts, devoted, respectively, to God as Light (*Das Lichtwesen*), Plant and Animal (*Die Pflanze und das Tier*) and the Artificer (*Der Werkmeister*). Hegel describes the trajectory of these three moments in terms of the familiar triad of immediate consciousness, self-consciousness, and the unity of both in the shape of being-in-and-for-itself (PS 9.368/¶683).

Although the concern of the *Lichtwesen* section with 'the pure I' would seem to be abstractly divorced from considerations of beauty (given beauty's inherent connection to concrete shape and specificity), it is remarkable how much Hegel's account draws nonetheless on a noticeably aesthetic vocabulary—even when his goal is to describe that very abstractness itself. In the second paragraph of this section, in fact, Hegel draws already on aesthetic categories to describe the abstract purity of this 'I': "the essential simplicity of its thought moves aimlessly about in it without stability or intelligence, enlarges its bounds to the measureless, and its beauty [*Schönheit*], heightened to splendor [*Pracht*], is dissolved in its sublimity (*Erhabenheit*)" (PS 9.371/¶686). Hegel's striking appeal to these three aesthetic categories (and not just the mere Kantian duality of beauty and sublimity) could well, of course, be taken as evidence of an appeal of his to the wider English aesthetic palate in the tradition of Addison and Burke. But, in the context of the developing aesthetic vocabulary of the *Phenomenology of Spirit*, his language is striking: *Erhabenheit* appears only in two other sections of the *Phenomenology*, most prominently in Hegel's description (at the end of the previous chapter) of the 'moral genius' (PS 9.352/¶655), a form of conscience where ethical and aesthetic categories are notoriously fused.[11]

Hegel's appeal to aesthetic terms here is rooted, one might suggest, in the inherent project of the "Religion" chapter, where, as Hegel puts it, every shape of religion contains neither the existence of "Spirit as Nature that is free from thought" nor "thought that is free from existence," but is rather "an existence that is preserved in thinking [*das im Denken erhaltene Dasein*], and also something thought that is objectively present in it [*so wie ein Gedachtes das da ist*]" (PS 9.369/¶684). Even the most abstract form of religion, then, has some *shape*, and that shape—so it appears—is rendered accessible through aesthetic terms. Thus, in thinking about the 'pure I' of the *Lichtwesen*, Hegel draws on the rich language of an idea's complete 'penetration' of an object (*Durchdringung*), which is central to his philosophy of art. Compare, for example, Hegel's description of the pure 'I' ("which, in its externalization has within itself as *universal object* the certainty of its

---

[11] The other place *Erhabenheit* appears in the *Phenomenology* is in the section on phrenology (PS 9.186/¶335), where Hegel may well be mirthfully playing with the falsely elevated language of phrenologists—for whom sublimity itself, one might say, has been turned into a mere bump on the head: "denn weder ist der Mörder nur dies Abstraktum eines Mörders, noch hat er nur *eine* Erhabenheit und *eine* Vertiefung [for the murderer is neither merely this abstraction of a murderer, nor does he have only one bump and one hollow]." The reference to the 'moral genius', by contrast, is part of Hegel's larger and more serious task in the *Gewissen* chapter to show that the moments of Absolute Spirit (treated properly in the moments of self-consciousness within the "Religion" chapter) also make their appearance within conciousness itself. On this point and Hegel's overall tasks in the *PhG* from the end of Spirit to Absolute Knowing, see Moyar, "Reply to Howard, DeNys and Speight," 160–161, and Chapter 8 in this volume.

own self, or, in other words, this object is for 'I' the penetration [*Durchdringung*] of all thought and all reality" [PS 9.371/¶685]) with his definition of beauty in the Heidelberg *Encyclopedia* ("the penetration [*Durchdringung*] of intuition or image [*Anschauung, Bild*] through thought" [E1817, §460]).[12]

While even the most abstract moment at the beginning of Natural Religion, then, can be said to be described or interpreted through aesthetic categories, art's interpretive efforts begin to play an even more explicit role as the section moves forward. The following two sections (Plant and Animal, the Artificer) describe the growing power— over the manifold natural organic shapes that characterize this mode of religious experience—held by a figure Hegel refers to somewhat obliquely as the Artificer (or 'artisan' [*Werkmeister*]; on its first appearance, ¶PS 9.372/¶690, cited however merely as 'the worker' [*der Arbeitende*]). It is the artificer who brings together these shapes—first the more inert (*unschuldig*) forms of plant life and then the full seriousness (*Ernst*) of warring animal figures representative of various forms of national life—in such a way that what is really produced is the producer himself, a "self-consuming self, i.e., the self that becomes a Thing" (PS 9.372/¶690): "The artificer [*der Arbeitende*] therefore retains the upper hand over these mutually destructive animal spirits" (PS 9.372/¶690).

The emergence of the artificer—located by Hegel in the pyramid- and monument-fashioning Egyptian religious realm—marks the transition to the artist's role proper as natural religion gives way to the religion of art itself. Hegel's (often neglected) account of the role of this transitional but decisive figure stresses the move away from a blending of natural and human forms and from an instinctual to a more self-conscious mode of artistic creation, as the interpreter of the natural world becomes explicitly a self-interpreter.[13] Within the context of Egyptian religion, the artisan produces creatures like the Sphinx, an "ambiguous being which is a riddle to itself, the conscious wrestling with the non-conscious, the simple inner with the multiform outer, the darkness of thought mating with the clarity of utterance, these break out into the language of a profound, but scarcely intelligible wisdom" (PS 9.375/¶697). But the artisan's production of the riddling Sphinx has the significance of being the "end of instinctive effort" and affords the artisan finally a recognition where his own active self-consciousness can be met with self-consciousness in the object. Thus the partly human, partly animal "monsters in shape, word and deed" that are central to this moment of the artisan are "dissolved into spiritual shape" in the newly self-conscious activity of the artisan as he is transformed into an artist proper: now we have "an outer that has retreated into itself, and an inner that utters or expresses itself out of itself and in its own self"; we have "thought which begets itself, which preserves its shape in harmony with itself and is a lucid, intelligible existence"—hence, as Hegel signals the transition, finally an Artist (PS 9.375/¶698), or a 'spiritual worker' (*geistiger Arbeiter*) in a self-conscious sense.

---

[12] On Hegel's use of this term in the later Berlin philosophy of art, see Speight, "Philosophy of Art," 113, n. 1.

[13] For a fuller account of the role of the artisan in Hegel's philosophy of art, see Speight, "Artisans, Artists and Hegel's History of the Philosophy of Art."

7.3. ART-RELIGION AND ARTISTIC
SELF-INTERPRETATION

With the transition to art proper, the artist's interpretive activity now becomes decisively *self*-interpretive. The three sections of the Art Religion section—devoted, respectively, to what Hegel calls 'abstract', 'living', and 'spiritual' works of art—map a trajectory that runs from modes of art where the creative process and the resulting artwork are separated items (the 'abstract' forms of the statue, hymn, oracle, and cultic sacrifice) to the 'living' forms of human participation in which there is a kind of living absorption (in the mysteries and athletic competitions of Greek civic life), and finally to the unification of work and spontaneity in the forms of poetry (which itself moves from a form in which the bardic artist is separate from the enacted work, to the highest form, the drama, where the enacting artist as actor/agent stands in front of the audience in real-time performance of his work). Among the hallmarks of this movement is the emergence of speech (*Sprache*) as the mode in which the self "exists as self"—in contrast with the muteness that had pertained in the Egyptian world of the artificer, where the work produced by his *Arbeit* was still only 'soundless' ("mere noise and not speech," revealing only "an outer, not the inner self" [PS 9.375/¶695]). Increasing expressiveness is key to this movement: oracular speech gives way to a "further developed self which rises to become a *being-for-self*" and hence "master ... over the objectivity of the Light of Sunrise"—again a term with reference back to the initial form of *Lichtwesen* in natural religion) (PS 9.381/¶712).[14] Likewise, the hiddenness of mysteries must give way to unconcealment and self-awareness—an experience that Hegel notes involves "only the mystery of bread and wine, of Ceres and Bacchus, not of the other, the strictly higher, gods whose individuality includes as an essential moment self-consciousness as such. Therefore, Spirit has not yet sacrificed itself as *self-conscious* Spirit to self-consciousness, and the mystery of bread and wine is not yet the mystery of flesh and blood" (PS 9.387/¶724).[15]

The complexity of the *Phenomenology*'s account, particularly with its merging of what will become for Hegel two different genealogical accounts (one for Greek religion and one for Greek art), means that there are some interesting differences of stress and organization in comparison with the treatments of Greek religion and art that appear in the Berlin lecture series. The role of the statue in the *Phenomenology* account as only that of an initial and abstract (not yet 'living') artistic moment is at some odds with the high

---

[14] Hegel here has the inner self-awareness associated with Antigone in mind: this self "knows that simplicity of truth as *essential being* which does not have the form of contingent existence through an alien speech [such as that of the oracle], knows it as the *sure and unwritten law of the gods, a law that is 'everlasting and no one knows whence it came'*" (PS 9.381/¶712).

[15] See the account in Häussler, *Der Religionsbegriff in Hegels 'Phänomenologie des Geistes,'* who sees this as one of the 'Judaic' elements within Hegel's "Religion" chapter.

role given to sculpture as the very embodiment of concreteness and plasticity and art in the *Lectures on Fine Art*.[16] The more cultic moments within 'living' art are taken up in the *Lectures on the Philosophy of Religion* but are not given a codified place in the art lectures (which after all must give an account of the artistic genres that runs across cultural lines), while the treatment of Greek poetry and especially drama are more fully taken up in the art lectures. And Hegel's account of poetic modes in the art lectures will feature more prominently (particularly with an eye to his notion of the distinctive needs and modes of 'modern' art) the role of lyric between epic and drama.

Despite the accusation against him for fusing art and religion in this section, Hegel actually makes use of the single narrative of development to effect two critical separations: the first between ethical life as such and the self-consciousness that art has acquired; and the second between art and religion. Both emphasize the new status that the artist as such has taken on in ancient Greek culture. The new distance that the artist has in his self-awareness over his culture is striking: Hegel characterizes it both as a *mastery* of sorts over the people (PS 9.380/¶709)—a side that runs in the direction of the levity of comedy—and as a *withdrawal* ("The religion of the ethical Spirit is, however, its elevation above its real world, the withdrawal from its truth into the pure knowledge of itself" [PS 9.376/¶701])—a side that runs in the direction of the tragic continuance of the diremptions of the Unhappy Consciousness. As Hegel puts it, "This simple certainty of Spirit within itself has a twofold meaning: it is a serene, stable existence and settled truth, and also absolute unrest and the passing-away of the ethical order." Spirit both "mourns over the loss of its world" *and* "creates its own essence which is raised above the real world" (PS 9.377/¶701).

The artist's (tragic *and* comic) separation from the ethical culture in which he has lived leads likewise to the formal separation—not yet assumed as a separate mode of Absolute Spirit, but in the context of the *Phenomenology* viewed as an achievement—between art and religion. "In such an epoch" as that where the artistic spirit can mourn over the loss of the ethical order, Hegel says, "absolute art makes its appearance" (PS 9.377/¶702). Hegel appears to mean by this not merely that the instinctive fashioning of religious symbols characteristic of the artisan has given way to a fully spiritual mode of creativity but, more deeply, that

> Spirit transcends art in order to gain a higher representation of itself, viz., to be not merely the *substance* born of the self, but to be, in its representation as object, *this self*, not only to give birth to itself from its Notion, but to have its very Notion for its shape, so that the Notion and the work of art produced know each other as one and the same. (PS 9.377/¶702)

---

[16] Sculpture, in Hegel's view, is an art that "presents us with man as he is, with spirit completely in the shape of the body" (*HW* XIV.352, *LFA* II.702). Yet even more expressive—because involving the 'living' statues of actors performing their roles—is the drama. On the relation between sculpture and drama, see the differing viewpoints of Houlgate, "Hegel on the Beauty of Sculpture," and Rutter, *Hegel on the Modern Arts*.

This more complete transition represents the move from art-religion to the third and final section of the *Phenomenology* "Religion" chapter, in which Hegel describes a form of religion that he understands as making a more universal claim than the ethnically rooted forms of religion Hegel has described up to this point: what he terms the 'manifest' or *offenbar* religion, or as the *Lectures on the Philosophy of Religion* will describe it, the 'consummate' religion, which claims to be more than an ethnic religion (PS 9.400 ff/ ¶748 ff).

Hegel's account in these key paragraphs introducing the separations (PS 9.376–377/ ¶¶701–702) suggests that it is *because* we have a split between *Sittlichkeit* and religion— and a consequent loss of the ethical world—that there is the possibility of the independent emergence of *art* as distinct from religion. This is a key (and often unremarked) moment in the reading of Hegel's understanding of the role of art in *modernity*—the story of art's emergence as an independent mode of absolute spirit is, on Hegel's terms, something that cannot be separated from a tragic context: insofar as the artist emerges in a self-conscious way, he is already heralding the loss of his ethical and social world.

7.4. The 'End' of Art Religion and the Transition to Philosophy

We have seen that the key transitions within both natural religion and the art-religion itself are marked by increasing expressiveness on the part of the interpretive artists who provide the relevant terms in which religious experience can be understood. In the transition to the 'manifest' or 'revelatory' religion, Hegel constructs a figure that seems to combine at once the withdrawn but self-aware Greek dramatic artist with the human-and-divine Jesus. As he sets up the dramatic scene for this transition, Hegel brings together the dramatic artist's concomitant sense of both mastery over and loss of the Greek world with the decisive moment of betrayal that ushered in the emergence of a new religious worldview: the artistic activity in which Spirit has brought forth itself as object is "pure form, because the individual, in ethical obedience and service, has worked off every unconscious existence and fixed determination . . . This form is the night in which substance was betrayed and made itself into Subject. It is out of the night of pure certainty of self that the ethical Spirit is resurrected as a shape freed from Nature and its own immediate existence" (PG 9.377/¶703).

Hegel links not only the dramatic *situation*, as it were, but also the tragic suffering experienced by the

> individual which Spirit selects to be the vessel of its sorrow. Spirit is present in this individual as his universal and as the power over him from which he suffers violence, as his 'pathos', by giving himself over to which his self-consciousness loses its freedom. But that positive power of universality is subdued by the pure self of the

individual, the negative power. . . . Becoming its master, it has made the 'pathos' into its material and given itself its content, and this unity emerges as a work, universal Spirit individualized and set before us. (PS 9.378/¶704)

What exactly Hegel is up to in his description of this transition is not fully clear.[17] But one thing that does seem clear is that, just as natural religion required the interpretive efforts of art, so the religion that Hegel calls 'manifest' could not have emerged in the form it does without having passed through the moment of artistic self-awareness in which an individual is set over his world. The importance of this Greek and artistic passage to Christianity has been discussed in terms of the larger demythologizing project Hegel takes up in the third section of the "Religion" chapter's critique of *Vorstellung*—a reading which bolsters the account we have given of art's presence in the chapter.[18]

There are a number of remarkable elements in the overall transition to philosophy that occurs within the "Religion" chapter, but perhaps most striking for our purposes is the degree to which the demythologization that takes place is not something imposed by later philosophical or religious critique but rather (as one would expect, given the importance of internal critique in the *Phenomenology*) something that takes place within—and is thus *initiated by*—the interpretive activity of art itself. As the previous section suggests, this interpretive artistic activity has both a tragic and a comic aspect.

Already within the experience of the ancient Greek art form of tragedy, for example, Hegel has heralded not just a transition to a new form of *religion*, but more directly a transition to *philosophy* itself. A work like Aeschylus's *Oresteia*, for example, portrays in Hegel's view a conflict between ethical forces—the urge to avenge the murder of blood-kinsman, on the one hand, and the claims of civic and marriage oaths between non-blood relatives, on the other hand—as a conflict between two divine forces, the Furies and Apollo. As Hegel presents the tragic denouement that emerges in this conflict, there is a canceling out or resolution of these divine forces in such a way that what is left is a power of a different order: not just one more figure within the pantheon of the Greek religious imagination, but the notion of tragic Fate itself (the 'Zeus' that is appealed to in the end of Aeschylus's trilogy, understood not merely as another figure within the Greek pantheon but as a power that ultimately controls such conflicts [PS 9.396/¶740]):

This Fate completes the depopulation of heaven, of that unthinking mingling of individuality and essence. . . . The expulsion of such shadowy, insubstantial picture-thoughts which was demanded by the philosophers of antiquity thus already begins in [Greek] Tragedy in general through the fact that the division of the substance is controlled by the Notion. . . . (PS 9.396/¶741)

---

[17] On the oddness of the fused imagery, see Donougho, "The Pragmatics of Tragedy."
[18] On this issue, see Lewis, "Religion and Demythologization in Hegel's *Phenomenology of Spirit*."

The tragic dissolution of the pantheon of the conventional Greek religious imagination has a comic correlate with a further dimension, one which Hegel sees captured in the plot of Aristophanes' *Clouds*:

> Rational *thinking* frees the divine Being from its contingent shape and, in antithesis to the unthinking wisdom of the Chorus which produces all sorts of ethical maxims and gives currency to a host of laws and specific concepts of duty and right, lifts these into the simple Ideas of the Beautiful and the Good. The movement of this abstraction is the consciousness of the dialectic contained in these maxims and laws themselves and, consequently, the consciousness of the vanishing of the absolute validity previously attaching to them. With the vanishing of the contingent character and superficial individuality which imagination lent to the divine Beings, all that is left to them as regards their *natural* aspect is the bareness of their immediate existence; they are *clouds*, an evanescent mist, like those imaginative representations. (PS 9.398–399/¶746)

The pure thoughts of the Beautiful and the Good thus "display a comic spectacle."

If the cancellation of divine forces in Greek tragedy initiates a dialectical movement that culminates in the demands of Socratic philosophy, the corresponding movement within comedy brings Socratic philosophical concepts directly on stage, as it were. Philosophy thus makes its first appearance *as* a phenomenon within the 'Art-Religion'—a point which might be interestingly read in connection with Socrates' reference in the *Apology* to Aristophanes as the one who really hands up the 'first indictment' against him (and hence of the civic context for the 'examination' of philosophy in the city).

The consequence of these tragic and comic moves toward philosophy is, within the context of Hegel's larger narrative, to bring together divine essence and individual human self-consciousness (PS 9.399/¶747). At the level of the dramatic artform, this development means the convergence of individual actor and the *persona* he plays, as well as the collapse of the spectator-spectacle divide, since the comic spectator happily recognizes himself in the comic actor/persona (PS 9.399/¶747). The comic self-awareness of this convergence can be expressed in philosophical terms as the claim that "the self is absolute essence" (PS 9.400/¶748), or, in a phrase that helps underscore the peculiar role of art in the development of the 'revelatory' religion within the "Religion" chapter, what Hegel calls "the becoming-human of the divine essence [*die Menschwerdung des göttlichen Wesens*]" (PS 9.400/¶748).

As Jaeschke has pointed out, this notion of *Menschwerdung* plays a stronger role within the *Phenomenology of Spirit* than it does in the later *Lectures on the Philosophy of Religion*.[19] But *Menschwerdung* is, as I have argued elsewhere, a decisive trope within the later *Lectures on Fine Art*—in fact, particularly for giving a perspective on the notion of the 'end of art' and the transition from art to religion.[20]

---

[19] Jaeschke, *Religion in Reason*, 204.
[20] Speight, "Tragedy and the Human Image: German Idealism's Legacy for Theory and Practice."

The importance of these developments within the trajectory of the "Religion" chapter is that the development from the ultimate or 'absolute' form of religion (PS 9.405/ ¶759) to 'absolute' or speculative knowing, if it is to work, must hinge precisely on an understanding of what Hegel sees as a key inheritance of the art religion for 'absolute' religion: the notion of a religion that could somehow be called 'manifest' or 'revelatory' (*offenbar*) religion (*not*, as many have pointed out, 'revealed' religion)—that is, one whose very "being manifest consists in this, that *what it is*, is *known*" (PS 9.405/¶759). Hegel affirms that knowledge of such a form of religion *is* speculative knowledge (PS 9.407/¶761)—admittedly, still a form of religion and hence in an only implicit unity that needs to be further overcome in the transition to 'absolute knowing' itself (PS 9.422/ ¶788), but one that offers Hegel some distinctive resources (as I will claim in the final section) in comparison with both earlier and later perspectives on the relation between philosophy and the other modes of absolute spirit.

7.5. QUESTIONS AND CONCLUSIONS

A number of questions that arise from examining Hegel's project in the "Religion" chapter concern whether his account in the end confuses the relations among the modes of absolute spirit. Is this account too art-centered to make sense of religion or philosophy? Does the existence of simultaneous narratives of both the history of art and the history of religion unduly complicate the conceptual task of marking off the three modes? And what does this (con)fused account in the *Phenomenology* offer if we compare it to other attempts that Hegel makes to address similar issues?

With respect to the first question, the reply might be that Hegel's task in the *Phenomenology* chapter is to reconstrue religion and religious experience in a way that challenges certain conventional conceptions of it as essentially passive, even quiescent. By stressing the importance of the interpretive activity of art both for the development of earlier religions and for the ultimate task of demythologization in the transition from religion to philosophy, Hegel offers grounds for a revision of the understanding of religious thought: religion may indeed be a somewhat more actively shaped part of cultural and human self-understanding than is often claimed. (As Hegel put it in another context in the *Lectures on the Philosophy of Religion*, "Theologians are like the Englishman who didn't realize that he was speaking prose; because they work exegetically and (so they believe) in a passively receptive way, [they] have no inkling of the fact that they are thereby active and reflective.")[21]

With respect to the second question—whether the account of art here is one that is inordinately constrained by its association with religion—we might think about Hegel's project in the *Phenomenology* as particularly concerned not with the topic so

---

[21] *LPR* III.261.

familiar from the *Lectures on Fine Art*—the *end* of art—but rather with one that also runs through much of Hegel's thought about the philosophy of art but is much less frequently explored: the question of the *origin* of art. From this perspective, we might return to the earlier quotation cited earlier from the *Lectures on Fine Art*: Hegel's claims that the "universal and absolute need from which art (on its formal side) springs has its origin in the fact that the human being is a *thinking* consciousness, i.e., that the human being draws out of herself and puts *before herself* what she is and whatever else is." In the remarks that follow this passage, Hegel says that human beings acquire this consciousness both theoretically and practically; in explicating the latter sense, Hegel uses a striking analogy—one that has drawn the attention of many readers of Hegel's aesthetics, including Michael Fried in his book on Courbet, as well as Benjamin Rutter in his book on the modern system of the arts: "Even a child's impulse involves . . . practical alteration of external things; a boy throws stones into the river and now marvels at the circles drawn in the water as an effect in which he gains an intuition of something that is his own doing. . . ." As Fried has nicely put it in his discussion of this passage, "artistic production is at bottom a form of self-representation . . . but self-representation here involves something other than a simple mirroring of the self."[22] The stress in the "Religion" chapter on the artist's interpretive activity as *self*-interpretive fits nicely with this non-Narcissistic understanding of Hegel's view of the artist and the impulses that lie behind his work. Hegel's insistence that we must begin, for an account of the origins of art, with the artist's production (and not with an account of aesthetic receptivity and sensibility) does not lead him to posit a romantically inspired genius or to undertake an investigation of the conditions of artistic production, but rather to focus on the *meaning* of the activity undertaken by someone who is interpretively making use of the social achievements around him. In the case of the historical examples Hegel takes up in the "Religion" chapter, it can be said that, without the collective efforts of the Greeks to create a society where democratic rather than tyrannical forms of rule hold sway, Greek art as an interpretive effort to construe the significance of this change (in anthropomorphic statues and tales of the gods) would never have emerged.

With respect to the third question, in thinking about the transition to philosophy as a mode of absolute spirit, Hegel frequently wrestled with a concern about the potential *emptiness* of a philosophical system that he cast at several memorable points in his development in terms of a temptation toward *irony*. One famous statement of this comes in the key moment of transition to philosophy within Absolute Spirit in the Berlin *Encyclopedia*: as Hegel puts it there, if a notion of 'realized' Spirit—that is, Spirit in which "all mediation has superseded itself"—is taken in a merely formalistic (contentless) way, the result is not the contentful unity of what art and religion sought in imagistic form,

---

[22] Michael Fried, *Courbet's Realism* (Chicago: University of Chicago Press, 1990), 276. While this is certainly an interesting passage for comparing the standard version of the *Lectures* as edited by Hegel's student Hotho to what we have of the lecture transcripts (the published 1823 transcript, for example, lacks the specific "stones in the river" part of the passage), the larger philosophical points raised here remain crucial in any case.

but rather irony, which, Hegel says, "knows how to reduce every objective content to nothing, to a *vanity*" (E §571). In the *Phenomenology's* "Religion" chapter, Hegel links the notion of irony achieved by the comic consciousness with the alienation felt first by the Unhappy Consciousness and connected to the tragic fate we have seen develop in Hegel's notion of the art-religion: the loss felt by the Unhappy Consciousness is, Hegel says, "the counterpart [*Gegenseite*] and completion [*Vervollständigung*] of the comic consciousness that is perfectly happy within itself" (PS 9.401/¶752). Hegel's stress on the complementarity of these comic and tragic sides suggests that one insight we might derive from the *Phenomenology's* distinctively *artistic* treatment of irony is that such a perspective can only come from the embodied account of *Menschwerdung* that we have seen serves as the narrative backbone of the "Religion" chapter. Without the narrative of embodiment that precedes the emergence of comedy as the ultimate emergence of the art religion—without, that is, the experience of the human attempt to give shape precisely to the deepest meaning *of* the human that characterizes the impulse toward art in its origin, according to Hegel—irony in its contentlessness is always a risk of systematic philosophy.[23]

From these perspectives, the "Religion" chapter might be said to offer not simply a confused account of the modes of Absolute Spirit, but rather a crucial insight into important elements of what these moments involve for the mature Hegel. Art can be said to offer a key to construing religion in its connection with human activity, while an understanding of the religious background to art makes clear why art requires us to give a larger account of its social meaning—the concerns in both cases providing an indispensable point of departure without which philosophy (as Hegel worried) might only spin in infinite circles of irony.

WORKS CITED

Primary Texts

Hegel, G. W. F. *Encyclopedia of the Philosophical Sciences in Outline and Critical Writings* [E1817], edited by Ernst Behler. New York: Continuum, 1990.

Hegel, G. W. F. *Hegel's Aesthetics: Lectures on Fine Art* [LFA], translated by T. M. Knox. Oxford: Oxford University Press, 1975.

Hegel, G. W. F. *Lectures on the Philosophy of Religion* [LPR], translated by R. F. Brown, P. C. Hodgson, and J. M. Stewart, edited by Peter C. Hodgson. 3 vols. Berkeley; Los Angeles: University of California Press, 1984–1987.

Hegel, G. W. F. *Phenomenology of Spirit* [PS], translated by A. V. Miller. Oxford: Oxford University Press, 1977.

[23] An interesting test of my claim here might be made by considering one of Hegel's earlier attempts simply to *equate* irony and religion: as he put it (according to Rosenkranz) in the conclusion of his *System of Ethical Life*, "irony toward the mortal and profitable activity of men is reconciliation, the basic Idea of religion" (translation in SEL, 180).

Hegel, G. W. F. *Philosophy of Mind* [E], translated by W. Wallace and A. V. Miller, revised by Michael Inwood. Oxford: Oxford University Press, 2007.

Hegel, G. W. F. *System of Ethical Life and First Philosophy of Spirit* [SEL], edited and translated by H. S. Harris and T. M. Knox. Albany: State University of New York Press, 1979.

Secondary Literature

Crites, Stephen. *Dialectic and Gospel in the Development of Hegel's Thinking*. University Park: Pennsylvania State University Press, 1998.

Donougho, Martin. "The Pragmatics of Tragedy." *Idealistic Studies* 36, no. 3 (2006): 153–168.

Gethmann-Siefert, Annemarie. *Einführung in Hegels Ästhetik*. Munich: Fink, 2005.

Gethmann-Siefert, Annemarie. *Lectures on the Philosophy of Art: The Hotho Transcript of the 1823 Berlin Lectures*, translated by Robert F. Brown. Oxford: Oxford University Press, 2014.

Häussler, Matthias. *Der Religionsbegriff in Hegels 'Phänomenologie des Geistes.'* Munich: Karl Alber, 2008.

Jaeschke, Walter. *Die Religionsphilosophie Hegels*. Darmstadt: Wissenschaftliche Buchgesellschaft, 1983.

Jaeschke, Walter. *Religion in Reason: The Foundations of Hegel's Philosophy of Religion*, translated by J. Michael Stewart and Peter C. Hodgson. Berkeley: University of California Press, 1990.

Jamros, Daniel P. *The Human Shape of God: Religion in Hegel's 'Phenomenology of Spirit.'* New York: Paragon House, 1994.

Leuze, Reinhard. *Die ausserchristlichen Religionen bei Hegel*. Göttingen: Vandenhoeck and Ruprecht, 1975.

Lewis, Thomas A. "Religion and Demythologization in Hegel's *Phenomenology of Spirit*," in *Hegel's 'Phenomenology of Spirit,'* edited by Dean Moyar and Michael Quante. Cambridge: Cambridge University Press, 2008, 192–209.

Pinkard, Terry. *Hegel's Phenomenology: The Sociality of Reason*. Cambridge: Cambridge University Press, 1994.

Pöggeler, Otto. "Die Entstehung von Hegels Ästhetik in Jena," in *Hegel-Studien Beiheft* 20, edited by Dieter Henrich and Klaus Düsing. Bonn: Bouvier, 1980, 249–270.

Pöggeler, Otto. "System und Geschichte der Künste bei Hegel," in *Hegel-Studien Beiheft* 27, edited by Annemarie Gethmann-Siefert and Otto Pöggeler. Bonn: Bouvier, 1986, 1–26.

Rutter, Benjamin. *Hegel on the Modern Arts*. Cambridge: Cambridge University Press, 2010.

Speight, Allen. "Artisans, Artists and Hegel's History of the Philosophy of Art." *Bulletin of the Hegel Society of Great Britain* 34, no. 2 (October 2013): 203–222.

Speight, Allen. *Hegel, Literature and the Problem of Agency*. Cambridge: Cambridge University Press, 2001.

Speight, Allen. "Philosophy of Art," in *GWF Hegel: Key Concepts*, edited by Michael Baur. London: Routledge, 2015, 103–115.

CHAPTER 8

....

ABSOLUTE KNOWLEDGE AND THE ETHICAL CONCLUSION OF THE *PHENOMENOLOGY*

....

DEAN MOYAR

To comprehend "Absolute Knowledge" we must read it with an eye forward to *The Science of Logic*, and with an eye backward to the long road that brought the *Phenomenology of Spirit* to its concluding chapter. Most of the actual text is best understood in the latter, retrospective mode, and most of this chapter will be concerned with understanding how Hegel unifies the previous seven chapters of the *Phenomenology* by aligning what can be called the theoretical and practical accounts of objectivity. To understand "Absolute Knowledge" one must understand each part of the book, and so it seems that an explanation of AK (I will henceforth use AK to refer to the chapter and 'absolute knowledge' to refer to the knowledge itself) can only be given at the end of a long commentary on the whole book, not as a freestanding essay.[1] In what follows, I do say something about each part of the book, though in most cases only a little, and for a more adequate view I recommend that the interested reader consult the previous five chapters of this *Handbook* and the many excellent commentaries on the *Phenomenology* as a whole.

8.1. THE *PHENOMENOLOGY* AS THE DEDUCTION OF THE CONCEPT

....

In this opening section I focus on the purpose of AK with regard to *The Science of Logic*, outlining what Hegel took to be the *Phenomenology*'s basic task and how he arrived at

---

[1] The best accounts at the end of excellent full-length commentaries are Pinkard, *Hegel's Phenomenology*; Siep, *Hegel's Phenomenology of Spirit*; and Stewart, *The Unity of Hegel's Phenomenology of Spirit*.

that task through a critique of previous forms of idealism. The most compact summaries of the task occur in two passages in the Introduction to *The Science of Logic*, where Hegel emphasizes the *Phenomenology*'s role in the justification or deduction of the concept of science.[2] Here is the first passage:

> In the *Phenomenology of Spirit* I have presented consciousness as it progresses from the first immediate opposition of itself and the object [*Gegenstandes*] to absolute knowledge. This path traverses all the forms of the *relation of consciousness to the object* [Objekte] and its result is the *concept of science* [den Begriff der Wissenschaft]. There is no need, therefore, to justify this concept here (apart from the fact that it emerges within logic itself). It has already been justified in the other work, and would indeed not be capable of any other justification than is produced by consciousness as all its shapes dissolve into [*sich auflösen*] that concept as into their truth. (SL 21.32/28)

The *Phenomenology* is designed to examine consciousness, which is defined by an opposition of subject and object, starting from its most immediate conception of knowledge ("Sense-Certainty") and ending with the complete resolution of the subject-object dualism in AK. From this passage we can gather that the aspiration is to consider 'all the forms' of consciousness, so that in the end we have a *complete* and *comprehensive* overcoming of the opposition of subject and object. This is a justification of 'the *concept of science*', where Hegel means the Concept. (I will use Concept with a capital 'C' to refer to what Hegel also calls the concept of science or the absolute concept.) For our purposes, it is important to see that Hegel aims to reduce the separation or opposition in all shapes of consciousness to a basic *internal difference* or separation that is contained within the Concept itself. The shapes of consciousness are dissolved into, or resolved into, the basic form of conceptuality, which thus proves to be the *truth* of those shapes.

Hegel's deduction claim is that the Concept is the basis of a 'pure science' because it is the truth of all the shapes of consciousness, where this claim for justification can be cast in more epistemological terms as an anti-skeptical strategy for grounding knowledge. The *Phenomenology* overcomes the skepticism that one could have toward the identity of subject and object, thought and being, because every claim to knowledge of an object contrasted with the subject's knowledge proves to be dependent on a conceptual form common to both subject (thought) and object (being). In the second passage from the *Science of Logic*, he casts the *Phenomenology* in terms of *certainty* and truth:

> The concept of pure science and its deduction is therefore presupposed in the present work in so far as the *Phenomenology of Spirit* is nothing other than that deduction. Absolute knowledge is the *truth* of all the modes of consciousness because, as the course of the *Phenomenology* brought out, it is only in absolute knowledge that the separation of the *object* [*Gegenstandes*] from the *certainty of itself* is completely

---

[2] For a detailed inventory of the tasks of the *Phenomenology*, see Forster, *Hegel's Idea of a Phenomenology of Spirit*, Parts One and Two.

resolved [*sich aufgelöst hat*]: truth has become equal to certainty and this certainty to truth. (SL 21.33–34/29)

This passage casts absolute knowledge in the terms of the *Phenomenology* Introduction, where Hegel presented the process of consciousness 'testing' itself. The moment of the object is the moment of 'truth' or the 'in-itself' that is supposed to be independent of the subjective activity of consciousness, which Hegel identifies with the subject's 'certainty' or 'for-itself'. We can thus reformulate the trajectory of the *Phenomenology* as a path through every form of *limited* or *relative* truth, where each of those relative truths finds its ultimate truth in absolute knowledge. The main issue, then, is to understand how in absolute knowledge both certainty and truth are equal to each other *as the Concept*, and how absolute knowledge is thereby the truth of all the previous shapes. Absolute knowledge must contain the conceptual core of all the previous shapes, demonstrating that their objectivity (truth) and our knowledge of that objectivity (certainty) are united. How is this possible, and how did Hegel arrive at such a justificatory enterprise?

Hegel's project is deeply informed by the development of Kant's transcendental idealism in the hands of Reinhold and Fichte. Reinhold's 'principle of consciousness' and Fichte's 'self-positing I' are the precursors to Hegel's Concept. All three philosophers attempt to demonstrate that a *single* principle can provide a unified ground, immune to skeptical attacks, for all the branches of the idealist system that Kant had laid out but (in their view) had failed to properly ground. The issue of the unconditioned was central to Kant's attempt in the first *Critique* to provide *both* an account of knowledge of appearances (in the Transcendental Analytic) and a critique of the search for the unconditioned through thought alone (in the Transcendental Dialectic).[3] The Analytic showed that representations are conditioned by the unity of self-consciousness, but also that our conceptual knowledge is conditioned by the forms of sensible intuition. One can read Kant's attack on rationalism as saying that conceptual knowledge must be mediated by sensible intuition (and vice versa), so that we cannot attain knowledge of the unconditioned in the domain of theoretical knowledge.[4] The only genuine knowledge of the unconditioned comes from the practical side, in our knowledge of the moral law and our duties. But this leaves at least two dichotomies in Kant's system: (1) between sensible intuition and the concept, and (2) between the theoretical and practical domains. Kant himself suggested that freedom would be the master concept that provided the unity of the system, but it is hard to make out that unity from the rather baroque architecture of his system.

The philosophical system that Fichte developed in the 1790s, which has come to be known as the Jena *Wissenschaftslehre*, is the bridge from Kantian idealism to Hegel's system. I will focus on Hegel's difference from Fichte, but the positive influence on Hegel's project is deep and pervasive. Fichte had taken over from Reinhold the idea that

---

[3] See Kreines, "From Objectivity to the Absolute Idea in Hegel's *Logic*," Chapter 14 in this volume.

[4] On Kant's own definition of the term 'absolute' in Kant, *CPR*, see A324–326/B380–383. For a discussion of this passage in relation to AK, see Nuzzo, "The Truth of *Absolute Wissen*," 270–271.

one needed to start from a first principle, and he held that an original act of self-consciousness, a *Tathandlung* or fact-act, was the only possible candidate for such a first principle. This principle expressed the freedom or spontaneity of self-consciousness, while also including an original synthesis that could ground the *necessity* of our claims to knowledge of the objective world. Fichte held that only by starting from the subject could we hope to explain *both* our own activity as self-conscious beings *and* the objective world that we encounter outside of us. In his two famous 1797 Introductions to the *Wissenschaftslehre*, he argues that the only other possible philosophical system, which he thinks of as a *realist Spinozism*, seeks to explain everything starting from the domain of objects, but that it simply cannot explain freedom on that basis, and that it ends up endorsing a kind of *fatalism*. Fichte admits that there is a standoff of sorts between the two systems, with neither able to refute the other, but he argues that the idealist, subject-oriented system proves its superiority over the realist, substance-oriented system, because of its ability to explain human freedom. Opponents of Fichte's idealism will counter that any system that remains on the side of the subject cannot actually get beyond the domain of appearances limited by the subject's finite cognitive powers, and thus can never really comprehend substance.

Hegel's conception of philosophy as science, *Wissenschaft*, is quite similar to Fichte's, and Hegel's Concept is in fact rather similar to Fichte's self-positing 'I' if the latter is taken in logical rather than psychological terms. In the continuation of the second passage quoted earlier from *The Science of Logic*, Hegel actually goes on to write, "As *science*, truth is pure self-consciousness . . ." (SL 21.33/29), which indicates that he is taking the starting point of science proper to be the domain of pure thought conceived as pure self-consciousness.[5] But the whole *Phenomenology* is required to reach that point—a point at which the idealist system can commence without the specter of skepticism and without the admixture of psychological elements contained in Fichte's system. Hegel indicates in the Preface to the *Phenomenology* that the aim must be to overcome the standoff between subject-oriented idealism and substance-oriented realism. He writes, "In my view, which must be justified by the exposition of the system itself, everything hangs on apprehending and expressing the truth not as *substance* but also equally as *subject*" (PS 9.18/¶17). This point goes together with his holism, according to which the truth cannot be either subject or substance, conceived in an original way, but rather must be the whole that *results* from the dialectical interplay of the two. Hegel famously writes, "The true is the whole. However, the whole is only the essence completing itself through its own development. This much must be said of the absolute: It is essentially a *result*, and only at the *end* is it what it is in truth. Its nature consists precisely in this: To be actual, to be subject, that is, to be the becoming-of-itself" (PS 9.19/¶20). Hegel's language here gives us some indication of how in AK we complete the justification of the Concept by understanding how the Concept was at play all along in the earlier development. The

---

[5] See Pippin, *Hegel's Idealism*, for the classic account of Hegel's philosophy as focused on the theme of self-consciousness.

Concept is 'the essence completing itself', or the 'subject' that is 'the becoming-of-itself' through the process of overcoming the immediacy and externality of appearance.

Let me put the point once more in the terms of truth and certainty that Hegel uses in the Introduction to the *Phenomenology* and that he foregrounds in the passages from *The Science of Logic*. The process is a self-testing of the knowledge of consciousness in which that knowledge is compared by consciousness with the standard of truth, the 'in-itself', that consciousness has taken to be independent. The endpoint of this process comes when concept and object, certainty and truth, are no longer separate. We can see this as a deduction of self-consciousness (subject) as the ground of all objectivity insofar as the process aims to incorporate all of the in-itself or the 'real' (substance) within certainty or subjectivity. This movement is clear enough in the trajectory of the first three chapters, for those chapters culminate in 'inner difference', which he also identifies with 'infinity, the simple concept', and finally with self-consciousness. One might think, in fact, that the initial culmination at the end of Chapter III would already be absolute knowledge. If that conclusion really does show that the certainty of self-consciousness is equal to the truth of objectivity, why isn't this standpoint already absolute? The short answer is that the Concept has to be shown to be the truth not only of theoretical consciousness (Chapters I–III), but of *all* shapes of consciousness, which Hegel takes to include the ways in which we confront *each other* as natural beings and the way that we live with each other in social and religious institutions. The longer answer, as we shall see, is that we have to show that the practical world has replicated the structure of objectivity for self-consciousness itself, and that it has done so in actual history, rather than simply in an idealized reconstruction of experience.

8.2. Living with the Concept and Hegel's Ladder to Science

A curious feature of the above passages from *The Science of Logic* is that they make no reference to the specifically *practical* project carried out in much of the *Phenomenology* after Chapters I–III, and the project that dominates the actual text of AK. In this respect the passages follow the *Phenomenology* Introduction, which is a clear expression of the method but which was written with a less comprehensive project in view. Having completed the *Phenomenology*, with its long chapters on "Spirit" and "Religion," Hegel could in *The Science of Logic* have summed up absolute knowledge with a claim about the knowledge of ourselves *as free agents* who are not simply determinations of substance but are rather self-determining subjects. This not only would have shown that the *Phenomenology* aimed to overcome the standoff between Fichte and Spinoza, but also would have situated his project as an answer to Kant's split between *conditioned* theoretical objectivity and *unconditioned* but theoretically inaccessible practical freedom. I suspect that he thought that the comprehensive introduction to the system that he gave in the Preface to the *Phenomenology* dealt adequately with the practical and that the *Logic* should stick to theoretical matters. But I think that Hegel's argument in AK is in fact a response to the Fichtean and Kantian issues with freedom. The method of the *Phenomenology* Introduction does fit the expanded project, for one can include with *all* shapes of consciousness the ethical and religious attitudes toward the world. Hegel holds that science must be justified *to* the individual, *for* the individual, and the *Phenomenology* takes up this task for the entire extent of our conscious experience. In the end the *Phenomenology* is not just an epistemological text, but an ethical, political, and religious text as well, for those practical domains cannot be left out of the Concept's justification if the Concept is going to be accepted as the basis of their objectivity as well.

The famous passage in the Preface (written after AK) in which Hegel describes the *Phenomenology* as a ladder to science complements the two passages from *The Science of Logic* in emphasizing the justification of science to the epistemic subject *and* to the living, ethical agent. Hegel states the abstract principle of idealism—"[p]ure self-knowledge in absolute otherness," which I take to be a basic statement of the Concept as identity with otherness or difference. He continues,

> The beginning of philosophy presupposes or demands that consciousness feel at home in this element. However, this element itself has its culmination and its transparency only through the movement of its coming-to-be.... For its part, science requires that self-consciousness shall have elevated itself into this ether in order to be able to live—and [actually] to live—with science and in science. (PS 9.22–23/¶26)[6]

With this reference to life, Hegel already places the project of the *Phenomenology* on a practical plane and thus moves beyond the dynamics of 'Consciousness' explored in Chapters I–III. Indeed, he points us to the very first sections of Chapter IV in which he focuses on the concept of life and its relation to self-consciousness. Hegel's demand on the individual self-consciousness is complemented by a strong claim of the individual's right against the authority of philosophical science:

> Conversely, the individual has the right to demand that science provide him at least with the ladder to reach this standpoint. The individual's right is based on his absolute self-sufficiency, which he knows he possesses in every shape of his knowledge, for in every shape, whether recognized by science or not, and no matter what the content might be, the individual is at the same time the absolute form, that is, he possesses *immediate self-certainty*; and, if one were to prefer this expression, he thereby has an unconditioned *being*. (PS 9.23/¶26)

Hegel is emphasizing the individual I, saying that we cannot simply begin as Fichte did with a transcendental or universal I. When Hegel writes that the demand of "absolute self-sufficiency" is present "in every shape of his knowledge," he is saying that the challenge of reconciling the individual with the standpoint of science must be answered for

---

[6] I am adopting here Miller's translation of the very end of the passage.

the whole of science. In acknowledging the claim of the individual as that of 'uncondi-tioned being', Hegel is recognizing the claim of immediate self-consciousness *against* the pure mediation of the Concept. The 'element' of science expresses the complete mediation of the self through otherness and the otherness through the self, whereas the ordinary self-consciousness views itself as certain *over against* an independent world of objects.

Hegel acknowledges that the ordinary standpoint and the standpoint of science—which we can identify with the standpoints of naïve realism and philosophical idealism—seem to be the opposite of each other. He writes, "Each of these two parts seems to the other to be the inversion of the truth" (PS 9.23/¶26). He emphasizes that philosophical science must demonstrate that the realistic standpoint is implicated in the ideal, and that the idealist standpoint can account for the real. He is describing the task of the *Phenomenology* as the task of uniting natural consciousness and science:

> Science may be in itself what it will, but in its relationship to immediate self-consciousness it presents itself as an inversion of the latter, or, because immediate self-consciousness is the principle of actuality, and since, for itself, immediate self-consciousness exists outside of science, science takes the form of non-actuality. Accordingly, science has to unite that element with itself or to a greater degree to show both that such an element belongs to itself and how it belongs to itself. Lacking actuality, science is the *in-itself*, the *purpose*, which at the start is still something *inner*, which exists at first not as spirit but only as spiritual substance. Science has to express itself and become for itself, and this means nothing else than that science has to posit self-consciousness as one with [science] itself. (PS 9.23/¶26)

For philosophy, the opposition of subject and object is the loss of spirit, since spirit is defined (in an idealist manner) as the unity of subject and object. But for *consciousness*, a 'scientific' standpoint that bars consciousness from contrasting itself with objects, a standpoint in which objects were logically defined rather than given in immediate rep-resentation, would be a spectral world without actuality. Science says that "everything has its truth in the Concept" and "everything is conditioned by the Concept." Immediate self-consciousness thinks that these claims are ridiculous (because there just is a hard external world) and undesirable since they seem to take authority from the individual experiencer. The solution is to show that self-consciousness not only *is* the Concept—which is essentially Fichte's claim—but also that the *actuality* of the individual self and her world is already secured through the Concept.

In the preceding passage Hegel seems to equate 'natural consciousness' and 'self-consciousness', and this is confusing because, as I mentioned, the goal seems to be to show how consciousness is led through its own internal dialectic *to* self-conscious-ness. The key point here is that in the preceding passage Hegel is talking about *imme-diate* self-consciousness, which he also describes as "knowing itself to be opposed to [objective things]." He is taking realistic consciousness and realistic (or immediate) *self-*consciousness as part of *the same initial standpoint* that is to be elevated to science. The task of the *Phenomenology*, then, is to show *both* that the objects (that are putatively opposed to the subject) are in fact a function of conceptual mediation, *and* that the putatively immediate self-consciousness is in fact a *conceptually mediated self-consciousness*. This means that after showing that consciousness is dependent upon self-consciousness, Hegel then will need to show that self-consciousness is not immediate self-certainty, but rather is constituted by relations to other self-consciousnesses *through practical activity*. From his initial claim that "self-consciousness is *desire* in general" (PS 9.104/¶167) to his claim toward the end of "Spirit" that the language of moral conscience is "self-consciousness existing *for others*" (PS 9.351/¶652), Chapters IV–VI portray self-consciousness objectifying itself through practical activity. In this progression, Hegel shows that the conceptual mediations of consciousness and self-consciousness *are the same*, have the same structure. He thus shows that consciousness (in the narrow sense as the relation to objects outside of us) and self-consciousness (as our relation to our own activity) both take the form of the Concept and thus are "posited as one" with science.

Once we appreciate how consciousness (in the narrow sense) is standing in for the theoretical domain and self-consciousness is standing in for the practical domain, we are in a good position to see how absolute knowledge is supposed to accomplish the unity of the theoretical and practical. In AK, Hegel summarizes the unity as "the reconciliation of spirit with its own genuine [*eigentlichen*] consciousness" (PS 9.424/¶793) and as "[t]his reconciliation of consciousness with self-consciousness" (PS 9.425/¶794). I will argue in the next two sections that these summary statements are meant to show that with absolute knowledge the domains of theoretical reason and practical reason are united. Hegel develops consciousness into an objective totality of conditions governed by the Concept (what I call 'inferential objectivity'); self-consciousness and spirit are reconciled *with consciousness* in that they have produced an ethical world in which that same structure—of an objective totality of conditions—is embodied in the actions of ethical individuals. To know this ethical world as meeting the criterion of full objectivity, and to see how it thus achieves the aspirations of religion, is to have absolute knowledge.

8.3. OVERCOMING THE OBJECT

Hegel describes the main task of AK as following from a certain deficiency in the Chapter VII account of "Religion." While celebrating Christianity as the 'absolute religion', Hegel argues that there remains a gulf between religious consciousness and the world. For religious consciousness "actuality is still broken" (PS 9.42/ ¶787), and the 'reconciliation' of the human and the divine is only in the 'heart' (PS 9.42/ ¶787), rather than being an object for consciousness, an actuality present to consciousness. This divide should have been overcome in Christianity, since the idea of God becoming man and being unified in the Holy Spirit does involve a transfiguration of the world and of our relation to it. But the form of religious practice, as worship and feeling rather than as knowing, contradicts this content.[7] Hegel writes that moving beyond religion will require "sublating [*Aufheben*] the form of objectivity" or the "overcoming [*Überwindung*] of the object of consciousness" (PS 9.422/¶788). The form of objectivity is none other than the objectivity developed in Chapters I–III, and Hegel sets out to overcome it by recapitulating how the same structure is reproduced in a practical mode, *as* and *for* self-consciousness, in Chapters V and VI. The idea is that by showing that "the form of objectivity" has *already* been overcome in reason and spirit *for the subject*, we can leave behind the brokenness of the religious point of view because we will know the divine *in the world*.

Viewing the main account in "Absolute Knowledge" as the uniting of the theoretical account of Chapters I–III with the practical account of Chapters V–VI raises an obvious question: What role does the famous Chapter IV account of self-consciousness play in the unification of the theoretical and practical? Many commentators have rightly viewed that chapter's account of desire and the master-servant struggle as a turning point in the *Phenomenology*, so it stands as one of the great puzzles of AK that Hegel leaves out exactly that chapter, and that one alone, from his recapitulation.[8] Yet when we look closely at Hegel's opening description of the task of "Absolute Knowing," we see that he *does* address the end of Chapter III and the achievement of Chapter IV before he describes the movement we have to recollect from Chapters V and VI. He writes,

> The overcoming of the object of consciousness is not to be taken one-sidedly, that is, as showing that the object is returning into the self. Rather, it is to be taken more determinately, namely, that the object as such was exhibited to consciousness to be as much in the act of vanishing as, to a greater degree, the alienation of self-consciousness turned out to be what posits thinghood.[9] This alienation has not only a negative meaning but a positive one as well, and not only for us, that is, in itself, but also for self-consciousness itself. (PS 9.422/¶788)

The first sentence tells us that we cannot simply read the end of Chapter III, in which the object returns into the self, as sufficient for overcoming the object. The next sentence describes the movement of Chapter IV in which the object is exhibited "in the act of vanishing." He had portrayed this vanishing in IV.B in the shapes of skepticism, stoicism, and the unhappy consciousness. The first main move from alienation to positing

---

[7] There is a good description of this by Mitchell Miller, Jr.: "the subject as religious knower remains opposed to what, through religious knowledge, he knows himself to be" (Miller, "The Attainment of the Absolute Standpoint," 429).

[8] Allegra de Laurentiis argues the 'self-consciousnss' in Chapter IV is already a kind of absolute knowledge. See de Laurentiis, "Absolute Knowing."

[9] *Entäußerung* is especially difficult to translate. Most of the time the bland 'externalization' fits, but it does not convey the fact that it is *self-consciousness* that is active in this way. In the *Philosophy of Right* it is usually translated as 'alienation' in the sense that one can alienate a piece of property. In the current passage the deficiency of 'externalization' is obvious if you consider that Hegel is assuming that the natural reading of *Entäußerung* is for it to have a 'negative meaning.'

'thinghood' happens when the individual of medieval Christianity alienates himself completely in relation to God, but also (through the mediating activity of the priest) prepares the way for the positing of thinghood in the practice of 'observing reason'. The turn to 'Reason' *is* the turn from alienation having a negative meaning to alienation having a positive meaning. The move *within* Reason from a theoretical posture to a practical posture, from Reason A to Reason B, is the move to having positive meaning 'for self-consciousness itself'.

Let me back up a moment, though, to say a few more words on the theory-practice relation in Chapter IV and the transition to 'Reason'. There remains much disagreement about the import of Hegel's introduction of practical themes at the outset of the Chapter IV account of 'Self-consciousness'.[10] Hegel identifies self-consciousness with *desire* and with *life*, gives a detailed description of the intersubjective structure of mutual recognition necessary for the *satisfaction* of self-consciousness, and then portrays a struggle to the death between two agents that ends in the master-servant relation and a discussion of the significance of the servant's *work*. By contrast, much of the second part of the chapter (titled "Freedom of Self-Consciousness") returns to relatively familiar epistemological issues dealt with by the ancient stoics and skeptics. But in the 'unhappy consciousness' section, and the transition to 'Reason', we are forced to confront the *relevance* of the practical themes to the epistemological issue of skepticism, and how the complete alienation of the medieval Christian individual eventuates in the modern conception of theoretical, 'observing' rationality. My view, which I can only give here in slogan form, is that the chapter makes sense when we take self-consciousness to be from the beginning essentially *evaluative*.[11]

Hegel presents immediate self-consciousness at the opening of Chapter IV as desire, and if we disentangle this move from the many layers in which it is embedded, we can notice that it picks up on the fundamental ambiguity in the *object of desire*: Do we desire an object because it is good, or is it good because we desire it? Initially all that self-consciousness knows is that it must unite the object with itself, but the goodness of what is desired can only be a relatively opaque question mark. The only clearly good object is one that possesses the unifying capacity itself, namely another self-consciousness. In the master-servant relation that results from the clash between these two over who sets the standard of goodness, the servant's work is more significant than the master's dominance because in the formative activity of work one actually 'posits thinghood'. The big move from IV.A to IV.B is that the standard for the object is set by *thought*. This move is exemplified by the Stoic sage who is confident in his evaluation of the world. As Hegel writes, "Consciousness is the thinking essence and that something only has essentiality for consciousness, or is true and good for it, insofar as consciousness conducts itself

---

[10] See Jenkins, "Self-Consciousness in the *Phenomenology*," Chapter 4 in this volume.
[11] This is not too far from Charles Taylor's claim that Hegel's key insight is that we are 'self-interpreting' animals. But by putting the emphasis on evaluation rather than interpretation, I think we get a clearer sense of the continuity of the theoretical and practical.

therein as a thinking creature" (PS 9.117/¶198). But what, then, of the claim at the end of Chapter IV that the practices of self-denial of the Christian supplicant flip the alienation of self-consciousness over into the positive meaning of Reason? How does the giving up of one's own evaluative capacities to God, one's declaration of one's utter dependence, pave the way for Reason? The religious *practice* is supposed to have serious implications for the grounding of the *observational* sciences that we recognize as distinctive of the modern period. My claim is that the standpoint of the immediate evaluative individual is important throughout Chapter IV. Medieval Christianity is especially important because in it the immediate individual gives up his individual evaluative standpoint (which was still the basic locus of evaluation in stoicism and skepticism), and simultaneously invests a universal priestly class with the role of interpreting the world as it is. Religion in this sense helps the individual get out of his own way, so to speak, by getting him to devalue his desiring power and formative powers and even this thinking powers (insofar as those thinking powers lead to a denial of the world's reality). The priests are the forerunners of the modern natural scientists who have the goal of comprehending God's creation.

Hegel's summary of the lessons of Chapter IV when he introduces 'Reason' sheds a good deal of light on the rather cryptic commentary on 'Reason' in AK. The introductory paragraphs of 'Reason' are also important for AK because in them Hegel reflects on the moves that have led to a standpoint that he identifies with 'idealism'. He clearly aligns this view with Kantian and Fichtean idealism and to some extent with his own ultimate position. In a passage that is echoed in the AK claim for 'positive meaning', Hegel writes of the achievement of the standpoint of Reason that it has overcome the merely negative stance to otherness:

> Since self-consciousness is reason, what had so far been its negative relation to otherness is now converted into a positive relation. Until now it had occupied itself only with its self-sufficiency and its freedom in order to save and preserve itself for itself at the cost of the *world* or its own actuality, both of which appeared to it as the negative of its own essence. However, as reason assured of itself, it has come to be at rest with regard to both of them, and it can sustain them, for it is certain of itself as being reality. That is, it is certain that all actuality is nothing but itself, that its thought itself is immediately actuality, and it is therefore as idealism that it conducts itself in relation to actuality. (PS, 9.132/¶232)

This close identity of truth and certainty may look rather solipsistic in its certainty, but the opposite is the case.[12] The achievement of Reason is that it can let the world be, not have to consume it or form it or fight it in order to find unity with it. In evaluative terms, we can say that in Reason the world is good as an independent object to be discovered through observation. The certainty is a confidence that the world is intelligible to us. That the world is *open to* comprehension is the claim of Reason, but Reason does not aim to

---

[12] See Bristow, "Reason, Self-Transcendence, and Modernity in Hegel's *Phenomenology*," Chapter 5 in this volume.

project itself into the world, or set itself up as a standard *against* the world. Hegel formulates the 'positive meaning' in terms of *interest*:

> Since self-consciousness grasps itself in this way, in its own eyes it is as if the world had only now come to be for it for the first time. Formerly, self-consciousness did not understand the world; it desired it and worked on it, withdrew itself from it, took an inward turn back into itself away from it, and abolished the world for itself and itself as consciousness . . . self-consciousness discovers here for the first time the world as *its* newly actual world. In its continuing existence, this world **interests** it in the way it previously was only interested in the world's disappearance, for that world's *durable existence* comes to be in its eyes its own *truth* and *present moment*, and self-consciousness is certain that it experiences only itself within it. (PS 9.132–133/¶232, my bold)

Even with this claim, though, we have reached 'the positive meaning' only for consciousness, not for 'self-consciousness itself', in the initial phase of 'Observing Reason'. The passive stance of observation becomes explicitly self-conscious of the world as the world posited *by it* only with the transition to 'active reason', an explicitly practical stance that brings back the structure of desire and recognition from the opening of Chapter IV.

The task of 'overcoming the object' is thus a task of showing that our world, the world that expresses our freedom, does not fall short of objectivity. We achieve evaluative objectivity through acting in an ethical world that has the same structure or form as the gold standard of objectivity that was deduced in Chapters I–III. In AK, Hegel presents this overcoming as having already happened, and he recollects the moments of the practical activity of self-consciousness and spirit from Reason B through the end of Spirit. But what does it really mean to think of a practical form of objectivity that would parallel the theoretical form of objectivity? As I read it, Hegel's goal is to show how ethical activity (in a broad sense) leads to practical knowledge with the same form or structure of objectivity as the (already deduced) knowledge of the material world. As *active* or *practical*, the object in question has to be a *purpose*, an action that is subject to a criterion of successful realization, rather than confirmation by evidence. To continue the parallel with theoretical knowing, whose object is the *truth*, the object of ethical activity is *the good*, or *valuable action*. This switch to value is easy to miss, but Hegel does point us toward his conception of value in the tricky final sentence of the opening paragraph of "Absolute Knowledge." He writes, "This totality of its determinations makes the *object in itself* into a spiritual essence, and for consciousness, it becomes this in truth through the act of apprehending each of its individual determinations as a determination of the self, that is, through the spiritual conduct mentioned above" (PS 9.422/¶788). I take the 'spiritual essence' claim to be a reference to the end of Reason C.a., where Hegel introduces the 'spiritual essence' (9.227/¶418) in connection with the 'honest consciousness' (9.225/¶414) and 'the thing that matters [*die Sache selbst*]' (PS 9.223/¶409). I understand that earlier version of the spiritual essence as a conception of value that arises through a social process in which the agent learns that the meaning of her action depends on a world of value that she cannot manipulate at will.[13]

Even with this framing in terms of practical value, one might still wonder in analyzing the task of AK what happened to the Chapter IV account of intersubjectivity, of mutual recognition. I think that Hegel claims that the world of value is a social product, and the alienation of self-consciousness is a social process, but also that we should be able to give a structural account of social reality that focuses on the object of action rather than on the intersubjective processes that condition the action. Part of the reason for this goes back to the ladder passage and the need to demonstrate *to* the individual self-consciousness. The whole thrust of the account is to demonstrate the dependence of the individual on the social, but the justification still has to work *for the individual*. In this respect my interpretation is somewhat different from Terry Pinkard's influential 'social' reading of the *Phenomenology*. Pinkard holds that Hegel is talking about 'communal self-reflection' in AK, namely about the self-grounding character of the social practices that have developed in modernity.[14] I am sympathetic to this reading, but I think that for comprehending Hegel's exact moves it is important to put some distance between sociality or recognition, on the one hand, and the account of practical objectivity that he is reconstructing, on the other. I think that the theme of recognition is elided in the opening statement of AK (though not in the full recapitulation, as we shall see) because Hegel is focused on the practical *object*, which he gives—right up until the very end of his recapitulation—in terms abstracted from the intersubjective struggle over the meaning of the object. His account of value and his account of recognition are deeply intertwined, but by focusing on value we can get a more detailed sense of just how Hegel thinks that theoretical reason and practical reason are united. It is by replicating the structure of the true in the structure of the good that modern social practices attain their absolute status. By *knowing* the absolute content (which religion also possessed) as achieved by human, self-conscious agents, we will know the absolute content in the absolute *form* of the Concept. By stressing the role of value in this knowing, I aim to highlight the ethical character of knowledge and philosophy for Hegel.

---

[13] Contrary to my reading of this opening paragraph, H. S. Harris has argued that the description of the 'movement of consciousness' quoted earlier must be seen "as a review only of the *repetition* of the whole journey on the part of 'the Infinite' in chapter VII." Harris claims that this passage is unintelligible without assuming that the prior description is a recapitulation of the shapes of 'Religion': "For it is only after Chapter VI (*Spirit*) that the consciousness we are observing can have a *spiritual* relationship to its 'determinations'" (Harris, *Hegel's Ladder*, vol. 2, 713).

[14] "Absolute knowledge is *absolute* in that it has no 'object' external to itself that mediates it in the way the natural world mediates the claims of natural science. Absolute *knowledge* is thus the way in which absolute *spirit* articulates itself in modern life; it is the practice through which the modern community thinks about itself without attempting to posit any metaphysical 'other' or set of 'natural constraints' that would underwrite those practices. Absolute knowledge is the internal reflection on the social practices of a modern community that takes its authoritative standards to come only from within the structure of the practices it uses to legitimate and authenticate itself" (Pinkard, *Hegel's Phenomenology*, 262).

|

8.4. Inferential Objectivity in Theory and Practice

As we saw at the outset, Hegel claims that the *Phenomenology* is a justification of the concept of science because in it all the shapes of consciousness "dissolve into [*sich auflösen*] that concept as into their truth" (SL 21.32/28). The Concept can be expressed in a simple form, as when Hegel identifies it with 'infinity', or in *The Science of Logic* when he identifies its three moments as universality, particularity, and individuality. But the whole movement that Hegel lays out in AK is premised on *not* taking the Concept in its simplicity, but rather taking it in its expanded 'form of objectivity'.[15] The form of objectivity must be an expression of the Concept in order for Hegel's various claims about absolute knowledge to hold together. On my reading, this form of objectivity is best captured in Hegel's description of it as an *inferential whole* or a set of inferences linking together the moments of universality, particularity/determinacy, and individuality.[16] In this section I go through Hegel's recapitulation of the theoretical version of this form and the initial recapitulation of the practical form. Only in recognizing that this *expanded* version of the Concept is the 'truth' of the earlier shapes can we fully appreciate the positive achievement of the *Phenomenology*.

8.4.1. The Recapitulation of Theoretical Objectivity

The first three 'moments' in Hegel's theoretical description of the form of objectivity are a fairly straightforward presentation of the first three chapters. Each of those chapters is oriented by a single capacity (the senses, perception, the understanding) and a limited conception of the object. Each shape of consciousness takes itself to be complete, and each shape is undone by challenges that expose its limitations. But the *logical core* of each of these shapes is retained in the ultimate form of objectivity; each form of *judgment* retains a limited validity for constituting objectivity.[17] He writes of the first, "The

---

[15] When one compares AK to "C. Die Wissenschaft," a striking difference is that AK renders the object as an inferential whole whereas "C. Die Wissenschaft" is concerned only with the simple Concept.

[16] In focusing here (and in my essay "The Inferential Object") on the inference, I am concurring with the main thrust of the interpretation of Hegel by Robert Brandom. See especially Brandom, *Tales of the Mighty Dead*, Chapter 6. One of the few other scholars to pick up on the importance of the inference for AK is Allegra de Laurentiis. She writes, "To investigate the dynamic structure of an object of thinking by abstracting from its temporal or developmental features, according to Hegel, is tantamount to investigating its 'logic.' This is analogous to the way in which we think of an inference as opposed to the psychological event of inferring: an inference is an atemporal process despite the fact that the term does refer to a flow or 'movement' of thought. If, now, the object of thinking is thought itself, their dynamic structure or logic will be one and the same" (De Laurentiis, "Absolute Knowing," 250; see also 254–255).

[17] I have analyzed the first three chapters in terms of judgment and inference in Moyar, "The Inferential Object."

object is therefore in part *immediate* being, that is, a thing per se, something which corresponds to immediate consciousness" (PS 9.422/¶789). The account begins with the immediate sensing of individuals, and while Hegel's main goal in "Sense-Certainty" is to show that such immediacy must give way to mediation and universality, the 'thinghood' that we associate with spatiotemporal individuals is preserved. In the second phase, Hegel focuses on 'the thing of many properties' (PS 9.71/¶112), which he associates with perceptual understanding's attempt to stabilize the thing in its determinate relations to other things and properties. He writes of this second moment, "In part, it is a coming-to-be-the-other of itself, its relation, that is, *being for an other* and *being-for-itself*, the determinateness which corresponds to *perception*" (PS 9.422/¶789). At the end of "Perception" Hegel shows that the perceptual object on its own perishes from the contradiction inherent in its dual status as self-related and related to others. The downfall of perception leads to the idea of a supersensible ground, or essence, that Hegel associates closely with natural scientific laws of force. In AK he writes, "in part, it is *essence*, that is, the universal which corresponds to the understanding" (PS 9.422–423/¶789). The end of Chapter III is among the most difficult parts of the book, but Hegel's critique of the concepts of law and the kind of explanation that goes with it is fairly clear. He thinks that laws that are generalized from observations do not actually do much more than restate the observational phenomena in which those laws are expressed. The restatement through universal laws *is* important for Hegel, but he thinks that it is not sufficient for determining actual individual objects.

At the end of Chapter III, Hegel introduces 'the simple infinity or the absolute concept' (PS 9.99/¶162) as the conceptual core of the previous shapes. In light of what he says in his recapitulation of this move in AK, we can see that the absolute concept (= the Concept) is supposed to capture the *complete* form of objectivity because it is what ties together the *inferences* that form the whole of the determinations of the object. The Concept determines objects not simply as an abstract universality or unity, but through a specific *inferential form of objectivity*. That form unites the three main discrete moments of the Concept, such that objectivity is a totality of conditions inferentially articulated through the Concept.[18] In the definitive restatement of the achievement of Chapters I–III, Hegel describes the 'object as a whole' in this way in "Absolute Knowledge":

> The object as a whole is the inference or the movement of the universal through determination to individuality, as also the reverse movement from individuality through individuality as sublated, or through determination, to the universal. (PS 9.423/¶789)

This is supposed to capture both the sense in which universal laws determine individuals and the way in which individuals in concrete circumstances determine the nature of the laws themselves (the role of law-constituting individuals is easier to see in the Supreme Court than in the physics laboratory). Hegel thinks he has achieved in a single

---

[18]   See Rand, Chapter 17 in this volume, for how this model informs the philosophy of nature.

activity of reciprocal determination the *compression* of the Concept and the *expansion* of the conceptual that can account for complex systems. What becomes much clearer in the account of objectivity in *The Science of Logic*, as well as in the practical version that we are about to see, is that this form of objectivity is a *standard*, a *normative* conception of what an object has to be in order to be a self-determining whole. His full model is life, the organic (as he says already in ¶162), a self-sustaining and self-reproducing whole.

Hegel's doctrine of the inference is less exotic than it seems, for it is an expanded version of the idea of *definition through conditionals*. We can ask, what determines this object as a knife? It is the kind of object that *if* you were to bring its blade down onto this apple, *then* it would cut it in half. *If* you were to run your finger across its edge, *then* you would bleed. This thing, the individual knife, *relates* to other things, such as fruit, through the act of cutting, such that if there were a world in which it did not relate to other things in that way (in which nothing could be cut), it would not be the knife that it is. The general conditionals that we state of the knife are its 'essence': "*if* it is brought with certain force at a certain angle against material of a certain quality, *then* it will cut that material." When it is dull enough that this conditional no longer holds, it will cease to meet the normative standard of knifehood. This individual knife has *proven itself* in practice (as an inference from individual to universal), but we can also subsume it under the universal character of knifehood (the inference from universal to individual). Hegel likes to use the example of criminal action to illustrate the kind of inferential whole he is getting at here (see PS 9.98/¶159). A knife can also be used to stab someone. Shifting examples, we can think not of the consequences to the material cut by the knife, but of the consequences to the individual wielding the knife, whose action is defined in part by the laws that determine the punishment (the consequences) of the crime.

8.4.2. The Recapitulation of the Practical

Hegel's recapitulation of the practical is highly selective and does not map neatly onto the main stages of Reason or Spirit. The first moment is in some ways the trickiest, for with it Hegel aims to summarize the "Reason" chapter and set it into relation to the "Spirit" chapter.[19] According to this recapitulation, the pivotal moment is the transition from observing reason to 'active reason' (Reason B), for it is in that transition that the alienation's negative meaning first takes on a "positive meaning for self-consciousness itself." The negative meaning of this alienation is the case of the pseudoscience of phrenology (reading character from the bumps on one's skull), the turning of self-consciousness (character) into a thing (the skull bone). Hegel interprets phrenology as forfeiting and

---

[19] There is a case to be made that Hegel's reconstruction of this first moment is partly a hangover from the earlier plan of the book; "Observing Reason" is the one moment that is mentioned in "C. Die Wissenschaft" (PS 9.439), which was probably written for the end of the "Reason" chapter before Hegel decided to expand the book by adding the "Spirit" and "Religion" chapters. See Förster, *The Twenty-five Years of Philosophy*, for the argument that "C. Die Wissenschaft" was originally written for the end of "Reason."

externalizing self-consciousness, but also as leading to the move that *invests* thinghood *with* self-consciousness. Self-consciousness engages in pseudo-science in phrenology, alienating itself to try to bring the study of character into the form of rational science, to reach self-understanding with the tools of observational anatomical science. But in the reversal that leads to Reason B, the objectifying of self-consciousness is inverted such that what *counts as real* is henceforth the world as it presents itself to human *agents*.[20] In Hegel's recapitulation, the switch is from a theoretical, pseudo-scientific understanding of self-consciousness *as an object*, to a practical self-understanding of the objective world as subordinate to, a context for, free action. That is, the world is reappropriated at the higher level of practical reason.

Hegel's statements about the first moment in AK are obscure enough to warrant looking to the transitional text itself to see why he accords it such importance. In the opening paragraph of "The Actualization of Rational Self-Consciousness Through Itself" (Reason B), Hegel thematizes 'objectivity' in a way that clearly prefigures the AK discussion:

> Self-consciousness found the thing as itself and itself as a thing [*das Ding als sich, und sich als Ding*]; i.e., *it is for self-consciousness* that it is *in itself* objective actuality. . . . it is the kind of certainty for which the immediate as such has the form of what has been sublated, and it has been sublated in such a way that the *objectivity* of the immediate now counts as the merely superficial, whose innerness and essence is *self-consciousness itself*. (PS 9.193/¶347)

The 'merely superficial' character of the objectivity (an indication that we here witness a key move in the overcoming of the object) is the transformation of an observed physical object into an evaluatively loaded context for meaningful action. The skull bone had been used to make claims about the potential action of the person (e.g., whether or not he might be a criminal), and while Hegel finds these claims absurd, he thinks that phrenology prepares the way for the decisive reversal to thinking of the physical world as a function of the evaluative. The point that Hegel emphasizes here, and that he suppresses somewhat in his recapitulation, is that this first moment is the rendering of objectivity into a social, ethical register. He continues,

> Hence the object to which self-consciousness positively relates itself is a self-consciousness. The object is in the form of thinghood, i.e., it is *self-sufficient*. However, self-consciousness has the certainty that for it this self-sufficient object is nothing alien. It thereby knows that it is *in itself* recognized by the object. Self-consciousness is *spirit* that has the certainty of having its unity with itself in the doubling of its self-consciousness and in the self-sufficiency of both self-consciousnesses. (PS 9.193/¶347)

---

[20] Hegel references the scene in which Hamlet considers the skull of Yorick, the former court jester, in order to bring out the duality of Spirit as a bone and Spirit as a living, active individual (PS 9.184/¶333). See Harris, *Hegel*, 54.

Here Hegel clearly turns back to the issue of recognition, the intersubjective moment in which subjects identify with the object insofar as the object is another subject. The introduction to Reason B goes on to discuss ethical life and its immediacy, so that what is now objective is the happy ethical life of a free people. This highlights one of the odd structural features of the book, namely that the happy ethical life of the Greeks is thematized *both* at the beginning of Reason B and in Spirit A. For our purposes, one lesson is that Hegel is attempting in AK to include the "Reason" chapter within his recapitulation for the sake of the unity of the book as a whole; but we should also bear in mind that one can read Hegel's practical recapitulation as replaying the three main sections of "Spirit" itself. In the second moment of the practical recapitulation, Hegel jumps ahead to the discussion of the Enlightenment in the "Spirit" chapter. His reference to phrenology thus reads as a somewhat awkward attempt to get the "Reason" chapter into the overall recapitulation. Hegel's recapitulation would have been more straightforward if he had mapped the theoretical form of objectivity onto the "Spirit" chapter, for as it stands the first moment is located in Reason B, whereas the second, third, and comprehensive final moment are located in Spirit B and C. Once we appreciate the proximity of the first moment of the recapitulation to the first shape of "Spirit," Hegel's move in AK to the *second moment* of the recapitulation is less jarring. We see that he could have identified the first moment with Greek immediate ethical life, and the immediate ethical individual, and then moved to the alienation of culture and onto utility.

The second moment of objectivity brings out even more clearly Hegel's switch to a world of value, for he invokes a parallel between the theoretical shape of perception and the practical shape of *utility* that arises from the self-alienated culture of pre-revolutionary France. Announcing the transition from the first recapitulated moment to the second, he writes, "The thing is nothing in itself; it only has any meaning in relationships, only *by virtue of the I* and *its relation* to the I" (PS 9.423/¶791). Utility is the form of the good that represents "the truth of the Enlightenment" (PS 9.311/¶574). Like the object of perception, the object of utility is a unity through relation, in practical terms a purpose *defined as good* through a determinate benefit *for* another. In the world of utility, something is good because it is useful *for* someone or *for* some other end. In his treatment of utility, Hegel writes of a sense of loss when the world is disenchanted by the Enlightenment, once the intrinsic goodness of the world has fallen to instrumental rationality. Hegel calls this shape 'the *unsatisfied* Enlightenment' (PS 9.310/¶573), which is a version of the claim that the object has disappeared for consciousness but only with a negative meaning. The full-blown shape of utility arises once that sense of loss is itself lost, and utility takes on a positive meaning *for self-consciousness itself* (PS 9.314/¶579). This is the moment he identifies in his recapitulation with the moment of relation in objectivity; it is a conception of the good that has resulted from the alienation of self-consciousness in culture and from the struggle of modern science with religion. One might wonder if the concept of 'utility' is really fit to play this pivotal role in Hegel's account. We should recall, however, the momentous pronouncements that surround this move. In relation to religion, Hegel writes that in the victory of utility over faith, "Both worlds are reconciled, and heaven is transplanted to the earth below" (PS 9.316/

¶581), with the result that the modern world is characterized by practical rather than religious metaphysics.[21] Like the perceptual object, utility is ultimately contradictory, for the identity of the purpose 'for-itself' dissolves into the relations 'for another', with the result that nothing has value any longer unless it can be grounded in the universal will.

The third moment in Hegel's practical recapitulation is 'universality'. In the spiritual domain, this moment comes on the scene first with the general will of the French Revolution, but in Hegel's official recapitulation it is definitively represented by the will as the inner ground of action in the Kantian moral worldview (PS 9.424/¶792). For Kant the good is defined through the universal moral law; the unconditionally good will is the will that wills universality for the sake of universality. Of course this is not all that Kant has to say about the good, and Hegel had engaged since his student days with Kant's treatment of the Highest Good. Hegel ultimately thinks that Kant's attempts to reincorporate the ends of happiness into the moral picture through the idea of the Highest Good lead to a shifty moral stance that he calls 'dissemblance [*die Verstellung*]'. The problem arises because action is supposed to have value solely through the motive of duty, and yet finite ends are also supposed to get into the picture because we are beings who are necessarily oriented by the drive for happiness. Hegel's basic charge is that Kant has no way to stabilize the relationship between the moral value based on duty and the ordinary value based on happiness.

The hero of Hegel's practical recapitulation is, somewhat surprisingly, a version of post-Kantian *conscience*. With his new conception of conscience, one derived from Fichte's but differing in important ways, Hegel thinks he has achieved a holistic conception of practical reason that can stabilize the relationship between duty and interest, between objective and subjective value. Much of the confusion around AK stems from the dialectical complexity of Hegel's treatment of conscience in the "Spirit" chapter, for it seems incredible that Hegel would celebrate conscience in AK when he had strongly critiqued it earlier in the text. Yet in his recapitulation of the productive alienation of self-consciousness, Hegel follows the presentation of the three individual moments (corresponding to the three individual moments of the object) with an emphatic statement of the place of conscience as the completion of the form of objectivity:

> As conscience, it finally no longer switches back and forth between taking a position, then hedging about its position, and then dissembling about existence and the self. Rather, it knows that its *existence* as such is this pure certainty of itself. The objective element into which it injects itself [*sich hinausstellt*] when it acts, is nothing but the self's pure knowledge of itself.

---

[21] "In fact, what is now present is nothing more than an empty semblance of objectivity which separates self-consciousness from possession. In part this is so because all the durable existence and validity of the determinate members of the organization of the actual world and the world of faith have, as such, returned into this simple determination as their ground and their spirit, but in part it is because this objectivity possesses nothing more of its own for itself, and it is now to an even greater degree pure metaphysics, the pure concept or knowledge of self-consciousness" (PS 9.316/¶583).

These are the moments out of which the reconciliation of spirit with its own genuine consciousness composes itself. For themselves, those moments are individual,
and it is their spiritual unity alone which constitutes the force of this reconciliation.
However, the last of these moments is necessarily this unity itself, and, as elucidated
[*wie erhellt*], it in fact combines them all into itself. Spirit certain of itself within its
existence has as the element of its *existence* nothing but this knowledge of itself, that
is, nothing but its articulation [*Aussprechen*] that what it does, it does out of the conviction of duty, and that this, its language, is *what makes* its action *count as valid*. (PS
9.424/¶¶792–793)

Hegel's claim that conscience is the 'spiritual unity' of the moments is a reference especially to ¶641 (PS 9.345), in which Hegel described conscience as the 'negative essence'
of the earlier moments.[22] The conscience that Hegel refers to here is a complex whole
of determinate factors, not simply a feeling of certainty about my duty. Conscience
includes the moment of *recognition* by others and the moment of utility that Hegel conceives as a specific purpose or interest of the subject. It also includes the universality of
the Kantian moral law, but as a holistic process of deliberation that results in a specific
action, conscience is recognized and thus not guilty of the empty formalism of the moral
law.[23] In the earlier dialectic of conscience, Hegel had derived the *language of conscience*
from the initial indeterminacy of the holism of conscience, from the fact that its spiritual unity could conceal a tendency to favor self-interest over the universality of duty.

So how is Hegel's agent of conscience the holistic embodiment of the inferential objectivity that sets the standard for theoretical reason? Rather than an ordinary physical
object or physical system, the practical object is the object of intentional action, the *purpose* that one intends to carry out as an ethical agent. The action is an individual event
in space and time, but what really constitutes the action is the thinking—along with its
inferential form—that goes into the deliberation of which the action is the conclusion
(bracketing for the moment the important issue of the actual reception of the action by
others). In elevating conscience to the level of the holistic conclusion of the ethical form
of objectivity, Hegel is actually assuming quite a lot about the social context for the action
of conscience. This is important because if one thinks that Hegel is just describing conscience in a normative void, then his account of conscience as objectivity will seem rather
far-fetched and just as open to criticism as the debased versions of conscience that Hegel
sometimes ridicules. In the passage that Hegel refers to here (PS 9.344–345/ ¶¶640–641),

---

[22]   His recounting of the moments in ¶641 is slightly different but basically the same. Instead of a
reference to thinghood (the outset of Reason B) we have a reference to substance (beginning of Spirit)
as the first moment. Taking substance as the first moment fits better with my claim that these moments
of the object are moments of the *good*. The *immediate* ethical life of the Greeks, reading the good as what
is, the immediate substance of the people, is a clearer ethical moment than the one that Hegel stresses,
namely the move to 'active Reason' from observing Reason. The AK version puts more weight on the
practical character of the transition rather than its specifically *spiritual, ethical*, or *historical* character.
But given that Hegel actually introduces Greek ethical life already in the introduction to Reason B (PS
9.193–195/¶¶347–352), the difference between the two recapitulations is less than it seems.

[23]   For a fuller explication of this account, see Moyar, *Hegel's Conscience*.

he is clear that conscience includes the element of *recognition* or *substantiality* of ethical life. In fact, in the earlier shape, Hegel identifies that substantiality as the first of the three moments (the one corresponding to immediacy).

The picture of action on conscience is complex, yet it is not hard to locate its affinity with the two sorts of inferences (from individual to universal and from universal to individual) in the 'object as a whole'. As an individual, I deliberate about an action in a world suffused with recognized value (the moment of immediate ethical life), on a specific purpose that fits into my overall plans (the moment of utility), and according to principles that make my action my duty (the moment of universality). As a holistic deliberative structure, I am able to synthesize a host of morally relevant factors within a given decision. Perhaps most important, I am able to act on my own interests while also maintaining the subordination of those interests to the ethical purposes that provide the overarching value context for my action. In language I express my commitment to the action as my duty, as an individual act with the rationality of a universal. My individual action depends on the universal, and the universal depends in turn on the actions of individuals. In both directions of inference, my action is mediated by the particular or determinate purposes that bring my individual action into a relational nexus with other actions that stand under the universal.

8.5. THE CONVERGENCE OF ETHICAL ACTION, RELIGION, AND SCIENCE

In the world that Hegel has reconstructed as the world of ethical conscience, *the form of goodness* has the same *form of objectivity* that the object as whole had achieved by the end of Chapter III. The reconstruction has shown that the good achieves the same rational standard as the true and that the two domains are therefore united in that standard (the Concept). This is a convergence of knowledge and action: one acts only on one's knowledge of the good (and the good is defined in terms accessible to knowledge or truth). While the element of recognition is built into the conception of conscience, this shape of spirit is still distinct from absolute knowledge itself because the medium of practical activity is the finite ethical world. Hegel's own conception of philosophy does involve a conception of philosophy as action, but it is action within the domain of knowledge and interpretation. Hegel makes this point in AK in recounting the dialectic in the "Spirit" chapter and comparing the result to his conception of religion.

8.5.1. Recognized Conscience as Absolute Knowledge

The holistic conception of individual conscience is not quite the final word on how ethical objectivity reproduces and thereby overcomes the form of objectivity. There is a final move in which conscience splits into judging and acting sides, each representing the priority of one direction of inference (from universality judging the individual, and from the individual's interests determining what one counts as duty). It is only in the confession and forgiveness of these two agents that we have Hegel's full version of *mutually recognized conscience* as the ethical version of inferential objectivity. To translate the terms into the ethical register, conscience represents *inferential goodness*, or the agent has at her disposal a whole of value relations partly determined by previous history but united in the present by self-consciousness of their totality. An ethical world of agents of conscience, with the holism and recognition Hegel works into the view, *is* the world of freedom essentially determined by the form of the Concept and realized (Hegel thought and hoped) in modern Europe.

Hegel acknowledges the priority of the universal in ethical action, but he aims to do so without compromising the integrity and vitality of the individual. He also aims to demonstrate, in line with his inferential description of the 'object as a whole', that ethical life is a complex whole of mutually reinforcing inferences. The knowledge of this complex whole, as with all expressions of self-consciousness in Hegel, must be exhibited in a scene of mutual recognition. The reciprocal relations between the 'extremes' of individuality and universality must be mediated by a process of recognition that is manifest for the agents *as such a process*. The inferential form lies within conscience as individual conscience, but the full inferential objectivity is only secured when that form—the interrelation of universal and individual—becomes explicit between two self-consciousnesses.

His last argument in "Spirit" is thus a confrontation between two versions of the individual conscience. In AK he recounts this scene twice, and in between he attempts to clarify the relation of this scene to the philosopher's knowledge by aligning the philosopher with the figure of the beautiful soul. He writes, "The beautiful soul is its own knowledge of itself within its pure and transparent unity—the self-consciousness which knows this pure knowledge of *pure inwardly-turned-being* as spirit—not merely the intuition of the divine but the divine's self-intuition" (PS 9.425–426/¶795). The problem with that shape of consciousness is its stubborn interiority, its sense that any expression of itself in the finite world would compromise its purity. Hegel identifies the beautiful soul with one of the characters (the judge) in the dialectic of confession and forgiveness. He thus seems to say that the philosopher should be thought of as implicated in that same process, and that the philosophic perspective must be united with the perspective of action.[24]

The final scene of recognition comes about when the beautiful soul turns into the hard-hearted *judge* who enters a process of recognition with the *agent* of conscience.

---

[24] Pippin takes this character's focus on purity to define Hegel's paradigm of the view of agency he is trying to overcome: "The paradigm picture Hegel keeps reverting to is of an acting subject so stubbornly insistent on the decisive role played by his subjectively formulated intention, so insistent on the individual authority to determine the determinate content of what was done and what scope the action should include, that the actual transition from intention to action is experienced as a regrettable qualification and intrusion on such purity" (Pippin, 'The 'Logic of Experience' as 'Absolute Knowledge," 223).

The judge represents the inference from universal to individual, for the judge thinks that there are universal laws or principles that hold without exception, and he thinks that any admixture of particularity in the action vitiates its worth. His typical inference excludes actions from counting as ethical: "If the action produces any advantage for the agent, then it does not count as ethical." In fact, it must count as evil, for the only alternative to pure universality is the evil of particular individuality. The *agent* represents the individual to universal direction of inference because his deliberation is shaped through the priority that he gives to his own individuality. He eventually has to confess that he represented himself as purer than he actually was, though this is more a confession of a misconceived purity than an accusation against action in general. Every action has to be circumscribed insofar as it is determinate, and the individual's interest is typically a major factor in narrowing the field of action and determining which specific action is taken. Hegel thinks that selfless action is something of an oxymoron. There is *talk* about selfless action and *judgment* based on such an ideal, but action itself typically includes an investment by the self in the purpose.

The decisive move in Hegel's portrayal of the agent and judge is the analysis of self-righteous judgment as itself an action based on particular motives. This leads the agent to recognize himself in the judge and to confess his own prioritizing of particularity. Hegel concludes the retelling of the story in terms that bring out the structure of the Concept:

> One of the two parts of the opposition is the disparity between *inwardly-turned-being-in-its-individuality* [*In-sich-in-seiner-Einzelnheit-seins*] and universality—the other is the disparity between its abstract universality and the self. The former dies back [*stirbt . . . ab*] from its being-for-itself and alienates itself and confesses; the latter disavows the rigidity of its abstract universality and thereby dies back from its lifeless self and its unmoved universality. The result is that the former completes itself through the moment of universality which is the essence, and the latter completes itself through the universality which is the self. (PS 9.426–427/¶796)

Confession and forgiveness are the proper movements or inferences of the Concept because they arrive at the fundamental mediation and unity from each of the two opposed directions, one as the agent giving up its individuality and the other as the self-righteous judge giving up its 'unmoved universality'. In the reconciliation of the two self-consciousnesses, there is a mutual recognition that is an awareness of the inferential whole of the Concept, the basic structure realizing itself as the whole of the ethical world, existing in the knowledge of the two reconciled agents.[25]

---

[25] When Hegel first introduces the two directions of inference in "Force and the Understanding," he illustrates his theoretical point with the practical example of crime and punishment (¶159). This is a lower level of practical inferentialism, but in its basic similarity to the scene of conscience—as action-reaction-resolution through individual (criminal) and universal (law)—the example does bring out the unity of the end of Chapter III and the end of Chapter VI.

After his third recapitulation of confession and forgiveness in "Absolute Knowledge," Hegel writes of the reconciliation of judge and agent as the culmination of the determination of substance as subject. He writes, "For this concept is, as we see, the knowledge of the self's activity within itself as all essentiality and all existence, the knowledge of *this subject* as *substance* and of the substance as this knowledge of its activity" (PS 9.427/¶797). Clearly Hegel is writing here about *ethical* substance, and the fact that he does not qualify it as such is just one indication that the ethical project has come to take precedence over a more theoretical metaphysical project. Absolute knowledge is the self-knowledge of ethical substance that knows its norms as self-generated and as fulfilling the form of objectivity that theoretical reason had already discovered within the physical world. We can thus describe Hegel's philosophy as a *practical metaphysics*, not in the sense that metaphysical claims about God and immortality are practical postulates, but in the sense that the *reality of the ethical domain* is held to be a superior reality to the merely natural reality described by natural science.

8.5.2. The Affirmation of Ethical Action over Religious Consciousness

At this point a question remains: How exactly does our knowledge progress to absolute knowledge simply through a recapitulation of the earlier development? The question concerns the possibility of advancing in the account simply by looking back to what has already happened. If the sublation of objectivity has really already taken place for self-consciousness, how is it possible that self-consciousness did not know it as such? Can a later redescription of the previous movement really *transform* the earlier knowledge without thereby moving beyond it? Moreover, given that the problem seems to be a problem with *religion*, why should we think that a recollection of *spirit* would provide the solution, when the account had previously made a transition *from* spirit *to* religion?

Part of the answer is that in AK Hegel has explicitly united the theoretical and practical deductions of the form of objectivity, and that moral conscience was not previously self-conscious of the fact that it instantiates the form of objectivity developed in Chapters I–III. This answer is correct as far as it goes, yet by itself this would be a rather weak addition, since it is surely part of conscience and its movements that it knows its own objectivity *in some sense*. Conscience may not know objectivity in terms parallel to the shapes of sense-certainty, perception, and the understanding, but that doesn't seem to fundamentally alter its achievement.

A much bigger difference, and I think the real answer to the question, is that in AK conscience is explicitly compared with religion. Understanding both conscience's fundamental similarity to religion and the superiority of ethical action to religious practice is what elevates the knowledge of reconciled conscience to *absolute* knowledge. The Concept has now become the 'form of objectivity' that exists in the recognition of reconciled agency, so religion's opposition to a 'broken' world has been overcome. When he is presenting the movement of conscience as achieving objectivity, Hegel does mention the way in which religion almost reaches the same level, but in five straight paragraphs (PS 9.425–428/¶794–798) he thematizes the contrast with religion. He writes that "the unification of the two sides" (PS 9.425/¶794) is the only task that remains for the account, and he explicitly notes the way in which conscience surpasses religion. Hegel writes that the unification has already happened 'in-itself' in the movement of Protestant Christianity, whose worship did in fact involve a form of mutual recognition among members of the congregation (PS 9.419–420/¶786). But he is also quick to point out that this unification is inadequate since it stands opposed to "the movement of self-consciousness" (PS 9.425/¶795). Hegel claims that the unification must in fact take place in the element of self-conscious action, on the side "that contains both its own self and its opposite, not only *in-itself* or in a universal way, but rather *for itself* or in a developed and differentiated way" (PS 9.425/¶795). The key points of emphasis are on the superior attention to *form* rather than *content* in conscience, and on the active character of conscience against the passive or withdrawn character of religious devotion.[26] He writes, "the form is the self itself, since it contains the self-certain *acting* spirit, the self accomplishing the life of absolute spirit [*das Selbst führt das Leben des absoluten Geistes durch*]" (PS 9.426/¶796). The implication here is that philosophy itself must be conceived as action and realization, and thus be more like ethical action than religious devotion.[27]

In the main argument of "Absolute Knowledge," Hegel thus comes out strongly in favor of aligning philosophy with ethical action. But what does this mean? It certainly does not make Hegel into Marx, for Hegel does not think that philosophy's main aim is to change the world rather than to interpret it. Philosophy remains an interpretive discipline for Hegel, though one with an ethical purpose and one whose activity engages with the here and now, with actuality, in much the way that action on an ordinary ethical purpose does. The clearest discussion of this issue comes in §270 on the *Philosophy of Right*, in which Hegel deals with the relationship of the ethical state to religion. One of the main points of that discussion is that religion cannot claim to have a special authority over and above the laws of the state. Hegel holds that to the extent that the state needs an extralegal justification and legitimation, it is philosophy rather than religion that can provide it.[28] He thinks of the domains of ethics (centered on the state) and philosophy as sharing the medium of law, concepts, and knowledge: "Thus, *science*, too, is found on the side of the state, for it has the same element of form as the state, and its end is *cognition*, by means of thought, of *objective* truth and rationality" (PR §270R). To the extent

---

[26] Siep writes, "Hegel apparently considers the crucial point to be that the experience of moral consciousness 'individually performs,' as it were, a process which is also constitutive of the object of perfected religion: the individualization and externalization of a self-consciousness which appears in morality as at once universal law and 'communal consciousness.' It is the very same 'spirit' process which is thought, or faithfully believed, in the dogmas of the Trinity, creation, and salvation and which is to be found in the moral action of autonomous, conscientious consciousness" (Siep, *Hegel's Phenomenology of Spirit*, 230).

[27] For a reading that gives more importance to religion, see Lauer, *A Reading of Hegel's Phenomenology of Spirit*.

[28] See Siep, "Hegel's Liberal, Social, and 'Ethical' State," Chapter 23 in this volume.

that religion is rational, it will not contradict the (rational) state, so Hegel does think that religion and philosophy are compatible. For Hegel the realization of God is the actual ethical world, and our ethical action in that world is the realization of the divine, the accomplishment of the good.[29] Of course he is not claiming that everything is as it should be. He is to some extent lowering—or at least revising—expectations in relation to the idea of religious salvation and transfiguration. It is a picture of a "rose in the cross of the present," to borrow the phrase from his Preface to the *Philosophy of Right*, not a picture of a sanctified present with no crosses.

It is also the case that Hegel is not giving up on religion, or even entertaining the idea that that is possible. He is advocating a convergence of the ethical, religious, and philosophical, with the ethical and philosophical having a rather higher status but one that is nonetheless supposed to complement religion. This alignment of the perspective of conscience with religion and philosophy is not a one-off claim by Hegel. There is another important place in his corpus where he presents his case for this systematic convergence around conscience, namely in the *Encyclopedia* account of "World History" (E §552). There he claims a convergence of ethical conscience, religion, and philosophic knowing, and he does so in a remark added for the 1830 edition, thus reaffirming his position from almost twenty-five years earlier.

8.6. THE STANDPOINT OF PHILOSOPHICAL SCIENCE AND THE INCORPORATION OF REALISM

In my view, the main task of "Absolute Knowledge" is completed with the recapitulations of "Spirit" and the comparisons with "Religion." Hegel's reflections in the rest of the chapter have attracted more attention because he makes a number of sweeping claims about science, time, and history.[30] Hegel argues that it is only now, after the French Revolution and with the birth of Kantian and Fichtean moral philosophy, that science can appear. This is how I take the claim that "*science* does not appear in time and in actuality until spirit has come round to itself as being this consciousness about itself" (PS 9.428/¶800). Only once ethical life has reached a level of transparency to itself, consciousness of its own freedom, can philosophical science as a system of freedom emerge.[31] But Hegel is quick to deny that science is therefore *conditioned by* temporality.

---

[29] See Lewis, "Religion and Demythologization," and his Chapter 26 in this volume.

[30] For an account that focuses on these later sections, see Baptist, "Das absolute Wissen."

[31] See also Pinkard: "It is only when the form of life has incorporated into its essential self-understanding a conception of self-reflection on ourselves as cultural beings—only in a *self-grounding, reflective historicist* culture when the social practices of reason-giving have been turned on themselves—that such absolute reflection is possible and that this type of dialectical philosophical reflection can appear and can understand itself for what it is" (Pinkard, *Hegel's Phenomenology*, 266).

He claims that the completion of spirit's temporal development results in *a concept that negates the temporality of the development.*

The claim of Hegel's idealism is that the Concept is prior to, and in fact can generate, the forms of sensible intuition (space and time) through which objects appear to us. But the Hegelian claim is more complex than the rather similar Fichtean thesis because Hegel argues that we must work *through* the realist consciousness, critique it from within, in order to arrive at the Concept. In the key passage, in which the aim of overcoming Kant's intuition-concept dualism is fully on display, he writes:

> *Time* is the *Concept* itself that *exists there* and is represented to consciousness as empty intuition. Consequently, spirit necessarily appears in time, and it appears in time as long as it does not *grasp* its pure concept, which is to say, as long as it does not annul time. Time is the pure self *externally* intuited by the self but not *grasped* by the self; time is the merely intuited concept. In that this concept grasps itself, it sublates its temporal form, comprehends the act of intuiting, and is intuition which has been conceptually grasped and is itself intuition which is comprehending [*und ist begriff-nes und begreifendes Anschauen*]. (PS 9.429/¶801)

Hegel is thinking of the Concept as determining what *follows from* what. Insofar as time presents things following one after the other, it can also be thought of relationally. But time is external in the sense that there is no *inner* or *essential* relation of the moments to each other.[32] Time appears as 'fate' (PS 9.429/¶801) when the connection between the successive moments is not comprehended. But when the pure Concept grasps itself as the source of all relationality, by witnessing the object of consciousness becoming subject and the religious substance being reproduced by ethical subjectivity, then science can assert its own necessity or self-sufficiency against the accidents of time, as conditioning time rather than being conditioned by it.

Against those commentators who think that the standpoint of philosophical science—the *Science of Logic* and the whole *Encyclopedia* project—renders the *Phenomenology* dispensable, I argue that we should take seriously Hegel's claim that the *Phenomenology* exhibits the *reality* of the concepts developed in the *Logic*. The whole point of an immanent critique, starting from within shapes of consciousness in which the object is opposed to the subject, is to justify the concept of science by showing that it is the truth of the realist perspective of consciousness. The process undermines the *absoluteness* of the realist perspective, while preserving the moments of being and otherness that allow us to distinguish the world from our self-conscious activity. The *Phenomenology* negates the immediacy of the shapes of consciousness, and in that sense the real world goes missing. But the world is regained and put on solid footing within the phenomenological process itself. This is why Hegel writes, after emphasizing the logical character of science proper,

---

[32] See the discussion in Siep, *Hegel's Phenomenology of Spirit*, 232–235.

Conversely, to every abstract moment of science, there corresponds a shape of appearing spirit per se [*überhaupt*]. Just as existing spirit is not richer than science, so too spirit in its content is no poorer. To take cognizance of the pure concepts of science in this form, namely, in which they are shapes of consciousness, is what constitutes the aspect of their reality. In terms of that reality, their essence, the concept, which is posited in that reality in its *simple* mediation as *thought*, breaks up and separates the moments of this mediation and exhibits itself in terms of their inner opposition. (PS 9.529/¶805)

The 'pure concepts of Science', which correspond in a very rough way to the Kantian 'pure categories', do not take the form of postures *toward* objectivity (as the shapes of consciousness do). But this does not mean, Hegel says here, that we as living agents have ourselves somehow 'crossed over' into beings who do not need consciousness. While speculative philosophy can now present the content as self-developing, from simplest to most comprehensive, that does not mean that consciousness is 'lost' within the whole, or that the individual is swallowed within the System, as the caricatures of Hegel would have it. Rather, as "in its content no poorer," the existing [*daseiende*] spirit displays the richness of the scientific concepts, but seen from the side of 'the antithesis', from the opposition necessary to conceive of ourselves as subjects conscious of a world.

The final paragraphs of AK provide a short summary of the *Encyclopedia* project of moving from Logic to Nature to Spirit. One can view this as a portrayal of how philosophy itself can replicate the traditional representation of God, and thus prove that it supplants religion in conceptual form. Another, more sober way, would be to see it as Hegel's answer to the challenge set by Kant's idealism that I mentioned at the outset: how to establish a unitary and unifying ground prior to the conditions of space and time, so that space and time are not a separate, merely presupposed, root of knowledge. The goal of the *Phenomenology* is to justify the Concept, to deduce the starting point of *The Science of Logic*. He describes the logic as "*the exposition of God as he is in his eternal essence before the creation of nature and of a finite spirit*" (SL 21.34/29). The philosophy of nature, then, is the knowledge of that creation as it unfolds into the living organism and eventually into the human mind.[33] After the bold claims about philosophy's access to pure science as the 'eternal essence' and to nature, the step to the comprehension of spirit almost seems easy, and even modest, by comparison. In one sense he is just appealing to the temporal form through which we know ourselves by studying the history of spirit, which is just what the *Phenomenology* has done. The tricky issue here is how the account of conceptualized history is supposed to match up with the normative domains

---

[33] In AK he writes of the alienation of knowledge into time and space: "Knowing is acquainted not merely with itself, but also with the negative of itself, that is, its limit. To know its limit means to know that it is to sacrifice itself. This sacrifice is the alienation [*Entäusserung*] within which spirit exhibits its coming-to-be spirit in the form of a *free contingent event*, and it intuits outside of itself its pure *self* as *time* and likewise intuits its *being* as space. This final coming-to-be, *nature*, is its living, immediate coming-to-be. Nature, that is, alienated spirit, is in its existence nothing but this eternal alienation [*Entäusserung*] of its *durable existence* and the movement which produces the *subject*" (PS 9.433/¶807).

developed on a scientific basis in the *Philosophy of Spirit*. Hegel is forthright that there is contingency in this process; the philosopher's action of recollection [*Erinnerung*] is a way of taking into knowledge the contingent externalities of the past. The claim of absoluteness in the end is the claim that we can render all experience intelligible in the form of the Concept, Hegel's non-psychological version of the synthetic unity of self-consciousness. It is essential to this knowledge that it be able to adapt to contingency by incorporating it into an ethical interpretation of our form of life and its trajectory, rather than holding the conceptual judgmentally against the new and the different. In that interpretation we *understand* or *know* ourselves in our history, not through mere observation, but rather through an *evaluation* of who we have become, and who we should be.

WORKS CITED

Primary Texts

Hegel, G. W. F. *Elements of the Philosophy of Right* [PR], translated by H. B. Nisbet and edited by Allen Wood. Cambridge: Cambridge University Press, 1991.

Hegel, G. W. F. *Phenomenology of Spirit* [PS], translated by Terry Pinkard. Cambridge: Cambridge University Press, 2017.

Hegel, G. W. F. *The Science of Logic* [SL], translated by George di Giovanni. Cambridge: Cambridge University Press, 2010.

Kant, Immanuel. *Critique of Pure Reason*, edited and translated by Paul Guyer and Allen W. Wood. Cambridge: Cambridge University Press 1998.

Secondary Literature

Baptist, Gabriella. "Das absolute Wissen. Zeit, Geschichte, Wissenschaft," in *G.W.F. Hegel, Phänomenologie des Geistes*, edited by Dietmar Köhler and Otto Pöggeler. Berlin, Akad. Verlag, 1998, 245–262.

Brandom, Robert. *Tales of the Mighty Dead: Historical Essays in the Metaphysics of Intentionality*. Cambridge, MA: Harvard University Press, 2002.

De Laurentiis, Allegra. "Absolute Knowing," in *The Blackwell Guide to Hegel's Phenomenology of Spirit*, edited by Kenneth Westphal. Oxford: Blackwell, 2009, 246–264.

Forster, Michael. *Hegel's Idea of a Phenomenology of Spirit*. Chicago: University of Chicago Press, 1998.

Förster, Eckart. *The Twenty-Five Years of Philosophy: A Systematic Reconstruction*, translated by Brady Bowman. Cambridge, MA: Harvard University Press, 2012.

Harris, H. S. *Hegel: Phenomenology and System*. Indianapolis: Hackett, 1995.

Harris, H. S. *Hegel's Ladder II: The Odyssey of Spirit*. Indianapolis; Cambridge: Hackett, 1997.

Lauer, Quentin. *A Reading of Hegel's Phenomenology of Spirit*. New York: Fordham University Press, 1976.

Lewis, Thomas A. "Religion and Demythologization in Hegel's *Phenomenology of Spirit*," in *Hegel's Phenomenology of Spirit: A Critical Guide*, edited by Dean Moyar and Michael Quante. Cambridge: Cambridge University Press, 2008, 192–209.

Miller, Mitchell H., Jr. "The Attainment of the Absolute Standpoint in Hegel's *Phenomenology*," in *The Phenomenology of Spirit Reader*, edited by Jon Stewart. Albany: State University of New York Press, 1998, 427–443.

Moyar, Dean. *Hegel's Conscience*. Oxford: Oxford University Press, 2011.

Nuzzo, Angelica. "The Truth of *Absolutes Wissen* in Hegel's *Phenomenology of Spirit*," in *Hegel's Phenomenology of Spirit: New Critical Essays*, edited by Alfred Denker and Michael Vater. Amherst, NY: Humanities Books, 265–294.

Pinkard, Terry. *Hegel's Phenomenology: The Sociality of Reason*. Cambridge: Cambridge University Press, 1994.

Pippin, Robert. *Hegel's Idealism: The Satisfactions of Self-consciousness*. Cambridge: Cambridge University Press, 1989.

Pippin, Robert. "The 'Logic of Experience' as 'Absolute Knowledge' in Hegel's *Phenomenology of Spirit*," in *Hegel's Phenomenology of Spirit: A Critical Guide*, edited by Dean Moyar and Michael Quante. Cambridge: Cambridge University Press, 2008, 210–227.

Siep, Ludwig. *Hegel's Phenomenology of Spirit*, translated by Daniel Smyth. Cambridge: Cambridge University Press, 2014.

Stewart, Jon. *The Unity of Hegel's Phenomenology of Spirit: A Systematic Interpretation*. Evanston, IL: Northwestern University Press, 2000.

PART III

THE SCIENCE OF LOGIC

CHAPTER 9

....

HEGEL ON LOGIC AS METAPHYSICS

....

ROBERT B. PIPPIN

PARAGRAPH §24 of the *Encyclopedia Logic* raises the first and most important issue one faces in trying to determine what Hegel thinks a *Science of Logic* is. It is also a claim that lands one in the middle of a number of long-debated interpretive controversies.

> Thus *logic* coincides with *metaphysics*, with the science of *things* grasped in *thoughts*, which used to be taken to express the *essentialities of the things*. (T) [Die *Logik* fällt daher mit der *Metaphysik* zusammen, der Wissenschaft der *Dinge* in *Gedanken* gefaßt, welche dafür galten, die *Wesenheiten der Dinge* auszudrücken]. (E §24)[1]

It is especially important that Hegel does not say that metaphysics has a subject matter that requires a speculative logic in the Hegelian sense, but that this new metaphysics *is* logic. However, what he means by implying that logic can only *now* coincide with metaphysics, after we have somehow passed beyond the traditional metaphysical view that 'thoughts [*Gedanke*]' are to be considered the 'essentialities of things [*Wesenheiten der Dinge*]' is quite a compacted claim, to which we shall return. But there is first the large issue of the logic-metaphysics relation itself.[2] What I propose to do is to say something first about the historical context of logic in and after Kant, and present a few of the terms of art with which Hegel explains the substance of the claim that logic is now

---

[1] T will indicate alterations in the translation listed in Works Cited.

[2] This topic can obviously get very complicated very quickly, because the question of the nature of metaphysics is controversial in itself. In this chapter I want to put Hegel in conversation mainly with Kant and Aristotle, and more generally with the tradition of philosophical logic. But as Koch, "Metaphysik und Spekulative Logik," has shown, it can also be illuminating to compare and contrast Hegel's approach with contemporary versions of metaphysics, like David Lewis's, Peter van Inwagen's and Donald Davidson's. (Because of the many ambiguities in the notion of 'metaphysics', and because Hegel announces himself as a critic of modern rationalist metaphysics, and because Hegel's new understanding of metaphysics will include his *Realphilosophie*, the Philosophy of Nature and of Spirit, Koch suggests that it might be better to think of Hegel's speculative project as 'first philosophy'.)

metaphysics; then I speculate on what he might thereby mean by metaphysics, propose an interpretation of the substantive identification of logic with metaphysics by contrast with Kant, and briefly assess some of the implications of this way of looking at things for an interpretation of *The Science of Logic* as a whole.

9.1. The 'Logic' in 'Logic as Metaphysics'

We need to say something first about the historical context into which Hegel's §24 claim must be located. And that concerns the central issue introduced into theories of logic by Kant: the relation of concept to object.[3] Then there is the question of Hegel's relation to that innovation.

The innovation is Kant's most famous and important, and concerns general logic [*allgemeine Logik*] understood as an a priori reflection on the relations of ideas. Kant's view is a critique of past claims made on behalf of that reflective activity. Logic emerged in Kant as something much more than the study of valid forms of inference, but very different from an account of the laws that thinking does or ought to obey (as in the *Port Royale Logic*), or as transparently reflecting the basic ontological structure of reality (as in Wolffian and scholastic accounts of logic). For Kant, logic states the conditions of any possible sense, the distinctions and relations without which sense would not be possible, and so covers not only truth-functional assertions, but also imperatives and aesthetic judgments.

So where should we place Hegel? In this, as in so many other respects, he is, I would argue, firmly in the post-Kantian world, something already indicated by his distancing himself in §24 from how metaphysics had been understood—that is, simply (or non-speculatively) identifying thoughts with the 'essentialities' of things, as if empirically unaided thought were transparent to the conceptual structure of the real. There is no question that this is how Hegel viewed himself. As he states in the *Logic*'s Introduction:

> I should point out that in this work I make frequent references to the Kantian philosophy (which to many might seem superfluous) because, whatever might be said here or elsewhere of its distinctive character or of particular parts of its exposition, it constitutes the foundation and the starting point of the new German philosophy, and

---

[3] Förster (*The Twenty-Five Years of Philosophy*) has recently argued for the importance of distinguishing the early critical question of the possible relation between pure concepts and objects, and the later formulation of the problem of synthetic a priori judgments. They are certainly two different questions: How could a predicate not analytically contained in the subject be attributed to the subject a priori? vs. Does a pure concept have an object? But at the end of the day, the 'third thing', as Kant puts it, the 'condition', that allows that connection *is* a relation to an object, via the pure forms of intuition, and this to all possible sensible objects. The issue of whether this is an important distinction for the moral and aesthetic philosophy is too complicated for treatment in this context.

this is a merit of which it can boast undiminished by whatever fault may be found in it. An added reason for these frequent references in the objective logic is that Kantian philosophy delves deeply into important, *more specific* aspects of the logic, whereas later philosophical expositions have paid little attention to these aspects and in some instances have even expressed crude—though not unavenged—contempt for them. (SL 21.47/40)

Another typical and even stronger remark from the *Encyclopedia Logic*:

Nowadays, the Kantian philosophy has been left behind, and everybody wants to be at a point further on. To be further along, however, has a double meaning: both to be further ahead and to be further behind. Looked at in clear light, many of our philosophical endeavors are nothing but the method of the old metaphysics, an uncritical thinking along in a way everyone is capable of. (E §41RA)

Although it seems to have become oddly controversial among some Hegel scholars, I will assume that Hegel means what he says when he rejects this 'old metaphysics', that is, "the former metaphysics which was supposed to be the scientific edifice of the world as constructed by thoughts alone" (SL 21.48/42), and that he is proposing a speculative logic as a new metaphysics.

With general logic understood as it was in the Port Royal and the Wolffian traditions, and so with metaphysics understood as based on conceptual relations of 'containment', or analysis,[4] Hegel agrees that logical reasoning, understood *in that way*, does not provide knowledge of objects. He especially agrees that reason and the understanding are discursive activities, not passively 'illuminated' by means of a distinct, separate faculty. As "that great foe of immediacy," in Sellars's phrase, there is no mention of or reliance on such a distinct, intellectually receptive intuition in an a priori enterprise.[5]

Hegel also says such Kantian things as "the concept is the ground and the source of all finite determinateness and manifoldness" (SL 12.23/520),[6] and, given that he accepts that there is no way that a determination of the logically possible alone can contribute to any

---

[4] This is the heart of the 'metaphysics' Kant attacked, and extends to all attempts to derive 'object-implicating' conclusions from such conceptual relations alone. (This is how Anderson, *The Poverty of Conceptual Truth*, characterizes the strategy of the pre-Kantian tradition.) What I am trying to show in this chapter and in the book project of which it is a part is that Hegel wholeheartedly accepted the Kantian critique of *that* tradition, but argued that that form of inquiry hardly exhausted what could properly be called a 'speculative' metaphysics.

[5] Ultimately, Hegel wants to show that the abstract opposition between the intuitive and the discursive is overcome in speculative thought. Overcoming a strict opposition is not the same as obliterating or collapsing a distinction, though. Understanding properly the inseparability of these moments in such a form of thought is the supreme desiderata in trying to understand anything in Hegel's philosophy.

[6] I agree with Peter Rohs, when he notes that this formulation is the counterpart to Kant's claim at B130 in the *Critique of Pure Reason* that all combination should be understood as an "activity of the understanding," a *Verstandeshandlung*. Rohs, *Form und Grund*, 4. It is apparently necessary to note, when one highlights these Kantian passages, that this will not lead Hegel to any form of subjective idealism or noumenal skepticism.

knowledge about what is 'other than thought', whether a determination of what exists, or of that by virtue of which anything can be the determinate thing it is, he must understand that claim in a revised post-Kantian way, or at the very least not as an appeal to any 'conceptual truth', as it would have been understood by Descartes or Wolff.

Finally, for both Kant and Hegel, the unit of significance for any logic is not the proposition or any static formal structure, but acts of reasoning and assertion, and so the logic that is a model for both transcendental logic and Hegelian science is still a judgmental logic, raising as an inevitable question the status of 'subjectivity' (or 'psychology') in logic, the issue that so bothered Frege.

Here, then, is a typical account by Hegel of the subject matter of *The Science of Logic*. Hegel tells us only that the work concerns "the science of pure thinking" and he goes on in that passage to say that it is

> ... (t)he science that has *pure knowledge* for its principle and is a unity which is not abstract but living and concrete, so that the opposition of consciousness between *a being subjectively existing for itself*, and another but objectively *existing such being*, has been overcome in it, and being is known to be in itself a pure concept and the pure concept to be true being. These, then, are the two *moments* contained in logic. But they are now known to exist *inseparably*, not as in consciousness, where each *exists for itself*; it is for this reason and this reason alone, because they are at the same time known to be *distinct* [*unterschiedene*] (yet not to exist for themselves), that their unity is not abstract, dead and inert, but concrete. (SL 21.45/38–39)

Everything distinctive about Hegel's approach is contained in that paragraph, so we should proceed slowly, especially with respect to its key claim, which comes in two parts: (1) first, a double claim of identity—that being is itself a pure concept, and such a pure concept is being. That would certainly establish a relationship between logic and metaphysics—one of identity. Yet, this is supposed to be so even as (2) he warns us that this identity is of quite a special sort, one paradoxically compatible with their continuing distinctness. Such an insistence on distinctness at least makes it immediately clear that he cannot be saying that what there is is an abstract, immaterial entity or entities, in the way a realist might understand universals, or an idea-monist or a pantheist would understand everything, or a Platonist might understand ideas (i.e., that in thinking pure thinkings [*Gedanke*] we are thinking what there is, such ideal entities). Then there would just or only *be* such universals or ideas, or mind, really or in truth; there would be no continuing 'distinctness', nothing '*unterschiedene*'. (Not to mention that this identification would be exactly what Hegel has explicitly rejected: "the [supposed] scientific edifice of the world as constructed by thoughts alone.")

An earlier specification in the *Logic's* Introduction of this identity gives us a deeper clue about how to proceed and raises a theme that is interwoven everywhere in the *Logic*, but which, I would claim, still has not been successfully interpreted. The passage involves a much more Hegelian specification of what he meant by 'being' in that 'being-concept' identity claim:

As *science*, truth is pure self-consciousness as it develops itself and has the shape of the self, so that *that which exists in and for itself is the known* [gewußte] *concept and the concept as such is that which exists in and for itself.* (SL 21.33/29, my bold)[7]

"[W]hich exists in and for itself" obviously introduces many more complications than reference to mere 'being'. What could it be for something to exist 'for itself'? That alone is supposed to be what is identical to the 'known [*gewußte*] concept'? And what does he mean by adding that 'known' to the 'concept'? (Why not just say identical to the concept, as he would if he were a concept realist?)

The situation is immediately quite complicated. To some extent, part of Hegel's debt to Aristotle emerges here. (In general terms, so general they are not immediately helpful, *an sich* and *für sich* are Hegel's translations of *dynamis* and *energeia*.) Entities are the determinate entities they are 'in terms of' or 'because of' their concept or substantial form or true actuality (their formal causes).[8] Such a form accounts for such determinacy. Such entities embody some measure of what it is truly to be *such* a thing, and instantiate such an essence to a greater or lesser degree. A wolf is not simply, in itself, a wolf, but to some degree or other; if one is more Platonically inclined, a better or worse exemplification of such a concept 'for itself'; or in a more Aristotelian vein, the organic being is 'on the way' toward its full mature realization, or to becoming a weaker such realization with age. The main point is this: the object is not just 'as it is'; it is 'for' (here, in some sense of, 'for the sake of') its concept and thereby itself. A merely 'existing' particular wolf about which we can make a number of empirical claims will not tell us what an 'actual' wolf is. The latter would involve truly being in and for itself, the realization of wolfness. Hegel will tell us later that the subject matter of the *Logic* is 'actuality' [*Wirklichkeit*], not existence, and that will be treated later.[9] To say that an object is 'for its form' is just to say that there is an intelligible dynamic in its development, in its striving to become what it is. This intelligible dynamic is its concept and is not something that 'exists' separate from or supervening on some physical attributes and on efficient causation. It is just *the intelligible way* a development develops; there is nothing 'over and above' the development.[10] We also come close here to the most important general claim made in the *Logic*. Rendering a thing intelligible has many interconnected moments and depends on the sort of thing it is, the sort of account-giving appropriate to it. These are the differences between the different modalities of judgment, different forms of thought—between the intelligibility of atomic particulars in their qualitative and quantitative distinctness, particulars as

---

[7] There are passages like this from the *Phenomenology of Spirit*: "was *gedacht* ist, *ist*; und daß, was *ist*, nur *ist*, insofern es Gedanke ist" (E ¶465). But it is clear that by this point in the *Encyclopedia*, Hegel is not talking about what merely exists, and suddenly turning into Bishop Berkeley by claiming *esse est percipi*. What a thing truly is, is its concept, and a concept is not a self-standing 'thought' but a moment in a network of mutually inter-defining rules of determination.

[8] That is, each depends on its own individual form and its species form to be what it intelligibly is, and so on form itself, on such formality in various dimensions. The latter (what such formality amounts to) is the subject matter of the *Logic*. The *Logic* thus concerns The Concept, not individual concepts.

[9] The unity of concept and 'Realität' is what Hegel means by Wirklichkeit, actuality. See E ¶215.

[10] See Jonathan Lear, *Aristotle*, 41–42.

appearances of essence, and particulars judged 'according to their concept'. Hegel wants to understand both the distinctness and the interrelation of 'that horse is brown'; 'horses have four legs'; and 'that is a good horse.' In this last case, the concept has become reflexively transparent to itself, a particular is considered 'for itself' explicitly in the light of its concept, within an overall reflection about conceptual determination itself. This is the basis of the three books of the *Logic*.[11]

So we are trying to understand in what sense Hegel means us to understand a speculative identity between 'that which exists in and for itself' and 'the concept'. The dimension that we are on about now, about actuality and philosophy, is an unusual but still familiar claim about philosophy and we should pause to consider it for a while.

That is, whenever Hegel tries to explain the subject matter of the *Logic*, he makes clear that he is not talking about deducing the great multitude of empirical content, the intuited manifold, or just about thought-content in the sense of logical content, like subject-predicate. He says the following:

> By thus introducing content into logical consideration, it is not the *things*, but what is rather *the fact* [*Sache*], the *concept* of the things, that becomes the subject matter. (SL 21.17/19)

'Fact' doesn't help much as a translation; he doesn't seem to mean anything like *Tatsache*, or what is the case. He is moving in the opposite direction from anything empirical, anything having to do with particular things, or facts about existence. He becomes a little clearer when he says about the concept of such a content,

> This concept is not intuited by the senses, is not represented in imagination; it is only subject matter [*Gegenstand*], the product and content of *thought*, the fact that exists in and for itself [*die an und für sich seyende Sache*], the logos, the reason of that which is, the truth of what we call things; it is least of all the logos that should be kept outside the science of logic. (SL 21.17/19)[12]

This "reason of that which is" means that Hegel cannot be talking about logical content (like 'subject term', 'disjunct', or 'antecedent'), and that is stressed in other ways throughout SL and in the EL.

---

[11] Koch, "Metaphysik und Spekulative Logik," 49 is helpful here in distinguishing the first two books of the *Logic* as an *Objektlogik*, the heart of traditional metaphysical account of object determinacy, and the Concept Logic as a *Hintergrundlogik*, a meta-theory of the theoretical determinations in the earlier books.

[12] Cf. "This objective thinking is thus the *content* of pure science. Consequently, far from being formal, far from lacking the matter required for an actual and true cognition, it is its content which alone has absolute truth, or, if one still wanted to make use of the word 'matter', which alone is the veritable matter—a matter for which the form is nothing external, because this matter is rather pure thought and hence the absolute form itself" (SL 21.34/29).

When thinking is taken as active with regard to objects as the thinking over [*Nachdenken*] of something—then the universal, as the product of this activity—contains the value of the matter [*Wert der Sache*], what is essential [*das Wesentliche*], inner, true. (E §21)

This is the kind of issue that arises when we ask if some practice is 'actually' religious—peyote smoking, say, or Scientology. We don't doubt that the practice exists; we want to know its 'essentiality', *Wert, Sache an sich selbst*, and so forth. We don't doubt that animals exist and have various capacities; we want to know if they are actually rights-bearers. We know computers can play chess and win, perhaps one day could even pass Turing tests, but we want to know not whether these *facts* are true, but whether the computer is actually thinking. A gallery opens and some objects, clothes strewn around a floor, are displayed. Is it actually art? (And of course: What 'actually' is an object of experience? What is its actuality? Perhaps, "that in the concept of which the manifold is united.") As Quine pointed out, the answer to the question "What is there?" is easy: everything. But not everything is an actuality.

With the right qualifications in place, what Hegel means by actuality and all its synonyms is congruent with what Kant meant by categoriality (at that level of generality, in other words), and that helps explain his otherwise bewildering claim that the concept (in this sense) *gives itself* its own actuality. This has nothing to do with some neo-Platonic self-causing process, out of which concepts pop, like toast from a toaster. The claim means that the sort of questions posed in the preceding are in no sense empirical questions, answerable by some fact of the matter. If that is so, there is no reason we cannot speak Hegelese, and say that thought determines for itself what is actual—gives itself its own actuality. How then to account for the *determinate* actualities treated in the Logic? In answering this, Hegel seems to place a lot of faith in some sort of derivability of such essentialities from the conditions for the possibility of discursive intelligibility as such. The paradigmatic form of such sense-making is predicative, but only paradigmatically, not exclusively, assertoric categorical judgments. (A similar form of reasoning in Frege: a language *cannot* contain a representation of objects, unless it also contains predicative expressions. This also means that an intellect cannot have the power of apprehending objects unless it has the power of thinking something of them, of apprehending Fregean concepts.[13] This is already a metaphysics of objects and concepts. Frege will add relations and down the line, numbers.)[14]

We shall see how and why his attempt differs a great deal from Kant's similar one in the Metaphysical Deduction, but the point now is the similarity. The Concept gives itself

---

[13] These are Thompson's formulations. Thompson, *Life and Action*, 56–57.

[14] In this respect, compare Davidson, "The Method of Truth in Metaphysics," on the general problem we are discussing, expressed in his linguistic terms ("Why must our language—any language—incorporate or depend on a largely correct, shared view of how things are?" 199), on the task of "ontology . . . forced into the open" through an analysis of language (210), and on the specific example of the relation between the functioning of adverbs and an ontology of events (212). There is a useful discussion of the Davidson-Hegel relation in Koch, "Metaphysik und Spekulative Logik."

its own actuality. The answers to any type of question like those posed earlier are not empirical. Empirical questions depend on, would not be possible without, the determination of the intelligibly actual.

I have said that Hegel agrees with Kant that thinking is basically discursive. Again, a science of logic is a 'science of pure thinking'. What any thinking does is to render something intelligible, a task that has many different dimensions. But to say what something is, or to explain why something happened, or to understand the point or purpose of anything, is not just to present a picture or grasp a content, is not an intuitional grasp. It is to assert something that is always open to challenge and interrogation. This means that a science of thinking is also a science of 'reasons', of ways of giving reasons in rendering anything genuinely or properly intelligible. But this agreement about discursivity has to be immediately qualified. Understood as Kant does, it means that thought can give itself *no* content, *only* think about content 'supplied' *extra-conceptually*. Thinking is not, for him, a receptive power. Kant reasoned that the only available sort of extra-conceptual receptivity known to us is sensible; hence the fundamentality of the concept-(sensible) intuition divide. If that is the inference, then *'the discursivity of thought thesis'* immediately prohibits anything anywhere near the neighborhood of a *'concept gives itself its own actuality'* thesis, even if interpreted in the way suggested in the preceding. Such a prohibition is the whole point of the discursivity claim. (This would all not exhaust all the alternatives if by thinking, thought could produce, in the sense of create, its own objects—if there were 'intellectual intuition', something Kant reserves only for God. It is thus understandable that for some commentators what Hegel must mean by concepts giving themselves their own actuality must refer to such a power by Absolute Spirit. But this is not Hegel's view.)

But for Hegel, Kant had already himself indicated that discursive thought must have an 'intuitive moment' in itself in being able to lay out the elements of the Metaphysical Deduction. Thought must be able to determine its own determinate moments or form, not conceptualize an alien content. There can be no great tension in the two claims, because Kant is quite interested in what he says our "cognitive faculty . . . provides out of itself."[15] According to Hegel, Kant did not have a handle on his own thinking and seemed to pick up the categories from logic textbooks, but the fact that the concept of judgment itself could, at least putatively, "determine itself" in these moments, already gives Hegel his stalking horse. This moment is not anything like the 'seeing' of thought's nature as an object; it is, rather, spontaneous, productive. But neither is it the discursive application of a predicate to an object.

It is also the case that Kant himself had already shown, had made the 'logical point' in his account of space and time as both forms of intuition and pure intuitions, that a form could be a form of apprehension and itself a content at the same time. In the Addition to E §41, Hegel remarks that Kant himself, in formulating reason's critique of itself, treats forms of cognition as objects of cognition, thus being committed to the unity of "the activity of the forms of thinking" and "the critique of them." He calls this feat 'dialectic'.

[15] Kant, *Critique of Pure Reason*, B1.

Mathematical construction in mathematical proof makes essentially the same point, although the points about pure intuition are only analogues of the general point Hegel would want to make; they are not invoked as such in the *Logic*. And most suggestively for the entire enterprise of the *Logic*, practical reason can determine the form of a rational will that is also itself a substantive content. The self-legislation of the moral law is not volitional anarchy, but practical reason's knowledge of 'what' to legislate.

So it is perfectly appropriate to say that for Hegel reality "has a conceptual structure" or that "only concepts are truly real," as long as we realize we are not talking about entities, much less separable, immaterial abstract entities, but about the 'actualities' of beings, their modes or ways of being what determinately and intelligibly they are.[16] It is hard to understand what Hegel means by claiming that the determination of such actuality is a product of thought's self-determination, and that it is non-empirical, but at least we know he is not talking about the divine intuition of existences, and that his case is one parallel to, not orthogonal to, Kant's demonstration that actuality (but only phenomenal actuality) must have a causal structure, say.

And here again, Hegel's model of metaphysics, as is indicated by his frequent invocation of this German term for *energeia*, *Wirklichkeit*, is Aristotelian. And Aristotle's metaphysics is not modern dogmatic metaphysics, does not concern a 'supersensible' reality knowable only by pure reason. In many respects it is a metaphysics of the ordinary: standard sensible objects, especially organic living beings, and artifacts. This means that in many respects Kant's critique of rationalist metaphysics in effect 'misses' it, or intersects with it only marginally. Aristotle, for the most part, is not interested in the special, non-sensible objects that Kant was concerned with, but about the intelligibility conditions of ordinary objects. To say this is not to say that he is interested just in epistemology or the priority of epistemology. It is to say, as Hegel would, that he is interested not simply in how we make sense of things, but how things are such that they can be made sense of; and how could the questions be separated? Hegel's project, I am trying to suggest, has much more to do with this enterprise than either a neo-Platonist theory of ultimate reality, or an attempt to determine the furniture of the universe available only to pure reason, like a monistic substance or monads or ideas.

He has his problems with Aristotle, serious ones, the pursuit of which would take us far afield. He would not say that the mind can in some way 'become all things', or he has difficulties with any sort of passive intellectual intuition, but the similarities are much more important for our purposes here.[17]

Returning now to the main theme: we should of course be wary of attributing to Hegel psychologism or subjective idealism, but we should not be so wary that we lose touch completely with the fact that *The Science of Logic* is the science of such acts, construed

---

[16] See Falk, *Das Wissen in Hegels Wissenschaft der Logik*, for a good statement of this point, 170–171.

[17] Hegel admires what he takes to be the Aristotelian identification of 'thought' with 'objects in their truth' (or *Wirklichkeit*), but he complains that Aristotle's account of this identity is imprecise and confusing. So we never know, in thinking about the thoughts by virtue of which reality is determinately what it is, whether we are thinking the thoughts (the thought that . . .), or what the thoughts are about. See the important discussion in Redding, "The Role of Logic," 3–6.

'logically', that is, with respect to rendering anything properly intelligible, giving its proper sufficient reason to be as it is. There are of course many various sorts of such sufficient reasons, and so the task of the *The Science of Logic* must be quite ambitiously comprehensive, especially since Hegel will object to any claim of radical incommensurability among such grounds. Hegel is a monist in this sense—a logical monist. There are no incommensurable spheres of rational intelligibility—cognitive, moral, aesthetic—as there are, say, in Kant.[18] (And even Kant struggled to appeal to the same general logical framework of intelligibility in presenting both the second and third critique.) But the initial, simple point at issue now is that anything's being at all would be mere indeterminate and indistinguishable being, were it not conceptually determinate, articulable—in the simplest sense, an instance of a concept. As in Aristotle's *Metaphysics*, to be anything is to be a determinate something, and that principle of determination can be considered 'for itself'. It is what Hegel calls 'the Concept' (what Aristotle called 'substantial form'). And this raises Hegel's main question in the *Logic*: how to account for conceptual content (or as he would put it, conceptual determinacy), given the variety of ways of objects' being intelligible as what they are in themselves.

9.2. THE 'METAPHYSICS' IN 'LOGIC AS METAPHYSICS'

So, to return to the identity claim, what could we mean by 'metaphysics', given what has just been shown about logic, and about what Hegel has rejected? Adrian Moore has recently suggested that, given the variety of metaphysical projects, we define the subject matter as capaciously as possible, and he suggests, as a working definition of metaphysics: "the most general attempt to make sense of things."[19] And he rightly notes that this is the way Hegel describes his enterprise. For example,

> . . . metaphysics is nothing but the range of universal thought-determinations, and as it were, the net [*das diamantene Netz*] into which we bring everything to make it intelligible [*verständlich*]. (E §246A)

And Moore appropriately notes that the notion of making sense can range widely (as it does in Hegel, especially given the various 'logics' and their different assumptions) over "the meaning of something, the purpose of something, or the explanation for something,"[20] or in Hegel's most ambitious version, it can include an account of the

---

[18] This is not to say that there are not distinct modalities of intelligibility for Hegel (philosophical, aesthetic, and religious, for example), just that they are not incommensurable. See the discussion in Pippin, "Reason's Form," for the aesthetic dimension's 'modality'.

[19] Moore, *The Evolution of Modern Metaphysics*, 6.

[20] Moore, *The Evolution of Modern Metaphysics*, 5.

determinate identifiability of anything as just what it is and not anything else. And, understood in this way, it is clear that metaphysics, while it has adequacy or satisfaction conditions, does not have the kind of truth-conditions that a matter of fact assertion has. Determining *when sense has truly been made* is not of the same order of tasks as "what caused the fire to start?" or "why does water freeze?". And finally, obviously, not every attempt to make sense of something is metaphysics. We must be talking about ways of making sense (understanding the possibility of determinate intelligibility) at the highest level of generality, without which nothing else would make sense: the sense of identity through change, individuality within common class membership, the relation of discrete moments to their continuum, and so forth. This formulation by McDowell captures well the general point:

> The concepts of propositional attitudes have their proper home in explanations of a special sort: explanations in which things are made intelligible by being revealed to be, or to approximate to being, as they rationally ought to be. This is to be contrasted with a style of explanation in which one makes things intelligible by representing their coming into being as a particular instance of how things generally tend to happen.[21]

Being revealed to be a manifestation of some order of reason will require that we understand how there could be such an order of reason and what it consists in. That is the task of *The Science of Logic*.

For our purposes, what is also interesting is that Moore goes on to distinguish between making sense of things (rendering them intelligible, something we have to work at in any of the modalities described) from *making sense of sense*, which he ascribes to logic and the philosophy of logic. And this fits Hegel's 'logic' to some degree on this reading. He is also making sense of how we make sense of things, but, given that he does not think of such sense-making as a species-specific 'subjective' capacity, but as constitutive of possible sense, he would not say that this is irrelevant to or even separate from 'making sense of things.' Logic has emerged in Kant as stating the conditions of possible sense, the distinctions and relations without which sense would not be possible. The questions that emerge from Hegel's 'expansion' of Kant's logic are how we determine what those conditions are and whether they can be rightly confined to what the avoidance of logical contradiction will allow, whether the 'emptiness' that Kant ascribes to these forms can be maintained.

This—the inseparability of the questions, the fact that we cannot *make sense of sense-making* without it being the case that ways of making sense have actually *made sense of things as they are*—is, I want to propose, what he means by saying that logic *is* metaphysics, or that being in and for itself *is* the concept. Once we understand the role of, say, essence and appearance as necessary ways of making sense, we have *thereby made sense* of essences and appearances, and therewith, the world in which they are indispensable.

---

[21] McDowell, "Functionalism and Anomalous Monism," 328.

(We have not made sense of some species-specific feature of human sense-makers, but of the sense the world could make.)

The basic unit of sense-making, in Aristotle, in Kant, and in a revised way in Hegel, is the predicative act. In making sense of *this* way of sense-making, its presuppositions and implications, we *are* making sense of what there is, the only sense anything could make. What there is must be determinate, and its 'determinations' are just its predicates, the content of which depends on their roles in possible judgments, the forms of which begin the cumulative moment of the *Logic*.[22]

Now, this level of abstraction can obscure a number of important differences. One sense of 'making sense of sense'—and this may be what Moore is thinking of—could involve only that notion of logic as contentless in Kant's sense, perhaps tautologous in the early Wittgensteinian sense, the minimum structure of any logical grammar of possible sentences, the negation of which is not in any carefully considered sense *at all* conceivable.[23] When Kant called logic "the science of the rules of understanding in general"[24] he also meant to set out what constitutes *possible thought as such*, not what we, as human beings, could make sense of, or the rules we ought to be following, but just what *could be* sense. But what interests Hegel about any such delimitation is what interests Kant, too: it is the general idea of the suitability of such absolutely universal forms of sense, no matter our actual theory of formal or mathematical logic, for a consideration of any possible thought of objects (in Kant the relation between General and Transcendental Logic). (Here again, the importance of their commitment to a judgmental logic, and so the conditions for possible sense-*making*, and not mere logical architecture, is crucial.) This involves the immediate bearing of such logical form on the question of any possible thought of objects: the bearing, say, of the subject-predicate form for the thought of substances and properties; the bearing of antecedent-consequence relations for the thought of necessary connections among events. This notion of such an immediate bearing is proposed by Kant independently of any transcendental deduction, and one can understand a great deal of Hegel as emanating from a claim about Kant's so-called Metaphysical Deduction—to wit, that there is a lot of philosophy already involved in such a 'deduction' and that it is an achievement. This means that for Hegel, the direct bearing of a General Logic on any possible Transcendental Logic is actually another way of stating the identity claim in §24 of the EL, and is not a mere restating or reorganizing of logical facts of the matter. (In Kantian language, the claim of EL §24 would be that functions of judgment *are* categories, *the* forms of the thought of any object.) It involves

---

[22] The judgment is the basic, or most familiar unit of significance. It is ultimately significant itself in a way that depends on its possible roles in inferences, and these inferences are to be understood in their systematic interconnection. So the ultimate unit of significance is 'the whole'. But for the most part, the inferential and systematic implications are not necessary for the sense required in any local context to be made out. Finally, what Hegel famously calls 'the speculative sentence' is not formulable in any fixed, standard logical form.

[23] In the senses (in Kant, Frege, and Wittgenstein) traced by Conant, "The Search for Logically Alien Thought."

[24] Kant, *Critique of Pure Reason*, A52/B76.

the intimation on Kant's part of the speculative 'identity' Hegel had announced, quoted earlier, and so it is of much greater importance than Kant admitted to understand the proper philosophical specification of these forms of thought, especially in their interrelation to each other. (Or it can be so read when we realize that the 'subjectivity' referred to in the "conditions for the possibility of experience" clause refers to what Hegel would call an 'absolute' subjectivity, one that refers to an unlimited or unbounded notion of subjectivity, not Kant's official 'finite' subjectivity.)[25]

So it is of some significance in Kant that the forms of possible thought already determine, already in some sense are, the only possible forms of the thought of things, that the logical constitution of possible sense is the form of the only possible sense that can be made of things; or of some direct significance that the subject-predicate form should have anything to do with substances and properties in the world. It is, let us say, the intimacy, or even inseparability between General and Transcendental Logic that interests Hegel.[26] Ultimately, Hegel will want to claim that it is not the case that General Logic as Kant understands it should be seen as something like a basic form to which content is 'added'. Rather, the basic form of possible thought, rendering intelligible, is content-directed, even content-determining, and any General Logic is an abstraction *from* such modes of thinking.

Stated in Kant's terms, the Metaphysical Deduction can be established before we supposedly learn, as a result of the Deduction, that given our sensible forms of intuition, all that being a substance bearing properties could be 'for us' is the permanent in time undergoing temporal alterations, or all that necessary connection between events could amount to 'for us' is necessary succession according to a rule. And Hegel will give us other reasons for thinking of the relation between General and Transcendental Logic; in Moore's terms, making sense of sense, and making sense of things, is much more an interrelation than had been realized.

9.3. KANT AND TRANSCENDENTAL LOGIC

Kant's notion of the emptiness of logic does not of course mean that the notions in a general logic are or could be treated as mere uninterpreted symbols; Kant's logical functions of judgments are clearly determinate kinds of discrimination and affirmation (How much? Of what sort? Is so or is not so? Either so or not so? If such and such, then this

---

[25] The actual Kantian statement of this 'identity' is The Highest Principle of Synthetic Judgments and it invokes the same thought: that the conditions for the possibility of experience *are at the same time* the condition for the possibility of objects of experience. See the discussion in Pippin, *Hegel's Idealism*, on 'Identity theory', 79–88.

[26] It is also what gets Kant into trouble with some commentators and historians, as if it is already 'contaminating' logic as such. See Kneale and Kneale, *The Development of Logic*: "For it was he [Kant] with his transcendentalism who began the production of the curious mixture of metaphysics and epistemology which was presented as logic by him and other idealists of the nineteenth century" (355).

or that)[27] but their domain is completely unrestricted, not tied to any sort or range of objects. But this already complicates that relation between general logic and "the forms of thought considered with respect to any possible experiential object," or transcendental logic, because it is part of Kant's epistemology, not a theorem in his logic, that content can only be provided receptively for finite knowers, and for us that means sensibly.[28] (Although he is relying on Aristotelian logic, this is not a distinction that would have occurred to Aristotle. *The basic kinds of being there are* just show up in sortal predications, in the way 'Socrates *is a man*', 'that *is a stone*', sort *substances*, and 'is white' and 'is musical' designate *quality*, the qualitative *modes of being*. This may have been what Hegel meant by saying that the old metaphysics simply assumed that thoughts were the 'essentialities' of things, or that things were substantial entities.)[29]

In the traditional reading of Kant, it would appear that Kant wants to introduce a step here, as if skeptical about why 'our' ways of sorting things should have anything to do with 'sortal realism', in the world. But this way of looking at Kant's treatment of the relation between General and Transcendental Logic—which we are exploring as a possible perspective on that §24 identification—is implicated in a much broader set of interpretive claims that themselves raise problems of major dimensions.

The issue will be familiar to anyone familiar with a textbook Kant; call it the two-step picture. On this picture, there must 'first' be sensible receptivity (according to 'our' distinct, non-conceptual pure forms of intuition), and 'then' there is conceptual articulation/synthesis, which is possible because of the a priori 'imposition' of categorical form.[30] To some extent, this requirement can seem a consequence of Kant's view of judgment—that some component of the judgment must be a way of referring to objects, and another a way of saying something about the object. But since, for Kant as well as for Frege, interpreted concepts determine extensions, this picture of strict separability and independent contributions to knowledge looks problematic. That is, if this idea of some possible independent contribution from sensibility is dubious, either as a reading of Kant or in itself (if the two sources of knowledge are notionally distinct, but inseparable), then the general/transcendental logic distinction, which depends on this understanding of 'contentless' versus

---

[27]   Another way of putting what Kant is doing: he takes the logical constants essential for evaluating the success of any inference—all, one, some, is, is not, is-non, if-then, either/or—the so-called syncategorematic expressions, and understands them as *terms* (categorematic, or having referential significance), or 'pure concepts of the understanding'. This sets him up for a 'move' Hegel thinks is already just thereby made: how to get from the table of logical functions of the understanding to the table of categories, concepts of possible objects.

[28]   This is stressed by McFarlane, "Frege, Kant and the Logic of Logicism." The innovation in question—that for Kant, general logic was 'empty of content'—is not straightforward, however, as I discuss in a moment, and the claim that for 'pre-Kantian' logicians logic simply coincided with ontology (rather than being about a special object—thinking) is controversial (with regard to the Port-Royal logicians anyway). I am indebted here to Clinton Tolley (correspondence).

[29]   Cf. the discussion of Aristotle as the founder of the science of logic in the Addition to E ¶20.

[30]   For a rejection of this two-step and impositionist interpretation as the correct interpretation of Kant, in either his practical or theoretical philosophy, see Pippin, "Reason's Form."

'having content' or 'being provided with content exogenously' would have to be rethought as well.[31]

By the need to rethink the general/transcendental logic distinction, I mean the following. None of what we have seen about General Logic amounts to a theory of what would be recognized today as a theory of logical truth or falsity. It is, in the sense already sketched for Hegel, a logic of general intelligibility. (Failing to observe the 'norms of thinking' is not mistakenly thinking, making an error in thinking; it is not thinking at all, not making any sense. The prospect of objects 'outside' something like the limits of the thinkable is a non-thought, a *sinnlose Gedanke*.)[32] But just because it is, the strict distinction between a prior, content-free general logic and an a priori transcendental logic, the forms of possible thoughts about objects, can hardly be as hard and fast as Kant wants to make it out to be.[33] For one thing, as just noted, that depends on a quite contestable strict separation between the spontaneity of thought (as providing formal unity) and the deliverances of sensibility (as the sole 'provider of content').[34] If that is not sustainable, and there is reason to think even Kant did not hold it to be a matter of strict separability, then the distinction between forms of thought and forms of the thought of objects cannot also be a matter of strict separability.[35] To consider beings in their intelligibility (what Hegel called "the science of things in thought") is not to consider them in terms of some species-specific subjective capacity, anymore than considering truth-functional relations between sentences in a logic is a consideration of how we happen to go on with sentences. To be *is* to be intelligible—the founding principle of Greek metaphysics and philosophy itself.

So to put Hegel's idealism in summary form. Logic is the science of pure thinking. Pure thinking's object is, and only is, itself. But this "object" is not a nature, an object. The *Logic* has nothing to do with "the mind" as a substance or thing. (Hegel is following *both* Aristotle here when he says that mind has no actual existence before it thinks, *and* Kant, for whom the claim that the "I think" must be able to accompany all my representations is a logical point, expresses the form of thought, is not a claim about how the mind operates.) If that were the case, and Hegel were making a claim about the mind's nature, knowledge would

---

[31] We should also heed here the warning of Michael Wolff. He notes that just as we should not over-interpret Kant's claim that general logic has *no* content, we should be careful about Hegel's positive claims about logical content. The *Science of Logic* is not, does not have the content of, the philosophy of nature of the philosophy of spirit (another reason not to think of it as substantive, 'furniture of the universe' metaphysics). Wolff, "Science of Logic." For very strong (and I think, compelling) formulations of the interpretation that holds that Hegel has no doctrinal position of his own, no substantive metaphysics, see Falk, *Das Wissen in Hegel's Wissenschaft der Logik*, and Koch, "Metaphysik und Spekulative Logik."

[32] I am convinced here by Tolley, "Kant on the Nature of Logical Laws." For more on the same point, see Wolff, "Der Begriff des Widerspruchs," 186. And on the mere 'Schein' of sense, see Conant, "The Search for Logically Alien Thought."

[33] This is noted, for different reasons, by Wolff, "Science of Logic."

[34] I hasten to note that the denial of strict separability is not a denial of distinguishability, as if Hegel thought there was no sensible receptivity, no intuitions, there were infima species or 'concepts' of individuals. See Pippin, "Concept and Intuition."

[35] Wolff suggests that we think, with Hegel, of the relation between formal or general logic and transcendental logic not as '*vorgeordnete*' but as '*beigeordnete*' and that seems wise. "Der Begriff des Widerspruchs," 196. He also suggests that the general-logical formulation of 'the law' of non-contradiction' means it cannot have unconditional, but only conditional validity.

be limited by its "instrument," something Hegel had been denying since the Introduction to the *Phenomenology*. In knowing itself what pure thought knows is the intelligibility, the knowability, of anything that is. But the intelligibility of anything is just what it is to be that thing, the answer to the "what is it" (*tode ti*) question definitive of metaphysics since Aristotle. So in knowing itself, thought knows of all things, what it is to be anything. Again, as for Aristotle, the task of metaphysics is not to say of any particular thing what it is. It is to determine what must be *true* of anything at all, such that what it is in particular *can* be determined (or: what is necessarily presupposed in any such specification).

Now, this all places enormous pressure on what amounts to a kind of operator in Hegel's *Logic* on which all the crucial transitions depend; something like "would not be fully intelligible, would not be coherently thinkable without. . . ." What follows the 'without' is some more comprehensive concept, a different distinction, and so forth. Excluding logical contradictions would be one obvious instantiation of the operator. But—and here everything in the possibility of Hegel's logical enterprise depends on this point—*the range of the logically possible is obviously far more extensive than the range of what Kant called the 'really possible'*. The latter is what we need if we are to have a logic of the real. And Hegel cannot avail himself of Kant's non-conceptual forms of intuition to establish a priori the sensible conditions that set the boundaries of 'the really possible'. However, to pick a strange ally at this point, Strawson, in *The Bounds of Sense*, showed how to demonstrate that the really possible *can* be determined without what he considered Kant's subjective idealism (the subjective forms of intuition), and this—revealingly for our purposes—by a reflection on whether a candidate notion of experience *could be said to make sense*.[36] Moreover, the key issue in Hegel's account is not logical contradiction and logical possibility, but the possibility of the intelligible determinacy of non-empirical conceptual content presupposed in the determination of empirical content. He would also point out that it is already the case in Kant that he seems to assume that he is showing how the minimal intelligibility of judgment could not be possible without his version of the necessary logical functions, the twelve moments of the Table of Pure Concepts. That is already a kind of determination of the really possible.

This all would not of course mean that we could not still artificially mark out a formal logic in the modern sense of, say, forms of valid logical inference, which, when instantiated by variables, will yield valid results. It is just to say that the link between inferential and conceptual forms in general and forms of the thought of objects is an intimate and a priori one. That deeper connection means that such forms are, *at the same time*, possible forms of well-formed judgments and proper inferences, *and* forms of the thought of objects, of objects considered in their intelligibility. These latter constitute all that objects could be. They are the forms of objects, and without Kant's 'only for us' restriction (without his reliance on non-conceptual forms of sensibility to establish that claim).

By contrast, Kant seems to think that he is faced with two exclusive alternatives. Either concepts, qua concepts, have objects, or their objects are provided exogenously. Hegel is providing a third alternative: that a strict separability between concept and intuitively apprehended object is impossible, even though the moments are distinguishable. The

---

[36] Strawson, *The Bounds of Sense*.

forms of the thought of an object can be considered the forms of objects (in Kantian language, the forms of sensibility) if it can be shown that the thought of anything at all, any way of making sense, would fail without some form or other. And so Kant's appeal to the form of the extra-conceptual as if to a distinct contributor is misleading and unnecessary.

He agrees with this remark by Kant, in other words, but merely disagrees that Kant must then go on to prove that there must be such manifolds.

> The pure categories, however, are nothing other than presentations of things insofar as the manifold of their intuition must be thought through one or another of these logical functions.[37]

Kant of course wants that reference to the 'manifold of intuition' to be doing some necessary, extra–General Logic work, especially in the Transcendental Deduction of the second edition. For example, when we realize that such a manifold has a pure, non-conceptual form—time—we have a way of showing how categories provided by the understanding from itself could be the forms of objects that exist independent of thought. By being modes of time-consciousness, they are thereby the forms of any intuitable content, and can be considered extra-conceptually as a way of getting into view all possible sensible content. But for Hegel this specification by thinking of the temporal modality of its forms must be a *further specification by thought of its own activity*.[38] Otherwise the relation to objects in question turns out to have a quasi-empirical answer. The answer would have to be: in what sense the forms of thought relate to objects "for creatures built like us."[39] More broadly, we can say that Mary Tiles is right that "categories [and for me this means categories *alone, RP*] are the concepts which *frame* objects in this way," and they do this already, as forms, without reliance on extra-conceptual forms of sensibility.[40]

Kant's view seems to be that, first, all thinkings, all representations, have intensional content, so it is possible to consider pure thinkings in terms not just of intensional content (that *logical content*, like 'the subject-predicate form'), but also in terms of real or objective extensional content (substances and properties). We can thus formulate 'categories'. For Hegel we are thereby already in the heart of speculative philosophy. But since we are for Kant dependent in experience on non-conceptual forms of intuition, these must be *merely putative categories*. We cannot know without further ado that or how such 'transcendental content' bears on content so enformed. (Because of the

---

[37] Kant, *Critique of Pure Reason*, A245/B303.

[38] John McDowell, "Hegel's Idealism as Radicalization of Kant," has argued that Kant did not need 'completion' by Hegel to see this point himself, that in the B Deduction "[t]he essential move is to deny that the Transcendental Aesthetic offers an independent condition for objects to be given to our senses" (73). I think there are passages that certainly suggest that Kant saw the problems caused by too strict a separation between intuition and concept but that by and large he bit the separability bullet, and accepted the 'subjective' idealism, the ignorance of things in themselves idealism Hegel charged him with.

[39] This is what McDowell calls Kant's tendency to refer to our forms of intuition as "brute facts" about us. "Hegel's Idealism as Radicalization of Kant," 76.

[40] Tiles, "Kant: From General to Transcendental Logic," 109. See also her interesting suggestion that a transcendental logic understood this way could count "delimitation of domains of possible interpretation as being within its scope" Ibid.

independent status of pure forms of intuition, there is supposed to be no guarantee that sensible objects *can* be possible objects of the pure understanding, whatever the understanding's 'own' content is.) The 'further ado' (in this traditional way of reading Kant) is the transcendental deduction, after which we supposedly know that in our experience there are, must be, substances in the sense of that which is permanent through time and alterations, underlying such change, in which properties inhere. This, supposedly, proves that transcendental content is not *merely* intensional—that objects sensibly apprehended correspond to it. But again, if Kant's own indications that there cannot be any strict separability between concept and intuition hold, such a strategy is misconceived. This is Hegel's claim, and partly explains why the *Logic* looks the way it does.[41] Kant thinks: we cannot know *that there is anything* that instantiates what the pure categories determine (substances, say). We need the Deduction to establish that there are. But for Hegel, since the forms of thought cannot but determine what *could be* an object, Kant's question is simply asking how we know there are objects at all, and that is not a question either Kant or Hegel is interested in. It is a question that depends on assumptions they would both reject.

Finally, it is often pointed out by those who object to an interpretation of Hegel as what has come to be called, after Klaus Hartmann,[42] a category theorist, that Hegel's aim in the Logic is *truth*, understood in the so-called ontological sense.[43] His interest is in what really is, what there is 'in truth', what *'wahhaftes Sein'* is, not what we are in general committed to in understanding the finite empirical world. And, according to Hegel, what there is in truth, that is, what 'the Absolute' is, is the Idea, understood as the unity of concept and reality, or true actuality (*Wirklichkeit*). I have suggested that Hegel has an Aristotelian model for the metaphysics involved, and a post-Kantian model of logic (apperceptive judgment and therewith actuality self-determined by thought, the latter of which requires a great deal more exposition).[44] Finite existent objects do not count as 'what there is in truth' because they do not fully correspond with their concept, and in that sense are incompletely intelligible. A 'bad' house (and even any merely finite house, because always 'bad' in some sense) is not adequate to its concept. But it also is in some way, or it would not be a house. It is in this sense, that it is both identical with itself, is what it is, and not identical with itself, is not what it actually is, that it exists in a kind of contradiction.[45] (As Theunissen points out, this is already an indication that Hegel's famous notion of contradiction does not violate Aristotle's law of non-contradiction.)[46] And this suggestion of true reality residing in a thing's concept—and, since each finite concept,

---

[41] See Kant, Prolegomena §9, for clear formulations of the issue in these terms.

[42] Hartmann, "Hegel: A Non-Metaphysical View."

[43] Horstmann, *Ontologie und Relationen*, 45.

[44] It is not lost on me that trying to integrate the Kantian conception of logic without independent forms of sensible intuition, and with thinking understood as spontaneity, with an Aristotelian conception of first philosophy, without reliance on *noesis* or any receptive intellect, is like trying to square two circles at one time. But that is the problem Hegel poses for himself (and for us).

[45] Theunissen, "Begriff und Realität," 348.

[46] The sense in which a man is not a man (not fully or perfectly what a man is) is not the same sense in which he is a man (the individual may be subsumed under that concept). Ibid.

by virtue of being finite, does not perfectly express conceptuality (intelligibility) itself—seems to indicate that we have in Hegel a recognizable 'degrees of reality' Platonism.

But the point of Hegel's denying to finite, empirical reality the gold standard badge of true actuality, is not to say that it 'possesses' a lesser degree of *existence*, whatever that might mean. It is to say that finite objects *viewed in their finitude* can never, so isolated and interrogated, reveal the possibility of their own intelligibility. An empirical attention to the finite details will provide us only with lists of properties, successions of events, mere associations, nothing that would get us close to the basis of the possibility even of identifying those determinate properties and events. For that we need to understand such finite objects in the light of the concepts required for their intelligible apprehension and explanation, and we will never achieve that in empirical observation, and, given Hegel's attack on immediacy in all its forms, not by any intellectual intuition either. This process of thought's determination of its own possibility may still be, is, pretty vague, and the isolation and identification of the *necessary* moments of such self-determination will place a great deal of stress on that notion of necessity (and so on the process of internal self-negation by which they are identified), but those problems amount to the task Hegel's approach gives us. And this sort of interpretation allows one to see one sense in which it is close to Kant on the a priori specification of content by, exclusively 'thought', but without distinct, separable forms of receptivity, and without any appeal to an intuitive intellect 'creating' everything it thinks by thinking. At any rate, this is all we need for a beginning in trying to understand Hegel's *Science of Logic*.

WORKS CITED

Primary Texts

Hegel, G. W. F. *The Encyclopedia Logic* [E], translated by T. F. Geraets, W. A. Suchting, and H. S. Harris. Indianapolis: Hackett, 1991.

Hegel, G. W. F. *The Science of Logic* [SL], translated by George Di Giovanni. Cambridge: Cambridge University Press, 2010.

Kant, Immanuel. *Critique of Pure Reason*, edited and translated by Paul Guyer and Allen W. Wood. Cambridge: Cambridge University Press, 1998.

Secondary Literature

Anderson, R. Lanier. *The Poverty of Conceptual Truth: Kant's Analytic/Synthetic Distinction and the Limits of Metaphysics*. Oxford: Oxford University Press, 2015.

Conant, James. "The Search for Logically Alien Thought: Descartes, Kant, Frege, and the *Tractatus*." *Philosophical Topics* 20, no. 1 (1991): 115–180.

Davidson, Donald. "The Method of Truth in Metaphysics," in *Inquiries into Truth and Interpretation*, edited by Donald Davidson. Oxford: Clarendon Press, 1984, 199–214.

Falk, Hans-Peter. *Das Wissen in Hegels Wissenschaft der Logik*. München: Karl Alber, 1983.

Förster, Eckart. *The Twenty-Five Years of Philosophy: A Systematic Reconstruction*. Cambridge, MA: Harvard University Press, 2012.

Hartman, Klaus. "Hegel: A Non-Metaphysical View," in *Hegel: A Collection of Critical Essays.*, edited by Alasdair MacIntyre. Notre Dame, IN: Notre Dame University Press, 1976, 101–124.

Horstmann, Rolf-Peter. *Ontologie und Relationen.Hegel, Bradley, Russell, und die Kontroverse über interne und externe Beziehungen.* Königstein: Athenaum, 1984.

Kneale, W., and M. Kneale. *The Development of Logic.* Oxford: Oxford University Press, 1962.

Koch, Anton. "Metaphysik und Spekulative Logik," in *Metaphysik heute: Probleme und Perspektive der Ontologie,* edited by Matthias Lutz-Bachmann and Thomas M. Schmidt. Freiburg/München: Verlag Karl Alber, 2007, 40–56.

Lear, Jonathan. *Aristotle: The Desire to Understand.* Cambridge: Cambridge University Press, 1988.

McDowell, John. "Functionalism and Anomalous Monism," in *Mind, Value, and Reality,* by John McDowell. Cambridge, MA: Harvard University Press, 1998, 325–340.

McDowell, John. "Hegel's Idealism as Radicalization of Kant," in *Having the World in View: Essays on Kant, Hegel, and Sellars,* by John McDowell. Cambridge: Harvard University Press, 2009, 69–89

McFarlane, John. "Frege, Kant and the Logic of Logicism." *Philosophical Review* 111, no. 1 (2001): 25–65.

Moore, A. N. *The Evolution of Modern Metaphysics: Making Sense of Things.* Cambridge: Cambridge University Press, 2012.

Pippin, Robert. "Concept and Intuition: On Distinguishability and Separability." in *Hegel-Studien* 40 (2005): 25–39.

Pippin, Robert. *Hegel's Idealism: The Satisfactions of Self-Consciousness.* Cambridge: Cambridge University Press, 1989.

Pippin, Robert. "Reason's Form," in *The Impact of Idealism: The Legacy of Post-Kantian German Thought,* Vol. 1, edited by Nicholas Boyle, Liz Disley, and Karl Ameriks. Cambridge: Cambridge University Press, 2013, 373–394.

Redding, Paul. "The Role of Logic 'Commonly So-Called' in Hegel's *Science of Logic.*" *British Journal of the History of Philosophy.* 2014. http://dx.doi.org/10.1080/09608788.2014.891196.

Rödl, Sebastian. "Logical Form as a Relation to the Object." *Philosophical Topics* 34, no. 1–2 (2006): 335–369.

Rohs, Peter. *Form und Grund. Interpretation eines Kapitels der Hegelschen Wissenschaft der Logik.* Bonn: Bouvier, 1982.

Strawson, Peter F. *The Bounds of Sense: An Essay on Kant's Critique of Pure Reason.* London: Methuen, 1966.

Theunissen, Michael. "Begriff und Realität. Aufhebung des metaphysischen Wahrheitsbegriff," in *Seminar: Dialektik in der Philosophie Hegels,* edited by Rold-Peter Horstmann. Frankfurt: Suhrkamp, 1978, 324–359.

Thompson, Michael. *Life and Action: Elementary Structures of Practice and Practical Thought.* Cambridge, MA: Harvard University Press, 2008.

Tiles, Mary. "Kant: From General to Transcendental Logic," in *Handbook of the History of Logic,* edited by D. M. Gabby and J. Woods. Amsterdam: Elsevier, 2004, 85–130.

Tolley, Clinton. "Kant on the Nature of Logical Laws." *Philosophical Topics* 34, no. 1–2 (2006): 371–407.

Wolff, Michael. "Der Begriff des Widerspruchs in der 'Kritik der reinen Vernunft,'" in *Probleme der Kritik der reinen Vernunft,* edited by Burkhart Tuschling. Berlin: de Gruyter, 1984, 178–202.

Wolff, Michael. "Science of Logic," in *The Bloomsbury Companion to Hegel,* edited by Allegra de Laurentis and Jeffrey Edwards. New York: Bloomsbury, 2013, 71–102.

CHAPTER 10

....

SELF-DETERMINATION AND IDEALITY IN HEGEL'S LOGIC OF BEING

....

BRADY BOWMAN

10.1. SELF-DETERMINATION AND IDEALITY

HEGEL's *Science of Logic* proposes to begin with no determinate, presupposed content whatsoever, and then, purely by dint of a methodically controlled reflection on the 'movement' of thinking itself, to generate a demonstrably complete list of categories and forms of thought.[1,2] Like other of his contemporaries, Hegel regarded Kant as having neglected to provide a derivation of the categories he identified as constituting the structure of objectively valid experience (cp. SL 21.48/41, 12.44/541). *The Science of Logic* is intended to provide such a derivation and, in doing so, to improve upon similar attempts by Hegel's predecessors, especially Fichte and Schelling.

Kant's transcendental idealism is not the only philosophy with which *The Science of Logic* stands in critical dialogue. Equally important is the confrontation with Spinoza's substance monism. Indeed, the so-called Objective Logic, comprising the first two main

[1] In preparing this chapter I have profited from the writings of more scholars than can be mentioned here. I would like to acknowledge my indebtedness to Andreas Arndt, Dieter Henrich, Anton Friedrich Koch, and Robert Pippin, whose insights have helped shape my account, as much as it surely departs in particulars, and especially to Stephen Houlgate for his constructive comments on a draft of this chapter. I owe a special debt of gratitude to Birgit Sandkaulen, who hosted my tenure as a Humboldt Research Fellow in 2014/2015 at the Forschungszentrum für Klassische Deutsche Philosophie (Ruhr-Universität Bochum); our regular discussions on Hegel and post-Kantian philosophy have been a source of inspiration. The research that went into writing this article was generously supported by the Alexander von Humboldt Foundation.

[2] On Hegel's Logic as a theory of categories see Hartmann, *Hegels Logik*.

parts of the work (viz., the Doctrine of Being and the Doctrine of Essence), culminates in what Hegel proclaims to be "the one and only true refutation of Spinozism" (SL 12.15/ 512). The project of supplying a rigorous deduction of the categories is thus intertwined with that of vindicating "the freedom and the independence [*Selbständigkeit*] of a self-conscious subject" (SL 12.15/512) over against Spinoza's one-sided, 'realistic' monism of substance.[3]

To understand why Hegel found it promising to confront Spinoza's philosophy of substance with Kant's philosophy of subjective spontaneity, it is helpful to focus on the concept of *synthesis*, and more particularly on the concept of an *original synthetic unity*. Robert Pippin places Kantian apperception at the center of his groundbreaking study of *Hegel's Idealism*, noting Hegel's own association of 'the Concept' (i.e., the Logic's main and, in a certain sense, only topic) with the transcendental unity of apperception.[4] One of the keys to understanding Hegel's Logic is to see, first, that he conceives the triadically structured 'movement' of 'the Concept' through the successive stages of its exposition as the activity of a priori synthesis itself; and then, second, that he conceives this activity as generating a unified but internally differentiated, and in that sense *concrete*, content—namely, the content of the categories themselves.[5]

Because this originally synthetic activity is (for Hegel as for Kant) the defining feature of *thought*, we can aptly characterize it as *ideal*. But insofar as it is an actual activity that is, moreover, productive of its own content, we are equally entitled to consider it *real*—in the sense of producing objective 'whatness' (*realitas*), as well as in the more common sense of having independent existence. In a conceptual move that at once both runs counter to Spinoza's prioritization of substance and reinterprets his notion of the *causa sui* through the structure of self-consciousness, Hegel puts the idea of an originally synthetic, equally real and ideal, 'spiritual' (*geistig*) activity at the center of his philosophical system. We should also recall, however, that (for Hegel as for Kant) synthesis is *spontaneous, self-causing*, and *self-determining* activity. The project of the Logic is thus to vindicate the "freedom and independence of a self-conscious subject" by demonstrating, in a single, continuous, conceptual 'movement', that pure, spontaneous, synthetic unity—'pure knowing' or 'pure thinking', as he calls it (SL 21. 45/ 38–39)—is sufficient to determine itself by generating, in a completely autonomous manner, its own *content* or *reality*. That is the idealist argument of Hegel's *Science of Logic*.

---

[3] On the impact of Spinoza, see the contributions by Sandkaulen, Ng, and Zambrana (Chapters 1, 12, 13) in this volume. Cf. Beiser, *Fate of Reason*; Förster and Melamed, *Spinoza and German Idealism*.

[4] See Pippin, *Hegel's Idealism*, esp. 17–24; cp. SL 12.17–18/514–515.

[5] In one sense, the progress of the Logic is analytic in character, "merely the positing of that which is already contained in a concept" (E §88R). However, the content that is there to be posited is the product of an original, productive synthesis.

10.2. THE KANTIAN TEMPLATE

Given Hegel's intention to improve on Kant's presentation of the categories, we may expect a degree of overlap between *The Science of Logic* and the relevant portions of the First Critique. Kant structures his table of categories according to four headings: quantity, quality, relation, and modality (CPR B106). When we compare the main divisions in first part of the Logic, the logic of 'Being', we find them to deviate only slightly from the Kantian template: Hegel reverses the order of the first two headings, putting quality before quantity, and he introduces an additional heading, *measure*, which he conceives as the synthesis of the first two.[6] Under the heading *quality* we might therefore again expect to find categories that hew closely to the First Critique (viz., reality, negation, and limitation). Instead, we find the exposition of quality subdivided into three chapters devoted to Being, Being-Determinate (*Dasein*)[7], and Being-for-Self, respectively— terms that bear no obvious relation to the ones proposed by Kant. However, while this terminological deviation does signal deeper, more substantive differences, we can still discern an illuminating parallel with Kant's ordering of the categories.

For Kant, the pure concept of *reality* denotes 'mere affirmation' (CPR B328), 'positing' (CPR B625), or 'position' (CPR B630), a category he correlates with the form of affirmative judgment (cp. CPR B95). Correspondingly, Hegel uses *being* to denote an essentially affirmative aspect or 'moment' of all the categories derived under the heading of quality, and the first chapter is devoted to its exposition. Kant understands *negation* to require some affirmative term from which to be distinguished and in relation to which its content can be fixed (cf. CPR B602–603). Correspondingly, Hegel devotes

[6] Hegel adopts the triadic organization of the categories from Kant: cp. B 110; SL 21.324/283. In the same passage, he explains his addition of the category of *measure*.—Kant's categories of relation and modality find their analogues in the logic of 'Essence'.

[7] Hegel's term *Dasein* presents the translator with challenges. In ordinary non-Hegelian usage, the term usually translates as 'existence', though in many contexts 'to be present' or 'to be there' is more appropriate. Hegel himself points to the etymological meaning of the word as "being [*Sein*] in a certain place," but hastens to add that "the idea of space [*die Raumvorstellung*] does not belong" in the context of his logical analysis of the category (SL 21.97/83–84). In English we can similarly say that "there is someone coming," for instance, or speak of what it is "for there to be" something of a certain kind. 'There' functions as an empty placeholder that, despite the explicitly spatial metaphor, marks existence but has no distinctively spatial import. Hegel uses the word this way when he says of 'affirmative infinitude' that "it *is*, and *is there*, present, at hand [*es ist, und ist da, präsent, gegenwärtig*]" (SL 21.136/119). I will occasionally exploit this resource of the English language to render *Dasein* (e.g., in section 10.4.2).

However, neither 'being-there' nor 'existence' recommends itself as the primary rendering of the Hegelian term. Besides the fact that 'being-there', as an English term of art, is firmly associated with Heidegger's quite different notion of *Dasein*, neither does it serve well to track the more general Hegelian concept of which it is a special instance, namely *determinate being* (*bestimmtes Sein*; SL 21.96/83; cf. Houlgate, *The Opening of Hegel's Logic*, 298). 'Existence', in turn, ought to be reserved as a translation for the related but distinct Hegelian term, *Existenz* (cp. SL 11.324–34/420–430). I have opted to render *Dasein* as *being-determinate*, partly to bring it into line with related terms such as *being-in-itself* and *being-for-itself*, partly also to emphasize its adverbial character as a mode of being in contrast to the adjectival relation of a property (say) to an underlying entity that is thereby rendered determinate.

the second chapter to the category of *being-determinate*, at the heart of which lies the negative (contrastive) relation of 'something' and 'other'.[8] Kant analyzes the concept of limitation, finally, as bringing together the concepts of reality and negation (CPR B111). Correspondingly, Hegel introduces the concept of *being-for-self* in chapter 3 as the complete 'integration' [*Einbildung*][9] of negation into being (cf. SL: 21.144/126): something is said to be 'for itself' to the extent that it has "interrupted and repelled its relation and community with what is other and abstracted from it" (SL 21.145/126–27); rather than being limited from the outside, by something else, the very character (the reality) of whatever is for itself is defined by its own self-limitation.

There is thus a discernible correspondence between Kant's identification of the qualitative categories and Hegel's treatment of quality in the *Science of Logic*. However, we should be aware that a degree of simplification is involved in mapping Hegel's division of quality onto the corresponding terms in Kant's table of categories. We need only glance at the table of contents to see that, in addition to serving as the heading for the entire first section of the Logic, quality is itself also a subordinate determination of the category being-determinate (SL 21.98/84). Furthermore, reality and negation are not straightforwardly identified with being and being-determinate; rather, they are themselves subordinate aspects of the concept of quality (SL 21.98/85), while the category 'limit' falls under the subheading 'finitude' (SL 21.113/98), well before the transition to being-for-self. What, then, is the use of trying to map the Hegelian concepts onto what now appear to be but very inexact Kantian equivalents?

Hegel himself understands Kant to have conceived 'reality' as a purely *affirmative* category containing no negation (SL 21.99/86). But that, according to Hegel, is to *misconceive* the category of reality: to be determinate *just is* to contain negation, so reality as conceived by Kant is something utterly empty and indeterminate, tantamount to what Hegel criticizes as 'abstract being' in the opening chapter of the Logic (SL 21.100/86–87). Indeed, one of Hegel's chief argumentative goals in this first part of the Logic is to show that reality and negation can only be understood as in any sense determinate when the concept of a determining limitation (and ultimately, in being-for-self, a *self-limitation*) is prioritized, so that reality and negation are conceived as secondary, subordinate aspects abstracted from the higher, more concrete category. So Hegel's exposition can be read as *polemically identifying* Kant's 'reality' with 'abstract being', in order *progressively to rearticulate* reality as the internally self-limiting (and to that extent self-determining) 'being-for-self' that Hegel will eventually go on to identify with 'infinitude' or 'reality in a higher sense' (SL 21.136–37/119).

Mapping the divisions of 'Quality' onto their Kantian counterparts is thus useful for recognizing the precise manner in which *The Science of Logic* undertakes a critical transformation of Kant's doctrine of the categories.

---

[8] For Kant's view of negation as the source of determinateness among different 'somethings' or 'realities', cf. B 605–607; also cp. AA 2.30–31.

[9] Di Giovanni's translation of the *Logic* has occasionally been modified.

Something similar is true of being-determinate and its correspondence with the concept of negation. The main thrust of chapter 2, "Being-Determinate," is to argue that so long as we take a purely affirmative notion of being (e.g., Spinoza's 'substance') as our starting point, such that determinate existence can only be conceived as the result of negative limitations that are somehow externally imposed on an intrinsically undifferentiated substrate, we are inexorably led to a nihilistic conception of determinate existence: we have no alternative but to grasp it as purely relational, defined purely through contrastive relations that have no positive grounding in the individuals themselves. Being-determinate, thus conceived, turns out to be coextensive with what Hegel calls *finitude*: "When we say of things that *they are finite*, what we understand by this is that [. . .] non-being constitutes their nature, their being. [. . .] The hour of their birth is the hour of their death" (SL 21.116/101).

Hence, even though negation is not identified with being-determinate at the level of terminology, it is clearly Hegel's intention to argue that anyone who (like Kant or Spinoza) assumes the priority of affirmative being and accords negation a secondary, dependent status is forced to conceive determinate being as effectively coextensive with negation. Mapping the second division of the Logic onto negation as it figures in Kant's table of categories is thus useful for bringing out one of the most innovative aspects of the Hegelian agenda: the development of an alternative conception of negation and determination that evades nihilism and provides a logico-ontological foundation for the philosophy of self-determination.

As we will see in more detail later, the critical thrust of Hegel's analysis of the category of finitude is to expose a natural preconception that renders it logically self-undermining. To be finite is, minimally, to be limited. Yet the 'logic' of the limit is such that *what* is limited (viz., the finite) inexorably tends toward self-negation or annihilation when taken in its totality. In the 'nothing' that remains, there can be no limit. When we view the matter thus, it appears that the passing away of what is limited is tantamount to the emergence of what is *unlimited*: the non-finite, the *infinite*. But an infinite whose being consists in nothing more than just the non-being of the finite is itself precisely—*nothing*. So the seemingly natural assumptions governing the logic of being-determinate (viz., that reality is purely affirmative, and that determination arises by virtue of external relations of negation or mutual limitation) tend to do away with the notion of reality and limitation altogether.

Accordingly, even though the concept of limitation occurs relatively early in Hegel's exposition, we do not encounter a logically stable instantiation of the concept until we move into the territory of being-for-self (i.e., the territory of an internally self-relating, self-limiting structure). Thus it is helpful to keep in mind the corresponding concept in Kant's table of categories. For as surely as Hegel agrees with Kant's analysis of limitation as the unity of reality and negation, he is just as surely committed to developing a more compelling account of such unity and the associated metaphysical stakes.

The structure of Hegel's exposition of 'Quality' thus implicitly reflects the structure of the corresponding division in Kant's table of categories at the same time that it explicitly displaces and rearticulates the concepts and conceptual relations that constitute the true framework of Kant's account.

10.3. Being–Nothing–Becoming

As indicated earlier, chapter 1 ("Being") pursues the critical goal of showing that a purely affirmative notion of being is thoroughly indeterminate and hence indiscernible from the thought of nothing [*Nichts*]. At the same time, Hegel seeks to derive a positive result that can serve as the basis for the derivation of further categories. However, the reader should be aware that this opening 'dialectic' of being–nothing–becoming is among the most challenging of Hegelian texts and also the one that has invited the most criticism.[10]

Apart from its compactness, the main difficulty of the text stems from Hegel's insistence that the beginning of the Logic is wholly without presuppositions, and more especially that his demonstration does not rely on any 'concepts of reflection' such as identity and difference, agreement and contradiction, or form and content (e.g. SL 21.55–56/ 47, 78–79/67, 90/78).[11] Because we are proscribed from using these concepts as part of the positive exposition, it becomes difficult to reconstruct anything like an 'argument' showing that being and nothing are (in some sense) both identical and different. Not only do these terms themselves belong on the list of prohibited concepts; the very indeterminateness of pure being and nothing precludes any distinction of aspects (such as form and content) with respect to which we could compare being and nothing. So how should we understand the method and aim of this opening 'dialectical' exposition?

A full-blown analysis of Hegel's exposition is beyond the scope of this contribution. However, the following two observations are intended at least to increase the *prima facie* plausibility of the beginning of Hegel's 'speculative science' of logic.

In the first place, why must the Logic begin with the thought of *being*? One way to approach this question is to connect it to Kant's theory of mental activity, according to which the defining character of thought is *synthesis*. Indeed, Kant identifies the "highest point, to which we must attach all use of the understanding, even the whole of logic" (CPR B134) as the "original synthetic unity of apperception" (CPR B134). The idea of an *original* synthetic unity will necessarily seem problematic if by 'synthesis' we understand the bringing together of two or more distinct and separately existing terms, already 'there' prior to their synthesis.[12] Understood thus, all synthesis is necessarily *derivative*, presupposing distinct terms, each of which would have to exhibit its own prior (and,

---

[10]   On the early reception see Burkhardt, *Hegels 'Wissenschaft der Logik.'* Classical and contemporary criticisms are covered in Houlgate, *The Opening of Hegel's Logic*, esp. 29–102.

[11]   For Kant's account of the concepts of reflection and their role in concept-formation, see CPR B316–324, together with AA 9.94–95.

[12]   Cp. SL 21.78, 82–85; also cp. GW 4, 327.

somewhere down the chain of composition, non-synthetic) unity. For without such unity, it would not be a term or indeed anything at all.

Accordingly, if we are to speak of *original* synthesis at all, we must conceive it as concomitant with the very emergence of the terms it embraces; it would have to be, in some sense, the origin both of the relation and of the very difference whose unity the relation constitutes. The opening of the Logic can be understood as an attempt to resolve the conceptual difficulty involved in the notion of original synthetic unity. The underlying strategy can, roughly, be construed as follows: Assume that all synthesis is derivative (i.e., that all synthesis presupposes some prior, originally non-synthetic unity). If this thought is to have any content, then it must be possible to conceive some term, reality, or unity that is absolutely independent and separable, involving no constitutive relation to anything else. Such a term, reality, or unity would thus also be incapable of being differentiated in itself since any difference (i.e., any determination) would entail either the relation of different parts or aspects internal to it or the relation to something distinct from it. In short, synthesis, being a *relation*, would seem to require something utterly non-relational (call it *being*) as its precondition.

Now make good on this assumption in earnest: think, if you will, *being* in the sense just indicated. Thereupon (as will be spelled out shortly in more detail) you will find that the thought of being is itself the thought of a *pure* relation, in the sense of a *relating* that is prior to and independent of any relata. Or in slightly different terms, you will find that the single thought of being immediately involves the mind in an awareness of two distinct 'directions' or 'values': the negative (empty) character of being as 'vanishing' into nothing, and the self-negating character of nothing as 'reverting' to being in virtue of being thought, even as the being that has thus interposed itself into or in front of the thought of nothing nonetheless transports that negation in *failing* to be the thought of nothing.

This awareness, which has arisen through the attempt to think being in the sense just indicated, is nothing other than the immediate awareness of original synthetic unity. The thought of being is inseparable from the awareness of an original and irreducible duality between affirmation and negation. In its most native and original instantiation, pure a priori synthesis, the constitutive act of the mind, appears as a spontaneous act of self-differentiation into the opposed but inseparable 'moments' of affirmation and negation, the basic operations of logic.

To the extent this strategy succeeds, Hegel may be said to demonstrate the *possibility* of an original synthetic unity by inducing an exceptionally pure, *actual instance* of it. Thus, the Logic begins with what may rightly be said to be the beginning of logic as such: affirmation and negation as dual aspects of a single, self-differentiating, originally synthetically unified act of thinking. It thereby meets Hegel's conception of an ideally rigorous science of thought: "The principle ought to be also the beginning, and that which has priority for thinking [*das Prius*] ought to be also the first in the process of thinking" (SL 21.54/46).

The second of our two observations bears precisely on this synthetic unity of being and nothing, which Hegel infamously proclaims as the result of his exposition. How are we to understand it?—The key point in all Hegel's discussions of being and nothing is that they are indiscernible as putative *contents* of thought.[13] By contrast, the *act of thinking* being and nothing exhibits a determinate structure. Although there is no determinate content to be grasped when I undertake to think *being* in its 'indeterminate immediacy,' I do become aware of the negative character of being precisely insofar as I fail to grasp any content. (Hegel identifies being with "this pure empty intuiting [or thinking] itself" [SL 21.69/59].) Being is nothing.

Let us draw once more on Kantian resources to elucidate this idea further. Kant treats the concepts associated with the term 'nothing' in the same chapter as the concepts of reflection, explaining,

> The supreme concept with which it is customary to begin a transcendental philosophy is the division into the possible and the impossible. But since all division presupposes a concept to be divided, a still higher one is required, and this is the concept of an object in general [*Gegenstand überhaupt*], taken problematically, without its having been decided whether it is something or nothing. As the categories are the only concepts which refer to objects in general, the distinguishing of an object, whether it is something or nothing, will proceed according to the order and under the guidance of the categories. (CPR B346)

In other words, the categories constitute the basic forms of reference in general, and the 'table of nothing' that follows on this explanation enumerates the various respects in which concepts can *fail to refer*.

Depending on the specific category within which a given concept fails to refer, 'nothing' can apply (1) to a concept whose content is logically possible, but fails to pick out any corresponding object in experience (*ens rationis*); (2) to a concept that has determinate content, but such that its object is determined merely as the absence of some positive quality, as dark is the absence of light (*nihil privativum*); (3) to a mere form of intuition that cannot be intuited separately and for itself (*ens imaginarium*); or (4) to a concept whose content is impossible in itself and which therefore could not pick out any object (*nihil negativum*) (CPR B348).

At the opening of Hegel's Logic, 'being' might be said to fail in all these ways. Having no specific content ("it is pure indeterminateness," SL 21.69/59), it cannot be internally inconsistent, but neither does it pick out anything: it is an *ens rationis*. Once again, having no specific content ("it is pure [...] emptiness," SL 21.69/59), it is the negation of all content: *nihil privativum*. Since it is "only this pure empty intuiting itself" (SL 21.69/59), it cannot be intuited separately and for itself: *ens imaginarium*. Finally, in proving thus to be nothing in all these three senses, the thought 'being' is indiscernible from nothing; it is the same as its categorical negation, and in this way it is self-contradictory after all—not because its content is inconsistent, since it has none, but

---

[13] Cp. SL 21.72–73/62, 79–80/68.

because it is a self-undermining act of referring and thus a kind of performative self-contradiction: *nihil negativum*.

Do we violate the prohibition on concepts of reflection in thus explaining how the thought of being is the same as the thought of nothing? The obvious answer would be yes. This distinction and comparison among aspects in which the thought 'being' fails to refer is a paradigm case of reflection. But on second thought, is it not rather a special case? Here all four aspects are collapsed into one another and are themselves only artificially distinguishable. In fact, all four categories in which referential failure can occur all make at least a minimal presupposition, namely that of 'an object in general' *to which* reference may be made, and, concomitantly, an act of referring. So just as Kant goes the tradition one better in replacing the concept of a 'possible object' with the 'higher concept' of an 'object *überhaupt*', Hegel may be seen as going Kant one better and replacing that concept with the mere thought: *überhaupt*. This would in any case be in line with his notion of 'pure knowing' as having 'merged with itself' into an absolute unity, lacking any distinction of subject and object, in which "all reference to an other and to mediation has been sublated; it is distinctionless [*das Unterschiedslose*], and as such it itself ceases to be a knowing; only simple immediacy is present" (SL 21.55/47).

In the case of the determinate concepts Kant has in mind, their emptiness is not immediately apparent. They *appear* to refer to something, and it is only through comparative reflection that we recognize their actual emptiness, be it through comparison with what we find in experience (*ens rationis*), with the metaphysical nature of the referent (e.g., cold as the mere deprivation of heat rather than as a positive quality in itself), comparison of the concept's component contents with themselves (*nihil negativum*), or comparison of the empty form with the substantial content on which it depends in order to appear as something in the first place (*ens imaginarium*). *Being*, by contrast, is utterly transparent in its emptiness, rendering reflective comparison superfluous. It is impossible to think the thought *being*, without immediately perceiving its emptiness, its lack of a referent, and hence its 'untruth' (SL 21.71/61). It is a thought whose directedness toward something other than itself (a content) has, so to speak, been captured and held back; its referential import is transparently void. Precisely for this reason, it is predestined to be the first thought of the 'pure knowing' with which the Logic begins and in which "all reference to an other and to mediation has been sublated," such that "only simple immediacy is present" (SL 21.55/47). Pure knowing, as Hegel conceives it, *is* the thought of *being*.

Being is thus *the same as nothing*. However, what we have to recognize is that this transparent lack of reference, in virtue of which the thought of being effectively cancels itself out *as a thought*, is at the very same time the *thought* that I am engaged in thinking. My awareness of this transparent emptiness immediately invests it with an affirmative character. Just as *being* immediately manifests the simple immediacy of 'pure knowing', *nothing* immediately manifests the relationality or referentiality that is inseparable from thought. (As in the case of being, Hegel also identifies nothing with the "empty intuiting or thinking itself" [SL 21.69/59].) On the other hand, thinking stands to this nothing in the relation of cognitive reference: "To intuit or to think nothing has therefore a reference [*Bedeutung*]" (SL 21.69/59). So nothing immediately proves to have a relation, namely to the affirmative, being-like (*seiend*) character conferred on it in the act of thinking.[14]

Thus we re-arrive at *being*. But with a difference. In transparently exhibiting its sameness with being, nothing has effectively canceled itself out *as nothing*. Though in thinking *being* I have, in one sense, been *thinking nothing*, my thinking *of* nothing has at the same time (as it were, immemorially) failed to grasp it, as though the very act of thinking it were pushing it away. And yet my awareness of *this* failure to refer immediately *presupposes my grasp of the nothing* I am failing to think. As much as being manifests itself as 'always already' taking the place of nothing, nothing continuously evades, escapes, and opposes being, differing from it in what can only be called an absolute way.

This character of the thoughts of being and nothing, namely the fact that each is eternally returning into itself even as it vanishes into its other—this character of being and nothing immediately manifests the restless unity of pure thinking itself as original synthetic unity. Hegel terms this 'becoming' (SL 21.69/59).

10.4. THE LOGIC OF BEING-DETERMINATE (*DASEIN*)

10.4.1. Being-Determinate

As we have just seen, in my attempt to think *nothing*, nothing 'reverts' to being: it *is* (exists) as the referent of my thinking. But in thus thinking being *instead of nothing*, I am aware of my failure to think nothing: being is *not nothing*. In this way, both nothing and being are present in a single thought *as distinct*, and being takes on a first, minimal determinacy, that of being *not-nothing*. Being as not-nothing is what Hegel calls 'being-determinate'. This is not to say that being is internally differentiated (though thinking now is differentiated, insofar as it encompasses the difference between affirmation and negation). Nor can being really be said to be externally limited by nothing, since *nothing* is no kind of limit at all.

Inasmuch as this incipient determinacy represents the first, original emergence of determinateness, Hegel also calls it 'determinateness as such' (SL 21.97/84). In the course of the Logic we will encounter further forms or instantiations of determinateness (e.g., quantitative determinateness). In anticipation of those further forms, then, we distinguish this initial form in which determinateness as such first arises by calling it *quality* (SL 21.98/84). Quality is the determinateness belonging to *being* by virtue of its being *not-nothing*, two aspects that Hegel now further specifies by calling them *reality* and *negation*, respectively (SL 21.98/84).

---

[14] The argument of Parmenides is discernible in the background: see DK 28/B2.7–3.1, B6.1–2; cp. SL 21.88/76–77.

Here two clarifying remarks are in order. First, it is easy to relapse into treating being and nothing as though they were distinct *contents* of thought, with being on the one side (so to speak) and nothing on the other, each with its own quality ('beingness', say, and 'nothingness'), each somehow external to the other, limiting it. But it is easy to see that nothing, or negation as such, is not suited to define or determine anything at all; how could it be? Hence we must not think of quality, at this initial stage, as *some way* being is, such that it thereby differs from nothing. What we have in 'being-determinate' *just is* quality, a *differing* pure and simple, without reference to anything other than itself *from which* or *in relation to which* it differs. (As we might also phrase it, 'being there'—existence itself, in the broadest sense of the term—is, after all, just being that *differs from nothing*.) So rather than conceive of being-determinate as a quality-less substrate adjoined to a quality that is somehow distinct from it, we must conceive it rather as a concretely unified, quasi-adverbial *being-qualitative*. Hegel uses the word 'something' (*Etwas*) to denote this unity of being-there and quality, which he characterizes as "the first negation of negation, as simple, affirmative [*seiend*] relation to itself" (SL 21.102/88).

Second, since nothing or negation as such is not a real difference, the sense in which something is an immediate or simple 'oneness of being and nothing' (SL 21.97/83) is incomplete. As long as negation remains thus submerged in being-determinate, we have not yet actually fully formed the thought of *something*. At the same time, moreover, the opening of the Logic—indeed, its whole first volume, the Doctrine of Being—is governed by the 'one-sided' priority of being over negation (cf. SL 21.97/83). Therefore, wherever negation is present (and it is present throughout), it must also manifest itself 'in the form of being' (SL 21.97/83). Accordingly, to complete the thought 'something' we need to think of the moment of negation that is still present only in the submerged form of a simple unity of being and nothing (viz., being-determinate) as 'coming out into the open' and setting itself over against something as a *real* difference. Since the whole development here is unfolding 'in the form of being', negation too will emerge in an *affirmative*, being-like (*seiend*) guise, namely as 'something other' (SL 21.104/90).

Hegel's discussion of 'being-determinate as such' thus culminates in a transition: Being, or rather being-determinate, seems to be truly determinate only insofar as it stands in a relation of contrast to an *other* being-determinate, an other *something*. This 'other' something constitutes the limit, the terminus, or *the end* of the 'first' something. Hegel accordingly places this new sphere of dual, contrasting, limiting relations under the general heading 'finitude' (German: *Endlichkeit*) (SL 21.104–105/90).

10.4.2. Finitude

Omnis determinatio est negatio.[15] In Hegel's reformulation, "Determinateness is negation posited as affirmative" (SL 21.101/87). That is the core principle of finitude and it

---

[15] Hegel follows Jacobi in attributing this principle to Spinoza (cf. SL 21.101/87). For critical discussion

is central to the argument of 'Quality' in its entirety. Continued analysis of the relation of 'something and other' soon leads Hegel to the conclusion that qualitatively determinate beings are what they are only in virtue of their *limits*. If a quality may fittingly be described as whatever makes a difference, then qualitative beings have an existence that is purely differential, constituted by—but also exhausted in—their mutual contrasts. It is therefore not sufficient to say that qualitative beings are determinate in virtue of *having* limits; their limits are themselves "the principle of that which they delimit" (SL 21.115/ 100). Every limit is at once both a threshold of constitution and a site of mutual alteration. The sphere of qualitative being is thus constituted both as a heterogeneous continuum and as a perpetual flux in which nothing is actual except by differing.

Hegel is thereby suggesting not only that finite things are constituted by mere relations, above and beyond which they have no positively affirmative being of their own, but also that even in order to be what they are, they are bound to alter and destroy themselves.

> When we say of things that they are finite, we understand by this not merely that they are determinate, not merely that their quality is a reality and a determination that has being in itself, not merely that they are limited and hence still have a being this side of their limit—but rather that their very nature, their being is constituted by non-being. Finite things are, but in their self-relation they relate to themselves negatively, propelling themselves beyond themselves, beyond their being, by virtue of this very self-relation. [. . .] (SL 21.116/101)[16]

To capture this aspect of the finite, Hegel introduces the concepts of 'restriction' and 'the ought' as further specifying the concept of limit. To grasp the concept of restriction, it is helpful to focus on the dual role of the limit in defining a qualitative being. From a static, one-sided perspective, the limit is simply where one qualitative being *ends*; so at first glance it might seem as though something could remain whatever it is—maintain its defining quality—by remaining within its limit. On a more comprehensive, dynamic view, however, the limit is clearly defined as the interface between two 'contiguous' qualitative beings, each of which acts to limit (and thereby determine) the other. In order to 'be there' as *what it is*, each qualitative being has to interact with and thereby expose itself to *modification* or *alteration* by the other. But since a qualitative being is indeed defined by its quality, any alteration to it is tantamount to its negation or destruction. The qualitative being consumes and destroys itself, therefore, in its very realization.

In further unpacking this idea, we should keep in mind that what is at issue here are not primarily spatial or temporal limits, but *qualitative* limits. Hegel gives two examples: the limit beyond which something ceases to be a field and becomes a meadow, and the limit beyond which something ceases to be red and becomes a different hue (cp. SL

see Melamed, "Omnis determinatio est negatio." Cp. Stern, "Determination Is Negation."

[16] On the difference between limitation and finitude and the contrast with Spinoza cp. Houlgate, *The Opening of Hegel's Logic*, 370–375.

21.174/153). An instructive illustration can be drawn from the case of simultaneous contrast, where for example contiguous fields of blue and red interact, shifting the perceived hues toward green and orange, respectively. In a case like that, *what* the one qualitative being *is*—its defining quality—is determined not by 'itself', but by the efficacy of *another* qualitative being and *its* defining quality. Thus, the way a qualitative being 'is there' is a function of its surroundings; any *given* presentation of its defining quality is modified by the defining quality of the being or beings that limit it, as they are in turn modified through what they limit.

Thus, since the defining quality of a qualitative being (its 'determination', *Bestimmung*; SL 21.110/950) is essentially contrastive or differential, it 'is there' only to the extent that it is juxtaposed with another quality. That is the one side. But such juxtapositions are not inert; depending on what the other quality is, the first will 'be there' in one or another determinate *modification [Beschaffenheit]*, just insofar as it "preserves itself in its self-equality and asserts it [*geltend machen*] in its being-for-other" (SL 21.111/96).[17] That is the other side. Hence the specific surroundings both *constitute* a finite being's defining quality (its 'determination') and *modify* or *alter* the way it 'is there'.

An elemental tension is thereby introduced into finite qualitative beings. In order to be there at all, the defining quality must differ from and thereby limit some other quality; but depending on what the other quality is, the defining quality will (so to speak) be colored by it and made to take on some determinate hue. As long as it stands in that particular relation of mutual limitation, it will be *restricted* to 'being there' in that single modification (cp. SL 21.122/106–107). Limited by a different contrasting quality, it will be modified accordingly, thereby passing beyond one restriction, albeit only to be restricted in a new way. This tension between something's 'determination' and its various 'modifications' is what Hegel calls 'the ought [*das Sollen*]' (SL 21.119/104).

We are now in a better position to appreciate why Hegel says of finite beings that "the hour of their birth is the hour of their death." They realize their defining quality, or what they are, only by undergoing some alteration of their defining quality, that is, by ceasing to 'be there'. To all appearances, *that* is the implication of the principle *omnis determinatio est negatio*, and the entire field of qualitative determinateness falls within its scope. It does not take much to see, however, that qualitative being must be utterly without any grounding or ontological footing if it is truly constituted in the thoroughly differential manner indicated by the principle. We can see this more clearly by considering that there are two conditions on qualitative being: (1) no single qualitative being stretches any further than its actual 'being there'; (2) the 'being there' of a qualitative being can never count for more than a *restriction* of what it is in itself, so that, insofar as it (merely) *ought to be*, something is constantly in transcendence of its own limit (i.e., the way its

---

[17] Hegel's term *Beschaffenheit* is sometimes rendered as 'constitution', a word suggestive of something's inner makeup or fixed character. This connotation clashes with Hegel's use of the term to denote "what belongs to something outwardly [*was das Etwas* an ihm *hat*: cp. SL 21.108/93], *but not to its being-in-itself*" (SL 21.111/96, emphasis added). McTaggart's translation, 'modification' (*Commentary*, 26), is preferable in suggesting a quality something has in virtue of interacting with something else.

determinateness 'is there'). Now, these two conditions apply symmetrically to all qualitative beings; consequently, qualitative being in its entirety consists in nothing other than its own self-negation and perishing, part and whole alike. Non-being is the only true being of a qualitative sphere constituted solely by mutual restriction.

In a word, finite being-determinate negates itself. Its basic quality was, after all, first introduced as "the simple oneness of being and nothing" (SL 21.97/83); the successor notion of 'somethings' in relation to 'others' was introduced purely as a means of separating off the moment of negation so as to posit what we thought we could consider 'real' differences. As it turns out, however, what we find is that this whole way of 'translating' the simple unity of affirmation and negation into a sphere of real differences dead-ends as a form of nihilism. As a totality of mutually restricting and thus *merely restricted* qualities, 'being-determinate sums up to *nothing*. And that leaves us with nothing but a conception of being whose sole determination lies in the fact that, in contrast to the finitude of 'being-determinate,' it is *not nothing*. So we are back at square one. Or so it would seem until we take a broader and categorially richer view of 'finitude' and its role in the self-determination of being.

10.4.3 Infinity

'Finitude' represents the attempt to conceive determinateness as arising through the mutual restriction (negation) of otherwise affirmative qualities. The failure of that attempt teaches us that simple relations of negation between qualitatively distinct beings are insufficient to generate a system of determinate entities. If we allow ourselves to be guided by such a conception of negation in thinking through the principle *omnis determinatio est negatio*, we end up with a form of nihilism in which the 'world' of determinate existence 'vanishes' into an utterly simple and indeterminate 'being'. But the story is not over. In the transition to 'Infinity', Hegel takes up what is, to all appearances, a disastrous result, and subjects it to further, ultimately redeeming analysis.

To begin, a simple observation: Being as not-nothing is the way we initially introduced the concept *Dasein* (i.e., 'being there' or being-determinate). So in the (self-) negation of the finite, we have fallen back not quite to the very beginning of the Logic, but rather to its first properly determinate category. Furthermore, the initial analysis of 'being there' led us (*via* the concepts of quality, something, and something other) to the concepts of finitude, limit, and restriction as its entailments. Therefore, when we arrive at the result that the finite *is as nothing*, leaving us with the thought of being as simply *not-nothing*, we have in one respect re-arrived at our original point of departure and are poised to repeat the very same cycle of self-negating negative determination.

In another respect, however, the situation has changed. At the beginning of chapter 2, being and non-being (nothing) were present in 'simple unity', rather than in the stark contrast that emerged by the end of the section on 'finitude'. Consequently, being and non-being (nothing) now stand to each other in the more determinate relation of mutual limitation, each being what the other is not: the finite has revealed itself to be non-being, determining being accordingly as the non-finite, that is, as the *infinite*. But as Hegel is quick to point out, *this way* of grasping the concepts of the finite and infinite places them to each other in the characteristic relation of finitude (viz., mutual limitation or restriction). The same 'dialectic' that drove us to acknowledge the nullity of the finite will therefore repeat itself in the relation of the finite and the ('finitized') infinite— but this time with a more positive result.

By virtue of its purely differential constitution, the finite negates itself: that is the lesson of the previous section. In negating itself, the finite gives rise to (or perhaps more aptly, *gives way to*) the non-finite (cp. SL 21.109, 126/94, 110; SL 11.291/385). On closer inspection, however, this way of speaking might seem to be no more than mere word-play. The non-being of the finite is just that: *non-being, nothing*. In the absence of being-determinate in the sense of presence or 'being there' (*Dasein*), there *simply is nothing there* to which the finite could 'give way' in its perishing. The non-finite is only 'there' to the extent that it stands in contrast to the finite. But that lands us in a predicament. In order to 'be there' and stand in contrast to the non-finite, the finite has to persist or endure; otherwise the non-finite loses all determinateness and itself collapses into nothingness (the lesson of the Logic's opening chapter). So if the finite is nothing, so is the non-finite. Yet we have just established that the very essence of the finite is not to persist but to perish; for it to persist as the infinite's contrasting pole is thus for it to be non-finite itself. So if the infinite is not nothing, then it is the finite. There seems to be no way of keeping the infinite apart from the finite that does not end up either conflating them or destroying both (cp. SL 21.131/114).

Hegel sets out to resolve this difficulty by noting, first, that it is occasioned by the fact that we have started from a merely negative conception of the infinite as the non-finite. As surely as the infinite emerges as the self-*negation* of the finite, the infinite must also *posit* the finite in order to ensure for itself the degree of determinateness that is required to qualify it as any kind of *being* at all. To this extent, the infinite is inseparable from the finite. In the very moment the finite meets its destiny to undergo annihilation, the non-finite (the being that is not-nothing) restores it to existence as being-determinate. This much is guaranteed by the developmental sequence that began with 'pure being': the purely indeterminate being, left over after the finite vanishes, collapses into the 'pure' being of the beginning, which we have seen to unfold in a sequence that leads precisely to the finitude of 'being-determinate' and its self-negation. So we find ourselves in a repetitive cycle in which the infinite posits the finite, which negates itself and passes over into the infinite, which in turn posits the finite, and so on and so forth.

This cycle of negation and renewed positing, which Hegel famously dubs 'bad infinity' or the 'progress to infinity' (SL 21.129/113), is a crucial preliminary step toward resolving the difficulties outlined in the preceding. We have seen the cycle of bad infinity to involve 'moments' of both negation and affirmation (positing). Hegel develops the concept of 'true' or 'affirmative infinity' by comparing the way these two moments are at work from the perspectives of the finite and the infinite in turn. The result of his comparative analysis will be an expanded notion of negation that is able to do the work of both simple affirmation and 'simple negation' as they are present in the dialectic of bad infinity.

Hegel begins by considering what he variously calls 'simple', 'first', or 'immediate' negation from the perspective of the finite (e.g. SL 21.114/99, 127/111). When we take the finite in isolation, we find that its essential determination ('the ought') is to pass beyond its limit and thereby negate itself, thereby positing the infinite; but since the infinite is constituted as a being over against (i.e., limited by) the finite, it is in fact negated even as it is posited. When in turn we take the finite as standing in a limitative relation to the infinite, we are forced to acknowledge that the infinite, thus conceived, is subject to the same logic of 'the ought' and restriction that characterizes such relations generally; the infinite must therefore equally surpass *its* limit and pass over into the finite, thereby positing it anew. Hence in both cases, the finite is reproduced in its negation: the movement closes on itself and "merges with itself" in passing beyond or negating itself (SL 21.123, 134/108, 117).

Starting in turn from the infinite, we note its determination as the negation of the finite (viz., as the *non*-finite). It is thus determined as *beyond* the finite and consequently as limited by it. But such a limited infinite is itself finite and subject to the dialectic of the ought and restriction: it passes beyond the limit, negating itself, and the infinite is reproduced. The infinite thus exhibits the same cycle of negation and concomitant self-affirmation. Both the infinite and the finite constitute a single, identical movement of returning-to-self, a single process of 'becoming' (SL 21.135–136/118–119).

Upon reflection, then, we find that the finite and infinite do not in fact stand to each other in the relation of *simple* or *immediate negation* characteristic of 'being-determinate' as we initially came to understand it. Instead of each being the negation of the *other*, each is the negation of *itself* and thereby the renewed positing, reproduction, or reaffirmation of itself: *double negation* or the *negation of negation*.

Hence neither the finite nor the infinite can be understood as instances of simple, immediate being-determinate; they are instead internally self-mediated results, each arising from the identical movement of self-negation. The finite's (infinite) return to itself is itself the return of the infinite into itself. In the 'true' infinite, therefore, the logic of quality reaches a preliminary culmination. As a returning-to-self or self-relation, the true infinite exhibits the moment of immediacy that is characteristic of all determinations of 'being' in the technical sense of Hegelian logic. But as self-negation (and hence as a differing-from-self), the infinite exhibits the otherness or determinateness that is constitutive of determinate being. Hegel can therefore claim to have retrieved the notion of the infinite from its otherworldly sphere as what is merely beyond actual existence, proclaiming that "it *is*, and *is there*, present, at hand" (SL 21.136/119).

10.5. BEING-FOR-SELF

Hegel's analysis of 'true infinity' culminates in a transformed conception of reality, negation, and limitation. The categories of finitude were structured by what Hegel calls 'simple' or 'immediate' negation: *Dasein* is a heterogeneous continuum or manifold of qualities, each of which is supposed to constitute an *immediate* (i.e., independently graspable) reality and yet to be what it is only insofar as it represents the *negation* of (i.e., insofar as it differs from) some other quality external to it. This conception of reality and negation harbors a latent contradiction that Hegel's analysis of 'finitude' makes increasingly explicit: a world of qualities determined solely by mutual limitation could not be a world at all.

Hegel avoids this unacceptable conclusion by reconceiving negation. What is logically and metaphysically primary is an 'absolute' activity of self-negating negation. While it is right to think of this 'double negation' or 'negation of negation' as an original division, we must not imagine it as introducing difference into a preexistent unity ('substance' or 'being'). Division (self-negation) and unity (affirmation) are strictly concomitant. (It is easy to see that this is simply a further specification of what we said about *original* synthetic unity.) The concept of self-negating negation is intended to capture this paradoxical idea of a reality that divides itself in order to be one and that differs from itself by virtue of merging with itself.[18]

Such a reality can be said to be 'affirmatively infinite' in the sense that it is qualitatively determinate (it 'is there'), but not in virtue of being limited by any qualitative being external to it. Its determinateness is the result of self-limitation, that is to say, of self-determination. It is at once both a unity *for itself*, over against its manifold, finite determinations, and the unity of itself together with the manifold, finite determinations that are there *for it*.

At this point, it is natural to ask how and where we are supposed to find such a self-negating and thereby affirmatively self-determining reality to be instantiated. What claim to plausibility can be made on its behalf?

The beginning of an answer lies in Hegel's discussion of 'being-for-self', the topic of the third and final chapter of 'Quality.' By *being-for-self*, he means something closely analogous to the unified subject of apperception (cp. SL: 21.145/127, 12.17–19/514–516). It is important to emphasize, however, that the subject of consciousness is never encountered as a bare unity, but always as a unity saturated with the rich and particular content whose being is characterized by 'intentional inexistence,'[19] or what Hegel calls *being-for-one* (SL 21.146/128). Obviously, consciousness and its content are *realiter* inseparable. Yet they are also obviously distinct: within the unity of consciousness, there is a distinct and immediate *consciousness of unity* that persists through the flux of conscious content. As this consciousness of unity, being-for-self remains "at one with itself" (*bei sich*; SL: 21:145/127), notwithstanding its inseparability from the contents that are given to it as its modes.

Now, in Hegel's technical use of the term, 'consciousness' refers to a specific instance of the unity of being-for-self and being-for-one, in which the heterogeneity and externality of the unified content compromises the consciousness of unity as such (cf.

---

[18] Cp. Henrich, "Grundoperation."
[19] According to Brentano (*Psychology*, 88), the hallmark of mental phenomena.

SL: 21.145/127). By contrast, *self-consciousness* illustrates being-for-self in its purity. Here the difference in content that characterized being-for-one in the case of consciousness (sensations, intuitions, etc.) is canceled, and consequently the *Dasein*-like relation of being-other between distinct and independent 'somethings' also falls away. Being-for-one is, identically and indivisibly, also being-for-self; indeed, as self-consciousness, being-for-self can be said to obtain only insofar as it is itself being-for-one: being-for-self is *itself* the being-for-one *of* being-for-self (SL: 21.147/129).

We must therefore avoid the temptation to understand the content of self-consciousness as being *(merely) ideal* in contrast to the *reality* of the underlying 'subject' that grasps itself in it (SL: 21.147/129). Properly understood, being-for-self cannot be separated even notionally from the determinateness it has as being-for-one. In Hegel's words, "Ideality consists precisely in the fact that it is equally true of both [being-for-self and being-for-one] that they have being and validity only insofar as they are *for-one*, which is at one and the same time indistinguishably both ideality and reality" (SL 21.147/129).

The 'self-negating' character of true infinity and its categorial twin, being-for-self, does therefore find a plausible instantiation in the structure of self-consciousness, a unity which *is there* only to the extent that it simultaneously distinguishes itself *from itself* and identifies what is thus distinguished *with itself*. Nonetheless, being-for-self is explicitly not to be identified with self-consciousness, even though the two share the same basic structure.

The state of play at the opening of the chapter "Being-for-Self" is namely such that the manifold of qualities that populated the chapter "Being-Determinate" or *Dasein* has not yet reappeared after having vanished into nothingness along with finitude as such. The analysis of true infinity has merely shown us *how* qualitative being must be constituted in order not to succumb to the nihilistic logic of 'simple' negation, and being-for-self represents a corresponding reconception of the being-determinate that was the root of finitude. But being-for-self as such still has to undergo a process of development and realization parallel to the preceding development and realization of *Dasein*, whose successor-concept it is. Far from exhibiting the concretion of real self-consciousness, at this initial stage being-for-self is little more than a *principle* of self-determination, still lacking any concrete determinations that could anchor its abstract differentiation into being-for-self and being-for-one. It is, at this initial threshold of development, merely 'one [*Eins*]' (SL 21.150/132).

Accordingly, the remainder of 'Quality' is devoted to the successive unfolding of this 'one', by the agency of its negative self-relation. Because the one is *negative* self-relation, it *repels* itself from itself, thereby positing an unordered manifold of 'many ones' (SL 21.151–57/132–137). However, insofar as the one is negative *self*-relation, it is also the thoroughgoing *attraction* of those many ones. The result is a single, internally differentiated whole ('the one One'): "Since it contains repulsion in its determination, the latter equally preserves the ones as many within it; by its attracting, it musters, so to speak, something before it, gains a comprehension [*Umfang*] or a filling" (SL 21.162/141). Like all the subordinate triads within the *Science of Logic*, however, this one too concludes with a logically incomplete state of affairs that is, by consequence, ambivalent.

Over the course of the chapter, Hegel works out this conceptual tension, arguing that being-for-self acquires real determinateness only as the relation of many ones contained within a single One that is distinguished from them solely by its functional role as the unifying whole. The chapter ends with the insight that a relation like this is not yet sufficiently determinate to sustain a real distinction between the positive aspect of the one-many relation (the 'attraction' of the many exactly similar ones to the 'one One' (i.e., their *continuity* with it) and the negative aspect of the relation (the 'repulsion' of the many exactly similar ones, the *discreteness* that goes along with the very notion of plurality). The section on quality concludes with this notion of a quantum that is (in contrast to the heterogeneity of qualitative being) equally amenable to being construed as either a *homogeneous continuum* or a *homogeneous manifold* of discrete, but exactly similar 'ones', *units*. The transition to the next major division of the Logic of Being, 'Quantity' (SL 165–166/145, 173–174/152–153), is thus effected.

10.6. HEGEL'S IDEALISM

"Every philosophy is essentially idealism" (SL 21.142/124).—Understanding this statement is key to understanding the sense in which Hegelianism is idealism. The 'Remark' in which it occurs (SL 21.142/124) follows on the 'transition' from 'affirmative infinity' to 'being-for-self' and begins thus:

> The proposition that the finite is ideal [*ideell*] constitutes idealism. The idealism of philosophy consists in nothing other than in recognizing that the finite is not a true being [*ein wahrhaft Seiendes*]. Every philosophy is essentially idealism or at least has idealism for its principle, and the question then is only how far this principle is carried out. [. . .] The principles of ancient as well as modern philosophies, be it 'water', 'matter', or 'atoms', are *thoughts*, universals, ideal entities [*Ideelle*], not things as they are immediately given, i.e. in sensuous singularity. Not even the 'water' of Thales is that, for not withstanding the fact that it is also empirical water, it is besides that the in-itself or essence of all other things, which are thus not independent beings [*Selbständige*], self-grounded, but rather *posited* on the basis of an other, of 'water', i.e. they are ideal entities (SL 21.142/124).[20]

The first thing to notice here is Hegel's identification of ideality with (ontological) *dependence*, though not dependence on an 'other' that is external to itself. For something to be ideal is for it to be grounded in a process of which it is a moment and which it thus serves to realize. By implication, a 'true being' is (ontologically) *independent*,

---

[20] On the 'idealism of the finite', see Stern, *Hegelian Metaphysics*, 57–77.

self-grounded, self-determining, insofar as it constitutes the dynamic whole of its individual 'moments'. Insofar as the finite constitutes a sphere of mutually delimiting qualitative entities, clearly nothing within that sphere meets this criterion of 'true being'; but insofar as the finite as such proves to be inseparable from the infinite, neither does finitude in its affirmatively revised conception meet the criterion. As a 'moment' within the process or becoming of the true infinite, finite things retain their status as *merely ideal*.

Second, we should note that, *with respect to their specific content*, the principles Hegel adduces in illustration of his point ('water', 'matter', 'atoms') constitute classical varieties of *materialist monism*. Their material (i.e., non-mental) content serves to underline Hegel's contention in the same passage that "the opposition between idealistic and realistic philosophy is [. . .] without meaning" (SL 21.142/124). Instead, the decisive point concerns their *formal character* as *monistic* principles: 'water', 'atoms', and so on, are intended to constitute the unique, homogeneous basis for a system of real constitution. Everything that exists or 'is there' is to be grasped as a particular modification of that single underlying reality, separable from it only in thought, and to that extent *merely ideal*.

In the third place, we may observe that Hegel uses the term 'ideal' to characterize both the dependent, finite derivata and the independent, non-finite principles from which they are derived. 'Water', 'matter', and so on, are determinate '*thoughts*', and thus also *derived*; indeed, they are derived from the very finite derivata they are intended to explain. Their whole purpose, as *principles*, is to reveal how the determinate contents of finite, qualitative entities are posited; yet they are themselves, insofar as they exhibit the *form* of principles, posited through an act of thinking that has already taken the ideality of the finite contents as its point of departure. We can therefore recognize here an illuminating instance of the unity and inseparability of the finite and infinite that Hegel makes so much of in the main text. Furthermore, and perhaps more importantly, there is something about the very presence here of determinate content that renders it finite, *merely ideal*, to the extent that it differs in kind from the categorial content the Logic is meant to derive. 'Water', and any principle like it, is incapable of exhibiting the (original synthetic) unity of the real and the ideal that marks out infinitude as "reality in a higher sense" (SL 21.136/119; cp. 21.147/129, quoted earlier).

In this connection, it is instructive to consider Hegel's criticism of subjective idealism in the same 'Remark' (SL 21.143/125): To 'idealize' the contents of consciousness merely by denying their mind-independent existence is to fail to supply a principle of derivation by which to demonstrate their dependence (in terms of constitution) on the unity of the mind itself. Significantly, Hegel is also committed to the view that certain kinds or strata of mental content are insusceptible to such derivation: "the content, as taken up in sensation, intuition, or also in the more abstract element of representation and thought, contains a plethora of such finitudes, and these, by the exclusion of that one mode of finitude alone (of the form of subjective and objective), are still not done away with, and even less have they fallen off on their own" (SL 21.143/125).

This view grounds a specifically Hegelian form of *content-idealism*: only certain sets of cognitive contents—one prominent example being the contents of *The Science of Logic*, another being the contents of Hegel's speculative theories of nature and spirit—are fit to stand in the required relation, such that the contents are fully deriva-ble from the principle ('pure thinking') and the principle is fully realized in the contents ('pure thought-determinations').

The distinguishing feature of such content is that it exhibits (or can exhibit) within itself the actively synthetic, original unity *that is thinking itself*. In turn, the sequence and hierarchy of such content—in the case of the Logic: the categories or 'pure-thought determinations'—are determined *by the degree* to which the specific content *clearly and distinctly* exhibits, realizes, or objectively manifests that unity, the unity of what Hegel calls 'the Concept'. The categories of infinity and being-for-self, in which the logic of quality culminates, owe their special status precisely to the fact that they exhibit, in a rel-atively more explicit form, the active synthetic unity that was present merely implicitly at the Logic's beginning in the thought of being and nothing.

It is hardly coincidental, then, that Hegel chooses the transition between 'infinitude' and 'being-for-self' to enunciate the principle of idealism, to exemplify it in the naïve cosmologies of the Presocratics, and to criticize subjective (e.g., Berkeleyan) idealism as a spurious form of it. We have already recognized the structural affinity between the original synthetic unity of apperception and affirmative infinity/being-for-self. Now we see that all scientific striving, especially all philosophical striving, is 'idealistic' in the sense that it responds to a norm ('the ought') implicit in finite rational consciousness as such: namely, to realize itself by positing the 'stuff' by which it is determined in its immediate, qualitative (sensuous) existence as *merely ideal*, as having a merely deriva-tive being-for-one.

In contrast to subjective idealists, who erroneously imagine themselves already to have fulfilled this task merely by embracing the thought that nothing exists except by virtue of belonging to 'my' consciousness, Hegel urges what is essentially a version of Kant's transcendental ideal. Kant defines the ideal as "the idea, not merely *in concreto*, but *in individuo*, i.e. as an individual thing, determinable or indeed determined by the idea alone" (CPR B 596). In short, the 'transcendental ideal' represents the ideal of abso-lute self-determination. Viewed from one perspective, the culminating passages of 'Quality' are still far from delineating this ideal; after all, fully eight substantial sections of equal complexity still separate 'true infinity' and 'being-for-self' from Hegel's con-cluding exposition of the 'absolute idea'. To that degree, 'the ought' still predominates over the finite thought-determinations we encounter here. And in a larger sense, that is true of all finite thought, destined as it is to wrestle with an unruly environment of tran-sient, but nonetheless importunate qualities. From a different perspective, however, and in pointed contrast to Kant's gesture of humility and self-denial, the active orientation toward that ideal within the finite realm—the 'ought' as such—is itself already the pres-ence and reality of the ideal. Hence the emphatic expressions with which Hegel evokes the infinite, in another context, as the 'simple essence of life', the 'soul of the world', the 'native realm of truth' (PhenS 9.99, 103/¶¶162, 167). Wherever the mind strives for intel-lectual self-determination, it has, in the most basic sense, already determined itself to such striving. There the unity not only of apperception, but of reason itself, is present in full. That is the meaning of the unity of the finite and the infinite. Though we must strive for the ideal in order for it to exist, it exists and is present in our very striving. Reason is truly alive only in and through the finite; Hegel's idealism is practical.

WORKS CITED

Primary Texts

Brentano, Franz. *Psychology from an Empirical Standpoint*. London: Routledge 1995.

Hegel, Georg Wilhelm Friedrich. *The Science of Logic* [SL], translated by George Di Giovanni. Cambridge: Cambridge University Press, 2010.

Hegel, Georg Wilhelm Friedrich. *Wissenschaft der Logik: Die Lehre vom Sein (1832)*. In *Gesammelte Werke*, edited by the Academy of Sciences of Nordrhein-Westfalia, in cooperation with the Deutsche Forschungsgemeinschaft. Hamburg: Meiner, 1968 ff. Vol. 21.

Kant, Immanuel. *Critique of Pure Reason*, translated by Norman Kemp Smith. London: McMillan 1929.

Kant, Immanuel. *Gesammelte Schriften*. Akademie Ausgabe. Berlin: Reimer, later de Gruyter, 1900 ff.

Secondary Literature

Beiser, Frederick. *The Fate of Reason: German Philosophy from Kant to Fichte*. Cambridge, MA: Harvard University Press, 1987.

Burkhardt, Bernd. *Hegels 'Wissenschaft der Logik' im Spannungsfeld der Kritik: Historische und systematische Untersuchungen zur Funktion und Leistungsfähigkeit von Hegels 'Wissenschaft der Logik' bis 1831*. Hildesheim; Zürich; New York: Olms, 1993.

Förster, Eckart, and Yitzhak Y. Melamed (eds.). *Spinoza and German Idealism*. Cambridge: Cambridge University Press, 2012.

Hartmann, Klaus. *Hegels Logik*, edited by Olaf Müller. Berlin; New York: De Gruyter 1999.

Henrich, Dieter. "Hegels Grundoperation," in *Der Idealismus und seine Gegenwart. Festschrift für Werner Marx*, edited by Ute Guzzoni, Bernhard Rang, and Ludwig Siep. Hamburg: Felix Meiner, 1976, 208–230.

Houlgate, Stephen. *The Opening of Hegel's Logic: From Being to Infinity*. West Lafayette, IN: Purdue University Press, 2006.

Koch, Anton Friedrich, Friedrike Schick, et al. (eds.). *Hegel: 200 Jahre Wissenschaft der Logik*. Hamburg: Meiner, 2014.

McTaggart, John Ellis. *A Commentary on Hegel's Logic*. Cambridge: Cambridge University Press, 1910.

Melamed, Yitzhak. "'Omnis determinatio est negatio': Determination, Negation, and Self-Negation in Spinoza, Kant, and Hegel," in *Spinoza and German Idealism*, edited by E. Förster and Y. Melamed. Cambridge: Cambridge University Press, 2012, 175–196.

Pippin, Robert. *Hegel's Idealism: The Satisfactions of Self-Consciousness*. Cambridge University Press 1989.

Pippin, Robert. "Die Logik der Negation bei Hegel," In *Hegel: 200 Jahre Wissenschaft der Logik*, edited by A. Koch, F. Schick, et al. Hamburg: Meiner, 2014, 87–107.

Stern, Robert. "'Determination Is Negation': The Adventures of a Doctrine from Spinoza to Hegel to the British Idealists." *Hegel Bulletin* 37, no. 1 (2016): 29–52.

Stern, Robert. *Hegelian Metaphysics*. Oxford: Oxford University Press 2009.

SELECTED FURTHER READING

Arndt, Andreas. "Die anfangende Reflexion: Anmerkungen zum Anfang der *Wissenschaft der Logik*," In *Hegels Seinslogik: Interpretationen und Perspektiven*, edited by Andreas Arndt and Christian Iber. Berlin: Akademie Verlag 2000, 126–139.

Henrich, Dieter. "Anfang und Methode der Logik," in *Hegel im Kontext* by D. Henrich. Frankfurt am Main: Suhrkamp, 1967.

Horstmann, Rolf-Peter. "Der Anfang vor dem Anfang. Zum Verhältnis der Logik zur *Phänomenologie des Geistes*," in *Hegel: 200 Jahre Wissenschaft der Logik*, edited by A. Koch, F. Schick, et al. Hamburg: Meiner, 2014, 43–58.

Koch, Anton Friedrich. "Sein—Nichts—Werden," in *Hegels Seinslogik. Interpretationen und Perspektiven*, edited by Andreas Arndt and Christian Iber. Berlin: Akademie Verlag 2000, 140–157.

Redding, Paul. "The Relation of Logic to Ontology in Hegel," in *Categories of Being: Essays on Metaphysics and Logic*, edited by Leila Haaparanta and Heikki Koskinen. Oxford: Oxford University Press, 2012, 145–166.

Winfield, Richard Dien. *Hegel's Science of Logic: A Critical Rethinking in Thirty Lectures*. Lanham, MD: Rowman & Littlefield, 2012.

CHAPTER 11

THE LOGIC OF ESSENCE AS INTERNAL REFLECTION

MICHAEL QUANTE

TRANSLATED BY JOSHUA MENDELSOHN

HEGEL presents the Logic of Essence in his *Science of Logic* as a necessary outcome of the collapse of the Logic of Being. The self-contradictions of the ontology of a logic of being lead to a new program in which the constitutive function of subjective capacities is explicitly recognized. It was precisely the suppression of these capacities that hindered the Logic of Being from doing justice to the claim to truth and knowledge immanent to each act of thought. Read systematically, Hegel's analysis of the failure of the Logic of Being can be interpreted as a critique of any program of naturalism that attempts to flatten the difference between being and essence, conceived as one of facticity and legitimacy, into a unidimensional conception of the absolute. Eliminative or reductionistic programs cannot, Hegel is convinced, do justice to the constitutive capacities of subjectivity.

If, against this, one develops a conception in which these constitutive subjective capacities become explicit, then one crosses over, in Hegel's terminology, from the paradigm of Being into that of the Logic of Essence. It is illuminating, from a systematic point of view, to reconstruct Hegel's Logic of Essence by means of a Fichtean analysis of self-consciousness in the form of first-personal reference.[1] *Qua* presupposition, the 'I' is activity—Fichte speaks of a fact-act (*Thathandlung*)—and does not exist in the manner of a thing. *Qua* self-consciousness, this fact-act is self-referential, and *qua* claim to knowledge or cognition, it is available in a propositional, and therefore linguistic, form. This activity is a linguistic act of reference to itself. With the word 'I', the speaker refers to herself and the speaker knows, if she uses 'I' competently, that she thereby refers exclusively to herself. If we consider this structure as a whole, we see that it is a matter of

---

[1] I would like at this point explicitly to leave open the possibility that there are other models for Hegel's logic of essence, as Klaus Hartman's assessment recommends: "Hegel's conception of essence is a structural abstraction which covers a variety of cases" (Hartmann, *Hegels Logik*, 165).

conceptual self-determination, a structure in which self-reference and the object of this self-reference are the same. The one referring to itself and that other referred to in the first-personal mode are identical. At the same time, a difference must be contained in the structure because self-reference and the object of reference are two roles that the speaker of the first-personal expression occupies. When, by uttering 'I', I constitute myself and at the same time tag myself as the speaker and the author of this utterance, I perform a speech act in which the two roles become distinguishable as moments of an underlying unity (the speech-act itself), while at the same time remaining in a relationship of reference to one another. Hegel unfolds this movement in his conception of reflection and also develops a program of deduction categories that he calls 'determinations of reflection'.[2]

In this ontology of self-consciousness, being is no longer what is primary. Rather, within the reflection-logical self-unfolding of essence, being has the status of illusion, or 'shine [Schein]'. This is to be spelled out both epistemologically and ontologically.[3] If one views the Logic of Essence as an anti-realistic paradigm and takes the model of self-consciousness as the yardstick for this, then these two dimensions cannot strictly be separated from one another. Just this move is what the development from the Logic of Being to the Logic of Essence consists in. The defect that stems from the obscuring of subjective capacities, which the Logic of Being brought to a breaking point, gives way to a challenge to adequately preserve the aspect of being within the anti-realism of the Logic of Essence. In light of contemporary debates, one can think of the moves of the Logic of Essence on the whole as attempts to stop an idealistic rationalism based on the constitutive contributions of subjectivity from falling into a contentless 'spinning in the void' in which the world goes missing, while also not falling back into any of the being-logical variations on eliminating this self-determining subjectivity.[4]

In what follows, I will explicate the main current of the conceptual development in the first section of the Logic of Essence, "Essence as Reflection Within Itself."[5] Since Hegel prefaces this section with an introduction to the entire second book of the Logic (The Doctrine of Essence), I (1) consider this overarching determination of the text's starting point, an analysis that will reveal why Hegel himself viewed the Logic of Essence as the most difficult part of the logic.[6] The subsequent discussion (2) follows the division of Hegel's text and maps out the structure of the conceptual development, and I also briefly thematize (3) the second section ("Appearance").

---

[2] Compare on this point Houlgate, *Opening*, Ch. 1.

[3] By contrast, his conception of logic as a whole should be thought of as a "theory of absolute subjectivity" (Düsing, *Subjektivität*, 213).

[4] On this, see McDowell, *Mind and World*, and Quante, *Wirklichkeit des Geistes*, ch. 2.

[5] *Translator's note:* This translates "Das Wesen als Reflexion in ihm selbst," which di Giovanni translates as "Essence as reflection within." "Reflexion in ihm selbst" is also the phrase that is rendered less technically in the title of the essay as 'internal reflection'.

[6] See GW 20, 145, 14 (E 179); the characterization of "this part of the Logic" as "the most difficult one" is also found in the second edition (E1827 §114 A = GW 19.112, 27), but is absent from the first edition of 1817.

11.1. THE INTRODUCTION TO ESSENCE[7]

Hegel opens the second book of his *Science of Logic* with a short introduction concerning the whole Doctrine of Essence. In a tone resembling the paratactic opening of the Logic of Being, he begins by summarizing the conceptual development of the Logic of Being as a whole: "The truth of being is essence" (SL 11.241, 3/337). As a justification for this claim, Hegel states that knowledge cannot remain at the determination of being any more than it can remain at being as the immediate. Therefore, the claim to cognition made with the claim to knowledge entails a 'presupposition' (SL 11.241, 7/337), which Hegel elaborates using the image of a 'background' and characterizes as 'mediated knowledge'. Cognition of the mere datum finds that "*behind* this being there is still something other than being itself" (SL 11.241, 7/337). This "constitutes the truth of being" (SL 11.241, 8/337). This cognitive or argumentative operation is necessary in order for cognition of being to take place and for it to 'find' essence (SL 11.241, 13/337). Hegel justifies this connection by playing on the grammatical relationship of 'to be' (*sein*) and its past participle (*gewesen*), but not without clarifying that the spatial or temporal constellations are only illustrations of the logical relationship between being and essence.[8] For "essence is past, but timelessly past, being" (SL 11.241, 15/337): the structure is a logical one in the space of reasons.

Hegel also rebuffs, with reference to the Logic of Being, the notion that the transition from being to essence is an "activity of cognition" (SL 11.241, 18/337) that remains external to being and only takes place in the "activity of cognition" (SL 11.241, 18/337). The transition of being to essence is the "movement of being itself" (SL 11.241, 20/337) because it "is being's nature to recollect itself, and [. . .] becomes essence by virtue of this interiorizing" (SL 11.241, 21f./337). The transition from an immediate claim to knowledge to a justified cognition is "a mediated knowledge" (SL 11.241, 9/337).

After this retrospective opening, Hegel turns now to the point of departure of the Logic of Essence:

> If, therefore, the absolute was at first determined as being, now it is determined as essence. (SL 11.241, 22f./337)

In order to reveal the fundamental makeup of essence at a deep structural level, Hegel develops a distinction between a being-logical conception of essence, which he brings into connection with the "sum total of all realities" and characterizes as "pure essence" (SL 11.242, 3/338), and the essence-logical conception of essence. On the basis of its claim to knowledge, cognition cannot remain at the level of reports of particular states of affairs, at the "manifold of existence" (SL 11.241, 23/337). It must rather press ahead to

---

[7] Citations are given from the German and the English text. English citations follow the di Giovanni translation.

[8] *Translator's note*: The past participle of *sein*, *gewesen*, contains the German word for essence, *Wesen*.

"pure being" (SL 11.241, 25/337); but it also does not obtain a stable foothold there, since this pressing ahead itself "presupposes a recollection and a movement which has distilled immediate existence into pure being" (SL 11.241, 27f./337).[9] According to Hegel, through this process of purification, being is "determined as essence" (SL 11.241, 29/337), and yet this purification, in which "everything determined and finite" in being "is negated" (SL 11.241, 29/337), remains deficient from the point of view of the Logic of Essence. The most pronounced shortcoming consists in the fact that this purification or negation only takes place in an 'external manner' (SL 11.241, 31/338) by means of a 'external' negation and an 'abstraction' (SL 11.242, 6/338). Conversely, one could say it has not come about through a negative activity of essence itself: "to this unity the determinate was itself something external and, after this removal, it still remains opposite to it" (SL 11.241, 31–242, 1/338).

The error of this being-logical conception of the essence of pure being consists in a deficient conception of the movement of reflection, which, as an 'abstraction' and merely 'external' negation (SL 11.242, 6f./338), remains external to its object. In this way, however, essence becomes merely a product and only an object "for *another*, namely for abstraction" (SL 11.242, 13/338). Its only determination is, *qua* pure being, to be "a dead and empty absence of determinateness" (SL 11.242, 13/338). The method of subtraction on which cognition relies in its being-logical form thus generates a constellation of pure and determinate being, which displays a twofold deficiency. On the one hand, both of the poles generated by external reflection—determinate being and pure being—are considered as independent unities whose being is left untouched by this abstraction. On the other hand, the whole constellation is understood as a product of something that is itself an external operation. Cognition thereby takes itself to be no longer relevant, merely an external magnitude, and does not conceive of the movement of reflection as pure being's own activity.

If, however, the transition of the absolute from being to essence is itself to be thought of as an immanent movement of being, then this being-logical conception of essence cannot be adequate. The reflection of internalization (*Erinnerns*) must not be understood as external reflection, and likewise negation must not be understood as "external abstractive reflection" (SL 11.242, 10f./338). Hegel uses the next part of his introduction (SL 11.242, 14–21/338) in order to characterize an adequate essence-logical conception of essence and the determinations of reflection inscribed therein, as well as to characterize the relationship of essence to determinacy.

The development of the Logic of Being as a whole shows that the essence-logical conception of essence comes about by an immanent development of being itself, not through "a negativity foreign to it" (SL 11.242, 14f./338): It is *being-in-and-for-itself* (SL 11.242, 16/338). Hegel characterizes this structure as "absolute *in-itselfness*" (SL 11.242, 16/338). By this he means the negation of all determinacies and thus an autonomously effected purification. This is an autonomous negation,[10] standing in need of no manner

---

[9] Hegel uses the term 'reflection' here (SL 337 / 241, 26) in the sense of external reflection.

[10] Dieter Henrich viewed this as "Hegel's fundamental operation." See Henrich, "Hegels Grundoperation"; cf. also Koch, *Evolution des logischen Raumes*, ch. 6 and 7.

of external reflection, so that "otherness and reference to other have been sublated" (SL 11.242, 17f./338). Since essence, as the Logic of Essence conceives it, is the self-negation of being, it cannot be "only this in-itselfness" (SL 11.242, 19/338), because that would make it once again "only the abstraction of pure essence" (SL 11.242, 19/338). As 'for-itselfness', it achieves self-determination on its own and is itself therefore, in Hegel's terminology, "this negativity" (SL 11.242, 20/338); the externality or foreignness of merely given determinacies is itself negated by essence. The essence of for-itselfness is, according to Hegel, in fact nothing other than "the self-sublation of otherness and of determinateness" (SL 11.242, 21/338). We will see in the course of our analysis how Hegel continues to develop the result that the essence of essence must be the negativity of the sublation of given determinacies, since it is the self-negation of being. It will also be seen that the fact of its origin in being is likewise constitutive of the course of thought's further development.

Because essence has sublated all the determinacies of being into itself, it is "first [. . .] indeterminate essence" (SL 11.242, 22f./338). While it contains the determinacies (as sublated) "in themselves," it does so, as Hegel emphasizes, "without their being posited in it" (SL 11.242, 24/338). Here it already becomes clear that Hegel wishes to differentiate the relations between being and determinacies (*Bestimmtheiten*), on the one hand, and essence and determinations (*Bestimmungen*), on the other, so as to be able to distinguish the essence-logical conception of the absolute from the being-logical one.[11] On the basis of this modified relation, "absolute essence in this simple unity with itself has *no determinate being*" (SL 11.242, 24/338).[12] Yet, since essence is determined as being-in-and-for-itself, it is not able to remain in this constellation of determinacies that are merely found in themselves: essence "must pass over into determinate being" (SL 11.242, 25f./338). Hegel expresses this as follows: "it *differentiates* the determinations which it holds *in itself*" (SL 11.242, 26f./338).

There are three things to note about this expression. First, Hegel's formulation leaves it open whether essence differentiates the determinations from itself or whether it differentiates the various determinations from one another. Second, Hegel's locution switches from speaking of 'determinacies [*Bestimmtheiten*]' to 'determinations [*Bestimmungen*]'. Third, the transposition of the relation from the mode of 'in-itself' into the mode of 'posited in it' is of a piece with this movement.

In the text directly following, Hegel offers a decisive characterization of essence, which lays bare the motor of Hegelian conceptual development:

> Since it is the repelling of itself from itself or indifference towards itself, *negative* self-reference, it thereby posits itself over against itself and is infinite being-for-itself only

---

[11] Determinacies (*Bestimmtheiten*) are characteristics conceived in a being-logical manner, characteristics that the bearer 'has'(this is a passive model that presupposes the ontological independence of the features). Determinations (*Bestimmungen*) are by contrast essence-logical features that the essence ascribes to itself and that are actively produced in this ascription.

[12] Translator's note: I have changed Giovanni's "existence" for *Dasein* to "determinate being" throughout.

in so far as in thus differentiating itself from itself it is in unity with itself. (SL 11.242, 27f./338)

Coming originally from being, essence is absolute in-itselfness because it has freed itself from all the determinacy of being. At the same time it is *"being-for-itself* [...] essentially" (SL 11.242, 20/338) in the sense that it sublates this determinacy itself, as well as its being-other (*Anderssein*). If its essence is determined as absolute being-in-itself, then the self-determination that Hegel characterizes here as negative reference to itself is an activity which goes back to essence itself (and not the product of an external reflection), and which is at the same time indifferent to the determinacy of being absolute being-in-itself. For if this autonomous determining is meant to be self-referential and in this sense 'infinite being-for-itself', then it must express this being in-itself (or, in its culmination, realize it) and in its culmination negate itself. This is because it behaves as a being-for-itself toward its being-in-itself. Essence can only realize its overall structure of 'being-in-and-for-itself' autonomously, as coming from itself, if it turns out to be a unity of two different roles. By relating to itself through two oppositely determined roles, however, it repels itself from itself in the mode of being-in-itself. It does this, however, in order to realize itself in the mode of being-for-itself. This realization—and here its unity lies beyond this difference—is thereby essence itself *qua* reflection.

Hegel now discusses the respect in which the relation between essence and its determinations differs from a being-logical relation. Because the difference between essence and its determinations remains fundamentally unified in self-determination, in the process of '*negative* self-reference' (SL 11.242, 27/338) neither the essence nor these determinations change in the sense of coming to be and passing away characteristic of the Logic of Being. Rather, they are 'self-subsisting' (SL 11.242, 36/339) in the face of such modifications. At first glance, this is a paradoxical result. Because the transitions in essence remain the results of their own negative relation to themselves, one might assume that both sides of this relation—essence and determinations—would lose their independence. Hegel, however, claims that the integration of the relata into a unity that encompasses both of them supports their mutual stability: "they are self-subsisting but, as such, at the same time conjoined in the unity of essence" (SL 11.242, 36f./338–339).

Hegel uses the rest of the introduction (SL 11.243, 1–28/339) to characterize the intermediate position of the Logic of Essence. The task is now to "posit in its sphere" (SL 11.242, 38f./339) the determinacy that belongs to it due to its origin in being. That is, essence, which is "at first *simple* negativity" (SL 11.242, 37/339), must go from a determinacy that it "contains in principle only in itself" to a determination that it posits for itself, in order "to give itself determinate being and then being-for-itself" (SL 11.242, 39. cf. also 243, 13f./339). The completion of this movement consists in "giving itself *determinate being* and becoming as infinite being-for-itself what it is in itself" (SL 11.243, 15f./339). It will then have become, as Hegel says looking forward, 'concept' (SL 11.243, 17/339). Before that point, essence will pass through various stages of development, which can be thought of as a series of different essence-logical conceptions of the relation between essence and its determinations. The decisive difference from the being-logical sphere is that the following now remains constant:

> The negativity of essence is *reflection*, and the determinations are *reflected*—posited by the essence itself in which they remain as sublated. (SL 11.243, 7–9/339)

It would not stretch the text to read Hegel's entire Logic of Essence as his ontology of self-consciousness, in the sense of a grammar of self-determination. Within the program of the Logic of Essence, the thought of an active determination dominates in contrast to the passive reception of determinacies. The underlying model for this is self-referentiality, since this represents, in Hegel's view, an alternative to the internal collapse of the Logic of Being, which had attempted to establish a system of independent determinacies from the perspective of an uninvolved observer, that is, to establish them purely descriptively. The Logic of Essence is Hegel's conception of autonomous self-determination as the fundamental organizing structure of a system of categories and ontological models. By accentuating active self-determination, the prescriptive character of positing gains primacy; at the same time, it is one of Hegel's most fundamental assumptions that there can be no self-determination without contentful determination, even if the latter needs to be made comprehensible as a result of the former. While the basic problem of the Logic of Being consisted in integrating the active constitution of the system of categories and thus the subjective character of the absolute, the crucial task of essence consists in retaining a place for the aspect of being within a conception of autonomous subjectivity. The three sections of the Logic of Essence—the relations of reflection, appearance, and actuality—represent ever more complex and stable constellations of the mediation of self-determination and the determinacy of essence.

This first section is among the most difficult passages of the *Science of Logic* because Hegel here describes the implicit grammar of this mediation, its most unstable and, as an internal structure of self-relation, most complete form of mediation and immediacy.[13] If it is nevertheless the case that no conception of the absolute that ascribes to this a rational, philosophically explicable structure can get by without assuming that this is absolute subjectivity and the knowing subject is active in the structure to be explicated, then we can appeal to Hegel's conception of self-determination in the structure of essence "as reflection within itself" (SL 11.244, 2/340). This basic conception manifests

---

[13] According to Henrich, "Hegel was able to write some of the most dense speculative passages of his work [here]. Unfortunately, they are also among the passages whose hermetic character most quickly drives an interpreter to despair. Hegel himself provides practically nothing to clarify the logical relationships which he moves through with unreflective virtuosity" ("Logik der Reflexion," 114) [*Translator's note*: My translation]. As much as I agree with Henrich that the reader of this text might begin to despair at the task of its interpretation, I disagree with his claim that Hegel is unreflective here. If, in these sections, Hegel is explicating the grammar of all acts which we use to make normative claims to validity, then it is not possible for him to reflexively explain the method underlying this explication itself, because that would itself be a case of what is being represented. Hegel's seemingly unreflective virtuosity in these sections is due to the nature of the subject matter, which can only be enacted and thus shown, but not said.

itself in phenomena that aim at normative legitimacy, such as desire and cognition (as the basic modes of self-consciousness), as well in phenomena that are directed at truth and justification, such as giving and asking for reasons.

11.2. Essence as Reflection within Itself

Since essence arises from the failure of the Logic of Being, its specific character of being in-and-for-itself is not immediately available as a presuppositionless initial condition, but rather is a "result of that movement" (SL 11.244, 4/340). Because we are here dealing with a change in the fundamental model, the conception of essence must also be thought of as a new and, in this sense, immediate point of departure. There are now two opposing paradigms that can be thought of as independent of one another. In this way, essence has gained "specific determinate being [*bestimmtes Dasein*] to which another stands opposed," so that it "is only *essential* determinate being, as against the *unessential*" (SL 11.244, 6/340).

11.2.1. Shine

By way of introduction, Hegel summarizes the tense internal relationship between being and essence: "As it issues from being, essence seems to stand over against it" (SL 11.244, 17/341). Yet this appearance is deceptive. The claim that being can be thought of as something separate from essence and at the same time reduced to 'the *unessential*' (SL 11.244, 18/341) cannot be reconciled with the fact that essence is being that has attained being-in-and-for-itself. The demotion to the unessential of the being that stands opposed to essence is too weak and leaves being with too much independence. As essence's other, it is "being void of essence" (SL 11.244, 19/341) in which no degree of independence remains, because essence allows nothing to stand over against it. Thought of in this way, that which stands opposed to essence is merely 'shine'.[14] Yet it is indisputable that essence is related to being because of its origin. Furthermore, it is supposed to be being-for-itself in the sense of complete self-determination. On this basis, shine is not allowed to be "something external, something other than essence" (SL 11.244, 21/341). If essence is being-in-and-for-itself, then shine must, as a product of its own activity, turn out to be "essence's own shining" (SL 11.244, 22/341). Hegel calls this constellation "the shining of essence within itself," which he characterizes as the basic structure of 'reflection' (SL 11.244, 22/341).

---

[14] *Translator's note:* The German word *Schein*, which, following di Giovanni's translation, I rendered here as 'shine', can also mean 'illusion'.

In what follows, we will explicate this structure and consider its content. We can, however, already say with confidence that the model in the first subsection represents a deficient conception that sells short the result of the Logic of Being (it thus corresponds structurally to the being-logical conception of essence, which Hegel discussed in the general introduction to the Logic of Essence [SL 11.242, 2ff./338]). Shining and reflection will, on the other hand, turn out to be constitutive aspects of essence, aspects which themselves demand and can be given an essence-logical explication.

11.2.1.1. *The Essential and the Unessential*

If the difference between being and essence is characterized by means of the distinction between essential and unessential aspects of a thing, we have "made essence relapse into the sphere of determinate being" (SL 11.245, 17f./341), because these are only distinguished from "some external standpoint" (SL 11.245, 29/342). This distinction would be a "separation which falls on the side of a *third*" (SL 11.245, 27/342), with the result that essence's character of being-in-and-for-itself would go missing. Hegel marks the inadequacy of this being-logical conception by distinguishing forms of negation: in the shape of the essential, essence is only a 'determinate negation' (SL 11.245, 9/341), which, as the 'first' (SL 11.245, 33/342) negation is still a '*determinateness*' (SL 11.245, 34/342).

11.2.1.2. *Shine*

Because being has sublated itself into essence, it can be nothing completely independent over against essence. At the same time, because essence is determined as issuing from being, it must leave its mark in essence. And because essence is being-in-and-for-itself, this mark must, in the end, be essence itself.

The first attempt to do justice to this requirement fails because, as the unessential, being had been accorded too much independence, and the differentiation between being and essence had been generated by an external 'standpoint' (SL 11.245, 26/342). On the second pass, this task is to be carried out by ascribing to being the character of a mere illusion: "*Being is shine*" (SL 11.246, 8/342).[15] Here, shine is thought of as a 'nothingness' (SL 11.246, 9/342) whose character as being consists solely "in the sublatedness of being" (SL 11.246, 8f./342).

Hegel carries out his argument in two steps. In the first step (SL 11.246, 8–247, 23/342–343), Hegel explains the diminished potency of being that results from the progression from the unessential to shine. In a second step (SL 11.247, 24–249, 18/343—345), Hegel traces out the way that the aspect of independence remains and is preserved in the model of 'being as shine'. Both steps are necessary for fulfilling the adequacy conditions of an essence-logical conception of essence that accounts for the origin of essence in the sublation of being. Between these two steps of the explication, Hegel inserts an excursus (SL 11.246, 24–247, 33/343), which introduces the skeptical conception of the phenomenon and the idealistic conception of appearance as two variants of shine. The first makes no claim to truth whatsoever; the second denigrates appearances because it does

---

[15] *Translator's note*: see note 11.

not "permit itself to regard cognitions as a knowledge of the thing-in-itself" (SL 11.246, 27f./343). Its character as being is located entirely in its "connection with the subject" (SL 11.246, 26f./343). At the same time, these conceptions ascribe determinations to essence *'immediately'* (SL 11.247, 1/343), and thus the determinations are not acknowledged as products of the subject. Neither shine nor the subject is viewed as bringing forth these determinacies. Hegel diagnoses what is wrong with these conceptions as consisting in the fact that neither shine nor the subject counts as the "generating and controlling force" (SL 11.247, 13/343) which posits the determinacies of shine as its determinations. Even Fichte, whose conception of self-consciousness manages to avoid the idea of a thing-in-itself, requires a passive element: 'the infinite obstacle' (SL 11.247, 17f./343) does not come from the spontaneity of the 'I', so that, for Fichte, there remains an 'externality' (SL 11.247, 20/343) to be sublated in self-consciousness. For this reason, according to Hegel, Fichte's conception of self-consciousness entails "an immediate non-being of it" (SL 11.247, 23f./343).

In the first step of the explication, shine is determined as "all that remains of the sphere of being" (SL 11.246, 12/342). Standing in opposition to essence, it still "seems [*scheint*]" (SL 11.246, 13/342) to have "an immediate side which is independent of essence" (SL 11.246, 13f./342). With its potency thus diminished, shine is left "only the pure moment of non-existence" because the errors of the model of determinate being [*Dasein*] have turned out to be the central shortcoming of the conception of the essential and the unessential. Hegel characterizes the independence that results from an externally induced absolute loss of potency as *'reflected* immediacy' (SL 11.246, 21/342). This is because the independence of shine *qua* immediacy "has determinate being only with reference to another, in its non-determinate being [*Nichtdasein*]" (SL 11.246, 18f./342).

On Hegel's conception of essence, the autonomous self-referentiality of the 'I' is thus characterized as absolute negation in the sense of a self-determination that stems only from itself. Hegel thereby also delineates what is to be proven next: because shine is already determined as 'non-determinate being [*Nichtdasein*]' (SL 11.246, 17/342), the task is now "not to demonstrate that it sublates itself" (SL 11.247, 26/343), but rather the "task is to demonstrate that the determinations which distinguish it from essence are the determinations of essence itself" (SL 11.247, 28f./343). This is one of the adequacy conditions for the development to come; furthermore, the essence's character as being-in-and-for-itself needs to be preserved. The second goal is therefore to show "further, that this *determinateness of essence*, which shine is, is sublated in essence itself" (SL 11.247, 29f./343–344).

The character of shine as being results from the 'immediacy of *non-being*' (SL 11.247, 31/344). This in turn arises from the fact that shine represents a structural feature of essence itself, 'essence's own absolute in-itself'. Thus the absolute mediation of essence with itself contains a 'reflected immediacy' (SL 11.248, 3/344) and thereby 'being as [a] moment' (SL 11.248, 5/344). Shine is therefore a structural feature of essence, not something distinct from essence as a specific 'mode' of immediacy (in the way that appearance as the way of the thing-in-itself being given for us might be). Shine is instead the *'shine of essence itself'* (SL 11.248, 11f./344).

Hegel shows how this determinacy "is sublated in essence itself" (SL 11.247, 30/344) in two steps: first (SL 11.248, 13—24/344) from the side of essence, and then from the side of shine (SL 11.248, 25–32/344–345). The determination that applies to essence immediately is absolute negativity, autonomous self-determination. It does not do justice to essence or this movement of essence to be, as immediacy, only *in* essence. Immediacy is, in Hegel's considered opinion, itself the 'negative or determinate' (SL 11.248, 21f./344) as against the basic structure of essence. The indeterminate in this constellation thereby plays the role of being 'absolute negativity' (SL 11.248, 18/344). By taking over a definitive function of essence, immediacy becomes 'negativity' and 'sublation itself' (SL 11.248, 22f./344), for the completed act of determination negates the content of the act, namely the fact of immediacy. This relation itself thus has the structure of absolute negativity, so that it turns out to be structurally identical to essence itself. This determination is hence "a turning back into itself" (SL 11.248, 24/344). By presupposing an illusion proceeding from the immediacy of its structure, the fact-act (*Thathandlung*) establishes the total structure appropriate to it.

On the side of shine, too, we observe the same result: because shine, *qua* dependent, relates to itself negatively, it posits its dependence as dependence. This "reference of the negative or the non-subsistent *to itself*" is its '*immediacy*' (SL 11.248, 28f./344), because shine has here precisely the character of being, namely the character of having determinateness "over against it" (SL 11.248, 30/345) and thereby having "an other than it" (SL 11.248, 29f./344) in opposition to it. The object constituted in the fact-act, determined as the negative or shine, has the requisite diminished independence. Its being consists exclusively in essence's positing this structure in-itself but not yet for-itself. Seen in this way, shine is negative self-relation, the "absolute sublation of the determinateness itself" (SL 11.248, 32/345) and thereby the realization of the structure of essence.

In the final paragraph of section B (SL 11.249, 4—18/345), Hegel identifies what is lacking in the conceptions of the unessential and in that of shine as consisting in the fact that essence is "taken at first as an *immediate*" (SL 11.249, 9f./345). Having proven that we are dealing with essence's own "shining of itself within itself" (SL 11.249, 17f./345), this deficit is lifted and we reach the structure of reflection within itself which essence for the first time achieves a conception of itself that is adequate to the Logic of Essence.[16]

11.2.1.3. *Reflection*

The structure of the first chapter of the Logic of Essence is reproduced in the construction of the subsection C, in which Hegel explicates 'reflection' (SL 11.249, 20/345). The first two levels of development, positing and external reflection, are inadequate

---

[16] According to Hegel's own methodological self-conception, it remains to be seen whether these deficient self-conceptions of essence can be shown to be necessary moments of its development. On this point, see Henrich, "Logik der Reflexion: Neue Fassung," 229, who diagnoses these as "detours on the way to the concept of essence" [*Translator's note*: My translation]. If they are not, then these sections, up to the initial development of a conception of essence meeting the essence logic's standards, would either not form a part of the argument or else something added by the observer would be constitutive of the course of development as a whole; on this, see also Wirsing, "Grund und Begründung."

conceptions of essence that are brought together and demoted to moments of determining reflection in the first adequate conception of reflection.[17] From the determinacy of essence arises the following adequacy condition: it must give itself its determinations in order to transform its own determinacy, its autonomous negativity, from the mode of being-in-itself into the essence-logical mode of being-in-and-for-itself. By way of introduction, Hegel again attempts to provide an essence-logical account of the basic structure of essence, while at the same time preserving the moment of being in essence properly conceived. The movement of essence *"from nothing to nothing and thereby back to itself"* (SL 11.250, 3f./346) can be made intelligible using the model of self-consciousness. As autonomous self-determination, essence is the negation of being and at the same time an absolute, spontaneous beginning that proceeds 'from nothing'. This connection generates the object of its reference, which is determined as a nothing because it is only an internal moment of essence itself. In this self-reference the identity of essence produces itself for itself because in pure negativity it refers to itself *qua* shine (i.e., in the form of pure negativity). Because, Hegel's thinking continues, the 'negation of nothingness' (SL 11.250, 7/346) lies ready to hand, two aspects of being remain preserved: that it is a negation of nothingness and that it has immediate self-reference in the negation of shine. Properly understood, self-consciousness is essence as 'this pure absolute reflection' (SL 11.250, 12/346). Its task of bringing this being-in-itself to its own being-for-itself does not succeed until determining reflection, which thus counts as the first conception that is adequate to the Logic of Essence.

In the remark that Hegel inserts between the second and third steps of the explication, he clarifies how he understands 'reflection'. For Hegel, the issue is "neither the reflection of consciousness, nor the more specific reflection of the understanding that has the particular and the universal for its determinations," but rather "reflection in general" (SL 11.254, 23–25/350). With reference to Kant's conception of the power of judgment, Hegel highlights the fact that reflection is "usually taken in a subjective sense" (SL 11.254, 7/350) or conceived of as 'external reflection' (SL 11.254, 36/350) in which a subject relates something particular to something general, the latter being taken as "the principle or the rule and law" (SL 11.254, 29/350). Even if reflection "applies itself to the immediate as to something given" (SL 11.254, 27f./350) and thereby lacks reflection's essential character, Hegel finds something of lasting philosophical value in these defective models, which in his own system appear under the name of '*external* reflection' (SL 11.254, 27/350). By treating "the universal, the principle or the rule and law" (SL 11.254, 29/350) as the "essence of the immediate" (SL 11.254, 30/350), this conception already implicitly contains "the concept of absolute reflection" (SL 11.254, 29/350). Nevertheless, this reflection remains deficient because it proceeds from "something immediately given that is alien to it" (SL 11.255, 3/350) and thereby conceives of itself as "a merely formal operation that receives its material content from outside" (SL 11.255, 4f./350). This passive self-interpretation of

---

[17] This structure corresponds to the relationship between universality, particularity, and singularity that will be determined in the Logic of the Concept. This becomes especially clear in Hegel's conception of the will in the *Philosophy of Right*; on this, see Quante, *Wirklichkeit des Geistes*, ch. 7.

reflection fails to recognize its own spontaneous character and considers its being-for-itself as a 'movement conditioned' (SL 11.255, 5f./351) by some content that is given in advance.[18]

Positing reflection: Within essence, shine preserves its "own equality with itself" (SL 11.250, 24/346), which is nothing other than the reflection of essence itself. Hegel calls this structure 'absolute reflection' (SL 11.250, 25/346) because essence only requires itself for its realization. Because the aspect of being in shine that constitutes itself via the negative self-relation of negativity (through the self-correspondence contained in that self-relation) is simultaneously the *negation* of the absolute negativity of essence, absolute reflection is determined as self-contradictory:

> It consists, therefore, in being *itself* and *not being itself*, and the two in *one* unity. (SL 11.250, 29f./346)

Self-consciousness is accordingly faced with a self-contradictory structure. Absolute reflection is the 'turning back' (SL 11.251, 4/347) of essence determined as negativity from its internally generated immediacy. Hegel introduces the term '*positedness* [*Gesetztsein*]' (SL 11.251, 7/347) for an immediacy that reflection cannot start from because it first comes into being in the act of reflection. In order to further explicate this structure, Hegel introduces the pair of concepts 'positing [*Setzen*]' and 'presupposing [*Voraussetzen*]'. Because absolute reflection is fundamentally an internal structure, it cannot refer to something separate from it. This has the result that the immediacy which emerges must be a positing, a product of reflection. As equality of the negative with itself, positing cannot stand on its own. As an internal moment of the movement of reflection, it remains dependent on presuppositions made in the act of positing. The structure of essence only becomes actualized if an autonomous positing takes place whose presuppositions are posited with it at the same time. Since essence is being-in-and-for-itself, it can only presuppose itself (i.e., its structure) in the activation of its essence. Essence is not a substance but rather 'self-movement' (SL 11.252, 18/348) that takes place spontaneously and is not induced from without. Hegel characterizes this as '*absolute internal counter-repelling*' (SL 11.252, 11f./348).

Positedness is a structural characteristic of essence in the double sense of being a negation (the result of a positing) and being an immediacy (a harmony with itself arising from this negation). Even so, essence is also determined in this constellation as "immediately in opposition to something, and hence to an other" (SL 11.252, 27/348). Absolute reflection is determined by the fact that something presupposed forms a part of its positing.

External reflection : Insofar as reflection presupposes "only shine, only positedness" (SL 11.252, 34/348), its determinacy as positedness brings to expression the primacy of

---

[18] Hence this concerns not the epistemic activity of a subject, but rather a reflection that first constitutes a subject.

active reflection. This goes missing in external reflection; here reflection posits itself "as sublated, as the negative of itself" (SL 11.252, 36/348). This structure is robust, because the contradictoriness of the 'one unity' of absolute reflection is dissolved insofar as the conflicting determinations are split into two relata conceived as independent presuppositions, characterized by Hegel as 'extremes' (SL 11.252, 23/349).

By determining itself as external, reflection presupposes that the thing to be determined is self-standing. Determinateness then only counts as an 'external reflection' (SL 11.253, 15/349) placed on it by something else. Hegel justifies this fall back into the Logic of Being on the grounds that, within this constellation, the "negative is thereby sublated as negative" (SL 11.253, 7f./349) and reflection thus makes an *immediate presupposition* (SL 11.253, 9/349) which it 'finds' (SL 11.253, 9/349) and from which it can proceed as reflection.[19] This obscures the fact that the thing presupposed can play the role of a point of departure for reflection because it is thus posited through reflection (this aspect is only brought to expression in positing reflection).

If one also takes into consideration that the presupposition is, as a presupposition, itself something posited, then it becomes clear that what is immediate in external reflection, "from which it seemed to begin as from something alien," exists only in "its beginning" (SL 11.253, 29/349). External reflection is thus at the same time "just as much the immanent reflection of immediacy itself" (SL 11.254, 2f./349–350). The result that reflection posits "essence existing in and for itself" (SL 11.254, 4/350) as its presupposition is thus achieved in itself, even if not for the reflection that is rooted in the model of external reflection. Reflection thus develops into determining reflection and for the first time attains a structure that meets the adequacy conditions of an essence-logical conception of essence.

Determining reflection : Determining reflection is hence "in general the unity *of positing* and *external* reflection" (SL 11.255, 19f./351), the unity of two conceptions whose strengths and weaknesses were complimentary. External reflection "begins from immediate being" (SL 11.255, 21/351) but presupposes that this other has the structure of essence. Unlike external reflection, positing reflection does not forget its own activity, but rather misapprehends the 'presupposition' (SL 11.255, 24/351) immanent to it *qua* essence. Hegel sees the shortcoming of positing reflection as consisting in the fact that, for it, this posited thing remains something 'other' than the movement of reflection itself. Thus positedness corresponds to being-logical determinate being, though since it develops within the Logic of Essence it has its immediacy only as a moment within reflection and essence. Thus positedness represents the 'middle term' (SL 11.256, 2/351) between determinate being and essence, because it 'conjoins' the two of them (SL 11.256, 3f./351).

Hegel now introduces the concept of a 'determination of reflection [*Reflexionsbestimmung*]' (SL 11.256, 13/352) as the further development of the conception

---

[19] Hegel sees a regression in this conception, which he likens to the logic of being (SL 11.253, 18, 20 ff./349).

of positedness. This conception arises by thinking of determining reflection as a unity of positing and external reflection. External reflection had already ascribed to the immediate, albeit implicitly, an internal essence-structure. This implicit ascription must be made explicit by the determination of reflection in positedness. Unlike positedness, the determination of reflection shows that 'immanent reflectedness' (SL 11.256, 24/352) is the aspect that ensures immediacy. The structural characteristic that implicitly preserved the independence of the object of reference in external reflection is now developed within the conception of a determination of reflection until that characteristic becomes the explicit basis for its own subsistence, that which "gives subsistence to it" (SL 11.256, 34/352).

11.2.2. The Essentialities or Determinations of Reflection

In the second chapter, Hegel develops the concept of a determination of reflection, thereby continuing his deduction of the central categories of self-consciousness from the first-personal mode of self-reference of the 'I'.[20] The conceptual development takes place by showing that these "essentialities or the determinations of reflection" (SL 11.258, 2–4/ 354) have the internal structure that Hegel developed in determining reflection. Self-identity based on negation is what makes determinations of reflection appear as '*essentialities*' (SL 11.256, 37/352) that admit of no further explication. Since determinations of reflection are also shine (insofar as they are posited), reflection here attains the status of 'essential shine' (SL 11.257, 2/352), which appears to be something that develops its content from out of itself. At the same time, in the conception of determinations of reflection, the prior conception of determining reflection has been completely "lost in the negation" (SL 11.257, 4/352), because the structure of first-personal self-determination is nothing other than the system of determinations of reflection.

The way that the determinations of reflection appear—as "free *essentialities*, sublated in the void without reciprocal attraction or repulsion" (SL 11.256, 36/352)—is in fact what is defective about them. For in the conception of a determination of reflection, the systematic connection of all determinations of reflection remains undeveloped, with the result that it can seem as if the individual essentialities each evolve in their content independently of one another. Furthermore, the relationship between self-determining reflection and the system of essentialities is neither explained nor integrated into the content of either of them.

In the third step of the argument, Hegel further develops the basic structure of the determination of reflection: on the one hand, it is "a non-being as against another, namely, as *against* the absolute immanent reflection or as against essence" (SL 11.257,

---

[20] Parallels to the first part of Fichte's 1794 *Foundations of the Science of Knowledge*, in which the three laws of identity, opposition, and ground are derived from the fact-act of the 'I', are clearly visible here. On Hegel's references to Fichte, see also Schmidt, *Hegel*.

18 f./353). Determinations of reflection are nothing other than products of the self-determining negativity of self-consciousness. At the same time, they achieve independence, since each determination of reflection is "reflected within itself" (SL 11.257, 20/353). Because both aspects must be held apart from one another as 'distinct' (SL 11.257, 21/353), their relation to their structurally identical counterpart, reflection, is only 'in it [an ihr selbst]' (SL 11.257, 24/353), not for the thing itself. This shortcoming is to be fully corrected by the development through the determinations of reflection: identity, difference (including the internal differentiation of 'absolute difference' [SL 11.265, 31/360], 'diversity' [SL 11.267, 8/362], and 'opposition' [SL 11.272, 17/367]), and contradiction.

In the first remark, Hegel brings out the specific difference between the being-logical understanding of a 'determinacy of being' (SL 11.259, 6/355) and the determinations of reflection. While the former are, as qualities, a 'transition into the opposite' (SL 11.259, 6 f./355), the determinations of reflection claim to be independent because they possess the internal structure of reflection; they "consequently abstract from the determinateness of others" (SL 11.259, 17 f./355). At the same time, Hegel holds that the determinations of reflection are "to be regarded in and for themselves" (SL 11.259, 33/355) and are not to be presented in the usual manner as 'universal laws of thought' (SL 11.258, 23/355). His reason for this derives from the fact that they are partially independent. Taking a linguistic-critical turn, Hegel criticizes the 'drawback' (SL 11.259, 33 f./355) of such propositions, namely that they are grammatically expressed using quantifying formulations ("everything is equal to itself"; SL 11.258, 28/354) that "have 'being', 'everything', for subject" (SL 11.259, 34/355). Hence they are expressed in a being-logical way: "They thus bring being into play again, and enunciate the determinations of reflection (the identity, etc., of anything) as a quality which a something would have within [an ihm]" (SL 11.259, 36/355).

This falls short of the basic essence-logical constellation in two respects. First, the form 'something is p' suggests that "something, as subject, persists in such a quality as an existent" (SL 11.259, 37/355). Second, this being-logical conception of predication obscures the possibility of developing the relatedness of the determinations of reflection to one another as a system of internal relations. This is because, as qualities, they are decoupled from the internal progression of essence's development. Against both of these, Hegel posits a conception in the 'speculative sense' (SL 11.259, 36 f./355), a conception in which essence "has passed over into identity (etc.) as into its truth and essence" (SL 11.259, 38 f./355).[21] The ontology of essence is not an ontology of things, but rather one of autonomous self-determination; the determinations of reflection are not properties that the 'I' has, but rather modes of its reflection; the 'I' is not a substrate, but rather

---

[21] In the second remark on the law of identity, Hegel makes the claim that "[m]ore is entailed, [. . .] in the form of the proposition expressing identity than simple, abstract identity' (SL 11.264, 24 ff./360) (by which he means numerical identity): "Entailed by it is this pure movement of reflection" (SL 11.264. 25 ff./360), Hegel claims, bringing in his conception of essence. We can say with Wittgenstein that the form of this sentence shows more than the sentence itself says.

the activity that exists in the self-generation of the system of determinations of reflection, that is, the system of the development of the system's essence.[22]

As self-consciousness, essence is 'simple self-*identity*' (SL 11.260, 25/356), which as a fact-act is "a pure production, from itself and in itself" (SL 11.260, 29/356). In contrast to numerical identity, which Hegel calls 'abstract identity' (SL 11.260, 30/356), this '*essential* identity' (SL 11.260, 30/356) does not come about through "a relative negation preceding it [. . .] *existing* outside it" (SL 11.260, 31/356). Identity is thereby in fact not a determination that essence might have, but rather it is "in the first instance, essence itself" (SL 11.261, 25/357). In the act of first-personal self-reference, the object is constituted and at the same time identified with the self-relating, so that the identity is with "the entire reflection, not a distinct moment of it" (SL 11.261, 25/357).

Understood in this way, the identity is "immanent reflection, reflection which is such only as inner repelling, and it is this repelling as immanent reflection, repelling that immediately recovers itself" (SL 11.262, 3–5/357). Both the differentiation between subject and object and knowledge of their identity are constitutive of a self-consciousness; this self-reference constitutes identity via the sublation of internally generated 'absolute non-identity' (SL 11.262, 10/357). With this, the internally generated non-identity, as a distinguishable moment, stands opposed to the movement of the reflection of identity as a whole. Thus identity and difference, which both proceed from autonomous reflection, arise as mutually independent determinations of a structural whole.

Difference is hence developed as a second determination of essence and is determined as "the negativity that reflection possesses in itself" (SL 11.265, 32/361). As autonomously generated, it is '*absolute* difference' (SL 11.266, 1 f./361) that does not come about through an external comparison. Hegel explains this second determination of reflection by way of three aspects: First, it is 'difference of reflection' regarding 'the other in and for itself' and 'simple determinateness in itself' (SL 11.266, 9 ff./361). In contrast to the sphere of being, however, it makes itself manifest not only "as the transition of a determinateness into the other"; rather "here, in the sphere of reflection, difference comes in as reflected" (SL 11.266, 17 ff./361). Second, Hegel claims that a moment of identity belongs to difference because of this internal structure of reflection, which makes it 'not itself but its other' (SL 11.266, 21/361). This other of the difference is identity, so that it is "therefore [. . .] itself and identity" (SL 11.266, 22 f./361). This structure, which one can also express in the formula of 'the identity of identity and non-identity', gives adequate expression to essence: "This is to be regarded as the essential nature of reflection and as *the determined primordial origin of all activity and self-movement*" (SL 11.266, 28 ff./362). Because difference and identity are thus determined in opposition to one another, both have internal reference to their opposite and, as '*positedness*' (SL 11.267, 2/362), attain their own 'determinateness' (SL 11.267, 2/362).

---

[22] It is surprising that Hegel buries this consideration, one that is so central to his entire approach, in a remark instead of presenting it as the introduction to the second chapter (this would still not make it an internal component of the explication, which, on Hegel's self-conception, it cannot be).

Owing to this moment of identity, both determinations possess an independence that Hegel explicates under the heading of 'diversity'. Identity and difference no longer spill over into one another, as in the Logic of Being. Rather, in reflection, they can be taken as diverse things related to one another and at the same time stable in opposition to one another. One structure that preserves a facet of being is thereby identified in the Logic of Essence. The price of the stability of the determinations thus attained is, however, that reflection becomes '*external*' (SL 11.267, 32/363); somewhat later, Hegel also speaks of "reflection [. . .] alienated from itself" (SL 11.269, 1/364). By contrast to 'reflection in itself' (SL 11.268, 10/363), which should be thought of as internal self-movement, '*external reflection*' (SL 11.268, 16/363) falls short of its essence, which is to be 'absolute reflection' (SL 11.268, 17/363). It attaches diversity to the determinations in the manner of an external appendage, and it at the same time presupposes that the identity of the determinations is not affected by this comparison.

The identity thus diminished to equality is, however, like the difference demoted to inequality, unstable. Because external reflection holds these apart as different aspects or perspectives, it destabilizes what is supposed to be preserved, since both only achieve stability thanks to their internal relation to one another: "this keeping of likeness and unlikeness apart, is their destruction" (SL 11.269, 12 ff./364). There is a double failure in the strategy of avoiding contradiction via the epistemic self-interpretation of reflection as external. First, it destroys the determinations of reflection that were supposed to be preserved, those for which their relation to one another is essential and which "have no meaning outside" this relation (SL 11.269, 16/364). Second, the contradiction is only deflected into reflection itself, which simultaneously holds these aspects apart and relates them: "But it is this reflection which, *in one and the same activity*, distinguishes the two sides of likeness and unlikeness, by the same token contains them *in one activity*, and lets the one shine reflected into the other" (SL 11.272, 7 ff./367).

With this result, 'determining reflection' comes into play and "difference [. . .] is brought to completion" (SL 11.272, 18/367). Hegel calls this constellation 'opposition' and analyzes it as "[t]he positedness of the sides of external reflection" (SL 11.272, 27/368). The 'moments of opposition' are interlocked: equality is generated by a reflection that aims at inequality, while inequality is constituted by a negative relationship to equality: "Each of these moments, in its determinateness, is therefore the whole" (SL 11.272, 36/368). At the same time—and this constitutes their character as determinations of reflection—each moment is "the whole because it also contains its other moment" (SL 11.272, 37/368). Since this other is at the same time posited in this constellation of reflection as something independent, as "an indifferent existent" (SL 11.273, 1/368), 'the whole' becomes posited as "essentially referring to its non-being" (SL 11.273, 2 f./368). Both of these moments, conceived in this manner as a whole, are what Hegel calls 'the *positive*' (SL 11.273, 5/368) and 'the *negative*' (SL 11.273, 6 ff./368). The first is the successor of the moment of equality; the latter denotes the moment of inequality.

The positive and the negative are 'simply *opposites*' (SL 11.273, 37/369). That is, they are not opposed only in certain respects, but they are "*first, absolute moments* of opposition" (SL 11.273, 34 ff./369), which subsist 'inseparably' (SL 11.273, 35/369). Due to the aspect of identity that lends them stability, both moments are also independent of one another, so that the determination of being positive or negative remains external to them. As 'merely diverse' (SL 11.274, 11 f./369), their role of being positive or negative can be 'interchanged' (SL 11.274, 15 f./369). As a "self-subsistent unity existing for itself" (SL 11.274, 27/370), each determination, which is able "to exclude" the opposite which is constitutive of it, is positive or negative "not just in themselves, but in and for themselves" (SL 11.275, 7 f./370).[23]

In the remark to the section on diversity, Hegel had, looking forward, mentioned that by distinguishing aspects, the "contradiction is not thereby dissolved but is rather shoved elsewhere, into subjective or external reflection" (SL 11.272, 11 ff./367). With the positive and the negative, the first "*self-subsisting determinations of reflection*" (SL 11.279, 7 ff./374), the first 'posited contradiction' (SL 11.279, 27/375) is attained.

The positive and the negative likewise suffer from a contradictory composition: "the positing of both in *one* reflection" (SL 11.280, 9/375). At the same time, Hegel marks an asymmetry. Although it is "the same contradiction" (SL 11.280, 22 f./375) in both cases, the positive is "only *implicitly* this contradiction" (SL 11.280, 22 f./375), because it relates to itself as something identical. The negative, "on the contrary, is the *posited* contradiction" because, being something negative, it is determined to be "a negative which is identical with itself" (SL 11.280, 24 f./375). Essential identity has turned out, according to Hegel's explication, to be the identity of identity and non-identity. The negative, it turns out, "is therefore the whole opposition—the opposition which, as opposition, rests upon itself" (SL 11.280, 28 ff./376).

The contradiction, however, is not stable but rather "resolves itself" (SL 11.280, 33/376). The first result that comes about in this way "is the *null*" (SL 11.280, 39/376), which Hegel refers to as "this internal ceaseless vanishing of the opposites" (SL 11.280, 27/376). Yet this '*first unity*' (SL 11.280, 38/376), which shows up in this vanishing, only gives expression to the negative moment. Because the positive moment also forms a part of this paradox, this instability has a positive result: "It is this *positedness* [of the self-subsistent] which in truth founders to the ground in contradiction" (SL 11.281, 5 f./376). The second negation is thus not the return to the condition that was given before the first negation. The sublation of this positedness is "not, therefore, once more positedness as the negative of an other, but is self-withdrawal, positive self-unity" (SL 11.281, 32 ff./376).

Because essence retains its self-subsistence in this sublation, the opposition "has not only foundered" (SL 11.282, 1/377) in the contradiction, but rather "in foundering it has gone back to its foundation, to its ground" (SL 11.282, 2/377). In this movement, "*essence is as ground a positedness, something that has become*" (SL 11.282, 16 ff./377). And yet since it concerns the internally persisting movement of reflection, the ground of autonomous self-determination does not lie outside it: "Ground is essence as positive

---

[23] In the remark to this section, Hegel establishes a connection to 'arithmetic' (SL 11.275, 26/371) and the conceptions of positive and negative found there. For more detail on this, see Wolff, *Begriff des Widerspruchs*, ch. 5.

self-identity [. . .] and essence is ground, self-identical in its negation and positive" (SL 11.282, 33 ff./378).

11.2.3. Ground

With ground, the development of the determinations of reflection comes to a close.[24] Hegel opens this chapter with another extensive introduction and a remark. In the remark he draws attention to the proposition "everything has a sufficient ground or reason" (SL 11.293, 3/388), which states that nothing should be considered to exist "as an *immediate*" (SL 11.293, 4/388) but rather should be considered "as a *posited*" (SL 11.293, 5/ 388). Simultaneously, Hegel uses a reference to Leibniz as an occasion to introduce the distinction between the teleological understanding of ground (*'final causes'*; SL 11.293, 31/388) and the idea of "causality taken in its strict sense as mechanical efficiency" (SL 11.293, 20 f./388). The Logic of Essence cannot be about causality "in a teleological sense" (SL 11.293, 32 f./388). Rather, "taken one by one, the determinations are comprehended through their causes" (SL 11.293, 23 f./388), for which reason, Hegel claims, the "unity of the determinations" (SL 11.293, 28 f./388) cannot be attained, since for Hegel this occurs "only in the concept, in the purpose" (SL 11.293, 27/388). The principle of sufficient reason is thus conceived teleologically, and finds its place in the Logic of the Concept. On this reading, Hegel's remark serves to keep apart the concept of a final cause from the essence-logical determination of ground.

The introduction to the third chapter recapitulates the development of essence through the end of the development of the determinations of reflection. Ground, which essence determines itself to be, is the last determination of reflection and only expresses the 'determination' that it is 'sublated determination' (SL 11.291, 17 ff./386). By determining itself in this way, it gives rise to the 'true meaning' (SL 11.291, 19/386) of the determination of reflection, that it is "the absolute repelling of itself within itself" (SL 11.291, 19/ 386). Absolute self-determination, as the essence of essence, is thus adequately realized through the positing of the essence.

In contrast to reflection, which as "*pure mediation* in general" (SL 11.292, 10/387) through shine continued to refer to an other that in its independence was not completely sublated, ground represents "the *real mediation* of essence with itself" (SL 11.292, 10 f./387). This "pure mediation is only pure reference, without anything being referred to" (SL 11.292, 16 f./387). The relatedness of the relata remains unstable and thus remains something external to the relating as an unsublated aspect of being. Ground, on the other hand, is "mediation that is real, since it contains reflection as sublated reflection" (SL 11.292, 19 f./387). The relationality of the things related thus contains its own

---

[24] Within the ontology of self-consciousness, the double-meaning of 'ground' (an ontological basis, such as a cause, on the one hand, or rational justification, on the other) need not be detrimental, because the distinction between ontological and epistemological aspects is not to be conceived as a dualism. The best commentary on this aspect of Hegel's logic is still Rohs, *Form und Grund*.

immediacy, in which their self-subsistence exists apart from their being related. The relation thus manages to be a real relation between relata, whose relationality forms a part of their own determination.

11.2.3.1. *Absolute Ground*

Ground is "essence determined through itself" (SL 11.294, 12/389) and is for this reason absolute; but it determines itself "as *indeterminate* or as sublated positedness" (SL 11.294, 12f/389). This double role of essence leads to the constellation "of the *ground* and of the *grounded*" (SL 11.294, 16/389). In the case of autonomous self-determination, essence takes on both roles simultaneously. But each determination, and each self-determination, requires an identifiable content, something that essence determines itself as. Reflection is the structure of essence, though not a determination that essence merely has, but rather it is the activity in which it realizes itself. Hegel calls this structure '*form*'. Only in ground does essence gain the character of a substrate with determinations, and it thereby gains a self-subsistence that makes it possible to say that essence carries out the positing. Before the attainment of the reflection-determination of ground, there arises for the exposition the problem that one must describe the structure of essence in an inauthentic manner:

> Essence *has* a form and determinations of this form. Only as ground does it have a fixed immediacy or is *substrate*. Essence as such is one with its reflection, inseparable from its movement. It is not essence, therefore, through which this movement runs its reflective course; nor is essence that from which the movement begins, as from a starting point. It is this circumstance that above all makes the exposition of reflection especially difficult, for strictly speaking one cannot say that *essence* returns into itself, that essence shines in itself, for essence is neither *before* its movement nor *in* the movement: this movement has no substrate on which it runs its course. A term of reference [*Ein Bezogenes*] arises in the ground only following upon the moment of sublated reflection (SL 11.295, 7 ff./390).

Qua ground, essence is a substrate and "has form as essence" (SL 11.295, 17/390). Whereas quality "is one with its substrate, being" (SL 11.295, 26 ff./390), form has its self-subsistence over against essence, which is its substrate, and is "positing and determining" (SL 11.296, 11/391), while "simple essence, on the contrary" is the "indeterminate and *inert* substrate" (SL 11.296, 11 f./391). By determining essence, form sublates the distinction presupposed between itself and its foundation: "These distinctions, of form and of essence, are therefore only *moments* of the simple reference of form itself" (SL 11.297, 1 ff./392). If form is completely abstracted from it, "essence becomes matter" (SL 11.297, 11/392); at the same time, "form *presupposes* a matter to which it refers" (SL 11.297, 25/392). The contradiction consists in the fact that form and matter, presupposed to be self-subsistent, refer to one another in their self-subsistence and "*pre*-suppose each other" (SL 11.298, 36/393). Like symmetric determination of form and matter, "the original unity of the two is, on the one hand, restored; on the other hand, it is henceforth a *posited* unity" (SL 11.300, 11 ff./395). As posited, this unity is determined; as a unity, a moment of self-subsistence pertains to it over against form, which Hegel refers to with the term '*content*' (SL 11.301, 10/396): "Content has, *first*, a form and a matter that belong to it essentially" (SL 11.301, 21/396) and "is, *second*, what is identical in form and matter" (SL 11.301, 28/396).

11.2.3.2. *Determinate Ground*

In this constellation, ground becomes 'determinate ground'; it not only stands in opposition to content generally, but also retains a determinate content whose ground it is. Since the content is what is identical in the opposition of essence and form, it occurs in two ways: "once in so far as it is *ground*, then again in so far as it is *grounded*" (SL 11.303, 15 f./398). But this only captures "formal ground" (SL 11.302, 23/397) because this is an analytic connection that relies on a presupposed identity of content. In his remark on this, Hegel therefore speaks of a 'mere formalism' and 'empty tautology' (SL 11.304, 12 f./399) and gives as an example the dispositional explanations of physics such as '*attractive force*' (SL 11.304, 20/399). These are, according to Hegel, not informative, so that a philosophical question arises as to why "the explaining is not set aside and the facts are not taken as they simply stand" (SL 11.307, 9 ff./402). In an explanation, according to Hegel, one requires that "ground and grounded have a diverse content" (SL 11.307, 28/403), and thus one requires a real ground and not a formal one. The diversity needed "is therefore the *reference to another*" (SL 11.309, 2/404). As Hegel discusses in the remark on this section, from this structure there arises a 'manifold' (SL 11.310, 9/405) of determinations that can be offered as real grounds. A variety of 'formalism' (SL 11.310, 15/405) thus shows up again in this schema of explanation because no real ground can be a '*sufficient ground*' (SL 11.312, 2/407).

11.2.3.3. *Condition*

The fluctuation between the formality of a tautology and the formality of the perpetually insufficient real ground shows that determinate ground cannot achieve the 'totality' (SL 11.314, 15/409) that is the aim of explanation. Because of this failure, the requirement to capture "the total ground-connection" must be weakened. Hegel introduces the category of the condition for the form of explanation that relies on this weakened connection. The real ground is now referred to another, to its condition. On the basis of its presupposed self-subsistence, a being is 'indifferent' to the determination of "*being a condition*" (SL 11.315, 10/410), so that the being at the same time "constitutes the *presupposition* of ground" (SL 11.315, 11 f./410). Thus arises the "contradiction, that they are indifferent immediacy and essential mediation, both in one reference" (SL 11.318, 10 f./413). The "absolutely unconditioned" (SL 11.318, 27/414), which Hegel later also calls "the *truly unconditioned; the fact in itself*" (SL 11.318, 17 ff./413),

is in its movement of positing and presupposing only the movement in which this *shine* [the relationship of condition and ground; MQ] sublates itself. It is the fact's own doing that it conditions itself and places itself as ground over against its conditions. (SL 11.319, 5 ff./414)

The fact is thus its own ground and at the same time its own condition, since, as something absolutely unconditioned, it has no external presupposition, but rather presupposes all of these through its own positing, by positing the very fact that it is posited. "*When,*" Hegel continues, "*all the conditions of a fact are at hand,* the fact steps into concrete existence" (SL 11.321, 5 ff./416). Because essence, as ground and condition, itself brings about these preconditions of its existence, the ontological status of being applies to them before their existence: "The fact is, *before it exists*" (SL 11.321, 6/416).

Just like a disposition is absorbed into its manifestation and does not remain behind as a substrate, so also the self-subsistence of ground stays behind only as a posited shine of essence determining itself:

> If, therefore, all the conditions of the fact are at hand, they sublate themselves as immediate existence and as presupposition, and the ground is equally sublated. (SL 11.321, 22 ff./417)

The self-positing fact-act of the 'I' brings essence to existence and is thus its own ground and its own condition. This "coming forth is thus the tautological movement of the fact to itself: its mediation through the conditions and through the ground is the disappearing of both of these" (SL 11.321, 26 ff./417). The essence-logical reflection-framework of positing and presupposing can be explicated philosophically. The autonomous negation completed by the 'I' generates in this act its own identity through difference and thereby posits the totality of all of its conditions, the complete system of determinations of reflection, in one act: "The coming forth" of essence "into concrete existence is therefore so immediate, that it is mediated only by the disappearing of the mediation" (SL 11.321, 27 ff./417). The free decision of an autonomous subject, which in Hegel's view has the fact-act of the 'I' as its prototype, therefore must be conceived in its proper meaning as 'the *groundless*' (SL 11.322, 3/417).

11.3. APPEARANCE

If one reads the first section of the Logic of Essence as an ontology of self-consciousness in the sense of an *genitivus objectivus*, then a good interpretive hypothesis is that the second section can be read as an ontology of self-consciousness in the sense of a *genitivus subjectivus*. In this second section of his Logic of Essence, Hegel develops an ontology of the object in which the constitutive epistemic capacities of self-consciousness are contained in a form that becomes increasingly reflexive.

By the end of the first section, the self-mediation of essence (which vanishes in the constellation of ground and condition) has given rise to the category of existence

(*Existenz*) as an essence-logical successor of shine. The motor of this development is the contradictoriness of essence, which determines itself in ever more complex constellations through its autonomous negation. If this development at the end of the first section brings to light the aspect of being in the form of existence as a starting point, then two things are to be expected in the development of the second section. First, the aspect of negativity will again be expressed as Hegel works through the contradictoriness of the constellations that capture the aspect of being. Second, ontological constellations will arise in the course of the development that increasingly bring to expression the constitution of essence as autonomous negation.

'Essence must appear' (SL 11.323, 3/418); with this famous phrase, Hegel introduces the subsequent development of the Logic of Essence. In saying this, he claims that existence cannot be a stable endpoint for essence. The immediacy attained "is, *first, concrete existence*, and a concrete existent or *thing*" (SL 11.323, 22/418), yet it remains deficient: "The thing indeed contains reflection, but its negativity is at first dissolved in its immediacy" (SL 11.323, 24 ff./418). This is Hegel's reconstruction of the 'thing-in-itself' (SL 11.323, 28 f./418). But since reflection is constitutive of the Logic of Essence, this immediacy must become explicitly the result of a positing. In the first chapter, "Concrete Existence" (SL 11.324, 8/420), Hegel traces the "dissolution of the thing" (SL 11.336, 15/432) that takes place via this explication. Because the thing in itself and reflection (or the epistemic capacities of the subject) were related to one another only externally, the thing in itself became alienated from its essence:

> It is for this reason also self-repelling thing-in-itself which *thus relates itself to itself as to an other*. Hence, there are now a *plurality* of things-in-themselves standing in the reciprocal reference of external reflection. (SL 11.328, 37 ff./425)

The determinateness of the thing-in-itself brought to light thereby is the "*property of the thing*" (SL 11.329, 39/426). And yet the thing-property ontology is also incapable of dissolving the contradiction between the ontological interdependence of the relata and their simultaneous self-subsistence. The things-in-themselves are differentiated through their properties, "not because of some viewpoint alien to them" (SL 11.332, 31 ff./429). Thus the "reciprocal action of things" (SL 11.332, 27/429) becomes their essence, which thus transitions from thing into property.[25] If these properties are thus reified as 'matter' (SL 11.334, 11/430), the fundamental contradiction returns. Furthermore, the thing is thus reduced to matter and thereby the "dissolution of the thing" (SL 11.336, 15/432) is brought to a completion.

According to Hegel, the thing-in-itself is determined as a 'positedness' (SL 11.323, 27/418) and thus as an 'appearance' (SL 11.341, 3/437) in this development. This "is what the thing is in itself, or the truth of it" (SL 11.323, 28 ff./418). Because this ontology of a "world of appearance" (SL 11.323, 30 ff./419) only arises as the result of the negation of immediacy,

---

[25] One can understand this as the switch from an ontology of intrinsic essences to an ontology that conceives of essential properties as relations; on this, see also Yeomans, *Freedom and Reflection*, 51.

as mediation, the reference to its other—to "the *world* that *exists* in itself reflected into itself" (SL 11.323, 31/419)—remains constitutive of it. Content applies here to both sides as an identical moment in the form of a law: "The law, therefore, is not beyond appearance but is immediately *present* in it; the kingdom of laws is the *restful* copy of the concretely existing or appearing world" (SL 11.345, 20 ff./441). It gives expression to the invariant structure—Hegel speaks of it as "unchanging" (SL 11.348, 31/444)—of the manifold grasped as a perpetual subject of change. It is not, however, only an external description of this, but rather constitutive of it as a law: "Law is this simple identity of appearance with itself" (SL 11.347, 12 ff./443). Thus laws are "the *determinate* ground of the world of appearance" (SL 11.351, 3 ff./447); and yet at the same time, "it is precisely in this opposition of the two worlds that *their difference* has disappeared" (SL 11.351, 13 ff./447). In the manifold of existence, the law is '*realized*' (SL 11.352, 19/448) and its reality is to be a manifold: " 'World' signifies in general the formless totality of a manifoldness; this world has foundered both as essential world and as world of appearance" (SL 11.352, 27/448).

The dualism of this constellation remains unstable and gives expression in turn to the contradictoriness of essence: "what appears shows the essential, and the essential is in its appearance" (SL 11.324, 2 ff./419). The tension alluded to through "to show [*zeigen*]" and "is [*ist*]" ends in a complex constellation that Hegel develops in the third chapter of the second section: "The truth of appearance is the *essential relation*" (SL 11.353, 3/449). From the very beginning, Hegel makes clear that it is "not yet the true *third* to essence and to *concrete existence*" (SL 11.353, 16 ff./449); this will be 'actuality' as "the unity of essence and *concrete existence*" (SL 11.369, 3/465). But the essential relation "already contains the determinate union of the two" (SL 11.353, 17 ff./449). It is, however, "something internally fractured" (SL 11.353, 29/449), because it is "a totality which, however, essentially has an opposite or a *beyond*" (SL 11.353, 26 f./449). The first constellation of this self-contradicting unity is the "relation of the whole and the parts" (SL 11.354, 28/450). In this constellation, "*immediate* self-subsistence" (SL 11.354, 33/450) and an essential relation to one another are features of both the whole and its parts, thus also of "their sublatedness no less" (SL 11.354, 33/451). Then, in the "relation of force and its expression" (SL 11.359, 19/455), the dynamic of this essential relation is registered as the positing and presupposing of essence. Essence is thus "the truth of that first relation" (SL 11.359, 21/455) because the relation of both sides to one another is given expression as the activity of essence itself. The shortcoming of this essential relation is twofold. On the one hand, it consists in the fact that force, as a property, is conceived as a "*quiescent determinateness of the thing* in general" (SL 11.360, 26 ff./456) and thus immediacy's character as being becomes once again dominant. On the other hand, force is the expression of the side of activity, and the other made available by its character as being can only be "*another force*" (SL 11.362, 7/457), so that one force "is reciprocally a *stimulus* for the other force against which it is active" (SL 11.362, 18 ff./458). The whole relation is therefore infinite in the sense of a relation of force that remains internal. The external relationship of one force to another is structurally identical with force's self-relation. Force determines itself as a dynamic relation in the entire system of forces, whose "stimulus by virtue of which it is solicited to activity is its own soliciting" (SL 11.364, 16 ff./459). In the third essential relation "of the outer and the inner" (SL 11.364, 23/460), the way that this difference is stabilized into a dualism also turns out to be unstable: "the two, however, are only one identity" (SL 11.365, 7/460). At the same time, the relata of inner and outer are determined in this essential relation in such a way that each, through its own structure, "points to the totality of both" (SL 11.366, 16 ff./461). The category that sublates the deficiency that essence is only inner, and the complimentary deficiency that appearance is only the outer of essence, is actuality, the "identity of appearance with the inner or with essence" (SL 11.368, 36 ff./464).

The grammar of subjectivity, in particular in the form of self-consciousness, belongs to this day to the most difficult objects of philosophy. This holds both in the philosophy of German Idealism as well as in analytic philosophy. On the one side, this grammar supplies the basic structure of all fundamental epistemological conceptions. On the other side, the metaphysical aspect of this grammar is itself the object of various ontological interpretations. Hegel's analysis of essence as internal reflection is one of the most rigorous analyses of this grammar of subjectivity. His conception has two main strengths: first, the approach operates at such a fundamental level that the distinction between the epistemological and the ontological dimension is itself conceived as an element of this grammar. Second, Hegel succeeds in unfolding the complexity of this grammar out of a single principle by means of a self-referential movement of the Concept.

WORKS CITED

Primary Texts

Hegel, G. W. F. *Enzyklopädie der Philosophischen Wissenschaften im Grundrisse (1827)* (= *Gesammelte Werke, Band 19)* [E1827] [cited as GW 19, page, line], edited by Wolfgang Bonsiepen and Hans-Christian Lucas. Hamburg: Felix Meiner Verlag, 1989.

Hegel, G. W. F. *Enzyklopädie der Philosophischen Wissenschaften im Grundrisse (1830)* (= *Gesammelte Werke, Band 20)* [E].

Hegel, G. W. F. *The Science of Logic* [SL], translated by George di Giovanni. Cambridge: Cambridge University Press, 2010.

Hegel, G. W. F. *Wissenschaft der Logik. Erster Band: Die objektive Logik (1812/1813)* (= *Gesammelte Werke, Band 11)* [cited as GW 11, page, line], edited by Friedrich Hogemann and Walter Jaeschke. Hamburg: Felix Meiner Verlag, 1978.

Secondary Literature

Düsing, Klaus. *Das Problem der Subjektivität in Hegels Logik*. Bonn: Bouvier, 1976.

Hartmann, Klaus. *Hegels Logik*. Berlin: Walter de Gruyter, 1999.

Henrich, Dieter. "Hegels Logik der Reflexion, " in *Hegel im Kontext* by Dieter Henrich. Frankfurt: Suhrkamp Verlag, 1971, 95–157.

Henrich, Dieter. "Hegels Grundoperation," in *Der Idealismus und seine Gegenwart*, edited by Ute Guzzoni, Bernhard Rang, and Ludwig Siep. Hamburg: Felix Meiner Verlag, 1976, 208–230.

Henrich, Dieter. "Hegels Logik der Reflexion. Neue Fassung," in *Die Wissenschaft der Logik und die Logik der Reflexion*, edited by Dieter Henrich. Bonn: Bouvier, 1978, 203–324.

Houlgate, Stephen. *The Opening of Hegel's Logic*. West Lafayette, IN: Purdue University Press, 2006.

Koch, Anton F. *Die Evolution des logischen Raumes*. Tübingen: Mohr Siebeck, 2014.

McDowell, John. *Mind and World*. Cambridge, MA: Harvard University Press, 1994.

Quante, Michael. *Die Wirklichkeit des Geistes*. Frankfurt am Main: Suhrkamp Verlag, 2011.

Rohs, Peter. *Form und Grund*. Bonn: Bouvier, 1969.

Schmidt, Klaus J. *G. W. F. Hegel: 'Wissenschaft der Logik—Die Lehre vom Wesen.'* Paderborn: Ferdinand Schöningh Verlag, 1997.

Wirsing, Claudia. "Grund und Begründung. Die normative Funktion des Unterschieds in Hegels Wesenslogik," in *Hegel: 200 Jahre Wissenschaft der Logik*, edited by Anton Friedrich Koch, Friedrike Schick, Klaus Vieweg, and Claudia Wirsing. Hamburg: Felix Meiner Verlag, 2014, 155–178.

Wolff, Michael. *Der Begriff des Widerspruchs*. Frankfurt am Main: Frankfurt University Press, 2010.

Yeomans, Christopher. *Freedom and Reflection*. Oxford: Oxford University Press, 2012.

CHAPTER 12

....

FROM ACTUALITY TO CONCEPT IN HEGEL'S *LOGIC*

....

KAREN NG

THE concept of actuality (*Wirklichkeit*) is omnipresent throughout Hegel's system and is widely recognized to be of utmost importance for understanding the key tenets of his philosophy. Although much has been written about this concept in the context of Hegel's social and political philosophy, its significance and place in *The Science of Logic* remains obscure and is less well understood. What is actuality in the context of the *Logic*?

As the third and final section of the Doctrine of Essence, actuality provides a conclusion not only for this second book of the *Logic*, but also for the Objective Logic as a whole, presenting the transition to the Subjective Logic, or the Doctrine of the Concept. In order to serve as such a transition, actuality has to fulfill at least two related and essential functions. First, it must provide what Hegel calls the genesis of the Concept.[1] Like so many of Hegel's ideas, the genesis of the Concept can in part be understood both in comparison and in contrast with Kant. We can compare this section of the *Logic* with Kant's transcendental deduction, insofar as what Hegel is trying to show is the necessity of the Concept—his highly altered version of Kant's 'I think', or the original synthetic unity of apperception—as the self-determined ground or foundation of the categories that have already been generated in the Doctrines of Being and Essence.[2] Actuality must show that the unity of the Concept, a kind of self-actualizing form, is necessary for the determination of anything as *actual* (*wirklich*), for the determination of anything that has a sufficient reason or self-determined *end* (*Zweck*). From here we can already begin to see some of the differences from Kant, for Hegel's deduction appears to be much more demanding. Whereas Kant's deduction only aims to establish the necessary

---

[1] "*Objective logic* therefore, which treats of *being* and *essence* constitutes properly the *genetic exposition of the Concept.* . . . the Concept has substance for its immediate presupposition. . . . Thus the *dialectical movement* of *substance* through causality and reciprocity is the immediate *genesis* of the *Concept*, the exposition of the process of its *becoming*" (SL 12.11/577).

[2] See SL 12.17–18/584. For the classic interpretation of Hegel that takes this passage as definitive, see Pippin, *Hegel's Idealism*.

conditions for the *possibility* of experience (more specifically, the deduction establishes the legitimacy of the a priori applicability of the categories to objects),[3] Hegel's deduction aims to determine the conditions for *actuality* (but importantly, *not existence*) and *actual* knowledge. Far from being an extravagant form of idealism, we can read Hegel's deduction here as an argument for the priority of actuality over possibility in our knowledge claims. We can also identify a further difference at the level of method: in contrast with Kant's *transcendental* deduction, Hegel refers to his genesis of the Concept as an "immanent deduction" (SL 12.16/582). Specifically, Hegel attempts to develop the basic determinations of the Concept immanently from the idea of substance as it has been understood in modern philosophy, particularly in Spinoza. If successful, Hegel's deduction should bring us from substance to subject.

In connection with the transition from substance to subject, the second function that actuality must fulfill is the transition from necessity to freedom. Proceeding immanently from the Spinozist conception of substance, the section on actuality aims to determine a kind of self-relating, self-actualizing form—the form of freedom itself—making good on Spinoza's definition of substance as *causa sui*.[4] Actuality provides the argument for Hegel's important and oft-cited claim that with the Concept "we have opened up the realm of *freedom*" (SL 12.15/582). Given that the Doctrine of Essence is a study of relations and relational determinations of being, at its conclusion, Hegel aims to secure a form of self-relation that can be characterized as self-determination, a kind of relationality that can properly be called free. Hegel's turn to the notion of actuality hinges on his interest in determining the form of self-actualization as such, and his argument will attempt to resolve, or perhaps better, dissolve, one of the biggest debates in modern philosophy in a distinctively post-Kantian vein, namely, the opposition between necessity and freedom and the threat this poses to the latter determination in particular. Of particular importance here is the overcoming of mechanism as the definitive and exclusive mode of causality and a vindication of the relational mode of *Wechselwirkung*, reciprocity, or reciprocal action. In determining a self-relating reciprocity between causes and effects akin to Kant's notion of inner purposiveness, Hegel hopes to philosophically demonstrate not only the possibility of freedom, but also its actuality.[5]

---

[3] See Kant, *Critique of Pure Reason*: "The explanation of the manner in which concepts can thus relate a priori to objects I entitle their transcendental deduction" (A85/B117).

[4] "[S]ince substance has *necessity* for its particular relational mode, freedom reveals itself as the *truth of necessity* and as the *relational mode of the Concept* [*die* Verhältnisweise des Begriffs]" (SL 12.12/577–578).

[5] On the idea of intrinsic purposiveness, see Kant, *Critique of Judgment*, §§63, 66. Hegel refers to the notion of inner purposiveness as "Kant's great service to philosophy." See SL 12.157/737. In *Freedom and Reflection*, Yeomans offers a detailed account of how the categories of Hegel's *Logic*, and in particular, the treatment of modality, mechanism, and teleology are essential for understanding the notions of agency and the free will that are generally viewed exclusively as elements of his practical philosophy. Although Yeomans is not primarily concerned with interpreting what Hegel means by the Concept, his arguments clearly demonstrate the significance of these categories of the *Logic* for understanding the Hegelian conception of free activity and are highly instructive in addressing questions in the philosophy of action.

Having dived right into the thick of the *Logic*, we can already see that Hegel places a huge burden on the concept of actuality, particularly as it appears in these highly condensed pages that bring us to the Doctrine of the Concept. In order to argue that the 'actuality' section in the *Logic* fulfills the two preceding functions—namely, the genesis of the Concept and the determination of the form of freedom—I will begin with a brief overview of the concept of actuality as it appears in Hegel's system and its place in the *Logic* in particular (section 12.1). I will then build Hegel's argument through the three chapters that comprise the section on 'actuality': "The Absolute," "Actuality," and "The Absolute Relation" (sections 12.2, 12.3, and 12.4). What will emerge in the development of these moments is the significance of purposiveness in bringing us from actuality to the Concept. In particular, I will argue that Hegel arrives at the self-relation of the Concept by first determining the self-relating activity of living beings, presenting the self-conscious Concept as an actualization of living activity (section 12.5). In order to present the trajectory of all three final chapters of the Objective Logic, each of which could be the topic of independent studies of their own, this essay will inevitably overlook certain details of each chapter and does not aim to be an exhaustive account of the section on 'actuality'. My goal is to establish the overarching philosophical importance of this idea for understanding Hegel's Concept, and to situate this idea within the *Logic* as a whole.

12.1. What Is Actuality?

Actuality is Hegel's appropriation of Aristotle's notion of *enérgeia*, and is generally employed to combat dualistic ways of thinking in philosophical conceptions of nature, spirit, and logic. What brings Hegel to return again and again throughout his system to the notion of actuality is his interest in articulating a determinate conception of *activity*, or more specifically, an activity of form (*Formtätigkeit*) in which form and matter, inner and outer, are not opposed.[6] Hegel explains actuality in Aristotle in his *Lectures on the History of Philosophy* as follows:

> There are two leading forms, which Aristotle characterizes as that of potentiality (*dúnamis*) and that of actuality (*enérgeia*); the latter is still more closely characterized as entelechy (*entelecheia*), which has the end (*tò télos*) in itself, and is the realization of this end. . . . To Aristotle, the main fact about Substance is that it is not matter merely . . . matter itself is only potentiality, and not actuality—which belongs to form—matter cannot truly exist without the activity of form. With Aristotle *dúnamis*

---

[6] Hegel first refers to the activity of form as well as absolute form in the *Logic* in the chapter titled "Ground." See SL 11.296, 298–300/449, 452–454. Activity of form will come up again at a crucial moment in Hegel's discussion of the hypothetical syllogism (SL 12.123/700), one that mirrors in important ways his analysis of actuality. See also E §§150, 151, 212. In *Hegel's Critique of Metaphysics*, Longuenesse also argues that the outcome of Hegel's discussion of actuality is a concept of activity (*Tätigkeit*) (see 151–162).

does not therefore mean force (for force is really an imperfect aspect of form), but rather capacity which is not even undetermined possibility; *ènérgeia* is, on the other hand, pure efficaciousness out of itself [*die reine Wirksamkeit aus sich selbst*]. (LHP 19.154/2.138–139)

Matter, being, especially substance, cannot exist without the activity of form; in fact, matter taken 'in itself' is simply an abstraction from the activity of form that gives shape and determinacy to anything identifiable as such. Activity of form not only brings form to matter but can also be characterized as an activity of *determination*, insofar as the lack of form entails indeterminacy, indefiniteness, vagueness, abstraction, and in general, something unknown. We can think of *Formtätigkeit* here in one of two ways. First, activity of form brings form and determinacy to *objects*. When Aristotle suggests that matter cannot exist without the activity of form, he is arguing against the idea of 'pure matter', suggesting that 'matter' can only be something determinate insofar as it has form— either a form given externally or a form that is the result of its own activity. Form that is the result of a thing's own activity is, secondly, a kind of activity that also forms and determines a *subject* of activity. This kind of activity brings determinacy to and is formative of a self, in addition to or alongside the activity of determining objects. Activity of form is therefore what makes a thing (an object or a subject) *actual*, for without it, matter remains indeterminate and not even an "undetermined possibility."

Thus, although Hegel famously identifies the rational and the actual in the preface to his *Philosophy of Right*, it might be more accurate to identify actuality with formative activity that constitutes an end in itself. Of course, rational activity is certainly exemplary here, but note that Hegel's characterization is in fact much broader than what would generally be construed as rational. We can consider for a moment how Hegel takes up the issue of form-activity from three distinct but related perspectives, which make up the keystones of his philosophical system. First, from the perspective of *nature*, what exemplifies the unity of form and matter characteristic of the 'actual' is the activity and productivity of living nature, and in particular, of animal organisms. In the *Philosophy of Nature*, Hegel discusses the totality of the earth as an implicit process of formation (*Bildungsprozeß*), which is fully realized only in animal activity, for the animal is nothing but the product of "its own self-process" (E §339A). Reminding us that Kant had defined the animal as an end-in-itself, Hegel follows suit by describing the animal as a *Selbstzweck*, insofar as the animal produces itself from its own activity: whereas the earth merely *endures* (dauert), undergoing transformations due to external forces, the animal produces and reproduces itself and its species through its own formative activity. In the productivity of organisms, form and matter, inner and outer, are not opposed, but exist in a necessary, internal relation of self-production.[7] The productive activity of animal organisms in the natural world exemplifies for Hegel the kind of activity that, with further determinations, will be ultimately characterized as free. The idea of

---

[7] "Whenever inner and outer, cause and effect, end and means, subjectivity and objectivity, etc., are one and the same, there is life" (E §337A).

"pure efficaciousness out of itself" finds its first actuality in the self-production of living beings.

Second, from the perspective of *spirit*, Hegel defines *Geist* itself as "*manifestation*" and "absolute *actuality*" (E §383). As the collective intellectual and material history of individual and social agents, spirit, as has been noted by Robert Pippin, is "not a thing."[8] Rather, spirit is nothing but its ongoing activity, and we determine what spirit *is* by attending to what it *does*. Using the terms of Hegel's *Logic*, we can say that understanding what spirit is (the *being* of spirit) is to understand the formative activity that constitutes its *essence*; put somewhat differently, we could also say that understanding the determinate practices, institutions, customs, laws, and culture of spirit is to understand them as manifestations of spirit's free activity. Spirit itself, and particularly its development as traced in the *Phenomenology*, is often described as a process of *Bildung*, here understood as the social and historical activity of cultural formation. In the domain of spirit, actuality is a key concept for understanding both the philosophy of action and Hegel's social philosophy, where the latter attempts to assess the rationality of our institutions on the basis of the degree of individual and collective freedom they enable, the degree to which they provide the conditions for spirit's self-actualization, thereby allowing agents to be "at home with one self in one's other" (E §24A).[9] We can thus understand the rationality of the actual both as a critical method for coming to self-knowledge of our present age, and as a thesis concerning the conditions for the reality of freedom. Grasping spirit as absolute actuality and being at home in the world requires that we not only view the world as the product of our own activity, but further, that the products of our activity provide further conditions for and continue to enhance our ongoing self-realization.

Finally, from the perspective of *logic*, which will be our focus here, actuality takes up the problem of the unity of essence and appearance at the highest level of formality, the most developed version of which is discussed by Hegel under the heading of the relation of inner and outer. It is important to note that at the beginning of the section on actuality, the form-activity characteristic of freedom has not yet been fully determined. Instead, Hegel describes the unity of inner and outer as a kind of self-revealing and self-expression. The key concept that brings us to actuality is the idea of *manifestation*: on the one hand, essence must appear, essence must manifest itself in appearances; on the other hand, appearances themselves are nothing but the manifestations of essence. In determining this essential relation between the inner and the outer in terms of manifestation, Hegel begins to move away from the dualistic framework presumed in the very distinction between essence and appearance. Again, we can see why the appropriation of Aristotle's notion of actuality can be helpful in this context: just as Aristotle protested the Platonic separation of ideas (intelligible essence) from their instantiations (sensible appearances), Hegel is protesting Kantian versions of this separation throughout his presentation of the categories of essence.[10] Once Hegel has established the essential

[8] Pippin, *Hegel's Practical Philosophy*, 41.

[9] For readings that present Hegel's practical philosophy as a social theory, see Neuhouser, *Foundations of Hegel's Social Theory*; Honneth, *The Pathologies of Individual Freedom* and *Freedom's Right*.

[10] See E §142A; and Longuenesse, *Hegel's Critique*, 113.

relation between the inner and outer as manifestation, we arrive at the logical determination of actuality.

12.2. THE ABSOLUTE

Hegel begins the final section of the Doctrine of Essence with a chapter titled "The Absolute." Proceeding from the categories of reflection and appearance and immediately following the categories of the essential relation (whole and parts, force and its expression, inner and outer), the arrival of the absolute at this juncture immediately presents at least two interpretive puzzles. The first is simply, why have we reached the absolute at this point? Initially, it appears to be a rather uncharacteristic place for the absolute to make an appearance, given that Hegel usually reserves the denomination for the conclusion of his texts. The second puzzle concerns the status of the absolute at this juncture and its connection to actuality. Why is the absolute the first moment or determination of the actual? How does the absolute function here as a step toward the development of the idea of form-activity?

To address the first puzzle, we can begin by noting that Hegel's use of the term at this particular moment in the *Logic* is self-consciously ambivalent. There is something clearly premature about the announcement of the absolute in the Doctrine of Essence, and yet, there are good reasons for its appearance as the first moment of actuality. One clue that the absolute presented here is premature can be found in Hegel's use of absolute in the nominative, which, while not by any means unprecedented, is unusual, and deviates from his more official uses of the term. Within Hegel's system, the term 'absolute' usually appears in an adjectival form, describing a specific determination of something—*Wissen, Form, Idee, Geist*—rather than denoting something substantial in itself.[11] Our form of knowing is absolute, for example, when it is self-consciously determined and carried out in a certain way, mode, or manner, something that is only possible as the result of a particular development. Absolute spirit—art, religion, and philosophy—consists of specifically defined modes of self-knowledge that are essential for understanding human freedom. *The* absolute, then, as a substantive, is something rather empty and indeterminate, and "the absolute itself [at first] appears only as the negation of all predicates and as the void" (SL 11.370/530). To develop the concept of the absolute into something determinate and actual, Hegel will ultimately conclude the chapter by turning to the mode (*Modus*) of the absolute as the absolute's "way and manner," the way and manner in which the absolute comes to be manifest (SL 11.374/535).[12]

---

[11] On some of the different uses of the term 'absolute' as an adjective, see Nuzzo, "The Truth of *Absolutes Wissen*."

[12] The *modus* of the absolute will ultimately lead Hegel to conclude the *Logic* with an absolute *method*. See SL 12.237/825ff.

The utter abstractness and obscurity of *the* absolute in its initial pronouncement is thus no accident, for we do not yet know exactly what it is that is being described as absolute.

Nonetheless, Hegel has good reasons for introducing the absolute at this moment in the Doctrine of Essence, for it is an important marker of both an end and a beginning at once. As the marker of an ending, the absolute is the result of the cumulative determinations of the *Seins-* and *Wesenslogik* which make up the first volume of the *Science of Logic*. The absolute is thus a "negative outcome," and we can read the progression of the *Logic* thus far, the entire movement through the categories of being and essence, as "the *negative exposition* of the absolute" (SL 11.370–371/530–531). As negative, the absolute denotes the end of the Objective Logic (which corresponds in part with Kant's transcendental logic),[13] and can be viewed as a refutation of the modes of thinking expounded by its categories, in particular, the metaphysical realism of being and the irreconcilable, unself-conscious dualisms of essence.[14] The absolute is "the ground in which [the previous determinations] have been engulfed," expressing at once the insufficiencies of an Objective Logic, as well as providing the true basis presupposed by being and essence, a presupposition that has now been posited and made explicit through the exposition of the prior categories. However, as ground, the absolute is not only something negative, but "this exposition has itself a *positive* side" and also represents a new beginning (SL 11.372/532). The beginning for which this section provides the transition is, as mentioned earlier, the Doctrine of the Concept or the Subjective Logic, the final book and undoubtedly the key to the *Logic* as a whole. In laying the ground for the determination of the Concept, the absolute in the beginning of its exposition is not only abstract, but further, can only be spoken of from a limited, external perspective. If, as suggested by the opening section of the chapter, the absolute is nothing ahead of displaying and exhibiting its content, nothing ahead of the very process of its own exposition (*Auslegung*), then at the outset, and in referring to it as a substantive rather than exhibiting it as a mode, the beginning can only be "the *absolute of an external reflection*" (SL 11.372/533). *Qua* beginning, the absolute is not yet actual, but a mere seeming (*Scheinen*), a merely relative absolute that is as yet premature.[15]

Turning to the second interpretive question concerning the status of the absolute and its connection to actuality, it is important to recall Hegel's oft-cited claim that the absolute must be grasped not only as substance but equally as subject.[16] Determining the absolute as both substance and subject *is* to determine the actuality or true reality of the absolute. Perhaps more than in many other places where Hegel attempts this transition, the development presented in the *Logic* is quite literal: the absolute represented by Spinoza's substance must be actualized into a mode of post-Kantian subjectivity

---

[13] SL 11.31/61–62.

[14] Pippin argues that the Doctrine of Being presents an argument against classical metaphysical realism, whereas the Doctrine of Essence argues against notions of 'reflected being' while beginning to present Hegel's own idealism by attempting to reconcile traditional dualisms between essence and existence. See his *Hegel's Idealism*, 181.

[15] See also PS 9.21–22/¶24.

[16] See for ex. PS 9.18/¶17.

represented by the Concept (*der Begriff*). Thus, the trajectory of the "Actuality" section brings us from *the* absolute (which Hegel wryly and absurdly refers to as the "absolute absolute" [SL 11.373/533]), the absolute attribute, and the mode of the absolute (the three moments of Spinoza's substance metaphysics), to an absolute self-relation of universality, particularity, and individuality, the three moments of Hegel's Concept. To make this transition plausible, Hegel must develop a philosophically defensible notion of self-actualization, a mode of activity that is proper to self-determining subjectivity. If the absolute is to be actual, and not merely an empty definition or dogmatic concept, it must show itself to be the result of its own activity of self-production, it must reveal its actuality to be a process of self-actualization.

Although there are hints that this is where Hegel is heading (he refers to the "act" of the absolute as well as to absolute form), we have reason at this point to be skeptical. The chapter on the absolute is obscure even by Hegelian standards, providing few arguments toward developing the idea of activity, and at most, attempts to present two objections against Spinoza's conception of substance, which appear most clearly in the "Remark" that concludes the chapter.[17] The first is that Spinoza's axiomatic, geometric method, which begins with a series of assumed definitions, fundamentally regards substance from the perspective of external reflection rather than immanently determining the inner necessity of the matter at hand. To complete this argument, it will in fact take Hegel the rest of the *Logic* to present his own immanent exposition of the absolute, and further, the presentation of his alternative account of method will only come at the very end of the *Logic*, concluding the text as a whole. The second complaint is captured by Hegel's famous remark that substance lacks individuality or personality [*Persönlichkeit*]. By defining substance *without* subject as absolute, Spinoza cannot adequately account for the determinations of subjectivity and self-consciousness that are essential to substance according to Spinoza's own exposition. More specifically, Hegel contends that the typology of substance, attributes, and modes cannot adequately account for the determination of thought within its prescribed tenets as not only actual and necessary, but most important, as free. In order to develop his own conception of free subjectivity, Hegel turns directly to the determination of modes that display the very power of substance as absolute. In the second chapter titled simply, "Actuality," Hegel further explores the idea of the mode of the absolute by turning to the modal categories and, in particular, the modality of necessity.

---

[17] It is beyond the aims of this chapter to assess Hegel's critique of Spinoza, which, like his critique of Kant, is a matter of much debate. One of the central issues in the debate between Hegel and Spinoza is whether or not Spinoza is guilty of 'acosmism'—the denial of the existence of finite individuals and the belief that only God is real. See Hegel's treatment of Spinoza in LHP 20.157–198/3.252–290; see also Schmusli, "Hegel's Interpretation of Spinoza's Concept of Substance"; Parkinson, 'Hegel, Pantheism, and Spinoza'; Melamed, "Acosmism or Weak Individuals?"; Machery, *Hegel or Spinoza*; Ravven, "Hegel's Epistemic Turn—or Spinoza's?"; and Newlands, "Hegel's Idealist Reading of Spinoza."

12.3. MODALITY AND ABSOLUTE NECESSITY

Hegel's chapter on the modal categories consists of his most direct treatment of the relation between the actual, the possible, the necessary, and the contingent. The crux of the chapter is to develop a conception of absolute necessity, one that will both return us to the problem of substance as well as lay the ground for reconciling necessity and freedom. To begin, it will help to unpack two theses that underlie Hegel's treatment of actuality as the mode and manifestation of the absolute. The first is that actuality is not simply what exists, what is contingently there, what is tangible; not everything that *exists* is *actual*.[18] Actuality has a particular kind of self-determined, rational form; things that are actual must live up to their own inner principle or standard of truth and activity: a body separated from its soul or life exists, but is not actual; a state that does not live up to its own constitution surely exists, but is also not actual. Actuality is self-manifestation, a necessary relation between inner and outer, form and content, as self-expression. In order to be *self*-expression, actuality must be inherently divided against itself; it is not merely contingent existence, but "self-distinguishing and self-determining movement," a "form-unity" of existence *and* essence, and hence, "the determination of *immediacy* over against the determination of reflection-into-self" (SL 11.381/542). More specifically, the negativity of actuality is expressed as "an *actuality as against a possibility*," that is, actuality is more than what it is and already contains within itself a relation between actuality and possibility. Understanding how actuality is more than itself, goes beyond itself, and contains potentiality within itself to become something else, to produce a new actuality, is what it means for actuality to be absolute.

Second, Hegel argues for a priority of actuality over possibility; in fact, properly speaking, there is only one modality out of which all other modes are determined, namely, actuality (one reason that "Actuality" is simply the title for the whole last section of the *Wesenslogik*).[19] The claim here is, unsurprisingly, thoroughly Aristotelian: only actuality can 'beget' another actuality, meaning that understanding potentiality, the "conditions of possibility," the power of some reality to bring about, express, and determine another reality, is to understand something about actuality as a dynamic process of the actualization of its own potentialities. As Aristotle writes in *Metaphysics*, "it is by *actuality* that the potential becomes *actual*."[20] In effect, possibility, contingency, and necessity are all

---

[18]   See, for example, E §§6, 142A, SL 11.380–381/541–542. Hegel writes, "In common life people may happen to call every brainwave, error, evil and suchlike 'actual', as well as very existence, however wilted and transient it may be. But even for our ordinary feeling, a contingent existence does not deserve to be called something-actual in the emphatic sense of the word; what contingently exists has no greater value than that which something-*possible* has; it is an existence which (although it is) can just as well *not be*" (E §6A).

[19]   Hegel writes of Kant's categories of modality, "Possibility should come second; in abstract thought, however, the empty conception comes first" (LHP 20.345/3.439).

[20]   Aristotle, *Metaphysics* 1051a30. See also *Metaphysics* 1049b25–30: "For it is always by a thing in *actuality* that another thing becomes *actualized* from what it was potentially; for example, a man by a man and the musical by the musical. . . . We have stated in our discussion of substance that everything

modes or determinations *of* actuality, ways in which actuality comes to be determined. Substance must be posited as actuality, as containing potentiality and power within itself to produce new actualities, and it is in unpacking the movement of this process that Hegel comes to the idea of self-actualization. Hegel thus uses Aristotelian *ènérgeia* to read Spinoza,[21] and the appropriation of *ènérgeia* is required for and anticipates Hegel's account of substance as power and reciprocal causality (*Wechselwirkung*), or substance as inner purposiveness of form. Before we get there, let us turn briefly to the details of Hegel's analysis of modality.

Hegel moves swiftly in this chapter through three moments of actuality: formal modality (or contingency), real modality (or relative necessity), and absolute necessity.[22] Although Hegel is often thought of as a necessitarian who preaches the cold march toward history's end, here it becomes clear that he is in fact not only attuned to the role of contingency in the course of actual events, but further, that understanding the constitutive role of contingency is central to his account of necessity.[23] Nonetheless, Hegel does begin his argument by presenting a critique of a *certain* understanding of contingency, one that finds its beginnings in a merely formal (or logical) notion of possibility. According to formal possibility, anything that is not self-contradictory is possible. This leaves the realm of formal possibility open to a "boundless multiplicity" (SL 11.382/543): the moon could be made of cheese, I could be six feet tall, rotary phones could come back into fashion, the list of possibilities in the formal sense is potentially endless. To make matters worse, contradiction, a category presented earlier in the Doctrine of Essence, is in fact essential to the reflected determination of all finite things, meaning that everything is in fact self-contradictory, and hence, nothing is possible.[24] Hegel is suggesting that understanding the relation between the actual and the possible according to a formal conception of possibility amounts not to a determination of actuality at all, but rather, amounts only to a determination of contingency or mere existence. He writes, "The contingent is an actual that at the same time is determined as merely possible, whose other or opposite equally is" (SL 11.383–384/545). We could call this initial, merely formal sense of contingency a naïve or unself-conscious contingency—the

which is being generated is being generated from something and by something, and the later is in the same species as that which will be generated."

[21] Spinoza's substance/God is not only absolutely necessary, but also absolute actuality: "God's omnipotence has been actual from eternity and will remain in the same actuality to eternity" (*Ethics* 1p17s1).

[22] Longuenesse notes that the three moments of actuality (formal, real, absolute) mirror the three moments of determinate ground. See *Hegel's Critique*, 121; and SL 11.302–314/456–469.

[23] Hegel's idea of the necessity of contingency is a topic of much debate. See, for example, Henrich, "Hegels Theorie über Zufall"; Houlgate, "Necessity and Contingency in Hegel's *Science of Logic*"; di Giovanni, "The Category of Contingency in the Hegelian Logic"; Lampert, "Hegel on Contingency, or, Fluidity and Multiplicity"; and Burbidge, *Hegel's Systematic Contingency*.

[24] See SL 11.279–290/431–443. Hegel writes, "Finite things, therefore, in their indifferent multiplicity are simply this, to be contradictory and *disrupted within themselves and to return into their ground*" (SL 11.289/443).

thought that everything that exists could equally well not exist, the thought that every-thing is determined *only* by chance.

It is important to note that Hegel does not deny that even this unself-conscious form of contingency has a place in the world, and even a place in our own sense of self-understanding. Contingency "deserves its due in the world of objects," both when we are considering the realm of nature, where contingency has a certain degree of "free rein," and when we are considering the realm of spirit, where arbitrariness or freedom of choice (*Willkür*), despite its limitations as a determination of freedom, is an irreduc-ible element of the human will (E §145A). Nonetheless, contingency as it arises out of the notion of formal possibility remains caught between two one-sided moments that cannot cohere into a plausible determination of actuality. When we refer to an event, act, or state of affairs as merely contingent, what we mean to say is that it has no ground, that it has no sufficient reason for being one way rather than another. However, as a pos-sible event, act, or state of affairs, it must have *some* ground, it must have arisen from some other event, act, or state of affairs, otherwise it would not be possible at all. Hegel writes, "The contingent, then, has no ground because it is contingent; and, equally, it has a ground because it is contingent" (SL 11.384/545). In fluctuating between these two determinations, we come to realize that this back-and-forth between groundlessness and groundedness is in fact necessary for grasping this form of unself-conscious contin-gency. Contingency as this "*absolute unrest*" is *necessary* for the determination of actual-ity according to this formal account of modality.

For Hegel, the shortcoming of this initial understanding of the necessity of contin-gency is its lack of awareness concerning the content of its own claim. In claiming that the fluctuation between groundlessness and groundedness is necessary, what one is really saying is that one lacks sufficient knowledge concerning the grounds in ques-tion, that one does not know the real conditions and circumstances that brought a particular actuality about. Thus, although Hegel acknowledges that sheer chance cer-tainly plays a role in the determination of the actual, formal contingency operating as a *complete* determination of actuality is disingenuous insofar as it stops short of doing the work of understanding how particular events, acts, or states of affairs came to be actualized. This brings us to the second moment of real modality, which moves beyond the determination of formal possibility into considering real possibility, the concrete conditions that bring some actuality into being. Hegel describes real possi-bility as follows:

> What is actual *can act* [*Was wirklich ist*, kann wirken]; something announces its actuality *through that which it produces*. . . . if one brings into account the determi-nations, circumstances, and conditions of something in order to ascertain its pos-sibility, one is no longer at the stage of formal possibility, but is considering its real possibility. . . . The real possibility of something is therefore the existing multiplicity of circumstances which are connected with it. This existing multiplicity is, therefore, both possibility and actuality. . . . real possibility constitutes the *totality of conditions*, a dispersed actuality. (SL 11.385–386/546–547)

Real possibility as the totality of conditions necessary for bringing something about determines actuality as something that can act, as something that can produce effects, only insofar as it is a process of actualization resulting from a determinate set of real conditions and circumstances. Thus, for the time being, it is not *really* possible—that is, the totality of real conditions are not present—for the moon to be made out of cheese or for me to be six feet tall. Moving beyond formal possibility as mere non-contradiction, but also beyond what Kant would call transcendental conditions of possibility, real modality determines the identity and difference of the actual and the possible by taking up actuality as a set of concrete, dispersed potentialities, as containing *within itself* the possibility of becoming a new configuration of conditions, and hence, a new actuality. In the "movement of translating" real conditions and circumstances into new actualities and translating existing actualities into new, concrete conditions of possibility, Hegel is already beginning to present his notion of activity (*Tätigkeit*) (E §148).[25] Conceiving of actuality as the process of actualizing real possibilities is to determine actuality as a movement that can produce effects, as a movement that "can act," as a kind of form-activity that produces and transforms itself on the basis of existing potentialities that are identical with itself. Once we move beyond formal possibility and contingency and do the work of determining and assessing the totality of conditions, actuality is seen not exclusively as the result of sheer chance, but as a dynamic process of activity in which real conditions bring about real results.

In assessing the notion of activity Hegel is presenting here, we now can draw a distinction between activity as *absolute necessity* and activity as *purposive or free*. Although activity in the latter, fully developed sense will only be presented as the final moment in the transition to the Subjective Logic, it is helpful to have this goal in mind as we ascertain the significance and limitations of absolute necessity. To complete his account of real modality, Hegel writes, "When all the conditions of something are completely present, it enters into actuality" (SL 11.387/548). And perhaps even more emphatically in the *Encyclopedia*: "When *all conditions* are present, the matter *must* become actual" (E §147). In effect, real possibility is already real necessity because the totality of conditions is identical with a realized actuality, and thus, given a certain set of conditions, a certain actuality *necessarily* follows. Here again, however, Hegel shows himself to be attentive to the role of contingency in the determination of the actual, for in fact, this kind of necessity remains relative because "it has its *starting point* in the *contingent*" (SL 11.388/549). Although given a certain set of conditions a certain actuality necessarily follows, the multiplicity of existing circumstances are themselves contingent, leading to the necessity of contingency now in a deeper, self-conscious, and self-determined sense. Unlike the formal determination of contingency as a fluctuation between groundlessness and groundedness, the real determination of contingency requires us to grasp the constitutive role of contingency in the necessary progression of conditions into that which is actualized. What Hegel calls absolute necessity is simply the self-consciousness of

---

[25] The notion of activity is even more explicitly highlighted in the *Encylopedia Logic* account of modality. See esp. E §§147–151.

contingency as constitutive in the process of actualization, that the progression of contingent conditions is "necessity's *own becoming*" (SL 11.390/551). Contingency is necessity's own becoming because it is constitutive of—that is, *absolutely necessary* for—the determination of actuality and its ongoing process of actualizing potentialities.

In the conclusion of the "Actuality" chapter, Hegel goes on to suggest that absolute necessity is "blind" and "light-shy" (SL 11.391, 392/552, 553). The progression of absolute necessity is blind, insofar as

> *purpose* [Zweck] is still not present *for-itself* as such in the process of necessity. The process of necessity begins with the existence of dispersed circumstances that seem to have no concern with one another and no inward coherence. These circumstances are an immediate actuality that collapses inwardly, and from this negation a new actuality emerges. . . . hence the necessity that constitutes this process is called 'blind'. By contrast if we consider purposive activity [*zweckmäßige Tätigkeit*] . . . this activity is not blind but sighted [*sehend*]. (E §147A)

There are two claims here that should be highlighted. First, the notion of activity present in absolute necessity is limited and incomplete. Purpose, a sense of goal-directed activity or activity that aims at an end is not yet explicitly present, is not yet present in a fully developed or self-determined sense. That purposiveness is not yet present *for-itself* implies that at the stage of absolute necessity, purposiveness or activity is only present *in-itself*, that is, in an implicit or yet-to-be-developed sense. Absolute necessity is blind because the progression of contingent conditions has no self-determined purpose or goal, and further, the conditions and circumstances themselves are only indifferently related to one another in their ongoing progression. Second, purposive activity, where purpose is present *for-itself*, results in a form of activity that is *not blind*, but sighted. What exactly does Hegel mean by "seeing" here? Purposive activity is a form of seeing activity insofar as its ends and goals are self-determined. Conditions are actively shaped such that they are not indifferently related and have an internal coherence; the progression of conditions are goal-directed and self-organized. Nonetheless, although purposive activity determines its own ends, "seeing" here does not entail that the totality of conditions and circumstances are fully in view in advance of, or in the midst of, carrying out an end. Even in the most conscientious activity, prospectively, we never have complete knowledge of the circumstances and conditions surrounding any particular act.[26] This lack of complete knowledge of the totality of conditions is simply a part of our self-consciousness regarding the necessity of contingency in the progression of conditions into effects. Behind this thought is a familiar Hegelian theme, namely, that the totality of conditions can only be recollected retrospectively, that the actual is truly determined and grasped as rational only after the fact. Here, on the cusp of the transition to freedom

---

[26] Hegel writes in the *Phenomenology*, "This actuality is a plurality of circumstances which breaks up and spreads out endlessly in all directions, backwards into their conditions, sideways into their connections, forwards into their consequences. The conscientious mind is aware of this nature of the thing and of its relation to it" (PS 9.346/¶642).

or the Concept, Hegel reminds us that self-actualization must be grasped not only from a forward-looking perspective, with conditions marching ever onward into their results. Rather, self-actualization must also be grasped, and in fact, can only be fully grasped, from a retrospective, backward-looking perspective, one that carefully gathers up a dispersed actuality and determines it as the rational result of purposive, free activity.

12.4. THE ABSOLUTE
RELATION: RECIPROCITY

The problem of the third and final chapter, titled "The Absolute Relation," is how to make the transition from a notion of activity where purpose is implicit (absolute necessity) to a notion of activity where purpose is explicitly self-determined and constitutes a relation-to-self. Establishing the latter completes the final stage of the genesis of the Concept; in fact, Hegel suggests that a self-determining, purposive self-relation simply *is* the Concept. Initially, Hegel's strategy in this chapter can appear somewhat artificial: he returns first to the problem of substance (the absolutely necessary), taking up the relation between substance and accidents; next, he takes up the relation of causality, in particular, the causal relations characteristic of mechanism; finally, Hegel concludes the Objective Logic with the category of reciprocity or reciprocal action (*Wechselwirkung*), a reciprocal relation between causes and effects posited as a self-relation, determining purposive activity as the relation that is absolute.

Despite a certain artificiality in Hegel's progression here, the final chapter of the Doctrine of Essence in fact takes up all three of Kant's categories of relation and can be read as an attempt at rewriting the analogies of experience found in the first *Critique*.[27] There, Kant claimed that "[t]he general principle of the three analogies rests on the necessary *unity* of apperception,"[28] and Hegel too, is suggesting that the determination of actuality outlined thus far rests upon the self-relation of the Concept. However, there is also a decidedly un-Kantian moment in Hegel's final step of the genesis or deduction of the Concept. Hegel claims that with reciprocity, the relation of finite or external causality called mechanism "is sublated" (SL 11.407/569).[29] The determination of the Concept

---

[27] See Kant, *Critique of Pure Reason*, B106 and A176/B218–A218/B265. A helpful reconstruction of this chapter that also discusses Hegel's rewriting of Kant's analogies can be found in Houlgate, "Substance, Causality, and the Question of Method." See also Iber, "Übergang zum Begriff."

[28] Kant, *Critique of Pure Reason*, B220.

[29] "In der Wechselwirkung ist nun dieser Mechanismus aufgehoben" (SL 11.407/569). It is certainly not the case that the third analogy sublates the second analogy; Kant takes them to be compatible and complementary, and reciprocity is by no means an overcoming of mechanism. On the connection between the second and third analogy, see Watkins, *Kant and the Metaphysics of Causality*, ch. 3 and 4. As Watkins notes, "mutual interaction [occurs] in light of Newton's law of the equality of action and reaction, the action of the repulsive force of the one corresponds to the reaction of the repulsive force of the other" (137). See also ibid., 249–250, and the section on mechanics in Kant, *Metaphysical Foundations of Natural Science*, 84–92.

hinges on the demonstration of a purposive self-relation that can be said to be the *cause and effect of itself*. There are two points of reference here that are important to note concerning the idea of self-cause. First, despite the latter being Spinoza's definition of substance, Hegel is suggesting again that the self-relation of being the cause and effect of oneself presupposes and requires the determination of subjectivity as coextensive with substance.[30] The absolute must be determined not only as substance, but equally as subject because the notion of *causa sui* is unintelligible without some conception of the self. Commenting on Spinoza's philosophy, Hegel writes, "Absolute substance is the truth, but it is not the whole truth; it must also be thought of as in itself *active and living* [*in sich tätig, lebendig*], and by that very means it must determine itself as mind [*Geist*]" (LHP 20.166/3.257). The connection between *active* and *living* is key: only living activity suffices for determining the purposiveness characteristic of subjectivity. The second point of reference is in some ways even more important, and has been rarely pointed out by scholars and is less well understood. In the third *Critique*, Kant defines a natural purpose (*Naturzweck*)—a living organism—as "both cause and effect of itself."[31] However, according to Kant, the self-organizing causal connections involved in the determination of natural purposes cannot be fully captured by the causality operating according to mechanism, and troublingly, require us to attribute *intrinsic purposiveness* to such beings. For Kant, ultimately, the attribution of this kind of purposiveness remains a regulative principle for judgment rather than constitutive of actual objects, a claim that Hegel must reject. It is this nexus of problems that frames Hegel's consideration of reciprocity as the absolute relation that will bring us to the Concept: in order to determine the notion of subjectivity adequate to absolute substance, the causality characteristic of living beings must first be determined as the first actuality of freedom, forming the basis for any possible determination of selfhood.

Although this may seem like a tall order, Hegel's argument here is continuous with the development of the concept of actuality we have been tracking thus far. Returning to the question of actualizing conditions into their effects, Hegel introduces the shortcomings of mechanistic causal determination by highlighting the limits of this framework for our understanding:

> [A]bove all, we must note the *inadmissible application* of the relation of [mechanistic] causality to *relations of physico-organic* and *spiritual life*. Here, what is called cause certainly reveals itself as having a different content from the effect; *but the reason is that* that which acts on a living being is independently determined, changed, and transmuted by it, *because the living thing does not let the cause come to its effect*, that is, it sublates it as cause. Thus it is inadmissible to say that food is the *cause* of blood, or certain dishes or chill and damp are the *causes* of fever, and so on; it is equally

---

[30] "The only possible refutation of Spinozism must therefore consist, in the first place, in recognition its standpoint as essential and necessary and then going on to raise that standpoint to the higher one through its own immanent dialectic. The relationship of substance considered simply and solely in its own intrinsic nature leads on to its opposite, to the Concept" (SL 12.15/581).

[31] Kant, *Critique of Judgment*, §§64, 65.

inadmissible to assign the ionic climate as the *cause* of Homer's works, or Caesar's ambition as the *cause* of the downfall of the republican constitution of Rome. In *history* generally, spiritual masses and individuals are in play and reciprocal determination [*Wechselbestimmung*] with one another; but it is rather the nature of spirit, in a much higher sense than it is the character of the living thing in general, not *to receive into itself another originating thing*, or not to let a cause continue itself into it but to break it off and to transmute it [*sondern sie abzubrechen und zu verwandeln*]. (SL 11.400–401/562)

Hegel speaks here of the inadmissibility of mechanism for the determination of both organic and spiritual life, an inadmissibility that hinges on how causes and effects are to be understood in the process of actualization. Living things, especially self-conscious living things, are not only passive substances along a causal chain (think: billiard balls), but rather, such beings break off and transform their conditions according to self-determined ends. In the flow of causes and effects determined according to mechanism, however, we remain at the level of blind contingency: conditions are dispersed, external, and indifferent to one another, expressing no internal coherence. Consider another example offered by Hegel in this context: Suppose a man developed a talent for music—how do we understand the causes of his talent? (SL 11.400/561–562). The talent was developed as a result of the man losing his father, so his father's death was the cause of his talent. But his father was shot while at war, so the shot, and then the war, were the causes. This kind of reasoning is potentially endless, and can include all sorts of other contingencies, such as the gun was made with steel, so steel caused the man's talent; his father was shot on a foggy day, so fog was the cause of his talent; an overzealous monarch caused the war, and so he in fact caused the man's talent. Hegel contends that what we are speaking of here "is not a cause at all but only a single *moment* which belonged to the *circumstances of the possibility*" (SL 11.400/562). When actuality is understood exclusively according to the causal connections of mechanism, the totality of conditions that constitute a given actuality are forever under- and overdetermined in such a way that actuality cannot be determined as something that "can act," as something that can display its power to produce effects. Mechanism underdetermines because there is an infinite regress of causes, so the set of conditions is never complete; mechanism overdetermines because there are too many causes and provides no criteria with which to distinguish genuine, essential causes from accidental, non-essential ones. In the preceding example, what mechanism cannot grasp is the development of musical talent as, irreducibly, a matter of self-determination, even while it takes place in the midst of a plurality of circumstances and events that provide a context of action.

Hegel refers to the external determinations of mechanism as a form of violence: "Violence is the *appearance of power*, or *power as external*" (SL 11.405/567). Although this might sound like Hegelian dramatic flair, external power appears as violence because it does not allow actuality to be determined as something that *can act*, destroying the determination of actuality as something with the power to determine itself. In the mechanistic determination of causes and effects, actuality is determined as something acted upon by a variety of indifferent causes, a passive substance that "suffers *violence*" from causes acting as external powers. Insofar as it suffers violence, what is presupposed is a cause that can be an "*act* of violence . . . an *act* of power."[32] It appears that even according to mechanism's own determinations, an external cause must be determined as a cause with the *power* to act upon some effect, the effect has to *suffer* some alteration, otherwise neither cause nor effect would be what they are along the descending mechanistic chain of causes to their effects.[33] In cause, a power to act is presupposed that is only realized or posited in the effect; in the alteration suffered in the effect, what is again presupposed is a power to act again as cause. Substance is thus determined as both active and passive, as actuality that can be both an act of power and vulnerable to acts of power. Notice here how Hegel is already demonstrating a reciprocity at work between cause and effect, agent and patient, within the paradigm of mechanism itself: a cause would not be able to act as cause without at the same time having the 'capacity' to passively suffer some alteration by another cause; an effect cannot be an effect unless the alteration it suffers is again a power to act as some new cause. At first, the power of passive substance to act again as cause is determined as a *reaction*: as reaction, passive substance is divided as both the effect of a previous cause, and displays itself as its own power of causality. It is both passive substance and reactive substance at once. Now the difference between reaction and self-determined action, like the transition from real to absolute necessity, is not only subtle, but in fact, "the hardest" (EL §159).[34] In reciprocity, causality is "*bent round* and becomes an action that returns into itself" (SL 11.407/569). In bending around and turning back, passivity is taken up as a product of self-activity, and the entire series of conditions acting upon passive substance are broken off and transmuted into the active becoming of substance itself. Substance as reciprocity is

> both passive and active. . . . is mediated *by itself*, is produced by its own activity, and is thus the *passivity posited by its own activity*. Causality is conditioned and

---

[32] My emphasis.

[33] In stating that in causality we presuppose a power (*Macht*) to act, there is an important argument that Hegel is assuming here from earlier sections of the Doctrine of Essence, namely, that the positing of laws and forces within the mechanistic paradigm do not help to explain or determine the matter at hand with necessity, or as a matter of *essence* (see the chapter "Appearance," SL 11.341–352/499–511; and the section on force and its expression and its resolution in the unity of inner and outer, SL 11.359–368/518–528). This argument is also famous from the "Force and Understanding" chapter in the *Phenomenology*. Laws and forces belong to a previous shape of essence called 'appearance'; they were posited as two different shapes of essence that belonged to a view in which existence was determined merely as appearance, with forces and laws standing behind appearances as their truth. They do not belong to the sphere of actuality because in actuality, we have already achieved the standpoint of the unity of inner and outer as expression and manifestation, meaning that laws and forces that stand behind appearances are no longer valid as explanatory for actuality. The unity of inner and outer is what allows Hegel to suppose that a power to act is presupposed in the expression of a cause. The problem of laws and forces is extremely complex—one of the most difficult in all of Hegel—and I cannot do justice to the relevant arguments here. For a clear and insightful account of the issues at stake, see Kreines, "Hegel's Critique of Pure Mechanism," 46–50.

[34] "The passage from necessity to freedom, or from the actual into the Concept, is the hardest one."

conditioning ... cause not only *has* an effect, but in the effect it stands, *as cause* in relation to itself. Causality has hereby returned to its *absolute Concept*, and at the same time has attained to the Concept itself. ... In reciprocity, originative causality displays itself as an *arising* from its negation, from passivity, and as a *passing away* into the same, as a *becoming*. (SL 11.407–408/569–570)

Two things are happening at once in the logic of reciprocity, the logic of bending around and turning back: the first is the explicit determination of *purpose* in the reciprocity of active and passive substance; the second is the determination of the self-conscious Concept insofar as it turns back on the first relation and thereby determines its own reciprocity—its freedom—as both substance *and* subject. How is it that the determination of reciprocity realizes both relations at once?

12.5. LIFE AND CONCEPT

The transition from reciprocity to freedom can appear hasty, but we can turn to two other places in Hegel's work in order to better understand what is taking place. Both in the *Phenomenology of Spirit* and in the "Phenomenology" section of the *Philosophy of Mind* that forms the third part of the *Encyclopaedia*, Hegel suggests that there is a necessary connection between the self-relation characteristic of living things and the self-relation characteristic of self-consciousness. In the phenomenological context, Hegel suggests that self-consciousness is "ignited" in its contemplation of the living: it is in grasping the purposive form of the organism that self-consciousness comes to determine its own self-relation as an 'I'.[35] Bracketing here the similarities and differences between these two accounts, and acknowledging that many details of Hegel's suggestions in those contexts are both complicated and obscure (and cannot be explored in more detail here), I want to claim nonetheless that Hegel's overall argument is both important and instructive. First, at a very general level, Hegel is suggesting that there is what he calls a "speculative identity"—namely, an irreducible identity and difference—between how we understand the self-relating activity of the living thing and the self-relating activity of self-consciousness. The identity and difference at stake here is not merely trivial or accidental, but essential to the way we determine our activity as free. On the side of identity, Hegel is suggesting that the self-relation of the merely living being and the self-conscious living being have the same formal structure: both are forms of purposiveness that we grasp as causes and effects of themselves; both are forms of activity that, as self-caused, can be determined as a relation of self-constituting subjectivity. On the side of difference, what separates the living being from the self-conscious living being

---

[35] See E §§418A, §423; see also E 9.107/¶¶172–173. For an excellent account of this transition in the *Phenomenology of Spirit* that analyzes the structural homology and difference between life and spirit, see Khurana, "Die Geistige Struktur von Leben und das Leben des Geistes." See also Ng, "Life, Self-Consciousness, Negativity: Understanding Hegel's Speculative Identity Thesis."

is self-conscious mediation: the activity of the living thing is immediate, unconscious, and blind in contrast with our own self-conscious, intellectually and conceptually mediated activity. This identity and difference allows Hegel to determine self-consciousness as an *actualization* of natural life without in any way reducing self-consciousness to its merely natural existence. Although the specific determinations of this identity and difference take many different forms, bringing both satisfaction and dissatisfaction for self-consciousness, the overarching Hegelian claim is that self-conscious self-actualization takes place in the development of this identity and difference.

Second, and now returning to the specific context of the transition from reciprocity to freedom or the Concept in the *Logic*, I want to suggest that Hegel is leveraging this same identity and difference between living and self-conscious reciprocity, and arguing further for the reciprocity (an absolute relation) between these two modes. Now in the *Logic*, of course, what is at stake is not the "ignition" or phenomenological determination of self-conscious experience. Rather, what Hegel aims to provide here is first, the *logical form* of the Concept as self-determination, and second, the *basic categories* of that logical form from which the categories of the Subjective Logic will be developed. Now the logical form of self-causation identified by Hegel is the reciprocity of causes and effects posited as a self-relation. Once reciprocity is grasped *as* reciprocity, or, once reciprocity is self-consciously comprehended (*begriffen*), posited *as* a determination of thought, then we have already attained the standpoint of self-conscious subjectivity, or the self-conscious Concept.[36] In terms of providing the basic categories entailed by the actuality of reciprocity, Hegel will suggest that the Concept determines itself as the self-relation of *universality, particularity*, and *individuality* (or singularity, *Einzelheit*), replacing the Spinozist metaphysics of substance, accidents, and modes. Far from pulling these determinations out of thin air, these three categories are necessarily produced through the self-actualizing activity of subjects in the broad sense, covering both non-spiritual and spiritual *selves*. As causes and effects of themselves, subjects reproduce themselves as universal, or in reference to a species or genus (*Gattung*). Through their ongoing activity, they further determine themselves as a particular, or as one member among many others within a species. As particulars, they share many essential features common to their species, relate to the whole as a part, as well as maintain a part/whole relation within themselves that is reciprocally determined by the members of the species. Finally, the self-relating activity of subjects produces them as singular, distinguishable individuals distinct from both the universal and other particulars.[37] Although much more can be said about these three determinations (Hegel begins the Subjective Logic by developing these categories), what is important here for understanding Hegel's aim is that the three categories are necessary for grasping any form of self-determining activity as something *actual*. Coming full circle, we can say that determining something as actual, rather than as merely possible or contingent, means that we grasp it in its

---

[36] See E §156A.

[37] These three determinations can also be found in Kant's explication of the natural purpose. See Kant, *Critique of Judgment*, §64.

Concept—in its self-relation as universal, particular, and individual at once. What can appear as an equivocation in Hegel's use of terminology—for example, in referring to the universal as *genus*, and employing it to refer to concrete and conceptual generalities— is in fact a claim about the ground of these categories: universality, particularity, and individuality are the objective categories of self-actualizing form, which are determined *immediately* in the activity of living beings, and self-consciously mediated in the activity of self-conscious living beings. In a passage that may be one of the most important for understanding the transition to the Subjective Logic, as well as Hegel's philosophy as a whole, the determination of the Concept is summed up as follows:

> [T]he Concept is to be regarded not as the act of the self-conscious understanding [*Verstandes*], not as the *subjective understanding*, but as the Concept in and for itself which constitutes a *stage* of *nature* as well as of *spirit*. Life, or organic nature, is the stage of nature at which the Concept emerges, but as blind, as unaware of itself and unthinking; the Concept that is self-conscious and thinks pertains solely to spirit. (SL 12.20/586)

12.6. Conclusion

In this chapter, I have argued that actuality in the context of Hegel's *Logic* should be understood as the immanent deduction of the Concept, one that also serves the function of determining the form of freedom. I suggested that for Hegel, the main issue revolved around developing a notion of activity that could be characterized as self-relating and self-caused—in short, Hegel's aim was to develop a notion of self-determining activity adequate to subjectivity. One advantage of emphasizing the importance of purposiveness and the activity of living beings in Hegel's account is that it allows us to see the ongoing influence of both Kant and Aristotle for Hegel's thinking, as well as his innovative appropriation of their ideas, without overemphasizing one strand at the expense of the other.[38] In aligning his concept of the Concept with Kant's notion of self-consciousness, Hegel also aimed to determine the activity and freedom of self-consciousness as an *actualization* of the self-producing activity of living beings—an activity that provides the basis for understanding the necessary and internal relationship between the inner and outer, form and matter. A further advantage of this interpretation is that it anticipates and provides a framework for understanding the culminating and concluding moment of *The Science of Logic* in the determination of the Idea. Hegel arrives at the Idea as the immediate result of his treatment of the categories of mechanism, chemism, and teleology, ultimately presenting

---

[38] I would argue that interpreters such as Pippin and Longuenesse (cited earlier) overemphasize Kantian influences in their reading of actuality, whereas Ferrarin overemphasizes the Aristotelian influence. See Ferrarin, "Hegel on Aristotle's *Ènérgeia*."

the first determination of the Idea as life, followed by the Idea as self-consciousness or cognition. Although it is beyond the aims of this chapter to elaborate on these further developments in the *Logic*, I hope that the interpretation of actuality presented here, in addition to helping us understand the transition to the Subjective Logic, also provides us with some resources for that endeavor.

WORKS CITED

Primary Texts

Aristotle. *Metaphysics*, translated by Hippocrates G. Apostle. Bloomington: Indiana University Press, 1966.
Hegel. G. W. F. *The Encyclopaedia Logic* [E], translated by T. F. Gereats, W. A. Suchting, and H. S. Harris. Indianapolis: Hackett Publishing, 1991.
Hegel. G. W. F. *Lectures on the History of Philosophy* [LHP], translated by E. S. Haldane and Frances H. Simson as *Lectures on the History of Philosophy*, Vols. I and III. Lincoln; London: University of Nebraska Press, 1995.
Hegel. G. W. F. *Phenomenology of Spirit* [PS], translated by A. V. Miller. Oxford: Oxford University Press, 1977.
Hegel. G. W. F. *Philosophy of Nature* [E], translated by A. V. Miller. Oxford: Oxford University Press, 1970.
Hegel, G. W. F. *The Science of Logic* [SL], translated by George di Giovanni. Cambridge: Cambridge University Press, 2010.
Hegel. G. W. F. *Vorlesungen über die Geschichte der Philosophie, Werke*, Vols. 18–20, edited by Eva Moldenhauer and Karl Markus Michel (based on Michelet's edition). Frankfurt am Main: Suhrkamp, 1969–1972.
Kant, Immanuel. *Critique of Judgment*, translated by Werher S. Pluhar. Indianapolis: Hackett Publishing, 1987.
Kant, Immanuel. *Critique of Pure Reason*, translated by Norman Kemp Smith. New York: Palgrave MacMillan, 2003.
Kant, Immanuel. *Metaphysical Foundations of Natural Science*, translated by Michael Friedman. Cambridge: Cambridge University Press, 2004.
Spinoza, Benedict de. *Ethics*, translated by Edwin Curley. New York: Penguin, 2005.

Secondary Literature

Burbidge, John. *Hegel's Systematic Contingency*. London: Palgrave Macmillan, 2007.
di Giovanni, George. "The Category of Contingency in the Hegelian Logic," in *Art and Logic in Hegel's Philosophy*, edited by Warren E. Steinkraus and Kenneth L. Schmitz. New York: Humanities Press, 1980, 179–199.
Ferrarin, Alfredo. "Hegel on Aristotle's *Energeia*." *Bulletin of the Hegel Society of Great Britain* 53 (2006): 69–80.
Henrich, Dieter. "Hegels Theorie über den Zufall," in *Hegel im Kontext* by Dieter Henrich. Berlin: Suhrkamp, 2010, 158–187.
Honneth, Axel. *The Pathologies of Individual Freedom: Hegel's Social Theory*, translated by Ladislaus Löb. Princeton, NJ: Princeton University Press, 2010.

Honneth, Axel. *Freedom's Right: The Social Foundations of Democratic Life*, translated by Joseph Ganahl. New York: Columbia University Press, 2014.

Houlgate, Stephen. "Necessity and Contingency in Hegel's *Science of Logic*." *The Owl of Minerva* 27, no. 1 (1997): 37–49.

Houlgate, Stephen. "Substance, Causality, and the Question of Method in Hegel's *Science of Logic*," in *The Reception of Kant's Critical Philosophy: Fichte, Schelling, & Hegel*, edited by Sally Sedgwick. Cambridge: Cambridge University Press, 2000, 232–252.

Iber, Christian. "Übergang zum Begriff: Rekonstruktion der Überführung von Substantialität, Kausalität und Wechselwirkung in die Verhältnisweise des Begriffs," in *Der Begriff als die Wahrheit: Zum Anspruch der Hegelschen 'Subjektiven Logik*,' edited by Anton Friedrich Koch, Alexander Oberauer, and Konrad Utz. Paderborn: Ferdinand Schöningh, 2003, 49–66.

Longuenesse, Béatrice. *Hegel's Critique of Metaphysics*, translated by Nicole J. Simek. Cambridge: Cambridge University Press, 2007.

Khurana, Thomas. "Die Geistige Struktur von Leben und das Leben des Geistes." *Hegel-Jahrbuch: Geist? Erster Teil* (2010): 28–33.

Kreines, James. "Hegel's Critique of Pure Mechanism and the Philosophical Appeal of the Logic Project." *European Journal of Philosophy* 12, no. 1 (2004): 38–74.

Lampert, Jay. "Hegel on Contingency, or, Fluidity and Multiplicity." *Bulletin of the Hegel Society of Great Britain* 5, no. 1–2 (2005): 74–82.

Machery, Pierre. *Hegel or Spinoza*, translated by Susan M. Ruddick. Minneapolis: University of Minnesota Press, 2011.

Melamed, Yitzhak Y. "Acosmism or Weak Individuals? Hegel, Spinoza, and the Reality of the Finite." *Journal of the History of Philosophy* 48, no. 1 (2010): 77–92.

Neuhouser, Frederick. *Foundations of Hegel's Social Theory: Actualizing Freedom*. Cambridge, MA: Harvard University Press, 2000.

Newlands, Samuel. "Hegel's Idealist Reading of Spinoza." *Philosophy Compass* 6, no. 2 (2011): 100–108.

Ng, Karen. "Life, Self-Consciousness, Negativity: Understanding Hegel's Speculative Identity Thesis," in *The Freedom of Life: Hegelian Perspectives*, edited by Thomas Khurana. Berlin: August Verlag, 2013, 33–67.

Nuzzo, Angelica. "The Truth of *Absolutes Wissen* in Hegel's *Phenomenology of Spirit*," in *Hegel's Phenomenology of Spirit*, edited by A. Denker. Amherst: Humanities Press, 2003, 265–294.

Parkinson, G. H. R. "Hegel, Pantheism, and Spinoza." *Journal of the History of Ideas* 38, no. 3 (1977): 449–459.

Pippin, Robert. *Hegel's Idealism: The Satisfactions of Self-Consciousness*. Cambridge: Cambridge University Press, 1989.

Pippin, Robert. *Hegel's Practical Philosophy: Rational Agency as Ethical Life*. Cambridge: Cambridge University Press, 2008.

Ravven, Heidi M. "Hegel's Epistemic Turn—or Spinoza's?" *Idealistic Studies* 33, no. 2–3 (2003): 95–202.

Schmusli, Efraim. "Hegel's Interpretation of Spinoza's Concept of Substance." *International Journal for Philosophy of Religion* 1, no. 3 (1970): 176–191.

Watkins, Eric. *Kant and the Metaphysics of Causality*. Cambridge: Cambridge University Press, 2005.

Yeomans, Christopher. *Freedom and Reflection: Hegel and the Logic of Agency*. Oxford: Oxford University Press, 2012.

CHAPTER 13

SUBJECTIVITY IN HEGEL'S *LOGIC*

ROCÍO ZAMBRANA

IN what is perhaps the most famous passage of his dense and difficult corpus, Hegel argues that everything hinges on understanding substance as subject (PS 9.18/¶25). The passage, which appears in the Preface to the *Phenomenology of Spirit*, is the *locus classicus* for specifying the status of Hegel's idealism. Yet many have failed to notice its crucial iteration in the transition from the Objective Logic to the Subjective Logic in Hegel's monumental *Science of Logic* (SL 12.11/509). This transition is particularly important for establishing the status of Hegel's idealism. In it, Hegel recapitulates the critique of Spinoza pursued in the Doctrine of Essence and begins a seminal critique of Kant that spans the Doctrine of the Concept. In the Doctrine of the Concept, Hegel transforms Kant's notions of subjectivity, objectivity, and the idea. Key here is Hegel's move away from the first-person perspective of Kantian epistemic or moral subjectivity toward understanding subjectivity as the rationality of 'matters themselves'.[1] Hegel thereby elaborates his own brand of post-Kantian idealism, which culminates in the last chapter of the book, entitled "The Absolute Idea."

This chapter considers the preface to the Subjective Logic, "On the Concept in General," and the first section of the Doctrine of the Concept, "Subjectivity," which is composed of chapters on the Concept, Judgment, and the Syllogism. These discussions clarify Hegel's notion of subjectivity and provide a rubric for specifying the status

---

[1] Hegel's '*die Sache Selbst*' has been translated as 'the thing itself', 'the real thing', 'the matter at hand', 'matters themselves', 'the subject matter', 'the heart of the matter', 'the thing that matters', and most recently, 'reality'. This elusive notion is central to Hegel's theoretical and practical philosophy. With it, Hegel distances himself from the notion of a 'thing' (*Ding*) as well as Kant's notion of the 'thing in itself' (*Ding an sich*). Things themselves—from an action to a concept—unfold through their own activity and in light of their own content. An account of matters themselves thus rejects Kant's insistence on restricting any account to what can be known or what can be consistently thought. For helpful discussions of '*die Sache Selbst*', see Inwood, *Hegel Dictionary*, 288–290; Pinkard, *Hegel's Phenomenology*, 380–381, n. 93; and Bowman, *Metaphysics of Absolute Negativity*, ch. 6.

of Hegel's idealism. I begin with a brief overview of recent debates about Hegel's idealism, since they help contextualize the stakes of Hegel's rewriting of Kant's notion of subjectivity. I then discuss Hegel's critiques of Spinoza and Kant in "On the Concept in General." Finally, I examine the chapters on the Concept, Judgment, and the Syllogism and assess the notion of concrete universality crucial to Hegel's distinctive understanding of subjectivity.

13.1. Beyond the Metaphysical and Non-Metaphysical Debate

Since the 1970s, the dominant debate in Hegel scholarship has centered on the status of Hegel's idealism.[2] The debate developed as a result of readings divided on the question whether Hegel's idealism is metaphysical or non-metaphysical.[3] The details of each reading within both interpretive trends differ, to be sure. Nevertheless, commentators working within each camp share basic inclinations about Hegel's relationship to Kant and ideas about what counts as metaphysics given Kant's own influential critique.

By and large, metaphysical readings have argued that Hegel's critique of Kant amounts to a radical break with the critical project. A critical rather than dogmatic philosophy, Kant argued in the *Critique of Pure Reason*, rejects giving an account of the relation between thought and being in favor of considering the relation between cognition and object. Getting clear on the limits of human knowledge, he maintained, allows us to properly specify the status of traditional metaphysical questions that arise from reason's demand for an ultimate explanation. Principles of reason are no longer understood as constitutive—they no longer play a role in the determination of objects of experience. Hence, they no longer apply to reality as it is in itself. They are now understood as regulative, playing a necessary but merely organizing role within systematic bodies of knowledge. Hegel rejects Kant's insistence on the limits of human cognition, metaphysical readings have argued, thereby pledging allegiance to a Spinozist or Leibnizian view of philosophy.[4] Hegel's idealism is a metaphysics in line with pre-critical rationalism, since it not only purports to establish the relation between thought and being. It defends the view that the structure of thought and being are essentially the same. Consequently, among metaphysical interpretations we find that *Geist* (spirit) is understood as a 'cosmic entity', categories of thought are understood as 'structures of being', knowledge of reality is understood as accessible to finite beings given their capacity for intellectual intuition.[5]

---

[2] For helpful summaries of the debate, see Kreines, "Hegel's Metaphysics"; Lumsden, "Rise of Non-metaphysical Hegel"; and also Horstmann, "Hegel's Legacy."

[3] Hartmann's "A Non-Metaphysical View" initiated the interpretive trend.

[4] For a Spinozist reading of Hegel, see Beiser, *Hegel*. For a Leibnizian reading of Hegel, see Longuenesse, *Hegel's Critique of Metaphysics*, ch. 5 and 6.

[5] See Taylor, *Hegel*; Houlgate, *Opening of Hegel's Logic*; and Longuenesse, *Hegel's Critique of Metaphysics*.

Non-metaphysical readings of Hegel, in contrast, have rejected the claim that Hegel breaks with Kant.[6] Albeit in different ways, commentators who defend the non-metaphysical view have argued that Hegel seeks to 'complete' the critical project.[7] These readings thus strive to read Hegel's pre-critical language in light of post-critical commitments. Hegel's notion of *Geist* is not seen as a cosmic entity, but rather as Hegel's key concept for elaborating the "sociality of reason."[8] Hegel's account of categories of thought is not seen as a claim about being, but rather as a way of developing further the "apperception theme" in Kant's critical epistemology.[9] Hegel's insistence on going beyond the human standpoint is not an affirmation of the epistemic subject's capacity for intellectual intuition. It is rather a feature of Hegel's commitment to the "autonomy of reason"—to the fact that reasons, rather than a given, determine what counts as evidence about the nature of things.[10] Hegel's idealism is decidedly non-metaphysical, then, since it works within the strictures of Kant's critique of metaphysics in order to develop the critical project more consistently.

Recently, however, a number of scholars have argued that the more fruitful approach is going beyond the metaphysical/non-metaphysical divide. Granting that Hegel's post-critical idealism indeed involves metaphysical claims, some have argued, frees up interpretive space to consider what type of metaphysics Hegel develops. The focus is thereby shifted to an assessment of specific problems raised by Hegel's theoretical or practical philosophy. On one version of this argument, Hegel's idealism is more productively assessed if we consider what counts as a reason or ground of explanation, given Hegel's emphasis on the independence [*Selbstständigkeit*] of a satisfactory ground.[11] The debate is thus shifted to considering whether Hegel's commitment to a principle of activity intrinsic to matters themselves is an issue of a philosophical principle that is self-justifying, or of the justifiability of reasons within a historically specific shape of *Geist*. On a different version of the argument, Hegel's metaphysics is thought to be "emphatically revisionary," since it aims to develop concepts that explain the structure of reality by showing both the necessity and inadequacy of traditional ontological concepts.[12] Hegel's key concepts—the concept (*der Begriff*), absolute negativity (*absolute Negativität*)—represent a critique and indeed overcoming of traditional ontology. Hegel's speculative science is thus a metaphysics that lacks an ontology. Here the debate is shifted to questions about the structure of the concept as absolute negativity and to assessing Hegel's claim that absolute negativity elaborates a logic of content (or reality).[13]

---

[6] Although Hartmann initiated the interpretive trend, Pippin's *Hegel's Idealism* set the parameters for the debate.

[7] Ibid.

[8] See Pinkard, *Hegel's Phenomenology*.

[9] See Pippin *Hegel's Idealism*.

[10] See Pippin, "Hegel, Modernity, and Habermas."

[11] Kreines, "Learning from Hegel."

[12] See Bowman, *Metaphysics of Absolute Negativity*, 7.

[13] Cf. De Boer's account of negativity in *On Hegel*.

My own view is that going beyond the metaphysical/non-metaphysical debate is fruitful. It is clear that, for Hegel, to be is to be intelligible. Hegel gives the commitment to intelligibility a distinctively post-Kantian twist. He moves away from Kant's insistence on the first-person perspective for an account of knowledge, truth, and moral worth. Intelligibility, for Hegel, is the result of historically specific practices and institutions of rendering intelligible—what he calls *Geist*. *Geist* is a notion that privileges history for understanding the nature of intelligibility. Rendering intelligible is based on making and remaking distinctions within science, philosophy, the institutions of modern ethical life, and so on, that establish the nature of nature, self, and society at a specific moment in time. Privileging history when specifying the nature of intelligibility, however, involves an ahistorical account of intelligibility. It involves an account of the necessary historicity of intelligibility, which is established by showing that intelligibility is a matter of the rationality of matters themselves. Hegel develops such an account in *The Science of Logic* and pursues its consequences in his treatment of nature and subjective and objective *Geist* further along in the system. Moving away from the debate concerning the metaphysical or non-metaphysical status of Hegel's idealism, then, allows us to assess the character of Hegel's distinctive transformation of Kantian subjectivity crucial to his insistence that intelligibility is a matter of *Geist*.[14]

13.2. Spinoza's Lack, Kant's Formalism

Everywhere in his corpus, Hegel establishes that substance is subject by developing his distinctive understanding of negativity (*Negativität*). It is helpful to briefly consider Hegel's discussion in the *Phenomenology*, since it helps us see why negativity is central to Hegel's notion of subjectivity. In the Preface, Hegel elaborates his conception of reason in light of a logic of actualization (*Verwirklichung*). Hegel characterizes reason as 'purposive activity' (PS 9.20/¶22). Yet he does not conceive purposiveness in terms of a goal that is unambiguously actualized, thereby affirming a classical teleology of reason. Reason is purposive, Hegel writes, "in the sense in which Aristotle also determines nature as purposive activity." Purpose is what is 'self-moving', that is, what is '*subject*'.[15] Reason is purposive activity in being nothing but a thing, event, idea's 'power to move'. The thing's power to move—its being-at-work—is its subjectivity.[16] What does this mean?

In the Preface, Hegel speaks of subjectivity as "pure *simple negativity*" (PS 9.18/¶18). He clarifies that it is "the bifurcation of the simple." As such, "it is the doubling which sets up opposition, and then again the negation of this indifferent diversity and its

---

[14] For a full account, see my *Hegel's Theory of Intelligibility*. Cf. Pippin "Idealist Theories of Logic."
[15] Emphasis is mine.
[16] See Ferrarin's *Hegel and Aristotle* for an understanding of Hegelian subjectivity as Aristotelian *energeia*.

antithesis." Negation divides what appears to be immediate, a self-standing identity. This division, however, is a *self-negation*. It is the dispersal of that simple identity or unity into an opposition. This division, then, is the institution of an opposition. Yet this opposition reveals that the externality of what was seen as an immediate identity ('the simple') is essential to it. It reveals that such identity, which comprises a thing's intelligibility, is in fact the result of a totality of existent conditions that exceed it. In dividing the simple, then, negativity makes possible an alternative determination. It makes possible negating the 'indifferent diversity' of a dispersed unity. Division, to be more precise, establishes a *concrete* unity. The identity is no longer an identity given its self-sufficiency. Rather, it is an identity in light of the totality of conditions that produced it in the first place.

The "tremendous power of the negative," then, is the capacity of a thing to unfold in and through conditions that produced it in the first place. Matters themselves unfold in light of their own content. Because a new determination is established, negativity should be understood as an activity that returns-to-self. It is precisely because negativity establishes a new determination that it can be understood as a process of actualization—a process whereby a thing, event, idea "becomes other" thereby "returning-to-self."[17] Negativity, in a word, makes possible '*being-for-self*' (PS: 9.20/22). Through this process of actualization, the thing itself exhibits its own rationality. Matters themselves are produced by a totality of existent conditions, yet they nevertheless express *rational form* or, more precisely, a *form of rationality*. As we will see, the universality that matters bear in their singularity depends on particular conditions at hand. Actuality should therefore be understood as a concrete form of rationality. Now, because the intelligibility of any thing depends on conditions that produce it in the first place, its form of rationality should be understood in terms of its self-determination. The form of rationality that things express is thus their subjectivity. Because things themselves have the power to move themselves, to develop themselves through their own self-negation, they *are* forms of *subjectivity*.

'Subject', then, does not refer to a single epistemic, moral, social individual. It is the process of actualization of things themselves. Becoming-other and returning-to-self is the process whereby, as Hegel writes, "being is absolutely mediated" and therefore it is "equally immediately the possession of the I, is self-like, that is, is the concept" (PS 9.30/ ¶37). Actualization is thus a process of 'mediation [*Vermittlung*]'. The unity, rationality, and hence intelligibility of the thing itself is a matter of its own unfolding given its

---

[17] The easiest way to understand Hegel's very abstract notion of actualization is to think of action. As Pippin argues in *Hegel's Practical Philosophy*, Hegel understands action as the inseparability of an intention and the publicly performed deed. To act is to attempt to express an intention publicly. This means that the determinacy of an action is not fully up to the agent. It is a matter of its 'externality'—its publicity. Action entails 'self-negation', then. The determinacy of deeds, moral worth, even intentions can only be established in light of the temporal extension and intersubjective character of action—in light of misfires, competing interpretations, unforeseen consequences, normative expectations, and so on, that exceed the intentions of the agent. What was done, as well as who I am in light of what I did, then, can only be established ex post facto. For this reason, an intention is indeterminate—'the simple'. An action as well as an intention is only 'concrete' as a result of a process of actualization that necessarily includes all the elements that exceed it.

constitution, given the totality of conditions that produced it in the first place (PS 9.19/
¶20). That being is mediated warrants that it is understood as subject. It determines or
articulates itself through a process of actualization.[18] Substance should be understood as
subject. Now, in the Preface, Hegel clarifies that subjectivity is to be understood not only
as negativity itself, but also as *Geist* (PS 9.22/¶25). A concrete form of rationality is the
result of historically specific distinctions that establish what some thing, event, idea, or
institution is and what it should be on the basis of what it is not. These distinctions are
sustained or debunked by material, social, and historical conditions that produce them
in the first place. Being, then, is always already historically mediated. It is only, however,
through an account of the concept as negativity that being can be understood as always
already historically mediated, that substance can be said to be subject. More precisely,
it is only with Hegel's account of the idea offered in the closing section of the *Logic* that
intelligibility can be understood as a product of distinction making and remaking by
and within specific shapes of *Geist*.[19] In the interest of focus, let us set aside the role of
Geist in Hegel's understanding of subjectivity.

In "On the Concept in General," the preface to the Subjective Logic, Hegel reiterates that in being "absolute power or self-referring negativity," substance is best understood as subject (SL 12.12/509). As self-referring negativity, it is the "consummation
of substance" in "something higher," namely, "the concept, the subject" (SL 12.14/511).
Here Hegel recapitulates the critique of Spinoza laid out in an important remark in the
Doctrine of Essence. In the remark, Hegel agrees with Spinoza that "determinateness
is negation" (SL 11.376/472). The unity, determinacy, or identity of matters themselves
depends on distinctions that contrast it from what it is not. It is a matter of opposition,
which Hegel understands in terms of negation. For Spinoza, however, negation is only
a feature of the finite. Unlike the finite, Spinoza maintains, substance, the infinite, is a
matter of positive affirmation. The distinction between attributes, for instance, is understood without opposition. Hegel argues, in contrast, that the infinite is also matter of
negation.[20] The infinite, Hegel maintains, is nothing but "self-negating negation" (SL
11.376/472). Spinoza's notion of negation is lacking, Hegel insists, since it cannot account
for the activity of substance and hence for its status as the absolute ground of existence,
indeed of itself. Spinoza's notion of substance, Hegel writes, "is the absolute unity of
thought and being or extension; it therefore contains thought itself, but only in its *unity*
with extension, that is to say, not as *separating* itself from extension and hence, in general, not as a determinative and formative activity, not as a movement of return that

---

[18] Hegel writes, "the living substance is the being that is in truth *subject*, or, what amounts to the
same thing, it is in truth actual only insofar as it is the movement of self-positing, that is, that it is the
mediation of itself and its becoming-other-to-itself" (PS 9.19/¶20).

[19] With the claim that reason is autonomous, Kant and post-Kantian (specifically Fichtean)
metaphysics makes possible understanding society and history as a matter of distinction making and
remaking. See my *Hegel's Theory of Intelligibility*.

[20] See Melamed, "Omnis determinatio est negatio."

begins from itself" (SL 11.376/472; T). The ground that Spinoza fails to explain is the very logic of actualization that we have seen.[21]

Hegel famously argues that Spinoza's notion of substance "lacks the principle of personality" (SL 11.376/472). Hegel returns to the notion of personality in a crucial passage at the closing of the *Logic*, in the chapter on the Absolute Idea. *Persönlichkeit* is intimately related to but not the same as *Subjektivität*. In both cases, Hegel argues that intelligibility is grounded in *freedom* [*Freiheit*]. The closing of the *Logic* elaborates freedom in light of Kantian autonomy and Fichtean self-determination, thereby establishing that intelligibility is a matter of normative authority. In describing the absolute idea as personality, Hegel suggests that binding is the structure of intelligibility. As the unity of the theoretical and the practical, the absolute idea is the category that expresses that the intelligibility of matters themselves is a question of currency.[22] The chapters on Subjectivity elaborate freedom in a slightly different way by emphasizing self-negation as the structure of actualization. These chapters directly respond to the failure of Spinoza's metaphysics and develop the notion of substance in light of negativity—substance as subject, substance as concept. Rather than autonomy or self-determination, the concept as freedom in these chapters refers to Hegel's conception of *form* as negativity. More precisely, Hegel develops the notion of 'absolute form [*absolute Form*]', which accounts for the inseparability of form and content that replaces Spinoza's substance. The notion of absolute form is key to Hegel's understanding of subjectivity as the rationality of matters themselves. In order to develop the notion of absolute form, however, we must not only overcome Spinoza's notion of substance. We must transform Kant's notion of subject.

In "On the Concept in General," Hegel reiterates the failure of Spinoza's notion of substance and argues that its "genuine refutation" requires articulating how it necessarily "passes over" into the notion of the concept (SL 12.15/512). The "inner necessity" of Spinoza's notion of substance already expresses that substance is to be understood as "*positing itself* through the moment of absolute negativity." As a figure of internal necessity, substance can only be consistently understood as "self-referring negativity." For this reason, it is self-subsistent and hence should be understood in terms of "*freedom*[,] which is the identity of the concept" (SL 12.15/512). Freedom is here appropriate because we are speaking of "an identity that exists in and for itself" (SL 12.15/513). As self-referring negativity, this identity is the result of the process of self-negation and return-to-self that we have seen. It is not 'in-itself' or merely implicit, a simple identity. Nor is it merely for-itself, an identity that has been made explicit through its unfolding. As self-referring negativity, freedom is in and for itself; it expresses or manifests its unfolding as essential to it. It is therefore concrete. Hegel here preliminarily explains "the concept of the concept" along these lines. By referring only to itself, Hegel writes, the concept is "no

---

[21] Hegel's argument is thus not an 'inverted Spinozism'—one in which thought, the idea, or *Geist*, is the immanent principle of substance or being itself. It is rather that the rationality or intelligibility of concrete conditions is articulated by those conditions themselves. See Moyar, "Thought and Metaphysics" and Pippin *Hegel's Idealism* for discussions of this issue.

[22] Going beyond the *Logic*, currency or bindingness is a matter of the development of a practice or institution that expresses a specific form of rationality.

less simple identity." In its equality with itself, the concept is the *universal*. Such universality, such simple identity, is nothing but negation, however. It has the "determination of negativity," Hegel says. So the concept is, in truth, *singular*. It must be understood as a *concrete totality*. As simple universality, the concept is but an abstraction. It is indeterminate. As mediated by its unfolding, it is singular. It is determinate, concrete. This is all very abstract, Hegel realizes (see SL 12.17/514). So he moves on to clarify how the concept, as a figure of freedom, transforms the structure of Kant's notion of transcendental subjectivity.

"The concept," Hegel writes, "when it has progressed to a concrete existence which is itself free, is none other than the 'I' or pure self-consciousness" (SL: 12.17/515). I certainly *have* concepts, he clarifies, but this is *not* what is meant by *the* concept. The concept is the structure of self-referring negativity—self-relation through negation. What Kant describes under the banner of the transcendental unity of apperception, the 'I think' that must accompany all my representations, bears this very structure. The 'I think' can be understood as 'simple universality'. In "withdrawing from all determinateness and content," the 'I' is subjectivity in general. It is a universal structure of self-relation necessary for experience. It is the activity of synthesis that makes possible the determinacy of the object of experience, as well as the unity of experience. In this sense, Hegel notes, the 'I' is but an abstraction. It is free from the content of the manifold given in intuition, which it in fact determines. But when we take a closer look, we see that the 'I' should be understood as 'absolute determinateness'. The 'I' is the unity of the activity of self-consciousness ("the absolute positedness," Hegel says, borrowing Fichtean language) and the content of its synthesizing activity ('the positedness'). Self-consciousness is here 'singularity', 'individual personality'.[23] When examined more closely, then, the 'I' cannot be understood as free from content. The activity of the "I think', apperceptive judging, can only be properly understood in light of its synthesis of a manifold of intuition (SL 12.17–18/515). The freedom of the concept, of the 'I', is not compromised by its dependence on content, Hegel will go on to argue. It is rather a matter of the unity of form and content—the unity of the synthesizing activity of the 'I' and the 'not-I'.

Hegel is here beginning to develop his notion of *absolute form*. Form is nothing but negation, negativity. Negation requires content in order to be negation.[24] Rather than an external operation of an epistemic subject, however, negation, *form*, is the "indigenous coming-to-be of the concrete content itself [*die Form das einheimische Werden des konkreten Inhalts selbst ist*]" (PS 9.41/¶56). It is the unfolding of matters themselves through a process of actualization. To be sure, Hegel argues, Kant intimated the unity

---

[23] Note that Hegel here uses the term 'personality', which I argued earlier should be distinguished from subjectivity. Again, both are crucial, but we should distinguish between the structure of autonomy of the idea and the structure of the concept as negativity. The concept as negativity establishes the dialectical relation between form and content, which impacts how we understand the idea as a structure of bindingness. See my *Hegel's Theory of Intelligibility*.

[24] Even if we argue, like Dieter Henrich has, that for Hegel negation negates itself (it is 'autonomous'), then the very activity of negation is the content of negation. See Henrich, "Hegels Grundoperation." See also SL 12.33/530.

of form and content. He introduced "the extremely important thought that there are synthetic judgments a priori," thereby arguing that we must be able to account for the conceptual extension of knowledge by elaborating the relation between form and content (in Kant, concept and intuition) from the side of form (in Kant, as a matter of the strictures of human cognition) (SL 12.17–18/515 and also 22–23/520). And he proposed "one of the most profound principles for speculative development," namely, the "original synthesis of apperception," thereby finding the ground of the relation between form and content (concept and intuition) in the synthesizing activity of form itself (the 'I think'). Yet because he conceived apperception in narrow terms, as the activity of an epistemic subject, he misunderstood his brilliant insight (SL 12.17–18/515 and 12.19/516). In maintaining that receptivity and spontaneity, sensibility and the understanding establish the possibility of synthetic a priori judgments, Kant merely offers a faculty psychology (SL 12.22–23/520).

The problem here is that, in merely sketching the work-in-concert of heterogeneous capacities (receptivity and spontaneity), in thereby conceiving of concept and intuition as heterogeneous elements, Kant cannot account for the objectivity of any determination. Concept and intuition are merely externally combined. Unity is merely "*external unity*," a "*mere combination* of entities that are *intrinsically separate*" (SL 12.23/520; my emphasis). Kant's notion of apperception is thus an "*empty identity or abstract universality*" that can only impart external unity. Now, Hegel is here not interested in establishing the strictures of epistemic objectivity. Rather, he is calling into question Kant's *philosophical strategy*, which privileges the problem of 'representation', as he puts it. Kant's strategy, according to Hegel, occludes an account of the relation between form and content implicit in any account of epistemic objectivity. Kant holds, for instance, that "the understanding . . . obtains reality only by virtue of that given content," yet at the same time that the understanding "abstracts from it [reality], that is to say, discards it as something useless" (SL 12.20/518). Such inconsistencies derive from his insistence on epistemic subjectivity. For Hegel, we must abandon the idea that "intuition and representation, is at first just there by itself" and that "the understanding then comes into it, brings unity to it." We must give an account of the determinacy of matters by giving a proper account of the relation between form and content.

While Kant had within his reach concepts that could account for the inseparability of form and content—original apperception, synthetic a priori judgments—he restricts the power of these concepts by understanding them to be about epistemic subjectivity.[25] Hegel takes Kant's insights in a different direction by shifting the ground of these concepts from the first-person perspective to an account of intelligibility in general. He moves away from Kant's critical epistemology to what he calls a "science of absolute form" (SL 12.25/523). A science of logic is a science of form—of *negativity*—that must be understood as the "coming-to-be of content." You may call this science of absolute

---

[25] See Hegel's treatment of Kant's notion of the intuitive understanding in SL 12.25/522 and in *Glauben und Wissen*, translated as *Faith and Knowledge*. See also Förster, *The Twenty-five Years of Philosophy*.

form a metaphysics, but it is crucial to note that it is not an ontology. It is a theory of intelligibility.

We must understand content here in two ways. A science of absolute form is a science of the becoming of content, first, in a narrow sense.[26] It pursues an immanent critique of metaphysical concepts (being, essence, concept), which are the immediate content of a speculative logic. This philosophical critique, however, establishes the necessity to go beyond or, more precisely, outside of itself. Therefore, second, a science of absolute form establishes the need to move from a philosophical account of intelligibility to an account of the intelligibility of nature, self, and society in a *Realphilosophie* (SL 12.253/752–753). Content here is no longer a matter of the character and status of the metaphysical concepts examined in the Doctrines of Being, Essence, and Concept. Rather, it is a matter of concepts that articulate the nature of nature, self, and society. *Pace* Kant, the concept, the 'I', subjectivity is "not a trivial, empty identity" that determines content externally. In being nothing but negativity, it is the "coming-to-be of content" in these two senses.

13.3. Concrete Universality

Hegel's rejection of Spinoza's metaphysics and Kant's critical epistemology is key for understanding the concept of reason developed in the Doctrine of the Concept. Rather than an ontological principle or epistemic faculty, reason is the form of rationality distinctive of matters themselves. Things themselves, Hegel shows in the Doctrine of Essence, are produced by a totality of existent conditions. Nevertheless, he shows in the Doctrine of the Concept, they express rational form. The universality that matters bear in their singularity depends on particular conditions at hand. Hegel's conception of reason, then, requires a concrete understanding of universality. The chapters on the Concept (*der Begriff*), Judgment (*das Urteil*), and the Syllogism (*der Schluß*) that comprise the section on Subjectivity develop the notion of *concrete universality* central to Hegelian rationality. Indeed, understanding Hegel's distinction between abstract and concrete universality is necessary for grasping his provocative claim that "the syllogism ... is the rational" or that "everything rational is a syllogism" (SL 12.90/588).

Before discussing the notion of concrete universality, it is important to note Hegel's starting point, particularly in the chapter on the Concept. Hegel frames his discussions of the Concept, Judgment, and the Syllogism by displacing Kant's claim that their function refers to epistemic faculties. "The faculty of concepts," Hegel writes, "is normally associated with the *understanding* [*Verstand*], and the latter is accordingly distinguished from the *faculty of judgment* and from the faculty of syllogistic inferences which is formal *reason* [*Vernunft*]" (SL 12.32/529). This frame deepens the critique pursued in "On the Concept in General." Earlier I argued that, in "On the Concept in General," Hegel takes issue with Kant's philosophical strategy. Kant's attempt to secure objectivity by

---

[26] It has "a content or reality of its own," Hegel says (SL 12.25/523).

tracing the work of the concept to the understanding and the givenness of intuition to sensibility fails. The empiricist impulse in Kant's idealism not only both affirms and denies the significance of reality. It neutralizes the power of the deduction. An account of the activity of the mind cannot definitively establish the applicability of concepts to intuitions conceived as external, as given.[27] For Hegel, this means that Kant thinks of concepts abstractly, formally—to be applied to a reality ultimately beyond their reach.

In the opening of the chapter on the Concept, Hegel adds that Kant's abstract, formal understanding of concepts follows from his commitment to the perspective of the understanding.[28] Indeed, it is Kant's commitment that reduces an account of intelligibility to an account of representation. Famously, Hegel takes issue with Kant's distinction between *Verstand* and *Vernunft*, the understanding and reason. While the understanding is the faculty of cognition, reason is the faculty of principles. The understanding synthesizes manifold representations into one cognition.[29] Concepts are therefore "functions of unity."[30] Accordingly, the understanding is the faculty of judgment—the capacity to combine concepts or to subsume intuitions under concepts. Reason, in contrast, infers premises for any given conclusion. Ideas of reason systematize (unify) bodies of knowledge, yet they do so appropriately when understood as merely regulative. Hegel begins his account of subjectivity by dispelling conceptions of the concept, judgment, and syllogism as "a thing of the understanding [*Verstand*]" (SL 12.32/529). As a thing of the understanding, a concept is a function that unifies a manifold given in intuition, which is to say, whose content is external to it. Judgment combines 'self-subsisting' concepts whose self-subsistence is a matter of their material marks. Syllogism infers from judgments ultimately depending on the material marks of the concepts combined in said judgments. To be sure, these are appropriate ways of thinking of the concept, judgment, and the syllogism if we are asking epistemological, anthropological, psychological, or logical questions.[31] However, according to Hegel, they are insufficient for an account of intelligibility or rationality as such.

Earlier I suggested that, in "On the Concept in General," Hegel argues that implicit in Kant's account of apperception is a notion of form that can appropriately account for the relation between form and content. In the chapters on the Concept, Judgment, and the Syllogism, Hegel argues as well that Kant's treatment intimates a proper understanding of the concept and its relation to judgment and the syllogism. By understanding the concept as a 'function of unity', judgment as a matter of 'synthesis', and syllogism as a matter of 'inference', and by understanding all three as germane to a faculty, Kant inadvertently suggests that these are activities whose content refers not to external reality, but to their own activity. Activity should not be understood as a matter of cognition, then. It should be thought of as the production of content itself. Even for Kant,

---

[27] See Bowman, *Metaphysics of Absolute Negativity*, 91 ff., and Pippin, "Idealist Theories of Logic," 19.

[28] See Bowman, *Metaphysics of Absolute Negativity*, 86ff., for an account of Hegel's critique of Kant's *Verstandesmetaphysik*.

[29] CPR B103/A77.

[30] CPR A68–69/B93–94.

[31] Logic here would be what Hegel calls 'formal logic'—matters of validity.

the concept 'gives content to itself', since its content derives from its role in judging and inferring.[32] Developing this thought further, however, requires abandoning the problem of representation and focusing on the strictures of reason. Reason is nothing but the necessary relation between or, more precisely, the interrelatedness of concept, judgment, and syllogism. Reason, in other words, is the becoming of content by virtue of a totality of relations that makes said content what it is. For Hegel, this gets us closer to a satisfactory account of the relation between form and content necessary for an account of the rationality of matters themselves. By shifting our commitment to reason, the concept is no longer abstract, something to be applied to material, sensuous reality beyond it. It is rather concrete—a matter of its own unfolding.

Having clarified that the discussions that follow move away from Kant's commitment to the perspective of the understanding, Hegel sets out to show that *the* concept is nothing but negativity. Indeed, the concept is *absolute negativity* (SL 12.35/532).[33] As absolute negativity, the concept is a matter of development [*Entwicklung*], first, from universality [*Allgemeinheit*], to particularity [*Besonderheit*], to singularity [*Einzeinheit*] and, second, from concept, to judgment, to syllogism.[34] It is important to note that in each chapter and in the section on Subjectivity as a whole, the argument moves in the form of a *reductio*. Hegel begins the section by arguing that the concept can be understood atomistically, independent from judgment and syllogism. In the course of the discussion, however, we realize that an atomistic understanding of the concept is untenable. Similarly, he begins the chapter on the Concept arguing that universality can be understood independent from particularity and singularity. Yet the discussion shows that such a claim is untenable. Hegel's distinction between abstract and concrete universality functions accordingly. It addresses the 'misconception' that universality, particularity, and singularity are to be understood "apart from each other."[35] They are rather 'moments' [*Momente*] of the concept (SL 12.32/529). The concept is concrete through its unfolding, furthermore, by virtue of its self-differentiation in judgment and its return-to-self in the syllogism. By the end of the section, Hegel has established that the syllogism is 'mediation' or "the complete concept in its positedness" (SL 12.126/624). The syllogism is the truth of the concept, since it is the holistic structure that can do justice to the unity of universality, particularity, and singularity expressed by concrete universality.

The abstract universal, Hegel argues, is "opposed to the particular and the singular" (SL 12.33/531). It is abstract, since its content is "imported . . . from outside." Within a Kantian framework, as we have seen, content is a matter of intuition. It is a matter of the material marks of concepts that ultimately refer to the sensible given. In contrast, Hegel maintains that the universal is concrete when, in being nothing but negativity, it is nothing but the development of its *own* content. First, as "immediate negation,"

---

[32] Cf. Pippin, "Idealist Theories of Logic," 17.

[33] Hegel adds that as absolute negativity, the concept is the "informing and creating principle" of matters themselves (SL 12.35/532).

[34] See Stern, "The Curious Case of the Concrete Universal," 126.

[35] Ibid. Hegel writes, "one cannot speak of the universal apart from determinateness which, to be more precise, is particularity and singularity" (SL 12.35/532).

universality is determinate as particularity. Second, "as the negation of negation," universality is singularity, hence concreteness. For this reason, Hegel argues, the universal is "the totality of the concept" (SL 12.35/532). He adds, "what is concrete, is not empty but, on the contrary, has content by virtue of its concept." Now, I have argued that the concrete concept is concrete insofar as it has unfolded in and through a totality of conditions that exceed it, yet produced it in the first place. It is concrete, in other words, only through an other. Notice that Hegel here argues that the universal is simply 'self-reference [*Selbstbeziehung*]', 'absolute self-identity [*die absolute Identität mit sich*]', the "soul of the concrete which it inhabits, unhindered and equal to itself in its manifoldness and diversity" (SL 12.33/530, 34/531). The universal is concrete when it maintains itself unscathed in its own negation. What does this mean?

The universal is concrete insofar as it is identical with itself by virtue of the difference it posits in being what it is.[36] The very notion of *organism*, for example, is *necessarily* "pregnant with content" other than a reference to itself. In order to be universal, universal concepts, genera, must be differentiated into *particular* determinations, species. The genus *organism* is differentiated into the species *animal, plant,* or *single-celled life form*. Genera retain their identity as universals in "remain[ing] unaltered" throughout their differentiation in species (SL 12.37/534). The very notion of *organism* remains self-identical because of its differentiation into particulars, but also because a universal can be the species of higher genera, thus, *life form*. Species, in turn, are "not different from the universal but only *from each other*" (SL 12.37/534). We are therefore speaking of singularity, rather than particularity. Through this self-related negativity—the division implied by the differentia that differentiates the genus into species—the universal and particular can in fact be described as the being-for-self of this singular (SL 12.51/548). Note that Hegel is not speaking of concepts here—empirical or otherwise. Hegel's aim is rather to account for the very work or function of a universal. Hegel's point is that the universal can only function as a universal by virtue of its relation to particularity and singularity.

Although Hegel has shown that universality can only function as such by virtue of particularity and singularity, the discussion of the concept is not sufficient for articulating concrete universality. In isolation, the chapter cannot account for the development of the concept. The concept is concrete only insofar as it is understood in relation to judgment and the syllogism. As mentioned previously, its development is nothing but its self-differentiation in judgment and return-to-self in the syllogism. In isolation, the chapter on the Concept offers an atomistic account of determinacy. To be sure, Kant already understood judgment rather than the concept as the minimum unit of determinacy.[37] Whether the unification of subject and predicate or concept and intuition, the unity of the object, as well as the unity of experience, is the result of apperceptive judging. Hegel takes Kant's argument further by arguing that syllogism, rather than judgment, is the minimum unity of intelligibility. Unity is the result of a form of rationality.

---

[36] Winfield, *From Concept to Objectivity*, 80.
[37] See Brandom, *Making It Explicit*, 79.

Against Kant, then, Hegel argues that to "restore again the identity of the concept, or rather to posit it is the goal of the movement of judgment" (SL 12.59/556). Judgment is the truth of the concept. However, when the copula is "posited as the determinate and fulfilled unity of subject and predicate," we are speaking of "the conclusion of the syllogistic inference" (SL 12.59/556). The truth of judgment, accordingly, is the syllogism. As a figure of mediation, the syllogism is the truth of the concept. Universality is concrete by virtue of its role in inference or, to be more precise, its inferential structure.

Unlike Kant, who conceives judgment as an activity of combination or unification, Hegel understands judgment as a matter of separation or division (*Teilung*).[38] That the universal already contains difference within itself means that it is implicitly divided. Hegel characterizes this division as the "realization of the concept," and he points out that this division is a "positioning of its determinations over against each other" (SL 12.53/550). This becoming-other is its "own determining." We must resist, however, understanding this positioning along Kantian lines. What is partitioned appears as "determinate totalities," which "go under the name of subject and predicate" (SL 12.53/550). In a judgment S is P, the concepts in the subject and predicate positions are just as much "essentially disconnected, indifferent to each other, as mediated through each other" (SL 12.53/550).[39] Problems arise when, along Kantian lines, they are considered as 'self-subsistent' and their relation is understood as a matter of 'connection' or 'combination' performed by a subject (SL 12.55/552). "Combination," Hegel argues, is here a "vague expression" for unity, given that it depends on an "external copula" (SL 12.56/553).[40] It is an abstract connection established "in someone's head," Hegel says. Recall Kant's central issue in the first *Critique*—synthetic a priori judgments. Propositions central to scientific inquiry whose predicate is not contained in the subject—for example, "Every event has a cause"—can nevertheless be considered universal and necessary given the strictures of human cognition. The objective ground of such combination, in other words, is cognition itself. We have seen that this strategy is insufficient, according to Hegel, since it retains an empiricist impulse in tension with the deduction. Rather than cognition, Hegel argues, the "ground of judgment" is the concept (SL: 12.56/554). As absolute negativity, it is the necessary division that follows from the fact that concepts must refer to other concepts to have determinate content. Judgment, along these lines, is not an activity of combination, but rather the differentiation that makes a concept what it is.

---

[38] Hegel follows Hölderlin and argues that judgment is an activity of separation or division—it is a *Teilung*. See Hölderlin, *Über Urtheil und Seyn (On Judgment and Being)*, in Harris, *Hegel's Development*. See also Henrich, *Hegel im Kontext* and *Between Kant and Hegel*.

[39] Cf. Hegel's discussion of the speculative proposition in the *Phenomenology*. There he argues that Kant's view of judgment is essentialist. In a judgment S is P, the concept in the subject position is "made into the ground." Yet the very act of predication establishes the predicate, rather than the subject, as the ground. When we say that "God is being" or "The actual is the universal," Hegel argues, 'being' and 'universal' are the "substantial meaning in which the subject melts away." The essence is in fact the predicate. This reveals that what is taken to be the ground—the subject—essentially depends on the very act of predication. Predication, then, articulates or unfolds the subject. See PS 9.42–4/¶¶60–62.

[40] Here again Hegel reminds us that what is really meant is "determinations of representations."

The universal at work in each type of judgment Hegel discusses clarifies his understanding of judgment as a *Teilung*.[41] The judgment of the concept (*das Urteil des Begriffes*) is most relevant to our discussion, since it contains the concrete universal. Here, concrete universality is a matter of normativity. The judgment of the concept is a normative judgment not in the sense that it addresses what ought to be the case, but rather in the sense that it bears the ought structure (SL 12.84–85/581–582). Hegel, to be sure, stresses that the concrete universal pertains to normative assessments that contain as "predicates *good, bad, true, beautiful, correct*, etc." (SL 12.84/582). The point, however, is that the judgment of the concept considers a thing *according to its own proper concept*.[42] Here again, Hegel clarifies that this is not a matter of a 'subjective' 'thought' determining whether reality does or does not conform to a concept. It is rather a matter of the concept's own content (SL 12.84/582). The normative structure of the judgment of the concept articulates universality in light of the constitution of matters themselves.

Hegel discusses the judgment of the concept as assertoric, problematic, and apodictic. Assertoric judgments are those in which predicates can be asserted of subjects immediately: "The subject is concrete singular in general, and the predicate expresses this same as the *relation* of its *actuality*, determinateness, or *constitution* to its *concept*"—e.g., "This house is *bad*, this action is *good*" (SL 12.85/583). Insofar as it remains an assertion without justification, however, it remains problematic. It could or could not be the case that the house is bad or that the action is good (SL 12.86/584).[43] The judgment remains contingent—*contingent on* or "*according to*" the constitution of the house (SL 12.86/584). Such justification is provided by a consideration of the constitution of a particular in light of the universal. This singular house is shown to necessarily be good or bad, given its particular constitution yet in relation to its universal aspect, its concept. This is not to say that the particular is subsumed under the universal. Universality is rather the thing's own articulation given its constitution—"the house constituted so and so is good" (SL 12.87/585). In being able to establish that the constitution of a given matter is in accordance with its own concept, the apodictic judgment determines the necessity or *actuality* of the determination. The apodictic judgment is thus the "truly objective"—the "subject and object correspond to each other" (SL 12.88/585).

For Hegel, this means that we are no longer speaking of judgment, but rather of the syllogism. Judgment "has perished," given that "the *determinate* and *accomplished* [*erfüllte*] copula which hitherto consisted in the abstract 'is' . . . has now further developed into *ground in general*" (SL 12.88/586). We are no longer considering the copula. We are rather considering the middle term. The middle term, "the essential element of the syllogism," is the totality of the concept (SL 12.91/589). Now, it is crucial to note that syllogisms are determinations of *absolute form*. As such, they are the becoming-of-content. They are not static judgments that rely on isolated concepts to be unified. Their ground is the concept in its unfolding. The concept unfolds through various judgments, manifesting its inferential structure. As

---

[41] Winfield, *From Concept to Objectivity*, 92–94.
[42] I am here paraphrasing Longuenesse, *Hegel's Critique of Metaphysics*, 213.
[43] See also ibid.

the middle term, then, the concept is a figure of *mediation*. For our purposes, the syllogism of necessity (*der Schluß der Notwendigkeit*) is most relevant, since it articulates mediation as a totality of relations. The middle term is "full of content," Hegel says (SL 12.118/617). The syllogism of necessity overcomes Kant's formalism, making possible an account of the rationality—the subjectivity—of matters themselves. Indeed, in the syllogism of necessity, "the mediating element is the objective nature of *die Sache*" (SL 12.92/590).

Under the heading of the syllogism of necessity, Hegel examines categorical, hypothetical, and disjunctive syllogisms. The transition from the hypothetical to the disjunctive syllogism is key. It clarifies the status of the middle term, first, as mediation and, second, the self-mediation of the thing, the matter at hand—*die Sache*. The hypothetical syllogism announces that mediation is irreducible by stressing the role of negativity. The hypothetical syllogism expresses a "necessary *relation*"—if A is, B is (SL 12.121/620). The necessary relation between the terms is a matter of "translating the conditioning into the conditioned actuality" (SL 12.123/622). The point here is that specifying the relation between ground and consequent establishes that the terms are reciprocally determined, and therefore mediated. Mediation here, however, is a matter of relations of dependence that betray that those relations depend on exclusion. Hegel notes that "the being of A is also not its own being but that of B and *vice versa*" (SL 12.123/622). To say that "if A is, B is" is to state that the 'being' or determinacy of one is dependent on the other, which is to say, on what it is not. The hypothetical syllogism, then, makes explicit that the relation between condition and conditioned, ground and consequent, is a matter of negation rather than connection. It also reveals that this negativity, this form activity (*Formtätigkeit*), is necessarily a matter of content. The syllogism is a matter of form *and* content—*absolute form* (SL 12.123–124/622). At this point, however, we have already transitioned to the disjunctive syllogism.

The disjunctive syllogism represents the *collapse* of the syllogism and the transition to the section entitled "Objectivity." "What is posited in the disjunctive syllogism is thus the truth of the hypothetical syllogism," Hegel writes, "the unity of the mediator and the mediated, and for that reason the disjunctive syllogism is no longer *a syllogism at all*" (SL 12.124/623). As disjunctive, the syllogism effectively collapses because no mediation understood as the connection between two independent terms is occurring. When considering the disjunctive form—"A is either B or C or D"—we are speaking of a system of relations. To be clear, while the disjunctive syllogism is a collapsed syllogism, mediation itself is not canceled. On the contrary, elements in a syllogism are related by way of exclusion, which establishes the concrete content that they share. Notice, however, that in the disjunctive syllogism, "the middle term is . . . a *universality replete with form*" (SL 12.123/622). The middle term is constituted by 'form activity'. The totality is not a set of relations between fixed determinations. It is rather the inferential process of negation.[44] Negativity here is the very inferential moves that coextensively institute the totality of relations involved in the inference itself. The middle term is for this reason 'complete

---

[44] See Brandom, *Making It Explicit*, and Pippin "Brandom's Hegel." Cf. Rosen, *The Idea of Hegel's Logic*, 22–23.

determinateness'. It is the totality of the concept. Universality can now be considered concrete. Mediation is now understood in holistic terms. The concept is grasped as an inferential structure (SL 12.125–126/624). The collapse of the syllogism indeed means that "the concept as such has been realized" (SL 12.125/624).

The concept, then, is a figure of mediation or, rather, is nothing but the activity of mediation. This makes possible Hegel's distinctive understanding of mediation as the self-mediation, self-determination, *subjectivity* of *die Sache*. With the collapse of the syllogism, Hegel argues, the distinction of mediating and mediated has "fallen away" (SL 12.125/624). "That which is mediated," he writes, "is itself an essential moment of what mediates it, and each moment is the totality of what is mediated." This understanding of the concept overcomes the main assumptions underlying Kant's critical epistemology. It overcomes Kant's insistence on bridging what mediates (concept, the 'I') and what is mediated (manifold of intuition, the 'not-I'). Indeed, it overcomes Kant's understanding of mediation as 'bridging', 'connecting', 'unifying' heterogeneous elements. In being nothing but the self-mediation of matters, concrete universality makes possible an account of *objectivity*. This is not an account of the objectivity of the relation between 'I' and 'not-I', concept and intuition. It is an account of matters themselves. At this point, Hegel maintains, the concept "has obtained a reality that is *objectivity*." Hegel thus turns to modes of account-giving that follow a logic of the object under the rubric of Mechanism, Chemism, and Teleology in the section on Objectivity.

13.4. Conclusion

In this chapter, I have argued that the key to Hegel's idealism is his understanding of subjectivity. Things, events, ideas, and institutions can be said to be forms of subjectivity, since the rationality that they express is the result of their own actualization. More precisely, the universality that singularities bear is the result of their unfolding through particular conditions that produce them in the first place. In order to give an account of the rationality or subjectivity of matters themselves, we must overcome Kant's commitment to the first-person perspective of epistemic subjectivity, since it reduces an account of intelligibility to a matter of representation. Overcoming the main assumptions and tensions in Kant's critical idealism is the task of the Doctrine of the Concept as a whole. Indeed, we only arrive at the proper Hegelian understanding of the relation between concept and reality, subjectivity and objectivity, with the account of the idea. We have seen, however, the first step toward Hegel's post-critical idealism. In the section on Subjectivity, Hegel shifts our understanding of the concept and, with it, our understanding of mediation. As absolute negativity, the concept must be understood as concrete. Mediation must accordingly be conceived as a matter of the self-determination of *die Sache*.[45]

---

[45] This discussion should be brought to bear on Hegel's distinction between reality (*Realität*) and actuality (*Wirklichkeit*). My aim in this chapter is not to deny such a distinction by arguing that all matters at hand are actual, *wirklich*. On the contrary, reality that lacks actuality is one whose unfolding in

WORKS CITED

Primary Texts

Hegel, G. W. F. *Phenomenology of Spirit* [PS], translated by Terry Pinkard. http://web.mac.com/titpaul/Site/About_Me.html.

Hegel, G. W. F. *The Science of Logic* [SL], translated and edited by George di Giovanni. Cambridge: Cambridge University Press, 2010.

Kant, Immanuel. 1999. *Critique of Pure Reason*, translated and edited by Paul Guyer and Allen Wood. Cambridge: Cambridge University Press.

Secondary Literature

Beiser, Frederick. *Hegel*. London: Routledge, 1995.

Bowman, Brady. *Hegel and the Metaphysics of Absolute Negativity*. Cambridge: Cambridge University Press, 2013.

Brandom, Robert. *Making It Explicit: Reasoning, Representing, and Discursive Commitment*. Cambridge, MA: Harvard University Press, 1998.

De Boer, Karin. *On Hegel: The Sway of the Negative*. London: Palgrave, 2010.

Ferrarin, Alfredo. *Hegel and Aristotle*. Cambridge: Cambridge University Press, 2007.

Förster, Eckart. *The Twenty-five Years of Philosophy: A Systematic Reconstruction*. Cambridge, MA: Harvard University Press, 2012.

Harris, H. S. *Hegel's Development: Towards the Sunlight, 1770–1801*. Oxford: Clarendon Press, 1972.

Hartmann, Klaus. "Hegel: A Non-Metaphysical View," in *Hegel: A Collection of Critical Essays*, edited by Alasdair MacIntyre. Notre Dame, IN: University of Notre Dame Press, 1977, 101–124.

Henrich, Dieter. *Between Kant and Hegel: Lectures on German Idealism*, edited by David S. Pacini. Cambridge, MA: Harvard University Press, 2003.

Henrich, Dieter. *Hegel im Kontext*. Frankfurt am Main: Suhrkamp, 1971.

Henrich, Dieter. "Hegels Grundoperation," in *Der Idealismus und seine Gegenwart. Festschrift für Werner Marx*, edited by U. Guzzoni, B. Rang, and L. Siep. Hamburg: Felix Meiner Verlag, 1976, 208–230.

Horstmann, Rolf Peter. "What Is Hegel's Legacy and What Should We Do with It?" *European Journal of Philosophy* 7 (1999): 2.

Houlgate, Stephen. *The Opening of Hegel's Logic: From Being to Infinity*. West Lafayette, IN: Purdue University Press, 2005.

Inwood, Michael. *A Hegel Dictionary*. London: Blackwell, 1992.

Kreines, James. "Hegel's Metaphysics: Changing the Debate." *Philosophy Compass* 1 (2006): 5.

Kreines, James. "Learning from Hegel What Philosophy Is All About: For the Metaphysics of Reason and Against the Priority of Semantics." *Verifiche XLI* (2012): 1–3.

and through material, social, and historical conditions maintains separate universality, particularity, and singularity. Consider, for example, Hegel's claim in the *Philosophy of Right* that a state is real yet not actual if it does not in fact fulfill its purported normative commitments (freedom). Consider as well Hegel's analysis of the Terror in the *Phenomenology of Spirit*, where a commitment to absolute freedom fails to recognize the particularity of the political situation.

Longuenesse, Béatrice. *Hegel's Critique of Metaphysics*, translated by Nicole J. Simek. Cambridge: Cambridge University Press, 2007.

Lumsden, Simon, "The Rise of the Non-metaphysical Hegel." *Philosophical Compass* 3 (2008): 1.

Melamed, Yitzak. "'Omnis determinatio est negatio': Determination, Negation, and Self-Negation in Spinoza, Kant, and Hegel," in *Spinoza and German Idealism*, edited by Eckart Förster and Yitzhak Y. Melamed. Cambridge: Cambridge University Press, 2012, 175–196.

Moyar, Dean. "Thought and Metaphysics: Hegel's Critical Reception of Spinoza," in *Spinoza and German Idealism*, edited by Eckart Förster and Yitzhak Y. Melamed. Cambridge: Cambridge University Press, 2012, 197–213.

Pinkard, Terry. *Hegel's Phenomenology: The Sociality of Reason*. Cambridge: Cambridge University Press, 1994.

Pippin, Robert. "Brandom's Hegel." *European Journal of Philosophy* 13 (2005): 3.

Pippin, Robert. "Hegel, Modernity, and Habermas." *Monist* 74 (1991): 3.

Pippin, Robert. *Hegel's Idealism: The Satisfactions of Self-Consciousness*. Cambridge: Cambridge University Press, 1989.

Pippin, Robert. *Hegel's Practical Philosophy*. Cambridge: Cambridge University Press, 2010.

Pippin, Robert "The Significance of Self-Consciousness in Idealist Theories of Logic." *Proceedings of the Aristotelian Society* 11 (2014): 145–166.

Rosen, Stanley. *The Idea of Hegel's* Science of Logic. Chicago: University of Chicago Press, 2014.

Stern, Robert. "Hegel, British Idealism, and the Curious Case of the Concrete Universal." *British Journal for the History of Philosophy* 15 (2007): 1.

Taylor, Charles. *Hegel*. Cambridge: Cambridge University Press, 1975.

Winfield, Richard. *From Concept to Objectivity: Thinking Through Hegel's Subjective Logic*. London: Ashgate, 2006.

Zambrana, Rocío. *Hegel's Theory of Intelligibility*. Chicago: University of Chicago Press, 2015.

CHAPTER 14

....

FROM OBJECTIVITY TO THE ABSOLUTE IDEA IN HEGEL'S *LOGIC*

....

JAMES KREINES

HEGEL is difficult to interpret, and *The Science of Logic* especially difficult. The conclusion of the book centers on the transition to the last section, "The Idea," and the transition to the last chapter in that section, "The Absolute Idea." Of course, Hegel's own terminology is among the considerable difficulties. But I think that it is possible to understand the arguments here, to give an account in independently accessible philosophical terms, and to uncover some strengths of lasting philosophical interest. I argue that there are two keys.

First, the *Logic* takes a kind of metaphysics as fundamental within philosophy. This is not to deny that Hegel addresses other topics, such as epistemology. But the *Logic* ultimately argues that other issues should be understood and addressed in metaphysical terms. So the *Logic* does not seek an epistemologically specified ultimate end, such as that of indubitable and foundational *knowledge*—making secondary the question of what, if any, metaphysics would serve that end. And the problems the *Logic* takes as basic, in the end, do not descend from those Kant seeks to resolve by means of the deductions of the Transcendental Analytic of the first *Critique*, concerning the relation between cognition or concepts and objects. The *Logic* will give priority, rather, to metaphysical problems drawn from Kant's Transcendental Dialectic, and this provides the unity and philosophical force of the arguments that conclude the *Logic*.

Second, those who see a metaphysics in Hegel tend to see one that is specifically monistic, descended from Spinoza's or from neo-Platonism. But I argue that the metaphysics at the end of the *Logic* is very different. I take 'metaphysical foundationalism' to be the view that there is some sufficient reason or ground for everything, on which everything depends, while it depends on nothing. Metaphysical monism is a specific version: the foundation is the One that everything is 'in'. But Hegel's own conclusions, I will argue, are no form of metaphysical foundationalism at all—neither a scientistic, theological, nor monistic form. There is, to be sure, something that is first in metaphysical priority: the absolute idea. But, as Hegel often says, the end is what is first: what is most mediated and even, in a sense, dependent (the end) is also first, or of highest metaphysical priority. But this claim is difficult, and requires much preparation.

14.1. Kant's Dialectic and Hegel's Metaphysics of Reason

In this section, I want to work from a connection to Kant toward a way of explaining the topic addressed by the end of the *Logic* in independently accessible philosophical terms. I begin with Kant's account of the 'faculty of reason [*Vernunft*]' in the Transcendental Dialectic of the first *Critique*. Kant here argues that we have an ineliminable need for a goal to guide or regulate the use of our theoretical faculties. The faculty of reason is supposed to provide this, insofar as it directs us away from incurious satisfaction with the surface of things, demanding that we instead assume for the sake of inquiry that things have further explanations, and to seek to find the *conditions* or grounds in terms of which they could be explained—and ultimately *the unconditioned*, where this is the notion of something to which one could appeal in explaining *completely*, or a complete explainer.[1] In the Dialectic's technical terms, 'ideas' are specifically ideas of the unconditioned (CPR, A334–337/B391–394). And Kant concludes, given the ineliminable guiding role of reason, that metaphysical questions about such ideas are inescapable for us (CPR, A421/B449). So there is an inescapability of questions on the domain of the *metaphysics of reason*, as I will call it; those who pretend indifference to them are unknowingly assuming answers, if they continue to think at all (CPR, Ax).

But Kant also argues that we cannot answer those questions. He does so by arguing that all of the obvious approaches to the inescapable topic are unacceptable. *First*, we could hold that there must always be unconditioned grounds. This is one specific way of pursuing the metaphysics of reason: the rationalist way, built around the principle of sufficient reason (PSR).[2] Kant seeks to explain a kind of inevitable rational appeal of metaphysical rationalism, but in a manner demonstrating that philosophy should never assert such a view or draw such conclusions. For the Antinomy of Pure Reason argues that this view generates contradictions; rationalism can escape direct self-contradiction only in versions that both rest on principles like the PSR and yet would equally be undercut by those same principles—only in a "dogmatic stubbornness, setting its mind rigidly to certain assertions without giving a fair hearing to the grounds for the opposite" (CPR,

---

[1] E.g., *CPR*, A307/B364. I defend Kant's argument on this score in my 2015, ch. 4. For other accounts in terms of *explanation* see Grier, *Transcendental Illusion*, 145; Allison, *Transcendental Idealism*, 331; and Rohlf, "Ideas of Pure Reason," 206. And see Proops, "Kant's First Paralogism," 455, on Kant's focus on worldly 'conditions' or 'grounds', and the connection to why-questions.

[2] See my "Hegel: Metaphysics without Pre-Critical Monism" on the connection to the PSR.

A407/B434). *Second*, there are negative responses. But to deny the existence of any and all forms of the unconditioned would merely be the opposite form of dogmatism (CPR, A471/B499). And other forms of skepticism or indifferentism concerning the unconditioned are, Kant says, impossible, and anyway an unacceptable "*euthanasia* of pure reason" (CPR, A407/B433–434). So Kant concludes that a *third* response is necessary, one that is supposed to be radical and new. The full story of this resolution of the antinomy problems is the package of views that comprise transcendental idealism (CPR, A491/B519). For our purposes, the crucial part of this package is the conclusion that we have strict epistemic limits—fixed by our sensibility and its pure forms, space, and time. For from this it will follow that philosophy can legitimately conclude neither that there are any unconditioned grounds, nor that there are none. Thus philosophy cannot answer metaphysical questions, at least in this sense of 'metaphysics' that is supposed to be of most direct and inescapable rational interest.[3]

Kant's aim here is not to give up on theoretical philosophy; it is to transform it into a new kind of project—as pursued, for example, in the Transcendental Analytic consideration of the necessary conditions of the possibility of cognition of objects. (We need not resolve, for our purposes, whether the basic topic there is more narrowly epistemological—concerned with knowledge, justification, and so on—or more broadly about issues we might now call 'semantic', concerning the very possibility of aboutness, objective purport, intentionality, or similar.[4] For the sake of having a term, I call all such issues about relations between cognition and objects 'broadly epistemological'.) What is important is that there are senses in which the new project is supposed to be a transformed version of 'metaphysics'. For example, it is not empirical; it offers, in the face of doubts, a justification of the synthetic a priori.[5] So the new project seeks to "transform the accepted procedure of metaphysics" (CPR Bxxii), and will take as basic such broadly epistemological notions as a priori. But note that the Dialectic does not merely *presume* anything like this priority of epistemology. It does not, in particular, argue *from* claims about our epistemic limits, because it could not then *support* such claims.[6] It argues that a more direct engagement with metaphysics is necessary, but then comes into conflict with itself, calling itself into question.

Now Hegel will take on board much from Kant, before diverging: yes, it is necessary to directly engage the metaphysics of reason; skepticism or indifferentism about reason is unacceptable; metaphysics generates necessary conflicts; and these conflicts do end the prospects for pre-Kantian metaphysics. *But* Hegel will argue that the considerations of Kant's Dialectic nonetheless support no epistemic limitations, and no exit

---

[3] On metaphysics and unanswerable questions, see the A-Preface to the *Critique*. My formulation saves room for other contexts aside from such philosophy, including practical contexts, in which we have (Kant holds) justification for conclusions about the unconditioned.

[4] There may be other great differences between projects taking the narrowly epistemological or the semantic as fundamental. Still, the project concluding at the end of the *Logic*, is (I argue) neither.

[5] See, e.g., Kant on the importance of doubt about metaphysics at Proleg 4:256.

[6] Kant notes the need for support from the Dialectic at *CPR*, B xix.

from direct consideration of the metaphysics of reason—no transformation after which metaphysics would be engaged from the perspective of broadly epistemological issues. Considerations in Kant's Dialectic are rather supposed to support a new and different constructive metaphysics of reason.

And so we can give an explanation of the topic at the end of the *Logic*, in a manner that clarifies Hegel's terminology in independently accessible philosophical terms. The topic is metaphysics, in the sense of general and direct questions about the *why* or *because* of things, about that in the world to which one would have to appeal in explaining and ultimately explaining completely. It concerns what Hegel calls 'reason [*Vernünft*]' or 'the rational [*das Vernünftige*] in the world'.[7] For example, according to this *metaphysics of reason* conception, the point of a *materialist* metaphysics would be this: reason is in the world only in a way in which everything real is (the materialist claims) grounded in basic matter, which is itself brute, lacking any further reason or grounds. But Hegel's own specific view will not be materialist. Hegel seeks to argue that there is a more complete form of reason, or something to which one could appeal in explaining completely. Hegel, borrowing from Kant, calls this 'the idea'. Kant would call it 'the unconditioned', and while Hegel sometimes borrows this last term, he also worries about it (E §45). In part, Hegel worries that this term makes it too easy for Kant to connect the topic with specifically rationalist notions—such as substance as a substrate with attributes 'in' it. To bring the overall ambition together in a main point, Hegel wants to argue that 'the idea', or completeness of reasons, must be understood in terms of unconditionedness in the different sense of a kind of active self-determination. Thus

> [t]he idea is the *rational* [*Vernünftige*];—it is the unconditioned, because only that has conditions which essentially refers to an objectivity that it does not determine itself. . . . (SL 12:173/671)

And Hegel will argue that, once 'the idea' is better understood in this way, there will no longer be grounds for Kant's claim that it is unknowable for us, and no sense in which attention to reason suggests any in principle limits to our knowledge at all.

Understanding the details requires traveling a long road. What is crucial at the start is that we resist the temptation to epistemologize the notion of 'reason' and the corresponding project. For Hegel's aim is to show that the Dialectic fails *before* it justifies Kant's transformation of metaphysics, or the shift onto broadly epistemological ground, or ground of Kantian deductions, or similar. So 'reason' here is precisely not *at base* given content by notions like that of justification, as for example where one might give someone a justification for one's claim, or ask for such justification, or similar. And

[7] See, e.g., E §24, and similar at SL 21.35/30; VPG 12:23; VGP 18:369, 19:262. On this point I follow Horstmann (e.g., *Grenzen der Vernunf*, 175 ff.) and Beiser (e.g., *Two Concepts of Reason*), but draw conclusions both would reject.

Hegel's project is in this respect unlike one that would begin with a sense of 'reasons' resting on a supposedly basic contrast between reasons and causes, or the normative and the nomological, or similar. Hegel's arguments have implications concerning these topics—for what we would call 'normativity', for example—but he addresses these in terms of an underlying metaphysics, including issues about whether and how it might be possible to account for and justify a distinction between normative and non-normative forms of *reason in the world*, and a metaphysical priority for the former. Similarly, the ultimate aim is not epistemologically specifiable—for example, as a priori results, independent of the empirical; the ultimate end lies more directly within metaphysics, even if the means must be in some senses an a priori method. And, finally, my point of stressing reason *in the world* is not to suggest any priority of either world or mind in addressing broadly epistemological questions about the possibility of cognition of objects; the point is that the basic issues lie elsewhere, with this at base metaphysical rather than epistemic notion of reason.

To be sure, Hegel does agree with Kant that pre-Kantian philosophy is unacceptably dogmatic. But Hegel's point is not what we would ordinarily expect from such agreement. It is not that the topic of Kant's deductions is so fundamental that any philosophy without them implicitly assumes an unacceptably immediate identity of cognition and reality. It is not that pre-Kantian philosophy fails because it is not yet properly set on the basis of such deductions. Rather, Hegel finds pre-Kantian philosophy dogmatic because it does not face directly its own assumptions about the metaphysics of reason in the world, and the ways that these generate the conflicts uncovered by Kant's Dialectic. This emphasis on the Dialectic contradictions is what Hegel means in approaching metaphysics under the heading 'logic': "the dialectic makes up the very nature of thinking," and "a cardinal aspect of logic" (E §11R). And so Hegel's *Logic* sees in Kant an 'insight' crucial to an "elevation of reason to the loftier spirit of modern philosophy"; but this is *not* any insight about any need for Kant's Analytic deductions; it is "insight into the *necessary conflict*" (SL 21.30/25–26)—the topic of the Dialectic. In some senses the *Logic* tests, at earlier points, projects more like Kant's positive project; but these are supposed to fail until and unless they are finally reshaped or transformed by the way the end of the *Logic* recognizes a priority of metaphysics.[8]

So the project concluding at the end of the *Logic* will neither be a version of Spinoza's rationalism, nor of Kant's positive project in the Transcendental Analytic. It is more distinctively Hegel's own: it is to use the supposedly negative or destructive considerations of Kant's Dialectic critique of metaphysics for the purposes of reconstruction—to rebuild metaphysics on the grounds of the strongest criticism of it.

[8] For example, Hegel says that the *first two* parts of the *Logic* (the 'objective logic'), rather than its actual conclusion, are comparable to Kant's 'transcendental logic' (SL 21.46–49/40–43). *The Science of Logic* is cited here according to the volume and page number of the *GW* edition.

14.2. Defense and Application of the Concept Thesis: Mechanism and Teleology

The final sections of *The Science of Logic* are as follows:

The Doctrine of the Concept

. . .

B. Objectivity

  (a) Mechanism

  (b) Chemism

  (c) Teleology

C. The Idea

  (a) Life

  (b) The Idea of Cognition

  (c) The Absolute Idea

Here Hegel is, in part, concluding his defense of a basic thesis, which I would name and express in this way:

> *The concept thesis*: the reasons that explain why things are as they are and do what they do are always found in immanent 'concepts' (*Begriffe*), akin to immanent universals or kinds (*Gattungen*).[9]

Hegel will apply this thesis in such a manner as to distinguish different logics of different forms of reason in the world, or different sorts of immanent concepts or *Begriffe*. First, take something that behaves lawfully, as with the rotation of the planets discussed in "Mechanism": Why does it do what it does? On account of immanent 'concepts' in the sense of the natures of such things that make them what they are, and more specifically the powers that such things have in virtue of this nature of their kind. For example, the planets rotate on account of gravitation being the nature of matter, or because "gravitation is the true and determinate concept of material corporeality" (E §269). Second, take a living being, as discussed in "Life": Why does it do what it does? On account of the 'concept' in the sense of the biological species or kind, and more specifically the

---

[9] With respect to the notion that objects are what they are owing to their 'concept', nature, or form, it is essential to note Westphal, *Hegel's Epistemological Realism*, ch. 10, and Stern, *Structure of the Object*; I am greatly indebted to them. On this topic, see also my "Between the Bounds" and "Hegel: Metaphysics without Pre-Critical Monism." But later I will also diverge from Stern and Westphal in many other ways.

distinctive ways in which its species seeks the immanent end of self-preservation. Third, take the sorts of beings who can more specifically grasp concepts and so engage in *cognition*: Why do we do what we do? On account of our immanent 'concept', the concept of 'spirit', which turns out to be not just any concept but 'the concept', and whose content turns out to be *freedom*.

On this account, immanent concepts—at least in the case of nature—are discovered by the natural sciences. But defense of the concept thesis itself is a different matter. Here Hegel gives, within metaphysics, a distinctly philosophical defense, arguing that the thesis is inescapable for any possible philosophy: the considerations that most seem to threaten it will in fact turn out to support it. For Hegel, the most important such case comes near the conclusion of the *Logic*, in the "Mechanism" chapter. But the way to understand this is as concluding a line of argument begun earlier, excluding different ways of avoiding the concept thesis:

First, Hegel draws everywhere on the idea that explanation must be, at least in part, subject to a kind of worldly constraint. Explaining why things are as they are or do what they do requires more than formulating a way of describing things that seems explanatory to some audience. This is perhaps clearest where Hegel notes kinds of accounts—like those in astrology or phrenology[10]—which might seem compelling in context of some audiences, but cannot truly explain in any context at all.

Second, one of course might try to understand the worldly constraint on explanation without any appeal to reason in the world at all. One might understand explanation rather in terms of what Hegel calls, earlier in the *Logic*, 'formal ground'. On this kind of view, successful explanation would not require anything in the world over and above what happens or how things actually develop—or the facts that make true a description with a certain *form*, such as that of a universal generalization. But the *Logic* argues that such grounds would have to be "a mere formalism, the empty tautology of repeating," where nothing is "explained by this formalism" (SL 11.305/400). For noting that something regularly happens is not to explain why it happens, but just to repeat that it happens in this case as well as others. So there are grounds to conclude, with Hegel, that the worldly constraint on explanation would have to be understood in terms of something over and above the happenings or developments to be explained—in terms of a *reason* for them. Reason in the world, then, is the metaphysical side of explanation.[11] For example, take accounts of our behavior in terms of bumps on skulls. Someone might gerrymander their way to correlations between certain bump-shapes and certain behavior. But no such correlations would explain, regardless of audience, because they fail to identify any real form of reason in the world; behavior is in fact 'indifferent [*Gleichgültig*]'[12] to gerrymandered bump-shapes on the skull, where 'indifference' means the lack of any form of reason in the world.

---

[10]   Respectively, VGP 19:319/2:297 and PS ¶321.

[11]   This allows another side, with any number of other constraints on explanation that are epistemic, contextual, etc.

[12]   PS ¶321.

Third, one could grant an understanding of explanation in terms of reason in the world, but seek to avoid the conclusion that the reasons for things are specifically concepts. This is where Hegel sees a crucial competitor in appeals to mechanism. The idea would be what I call 'pure' or 'conceptless' mechanism: for any whole object, a supposed nature or concept of this kind of whole will be of no explanatory relevance to what it does; all the explanatory work would be done insofar as every whole is mechanistic, or (in Kant's terms) the "product of the parts and of their forces and their capacity to combine by themselves" (CJ 5:408). But Hegel argues that pure mechanism undercuts its own coherence. With pure mechanism each and every object

> ... points for its determinateness outside and beyond itself, constantly to objects for which it is however likewise a matter of indifference that they do the determining. . . . (SL 12.135/633)

So no way of redescribing, breaking things down into wholes and parts, would be privileged over or better than any other when it comes to explaining, and all would be equally arbitrary or a matter of subjective preference. All would be equally *indifferent*. Note that Hegel's argument does not assume that everything can be explained completely, and then criticize mechanism with this assumed but question-begging standard.[13] Pure mechanism sets the standard by which it fails, in arguing that appeal to immanent concepts are superfluous *because the real explanation is rather always mechanistic*. No one can coherently make that proposal, because by his own lights, ". . . to *explain* the determination of an object, and to this end to extend the representation of it beyond it, is only an *empty word*" (SL 12.135/633).[14]

Fourth, one might think that this mechanism argument leaves open the real competitor to Hegel's immanent concepts, namely, mechanistic *forces* or *laws* as a kind of 'real ground' *external* to what they explain. But the *Logic* has already shown that this is the other side a dilemma, along with 'formal ground', noted earlier. The point is that it is impossible to make sense of the reasons for things—and so of explanation—at this earlier stage of the *Logic*, prior to the development of the metaphysics of immanent concepts concluding the *Logic*. We would in particular need immanent concepts *of* such external forces or laws themselves, if we are to account for the explanatory import of these. So avoiding immanent concepts by positing forces or laws as real or external grounds makes no progress, and would leave us wanting to posit unknown further grounds for grounds, and so on forever (SL 11.307/402).

Thus Hegel draws his metaphysical conclusion: there are reasons for things, over and above what happens (contra 'formal ground'), but (contra 'real ground') they are rooted in immanent concepts. With respect to mechanistic cases specifically, the result is what I call 'reasonable' mechanism: some things (not all) are explicable in mechanistic terms,

---

[13] Compare Inwood's reading on which Hegel does sometimes require such a premise (*Hegel*, 63–64).
[14] Following my "The Logic Project."

in terms of laws, in virtue of the immanent concept of *matter*. Hegel's central example is the rotation of the solar system. First, this has a reason in the world ('its reason'):

> The movement of the solar system is governed by unalterable laws; these laws are its reason. But neither the sun nor the planets which revolve around it are conscious of them. . . . [T]here is reason in nature. . . .[15]

And the law that is its reason is rooted in the immanent concept of matter, which is gravitation. With respect to these rotating material bodies, then, "law is indeed immanent in them and it does constitute their nature and power," as Hegel puts it at the end of "Mechanism" (SL 12.146/644).

With this sketch of the *defense* in hand, we can now turn to the *application* of the concept thesis. The most important issues concern the possibility of a teleological and so normative form of immanent concept. Hegel raises the central problem here in the 'Teleology' chapter, near the conclusion of the *Logic*. We tend to think that it is enough, to introduce teleology into an otherwise lawful or necessity-governed world, to introduce conscious representations of purposes or ends as efficient causes. And since the rise of the modern sciences, philosophers have tended to want to restrict teleology to cases involving such representations. But Hegel argues for the contrary view, which he traces to Aristotle:

> With regard to the purpose, one should not immediately or should not merely think of the form in which it is in consciousness . . . in the representation. (E §204R)

Hegel, drawing on a distinction from Kant, calls this 'external' teleology. And Hegel argues that, *if* the world were otherwise entirely necessity-governed, then the addition of external teleology, or 'the subjective purpose', would be a matter of 'objective indifference [*Gleichgültigkeit*]' with respect to what happens (SL 12.161/658)—such purposes would not be the reason for anything at all. So *if* there are any teleological forms of reason in the world (including the purposive behavior of intelligent agents), then there must be at least some form of teleology independent of such causation by external subjective representations of ends—there must be *also* what Kant calls 'inner purposiveness'.[16]

This is to raise a problem, because Kant's own point about this is largely skeptical. True, Kant argues that we judge organisms in terms of inner purposiveness, or as 'natural purposes [*Naturzwecke*]', and that such judgment plays an ineliminable guiding role;

---

[15] VPG 12:23/34. Hegel here glosses a view Anaxagoras "was the first" to hold; Hegel adopts the view but puts it to his own very different purposes.

[16] In effect, whatever the role for subjective purposes is, purposive agents acting on mechanistic objects would also require bodies that are organized teleologically independent of subjective purposes. See also Pippin, *Hegel's Idealism*, 245, and de Vries, "Dialectic of Teleology," 57–58.

but it is impossible (Kant argues) for us to know whether there is any such thing as a *Naturzweck* or any real inner purposiveness.[17]

Crucial to Kant's case is his insight that we cannot analyze teleology in metaphysically deflationary terms—say, as just one among many of our explanatory practices, or ways of describing the structure of things or how they in fact develop. To simplify Kant's example, the arctic ecosystem developed in such a way that seals benefit humans. Deflationary accounts constraining only structure or development will be subject to examples like this, where they can be forced to hold that this development of benefit justifies finding a teleological kind of intelligibility, concluding that the *telos* of seals is to benefit humans. But the fact of benefit justifies no such teleology (CJ 5:369). This is clearest in considering the normativity that comes with teleology (EE 20:240): clearly benefit does not justify the conclusion that seals have the normative function of benefiting humans, so that those evading capture are malfunctioning. Thus for real teleology, something is required over and above a structure with benefits, namely a specific kind of *reason* for this structure: beneficial parts must be present *because* of their benefit in relation to the whole.[18] The obvious way that this requirement could be met is by artifacts that are the product of external design. For example, a gear in a watch comes to be present because of its benefit in relation to the way the whole serves the designer's end of reliable indication of the time (CJ 5:374). This makes the watch a purpose, or *Zweck*. But for the <u>inner</u> purposiveness of a <u>*Naturzweck*</u>, there is a second requirement: purpose must be not imposed from without, but stem from the parts within the system.[19]

The problem is that we cannot, Kant argues, know these two requirements to be jointly met. With respect to organisms specifically, it is obvious but entirely insufficient that they in fact develop a structure in which the parts benefit the self-preservation of the whole. What matters is rather the reason why, or the because responsible for this development. The candidate systems that we know about come into existence in a temporal process, and the beneficial relation of parts to whole does not exist prior to that process. The problem is, then, how parts can initially come to be present *because* of their later relation to the whole. The analysis of teleology does not require this 'because' to be any kind of efficient causality. But, *with the temporal origin of the systems we know about*, the analysis can be met (Kant argues) only where a system is the product of design, or some prior intelligent *representation* of the role to be played by the parts.[20] Further, *inner* purposiveness, given that the systems we know about are made of matter, would then require matter itself to represent ends and organize itself in accordance—which is impossible (CJ 5:383). There is no evading this argument by returning to a deflationary

[17] The concept of a *Naturzweck* is 'problematic', so that when employing it "one does not know whether one is judging about something or nothing" (CJ 5:397). Also EE 20:234 and CJ 5:396. On CJ on teleology, I follow here my 2005 and 2013.

[18] "[P]arts . . . are possible only through their relation to the whole" (CJ 5:373). See also Kant's stress on the because—*darum* and *weil*—in arguing that benefit is not enough (CJ 5:369).

[19] Kant's formulation folds the two requirements together: the parts must be "combined into a whole by being reciprocally the cause and effect of their form" (CJ 5:373).

[20] See CJ 5:372 and Zuckert, *Kant on Beauty and Biology*, 136.

analysis which does not constrain the reason that the parts are present, given cases like the arctic, described earlier. So Kant concludes that we cannot know that any system has true inner purposiveness. We can only think that a higher form of intellect might have knowledge of "supersensible real ground of nature" (CJ 5:409), and think that this ground might make possible an inner purposiveness that we could neither understand nor know.

Hegel will respond in the "Life" chapter at the conclusion of the *Logic*.[21] The chapter's three sections consider systems meeting three requirements: systems (1) organized in a manner that supports self-preservation in the senses of (2) extracting something needed from outside itself, and (3) the reproduction within kind or species [*Gattung*].[22] Hegel agrees with Kant that we do in fact think of organisms, which meet these criteria, in terms of inner purposiveness. But the key is that we also take the nature of the reproducing type, kind, or species as the very substance of the token or individual. And this species or kind (Hegel argues) would be a distinct teleological form of 'concept [*Begriff*]'.[23] So inner purposiveness will seem to be an 'incomprehensible mystery', until and unless we "grasp the concept . . . as the substance of life" (SL 12:181/678). For if the kind or concept is the substance of an organism, then there is a sense in which we can know organisms to be self-producing: they are the product of something the same in kind or concept.[24] And a token part or 'member' of such an organism will be the product of its own role in the whole—the product of the beneficial work of its own part (type) in the whole (type). So this type/token intimacy—the sense in which the kind is the very substance of the instance—would make such systems meet Kant's analysis of inner purposiveness.

Granted, *that* we think in such terms about organisms would be no proof that they are so. But what Hegel shows is that the best reason to doubt inner purposiveness—Kant's skeptical argument—in fact supports it. For Kant's argument looks to artifacts to establish a demanding standard for teleology. If Kant says that a gear in a watch is present because of *its* contribution within the whole, then the 'its' can refer at once to the *token* gear and the designer's representation of its *type*. And this type-token intimacy (Hegel shows) also establishes real and knowable inner purposiveness. Strictly speaking, the *Philosophy of Nature* discusses empirical facts about actual living beings; but what is needed for this *Logic* argument will be uncontroversial, since organisms clearly do assimilate and reproduce.

Hegel's conclusion is a kind of compatibilism: within living beings there is stuff that does what it does because of its *lawful*, non-teleological natures or concepts; there is an 'indifference' to 'purpose' (SL 12:188/685). But there is a *further* teleological reason that just such stuff is present in just such an arrangement—namely, the contribution made

[21] I follow my "The Logic of Life" on this material.

[22] "A. The Living Individual," "B. The Life Process," and "C. Kind (*Gattung*)," respectively.

[23] "[T]he realized species (*Gattung*)" here "has posited itself as identical with the concept" (SL 12.191/688).

[24] See, for example, Hegel on Aristotle: "That which is produced is as such in the ground, that is, it is an end, kind [*Gattung*] in itself, it is by the same token prior, before it becomes actual, as potentiality. Man generates men; what the product is, is also the producer" (VGP 19:176).

to the inner purpose or *telos* of self-preservation. So this defense of natural teleology requires no claim that all *matter* as such is teleological, nor any claim to know anything like a supersensible substrate of all matter or nature.

But this is not to say that Hegel's view is non-metaphysical or entirely deflationary. Hegel does not dismiss or unask the metaphysical questions concerning something over and above the structure of a system or development—namely, the *reason* for this structure or development; he does not, in particular, mistakenly say that the metaphysical questions could concern only efficient causes, or only something irrelevant to teleology.[25] Hegel's view is that the metaphysical issues must be faced, but can be resolved with a case for a metaphysics of immanent concepts that are teleological, and so a teleological—and normative, in the associated sense—form of reason in the world.

14.3. THE IDEA: EXPLANATORY COMPLETENESS

The metaphysics of Hegel's concept thesis, however, leaves us still short of the extent of his metaphysical ambitions. For the purposes of understanding these ambitions, we tend nowadays to worry both too much and also too little about the kind of metaphysics described earlier. We worry too much in that we overestimate the threat from fundamentally epistemological concerns, such as the worry that we could not have knowledge in metaphysics, or that our concepts in metaphysics have not been (or could not be) shown to have any genuine relation to objects. Hegel has powerful reasons for brushing such worries aside: First, such worries should generalize, affecting equally any other domain: they will be no reason to prefer epistemology, transcendental reflection, natural science, or anything else over metaphysics.[26] For example, taking such worries to require Kantian deductions as a basis for metaphysics would be like, Hegel says, wanting to learn to swim before getting in the water (E §10R). A second reason for brushing such concerns aside is that the supposed alternatives to metaphysics (Hegel argues) are in fact built on metaphysical assumptions. For example, it is a "fundamental delusion in scientific empiricism" is that it merely presupposes its own empiricist metaphysics (E §38R).

But we also worry too little, in that we tend nowadays to underestimate the threat from Kant's Dialectic. Kant's argument calls metaphysics generally into question. It does not only target the metaphysics of otherworldly objects, like immaterial souls or gods, or the supersensible in that specific sense.[27] Even a metaphysics of ordinary objects is

---

[25] See Yeomans, Ch. 21, for a similar point applied to Hegel's philosophy of action: the retrospective element of Hegel's theory is not the whole; Hegel recognizes a "productive relation between the agent and her action," so that traditional problems about free will must be engaged rather than dismissed.

[26] See, for example, Hegel's reply to empiricist attempts to use skepticism against metaphysics (E §39R).

[27] Contrast Beiser, "Two Concepts of Reason," 55.

supposed to involve claims about the reasons rendering them explicable, and thereby also (at least implicitly) raising questions about the completeness of such reasons. But such issues lead to conflicts internal to metaphysics, even—as in the first two or 'mathematical' antinomies—where the topic is limited to the spatio-temporal (CPR A530/B558). Kant's claim is that the only solution must involve his epistemic limits, preventing philosophy from answering some questions that it inescapably raises.

Taking this Kantian worry so seriously is the basic reason that Hegel needs a systematic metaphysics that relates everything to the completeness of reason—or 'the idea'. To instead claim to sidestep the worry of the antinomies would be, on Hegel's view, a pre-critical reversion from Kant. Thus Hegel, although following Aristotle on many particulars, also holds that everything in metaphysics must be reconstructed, as an organized whole, on grounds drawn from Kant's Dialectic. So it is no surprise that Aristotle is supposed to lack the required systematicity (e.g., VGP 19:133/2:118).

And Hegel takes the problem to require a distinctive method in response: we must directly consider incomplete forms of reason in the world, which trigger antinomy problems. But we must not conclude that a contrasting completeness of explanation would be wholly other or beyond this, and knowable or understandable only by a higher intellect. This would be a kind of 'abstract negation', as opposed to Hegel's favored determinate negation.[28] We must rather draw, out of the problem with incomplete reasons, incrementally better candidate accounts of more complete forms of reason.

I turn, then, to Hegel's account of a form of incomplete reason, in the "Chemism" chapter.[29] Hegel is not here addressing what we think of as chemistry specifically[30]; he is addressing whatever kinds or concepts fundamentally interact lawfully.[31]

Hegel argues that to be this kind of thing is to interact lawfully in certain ways with other kinds; each kind of lawful thing, then, "is not comprehensible from itself, and the being of one object is the being of another" (SL 12:149/646). From here, Hegel quickly reaches a kind of metaphysical holism of the lawful: to be lawful kind X is to react with Y, and so on to Z and a whole interconnected network of kinds and laws. The 'determinateness' of anything lawful is just one 'moment' of a larger 'whole' or concept of the whole: it "is the concrete moment of the individual concept of the whole which is the universal essence, the *real kind [Gattung]* of the particular objects" (SL 12:149/646).

The philosophical pressure toward this kind of metaphysical holism has often been noted more recently, even while holism is often resisted. Chalmers is an example:

> . . . physical theory only characterizes its basic entities *relationally*. . . . One might be attracted to the view of the world as pure causal flux, with no further properties for the causation to relate, but this would lead to a strangely insubstantial view of the physical world.[32]

---

[28] For example, on responding to the Antinomies with 'abstract negation' (SL 12.245–246/745).
[29] On this chapter, I follow my "Logic of Life."
[30] SL 12.148/645.
[31] "Both, mechanism as well as chemism, are . . . included under natural necessity" (SL 12.148/652).
[32] *Conscious Mind*, 153. Compare also Russell, *Analysis of Matter*, 325.

|

And there is in fact a kind of antinomy here. The thesis would demand, as Chalmers does, that there must be something more to reality than just relations. The antithesis would deny that there can be anything more.

To understand Hegel's response to the problem, we need to note how he argues throughout earlier parts of the *Logic* against the positing of metaphysical 'substrata'. In short, metaphysicians tend to think that substrata are needed in order to support things. But substrata would (Hegel argues) turn out to be merely 'indifferent [*Gleichgültig*]', or no form of reason in the world, and no support for anything.[33] For example, we expect a substratum of any lawful X to be required to support the possibility of X standing in lawful relations with any Y. But this appeal would justify, at most, more relations: the relation of *support* between the substratum and X's relation to Y. The substratum itself remains indifferent, and no need for support, or any kind of reason, justifies positing it. The demand for substrata always rests, rather, on a demand that reality must include something to correspond to the subject of subject-predicate judgment. This Hegel takes to be the root of early modern metaphysics of substance, taking substance to be a kind of 'subject' (as in subject-predicate judgment) that attributes can be 'in'. Hegel calls this "the metaphysics of the understanding," or of the faculty of judgment.[34] But, first, such metaphysics provides no justification for the demand that reality correspond to judgments (EL §28R). Furthermore, Hegel argues that the pre-Kantian metaphysics raising antinomy problems must persist so long as we confuse the demands of the understanding (for correspondence to the form of judgment) and of reason (for complete reasons):

> The *metaphysics of the past* . . . is always on hand, as the *perspective of the understanding alone* on the objects of reason. (E §27)

Hegel argues that Kant's response to the antinomies is a retreat back to the perspective of the understanding, which then requires Kant to restrict reason. But Hegel engages directly with the form of metaphysics considered in Kant's Dialectic account of reason, and finds no grounds for letting the perspective of the understanding stand in the way of resolving those problems from the perspective of reason alone.

We can now see the distinction between two kinds of responses in Hegel to worries about the insubstantiality of lawful reality:

> *First*, with respect to substrata: Lawful reality is perfectly real—it is not an illusion—but any lawful X lacks a substratum of lawful relations with others, and is insubstantial in this respect.

> *Second*, there is the very different issue of whether there is anything to X in itself that is a reason why X reacts specifically as it does with Y, and so on. Here Hegel's response is more complicated. On the one hand, Hegel again answers in the

---

[33] For example, SL 12.57–58/554–555.
[34] Cf. CPR A69/B94.

negative: within the lawful, the search for the reason proceeds out of X, to Y, and so on, without completion of the regress. There is no completion even in the whole. For even the whole web of lawful relations is itself dependent on there being ('posited') differentiated parts (SL 12.149/646). This is a real incompleteness of reason. It is a counterexample to the rationalists' PSR.[35] On the other hand, however, Hegel does see here a real problem—some truth to the other side of the antinomy problem. For theoretical inquiry seeks a complete reason, and must presuppose for the sake of inquiry that there is such a thing. So theoretical inquiry must conclude that there is at least something else with the determinate features, lacking in the lawful, which would make for greater explanatory completeness. This is the systematic ground that *requires* the *Logic* to turn, after "Chemism," toward teleology.[36]

We saw earlier Hegel's arguments that teleology requires inner purposiveness ("Teleology," the last chapter before "The Idea" section), and defending inner purposiveness ("Life," the first chapter in "The Idea" section). Now we know the point of this ordering: the inner purposiveness of life first provides any explanatory completeness. Or, "the idea is, *first of all, life*" (SL 12.177/675). To see why, contrast Hegel's account of a living being with the explanatory regress of the lawful. Why does a tiger, for example, have the capacity to catch the deer that it eats? It is not the case that the only answer is: all that it is to be this kind of tiger is to catch deer of this kind. Nor is the only answer the one that would follow the regress into the underlying lawful kinds of stuff and a network of laws. For there is a kind of explanatory anchor with the tiger itself: it has claws, and the power to slice, and this underlying constitution, *because* of the contribution that all this makes to the tiger's own immanent end of self-preservation. The inner purposiveness of an organism allows its nature to be found in the determinate ways that it relates to the environment, without its nature being merely dissolved away into external relations. And so it allows for greater explanatory completeness, and a kind of greater substantiality in this respect. Thus the *Phenomenology* says that an animal is "the real end [*Zweck*] itself. . . . [I]t preserves *itself* in the relation to an other" (PS ¶256); a lower-level thing "gets lost" (PS ¶246). The *Logic* says that 'cause' in the sense of 'blind necessity' must "pass over into its other and lose its originality":

> The purpose, by contrast, is posited as *in itself* the determinacy . . . does not pass over
> . . . but instead *preserves itself*. . . . (E §204R).

From the account of the immanent purposiveness of life, then, we can abstract our way to an understanding of Hegel's more general account of explanatory completeness or 'the idea'—and with it his replacement for substrata accounts of the metaphysics of substance. We need only abstract away from life's *specific* inner purpose of self-preservation.

---

[35] Note also Hegel's explicit criticisms of the PSR at (SL 11.293–294/388).
[36] On the sense in which this leaves contradiction in the world, see my *Reason in the World*, ch. 6.

In *general*, only some inner purpose is required. I would express the resulting theory in this way:

> *The idea* = a reciprocal process of concept and individual instances sufficient to establish the concept as the substance of an individual, and thereby some inner purpose.

So the idea in general requires an account of a concept with the special relationship to individual instances in which it gives them their substance. And that is why 'the idea' cannot be understood as *only* one-half of that relationship. Thus the canonical formulations of the material introducing the section titled "The Idea": "the idea is the unity of the concept and objectivity" or "the unity of concept and reality."[37] In general, the idea involves

> the concept that distinguishes itself from its objectivity—but an objectivity which is no less determined by it and possesses its substantiality only in that concept. (SL 12.176/673)

Recall that life is (on Hegel's account) something *dependent* in a certain respect: life is dependent for its existence on something underlying with an "indifference ... to purpose" (SL 12.188/685), and so not something interfering with the explanatory completeness of teleology. This carries several important implications about 'the idea' in general.

First, it means that Hegel is *not* arguing that everything real is just a realization of the idea. The idea, as in the case of life, is realized in *what is not the idea*. There is reality that is 'finite', specifically in the respect that it does not involve the previously noted unity of concept and objectivity, or falls short of the idea. This, Hegel says, is the topic of the "Objectivity" section prior to "The Idea":

> Finite things are finite because, and to the extent that, they do not possess the reality of their concept completely within them but are in need of other things for it. . . . (SL 12.175/672)

Further, Hegel is arguing against a conception of explanatory completeness as that which is depended upon without itself being dependent—as something like a substance in the sense of a substratum. He is aiming for a more positive conception of reason and its completeness: not in terms of a *lack of dependence*, but in terms of *concepts with explanatory import of their own*—a kind of self-determination. If the latter standard is met, then dependence on an indifferent substrate does not matter.

And, more radically still, Hegel is arguing not just that life or this or that actual form of the idea is in fact dependent; he is arguing for the philosophical conclusion that anything completely explicable *must necessarily* be dependent. Inner purposiveness

---

[37] SL 12.174/671 and 12.176/673, respectively.

depends on or is 'mediated' by an indifferent, realizing substrate. The lawful substrate gets lost in relations. Inner purposiveness must use this substrate. If inner purposiveness were instead supposed to have a primitive or 'immediate' power to interact with certain chemical substances, then it would itself be drawn into the mere regress of the lawful, losing its explanatory completeness:

> In an *immediate connection* with that object, purpose would itself enter into the sphere of mechanism and chemism and would therefore be subject to accidentality and to the loss of its determining vocation. (SL 12.166/663)

That is why the idea in general, and not just in the case of life, must be a process, dependent on there being some substrate indifferent to the idea, in order to realize the process (SL 12.176–177/674).

On my view, then, there can be no route back from Hegel's arguments to a rationalist monism, on which there is a sufficient reason for everything provided by a substance that is a substrate in which everything inheres, but itself depends on nothing. Metaphysics, Hegel argues, cannot rest on any such notion of substance that it might take as basic, as in the accounts considered at the end of the Doctrine of Essence.[38] On the contrary, substance too must be reconsidered, accounted for in terms of 'the concept' and ultimately 'the idea', or explanatory completeness. But to say that the idea is the substance of things is, again, not to say that it is everything. As we have seen, lawful reality is insubstantial even though it is real—not a mere subjective illusion or semblance. The substantial begins when we come to life. And Hegel's point is that all substance must be built out of the insubstantial. This is one form of the proposal that what is metaphysically prior comes at the end, and is mediated or dependent on something earlier.

Similarly, "*something has truth only in so far as it is idea*" (SL 12.173/670). But Hegel distinguishes 'correctness' from the special notion of 'truth' that he reconstructs in terms of the metaphysics of reason (SL 12.65/562). So, in short, we find *the idea* where we have an inner purpose, and so a normative standard, set by a concept so intimately related to particular individuals that it gives them their substance; 'truth' is agreement of an object with its own immanent standard. Some things are not the idea, having no immanent concept as standard, so there cannot even be any question of their being 'true'. So where "finite things are finite," because they do not have concepts providing their very substance, this is their '*untruth*' (SL 12.175/672).

Also similar is Hegel's claim that we must "regard everything *as being* actual only to the extent that it has the idea in it and expresses it" (SL 12.174/671). But the term 'actual' does not mean everything that happens to exist; Hegel's term "discriminates . . . what truly merits the name '*actuality*'" (E §6). 'The actual [*das Wirkliche*]' is supposed to be what is effective or what produces [*das Wirkende*] (E §163R). Lawfully interacting kinds,

---

[38] See also Ng, Ch 12 of this volume, and Zambrana, Ch 13 of this volume, on Hegel's critique of Spinoza and its role in the transition from 'Substance' at the end of The Doctrine of Essence to The Doctrine of the Concept.

for example, exist but have only the barest trace of borrowed actuality, since each is an effective reason only on account of relations to others—they are but the barest trace of the idea. Only full forms of 'the idea' are fully actual.

14.4. The Absolute Idea, Method, and the Conclusion of the *Logic*

There are two especially important openings for rejoinder. The first concerns Hegel's metaphysics itself: the Kantian might object that all this so far concerns only explanatory completeness that is *relatively* greater. But the Transcendental Dialectic is ultimately concerned with *absolute* endpoints of inquiry. Perhaps a Hegelian could respond that explanatory completeness greater than anything allowed in Kant's Antinomies is enough to counter Kant. But Hegel himself clearly accepts the challenge, seeking to account for the metaphysics of what he calls 'the absolute idea'.

The case of life makes the problem clear, because there are clearly limits to its explanatory completeness. There are many different ways in which different species could seek the end of self-preservation. And the general idea of life does nothing to explain why *multiple, diverse* forms or species should be actually realized in the world, nor which ones should be; this has no explanation or reason, on Hegel's account.[39] One could *imagine* that something more powerful might somehow close those explanatory gaps. But Hegel's challenge is to provide an explanation of how.

The *Logic*'s first proposal, in "The Idea of Cognition," is that explanatory completeness might be provided by an individual, X, with the capacity for theoretical cognition. But if we leave it at that, then what would do the philosophical work of privileging X would not be X itself, but rather a special, supposedly higher object beyond it: 'the true' (SL 12.199/ 697 ff.). The same applies to a special power of willing, and a special supposed object of it, the good (SL 12.231/729 ff.). Either way, the metaphysical priority of X would not be explained, but only presupposed in positing the higher object.

The *Logic*'s solution, in the final chapter, "The Absolute Idea," is this: go back to the idea as life and add a sort of thinking *of itself* which (Hegel argues) thereby makes the immanent purpose no longer *self-preservation* but rather a sort of *freedom*. So:

> The absolute idea = any reciprocal process of concept or kind and individual where thinking or reflection establishes freedom as immanent purpose.

The freedom here is a sense in which realizations of this concept would be not merely determined by that concept—their substance—behind their back, as it were; such a case would be what it is because its concept or *Begriff* would not just be *in itself*, in that last

---

[39] E.g., E §248R.

sense, but also *for itself.* So, relative to the initial proposals about the good and the true, the *Logic* needs "a turning back to *life*," but without the 'immediacy' of life or its lack of the *for itself.* This is supposed to make possible a variety of 'the idea', which now, unlike life, explains diversity out of itself, or "harbors the most extreme opposition within" (SL 12.236/735). And this absolute idea is what just what was missing in 'Life': "the *free kind* [*Gattung*] *for itself*" (E §222).

One *illustration* of the gist here will come later in the *Encyclopedia*, with the theory of spirit. There we will get a case that the concept, or *Begriff*, of human beings is freedom, and that this explains from itself, first, the emergence of conflict and so diversity in the way in which human beings organize themselves, and, second, a kind of directionality to our development toward forms of social life that realize freedom.[40] But for the *Logic*, nothing specifically about *human beings* as such matters. What is important is rather the case of *whatever* might think through the argument of the *Logic* itself. So the *Logic* distinguishes the topic that "belongs to the doctrine of spirit proper" from "[t]he *idea of spirit* which is the subject matter of *logic*," or "the logical idea of spirit" (SL 12.198/695– 696). Spirit (in this logical sense) is what thinks, and so entangles itself in the problems of philosophy, and in this way generates from itself the distinctions between different steps along the way of the *Logic*, until it comes to the conclusion that its kind or concept is a free thinking that realizes the absolute idea. If we can think through this process, then the absolute idea is real.

This is also what Hegel means in emphasizing the definite articles in *the* idea (*die Idee*), and *the* concept (*der Begriff*). There are many forms of concept, but others turn out to be lesser forms of the absolute case of *the* concept, the concept of freedom: "The concept is the *free*, as the *substantial power that is for itself*" (E §160). And all forms of the idea are lesser forms of this absolute form: 'the idea' is "the free concept, the concept determining itself and thereby determining itself as reality' " (E §213R).

And this is what is meant by Hegel's famous claims that substance must be understood as subject or spirit.[41] The point is not to accept Spinoza's claim that there is a single substance/substrate 'in' which everything real inheres, adding only that this is a subject or spirit. For Hegel's absolute idea is no substrate at all. Nor is it an individual. It is a process or movement, and one connecting a universal kind and particular individuals. And Hegel denies that everything real is just a form of the absolute idea, holding that this process is realized in something not the absolute idea, or spirit in the logical sense.

But there is a second obvious opening for rejoinder. And this is now a distinctive form of *epistemological* problem raised by Hegel's metaphysics. In short, the issues raised in Kant's Dialectic concern, on Kant's account, the ideas of reason as guiding theoretical inquiry. Hegel responds with a metaphysics on which it is not the case that everything truly realizes the absolute idea. But from Kant's point of view, then, the guidance of

---

[40] See Pinkard, "Hegel's Philosophy of History as the Metaphysics of Agency," Chapter 24 in this volume.

[41] E.g., E §213R, and lecture notes here: "the idea is subject. Substance, if it is to become true, must be apprehended as subject" (VL 208/212).

reason would seem to leave inquiry on some domains, such as that of the lawful, simply hopeless—in that it could not possibly reach its guiding goal.

Note, however, that Kant faces a similar problem. On Kant's view, we can never reach knowledge of anything unconditioned. Why then is inquiry not hopeless? Kant argues that our inquiry can at least make progress, heading in the direction that would, if we could follow completely, satisfy reason—progressing "asymptotically, as it were, i.e., merely by approximation" (CPR A663/B691).[42]

Now reconsider the problem for Hegel: True, Hegel's metaphysics allows the lawful neither to be nor to metaphysically depend upon the absolute idea. Still, Hegel's account opens up a different way of accounting for the *epistemological* side of explanation—the sense in which finding explanations should produce *insight* into or *understanding* of the world.[43] For explaining in lawful cases could produce such understanding in virtue of an approximation of the lawful, for example, to the absolute idea. So even chemism falls short in the way shown, in the *Logic*, to suggest the right direction, or being on the way: chemism "is not yet for itself that totality of self-determination" (SL 12:148/645).

In the end, then, Hegel advocates two different forms of the priority of the absolute idea:

> *Metaphysical priority*: the absolute idea is the absolutely complete form of reason in the world, and so prior in a metaphysics of reason.

> *Epistemological priority*: all intelligibility of everything depends on the intelligibility of the absolute idea.

If 'idealism' refers to any claim for a priority of any form of idea or mind, then these are both a metaphysical and an epistemological form of 'idealism'. The latter view is also a form of epistemological monism, because it requires that the intelligibility of anything requires its fitting a system of knowledge that would relate everything to the absolute idea. The conclusion of the *Logic* gives this epistemological monism a striking formulation in claiming that 'the method' discussed here is that of theoretical inquiry generally. The point is this: in pursuing theoretical inquiry on some domain, we are seeking the rational or the absolute idea there. We can reach explanatory satisfaction to different degrees on different domains. But no limit here is an epistemic limit of ours; it would stem from the metaphysical incompleteness of some domains. And whatever satisfaction we reach anywhere will be only in finding there at least an approximation of the idea. Finding laws of nature would be *one* step in a process that, if carried farther through, would have to turn into an inquiry looking very different on the surface: it would have to find in its results contradictions, which point to something more complete, until we come to the absolute idea thinking itself. There is supposed to be a natural

---

[42] See Kitcher's "Order of Nature" and my "Kant on the Laws of Nature" for an alternative account of this.

[43] That explanation has a metaphysical side, emphasized earlier, does not preclude it from also having this epistemological side. Compare Kim "Explanatory Knowledge."

progression here from what would begin as empirical, and end up a priori, in the sense that the method in the *Logic* and its results would be independent regardless of any initiating empirical details. So physics may be complete *relative to its own purposes*, but it also raises further questions that *reason* cannot ignore. Thus, the *Logic* pursues

> ... the method proper to each and every fact. ... It is therefore not only the highest *force* of reason, or rather its *sole* and absolute *force*, but also reason's highest and sole *impulse* to find and recognize *itself through itself in all things*. (SL 12.238/737)

Note the way in which this explains Hegel's famous claims about circular structure: Philosophy itself is a form of rational inquiry; so it seeks the end of reason, or complete reason in the world.[44] Thus it must necessarily begin by at least by presupposing, for the sake of inquiry, that there is some complete form of reason to be sought. The *Logic's* final account of the absolute idea and philosophical method is supposed to justify (and in this sense *mediate*) that initially unjustified (or immediate) presupposition:

> By virtue of the nature of the method just indicated, the science presents itself as a *circle* that winds around itself, where the mediation winds the end back to the beginning. (SL 12.252/751)

But the point here crucially concerns *epistemic* necessity. There is no claim for the existence of the rationalists' metaphysically necessary substance, a subject containing the predicate of existence, as a beginning or ground on which everything depends. Rather, the point is that the beginning is not arbitrary, but a standpoint *necessary* for philosophy as a form of theoretical inquiry; and this *must* lead, through contradictions, to their resolution with the absolute idea.

Finally, this overall argument of the *Logic* is supposed to establish a kind of 'absolute knowledge'. The point is that there is no in-principle limit to our access to explanatory knowledge. So the view is not that we can know every fact all at once—let alone just by reading the *Logic*.[45] We can, through reading the *Logic*, gain knowledge of a form of absolute idea—of spirit, in the logical sense involving thinking through the *Logic* itself; this is knowledge of "the *concept that comprehends* itself *conceptually*" (SL 12:252/752). And in all other cases that fall short of this, including the rotation of matter in the solar system and the growth of living beings, there are contradictions that connect consideration of them back to the absolute and the case of spirit. This need not include a supposed explanation for anything like a complete reason for the location and features of every material particle in the universe. For Hegel denies that there is always complete explanation for everything, leaving no reasons unknowable where there are no reasons. Still, whatever follows and comprehends the path of the *Logic* can know itself as spirit in the

---

[44] See the *Encyclopedia Logic, Werke* 8:13/Brinkmann and Dahlstrom, 6–7, and 8:38/26.
[45] Cf. "it is quite improper" to try to "deduce" the "contingent products of nature" (E §250R).

logical sense and the absolute idea. Thus, Hegel says, where he glosses the point to be made in the last chapter of the *Logic*:

> spirit recognizes the idea as its *absolute truth* ... the infinite idea ... which is the absolute knowledge of itself. (SL 12.178/675)

14.5. Conclusion

We can now consider the bearing of this material, from the conclusion of the *Logic*, on other recently popular interpretative approaches to Hegel. I have many debts to members of all of the groups I will mention, which I have tried to note in the preceding. But I have argued that understanding the end of the *Logic* requires rejecting a point on which most everyone seems to agree, namely: Hegel's engagement internally with Kant's philosophy would have to involve taking as a basis any broadly epistemological concerns, from Kant or otherwise. Some, a first group, think that Hegel fails to so engage with epistemological concerns, and so begs the question against Kant; they usually take Hegel to be a metaphysical monist.[46] Others think that Hegel does manage to argue from epistemological considerations. Some, a second ground, think that he gives an epistemological argument for metaphysical monism. For example, knowledge would require no gap between subject and object, which would both have to be in the One.[47] Others still, a third group, see Hegel as basing his project on more deflationary epistemological considerations, arguing for an epistemological fallibilism and/or coherentism, which is supposed to lead to a more modest form of ontological holism.[48]

It is worth saying something more about a fourth kind of approach, descendent from Pippin's breakthrough *Hegel's Idealism* (1989). Of the alternatives, this best captures something I think crucial: the way Hegel's project draws its considerable philosophical strengths from the way it is unified by a metaphilosophical commitment, about what is *basic* in philosophy. But, compared to my proposals in the preceding, this Kantian account sees the opposite metaphilosophical details: Hegel is supposed to take as "basic to his project" issues with a unifying "common theme"—"the argument that any subject must be able to make certain basic discriminations in any experience in order for there to be experience at all."[49] More recent versions might substitute for 'experience' a concern with conditions of the possibility of any relation between concept and object, of the

---

[46] E.g., Guyer, "Thought and Being," 171–172; Düsing, *Das Problem der Subjektivität*, 119; Düsing, "Constitution and Structure of Self-Identity," 421; Siep, *Phänomenologie des Geistes*, 18–21.

[47] E.g., Beiser, "Problem of Metaphysics," 15. Horstmann sees in Hegel an argument resting on epistemology, but not a primary interest in epistemology; "Ordnung der Dinge", 23. I think that the correctness and importance of his latter point justifies denying the former, and revising our understanding of the metaphysics itself.

[48] E.g., Westphal *Hegel's Epistemological Realism*, ch. 10, and Stern, *Hegelian Metaphysics*.

[49] Pippin, *Hegel's Idealism*, 7–8.

normativity of concept use, of objective purport, and so on. All such versions agree that Hegel's project aims to extend Kant's positive project from the Transcendental Analytic. It is a mistake to object that this Kantian approach precludes recognition of Hegel as metaphysician, or limits Hegel to subjective idealism. The Kantian approach can allow Hegel to pursue metaphysics, so long as metaphysics itself is understood through the lens of the supposed fundamentality of issues descended from Kant's Analytic. And one might argue that Hegel seeks, by accounting for the conditions of the possibility of cognition, to account for *objects* of cognition themselves, and even to eliminate any Kantian worries about any unknowability of objects in themselves; one might argue that this is a kind of metaphysics.[50]

But while I see how one might get *a* metaphysics in this way, it doesn't seem to me to be *the metaphysics of the end of the Logic*. Consideration of the possibility of cognition of any object might get you a metaphysics of what is common to all objects. Or it might get you a metaphysical priority of one side of a dualism over the other: of the judging *subject* over the *objects* of its judgments.[51] But I don't see how it could get you Hegel's tight focus on a metaphysics *of reason*, so clearly suggested by borrowing the crucial terminology here—'the idea', 'reason', and so on—specifically from Kant's Dialectic. And I don't see how it could get you Hegel's complex development of multiple steps of metaphysical priority of reasons in the world. For example, Hegel's point about the inner purposiveness of life is not that *every* object is alive in the full sense, or that this is a necessary condition of the possibility of judgment about any object. The metaphysical priority of teleological to non-teleological forms of reason in the world is crucial. Nor is the point that anything with inner purposiveness would engage in acts of judgment or cognition in the full sense. A metaphysical priority of the absolute idea over the idea generally is also crucial. Perhaps the Kantian deduction approach, if focusing specifically on the end of the *Logic*, would best argue that any 'object-level' metaphysical ambitions here are not "playing any significant role in the position defended," which is more 'metalevel'.[52] But the arguments themselves in this stretch of text, I have tried to show, do have such direct metaphysical import—as, for example, about objects structured by inner purposiveness.

True, Hegel engages even here with epistemological problems, but he does so specifically as these are radically reshaped by his taking the metaphysics of reason as more fundamental; this is why the epistemological issues come to be those raised specifically by Hegel's metaphysics of explanation—concerning the possibility of intelligibility or understanding, in that sense, rather than anything like relations between acts of cognition or judgment and objects of cognition or judgment. That is why I think it better to place the considerable insights of the Kantian approach in context of the opposite reading of Hegel's unifying aims. Sticking to the Kantian deduction approach, at this

---

[50]   See Pippin's use of Kant's A158/B197 both at *Hegel's Idealism*, 33 and, more recently, "The Significance of Self-Consciousness," 148.

[51]   Perhaps by way of Pippin's powerful (*Hegel's Idealism*) argument that Kant's own epistemology pushes against Kant's claim to metaphysical neutrality, toward a robust metaphysics of the spontaneity of the subject.

[52]   Pippin, *Hegel's Idealism*, 247.

point, would seem to require a transition principle. For example, one might see a basis in a deduction of a priori necessary conditions of intelligibility, and then transition by means of a principle requiring that anything real must be intelligible. But that principle defines the rationalism Kant's Dialectic rejects; and Hegel follows, taking Kant's "insight into the necessary conflict" to leave *that* sort of metaphysics hopeless, a reversion from the "loftier spirit of modern philosophy" (SL 21:30/25–26). The modern options would then be *either* Kant's restrictions *or* Hegel's reconstruction of metaphysics on grounds from Kant's Dialectic. If the latter works, then it leaves no support for Kant's attempt to transform metaphysics by placing it on the basis of deductions like those of the Transcendental Analytic. And this is why I think that the real Hegel is in a philosophically stronger position than either any either Kantianized or epistemologized Hegel could be: the real Hegel needs no transition principle from any supposed basis to metaphysics; rather, *Logic* knocks out other options until concluding that theoretical philosophy should always already be direct engagement with the metaphysics of reason.

Finally, I think that the conclusion of the *Logic* is philosophically strong enough to suggest the lasting importance of some questions relatively neglected today:

First, consider those today who would prefer to pursue a version of Kant's transformed theoretical philosophy, taking as basic to their projects broadly epistemological issues about the relation of cognition and objects. But why? To judge by Hegel, the attractive option here will not be any claim that metaphysics is a matter of indifference. Kant already sees this as hopeless (CPR Ax). And if metaphysics is not a matter of indifference, then how to justify the broadly Kantian transformation? Hegel shows that no arguments from a broadly epistemological basis can work; they would presume the authority or fundamentality of epistemology in trying to defend it. So even though Kant's Dialectic is relatively neglected today, reading Hegel suggests that *it* is what should be most crucial for Kantians today. Can contemporary Kantians defend the Dialectic argument itself? Or can they replace it with some new way of arguing that metaphysics goes awry from within?

Second, consider those who would still pursue metaphysics today. To judge by Hegel, the attractive option here is not to dismiss all worries about metaphysics as irrelevant because they are merely epistemological. For Hegel shows that even fans of metaphysics should recognize the importance of very different challenges like those of Kant's Dialectic. And Hegel's response suggests an essential question here about metaphysical foundationalism. As contemporary philosophy turns back toward metaphysics, it develops just as Kantians and Hegelians should expect: it begins to focus on metaphysical *conditions*—like the 'grounds' now considered under the heading of 'metaphysical grounding'; and then it begins to focus on forms of the unconditioned, ultimate grounds, and new forms of what is now called 'metaphysical foundationalism'.[53] The question suggested by the conclusion of Hegel's *Logic* is whether metaphysics can defend some form of foundationalism against the problems raised by Kant's Dialectic

---

[53] See especially Schaffer's defense of monism on grounds of foundationalism ("Monism," 37).

and Hegel? Or is it better for metaphysicians to seek, with Hegel, a principled alternative to metaphysical foundationalism?

In any case, the end of Hegel's *Logic* shows that his basic aim is to rebuild metaphysics on grounds of the strongest worry about it. Because of this, he can still help us to engage with one another philosophically, even across the chasm separating those who would travel in contrasting philosophical directions. For Hegel offers us a single metaphilosophical framework that can bring into focus at once both powerful worries about metaphysics, and also continuing prospects for its defense.

WORKS CITED

Primary Texts

Hegel, G. W. F. *Encyclopedia Logic* [E], translated by K. Brinkmann and D. O. Dahlstrom. Cambridge: Cambridge University Press, 2010.

Hegel, G. W. F. *Hegel's Philosophy of Nature* [E], translated by W. Wallace and A. V. Miller. Oxford: Oxford University Press, 1970.

Hegel, G. W. F. *Lectures on the History of Philosophy* [VGP], 3 vols., translated by E. S. Haldane and Frances H. Simson. Lincoln: University of Nebraska Press. *Werke* vol. 18–20.

Hegel, G. W. F. *Lectures on the Philosophy of World History; Introduction: Reason in History* [VPG], translated by H. B. Nisbet. Cambridge: Cambridge University Press, 1975. *Werke* vol. 12.

Hegel, G. W. F. *Phenomenology of Spirit* [PS], translated by A. V. Miller. Oxford: Oxford University Press, 1977.

Hegel, G. W. F. *The Science of Logic* [SL], translated and edited by George di Giovanni. Cambridge: Cambridge University Press, 2010.

Hegel, G. W. F. *Vorlesungen über Logik* [VL], transcribed by Karl Hegel, edited by U. Rameil and H. C. Lucas. Hamburg: Meiner, 1831.

Hegel, G. W. F. *Werke in zwanzig Bänden*, [Werke] ed. Eva Moldenhauer and Karl Markus Michel (Frankfurt am Main: Suhrkamp Verlag, 1970).

Kant, Immanuel. *Critique of Pure Reason* [CPR], translated by P. Guyer and A. Wood. Cambridge: Cambridge University Press, 1998.

Kant, Immanuel. Postumously published first introduction to *Critique of the Power of Judgment* [EE], translated by P. Guyer and E. Matthews. Cambridge: Cambridge University Press, 2000. *Werke* vol. 12.

Kant, Immanuel. *Critique of the Power of Judgment* [CJ], translated by P. Guyer and E. Matthews. Cambridge: Cambridge University Press, 2000.

Secondary Literature

Allison, H. E. *Kant's Transcendental Idealism*. Revised and Enlarged Edition. New Haven, CT: Yale University Press, 2004.

Beiser, F. C. "Introduction: Hegel and the Problem of Metaphysics," in *The Cambridge Companion to Hegel*, edited by F. C. Beiser. Cambridge: Cambridge University Press, 1993, 1–24.

Beiser, F. C. "Two Concepts of Reason in German Idealism." *Internationales Jahrbuch des Deutschen Idealismus/International Yearbook of German Idealism* 1 (2003): 15–27.

Chalmers, D. *The Conscious Mind*. New York: Oxford University Press, 1996.

DeVries, W. "The Dialectic of Teleology." *Philosophical Topics* 19 (1991): 51–70.

Düsing, K. "Constitution and Structure of Self-Identity: Kant's Theory of Apperception and Hegel's Criticism." *Midwest Studies in Philosophy* 8 (1983): 409–31.

Düsing, K. *Das Problem der Subjektivität in Hegels Logik. Hegel-Studien* supp. 15, Bonn: Bouvier, 1976.

Grier, M. *Kant's Doctrine of Transcendental Illusion*. Cambridge: Cambridge University Press, 2001.

Guyer, P. "Thought and Being: Hegel's Critique of Kant's Theoretical Philosophy," in *The Cambridge Companion to Hegel*, edited by F. Beiser. Cambridge: Cambridge University Press, 1993, 171–210.

Horstmann, R. P. *Die Grenzen der Vernunf. Eine Untersuchung zu Zielen und Motiven des Deutschen Idealismus*. Frankfurt: Anton Hain, 1991.

Horstmann, R. P. "Hegels Ordnung der Dinge. *Die Phänomenologie des Geistes* als 'transzendentalistisches' Argument für eine monistische Ontologie und seine erkenntnistheoretischen Implikationen." *Hegel-Studien* 41 (2006): 9–50.

Inwood, M. *Hegel*. London: Routledge, 1983.

Kim, J. "Explanatory Knowledge and Metaphysical Dependence." *Philosophical Issues* 5 (1994): 51–69.

Kitcher, P. "Projecting the Order of Nature," in *Kant's Philosophy of Physical Science*, edited by R. E. Buts. Dordrecht: Reidel, 1986, 201–235.

Kreines, J. "Between the Bounds of Experience and Divine Intuition: Kant's Epistemic Limits and Hegel's Ambitions." *Inquiry* 50, no. 3 (2007): 306–34.

Kreines, J. "Hegel: Metaphysics without Pre-Critical Monism." *Bulletin of the Hegel Society of Great Britain* 57 (2008): 48–70.

Kreines, J. "Hegel's Critique of Pure Mechanism and the Philosophical Appeal of the Logic Project." *European Journal of Philosophy* 12, no. 1 (2004): 38–74.

Kreines, J. "Kant on the Laws of Nature: Laws, Necessitation, and the Limitation of Our Knowledge." *European Journal of Philosophy* 17, no. 4 (2009): 527–558.

Kreines, J. *Reason in the World: Hegel's Metaphysics and Its Philosophical Appeal*. Oxford: Oxford University Press, 2015.

Kreines, J. "The Logic of Life: Hegel's Philosophical Defense of Teleological Explanation in Biology," in *The Cambridge Companion to Hegel and Nineteenth-Century Philosophy*, edited by F. Beiser. Cambridge: Cambridge University Press, 2008, 344–77.

Pippin, R. *Hegel's Idealism*. Cambridge: Cambridge University Press, 1989.

Pippin, R. "The Significance of Self-Consciousness In Idealist Theories of Logic." *Proceedings of the Aristotelian Society* CXIV (2014): 145–166.

Proops, I. "Kant's First Paralogism." *Philosophical Review* 119, no. 4 (2010): 449–495.

Rohlf, M. "The Ideas of Pure Reason," in *The Cambridge Companion to Kant's Critique of Pure Reason*, edited by P. Guyer. Cambridge: Cambridge University Press, 2010, 190–209.

Russell, B. *The Analysis of Matter*. London: Kegan Paul, 1927.

Schaffer, J. "Is There a Fundamental Level?" *Noûs* 37 (2003): 498–517.

Schaffer, J. "Monism: The Priority of the Whole." *Philosophical Review* 119, no. 1 (2010): 31–76.

Siep, L. *Der Weg der Phänomenologie des Geistes*. Frankfurt: Suhrkamp, 2000.

Stern, R. *Hegelian Metaphysics*. Oxford: Oxford University Press, 2009.

Westphal, K. R. *Hegel's Epistemological Realism*. Dordrecht: Kluwer, 1989.

Zuckert, R. *Kant on Beauty and Biology: An Interpretation of the Critique of Judgment*. Cambridge: Cambridge University Press, 2007.

PART IV

THE *ENCYCLOPEDIA* PROJECT, *PHILOSOPHY OF NATURE*, AND SUBJECTIVE SPIRIT

CHAPTER 15

HEGEL'S *ENCYCLOPEDIA OF THE PHILOSOPHICAL SCIENCES IN OUTLINE*

ANGELICA NUZZO

THE comprehensive, all-embracing, and exhaustive systematic form that Hegel confers to his philosophy has been at the center of the debate on his work since the very beginning. And there is no doubt that the unique system in which Hegel programmatically structures his philosophy—in Kant's aftermath and in contrast with the work of contemporaries such as Fichte and Schelling, Friedrich Schlegel, and Novalis—is one of his most enduring legacies. This can be ascertained by simply looking at the wide range of reactions that Hegel's systematic idea of philosophy has generated and continues to generate in our time. And yet among all the published works of the Hegelian *corpus*, there is only one book that directly and fully contains Hegel's 'system of philosophy' in its entirety, that is, as a 'system' and not as one of its parts, and that explicitly thematizes the structure of that system in its internal constitution. This is the *Encyclopedia of the Philosophical Sciences in Outline*, published in three editions (successively revised and augmented) in 1817, 1827, and 1830. The encyclopedic format is no novelty in the philosophical tradition, in particular in the aftermath of the European Enlightenment, which not only produced Diderot's *Encyclopédie*—the most celebrated "reasoned dictionary of the sciences, arts, and crafts"—but also consolidated the German custom of writing thematic encyclopedias to be used by professors as didactic tools on the basis of which they developed their lectures. Both with regard to the discipline of philosophy and with regard to the particular arts and sciences, encyclopedias displayed different ways of externally arranging their materials, ranging from the alphabetical order in distinct entries to a more or less logically organized succession of brief, compact paragraphs to be expanded during the oral presentation. In none of these cases, however, is systematicity connected with the encyclopedic form. Hegel's *Encyclopedia*, while historically inscribed in the German tradition of the second half of the eighteenth century, and externally occasioned by didactic needs (first in Nürnberg, then in Heidelberg, and finally in Berlin), brings this format to bear in a fundamental and programmatic way on his very idea of philosophy as a 'science' and as a 'system'. For Hegel, at stake in the presentation of the "encyclopedia of the philosophical sciences" is the central issue of the scope, function, content, and method of philosophy. Thus, the account of the peculiar nature of the encyclopedic form in which Hegel structures his mature philosophy in the *Encyclopedia* and the thematization of its internal development and immanent divisions in their necessity, which are the tasks attempted in this chapter, ultimately imply a metaphilosophical reflection on Hegel's idea of philosophy itself.

I shall now examine the *Encyclopedia* in light of the claim that Hegel's conception of the internal structure and necessary divisions of this work is ultimately identical with his conception of philosophy as 'science' and 'system'. I begin by briefly discussing the place of the *Encyclopedia* within the development of Hegel's philosophy. I shall do so in order to introduce the main issue concerning the relationship between the idea of philosophy as science, its systematic structure, and the encyclopedic form as this connection emerges in the Introduction to the 1817 and 1827–1830 *Encyclopedia* (E1817 §§6–10; E.§§13–14, 16). I then proceed to examine the topic of the philosophical encyclopedia and the root of its internal division in the three spheres of the Logic, the Philosophy of Nature, and the Philosophy of Spirit (E §§1–8, 15–18); and most important, I address the peculiar 'method' or the inner logic that governs the unfolding of this division in its necessity, the method that structures its progressive dynamic and dialectical development in the forms of a "circle of circles" (E §§15, 17). I shall look at the crucial 'transitions' among the different spheres or parts of the *Encyclopedia* in order to bring to light the reciprocal relation between the whole and the parts that shapes this work in a unique dialectical way. For, counter to the common, merely external, and arbitrary ways of organizing the materials of traditional encyclopedias, Hegel's contention is that the method in charge of developing the encyclopedic whole is given internally by the very content presented therein. The whole and the parts mutually determine each other, so that the systematic whole is produced, circularly, by the overall process that first institutes its parts as parts of—and in—that encyclopedic whole. At stake in the thematization of the method of the *Encyclopedia* through its transitions is the way in which the Logic as the first part of the system leads in its conclusion immanently and necessarily to the Philosophy of Nature; the way in which the dialectical account of nature in turn transitions into the Philosophy of Spirit; and finally, the way in which Hegel argues for the circular syllogistic structure of the whole whereby its three main spheres ultimately constitute the self-grounding, recursive, indeed 'encyclopedic' whole that is philosophy. Taking seriously the cyclical sense implied by the etymology of 'encyclopedia', Hegel shows how in the end we return back to the beginning—although in a different, thoroughly mediated perspective. The Logic is both the first and the last science of the system, although, as we shall see, Hegel leaves the last word of the *Encyclopedia* to Aristotle.

The problematic framework within which I shall discuss Hegel's *Encyclopedia* can be summarized in the following questions. What is the relation between the 'speculative method' (E §238) presented in the conclusion of the Logic and the method that guides the entire circular progression of the systematic whole of the *Encyclopedia*? Is the logical method the same as the 'necessity of the concept' that produces the encyclopedic division? To put the issue differently, is the dialectic-speculative method of the Logic both necessary and sufficient to understand the major systematic transitions—the *Übergang* from Logic to Nature, from Nature to Spirit, and the final conclusion of the *Encyclopedia* as a whole? Or are further assumptions necessary to integrate within the logical method the particular conditions pertaining to the specific object at issue in each systematic sphere? This is the long-standing problem that the literature continues to debate under the heading of the relation between Hegel's Logic and the *Realphilosophie*. Far too often, however, this debate loses sight of the fact that this is a problem that Hegel uniquely poses within the systematic framework of the *Encyclopedia*—from which it follows that the solution should also be sought within Hegel's *encyclopedic* idea of philosophy.

15.1. PHILOSOPHY AS 'SCIENCE' AND AS 'SYSTEM': 'PHILOSOPHICAL ENCYCLOPEDIA' AND *ENCYCLOPEDIA OF THE PHILOSOPHICAL SCIENCES*

Kant's transcendental philosophy sets the post-Kantian reflection on the path of an ongoing conflicted confrontation with the idea of systematicity. While Kant promotes the idea of system—precisely as an 'idea' of reason and as the most proper form and constitution of reason itself—to one of the central endeavors of philosophical cognition, he also denies that the system of cognition, being as such a necessarily complete whole or totality, is ever attainable as an actual possession of reason (i.e., as something more than a 'regulative' idea). And in this regard the transcendental and critical doctrine consigned to the *Critique of Pure Reason* is famously declared to be not the system of philosophy itself, but only the preparation for or propaedeutic to it.[1] On the other hand, however, the Kantian claim that human knowledge is grounded in and indeed made possible by a set of a priori concepts that are originally proper to our mental faculties and can be comprised in a complete and exhaustive 'table of categories' opens up to the idea of an encyclopedia that, unlike any open-ended collection of merely empirical observations and concepts (but also unlike a merely regulative endeavor of reason), may in fact lead to an exhaustive and actually complete system of cognition. This conflicted Kantian legacy shapes the development of German philosophy in the first decade of the nineteenth century.

In his well-known letter to Schelling of November 2, 1800, Hegel sketches out his early philosophical education as a trajectory leading from his empirical inquiries into the 'lower human needs', that is, into historical, social, and political themes (to which

---

[1] KrV B25/A11; see Horstmann, "The Unity of Reason and the Diversity of Life."

his interest in theological issues should be added), to 'science', that is, to philosophy. This turn, Hegel programmatically acknowledges, finally requires the transformation of the "ideal of his youth" into a 'system'.[2] To be sure, Hegel's contemporaries were as concerned with the idea of the philosophical system as he was. In his Jena project of the *Wissenschaftslehre* (the 1794 *Concerning the Concept of the WL* and the 1794–1795 *Foundations of the Entire WL*), Fichte conceives the system of the 'doctrine of science' as a deductive system of principles that proceeds from a first principle posited as the ultimate foundation of science. Schelling, for his part, thinks of the whole of philosophy naturalistically, not according to a linear and deductive logic, but according to the circular teleological logic embodied in the living organism. Fichte's and Schelling's views of systematicity are connected to different ways of envisioning a possible philosophical encyclopedia—alternatively as a deductive linear and strictly logically organized encyclopedia, or as an organic, circularly growing whole, the model of which is no longer the traditional 'tree of knowledge' but a circle of interacting causes and effects. To these efforts we must add Novalis's and F. Schlegel's idea of an encyclopedia that, arising from poetic and artistic inspiration rather than logic and scientific knowledge, ultimately—and contradictorily—converges into the notion of the 'fragment' to form the oxymoric idea of a 'system of fragments'.[3]

Hegel's Jena itinerary toward the philosophical encyclopedia develops in connection with his reflection on the systematic form of philosophy. However, Hegel's idea that philosophy is a 'science' that has (or rather ought to have) scientific form, hence should be developed in the structure of a 'system', first emerges in connection with the thesis that draws the concept of *Geist* or 'spirit' to the center. Both claims—the one concerning the systematic nature of philosophy or the idea that philosophical 'truth' is a 'whole', and the one concerning spirit as the unique 'subject' of the philosophical science—are famously presented in the preface to the 1807 *Phenomenology of Spirit*. As the subtitle of this work reveals, they are the topic of a phenomenological "science of the experience of consciousness." The *Phenomenology* is conceived as "the first part of the system of the science" (E §25A) or rather as the 'introduction' to the system proper.[4] In its conclusion in the position of Absolute Knowing, having exhausted the entire spectrum of 'figures' of consciousness and spirit (hence being itself systematic in its exhaustive character), the science of the experience of consciousness leads to the threshold or to the 'standpoint' of science, which is the logic.[5] At this time, however, given that the actual system is not yet in place, Hegel seems to leave us with a variant of the Kantian tension at play between transcendental philosophy—which announces the system but is still positioned outside of it as its preparation—and the system itself, which, in turn, is either declared in principle unattainable (for Kant, a regulative idea of reason) or is

---

[2] Hegel, *Briefe*, 59; see Jamme and Schneider, *Der Weg zum System*; Baum, *Die Entstehung der Hegelschen Dialektik*.

[3] See Dierse, *Enzyklopädie*.

[4] See, as a general introduction, Moyar and Quante, *Hegel's Phenomenology of Spirit*; also Forster, *Hegel's Idea of a Phenomenology*; Westphal, *Hegel's Epistemology*.

[5] See Nuzzo, "The Truth of 'absolutes Wissen.'"

announced as a future project. In fact, when Hegel's system eventually takes form in the first *Encyclopedia* (1817), the idea of a phenomenological introduction is dropped. While the function of introducing the system is herein taken by a *Vorbegriff* or 'pre-concept' of the Logic, an entirely transformed Phenomenology is integrated into the philosophical systematic of subjective spirit.[6]

It is an external event that precipitates Hegel's thinking of philosophy—already viewed as science and system—specifically in terms of a 'philosophical encyclopedia'. In 1808 Immanuel Niethammer appointed Hegel to the double post of rector of the Gymnasium in Nuremberg and of professor of philosophy in the preparatory classes. The Bavarian educational directive of the time prescribed that all speculative and philosophical themes taught in the lower levels of the gymnasium be collected for the upper classes in a 'philosophical encyclopedia'.[7] At this point, Hegel's broader program concerning the systematic structure of philosophy as a science begins to converge with his work on a philosophical encyclopedia to be used in his lectures. In the Nuremberg years (1808–1816) Hegel's different drafts of *Philosophical Encyclopedia* or 'propaedeutic' for use in his classes not only aim at offering an easily accessible exposition of particular philosophical disciplines, but aim also, and for the first time in Hegel's development, at presenting a reflection on the general overall structure of the whole of philosophy itself.[8] At this time Hegel not only further investigates the separation between non-philosophical consciousness and the speculative standpoint already at stake in the *Phenomenology*. He now explores the difference between 'usual encyclopedias' and what is instead a 'philosophical encyclopedia'; and he presents his conception of the internal division of the philosophical science as an *encyclopedic* division. As Hegel makes clear in his 1812 *Privatgutachten* to Niethammer, the whole of philosophy encyclopedically structured—or the 'general content of philosophy'—comprises three 'main sciences', namely, "1. the logic, 2. the philosophy of nature, and 3. the philosophy of spirit." All other sciences, which are necessarily 'non philosophical', are already included within the philosophical sciences with regard to their 'beginnings' and first principles. In a philosophical encyclopedia, Hegel maintains, they should be considered in these beginnings only (and not, for example, in their empirical developments: TW 4, 407f.). The logic is the only 'pure science' or the science of the pure essence considered as simple and in itself, while the philosophy of nature and spirit are 'applied sciences' that have as their object the pure essence respectively in its 'alienation' and in the return in itself from this alienation. This disciplinary partition, already latently present in the Jena system-drafts,[9] is now

---

[6] This crucial change in the systematic role of the Phenomenology as a discipline—and of the *Phenomenology of Spirit* book—has been at the center of important debates in the literature. See the classic Fulda, *Das Problem einer Einleitung*; Nuzzo, "Das Problem eines 'Vorbegriffs'."

[7] It is the 1808 *Allgemeine Normativ der Einrichtung der öffentlichen Unterrichtsanstalten* to which Niethammer had collaborated. See Verra, "Introduzione," 12.

[8] See Rameil, *Philosophische Enzyklopaedie.*

[9] In Jena, logic functions as the introduction to a separate metaphysics (in 1802) or to a *Realphilosophie* internally divided into a philosophy of nature and a philosophy of spirit (in 1803–1804, 1805–1806).

explicitly an encyclopedic division and, most important, is brought back to the dynamic of an inner, necessary development (the pure essence in itself, in its alienation, in the overcoming of its alienation).

In the Introduction to the 1817 *Encyclopedia* (E1817 §§6–10) Hegel institutes the identity between the science of 'philosophy', the 'philosophical encyclopedia', and the idea of an 'encyclopedia of the philosophical sciences'. The basis of such identity is the systematic character of philosophy. That "philosophy is encyclopedia of the philosophical sciences" has two general implications: first, philosophy is the *encyclopedia* of *all* the particular philosophical sciences since the presentation of the whole can only take place through the determinate account of each of its parts; second, the encyclopedia here at stake is *'philosophical'* to the extent that the separation and interconnection of its parts follows "the necessity of the concept" (i.e., is not an arbitrary division as in common encyclopedias; E1817 §6). The first implication confirms Hegel's long-standing conception of the *discursive* nature of philosophical thinking: philosophy is not a homogeneous monolithic totality of knowledge, accessible by a sort of intellectual intuition capable of immediately grasping the whole. The second implication points to the fact that the encyclopedia is properly 'philosophical' when its structure is brought back to the "necessity of the concept" and this, in turn, is the basis on which both the *separation* of the different parts of the whole and their *coordination* is established. This constellation offers the fundamental difference between Hegel's philosophical encyclopedia and 'ordinary encyclopedias': the latter are a mere 'aggregate' of empirically collected and extrinsically ordered parts, while only the former presents the true necessary system of the sciences (E1817 §10A; E §16A). But in addition, Hegel insists that "philosophy is also *essentially* encyclopedia"—which means that philosophy is 'necessarily system' or 'essentially system' (E1817 §7; E §14)—from which it follows, analytically, that "a philosophizing without system can be nothing scientific" (E1817 §7A; E §14A). And here Hegel offers a variation on the well-known claim from the preface to the *Phenomenology* ("truth is the whole"; but the whole is actual only as 'system': TW 3, 24, 28). He now maintains that truth "can only be totality" and this, again, means that only a structured whole constituted through "differentiation and determination of its differences" (E1817 §7) can guarantee the 'necessity' but also, significantly, the 'freedom' of the whole (E1817 §8; E §14A). Freedom is achieved by a movement of immanent *self*-differentiation brought about by the concept, or by thinking itself.

However, if the philosophical encyclopedia is philosophy developed as a system, this system should not be brought back to an isolated "particular principle separated from all other principles." On the contrary, "the principle of a truer philosophy is to contain in itself all the particular principles" (E1817 §8). This holds true, Hegel argues, in two respects. On the one hand, this principle is displayed in the philosophical encyclopedia to the extent that each encyclopedic discipline appears as the branch of a unique totality. On the other hand, however, with this claim we meet the specific additional dimension that connects Hegel's idea of systematicity to the project of the encyclopedia, namely, the *historical* dimension of philosophy. In this regard, the history in which philosophy manifests itself in a multiplicity of different, often antagonistic philosophies, once taken up in the encyclopedic whole, shows each philosophy to be the manifestation of the same 'one philosophy' developing historically through different stages (E1817 §8; E §13). Philosophy is not just one among the many particular systems of scientific cognition; and the philosophical encyclopedia is not just the form of the 'truer philosophy' among many competing philosophies. Hegel's strong (and often contested) claim is that only *that* philosophy which achieves the form of philosophical encyclopedia or of actual system is the philosophy that assumes as its principle not a particular principle but the 'meta-principle' of including in itself all particular principles and philosophies. In other words, only the philosophy that finally comprehends in itself *all* the *historical* manifestations of philosophical thinking is successfully systematic and truly encyclopedic because it thereby proves to have gone through all the stages of philosophy's historical development, to have learned the lesson of past mistakes, and on this basis is now able to move on, carrying this entire history to a new level. This is precisely the stage in which all previous partially true (or particular) principles are embraced in their partiality in the most comprehensive 'encyclopedia'. As partial moments, they are now reconnected among themselves and reorganized within a different and new systematic totality (according to the 'necessity of the concept') to form the idea of Hegel's dialectic-speculative philosophy (E1817 §8; E §13). Thereby Hegel presents his own solution to the tension implicit in Kant's idea of the system—that it is, at the same time, necessary to reason and unattainable by it. The philosophical encyclopedia (or the true system) has been historically unattained (and unattainable) until philosophy, in Hegel's present time, has fulfilled the retrospective, historical task of embracing all past philosophical principles in itself, moved by the encyclopedic (meta-) principle of *historical completeness* (i.e., by the necessity of including in itself all particular principles). This thought has often been taken by interpreters as a sign of the *hubris* implicit in Hegelian systematicity.[10] However, it is important to underscore how the principle of historical completeness, viewed as a necessary implication of Hegel's idea of philosophical encyclopedia, should be taken rather as a sign of the historical rootedness of Hegel's reflection on the aims and task of philosophical thinking, and as Hegel's recognition of the essential debt that his encyclopedia owes to the history of philosophy. Finally, this point offers an example of how Hegel fundamentaly transforms the encyclopedic form: the history of the discipline is no longer, as it was in traditional encyclopedias, an 'external history' instrumentally and extrinsically used to introduce the reader to the main issues; it is, by contrast, the inescapable dimension displayed by the content itself (E §13).

After having established the identity of 'philosophy', 'philosophical encyclopedia', and the 'encyclopedia of the philosophical sciences' on the basis of the idea of systematicity, Hegel distinguishes the encyclopedic account of the philosophical sciences from the specific independent developments of its parts. And although Hegel's main

---

[10] See, as introduction to the topic, Duquette, *Hegel's History of Philosophy*. More recently, the issue of the closure of Hegel's system goes back to Derrida's Hegel interpretation (Derrida, *Margins*); see Malabou, *The Future of Hegel*, and De Boer, *The Sway of the Negative*, for a response to Derrida and to the issue in general.

objective is to present an additional argument in support of the specifically *philosophical* nature of his *Encyclopedia*, he implicitly offers an important insight into how we should frame the structural and formal difference that separates, for example, the account of logic given in the *Encyclopedia* Logic from that offered in the thematically corresponding published work, the *Science of Logic*, or distinguishing the encyclopedic account of the Philosophy of Objective Spirit from that offered in the *Philosophy of Right*. Such an insight is also important in order to frame the significant distance separating the encyclopedic presentation of the forms of Absolute Spirit—namely, art, religion, and philosophy—from the development of the same topics in the corresponding *Lectures* on art, religion, and the history of philosophy. Hegel maintains that "[a]s an encyclopedia this science [i.e., philosophy] shall not be presented in the extensive development of its particularizations but has to be limited to the beginnings and the fundamental concepts of the particular sciences" (E1817 §9; E §16).[11] It is not only a matter of how extensively a discipline is developed, that is, in its fundamental concepts, principles, and beginnings in the *Encyclopedia* as opposed to the detailed presentation often recurring to the historical wealth of empirical sources that Hegel uses in the *Lectures*. There is, in addition, an important methodological difference. Unlike the independent thematization of the parts of the system (*The Science of Logic, Philosophy of Right*), the encyclopedic presentation always keeps the relationship between the whole and the parts in view. This means that the immanent development of a particular systematic sphere is always accompanied by the awareness of *where* we stand, exactly, within the encyclopedic whole (i.e., by awareness of the necessary connection with both a preceding and a following sphere within the structured whole). For, it is precisely the advancement made in the consciousness of such a connection—*a parte ante* and *a parte post*—that first produces the whole as an encyclopedic totality. This point will be clearer in the next sections as we move on to an account of the inner division of the *Encyclopedia* and its peculiar 'method'.

15.2. CONTENT AND DIVISION OF THE *ENCYCLOPEDIA*

In the Introduction, setting out to present the content of the *Encyclopedia*, Hegel addresses the question of what is the 'object' proper to philosophy. And the first relevant point is precisely the fact (or indeed the 'inconvenience': *das Unbequeme*; E1817 §2) that distinguishes philosophy from all the other sciences. Unlike all other disciplines, philosophy cannot take for granted that its object is already and immediately given, determinately circumscribed, and acknowledged in common representations and by common

---

[11] See the cited 1818 *Privatgutachten* to Niethammer TW 4, 408. In the Preface to the 1817 edition, Hegel adds that although the encyclopedia is an 'outline' (*Grundrisse*), it does not exclude an exhaustive elaboration of the content; its central concern, however, is with the 'systematic derivation' or proof of such content.

sense (HEnz.§1–2, E §1). The same holds true for the 'method' according to which philosophy should investigate its assumed object—the method that would determine its 'starting point' and the proper way of 'advancing' (HEnz.§3, E §1). The first task of the Introduction then, is to give an account of the objective realm proper to the philosophical science. The issue is particularly relevant since the division or internal organization of the work, having to follow, as we have seen, the 'necessity of the concept' in order to produce a properly *philosophical* encyclopedia, is the division immanently required and yielded *by the content itself* and not by some external way of arranging and considering it. Thus Hegel's account of the thematic object of philosophy will also shed light on the meaning of the 'necessity of the concept' as the organizing principle of the *Encyclopedia*.

Hegel begins by addressing the issue of philosophy's content in a *formal* way. The first and most general claim is that philosophy, just as religion, has 'truth'—and "truth in the highest sense" as its object (for, "god, and only god is the truth"; Enz.§1). Truth is manifested both in the realm of the infinite and in that of the finite, where our common representations seem to have a concrete grasp of their objects. The realm of the finite embraces nature, the human spirit, and their "relation to each other and to god as to their truth" (E §1). Philosophy, however, is defined not by the material type of objects it considers, but by the specific way in which it considers them. And here lies not only the difference between philosophy and the common representation of things, but also the difference between philosophy and religion (E §4). Since at stake in philosophy are not 'representations' but 'concepts', the task is to understand how thinking and 'conceptual knowledge [*denkendes Enkennen*]' in confronting their object move from common representations to concepts (E §§1, 5). From this, a first working definition of philosophy is reached. Philosophy is "the consideration of objects in thinking [*denkende Betrachtung der Gegenstände*]" (E §2).[12] Thereby philosophy is formally defined by the way in which it considers its objects, namely, through thinking (and not, in the first place, by the material type of objects it considers). This accounts, among other things, for the comprehensive character that the philosophical encyclopedia displays in relation not only to the particular sciences, but also to other types of encyclopedias. In principle, any object can be a topic of philosophical investigation insofar as it is an object of thinking.[13] And yet, while philosophy is a mode of thinking, it is also a "peculiar mode of thinking," the specific difference being indicated by that through which thinking "becomes knowledge and conceptual knowledge [*begreifendes Erkennen*]." Herein we meet the important distinction between the manifold 'forms of thinking'—such as 'feeling, intuition, representation' (E §2), as well as images, purposes, and desires, which populate our ordinary consciousness (E §3) and constitute our different attitudes toward things—and 'thinking *as form*' (E §2). Significantly, it is the latter that circumscribes, at the most general level, the realm of philosophy and the domain of the philosophical encyclopedia as the realm of properly 'conceptual knowledge'.

---

[12] Hegel italicizes *denkende Betrachtung*.
[13] This is the point made in HEnz. §9, E §16, and discussed earlier.

Once the domain of philosophy has been *formally* defined through the specific modality of 'conceptual knowledge' and inscribed in the highest dimension of 'thinking *as form*', Hegel moves on to integrate the *content* into this domain, thereby establishing the comprehensiveness of the system of philosophy on the objective side as well. And it is here that we can discern Hegel's appropriation and transformation (in the aftermath of Kant's criticism) of the topics of traditional metaphysics (as *philosophia prima*), and at the same time their reconciliation (this time, beyond Kant's transcendentalism) with a new conception of experience. Hegel underscores that philosophy should conceive of the peculiarity of its object not only in contrast to the other sciences, but also in contrast to what the tradition has considered the topic of philosophical speculation, seeking it either beyond experience (metaphysics) or in an experience that was assumed by definition as separated from all matters spiritual (empiricism and Kant).[14] In fact, Hegel claims that philosophy's "topic [*Inhalt*] is none other than the basic content [*Gehalt*] that has originally been produced and that produces itself in the realms of the living spirit, a content [*Gehalt*] made into a *world*, namely, the outer and inner world of consciousness." In sum, Hegel concludes, "the topic [*Inhalt*] of philosophy is *actuality* [*Wirklichkeit*]." And he significantly adds: "Experience is the closest consciousness of such a topic" (E §6). Traditional ontology—or the idea of philosophy as the science of being *qua* being—is thereby transformed into an immanent conception of reality, where reality is the constructed and self-produced actuality of the 'living spirit', realized and wholly manifested in the objectivity of a 'world'. Such a world, however, far from being a transcendent (cosmological) object or an antinomic idea set beyond the limits of experience (as for Kant), is constitutively permeated by consciousness—it is consciousness's own, self-produced internal and external reality—and is accordingly always an experienced world. Indeed, if 'objects' such as 'freedom, spirit, god' are certainly not given in *sensible* experience, in professing a less limited conception of experience than Kant, Hegel now reclaims these objects to consciousness. These objects are, in fact, present to consciousness, they are its very content, and "what is in consciousness in general is experienced"—this is, Hegel observes, a simple 'tautological proposition' (E §8). It follows that what philosophical or conceptual knowledge reveals (and may remain instead hidden to other forms of representation) is the necessary convergence and agreement (the *Übereinstimmung*) of 'actuality and experience'. Indeed, appropriating the traditional definition of truth as correspondence, Hegel claims that this agreement "may be regarded as at least an external measure of the truth of a philosophy." But he carries this point a step further by turning it into the defining task of philosophical knowledge. "It must be regarded as the highest final goal of science to bring about through the cognition of this agreement [i.e., of actuality and experience] the reconciliation [*Versöhnung*] of reason that is self-conscious [*selbstbewusste Vernunft*] with reason that *exists* [*seiende Vernunft*], namely, with actuality" (E §6). If truth is the chief topic of philosophy (E §6), truth is a relation of correspondence and agreement that has reason as its protagonist.

---

[14] Clearly, E §§6–8 contain, *in nuce*, the thought that Hegel will develop in the Positions of Thinking toward Objectivity in the *Vorbegriff* to the Logic.

For, reason displays different forms that, despite their seeming opposition (at least for ordinary consciousness), are instead manifestations of the one *Vernunft*. This is 'self-conscious reason', present and at work, subjectively, in the experience of the world as well as in the production (and self-production) that is the world itself. But reason is also, objectively, the deeper rational dimension of actuality itself—of *Wirklichkeit* insofar as actuality is the existent form assumed by reason as '*seiende Vernunft*'. To be sure, the convergence—which is both correspondence and conciliation, *Übereinstimmung* and *Versöhnung*—that Hegel indicates with this program is also the convergence of the the-oretical and the practical function of philosophy.[15] Science, just as truth, is a rational activity in which the theoretical and practical dimensions converge: to recognize and to know that actuality and experience constitute a unity (*Übereinstimmung*), to recognize and to know that reason is one and the same reason in its self-conscious and in its exist-ent manifestations, is to produce or 'to bring about' the 'reconciliation' of the two sides, that is, it is to bring into existence a new and higher—indeed a reconciled—form of actuality, a new 'world'. Technically, for Hegel, the term *Wirklichkeit* indicates precisely this multilayered, constructed convergence. *Wirklichkeit* is the sediment or the objecti-vization of reason's activity, the solid reality assumed by an 'activity' (*Wirken*) that has shown and continues to show its *efficacy* (*Wirksamkeit*) in the world precisely by consti-tuting and reconstituting this world. The historicity of philosophical thinking goes hand in hand with the historicity of the world as constituted by reason's most proper activity. As philosophy's task is the rational or conceptual comprehension of actuality, this task expresses the practical efficacy of reason in the world.

It is relevant that in the 1827 edition Hegel adds a remark to Enz. §6 on the concept of *Wirklichkeit*, clarifying the misunderstandings generated by the famous passage of the Preface to the *Philosophy of Right*, which claimed the rationality of the actual and the actuality of the rational.[16] In both texts Hegel presents the same thought regarding the function and content of philosophical knowledge. The core of Hegel's remark regards the object of the philosophical science, namely, *Vernunft* that possesses *Wirklichkeit*, as one of the most proper forms of activity and as its objective worldly manifestation. It is just as false to claim that reason does not have the power of actualizing its ideas (i.e., that reason remains a mere unreal and unfulfilled 'ought to') as it is to claim that every-thing that is (for the simple fact of existing) is rational. For, as the Logic teaches, 'actual-ity' is not the same as 'appearance' or as 'existence'—*Wirklichkeit* or the actuality of the rational is not *Erscheinung*, is no indistinct *Dasein*, and no mere *Existenz* (E §6A). The latter lack precisely that necessity and self-affirming efficacy that reason confers to the former and to this alone.

In the 'preparatory concept' or *Vorbegriff* of the Logic, Hegel confirms this general view of the nature of philosophical rationality by introducing the notion of 'objective

---

[15] The former term indicates, as I already have mentioned, the traditional problem of truth; the latter has an important religious (and Christian) connotation, indicating the conciliation of the divine and the world brought forth by the figure of Christ.

[16] For a recent reading of this passage, see Stern, *Hegelian Metaphysics* (part I).

thinking' (*objektiver Gedanke*) (E §§24–25; TW 5, 43).[17] "The expression of *objective thinking* indicates the *truth*, which ought to be the absolute *object*, and not only the *aim* of philosophy" (E §25). Truth is the immanent 'absolute object', or the dimension within which philosophical thinking is always and necessarily inscribed. It is not a separate, external 'aim' toward which thinking strives (and may or may not reach or simply approximate)—thinking remaining, in this way, merely subjective thinking or a position of consciousness (like the series analyzed in the *Phenomenology*; E §25A). Truth is instead 'objective' thinking because it is not merely the truth of *self-conscious* reason, but brings to light the objective rationality or 'essentiality' *of things* themselves (it is the truth of *seiende Vernunft*, as claimed in E §6). Moreover, Hegel explains that "the expression 'objective thinking' means the same as the claim that understanding, reason is in the world" (E §25A). Thinking is *objective* because rationality does not remain separated from things (as in Kant's transcendentalism), but immanently shapes the structure and the historical manifestations of the world itself. This is, to be sure, precisely the meaning of the much-contested claim of the Preface to the *Philosophy of Right* regarding the actuality of reason and the rationality of actuality.

In Hegel's presentation of the content of philosophy in E §6, we already have the full indication of how he conceives the content of the *Encyclopedia* in its internal divisions. Reason and its actuality are the object of the conceptual knowledge proper to philosophy; but reason is also the subject of (or the subject doing) such knowledge. Accordingly, given the nature of a properly *philosophical* encyclopedia, it is rationality itself (or 'objective thinking') in its internal constitution that should produce the partition of the system so that, *vice versa*, the partition of the encyclopedic system can be taken, directly, as the philosophical manifestation of the systematic structure of reason. Thus, in construing the encyclopedia of the philosophical sciences, reason thematizes or thinks itself, as it were, in its necessary systematic development. This explains why in 1827–1830 Hegel concludes the entire *Encyclopedia* with a passage from Aristotle's *Metaphysics* XII,7 concerning the concept of *noesis noeseos* or 'thought thinking itself'. Having reached its conclusion, and from the height of this conclusion, the *Encyclopedia* appears as the objective manifestation of thinking that thinks (and has thought) itself in its inner immanent development.

Since "the whole of the science is the presentation of the idea, its *partition* [*Einteilung*] can first be conceived only from the idea" (HEnz. §11; E §18). Now, "the idea is the self-identical reason that, in order to be for itself, sets itself in front of itself [*sich gegenüberstellt*] and is an other to itself, but then in this other it is identical to itself" (HEnz. §11). Thereby Hegel concisely renders the necessary unfolding of the partition of the *Encyclopedia* thought in the main divisions of the *Logic*, the Philosophy of Nature, and the Philosophy of Spirit. The 'idea' as self-identical reason is the protagonist of this partition. In order to be what it is in a self-conscious, actualized way (i.e., to be 'for itself'), reason reflectively sets itself in front of or against itself becoming the 'other of itself' in an act of self-alienation. In this otherness, however, reason ultimately

---

[17] See Jaeschke, "Objektiver Gedanke."

recognizes itself and is thereby truly free in the sense of being-at-home in its otherness. The Logic as the first, foundational sphere of the system gives an account of reason considered 'in and for itself' (E §18) in its pure structures (i.e., offers an account of 'thinking' as such or of the 'idea' taken in the complete development of its pure forms); but the Logic also gives an account of the real examined in its internal logical distinctions (i.e., considers that which distinguishes, logically or formally, *Realität* from *Dasein, Existenz* from *Erscheinung* and *Wirklichkeit*). Hegel's dialectic-speculative logic now 'replaces' (or succeeds) both traditional ontology and the critical transformation of ontology that has taken place in Kant's transcendental logic (TW 5,45; E §25). On a general level, the *Encyclopedia* Logic can be seen as a compressed version of *The Science of Logic* first published in 1812 and 1816, before the first edition of the *Encyclopedia*.

The apparent separation of reason from its actuality—reason's 'otherness' (E §18) and 'alienation', as Hegel intimates already in the Nürnberg *Encyclopedia*, or its becoming other (E §18A: *Entäußerung*)—is the topic of the second main division of the work, the Philosophy of Nature. This is Hegel's dialectic-speculative transformation of metaphysical cosmology, as well as an account of the philosophical cognition of nature conducted in a close confrontation with the natural sciences of the time and with past philosophical views of nature.

Finally, the process of reason's 'reconciliation' with actuality, namely, the reconciliation of 'reason that exists' and 'self-conscious reason', or the idea's 'return to itself from its otherness' (E §18), takes place in the development of the Philosophy of Spirit. This latter, in its first division, the Philosophy of Subjective Spirit, completes the transformation of metaphysics and the overcoming of Kant's criticism by offering a dialectic-speculative account of psychology (along with anthropology and phenomenology). The second division of the Philosophy of Spirit is dedicated to spirit's actualization in the social, political, historical world. In the sphere of 'objective spirit' Hegel addresses, again in compressed form, the themes to which the *Philosophy of Right* (1820) is dedicated. Systematically, this sphere also contains a fundamental reflection on the topic extensively developed in the *Lectures* on the Philosophy of History, namely, 'world-history'. Finally, the last sphere of this main division, 'absolute spirit', thematizes the 'absolute' yet fundamentally historical productions of art, religion, and philosophy. These are the topics that Hegel explores in a less systematic and generally more historically oriented perspective in his *Lectures* on the Philosophy of Art, Religion, and the History of Philosophy.

15.3. STRUCTURE AND METHOD OF THE *ENCYCLOPEDIA*: THE METHOD OF THE SYSTEM AND ITS TRANSITIONS

The overall structure of the *Encyclopedia*, just like the structure of reason in its dynamic development, is not a linear progression leading from the logical account of the idea's pure forms on to its first alienation in nature, and then, even further away from the Logic, on to its spiritual reconciled manifestations in the sphere of spirit. As the etymology already suggests, the *Encyclopedia* displays a cyclical, circular structure—it is a progression that comes back to itself and grows on itself in the form of a circle. Famously, Hegel claims that in the encyclopedic presentation "philosophy manifests itself as a circle that goes back to itself" (E §17). More properly, however, given the homogeneity of the parts to the whole that characterizes the system,[18] the philosophical encyclopedia describes the structure of a 'circle of circles': it is a circular whole whose moments are themselves circles or recursive processes (E §15). Accordingly, in the whole that is the *Encyclopedia*, the end goes back to the beginning, so that the Logic appears as both the first and the last of the encyclopedic sciences. But then also within each systematic sphere or circle, the end is attained in the point in which the movement goes back to the beginning, and this, significantly, in order to produce the proper beginning of the new and successive sphere. Two general points must be made in this regard. First, on the basis of the process whereby circularity reconnects the end to the beginning (of the whole and of each sphere), the initial moment to which thinking conclusively returns is no longer the exact same moment that we had at the beginning; it is, rather, the beginning transformed (or mediated) by the process it has gone through. The Logic that as the first science of the system is an abstract discipline depicting pure thinking's progression in the 'realm of shadows' (TW 5, 55), at the end of the *Encyclopedia* appears as the science in which thinking's pure forms have gained natural and spiritual content—or actual and concrete truth—by having gone through the entire encyclopedic process (E §574). At the end of the *Encyclopedia*, the Logic is a science whose truth has been fully demonstrated by and instantiated in the manifold forms presented in the philosophy of nature and spirit. Now, what is valid for the whole of philosophy is valid for each of its parts. Hence, if we consider one part of the whole, for example the Logic, we see that the end of the logical process goes back to its immanent beginning, namely, to the pure immediacy of 'being'. But as it goes back to 'being' this time as it has been immanently transformed by the logical process of mediation, the circular movement produces the first step of the new sphere of Nature in which the idea simply 'is', this time in its *natural* immediacy, exteriority, and otherness: 'being', at this point, is the immediacy of natural exteriority (E §§244, 247).

Hegel describes the complex structural process that distinctively constitutes the encyclopedic totality as follows:

> Each part of philosophy is a philosophical whole, a circle that closes on itself; but the philosophical idea is, in each circle, in a particular determinateness or element. In addition, each single circle since it is in itself a totality breaks the limit of its element and grounds a further sphere. Thereby the whole presents itself as a circle of circles,

---

[18] In a system, the parts and the whole have the same nature, i.e., the parts of the whole are themselves wholes of parts: the whole is a circle of circles.

each one of which is a necessary moment, so that the system of all their specific elements constitutes the whole idea that appears in each one of them. (E §15)

At stake herein is the dynamic process that institutes the systematic whole of the idea (or the 'whole idea') as a totality of totalities. Each part, being homogeneous to the whole, is a circle that displays the idea, which, in turn, is omnipresent and immanent in each part. Each circle, however, is uniquely characterized by the specific modality—the 'determinateness'—in which the idea determines itself in successively specific manifestations (i.e., alternatively, logical, natural, and spiritual manifestations). Hegel describes this determinateness as the 'element' in which the specific determination-process of the idea takes place in each sphere. This element is the *medium* in which the comprehensive reality of the idea successively (and partially) 'appears' in each sphere. But it is also the *medium* that fundamentally *determines* the way in which the idea respectively shapes itself in each sphere. Moreover, the crucial point is that the conclusive step of the movement that, in each sphere, is responsible for closing the circle is also the very step that, breaking the limits of its own 'element', inaugurates the beginning of a new systematic circle (i.e., leads *outside* of the circle into a different manifestation of the idea). We have now to understand how this spiraling movement takes place; namely, in sum, what is the 'logic' or the 'method' that structures the act with which thinking closes one circle, thereby breaking, at the same time, the continuity of its element and grounding a new systematic sphere? What is the 'logic' according to which different 'elements' shape different manifestations of the idea and succeed one another to form the movement of the encyclopedic whole? This is the issue of the specific encyclopedic 'method' to which I presently turn.

At the most fundamental level, the circular recursive structure of the system must be brought back to the trajectory of the 'method' of Hegel's dialectic-speculative philosophy—the method or the 'logic' that immanently shapes the unfolding of the whole of philosophy in its internal necessary partition throughout the three main divisions (Logic, Nature, Spirit) and then within these main divisions themselves. But what is this method and where do we find Hegel's account of it? The Logic is an obvious and privileged candidate when looking for an answer to this question. And not only because, in the conclusion of the Logic, Hegel explicitly thematizes, retrospectively, the 'speculative method' that has guided the immanent unfolding of the first systematic sphere and that constitutes the very method of 'cognition' (E §§238–243)—the philosophical cognition that will be then seen at work within nature and the different levels of spirit's reality—but also because of the double position that the Logic occupies within the encyclopedic whole. The fact that the Logic is uniquely present in the beginning and in the end of the most extensive circle of philosophy elicits the assumption that the *logical method* (namely, the 'method' that internally structures the development of the first systematic circle from the Logic of Being through the Logic of Essence up to the Logic of the Concept) may be at work throughout the development of the encyclopedic whole, being responsible for its immanent unfolding. After all, the Logic shows that "the method [. . .] is not external form but is the soul and the concept of the content" and is distinguished from such content only by the fact that the 'moments of the concept' in the method are taken into account in their own right (E §243). Hence the question under which I propose to investigate the issue concerning the method of the *Encyclopedia* as a whole regards the relation between the 'speculative method' (E §238) presented at the end of the Logic and the systematic and encyclopedic method that guides the circular progression of the *Encyclopedia*. Is the logical method the same as the 'necessity of the concept' that produces the encyclopedic division? In this way, I will address, indirectly, the long-standing issue of the so-called relation between Hegel's Logic and the *Realphilosophie*.[19] My chief concern herein is to bring this discussion back to the unique *encyclopedic* context in which Hegel frames the issue.

I shall sum up my general claim and then proceed to its discussion by taking on the two cases of the 'transition' from the Logic to Nature, and the 'transition' from Nature to Spirit. The method or the 'logic' of the encyclopedic presentation is the dialectic-speculative method that Hegel thematizes in the conclusion of the Logic as the method that has successively produced the immanent logical development so as to ultimately close up the first circle of the encyclopedic whole.[20] The logic of the encyclopedic whole, however, is this *logical* method *as it is successively modified*—that is, specified and expanded—by its interaction with the different 'elements' characterizing the thematic objects proper to each sphere and successively produced by the immanent development (each one being the result of the previous sphere: nature and its 'element' being the result of the logical idea's first alienation [E §247]; spirit and its 'element' being the result of nature's transition to its 'truth,' i.e., to the 'subjectivity of the concept' in which the overcoming of nature's alienation first begins [E §376]). Thus, the method of the development, respectively, of the sphere of Nature and Spirit displays two components: (1) the pure logic that reveals the fundamental structures respectively of nature's and spirit's reality and its forms of cognition as displayed by the method of the Logic; and (2) the *modification* of this pure logical method that is produced by its interaction with the specific 'element' characterizing respectively nature and spirit. Such 'element' is the *medium* in which rationality is successively considered—nature being the idea in the exteriority of its space and time determined 'otherness', spirit being the idea free in the return from this alienation. The 'element' of nature and spirit in which the logical concept or idea is successively to be considered is constituted by the manifold representations that accompany our attitudes—cognitive and practical—toward nature and spirit, as well as by the concrete modality determining the way in which nature and spirit display their forms (for example, the contingency and necessity that makes freedom impossible in nature's realm; E §248).

---

[19] Scattered references can be found in the Logic and the Introduction to the *Lectures* on the History of Philosophy, where Hegel suggests a sort of 'parallelism' between logical forms and systems in the history of philosophy (see Nuzzo, "The Truth of 'absolutes Wissen' "); the *Philosophy of Right* is a text that has been interrogated for possible answers to the problem (see Nuzzo, *Rappresentazione e concetto*).

[20] Henceforth I take 'method' to mean, minimally, the inner 'logic' of a process (which is both the process that constitutes the object and its cognition).

Given the difference that separates Hegel's systematic idea from foundationalist accounts of systematicity such as Fichte's,[21] we can suggest that for Hegel the Logic is the first sphere and the basis of the encyclopedic whole not because it provides the first principles from which to *deduce* the propositions of the other sciences, nor because it presents the a priori concepts which should then be *applied* to concrete cases offered by experience and the sciences. The *logical method* is nothing else but the immanent formal process that actually generates (and, when viewed retrospectively from the conclusion of the science, has *de facto* generated) the Logic as a whole. Now, the Logic is the *formal* presentation of the *same* realm of 'objective thinking' or of the *same* rational 'actuality' that we encounter in a different modality, namely, in alienated form and in self-conscious form, respectively, in the spheres of Nature and Spirit. It is accordingly fitting that the logical process—or the logical method—will be found again underlying the unfolding of objective thinking when those other modalities in which rationality manifests itself are taken into account. This is precisely the meaning of Hegel's gesture that sets the Logic as the first foundational sphere of the system. The Logic is *methodologically* the first science in that it maps out the road that in its entire length constitutes the 'circle of circles' of the *Encyclopedia*. However, if method is, etymologically, the reflection on the road traveled *after* the road has been traveled, the Logic does indeed disclose the road to systematicity. But as it does so, it also makes us realize that there is much more distance ahead to be traveled. The Logic is the first step but is also still *only* a first step; it is a *necessary* condition for the constitution of the encyclopedic whole, but not a *sufficient* condition. The logical method must be further expanded and specified in interaction with the elements, respectively, of nature and spirit.

Let us now consider how Hegel programmatically discloses the necessary modification of the logical method, first in the transition from the Logic to Nature, and then in the transition from Nature to Spirit. Notice that the 'transition [*Übergang*]' is the crucial 'knot' in the systematic process responsible for (1) closing up one systematic circle; (2) breaking its specific element by producing a new element and object as its result; and finally (3) indicating the specific beginning of the new sphere precisely as a *new* systematic beginning [E §15].

15.3.1. The 'Transition' from the Logical Idea to Nature and the Logic of Nature

The Logic as the first encyclopedic circle reaches its conclusion when the account of the 'method' circularly leads to the self-thematization and self-comprehension of the pure 'idea'. The logical science ends at the moment in which it comprehends its own concept (i.e., in the moment at which it conceives of itself "as the pure idea for which the idea is"; E §243). This identity (the idea 'in itself' and 'for itself', or the idea and that for which

---

[21] See Rockmore, *Circular Epistemology.*

the idea is) has been reached by the development of *discursive* thinking throughout the process of logical determination. Now, however, when viewed as a result of the logical method, this identity displays the undifferentiated immediacy belonging to 'intuition'. In its 'unity with itself', the idea simply and immediately intuits itself as itself, (i.e., as the fulfilled and complete actuality of logical truth). At this point, Hegel names this identity in a way that allows him both to conclude the first systematic circle and to break the continuity of its element, thereby producing the 'transition' to a new circle and a new beginning (E §15). The 'intuiting idea', Hegel maintains, is 'nature' (E §244). The claim that posits the identity of intuiting idea and nature explains the 'absolute freedom' now attributed to the logical idea (E §244). This is the freedom of an absolute 'decision'—of a *Sich Entschliessen* that can only manifest itself by embracing its radical opposite and producing a radical break. Hence Hegel contends that the idea neither simply 'transitions into life', nor does it reflect on life in forms of 'finite cognition'—which would be a merely *natural* transition and not a real manifestation of freedom. Rather, the idea expresses its freedom by embracing and disclosing 'its absolute truth', that is, by letting this truth simply be in its utter immediacy. And the truth at this point is that the idea, being merely logical and pure idea, is "in a one-sided determination" By embracing this predicament—which is indeed the opposite of its alleged 'absoluteness'—by letting this predicament be what it truly is, the idea makes itself into its own 'otherness', into its 'specular opposite [*Widerschein*]' (i.e., 'nature'; E §244). Thus, the act of disclosing its truth—or *Sich Ent-schliessen*—leads the absolute idea to the free letting be (or letting go) of nature as its other, to the *Ent-lassen* of nature. Thereby the transition from the Logic to Nature is accomplished—and is accomplished in a properly 'dialectical' (and not in a deductive) way. At the same time, this transition produces the beginning of the new systematic sphere to which the Philosophy of Nature is dedicated.

Since Hegel insists that the philosophical encyclopedia must provide the necessary 'beginnings' (and the *Grundbegriffe*) of the different philosophical sciences (E §16), we should look at how the beginning of the Philosophy of Nature is made once the 'transition' from the Logic is accomplished. For, the opening of the new systematic sphere determines, methodologically, the way in which the Philosophy of Nature will proceed in its immanent development. Hegel opens the Philosophy of Nature presenting two lines of argument. First, he introduces the idea of 'nature' by addressing the different modalities in which we relate to it—practically and cognitively—as well as the different common and scientific representations that we have of nature. Thereby, the identity between the 'intuiting idea' and 'nature' that has concluded the previous sphere (E §244) is confirmed and fleshed out, this time in a non-logical, concrete way. Second, Hegel brings the common understanding of nature thereby disclosed to bear on what is, more properly and scientifically, the 'Concept of Nature' that has arisen from the transition from the logical idea. In sum, the Philosophy of Nature begins by showing, first, how the 'concept' of nature actually corresponds to common, concrete, historical 'representations' and practices, and by showing, second, what is the properly philosophical 'concept' that, in interaction with the specific element of 'nature', will guide the immanent development of the new systematic sphere.

From the 'practical' attitude that we assume toward nature, which is disclosed by the 'finite teleological standpoint', we can infer the characters of immediacy, exteriority, and contingency that we generally attribute to what we call 'nature'; and we are led to the "correct presupposition that nature does not have its end in itself" (E §245). The 'theoretical' approach to nature, by contrast—the one proper to 'physics' and to traditional versions of the 'philosophy of nature'—being a "consideration *in thinking [denkende Betrachtung]*" of nature does not appeal to external determinations of its object as the practical attitude does, but rather aims at a 'cognition of the universal' in nature (i.e., to nature's laws, genera and species), which in its turn leads to a view of nature as an 'organization' of forms (E §246). While the beginning of the Logic is a beginning that rests on no presupposition at all, both the Philosophy of Nature and the Philosophy of Spirit systematically develop on the basis of presupposed representations of their respective objects. These representations are not only common ways of relating to their specific objects and historical notions of them, but also are implied by the intra-systematic conceptions yielded by the transition from the previous sphere. Accordingly, the end of the Logic posits nature as exteriority and otherness (with regard to the idea); the beginning of the Philosophy of Nature confirms this result, underscoring how those formal determinations of exteriority and otherness are implied in the practical and theoretical attitude of man toward nature. Hegel's point, however, is to insist that what the dialectic-speculative comprehension of nature must overcome is the one-sidedness of such common-sense un-scientific 'presuppositions' (E §245). Thus, in contrast to the *practical* attitude toward nature, at stake now is the 'method'—or the *Betrachtungsweise*—that, given by the very 'concept' of nature, immanently guides the unfolding of Nature as a whole (E §245); while in contrast to the *theoretical* attitude of 'physics' at stake in Hegel's new, speculative 'philosophy of nature' is the '*conceptual* consideration [*begreifende Betrachtung*]' (E §246) of the universal and necessary development of its object. This objective is achieved by endorsing a method guided by 'the proper, immanent necessity' of the concept of its object so that the articulation of the 'philosophy of nature' is ultimately the 'self-determination' of the concept of nature itself (E §246). This twofold claim now specifies, in the case of the object 'nature', the general contention that Hegel presented with regard to the overall method of the *Encyclopedia*, namely, that its divisions be produced by the 'necessity of the concept' (HEnz. §6; E §246). Now at stake is not the pure logical concept, but rather the concept *of nature* or the concept *that exists in and as nature.*

This leads directly to Hegel's thematization of the 'Concept of Nature' (E §§247–251). The 'concept' of nature is the result of the conclusion of the Logic, which is now repeated: "nature is the idea in the form of otherness." With regard to the task of developing this concept in its internal immanent determinations, this definition means not only that nature is exteriority with regard to the idea; it also now means that "exteriority constitutes the very determination in which the idea is nature" (E §247). Exteriority is the fundamental feature proper to 'nature' as the 'element' in which the concept develops (the first appearances of which are space and time and matter); hence it is one of the chief determinations that modify the logical method presented at the end of the first systematic sphere.

Accordingly, Hegel claims that immersed "in this exteriority the determinations of the concept have the appearance of an *indifferent subsistence* and of the *singularization* [*Vereinzelung*] against each other." The modality in which nature displays its forms of existence [*Dasein*] is 'necessity and contingency', not freedom (E §248). 'Contradiction' is present in nature as a contradiction in natural *existence*. At the most general level, what nature displays is the contradiction between the 'necessity' and lawfulness of its forms (the ground of which is the concept) and their 'contingency' and utter lack of regularity (E §250). Importantly, this is a contradiction that nature cannot resolve (this is nature's distinctive '*Ohnmacht*' or powerlessness; E §250A) but has its 'right' in it (E §250). Ultimately, this is the contradiction that leads the philosophy of nature to its end and to its transition to spirit.

The movement that articulates its successive levels and gives the inner method and division of Hegel's philosophy of nature, up to its transition to spirit, is the movement whereby "the idea *posits* itself as that which it is *in itself*," that is, the movement whereby the idea "from its immediacy and exteriority, which is *death*, goes into itself in order to be first as *living being*, and then to overcome this determination in which it is only life, and to produce itself in the existence of spirit." The latter is now disclosed as the "truth and final end [*Endzweck*] of nature" (E §251)—that end which the common-sense practical, teleological attitude toward nature correctly considers external to it (E §245).

15.3.2. The 'Transition' from Nature to Spirit and the Logic of Spirit

The Philosophy of Nature brings the development of the concept of nature to its conclusion by showing the way in which the contradiction that has animated nature throughout in the unfolding of its manifold forms (mechanical, physical, and organic) up to the existence of living animal 'subjectivity' finally brings the natural individual to its end (i.e., first to its 'illness' then to 'death'; E §371, §375). Natural death dialectically entails the 'transition' to—hence the beginning of—the new sphere of spirit. Illness already manifests the 'conflict [*Konflikt*]' and the unmediated contradiction taking place within the natural individual organism between its organic and inorganic nature, between the fluidity of the life of the whole and the fixation that is natural individuality, and more broadly between the universality of the genus and the individuality of the singular organism (E §371, §374). In its illness, the organism is suspended between the possibility of healing and the possibility of dying (E §374). But even the death of the individual does not overcome the fundamental 'inadequacy [*Unangemessenheit*]' that undermines natural existence as such. The 'universal inadequacy' that undermines the natural individual consists in the fact that "its idea is *immediate*, that as animal the individual is placed *within nature*, and that its subjectivity *is* only *in itself* the concept but not *for itself*" (E §374). What brings nature dialectically to its end is precisely its success, namely, the fact of having achieved the form of 'subjectivity'. Now, being *only* natural, this is a contradictory subjectivity, that is, it is a subjectivity that lacks precisely that which defines it as subjectivity: namely, first, reflective mediation (as natural, it is instead 'immediate' despite all the mediation received through the genus); second, the fact of being more than natural (instead it exists only 'within nature'); and finally, the capacity of display-ing its being 'for itself' (while it is only the concept 'in itself'). This fundamental inade-quacy (that is both 'universal inadequacy' [E §374] and 'inadequacy of the individual to the universal' [E §375]) is the 'original illness' of the individual, the 'seed of death' that more radically undermines all natural forms as such (E §375), and ultimately produces nature's self-overcoming in spirit. While the 'death of the natural' (E §376), reducing it to 'abstract objectivity' (E §375), institutes the true identity of individuality and univer-sality that the living individual was never able to assert, it also conclusively mediates the immediacy of nature, installing subjectivity, this time in the broader circle of the 'life of the concept' to which it truly belongs. This is the movement whereby nature finally over-comes that 'exteriority' by which it was defined already in the transition from the Logic (E §247, §376). Now the overcoming of exteriority is the movement whereby "nature has transitioned to its truth," namely, "to the subjectivity of the concept"—and this is the new 'element' in which the concept is now posited. Importantly, subjectivity now con-stitutes the *Dasein* within which the concept is set to develop its forms of 'corresponding reality' (E §376). This is the new level of spirit. Spirit is the sphere of reality—the element or the medium—in which the concept from now on will develop its forms.

The Philosophy of Spirit begins in a way that parallels the opening of the Philosophy of Nature. Hegel first presents common and historical representations of 'spirit' and dis-cusses different modalities of cognition of spirit in order to rectify them in the dialectic-speculative perspective of his own philosophy of spirit. Then he proceeds to expound the 'Concept of Spirit' that constitutes the methodological basis for the dialectic-spec-ulative development of spiritual reality throughout its three systematic spheres—Subjective, Objective, Absolute Spirit. The knowledge of spirit, Hegel announces at the outset, "is the most concrete and hence the most difficult." He sums up the formula for spirit's knowledge in the Socratic 'absolute command' of self-knowledge: "know your-self." The point is relevant: if the philosophy of spirit is knowledge of the activity and reality of spirit, then such knowledge is necessarily 'self-knowledge'. But Hegel warns against taking this formula either in the sense of traditional empirical psychology as an investigation into the particular functions, character, and inclinations of the individ-ual, or in the sense of traditional anthropology as an inquiry into the essence of man. For, in both cases, what is true and 'substantial' in the reality of spirit remains properly unknown (E §377). In the history of philosophy, Hegel considers the traditional meta-physical account of spirit offered by rational psychology to have been rightly overcome by Kant's criticism, but already to have been reduced to irrelevance by a confrontation with Aristotle's *De anima*. This remains for Hegel "the only work of speculative inter-est on the topic" so that, after Aristotle, the only aim of a philosophy of spirit can be 'to reintroduce' the speculative concept in the knowledge of spirit (E §378). Against the traditional ways of thematizing the reality of spirit that dissolve it into a manifold of separate and abstract "faculties, forces, and [...] activities," Hegel underscores the fundamental 'living unity' of *Geist*. But he also rejects the traditional dichotomies that constitute philosophy's usual way of posing the question of spirit, namely, the issue of freedom versus determinism, the opposition of mind and body. Thus, at stake is a new speculative reconceptualization (a '*speculative Betrachtung*') of the living unity of spirit's manifold reality, capable of encompassing all the problems previously addressed bringing their antinomic contradictions to a true solution (E §378).

Hegel's speculative 'concept' of spirit and the specific method that spirit's reality (as element) requires a speculative philosophy of spirit to assume, immediately follow these considerations. Methodologically, the 'concrete nature of spirit' offers a 'peculiar difficulty' in contrast to nature. Nature does not properly 'evolve' as a unitary whole since its different forms remain independent and separated from one another in 'particular forms of existence'. In the sphere of spirit, instead, we encounter what is properly the '*Entwicklung des Begriffs*'—the immanent and unitary development of the concept. According to the movement of *Entwicklung*, "the determinations and levels of spirit in contrast [to nature] are essentially only moments, states, determinations within the higher levels of development." This means that lower, more abstract determinations already contain in themselves higher determinations—albeit only in empirical, inadequate form—and can be considered 'anticipations' of those higher forms (for example, in 'sensation' one can recognize in abstract form more developed contents that belong to religious or ethical consciousness; E §380). Within the encyclopedic division (or 'for us') the 'concept of spirit' has nature as its 'presupposition'. Given the general meaning of Hegel's systematic transitions, spirit is now presented as the 'truth' of nature, and as its 'absolute first'. In the transition to spirit, nature 'has disappeared' in the unity of subjectivity and objectivity that is spirit in its concept; and yet nature remains the basis as spirit's necessary presupposition. Nature will accompany spirit's development from the natural subjectivity of anthropology through the geographical determination of world history up to the different modes of the artwork's relation to natural materials and forms. Systematically, spirit is the movement of 'coming back from nature' (E §381). Freedom constitutes spirit's most proper essence. Formally or negatively, this means that spirit can make abstraction from all exteriority—even from its own existence—and this constitutes spirit's universality (E §382)—the freedom and universality that nature (and the natural individual) could never achieve. Concretely, however, freedom is the movement of self-realization whereby spirit's universality becomes particular and concretely individual in its actual manifestations (E §383). Ultimately, the movement of actualization of spirit's freedom is the movement of 'revealing' or *Offenbaren* (i.e., the process through which spirit posits and creates nature as its own 'world'; E §384)—a world that is both the reality of spirit's subjectivity and the sign of its absoluteness.

Works Cited

Primary Texts

Hegel, G. W. F. *Briefe von und an Hegel* [Briefe], edited by J. Hoffmeister. Berlin: Akademie Verlag, 1970.

Hegel, G. W. F. *Encyclopedia of the Philosophical Sciences in Outline and Critical Writings* [E1817], edited by Ernst Behler. New York: Continuum, 1990.

Hegel, G. W. F. *The Encyclopedia Logic* [E], translated by T. F. Geraets, W. A. Suchting, and H. S. Harris. Indianapolis: Hackett, 1991.

Hegel, G. W. F. *Werke in zwanzig Bände* [TW], edited by E. Moldenhauer and H. M. Michel. Frankfurt am Main: Surhkamp, 1986.

Secondary Literature

Baum, Manfred. *Die Entstehung der Hegelschen Dialektik.* Bouvier: Bonn, 1986.

De Boer, Karin. *Hegel: The Sway of the Negative.* New York; London: Palgrave, 2010.

Derrida, Jacques. *Margins of Philosophy.* Chicago: University of Chicago Press, 1982.

Dierse, Ulrich. *Enzyklopädie. Zur Geschichte eines philosophischen und wissenschaftstheoretischen Begriffs* (Archiv für Begriffsgeschichte, Beiheft 2). Bonn: Bouvier, 1977.

Duquette, David (ed.). *Hegel's History of Philosophy: New Interpretations.* Albany: State University of New York Press, 2002.

Forster, Michael N. *Hegel's Idea of a Phenomenology of Spirit.* Chicago: University of Chicago Press, 1998.

Fulda, Hans Friedrich. *Das Problem einer Einleitung in Hegels Wissenschaft der Logik.* Frankfurt am Main: Klostermann, 1965.

Horstmann, Rolf-Peter. "The Unity of Reason and the Diversity of Life: The Idea of a System in Kant and 19th Century Philosophy," in *The Cambridge History of Philosophy in the 19th Century (1790–1870)*, edited by A. Wood and S. S. Hahn. Cambridge: Cambridge University Press, 2012, 61–91.

Jaeschke, Walter. "Objektiver Gedanke. Philosophiehistorische Erwägungen zur Konzeption und zur Aktualität der spekulativen Logik." *The Independent Journal of Philosophy* 3 (1979): 23–37.

Jamme, Christoph, and Helmut Schneider (eds.). *Der Weg zum System. Materialien zum jungen Hegel.* Frankfurt am Main: Suhrkamp, 1990.

Malabou, Catherine. *The Future of Hegel: Plasticity, Temporality, and Dialectic.* London; New York: Routledge, 2004.

Moyar, Dean, and Michael Quante (eds.). *Hegel's Phenomenology of Spirit: A Critical Guide.* Cambridge: Cambridge University Press, 2008.

Nuzzo, Angelica. "Das Problem eines 'Vorbegriffs' in Hegels spekulativer Logik," in *Der "Vorbegriff" zur Wissenschaft der Logik in der Enzyclopaedie von 1830*, edited by A. Denker and A. Sell. Freiburg: Alber, 2010, 84–113.

Nuzzo, Angelica. "Hegel's Method for a History of Philosophy: The Berlin Introductions to the Lectures on the History of Philosophy (1819–1831)," in *Hegel's History of Philosophy: New Interpretations*, edited by D. Duquette. Albany: State University of New York Press, 2003, 19–34.

Nuzzo, Angelica. *Rappresentazione e concetto nella 'logica' della Filosofia del diritto di Hegel.* Napoli: Guida, 1998.

Nuzzo, Angelica. "The Truth of 'absolutes Wissen', in Hegel's *Phenomenology*," in *Hegel's 'Phenomenology of Spirit'*, edited by A. Denker. Amherst, NY: Humanities Press, 2003, 265–294.

Rameil, Udo. *Philosophische Enzyklopaedie: Nürnberg 1812–13.* Frankfurt am Main: Meiner, 2002.

Rockmore, Tom. *Hegel's Circular Epistemology*. Bloomington: Indiana University Press, 1986.

Stern, Robert. *Hegelian Metaphysics*. Oxford: Oxford University Press, 2009.

Verra, Valerio. "Introduzione." *G.W.F. Hegel, Enciclopedia delle scienze filosofiche in compendio*, vol. 1, *La scienza della logica*. Torino: UTET, 1981.

Westphal, Kenneth. *Hegel's Epistemology: A Philosophical Introduction to the Phenomenology of Spirit*. Indianapolis: Hackett, 2003.

CHAPTER 16

....

HEGEL'S VORBEGRIFF TO THE *ENCYCLOPEDIA LOGIC* AND ITS CONTEXT

....

ROBERT STERN

WHILE fundamentally a systematic thinker, for whom "the true is the whole" (PS 9.15/ ¶20), Hegel is nonetheless well known for certain individual 'set pieces' in his work, such as the master-slave dialectic in the *Phenomenology of Spirit*, the transition from the categories of pure being to nothing to becoming in the *Logic*, and the Preface to the *Philosophy of Right* with is notorious claim that "[w]hat is rational is actual; and what is actual is rational" (PR 14,1.14/20). These parts of Hegel's texts, along with others of a similar distinctiveness and centrality, have been vigorously debated and discussed, and a large body of literature focusing on them has arisen as a result.

The 'Vorbegriff' or 'preliminary conception'[1] to Hegel's *Encyclopedia Logic*[2] is not generally considered a set piece of this sort, however. In the literature, explicit treatments of it are relatively rare,[3] and it is not the direct focus of any very heated ongoing debate

---

[1] The English translation does not fully capture the significance of this title, where, as we shall see, for Hegel the Concept or 'Begriff' is his highest and most significant category, which is discussed fully in the third and final part of the *Logic*. The 'Vorbegriff' is thus not merely a first conception, but also something that comes before the *Begriff* or Concept itself, as this is articulated later in the text, and toward which we here start to make our way.

[2] The Vorbegriff appears only in the *Encyclopedia Logic* (1st ed., 1817; 2nd ed., 1827; 3rd ed., 1830), though some of the introductory material to the *Science of Logic* (published in parts between 1812 and 1816) has a similar role, particularly the section entitled "With What Must Science Begin?" (SL 21.53–66 / 45–55). The 1817 edition of the *Encyclopedia Logic* had a much shorter Vorbegriff (E1817, §§12–36 /56–67), which nonetheless covers similar ground.

[3] A recent collection of articles on it is Denker, Sell, and Zaborowski (eds.), *Der Vorbegriff*. Earlier contributions include Fulda, *Das Problem einer Einleitung*; Flach, "Zum 'Vorbegriff' der Kleinen Logik Hegels"; Flach, "Die dreifache Stellung des Denkens zur Objectivität"; Fulda, "Vorbegriff und Begriff von Philosophie bei Hegel"; Westphal, "Hegel's Attitude towards Jacobi"; Lucas, "Der 'Vorbegriff' der enzyklopädischen 'Logik."

or controversy. Indeed, Hegel's very placing and naming of this part of the text seems designed to downplay its significance, as a mere steppingstone to the more substantial matters that are to come.

Nonetheless, appearances can be misleading. For the Vorbegriff in fact contains some very important material that can be extremely helpful in helping us to understand Hegel's views, and particularly in enabling us to locate his thought in relation to his predecessors, such as the ancient and rationalist traditions in metaphysics, as well as Kant's critical philosophy. It also contains some highly important discussions of central philosophical issues and concepts, such as what Hegel means by 'thought', the distinction between what is subjective and objective, the nature of truth, and the differences Hegel sees between 'understanding' and 'reason'. There are also systematic issues raised by this chapter, concerning what role such a Vorbegriff can play in relation to the main business of the *Logic* itself, and how it stands in connection to the *Phenomenology of Spirit*; for the latter was itself characterized as offering us a way into the *Logic* (cf. PS .9.19–21/¶26), where it is not clear what room there is for both texts as 'ladders' up to the system of philosophy, even assuming such a system can be given such a ladder at all.[4] Thus, while the Vorbegriff may not have the high profile of some of Hegel's other discussions, many fundamental issues in understanding his thought—which are substantive, methodological, and historical—can be explored and better grasped by closely studying this part of his work.

The chapter itself is relatively straightforward in its structure. As usual in the *Encyclopedia*, it is divided into sections, each of which has a main part and then some remarks written by Hegel himself, followed by additions taken from students' notes.[5] The chapter runs from §19 to §83, where it is preceded by a series of Prefaces and an Introduction, and is followed by the main text of the *Logic* itself, beginning with Hegel's account of 'pure being'. The Vorbegriff falls into three main parts: §§19–25 are largely devoted to explaining what Hegel means by 'thought', where we have already been told in the Introduction that "to begin with, philosophy can be determined in general terms as the *thinking consideration* [*denkende Betrachtung*] of things" (E §2). Then, in §§26–78, Hegel moves through three main ways in which previous philosophers have conceived of how thought may be taken to relate to such things, exemplified first in the rationalism of traditional metaphysics; second, in Kant's critical philosophy as it developed out of the empiricist critique of this rationalism; and third, in the anti-rationalism of F. H. Jacobi and others. Finally, in a brief but very important discussion that runs from §79 to §83, Hegel gives what he calls "a more precise conception and division of the *Logic*," where he draws a distinction between the three 'sides' of thought that are "*moments of everything logically real*" (E §80), which he calls the understanding, the negatively rational, and the

---

[4] For further discussion of this issue in relation to the *Phenomenology*, see Stern, *Routledge Guidebook to Hegel's 'Phenomenology'*, 22–30. For a classic more detailed discussion, see Fulda, *Das Problem einer Einleitung*. For a recent consideration of how these issues also relate to the Vorbegriff, with further references, see Nuzzo, "Das Problem eines 'Vorbegriff.'"

[5] In giving translations, I will largely follow the text of Hegel, *The Encyclopedia Logic*, translated by Geraets, Suchting, and Harris, though this will be amended where necessary.

positively rational, where it is largely out of this triadic structure that the Hegel legend of 'thesis-antithesis-synthesis' is born. In the very last section, Hegel also explains his threefold division of the *Logic* into The Doctrine of Being, The Doctrine of Essence, and The Doctrine of the Concept, and how this relates to his account of the 'sides' of thought that has gone before. It should thus be clear from this brief outline that the Vorbegriff is a vital part of this first installment of Hegel's philosophical system, and is rich in the kind of material that is required for a proper understanding of his views.

In what follows, I will begin by situating the Vorbegriff in the *Logic* and relating it in more detail to the Introduction (section 16.1). I will then trace through the three main parts of the chapter that have just been outlined (sections 16.2–16.4), before concluding with a consideration of what problems the text may seem to raise for Hegel and his overall project (section 16.5).

16.1. THE ROLE OF HEGEL'S VORBEGRIFF

As a philosopher committed to a systematic approach, Hegel was famously ambivalent about prefaces and introductions to his work. On the one hand, he saw the need that a reader might have for some sort of preliminary orientation and motivation; on the other, he worried that by offering brief summaries or unsubstantiated conclusions, his reader might be tempted into adopting a simplistic picture of his position that was insufficiently worked-through. For, if philosophy really does require a properly systematic elaboration to be set out and defended, then it is only *with* the system that it can be grasped: all preliminaries are at best mere hints of what is still to come, and at worst can be positively misleading and even intellectually corrupting, as complex views get reduced to labels and simple-minded caricatures. Hegel's ambivalence in this matter is reflected in several works, including the Prefaces to the *Phenomenology of Spirit* and the *Philosophy of Right*, as well as his discussion in the *Science of Logic* entitled "With What Must Science Begin?". Hegel shows a similar unease about such matters in the Vorbegriff. So, for example, in §79R where he sets out the three sides of thought, he reminds us that "[l]ike the division itself, the remarks made here concerning the determinations of the logical are only anticipations and historical at this point"; and in §25 he touches on the fraught relation between the *Phenomenology* and the system, where he says that the Vorbegriff faces a similar difficulty in that it too brings in historical content and so in some ways is not properly systematic, while it is still needed as a way into the formal system itself. In reading the Vorbegriff, therefore, it is important to bear these warnings from Hegel in mind, as many of his claims will only receive their full elaboration and defense when the full system is worked out in the main body of the text.

What can help, clearly, is if one *already has* some sense of the system to which these preliminary sections are an introduction, for then one will have a grasp of where this is meant to be taking us, and so will be less likely to go astray. Thus one arrives at the familiar Hegelian idea that the process of philosophizing is essentially circular, as one returns to the beginning with a deeper sense of what that beginning amounts to, having previously come to the end to which it points us. Hegel thus doubtless expects his readers to have *already read* the *Logic* before they can fully grasp the Vorbegriff, which is meant to precede it. What, then, is the text to which we are here being introduced?

Hegel's *Logic* is the first part of his system of philosophy, of which the subsequent two parts are the *Philosophy of Nature* and the *Philosophy of Spirit*. As such, it is a formal treatment of the fundamental categories of thought and thus (for Hegel) of metaphysics, such as 'being', 'quantity', 'cause', 'substance', and so on. Rather than merely consisting in a list of such categories in a random order, Hegel traces a development through them, in the course of which their various limitations and interrelations are brought out, in ways which Hegel hopes will overcome the deficiencies we may find in using them. The highest categories are those of the Concept (*Begriff*), which comprise universality, particularity, and individuality. Hegel argues for a particular way in which they should be best understood, which he thinks will then enable us to properly conceive of the natural world in his *Philosophy of Nature*, and the world of mind or spirit in the *Philosophy of Spirit*, which comprises our own minds both individually and collectively, as well as our cultural productions, religious thought, and philosophy itself.

Thus, from this brief outline of Hegel's system as a whole, we can already anticipate some of the central themes of the Vorbegriff, particularly: the nature of thought, as the vehicle for our categories; how that thought relates to the world and thus its metaphysical implications; how thinking develops and is structured; and how Hegel's view of all this relates to and differs from the views of his predecessors.

As well as setting the Vorbegriff in the context of what comes afterward, it is also useful to briefly set it in the context of what comes before, particularly the Introduction.[6] One important common theme is again the issue of *thought*: why this is so central to philosophy; how this relates to other capacities such as perception, imagination, emotion, and so on; and how because philosophy has thought as its object, it must proceed in a presuppositionless and systematic way, without taking anything for granted. As is often the case in his prefaces and introductions, Hegel here takes himself to be arguing against critics of philosophy who claim that it is overly abstract, abstruse, and remote from our real concerns, precisely because it seems to focus on pure thought over experience, feelings, and concrete representations. The result, Hegel fears, is a kind of anti-philosophy or misology, which rejects the discipline in favor of some apparently more tractable and usable alternative, such as empirical science, direct religious faith, or unreflective common sense. However, as he hopes to show in what follows, to go in these directions while leaving philosophy behind is a false step that is fraught with peril: for this approach exaggerates the difference between thought on the one hand and these other faculties on the other, while the categories that philosophy reflects upon play a role at all these levels, where without such reflection we can easily be led astray. Moreover, the Introduction also signals how the history of philosophy can help shed light on these

---

[6] The Vorbegriff is also preceded by two Prefaces and a Foreword, each relating to different editions of the *Encyclopedia*.

issues, insofar as it too can be understood in a systematic way, in tracing thought's conception of itself through time, and how this has developed. Having alerted the reader to these themes, and warned her about the difficulties we have mentioned, concerning how philosophy is to begin (E §17), we then move to the Vorbegriff itself, which again starts by focusing on the nature of thought.

16.2. "Logic Is the Science of *Thinking*"

Hegel assumes that he can count on the fact that "we are all agreed" that "*thinking* is the subject matter of logic" (E §19A2), where such thought has its own constitutive categories and laws "which thinking does not already *have* and find given within itself, but which it gives to itself" (E §19R). This makes logic difficult because it is highly abstract, just as thought appears abstract; but it may also seem to make logic easy, because it only concerns our own thinking and its fundamental categories, and so can be conducted by just turning inward, as it were. However, Hegel warns us not to be complacent on this score, as a major part of his inquiry will be to challenge the way in which we standardly think about such categories, where such a sense of familiarity will then get in the way of this investigation by encouraging us to believe that no such examination is needed, thereby mistakenly leading us to dismiss the *Logic* as redundant and a waste of effort (E §19R).[7]

Moreover, Hegel warns, opinions differ regarding the capacities of thought, and how well or badly it can get us to the truth. For some, the truth may be seen as unattainable, while for others it may be attainable but in a way that does not require thought at all, as it can be reached in some other fashion, for example through direct experience or feeling. On the other hand, people may hold that it is only through thought that we can come to understand the highest things, such as God. At the same time, some may therefore take logic to have little value, and to make no real practical difference to how we see the world, while others may believe that it is only via logic that thought attains its true potential and is at last "free, at home with itself" (E §19A2). Thus, "[p]eople can have a high or a low opinion of the science of thought, just as they can of thought itself" (E §19A2). Finally, Hegel notes, people have become suspicious of thought for the way in which abstract philosophizing has led to radical challenges to religious and political life, from Anaxagoras to Socrates onward, through to the French Revolution: "For this reason, a justification of thinking with regard to its results was demanded; and the inquiry into the nature and competence of thinking is just what has very largely constituted the concern of modern philosophy" (E §19A3). The opening of the Vorbegriff therefore echoes

---

[7] On my account, this issue is also one explanation for the need for the *Phenomenology*, whose role in part is to get consciousness to see why such an examination of the categories is needed, and thus to undertake the "strenuous effort" of the *Logic*. See Stern, *The Routledge Guidebook to Hegel's 'Phenomenology'*, 22–25.

the concerns voiced in the Introduction, that an exercise such as Hegel's *Logic*, with its close investigation of thought and its consequent commitment to the latter's value, is not necessarily in tune with the spirit of the times, where doubts about the limits, usefulness, and importance of thought have been raised.

Hegel now proceeds to consider thought in relation to what he calls 'subjectivity' and 'objectivity', where he moves in the next sections from the former to the latter (E §§20– 25). Unfortunately, he does not make clear at the outset exactly what he has in mind in drawing this distinction, but it becomes more evident as the discussion proceeds. Beginning in §20, he starts by considering thought in "its ordinary subjective signifi-cance, as one spiritual activity or faculty *side by side* with others such as sensation, intu-ition, imagination, etc. desire, volition, etc." Thus, this is subjective in the sense that it considers thought simply as one of the subject's capacities alongside others, where it is also said to be subjective because thought here is seen as producing abstract ideas, which belong merely to the mental life of the subject and subsist "in their heads"; rather than being parts of the concrete world, they are the subject's representations *of* that world to itself. As a result, thought comes to be set over against sensible experience, which appears to grasp things in their individuality, and thus as they are apart from thought.

However, for Hegel this view of thought is inadequate precisely because it dis-tances thought from the world and has the kind of mistaken conception of immedi-ate experience that he had earlier criticized in the *Phenomenology* under the guise of 'sense-certainty', where he briefly reprises the argument made there that in fact 'appre-hension' is impossible without 'comprehension'.[8] Hegel thus thinks he can show that, far from cutting us off from reality, it is in fact *by* thinking that we better come to understand reality through the process of "thinking things over [*Nachdenken*]", so that rather than leading us away from the world into the realms of abstraction and purely subjective representations, the universals employed by thought help us to grasp that world more fully and adequately. Hegel argues that this more positive view of thought is reflected in many aspects of our lives, such as when we tell children about gram-matical rules, or act for general purposes, or look for general moral principles, or see natural phenomena as falling into general kinds or as governed by universal laws (see E §21A), where in all these cases we treat thought as guiding us to "the value of the *mat-ter*, what is *essential, inner, true*" (E §21), so that "we must first *think it over* in order to arrive at the genuine constitution of the object, and that by thinking it over this [goal] is indeed achieved" (E §21R). The truth we are getting at here is not mere 'correctness' or representational adequacy, but rather the fundamental nature of things, to which those things ought to conform (E §24A2; cf. also E §213A). Once this is allowed, we have taken an important first step away from a merely 'subjective' to a more 'objective' conception of thought.

Hegel then turns to consider in a little more detail how exactly this "thinking things over" in fact does manage to get at the fundamental features of the world, where he

---

[8] E §20R; cf. PS 9.69–78 / §§90–110.

accepts that it does so by going beyond what is immediately given to us in sensation or intuition or representations. He acknowledges, of course, that this may then give rise to a skeptical worry, one that he thinks lies at the heart of Kant's critical philosophy, which is discussed in more detail later (E §§40–60): namely, that by transcending what is immediately given, or even altering it in various ways, we are cut off from things as they really are. However, he thinks at this stage he can appeal to common sense, which is happy to accept that thought takes us to the truth by proceeding in this manner, as "it has been the conviction of every age that what is substantial is only reached through the reworking of the immediate in our thinking about it," where to think otherwise is only the result of the "sickness of our time" (E §22A), which Hegel hopes his *Logic* will be able to cure.

Thus, while more will be said about this issue in his later discussion of Kant in the Vorbegriff, and where Hegel signals it is primarily Kant he has in mind here,[9] Hegel thinks that at this stage he can now ask a further question: namely, if skepticism can be rejected, what does that tell us about the nature of the world around us and in which we live? Hegel claims that it shows that this world is not *alien* to thought and thus to us as thinkers, so that in "thinking over the genuine nature [of the object]," the subject is also "*at home with itself*" and therefore free, where through its own activity of thinking the mind is able to rise above its own particularity as an individual thinker and come to know what holds universally, for all thinkers, so that "the worthiness that consciousness ascribes to itself consists precisely in the giving up of our *particular* opinions and beliefs and in allowing the *matter* itself [*die Sache selbst*] to hold sway over us" (E §23R).[10] In the light of this, Hegel holds, we are entitled to take thoughts to be not just subjective but also *objective*, in the sense of reflecting the fundamental nature of things themselves, so that logic tells us not just about the structure of *our* thinking but also about the structure of the world, whereby it is also a form of metaphysics. Hegel thus famously writes at this point, "Thus *logic* coincides with *metaphysics*, with the science of *things* grasped in *thoughts* that in return have been taken to express the *essentialities* of *things*" (E §24).

Here, then, we arrive at the picture of objective thought that Hegel wants to defend, which he here puts in a variety of ways that all amount to the same claim: namely, that thoughts are not just subjective ideas in our heads, but they also structure reality itself at a fundamental level, insofar as what is universal is also inherent in which is individual and particular.[11] Thus, Hegel thinks he is in entitled to say (in a preliminary way, which will be further defended when he comes to consider further the relation

---

[9] Cf. E §22A, where he refers to "the standpoint that has been maintained by the Critical Philosophy."

[10] On the issue of freedom, see also E §24A2.

[11] Cf. "To say that there is understanding, or reason, in the world is exactly what is contained in the expression 'objective thought'" (E §24R); "nature [is] a system of thought without consciousness, or an intelligence which, as Schelling says, is petrified" (E §24A1); "This meaning of thinking is more precisely expressed by the Ancients when they say that *nous* governs the world, or by our own saying that there is reason in the world, by which we mean that reason is the soul of the world, inhabits it, and is immanent in it, as its own, innermost nature, its universal" (E §24A1).

between universal, particular, and individual later on in the *Logic*), that "thinking constitutes the substance of eternal things," while at the same time, as thinking beings *ourselves*, "it is also the universal substance of what is minded [*des Geistigen*]" (E §24A1). Far from there being a skeptical *gap* between mind and world, therefore, the two are fundamentally in alignment, and as thinking beings ourselves, we are uniquely able to bring this conceptual structure of nature to consciousness, by knowing (in a way that objects in nature do not) that both we and they *are* indeed conceptually structured in this way. Thus, "[n]ature does not bring the *nous* to consciousness for itself; only man reduplicates himself in such a way that he is the universal that is [present] *for* the universal" (E §24A1). As a result, our investigations into nature and the workings of the mind itself (undertaken in the *Philosophy of Nature* and the *Philosophy of Spirit*, respectively) may be thought of as cases of "applied logic" (E §24A2), whereby we look for the conceptual structures we consider in their pure form in the *Logic* itself to see how they play out in the context of the natural world and our own 'mindedness' in which they are embodied.

This means, however, that there is a fundamental *normative* nature to the way in which these inquiries are conducted, for if things are taken to be exemplifications of universals, we can ask how *well* or *badly* they exemplify them, and thus whether they are 'true' or 'false' as individuals this sense—where again Hegel takes himself to have common sense on his side, which is happy to ask of someone whether they are a 'true friend', for example, meaning whether they properly instantiate the nature of friendship (E §24A2). However, where common sense may find things more challenging is that we can ask how adequately the categories of thought manage to capture the nature of things in a fundamental way without leading us into incoherence, where this deeper reflection may take us beyond our usual view of these categories and what we ordinarily mean by 'existence', 'cause', 'freedom', and so on. It is this investigation of the possible limitations of such 'finite' categories as leading to something more satisfactory that forms the focus of the main body of the *Logic* (E §24A3).

Hegel has thus given a sketch of the position he hopes to defend further in the *Logic* itself, as a form of *objective* idealism, in the sense that it is a realism about thought and thus concepts, which do not reside merely within subjects who are thereby cut off from the world by this capacity to conceptualize, but are rather brought closer to it.[12] However, Hegel recognizes that this is not the only view that may be taken of such matters, and that other options concerning the relation between mind and world are and have been upheld. At this point, therefore, he turns to offer a brief and systematic overview of the history of positions (*Stellungen*) that have been taken on the issue of objective thought, in order to bring out where his view differs from these alternatives, and how it constitutes a worthy successor to them.

|

---

[12] For further discussion, see Stern, "Hegel's Idealism."

16.3. THOUGHT'S VIEW OF ITSELF: A HISTORY

The next part of the Vorbegriff is the only place in which the history of philosophy is given any extended treatment within Hegel's systematic writings, and the only published account of that history that Hegel presented in his mature works. While well known for his views on the history of philosophy, these are expressed elsewhere, either in his posthumously published lectures, or in his early works such as the so-called *Differenzschrift*; and while various predecessors are alluded to in the *Phenomenology*, they are not given any explicit discussion, in accordance with the approach adopted in that text. These sections of the Vorbegriff are thus a very useful source for understanding Hegel's views on the historical development of the philosophical tradition.

Prior to beginning his account, Hegel makes plain why such historical discussions are not given more of a role within his mature published writings, which is that they cannot be conducted in a properly systematic manner. But as with the *Phenomenology*, there is said to be some value in this treatment nonetheless, as it shows the role that the categories can play in our view of fundamental matters such as knowledge and faith, where it is such categories or "thought determinations [*Denkbestimmungen*]" which (as we have seen) will be properly analyzed in the main part of the *Logic* itself. Thus, how we conceive of the categories is a fundamental focus of the historical discussion that Hegel offers here, as this will determine how we view thought itself and the positions that are taken up concerning its relation to the world.

From this perspective, Hegel takes us through three such positions on the objectivity of thought. The first standpoint is that of rationalist metaphysics,[13] which starts out with a naïve confidence in the ability of thinking to take us to the heart of things (E §26). As is often the case with Hegel's discussion of positions of this sort, he will in fact want to recapture something of the spirit of this outlook, but to do so in a more sophisticated and knowing way. For, as it stands, he recognizes that such metaphysics is vulnerable to the complaints raised against it by Kant's critical philosophy, which casts doubt on

---

[13] Although this discussion is more historically concrete than anything we find in the *Phenomenology*, Hegel still leaves it somewhat vague who exactly he has in mind here. In particular, while it is clear he is focusing on pre-Kantian metaphysics, and thus presumably the seventeenth- and eighteenth-century rationalists who were criticized by Kant himself, such as Leibniz and Wolff, it is not so clear if he also intends to include classical Greek metaphysics in the mix. Some of the views he attributes to the metaphysical position, particularly its confidence in reason, are (as we have already seen) views he often also attributes to the ancients; but there is a post-Christian focus to the metaphysical position he theorizes here, while in one Addition, he seems to include within it the Scholastics but not Plato and Aristotle (E §36A), where in general, Hegel's very positive view of the latter two would suggest they are not really to be brought under this position and its inadequacies.

this confidence. Hegel therefore makes plain that he hopes this positive attitude can be restored, but in a less simplistic manner.[14]

Where Hegel concedes that rationalistic metaphysics is vulnerable, and where he sees Kant as doing great service in revealing this vulnerability, is in its view of the categories that it tried to apply in this unquestioning way, without distinguishing between thought concerning ordinary finite objects and thought about the special objects it claims to grasp, such as God, the soul, or the world as the whole (which are the three transcendental ideas identified by Kant himself as central to the metaphysical tradition he criticizes).[15] Hegel thus claims that this metaphysics took both the ordinary categories and the ordinary forms of propositional thinking, and attempted thereby to theorize about such objects, without realizing that it is not possible to move from one level to the other: for example, God cannot be thought of as 'existing' in the same way as a table can, nor can we just apply predicates to him in the way we can to other things. As a result, Hegel admits, rationalistic metaphysics inevitability got itself into conceptual difficulties in a way that Kant was the first to recognize fully, as using these terms it was not possible to settle various questions and aporia that then seemed to arise. So, for instance, Hegel suggests that rational psychology made the category mistake of conceiving of the soul as a 'thing', which then led to all sorts of irresolvable puzzles (E §34A); equally, when thinking about freedom, the concept of necessity that is contrasted with this is taken from mechanics, and thus the two are rendered incompatible with one another (E §35A). The early promise of rationalist metaphysics is thus one that it finds impossible to fulfill, because it has not yet reflected hard enough on the forms of thought with which it proposes to engage with its inquiries, but has taken them up naïvely and in what turns out to be a limited manner.

As a result of this failure, philosophy undergoes a counter-reaction, and moves from rationalism to empiricism, where this takes us on to the second position that thought takes in relation to objectivity, of which empiricism is its first phase and Kantian philosophy its second. Empiricism turns away from the apparently empty theorizing of rationalism, while also questioning the capacity of thought to tell us about reality, as concrete sensible experience is now given epistemic priority over the abstract speculations of metaphysics (E §37). Hegel is happy to accept that this correction to rationalistic metaphysics was needed, and has some value in bringing us back into contact with the world around us.[16] Nonetheless, Hegel argues, empiricism is also naïve in its own way,

---

[14] "This science [of metaphysics] regarded the thought-determinations as the *fundamental determinations of things*; and, in virtue of this presupposition, that the cognition of things as they are *in-themselves* results from *thinking* of what *is*, it stood at a higher level than later critical philosophising" (E §28); "The presupposition of the older metaphysics was that of naïve belief generally, namely, that thinking grasps what things are *in-themselves*, that things only are what they genuinely are when they are [captured] in thought. . . . The standpoint of the older metaphysics referred to here is the opposite of the one that resulted from the Critical Philosophy. We can fairly say that this latter standpoint sends man to feed upon husks and chaff" (E §28A).

[15] Cf. *CPR* A334–335 /B391–392.

[16] "From Empiricism the call went out: 'Stop chasing about among empty abstractions, look at what is there for the taking, grasp *the here and now*, human and natural, as it is *here* before us, and enjoy it!' And there is no denying that this contains an essentially justified moment. The world, the *here and now*, the

in holding that it has somehow escaped from having any metaphysical commitments of its own, where as a result (like rationalistic metaphysics before it) it fails to reflect at all upon these commitments and subject them to philosophical examination. But no matter how much it simply tries to stick to experience, some thought and theorizing are inevitably involved in its inquiries, so that far from escaping metaphysics, empiricism simply engages in it unthinkingly, and in a way that is therefore just as problematic as the rationalist's approach turned out to be.[17]

The great insight of Kant's critical philosophy, for Hegel, is that it sees more clearly than anyone who came before him that there is no possibility of experience without thought (thus taking us beyond the naïveté of empiricism), while also recognizing that the categories of thought cannot be just taken for granted as putting us in touch with the world (thus taking us beyond the naïveté of rationalism), so that its role in "[s]ubjecting the determinations of the older metaphysics to investigation was without doubt a very important step" and "certainly involves the correct insight that the forms of thinking themselves must be made the object of cognition . . ." (E §41A). Hegel thus accepts that Kant's critical philosophy represents a crucial turning point in the history of philosophy; yet at the same time, he sees it as fundamentally flawed. For he thinks that in conducting this investigation into our categories, Kant was led to treat them as *merely* belonging to our thought in a subjectivist manner, thereby cutting thought off from the world as it is in itself and confining us to the world of appearances. According to Hegel, this is because Kant made a crucial mistake: while he rightly saw that the categories of rationalist metaphysics were flawed and limited in their capacity to capture the nature of things, he did not see that our categories of thought are not limited to these or the way the rationalist conceives them, so that Kant took thought to be stuck at this level of inadequacy. But for Hegel, this was itself an uncritical assumption, where Kant's inquiry falls fatally short; for what remains to be seen, and what the *Logic* itself will attempt to discover, is whether our concepts can be further refined in such a way as to overcome the puzzles that Kant thinks are insuperable for thought. In this way, then, something of the old confidence of rationalist metaphysics can be restored, but on a new and radically different basis, whereby the categories are then fundamentally reconceived and not just taken for granted. Once this has been achieved, we can accept the Kantian insistence that our experience is conceptually structured, but without succumbing to Kantian fears that this sets the mind apart from the world; rather, we can take it that these conceptual structures map onto reality and so can treat thought as objective, just as Hegel had urged

---

present, was to be substituted for the empty Beyond, for the spiderwebs and cloudy shapes of the abstract understanding. That is precisely how the firm footing, i.e., the infinite determination, that was missing in the older metaphysics was gained" (E §38A).

[17] "The fundamental illusion in scientific empiricism is always that it uses the metaphysical categories of matter, force, as well as those of one, many, universality, and the infinite, etc., and it goes on to draw *conclusions*, guided by categories of this sort, presupposing and applying the forms of syllogising in the process. It does all this without knowing that it thereby itself contains a metaphysics and is engaged in it, and that it is using those categories and their connections in a totally uncritical and unconscious manner" (E §38R).

earlier in the Vorbegriff, and as he thinks both rationalism and common sense are happy to allow.[18]

However, this is to get ahead of ourselves; for, before this Hegelian approach seems worth trying, another response to the Kantian viewpoint must be considered, which constitutes the third and final historical position that Hegel discusses. On this position, Kant's apparent skepticism is rejected, but not in the Hegelian manner, but rather by turning away from thought in favor of a kind of non-conceptual knowledge that is taken to be the highest form of cognition. On this account, which Hegel mainly associates with F. H. Jacobi, conceptual thought is said to be limited to comprehending things by seeking their conditions;[19] but this means that when it comes to making sense of an infinite and hence *un*conditioned being such as God, it is useless, so that "God, or what is infinite and true, lies outside the mechanism of a connection of this kind to which cognition is supposed to be restricted" (E §62R). As a result, it is argued, such mediated knowledge must be given up, and we must instead adopt a form of immediate knowing, or what Jacobi also calls 'faith [*Glaube*]', because it is not based on any argument or reasoning, or search for grounds.

Hegel's response to this outlook is to claim that it sets up a false opposition between immediate knowledge and philosophical inquiry, such that "immediate knowing adopts an *exclusionary* posture or, in other words, it sets itself against the doing of philosophy" (E §64R). But, Hegel argues, as Descartes' *Cogito* shows, philosophy can happily allow that there are forms of foundational and non-syllogistic knowledge, not based on any prior rational grounds (E §64R). When the proponents of immediate knowledge try to be more radical than this, Hegel claims, they are then led astray by adopting an overly simplistic characterization of the relation between the notions of mediation and immediacy. So, for example, he argues that while the well-trained inquirer (such as an expert mathematician) may seem to grasp truths immediately, this is in fact based on reasoning that is now simply habitual and largely unconscious, just as our unreflective actions as adults are nonetheless mediated by earlier training (E §66). Likewise, Christian faith itself is not fully immediate, but comes about through education and enculturation (E §67), while thought and being are themselves mediated by one another (E §70). Ultimately, Hegel argues, the proponent of immediate knowledge must therefore fail to draw a clear distinction between what is immediate and what is mediated, as both imply the other, where (in a claim that will become clearer after the next part of the Vorbegriff) "[i]t is only the ordinary abstract understanding that takes the determinations of

---

[18] "Now, although the categories (e.g., unity, cause and effect, etc.) pertain to thinking as such, it does not at all follow from this that they must therefore be merely something of ours, and not also determinations of objects themselves. But, according to Kant's view, this is what is supposed to be the case, and his philosophy is *subjective idealism*, inasmuch as the Ego (the knowing subject) furnishes both the *form* and also the *material* of knowing—the former as *thinking* and the latter as *sensing* subject" (E §42A3).

[19] Cf. Jacobi, *Concerning the Doctrine of Spinoza*, 373: "We comprehend a thing whenever we can derive it from its proximate causes, or whenever we have insight into the order of its immediate conditions. What we see or derive in this way presents us with a mechanistic context."

immediacy and mediation to be absolute, each on its own account, and thinks that it has an example of a *firm* distinction in them" (E §70).

Moreover, Hegel suggests, adopting this position can also have broader consequences that are to be avoided if possible. Thus, in epistemology, this appeal to immediacy can lead to a kind of subjective dogmatism, where what strikes an individual as self-evidently the case is taken to be valid for all (E §71). As a result, virtually any belief can be claimed to be true using this criterion, as well as any conception of good or evil, as no reason need then be given in support, as long as the view is strongly believed or sincerely held in an 'immediate' manner (E §72). Finally, when it comes to religious faith, because the knowledge of God is non-conceptualized, it must remain largely indeterminate and abstract, as any more concrete knowledge would require mediation through concepts; but then the result is just a conviction *that* God exists, but no grasp of *what* he is, in a way that is impoverished and empty (E §73). Jacobi might reply with what is his essential claim: namely, that God himself cannot be mediated, as that is to make him dependent on an other and hence finite. But Hegel's response is that what mediates God is not an *other* in a way that reduces him to finitude, but that rather he undergoes a form of *self*-mediation, and so contains mediation *within* his immediacy, in a way that makes him determinate and concrete while also allowing him to be unconditioned and infinite. This is the only way, Hegel holds, that immediate knowing can avoid the very abstractness of which it had accused theoretical philosophy (E §74). Thus, Hegel claims to have refuted immediate knowledge in an immanent manner, for where this form of knowing places great store on what is evidently the case or an indisputable fact, Hegel argues that it is precisely evident in this way that there is no purely immediate knowing, and that thinking involves both aspects, as the *Logic* itself will further demonstrate in its own procedure (E §75).

Finally, Hegel considers the relation between this position of immediate knowledge and the rationalist metaphysics with which we began (and for which, it will be remembered, Hegel expressed considerable sympathy). Viewed superficially, he allows, the two positions may appear rather close: for, as we have seen, Descartes' *Cogito* may be taken as a form of immediate knowing, while the rationalist may think there is a direct connection between the idea of God and his existence, and may also hold that sensible experience gives us access to things in their immediacy as bare particulars (E §76). But, Hegel insists, on closer inspection this similarity is less striking than the differences between the two standpoints. For Descartes may have begun with the *Cogito*, but he did not *stop* there, going on instead to reason from this basis up to a belief in God. The proponents of immediate knowledge, however, refuse to go any further, and their dissatisfaction leads them to give up reasoning altogether.

As Hegel himself allowed in his own critique of rationalist metaphysics, this dissatisfaction may to some extent be justified; but nonetheless he holds that it is a false step to move from this to abandoning reasoning as such, as the result can only be that this position "surrenders itself to the untamed arbitrariness of imaginations and assurances, to moral conceit and haughtiness of feeling, or to opinions and arguments without norm or rule" (E §77). By contrast, Hegel argues, philosophy in general and his *Logic* in particular will avoid any such dogmatic starting points, by beginning in a presuppositionless manner, where the idea that there is an antithesis between immediacy and mediation is one of many such assumptions that needs to be given up. This is not the same as beginning with *skepticism*, however, as skepticism itself makes its own assumptions regarding the nature of our categories and how we must think using them; though as we shall see in the final part of the Vorbegriff, skepticism is given some role in our inquiries in Hegel's account. But what we really want is a more positive form of presuppositionless investigation, which can be "fulfilled by the freedom that abstracts from everything, and grasps its own pure abstraction, the simplicity of thinking—in the resolve of *the will to think purely*" (E §78R). In other words, what we want is what Hegel has already promised he will give us in the *Logic*, namely thought thinking itself, unconstrained by prior assumptions—where, as we have seen, it is such fundamental assumptions that he thinks have vitiated the various positions he has worked through in this part of the Vorbegriff. So, for example, metaphysical rationalism took our ordinary categories for granted and did not inquire further into their limitations; Kant went on to highlight those limitations, but in turn assumed that we could not develop our categories any further; while Jacobi simply accepted an irresolvable opposition between the categories of immediacy and mediation, and took all concepts to fall into the latter camp.

The implicit lesson of this historical part of the Vorbegriff, therefore, is that it is assumptions of this sort that will be problematic to philosophy, where it is only if they are overcome that we can return to the optimism concerning objective thought with which metaphysics began. This lesson is then made more explicit in the final part of the Vorbegriff, in which Hegel offers his last preliminary discussion, focused on giving us a "More Precise Conception and Division of the *Logic*."

16.4. THE SCIENCE (AND ART) OF SPECULATIVE THINKING

In this short but very significant conclusion to the Vorbegriff, Hegel offers a key to the approach that he will take in what follows—though with his customary warning against any such preliminary statements and their potential to mislead.[20] The discussion rests on a distinction that he draws at the outset, between the 'sides' of thought as 'moments' of the 'logically real [*Momente jedes Logisch-Reellen*]', by which he means "every concept or everything true in general" (E §79R). These are "(α) *the side of abstraction* or *of the understanding*, (β) *the dialectical* or *negatively rational side*, [and] (γ) *the speculative* or *positively rational* one" (E §79).

---

[20] "Like the division itself, the remarks made here concerning the determinations of the logical are only anticipations and historical at this point" (E §79R).

The first stage, of the understanding, is characterized as a form of thinking that operates in terms of fixed antitheses and distinctions, while it also operates by abstracting its concepts from concrete particulars, and so is treated as opposed to experience and immediate intuition. It thus forms the basis for certain kinds of theorizing in empirical science, which draws important distinctions between natural phenomena using concepts like "matters, forces, kinds, etc.," while in practical matters it focuses on some things to the exclusion of others, and will insist that the practical world must involve important divisions, such as that between the executive and judiciary within the state. Likewise, in art, religion, and philosophy itself, the understanding will insist on drawing clear differences within and between things, so that confusion and indeterminacy are avoided (E §80A). Throughout this discussion, Hegel makes evident that this approach taken by the understanding is highly beneficial up to a point; what concerns him, however, is that "the understanding must not go too far" (E §80A), leading us to think that its view of the world is the full story.

For, Hegel argues, if we just stick to the understanding, we will inevitably enter the second or dialectical stage of thought, whereby the distinctions that it insists on making will draw us into seemingly irresolvable conceptual difficulties. So, for example, in separating the concept of freedom from the concept of cause, we will be led to think of freedom as mere arbitrariness lacking in any ground whatsoever, in a way that itself seems to *undermine* freedom by rendering it empty. Or, by separating God from his creation on the grounds that he is infinite and it is finite, we will limit God in a way that then makes *him* finite, as he is now bounded by the world he created. Or, by separating universals from the individuals in which they are instantiated, we treat the latter as propertyless and thus indistinguishable from each other after all, thereby undermining their status *as* individuals as they are no longer different from one another. In all these ways, and many others, the understanding can push us into seemingly irresolvable puzzles, akin to those that Kant identified in the antinomies and elsewhere in the dialectical section of the first *Critique*. But where Kant took the problem to lie in the attempt to use categories beyond the bounds of experience, for Hegel the problem lies instead in the way in which those categories are treated by the understanding, which grasps them in a way that is insufficiently sophisticated and complex.

Hegel holds that it is here that skepticism finds its natural place, for when the understanding is forced to see that its conceptual divisions lead thought into incomprehension and puzzlement, it may come to doubt that we can ever arrive at a satisfactory picture of how things are, and so cause us to give up our inquiries in despair. However, he insists that the results of the dialectical stage are not merely 'negative' in this way: rather, they lead to the third and final stage of *reason*, which "apprehends the unity of the determinations in their opposition, the *affirmative* that is contained in their dissolution and their transition into something else" (E §82).

Thus, after thought is forced to reconceive its concepts in such as way as to break down the 'abstract *either-or*' of the understanding (E §80A), it can arrive at a new way of conceiving of things, from which it can see how these divisions are simplistic and misleading, in a way that will overcome the skeptical aporia of the dialectical stage. So, for example, it will see how freedom is not opposed to causality, but that the latter can be incorporated into the former; that God can remain infinite while at the same time being embodied in his finite creation; and that universals can be instantiated in individuals in a way that enables the latter both to be distinguished from one another and not reducible to merely general properties. All this, Hegel accepts, will remain hard for the understanding to make fully intelligible to itself, so it will be drawn back to the earlier distinctions that caused the problems for thought in the first place; but he thinks that the speculative capacity of *reason* is capable of thinking in the way that is required, so that it is reason that in the end is required to make sense of the world for us, not the understanding—thus reversing Kant's priority of the latter over the former. Thus, as Hegel had put it earlier in the Vorbegriff, "[t]he struggle of reason consists precisely in overcoming what the understanding has made rigid"; and it is precisely in moving from the understanding to reason that we can advance over the mistakes of traditional metaphysics, into a metaphysics of a more successful and speculative form: "[t]he dogmatism of the metaphysics of the understanding consists in its adherence to one-sided thought-determinations in their isolation, whereas the idealism of speculative philosophy involves the principle of totality and shows itself able to overgrasp the one-sidedness of the abstract determinations of the understanding" (E §32A). In this way, we can see even more clearly how Hegel took pre-critical metaphysics to be naïve: it adopted a limited conception of the categories, which then led it into philosophical puzzles that cast doubt on its intellectual self-confidence. On the other hand, Kant was wrong in the diagnosis he offered of this puzzlement, precisely because he took it to be insuperable and thus as evidence of the limitedness of human thought, rather than seeing how it can lead us to adopt a new way of thinking that can be achieved by speculative reason. This will then restore to us the self-confidence of thought, but this time on a secure basis, which will also be invulnerable to Jacobi's critique, for that too was directed against the limited outlook of the understanding rather than reason itself.

Now, obviously, actually showing that speculative reason can indeed be triumphant in this way is an enormously ambitious undertaking, which aims at nothing less than the resolution of all the traditional problems of philosophy. It is this project, nonetheless, that Hegel sets out to realize in the *Logic*, as well as the *Encyclopedia* as a whole. Thus, in the main body of the text, Hegel seeks to demonstrate how the various categories of thought are interrelated in a dialectical manner, such that the conceptual oppositions responsible for our perplexities can be overcome and resolved. In fact, however, he thinks that this will prove easier in relation to some categories rather than others, so that in the final section of the Vorbegriff, he anticipates the structure of what is to come by distinguishing between the categories of Being, Essence, and the Concept. At the first level of Being, the relation between categories is one of "passing over" or "transition into the other [*Übergehen in Anderes*]"; at the level of Essence, it is a closer relation of "reflection and mediation" or "appearance in the other [*Scheinen in Anderes*]"; and at the highest level of the Concept, it is one of "development [*Entwicklung*]" (E §83; cf. also §161 and §161A). So, for example, while the categories of Being can be connected with one another, this connection may be simply one of negation (as when we conceive of nothing as that which is not, for example); but the categories of Essence are more internally related (as when we see that something can only be a cause if it has an effect, and vice versa, for example), and those of the Concept are yet further interrelated again (such that each of the categories of universal, particular, and individual can only be made sense of in terms of the others). The point here, therefore, is that it is only really at the end of the *Logic*, with the categories of the Concept, that true speculative thinking can really be achieved; for it is once these categories are properly grasped that the possibilities of "objective thinking" promised in the Vorbegriff can be vindicated, as we then move on in the rest of the *Encyclopedia* to make full sense of both the world around us and ourselves.

16.5. How Is Hegel's *Logic* Possible?

In conclusion, it seems appropriate to provide some critical assessment of what Hegel has achieved in the Vorbegriff. But of course, in many ways this is impossible: for as we have seen, the Vorbegriff is no more than an anteroom to the *Logic* itself, where Hegel makes clear than anything he claims in the former must stand or fall with the latter—and this is hardly the place to assess the *whole* of the *Logic*, much less the full *Encyclopedia* system of which it is part.

Perhaps, however, something more modest is achievable here, namely to consider how far it even makes sense for Hegel to *promise* what he does in the Vorbegriff concerning the *Logic*, even if we cannot here assess how far that promise may be fulfilled. Might we not already know, even before Hegel starts down this path, that he must surely fail? Are there not clear reasons to reject the project proposed in the Vorbegriff, even before it begins? Certainly a number of misgivings might legitimately be raised, of which I will here briefly consider four.

First, it might be said that insofar as this project promises to return us to a rationalist faith in the power of the human mind to attain a full grasp of reality, we can question any such faith at the outset, as we can be confident that our minds are limited in a variety of ways, where intellectual humility of this sort is no more than what is appropriate to the finite creatures that we clearly are.

Second, it could be argued that insofar as Hegel pushes for a more optimistic picture, he does so on blatantly circular and thus illegitimate grounds; for he takes what idealism tells us about the metaphysics of the world, namely that it is conceptually structured, and uses this to ground his confidence in our ability to comprehend it, while at the same time his idealist claims are themselves based on his faith in the power of thought—where ultimately this alignment that he claims between the mind and world can be taken as no more than a happy accident, if we reject the idealistic metaphysics that supposedly explains and underlies it.

Third, it could be said that the claims that Hegel makes in the Vorbegriff regarding the method he will pursue in the *Logic* are clearly unsupportable, particularly regarding its supposed presuppositionlessness. And finally, the worry might be raised that we have good reason to doubt that Hegel's attempt to follow the path of speculative reason can lead us anywhere, as such a dialectical dance can only take us into a world of sophistry and illusion, by violating the very rules and laws of thought that make such thinking intelligible, such as the law of non-contradiction.

Now, while all these worries are certainly legitimate, I believe that they can be addressed by the Hegelian, though I perhaps do not have the space to do so fully here—and where again, some of the replies will depend on how one views the main part of the *Logic* itself, not just what is said in the Vorbegriff. Nonetheless, I will here attempt a brief response to each of the concerns.

As regards the first worry, this can perhaps be addressed by drawing out some affinities that I think exist between Hegel's approach and those adopted later by pragmatists such as C. S. Peirce. Thus, while Peirce was a fallibilist, who was perfectly prepared to accept that there may well turn out to be limitations to the human mind and that our knowledge claims may always need revising, he was nonetheless hostile to the claim that our cognitive limitations could be known *in advance* of inquiry, and that this could be enough to cause us to give up on certain matters. This, he argued, would violate a fundamental principle that "deserves to be inscribed upon every wall of the city of philosophy": "*Do not block the road of inquiry.*"[21] Of course, this does not assume or guarantee that our inquiries *will* be successful: at some points, we may be compelled to give up, or at least suspend, further investigation pending new developments. But until we meet what appears to be an *actual* blockage, we should just inquire as best we can and not think *in advance* that we are debarred from doing so because of our cognitive limitations. Likewise, then, I believe that Hegel would hold that at the stage of the Vorbegriff, at least, nothing should prevent us in undertaking the kind of inquiry he promises in the *Logic*, though of course this does not guarantee the latter's success, or show in advance that it will not fail somewhere—but until we have actually *reached* that point of breakdown, nothing rules out the legitimacy of making a start, so at least the Vorbegriff itself can be vindicated at the outset. Of course, as we have seen, a Kantian might respond by saying that she *has* shown that an actual breakdown can and will occur, so that she is *not* just raising this as an abstract possibility. However, as again Hegel hopes the *Logic* itself will show, he believes that Kant was wrong in his diagnosis of what appears to go wrong with our inquiries, so again we are entitled to at least *start* the *Logic* to see how this goes, and thus to see whether Hegel's speculative approach can indeed improve on Kant's transcendental one.

Turning now to the second worry, the concern is here that Hegel's approach can only really be circular, as he bases his confidence in our reason on an idealist metaphysics, which itself assumes the efficacy of this reason. However, I think this worry can be addressed along the same lines as the response given in what we have just said. That is, I think one can argue that again Hegel is not guaranteeing at the outset that his inquiry will be successful, which would then require some suitably strong metaphysics

---

[21] Peirce, "The First Rule of Logic," 48.

to underpin it; rather, he is proposing that we begin his inquiry with some *hope* that this may be so, where *if it is* successful this in turn will vindicate the idealist metaphysics that would explain it, particularly if it turns out to result in a picture of the world that is itself idealistic in Hegel's sense—which is how Hegel claims things do indeed turn out at the end of the *Logic*. Both rationalist metaphysics and common sense, Hegel thinks, share this hope that our thought can fathom reality, as they again see no prior reason for doubt, while they also see that thought has at least had some success on this score; but this, Hegel would hold, is enough to justify the stance taken in the Vorbegriff, and to make starting the *Logic* at least a reasonable undertaking, without begging any questions from the beginning.

But this may bring us to the third worry, namely that by claiming not to start with any presuppositions in this way, Hegel is being absurdly naïve, as *all* inquiry must begin from somewhere and so make some assumptions, including his own. Now, again, when we look at the *Logic* itself, Hegel may or may not turn out to have violated his own rules at various stages, and so has taken for granted things he should not have. The question as regards the Vorbegriff, however, is whether it is absurd to even think that *in principle* any such approach is possible. It is probably impossible to fully address this concern here, as it will in part depend on getting clear exactly what is meant by 'presuppositionless', and thus precisely what this rules in or out.[22] But again, I think Hegel's main point would be that we cannot know *in advance* that such an approach is impossible or unworkable: all we can do is move from the Vorbegriff to the rest of the *Logic* itself, to see whether Hegel actually achieves it, so to that extent the limited role of the Vorbegriff again is adequately realized.

Finally, one may feel that the Vorbegriff sinks Hegel's project from the outset, for precisely in §§79–82 it offers us a conception of 'speculative thinking' that can only prove absurd, and lead us into nonsense. For, it can be argued that the distinctions that Hegel identifies with the understanding are in fact good ones, without which thought loses all determinacy and content, and in transcending which Hegel is forced to violate certain fundamental rules of thought, such as the principle of non-contradiction. From what the Vorbegriff tells us about his 'speculative science', we can thus know in advance that it is absurd and bound to fail.

Once again, this raises large issues that cannot be fully addressed here. First of all, while Hegel clearly expects his way of thinking to be difficult for us and fundamentally challenging, I think that some take his rather provocative comments on this too far, where I do not hold that he is hereby actually rejecting the principle of non-contradiction or related principles: in fact, it seems that without a basic allegiance to such principles, the dialectic could not be driven forward, as contradictions within a position could just be accommodated, thereby undermining the process of immanent critique that is made central to Hegel's approach. Of course, this does not mean that everything he says in the *Logic* is fully intelligible and easy to grasp, and there are certainly positions that will appear contradictory *to the understanding*; but this is not

---

[22] Cf. Houlgate, *The Opening of Hegel's 'Logic'*, 29–71, for further discussion of this issue.

because reason is licensed to assert contradictions as such, but because it can conceive of the categories in ways that show they are *not* in fact in contradictory to one another, despite how this appears to the understanding. Now, perhaps there are also points where Hegel's attempt to transcend dichotomies or to encompass different sides is unworkable, and the results lack cogency. But again, that is a matter that can only be decided by looking at the various positions laid out in the *Logic* itself, and *not* something that can be decided at the outset, from just the description that Hegel gives us in the Vorbegriff of speculative reasoning and its differences from the understanding.

It seems, then, that from what we learn about Hegel's project in the Vorbegriff, we are not entitled to abandon that project *in advance*. But of course, from what Hegel himself says about any such preliminary discussion, the Vorbegriff on its own cannot vindicate that project either. To do that, we must embark on the project itself—which is exactly what Hegel hopes his readers will do, once they have been properly oriented by the text we have been discussing.

WORKS CITED

Primary Texts

Hegel, G. W. F. *Encyclopedia of the Philosophical Sciences in Outline and Critical Writings* [E1817], edited by Ernst Behler. New York: Continuum, 1990.

Hegel, G. W. F. *The Encyclopedia Logic* [E], translated by T. F. Geraets, W. A. Suchting, and H. S. Harris. Indianapolis: Hackett, 1991.

Hegel, G. W. F. *Phenomenology of Spirit* [PS]. Translated by A. V. Miller. Oxford: Oxford University Press, 1977.

Jacobi, Friedrich Henrich. *Concerning the Doctrine of Spinoza in Letters to Moses Mendelssohn*, in *The Main Philosophical Writings and the Novel 'Allwill'*, translated by George di Giovanni (Montreal; Kingston: McGill-Queen's University Press), 1994, 173–251.

Peirce, Charles Sanders. "The First Rule of Logic," in *The Essential Peirce: Selected Philosophical Writings*, Volume 2: *1893–1913*, edited by Nathan Houser. Bloomington: Indiana University Press, 1998, 42–56.

Secondary Literature

Denker, Alfred, Annette Sell, and Holger Zaborowski (eds.). *Der 'Vorbegriff' zur Wissenschaft der Logik in der Enzyklopädie von 1830*. München: Karl Alber, 2010.

Flach, Werner. "Die dreifache Stellung des Denkens zur Objectivität und das Problem der spekulativen Logik," in *Die Wissenschaft der Logik und die Logik der Reflektion*, edited by Dieter Henrich. Bonn: Bouvier, 1978, 3–18.

Flach, Werner. "Zum 'Vorbegriff' der Kleinen Logik Hegels," in *Der Idealismus und seine Gegenwart*, edited by Ute Guzzoni, Bernhard Rang, and Ludwig Seip. Hamburg: Meiner, 1976, 133–146.

Fulda, Hans Friedrich. *Das Problem einer Einleitung in Hegels Wissenschaft der Logik*. Frankfurt am Main: Klostermann, 1965.

Fulda, Hans Friedrich. "Vorbegriff und Begriff von Philosophie bei Hegel," in *Hegels Logik der Philosophie*, edited by Dieter Henrich and Rolf-Peter Horstmann. Stuttgart: Klett-Cotta, 13–34.

Houlgate, Stephen. *The Opening of Hegel's 'Logic'*. West Lafayette, IN: Purdue University Press, 2006.

Lucas, Hans-Christian. "Der 'Vorbegriff' der enzyklopädischen 'Logik' doch als Einleitung im emphatischen Sinne?," *Hegel-Studien* 26 (1991): 218–224.

Nuzzo, Angelica. "Das Problem eines 'Vorbegriff' in Hegels spekulativer Logik," in *Der 'Vorbegriff' zur Wissenschaft der Logik in der Enzyklopädie von 1830*, edited by Alfred Denker, Annette Sell, and Holger Zaborowski. München: Karl Alber, 2010, 84–113.

Stern, Robert. "Hegel's Idealism," in *Hegelian Metaphysics*, by Robert Stern. Oxford: Oxford University Press, 2009, 45–76.

Stern, Robert. *The Routledge Guidebook to Hegel's 'Phenomenology of Spirit'*, 2nd ed. Abingdon, UK: Routledge, 2013.

Westphal, Kenneth. "Hegel's Attitude towards Jacobi in the 'Third Attitude of Thought Toward Objectivity'," *Southern Journal of Philosophy* 27 (1989): 135–156.

CHAPTER 17

HEGEL'S *PHILOSOPHY OF NATURE*

SEBASTIAN RAND

17.1. INTRODUCTION: NATURE AND SELF-DETERMINATION

ONE of the dominant themes of Hegel's philosophy is freedom, and in treating this theme he aims not only to develop a satisfactory concept of freedom, but also to show how developing such a concept is part of actualizing it, part of our being free. As is well known, Hegel devoted significant efforts to the ordering and articulation of the philosophical system he thought this goal demanded. So when we look at his most comprehensive systematic text—the *Encyclopedia*—and find at its literal center the *Philosophy of Nature*, we are justified in thinking that Hegel takes an examination of nature to be philosophically central to his larger freedom-oriented project.[1] Since for Hegel freedom is a kind of autonomy, pursuing this thought means explaining how the *Philosophy of Nature* contributes to the development of the proper concept of human autonomy, and why the actualization of that concept requires just such a contribution—explaining why, in Hegel's own phrase, the philosophy of nature is "the science of freedom" (NSR 24.8).

In terms of developing a concept of freedom, the need to think about nature can seem straightforward: humans are natural things; as self-conscious autonomy, human freedom requires self-understanding; thus human freedom requires an understanding of nature. But Hegel evidently has something more than this in mind when he says that the philosophy of nature brings about not just self-knowledge but "the freeing of nature"

---

[1] Nonetheless, the philosophy of nature has rarely been the focus of detailed commentary, and interpreters seldom draw on it to explain other parts of the system. Instead, they tend to draw on either the *Phenomenology*'s section on Observing Reason or the *Logic*'s on Mechanism, Chemism, and Teleology.

itself (E §246R). The study of nature not only tells us about our natural existence but reveals that other natural objects "have an existence just as justified and satisfied as ours," and are therefore "self-contained and rational," such that nature's "essence is our own, namely reason." Yet because "humans are free only insofar as those next to us are also free," knowing the rationality and hence freedom of nature partially actualizes our own freedom (NSR 24.5, 8). Lastly, since we are natural, the actualization of our freedom is also the actualization of nature's freedom, meaning that our knowing nature as free in fact completes nature's own freedom. [2]

Claims about nature being free are always striking, but especially so here, when we recall some of Hegel's more familiar claims contrasting the freedom of spirit with the necessity and 'externality' of nature.[3] These claims have encouraged the idea that for Hegel, we may begin as animals, but we become free—become spirit, or *Geist*—only when we succeed in taking ourselves to be, and thereby in making ourselves, non-natural.[4] This idea gets something right; after all, Hegel does make these more familiar claims, and the *Philosophy of Nature* is not the *Philosophy of Spirit*. But a few points about Hegel's conception of freedom can help us get a sense of how nature might be free in a way relevant to our freedom, while not being free precisely as we are free.

Consider Kant's claim in the *Groundwork* that we are autonomous to the extent that we can (rightly) regard ourselves as the 'original authors' of the laws to which we are subject (GrW 4:431). One popular interpretation of this original authorship criterion takes it to require that I be capable of a free act in which I legislate these norms to myself.[5] But if that legislative act is to be a free act—as it must be, on penalty of leading not to my autonomy but to my heteronomy—it must itself be done from a norm self-legislated by some prior act. The threatened regress or paradox here has prompted interpreters to attribute various proposed remedies to the post-Kantian idealists.[6] One alternate way of taking the original authorship criterion sees it as satisfied whenever the norms binding me either make up or follow from my essence—or in Hegel's own terms, my concept; on this interpretation I am their original author, and self-legislating, not through some imagined paradoxical act, but simply in that these norms are immanent to me, or

---

[2] It is "the determination and the purpose of the philosophy of nature that spirit should find its own essence, i.e., the concept, in nature. . . . So the study of nature is the freeing of spirit in her. . . . It is for the same reason the freeing of nature; nature is in itself reason, but this emerges as such into existence [*tritt als solche heraus in die Existenz*] in nature first through [*durch*] spirit" (E §246A).

[3] See, e.g., PR §146R.

[4] See Pippin, "Leaving Nature Behind," where he pits his anti-naturalism against the second-nature naturalism of McDowell's *Mind and World*. Neither Pippin nor McDowell gets Hegel's view of nature right. Briefly put: *contra* McDowell, an updated Aristotelian second nature is not natural enough to do the work Hegel needs done; *contra* Pippin, natural autonomy is free enough to do that work.

[5] As Kant says, the autonomous will "must be seen as *giving the law to itself* [selbstgesetzgebend] and precisely thereby subject to the law" (GrW 4:431).

[6] See Pippin, "Hegel's Practical Philosophy"; Pinkard, *German Philosophy*, 59–60 (but compare his later *Hegel's Naturalism*); and the essays collected in Khurana and Menke, eds., *Paradoxien der Autonomie*.

constitutive of me, as the kind of thing I am.[7] According to this view, being—and know-ing myself to be—immanently self-determined counts as being self-consciously auton-omous, even if the norms by which I determine myself prohibit me from doing things I am in some sense inclined to do.

The emphasis here on simultaneously being some way and knowing oneself to be that way implies that Hegelian ethical autonomy is actualized through robust (and, as it turns out, historically and socially mediated) relations of self-consciousness. Since according to Hegel such relations do not arise among non-human animals or among non-animal natural things, it can seem misleading to attribute a genuinely Hegelian freedom to such things (and thus to nature). But as Hegel's previously quoted remarks suggest, we need not regard ethical autonomy as the only species of autonomy. Even if the fact that they do not know themselves to be self-determined means that non-human natural things are not free in the way that we can be free, they can nonetheless actually be self-determined through their immanent concepts and thus free in a more limited sense—one in which they are in fact the 'original authors' of the laws to which they are subject, despite not regarding themselves as such (because they do not 'regard themselves' at all). Such a limited, natural autonomy, while distinguishable from ethical autonomy, is nonetheless relevant to it. This relevance consists not only in coming to grasp my environment as rational in the same basic way that I am rational, but also in my grasping my own natural life in a particular way. When we come to see some of our properties and dispositions as determinations we give ourselves in the course of living our lives as the sorts of animals we are, we see that they are neither externally imposed nor irrationally given.[8] And inso-far as our ethical autonomy depends on knowing ourselves to be self-determined, and thus on knowing ourselves, *qua* natural things, to be self-determined in the way natural things of our kind are, a study of nature that reveals its self-determination constitutes an essential step in achieving that autonomy.[9]

Put this way, and understood primarily in relation to living things, Hegel's take on nature's self-determination seems rooted in Kant's theory of natural teleology.[10] Drawing on Kant's distinction between mechanical and teleological forms, approaches

---

[7] See Rödl, *Self-Consciousness*, 114–120. Immanent conceptuality is front and center in some recent interpretations of Hegel's metaphysics; see Bowman, *Absolute Negativity*; and Kreines, *Reason in the World*.

[8] Of course, not all of my natural properties and dispositions will ultimately count as self-determined, according to Hegel; those not essentially related to being the *kind* of animal I am will not count as self-determined in the relevant way. Furthermore, many, if not all, of my naturally given determinations will conflict in some way with others, such that fully self-conscious autonomy will require what Hegel calls the "purification of the drives" (see PR §§19–21 and McCumber, *Hegel's Mature Critique*, 118–122).

[9] Consider episodes in which we accept aspects of ourselves—our capacities, looks, aversions, whatever—that we did not initially think conducive to the good life. Such acceptance is a kind of liberation, and it is assisted by the reflection, e.g., that I am the kind of animal that gets cranky when it doesn't get enough sleep.

[10] The recognition of this connection, and of the importance of the category of life to Hegel's thought in general, is at the center of some recent literature on Hegel's logic, ethics, and action theory. See, for instance, the essays collected in Khurana, ed., *The Freedom of Life*, particularly those by Ng and Haase; Thompson, *Life and Action*; Rödl, *Self-Consciousness*; and Rand, "Animal Defect."

to Hegelian natural autonomy emphasizing the special status of living things stress how, through their life-processes, they are self-determining in a way not manifested by inanimate nature. That is, they emphasize how living things' activity of making themselves into the things they are combines the active aspect of self-legislation with the immanence of natural kinds or essences, letting us have both interpretations of Kantian ('original authorship') autonomy at once. Such views thus yield a kind of natural autonomy limited to the living and encourage us to see such a living autonomy as a prerequisite to full-fledged human spiritual autonomy, while also letting us reinforce a distinction between the free and the unfree, now understood as an intra-nature distinction between organism and mechanism. But while Hegel undeniably privileges the living, his *Philosophy of Nature* quite clearly aims to vindicate the claim that all natural things—including the inorganic—are immanently self-determining. It is this global claim that I will consider in what follows.

17.2. THE TRANSFORMATION OF THE SCIENCES

17.2.1. Preliminaries

Even if the idea of a natural freedom consisting in the immanent conceptual self-determination of natural things is intriguing, it is not obvious that the sciences give us much evidence of such freedom; on the contrary, the nature they show us often looks anything but self-determining. Thus, despite the importance he attaches to the study of nature, and despite his affirmation of the modern mathematized experimental sciences as indispensable to that study, Hegel cannot simply take their results into his system as is. Rather, he must present in his own terms the self-determination of nature both discovered and obscured by natural-scientific modes of thought. This presentation begins by characterizing those modes of thought as according unquestioned authority to 'the understanding'. Operating under this authority, Hegel tells us, the sciences do not "consider nature as free in its proper vitality" (E §245A) but treat it as "mere externality, immediacy, [and] sensibility." The philosophy of nature, by contrast, grasps nature through reason and lifts it "up into the unity of the concept, into freedom, into being-for-self" (NSU 24.218) by carrying out an '*Umbildung*' or transformation of the results of the natural sciences that removes these results from the domain of the understanding.[11]

This transformation, then, is the method through which the *Philosophy of Nature* carries out its systematic task. At first glance, the method seems like a familiar one; put in Kantian terms, it seems to involve converting a posteriori knowledge into a priori knowledge by replacing empirical claims with purely rational ones (the latter derived,

---

[11] See, e.g., NSG 24.490.

presumably, from the *Logic*).[12] Although such a Kantian interpretation is initially plausible, it leaves Hegel in an awkward philosophical position. For even Kant's relatively modest ideas about what might be demonstrated a priori turn out not to have been modest enough, and more generally, any claim to derive natural laws a priori runs counter to the fallibilist spirit (and actual history) of the sciences. Neo-Kantian varieties of historicized and relativized apriority are designed to respond to these difficulties while maintaining a basically transcendental framework.[13] Applied to Hegel, a neo-Kantian approach would assimilate the philosophy of nature to his deep historicism, arguing that he aims, first, to lay bare the constitutive presuppositions of contemporary natural science; second, to show how those presuppositions structure the relevant empirical results; and third, to demonstrate their connection to other areas of human inquiry and action. Yet there are reasons to be skeptical of such an approach to Hegel: for instance, the absence of any real history of natural science in Hegel's system or lectures suggests that the *Philosophy of Nature* is emphatically a philosophy of nature and not a philosophical history of, or a historicist philosophy of, natural science. Thus while there may be room in a broadly Hegelian program for the historicist study of the natural sciences as human practices, what Hegel actually gives us in the *Philosophy of Nature* is something else entirely.[14]

We can avoid the Kantian and neo-Kantian readings of Hegel's transformational method by noticing their decidedly un-Hegelian commitment to some version of the a priori/a posteriori distinction. Given his relentless dialectical critique of traditional philosophical oppositions, it would be out of character for Hegel to leave the a priori/ a posteriori distinction intact, as even the historicizing strategy essentially must do.[15] Certainly if he were to deploy this distinction in his system—as he does many inherited distinctions from the history of philosophy—he would have to subject it to dialectical critique first. But aside from occasional (though consistent) ironic and dismissive remarks, we do not find any such critique anywhere in his works, notes, or lectures. And indeed, 'a priori' does not seem to be one of Hegel's terms. He rarely uses it, and he nowhere tells us how to distinguish—even in a provisional way or by examples— a priori from a posteriori concepts, claims, knowledge, or warrant. Moreover, when he does actually use either term (particularly in the *Philosophy of Nature*), it is almost

[12] For a recent Kantian reading of Hegel's philosophy of nature, see Posch, "Hegel and the Sciences"; for other broadly Kantian-aprioristic interpretations see Stone, *Petrified Intelligence*; Houlgate, *Introduction*; and Bowman, *Absolute Negativity*.

[13] See Friedman, *Dynamics of Reason*.

[14] For Hegelian historicism about the natural sciences, see Meyerson, *Explanation*, and Koyré (e.g., *Astronomical Revolution*), along with Kuhn, who in *Structure* acknowledges the influence of his French Hegelian predecessors (but not Hegel). See also Hegel's deceptively Kuhnian-looking claim that "all revolutions, in the sciences no less than in world history, come about only because spirit, in order to understand and take possession of what is its own, has altered its categories, grasping itself in a truer, deeper, more inner, and simpler way" (E §246A).

[15] See Sedgwick's similar line of thought about Hegel's critical orientation toward some (other) basic Kantian structural distinctions in her *Hegel's Critique*, which focuses on (among other things) Hegel's alleged endorsement of a form of intellectual intuition.

always to characterize a position he is about to attack.[16] The evidence thus suggests that Hegel is not much interested in appealing to this distinction to characterize any of his own claims—either as a priori or a posteriori. If we want to understand the relation Hegel articulates between the natural sciences and his own philosophy of nature, then, we do well to put the a priori/a posteriori distinction aside and draw instead on other resources.[17] Such resources are readily available; they offer both a Hegelian picture of the character of natural-scientific representations and the elements of a method for transforming these representations into properly systematic Hegelian concepts.

17.2.2. The Form of Natural Science

By characterizing the philosophical interpretation of the natural sciences as a transformation, Hegel emphasizes that the *Philosophy of Nature* will not augment, alter, or replace their content, but only put it in a new form. In the natural sciences themselves, and in the scientistic metaphysical interpretations that arise with them, that content has a form Hegel calls representational and associates (as we saw) with the understanding, in contrast to what he identifies as conceptual form properly so called, linked with reason.[18] But this representationally formed content, upon which Hegelian transformation will operate, is itself not simply given either to perception or to the understanding; it is rather the end product of a complex prior process of formation involving observation, experiment, and reflection. "In the first instance, we know about nature through the senses," or, in Kantian terms, "we intuit natural objects"; on this basis "our formal thinking then proceeds" (NSR 24.3). This thinking "should define the genera, classes, etc." or "determine them, [i.e.] the essential should be extracted from out of the mass of conditions that are found in immediate intuition" through "an activity of the understanding, an activity of abstraction" (NSU 24.189). Such abstraction brings about a reduction in the "naturalness, singularity, and immediacy of things" (E §246A), since it universalizes by treating determinations or properties not as they are found entangled with others in concretely existing things, but as separated and isolated in thought.[19]

---

[16] 'A priori' (in its various forms) appears four times in the *Philosophy of Nature* (at E §§267R, §275A, §293R, and §305R). In no instance does the term appear in a main body paragraph. In all but one instance, Hegel uses the term to describe the claims of others, rejects those claims, and either asserts or implies that their (spurious) a priori status is part of the problem. In the other instance (E §275A), the term appears in a passage generated posthumously by Hegel's editors. The situation is similar in all of Hegel's mature works. Hence the direct lexical evidence in favor of Hegelian apriorism is either weak or nonexistent.

[17] Of course, Hegel could be committed to a kind of crypto-apriorism, but his appropriation of most of the rest of the vocabulary of Western philosophy for his own systematic ends makes this idea implausible. Note that if I am correct, we are equally mistaken if we describe Hegel's claims as a posteriori: what he objects to is the distinction itself, and the dogmatic subjectivism that comes with it.

[18] See, e.g., E §182R.

[19] Many passages in his lectures (e.g., NSU 24.251) show Hegel's grasp of the varied and changeable factors, methods, and processes—often multi-generational and rarely the work of a single individual—involved in forming natural-scientific universals.

Hegel's conception of abstraction as an inherently universalizing operation is a component of his broader view that while natural things are singulars, and while much of our mental life deals in singulars, all thought properly so called is universal in form.[20] Hegel touches on this view in his Introduction to the *Philosophy of Nature* by discussing the role of singularity and universality in our practical and theoretical attitudes toward natural objects. When I adopt the practical attitude, I treat singular things as means to my ends; in consuming or altering them to bring about these ends, I negate or destroy them, either partially (as in milling trees into lumber) or completely (as in eating and digesting). This practical negation is sometimes simply an external, formal one (as when a bird arranges found sticks into a nest), sometimes a partially formal, partially contentful ('real') one (as with the lumber), and sometimes a more complete real and formal one (as when I metabolize what was an apple and nothing apple-like remains).[21] When I adopt the theoretical attitude toward things, I also negate, through abstraction, the singular form of what I sense, perceive, and intuit; when I take a thing as an instance of one of its properties, by focusing on, for example, this rose's weight, color, or smell, I turn what I first encountered in the form of a singular thing into something that could, formally or in principle, be the weight, color, or smell of some other object. But in contrast to practical negation, theoretical negation preserves, or at least intends to preserve, the content unaltered within the new universal form given to it by abstraction; the point of abstracting away the other features of the rose is, after all, to get or keep hold of the one I am focused on.

Yet there is reason to doubt that abstraction can preserve its content in its new form, since singularity, according to Hegel, is the only form natural existence can take. The universals produced in natural-scientific inquiry "do not fall in the domain of perception[,] only their expressions do" (NSU 24,189); natural things are "singulars, and the lion in general does not exist" (E §246A). But if natural things are singulars, we might well ask why thinking by means of abstractive universals should count as thinking about natural things at all. The difficulty is deeper than a worry about whether this or that procedure leads us to abstract out the right properties from the 'mass of conditions', for even if we resolve that worry, the output of our abstractive efforts will always be a universal, while we wanted our knowledge to be about natural objects—which are and must be singulars. Nor, it seems, can we reconstitute the singularity of existent natural things by concatenating multiple abstract universal representations: as long as the universals we are using are abstractive, and are thus the representations of isolated properties or relations supposedly intelligible independently of one another, no concatenation of them could recapture the simple unity in which they are found together in the thing's natural singular existence.[22]

---

[20] On mental form and content, see E §3. For the doctrine that thought is always (either abstractly or concretely) universal, see, e.g., the treatment of singularity in the *Logic* (SL 12.49 ff/546 ff). The interplay of universality and singularity in our sensory, perceptual, and experiential engagement with nature is discussed in E §§445–468.

[21] See E §362.

[22] Compare Hegel's attacks on this and related difficulties in the Perception section of the *Phenomenology* (PS 9.71–81/§§111–131).

17.2.3. The Form of the Philosophy of Nature

Hegel's method aims to give the sciences a form of generality that does not exhibit the short-comings of abstraction, by transforming the "unconceptualized concept" of the under-standing into an explicitly "conceptualized" one of reason (SL 12.40, 45/537, 542). As a *"conceptualizing* consideration" of nature, the philosophy of nature deals with "the same *universals*" produced by natural science, "but *for themselves*" (E §246); by means of a syn-thetically oriented thinking-through or *Nachdenken*, rather than an abstractive *Reflektion*, it "translates the universals delivered to it . . . into the concept" (E §246A).[23] This transla-tion is possible to the extent that the natural sciences "play into the hands of philosophy" (E §246A) by putting their formally isolated, abstractive representations to work in explan-atory and descriptive schemes. Such schemes do not just concatenate the representations they employ, but also display their determinate connections and distinctions—for instance, in genus-species hierarchies of natural kinds, in binary classifications (acid/base, positive/ negative charge), or through mathematical natural laws.[24] And such schemes are part and parcel of the terms occurring in them: we do not first develop our natural-scientific rep-resentations (e.g., 'mass', 'motion', 'element', 'plant') independently, only later organizing them into explanations. Rather, our universals always already function within some kind of organized explanation and description (relating, say, mass to velocity in momentum). What transformative *Nachdenken* looks for, then, is the way the content of our natural-scientific representations is implicitly elaborated beyond their simple abstract determinacy through their explanatory and descriptive roles. Hegel's method aims to present that content entirely in terms of such roles, whose determinate general logical forms are laid out in the *Logic*; so understood, the content has become 'for-itself' in the sense that it now has the form that coincides with the way it, as a conceptual—that is, rational—content is actually determined.

In Hegel's terms, properly conceptual generality is 'concrete', as opposed to the abstract universality of the understanding and its representations. The presentation of natural scientific content in a system of concrete universals is not, however, an end in itself, but rather a remedy for the mismatch between the singularity of natural existence and the representational form of the natural sciences, a mismatch resting not on gener-ality as such, but on the understanding's abstractive character. Yet that abstraction is still a necessary stage in arriving at the concrete concepts of the philosophy of nature, a point Hegel emphasizes by insisting that philosophy as a whole, and the philosophy of nature in particular, cannot develop without the sciences and their specific mode of investi-gation.[25] The simple unity of singular natural objects is undone by the elaborating and

---

[23] In the Introduction to the *Encyclopedia*, Hegel characterizes the activity of philosophy in general as a *Nachdenken*, or a re-thinking of what has already been thought, experienced, or known (E §§2–9). It is in this sense that Hegel later writes that "not only must philosophy be in correspondence with the experience of nature, but the *inception* and *formation* of philosophical science has empirical physics as its presupposition and condition" (E §246R).

[24] Of course, not all methods for organizing natural things into such structures are valid, on Hegel's view; see, e.g., his attack on various conceptions of natural series (E §249A).

[25] See note 23 and E §12.

abstractive power of the understanding, but the rational core of that unity is restored, as conceptual concreteness, in transformative systematization. Properly conceptual generality thus captures, in an explicit, concrete, 'for-itself' form, the very same unified content that appears in an implicit, simple, 'in-itself' form in natural existence, but only by first rendering it, via the understanding, into an abstracted array of apparently independent determinations.

But even the results of this transformative method are only intermediate ends, valuable for Hegel's project because of their contribution to our grasp of nature as self-determined and therefore autonomous. We see this contribution when we see that concrete unity and self-determination are two sides of the same coin. For concrete unity consists not in the various determinations of some existent thing jointly making up the concept of its kind through their mutual dependence. This dependence does not flow from some abstract logical or metaphysical principle, but is exhibited in the rationally structured explanatory and descriptive use to which the relevant representations are put—that is, exhibited in the content itself when it is rationally comprehended. The systematically articulated contents of a given concept thus express what we have discovered about the kind of natural thing in question, such that these contents are the properties and relations our study of nature has revealed to be jointly co-constitutive of individuals of the relevant kind. But if this is so, then for something to be an individual of that kind is just for it to have those determinations, and thus for all of them to count (jointly) as self-determined. Hence the determinations specified by the systematically articulated concept of a thing are those the instantiation of which in its natural existence actualize its natural freedom. To grasp nature as a domain populated and structured by naturally autonomous things determining themselves is to conceive of nature as "being an existence just as justified and satisfied" as ours and thus as "self-contained and rational."

17.2.4. Impotence, Self-Externality, and the System of Stages

Put in these terms, it seems that what Hegel regards as the content of the concrete concept of a thing is just what would traditionally be called its essence, and that for a determination to count as self-determined is just for it to be an essential one. But Hegel's characterization of conceptual self-determination as autonomy blocks this interpretation, since it commits him to the claim that natural things can be the kinds of things they are while failing to have determinations that, if they had them, would count as self-determinations. Hegel makes this commitment clear when he claims, for instance, that some ('mechanical') motions of a material body are free, or self-determined, while others are unfree, and then directly analogizes this distinction to the distinction between the ethical and unethical actions of a human agent.[26]

---

[26] "Thus while finite matter receives motion from outside, free matter moves itself. . . . Similarly, the ethical person is free in the laws, and they are only external to the unethical person" (E §264A).

Hegel's most striking characterization of the possibility of failure inherent in natural self-determination attributes an essential 'impotence' to nature (E §250),[27] an attribution built in to the systematic definition of nature as "the idea in the form of otherness [*Andersseins*]" (E §247). 'The idea' is one of Hegel's technical terms, designating the unity of 'the' concept—the total system of all properly conceptual determinations—and that system's actuality—its real existence, for instance as nature. In the 'form of otherness', these two sides of the idea remain other to one another, opposed and distinct—that is, in this form the idea's existence is characterized precisely by a failure to match up with its concept. Yet that existence is still the existence of the concept, and the concept is still the concept of that existence. Hence in Hegel's words, nature—considered as the unity of the concept and its existence—is necessarily 'self-external'.[28]

In saying that nature is self-external, Hegel is not saying that nature is essentially irrational or unknowable, nor is he saying that natural things are not self-determined.[29] On the contrary: to grasp nature as self-external is to know its concept, to know its existence, and to know the latter as failing to actualize the former. In other words, nature's failure here is not unspecified, such that Hegel could invoke it ad hoc to render his claims about nature irrefutable, but rather a specific one inflecting every aspect of natural existence in a determinate way. Hegel begins by arguing from nature's self-externality to its general spatiotemporal structure, in which each point and instant fundamentally has no other determination than that of being simply external to, or non-identical with, the others—from which it is otherwise indistinguishable. In giving a wholly general and yet determinate form to the essential non-correspondence of concept and actuality in nature, the self-external structure of space and time gives all natural things their characteristic singular existence, determining each as outside its neighbors and giving each thing's 'inner' properties and parts "the appearance of an *indifferent subsistence* and of *singularization* over and against each other" (E §248). When we grasp these properties and parts through the concrete concept of the thing in question, we know this indifference to be a function of nature's impotence, and thus to be 'only apparent'—we know that although the liver is a distinct organ, it is also essentially a member of the living organism and cannot survive excised from it. Yet the impotence of nature lies precisely in the necessity of this appearance and in the fact that although it is only an appearance, it is not an illusion: the liver is a distinct organ, and so can be separated from the body, destroying both.[30]

---

[27] "It is the impotence [*Ohnmacht*] of nature, that it maintains conceptual determinations only abstractly and exposes the completion of the particular to external determinability" (E §250).

[28] Self externality, Hegel says, "constitutes the determination in which the idea is as nature" (E §247). Thus the self-externality of nature is not an error theory but marks a necessary non-correspondence of concept and actuality.

[29] For the view that Hegel *does* take nature to be fundamentally irrational and unknowable, see Bowman, *Absolute Negativity*, Ch. 4.

[30] As it turns out, the kind of distinctness exhibited by organs in their unity with the rest of the body provides the basis for 'accidental' death but also for 'natural' death, through a process Hegel identifies with habit. For Hegel's conception of habit, see McCumber, "Hegel on Habit"; Lumsden, "Limits"; Malabou, *Future of Hegel*; and Malabou, "Hegelian Wolves."

In contrast to the self-externality of natural existence, conceptual form exhibits a unity of multiple mutually dependent determinations. The question, parallel to the one that arose earlier regarding abstract representations, is how a natural, spatiotemporally extended self-external thing can count as the existence of an inner conceptual unity it is incapable of fully actualizing. Hegel's answer is straightforward: a natural, self-external thing counts as self-determined when it exhibits, in its natural existence and activity, not mere spatiotemporal juxtaposition of parts or moments (equivalent to a concatenation of representations), but a unity of both its parts and its activity isomorphic to the unity of its concrete conceptual content. In other words, Hegel conceives of the variety of logical connections articulating the content of a concrete concept as corresponding to a variety of natural—that is, spatiotemporal—relations. So, for instance, material bodies move freely when their motions are determined by laws expressing the concrete unity of space and time constitutive of the concept of a material body as such. As it turns out, these laws determine the motion of a given material body only insofar as it is one in a system of bodies with a common center of gravity.[31] But if the only motion of a material body that counts as a self-determined motion is one in which it is determined as a subordinate part of a larger system, then a single material body, although self-determined in its motion, cannot count on its own as the full actualization of a spatiotemporal unity corresponding to the conceptual unity of its content. If anything in mechanics can do this, it is the total system of mechanical bodies (but then, such a system—if it exists—is not one material thing). By contrast, the body of a higher-order mammal—while dependent on its environment and other animals in many ways—exhibits a unity that is concrete to a high degree. Yet it, too, ultimately remains self-external—a fact Hegel illustrates by pointing to the sexual processes through which the individual and species are produced and reproduced.[32]

Now, although its singular existence is a more complete actualization of conceptual unity than the motion of mechanical bodies, the living animal is still self-external and thus susceptible to external determination, just as a material body is. All natural things, of whatever kind, share this exposure. But by differentiating among natural things in terms of the extent to which they exhibit fully concrete unity, and thus also in terms of the modes and degree of this exposure, Hegel is able to order the totality of nature into a "system of stages [*Stufen*]" (E §§249–251). In this system, stages or levels of nature (Mechanics, Physics, and Organics) are differentiated in terms of the general kind of concrete unity the concepts belonging to them exhibit, while within each level, kinds, laws, activities, and properties are ordered in terms of the degree to which they in fact are self-determined in the ways available in principle to things at their level.[33] So, for instance, all living things are capable of a more complete self-determination than bare

[31] See the discussion later in this chapter and note 41.

[32] See Rand ("Animal Defect") for a more detailed argument about the kind of individuality Hegel attributes to animal life and its relation to the logical unity of the concept. See also note 30 on habit, which arguably counts as a distinct basis on which the animal displays its self-externality.

[33] Although '*System von Stufen*' is usually translated as 'system of stages', Hegel is clear that the stages (or, alternatively, levels) are neither temporally nor causally ordered (E §249).

material bodies can achieve, but within the organic level, plants are ordered prior to ('lower' than) animals because plants exhibit the self-determination characteristic of living things to a lesser degree. The system of stages is thus Hegel's way of organizing the contents of the natural sciences in light of both the self-externality of nature and the systematic goal of exhibiting nature's self-determination.

17.3. CASE STUDY: COLLISION AND FALL

The bulk of Hegel's texts and lectures on the philosophy of nature are concerned not with laying out the method but with using the method to carry out the task of the philosophy of nature. Thus while the size of the present chapter makes a detailed account of Hegel's transformed vision of nature impossible, a satisfactory overview of his idea of the philosophy of nature demands that we examine at least one case. While taking a case from the Organics would allow us to focus on certain undeniably important aspects of Hegel's project and strategy—the relation between embodied life and spirit, his appropriation of Kantian teleology, and his attempt to differentiate his project from Schellingian *Naturphilosophie*—these topics are generally well represented in the recent secondary literature.[34] Less well represented are topics treated by Hegel in the Mechanics and Physics. But the Physics—covering a wide range of material from chemistry to electromagnetism to acoustics—demands familiarity with superseded theories and so is ill-suited for our present purposes.[35] The Mechanics, by contrast, avoids that obstacle, since many of its basic concepts are familiar from high school physics, and it has the added advantage of dealing with precisely those natural phenomena that seem least likely to exhibit the self-determination Hegel is after. Thus if we can make sense of Hegel's claim that mechanical objects and phenomena are self-determining, our prospects for understanding his similar claims in other, more promising cases are good.

Hegel's main argumentative line in the Mechanics traces the relationship between the concept of motion and the concept of a material body. These concepts, Hegel claims, are implicitly 'identical' in the sense that material bodies are essentially in motion and that whatever is in motion is a material body; according to his argument, when this identity is fully, concretely articulated, there turns out to be one kind of motion—'absolute' or gravitational motion—whose laws best express that identity. A body moving absolutely is therefore as self-determined as is possible for a natural thing at this stage or level of nature.

Hegel arrives at the claim that the concepts of matter and motion are implicitly identical through an analysis of the concepts of space and time meant to show that the concepts

---

[34] On the first, see Pinkard, *Hegel's Naturalism*; on the second, see the contributions to Khurana and Menke, eds., *Paradoxien;* on the third, see Rand, "Hegel and Schelling."

[35] On the Physics see Burbidge, *Real Process*, although the focus there is more on the logic of Chemism than on Hegel's interpretation of the details of contemporary chemistry.

of matter and motion both have the concepts of space and time as their contents; asserting that they have the same concepts as their contents is another way of asserting their
implicit identity.[36] In the course of this analysis, Hegel argues that the concepts of space
and time always come as a pair, in the sense that although space and time are qualitatively distinct kinds of quantitative multiplicity, neither can be assigned a determinate
quantitative value—that is, neither can be employed as a physical quantity—without reference to the other. Hegel's argument here is relatively compact, but the mutual dependence of time and space he is after can be seen directly in our practices of measurement,
in which we measure time elapsed by distance traversed and distance traversed by time
elapsed.[37] Matter and motion, as unities of time and space, are two distinct forms of this
mutual dependence: united as matter, space and time mutually determine each other's
identity or persistence; united as motion, space and time mutually determine each other's differences or changes.

Insofar as they are simply two distinct ways in which time and space can be unified,
matter and motion are independent, and a material body has no particular motion (or
rest) proper to it *qua* material body. This simple independence is the core of the conception of matter as inert, captured famously by Newton's First Law.[38] Yet Hegel's method
requires that he consider key theoretical terms not only as they are explicitly defined,
but as they are actually deployed in description and explanation—which in the case of
mechanics means considering how the defined terms relate to the physical quantities
appearing in the relevant equations. We find here, too, key quantitative determinations
that seem to express an external determination of motion. For instance, the quantitative
independence of speed (as a quantity of motion) and mass (as a quantity of matter) in
the equations expressing the basic laws of the inertial conception captures their essential 'indifference', according to this conception—that is, this quantitative independence
captures the fact that inert matter is not self-determined to any motion but rather determined wholly 'externally' (E §§264–265).[39]

[36] See E §§254–259; for commentary on details, see Wandschneider, *Raum, Zeit, Relativität*; Halper,
"Nature, Space and Time"; Winfield, "Space, Time and Matter"; and Houlgate, *Introduction*, Ch. 6.

[37] In the SI system, for instance, units for time are determined through frequencies or cycles, and thus
through spatial intervals; those for space are determined through distance traveled by light in a specific
time-interval.

[38] "Every body perseveres in its state of being at rest or of moving uniformly straight forward, except
insofar as it is compelled to change its state by forces impressed" (Newton, *Principles*, 416).

[39] 'Speed' translates Hegel's '*Geschwindigkeit*', which translates the Latin *velocitas*. We now reserve
'velocity' for the vector quantity and 'speed' for the scalar, but in Hegel's time the direction of a motion
was understood not as an aspect of its quantitative determinacy but as a qualitative determinacy.—As
a direct ratio of space to time, speed expresses a conception of motion on which space and time are
indifferent. Their determinate essential relation is expressed in acceleration, while the implicit unity of
matter and motion is expressed in momentum as a product of mass and speed (E §§267–268). It is harder
to say what quantitative relation of space and time Hegel thinks is constitutive of mass as a physical
quantity, though he appears to operationalize it in terms of the displacement of an arbitrary benchmark
object under some standardized collision conditions. See E §265 and Kluit, "Gravitational Mass."

17.3.1. Collision and Communication of Motion

Having laid out the concrete contents of some basic concepts—space, time, matter, and motion, among others omitted here—Hegel considers further precisely how the inertial conception specifies the external determination of motion. He argues that implicit in the standard inertial account is a different conception on which matter, while still exposed to externally determined motions, is self-determined to other motions.[40]

According to the inertial conception, he says, there is no state of motion or rest that is essential or immanent to any material body. Thus no matter what state of motion or rest a given body is in—and it must be in some such state—the inertial conception must understand it as having been externally determined to that state at some prior time by some other body. Consequently, the inertial conception cannot countenance the possibility of a lone material body existing by itself, and it follows from the inertial conception itself that any material body is both necessarily part of a system of such bodies and has had its current state of motion or rest determined externally by one or more of those other bodies.[41]

Hegel then considers the mode in which that necessary external determination happens. The simplest form of such determination, on his view, is the communication of motion in impact (*Stoß*). Hence Hegel begins by considering a highly idealized case: a perfectly elastic collision in one dimension with one of the bodies moving and the other at rest prior to impact.[42] In such a case, he says, the communication of motion from one body to another is to be understood as involving the unification of the two bodies into one body at the instant of impact,[43] and their motions after impact are determined by redistributing this body's unified motion between them in a ratio determined by their relative masses.[44] Its use of this procedure shows that the inertial conception,

---

[40] Certain passages (particularly in E §266R) suggest a stronger interpretation, on which matter's capacity to be subject to external determination by collision would depend on the specific way in which it is self-determined to other motions—a point someone other than Hegel might express by saying that mechanical phenomena are grounded in dynamical properties and relations.

[41] Thus Hegel speaks of "the inert body externally posited as in motion, which for this very reason is finite, and thus related to another . . ." (E §265). Hegel is probably not arguing from Galilean relativity of motion here, though such considerations arise elsewhere in his argument. He also does not consider forces operating independently of any bodies, for reasons relating to his critique of the concept of force (see PS 9.82–102/¶¶132–165, SL 11.359–364/455–459).

[42] Hegel's discussion here follows the presentation of collision in Gren, *Naturlehre*, which Hegel owned (see Neuser, "Hegels privater Bibliothek") and which was widely used in German universities of the period (see Frercks, "Disziplinbildung"). See Pfleiderer, *Physik*, for the kind of mechanics Hegel would have been taught in Tübingen.

[43] "The inert body, in motion externally . . . momentarily makes up *one* body [with the resting body it strikes] . . . the motion is in this way *one* of both bodies (*communication of motion*)" (E §265); "In the instant of impact, then, the bodies make up one body. The motion of the one is here also the motion of the other" (NSU 24.257).

[44] "But after the collision, in that the bodies are separated, the motion [i.e., the quantity of motion as momentum] remains the same as it was before the impact.—Thus if in the simplest case one body rests and another body, which is moved, collides with it, so each body retains its mass and the speed is divided then according to the relation of the magnitudes of weight" (NSU 24.257).

though superficially committed to the independence of mass and speed, is in fact implicitly committed to the idea that mass (as quantity of matter) and speed (as simple quantity of motion) stand in a determinate relation in any communication of motion.[45] And given the necessity of such communication for the inertial conception's understanding of material bodies, it follows that the inertial conception must in fact regard momentum—the physical quantity that captures or expresses this determination relation between mass and speed—as the most complete quantitative expression of matter and its motion.[46] Thus for the inertial conception to present mass and speed as 'in principle' independent is for it to prioritize an abstraction over its own explanatory/descriptive content.

Now, insofar as on this account communication of motion is understood essentially to involve the unification of the two bodies at impact, the account organizes its entire explanation of the communication of motion around what Hegel calls the system's 'center'. This orientation toward the center is evident from the way the motions of the bodies before and after impact are understood as directed toward and away from it, respectively. More precisely, the center in question is the center of mass of the unified body formed at the instant of impact, or what we would conceive as the origin point of the center of mass frame for the system made up of the two bodies. As this point, the center is non-identical with the center of either body taken on its own.[47] This is what Hegel is after when he points out that, although the communication of motion involves a unity of the two bodies, they remain two distinct bodies, and thus their unity is not complete or fully actualized. This overall situation is expressed by Hegel's description of the distinct motions of the bodies as 'striving' to occupy a common center,[48] and Hegel argues that for the inertial conception, even the resting body is in motion ('striving') in some sense.[49]

[45] For Hegel the individuality each material body retains is its "being-for-self" or "relative heaviness [*relative Schwere*]" which is "further particularized through the quantum of mass" and also known as "weight [*Gewicht*] as the *heaviness* [Schwere] of a quantitatively particular mass (extensive as a multiplicity of heavy parts [*schwerer Teile*]—intensive as a determinate *pressure*)" (E §265). For a careful treatment of Hegel's conception of mass in relation to Newton's, see Kluit, "Gravitational Mass"; and, more broadly, Ihmig's outstanding *Hegels Deutung*.

[46] For Hegel, the (inertial) mass "as the real determination makes up, with the ideal, with the quantitative determinacy of motion [as] speed, *one* determinacy (*quantitas motus* [momentum]), within which each can take the place of the other" (E §265).

[47] Compare our procedure of normalizing to the center of mass frame, in which the bodies have identical momentum (except for direction), and in which their motions prior to impact are explicitly taken as directed toward, and thus as organized or determined in reference to, the center of mass of the system (identical to the center of mass of the body formed by their unification at the moment of impact).

[48] "Impact and resistance, like the motion posited through them, therefore have a substantial ground in a *center* common to the single bodies and lying outside them, and their externally posited, accidental motion goes over into *rest*, in this middle point. At the same time, in that the center is outside the matter, this rest is only a *striving* for the center" (E §266). Compare here the Corollaries to Newton's Third Law.

[49] Although he does not invoke our center-of-mass frame normalization procedure (see note 47), Hegel insists that both bodies in a collision are moving (E §265A), indicating that his emphasis on their making up one body in collision is meant to assert that they constitute a single system of motion.

Thus by examining the standard procedure through which mechanics understands communication of motion, Hegel tries to show that the simple representation of matter as 'inert' in fact has a much more complex content, expressed in the ways the concepts of space, time, matter, mass, body, motion, velocity, momentum, impact, center, and so on, all relate to one another in the definitions, verbal formulas, and equations used to understand communication of motion. He concludes that, because the inertial conception requires that all states of motion or rest be 'externally' determined, and because it conceives of such external determination as communication of motion within a system of bodies where motion is essentially toward their common center, it ends up committed to an essential motion of all bodies with respect to the system of which they necessarily make up a part. But although this commitment is in some sense opposed to the conception of matter as inert, the resulting interpretation of the communication of motion does not require that we abandon any of the calculative procedures, equations, or major theoretical terms of the inertial conception, even as that conception gets transformed. In fact, Hegel retains them all, and his critical analysis displays the extent to which, and the basis upon which, they are valid. Thus Hegel's treatment of inertial motion provides a straightforward example of the method he employs to tease out the concrete content implicit in the understanding's natural-scientific representations. Through this analysis, that content—including the relevant laws, which are neither refuted nor rejected—is preserved in a new form.

17.3.2. Transition to Falling Motion

Hegel's analysis of the inertial conception, however, doesn't simply transform its content; it also reveals that the transformed contents require further distinct quantitative measures and laws for their full expression. More precisely, the analysis explicitizes the inertial conception's commitment to the claim that all bodies are self-determined to move toward a center outside themselves. Yet the mathematical laws governing the communication of motion and the physical quantities and measures appearing in these laws, although preserved in the transformation, do not themselves explicitly capture such a motion. But another law, discovered empirically and developed quite independently of Newton's conception of inertia, does capture such a motion: the Galilean law of fall.[50]

The law of fall states that the distances traveled by two falling bodies (or by the same body considered over two appropriate intervals) are proportional to the squares of the elapsed times of their fall.[51] Such motion, he says, is a '*relatively free*' one: free because it

---

[50] "This striving . . . is *fall*, the *essential* motion" (E §266). Note, however, that Newton himself, having discussed in the Corollaries to his three laws various points about conservation of momentum and inertial systems, asserts in the subsequent Scholium that Galileo's notion of fall follows directly upon that material. So Hegel's order of exposition here follows Newton closely.

[51] Hegel refers specifically to the "Galilean law *that the traversed spaces are related as the squares of the elapsed times*" (E §267).

is "posited through the *concept* of a [material] body" and therefore "immanent" to every such body; only relatively free because, as a motion essentially oriented toward a point or center outside itself, falling motion begins with the falling body subject to an "*externally* posited, *contingent* determination" of standing at some given distance from that center (E §267). The merely relative freedom here is just the brute givenness, and hence non-self-determination, of that distance. According to Hegel, then, falling motion is more self-determined than inertial motion, in which all the quantitative determinations are simply given as or in initial conditions, and in which the total quantity of motion does not change as a result of its communication from one body to another. But while in fall the quantity of motion is determined in part by brutely given factors—not only the distance of the falling objects from its center, but also the constant or unit of fall—it is also determined in part by a determinate quantitative ratio of distance to time, which, on Hegel's view, expresses quantitatively the essential conceptual relation between space and time themselves.[52] All motions, of course, involve a quantitative relation of space to time, but unlike the uniform velocity characterizing inertial motion (s:t), the ratio characterizing falling motion is not a direct ratio but a power ratio, the proportion s:t^2 (visible in the standard equation for fall, $s = 1/2gt^2$). Hegel's idea is that this power ratio expresses not a simple, immediate unity of space and time, but a mediated, determinate one, and that it therefore gives at least partial quantitative expression to the determinate qualitative unity of space and time making up the content of the concepts of mass and motion.[53] In sum, then, the essential motion toward a center implicit in the inertial conception of motion now gets its explicit quantitative expression in the law of fall, such that this law better expresses the concrete content of the concepts of matter and motion.

We can see Hegel's point here by looking briefly at the standard interpretation of fall. On that interpretation, falling motion is caused by an attractive force exerted on the (essentially inert) falling body by the resting body toward which it falls. This interpretation puts the focus on explaining and quantifying an attractive force, whose effect on the motion of the falling body is wholly independent of the falling body's mass. Newtonian theory understands this force's quantity as a function of both the mass of the resting body and the distance of the falling body from its center, and interprets the constant g in the standard equation for the law as a measure of that force.

Hegel's interpretation, by contrast, focuses not on identifying that dynamical cause of this motion, but on understanding the ratio of space to time in the motion itself. His interpretation is somewhat dense and depends in its details on a number of

[52] For Hegel the law of fall "has an aspect that is determined out of the *concept* of a body," and the connection between this concept and the Galilean law "is to be seen as simply lying in [the law] itself," in which "the conceptual determinations of time and space become *free* with respect to each other, i.e., their quantitative determinations are related just as their conceptual ones" (E §267R).

[53] Hegel holds that the concept of ratio links quality and quantity, and that power ratios are the most complete type of ratio (SL: 21.318–320/278–279). He also understands the calculus in terms of power series (SL: 21.275/236) and regards it as the branch of mathematics with the highest philosophical standing (e.g., SL: 21.241/207). See the connections drawn between power series, fall, and the calculus in Hegel's discussion of Lagrange's analytical treatment of fall, in a note to E §267R.

commitments we cannot consider here, but its basic gist is not hard to get. Recall that for Hegel, space and time come as a pair or are mutually dependent in some determinate way, and the Hegelian question regarding any type of motion is about what determinate relation of space and time it asserts and whether that relation is the one actually constituting their concepts. Now, in fall the distances traversed are proportional to the squares of the times elapsed, so that if in the first second of fall a body falls 15 Paris feet, in the first two seconds it falls not 30 ($= 15 \times 2$), but 60 ($= 15 \times 2^2$) Paris feet. In his analysis here, Hegel emphasizes that in the ratio determining fall, the same number plays two roles: it both measures the time elapsed and shows up squared as the coefficient of the fall value (15 Paris feet), yielding as product the space traversed.[54] In this proportion, then, what is called 'the square of the time' does not itself determine a quantity of time but expresses the way in which the quantity of space is determined in concert with the fall value (that is, the constant of fall interpreted not as a measure of force but as a simple distance).

Through the double duty done by this quantity in the determination of the motion of fall, says Hegel, the proportion $s{:}t^2$ or s/t^2 expresses the mutual conceptual dependence of space and time by expressing both their identity and their determinate difference at once. The fact that the term for time appears in the denominator or divisor expresses the qualitative role time plays with respect to space generally: the unbroken continuity of space can only be limited and thus determined by means of a principle of division of the sheerly self-external, and this principle is time. Time is therefore essentially a divisor of space.[55] But the constantly flowing series of discrete instants of time, in turn, can only be given a positive, measurable existence through a principle for the totalizing unity of the sheerly self-external, and this principle is space. Thus space, for its part, is an expansive or extending principle: it is that in which whatever is delimited and determined stands in an essential unity with another outside it, or it is that which goes beyond itself to make up a new unified multiplicity or totality. Now, a motion that adequately exhibits the concrete concept of space can do so only by showing that the space of that motion is determined as a function of the time. But the time that determines space in such a motion cannot simply be time, on its own, but must be time mediated by space, or time understood in a way that expresses its essential mutual determination with space. If space is an expansive principle, then, the time component of the motion of fall must not be constant—that is, must not determine a simple constant additive increase in the space traversed—but must serve to determine the increase in the increase of space in the motion. Yet for this time component to be self-determined, it must determine the increase in the increase through itself. And this is how Hegel understands the fact that in fall, the distance traversed is not a function of the time *simpliciter* but of the time squared—since the square of the time is the time increased by an amount determined

[54] The fall value is not the same as (though it is related to) *g* as normally interpreted; while *g* is a measure of force, the fall value is simply a distance. Like Newton, Hegel doesn't focus on our *g* (which they both express, in Paris feet, as 30 ft/s^2) but on the fall value, namely, the distance fallen in the first second (15 Paris feet).

[55] Hegel contrasts this case with the case of uniform velocity, in which time or space can function as divisor (E §267R).

by the time itself. [56] Hence the ratio $s:t^2$ expresses the qualitative conceptual relationship between space and time, and the motion determined (partially) through this ratio counts as a motion that expresses a relatively self-determined or free motion of matter.

17.3.3. Transition to Orbital Motion

In falling motion, then, we have a self-determined motion of matter, the law of which expresses explicitly the relations of space and time implicit in the inertial conception (and in the concepts of space, time, matter, and motion themselves). Hegel's interpretation of this law argues that a self-determined motion of matter is quantitatively determined through the qualitative conceptual relations constituting motion and matter as mutually determining unities of space and time. But the self-determination of falling matter is again limited or partial, insofar as it is still saddled with elements of givenness (e.g., the distance of the falling body from the center). Through a subsequent analysis, Hegel arrives at the conclusion that fall, too, implicitly involves a larger conception of matter and its self-determined motion (E §§268–271). According to this larger conception, the self-determined motion of material bodies is not a simple motion toward a center, but rather a motion of multiple bodies organized around, but not striving to become identical with, their common center—a motion in which both their 'ideal' unity with this center and their 'real' particular difference from it are given a determinate quantitative expression in the laws. For Hegel this motion is most directly expressed by Kepler's laws, which jointly determine orbital motions around a common center, relate the periods of those motions to the distances of the bodies from the center, and relate the speeds of the bodies along any portion of their orbital paths to a ratio of the distance traversed and the body's distance from the center. These laws, like the law of fall, are explicitly expressed as power ratios of space to time, though unlike the law of fall they are saddled with no constants representing sheerly given quantities.[57] If Hegel is right, then, Kepler's laws are quantitative expressions of the qualitative relations determining the concepts of motion and matter and thus capture a motion that is self-determined in the highest degree.

Although the very intriguing issues surrounding Hegel's relation to Newton are too complex to be treated adequately in the present format, it is worth mentioning that Hegel's frequent objections to Newton (on questions of both method and content) should not be overemphasized. It is true that Hegel attacks the brew of pure mathematics, metaphysics, and brute empirical fact that characterizes Newton's argument

---

[56]   See note 53 on power ratios and E §267R on this ratio in particular.

[57]   Kepler's first ('Ellipse') law states that the orbital paths of the planets around the sun are ellipses, whose equation includes two square/square power ratios; his second ('Area') law states that the areas swept out in equal times by a line connecting a planet and the sun are equal, and so relates time to an area, which is expressed as a power (units squared); his third ('Period') law states that the square of the period of the planet's orbit is proportional to the cube of the semimajor axis of its ellipse, and so relates two powers (square and cube).

style in the *Principia*, and it is also true that Hegel has few kind words for explanatory appeals to forces. But he also praises Newton as the discoverer of a properly *universal* attraction, specifically praises the insight his theory offers into orbital perturbations, and happily admits that Newton's equations are practically preferable in many circumstances (E §270R). Hegel's preference for Kepler's laws, then, is not to be understood as the claim that no progress has been made since Kepler—indeed, Hegel frequently refers to Lagrange's algebraic development of Newton's laws—but rather as the claim that Newton's way of conceiving of things does not deliver what we need philosophically: namely, a way to see the nature thus described as genuinely self-determining. Other, compatible laws, properly interpreted, do allow us to see nature that way, and if Hegel's arguments are correct, a philosophical focus on these laws does not require us to abandon anything of applied or technical importance.

The resulting Hegelian picture of material bodies and their motion is one on which the self-determined motion of any single body is always understood only within the context of the larger system of which it is a part. Absent the external determination of its motion in collision or fall—to which it is always exposed due to its being a spatiotemporally distinct single thing—it would self-determine to orbital motion. Yet in this orbital motion the body is not strictly self-determined as this single thing, but rather as one of many bodies differentiated from the others in its system. Thus the self-determination of matter in mechanics turns out to be the internal differentiation of a system of bodies into particular material bodies with specific determinations of their own, distinct from those of the other bodies in the system. For Hegel, matter's turning out to involve such an internal differentiating activity marks the transition from the mechanical to the 'physical' or chemical stage, so that the chemical view of matter and its actions and reactions appears as the unfolding of commitments inherent in the mechanical conception.

17.4. CONCLUSION

As this brief summary of some main points from Hegel's analysis of collision and fall suggests, his full argument for the self-determination of nature involves a complex and detailed engagement with contemporary scientific theory. But amidst the profusion of detail, the aim of the argument at each stage is clear: to show that the content of our best science can be given a new form that reveals nature to be thoroughly self-determining. This self-determination happens in many ways, culminating for Hegel in the self-maintaining life processes of higher-order mammals. Even self-determined human life is, of course, exposed to many kinds of contingent external determination. But whatever the sublation of this life into spirit may involve for Hegel—including the achievement of a form of activity and existence that no longer counts as essentially self-external—it cannot involve leaving nature behind. At most, it can show us how to take up our natural selves, and with them the entirety of the natural world in which they are embedded, in a new, self-internal way. Something like this seems to be suggested by the philosophical anthropology Hegel develops in the opening section of the *Philosophy of Mind* under the heading of 'natural soul'. But ultimately, such an embrace of nature within and without us can happen only through the kind of extended philosophical confrontation with the natural sciences that characterizes the *Philosophy of Nature* and makes it an indispensable part of the Hegelian project.

WORKS CITED

Primary Texts

Note: Translations of Hegel's texts are either my own, or are taken from the translations given here, frequently modified.

Hegel, G. W. F. *Elements of the Philosophy of Right* [PR], edited by Allen Wood, translated by H. B. Nisbet. Cambridge: Cambridge University Press, 1991 [Cited as PR, followed by section number].

Hegel, G. W. F. *Hegel's Phenomenology of Spirit* [PS], translated by A. V. Miller. Oxford: Oxford University Press, 1977 [Cited as PS, followed by GW volume and page/English paragraph number].

Hegel, G. W. F. *Hegel's Philosophy of Nature: Part Two of the Encyclopedia of Philosophical Sciences (1830)* [E], translated by A. V. Miller. Oxford: Oxford University Press, 1970 [Cited as E, followed by section number, with 'R' for Remarks. Section numbers followed by 'A' refer to Additions (*Zusätze*), omitted in GW but reproduced in: Hegel, *Enzyklopädie der philosophischen Wissenschaften in Grundrisse 1830: Zweiter Teil: Die Naturphilosophie, mit den mündlichen Zusätzen*. Frankfurt am Main: Suhrkamp, 1970].

Hegel, G. W. F. *Nachschrift zu Hegels Vorlesungen über die Philosophie der Natur* (WS 1823/24) [NSG], von Karl Gustav Julius von Griesheim (in GW 24,1).

Hegel, G. W. F. *Nachschrift zu Hegels Vorlesungen über die Philosophie der Natur* (WS 1819/20) [NSR], von Johann Rudolf Ringier (in GW 24,1).

Hegel, G. W. F. *Nachschrift zu Hegels Vorlesungen über die Philosophie der Natur* (WS 1821/22) [NSU], von Boris von Uexküll (in GW 24,1).

Hegel, G. W. F. *The Encyclopedia Logic: Part I of the Encyclopedia of Philosophical Science with the Zusätze* [E], translated by T. F. Geraets, W. A. Suchting, and H. S. Harris. Indianapolis: Hackett, 1991 [Cited as E, followed by section number, with 'R' for Remarks. Section numbers followed by 'A' refer to Additions (*Zusätze*), omitted in GW but reproduced in: Hegel, *Enzyklopädie der philosophischen Wissenschaften in Grundrisse 1830: Erster Teil: Die Wissenschaft der Logik, mit den mündlichen Zusätzen*. Frankfurt am Main: Suhrkamp, 1970].

Hegel, G. W. F. *The Science of Logic* [SL], translated by George di Giovanni. Cambridge: Cambridge University Press, 2010 [Cited as SL, followed by GW volume and page/English page].

Kant, Immanuel. *Groundwork of the Metaphysics of Morals*, edited by Mary Gregor and Jens Timmerman. Cambridge: Cambridge University Press, 2012 [Cited as GrW, by volume and page of Kant, *Gesammelte Schriften*. Berlin: de Gruyter, 1900–].

Secondary Literature

Bowman, Brady. *Hegel and the Metaphysics of Absolute Negativity*. Cambridge: Cambridge University Press, 2013.

Burbidge, John. *Real Process: How Logic and Chemistry Combine in Hegel's Philosophy of Nature*. Toronto: University of Toronto Press, 1996.

Frercks, Jan. "Disziplinbildung und Vorlesungsalltag: Funktionen von Lehrbüchern der Physik um 1800 mit einem Fokus auf die Universität Jena." *Berichte zur Wissenschafts-Geschichte* 27, no. 1 (March 2004): 27–52.

Friedman, Michael. *The Dynamics of Reason*. Stanford, CA: CSLI Publications, 2001.

Gren, Friedrich Albrecht Carl. *Grundriß der Naturlehre*. 4th ed. Halle: Hemmerde und Schwetschke, 1801.

Halper, Edward. "The Logic of Hegel's *Philosophy of Nature*: Nature, Space and Time," in *Hegel and the Philosophy of Nature*, edited by Stephen Houlgate. Albany: State University of New York Press, 1998, 29–49.

Houlgate, Stephen. *An Introduction to Hegel: Freedom, Truth and History*, 2nd ed. Malden, MA: Blackwell, 2005.

Ihmig, Karl-Norbert. *Hegels Deutung der Gravitation. Eine Studie zu Hegel und Newton*. Frankfurt am Main: Athenäum, 1989.

Khurana, Thomas, ed. *The Freedom of Life: Hegelian Perspectives*. Berlin: August, 2013.

Khurana, Thomas, and Christoph Menke (eds.). *Paradoxien der Autonomie*. Berlin: August, 2011.

Kluit, Peter Martin. "Inertial and Gravitational Mass: Newton, Hegel, and Modern Physics," in *Hegel and Newtonianism*, edited by Michael John Petry. New York: Kluwer, 1993, 229–247.

Koyré, Alexandre. *The Astronomical Revolution: Copernicus—Kepler—Borelli*, translated by R. E. W. Maddison. New York: Dover, 1992.

Kuhn, Thomas. *The Structure of Scientific Revolutions*. Chicago: University of Chicago Press, 1962.

Lumsden, Simon. "Habit and the Limits of the Autonomous Subject." *Body & Society* 19, no. 2–3 (June & September, 2013): 58–82.

Malabou, Catherine. "Who's Afraid of Hegelian Wolves?" in *Deleuze: A Critical Reader*, edited by Paul Patton. Malden, MA: Blackwell, 1996, 114–138.

Malabou, Catherine. *The Future of Hegel: Plasticity, Temporality, Dialectic*, translated by Lisbeth During. New York: Routledge, 2005.

McCumber, John. "Hegel on Habit." *The Owl of Minerva* 21, no. 2 (Spring 1990): 155–165.

McCumber, John. *Understanding Hegel's Mature Critique of Kant*. Stanford, CA: Stanford University Press, 2014.

McDowell, John. *Mind and World*. Cambridge, MA: Harvard University Press, 1996.

Meyerson, Émile. *Explanation in the Sciences*, translated by Mary-Alice Sipfle and David Sipfle. New York: Springer, 1991.

Neuser, Wolfgang. "Die naturphilosophische und naturwissenschaftliche Literatur aus Hegels privater Bibliothek," in *Hegel und die Naturwissenschaften*, edited by Michael John Petry. Stuttgart-Bad Cannstatt: frommann-holzboog, 1987, 479–499.

Newton, Isaac. *Mathematical Principles of Natural Philosophy*, translated by I. Bernard Cohen and Anne Whitman. Berkeley: University of California Press, 1999.

Pfleiderer, Christoph Friedrich von. *Physik. Naturlehre nach Klügel. Nachschrift einer Tübinger Vorlesung von 1804*, edited by Paul Ziche. Stuttgart-Bad Cannstatt: frommann-holzboog, 1994.

Pinkard, Terry. *German Philosophy 1760–1860: The Legacy of Idealism*. Cambridge: Cambridge University Press, 2002.

Pinkard, Terry. *Hegel's Naturalism: Mind, Nature, and the Final Ends of Life*. Oxford: Oxford University Press, 2012.

Pippin, Robert. "Hegel's Practical Philosophy: The Realization of Freedom," in *The Cambridge Companion to German Idealism*, edited by Karl Ameriks. Cambridge: Cambridge University Press, 2000, 180–199.

Pippin, Robert. "Leaving Nature Behind, or Two Cheers for 'Subjectivism,'" in *Reading McDowell: Mind and World*, edited by Nicholas Smith. New York: Routledge, 2002, 58–76.

Posch, Thomas. "Hegel and the Sciences," in *A Companion to Hegel*, edited by Stephen Houlgate and Michael Baur. London: Blackwell, 2011, 177–202.

Rand, Sebastian. "Stimulus-Response Relations and Organic Unity in Hegel and Schelling." *Internationales Jahrbuch des Deutschen Idealismus/International Yearbook of German Idealism* 8 (2010): 185–206.

Rand, Sebastian. "What's Wrong with Rex? Hegel on Animal Defect and Individuality." *European Journal of Philosophy* 23, no. 1 (March 2015): 68–86.

Rödl, Sebastian. *Self-Consciousness*. Cambridge, MA: Harvard University Press, 2007.

Sedgwick, Sally. *Hegel's Critique of Kant: From Dichotomy to Identity*. Oxford: Oxford University Press, 2013.

Stone, Allison. *Petrified Intelligence: Nature in Hegel's Philosophy*. Albany: State University of New York Press, 2005.

Thompson, Michael. *Life and Action: Elementary Structures of Practice and Practical Thought*. Cambridge, MA: Harvard University Press, 2008.

Wandschneider, Dieter. *Raum, Zeit, Relativität: Grundbestimmungen der Physik in der Perspektive der Hegelschen Naturphilosophie*. Frankfurt am Main: Vittorio Klostermann, 1982.

Winfield, Richard Dean. "Space, Time and Matter: Conceiving Nature Without Foundations," in *Hegel and the Philosophy of Nature*, edited by Stephen Houlgate. Albany: State University of New York Press, 1998, 51–69.

CHAPTER 18

HEGEL'S ANTHROPOLOGY

ANDREJA NOVAKOVIC

18.1. ANTHROPOLOGY FROM A SYSTEMATIC POINT OF VIEW

HEGEL's section entitled "Anthropology" appears, at face value, to be his contribution to the relatively new field of philosophical anthropology. It touches upon a number of topics usually treated in parallel accounts, including feeling, sleeping, dreaming, laughing, and crying. When Hegel began lecturing on these topics in Berlin in the 1820s, philosophical anthropology was emerging as an empirically informed discipline within philosophy, whose task was to determine human nature through reflections about (among other things) climate and geography, cultural differences, social behaviors, subjective faculties, and individual pathologies. Hegel's "Anthropology" can certainly be read as his version of such an account, and it is possible to take an independent interest in his conclusions. Even if many of them may not stand the test of time, they demonstrate a sincere effort to engage with the findings of his day, including research into animal magnetism and other occult phenomena, without compromising his picture of the human being as an essentially thinking creature.[1]

It is, however, important to keep in mind that Hegel's "Anthropology" also has a pressing systematic function to perform. Given its placement in his *Encyclopedia of the Philosophical Sciences*, this chapter tracks the transition from 'nature' to 'spirit', more specifically, the development of consciousness out of mere animal life. In its opening pages we find a living individual who exhibits the same degree of independence from her environment that all living beings do, but who is not yet aware of herself as an individual, and so not yet aware of her difference from her environment. The standpoint

---

[1] Hegel was actually enthusiastic about research into animal magnetism because he thought that it provided evidence in favor of his speculative philosophy. For a helpful discussion of his topic, see Magee, "Dark Side of Subjective Spirit."

of consciousness is marked by this awareness that the objective world I inhabit is not simply an extension of me. It is the standpoint treated explicitly in the "Phenomenology of Spirit," the section that follows the "Anthropology" and whose attainment the "Anthropology" is thus meant to explain. Because Hegel is introducing standard anthropological topics with this aim in view, his "Anthropology" cannot be understood adequately if abstracted from its particular position within his system.

Tracking the first steps in the transition from nature to spirit is not the only systematic aim of the "Anthropology" and does not exhaust its philosophical value for Hegel. Because this second aim is not as obvious at first glance, it is instructive to compare Hegel's "Anthropology" to Kant's *Anthropology from a Pragmatic Point of View*. Kant's textbook to his long-standing lectures, published after his retirement in 1798, served as an early model of a philosophical anthropology, one with which Hegel was familiar.[2] Although both texts deal with a similar subject matter, there is one noteworthy difference between them. Kant's "Anthropology" is empirically grounded in a more straightforward sense, and thus does not interfere with the transcendental investigation of his three Critiques. What Kant offers are a number of empirical generalizations derived by observing the behavior of human beings. He does not insist on the necessity of his conclusions, nor does he attempt to demonstrate their systematic connections. This does not seem to be true of Hegel's "Anthropology." As Murray Greene has argued in his *Hegel on the Soul*, Hegel is offering a 'speculative' anthropology precisely because he wants to demonstrate that this stage is a necessary one in the development from nature to spirit.

If this is true, it means that the empirical is going to have a more problematic status in Hegel's account than it had in Kant's. On the one hand, Hegel's Anthropology is part of what he calls *Realphilosophie* and so must reckon with the world as it happens to be. On the other hand, it must still be a 'scientific' work, which means that it is saddled with the task of drawing out the necessary dimension within the domain of the contingent. To put this differently, Hegel must show that the various transformations that human beings generally undergo are indispensable to the formation of objective consciousness. While he cannot deduce these transformations in an a priori manner, without examining how human beings as a matter of fact develop, his ambition is to show that we could not have turned out the way we did without them. According to Greene, this is Hegel's most radical departure from Kant. "If the Kantian Anthropology had been lost or never written, the Kantian metaphysic of knowledge would remain essentially unimpaired. If Hegel's Anthropology had been lost, the foundation would be missing in the logical structure of Subjective Spirit, which is an important part of Hegel's metaphysic of knowledge."[3]

While this may indeed be a significant difference between the respective functions of the two anthropologies, they have more in common than this makes it seem. One peculiar feature of Kant's "Anthropology" is that it is written from a "Pragmatic Point of View," and thus with a view to the ethical advantages and disadvantages of human

---

[2] Kant's "Anthropology" seems to have been explicitly referenced, according to the Addition to §395.

[3] Greene, *Hegel on the Soul*, ix.

nature. Kant defines pragmatic knowledge of the human being as "the investigation of what *he* as a free-acting being makes of himself, or can and should make of himself."[4] In short, it is not motivated by a neutral interest in natural facts about us, but investigates the extent to which those facts can positively assist the ends of ethics.[5] I believe that there are reasons to think that Hegel's "Anthropology" is also guided by a similar question, for Hegel is focusing on those human capabilities that, even if they enable the initial stages of our subjective development, are only fully realized in what he calls 'ethical life'—the province of Objective Spirit in his *Encyclopedia*. As we will see, he insists repeatedly that the relevant forms of subjectivity remain mere forms until they are filled with an objective content, which only ethical life can provide. The question then becomes which forms are more suitable to this content than others.[6]

Moreover, Hegel points out that the placement of the "Anthropology" (or of Subjective Spirit as a whole) cannot avoid seeming one-sided, for Subjective Spirit and Objective Spirit are two sides of the same coin. In his words, "One could say just as well that spirit is at first objective and should become subjective, as that spirit is at first subjective and has to make itself objective. Consequently the difference of subjective and objective spirit is not to be seen as rigid" (E §387A).[7] As I read this reminder, Hegel is noting that human beings become conscious subjects, not in the midst of brute nature, but in a social world that allows them to make the most of what nature has given them. In the following, I will clarify some of the ways in which Hegel's particular reflections about human nature serve his broader philosophical projects—from an explanation of how we are able to become conscious of a world over and above us, to an explanation of how we can become ethical agents who identify with our world, and so have succeeded in making the objective subjective in turn.

18.2. Spirit as (Natural) Soul

Hegel opens Subjective Spirit by echoing the Ancient Delphic demand for self-knowledge—*Erkenne dich selbst*—as its task. He claims that this demand is, on the one

---

[4] Kant, *Anthropology*, 7:119.

[5] There is for Kant an important difference between practical and pragmatic knowledge. Practical knowledge is knowledge about what is constitutive of ethics, thus knowledge of what our duties are and our motives ought to be. Pragmatic knowledge is knowledge about what can be useful to ethics, even if it is not constitutive of it. For example, we should avoid bad habits and foster good habits because those will interfere less with moral action. But this, for Kant, does not mean that we should seek to act morally out of habit.

[6] Here the distinction between pragmatic and practical is not as relevant, for Hegel does not think that these forms are only instrumentally valuable for the end of ethics.

[7] This comment is consistent with Hegel's broader methodological commitments to the circularity of his system. Because the story he is telling is not only a developmental one, but also reveals ever-deeper conditions for what comes before, it could also have been rewritten by starting with the conclusion and working backward to the beginning.

hand, the human being's own. In other words, it is we who demand self-knowledge of ourselves, rather than being asked to pursue it by someone or something outside of us. But this demand is, on the other hand, also an 'eternal' or 'divine' one, which means that it can only be satisfied once the human being overcomes her finite perspective. Finitude or limitation by something other than oneself plagues the early stages of Subjective Spirit, from the "Anthropology" to the "Phenomenology." Initially this limitation comes from the seamless dependence that human beings have on their material environment, including their own bodies. Later this limitation will come from an objective world that stands over, above, and against us as subjects. But spirit in its subjective form is already being defined as the effort to overcome these limitations, to become eternal or divine. And the suggestion is made that spirit becomes objectively eternal or divine when it attains self-knowledge, when we know ourselves to be spiritual beings.

While one might naturally assume that the "Anthropology" is going to have the human being as its object of investigation, Hegel claims that the subject matter of the "Anthropology" is going to be the 'soul', and it does not initially seem as if only human beings have it. As we will see, the 'natural soul' and the 'feeling soul' involve traits that we share with other animals. What we find out in the course of the "Anthropology," however, is that there is a sense in which only human beings have a soul, because the soul is only fully realized in them. In Hegel's terminology, only human beings have an 'actual soul'. But the distinctive features of human beings, those that relevantly set them apart from other animals, do not emerge until the end.[8]

Hegel characterizes the soul in three telling ways. He claims that (1) it can also be called 'natural spirit', or *Naturgeist* (E §387); (2) it is "the universal immateriality of nature, its simple ideal life" (E §389); and (3) it is the "sleep of spirit" (E §389A).[9]

First, the soul is the most natural form that spirit can take. At this stage of our spiritual development, we are directly influenced by the natural world and in this respect not significantly different from other animals. Hegel will accordingly emphasize this continuity between subjective activity and nature, and he will point out the numerous ways in which this activity is naturally determined.

Second, Hegel states that the soul is, unlike the body, immaterial: "The soul is not only for itself immaterial, but the universal immateriality of nature, its simple ideal life" (E §389). Before we can parse this definition, we need to consider what Hegel does *not* mean to say. As the additions to this paragraph make clear, Hegel is hoping to preserve important aspects of the soul (its immateriality and simplicity) as it was traditionally conceived without inheriting the confusion these tend to generate. In particular, Hegel wants to reject the picture of the soul in rational psychology, according to which the soul is an immaterial and simple *thing*. This picture produces countless puzzles about the community between body and soul, about how something immaterial can exert

---

[8] By adopting this language of the 'soul', Hegel means to put himself in conversation with Aristotle's *De Anima*. See Malabou, *The Future of Hegel*, 39–56; Ferrarin, *Hegel and Aristotle*, 234–283.

[9] All translations of Hegel are my own, with the help of the Wallace/Miller translation.

influence over something material, how it itself can change, and where its seat is to be found. According to Hegel, we go wrong as soon as we imagine the soul to be a 'thing' (*Ding*) at all, whether material or immaterial.

Instead, Hegel recommends that we think of the soul as a particular stage in the development of spirit, the stage of becoming a *self*. Attaining this stage requires undergoing a process of individuation, during which we acquire sufficient distance from everything that is external to us. It is at the end of this process that we truly possess a soul, that the soul is realized in us—in other words, that we have achieved a sense of ourselves as selves. But this process comes to an end only when we have also achieved a unity between our selves and our bodies, when our bodies have been reshaped so as to express our subjective activity. This means that the soul can never be something real or *actual* unless it is embodied.

But Hegel describes the soul nevertheless as 'immaterial', and that for two important reasons. One reason is that soul is a form of spirit, and as a form of spirit, it strives toward a standpoint from which it can distinguish itself from material nature, even if it can never dispense with it either.[10] The other reason is that the soul during its development is not yet individuated and so lacks contours, edges, and boundaries that could make it an object in the material world. In the material world, objects are external to each other, distinguished from each other by time and place. The soul, in contrast, belongs to a stage at which we do not recognize any such distinctions. This means that there are not yet individual 'souls' properly speaking, and it explains why Hegel does not claim that souls are immaterial, but that *the* soul is the "universal immateriality of nature." As Hegel clarifies, "The soul is the all-permeating [*Allesdurchdringende*], not simply existing in one particular individual . . . for it has to be grasped as the truth, as the ideality of everything material, as the completely universal, in which all differences are only ideal and which does not stand one-sidedly over and against the other, but encroaches [*übergreift*] on the other" (E §406A). What this means is that the soul is, on the one hand, amorphous, not yet particularized or individuated, and on the other hand, the 'ideal' side of all matter. It is the 'ideal' side of all matter because it first introduces the structure of spirit into the natural world. It is spirit's most basic expression.

Third, Hegel tells us that the soul represents the 'sleep' of spirit. In the "Anthropology" Hegel examines the state of being asleep and comments on its difference from waking. But when he calls the soul the 'sleep' of spirit, he means that in a broader, more metaphorical sense. He adds, the soul is "the form of un-differentiation, consequently of unconsciousness" (E §389A). In other words, the soul is not yet technically conscious, even when it is literally awake, because it has not gained the requisite distance from its environment to view it from an objective standpoint. The entire "Anthropology" represents the process of 'waking up' to this standpoint. So its proper subject matter is

---

[10] See, for example, Nuzzo, "Soul-Body Relation." She argues that the soul-body problem is not solved before the "Anthropology" opens, but that it is the central problem of the "Anthropology" itself. Given that the 'actual' soul turns out to be the identity of the inner and outer (E §411), she is right in saying that the relationship between body and soul persists as a problem throughout the "Anthology."

the 'unconscious', which for Hegel means the state of immediate continuity with the natural world.

The "Anthropology" is accordingly divided into three forms that the soul can take. It is important to note that these are meant to constitute stages in a process of development, even if none of them vanishes completely in it. In other words, Hegel is not simply outlining a number of different subjective faculties that exist alongside each other, the way that Kant did in his "Anthropology." He is showing these faculties (or, in his terminology, 'forms') as emerging out of one another, with each comprising a unified stage in this process. The three forms are the natural soul, the feeling soul, and the actual soul. I will consider them in turn.

The natural soul is the most immediate form that the soul can take, even if it is true that every form of the soul is in some sense immediate. What makes the natural soul most immediate is that it is thoroughly under the influence of its external conditions, with no subjective way of processing that influence. Hegel divides this soul in three further ways, outlining (1) the natural qualities, or the environmental, planetary, and geographical conditions that shape the mood and character of human beings; (2) the natural alternations, or the process of growth and decline that each human being nat-urally undergoes; and finally (3) sensation. The section on natural qualities is perhaps the most notorious, because in it (or, more accurately, in the additions) Hegel voices many cultural and racial prejudices of his age. For example, Hegel remarks that Africans constitute a '*Kindernation*' and let themselves be bought and sold, because they have no sense of right and wrong (E §393A). More locally, Hegel makes much of the difference among European nations, distinguishing, for instance, the intellectual predispositions of the English and the Germans. What all of these reflections are meant to illustrate is more generally that climate and other environmental factors affect our personalities.

Hegel's more persuasive point has to do with the relationship between natural advan-tage and *ethical* character. In the additions (to §395), Hegel hopes to dispel two familiar beliefs about character. One is the belief that some people are naturally predisposed to be good, that there are 'moral geniuses' who happen to be blessed with a gift akin to musical talent. The other is the belief that character is composed of idiosyncratic traits that set one individual apart from another. Hegel claims that there are no moral geniuses, because character is always an achievement, and one that can in principle be demanded of any-one, regardless of her natural dispositions. He also claims that, while it is true that people differ in their character, this is only because some have character and others do not, for to have character means to have achieved a 'firm determinacy [*feste Bestimmtheit*]'.

The most developed form of the natural soul is sensation, sensitivity, or sentience, which Hegel calls *Empfindung*.[11] When I awake from sleep, I find (*finden*) the world already there by means of sensation. It is my first waking experience and constitutes an important step in the direction of individuating myself and of relating to objects. As Hegel puts it, waking up gives us an indeterminate sense of our difference from

---

[11] There is no adequate English equivalent for this term, because it is meant to encompass both 'outer' and 'inner' sense. So it refers to sensory input that comes from outside of us. But it also refers to an inward sensitivity, captured by the expression '*empfindlich*'. It is clear that Hegel has both senses in mind.

the external world, whereas sensation gives us an increasingly determinate sense of this difference (E §399A). The main change is that I have become receptive to external impressions as external and that I can distinguish between those that come from my imagination and those that do not.[12] This development is due to the increasingly *mediated* relationship I have to what I sense. My sense organs provide me with tools for exploring objects, namely by touching them, tasting them, hearing them, and so on. And the reason that Hegel deems our faculty of sight to be our most spiritual sense is that it allows for the greatest distance between me and the sensed object, with the least physical impact of the object on me.

Sensation has a formative role to play in the developmental process that Hegel is tracking, but it is significantly limited. Although Hegel echoes Aristotle by stating that "everything is in sensation and, if one wants [to put it this way], everything that emerges in our spiritual consciousness and in reason has its source and origin in it" (E §400), he immediately clarifies that this refers only to the initial way in which spiritual consciousness and reason appear. He is especially concerned to dispel the misconception that sensation has any ethical significance. Here he is addressing himself to a conception of ethical life that takes the 'heart' to be the foundation of character or conviction.[13] He argues that the 'heart' cannot serve as a foundation, because it is far too flimsy and fickle to ground anything like character or conviction. While it might be a good thing to have a 'good heart' in addition to a firm character, the latter cannot have its basis in the former. One implication this has is that we cannot *justify* what we do by appealing to the dictates of our heart in the way that some of Hegel's contemporaries believed.[14] In fact, Hegel concludes with a decisively negative assessment of *Empfindung*, calling it the "the worst form of the spiritual, and that which can ruin even the best content" (E §402) by degrading it into this lower, non-rational form. This will not be his assessment of the "Anthropology" as a whole—that it only provides us with provisional forms of spirit. Unlike sensation, habit does not degrade its content. It even elevates this content by giving it a stable form.

18.3. Feeling, Madness, and Habit

Habit is the most developed form of what Hegel calls the feeling soul, which emerges out of the natural soul as a solution to the problem posed by sensation. Earlier I mentioned

---

[12] Hegel follows Kant in the criteria for distinguishing waking from dreaming impressions: when we are awake, our impressions hang together in a necessary and objective way, whereas when we are dreaming, our impressions are isolated and unrelated to each other (E §398A).

[13] Here we see this other sense of *Empfindung* than the one that is his primary focus, since it concerns inner rather than outer sense.

[14] Although Hegel is not very specific, he seems to have in mind people like Fries and Schleiermacher, both of whom made emotion or subjective conviction the foundation of religion and ethics. For more information about Hegel's references in Subjective Spirit, see the commentary by Petry, *Hegel's Philosophy of Subjective Spirit*.

what makes *Empfindung* limited from the ethical standpoint. But Hegel is also committed to showing that it turns out to be inadequate from the standpoint of our early spiritual development. In particular, sensation proves incapable of achieving an individual 'I', because sensations are on their own fragmented and ephemeral (E §402). They come and go in succession without leaving behind anything enduring. The 'feeling soul' develops as a higher stage in this process because it allows for a very basic form of self-awareness. I am taking a stance toward the material that is given to me. I discriminate among this material. I prefer some of it to others.

Hegel points out that, even though feeling (*Gefühl*) and sensation (*Empfinden*) tend to be treated as synonymous, they have significantly different connotations: sensations are something we 'find', whereas feeling already implies an active relation to what is merely found. This kind of soul is, more precisely, caught somewhere between activity and passivity—while it is still dependent on a naturally given content, it also does something, namely, *identifies* with this content. But my relationship to my feelings is at this point one of 'immediate identification'. Hegel also suggests that there is a further difference between sensation and feeling. Much of his discussion of the feeling soul in its more passive variations is dedicated to paranormal phenomena involving forms of influence that cannot be explained through sense-impressions. As he puts it, "feeling or the subjective way of knowing, dispenses wholly, or at least in part, with the mediations and conditions indispensable to an objective knowledge and can, for example, perceive visible things without the aid of the eye or with the mediation of light" (E §406A). One of Hegel's favorite cases of this is the connection between a mother and the fetus she is carrying, a connection in which the mother acts as a 'genius' who exerts 'magical' influence over her fetus, similar to the influence exerted upon a medium in a séance. As Hegel recounts, a mother injured during pregnancy, say, by breaking her arm, has been known to give birth to a child similarly injured (E §405A). Another example of it are cases of animal magnetism, in which people were put into a state of hypnosis or trance through another's direct influence. Hegel also discusses clairvoyance in this context without dismissing it as lacking credibility. Instead, he argues that the clairvoyant person might very well be onto something, and we often later discover that they were. The problem is that there is no way of telling whether or not she in fact knows, whether her feelings are guiding her correctly or leading her astray. Even she cannot be sure.[15] For that, she would have to adopt a more mediated relationship to the world in the way that her five senses allow.

What we discover is that a reliance on feeling for one's identity ('self-feeling') can lead to madness. Self-feeling is the most paradigmatic version of feeling soul. According to Hegel, the feeling soul in its most elementary form is purely passive and so thoroughly controllable by a genius. But as self-feeling, the feeling soul becomes engaged in the activity of taking up some of its feelings at the expense of others. The way that Hegel characterizes it is that the feeling soul identifies itself wholly with one feeling (or a handful

---

[15] Hegel compares clairvoyant people to animals that are guided by instinct, even if reliably so (E §406A).

of feelings) in particular, and so ignores the fact that they are particular. "It is immersed in the *particularity* of feeling and at the same time through the ideality of the particular it combines itself in them with itself as a subjective unity" (E §407). This kind of exclusive identification with some particular feelings can have pathological consequences, because it can lead to fixation and delusion. The self-feeling soul is prone to fixate on one emotional attachment in an exaggerated and damaging way,[16] or on one perception without putting it in an objective context and allowing it to be judged against other perceptions.[17] For Hegel this amounts to madness, or 'sleeping while awake [*wachend träumen*]' (E §408A). Hegel goes so far as to call madness a 'contradiction' at the heart of self-feeling (E §408), a contradiction between the particularity of the feeling and the exclusivity of my identification. If this feeling I am having is just one feeling among others, it does not merit this kind of single-minded devotion, and it is contradiction to treat it as if it were absolutely authoritative and exhaustive. But he also clarifies that madness is not a *necessary* stage in this developmental process.[18] It is merely an extreme case that reveals that general inadequacy of feeling, analogously to the way that crime reveals the inadequacy of purely contractual relations in Objective Spirit (E §408A).

Habit emerges as a cure to madness because it achieves the two goals of this developmental process. It introduces stability into our feelings and thus paves the way for perceptual consciousness and allows us to become individuated, to gain a sense of self. The way it achieves this is by significantly changing our relationship to our feelings, and by extension to the body as a whole. Here is Hegel's own definition of habit:

> Habit is the soul making itself into an abstract universal being and reducing the particularity of feeling to a mere determination of it. In this way the soul has the content in its possession and preserves [this content] in it, so that it is not sensitive [*empfindend*] in its determinations, not indistinguishable in its relation to them nor immersed in them, but has them in it in an insensitive [*emfindungslos*] and unconscious [*bewusstlos*] manner and moves within them. [The soul] is free from them to the extent to which it is not interested in them or preoccupied with them; by existing in these forms as its possession, [the soul] is simultaneously open for further activity and occupation—of sensation as well as of spiritual consciousness in general. (E §410)

In the first two sentences, Hegel is articulating the structure of this new relationship. Through habit I stop being immersed in my feelings, but become capable of distinguishing myself from my feelings, stepping back from them and seeing them for what they are. It is only in virtue of this distinction that my feelings become my 'determinations,'

---

[16] A helpful example is romantic obsession that comes at the expense of all other commitments. See Mowad, *Awakening to Madness*, 98.

[17] The example given in the additions to §408 is the delusion that I am king (even though there is ample evidence against it).

[18] "The subject finds itself in this way in a contradiction between the systematic totality in its consciousness and the particular determination that is not fluid and not properly ordered in this totality—*madness*" (E §408).

my possession. Simply put, they are now no longer *me*, but *mine*.[19] In the second and third sentences, Hegel indicates how habit is able to achieve this, namely, by making us 'insensitive' and 'unconscious'. In other words, I become liberated from my feelings by becoming so accustomed to them that they no longer demand my attention. That to which I am habituated recedes into the background, in this way enabling me to pursue other, more demanding projects, like philosophy.[20]

Hegel explicitly associates habituation with *liberation*, with an activity of detaching oneself from feeling. This has the upshot of shaping a new, more distanced relationship to the content of my experience. But habituation can only be liberating because it makes this content *unconscious* and in this way banishes it from view. This is why Hegel claims that there is a tension at the bottom of habit, a tension that is aptly captured in the phrase 'second nature':

> Habit is rightly called a 'second nature'—*nature*, for it is an immediate being of the soul—a *second*, for it is an immediacy posited by the soul, an impressing and moulding of corporeality, which enters into the determinations of feeling as such and into the representational and volitional determinations made corporeal. (E §410)

Hegel is pointing out that it is the process of habituation that is properly liberating, for habituation is unequivocally a kind of activity, an active impressing and molding through repetition and practice, and so a deliberate effort to take possession of my own body and make it conform more effectively to my will. Although habituation is not always intentionally undertaken, habituating myself does require the exercise of my intellect and the conscious control of my movements and limbs. Through practice and repetition, I alter some of my natural determinations (by learning to stand upright) as well as giving myself new determinations, produced by me (by learning to fashion and use a tool). This is what makes habituation the imposition of a *second* nature.

The outcome of the process is still, however, *nature* in a potentially problematic sense. Hegel does recognize that habituation produces lasting benefits by creating a background of stable feelings that no longer interfere with our activity. In general, "habit possesses the greatness to be freed from that to which one is habituated" (E §410). Hegel distinguishes between three types of habits: habits of hardening (*Abhärtung*), specifically to sensations; habits of indifference (*Gleichgültigkeit*), specifically toward the

---

[19] McCumber, "Hegel on Habit," 158.

[20] See, for example, "[Habit] is free from them [sensations, etc.] insofar as it is not interested in and preoccupied with them; by existing in these forms as its possessions, it is likewise open to further activity and occupation—of sensation as well as of the consciousness of spirit" (E §410). Hegel explicitly mentions the dependence of philosophy on habit in his addition to §151 of the *Philosophy of Right*, when he writes that "habit belongs to the ethical just as it belongs to philosophical thinking, since the latter demands that spirit be cultivated against arbitrary ideas and that these be eliminated and overcome so that rational thinking can have free reign."

satisfaction of desires; and habits of skill (*Geschicklichkeit*). So habits free us from the overwhelming and maddening imposition of sensations, from the distracting effects of drives and desires, and even from the mental exertion involved in acquiring skills like learning how to carve and throw a spear. The problem is that habits can only achieve this beneficial result by producing something that looks unconscious, or as Hegel also puts it, *mechanical*. When I become habituated, especially to a certain activity, I am no longer paying attention to what I am doing, and my body seems no longer guided by my will and intellect. This is the reason that habit can liberate only by putting a second 'nature' in place of the first—a set of fixed dispositions that determine our behavior 'blindly', so to speak.

Hegel's discussion of habit has received more scholarly attention than earlier sections of his "Anthropology." Most interpreters of this section have focused on habit's role in the transition from nature to spirit, attempting to explain how habit can contribute to the development of individuality and objective consciousness. One example is Simon Lumsden, who stresses the complex intermediary position that habit occupies, falling neither on the side of spontaneity nor on that of receptivity.[21] David Forman offers a particular illuminating explanation of this intermediary position, clarifying how it is that habits enable us to become conscious in the first place.[22] It is worth noting that both of their interpretations grapple with a McDowellian account of the mind-world relation, arguing that Hegel offers an alternative to McDowell's dualism of 'space of reasons' and 'space of causes', or of spontaneity and receptivity. But in doing so, Forman takes Hegel's point about second nature differently from the preceding. According to Forman, habit is meant to be a second 'nature' because it maintains a connection with the natural world through reliance on sensory input, and through an eventual consciousness *of* nature. This is a surprising rendering of this phrase, given that Hegel himself emphasizes the connection between nature and mechanism in the relevant passages. In other words, what makes habit a second 'nature' for Hegel is not that it continues to rely on nature, but that it produces something that looks natural, namely, unreflective forms of behavior. Thus Hegel's point does not seem to be primarily an epistemic one, but alludes to the effects of habituation on agency.

There is another strand in the scholarship that has also focused on the transitional place of habit, but has emphasized its consequent limitations. Such interpretations argue that habit represents a form of unfreedom and must be left behind by the further unfolding of spirit. These interpretations admit that habits can form a background to our conscious and deliberate activity, since certain habits need to remain in place in order for us to be able to engage in more demanding projects. But it is indisputable, they claim, that Hegel believes that freedom itself could never become habitual without ceasing to be freedom at all. One example is Thomas A. Lewis, who has argued that habit is

---

[21] Lumsden, "Between Nature and Spirit." Though Lumsden foregrounds the transitional place of habit, he does also suggest that habit forms an enduring part of 'lived experience'.

[22] Forman, "Second Nature and Spirit."

something we have to move away from and that language is what allows this move.[23] John McCumber offers an especially clear articulation of this approach.[24] According to McCumber, habit has merely the instrumental value of liberating us from our first nature, and to this end it does not matter which habits we develop. Even bad ones will do. But all habits reintroduce a form of compulsion from which we need to be liberated in turn. McCumber concludes that Hegel "views habit as, like falsity, a phenomenon of transition which, though not good in itself, can help bring about a better state of affairs."[25]

Both of these interpretive strands have philosophical merit and textual support. The first is in a position to explain how habit is meant to operate within the "Anthropology" itself, how it is supposed to achieve the desired results of individuation and consciousness. As Forman rightly points out, Hegel's interest in habit at this stage is first and foremost an interest in how we *become* spiritual beings (and not how we turn *back* into 'natural' beings).[26] The second is in a position to explain why the story does not end with habit, why spirit has further work to do, and how this work might be motivated by the limitations that habit imposes on us. But I think they are missing something important in Hegel's account. Habit, after all, makes a remarkable reappearance at another juncture in Hegel's system, in Objective Spirit. There he tells us that "self-conscious *freedom* has become *nature* again" (E §513). And in his more extensive *Philosophy of Right* he writes that

> [in] the simple identification of individuals with actuality [*Wirklichkeit*], the ethical [*das Sittliche*] appears as their general manner of conduct [*allgemeine Handlungsweise*], as custom [*Sitte*]—the habit [*Gewohnheit*] of the ethical appears as a second nature, which is put in place of the first purely natural will and which is the soul, meaning, and actuality permeating its existence. (PR §151)

The available interpretations have neglected to consider habit from a 'pragmatic point of view', and thus from the standpoint of its suitability to ethical life. Considering it from this standpoint might help us understand why ethical actions should become habitual, according to Hegel. Moreover, the picture of habit that has emerged so far makes it very difficult to see how habit could come to play this eventual role, if it is essentially a form of unfreedom. It also makes it difficult to see how Hegel can say in the

---

[23] Lewis, "Speaking of Habits." "While Hegel views habit as a key step in liberating us from determination by natural factors and immediate impulses, because acting out of habit is acting automatically, without consciousness, it is ultimately unfree in crucial respects" (25).

[24] McCumber, "Hegel on Habit."

[25] McCumber, "Hegel on Habit," 157.

[26] I am not as convinced that these two processes can be treated fully independently from one another. For Hegel we become fully spiritual beings only when we turn back into 'natural' beings, when we achieve immediacy in our comportment. This is why the process culminates in a second nature—an unreflective way of conducting ourselves that is not our default state, but is won through effort and cultivation.

"Anthropology" itself that "the form of habit encompasses all sorts and stages of spiritual activity" (E §410).

But Hegel has a richer—and more heterogeneous—picture of habit. This picture emerges in his analysis of skills, which comprise the third category of habits and which differ significantly from hardening and indifference. Skills are expressed in activities. Though they are acquired through conscious control of our movements, we truly have them only when our movements are no longer laborious and difficult for us and our bodies have become unresisting (*widerstandlos*) and fluid (*flüssig*). For Hegel this is a process by which our aims become integrated so thoroughly into what we do that our outer bodies come to mirror our inner aspirations. It is not only the process of habituation that is a spiritual one, but also habitual activity itself, for when I act habitually (and my habits are *good*), I am seamlessly expressing myself. There is no longer a gap between how I see myself and what my behavior reveals to be true of me.

Skills are the turning point of the entire "Anthropology," because they enable us to achieve a sense of self. We achieve this sense by detaching from the body, reshaping it, and identifying with the result of our effort. Skills also represent an enduring form of spiritual activity. For Hegel, ethical actions are going to be skills acquired through repeated practice—actions that reflect the quality of our frame of mind. It is for this reason that Hegel concludes his official account of habit with the following verdict:

> Habit is usually spoken of disparagingly and is taken to be something lifeless, arbitrary, and particular. Of course the form of habit, just like any other form, is capable of a completely arbitrary content, and it is the habit of life, which brings about death, or which, put abstractly, is death itself. And yet habit is most essential for the *existence* of all spirituality in the individual subject, so that the subject can be a *concrete* immediacy, an ideality of the soul, so that the content, religious, moral, etc. can *belong* to him as *this self*, to him as *this* soul, and be neither a latent possibility, nor a fleeting sensation or representation, nor an abstract interiority, separated from activity and actuality, but instead be in his being. (E §410)

In the first sentence, Hegel notes that habit has garnered the bad reputation of being lifeless, arbitrary, and particular. It looks like, when we act habitually, that we are acting mechanically, without control over or insight into our behavior.[27] This is also why

---

[27] This is actually Kant's own assessment of habit: "*becoming accustomed* (*consuetudo*) in fact makes the endurance of misfortune *easy* (which is then falsely honored with the name of a virtue, namely patience), for when sensations of exactly the same kind persist for a long time without change and draw one's attention away from the senses, one is barely conscious of them any more. But this also makes consciousness and memory of the good that one has received *more difficult*, which then usually leads to ingratitude (a real vice). *Habit* (*assuetudo*), however, is a physical inner necessitation to proceed in the same manner that one has proceeded until now. It deprives even good actions of their moral worth because it impairs the freedom of the mind and, moreover, leads to thoughtless repetition of the very same act (*monotony*), and so becomes ridiculous" (Kant, *Anthropology*, 7:148–149).

habit is taken to be a source of death, or even death itself.[28] In the second sentence, Hegel explicitly rejects this assessment. While there can be bad habits, just as there can be bad feelings, this for him does not discredit the form of habit as such. Moreover, Hegel concludes that it is by means of habit that any spiritual (including ethical) content gains concreteness, strikes root in us, belongs to us—that it becomes *mine*.[29]

18.4. THE ACTUAL SOUL AND THE HUMAN BEING

Habits of skill enable the transition from the feeling soul to the actual soul, thereby revealing that the soul has not been real until now. Why not? Why do the natural soul and the feeling soul not count as real? Hegel's answer is that the soul is not real until it is individuated, until it develops an 'I'. It must first 'awaken' to the 'I', as he puts it (E §412). And habituation is this process of awakening. It allows me to relate to myself as an individual with determinations that constitute my distinct identity. But the moment I develop a self-conception, I also adopt a different stance toward everything that is not me. So this process also puts me in touch with *objects* out there, a world that is external to my self. This is the standpoint of consciousness that is to be investigated in the next part of the *Encyclopedia*. Habits of skill enable individuation and consciousness because they change my relationship to my own body. It is my body that makes me a particular individual with a distinct point of view. It is my body that is not only one object among others, but also grants me access to the external world at large. And it is my body that, when successfully habituated, yields to my will and reflects my aspirations. So the soul only becomes real in and through the body.

We now see why it is potentially misleading to think of the soul as immaterial or as immateriality as such, even if we don't think of it as a thing. What we now learn is that the soul does not yet exist, strictly speaking, until it become materially actualized, realized, or *expressed*. Hegel opens his relatively brief discussion of the actual soul by redefining the soul as the "identity of the inner and the outer" (E §411), an identity that is won through the hard work of habituation. In its earlier versions, the soul was immersed in and indistinguishable from the material world. It was helpless against the world's sensory effect upon it. But this does not mean that the soul *identified* with this world. In fact,

---

[28] This is a worry that Hegel shares. In nearly every passage in which Hegel mentions habit, he indicates its connection to death. See, for example, PR §151A. As I read him, Hegel is not suggesting that habit is necessarily deadening, but that it can become deadening when it is never tempered by other, more reflective ways of acting. We can become excessively habituated. This does not mean that there is a way of acting that is better, more elevated than habit and that we should be striving for.

[29] See also Moland, "Inheriting, Earning, and Owning." In this paper she argues that Hegel's "Anthropology" tells the story of how we come to own or own up to those aspects of our practical identities that we did not choose, and that habituation in particular exemplifies this process.

it was too immersed in and indistinguishable from it to be in a position to identify with it. Through habit, it gains the needed distance to identify with at least one part of it—its own body. The body, according to Hegel, has become a sign (*Zeichen*) of the soul. "This unity, which is brought about but has become immediate, we call the reality of the soul" (E §411Z).

But not all kinds of habits—even habits of skill—are going to count as sufficient evidence of an actual soul. Standing upright, for example, is not, even though it is a learned behavior that expresses our will.[30] Hegel is interested in the habit of standing upright because it seems to be a habit that only human beings develop. As he reminds us, the orangutan does not stand on its hind legs. But Hegel also notes that these mute postures and movements of the human body—standing, laughing, crying, manual labor—are only extensions of our animal nature. "For the animal, the human form is what is highest, is how spirit appears to it. But for spirit it is only its *first* appearance, and language is instantly its complete expression" (E §411).[31] This statement makes clear that the acquisition of language introduces an innovation that sets the human being relevantly apart from the animal. Even animals can and do acquire habits and skill. But animals do not use words. This is admittedly not a shocking observation, and Hegel is certainly not the first to make it.[32] His original point, however, is that language sets us apart as human beings because it is the complete expression of a structure that is not to be found in the natural world—the structure of spirit.

It is helpful to consider Hegel's own example. In the additions (to E §410), there is mention of a seemingly different kind of habit—writing. Learning how to write is at face value the acquisition of a skill, like any other. I have to practice it in order to be able to do it. But the ensuing activity is not simply unconscious or mechanical.

> If the activity of writing has become a habit, then our self has so completely mastered all of the relevant details, has so infected them with its universality, that they are no longer present to us as peculiarities and we only have the universal before our eyes. Consequently we see that in habit our consciousness is simultaneously present in the subject matter, interested in it, and yet conversely absent from it, indifferent to it. (E §410A)

In short, in writing the mind is *both* present and absent, interested and indifferent. I am paying attention to what Hegel calls the 'universal' aspect of my activity—to the content

---

[30] "[T]he external, the spatial determination of the individual, that he stands upright, is made into a habit through his will, an *immediate, unconscious* position, which always remains a part of his enduring will; the human being only stands because and to the extent to which he wills it, and only so long as he wills it unconsciously" (E §410).

[31] Language is here making its first appearance, but we don't yet have all of the resources we need to make sense of its structure. It is worth keeping in mind that language becomes thematized again at other stages of the *Encyclopedia*, notably in the Theoretical Spirit section of his *Psychology*.

[32] A classic example is Descartes' proposal for how to distinguish human machines from real humans, in contrast with our criteria for distinguishing animal machines from real animals. He claims that language is one sure criterion. See Descartes, *Discourse on Method*, 32.

I am trying to communicate, but also to the means (words, sentences, paragraphs) available to me for doing so. At the same time, there are many irrelevant peculiarities that I have learned to disregard—the idiosyncrasy of my handwriting, the individual letters that compose the words that I am now so used to seeing written down. Hegel explains this frame of mind through the concept of a 'rule', since following rules requires simultaneous attention to commonalities and disregard for countless differences. What habits like writing achieve is to make following rules so easy that we are no longer relating to them as rules. We no longer have to think about rules of syntax and punctuation, even though we consistently adhere to them. This ease is what makes habitual rule-following appear like a second nature, too. So when Hegel writes that it is not our corporeal postures and movements that make us human, but language, he is not taking back his previous conclusion that habit actualizes the soul. Our use of language is a habit, albeit a spiritual one.[33]

Hegel's "Anthropology," as well as Subjective Spirit as a whole, is widely acknowledged to be a neglected part of Hegel's system. Although there are a few classic studies of the "Anthropology" and a growing number of essays on parts of it,[34] it has remained comparatively obscure. This is regrettable on several counts. Hegel's "Anthropology" is, after all, *the* point at which the pivotal transition from nature to spirit is supposed to take place, so it should be of obvious relevance to those interested in understanding this transition. Even those who find the developmental story itself unattractive or unpersuasive can still look to the "Anthropology" for an account of the important difference between nature and spirit, an account of what constitutes our irreducible gulf from other animals. Finally, I have stressed that Hegel's "Anthropology" has bearing on the development beyond Subjective Spirit, for Hegel is perpetually assessing subjective forms like talent, disposition, feeling, and habit from an ethical vantage point. The question he is asking is whether these can do justice to an objective content, or whether they are so underdeveloped that they are bound to ruin it. If we act ethically because we were born with a good disposition, or because our heart dictates that we should, or because we have been habituated to do it, is there ultimately something inadequate about what we are doing? These are questions of undeniable philosophical interest, and Hegel's "Anthropology" provides subtle, surprising, and fruitful answers.[35]

---

[33] Lewis in "Speaking of Habits" emphasizes the significance of language in relation to habit, arguing that it is the introduction of language that makes us free because it allows us to transcend 'mere' habit. But I believe that he has misconstrued this significance. First, he does not appreciate the extent to which habit is continuous with Hegel's account of language—that language is itself a habit of spirit. Second, it is far from clear why being able to speak about our habits, to put them into words, is supposed to make us free with respect to them. Although the capacity to reflect on our habits may be crucial, it is definitely not sufficient to liberate us from them in any actual sense. If I discover that I have developed a set of bad habits, what I need to do is to *rehabituate* myself, and so give shape to new, better ones.

[34] In addition to Greene's book, there are Willem deVries, *Hegel's Theory of Mental Activity*, and a collection of essays edited by Stern, Hegel's *Philosophy of Subjective Spirit*.

[35] I am grateful to Pierre Keller for helpful conversations and suggestions.

Works Cited

Primary Texts

Descartes, René. *Discourse on Method and Meditations on First Philosophy*, translated by D. A. Cress. Indianapolis: Hackett, [1637] 1998.

Hegel, G. W. F. *Philosophy of Mind* [E], translated by W. Wallace, A. V. Miller, and Michael Inwood. Oxford: Oxford University Press, 2007.

Kant, Immanuel. *Anthropology from a Pragmatic Point of View*, translated and edited by R. Lauden Cambridge: Cambridge University Press, 1798, 2006.

Secondary Literature

DeVries, Willem. *Hegel's Theory of Mental Activity: An Introduction to Theoretical Spirit*. Ithaca, NY: Cornell University Press, 1987.

Ferrarin, Alfredo. *Hegel and Aristotle*. Cambridge: Cambridge University Press, 2001.

Forman, David. "Second Nature and Spirit: Hegel on the Role of Habit in the Appearance of Perceptual Consciousness." *Southern Journal of Philosophy* 48, no. 4 (2010): 325–352.

Greene, Murray. *Hegel on the Soul: A Speculative Anthropology*. The Hague: Martinus Nijhoff, 1972.

Lewis, Thomas A. "Speaking of Habits: The Role of Language in Moving from Habit to Freedom." *Owl of Minerva* 39, no. 1–2 (2008): 25–53.

Lumsden, Simon. "Between Nature and Spirit: Hegel's Account of Habit," in *Essays on Hegel's Philosophy of Subjective Spirit*, edited by David S. Stern. Albany: State University of New York Press, 2013, 121–137.

Magee, Glenn Alexander. "The Dark Side of Subjective Spirit: Hegel on Mesmerism, Madness, and Ganglia," in *Essays on Hegel's Philosophy of Subjective Spirit*, edited by David S. Stern. Albany: State University of New York Press, 2013, 55–69.

Malabou, Catherine. *The Future of Hegel: Plasticity, Temporality, and Dialectic*. London: Routledge, 2005.

McCumber, John. "Hegel on Habit." *Owl of Minerva* 21, no. 2 (1990): 155–164.

Moland, Lydia. "Inheriting, Earning, and Owning: The Source of Practical Identity in Hegel's 'Anthropology.'" *Owl of Minerva* 34, no. 2 (2003): 139–170.

Mowad, Nicholas. "Awakening to Madness and Habituation to Death in Hegel's 'Anthropology,'" in *Essays on Hegel's Philosophy of Subjective Spirit*, edited by David S. Stern. Albany: State University of New York Press, 2013, 87–105.

Nuzzo, Angelica. "Anthropology, *Geist*, and the Soul-Body Relation: The Systematic Beginnings of Hegel's *Philosophy of Spirit*," in *Essays on Hegel's Philosophy of Subjective Spirit*, edited by David S. Stern. Albany: State University of New York Press, 2013, 1–17.

Petry, Michael John. *Hegel's Philosophy of Subjective Spirit*, Vol. 2: *Anthropology*. New York: Springer, [1978] 2013.

CHAPTER 19

......

HEGEL'S PSYCHOLOGY

......

HEIKKI IKÄHEIMO

DESPITE its central importance in Hegel's mature system, the Subjective Spirit part of his *Encyclopedia of Philosophical Sciences* has attracted relatively little attention in the reception history of Hegel's work. The most influential early readers of Hegel were mostly interested in other parts of Hegel's system; and relatively soon after Hegel's death, more empirically oriented approaches to the topics of Subjective Spirit won the day, displacing the overly 'speculative', armchair philosophical approach that Hegel was seen as representing. Hegel's direct disciples and moderate 'center Hegelians' Johann Karl Friedrich Rosenkranz and Karl Ludwig Michelet did write extensive commentaries on Hegel's Philosophy of Subjective Spirit,[1] but their influence paled in comparison to the more politically astute and independently creative Hegelian 'left', who mostly focused on the *Philosophy of Right* or the *Phenomenology of Spirit*, as well as in comparison to the Hegelian 'right', who were mostly interested in Hegel's views on religion and history. The long neglect of Subjective Spirit is evident even today in the curious way in which the recent revival of Hegel as an epistemologist and a philosopher of mind, or of 'mindedness',[2] has mostly ignored this text[3]—even if, systematically speaking, Subjective Spirit

---

[1] Rosenkranz, *Psychologie oder die Wissenschaft vom subjektiven Geist*; Michelet *Anthropologie und Psychologie*.

[2] For an early overview of this movement in Hegel studies, see Ameriks, "Recent Work on Hegel."

[3] For important exceptions, see deVries, *Hegel's Theory of Mental Activity*; and Halbig, *Objektives Denken*. General literature dealing with the Philosophy of Subjective Spirit includes, but is not limited to, Fetscher, *Hegels Lehre vom Menschen*; Greene, *Hegel on the Soul*; Drüe, *Psychologie aus dem Begriff*; Peperzak, *Selbsterkenntnis des Absoluten*; Henrich, ed., *Hegels philosophische Psychologie*; Eley, ed., *Hegels Theorie des subjektiven Geistes*; Hespe and Tuschling, eds., *Psychologie und Anthropologie oder Philosophie des Geistes*; Wolff, *Das Körper-Seele-Problem*; Ikäheimo, *Self-Consciousness and Intersubjectivity*; Schalhorn, *Hegels enzyklopädischer Begriff von Selbstbewusstsein*, Stederoth, *Hegel Philosophie des Subjektiven Geistes*; Inwood, *A Commentary of Hegel's Philosophy of Mind*; Rometsch, *Hegels Theorie des erkennenden Subjekts*; Winfield, *Hegel and Mind* and *The Living Mind*; Stern, ed., *Essays on Hegel's Philosophy of Subjective Spirit*; Herrmann-Sinai and Ziglioli, eds., *Hegel's Philosophical Psychology*.

is *the* part of Hegel's system where issues of knowledge and of the mind are explicitly at stake.

There is also a widespread view according to which Hegel was engaged in his Jena writings in a project of 'detranscendentalizing' the Kantian subject of knowledge and action problematically divided between the empirical and transcendental, or in other words of consistently conceptualizing it as a living individual human person embedded in the natural and social world, in language and in intersubjective interaction. According to this view, after Jena, Hegel for whatever reason gave up this project and in his later work regressed into a dubious metaphysics of a 'spirit', which obfuscates the concrete lived reality of the human individual.[4] Whatever the truth about Hegel's metaphysics,[5] this chapter aims to show that in the Philosophy of Subjective Spirit, Hegel develops a thoroughly 'detranscendentalized' account of the human person as the 'concrete' flesh-and-blood subject of knowledge and action, an account that deserves much more attention than it has so far received.

In short, whereas the section "Anthropology—Soul" of Subjective Spirit (see Chapter 18) deals with the bodily aspects of the concrete subject, the section "Phenomenology of Spirit—Consciousness" deals with the various dimensions of intentionality, or in other words, of the subject's theoretical and practical relation to objectivity, and finally the section "Psychology—Spirit" deals with the intrasubjective or mental processes and activities at work in the various object-relations. Eventually, all three sections contribute to a holistic picture of the human person as the 'concrete subject'[6] of knowing and acting, yet reconstructing this picture requires a proper understanding of the structure of the text, which at first sight, on a simple linear reading, appears rather fragmentary and thus confusing. This chapter focuses on the "Psychology" section, and the thematically closely connected "Phenomenology" section.

I will first reconstruct the 'parallel architectonics' of the "Phenomenology" and "Psychology," the understanding of which is essential for comprehending the substantial views Hegel puts forth in them. I will then draw on this reconstruction and introduce central elements of Hegel's account of the human person as the concrete subject of knowledge and action as it unfolds in the text.

19.1. The Structure of the Text

As soon as one starts studying Subjective Spirit, one easily gets the impression that the general neglect of and ignorance about this part of Hegel's work may have something to

---

[4] See Habermas, "From Kant to Hegel and Back."

[5] For a balanced rehabilitation of Hegel as a metaphysician, see Bowman, *Hegel and the Metaphysics of Absolute Negativity*.

[6] For Hegel's use of the terms 'concrete subject', 'concrete subjectivity', and 'concrete I', see E §§398, 400, 405, 456, and 457.

do also with the qualities of the text itself. There is at first sight something rather confusing and thus disappointing about it—namely, the apparently sporadic way in which closely connected themes are scattered here and there, without any apparent reason other than some excessively formalistic systematics that Hegel utilizes without ever really explaining it. For example, whatever exactly Hegel means by 'sensation', 'desire', and 'practical feeling', these seem to be closely connected themes, yet in the text they are for some obscure reason discussed very far apart from each other (see Table 19.1). Also, though broadly speaking Subjective Spirit begins (in the first section, "Anthropology") with simpler phenomena that humans share with non-human animals, and ends (in "Psychology") with more advanced or demanding phenomena unique to cultivated humans, on closer reading there are puzzling details in the thematic order of the text. Why, for example, does Hegel discuss 'intuition' after 'reason', or 'practical feeling' after 'thinking', even if in both cases he clearly means by the last mentioned member of the pair something more advanced or demanding than by the first?[7] Such questions about the thematic order of the text are related to a question about the relation of "Phenomenology" and "Psychology": they seem thematically closely interconnected, yet the precise nature of this interconnection seems unclear. All in all, even if what Hegel writes in the individual chapters of the text is often easier to follow than, say, most parts of the 1807 *Phenomenology of Spirit*, due to its puzzling architectonics the overall impression is fragmentary and confusing. Secondary literature on Subjective Spirit is scarce, and so far it has not been successful in solving these fundamental architectonic questions that are crucial for understanding the substantive content of the text.

Which architectonic principle or principles then organize the Philosophy of Subjective Spirit in general, or the sections "Phenomenology" and "Psychology" in particular? Two candidates immediately come to mind: developmental and logical. First, Hegel did not subscribe to evolutionism of any kind and thus did not have the evolution of the human species in mind, yet, as already noted, broadly speaking simpler phenomena seem to be followed by more complex or more advanced ones in the text. Hence, given its general topic, it seems not too far-fetched to expect that the text at least in some respects reflects the development of the human individual. Second, the logical concepts explicated by Hegel in his logic clearly have some important role to play in his discussion of the various phenomena at issue in this text, as they do in his discussion of everything in the *Realphilosophien*. For Hegel they are the logical structures of reality, and thus obviously at issue in a scientific or philosophical grasp of reality. Yet, neither of these candidates takes one very far. With regard to the developmental explanation, many of the details indeed actually defy the assumption of at least a simple, straightforwardly linear developmental ordering of themes in the text. As to the logical explanation, the problem is that there are simply too many logical categories at work in everything that Hegel writes,

---

[7] Vittorio Hösle voices these puzzles in Hösle, *Hegels System*, 348–349, 371, 389.

Table 19.1 The List of Contents of Subjective Spirit
in the *Encyclopedia of Philosophical
Sciences in Outline* (1830)

A. Anthropology. Soul. § 388
  a. The natural soul. § 391
    α. Natural qualities. § 392
    β. Natural alterations. § 396
    γ. Sensation. § 399
  b. The feeling soul. § 403
    α. The Feeling soul in its immediacy. § 405
    β. Self-feeling. § 407
    γ. Habit. § 409
  c. The actual soul. § 411
B. Phenomenology of Mind. Consciousness. § 413
  a. Consciousness as such. § 418
    α. Sensuous consciousness. § 418
    β. Perception. § 420
    γ. Understanding. § 422
  b. Self-consciousness. § 424
    α. Desire. § 426
    β. Recognitive self-consciousness. § 430
    γ. Universal self-consciousness. § 436
  c. Reason. § 438
C. Psychology. Spirit. § 440
  a. Theoretical spirit. § 445
    α. Intuition. § 446
    β. Representation. § 451
      1. Recollection. § 452
      2. Imagination. § 455
      3. Memory. § 461
    γ. Thinking. § 465
  b. Practical spirit. § 469
    α. Practical feeling. § 471
    β. Drives and willfulness. § 473
    γ. Happiness. § 479
  c. Free spirit. § 481

and none in particular seems to offer a key for understanding the overall thematic structure of the text.[8]

Where to turn then? We are best served by taking a lead from what Hegel writes in the introduction to the entire *Philosophy of Spirit* (including Subjective, Objective, and Absolute Spirit). On Hegel's broadly Aristotelian normative or evaluative essentialism, things have essences, which they can actualize to different degrees, and the more they actualize

[8] For an extended discussion of the relationship of the structure of the Philosophy of Subjective Spirit to Hegel's logic, see Stederoth, *Hegel Philosophie des Subjektiven Geistes*.

them the better or more perfect they are. In the Introduction to *Philosophy of Spirit*, Hegel declares 'spirit' as the "essence of man/the human [*Mensch*]," and 'freedom' as the "essence of spirit."[9] By saying that the essence of man/the human is spirit, Hegel is referring to the constellation of phenomena, structures, and relations that are the topic of *Philosophy of Spirit*, and is saying that they are what distinguish humans from merely animal beings. Since he means essence in a normative or evaluative sense, this means that the human *telos* and task is the actualization and perfection of these defining phenomena of humanity. By saying that the essence of 'spirit' is freedom, Hegel means that perfection for all of the distinctively spiritual phenomena, and thus for humanity, means an increase in their realizing freedom: becoming (increasingly) what we are, not merely animals (though we are that, too), but, as one would say in contemporary terms, persons, means our becoming free. The *Philosophy of Spirit* as a whole and thus also the sections of the text at issue here are organized and written with this immanent normative principle, *telos*, and task in mind.

To understand what this means more concretely, we need to understand what exactly Hegel means by 'freedom' here. He makes clear in the Introduction that he is not talking about freedom in the 'abstract' sense of freedom from determination, but rather in the 'concrete' sense of freedom in relation to what necessarily determines one.[10] The idea of freedom *from* determination by something whose determination is essential to what one is is obviously nonsense and on Hegel's account attempts to realize it are counterproductive, if not destructive. The only real or realizable freedom with regard to such essential determinants—internal and external nature, social institutions, and other humans—is freedom 'in relation to' or 'with regard to' them. Importantly, Hegel conceives of the structure of concrete freedom in terms of the concept of 'absolute negativity', 'negation of negation' (E §382), or 'double negation' (SL 12.34/531), where the first 'negation' means differentiation or distinction from something that determines one as one's opposite, and the second negation the overcoming of its alienness or hostility to one. Another formula for concrete freedom is "unity of unity and difference," and metaphorically Hegel characterizes it as "being with oneself in otherness," and more exactly as "being conscious of oneself in otherness."

The double-negation-structure of concrete freedom also provides the key for understanding many of the details of the architectonics of Hegel's text organized in triads (within Subjective Spirit A-B-C, a-b-c, and α-β-γ; see Table 19.1). Almost all of the triads forming the *Encyclopedia of Philosophical Sciences* are instantiations of the double-negation-structure of concrete freedom in the sense that the first member instantiates immediate unity, the second one differentiation or distinction that bifurcates the immediate unity (first negation), and the third a mediated unity incorporating the difference or distinction in question (second negation).

This is, of course, a very general structure and what it means more exactly to instantiate it varies greatly in each case, depending on the thematic content of the triad in question. Even the most general triad *Logic—Philosophy of Nature—Philosophy of*

---

[9] See E §382, VPG, 5–7, LPS, 58–60, 65–66; and Ikäheimo, *Anerkennung*, ch. 4.1.
[10] VPG, 13–15, LPS, 65–66.

Spirit forming Hegel's *Encyclopedia* instantiates it in a particular way, and so does the Subjective Spirit—Objective Spirit—Absolute Spirit triads forming the *Philosophy of Spirit*. As to our topic, "Subjective Spirit" instantiates the structure in the sense that the "Anthropology" discusses levels of organization of the concrete subject that are immediate in the more exact sense of pre-intentional; "Phenomenology" then discusses intentionality or the subject-object-relation, or in other words, the differentiation of the objective world and the subject for the subject itself; and finally, "Psychology" discusses psychological processes and activities responsible for the various aspects and dimensions of the subject-object-relation, and thus, taken formally, a unity that incorporates the difference.

However, though "Phenomenology" and "Psychology" are also both organized triadically, the 'immediate unity—differentiation—mediated unity' structure does not seem decisive for the most general triads organizing them, namely B.a. Consciousness as such—B.b. Self-consciousness—B.c. Reason, and C.a. Theoretical spirit—C.b. Practical spirit—C.c. Free spirit. Rather, here we find a more straightforwardly substantial organizing principle stemming directly from the thematic content of the chapters in question. As to "Phenomenology," the first chapter B.a. Consciousness as such discusses theoretical subject-object-relation, the second chapter B.b. Self-consciousness discusses practical subject-object-relation, and the third chapter B.c. Reason draws the results of these chapters together and provides the transition on the one hand to "Psychology," and on the other hand to Objective Spirit. The structure of "Psychology" is thematically analogous with that of "Phenomenology": the first chapter C.a. Theoretical spirit discusses the processes and activities of the mind corresponding to the various moments of theoretical intentionality, whereas C.b. Practical spirit discusses the processes and activities of the mind corresponding to the various moments of practical intentionality. Finally, C.c. Free spirit draws the results of the Theoretical spirit and Practical spirit together and provides another perspective to the transition to Objective Spirit. What this means is that the analogy or parallelism of the a.- and the b.-chapters of "Phenomenology" and "Psychology" is not merely structural, but also thematic, in that C.a. Theoretical spirit discusses the mental activities responsible for the forms of theoretical intentionality discussed in B.a. Consciousness as such, and C.b. Practical spirit discusses those responsible for the forms of practical intentionality discussed in B.b. Self-consciousness.[11]

This parallelism can be followed down to the details of the α.-β.-γ. sequences of each of the four a.- and b.-chapters of "Phenomenology" and "Psychology," and here it is both structural and thematic. As to the structural side, the immediate

---

[11] Iring Fetscher (*Hegels Lehre vom Menschen*, 105, 194) notes this parallel structure. Hösle (*Hegels System*) is aware of the various puzzles facing a linear reading (see note 7), but strangely never doubts that the thematic order of the text might not be purely linear. See Ikäheimo, "On the Role of Intersubjectivity." Michael Inwood (*A Commentary of Hegel's Philosophy of Mind*, xv–xvi) shows awareness of some kind of mutual dependence of the topics of "Phenomenology" and "Psychology," but does not follow this clue systematically in his in many places excellent commentary. Winfield, *Hegel and Mind* and *The Living Mind* are often very illuminating companions for reading of the Subjective Spirit, yet are harmed by an unquestioned linearity of reading.

unity—differentiation—mediated unity structure applies here again. Though at the level of the "Anthropology"—"Phenomenology"—"Psychology" triad, "Phenomenology" instantiates differentiation in the sense of the subject-object-difference; within "Phenomenology" both α.-sub-chapters Sensuous consciousness and Desire discuss modes or moments of intentionality that are in certain ways characterized by immediacy or lack of differentiation. Both β.-sub-chapters then introduce differentiations lacking at the α.-level, and finally the γ.-sub-chapters discuss modes of intentionality in which the differences in question are sublated into a mediated unity. The same goes, *mutatis mutandis,* for the two α.-β.-γ. sequences in "Psychology": in both cases the mental processes discussed in the α.-sub-chapter are characterized by immediacy or lack of differentiation, the β.-sub-chapters discuss processes or activities that involve different forms of differentiation lacking at the α.-level, and finally the γ.-sub-chapters discuss mental activities in which the differences are somehow sublated into a mediated unity.

But here there is also another organizing principle at work, giving the parallelism of the α.-β.-γ. sequences a more clearly thematic or substantial character. This is the developmental principle mentioned earlier. Though a simple, purely *linear* developmental reading of Subjective Spirit in general does lead to obvious problems of the kind mentioned earlier, a *parallel* developmental reading of the four α.-β.-γ. sequences of the "Phenomenology" and "Psychology" makes much better sense of the text. It also allows one to see something one desperately misses on the simple linear reading: the different chapters and sub-chapters contributing to a unified, holistic picture of the human person. It is, importantly, a picture that allows for development, and is thus true to the nature of the human person as the 'concrete', changing, and developing subject of knowledge and action.

This picture also involves a close intertwinement or mutual determination of the theoretical and the practical aspects of the being of this concrete subject. This becomes visible as soon as one sees the theoretical and practical α.-β.-γ. sequences thematically parallel to each other, or in other words, each α.-sub-chapter discussing different aspects of a closely interconnected whole. The β.- and the γ.-sub-chapters are similarly connected. In short, the four α.-β.-γ. sequences of the "Phenomenology" and "Psychology" can be read as describing one developmental sequence from four mutually complementary points of view. This developmental sequence is, to be sure, highly idealized, corresponding to real development of the human individual (or of the species, though this was not Hegel's concern) only in a very general, ideal-typical way (see Table 19.2).

There is one more crucial structural fact one needs to be aware of when reading and interpreting the actual content of the text. This is the fact that the sequence can be read from two mutually complementary 'directions': bottom-up and top-down. Read from the *bottom-up-direction,* the four α.-sub-chapters discuss intertwined aspects of a developmental level that can take place without the further β.- and γ.-level phenomena. The four β.-sub-chapters then discuss intertwined aspects of a second developmental level, which requires that the α.-level phenomena, but not the γ.-level phenomena, are in place. Finally, the γ.-sub-chapters discuss intertwined aspects of a third developmental level that presupposes both the α.-level and the β.-level phenomena. Read from the

Table 19.2 The Parallel Architectonics of Phenomenology and Psychology

Theoretical Moment		*Practical Moment*	
Intentionality	*Mental Activity*	*Intentionality*	*Mental Activity*
B. Phenomenology	C. Psychology	B. Phenomenology	C. Psychology
a. Consciousness as such	a. Theoretical spirit	b. Self-consciousness	b. Practical spirit
α. Sensuous consciousness	α. Intuition	α. Desire	α. Practical feeling
β. Perception	β. Representation	β. Recognitive s.-c.	β. Drives and willfulness
γ. Understanding	γ. Thinking	γ. Universal s.-c.	γ. Happiness
	c. Reason/c. Free spirit		

Or

Intentionality		*Mental activity*	
B. Phenomenology		**C. Psychology**	
Theoretical Moment	*Practical Moment*	*Theoretical Moment*	*Practical Moment*
a. Consciousness as such	b. Self-consciousness	a. Theoretical spirit	b. Practical spirit
α. Sensuous consciousness	α. Desire	α. Intuition	α. Practical feeling
β. Perception	β. Recognitive s.-c.	β. Representation	β. Drives and willfulness
γ. Understanding	γ. Universal s.-c.	γ. Thinking	γ. Happiness
c. Reason		c. Free spirit	

top-down direction, on the other hand, the 'lower' levels already presuppose or are intertwined with the 'higher' ones. This duality of directions immanent in Hegel's text reflects the temporal being of the human person, which ideally follows a developmental course beginning with simpler or 'lower level' phenomena or activities, gradually progressing to more complex or higher level ones, and ending up in a fully cultivated human person whose constitution the lower level phenomena are still part of, only now infused with the higher level ones and accommodated in a thoroughly cultivated unity. This, very schematically presented, is the course of the realization of concrete freedom and thus the human essence from the point of view of the Philosophy of Subjective Spirit, which is to say, abstracting from the social and institutional world discussed in Objective Spirit, in which the human person is of course embedded in reality.[12] Reflecting the duality of directions from which the text has been written and thus can be read, we find Hegel

---

[12] "We examine [in Philosophy of Spirit] the series of stages through which spirit liberates itself, and the goal is that spirit comes to be free, as free spirit" (VPG, 8, LPS, 61).

discussing, for example, both primitive intuition that can take place without the mental processes and activities discussed in the β.- and γ.-sub-chapters, and cultivated intuition influenced by or interwined with these higher level phenomena (see section 19.2 of this chapter).[13]

Unfortunately, Hegel makes none of these architectonic features of the text explicit to the reader, but as soon as one starts reading it with them in mind, pieces in the puzzle start falling into place, and the text sheds at least much of the impression of fragmentariness that inevitably burdens it on a simple linear reading.

19.2. A Holistic Account of the Human Person as the Concrete Subject of Knowledge and Action

In what follows, I will present a selective overview of the themes of the "Psychology" section, in their intertwinement with those of the "Phenomenology," utilizing the reconstruction of the text's structure presented earlier. The aim of this overview is to reconstruct the outlines of Hegel's account of the human person as the concrete subject of knowledge and action. To understand the wholly 'detranscendentalized' character on this account, it is eventually important to conceive of Hegel's discussion of the mental processes and activities that are the topic of "Psychology" in tandem also with his discussion of the bodily aspects or embodiment of the mind discussed in the "Anthropology," but here references to the "Anthropology" will be kept to minimum.

19.2.1. The α.-level Characterized by Immediate Unity: Primitive and Cultivated

In the "Anthropology," Hegel develops a highly elaborate account of the organization of the sentient body.[14] Both the "Phenomenology" and "Psychology" proceed from that discussion in that the four α.-chapters focus on the organization of the sensations (*Empfindung*) (E §§399–402) of the embodied subject into the intentional form, defining what Hegel calls 'consciousness [*Bewusstsein*]', or in other words, into a form in which the subject experiences the sensations as being *about* independent objects and thereby

---

[13] A similar duality of perspectives is present also, for example, in Hegel's discussions of sensation and habit in the "Anthropology." Hegel comments on this issue, though in a rather offhand way, in E §380.

[14] I refer by the 'α.-level' to the level or developmental stage of concrete subjectivity discussed from different perspectives in the four α.-sub-chapters. The same goes for my talk of the of 'β.-level' and the 'γ.-level'.

itself as distinct from those objects. The subject of consciousness, the 'I [*Ich*]' is in this sense, as Hegel puts it in the Introduction to the "Phenomenology" section, "one side of the [subject-object-] relationship, and the whole relationship" (E §413). Importantly, just as the subject of sentience that Hegel calls the 'self [*Selbst*]' in the "Anthropology," the 'I' as the subject of intentional consciousness is not transcendental in the Kantian sense; neither is it some sort of homunculus inhabiting the body. It is rather a structure or form of being of the concrete flesh-and-blood subject embedded in the world.

Hegel discusses in the "Anthropology" both 'external sensations', that is, the deliverances of the five senses, and 'internal sensations', that is, sensations or feelings of the embodied subject's internal states, including the hedonic value of 'the pleasant' and 'the unpleasant' which register the 'comparison', or accord or disaccord of the body's actual state with its needs or constitution (E §401). The outer and inner sensations, and the sensations of pleasure and displeasure, form a concrete interwoven whole of "the soul's natural life," and Hegel has the 'objectification' of all of these "content[s] of the natural soul" in mind in the following passage in the Phenomenology:

> [T]he content of the natural soul is object for this reflection that is for itself. Pure abstract freedom for itself discharges from itself its determinacy, the soul's natural life, to an equal freedom as an independent object. It is of this object, as external to it, that I is initially aware, and is thus consciousness. (E §413)

Consciousness at its most rudimentary level, discussed in the α.-chapters (read from the bottom-up perspective), is simply sensations, both external and internal, having attained an intentional form, or in other words appearances of external objects for the subject. By 'abstract freedom' Hegel refers here to what I call the 'first negation' of concrete freedom, in this case the originary division or '*Urteil*' (E §415) of objectivity from the subject, and thus the simultaneous setting free of subject and object from each other and their mutual determination as subject and object. 'Concrete freedom' will be eventually achieved by the 'second negation', which negates the object's alienness for the subject. The objectified form of external sensations is the topic of B.a.α. Sensuous Consciousness, whereas B.b.β. Desire discusses the objectified form of internal sensations, most importantly, felt needs. Though Hegel does not say this explicitly, as the external and the internal sensations form an interconnected whole, so do their objectifications discussed in these two chapters. The latter is the whole of the concrete subject's intentional relations with the world.

We grasp the general function of the "Psychology" section, when we understand that Hegel is not satisfied with leaving the forms or structures that consciousness or the subject-object-relation takes as 'facts of consciousness' which allow no further explanation.[15] On the contrary, he wants to scrutinize how they are produced by the mental activities of 'intelligence [*Intelligenz*]' and 'will [*Wille*]' of the concrete subject. This is the

---

[15] See Inwood, *A Commentary of Hegel's Philosophy of Mind*, 458 on 'facts of consciousness'.

general topic of the "Psychology" section. In the Addition to §441 in the Introduction to "Psychology" we read:

> when people speak of 'facts of consciousness' which for the mind are what is primary and must remain an unmediated given for it, it is to be noted on this that of course at the standpoint of consciousness a great deal of such given material is found, but the free spirit has to demonstrate and so explain these facts as deeds of the spirit, as a content posited by it, not leave them as independent things given to it. (E §441A)

It is these 'deeds of spirit' or of the mind discussed in "Psychology" that are responsible for bringing about both the 'first negation' of the subject-object-*Urteil* and the 'second negation' of a unity that incorporates the divide, or in other words, *both* grasping sensations as being about independent objects *and* doing away with their alienness. Overcoming the alienness of objectivity takes place on the one hand by comprehending its rational structure (intelligence, the theoretical aspect), and on the other hand by learning to will contents that are not simply given but mediated by rational reflection, and eventually institutionalized in the 'system of freedom' that is the state (will, the practical aspect). The development of intelligence and will, the respective general topics of Theoretical and Practical spirit, hence both contribute to the attainment of concrete freedom and thus the human essence, and Hegel thinks of them as closely intertwined (see his Remark to E §445), even if he does not explicitly work out the interconnections in any detail.

Again, the 'deeds of spirit' do not have any Kantian-style transcendental role as constituting or structuring the world, which otherwise would have no structure (at least one that we can know). This would be impossible since the subject really is a 'concrete subject' embedded in the world and thus, unlike the transcendental subject, not in a position to determine its structure. In the lecture-material included in the *Zusätze*, Hegel makes clear that on his account both spatiotemporal and conceptual structures are 'out there', independently of the concrete subject, and intelligence is merely its activity of comprehending them. As to space and time, we can read in the chapter on Intuition the following:

> [W]hen we said that what is sensed receives from the intuiting mind the form of the spatial and temporal,[16] this statement must not be understood to mean that space and time are *only subjective* forms. This is what Kant wanted to make space and time. However, things are in truth themselves spatial and temporal; this double form of asunderness is not one-sidedly imposed on them by our intuition, it has already been

---

[16] The reference here is to the main-text of §448, where Hegel writes, "Intelligence hereby determines the content of sensation as a being that is outside itself, casts it out into space and time, which are the forms in which intelligence is intuitive. According to consciousness the material is only an object of consciousness, a relative other; from spirit it receives the rational determination of being the other of itself" (cf. E §§247, 254). 'Being the other of itself' means having spatiotemporal structure, and Hegel

originally imparted to them by the infinite spirit that is in itself, by the creative eternal Idea. (E §448A)

Here we get a glimpse of Hegel's larger metaphysical picture in which the structure of both being and thought is ultimately the structure of 'the Idea' or 'infinite spirit',[17] and at the same time a clear statement that with regard to the finite spirit, or the existing concrete human individual, the spatiotemporal organization of the world exists independently of it. Saying that the pre-intentional contents of sensations 'receive' the spatiotemporal form "from the intuiting mind" is only saying that the mental activities Hegel discusses under the title 'intuition' grasp preexisting spatiotemporal structures of the world and thus organize it for the subject. Similarly with conceptual or 'rational' structures:

> what the intelligence seems to receive from outside is, in truth, none other than the rational and is consequently identical with the mind and immanent in it. The activity of mind has, therefore, no other aim than, by sublation of the ostensible being-external-to-its-own-self of the implicitly rational object, to refute even the semblance of the object's externality to mind. (E §447A)

Here again Hegel refers to his larger metaphysical picture in which the intelligible structures discussed in the logic are structures of both being and thinking. From the point of view of the human person as the concrete subject of knowledge about the world this means however that the world in which she lives and is confronted with in consciousness is intelligibly structured and that the goal of the theoretical activities of the mind (that is, of *her* theoretical or epistemic activities) is comprehending these structures and thus the world which she is part of.

This realism of Hegel's is at the same time compatible with a spatiotemporal and conceptual perspectivism or 'pragmatism'. The concrete subject does not occupy a 'view from nowhere' but is embedded in the world as a finite living being with particular needs that structure its relations with the world. This becomes explicit when one draws together Hegel's discussions in the four α.-sub-chapters. The simplest form of 'theoretical' givenness of objects, discussed in the chapter Sensuous consciousness, is the deliverances of the sense-organs being synthetised into spatiotemporally unified singular objects and thereby characterized as "being, something, existing thing, singular and so

---

refers here to paragraphs in his Philosophy of Nature on space and time. Note that this passage suggests that consciousness somehow independently gives sensations the form of objectivity, and that spirit or intelligence only gives this objectivity spatiotemporal form. Yet this is in contradiction with Hegel's explicit statements elsewhere that also the first task belongs to spirit ("the activity of intuition initially produces in general a shifting of intuition away from us"; §448Z.), and more broadly not in line with Hegel's general division of the roles of consciousness and intelligence in which all organizing activities belong to the latter, the former being the result of these.

[17] Absolute negation (and thus concrete freedom) is arguably also the central principle of Hegel's metaphysics. See Bowman, *Hegel and the Metaphysics of Absolute Negativity*.

on" (E §418), without yet appearing as things with multiple properties. In Desire, the α.-sub-chapter of Self-consciousness, Hegel discusses the practical aspect of the same level (or from the top-down perspective, element) of intentionality. The singular objects in question are objects of desire, or in other words, objects that the concrete subject instinctively experiences as promising satisfaction of its immediately felt bodily needs. These 'singular' (E §428) objects are "determined as nullity" (E §426) for the subject, which is to say that they have for it no other determinations than those relevant to satisfying its needs. This is what it means that an object is not at all differentiated for the subject as a thing with properties: it is, in the subject's perspective, simply identical with whatever sensed property or undifferentiated bundle of properties (say, a particular scent, pattern of movement, and so forth) makes the object desirable for it. Nothing else about the object, no other properties or relations, are of interest for the primitive subject, and thus they are not even present in its perspective. In other words, at the α.-level things are indeed given as objects for the subject, and thus there is a minimal differentiation between the object and the subject for the subject, yet objects still lack genuinely independent existence for the subject in that their 'meaning' and the qualities in terms of which they appear are fully determined by relevance for immediate need-satisfaction.[18]

Attention (*Aufmerksamkeit*) (E §448), discussed in Intuition, the α.-sub-chapter of Theoretical spirit, is arguably central in this primitive spatiotemporal object-constitution at issue in the α.-chapters (read bottom-up). That this is so is not immediately apparent in the text. In the published 1830 *Encyclopedia* text, Hegel seems in fact to be saying that attention and the spatiotemporal organizing of objects are two different functions.[19] Yet, on the other hand, in his lectures of 1827–1828 attention seems responsible for the spatiotemporal organizing of objectivity into singular objects.[20] Hegel's explicit statements on this issue leave room for uncertainty, perhaps signifying his own hesitation about it, but on a rational reconstruction it makes good sense to think that synthesizing the sensuous material of the five senses into singular objects requires grasping them as spatiotemporal wholes, and that this means attending to the clusters of sensations of the different senses that each spatiotemporally separate thing produces in the subject. As Hegel puts it, one needs "attention, the abstract identical direction of spirit in feelings [. . .] without which nothing has *being* for it" (E §448, my emphasis)—thus suggesting that it is attention that construes the deliverances of sensations (of

---

[18] See Redding, *Hegel's Hermeneutics*, 104–110; and Ikäheimo, "Animal Consciousness in Hegel's Philosophy of Subjective Spirit."

[19] E §448: "The one moment in this diremption of the immediately found [i.e., in the objectivation of sensational matter] is attention [. . .]. The other moment is, that intelligence posits [. . .] the feeling-determinations as something negative, as the abstract otherness of itself."

[20] VPG, 196–197, LPS, 212: "Space and time are the forms of the sensible, forms of intuition. [. . .] They are [. . .] ideal forms that do not belong to determinations of feeling as such. This is the activity of intelligence, *attention* to self, the act that posits this content outside of itself in order to make itself free" [Emphasis H. I.]. Note also (see note 16) that here Hegel grasps positing the sensational material as an object outside the subject, and giving it spatiotemporal order, as one and the same function. For a contrary view, see de Vries, *Hegel's Theory of Mental Activity*, 112.

the five senses) into objects of sensuous consciousness, characterized as "being, some-thing, existing thing, singular and so on" (E §418).

Related to this discussion, in the Introduction to Practical spirit Hegel talks of a 'dou-ble ought' of practical spirit, or of the practical dimension of mental activities. The first 'ought' is

> the opposition of the determinacy posited from out of itself to the immediate deter-minedness that thereby enters again, the opposition to its reality and condition, what in consciousness develops at the same time into the relationship towards external objects. (E §470)

What is at issue here is the felt unpleasant 'opposition' between what the living animal organism needs (nutrients) and its present condition (lack of them), and the develop-ment of this opposition into a desiring relation to 'external objects' in the environment that are instinctively identified, based on their sensed properties, as promising satis-faction. Though Hegel does not say it explicitly, it seems obvious that this, the topic of the extremely condensed sub-chapter Practical Feeling, is what provides motivation and orientation for the 'identical direction' of primitive attention, or in other words, for tracking interesting objects over time and in space while moving in ways that are appropriate for satisfying one's needs with the objects. A full reconstruction of Hegel's theory of object-constitution at this still basically animal level would require drawing also on his discussion of animal movement and the animal's relation to its environment (*Umwelt*) in the Philosophy of Nature, but this cannot be done here.[21] Suffice it to say that his reconstructed account is arguably compatible with contemporary 'enactive' accounts of perception that put a heavy emphasis on the role of movement and bodily action in object-constitution.[22]

As I hinted earlier, in the chapter Intuition Hegel speaks not only of 'intuition' as this simple, instinctive and thus basically animal form of spatiotemporal synthesis of objects, but also of cultivated intuition involving all the learning of a cultivated adult human being. Whereas the spatiotemporal synthesis alone grasps objects in terms of the simple logical determinations of "being, something, existing thing, singular and so on," or in other words, according to the conceptual structures Hegel discusses in the Logic of Being, cultivated intuition is seeing objects in light of the more complex conceptual structures which they also instantiate:

> Only by cultivation of the mind does attention acquire strength and fulfilment. The botanist, for example, notices incomparably more in a plant than one ignorant of botany does in the same time. The same is naturally true in regard to all other objects of knowledge. A man of great discernment and education has at once a complete

---

[21] See Ikäheimo, "Animal Consciousness in Hegel's Philosophy of Subjective Spirit" and "The Times of Desire, Hope and Fear."

[22] See Noë, *Action in Perception*; and Inwood, *A Commentary of Hegel's Philosophy of Mind*, 68.

intuition of what is at issue; with him sensation has the character of recollection throughout. (E §448A)

The scientifically cultivated person sees or 'intuits' objects in his environment immediately, that is to say habitually, in light of what he has learned about them through the tortuous path of scientific and philosophical education. For him, intuition of objectivity therefore has the character of 'recollection [*Erinnerung*]', or consciousness of something he already knows, and thus in a sense of consciousness of 'himself' in the objects. Analogously, Hegel also talks, in contrast to primitive practical feeling, which seeks satisfaction in immediately given objects of uncultivated desire, of cultivated practical feelings, which are motivationally affective felt qualities attached to mental contents that presuppose a higher level of mental processing (see E §472 and §472Z). The practical feelings of cultivated human persons are not limited to mere seeking of immediate satisfaction and thus to desires for immediately given objects promising it. Rather, they are mediated by the more refined forms of practical and theoretical processing that Hegel discusses in the β.- and γ.-sub-chapters of "Psychology," and the more refined kinds of object-relations at issue in the β.- and γ.-sub-chapters of "Phenomenology".

One of the recent philosophical debates concerning Hegel, and his relation to Kant, has turned around the question of whether all intuition is conceptually structured according to these thinkers, and in truth. Attempts to determine Hegel's view on the matter have mostly drawn on Hegel's discussion of 'sense certainty' in the 1807 *Phenomenology of Spirit*, where Hegel argues that trying to base knowledge-claims about the world, and eventually a philosophical system, on purely non-conceptual sensory givenness are self-contradictory. In the wake of John McDowell's *Mind and World*, an influential line of thought on this question has been that the world is given for individuals in intuition, mediated through conceptual structures embodied in their language and culture, and internalized in socialization as a habitual 'second nature'. As a result, the world given in intuition is structured according to the same conceptual structures in terms of which it is also thought and talked about, and this means that intuition can verify or falsify beliefs about the world. This, according to McDowell and others, is also Hegel's view on the matter.

These debates have arguably been doubly misconceived. First, Hegel's real theorizing on intuition is not to be found in the *Phenomenology of Spirit*, which is an introduction to his system, with a very particular argumentative task and method,[23] but in his actual 'real-philosophical' treatment of the theme in the Philosophy of Subjective Spirit— including his discussion of external and internal sensations in the "Anthropology," and the chapter titled Intuition in "Psychology," which I have argued needs to be

---

[23] A standard mistake in readings of the "Phenomenology" section of Subjective Spirit is projecting the method of the 1807 *Phenomenology of Spirit* onto it. The chapters and sub-chapters of the "Phenomenology" of Subjective Spirit do not describe 'patterns of consciousness' (*Gestalten des Bewusstseins*) in the sense central for the method of the *Phenomenology of Spirit* (see Emundts, Chapter 3 in this volume), but are structural descriptions of developmental layers (bottom up) and constitutive elements (top down) of the human person.

read in conjunction with the three other a.-sub-chapters of "Phenomenology" and "Psychology."

Second, Hegel's real view on the intuition question is more complex than the view attributed to him. That view only grasps the 'top-down' perspective on intuition exemplified by the Hegel's 'botanist', who immediately intuits the world according to conceptual structures in terms of which he has learned to think and talk about the world (of plants) through (botanical) education and which for him have become habitual 'second nature'. But as we saw, Hegel also thinks of intuition from the 'bottom-up' perspective prior to socialization. This, at the most rudimentary level, is the intuition of the (human) animal directed by immediate physiological needs. On Hegel's account, already this primitive intuition does indeed grasp the world in terms of conceptual structures, yet only very rudimentary ones discussed in his Logic of Being. These structures are structures of the world that the primitive subject needs to grasp in order to survive. There is thus a sort of epistemic normativity involved already at this rudimentary level, but not one of making and communicating epistemic claims about it, and thus not something to which the argumentation of the *Phenomenology of Spirit* applies.

19.2.2. The Differentiated β.-Level of Intentionality and the Corresponding Mental Activities

As we have seen, though in contrast to the pre-intentional layers of subjectivity discussed in the "Anthropology," the α.-sub-chapters do introduce differentiation in the sense of the subject-object-divide, the particular mode of subject-object-relation discussed in these sub-chapters is itself characterized by immediacy or lack of differentiation: the primitive α.-level mental processes and forms of intentionality constitute a sort of 'one-track-mind' incapable of distancing the concrete subject from the constraints of what immediate physiological need and instinct determine as salient in its environment (say, the breast for the human infant, or a particular plant or animal for a nonhuman animal). In contrast, in the chapter Representation (*Vorstellen*) in Theoretical Spirit, Hegel discusses mental processes and activities that achieve distance from the immediately given and thereby also a more comprehensive epistemic or cognitive grasp of the world. In the parallel chapter Drives and Wilfulness in Practical Spirit, Hegel analogously discusses modes of the 'will' that are more advanced than 'practical feeling' in that they involve freedom from determination by the immediately given felt needs. In short, 'willfulness [*Willkür*]' is the capacity to choose otherwise, or to choose between alternative motivations and courses of action, whereas 'drive [*Trieb*]' means in this context a temporally extended 'futural' mode of motivation whose content has some generality. Whereas the contents of 'desires' are fully determinate ("that desirable object over there") and thus no choice or 'wilfulness' is involved in relating to them, due to the generality of their contents or objects (say, "comfortable life at 50" or "bringing about the revolution"), the realization of 'drives' necessarily requires a choice between different specifications of the content and different means to achieve it.[24]

On a rational reconstruction it is clear that the theoretical and practical aspects of the mind are again closely intertwined. For one thing, whereas the spatiotemporal object-constitution discussed in Intuition is at the uncultivated level simply instinctive, the mental activities discussed in Representation involve increasing degrees of freedom of choice or 'wilfulness': any object has many properties and a multitude of internal and external relations, and part of the cultivation of the mind is to develop the capacity to wilfully change perspectives and choose what exactly in the object or objects to attend to. Second, the mental activities discussed in Representation require, *as activities* of the concrete subject (see E §445), a form of motivation that transcends the uncultivated immediacy of 'practical feeling' and thus 'desire'. Only a subject with at least some degree of the long-term future-directed mode of motivation (that Hegel calls in shorthand 'drive') has an interest in cognitively grasping anything else than the immediately given. Viewed from the opposite side, the capacity to choose presupposes the capacity to represent or imagine alternative states of affairs that are not given in present intuition. Similarly with the long-term form of practical motivation of 'drive': it involves experiencing possible future states of affairs as motivating ends and thus presupposes the capacity to represent them in the first place.

The sub-chapter titled Representation is perhaps the richest in content of all the sub-chapters of Subjective Spirit. Yet, read in abstraction from the other β.-sub-chapters, it seems in a certain way disappointing, painting a strangely atomistic picture of the mental activities it discusses—as if they were all uninfluenced by, or merely externally related to, other thinking, knowing, and acting human beings, or the social and historical world more broadly. This 'Cartesian' impression is largely due to the general division of labor between the Philosophy of Subjective and Objective Spirit: Subjective Spirit abstracts from the social reality to which the human person constitutively belongs, and Hegel mostly sticks to his architectonics, even if thematically this often seems rather contrived. And yet, he does make one highly significant deviation from this aspect of his architectonic strictures. This is the β.-sub-chapter of Self-consciousness, titled Recognitive Self-consciousness, and the subsequent γ.-sub-chapter Universal Self-consciousness. Here Hegel explicitly discusses the intersubjective mediation of human subjectivity and appears to give it a major role in the coming about and constitution of what he thinks of as a genuinely human form of practical intentionality. It is striking that Hegel makes this move, one that clearly violates his own architectonic strictures, at the exact center-point of Subjective Spirit—sub-chapter B.b.β.—and at the same time disappointing that he says barely anything about the significance of the intersubjective mediation discussed in this and the subsequent sub-chapter for everything else discussed in Subjective Spirit.

Some interpreters have concluded that everything that comes after B.b.β. Recognitive Self-consciousness involves intersubjective mediation, thereby assuming a purely linear

---

[24] See Yeomans, *Freedom and Reflection*, 30.

thematic development.[25] But this is too hasty, as the linear order of the text is not the order of its thematic development: the α.-level phenomena discussed in "Psychology" are no more developed than the α.-level phenomena discussed in "Phenomenology," and (from the bottom-up perspective) none of them necessarily involves intersubjective mediation or needs any input from the social and historical world. Yet, and though Hegel gives very little explicit indication of this in the text, on a rational reconstruction the intersubjective mediation explicitly introduced in Recognitive Self-consciousness is decisive for the difference between the α.- and the β.-level chapters in all of the four parallel chapters of "Phenomenology" and "Psychology" (Consciousness as such, Self-consciousness, Theoretical Spirit, and Practical Spirit). It is also essential for understanding the thoroughly detranscendentalized nature of Hegel's account of the concrete subject by clearly thematizing how the constitution of objectivity for the subject by its mental activities (discussed in "Psychology") is influenced by the world, which is robustly independent from it. Whereas the objects of desire are on Hegel's account incapable of resisting their reduction in the subject's viewpoint to what is relevant to the satisfaction of the subject's immediate needs (see E §427), and thus incapable of challenging its desiring one-track mind, another subject as a 'free object' (PS §429) will resist such reduction and thus thematize to the first subject its (the first subject's) viewpoint as a particular viewpoint. In addition to this 'decentering' of the subject for itself, the sub-chapter Recognitive Self-consciousness also discusses the intersubjective or social conditions in which the short-term temporality of desire is transcended in the long-term, future-directed, or plan-like temporality and practical orientation, which Hegel in Practical Spirit calls (perhaps somewhat counterintuitively) 'drive'. Hegel discusses this by means of the familiar figures of the 'master' and the 'bondsman', which illustrate the thematization of the subject's vulnerability for himself through the challenge and threat of another subject with a practical viewpoint (E §§432–433), and the consequent concern for future well-being, or as Hegel puts it "taking care and securing the future'" (E §434), which in the bondsman's case means working for the master. This also returns us to Hegel's talk of the 'double ought' in the Introduction to Practical Spirit (E §470): the first 'ought' of uncultivated practical feeling and desire is now subordinated under a second ought, which at this level means social normativity in the form of normative expectations by the relevant other subject or subjects—'the master'. The contents of the bondsman's 'drives', if he is to live, must be harmonious enough with the master's commands.[26]

These are concrete processes in the world that affect the subject from the outside, but Hegel does not allow himself enough leeway to thematize them in his "Psychology," the focus of which is strictly intrasubjective. He does give, however, one indirect hint of the importance of the intersubjective mediation for the transition from intuition to representation,

---

[25] See Hespe, "System und Funktion der Philosophie des Subjektiven Geistes."
[26] The master's commands are general in the same way as 'drives' are: they require specification and thus choice or 'willfulness' by the one who executes them.

even if only in the lecture material. In the Addition to §449 we read, "Only when I make the reflecion that it is I who have the intuition, only then do I occupy the standpoint of representation." When or why do I make the reflection? Hegel's answer in the parallel sub-chapter Recognitive Self-consciousness is clear: in being confronted with another subject with another perspective. It is the clash of perspectives that makes me aware of myself as a subject with a perspective, or as 'having an intuition'. This suggests what seems fairly clear otherwise, namely that whereas the mental processes that Hegel calls by the umbrella term 'intuition' are not necessarily intersubjectively mediated, the activities that he calls 'representation' are.[27] It is because the subject is now becoming conscious of itself as a subject that we are also witnessing a gradual transition in the text from unconscious mental *processes* to mental *activities* that the subject can in principle be conscious of and thus deliberately rehearse and cultivate—just as the bondsman is forced to cultivate its own capacities.

In the Representation-subchapter Hegel starts with the process or activity of storing contents given in intuition as 'images' and thus abstracting them from the place and moment in time in which they were originally present for the subject (E §452). He then continues by discussing the comparison of already stored images and new intuitions, and the gradual grasp of differences and similarities between them, or in other words, grasping 'what is universal' in them (E §454). He is describing here the simplest form of the mental processing that produces the mode of objectivity discussed in the sub-chapter Perception in the "Phenomenology," a mode in which objects are no longer identical with whatever feature makes them immediately desirable, but are things with many properties, and thus related with each other in terms of qualitative similarities and differences (E §§420–421). As Hegel puts it there (E §420), the subject is now making 'experiences [*Erfahrung*]', or in other words, learning about the world. The discussion of these mental processes or activities continues in "Psychology" with 'reproductive imagination', the first instinctive but gradually more willful cognitive handling of the stored images, of associating them and organizing them under empirical concepts, or under 'universal representations [*allgemeine Vorstellung*]' (E §§455–456), as he calls them. The perspectival and pragmatic nature of this organizing or subsuming of the given under empirical concepts is clear in §456, where Hegel says it is an activity of 'concrete subjectivity' with 'interest'—pointing to the fact that the world can be carved, or phenomena subsumed under empirical concepts, in many different ways, and that it depends on interest which way a subject will follow. This connects with Hegel's remarks in the parallel sub-chapter Drives and Wilfulness, where he says that "[t]he subject is [now, after having overcome the immediacy of the α.-level] the activity of satisfying drives," and that "nothing comes about [...] without interest" (E §475). This is to say, very much in a pragmatist vein[28] (or of Heidegger[29]), that we are constitutively engaged in

---

[27] This does not necessarily mean that they are linguistically mediated; see later discussion in this chapter.

[28] For a classical pragmatist reading of Subjective Spirit, see Dewey, "Hegel's Philosophy of Spirit: 1897."

[29] See Ikäheimo, "The Times of Desire, Hope and Fear."

goal-directed activities, and thus driven by ends that are our interest, and it suggests that the epistemic activities of carving the world in terms of empirical concepts are both motivated by and serve these drives and interests. Hegel does not allow himself (or bother) to say the obvious: that such interests in human persons are influenced by their social environment, and that any organized coexistence and communication—such as that between the illustrative figures of the master and bondsman—requires that subjects carve the world in similar enough ways and so can understand each other. The bondsman's life depends on understanding the master, and thus it is in his interest to try to carve the world similarly enough with him. The human infant learns the ways to carve the world particular to her culture from the adults, but it would learn nothing without suitable future-directed interests.

Hegel discusses next the production of symbols and signs (E §§457–460), mostly abstracting from the fact, of which he is of course aware,[30] that these are in reality social and historical processes and that each new generation is introduced into an already existing world of symbols and signs by the previous ones. Whereas symbolism depends on a similarity between the symbol and the symbolized, a sign's signification is ideally completely dependent on willfulness, or in other words, on convention. Hegel puts heavy emphasis on 'mechanical memory [*mechanische Gedächtnis*]' which is the capacity to bind words or 'names' to what they signify, and thus to operate in thought and speech with names without the need of actually recalling the referred representations (of different degrees of abstraction and complexity) from the 'nocturnal pit' of unconsciousness in which they are stored (E §453). Hegel's discussion of symbols, signs, and language is probably the part of "Psychology" most discussed in the secondary literature, and though Hegel's brief discussion does not really amount to a theory of language, attempts have been made to reconstruct Hegel's (or a Hegelian) theory of language from ingredients in what he writes.[31] This part of the "Psychology" has also attracted attention by authors who want to question Hegel's claims on the capacity (in principle) of philosophical language and thought to be independent of the perspectivity of intuition and representation and of the uncontrollable contingence of symbolic meaning—and thus its capacity to be 'pure' in the sense Hegel takes it to be in his Logic.

One of the important questions concerning the themes discussed in the sub-chapter Representation concerns the relation of language to the psychological processes and activities discussed earlier in the sub-chapter. Though from the 'top-down' perspective all of them may involve language (and of course already the 'botanist's' erudite intuition does), nothing in the text commits Hegel to the view that all of them *necessarily* do. Hegel is clearly not a 'linguistic a priorist' on human psychology. Whatever his explicit views on the difference between human psychology and that of non-human

---

[30] "That language is gradually formed and developed is self-evident" (VPG, 215, LPS, 229). See also E §459.

[31] See, for example, Bodammer, *Hegels Deutung der Sprache*; Vernon, *Hegel's Philosophy of Language*; and the collection Surber, ed., *Hegel and Language*.

animals,[32] the architectonics of his text makes his account in principle compatible with sophisticated contemporary views on pre-linguistic processes of thinking in great apes and human infants.[33] Humans are born as animals and have to be equipped from the beginning with psychological capacities that enable them to orient in their environment before learning language, and—centrally—make it possible for them to interact with adults in ways that enable learning a language and human culture and to thus develop the more refined, specifically human psychological capacities dependent on these.[34] The 'bottom-up' reading of Representation does justice to these developmental necessities.

19.2.3. Transcending or Accommodating Differences at the γ.-Level

The γ.-sub-chapters of "Phenomenology" and "Psychology" discuss finally mental activities and modes of intentionality where the various differentiations present at the β.-level are incorporated into an overarching unity (see E §465Z), and in which the relations between the different elements are conceived of as internal rather than external. Also, the perspectivity of the β.-level is left behind at the γ.-level, so that now we are dealing with perspective-independent determinations of things and processes in the world, or their 'interior' (E §420), as Hegel puts it in the parallel sub-chapter Understanding (*Der Verstand*), which discusses the form of objectivity that is the product of 'thinking', or more exactly of 'thinking over [*Nachdenken*]' (see later discussion in this chapter) objects of perception and their determinations. The analogy between the theoretical and the practical γ.-sub-chapters of "Psychology"—C.a.γ. Thinking and C.b.γ. Happiness— is, however, not perfect in this respect. Whereas Hegel's discussion of thinking is mainly positive, conceiving of it as a level of mental activity that achieves a genuine unity of differences and leaves behind particularity of perspective, his discussion of happiness is mainly negative, pointing out the inadequacy of 'happiness' as an end of willing in these regards.

Let me begin with thinking and the theoretical dimension. On Hegel's account, the cognitive or epistemic activities of 'representation' are only able to produce a comprehension of the world that is a 'mixture' of 'individuality' and 'universality', or in other words, a mixture of the thing conceived of as a singular thing, on the one hand, and its 'various properties', on the other hand (E §421). According to Hegel, this is "in general the standpoint of ordinary consciousness and more or less of the sciences" (E §420).

---

[32] See Ikäheimo, "Animal Consciousness in Hegel's Philosophy of Subjective Spirit."

[33] See Bermudez, *Thinking without Words*; and Tomasello, *A Natural History of Human Thinking*.

[34] Here I agree with Winfield, *The Living Mind*, 184. Winfield's purely linear reading commits him, however, to some highly artificial conclusions, such as that Hegel's account of the master and bondsman in the Phenomenology involves neither thought nor language (Winfield, *The Living Mind*, 213). After all, these themes are thematized only 'later' in "Psychology." On my reading, Hegel's architectonics is flexible enough to accommodate both prelinguistic and linguistically mediated 'master-bondsman relations'.

The point here is that the cognitive activities of 'representation' are incapable, or insufficiently capable, of grasping objects as unities of necessarily interrelated determinations. In Hegel's jargon, this is to say that they remain at the level of the 'abstract universal'. Things are different with the cognitive activities that he calls 'thinking': they are "intelligence comprehending the concrete universal of objects" (E §445A). In §465, the first paragraph of the Thinking-sub-chapter, Hegel refers back to paragraphs 5 and 21 at the beginning of the *Encyclopedia*, where he discusses thinking as the activity of 'thinking over' (*Nachdenken*) representations and thereby "generating concepts of them" (E §1). What he has in mind is ultimately philosophical comprehension of the world, which is what he is himself engaged in in his *Realphilosophien*, or in other words, the Philosophy of Nature and the Philosophy of Spirit.

In the Thinking-sub-chapter Hegel utilizes, in an extremely condensed form, his discussion of the concept, judgment, and syllogism in the Logic of the Concept (E §467). He does not explicitly introduce different kinds of concepts, judgment, and syllogism here, but it is clear that the internality of the relations between determinations of an object that is distinctive of 'thinking' comes in degrees and is achieved ideally only in the highest forms.[35] Merely 'qualitative judgments' and 'qualitative syllogisms' operate with accidental properties, such as when we say "this rose is red" (E §172), and they involve no necessary connection between the individual and the universal, or the thing and the property, nor establish anything concerning other properties of the thing, or its relations to other things. In contrast, judgments and syllogisms 'of reflection' operate with properties that imply something about the thing's other properties and its relations with other things, such as when we judge a particular plant, or some or all plants of a certain kind, as having healing powers (E §174). Further on the scale of concreteness in Hegel's sense are judgments and syllogisms 'of necessity' which connect an individual with a species concept, as in "Caius is a human being" (E §177A). The species concept is a 'concrete universal' establishing a concrete unity in many respects. It determines the individual's essential properties (say, rationality), generic judgments and related syllogisms that apply to individuals of that genus (say, humans are rational), and which properties of things of this kind have "value and meaning" (E §177A) (say, Caius being learned or brave). As Hegel says, it would make "no sense to assume that Caius could somehow not be human being, but be brave, learned, and so forth" (E §175A). The final form of judgment, 'the judgment of the concept' finally articulates explicitly Hegel's normative or evaluative essentialism. Judgments of this kind judge something as being "good or bad, true, beautiful and so forth" (E §178), which Hegel understands in terms of their correspondence to their concept which is their norm or 'ought' (SL 12.84/582). In other words, the species concept determines what it is to be a good or bad individual of that species, or to be 'true' in the ontological sense of truth as correspondence with the species concept. It is here that we reach a truly 'concrete universal' unifying exemplars of the species, allowing them to differ in their qualities (both in time and relative to each other), while at the same time being their norm or measure of goodness.

---

[35] See deVries, *Hegel's Theory of Mental Activity*, 179–202.

The relations of Hegel's telegraphic discussion in Theoretical Spirit of thinking as an activity that grasps the 'concrete universal' of objects, or their concept as their principle of unity and perfection, his more extended discussion of the forms of such thinking in the Logic of Concept, and his own actual philosophical 'thinking over' of the various realms of being in his *Realphilosophien* are not easy to determine. Suffice it to say that his essentialist treatment of subjective spirit in terms of the 'concept of spirit' is an example of what he means.[36] Thinking that adequately grasps the intelligible structure of things, or the 'objective reason' (E §441, §467Z) in them is the consummation of intelligence, not only by grasping things and their particular determinations and relations in their 'self-developing concept(s)' (E §467Z), but also in thereby achieving an "overarching unity of itself and its other, being" (E §465). In other words, philosophical comprehension of the world is the ultimate, though by no means self-sufficient, form of concrete freedom in cognition. It is not self-sufficient, since human life requires equally the α.- and β.-level cognitive activities, and since it only comes about by 'thinking over' the products of these 'lower' activities. Furthermore, as we saw in Hegel's discussion of intuition, philosophical comprehension does not remain in the proverbial ivory tower, but can and should be built into the everyday cognitive life of the cultivated human person.

Hegel's discussion of the γ.-level of Practical Spirit consists of two short paragraphs (E §§479–480) discussing happiness as a general end of willing. Here Hegel's architectonic breaks down somewhat as happiness is—analogically to the β.-level in the theoretical side—a "mixture of qualitative and quantitative determinations" (E §479). An individual may have various interests, and whether they can be integrated, or what is their ideal 'mixture', is highly contingent, dependent on external circumstances and subjective idiosyncrasy. As Hegel puts it, "[h]appiness is only the represented, abstract universality of the contents, a universality which only ought to be" (E §480). 'Actually free will' (E §480) does not have such indeterminate representations as its object, but rather the objective system of freedom, which is the topic of the Philosophy of Objective Spirit. The individual sheds his 'abstract individuality' and becomes a 'concrete subject' with a stable 'character' (E §482) in the practical dimension by willing contents that are in harmony with and contribute to the rational state whose goodness and rationality he recognizes in feeling and—if he is philosophically educated—in knowledge, thereby being 'conscious of himself' in it and thus concretely free with regard to it. Hegel's mainly negative discussion of 'happiness' thus introduces the necessity of the ideal state as the 'realm of actualized freedom' (PR §4) for the full realization of concrete freedom and thus the human essence. It is in the state that the 'second ought' of practical spirit ceases to be something which 'only ought to be', and takes the form of normative expectations built into the concrete social roles in which individuals lead their lives and realize themselves in harmony with and contributing to the whole.

In the parallel chapter Universal Self-consciousness, Hegel discusses the state of mutual recognition in which the asymmetry and coerciveness of the master-bondsman-type

---

[36] See also Hegel's discussion of this theme in the context of his *Philosophy of Nature* in PN1, 201–205.

relationship is overcome. He conceives of this "universal mirroring of self-consciousness," or in other words, mutual consciousness of oneself in each other in relations between persons, as the "substance of every essential spirituality—of the family, courage, of honor, of fame, as well as of all virtues, of love, friendship, courage, of honor, of fame" (E §436). In short, mutual recognition between individuals is that whereby ethical life (*Sittlichkeit*) realizes concrete freedom and thus the human essence. Hegel makes no reference here to vertical relations of recognition between individuals and the state, leaving this theme to the Philosophy of Objective Spirit.[37]

WORKS CITED

Primary Texts

Hegel, G. W. F. *Elements of the Philosophy of Right* [PR], edited by Allen Wood, translated by H. B. Nisbet. Cambridge: Cambridge University Press, 1991.

Hegel, G. W. F. *Encyclopedia of the Philosophical Sciences in Basic Outline. Part I: Science of Logic* [E], Translated and edited by Klaus Brinkmann and Daniel O. Dahlström. Cambridge: Cambridge University Press, 2010.

Hegel, G. W. F. *Hegel's Philosophy of Nature* [PN1] Vol. 1, edited and translated by M. J. Petry. London: Allen and Unwin, 1970.

Hegel, G. W. F. *Lectures on the Philosophy of Spirit 1827–8* [LSP], translated with an introduction by Robert R. Williams. Oxford: Oxford University Press, 2007.

Hegel, G. W. F. *Philosophy of Mind* [E], translated by W. Wallace and A. V. Miller, revised with an introduction by Michael Inwood. Oxford: Clarendon Press, 2007.

Hegel, G. W. F. *The Science of Logic* [SL], edited and translated by George di Giovanni. Oxford: Oxford University Press, 2010.

Hegel, G. W. F. *Vorlesungen über die Philosophie des Geistes. Berlin 1827/1828* [VPG]. Nachgeschrieben von Johann Eduard Erdmann und Ferdinand Walter. Georg Wilhelm Friedrich Hegel, Vorlesungen, Band 13. Hamburg: Felix Meiner, 1994.

Secondary Literature

Ameriks, Karl. "Recent Work on Hegel: The Rehabilitation of an Epistemologist?" *Philosophy and Phenomenological Research* 52, no. 1 (1992): 177–202.

Bermudez, José Luis. *Thinking without Words*. Oxford: Oxford University Press, 2003.

Bodammer, Theodoer. *Hegels Deutung der Sprache*. Hamburg: Meiner, 1969.

Bowman, Brady. *Hegel and the Metaphysics of Absolute Negativity*. Cambridge: Cambridge University Press, 2013.

deVries, Willem. *Hegel's Theory of Mental Activity*. Ithaca, NY; London: Cornell University Press, 1988.

[37] I wish to thank Andy Blunden, Filipe Campello, Luca Corti, Katerina Deligiorgi, Jack Ferguson, Cinzia Ferrini, Ilmari Jauhiainen, Ismael Magadan, Guido Seddone, Italo Testa and the other participants of an academia.edu-session on this paper in November 2015 for helpful comments and questions.

Dewey, John. "Hegel's Philosophy of Spirit: 1897," in *John Dewey's Philosophy of Spirit: With the 1897 Lecture on Hegel*, edited by John R. Shook and James A. Good. New York: Fordham University Press, 2010, 93–174.

Drüe, Hermann. *Psychologie aus dem Begriff, Hegels Persönlichkeitstheorie*. Berlin; New York, de Gruyter, 1976.

Eley, Lothar (ed.). *Hegels Theorie des subjektiven Geistes; in der "Enzyklopädie der philosophischen Wissenschaften im Grundrisse.*" Stuttgart: Fromman-Holzbook, 1990.

Fetscher, Iring. *Hegels Lehre vom Menschen; Kommentar zu den §§ 387 bis 472 der Enzyklopädie der Philosophischen Wissenschaften*. Stuttgart: Frommann-Holzboog, 1970.

Greene, Murray. *Hegel on the Soul: A Speculative Anthropology*. The Hague: Martinus Nijhoff, 1972.

Habermas, Jürgen. "From Kant to Hegel and Back: The Move Towards Detranscendentalization." *European Journal of Philosophy* 7, no. 2 (1999): 129–157.

Halbig, Christoph. *Objektives Denken* (Spekulation und Erfahrung, Abteilung II: Untersuchungen, Band 48). Stuttgart: Frommann-Holzboog, 2002.

Henrich, Dieter (ed.). *Hegels philosophische Psychologie*. Hegel-Studien/Beiheft 19. Bonn: Bouvier Verlag Herbert Grundmann, 1979.

Herrmann-Sinai, Susanne, and Lucia Ziglioli (eds.). *Hegel's Philosophical Psychology*. London: Routledge, 2016.

Hespe, Franz. "System und Funktion der Philosophie des Subjektiven Geistes," in *Psychologie und Anthropologie oder Philosophie des Geistes*, edited by F. Hespe and B. Tuschling. Stuttgart: Frommann-Holzbook, 1991, 490–521.

Hespe, F., and B. Tuschling (eds.) *Psychologie und Anthropologie oder Philosophie des Geistes*. Stuttgart: Frommann-Holzbook, 1991.

Hösle, Vittorio. *Hegels System*. Hamburg: Felix Meiner, 1987.

Ikäheimo, Heikki. *Anerkennung*. Berlin: De Gruyter, 2014.

Ikäheimo, Heikki. "Animal Consciousness in Hegel's Philosophy of Subjective Spirit," in *Hegel-Jahrbuch* 2010, edited by Andreas Arndt, Paul Cruysberghs, and Ardrzej Przylebski. Berlin: Akademie Verlag, 2011, 180–185.

Ikäheimo, Heikki. "On the Role of Intersubjectivity in Hegel's Encyclopaedic Phenomenology and Psychology." *The Bulletin of the Hegel Society of Great Britain* 49–50 (2004): 73–95.

Ikäheimo, Heikki. *Self-Consciousness and Intersubjectivity: A Study of Hegel's Encyclopedia Philosophy of Subjective Spirit (1830)*. Jyväskylä, Finland: University of Jyväskylä, 2000. Available online: https://unsw.academia.edu/HeikkiIkaheimo.

Ikäheimo, Heikki. "The Times of Desire, Hope and Fear: On the Temporality of Concrete Subjectivity in Hegel's Encyclopaedia." *Critical Horizons* 13, no. 2 (2012): 197–219.

Inwood, Michael. *A Commentary of Hegel's Philosophy of Mind*. Oxford: Oxford University Press, 2007.

McDowell, John *Mind and World*. Cambridge, MA: Harvard University Press, 1994.

Michelet, Carl Ludwig. *Anthropologie und Psychologie oder die Philosophie des subjektiven Geistes*. Berlin: Sanderschen Buchhandlung, 1840.

Noë, Alva. *Action in Perception*. Cambridge, MA: MIT Press, 2004.

Peperzak, Adriaan. *Selbsterkenntnis des Absoluten. Grundlinien der Hegelschen Philosophie des Geistes*. Stuttgart: Fromman-Holzbook, 1987.

Redding, Paul. *Hegel's Hermeneutics*. Ithaca; London: Cornell University Press, 1996.

Rometsch, Jens. *Hegels Theorie des erkennenden Subjekts: Systematische Untersuchungen zur enzyklopädischen Philosophie des subjektiven Geistes.* Würzburg: Königshausen & Neumann, 2007.

Rosenkranz, Karl. *Psychologie oder die Wissenschaft vom subjektiven Geist.* Königsberg: Gebrüder Bornträger, 1837.

Schalhorn, Christof. *Hegels enzyklopädischer Begriff von Selbstbewusstsein.* Hegel-Studien, Beiheft 43. Hamburg: Felix Meiner, 2000.

Stederoth, Dirk. *Hegel Philosophie des Subjektiven Geistes.* Berlin: Akademie Verlag, 2001.

Stern, David S. (ed.). *Essays on Hegel's Philosophy of Subjective Spirit.* Albany: State University of New York Press, 2013.

Surber, Jere Paul (ed.). *Hegel and Language.* Albany: State University of New York Press, 2006.

Tomasello, Michael. *A Natural History of Human Thinking.* Cambridge, MA: Harvard University Press, 2014.

Vernon, Jim. *Hegel's Philosophy of Language.* London: Continuum, 2007.

Winfield, Richard D. *Hegel and Mind: Rethinking Philosophical Psychology.* Basingstoke, UK: Palgrave, 2009.

Winfield, Richard D. *The Living Mind: From Psyche to Consciousness.* Lanham, MD: Rowan & Littlefield, 2011.

Wolff, Michael. *Das Körper-Seele-Problem: Kommentar zu Hegel, Enzyklopädie (1830), §389.* Frankfurt am Main: Vittorio Klostermann, 1992.

Yeomans, Christopher. *Freedom and Reflection: Hegel and the Logic of Agency.* Oxford: Oxford University Press, 2011.

PART V

OBJECTIVE SPIRIT

CHAPTER 20

HEGEL'S PHILOSOPHY OF LAW

THOM BROOKS

20.1. INTRODUCTION

G. W. F. HEGEL was neither a lawyer nor primarily a legal theorist, but his writings make a significant contribution to our understanding of legal philosophy. Hegel's primary contribution is his *Philosophy of Right*, although he provides us with important insights in other works, such as his *Philosophy of History* and even *The Science of Logic*. No survey of the history of legal philosophy is complete without Hegel. While there is no disputing his importance, there is disagreement about where Hegel's importance lies. Scholarly positions range widely, from the view that Hegel defends a theory of freedom to a philosophy of despotism.[1] There is further debate about which view about the nature of law best fits Hegel's legal philosophy.

I argue that Hegel's philosophy of law is best understood as a natural law theory. But what is interesting about Hegel's view is that it represents a distinctive alternative to how most natural law theories are traditionally conceived. Hegel's philosophy is remarkable for providing an entirely new way of thinking about the relation between law and morality than had been considered before. It is the distinctiveness of his legal philosophy that has rendered so difficult an easy categorizing into standard jurisprudential schools of thought. There is little that is standard in Hegel's innovative understanding of law.

The chapter proceeds as follows. I begin with an overview of leading natural law theorists from antiquity to today. Natural law is a wide tent composed of diverse views, but virtually all endorse some view of what I call *natural law externalism*: the idea that we determine moral standards for judging legal systems outside of them. The following section argues that Hegel supports *natural law internalism*: this is the view that we assess legal systems using moral standards found within them. Our moral assessment of law is

---

[1] See Paul Franco, *Hegel's Philosophy of Freedom*; and Karl Popper, *The Open Society and Its Enemies*.

internal and not external. This represents an important divergence from the natural law tradition that Hegel pioneered. The following sections consider implications of Hegel's jurisprudence for the relation of the judiciary to the public and his often misunderstood theory of punishment.

20.2. NATURAL LAW EXTERNALISM: OLD AND NEW

Natural law casts a large net, encompassing a wide array of theoretical perspectives. They are loosely bound together by a shared conviction that law and morality are interconnected: to say something is 'law' is to say something about its morality. Despite their many differences, natural law theories also understand the relation of law and morality in a particular way, as what I call *natural law externalism*. This is the view that we understand morality *externally* from the law and use our moral standard as an external measure of legal validity. This picture of the natural law tradition holds for most classical and contemporary natural law theorists. I explain this here in order to show in the next section that Hegel's philosophy of law represents an important break from this tradition because it conceives of law and morality in a different relationship.

Classical natural law is perhaps best stated by Cicero:

> True law is right reason in agreement with nature; it is of universal application, unchanging and everlasting; it summons to duty by its commands, and averts from wrongdoing by its prohibitions. And it does not lay its commands or prohibitions upon good men in vain, although neither have any effect on the wicked. It is a sin to try to alter this law, nor is it allowable to attempt to repeal any part of it, and it is impossible to abolish it entirely … there will not be different laws at Rome and at Athens, or different laws now and in the future, but one eternal and unchangeable law will be valid for all nations and all times, and there will be one master and ruler, that is, God, over us all, for he is the author of this law, its promulgator, and its enforcing judge. Whoever is disobedient is fleeing from himself and denying his human nature, and by reasons of this very fact he will suffer the worst penalties, even if he escapes what is commonly considered punishments.[2]

There are five central tenets of classical natural law that we can discern from this statement.[3] The first is that we can distinguish between 'law' and 'true law'. This is the difference between what is merely legal and what should always be legal. For example, it may be considered merely legal in this sense that a contract can allow a specific number of workdays during which it can be voided without penalty. It might be said that this

---

[2] Bix, "Natural Law Theory," 224.
[3] See Brooks, "Natural Law Internalism," 167–169.

is mostly a contingent matter because what is most important is the centrality of our consent to making any contract binding. Natural lawyers understand 'true law' as not a contingent or non-essential matter, but something more perfect. Not all laws share the same status: while all laws are part of a legal system, some are more central and ideal than others.

A second tenet of classical natural law is that we can make the distinction between law and true law by using a standard of moral justice. This links with a third tenet: that law is more 'true' the closer it coheres with a standard of moral justice. So we can distinguish between law and true law by considering how well law satisfies a moral standard. True laws more perfectly embody moral justice, and the merely legal occupy the opposite side of the spectrum. Morality is relevant for the study of law because it reveals how well the law meet standards of moral justice. Law should not be understood separately from morality and, more specifically, from a standard of moral justice.

Perhaps the greatest disagreement among classical natural lawyers concerns identifying the correct moral standard we should use in weighing up how 'true' our laws are. Most, if not all, follow Cicero's comments and identify true law as meeting some divine threshold. But where we should draw lines in confirming and applying these standards can differ virtually from one natural lawyer to the next.

A fourth central tenet of classical natural law is that the standard of moral justice is external and applied in our normative assessment of law. We are to consider first what should serve as a satisfactory standard of moral justice. Once this is identified, our moral standard is to be applied to our laws to see how 'true', or morally just, they are. But the standard we hold the law to is external to the law. We do not look first to the law to see what moral standards may already be embedded. Instead, we consider which moral standard the law should satisfy and then apply this external to the law standard to judge how just our laws are.

A final central tenet is specific only to classical natural law theorists. It is that the 'true' law is universally and eternally true. So for Cicero, the most just laws are applicable everywhere at all times without exception: what is a true law for Rome will be equally true for New York or New Delhi. This is the case whether we speak of the past, the present, or the future: the most perfect law is perfect for every people and every age; it does not change over time.

Contemporary natural lawyers agree with many of these tenets. Specifically, they agree that a standard of moral justice should be used to consider how just our laws are. This standard should be determined first externally to the law and then applied in our assessment of the law. Contemporary natural lawyers are deeply divided over what should serve as the most satisfactory standard, but they generally agree on an important break from natural law's classical tradition. This is that contemporary theorists do not tend to link the most just with the divine. One implication is that the majority may find a particular view of morality most justified, but few claim this supports the view that there is one and only one supremely just legal system everywhere at any time.

This can be explained partly by the Enlightenment's clear transition away from the view of all true law as divine to the idea of just laws grounded in compelling reasons.

This speaks to H. L. A. Hart's definition of natural law as "that there are certain principles of human conduct, awaiting discovery by human reason, with which man-made law must conform if it is to be valid."[4] Contemporary natural lawyers give greater weight to the use of reason in justifying the best standard of moral justice to assess the law.

For example, consider two different and influential contemporary natural law theories. The first is the natural law theory of John Finnis. His perspective is more traditional than most today. For instance, he claims that through reason we can identify seven basic forms of the human good. These include goods such as knowledge, play, and sociability.[5] Each is discoverable through our practical reflection on what basic forms of the good we might possess. These goods are understood as things worth having for a minimally decent human life. We undertake this task first before considering its legal application. Once we have identified these goods, this helps us structure our moral appraisal of law: "they lay down for us the outlines of everything one could reasonably want to do, to have, and to be."[6] So we determine basic forms of the good first, and then apply them in assessing law.

Of course, our use of practical reasoning may lead us to consider different forms of the good from those that Finnis identifies. Or we might disagree on how some forms come to serve as basic human goods. The points that I want to raise are, first, that our determining a moral standard is prior to our determining the relative moral justice of our laws and that, second, this standard is considered independently of the legal system we apply it to. Our moral standard is external to the law. Finnis is an example of one kind of what we might call natural law externalism, but so is Cicero because he has a view of divine justice first, which is then applied to law.

Now consider Lon Fuller's natural law approach as a second example of a contemporary natural lawyer whose view is compatible with natural law externalism in a different way. Fuller defends what he calls "the inner morality of law."[7] The inner morality he identifies is not, perhaps confusingly, a morality that is internal to the law. Instead, Fuller engages in practical reasoning to discover eight principles that he claims any legal system ought to satisfy.[8] These principles include the guarantee to "make the law known, make it coherent and clear . . . etc."[9] Fuller's principles require legal systems to provide general laws that are publicly accessible and not retrospective. If any of his eight principles is not met, then Fuller says that this "does not simply result in a bad system of law; it results in something that is not properly called a legal system at all."[10]

What Fuller calls law's 'inner morality' does not, in fact, emanate and develop from within a legal system. Law's morality is grasped externally by reason in response to circumstances. Fuller illustrates the application of morality to law with the example of our

---

[4]   Hart, *The Concept of Law*, 186.
[5]   See Finnis, *Natural Law and Natural Rights*, 85–90.
[6]   Finnis, *Natural Law and Natural Rights*, 97.
[7]   See Fuller, *The Morality of Law*, 42.
[8]   Fuller, *The Morality of Law*, 39–49.
[9]   Fuller, *The Morality of Law*, 42.
[10] Fuller, *The Morality of Law*, 39.

visiting a former minister of justice in Poland. The minister recounts how his government endeavored to make the law clear and well known by its citizens, but unfortunately this came at a hidden cost that making laws more understandable "rendered their application by the courts more capricious and less predictable."[11] Fuller argues that we should balance adhering as best we can to our moral principles in light of the changing circumstances that confront us. His is a project of determining these principles first, and then applying them to the law as a standard for law's moral assessment.[12]

Unsurprisingly, Fuller refers to his approach as "a procedural version of natural law theory."[13] For this reason, he can be understood to offer a more formalistic model of natural law. There is much of interest in Fuller's approach. One attraction is that his procedural approach in attempting to flesh out minimal moral conditions that any just legal system should satisfy addresses the criticism faced by many natural law views that they are too demanding because they are only satisfied when people act like angels. But two key points concern us here. One is that Fuller identifies a standard of moral justice first—that is to be applied later in a moral assessment of the law. Our moral standard for judging the justice of our laws comes prior to the laws themselves. Second, this standard is determined independently of our legal system.

In sum, this section provides important background about natural law theories old and new. Each accepts several tenets in common. They recognize that some laws are more morally satisfactory than others. They claim that this is to be determined through applying a standard of moral justice and, crucially, this standard is determined separately from the legal system to which it is applied.

My point is not to argue that the moral standards used lack any basis in real life and are always a product of speculation, but rather that the standards—however realistic or compelling—are not chosen on the basis of any particular moral standard found within a legal system. Instead, moral standards are determined externally to a legal system. Law and morality may be intrinsically linked, but they are also potentially separable. Natural law theorists may have different views on which moral standard is best, but most can recognize an immoral legal system as a legal system. Laws should aspire to compatibility with justice, but they can often fall far short. They remain law either way, even if some are more morally meritorious and just than others.

20.3. HEGEL'S NATURAL LAW INTERNALISM

The natural law tradition is a diverse array of different perspectives, rich in diversity. The previous section argued that both classical natural law and the leading contemporary natural law theorists share something in common: they all argue for an external

---

[11] Fuller, *The Morality of Law*, 45.

[12] See Fuller, *The Morality of Law*, 33–39.

[13] Fuller, *The Morality of Law*, 97.

understanding of morality that we then apply to our analysis of law as a standard of moral justice. There will be divergent approaches to how this shared practice is conducted. Cicero argues that we must grasp 'true reason' that is divine in nature, Finnis claims that we should identify basic forms of the human good through reason, and Fuller highlights moral principles that any legal system should embody. The point is that each identifies a moral standard first and then applies it to law afterward: we discern morality externally and then analyze law in light of this standard.

This discussion is important because it underscores the distinctive break from standard natural law theorizing that Hegel's legal philosophy represents. While his views are correctly understood by most as consistent with natural law, the precise connection between Hegel's views and the standard natural law tradition is overlooked or unnoticed: for most scholars, Hegel endorses natural law theory in an indistinctive way.[14] But this conclusion is a mistake.

The view that Hegel is an indistinctive natural lawyer is not shared by all commentators. Hegel's legal philosophy has been thought to belong to jurisprudential schools as diverse as the historical school of jurisprudence, Marxist legal theory, postmodern critical theory, and transcendental idealist legal theory.[15] This wide disparity of opinion is unique to Hegel. There is no similar disagreement about any other significant legal philosopher.

This disagreement arises from the fact that Hegel's legal philosophy does not fit traditional jurisprudential molds. This is because it defends a novel understanding about the relation of law and morality that has gone unnoticed. In short, Hegel offers what I will call a view of natural law *internalism*.[16] All natural law theorists claim that law and morality are linked, but while traditional natural law theorists first determine moral standards to then be applied in an assessment of law, the natural law internalism of Hegel assesses law through moral standards arising within the law itself. This section presents why Hegel's legal theory should be located with the natural law tradition—and why it provides us with an innovative understanding of how law and morality should relate that offers a distinctive break from other natural law theorists.

Hegel accepts a core tenet of natural law about law and morality. He argues, "To the Ideal of Freedom, Law and Morality are indispensably requisite" (PH, 41). Law and morality are not independent of each other, but instead interdependent. This puts Hegel

[14] See Brod, *Hegel's Philosophy of Politics*, 38, 79; Burns, *Natural Law and Political Ideology in the Philosophy of Hegel*; Knowles, *Hegel and the Philosophy of Right*, 128; Paton, *A Textbook of Jurisprudence*, 114–115; Pinkard, "Constitutionalism, Politics and the Common Life," 177; Rommen, "In Defense of Natural Law," 116; Thompson, "Institutional Normativity," 42; and Weinrib, "Legal Formalism," 338.

[15] See Brooks, "Hegel's Ambiguous Contribution to Legal Theory," 85–94; Curzon, *Jurisprudence*, 179, 212; del Vecchio, *Philosophy of Law*, 123, 125–129; Dias, *Jurisprudence*, 384–385; Douzinas, "Identity, Recognition, Rights or What Can Hegel Teach Us about Human Rights?," 379–405; Freeman (ed.), *Lloyd's Introduction to Jurisprudence*, 783–785; Hoffheimer, "Hegel's First Philosophy of Law," 823–874; Paton, *A Textbook of Jurisprudence*, 114–115; and Salter and Shaw, "Towards a Critical Theory of Constitutional Law: Hegel's Contribution," 464–486.

[16] See Brooks, 225; Brooks, "Between Natural Law and Legal Positivism: Dworkin and Hegel on Legal Theory," 513–560; and Brooks, "Natural Law Internalism," 167–179.

clearly at odds with positivists who claim that our study of law is about rules where morality may play no part.[17]

Like many traditional views of natural law, Hegel believes that law becomes more substantiated—or 'true' or 'actual'—when it better satisfies a moral standard by embodying a specific form of normativity. Some laws are more valid and authoritative the greater they cohere with this moral standard. Hegel says that "what is law [Geist] may differ in content from what is right in itself [an sich Recht]" (PR §212). So what is lawful might not be rightful. Slavery is an example of this. For Hegel, slavery was both legal and unjust (LNR, §8R). Laws become less unjust the more they achieve a 'realization [Verwirklichung]' of 'Right [Recht]' whereby the law better embodies justice (E §529).

Hegel's discussion of law plays on an ambiguity in his native German language using both Recht and Gesetz. Both words can be translated as 'law', but Hegel uses them in specific ways. He refers to law or a statute as Gesetz and reserves Recht for true law, or justice. Their difference is that only the latter is commensurate with justice. All other forms of positive laws (Gesetz) embody lesser forms of justice (Recht). They come together in the following way, Hegel says: "actual legal relationships presuppose laws founded on right [Rechtsgesetz] as something valid in and for itself" (LNR, §109). The recognition of a law is to assume it embodies some measure of justice. We do not then presume that our laws are inherently unjust. But it is a widely held concern that where laws are found to fall short of some compelling moral standard, this requires laws to be changed or terminated.[18] The discovery of unjust laws compels us toward making revisions so that our legal system moves closer toward justice.

Hegel argues that our understanding of law must start from the law itself. He says that "what is legal [gesetzmäßig] is . . . the source of cognition of what is right [Recht], or more precisely, of what is lawful [Rechtens]." So we are not to begin our appraisal—moral or otherwise—of the law until we first have an understanding about the law. We should discern what is right from the raw material that is the law itself: in other words, justice springs forth from the law. Our normative assessment of law develops from within the law internally: what is right (Recht) is instantiated from within what is lawful (Rechtens) (PR §3). Hegel says, "Law is part of the existing state of things, with Spirit implicit in it" (PH, 268). The law is not separable from its spirit. Our understanding of the law is therefore grounded in doctrine: it must be an account of "the present and the actual, not the setting up of a world beyond which exists God knows where" (PR 14,1.13/20). Hegel sees his view of natural law as embedded in our practices.

Hegel's natural law internalism occupies an interesting, and even novel, jurisprudential space. Like legal positivists, his focus is on the law itself. Hegel does not argue for assessing the law according to some standard that is outside and so external to the law.

---

[17] See Hart, The Concept of Law; and Kramer, In Defense of Legal Positivism

[18] This is a widely held view among the general public, but it is not commonly shared by most legal philosophers. While natural lawyers traditionally have dominated jurisprudence, legal positivism and legal realism are more popular among contemporary legal philosophers. This is not to say positivists and realists are unconcerned about injustice, but rather to draw attention to the fact that they share a different view about the importance and the place of morality in studying law.

Hegel's legal theory accepts natural law's commitment to claiming that our understanding of law is intrinsically bound with our normative assessment of law. But we can now see that Hegel's legal theory represents a distinctive break from this tradition insofar as only Hegel claims that the normative standard for assessing law is to be found within the law itself.

Hegel similarly understands legal development as an *internal* process. Robert Stern captures well how this should be considered:

> we can use here an "internal" notion of rationality, whereby it is rational to change from one outlook or theory to another *not* because the latter possesses the transcendental predicate of "truth" or "absolute validity," but rather because it represents a resolution of the problems, incoherences, anomalies, inconsistencies and limitations of the *previous* scheme or theory, and so constitutes an advance on it, in relative, but not absolute terms.[19]

This passage recommends a view about internal progress that speaks to Hegel's idea of law's immanent development over time. This legal progress is perhaps best understood as a series of resolutions, or inconsistencies and anomalies within the law. So the law does not simply 'develop' per se, but develops through overcoming its own incoherencies. Hegel recognizes that the law might instead appear to us as little more than "a collection without principle, whose inconsistencies and confusion require the most acute perception to rescue it as far as possible from its contradictions" (GC, 11) The law can look this way because of the contingencies about how it is forged. A state's legislation is rarely a seamless, coherent expression of a particular moral perspective. Instead, it is more commonly a product of political compromises peppered with statements about judicial doctrine and the rule of law from the judiciary's case law. These sources of law can sometimes be in tension, such as where an appointed judiciary finds unconstitutional—and so unlawful—legislation passed by elected representatives. Famous cases abound, such as *Brown v. Board of Education*, which ended the segregation of US students based on their race/ethnicity.[20]

The law resolves its own tensions and incoherencies arising from the law's contingent existence through particular statutes, secondary legislation, or authoritative case law. The law does this from within its own resources (PR §216). Hegel says,

> the *advance* from that which constitutes the beginning is to be considered only as one more determination of the same advance, so that this beginning remains as the underlying ground of all that follows without vanishing from it. (SL 21.58/49)

The kind of progress that Hegel has in mind here is a progressive comprehension. In this case, our focus is a progressive comprehension of law. Our comprehension develops

---

[19] Robert Stern, "MacIntyre and Historicism," 151.
[20] See *Brown v. Board of Education*, 347 U.S. 483 (1954).

from within the law's own normative content (PR §31). Its beginning does not 'vanish', but our understanding of it does as we develop clearer insights into law's normative content.

Law's internal development is a dynamic process. Hegel says that "the scope of the law [*Gesetz*] ought on the one hand to be that of a complete and self-contained whole, but on the other hand, there is a constant need for new legal determinations [*gesetzlicher Bestimmungen*]" (PR §216, and see §3R). In other words, the legal system is 'complete' insofar as a progressive understanding of its normativity need not warrant there be more laws imposed from outside itself. The law has all the resources it requires at the beginning for internal moral development. To grasp what shape this should take requires our looking more carefully at the laws we already have and not looking beyond to norms or laws we want to find.

Hegel clarifies these points further:

> an advance of the analytic intellect, which discovers new distinctions, which again make new decisions necessary. To provisions of this sort one may give the name of *new* decisions or *new* laws [*Gesetze*]; but in proportion to the gradual advance in specialization the interest and value of these provisions declines. They fall within the already subsisting "substantial," general laws, like improvements on a floor or a door, within the house—which though something *new*, are not a new *house*. (E §529)

Hegel's point is that as we solve internal incoherencies within the law according to its normativity and not from some external source, we may be mistaken into thinking we have created *new* laws. This view is mistaken because we are not creating new laws, but newly discovering what is already lawful—the law's previously unrecognized content. Hegel views the law as a seamless web. When we better articulate the law's internal normative content, our understanding of law becomes richer as these determinations are made explicit. The law progresses through resolving internal conflicts and by filling apparent gaps.

Law progresses toward justice. Hegel says that justice has its "existence [*Dasein*] in the form of law [*Gesetzes*]" and not "particular volitions and opinions" (PR §219). Law develops into justice through our "cognition of what is *right* [*Recht*], or more precisely, of what is *lawful* [*Rechtens*]" (PR §212R). We fill gaps and overcome incoherencies through codification. Hegel assumes that no political community will construct a timeless, unproblematic legal system on its first attempt. Legal codes are everywhere incomplete, although some are less finished than others (PR §211R).

A community's development of law is "the work of centuries," not to be completed overnight (PR §274A). Progressing our understanding of law toward justice is "a perennial approximation to perfection [*Volkommenheit das Perennieren der Annäherung*]" that we may never achieve fully (PR §216R). Hegel does not claim there is any one set of laws or legal system that is everywhere ideal at all times. Philosophy, for Hegel, is "a peculiar mode of thinking" (E §2) examining "*what is there before us*" (SL, 21.55/47). Philosophy allows us to better understand our past and gain insight into our present, but it is fundamentally historical: every individual is a "child of his time" and "philosophy, too, is its own time comprehended in thoughts" (PR 14,1.15/21). Any philosophical assessment is provisional and open to future revision over time.[21]

20.4. JUSTICE IN ROBES?

Hegel's understanding of natural law as a form of natural law internalism is a break from natural law's traditional externalism. But is Hegel's internalism preferable?

Natural law externalist theories expose themselves to the charge that they seek to impose a moral standard in determining law's validity, but their standards stand in need of further justification. This presents natural law externalism with two problems. The first is the need to justify that moral standards should determine legal validity. It might be countered that laws are valid if approved through agreed-upon procedures, but we can have unjust laws as valid laws. So what should serve as the appropriate moral standard? Natural lawyers are deeply divided over which is the most compelling. For example, Cicero might claim consistency with God's commands, Finnis favors compatibility of basic forms of human goods, and Fuller endorses our satisfying a threshold of his inner morality of law test, to name but three different types of external moral standards.

The problem is not only that each natural lawyer may well either defend different moral standards or apply these standards differently, but more centrally that each understands the study of law through moral philosophy. This is a problem because there may be practical limits to how far moral philosophy can and should go in our working out a legal system that is just. One example is Immanuel Kant's well-known division in *The Metaphysics of Morals* between the doctrine of right, where morality is relevant for forging and maintaining political and legal institutions, and the doctrine of virtue, where institutions become irrelevant.[22] So even if we could agree on a moral standard, there might be limits to its application in a legal system. But our focus remains on getting the moral philosophy right first: law might appear to almost get in the way of our enacting a preferred moral vision.

Hegel's natural law internalism rejects this approach. While he accepts that legal philosophy is about justice, the law is not an obstacle for achieving justice, but instead the necessary instrument through which justice can be forged. The central focus of Hegel's distinctive natural law theory is on the law itself as we try to grasp its own internal morality and foster it. So Hegel's theory avoids the problem of our being divided over which moral standard is best before we come to first consider the justice of a legal system. Hegel's concern is with making the law pure, not with trying to work law into a purer image derived from outside it.

[21] See Brooks, "History," 148–157.
[22] See Kant, *The Metaphysics of Morals*.

However, Hegel's avoiding this problem exposes him to another. This is the risk of misidentifying the 'right [*Recht*]' within a legal system. If law is to be morally developed from within, this requires our being able to correctly discern its inner morality. But we must do so in the absence of an independent criterion to avoid only 'finding' in the law what we were looking for in advance.

This point can be illustrated by considering this process in practice. For Hegel, our knowledge about justice must focus on identifying 'right [*Recht*]' and not on our mere personal convictions. This is because following our personal convictions causes our understanding of right to become tainted (PR §309). No one person's conviction of justice should prevail as we move toward a more communitarian, mutual recognition of the concept of right and its practical application in law (PR §§144, 260). This entails that judges should ensure that their personal views should not interfere with the content of their legal decision-making for fear that their decisions would be rendered 'arbitrary [*Willkür*]' (PR §211A). So courts should attempt to comprehend justice "in the particular case, without subjective feeling [*Empfindung*] of *particular* interest" (PR §219).

The issue is that there is no guarantee that our understanding of law accurately captures some important part of its internal morality waiting to be discovered, rather than one conjured from our imagination. Natural law internalism may represent a new understanding of natural law jurisprudence, but it suffers from an epistemological problem concerning our ability to identify correctly justice within the law.

This simple illustration of the obstacles any judge has in identifying the internal morality of law helps make the point about the problem Hegel's theory runs into, but it is inaccurate in an important respect. Hegel gives the public a key role in the administration of justice within the state. He held this view throughout his career and it can be found in his early writings as well:

> How blind are those who like to believe that institutions, constitutions and laws which no longer accord with men's customs, needs, opinions and from which the spirit has departed, can continue to exist, or that forms in which feeling and understanding no longer have an interest are powerful enough to furnish a lasting bond for a nation [*eines Volkes*]. (*M*, 2)

Our political and legal institutions lose some share of their moral legitimacy where they fail to accord with the community's shared convictions about public justice. This legitimacy is not majoritarian, but has an 'organic quality' (PR §302R). It is key that any legal system is accessible to the public, but without the requirement of a majority vote.[23]

---

[23] This raises some interesting parallels with Jean-Jacques Rousseau's political and legal philosophy. Rousseau was similarly concerned that true freedom—understood as the General Will—shaped the development of our laws and political institutions, rather than arbitrary decisions. The General Will is a similar core connection between citizens in a political community that work out in a deliberative way their shared view of justice. This is subject to constant revision over time. While Rousseau's thought is very different from Hegel's, it is likely these ideas had some influence on Hegel's thinking given his knowledge of and interest in Rousseau's writings. See Brooks (ed.), *Rousseau and Law*.

This view of the public and public justice are at the heart of Hegel's defense of the jury trial.[24] He says,

> knowledge [*Kenntnis*] of right and of the course of court proceedings, as well as the ability to pursue one's rights, may become the *property* of a class [*Stand*] which makes itself exclusive . . . by the terminology it uses, inasmuch as this terminology is a foreign language for those whose rights are at stake. (PR §228R)

Juries are important because they help ensure that individuals on trial are reasonably capable of understanding the proceedings and verdict. A defendant may well disagree with a jury's decision, but he or she should be able to have some inkling about how the jury came to their view in the trial. This is because the defendant is much like his peers serving on the jury. The alternative is to leave the decision exclusively in the hands of the trained judge. Hegel finds this problematic because it can run the risk that the proceedings and verdict may be conducted in a way that is inaccessible to a defendant, especially one who lacks a legal background. In that case, legal justice would become disconnected from the community it serves. It is through letting the public decide judicial outcomes through the jury trial that the link between the community and its legal system are maintained.

Nonetheless, letting juries determine outcomes may secure this link, but maintaining a connection between the public and their legal system is not necessarily the same as correctly identifying the morality internal to a legal system that should help guide how decisions should be made. My concern is that the two can easily come apart: the community's pursuit of its own sense of right may move in different directions than a pursuit following a view of right determined from careful examination of existing laws. Hegel seems to believe the two work in tandem, but this is unclear. Nor is it obvious that the community's pursuit of its sense of justice is coherent, or that the current legal system of any state has within it a discoverable and coherent internal morality.

Throughout his writings, Hegel was deeply critical of England's common law tradition. Hegel argues that a people's 'customary rights' will at first 'be characterized by *formlessness*, indeterminacy and incompleteness' when they are initially collected and set out in a legal code (PR §211R). But then this legal code should progressively self-develop by making itself more explicit through codification. And yet England's common law "is contained, as everyone knows" in an unwritten form: this is the cause of "enormous confusion which prevails in England" as "judges constantly act as *legislators*" (PR §211R). This is because it is they who help set out what the law permits in particular cases.

But it is unclear how strongly Hegel should criticize the common law system—notwithstanding his explicit rejection of it. This is because his argument for trial by jury—which originated in common-law jurisdictions—supports the flexibility of the people, giving expression to their sense of right. Hegel claims the law is living and evolving as it develops a conception of actualized right—it is not fixed or set in stone and thus

---

[24] See Brooks, "The Right to Trial by Jury," 197–212; and Brooks (ed.), *The Right to a Fair Trial*.

more fluid than the codified Roman law system prevalent in Germany then (as now). Hegel cannot both defend the case-by-case working out of right performed by jury trials while rejecting the case-by-case establishment of legal precedents by judges because the latter "retain a certain particularity" (PR §211A).[25] If working out how right can be understood concretely subject to revision and constant testing is how a people develop a more determinate sense of right, it is unclear why the common law cannot be used to achieve this end.

Hegel is also critical about the common law's adversarial system. Here he is on more solid ground. Hegel says, "In the English legal system, it is left to the insight or arbitrary will of the prosecutor to categorize an act in terms of its specific criminal character (e.g. as murder or manslaughter), and the court cannot determine otherwise if it finds his conclusion incorrect" (PR §225R). In the adversarial system, prosecutors on behalf of the state determine which crime a defendant will be prosecuted for. They may be in error—and they might also engage in some brinkmanship, prosecuting someone for a lesser charge that might be more certain to lead to a conviction. This is different from the German system of Hegel's time, where judges would lead courtroom deliberations, rather than lawyers for either side, without engaging in plea bargaining. This criticism does seem consistent with Hegel's legal theorizing because our goal is to determine what is right, rather than easier or more efficient paths to finding others guilty of offenses—especially where they might actually have committed a more serious, but more difficult to prove, offense.

In sum, Hegel defends a novel understanding of natural law that appears to avoid the problem of disagreement about which moral standard should be determined first and then applied to our normative appraisal of law as common with natural law externalism. However, Hegel appears to trade one problem for another. This is because natural law internalism lacks any guarantee that what we claim is law's internal morality is not our 'finding' a moral standard we had been looking for.[26]

---

[25] Part of Hegel's concern with common law trials is their creating case law. He appears to favor working out a legal system through a legislative process than through the courts. This might be explained by his nineteenth-century German view of the judiciary as a part of the executive branch: both the police and the judge apply universal laws to particular cases. A concern for Hegel is that he does not appear to accept that the finding in one case can be applied to another when determining justice. Instead, he seems to hold that we should remain transfixed on right [Recht] and not become distracted by how it may be thought established in particular cases. But this seems untenable for Hegel because common law precedents hold as *ratio*—what counts is not the particular facts per se, but the legal principles and distinctions that are worked out by courts over time and that are subject to constant revision. This again suggests that Hegel's stated opposition to English common law is perhaps misplaced—or at least underdeveloped. I am grateful to a Cara Cummings, graduate student in Dean Moyar's graduate class on Hegel's *Philosophy of Right* when I was a guest speaker at Johns Hopkins, for raising this illuminating issue.

[26] I have elsewhere argued that Hegel uniquely shares some core similarities with Dworkin's legal theory. Both apply a self-developing moral standard arising from within a community's shared sense of justice and right—they are both examples of natural law internalists. See Brooks, "Between Natural Law and Legal Positivism: Dworkin and Hegel on Legal Theory."

Moreover, Hegel claims that our discovering law's internal morality is a decision that juries are well placed to make because the determination of the application of justice in a particular case is their public conception of justice. It is unclear that the community's moral standard must be the same as law's internal morality. If it were so, then we might discover law's internal morality by looking more closely within ourselves without the need of looking within the law. This would render natural law internalism unstable, but we should recall that legal philosophy was not a major preoccupation for Hegel, despite his importance for the field. Hegel's philosophical outline and associated lectures may not illuminate some clear way out of this problem, but he does provide us with a new way of thinking about natural law and how the public can and should relate to justice.

20.5. THE UNIFIED THEORY OF PUNISHMENT

Perhaps Hegel's most significant and yet overlooked achievement is his identifying what we might call *the unified theory of punishment*.[27] In short, the unified theory is the view that punishment is neither retributive, nor a deterrent, nor rehabilitative; instead, it should be understood as bringing these different facets together. Thus punishment should not be seen as one or the other, but as some combination of all three. This section explains what is distinctive about Hegel's theory of punishment as a further example of the innovativeness of his legal philosophy more generally.

Philosophers typically defend one of the three main theories of punishment: retribution, deterrence, or rehabilitation. Retribution is the most popular of the three. It is generally understood as the view that offenders should be punished to the degree that they deserve for some immoral activity. Murderers should be punished severely, according to retributivists, because they deserve it on account of their moral responsibility for such an evil act and in proportion to the wrongfulness of their crime.

Retributivists have traditionally accepted a 'principle of equality' whereby an offender's punishment is proportionate to the corresponding crime.[28] This principle does not necessarily entail an eye for an eye, although some retributivists make statements in that direction.[29] Instead, it is usually a claim about comparative values: that the value of the criminal wrong should be proportionally equivalent to the severity of punishment. For example, if someone has performed an especially grave crime like murder, punishing it with an equality of value need not require the death penalty, although that is one possibility. But what is key—for the retribution as equivalence of value view—is that capital punishment would be justified not as an eye for an eye, but punishing a very serious

[27] See Brooks, "Hegel and the Unified Theory of Punishment."

[28] This phrase is taken from Kant. See Kant, MM 6:332.

[29] See Kant, MM 6:332: "whatever undeserved evil you inflict upon another within the people, that you inflict upon yourself. If you insult him, you insult yourself; if you steal from him, you steal from yourself; if you strike him, you strike yourself; if you kill him, you kill yourself." See Brooks, "Kant's Theory of Punishment."

crime with a very serious punishment. That murderers would be punished by death is more a coincidence than a requirement.[30]

Hegel is widely thought to support retributivism.[31] This common interpretation is not without some support in the *Philosophy of Right*. Hegel says that crime should be understood as an infringement of "the existence [*Dasein*] of freedom in its *concrete* sense—i.e. to infringe right as right" (PR §95R). It is the infringement of right, of justice, that is wrongful about crime. This requires a 'restoration of right' through punishment to reassert right's existence and confirm its importance (PR §99). Hegel calls this '*retribution*' with the important qualification of "in so far as [retribution], by its concept, is an infringement of an infringement" (PR §101). This means that crime is a violation of right because it attempts to negate it. In response, we should negate this negation: a crime is an attempt to violate our rights, and so punishment is an effort to undo this wrongful activity. Punishment is not to be a specific equality of like for like, but rather 'an approximate fulfillment' in value (PR §101R).

But this view of Hegel as a retributivist is flawed. One reason is that retribution presumes an account of moral responsibility and a legal system. We punish offenders because they have broken a law. However, Hegel's discussion here is in the section "Abstract Right," which is philosophically prior to the state and legal system. His claims about restoring right are specifically addressing the contractual stipulations arising through mutual recognition between self and other, not the more complex legal relationships that citizens develop over time in the state. There are no laws, no police, no courts, and no prisons at this point in his discussion. This is not to say his claims about crime as a violation of right where punishment aims to restore rights is meaningless. It is rather a foundational claim about the ground of punishment that helps structure his more complete theory of punishment that develops beyond "Abstract Right."

There are already strong indications that Hegel's theory of punishment departs from standard accounts of retribution, even in "Abstract Right." When discussing '*retribution*' with the important qualification already flagged in the preceding that by this he means "an infringement of an infringement" understood as a restoration of rights, Hegel says, "It is not the crimes or punishments which change, but the relation between the two" (PR §96A).

This is crucial because retributivists generally accept a fixed relation between crime and punishment: the moral wrongness of one is linked to the other, and this is a relationship that should not change if background conditions were different. Typically, retributivists like Kant were opposed to consequentialism, and so context should not factor into which punishment an offender deserves. But Hegel's first break with retributivists is that he accepts that context matters. Crimes may be public wrongs irrespective of circumstances, but they can make a difference in determining punishment.

---

[30] I am grateful to Brian O'Connor for first highlighting this distinction to me.

[31] Cooper, "Hegel's Theory of Punishment"; Findlay, *Hegel: A Re-examination*, 312–313; Inwood, *A Hegel Dictionary*, 232–235; Primoratz, *Justifying Legal Punishment*, 69–81; Stillman, "Hegel's Idea of Punishment"; and Wood, *Hegel's Ethical Thought*, 108–124.

Hegel's second break with retributivists is more explicit: he rejects the idea that punishment is no more than retribution. In a rarely quoted passage from his *Science of Logic*, he says,

> *Punishment*, for instance, has a variety of determinations: that it is retribution; and also a deterrent example, a deterring threat made by the law; and also a contribution to the self-awareness and betterment of the culprit. Each of these different determinations has been regarded as the *ground of punishment*, on the ground that it is the essential determination, and by default the others, since they are different from it, have been regarded as only accidental. But the one determination which is assumed as ground does not amount to the whole punishment. (SL 11.310/405–406)

These comments are crucial to understanding Hegel's theory of punishment.[32] They make clear that he does not believe we must choose to defend retributivism, deterrence, or rehabilitation. Instead, each is a part of what punishment is about. The ground of punishment is retributivist insofar as an offender must deserve punishment for it to be justified. But the purpose of punishment as a restoration of right can take different forms, including as a deterrent or rehabilitative project, if that serves that aim.

This passage is also not the only place where Hegel makes such remarks. In his *Natural Law* essay, he argues,

> in the case of punishment, one determinacy is seized upon—be it the moral improvement of the criminal, the damage caused, the awareness of the punishment before the crime was committed, or the need to give this awareness reality by carrying out the threat, etc.—and the detail in question is made the end and essence of the whole. It naturally follows that, since this determinacy has no necessary connection with the other determinacies which can also be brought to light and distinguished, endless agonising takes place to discover their necessary relationship or the dominance of one over the others. (NL 4.421–422/107)

This is a critique of our taking only one particular aspect about punishment as the punishment to the exclusion of others. Punishment is not one instead of another. Nonetheless, this thought is not obvious because different theories about punishment appear to clash at first glance. What an offender deserves may justify a very different punishment from what might best deter, for example.

---

[32] Philosophers who want to deny the importance of this passage must argue either that the *Philosophy of Right*'s discussion of punishment is incompatible with this explicit example from *The Science of Logic*—a text which Hegel clearly states several times informs and underpins the arguments of the *Philosophy of Right*—or that Hegel's example in the *Science of Logic* is inconsistent with his theorizing on grounds (and so must be incompatible with the *Philosophy of Right* on grounds of a false illustration of his *Logic*). It continues to surprise me that no other interpreter has picked up on this important passage, or even acknowledged it. I continue to be highly suspicious of counterarguments about Hegel's theory of punishment claiming it is some version of retributivism where they fail to acknowledge passages like this that so explicitly state that was not his view.

This leaves open the question about how punishment might bring together retribution, deterrence, and rehabilitation into a unified, coherent theory. While his comments indicate this is his position, he is less clear about the specific shape this should take. This is perhaps partly due to the fact that his comments on punishment are almost entirely in outline and require fleshing out.

Hegel leaves us some important clues. In the *Philosophy of Right*, he says,

> an injury to *one* member of society is an injury to *all* the others does not alter the nature of crime in terms of its concept, but in terms of its outward existence . . . its *danger to civil society* is a determination of its magnitude . . . This quality or magnitude varies, however, according to the *condition* of civil society. (PR §218R)

The nature of crime at a conceptual level is unchanged under different circumstances. In other words, murder and theft remain wrongful because they violate right and this is unaffected by context. It is in this sense that the ground is retributivist: all crimes are varieties of wrong at their heart.

But context matters for setting the relationship between crime and punishment. Hegel is explicit: "it is not the crimes or punishments themselves which change, but the relation between the two" (PR §96A). For example, the more that civil society is threatened by crime, the more severely it will seek to punish it. So for Hegel crimes can be punished more or less severely over time because they are seen as more or less of a threat to society. Examples he gives includes times of war or civil unrest (PR §218A). Crimes will be punished less severely during peacetime than during a war, not because the crime is conceptually different, but because we require a greater effort at restoring rights at such a time of conflict. Indeed, Hegel argues that as a state becomes more secure, we should expect the death penalty to "become less frequent, as indeed this ultimate form of punishment deserves to be" (PR §100A).

The important point is that this is no retributivist view: context can greatly influence penal severity, with circumstances influencing how problematic crimes are for society. Our individual desert for some action in the past might inform whether we have committed an offense. But it does not—by itself alone—determine how we should be punished. This is starkly different from traditional retributivist views whereby it matters only what someone deserves when punishing him, not whether it makes a society happier or more secure. Yet for Hegel the stability of society and its sense of self is a key factor in setting the severity—and perhaps even setting the criminal law.[33]

This leaves much to the imagination about how retribution, deterrence, and rehabilitation might work together to act as a restoration of rights. There is some indication offered by the British Idealists, sometimes called the British Hegelians. These figures,

---

[33] If society felt no threat by the performance of certain actions, then what might have once been crimes might begin to lose their criminal character. For example, witchcraft might have been seen as a serious threat to the community and punished accordingly. But where it loses that character, its punishment evaporates until there may be no reason to think it a crime, as it would not warrant punishment.

including T. H. Green, F. H. Bradley, and others, were heavily influenced by Hegel's philosophy, and most defend a similar view of punishment where retributivist, deterrent,
and rehabilitative features are combined into a unified theory of punishment. This may
not be an accidental coincidence given the strong influence of Hegel's philosophy, not
least his *Logic*, on their work.

The British Idealists help us spell out a bit more how a unified theory of punishment
might work.[34] The Idealist T. H. Green says, "the justice of the punishment depends on
the justice of the general system of rights" and "the proper and direct object of state-
punishment [is] . . . the general protection of rights."[35] Punishment is about societal
maintenance through the protection of rights. Crimes are rights violations that threaten
the community and require a response to restore the public recognition of rights possessed by individuals.

This is spelled out further by the Idealist James Seth:

> This view of the object of punishment gives the true measure of its amount. This
> is found not in the amount of moral depravity which the crime reveals, but in the
> importance of the right violated, relatively to the system of rights of which it forms a
> part . . . The measure of the punishment is, in short, the measure of social necessity;
> and this measure is a changing one.[36]

We punish crimes because they are violations of our rights, and these rights should be
restored through punishment. All crimes are rights violations, but some rights are more
central than others and so require more punishment. Theft may violate my property
rights and murder my right to life, but murder is more significant because violating this
right ends any possibility of my enjoying this or any other right.

These perspectives flesh out a bit more what a unified theory of punishment might
look like. Punishment must be deserved and its amount would vary depending on what
would be required to maintain and protect a system of rights. This could warrant more
deterrent punishments in some circumstances and more rehabilitative elements in others. Any clash between competing principles is governed by an overarching purpose of
rights protection.

This still leaves much more to be worked out and does not speak directly to individual
cases. But it should be clear that Hegel has once again done something remarkable. He
has offered us new insights into the nature of punishment and the possibility of a novel
alternative, the unified theory of punishment.

---

[34] See Brooks, "Punishment and British Idealism"; Brooks, "Is Bradley a Retributivist?"; and Brooks,
"On F. H. Bradley's 'Some Remarks on Punishment'", 223–225.

[35] Green, *Lectures on the Principles of Political Obligation*, §§189, 204.

[36] James Seth, *A Study of Ethical Principles*, 305. See Brooks, "James Seth on Natural Law and Legal
Theory."

20.6. CONCLUSION

This chapter has provided a survey of some key ideas in Hegel's philosophy of law. There is some debate about which jurisprudential school of thought best relates to his legal theory, although most commentators view it as an unexceptional natural law theory. But this is untrue. Hegel's philosophy of law uniquely creates a new distinction in the natural law tradition between natural law externalism and natural law internalism. The former represents most natural lawyers and it is the view that we are to determine a moral standard first and then apply it to the law to assess its overall justice. Hegel defends the latter and claims the moral standard we should use to assess the justice of a legal system is located internally to it. We look to the law first and ascertain its moral development from within.

This perspective is not without its problems. It is unclear how we can be sure that the moral standards we discover are not read into our interpretation of law's internal morality from outside. Nor is it clear how Hegel's clear support for the public having a say on matters of public justice, such as through the jury trial, can perform the task of developing the internal morality of law. But Hegel nonetheless provides us with a new understanding of the natural law tradition that has escaped his predecessors and offers an important, and to my mind convincing, defense of the jury trial.

Hegel presents us with an innovative theory of punishment. Instead of the traditional view that penal theorists must choose between defending retribution, deterrence, or rehabilitation, Hegel claims that punishment is not one of them, but all in combination. This opens his claim to the charge that these different theories clash with each other. But the key to unlocking this problem that was uncovered by the British Idealists inspired by Hegel's work in the late nineteenth century was that these three can be brought together under a new framework of societal maintenance through rights protection—an analysis that is consistent with Hegel's comments about punishment across his work. This has real contemporary importance because countries like the United States and the United Kingdom use sentencing guidelines that bring together retributivist, deterrent, and rehabilitative elements without a framework for employing them coherently. Hegel is the first to substantively contribute to the idea of the unified theory of punishment, and this offers a promising perspective for rendering more coherent the sentencing guidelines in force throughout many countries today.

Overall, these are remarkable achievements for a philosopher who was not trained in law and did not set out to be a philosopher of law per se. Hegel's work continues to inspire us with its rich insights into how we can better understand past thinking about key issues that still reap rewards for us today.[37]

---

[37] I am very grateful for comments by Dean Moyar and from students in his graduate seminar studying Hegel's *Philosophy of Right*. I further benefited from discussions about Hegel's legal theory with Chris Bennett, John Gardner, Stephen Houlgate, Dudley Knowles, Matthew Kramer, Peter Nicholson, Brian O'Connor, Bhikhu Parekh, Michael Rosen, Avital Simhony, Robert Stern, and Allen Wood.

WORKS CITED

Primary Texts

Hegel, G. W. F. *Elements of the Philosophy of Right* [PR], translated by H. B. Nisbet, edited by Allen Wood. Cambridge: Cambridge University Press, 1991.

Hegel, G. W. F. *Lectures on Natural Right and Political Science: The First Philosophy of Right: Heidelberg, 1817-18, with additions from the lectures of 1818-19* [LNR], translated by J. Michael Stewart and Peter C. Hodgson. Berkeley: University of California Press, 1995.

Hegel, G. W. F. "On the Scientific Ways of Treating Natural Law, on Its Place in Practical Philosophy, and Its Relation to the Positive Sciences of Right [NL]," in *Political Writings*, edited by Laurence Dickey and H. B. Nisbet. Cambridge: Cambridge University Press, 1999, 102-180.

Hegel, G. W. F. "The German Constitution [GC]," in *Political Writings*, edited by Laurence Dickey and H. B. Nisbet. Cambridge: Cambridge University Press, 1999, 6-101.

Hegel, G. W. F. "The Magistrates Should Be Elected by the People [M]," in *Political Writings*, edited by Laurence Dickey and H. B. Nisbet. Cambridge: Cambridge University Press, 1999, 1-5.

Hegel, G. W. F. *The Philosophy of History* [PH], translated by J. Sibree. New York: Dover, 1956.

Hegel, G. W. F. *The Science of Logic* [SL]. Translated and edited by George di Giovanni. Cambridge: Cambridge University Press, 2010.

Hegel, G. W. F. *Vorlesungen über Naturrecht und Staatswissenschaft*, Hegelberg 1817/18 (vol. 1 of *G.W.F. Hegel: Vorlesungen: Ausgewählte Nachschriften und Manuskripte*), edited by C. Becker, W. Bonsiepen, A. Gethmann-Siefert, F. Hogemann, W. Jaeschke, Ch. Jamme, H. Ch. Lucas, K. R. Meist, and H. Schneider, with an introduction by O. Pöggeler. Hamburg: Felix Meiner Verlag, 1983.

Kant, Immanuel. *The Metaphysics of Morals* [MM]. Translated and edited by Mary Gregor. Cambridge: Cambridge University Press, 1996.

Secondary Literature

Bix, Brian. "Natural Law Theory," in *A Companion to Philosophy of Law and Legal Theory*, edited by Dennis Patterson. Oxford: Blackwell, 1996, 223-240.

Brod, Harry. *Hegel's Philosophy of Politics: Idealism, Identity and Modernity*. Boulder, CO: Westview, 1992.

Brooks, Thom. "Between Natural Law and Legal Positivism: Dworkin and Hegel on Legal Theory." *Georgia State University Law University* 23 (2007): 513-560.

Brooks, Thom. "Hegel and the Unified Theory of Punishment," in Thom Brooks (ed.), *Hegel's Philosophy of Right*. Oxford: Blackwell, 2012, 105-123.

Brooks, Thom. "Hegel's Ambiguous Contribution to Legal Theory." *Res Publica* 11 (2005): 85-94.

Brooks, Thom. *Hegel's Political Philosophy: A Systematic Reading of the Philosophy of Right*, 2nd ed. Edinburgh: Edinburgh University Press, 2013.

Brooks. Thom. "Is Bradley a Retributivist?" *History of Political Thought* 32 (2011): 83-95.

Brooks, Thom. "James Seth on Natural Law and Legal Theory." *Collingwood and British Idealism Studies* 12 (2012): 115-132.

Brooks, Thom. "Kant's Theory of Punishment." *Utilitas* 15 (2003): 206-224.

Brooks, Thom. "Legal Positivism and Faith in Law." *Modern Law Review* 77 (2014): 139-147.

Brooks, Thom. "Natural Law Internalism," in Thom Brooks (ed.), *Hegel's Philosophy of Right*. Oxford: Blackwell, 2012, 167–179.

Brooks, Thom. "On F. H. Bradley's 'Some Remarks on Punishment.'" *Ethics* 125 (2014): 223–225.

Brooks, Thom. *Punishment*. New York: Routledge, 2012.

Brooks, Thom. "Punishment and British Idealism," in *Punishment and Ethics: New Perspectives*, edited by Jesper Ryberg and J. Angelo Corlett. Basingstoke, UK: Palgrave Macmillan, 2010, 16–32.

Brooks, Thom. "T. H. Green's Theory of Punishment." *History of Political Thought* 24 (2003): 685–701.

Brooks, Thom. "The Right to Trial by Jury." *Journal of Applied Philosophy* 21 (2004): 197–212.

Brooks, Thom (ed.) *Hegel's Philosophy of Right*. Oxford: Blackwell, 2012.

Brooks, Thom (ed.). *The Right to a Fair Trial*. Aldershot, UK: Ashgate, 2009.

Brown v. Board of Education. 347 U.S. 483 (1954).

Burns, Tony. *Natural Law and Political Ideology in the Philosophy of Hegel*. Aldershot, UK: Avebury, 1996.

Cooper, David E. "Hegel's Theory of Punishment," in *Hegel's Political Philosophy: Problems and Perspectives*, edited by Z. A. Pelczynski. Cambridge: Cambridge University Press, 1971, 151–167.

Curzon, L. B. *Jurisprudence*, 3rd ed. London: Cavendish, 1996.

del Vecchio, Giorgio. *Philosophy of Law*, 8th ed. Washington, DC: Catholic University of America Press, 1952.

Dias, R. W. M. *Jurisprudence*, 5th ed. London: Butterworths, 1985.

Douzinas, Costas. "Identity, Recognition, Rights or What Can Hegel Teach Us about Human Rights?" *Journal of Law and Society* 29 (2002): 379–405.

Findlay, J. N. *Hegel: A Re-examination*. London: George Allen & Unwin, 1958.

Finnis, John. *Natural Law and Natural Rights*. Oxford: Oxford University Press, 1980.

Franco, Paul. *Hegel's Philosophy of Freedom*. New Haven, CT: Yale University Press, 2002.

Freeman, M. D. A. (ed.). *Lloyd's Introduction to Jurisprudence*, 6th ed. London: Sweet and Maxwell, 1994.

Fuller, Lon L. *The Morality of Law*, revised ed. New Haven, CT: Yale University Press, 1969.

Green, T. H. *Lectures on the Principles of Political Obligation*. London: Longmans, Green, 1941.

Hart, H. L. A. *The Concept of Law*, 2nd ed. Oxford: Oxford University Press, 1994.

Hoffheimer, Michael H. "Hegel's First Philosophy of Law." *Tennessee Law Review* 62 (1995): 823–874.

Inwood, Michael. *A Hegel Dictionary*. Oxford: Blackwell, 1992.

Knowles, Dudley. *Hegel and the Philosophy of Right*. London: Routledge, 2002.

Kramer, Matthew H. *In Defense of Legal Positivism: Law Without Trimmings*. Oxford: Oxford University Press, 2003.

Paton, George Whitecross. *A Textbook of Jurisprudence*, 4th ed. Oxford: Clarendon, 1972.

Pinkard, Terry. "Constitutionalism, Politics and the Common Life," in *Hegel Reconsidered: Beyond Metaphysics and the Authoritarian State*, edited by H. Tristam Engelhardt, Jr., and Terry Pinkard. Dordrecht: Kluwer, 1994, 163–186.

Popper, Karl. *The Open Society and Its Enemies*, Vol. 2: *Hegel and Marx*. London: Routledge, 2002.

Primoratz, Igor. *Justifying Legal Punishment*. Atlantic Highlands, NJ: Humanities Press, 1989.

Rommen, H. A. "In Defense of Natural Law," in *Law and Philosophy*, edited by Sidney Hook. New York: New York University Press, 1964, 105–121.

Salter, Michael, and Julia A. Shaw. "Towards a Critical Theory of Constitutional Law: Hegel's Contribution." *Journal of Law and Society* 21 (1994): 464–486.

Seth, James. *A Study of Ethical Principles*, 9th ed. Edinburgh: William Blackwood & Sons, 1907.

Stern, Robert. "MacIntyre and Historicism," in *After MacIntyre: Critical Perspectives on the World of Alasdair MacIntyre*, edited by John Horton and Susan Mendus. Cambridge: Polity, 1994, 146–160.

Stillman, Peter G. "Hegel's Idea of Punishment." *Journal of the History of Philosophy* 14 (1976): 169–182.

Thompson, Kevin. "Institutional Normativity," in *Beyond Liberalism and Communitarianism*, edited by Robert R. Williams. Albany: State University of New York Press, 2001, 41–65.

Weinrib, Ernest J. "Legal Formalism," in *A Companion to Philosophy of Law and Legal Theory*, edited by Dennis Patterson. Oxford: Blackwell, 1996, 332–342.

Wood, Allen W. *Hegel's Ethical Thought*. Cambridge: Cambridge University Press, 1990.

CHAPTER 21

···

HEGEL'S PHILOSOPHY
OF ACTION

···

CHRISTOPHER YEOMANS

THERE are a number of questions, the answers to which define specific theoretical approaches to Hegel's philosophy of action. To begin with, does Hegel attempt to give a theory of free will that responds to the naturalistic skepticism so prevalent in the history of modern philosophy? Though some scholars hold that he is interested in providing such a theory, perhaps the majority view is that Hegel instead socializes his conception of the will such that the traditional naturalistic worries are no longer germane.[1] A second question is, does Hegel have a theory of action as such that competes with those found in the history of modern philosophy and more particularly in the Anglophone literature from the mid-twentieth century onward? Though perhaps the majority view is that Hegel does have such a theory of action, it is commonly held to be independent of any commitments to a conception of free will, and to take a form radically different from the other offerings in the literature in virtue of introducing an essentially retrospective rather than prospective relation between the agent and her action.[2]

On the one hand, the majority view emphasizes features of Hegel's theory of action that must be essential parts of a complete presentation of it: the social aspect, which makes the recognition of action by others an essential feature of action itself; Hegel's distinctive formulation of freedom as "being at home with oneself in the other"; and his denial that the category of causation can plumb the depths of intentional activity. On the other hand, Hegel thinks that there are objective structures of recognition, and these reintroduce many of the themes of the traditional free will debate; his technical formulations of the problem actually produce a plurality of models of agency that have yet to be

---

[1] See, e.g., Pippin, *Hegel's Practical Philosophy*, 15–16; Stekeler-Weithofer, *Philosophie des Selbstbewußtseins*, 355–357; and Westphal, "The Basic Context and Structure of Hegel's Philosophy of Right," 245. A related though sometimes distinct interpretive position is to see Hegel as a compatibilist.

[2] See, e.g., Quante, *Hegel's Concept of Action*, 120–138; Speight, *Hegel, Literature*, 4–5 and 44; and Pippin, *Hegel's Practical Philosophy*.

acknowledged in the literature; and among those models are versions of both the belief-desire and teleological accounts that dominate the contemporary literature.

21.1. THE UNAVOIDABLE PROBLEM OF THE EXPLICABILITY OF FREE ACTION

To take up this first point here—the existence of objective structures of recognition—is to ask what categories seem to be essential for our attribution of actions to free agents. We can set out some of these by attending to the terms in which one scholar, Alan Patten, argues for the legitimacy of seeing Hegel's social (rather than naturalistic) conception of freedom as a *bona fide* conception of free will. As Patten argues, Hegel's freedom is opposed to authority, rather than traditional free will, which is opposed to desires placed in the agent by her history or biology:

> Two parallel features of the cases suggest that Hegel's argument should be taken seriously. First, in each case, the agent allows the determination of some external agency or mechanism to be a sufficient reason or justification for his action. In the first case, the agent passively allows the instruction of the authority to stand as a justification of his final decision to act; in the second case, he passively allows the social and natural processes that determine what desires he experiences to count as a sufficient guide to what he should do. Secondly, in both cases, the agent *could* subject the problem of what to do to his own thought and reason.[3]

Here action that we do not recognize as fully attributable to the agent is understood in terms of the way in which it allows a *mechanistic cause* with respect to which the agent is *passive* to serve as an *external* explanation for action. By contrast, free action that is recognized as so attributable is explicitly understood as involving *alternate possibilities* (the agent could have used reason, but did not), and implicitly as involving an *internal* explanation in which the agent is *active* with respect to her own *goals*. The key then, is to provide an explanation of how we could produce actions in this second way, and that is largely a conceptual problem rather than either a scientific/naturalistic or social problem. We come to the same point by thinking through the second dominant aspect of contemporary presentations of Hegel's theory of agency, namely their emphasis on the retrospective identification of the intention of the agent subsequent to the action. The basis of such identification cannot be restricted to the agent's rational endorsement, since I can endorse many things that I do not do, such as others' actions or involuntary behaviors of my own such as digestion. Rather, that retrospective endorsement must go hand in hand with some productive relation between the agent and her action, and that

---

[3] Patten, *Hegel's Idea*, 70.

puts pressure on the categories we have for such relations (i.e., the italicized notions in the preceding).[4]

In Hegel, those categories are largely discussed in *The Science of Logic*. Here I want to pick up on just one form of this discussion, namely the discussion of the modalities (actuality, necessity, and possibility). A usual way of thinking about alternate possibilities is in terms of free choice (i.e., *Willkür* in German). On this conception, there is a range of opportunities that the world makes possible quite independent of the agent's activity, and that activity is limited to picking from among the given possibilities. On this conception there are a variety of different future paths extending from past conditions, and the agent chooses to walk one rather than the others. Hegel thinks that such a notion has a limited (though not unimportant) sphere of application, and as a metaphysical category he calls this 'real modality'. The deeper conception ('absolute modality') is one in which the very continuum of possibilities is established by the action itself, and comes to serve as the context for retrospective interpretation precisely because it is first discriminated as relevant by the action to be interpreted. On this conception there is only one necessary path from the past condition to the future, and yet that path, with its distinctive past condition and future state, is only one possible path from among others that connected different past conditions and different states. All of these paths lie along a continuum, and the contrasts provide the resources for interpretation by generating the contrasting fact that the agent took one path rather than another. It is not that nothing is given to the agent in this second conception, but the ratio of the given to the created (or constituted) shifts dramatically in the direction of the latter. Hopefully, the briefest of examples may help: consider agents assisting a child in need. On the model of real modality, we take the need as a given and then interpret agents' different responses to it as choices between options for response to that condition (e.g., does the agent help, or turn away, or call for someone else to help). But on the model of absolute modality, we take the need itself to be partially constituted by the response of the agent. One can see this in contrasting parenting styles: what counts as a need with respect to one style counts as an opportunity for the child to practice self-reliance with respect to another. Each choice of parenting style generates a matrix of possibilities for evaluation, for example the different kinds of bonds that might be formed through attachment parenting.

In what follows we will first set out in the most general way the given field of possibilities for agency by taking up Hegel's understanding of the three sub-projects of agency that combine to constitute free action (section 21.2). Then we will take up different ways of doing those three things at once (section 21.3), and these will be instances of absolute modality that define the continuum of alternate possibilities for action by prioritizing one of the three sub-projects.

---

[4] Yeomans, *Freedom and Reflection*, sec. 1.1.

21.2. THREE PROJECTS OF THE WILL

Buried in the middle of the Introduction to the *Philosophy of Right* are correlated lists of three different kinds of subjectivity and three different kinds of objectivity that Hegel takes to be relevant for understanding the basic project of willing. That latter project is the attempt to make subjectivity objective in such a way that the former can remain at home and recognizable in the latter (PR §§25–27). Each of these three correlations then characterizes a different aspect of that attempt, or defines a different constituent project of self-determination. Free action qua successful self-determination in general requires (at least partial) success at each of these constituent projects in particular.

The first correlation is between subjectivity as self-awareness and objectivity as the vocation and concept of the will. As a constituent project of self-determination, this is *self-appropriation*—we belong to ourselves in virtue of knowing our actions to be fitting for a being of a certain kind, and that means by doing those kinds of things. In Hegel's conceptual terms, this is the *universal* drive of the will, and so is naturally associated with a certain abstraction. At the limit of generality, we know ourselves as rational, planning agents, and so we own our actions as the kind of things that such creatures do.

The second correlation is between free choice (*Willkür*) and desire as forms of subjectivity, and objectivity as immersion in the particular features of one's experience. As a constituent project of self-determination, this is *specification of content*—we need to distinguish the signal from the noise of our lives. The most basic way that we do this is by pursuing and enjoying the objects of our desires in the face of obstacles to such satisfaction. In life this must be done at a relatively fine-grained level, and so it is not surprising that in Hegel's conceptual terms this is the *particular* drive of the will and is thus associated with a continuum of often minute or idiosyncratic differences in taste, habits, resources, and so on.

The third correlation is between subjective, unaccomplished ends and objective, accomplished ends. As a constituent project of self-determination, this is *effectiveness*— the need to see oneself as an agent rather than a patient, to see the world as embodying one of my purposes precisely because I have made it so. In Hegel's conceptual terms, this is the *individual* drive of the will, and is associated with strategies for taking the measure of that continuum of particular desires and histories by reference to the general or universal character of willing beings—that is, effectiveness requires planning, and planning requires a grip on the essential features of situations. It is the *individual* project both in the intuitive sense that here the agent makes her mark on the world and stands out in contrast to other agents, and in the technical Hegelian logical sense that it involves the relation of universality and particularity.

In sum, the basic picture arising from these sections in the *Philosophy of Right* is that in willing we are trying simultaneously to take possession of ourselves, to distinguish between what is central and what is peripheral in the events of our lives, and to make happen what we want to happen in those events. All action is an attempt to do these three things at once, but doing almost any three things at once is very difficult for most human beings. In many areas of our life in which we try to do multiple things at once (for example, musical performance), there are explicit training strategies designed to separate the requisite skills and train them individually before combining them. But no one has ever been taught first to take possession of themselves, then to distinguish the central from the peripheral, third to translate those central ideas to the world, and finally to put them all together in a complete performance of agency. It takes Hegel until the 1820s even to get clear on a theoretical description of the three skills of agency, and one shudders to think of the sort of practical training plan he might have devised for us. That said, at the same time that he is getting clear on these three skills, he seems to discover in the world of lived experience three general strategies for solving this problem implicit in the active lives of his contemporaries. He calls these three different forms of agency or accountability (*Zurechnungsfähigkeit*), each of which represents a conceptual distillation of common ways of life that are themselves attempts to manage this complexity on the ground, as it were.[5] And it will turn out that one of them is an (admittedly heterodox) version of the belief-desire accounts common in the Anglophone philosophy of action literature, and another a version of a teleological account. All three are forms of absolute modality in the sense that they are ways that an agent can herself set the context of alternate possibilities relevant for the interpretation of her actions.

21.3. THREE FORMS OF ACCOUNTABILITY

Hegel labels each of the forms of accountability by a different right of subjectivity: the rights of knowledge, intention, and insight into the good. These rights are each semi-autonomous conditions for the possibility of recognition of individual agents (i.e., they are different models for such recognition and thus organize different ways of life). So, for example, an agent exercises the first form of accountability when the agent legitimately expects to be held responsible for those and only "those aspects of its *deed* which it knew to be presupposed within its end, and which were present in its *purpose*" (PR §117). But there is also an aspect of the forms of accountability that is more difficult to grasp: each of the forms is equally a bait-and-switch routine in which the agent achieves something slightly different from what she means to achieve. This bait-and-switch is not a contingent feature of some particular interpersonal interactions (e.g., being conned by a salesman) but something essential to agency: we only act at all insofar as we mistake our goal for something that it isn't quite. Hegel seems to take this to be a conceptual fact about the project of finite willing as such. To take just a mundane example, I have seen the most experienced do-it-yourselfers motivate themselves for a new project on the basis of time and cost projections that they would not beforehand admit to be as unrealistic as they

---

[5] These forms of accountability also have legal connotations—Michael Quante translates *Zurechnungsfähigkeit* as 'sanity'—but this aspect is outside the scope of this chapter.

obviously are, and yet afterward would never actually judge their performance on the basis of those initial projections.

Hegel's terminology for this second aspect of action is 'the ought [*Sollen*]', since the standards for what we mean to do and the standards for what we actually do are not precisely the same and thus the latter have the form of an external requirement on the former. It is not just that we miss a given target; rather, we shoot at the target in one guise but hit it in another. It is not that we inevitably fall short of a high moral standard because of our human weakness; rather, we are bound to misunderstand or misperceive the standard we apply to ourselves. In this sense, the subjective rights are equally the conditions of possibility of *mis*recognition. Understanding Hegel's philosophy of action thus requires seeing how and in what respect each of the forms of accountability is a relative success and a relative failure at the general project of making subjectivity at home in objectivity. That is, understanding Hegel's philosophy of action requires understanding it as a philosophy of finitude.

We might therefore take some direction from Hegel's discussion of this paradoxical project in the *Logic*:

> The finitude of this activity [of willing] is thus the *contradiction* that, in the self-contradicting determinations of the objective world, the *purpose of the good* is both carried out and not carried out, and that it is posited as something inessential just as much as something essential, as something actual and at the same time as merely possible. This contradiction presents itself as the *endless progression* in the actualization of the good, that is therein established merely as an *ought*. (Here those contradictions come to the fore in which one stumbles around on the standpoint of morality—Addition) Formally, however, this contradiction disappears in that the activity supersedes the subjectivity of the purpose and thereby the objectivity, the opposition through which both are finite, and not only the one-sidedness of *this* subjectivity but subjectivity in general; *another* such subjectivity, that is to say, a *new* generation of this opposition, is not distinct from what was supposed to be an earlier one. This return into itself is at the same time the *recollection* of the *content* into itself, which is the *good* and the identity in itself of both sides,—the recollection of the presupposition of the theoretical stance (§224), that the object is what is substantial in itself and true. (The unsatisfied striving disappears if we know that the final purpose of the world has been brought about and to the same degree eternally brings itself about. This is generally the posture of the adult man, while the youth believes that the whole world is in a bad way and out of it a completely different world must be made. . . . This correspondence of is and ought . . . is not a frozen and inert correspondence; for the good, the final purpose of the world, *is* only in that it produces itself again and again . . . —Addition). (E §234 and §234A)

There is a lot going on here, but at a first pass we can say that satisfied action ("the posture of the adult") as much as the philosophical understanding of action require a kind of stereoscopic vision to see how the tensions within agency that appear to be crippling contradictions from one perspective could be the very way of going on from another.

The key here is the substitution of one subjectivity for another: successful action (1) translates subjectivity into objectivity only for (2) a new opposition between subjectivity and objectivity to arise, and the phenomenon holds together only because (3) this new subjectivity can somehow be identified with the first subjectivity. But then this latter identification appears to be just as much objective as subjective, since through that identification we take up again the theoretical stance that sees the truth primarily in the object rather than the subject.

Let us take a basic case as an example: an agent (1) satisfies her hunger by eating up a bit of the objective world; (2) hunger returns; and (3) she recognizes this new situation of being hungry as the same as the first, perhaps as part of a bit of practical planning. The agent may say to herself, "I'm always hungry at 9:30 a.m. so I should remember to bring a bagel with me to work"; or, more perspicuously (if slightly pedantically), "I'm the kind of person who is hungry at 9:30 every morning so bringing a bagel to work is fitting for me." In this way the agent treats herself as an object of a certain kind that has a feature (hunger at 9:30) that is independent of her subjective stance in the moment of her regarding herself as having that feature, even though the relevant feature is itself a subjective stance in the moment of her regarding the bagel as an object to satisfy her hunger. If hunger registers the difference or otherness between subjective desire and objective conditions, and connecting episodes of hunger by means of a typology that supports effective planning is a way of owning that otherness without eliminating it, then what we have here is an example of being at home with oneself in the other (i.e., of Hegelian freedom).

So far, so good. The example we just gave uses biological need to generate the renewed opposition between subject and object (i.e., hunger), just to try to bring the structure of the phenomenon into relief. One might think, then, that for more distinctively rational or abstract ends, such as justice or the good, the agent could transcend this cycle of renewed opposition and come to a final resting place. But as the preceding passage from the *Encyclopedia Logic* already suggests, such repose is not the destiny of agency of any kind. So we need to dig a little deeper to discover the more fundamental reason for this continual renewal of the opposition between subjectivity and objectivity.

To get at this reason, we need to back up a bit and say something about the general context of Hegel's most detailed discussion of action, which is in the Morality section of the *Philosophy of Right*. Hegel introduces morality as a way to prevent the generation of cycles of revenge in response to conflicting rights claims. The problem with revenge, he thinks, is not its content but its form. That is, it is in principle appropriate for someone to stand up for their rights by retaliating against another who has infringed them, but the personal nature of that retaliation makes it almost impossible for that other agent to accept it as appropriate to what she has done. The personal nature of revenge makes it difficult for the original perpetrator to own it as a fitting experience for her to undergo as the particular free agent that she is, since it is natural to see it as another injury that treats her as a thing, rather than as her own original action being reflected back upon her as just punishment under principles that she should otherwise endorse as protecting her own rights as well. In terms of the constituent projects of self-determination, revenge succeeds at specification of content, but fails at self-appropriation (PR§102).

This is important for our purposes only because it means that self-appropriation is the main problem of Morality and thus dominates and even deforms specification of content and effectiveness. And this deformation has consequences that are just as much objective as subjective, thus generating the contrast in standards that makes morality a 'mere' requirement. It is this deformation and its consequences that ensure the continual renewal of the opposition between subjectivity and objectivity, at the same time that it makes possible the renewal of their satisfactory identity.

This is the tale Hegel tries to tell in the prefatory sections of Morality (esp. PR §§108–113), though it must be said that his narrative technique leaves much to be desired. What is crucial, though not at all obvious, is that these sections represent a modification of the three forms of subjectivity and objectivity from the Introduction. To begin with, PR §109 presents the orientation of specification of content and effectiveness by self-appropriation, and then PR §111 traces the deformation of specification of content required by that orientation. This deformation is the heart of the first form of accountability.

21.3.1. The Right of Knowledge: "Relishing the Enjoyment of Pleasure"

In PR §111 Hegel says that regardless of the provenance of the particular conditions and desires of the will, we must consider that content "as the content of the will *reflected into itself* in its determinacy, and hence of the self-identical and universal will." We have seen this reflection into self already in our consideration of the *Logic*'s discussion of willing, in which a self-reflecting agent makes a kind of double identification. First, the agent identifies one desire with another (in our example, the two instances of hunger). Part and parcel of this first identification is the characterization of the agent as a certain type or kind of thing (in our rudimentary example, the kind of a person who is hungry in the morning). But, put another way, this is a second identification of the subject with an object of that kind (and thus the way in which it involves taking up the theoretical stance). This second identification comes out as an entailment of the self-reflection of the will: as a result, the will has "the inner determination of being in conformity with the will which has being in itself, or of possessing the *objectivity of the concept*."

Hegel means all of this rather literally: we reflect on ourselves and modify our subjective stances by means of seeing ourselves as a certain kind of object in the world. "[T]he will which has being in itself" clearly refers to the agent regarded from the theoretical perspective as an object having its own truth that can be known, but it is slightly more difficult to say why it should have the '*objectivity of the concept.*' The key here is that the agent is known to be a certain type or kind of object, which introduces generality or universality into the agent's self-relation. The key point here is that this generality is initially introduced into the project of specification of content because of the way in which this project is now colored by the project of self-appropriation. That is, in order for the content to be *my* content, it has to have a form consistent with the form of mineness as such—a form that qualifies it as an object that may be appropriated by an agent who can in principle then see herself in the particular positions of another (even if that other is just herself at a different time). Hegel spells this out nicely in his lectures:

> Now the content must be mine as it is accomplished, and as will it contains the deter-mination of the universality of the will, for the will which has being for itself is the infinite form, the infinite activity, and therefore the form which is at home with itself [*beisichseinde*], identical with itself, i.e., the universal. (GW 26.868/VPR III, 344)

The infinity of the form is connected with the "posture of the adult" in which precisely the repeated generation of opposition is seen as appropriate to the nature of the subject. It is infinite in the quite technical sense that such an agent knows that she will find her-self on the other side of that continually reappearing limit, so that there is a helical or cyclical shape to the process, rather than a linear progression.

The types or kinds that mediate this self-relation are not unrelated to the partic-ular content of desires and conditions; rather, the two sides arise out of one process, as Hegel is trying to make clear in the passage from the lesser *Logic* that we quoted at length earlier. In the greater *Logic* Hegel characterizes this process as a double reflec-tion or *Doppelschein* through which the universal and the particular come to have the distinctive content and significance that they do only in relation to each other (SL 12.35/533). So, in the preceding example, the self-identification as someone hungry in the mornings picks out certain motivational stances as particular desires that contrast with other desires and feelings experienced at the same time. The agent is a hungry person rather than a grumpy person, as the instances of hunger are picked out as the particular signal of the agent's life, whereas the instances of snapping at coworkers are explained as derivative on the failure to satisfy that hunger and thus as noise. There is, of course, ample opportunity for self-deception here, but that is just the way agency is. To take up the notion of absolute modality again, the hungry person frames the action along one continuum of alternate possibilities, whereas the grumpy person frames the action along another. For the former, the action contrasts with possible actions such as remembering to bring a snack or having forgotten breakfast entirely. For the latter, it contrasts with possible actions such as holding one's tongue or producing a more com-plete denunciation.

To briefly take stock, what we have so far is the orientation of specification of con-tent by self-appropriation, and not yet any sense of deformation (the possibility of self-deception aside)—that is, we have the way in which this particular relation of the projects of self-determination is a condition of the possibility of recognition, not yet of misrecognition. This is the positive side of what Hegel calls the 'right of knowl-edge', which consists in recognizing as my own in the content of my action those actual features of its public shape that give form to what I wanted to do (i.e., to my purpose [*Vorsatz*]) (PR §117–118). On the one hand, this is a common position in modern phi-losophy that defines accountable action by reference to the (causal) effectiveness of the agent's beliefs and desires. On the other hand, Hegel has a quite specific take on the way in which beliefs (i.e., the theoretical perspective) and desires (i.e., the practical perspective) are related to each other. This take is centered on the way in which beliefs specifically about the self are related to the self's active, practical stances toward the world (i.e., to desires). Hegel also has an interesting take on the way such desires are related to beliefs in general, and in particular to perceptual awareness of the external world. Let us first of all pick up on the positive aspect of this second element of Hegel's take before turning to the way in which both aspects generate the possibility of misrecognition.

The positive side of this second element can be found in Hegel's attribution of wholehearted enjoyment to this form of agency. In a revealing early manuscript when discussing the way of life of someone embodying this first form of agency (here, a farmer), he claims that it is characteristic of this figure that he "relishes the enjoyment of pleasure [*den Genuß des Vergnügens genießt*]" in contrast to the craftsman, who primarily appreciates the fact that he has made himself what he is, and the merchant, who is beyond any capacity for enjoyment (*Jenaer Realphilosophie* [GW 8.269]). And, adding more detail to this difference, Hegel says in his later lectures that "[t]his indifference [of craftsmen and merchants] to time and place, to the determinate, is alien [to the agricultural estate] . . . [T]he insatiability of profit is alien to it" (GW 26.1334/VPR IV, 516). We will put aside Hegel's social typology here; what is important for our purposes is his attempt to provide a conceptually robust defense of the value of basic desire satisfaction as a form of agency. Such satisfaction—that is, the accurate perception of the change in the objective world in accord with subjective desire, and the belief in the goodness of the conditions in which one finds oneself immersed—is a mode of being at home with oneself in the other and thus at least minimally solving each of the constituent projects of self-determination.[6] By perceiving self and world as in this relation, the agent has made at least part of the world her own, and in so doing has come to a kind of self-affirmation that is worthy of respect.

These two positive sides then give us the way in which this first form of agency constitutes a condition for the possibility of recognition. Self-identification as being of a certain type gives us a conception of what it is to be at home *with oneself*, and the enjoyment of the satisfaction of desire gives us a sense of how this is done *in the other*. But even in his initial formulations of the nature of morality, Hegel raises the possibility of misrecognition. More specifically, he raises the possibility of a mismatch between the particular, subjective content of the will and the objective truth of the will, and this possibility is what makes the correspondence between the two "only a *requirement*" (PR §111). Here we get to the deformation of the project of specification of content by that of form, specifically the form that arises from the project of self-appropriation. Thus we come to the deeper reason for the recurrence of the opposition between subjectivity and objectivity as it concerns this first form of agency. Unsurprisingly, we can see this

---

6 See also PS 9.199/¶362, where Hegel is clear that all successful action involves some kind of self-confirmation, even when that success is measured by 'the enjoyment of *pleasure*'.

deformation manifesting itself along the same two dimensions (i.e., in both the relation to the self and the relation to the world).

Recall from the previous section that Hegel initially thinks of the project of specification of content as the attempt, by means of free choice, to translate one's needs and desires into an immersive experience of the world. And we have just seen the way in which enjoyment is a kind of affective sign of that immersion. But we also saw the way in which the influence of self-appropriation on content interposed a type or general kind within the agent's relation to her particular desires. To put it structurally, a second kind of objectivity (formal or conceptual, rather than perceptual objectivity) intrudes itself into the formerly intimate relation between desire and its satisfaction.[7] As Hegel thinks of it, the bait-and-switch here is that I aim at perceptible pleasure, but what I achieve actually (or at least in addition) is a formal or conceptual status of counting as a certain type of person. To put it in the logical terms we used earlier, instead of a direct relation between particulars (i.e., between subjective desire and objective satisfaction in specific conditions), we get a relation between a particular and the whole conceptual process of the reflection of universal and particular (i.e., between a specific desire and the *Doppelschein* of particular desires and general type). But it is very difficult to know exactly what kind of relation the latter could be, and certainly it is very different from the relation at which the agent aimed and which served as the initial (if implicit) standard for success of the action.

The interpretive problem gets even worse. Hegel thinks through this conceptual problem by means of a technical, structural modification of the second form of objectivity—that is, the objectivity constitutive of the project of specification of content—but for that very reason his idea here has remained opaque to most readers, particularly those who think that he introduces the three forms of subjectivity and objectivity in the Introduction only to immediately reject two of them as irrelevant. Here is what is actually going on: In his first description of objective content in the Introduction as lacking the form of self-consciousness, there is no specific reference to *sensible* externality (PR §26[β]). Indeed, this initial conception of immersion in particular conditions included ethical norms and customs. But under the influence of the importance of self-appropriation within Morality, there is a move to understand those particular conditions as lacking the form of self-consciousness *because* they are sensible givens (PR §108). In Kantian terms, the initial confident immersion in the customary pattern of one's life is now being construed as heteronomy rather than autonomy. In the *Phenomenology*, the same thing happens in the struggle between faith and the Enlightenment: the latter re-characterizes the traditional content and devotional investments of faith as a merely sensible, perceptible externality (PS 9.312/¶576). In the actual practice of agency, this creates the possibility of misrecognition because it generates a need for justification and defense of certain actions where that need was not previously felt. Any agent caught in the midst of such a shift is bound to be defensive and somewhat flat-footed in the face of these new expectations.

---

[7] See GW 26.1200/VPR IV, 306 for a particularly clear statement of this.

So the interpretive problem follows a conceptual problem that is a real problem for agents, in Hegel's view. This is a reminder that we must take seriously Hegel's admonition not to indulge a "tenderness for worldly things" (E §48R): they are as full of tensions and problems and contradictions as thought itself. A good philosophy of action may need to replicate those tensions if it is to be descriptively adequate, rather than attempting to paper over them with a contrived solution. And yet the philosopher is not the first agent to face this problem—real agents in their own sociohistorical circumstances have faced the problems and cobbled together some partial solutions, so it is to Hegel's understanding of these that we now turn in an attempt to understand how these possibilities of recognition and misrecognition hold together as an integral practice of agency.

As Hegel understands agents embroiled in this historical mess, a common strategy is to re-describe that immersion as a tradition, and specific expectations as commands or promises.[8] Since this re-description characterizes immersion and expectations retroactively as specific kinds of laws or norms, new laws or norms can then be assimilated under the same rubrics. We can then complete our structural story as a conceptual analysis of these common strategies. For a more tenderhearted philosopher, one might expect the advocacy of a return to that earlier form of objectivity as immersion, or a restriction to it as the controlling form in the light of these tensions. But Hegel is nothing if not a post-Kantian in this respect, so rather than argue for an immediate return to the value of immersion, a *second* move is made to replace those sensible givens with the viewpoints of other self-conscious persons (PR§§112–113). He thus moves to thinking of the objectivity corresponding to the subjectivity of the agent's *Willkür* or contingent choice as now the wills of others. This external subjectivity is then a way in which subjectivity is at home in objectivity: "The external existence is the will, which becomes external as subject, a subject in general is generated, [and] I receive my subjectivity therein as object" (GW 26.868–869/VPR III, 346).

In our initial formulation of the problem of agency drawn from the lesser *Logic*, presented earlier, this is (3) (i.e., the moment of identification of the recurring instances of subjectivity with each other). But now we see this identification in a more radical sense than in the case of hunger, in which only instances of the same agent's intentional stances were identified. On the one hand, this move suggests a new other in which I can find myself at home, namely in the opinions and attitudes of fellow members of my society. On the other hand, this external subjectivity both highlights and challenges my own subjective *particularity*, which is the logical axis of specification of content: the opinions and desires of others are particular subjectivity, but subjectivity *external* to my own. Thus we also have a more radical sense in which the opposition between subjectivity and objectivity is necessarily rather than merely contingently recurrent.

If the first move of the shift (i.e., the characterization of immersive objectivity as merely perceived) opened up a gulf between that *for which* we are accountable (the specific perceptible features of our effective actions) and that *to which* we are accountable (the concept of the will as such), the second shift (i.e., the introduction of the opinions

---

[8]   Yeomans, *Expansion of Autonomy*, ch. 5.

and desires of others) attempts to cover some of the distance between these two senses of accountability. In this conception, that *for which* we are accountable are changes in the views of others:

> In the moral sphere, activity necessarily relates itself to the wills of others; these are in general the world in relation to which one is active. . . . In morality I generate changes also, there is an external material on hand, [but] it is not a matter of the alteration of the material, corporeal world; rather, the world in relation to which my subjectivity stands under the consideration of morality, is the subjectivity of others. (VPR IV, 307–308)

Furthermore, Hegel ambivalently describes the relevant external subjectivity both as the wills of others and as universal subjectivity, so the wills of others become a partial image of that *to which* we are accountable as well. We have a closing of the gap—the sense in which that *for which* and that *to which* we are accountable now have a more similar, if not precisely identical, form. If there is a single point in the *Philosophy of Right* at which one can locate Hegel's social reinterpretation of the problem of free agency, this is it; but he has buried it so well that it is easy to miss the extensive tensions within which it is embedded.

As we noted earlier, it is very difficult to know exactly what kind of relation that between particular desires and the whole conceptual process of the reflection of universal and particular could be. And that problem presented the first form of agency as a bait-and-switch in which we achieved a conceptual status when we aimed at pleasure. We now have Hegel's answer to the question of the nature of this relation: it is the expressive and interpretive relation between particular desire and the whole public world of opinion and evaluation. He then moves on to asking, what does agency look like that explicitly aims at such a conceptual status in the first place?

21.3.2. The Right of Intention

There are two particular features of this second form of agency that go directly to the question of the relation between the particular choice and the public world. The first is purposiveness, and the second is universality. Together these features define the right of intention (*Absicht*), which is the subjective right at the heart of this second form.

We can begin with purposiveness, which connects Hegel's view to the distinction we noted in the introduction to this chapter between causal and teleological theories of agency. We just learned that we have to aim at something, and one might think that the notion of aiming just is a notion of purposiveness. However one thinks of the conceptual proximity of these two notions, Hegel wants to draw some extensive consequences from the latter. In particular, this new (or newly explicit) characterization of the relation between subjectivity and objectivity introduces a distinction between ends and means into the nature of action:

> The intention [*Absicht*] is that which is mine in the action in a further determination [*in weiterer Bestimmung*] as the purpose [*Vorsatz*]. In terms of its content, the intention is something other than the mere purpose. The value that the action has for me, the intention, is a content, [and] this content is first of all the end [*Zweck*] of an action, and the action is the means for the end. This end [is] the content of my intention.... (GW 26.871/VPR III, 352)

Whereas the notion of purpose (*Vorsatz*) from the first form of agency emphasizes the temporal relation of priority between subjectivity and objectivity (both of which are objects of perception), the notion of intention (*Absicht*) emphasizes the priority of the goal over the conditions and resources for achieving that goal. So, on the one hand, this notion of purposiveness appears to be merely making explicit something that was implicit in the first form of agency. There are, of course, goals within that first form; but they are essentially taken as given ineluctably by circumstances (whether biological or social), rather than as produced by the process of agency and thus as something for which the agent can be held responsible. On the other hand, the notion of purposiveness appears to narrow the scope of agency or at least to reconceive its expressive center as being an end that animates the rest of the action as a means, rather than being a specifically mental stance than animates some succeeding physical realization.

Second, Hegel wants to emphasize the new universality of this second form of agency, and this he does in his very first presentation of it: "the truth of the *individual* is the *universal*, and the determinate character of the action for itself is not an isolated content confined to one external unit, but a *universal* content containing within itself all its various connections" (PR §119). To speak in terms of Hegel's logical theory, we might say that precisely because it is a *conceptual* status at which the agent aims, that status gathers together some particulars into a contrastive relation both internally and externally. Here this second feature (universality) contrasts with the first (purposiveness). Whereas the first seemed to restrict the scope of that for which the agent was accountable, the second seems to expand it.

Together, these two features help to specify this second form of agency as a form of absolute modality as we have characterized it. Specifically, the goal establishes a continuum of alternate possibilities in two senses: first, the goal contrasts with other related goals that might have been chosen; and second, the goal establishes a network of means that might be employed and resulting forms of achieving the goal.

In fact, these first two features are linked in the determinate negation of the first form of agency: "The transition from purpose to intention, is from the individuality of the immediate modification [of actuality] to the universality of action, to the interiority of the universality of the action" (GW 26.875/VPR III, 364). The "immediate modification" would be an external, perceptible change, whereas "the interiority of the universality of the action" would be the inherent teleological connections between that modification and other features of the extended context. It is important to see that the tension between these two features—the first contracting and the second expanding the scope of accountability—is essential to this form of agency and definitional of its integrity.

The easiest way to see this is in terms of the third feature. This form of agency aims not at just any conceptual status, but at the conceptual status of independence. Precisely by distinguishing between end and means and adopting a purposive relation with respect to the network of circumstances and processes that form the context of action, the agent claims to be an independent originator of action in the world: "By acting, the human being is reflected into himself, the action comes out of him, he is the beginner of the action. In this movement, which he performs, is a content" (GW 26.879/VPR III, 375). The universal conception of the end makes this possible, but also threatens it in the absence of a definite distinction between end and means. In moral theory, one can think of the doctrine of the double effect as a way in which this first feature is brought in to tame the second: At first I appear to be responsible for all of the manifold and extended consequences of my action in virtue of the fact that they obtain as part of the necessary and enabling relation that the specific circumstances of the world have to my purpose. But the mere fact that I foresaw some consequence does not make it a part of my *end* (i.e., it does not make it a part of the content of my intention) and so that fact is insufficient to define such a consequence as one for which I am accountable. This third feature, then, gives a general schema for all of the different forms of absolute modality that might be embodied by agents where one feature of the goal that defines the continuum of alternate possibilities is that its achievement establishes the independence of the agent.

Now we can return to our formulation of the problem of finite agency according to which such agency (1) translates subjectivity into objectivity only for (2) a new opposition between subjectivity and objectivity to arise, and the phenomenon holds together only because (3) this new subjectivity can somehow be identified with the first subjectivity. What we have so far is (1) for this second form of agency: someone exercising it translates a goal that is a universal end into objectivity by means of the whole network of conditions and resources in which they are embedded. The conception of the end as universal articulates one of the lessons learned from the first form of agency, which was the need to close the gap between that *for which* we are accountable and that *to which* we are accountable, but without erasing the particular subjective stance of the agent in contrast to her surroundings. Here that subjective stance is represented as the end or goal, "the interiority of the universality of the action," but because of that form it is inherently connected to the network of means, prominent among which are other agents and the productive resources developed cooperatively between them. Nonetheless, the tension between these two features is supposed to be productive, to make the third possible—the conceptual status of independence as an object of recognition.

But this is Hegel, so recognition and misrecognition go hand in hand. This is (2)—the way in which this second form is also a bait-and-switch routine, or a way in which we aim at something under one guise but hit it under another, with the result that our initial goal and our final achievement appear mismatched. And here we might divide the two forms of misrecognition into the theoretical and the practical (though this is not a label Hegel himself uses). What I mean by this is just that the first form of misrecognition concerns primarily the agents' understanding of the sources of their own motivation, and the second concerns the actual failure of agents to be embedded in objective systems of necessary resources for agency.

To get at the theoretical form of misrecognition, we have to come back to our three constituent projects of self-determination (self-appropriation, specification of content, and effectiveness). This form of misrecognition is driven by the idea that this new kind of inner effectiveness and this new model of the goal-directed self in terms of which agents appropriate their actions to themselves create deep problems for specifying the content of the subjective ends themselves:

> For the content of these ends, all that presents itself here is (α) formal activity itself, inasmuch as the subject *actively* commits itself to whatever it is to regard and promote as its end. . . . (β) But the as yet abstract and formal freedom of subjectivity has a more determinate content only in its *natural subjective existence*—its needs, inclinations, passions, opinions, fancies, etc. (PR §123)

That is, the characterization of self-appropriation as the mere formal ownership of effectiveness (α) imposes a kind of cost on the specification of content, namely that this content is now to be understood as naturally determined (β). Here is how Hegel puts the point in the Griesheim lectures:

> Here is first the found content, here is not yet the will which is in conformity with its concept; the concept only is the animating, that which generates content out of itself. . . . The content is here thus first something found. It still belongs to the natural subject, but it must at the same time be internal, it is formally that which is mine, but not the content of my freedom, of my concept; the positing of my freedom therein is just positing in general. (VPR IV, 331)

So I do not fully recognize myself—I am not in conformity with my concept—when I act in this second way. Even worse, this looks to replicate a problem we already saw in the first form of agency in which the content of purposes turned out to be a source of heteronomy rather than autonomy.

Here is why the problem recurs: in order to tame the potentially disastrous expansion of the scope of accountability introduced by the universality of the ends and contexts of agents, this form of agency insists on a formal feature of teleological processes, namely the distinction between ends and means. So it is by means of such a formal self-conception that agents appropriate actions to themselves, but the formality of the model of the goal-directed or end-setting self has a perverse and unexpected effect on the moral psychology in which it is taken to be of paramount significance. Specifically, it structurally highlights not the desired pure activity of the rational agent, but rather the particular, given contents of the subjective will. This widens the Kantian gap between the two aspects of the will in such a way that suggests that, at best, agents merely add their 'oomph' to goals that are already given to them by the teleological nexus in which they are embedded. To put the point in Kantian terms, this formal self-appropriation raises the specter that all practical reasoning is hypothetical rather than categorical, and thus the possibility that there is no autonomy at all. To put it in other terms, I aim at a conceptual status of independence but achieve a conceptual status of dependence on the sources of my goals, and this means that I achieve a status that is just as much achieved for me as by me: "the positing of my freedom therein is just positing in general."

But as we saw with respect to the first form of agency, there is a version of (3) here as well—that is, a way in which this reoccurrence of the divide between subjectivity and objectivity can be identified with the first in a conception of the agent as an object. In this second form of agency, this is done by way of the value of welfare, which is understood first as the satisfaction of the totality of the individual agent's needs and desires but then more broadly as the satisfaction of the totality of all agents' needs and desires. The broader, universal conception of welfare raises it to a distinctively *moral* value, on Hegel's way of thinking, and so articulates a way in which even this conceptual status of dependence is a dignified position worthy of respect. In this way, the formal rationality of the goal-directed (end-setting) self holds together the different instances of need not only across time in an individual agent, but across the experiences of different agents, and so holds together the conceptual statuses of dependence and independence. In Hegel's dialectic, however, this mitigating feature introduces another distinctive possibility of *practical* misrecognition.

In just the same way that Hegel ambivalently described the new form of objectivity arising in the first form of agency sometimes as universal subjectivity and sometimes as the choices and opinions of others, he ambivalently describes the value of welfare as both universal and as merely involving "*many other* particular beings in general" (PR §125) or even "the particular welfare of the individual" (PR §126R). In both cases, part of Hegel's point is to introduce contingency into the relation between the individual aiming at such a form of objectivity and that objectivity itself by showing that we aim at it under one guise but hit it under another. In this form of agency we have two guises of welfare—one formal and one material—and though Hegel has argued that in principle the two can be identified, we must nonetheless pick one and hope that by hitting it we hit both targets. The identity here is partial—it is like the overlap of two spheres in a Venn diagram. One could imagine an agent with color blindness who knew of this overlap, but couldn't visually make it out clearly because of its coloration. Such an agent would aim at the part she could see clearly and hope that by doing so she would hit the overlap. Hegel thinks that some of us have a moral vision in which the particular needs that constitute the content of welfare stand out in relief, and some of us have a moral vision in which the formal self-ownership of the goal-directed self (i.e., abstract property right) stands out in relief. Both groups try to hit the overlap between right and welfare, but the limitations of their perceptions make it the case that at least some of the time they fail to hit their target.

Hegel describes both kinds of misses, both kinds of practical misrecognition. In both cases, an initial form of subjectivity (either right or welfare) is successfully translated into objectivity, only for the other form of subjectivity to immediately crop up in opposition to the objectivity so transformed. His discussion of the first—aiming at the identity under the guise of welfare but missing its overlap with right—comes in PR §126. Hegel's example here is stealing leather to make shoes for the poor: welfare is made objective, but then the subjective claim to property right is legitimately raised against this new objective situation. However, he is more concerned about the second—aiming at the identity under the guise of abstract property right but missing its overlap with welfare. This form of misrecognition comes about when someone's abstract freedoms of ownership and contract are respected, but they are nonetheless deprived of the material basis of the satisfaction of their needs. So subjectivity in the form of abstract property right is translated into objectivity, only for the subjective claim of welfare to be raised in opposition to this new objective situation.

In his lectures, Hegel is quite clear about why he is more concerned about this second form: he takes a fundamental feature of his world to be the close proximity of the struggle for survival by the poor and the luxury secured by legitimate property claims of the rich (see GW 26.886–887/VPR III, 397–398 & GW 26.1221/VPR IV, 339). And so in the published text of the *Philosophy of Right*, he has rather little to say about mitigating structures for the first form of practical misrecognition, but more to say about mitigating structures for the second.

This mitigating structure goes under the name 'the right of necessity'. As Hegel initially presents it, it is the right of the person who is facing the catastrophic loss of her life itself to take what she needs to survive:

> The starving human being has the absolute right to violate the property of another. He violates the property of another only with respect to a limited content; it is inherent in the right of necessity, however, that he does not violate the right of the other as right. The interest is posited only in this little piece of bread; he does not treat the other rightlessly [*er behandelt den Anderen night rechtlos*]. (GW 26.1223/VPR IV, 341)

In order to see how this is a version of (3)—that is, a way in which the reoccurring gap between subjectivity and objectivity can be partially bridged—we must attend to the logical structure of Hegel's understanding here. It involves an explicit re-identification of welfare and right at their extremes, seemingly far removed from their overlap or partial identity. In his lectures he says, "Yes, the human being has a right to this unrightful action. For life is the totality of particularity, the entirety [*Gesamtheit*] of particularity reduced to its simple form. . . . Particularity has risen to the unity of the I" (GW 26.888/VPR III, 401). That is, any particular need of the agent would be insufficient to override a rights claim or provide the basis for a rights claim contrary to that of the property owner, but the totality of those needs shares the kind of formal selfhood had by the personality at the basis of the property claim, and so provides a competing rights claim. In this way, the new assertion of subjective opposition in the form of welfare can be partially identified with the original assertion of subjective opposition in the form of right.

But Hegel does not restrict this right of necessity to the immediate situation of the starving person; rather, he draws wide-ranging consequences from it:

> From the right of necessity arises the benefit of competence, whereby a debtor is per-
> mitted to retain his tools, agricultural implements clothes, and in general as much of
> his resources—i.e., of the property of his creditors—as is deemed necessary to sup-
> port him, even according to his estate [*sogar standesgemäß*]. (PR §127R)

This consequence brings the partial identity of welfare and right introduced by the
extreme case of the right of necessity back to the center, back to common structures
of life and the ordinary practice of moral judgment. It suggests, then, a third form of
agency that would explicitly aim to make just these kinds of judgments about what kinds
of needs are centrally related to the effectiveness of agency, and which are peripheral.

21.3.3. The Right of Insight into the Good

This third form of accountability is simpler, in a way, but only because its object has
become so complex that the resources of morality as such are only barely sufficient to
characterize it, even in outline. As we have already noted, this third form aims at objectivity in the form of the good, which means that it aims at an objective consistency of
right and welfare. But in the previous discussion of practical recognition, right and welfare showed up as essentially subjective claims (i.e., in the technical terms of the three
projects of self-determination, as the subjectivity of self-appropriation and the subjectivity of content, respectively). How is it that they now show up on the objective side of
the equation? The threefold pattern we have been following from the *Logic* gives us the
key: this third form of agency has taken up precisely that theoretical stance that identifies the two reoccurring forms of subjectivity with each other by identifying them as
shared features of a certain kind of object, and it does so as part of a practical process of
planning. This third form of agency aims at an objective form of existence in which these
two kinds of claims are in some sort of harmony with each other—this is its subjective
plan that it attempts to realize in the actual world.

That is the bait, but there is a switch as well:

> Every relationship (*Verhältnis*) contains an ought (*Sollen*) and even the good does
> not get beyond the ought. The abstract idea of the good should be realized. Freedom
> has the vocation [*Bestimmung*] of the good; freedom that is particularized in its own
> self—this should be realized. (GW 26.1227/VPR IV, 349).

With mention of the 'ought', we have moved on to (2)—misrecognition, or the way in
which the opposition between subjectivity and objectivity recurs. The obvious way that
this happens here is in the *Philosophy of Right*'s version of Hegel's so-called empty formalism objection to Kantian ethics. Here is Hegel's presentation from the Hotho lectures:

> Duty here is thus completely without content, genus but without further determi-
> nation to species [*Gattung noch ohne Fortbestimmung zur Art*]. But there should be

action [*Aber es soll gehandlet werden*], and so the question arises: where does the determining principle [*das Bestimmende*] fall? In duty, with respect to the objective we have nothing but this abstraction of the good. This is that which is without determination, so the determining falls on the subjective side. (GW 26.2.896/VPR III, 424)

We have a conception of the objective good that ought to be able to serve as the only needed aim or end of a form of agency, but is unable to do so. To put it in the Kantian terms suggested by the previous comparison, we have no mediating terms between the abstract formality of the law and the particular satisfactions that compose welfare. This lack of mediating terms undermines the goal of this form of agency, which is to make the kinds of judgments suggested by the benefit of competence—that is, to make judgments about the partial identity of right and welfare. The question then becomes, how do we get to (3)—that is, how does this form of agency hang together despite these difficulties? There can be no real hope of improvement on the subjective side—Hegel does not think that if we just think hard enough about the nature of teleology or the drive to achieve goals in general we will find any specific guidance here. The improvement has to be in the form we expect from (3), that is, by taking the theoretical attitude to the objective side and identifying these competing sides (right and welfare) by means of a mediating kind. But in searching for those mediating kinds, the resources of morality as such give out and we are forced, Hegel thinks, to look at the ways that these forms of moral agency are embodied at the intersections of different institutions and different ways of life. These institutions are the ones Hegel discusses in Ethical Life: family, civil society (i.e., all voluntary associations), and the state. The ways of life are described by Hegel as the *Stände* or the estates, some of which we have seen already. Each of these ways of life is a form of absolute modality, but Hegel's interesting point is that aiming at other ways of life as objects is itself a distinctive way of life and thus its own form of absolute modality.

21.4. CONCLUSION

Though Hegel has a strikingly pluralistic philosophy of action, we have seen that he intends philosophy to make good on a range of traditional commitments, running from the necessity of alternate possibilities through the value of desire satisfaction to the centrality of goal-directedness. It is of course true that many of those possibilities, desires, and goals are essentially social and even collective, and that determining their nature is a public and often retrospective interpretive act. But that determination must also take its cue from the interpretive direction proposed with the act by the agent herself, and the notion of absolute modality is Hegel's way of seeing that cue as consisting in the suggestion of a context of interpretation by way of marking out the contrast of the action with a certain range of other possible actions. There is a hermeneutic circle here, and one of Hegel's most unique contributions to the philosophy of action is his development of the public or social arc of that circle. This should not, however, lead us to overlook the extent to which he developed versions of the categories involved in the more traditional arc of that circle, such as modalities, desires, and goals.

Works Cited

Primary Texts

Hegel, G. W. F. *Elements of the Philosophy of Right* [PR], translated by H. B. Nisbet and edited by Allen Wood. Cambridge: Cambridge University Press, 1991.

Hegel, G. W. F. *The Encyclopedia Logic: Part I of the Encyclopedia of Philosophical Sciences with the Zusätze* [E], translated by T. F. Geraets, W. A. Suchting, and H. S. Harris. Indianapolis: Hackett, 1991.

Hegel, G. W. F. *Phenomenology of Spirit* [PS], translated by A. V. Miller. Oxford: Oxford University Press, 1977.

Hegel, G. W. F. *The Science of Logic* [SL], translated and edited by George di Giovanni. Cambridge: Cambridge University Press, 2010.

Hegel, G. W. F. *Vorlesungen über Rechtsphilosophie* [VPR], 4 volumes, edited by Karl-Heinz Ilting. Stuttgart: Frommann Verlag, 1974.

Secondary Literature

Patten, Alan. *Hegel's Idea of Freedom*. Oxford; New York: Oxford University Press, 2002.

Pippin, Robert B. *Hegel's Practical Philosophy: Rational Agency as Ethical Life*. Cambridge; New York: Cambridge University Press, 2008.

Quante, Michael. *Hegel's Concept of Action*, translated by Dean Moyar. Cambridge: Cambridge University Press, 2004.

Speight, Allen. *Hegel, Literature, and the Problem of Agency*. 1st ed. Cambridge; New York: Cambridge University Press, 2001.

Stekeler-Weithofer, Pirmin. *Philosophie des Selbstbewußtseins: Hegels System als Formanalyse von Wissen und Autonomie*. Auflage: Originalausgabe. Frankfurt am Main: Suhrkamp Verlag, 2005.

Westphal, Kenneth R. "The Basic Context and Structure of Hegel's Philosophy of Right," in *The Cambridge Companion to Hegel*, edited by F. C. Beiser. Cambridge: Cambridge University Press, 1993, 234–269.

Yeomans, Christopher L. *Freedom and Reflection: Hegel and the Logic of Agency*. New York: Oxford University Press, 2011.

Yeomans, Christopher L. *The Expansion of Autonomy: Hegel's Pluralistic Philosophy of Action*. New York: Oxford University Press, 2015.

CHAPTER 22

···

HEGEL'S MORAL PHILOSOPHY

···

KATERINA DELIGIORGI

DOES Hegel have anything to contribute to moral philosophy?[1] If moral philosophy presupposes the soundness of what he calls the 'point of view of morality [*Moralität*]' (PR §137), then Hegel's contribution is likely to be negative. As is well known, he argues that morality fails to provide us with substantive answers to questions about what is good or morally required and tends to give us a distorted, subject-centered view of our practical lives; moral concerns are best addressed from the 'point of view of ethics [*Sittlichkeit*]' (PR §137). Hegel's criticism of morality has had a decisive influence in the reception of his thought. By general acknowledgment, while his writings support a broadly neo-Aristotelian ethics of self-actualization, his views on moral philosophy are exhausted by his criticisms of Kant, whom he treats as a paradigmatic exponent of the standpoint of morality.[2] My aim in this chapter is to correct this received view and to show that Hegel offers a positive argument about the nature of moral willing.

---

[1] For their valuable comments on early versions of this essay, I want to thank Thom Brooks, Tim Carter, Stephen Houlgate, Dean Moyar, Andreas Schmidt, Klaus Vieweg, and Lambert Wiesing.

[2] That Hegel has an ethics is a consensus of relatively recent origin; in 1990 Wood saw the need to address the question "Does Hegel have an ethics?" (Wood, *Hegel's Ethical Thought*, 8) and argue against interpretations, which absorb Hegelian ethics into social or political theory; e.g., Walsh *Hegelian Ethics*, 11; though see too Brooks, *Hegel's Political Philosophy*. Wood's *Hegel's Ethical Thought* is a key statement of the neo-Aristotelean ethical naturalist interpretation; see too Taylor, *Hegel and Modern Society*; O'Hagan in Priest, *Hegel's Critique of Kant*, 135–160; Moyar, *Hegel's Conscience*; and Pinkard, *Hegel's Naturalism*, esp. 187–196. The literature on Hegel's criticisms of Kant's moral philosophy is vast. A classical source is Priest *Hegel's Critique of Kant*. Recent discussions include Pinkard, "Self-Understanding and Self-Realizing Spirit in Hegelian Ethical Theory"; Lottenbach and Tenenbaum, "Hegel's Critique of Kant in the Philosophy of Right"; Patten, *Hegel's Idea of Freedom*; Stern, *Understanding Moral Obligation*; Freyenhagen, "Empty, Useless, and Dangerous? Recent Kantian Replies to the Empty Formalism Objection"; Vieweg, *Das Denken der Freiheit*; Sedgwick, *Hegel's Critique of Kant*, esp. 2–7; and McCumber, *Understanding Hegel's Mature Critique of Kant*.

22.1. TEXTS AND INTERPRETATION

The primary text for the following discussion is the second part of the *Philosophy of Right*, "Morality."[3] Additional material comes from the paragraphs devoted to morality in the "Objective Mind" section of the *Encyclopedia Philosophy of Mind* and from the analysis of the idea of the good in the *Science of Logic*. The reason for focusing on these works is that, in contrast to the early writings and, to some extent, the *Phenomenology*, Hegel spends little time repeating his criticisms of Kant's moral philosophy. Instead, he devotes himself to the task of providing a positive characterization of moral willing.

Before we turn to these arguments, it is worth asking why morality is treated in a work entitled *Philosophy of Right*, which contains material about property rights, state constitution, and political economy. For readers whose expectations are shaped by contemporary discussions of morality, a historical comparison with Kant's *Metaphysics of Morals* will be useful, since this latter also contains a theory of right that covers property rights, contracts, marriage, state and international law, as well as a doctrine of virtue with advice about teaching and practicing virtue. Hegel's book starts with "Abstract Right," which deals with property, contracts and punishment, continues with "Morality," and concludes with "Ethical Life," a very wide-ranging section, which, besides a brief but significant discussion of virtue (PR §§150, 151), considers family and working life, politics, international law, and even world history. Despite their differences, both books show a shared concern to deal with political, judicial, moral, and social matters consistently and in the round, rather than in a piecemeal fashion.

Still it is striking that Kant subsumes his treatment of these various matters under 'morals [*Sitten*]', and Hegel under 'right [*Recht*]'. The extent to which Hegel considers political arrangements to be directly relevant to morals is illustrated in his retelling of the Pythagorean anecdote about a father who, in response to his request for advice regarding the ethical education of his son, is told: " 'Make him the *citizen of a state with good laws*' " (PR §153R). As we can see from the way Hegel organizes his argument in the book, however, the state with the good laws is already an *ethical* whole, and conversely, ethical life is politically organized. The unifying concept for the range of phenomena that Hegel treats in his book and which make up our practical lives, from the '*public laws*' and the '*public morality*' to '*religion*' (PR 14,1.7/11), is what he calls 'the

---

[3] In what follows I cross-reference the "Morality" section of the *Phenomenology* but do not focus on it. For an excellent discussion of morality in the *Phenomenology*, see Pinkard, *Hegel's Phenomenology*, 193–220. Hegel refers the readers of the *Philosophy of Right* to the *Phenomenology* for supplementary critical argumentation, but by the same token he shows that his interest has shifted to what remains vital about the moral standpoint. See the famous PR §135 paragraph, which contains critical discussion of Kant's moral philosophy: "The further antinomies and shapes assumed by this perennial *obligation*, among which the merely moral point of view of *relationship* simply drifts to and fro without being able to resolve them and get beyond obligation, are developed in my *Phenomenology of Spirit*" (PR §135R). For a discussion of the early writings that focuses on the relation to Kant, see Deligiorgi, "Religion, Love, and Law: Hegel's Metaphysics of Morals," 23–44.

ethical [*das Sittliche*]' (PR 14,1.10/15; 14,1.12/18).[4] Hegel's aim is to show that the ethical can be grasped in its 'rational form [*vernünftige Form*]' (PR 14,1.7/11). So his task is not just descriptive, to record what people take to be ethical phenomena. Indeed, he is quite scathing about such projects (PR 14,1.7–8/11–12). The book is a *philosophy* of right and as such is not concerned with mere narration of happenings (SL 12.22/519). To understand what the philosophical treatment of the ethical involves, we need to come to grips with Hegel's idealist and systematic commitments.[5]

Hegel's idealism is contested territory. Robert Pippin cites a number of possible contents for the term: romantic world-soul idealism, 'wild idealism' manifested in indifference to the world as in some sense arbiter of our notions, conceptual scheme idealism, and so on.[6] On Hegel's own definition, idealism amounts to treating the finite as 'ideal' in the privative sense of lacking 'true being' and then searching for the 'non-posited' on which the finite depends (SL 21.142/124). Applying this definition to Hegel's own philosophy needs to be done with care. Importantly, and as we shall presently see, the 'absolute' is not to be sought behind or beyond finite appearances.[7] The philosophical treatment of the ethical requires that we "recognize in the semblance of the temporal and transient the substance which is immanent and the eternal which is present" (PR 14,1.14/20).[8] Although 'temporal' and 'transient' are also finite, and therefore, on the privative definition of 'ideal', they lack true being, they are not nonentities, because they somehow form part of what Hegel calls 'the substance' and 'the eternal'. It may help here to distinguish between two senses of 'what is'. The first amounts to an ordinary claim that such and such entity exists or state of affairs obtains. A second sense, sometimes indicated by the qualifier 'true' (as in 'true being') but more usually by the term 'actual' and 'actuality', carries the idea of something that is *worthy* of being or rationally vindicated, as when Hegel announces that ethical 'content' is "justified to free thinking" (PR 14,1.7/11). This

---

[4] Knox translates *das Sittliche* as 'ethical life', and 'ethical order', Nisbett as 'the ethical'; see Wood, *Hegel: Elements of the Philosophy of Right*, 16.

[5] Following Houlgate, "Hegel, Rawls and the Rational State"; Vieweg, *Das Denken der Freiheit*; and Brooks, *Hegel's Political Philosophy*, I read the *Philosophy of Right* as a systematic text. However, I favor a reconstructive, rather than an immanent, reading, and so I am sympathetic to non-systematic interpretations; see Hardimon, *Hegel's Social Philosophy*; Franco, *Hegel's Philosophy of Freedom*; Patten, *Hegel's Idea of Freedom*; Neuhouser, *Foundations of Hegel's Social Theory*.

[6] Pippin, *Hegel's Idealism*, 61, 202, and 233. Pippin defends conceptual scheme idealism (*Hegel's Idealism* 8) and a version of anti-realism (ibid., 99). He does not seem concerned with the distinctiveness of moral philosophy, which can accommodate relatively easily commitments that may sound 'wild' from a theoretical perspective; for example, there is a significant constituency of defenders of aprioristic ethics, for whom moral notions are not derived from experience and are not reducible to empirical facts. For critical discussion of Pippin, see Ameriks, "Hegel and Idealism" and Stern, "Hegel's Idealism." I return to this issue in the last section.

[7] See too: "The true ideal is not what ought to be actual but what is actual, and the only actuality. If an ideal is held to be too good to exist, there must be some fault in the ideal itself, since actuality is too good for it" (LHP 95, 19:110), and more resonantly, that "nothing is actual except the Idea" (PR 14,1. 14/20).

[8] See too the 1818–19 Preface: "The genuine condition of the eternal cannot remain with the historicist view of legal conditions, for this view counts as just only that which prevails" (Brudner, "Prefatory Lectures 1818–19, 1822–23, 1824–5," 50) and the discussion of the 'historical treatment of law' (ibid., 67–69).

explains how Hegel can say both that philosophy is its time apprehended in thoughts and that its task is to grasp "*what is . . .* for *what is* is reason" (PR 14,1.15/21).

In the quote just given, if 'what is' and 'reason' are the same, then we have an unhelpful tautology; if they differ, the question is, how does a philosopher identify the actual from everything else that is? Just to call the actual 'rational' as in the famous assertion, "what is rational is actual; and what is actual is rational" (PR 14,1.14/20), does not help because we lack a measure of 'rational'.[9] Here is where Hegel's systematic commitments are relevant. Hegel does not spell out the criteria that we as philosophers may use to vindicate the practical phenomena that make up the ethical. The rational form of the ethical is to be discovered through his analysis of the concepts that map out this territory. This analysis is to proceed entirely immanently: different concepts are explicated and their use is justified in context by way of reciprocal relations established with other concepts. Stephen Houlgate, a key exponent of Hegel's holistic method, explains it thus: "a moment gains its character from the whole that it helps to constitute."[10] Each 'moment' or concept depends for its content and rationale on other such 'moments' or concepts in a structure of mutual support. But then it is unclear how in the absence of any content counting as basic, these concepts do not merely dissolve into relations.[11] The systematic question for us, then, is how relations among concepts can be explanatory and justificatory *for* these concepts, if all we have is just relations of explanation and justification. Although this question seems a long way away from morality, it will concern us in the later sections because how we resolve it will be crucial in getting the right measure of Hegel's claims about moral willing.

22.2. THE GOOD OF WILLING

A striking aspect of "Morality" in the *Philosophy of Right* is the near absence of what today is called normative ethics, that is, arguments about right and wrong, duties and

---

[9]   We followed here a rather ambitious interpretation of 'actual' as what has true being and is expressive of or identical with the 'Idea'. An alternative, more modest account is given by Allen Wood. Against Humean views that reason is idle or merely passive, Wood asserts the causal efficacy of reason and invites us to understand 'actual' as 'practical', pointing out that reason "constantly works changes in the world through human actions" (Wood, *Hegel's Ethical Thought*, 11). Both the ambitious and the modest interpretations, however, face the task of explaining what is to count as 'rational'.

[10]   Houlgate, *The Opening of Hegel's Logic*, 428. Houlgate discusses the *Logic* here. But his defense of holism is applicable to Hegel's other systematic works. Houlgate argues that ideality is about *being* a moment in a process, which gives us the "ontological structure of things" (ibid., 430). Stern argues that the idealist sees the world holistically, not as made up of atomic entities but "as parts of interconnected totality" (Stern, "Hegel's Idealism," 141). There is a debate about whether such holism is implausibly ambitious (Ameriks, "Hegel and Idealism") or quite modest (Stern, "Hegel's Idealism").

[11]   The argument, from Bradley, *Appearance and Reality*, 26, is that we cannot have *a* understood in terms of *b* and *b* in terms of *a* exclusively (nor *a* in terms of *b* in terms of *c* and so on until we are back to *a*); see Candlish, *The Russell/Bradley Dispute and Its Significance for Twentieth-Century Philosophy*, 167–170.

virtues. Instead, Hegel discusses intention, purpose, willing, action, deed—issues treated in contemporary action theory. The reason for this is that the topic of this part of the book is a certain conception of the will, which he introduces at the end of the previous section on "Abstract Right." So this is what we need to examine first.

The concluding discussion in "Abstract Right" concerns the conditions under which punishment for wrongdoing can be understood as justice, rather than as revenge.[12] At issue is not whether the concepts of revenge and of justice go together; revenge justice models show that they do.[13] Hegel is interested in how things look from the agent's perspective, how she can see her own punishment as justice, rather than as society's tit for tat. The concept that is needed, and which takes the discussion forward to "Morality," is of "a will [*Wille*] which, as a particular and *subjective* will, also wills the universal as such" (PR §103). Let us for the moment treat 'the universal' as indicating an expanded moral horizon and so as being roughly equivalent to 'morally right'; what Hegel seems to be saying here is that absent any sense of moral rightness, the wrongdoer simply lacks the resources to conceive of her punishment as justice.[14] The focus on the particular will is characteristic of the transition from abstract right to morality. Whereas in the earlier sections, 'will' is understood in terms of legally defined practices and the abilities these presuppose, in the sections we are about to examine, the topic is the nature of willing itself.[15] It is tempting here to think of 'will' as an executive function, part perhaps of our soul or mind, with a future-oriented temporal structure. As becomes clear in the course of the discussion, Hegel distances himself from such views of willing. The purpose of "Morality," he writes, is to analyze "the will's self-actualization" "[i]n accordance with *its* concept" (PR §104, emphasis added) and this concept is nothing less than the good.[16] The claim to be defended, then, is that moral willing, that is, willing "in conformity with the good" is basic (see PR §131).

[12] "[T]he cancellation of crime is primarily *revenge*, and its *content* is just so far as it constitutes retribution.... Thus revenge, as the positive action of a *particular* will, becomes *a new infringement*; because of this contradiction ..." (PR §102). "To require that this contradiction ... should be resolved ... is to require a justice freed from subjective interest ... that is, a *punitive* rather than an *avenging justice*" (PR §103).

[13] See Gerber and Jackson, "Retribution as Revenge and Retribution as Just Deserts."

[14] In the *Encyclopedia* transition Hegel describes 'morality' as the will that is reasonable and lets go the "wilfulness and violence of the state of nature" (E §502). Hegel qualifies 'universal' later on in the "Morality" section as 'substantive universal' (PR §141, and E §469), which is a more intriguing notion that we will seek to clarify later on.

[15] "[S]ubjectivity now constitutes the determinacy of the concept ... and more precisely ... the will of the subject, as the individual who has being for himself ..." (PR §106). See too the idea of will "as author of its own conclusions" (E §469 and E §503). As we shall see, the psychology of action is intimately connected with the good (see too E§54). Therefore the Quante and Pippin/Houlgate disagreement about whether this is action theory or ethics is easily resolved; see Quante, *Hegels Begriff der Handlung*; Pippin, *Hegel's Practical Philosophy*, 169; and Houlgate, "Action Right and Morality in Hegel's Philosophy of Right," 155–175. The material contains elements of both; see Moyar, *Hegel's Conscience*, 14 ff. on conscience as skilled agency. It also contains a meta-ethical argument that "for the truth of agency, more is needed ... than merely knowing the good" (Pinkard, *Hegel's Naturalism*, 93).

[16] "[T]hought determines itself into will and remains the substance of the latter; so that without thought there can be no will, and even the uneducated person wills only insofar as he has thought; the

Hegel defends this bold claim by focusing on what the will does. Instead of engaging in philosophical introspection, he considers the immediate context in which willing is philosophically important, and this is the context of doing things. The doing of the will is an action, *Handlung* (PR §113; see too E §113). An action has the character of something done, it "posits an alteration to this given existence [*Dasein*]" (PR §115; see too E §505). Hegel introduces the term 'deed [*Tat*]' to pick out this evental character of action: as deed, the action is also "an event, or a situation which has arisen" (PR §115R). If we ask, what makes an action different from an event—why it is *also* an event, rather than just an event—the simple answer is that action is *ex hypothesis* a product of the will. This is obviously unsatisfactory. What we want to understand is how invoking the will helps separate deeds from other events. This way of thinking about it suggests that the will adds something to what would otherwise be mere event, and so we obtain 'action'. Hegel proposes another way of thinking about it by asking how it is that a publicly observable performance can be attributed to and owned by a subject, or "be known by me in its externality as mine" (PR §113). If we allow that at least one function of will is to establish ownership of the deed, which makes sense in the context of morality to the extent that responsibility, praise, and blame are germane to our topic, then it is reasonable to concern ourselves with the ownership question. Most of "Morality" is devoted to answering this question (PR §§112–132). The argument roughly is that ownership can be settled provided we accept that the concept of the will is the good. In what follows I present a reconstruction of this basic argument, and in the subsequent section I examine whether the conclusion about will and the good is safe.

The main premises of Hegel's argument are as follows:

1. Deeds are actions, if deeds are intentional.
2. Deeds are intentional, if they realize some end presented to the agent as worth pursuing.
3. An end is presented to the agent as worth pursuing, if it links up with *the* good.

22.2.1. Deeds are actions, if deeds are intentional.

Hegel uses the inner/outer conception of what is in the mind and what is in the world, while also depriving it of metaphysical significance. So, for example, he states that an agent is able to 'objectify' her aims (PR §112), and describes this ability as 'expression' of the agent's will (PR §113). Objectification and expression aim to draw attention to the fact that whatever else an action is, it is also a public performance and as such an event. Hegel is not caught up in the concerns about actions and events that dominate

animal, on the other hand, because it does not think is also incapable of possessing a will" (E §468A). See Pinkard, *Hegel's Naturalism*, 31–33. Hegel treats the modern concept of the will as reducible to its manifestations: "the phenomenon of the will . . . sinks into itself" (E §512).

the contemporary debate. He simply assumes that when someone is doing something, at least for ordinary cases of 'doing' that involve moving one's limbs about, there is a publicly observable alteration. He then asks what is needed to connect the doing with the doer, so that it can properly be *hers*.

The first step is the claim that intention is a mark of action, a deed is an action if it is intentional. To get to the supporting argument, I will use throughout, adapted and expanded, Hegel's example about burning wood from PR §119. To burn the wood, the agent has to take into account the materials at her disposal. This taking into account has nothing to do with her and everything to do with the behavior of physical things— wood, fuel, and matches—when they interact. At the same time, if she is to claim the deed as hers, it must be possible to disentangle the event that is her doing from its "various attendant circumstances" (PR §115). While she is not responsible for the properties of the materials at her disposal, once she takes these facts into account and successfully lights the fire, she is the one burning the wood. We could of course say that the burning agent—along the lines of 'cleaning agent'—is the fire. This is true. Merely locating an agent within the "various attendant circumstances" does not allow for identification of the agent responsible for *setting up* the alteration in the environment.[17] The burning of the wood is the deed. We have an action only if we can establish that it is *her* burning of the wood (PR §113, E §469).

Establishing this is not easy:

> An event, or a situation which has arisen, is a *concrete* external actuality which accordingly has an indeterminable number of attendant circumstances. Every individual moment which is shown to have been a *condition*, *ground*, or *cause* of some such circumstance and has thereby contributed *its share* to it may be regarded as being *wholly*, or at least *partly*, *responsible* for it. (PR §115R)

What complicates things is not just the past causal history of a deed but also the causal chains it sets off; like any worldly occurrence, the deed has "its context in external necessity" and becomes "exposed to external forces" (PR §118) *as soon* as it is performed; for example, this wood burning may set the fence on fire. Deed attribution and demarcation of the bounds of the deed seem to go together, and,

---

[17] The deed, the burning of the wood, is also describable as an event of wood burning; the deed *qua* event is causally connected to environmental facts in the complex ways that events are. The subset of deeds that are intentional actions, which interests Hegel here, allows for an agent to be inserted in the description: the burning of the wood *by* her. Intentional actions have reasons as explanatory for the deed, and since the deed is something done, whatever brought it about must also count as causal, so in the Hegelian picture reasons are causal for deeds; I discuss intentional action in Deligiorgi, "Doing without Agency: Hegel's Social Theory of Action," 97–118. Note that Hegel is not concerned with the contemporary question of *how* reasons can be efficient causes, because he does not consider causality to be adequately captured as efficient causality only (see Schick, "Freedom and Necessity," 84–99) and is skeptical of the modern reason/cause dichotomy (see de Vries, *Hegel's Theory of Mental Activity*, esp. 4–7).

Hegel suggests, can be treated together through what he calls the '*right of knowledge*' (PR §117).

The 'right of knowledge' is the will's 'right' to recognize the parts of the deed that it is conscious of. There is a subjective side to this right, the 'right of intention', the '*universal* quality of the action' as is "*known* by the agent and thus [shall] have been present all along in his subjective will." And there is an objective side, the 'right of *objectivity*', the action "as known and willed by the subject as a *thinking agent*" (PR §120).[18]

Let us start with the right of intention and the subjective side. 'Universal quality of the action' means a general description of the action as a deed, as it might be available to any onlooker; the neighbor, for example, witnesses the burning of the wood (see PR §119). The right of intention means simply that the agent doing the deed 'owns' it insofar as she is doing it intentionally. It is presented as a right to *know* in the sense that while the agent is doing whatever she is doing intentionally, she knows *what* she is doing; she knows, for example, that she is burning wood. If we now look at the objective side, in this context, the right of objectivity allows us to add *that* she knows what she is doing as brought about by her. It is a 'right' insofar as the agent doing whatever it is she is doing intentionally can rightfully claim knowledge of it. This is not an item of theoretical knowledge, such as whether plywood is flammable; it is knowledge she has as the agent who is now burning the wood. Hegel presents intention and objectivity as elements in a single complex right to know because it allows the agent to assert ownership of her action as agent. She can say "the burning is mine, because I know I am doing it and I am, just now, in the process of doing it!"

Unfortunately, being in a position to assert this right does not answer the ownership question. The burning *qua* deed is and remains a stretch in a chain of external relations (PR §119R). In the *Phenomenology*, Hegel provides a critical argument about attempts to locate agential presence within stretches of causal chains and derides such efforts as 'vertigo inducing' (PS 9.333/¶617). Causal chains indeed have this characteristic that they can extend as far back as the explanatory demand goes; each causal stretch is qualitatively identical to any other and merely made relevant by its proximity to the deed. To firm up the gains achieved, we need a more robust conception of the agent not just as intentional doer, but also as thinker.

22.2.2. Deeds are intentional, if they realize some end presented to the agent as worth pursuing.

Agential intention can be firmed up only if it is supported by considerations that pertain to evaluations about what is 'worth' doing or is in the agent's 'interest' (PR §122), well-being, or happiness (PR §123).

---

[18] Again evaluative and action theoretical concerns are treated together, since description has moral and legal implications; 'tidying the backyard' warrants different judgments and attitudes than 'arson'.

The account presupposes that there is something the agent wants to achieve by her doing, yet nothing has been said so far about her willing of what she is doing. The burning of the wood does not come out of nowhere; someone is able to claim it as her doing, but this claim, the very assertion of the right to know, *also* does not come out of nowhere, it is a right the subject asserts "as a *thinking agent*" (PR §120). This shows how demanding willing is. It is not just a matter of "I want x." Willing involves having some ends one cares about. Wants make sense with reference to these ends (and so count as instances of willing). This demanding conception of willing is needed, Hegel suggests, because without it intention disintegrates. If the agent has no reasons *for* burning the wood, then she cannot properly lay claim to the action. Examples Hegel considers include "children, imbeciles, lunatics etc." who are unable to own their actions, because they are short of reasons. However, there is a range of attributable deeds that are reason-deficient, which Hegel does not consider, for example arational, purposeless, idle deeds ("No reason I just felt like it!") or those performed acratically ("I did not really want to do it, I hate myself for having done it"). The explanation is likely to do with the fact that these deeds are by their very description tenuously attached to the agent as *agent* (the agent is rather a patient).

The right of intention as we discussed it earlier is about the agent claiming her action: she knows what she is doing, she is burning wood. On this more robust conception of intention, she claims her intention as an end; her intention, to burn wood, is expressive of some interest she has in the realization of the end. That interest in turn is graspable by the agent in light of some view of her well-being or *Wohl* (PR §123).[19] She wants to burn the wood because she wants to tidy the garden, and keeping things tidy is a reason for her because the end satisfies her; this is how she sees her well-being. Her willing's orientation toward her conception of well-being is what gives her a reason for doing whatever she sets out to do. While *Wohl*-type considerations give reasons to any agent to pursue ends (PR §123), these are not infallible. The phenomenon of self-reproach (PR §125) illustrates this. *Wohl* then is not merely a subjective concept. *Wohl* shows an end as worth pursuing by showing it as *Wohl*-promoting or *Wohl*-expressive or *Wohl*-compatible. The difference between "end *e* looks to her worth pursuing" and "end *e* is really worth pursuing" allows Hegel to ratchet up the ownership conditions: if the agent gets her *Wohl* wrong, and realizes this, then she effectively disowns her action (this is why self-reproach matters), while if she gets it right, and knows this, then *Wohl* is a candidate at least for goodness or *das Gute* (PR §129). The question is how this connection to goodness can be established.

---

[19] *Wohl* has a subjective procedural side, reasoning about what makes the subject feel good, and an objective content-full side, about whether the upshot is *Wohl*-promoting/expressive/compatible. For Hegel, who is exploiting here an ambiguity in empiricist and eudaimonist conceptions of 'good', the two pairs are conceptually, not ontologically, distinct.

22.2.3. An end is presented to the agent as worth pursuing, if it links up with *the* good

Clearly reasoning about the *Wohl* can be good or not; in some borderline cases, bad reasoning may be practically indistinguishable from absence of reasoning. The key claim is that the agent's view of *her* good ties up with an objective conception of the good because good practical reasoning is sound reasoning about the good. Roughly, the thought seems to be this: either the agent gets the goodness of an end right, in which case it is not subjective, or she gets it wrong, in which case it is not good. The question is how we get objective worth or goodness from well-being.

First, though, let us start with a subsidiary issue: it looks as if we can disown all foolish and bad actions. If disowning is refusal of responsibility for the action, this would be troubling and would count against the account. But disowning can also be a matter of repentance, or at least an indication that the agent does not persist in affirming the foolish or wrong thing she did. I suspect that this sense is what Hegel is driving at. Ownership can be seen then as consonant with the earlier discussion about the actual: it implies rational vindication of the worth of the action, or conversely the availability to the agent of a better self, or "cognizance [*Kenntnis*] of the value which that action has in this objectivity" (PR §132). From this perspective, disowning would amount to confirming that some action the agent performed lacks worth.

With respect to the connection between well-being and good, the notion of 'subjective *value* and *interest*' (PR §122) is crucial. The agent lights a fire because she wants to burn some old wood. Her interest is in burning the wood. This interest is not final; she wants to burn the wood because she wants to tidy her garden. The interest in a tidy garden is in turn relative to some other end that has subjective worth for her. Just like the chains of causes, which tend to evacuate the agent from the deed, these chains of justifications tend to evacuate the end from the action, since they reduce the action to a mere 'means', insofar as the end "is a finite one, it may in turn be reduced to a means to some further intention, and so on in an infinite progression" (PR §122). The assumption is that if we reach no final reason, we have no justification for the action. For reasons to play their justificatory role, they must link up to some conception of the good that allows the series to end. Otherwise reasoning would end arbitrarily, or with a reason that is the equivalent of stomping one's foot: "I just want!" For Hegel this kind of brute fact about wanting threatens to corrode willing. Others may look at this more kindly and accept it as a fact of human desire. For our purposes, this argument against what he calls 'abstract', that is, content-neutral, practical reasoning matters because it introduces the idea of a final good into the account: "The relation of the good to the particular subject is that the good is the *essential* character of the subject's will" (PR §133).

22.3. The Good and the Actual

Two worries may arise regarding the relation between will and *das Gute* outlined in the previous section. The first is expressed in the following quote by Bernard Williams:

> In any ordinary understanding of *good*, surely, an extra step is taken if you go from saying that you want something or have decided to pursue it to saying that it is good, or (more to the point) that it is good that you should have it.[20]

Williams points out that wanting and judging something to be good, or good to have, are two different things. Although on Hegel's account, wanting and judging to be good can fall apart, they do so only in defective instances of actions. If Williams is right, these instances show something important about willing, that it has no essence, that it is mere want. The second worry is that *Wohl* need not connect to an objective, singular and terminal conception of the good, *das Gute*.

Among recent interpretations of Hegel's practical philosophy, Robert Pippin's 'self-constitution'[21] model offers a promising way to address these concerns. The position has obvious affinities to Christine Korsgaard's interpretation of Kant; both are constructivist and naturalist.[22] Pippin's naturalism requires accepting that "we simply have the wants and desires and passions and limitations that we do."[23] These are natural facts about human beings; they do not ground values and are not in themselves normative.[24] The constructivism of the self-constitution view requires that there are no mind-independent normative and evaluative facts. Evaluative concepts and norms do not exist apart from the practices to which they apply and which exemplify them. Such practices in turn exist because human societies and cultures exist that shape them and are shaped by them; "we alone (collectively, over time) can be responsible for the norms that direct our lives."[25] That human beings are what they make of themselves as social beings is stating a fact about what is necessary for human life, it is a natural fact with social content; this is crucial for Hegelian self-constitutivists.[26]

---

[20] Williams, *Ethics and the Limits of Philosophy*, 58; see too 210 n. 9.

[21] Pippin, *Hegel's Practical Philosophy*, 19.

[22] See Korsgaard, *Essays on Practical Reason and Moral Psychology*. For the basic commitments of self-constitution in Hegel, see Pippin, *Hegel's Practical Philosophy*, *The Persistence of Subjectivity*, and *Idealism as Modernism*; see too Speight, *Hegel, Literature and Agency*. The naturalism is consistent with Williams, *Ethics and the Limits of Philosophy*, 121–122.

[23] Pippin, *Hegel's Practical Philosophy*, 115

[24] It would be a 'fundamental misunderstanding' to take as the truth "the *starting point* in the *natural* development or the *history* of an individual in the process of self-formation" (SL 12.21–22/519). See also the discussion of life in E §221 and E §222. Hegel later both acknowledges organic life (E§350) and argues for an overcoming of nature by mind (E §376) that is simultaneously a recognition of our natural being (E §376A).

[25] Pippin, *Hegel's Practical Philosophy*, 150.

[26] See Pinkard, *Hegel's Naturalism*, 5 and 47; Yeomans, *Freedom and Reflection*, 57; Pippin, *The Persistence of Subjectivity*, 219; and Marmasse, *Force et fragilité des normes*, 45.

With these assumptions in place, the self-constitutivist can offer two different answers to Williams. The first starts with the observation that the wants of human beings *qua* natural beings originate and are satisfied within social contexts.[27] Social contexts are effectively normative contexts, given the self-constitutivist conception of the practices that make up societies and cultures. Given this, any expression of want, either in a statement, "I want this," or in a doing, can in principle and without exception be subject to evaluative and normative questioning by others just by virtue of the want's social, public aspect. On this view, to want is to be liable to evaluative and normative reflection, whether the desiring individual has undertaken that step herself or not; she cannot decline this liability without declining membership in the social context in which her wanting places her. In her answer to Williams, the self-constitutivist does not challenge the substance of Williams's claim, but merely its importance: what matters is that all wants are *apt* for evaluation about goodness.

The second answer straightforwardly contradicts Williams. It depends on an ontological claim about wants: no want is mere want, even if it appears as such to the desiring agent. The argument goes like this: social context is a condition for reflection about what is to count as appropriate or good, and such reflection guides individuals "to constrain or to elect to satisfy those urges."[28] Any want or urge, whether it explicitly appears as such to specific agents, has a value. Wants or urges have an integral evaluative aspect because agents constitute themselves as agents by reflecting about what counts as appropriate or good to want. Another way of saying this is that responsiveness to values and norms (and so possession and exercise of the capacity to make judgments of goodness) is a necessary condition for wanting by humans *qua* social beings; wanting is a practical achievement of 'minded' animals.[29] Although this view of human wants appears quite ambitious, it need not be, if we see it as contextualizing wants in human societies in a way that chimes with Williams's broader meta-ethical commitments without being overly theoretically taxing.

Let us grant that the self-constitutivist has the resources to respond to Williams, does she also show that the essence of willing is the good? If *das Gute* is whatever has the role of directing willing,[30] then it seems that the lines between what is good for the agent, what is satisfying for the well-socialized agent, and what is socially acceptable blend into one another, allowing no alternative conception of the objective good. We can have 'good for'—an agent or a collective—but no objective, singular, and terminal conception of the good. Given the denial of mind-independent normative and evaluative facts, the

---

[27] Pippin, *Hegel's Practical Philosophy*, 169; *Idealism as Modernism*, 425 and 448; and Pinkard, *Hegel's Naturalism*, 62–63.

[28] Pippin, *Hegel's Practical Philosophy*, 115. Both Pippin and Pinkard are interested in the normative rather than evaluative nature of such reflection; for this portion of the argument this does not matter since the reflection in question is about whether "any of the motivations of his animal nature deserve to be put to practice" (Pinkard, *Hegel's Naturalism*, 63).

[29] Pinkard, *Hegel's Naturalism*, 5 and 30.

[30] See Pippin, *Hegel's Practical Philosophy*, 19; *The Persistence of Subjectivity*, 219; and *Idealism as Modernism*, 163.

self-constitutivist can stand her ground and insist that it makes no sense to speak of the good outside *some* collective which gives the concept its application. For the Hegelian self-constitutivist, this is no obstacle to claiming that something is objectively good since the distinctions between subjective and objective, good and no good, are perfectly possible within particular instances of ethical life. The upshot of "Morality" is that we should abandon talk about the good and consider candidate goods within ethical life; we can only have goods and judge them as such relative to our *sittlich* concerns and situation.[31] To test this interpretation, we may turn to a text where Hegel discusses explicitly the idea of the good, in the penultimate chapter of *The Science of Logic*, "The Idea of Cognition," which consists of two sections, "The Idea of the True" and "The Idea of the Good."[32]

Hegel begins the section by stating that the good appears "with the worth of the universal because it is intrinsically itself the totality of the concept" (SL 12.231/729, translation altered). The self-constitutivist might seek to explain this characterization of the good by offering an aggregative interpretation of 'totality of the concept'. The summation of various local evaluations of goodness permits us to form a conception of *the* good without sacrificing the commitment to local *sittlich* concerns. The question is how we can identify mistaken evaluations in order to neutralize them in the summing up.[33] To do this, we need to know for sure that they are mistakes. This, however, would require prior knowledge of the good. Note, however, that we are not entirely bereft when it comes to judging goodness, even if we may not claim to possess the good in its totality. Here is how the self-constitutivist might cast the matter. An end is what appears as worth pursuing to an agent and it appears as worth pursuing because of some idea of goodness that structures the agent's willing. This idea of goodness in turn depends on the nexus of evaluations to which the agent is sensitive by virtue of her membership in the structures of ethical life. Of course, the availability of the self-constitutivist position presupposes successfully blocking pervasive skepticism about evaluations; in the language of the *Logic*, evaluations must *already* possess the "the worth of the universal" (SL 12.231/729). But then the self-constitutivist might ask whether pervasive skepticism even makes sense; from the worldly perspective we inhabit, we can only make sense of

[31] This seems to be Pippin's conclusion in *Idealism as Modernism*, 417–450. Moyar argues in a way that is more sympathetic and accommodating of Williams, by effectively absorbing *das Gute* into other considerations determining agential identity (*Hegel's Conscience*, 74–76).

[32] In the *Encyclopedia Logic* the structure is similar; however, there is greater emphasis on willing both in the introductory remarks on cognition (E §225) and in the analysis of the good proper (E §§233–234). In the *Philosophy of Right* Hegel writes about the concept of the will (PR §129) and then the essence of the will (PR §133) in a way that reverses the logical progression from essence to concept. This can be explained if we consider the progression of the argument within the *Philosophy of Right* where the aim is to move from 'the abstract character of the good' (PR §136) to a discussion of conscience (PR §137) and thence to ethical life.

[33] There are two further alternatives: all valuations are correct or acceptable, but this cannot be Hegel's view because it is a form of 'finitism', which he explicitly condemns; or the aggregative process is self-correcting (this is the view I associate with the rationalist interpretation of Hegel's conception of the good).

specific worries relative to this or that judgment about the good, this or that action, this or that practice. The position is consistent. The question is whether this interpretation captures the sense of universality Hegel attributes to the idea of the good as it 'appears' (*auftreten*).

To examine this, we need to look more carefully at Hegel's argument here. The main task of the section is to undermine the idea that the world is 'a nullity' devoid of worth (SL 12.233/732).[34] Hegel argues that this is the source of all conceptual mistakes about the good. On the one hand, we end up with valuations being thought of as merely subjective:

> [T]he *subjective attitude* of the objective concept is reproduced and perpetuated, with the result that the *finitude* of the good, with respect to both content and form, appears as the abiding truth. (SL 12.235/733)

One way out of the problem is to accept the perspectival nature of the good; after all, pervasive skepticism is most potent when the idea of the good as 'objective' is in play (SL 12.234/732). Hegel does not opt for this quick way out; rather, he diagnoses a problem in the objective concept's "own view of itself" (SL 12.235/733). The aim of objective notions of goodness is to connect it with truth.[35] One option is to say that goodness makes contact necessarily with non-evaluative 'given' features of the world (SL 12.231/731). Such non-evaluative features can be differently evaluated, however. This exacerbates the skeptical worry that valuing is something subjective and individual (SL 12.234/732).[36] So we need a different understanding of the relation between truth and goodness. What we want is for evaluations to be true *qua* evaluations and for human knowers to have the means to identify the true ones. At the same time, though, we want the idea of the good to direct practical thought, not just to be a matter of identifying something correctly; in Hegel's words, 'what is' must be seen as "altered by the activity of the objective concept" (SL 12.235/733). To conceive of what is as altered by the activity of the objective Notion, we need conception of actuality as the realization of the 'absolute end' (SL 12.235/733). This absolute end just is the idea of the good as neither subjective, and so not truth-evaluable, nor objective, and so potentially inert, but rather as the "Idea of the Notion that is determined in and for itself" or 'absolute Idea' (SL 12.235/733).

To assess the good in this its final incarnation, we need to get a better sense of the content conveyed through this highly abstract analysis. In the "Morality" section of the

---

[34] See too the criticism of direction of fit in the *Encyclopedia Logic*: 'The subjective idea . . . is the Good. Its drive to self-realization is . . . the reverse of the idea of truth and rather directed towards moulding the world it finds before it into a shape conformable to its purposed End. This Volition has on the one hand the certitude of the nothingness of the presupposed object; but on the other it presupposes the purposed End of the Good to be a mere subjective idea' (E §233).

[35] The idea of the good, Hegel says, "can find its completion only in the idea of the true" (SL 12.233/732). Hegel plays here with the idea of objective reality as given being a mere 'filling [*Erfüllung*]' (see also SL 12.231/729) and as true value realization or fulfillment *Ergänzung* of the good. Di Giovanni uses 'completion', Miller 'integration' for the latter.

[36] Hegel refers here to the act, not the valuing, but the valuing of the act parallels the valuing of the end.

Philosophy of Right, the discussion of willing the good is preparatory for the discussion of actual judgments of goodness made by more or less skilled judges in "Ethical Life." By contrast, in the *Logic*, the analysis of the Idea of the good abstracts from the contents of putative judgments in order to show how such judgments can be right or the 'Notion' of good objective. What connects the two is the thought that moral willing is basic: "The relation of the good to the particular subject is that the good is the *essential* character of the subject's will" (PR §133). The self-constitutivist makes sense of this demanding conception of willing by minimizing the force of the good in it: the good is partly a formal matter of self-constitution and partly acknowledgment of plural local goods that enable the agent to constitute herself as such. The final section examines whether this is the best way to capture the meta-ethical commitments of the discussion of 'absolute end'.

22.4. The End and the Idea

In the *Logic*, the absolute end is presented as a solution to the subjectivist/objectivist see-saw. The objectivist seeks to define the good as a feature of the world; the good-making features of willing correspond to or reflect this objective good. The subjectivist seeks to account for the practical aspect of goodness as an end realized by agents, which results in the identification of 'good-making' as 'willed' or 'pursued'. The absolute end bridges the gap with the thought of an end worth pursuing, full stop. There are at least four ways of spelling out the meta-ethical commitments of this position:

1. *Contextualist-particularist.* The very abstraction of the description of the absolute end shows that we can only speak sensibly about particular ends we judge to be worth pursuing. For each particular end there are going to be specific things to be said for or against it. The reasons agents adduce for doing things can be judged, criticized, and vindicated contextually, and this is all we can say about objective goodness.[37] There is no trans-historical absolute; the absolute is always some end that appears to some agent as worth pursuing, full stop.

2. *Valuing as attitude.* Granted that we should not seek to speak of goodness as such, abstracted from ends we deem worth pursuing. However, when we speak of particular ends as worth pursuing, we already do more than that. Implicit in practices of moral evaluation and normative justification is an action-guiding aspect, that what is judged as good or right is to be done, which is what Hegel seeks to convey by describing the Idea as self-determining.[38]

---

[37] That seems to fit (β) and (γ) in PR §113, and PR §141. On contextualism and particularism, see Moyar, *Hegel's Conscience*.

[38] Hegel acknowledges the relevance of 'interest' in moral willing, which captures subjective involvement but also commitment to the universal content of the aim (E §475); see too the description of ethical life as "a subjective disposition, but of that right which has being in itself" (PR §141R).

3. *Self-constitutivist.* Granted that when we speak of particular ends, which we judge to be worth pursuing, we already do more than that. What we do is constitute ourselves as agents; it is because we aim at this further end that we have the practical commitments we do, and conversely through our various practical pursuits we constitute ourselves as agents.[39] The Idea is self-determining, because it is the Idea of ourselves as minded agents.

4. *Rationalist.* Granted that when we speak of specific ends, which we judge to be worth pursuing, we already do more than that. We place our faith in our rational capacities and in a progressive rational teleology that supports the practices of criticizing and correcting our reasons for doing things, guaranteeing that we get it right in the long run. The Idea is actualized through such progressive teleology.

The first two positions would struggle with the idea of universality that Hegel associates with both good and willing (PR §103, §141; see too E §469, SL 12.231–2/730), the contextualist-particularist because the view is formulated in antipathy to universalist claims, the valuing as an attitude because it picks out a feature of evaluative and normative assessments, and it does not seem concerned with universality as content of the good or end of the will. This leaves us with the self-constitutivist and the rationalist interpretations. Each gives a different slant to Hegel's universalist commitments. To see this, we need to return to some of the larger issues about systematicity and idealism broached in section 22.1.

The attempt to explain the idealism and so the claim about the rationality of the actual led us to a holistic conception of philosophical vindication of specific phenomena by reference to their relation to other phenomena. We then encountered the problem of potential dissolution of any content presented for philosophical analysis and vindication into mere relations. On the self-constitutivist interpretation, relations are indeed primary in terms of what can be vindicated and asserted. The self-determining Idea states this truth economically and succinctly. In forming practical thoughts, we find ourselves in an axiological circle: the value concepts we use are the product of our collective self-authorship. Not all evaluations survive in the long run; some become obsolete, a loss retrospectively rationalized in the ongoing process of collective self-authorship. In other words, the activity of minded beings such as ourselves consists fundamentally in identifying, rejecting, and vindicating *prima facie* goods. Such vindication is never itself absolute; what matters is the activity, not the goods, since in the long run they all turn out to be *prima facie*. Universality is a feature of the process of self-constitution, not of the content of willing. The totality of the Notion is always relative; it means the sum of our best current judgments about the good, those that survive each retrospectively rationalizing episode or stage. The position is modest in that it does not presume to allow us to assert any content as good beyond our practices of practical judgment, which is just to restate that goodness is tied to practices.

---

[39] See: "the subject now exists as *free, universal self-identity*" (SL 12.235/733).

The rationalist, by contrast, sees the dissolution into relations as a serious problem and seeks to avert it by conceiving the Idea substantively as a rational end that shapes the entire system, "as an objective world whose inner ground and actual subsistence is rather the concept" (SL 12.235/734). The rationalist shares with the self-constitutivist the belief that values and norms address us as subjects; the issue is explaining what is a subject in this context. The rationalist has a somewhat more ambitious conception of subjectivity than the self-constitutivist. She starts with a conception of reality as a whole consisting of differentiated processes, including interaction of massive objects, organic generation, and episodes of practical thought. These are continuous and dynamically connected. There are no gaps. Subject is what becomes of this reality as a whole. What allows for this is a progressive teleology aimed at the realization of the absolute end. If we understand this as an ontological claim, it states that every layer of the whole is subject to normative forces and therefore appraisal. If we understand this as a statement within a closed system, then this progressive teleology is a conceptual process through which we attain ever more distinct and perspicuous evaluative and normative concepts. If we understand this as descriptive of a historical process that contains but also exceeds the system, the claim is that as rational animals we get better at appreciating where we stand within the whole in which we find ourselves, and so we get progressively better in our evaluations of our ends and in how best to bring them about. [40] In any case, the rationalist can assert universality as a feature of content of the absolute end, which amounts to saying that the good prevails.

It is not my purpose here to adjudicate between different versions of the rationalist interpretation, or between it and the self-constitutivist one. In different ways, each option leads beyond moral philosophy, which is the topic of this chapter. But it is paying attention to Hegel's positive argument about moral willing that led us here. We are now in a position to appreciate the role of that argument, not just as a steppingstone to the substantive ethics of "Ethical Life," but as essential to the larger project, which aims to show the actuality of the good.

WORKS CITED

Primary Texts

Hegel, G. W. F. *Encyclopedia of Philosophical Sciences* (*1830*) [E], *Part I, Logic*, translated by W. Wallace. Oxford: Clarendon, 1975.

Hegel, G. W. F. *Encyclopedia of Philosophical Sciences* (*1830*) [E], *Part III, Philosophy of Mind*, translated by A. V. Miller with the Michelet (1847) *Zusätze*. Oxford: Clarendon, 1971.

Hegel, G. W. F. *Lectures on the History of Philosophy* [LHP], translated by E. Haldane. New York: Humanities Press, 1968.

[40] Hegel leaves it to Aristotle to spell it out at the end of the *Encyclopedia*: "for the actuality of thought is life, and God is that actuality; and God's self-dependent actuality is life most good and eternal" (E §557, and *Metaphysics* 1073a12).

Hegel, G. W. F. *The Phenomenology of Spirit* [PS], translated by Terry Pinkard. 2010. Draft available online http://terrypinkard.weebly.com/phenomenology-of-spirit-page.html

Secondary Literature

Ameriks, Karl. "Hegel and Idealism." *Monist* 74, no. 3 (1991): 386–403.

Bradley, F. H. *Appearance and Reality*. Oxford: Clarendon Press, 1930.

Brooks, Thom. *Hegel's Political Philosophy: A Systematic Reading of the Philosophy of Right*. Edinburgh: Edinburgh University Press, 2012.

Brudner, Alan S. "The Significance of Hegel's 'Prefatory Lectures on the Philosophy of Law' followed by translations of the 'Prefatory Lectures 1818–19, 1822–23, 1824–5." *Clio* 8, no. 1 (1978): 41–70.

Candlish, S. *The Russell/Bradley Dispute and Its Significance for Twentieth-Century Philosophy*. London; New York: Palgrave Macmillan, 2007.

De Vries, W. *Hegel's Theory of Mental Activity*. Ithaca, NY: Cornell University Press, 1988.

Deligiorgi, K. "Doing without Agency: Hegel's Social Theory of Action," in *Hegel and Action*, edited by Arto Laitinen and Constantine Sandis. London; New York: Palgrave Macmillan, 2010, 97–118.

Deligiorgi, K. "Religion, Love, and Law: Hegel's Metaphysics of Morals," in *The Blackwell Companion to Hegel*, edited by Stephen Houlgate and Michael Baur. Oxford: Blackwell, 2012, 23–44.

Franco, Paul. *Hegel's Philosophy of Freedom*. New Haven, CT: Yale University Press, 2002.

Freyenhagen, Fabian. "Empty, Useless, and Dangerous? Recent Kantian Replies to the Empty Formalism Objection." *Hegel Bulletin* 63, no. 1–2 (2011): 163–186.

Gerber, Monica M., and Jonathan Jackson. "Retribution as Revenge and Retribution as Just Deserts." *Social Justice Research*, 26, no. 1 (2013): 61–80.

Hardimon, Michael O. *Hegel's Social Philosophy. The Project of Reconciliation*. Cambridge: Cambridge University Press, 1994.

Houlgate, Stephen. "Action, Right and Morality in Hegel's 'Philosophy of Right' in *Hegel and Action*, edited by Arto Laitinen and Constantine Sandis. London; New York: Palgrave Macmillan, 2010, 155–175.

Houlgate, Stephen. "Hegel, Rawls and the Rational State," in *Beyond Liberalism and Communitarianism: Studies in Hegel's Philosophy of Right*, edited by R. Williams. Albany: State University of New York Press, 2001, 249–273.

Houlgate, Stephen. *The Opening of Hegel's Logic*. West Lafayette, IN: Purdue University Press, 2006.

Korsgaard, Christine. *Essays on Practical Reason and Moral Psychology*. Oxford: Oxford University Press, 2008.

Lottenbach, Hans, and Sergio Tenenbaum. "Hegel's Critique of Kant in the Philosophy of Right." *Kant-Studien* 86 (1995): 211–230.

McCumber, J. *Understanding Hegel's Mature Critique of Kant*. Stanford, CA: Stanford University Press, 2014.

Marmasse, Gilles. *Force et fragilité des normes*. Paris: Presses Universitaires de France, 2011.

Moyar, Dean. *Hegel's Conscience*. Oxford: Oxford University Press, 2011.

Neuhouser, Frederick. *Foundations of Hegel's Social Theory: Actualizing Freedom*. Cambridge, MA: Harvard University Press, 2003.

Patten, Alan. *Hegel's Idea of Freedom*. Oxford: Oxford University Press, 2002.

Pinkard, Terry. *Hegel's Phenomenology: The Sociality of Reason.* Cambridge: Cambridge University Press, 1996.

Pinkard, Terry. *Hegel's Naturalism: Mind, Nature, and the Ends of Life.* Oxford: Oxford University Press, 2012.

Pinkard, Terry. "Self-Understanding and Self-Realizing Spirit in Hegelian Ethical Theory." *Philosophical Topics* 19, no. 2 (1991):71–98.

Pippin, Robert. *Hegel's Idealism: The Satisfactions of Self-Consciousness* Cambridge: Cambridge University Press, 1989.

Pippin, Robert. *Hegel's Practical Philosophy: Rational Agency as Ethical Life.* Cambridge: Cambridge University Press, 2008.

Pippin, Robert. *Idealism as Modernism: Hegelian Variations.* Cambridge: Cambridge University Press, 1997.

Pippin, Robert. *The Persistence of Subjectivity: On the Kantian Aftermath.* Cambridge: Cambridge University Press, 2005.

Priest, Stephen ed. *Hegel's Critique of Kant.* Oxford: Clarendon Press, 1987.

Quante, M. *Hegels Begriff der Handlung.* Stuttgard-Bad Canstatt: Frommann Holzboog, 1993.

Schick, Friderike. "Freedom and Necessity: The Transition to the Logic of the Concept in Hegel's *Science of Logic.*" *Hegel Bulletin* 68, no. 1 (2014): 84–99.

Sedgwick, Sally. *Hegel's Critique of Kant: From Dichotomy to Identity.* Oxford: Oxford University Press, 2012.

Speight, Allen. *Hegel, Literature and Agency.* Cambridge: Cambridge University Press, 2001.

Stern, R. "Hegel's Idealism," in *The Cambridge Companion to Hegel and to Nineteenth Century Philosophy,* edited by F. C. Beiser. Cambridge: Cambridge University Press, 2009, 135–173.

Stern, R. *Understanding Moral Obligation.* Cambridge: Cambridge University Press, 2011.

Taylor, Charles. *Hegel and Modern Society.* Cambridge: Cambridge University Press, 1979.

Vieweg, Klaus. *Das Denken der Freiheit. Hegels Grundlinien der Philosophie des Rechts.* Paderborn: Wilhelm Fink, 2012.

Walsh, W. H. *Hegelian Ethics.* New York: Garland, 1984.

Williams, Bernard. *Ethics and the Limits of Philosophy.* London: Fontana Collins, 1985.

Wood, Allen W. *Hegel's Ethical Thought.* Cambridge: Cambridge University Press, 1990.

Wood, Allen W., ed. *Hegel: Elements of the Philosophy of Right,* translated by H. B. Nisbet. Cambridge: Cambridge University Press, 1991.

Yeomans, Chris. *Freedom and Reflection: Hegel and the Logic of Agency.* Oxford: Oxford University Press, 2012.

CHAPTER 23

....

HEGEL'S LIBERAL, SOCIAL, AND 'ETHICAL' STATE

....

LUDWIG SIEP

MANY historians claim that the 'state' is something that belongs to the European modern age, and that it may come to an end with the end of that age.[1] With the first thesis Hegel agrees, although by distinguishing the 'modern' state (cf. PR §260) from the ancient he implicitly includes the latter in the concept of 'state'.[2] But he would consider the end of this state as a lapse into irrationality. He supports the modern state, yet he wants to correct modern, especially contractarian, concepts in political philosophy by drawing on the Aristotelian concept of 'polis'.[3] In PR §256 of the "Grundlinien" he certainly alludes to Aristotle's thesis that the state is '*physei proteron*', by nature prior to the individual and the family. He calls the state the 'true ground' and the 'first', both in reality and in the philosophical development of family, civil society, and the state in 'ethical life', the last part of the *Philosophy of Right*. This has a double meaning: 'in reality' here refers to the real historical life, where the state is the condition and guarantee of the normally peaceful existence of families and civil society. Even in the course of history itself, Hegel seems to assume that the state was prior to any sort of institutionalized family and civil—or market—society. But the second sense is even more important: the state is—like the Aristotelian polis—the 'telos', or 'destiny [*Bestimmung*]' of the less perfect unions or societies (*societates minores*) of family and civil society—or in the Aristotelian case of family (*oikos*) and village (*kome*). In Hegel's *Philosophy of Right* this has the sense of the state's being the fulfillment or 'realization' of the key concept of human society, namely freedom. The meaning of this thesis, however, remains controversial up to the present time. Is Hegel's state modern or traditional, liberal or authoritarian, or even

---

[1] Reinhard, *Geschichte der Staatsgewalt*, 535.

[2] The distinction occurs mostly in the lecture notes, see for instance the additions to PR §§182, 261, 279, 317.

[3] Regarding Hegel's reception of Aristotle's Politics, cf. Ilting, "Hegels Auseinandersetzung mit der aristotelischen Politik," 38–58; also Siep, "Hegels Rezeption der aristotelischen Politik," 59–76.

totalitarian? How does the state relate to the market economy and religion, its main rivals in modern times?

In the following, I will try to answer these questions by discussing the degree to which Hegel's state can be called liberal and social, and in which sense it is 'ethical'. The first attribute relates to the importance of individual rights and liberties—among them the market-liberties—in Hegel's state. The second concerns the way in which Hegel's state, particularly what he calls the state of 'necessity and understanding', has to care for the well-being of its citizens. Regarding this task, the state rivals and in some respects opposes the market society. The third attribute of the state, namely 'ethical', is a special term into which Hegel merges different meanings of 'custom', 'morality', and communal life. In that respect, the state has to come to terms with both the individual's social identity and her ultimate convictions. In this respect the state competes with religious institutions, especially churches, as sources of individual and social meaningfulness and as promoters of individual and common morality.

23.1. THE STATE AND THE RIGHTS OF THE INDIVIDUAL

In order to explain why and in what sense the state is the 'reality' or 'actuality [*Wirklichkeit*]' of 'concrete freedom', Hegel in PR §260 of the *Philosophy of Right* formulates a long and winding sentence of more than thirteen lines. I will draw on this sentence (three sentences in the English translation) in all parts of this chapter. Hegel writes,

> The state is the actuality of concrete freedom. But *concrete freedom* requires that personal individuality [*Einzelheit*] and its particular interests should reach their full *development* and gain *recognition of their right* for itself (within the system of the family and of civil society), and also that they should, on the one hand, *pass over* by their own activity into the interest of the universal, and on the other, knowingly and willingly acknowledge this universal interest even as their own *substantial spirit*, and *actively pursue it* as their *ultimate end*. The effect of this is that the universal does not attain validity or fulfilment without the interest, knowledge, and volition of the particular, and that individuals do not live as private persons merely for these particular interests without at the same time directing their will to a universal end [*in und für das Allgemeine wollen*] and acting in conscious awareness of this end. (PR §260)

For the first section I emphasize the first lines, namely the statement that concrete freedom consists in the complete development and recognition of the right of the personal individuality "within the system of the family and of civil society." To this right belongs the whole content of the first section of the *Philosophy of Right*, namely "Abstract Right," as well as the second, "Morality." In this latter section Hegel attempts a synthesis of two subjects that Kant had taken pains to distinguish and keep apart, namely right and well-being (*Wohl*). The furthering of both without an illiberal paternalism is the task of family, civil society, and the state, which are analyzed in the third section of the book under the title "Ethical Life [*Sittlichkeit*]".

Abstract right, as is well known, deals with the claim—both a right and a duty—of an individual to be treated as a 'person'. 'Person' in this context is an individual embodied actor, equally free as all other persons to act and use physical means according to his decisions. The freedom to 'lay one's will' in external objects is the core of the property rights that are mutually and by common institutions granted to every person.[4] These rights are independent of the actual use of the objects owned and of other limitations stemming from the owner's intentions. They include voluntary exchange (contract), but also the destruction of one's private property—following Roman law, Hegel regards the right of a person regarding her own property as limitless. Different from Roman law, however, there are no property rights regarding other persons (for instance, children and servants), not even relations "akin to right to Things" (Kant, MM, §§22 ff.).

The whole sphere of abstract right is developed, realized, and institutionalized within civil society. This is the subject of Hegel's chapter on the administration of justice [*Rechtspflege*] in the second section of "Civil Society." The freedom of trade within a market society, as well as the self-administration of professional estates, presupposes the general functioning of law in social life. 'General' here has to be distinguished from 'mechanical' in the sense in which Fichte or Schelling proposed the system of law to work—according to which the perfect sanctioning and preventing of violations of the law would in the end make them disappear altogether. Free spiritual life includes those violations and their 'reversals' by punishment and the reintegration of the criminal.[5] The way the administration of justice works, especially the judicial system, has to account for the personal and historical circumstances of a culprit (PR §§218, 223).

The rights of persons in civil society, however, extend much further. They include the development of one's 'particularity' by choosing a profession or establishing one's own enterprise. In this respect Hegel argues against Fichte's 'Closed commercial system' (1800) and his state-organized economy lacking a free market for jobs and commodities. Hegel's economic theory is much more liberal, even at the cost of greater risks of unemployment and crises in the market.[6] His concept of freedom demands this space of

---

[4] In general, every conscious and sane [*zurechnungsfähig*] human being qualifies as a person. However, Hegel distinguishes between human rights and both passive and active civil rights (cf. later discussion in this chapter). Regarding Hegel's conception of property rights, cf. Ritter, "Person und Eigentum," 55–72; Waldron, *The Right to Private Property*; Mohseni, *Abstrakte Freiheit*.

[5] As to Hegel's conception of penal law, cf. Mohr, "Unrecht und Strafe (PR §§ 82–104)," 83–110; and Primoratz, *Banquos Geist. Hegels Theorie der Strafe*. In my view, there is a lesson to learn from Hegel's conception of penal law for modern discussions on 'neuro-determinism' and its consequences for criminal law, but I cannot go into that here.

[6] Regarding Hegel's economic theory, cf. Herzog, *Inventing the Market: Smith, Hegel, and Political Theory*. For the development and ethical relevance of Hegel's economic thought, cf. Neschen, *Ethik und Ökonomie in Hegels Philosophie und in modernen wirtschaftsethischen Entwürfen*.

choosing and realizing a particular life plan. Although he realizes the necessity of state interference in the market, the individual rights that the state has to protect include economic freedom.

The self-realization of the particular individual in civil society comprises not only the individual's legal personality and the pursuing of her plans. Self-realization refers to the 'moral' personality as well. The moral personality has the right to act according to its own intentions and criteria of the good. As a rational being, these criteria are not 'solipsistic' but contain conceptions of the general good, including the well-being of everybody (PR §134). The pursuit of one's personal well-being and that of society are not mutually exclusive. Hegel agrees with the 'classical' economic theory that a market system within the framework of law and of some 'steering capacities' both by professional organizations and the state combines the pursuit of private interests and the common 'wealth'. This is *one* meaning of the claim in PR §260 that the individual and particular should "*pass over* by their own activity into the interest of the universal" (PR §260). Hegel refers not only to the invisible hand of market processes but also to the accommodation to customs of behavior and fashion and to the needs and demands of market participants.

However, this is only one side of the transformation of the self-realization of the particular person into a universal interest and will. The other side has to be carried out with her conscious will—or her moral personality. 'Becoming real' demands the acquisition of competences and virtue in order to be recognized in a group. The most basic type is the family, and the more developed type, requiring education and special skills, is the professional estate. Only as such a member can the moral concepts of the good be 'sustainably' realized and mutually recognized (cf. PR §207). On a higher level, the citizens of a state, and especially the members of its administration, actively and consciously pursue the common interest of an institutionalized community. Here the 'substantial spirit' of the community is recognized as the common goal. However, 'recognized' signifies that this is not a relation of obedience, but rather one of conscious agreement and support.

The two elements—namely the pursuit of one's own interests and conceptions of the good within the 'system' of a society organized by division of labor and market relations on the one hand, and the conscious and voluntary sustainment of the common tasks and spirit on the other—constitute what Hegel calls the 'enormous strength and depth' of the 'modern state'. It is modern in contrast to the ancient and feudal societies in which one's status is determined by birth (*Geburtsstand*) and in which one's roles and tasks are justified with reference to tradition. In this complex sense the Hegelian state is liberal: granting personal rights, the leeway to pursue one's interests and life plans, to realize one's conceptions of the good, and to give assent to required duties. All these rights and claims, however, are not without limits and counterparts, some of which, as we will see, are far from what we would call 'liberal' today.

23.2. THE STATE AND THE WELL-BEING
OF INDIVIDUALS AND GROUPS

At the end of the second section of "Morality" (PR §127), Hegel calls the 'totality' of the particular interests of the natural will of a person the 'personal existence as life'. This totality can clash with abstract right in cases where legal requirements of contract partners undermine the means to sustain this life. Hegel argues that it is justified in these cases to allow for an emergency law (as many legal systems do) to secure the debtor's means to sustain his life. In Hegel's interpretation, this shows that both strict private law and well-being are one-sided and 'finite'. Therefore on all higher levels of the *Philosophy of Right* both claims have to be mediated.

In consequence, all three levels of Ethical life—family, civil society, and state—have tasks regarding the welfare of their members. In the family the emphasis lies on the fulfillment of physical needs, and the meeting of emotional and intellectual demands, including the demand for recognition of one's natural properties and inclinations. In civil society, above all its professional estates and organizations, the well-being in question is that of gaining and securing the competences and means to sustain a respected life as a member. Since these means depend on physical well-being (especially health) and on some degree of independence from private and public catastrophes, professional security institutions—such as insurances, savings banks, chambers of commerce, and so on—are needed (cf. PR §§251–252). Without these means and securities, all legal claims remain 'on paper'.

However, as a follower of liberal economic theories, Hegel holds—for reasons explained earlier—that these institutions and organizations have to keep intact the basic rights of free choice of professions and enterprises. There is no way back to a strict limitation of the labor market by guilds, or forward to an illiberal future of state-directed economies. Only prudent advice from the oversight of the labor market is compatible with the freedom of the particularity (PR §§252, 254). In addition, the professional organizations get some influence in the state legislation—on the level of the constitutional state (PR §308). But the "monopoly of legal physical force" (Max Weber) remains with the state. Therefore a clash between property rights and the demands of the needy on this level can only be solved by the state.

Since Hegel is aware of the instability of the market society, its crises of overproduction and insufficient demand, which were elaborated for instance by Sismondi, it is clear to him that neither the family nor the professional organizations are able to deal with the 'social' tasks of liberal states. However, his solution is not simply a sort of liberal welfare state. Although his conception of the rational constitutional order of the state arises from a sort of synthesis and transformation of the family and civil society (cf. PR §256), this transformation has at least two aspects. The first is the stabilizing involvement of the state administration in the market society. In this respect, the state functions remain that of a—as he calls it—state of necessity and understanding (Not- und Verstandesstaat, PR §183). The second, and for Hegel higher, form of transformation is that of ethical life itself, including the mentality and 'identity' of its members, into that of the true life and mentality of an 'ethical' state. As will be seen later, from a contemporary view the former aspect is much more modern than the latter. But this was not the case in the age of the French Revolution and all its constitutional, social, and (civil) religious implications.

As to the first aspect, Hegel analyzes different forms of crises within civil society. The outcome may be that "a large mass of people sinks below the level of a certain standard of living" (PR §244). This process "makes it much easier for disproportionate wealth to be concentrated in a few hands" (PR §244). In addition to a lot of indirect measures supporting the market system—from the illumination of roads and the establishment of public hospitals (PR §242) through supporting foreign commerce (PR §§236, 247)—the social state has to protect the masses against[7] the 'particular interests and purposes' (PR §249). To this end it may interfere in private property by taxation ('poor rates' PR §245) or the fixation of prices for vital food (PR §236). However, the principal right of private property and the requirement to earn one's life by personal effort (PR §245) has to be maintained. In modern terms, we might classify this role of the state as 'social-democratic', even if in some respects the state as a second family transcends modern non-paternalistic measures and institutions (cf. PR §§241, 245): The state's public almshouses have the task of curing the 'rabble' of their laziness and other vices.

The more important ethical transformation, however, refers to the general mentality of self-interest that governs civil society. The implicit awareness of the common good and even the intentional activity of the professional associations and the state administration toward the common good are not sufficient in this respect. The view of the state as a means to secure one's long-term interest in self-preservation and the pursuit of happiness, the rationale of every contract theory of the state, is insufficient. It misses the true nature of humans as spiritual beings and their ethical 'destiny'. It confuses, in Hegel's famous words, the state with civil society (PR §258R). A state fulfilling the 'political nature', to put it in Aristotelian terms (or ethical freedom, as Hegel calls it), is one in which the "*union* as such is itself the true content and end, and the destiny [*Bestimmung*] of individuals [*Individuen*] is to lead a universal life" (PR §258R). In his Jena writings Hegel translated the Greek 'politeuein' as 'leading a life devoted to the public affairs'[8]—thus 'universal' is not to be taken as 'cosmopolitan', but rather as a particular polis or state.

That the 'true' state is not merely the social 'stabilization' of civil society does not mean, however, that it is external to civil society or even a different organization from the liberal and social state. In one sense, the state belongs to civil society and is incorporated in

---

[7] The German *von* in this context has the meaning of 'against' (this was mistaken in the Knox translation).

[8] In German, *dem öffentlichen ganz gehöriges Leben führen*. In Hegel, "Ueber die wissenschaftlichen Behandlungsarten des Naturrechts," 455.

it—in another, civil society is itself part of the state, not only a part of its order and sovereign power, but also a part of its 'idea'. There is no doubt that the administration that is necessary to make civil society work is the same which is from another point of view treated in the 'ethical' state as 'government [*Regierung*]'. This new point of view on the same institution and legal structure refers to its belonging to, and functioning within, the 'organism' of the state's constitution. At the same time, civil society and its 'inherent' state functions are a necessary 'moment' of the idea of the state (PR §256 R).

To clarify this relation, it is necessary to take a closer look at Hegel's remark to the final paragraph of civil society (PR §256 R). It contains some very fundamental and intricate formulations regarding the transition from civil society to the ethical state, or 'the state' as the full-blown result of its own teleological development.

In a piece of true Hegel terminology, this text claims that the idea of the state 'divides [*dirimiert*]' itself into family and civil society. To explain this statement one would have to go deeply into the 'science of logic', the method of which structures the argument of the *Philosophy of Right* (cf. PR §§2, 31, 141) as well as that of all other parts of the system. For my purposes I have to abbreviate this explanation. Just as 'the idea' within the logic is the self-reflection of the complete development of all fundamental categories of being and thinking, the idea of the state is the same self-reflection within the field of the 'determinations of freedom' (PR §§29–32). Determination here means at the same time (1) the unfolding of the implications of this concept, (2) its institutional realization (since 'social' freedom is possible only within institutions), and (3) its awareness in freely acting persons.

In all three senses, Hegel claims, family and civil society are themselves essential moments of the idea of the state, but at the same time their shortcomings as insufficient realizations of this idea prove the necessity to proceed to the true instantiation of the idea. They are both institutions mediating between the particular needs, interests, and rights of their members and the requirements of a lasting existence and function of the respective institution (or in the case of civil society, different interacting institutions). To devote themselves to the stability and 'flourishing' of the institution is an essential part of their members' destiny and fulfillment. But since the family—which in its modern sense[9] dissolves itself with the legal independence or the death of its members (PR §§177–180)—and civil society with its crises both are in need of an institution guaranteeing their stable functioning, this proves the necessity of the state. This necessity refers not only to the functional necessity but even more to the realization of the meaning of freedom. For the individuals and their 'political nature', freedom requires their 'public life' within an autonomous institution; for the all-encompassing institution of the state, freedom means a rational will directed at itself as its goal.

---

[9] As has often been remarked, Hegel deals with the modern bourgeois 'nuclear family' (*bürgerliche Kleinfamilie*), more or less limited to one or a few generations, not with the aristocratic family lasting for centuries or the large agricultural family whose 'oikos' (house, land, production) may also last for a long period of time. For a modern critical interpretation of Hegel's conception of the family, cf. Brauer, *Natur und Sittlichkeit, Die Familie in Hegels Rechtsphilosophie*.

Hegel calls the demonstration of this necessity the 'scientific proof' (PR §256) of the concept of state. Here he does not refer to the development of the logical categories 'behind' the presentation of the evolving forms of ethical life. However, the mutual presupposition of family, civil society, and state, and the latter's emergence as the 'true ground' and the overcoming of the diremption (*Entzweiung*) within civil society certainly follow a logical structure as well. It is important not to understand this overcoming as an institutional solution for the economic, social, and mental bifurcation of civil society—that is, the division between common property and private interests, the classes of the rich and the poor, the mentality of righteousness versus that of vicissitude and disloyalty, and so on. The 'ethical' state does not provide a more rational economy or some miraculous harmony between a capitalist economy and the 'family spirit' of social solidarity. Nor does Hegel envisage such a solution in his philosophy of history. The conflicts of civil society and its market relations persist within the ethical state and its rational constitution—as a "modern" state he has to grant the development of the principle of subjectivity and "personal particularity" (PR §260) in a stabilized but still fragile market economy. However, the impact of its crises on the citizens is considerably weakened. Their utmost concern—and for Hegel the overcoming of their petty self-interest—consists in the upholding of the constitution and the support for the strength, (international) influence, and flourishing of the ethical state. For this flourishing the material wealth of a state—including its 'human capital' (cf. PR §199)—is but the condition for the cultural and scientific life. The criteria for cultural life, however, are not just creativity and innovation, but common and individual self-reflection, culminating in philosophy. As we shall see, this cultural life is 'absolute spirit' and an end in itself, but the ethical state is not only the condition, but also a manifestation of this absolute and therefore an end in itself as well.

23.3. THE ETHICAL STATE

The development of Hegel's political philosophy shows a continual effort at reaching a view of the state unifying the protection of individual freedom with a strong identity of the spirit of the people (*Volksgeist*). This is in accordance with the impetus of the contemporary revolutions and their 'renaissance' of ancient Greek and Roman ideas of polis and imperium. Since his Berne years (1793–1796) Hegel followed both the Enlightenment's program of establishing the neutral state as sole source of civil rights— still partly held by the church and its sacraments[10]—as well as the 'classicist' idealization of the ancient republic.[11] This concerns less the 'constitutional form' of the Greek

---

[10] Citizenship depending on baptism or marital status on the sacraments of the churches. For Hegel's Critique in his manuscripts from the Berne period cf. Jaeschke, *Hegel-Handbuch*, 73.

[11] Although deeply influenced by Rousseau, Hegel, like Schiller and Hölderlin, followed the German preference for the Greek polis against the Roman republic.

polis—although he tried to modernize it in his essay on natural law (1802)—but rather its 'quasi-religious' form as source of social identity and meaningful life. As in the French Revolution, the sacralization of the state as the embodiment of 'divine' reason justifies at the same time its secularization or the emancipation from the churches. This extends to all functions of the churches as institutions dominating individual life and controlling important civil rights, as well as teaching the highest truths and mediating the final salvation. Unlike Fichte, Hegel did not remain true to the republican ideas of the French Revolution. Yet Hegel did transfer to his conception of a constitutional monarchy, developed in the Jena period (especially 1803–1806), the almost 'sacral' meaning of the state founded on reason in Rousseau, the French Revolution, and its German followers.[12]

In his mature philosophy Hegel developed a theory of the absolute as 'idea', that is, as all-encompassing, self-realizing, and self-reflecting thought. The rational state, then, has to be understood as a manifestation of this idea. As such, it is not subordinated to religion and its highest content, namely God. As a sovereign source of norms and their enforcement, it is above any religious authority. As the aim of all public activities, it is on an equal level with religious denominations, and the denominations themselves must remain within the legal norms of the state. In its constitutional 'architectonic' the state can be called a 'temple of reason'[13]—but not of a transcendent 'deity' of reason, as in some of the cults of the early French Revolution. In contrast, the state itself is absolute reason realized within the world of 'embodied' human beings and their natural needs. But since its essence is neither its physical power nor the human beings representing it, but its rational order and constitution, the state itself is a spiritual and 'immortal' being—in this respect transcending even Hobbes's 'mortal' god. One of the points to be clarified, however, concerns the relation of the particular historical nation states to the 'idea' (in a non-Hegelian sense) or concept of a state and its rational constitution.

Before tackling this question, however, I will support the preceding theses with reference to some key paragraphs of the section 'state'. To begin with, I (1) take a look at PR §§257–260; then I briefly discuss (2) Hegel's conception of 'constitutional' monarchy, (3) its concept of sovereignty (PR §§323–326), and finally (4) the relation of the ethical state to absolute spirit.

(1) According to PR §257, the state is a form of conscious 'substantial' will. It is conscious *within* the self-consciousness of individuals, but only insofar as this reflects the customs and the constitution such as the legislation, the jurisdiction of the courts, and so on. The constitution is generated within the development of the spirit of a people; its written fixation is important as an act of clarification, but not as the 'founding act' originating from the people's sovereignty, as for instance in the US tradition.[14] As we

---

[12] Cf. Siep, "Hegels praktische Philosophie und das 'Projekt der Moderne,'" 23 ff., and *Der Staat als Irdischer Gott*.

[13] This expression occurs in the lecture notes of Peter Wannenmann. Cf. *VNS*, 246.

[14] Cf. Siep, "Constitution, Fundamental Rights, and Social Welfare in Hegel's *Philosophy of Right*," 268–290, especially 272 ff.

shall see, Hegel is a defender of state sovereignty over the sovereignty of the people (PR §§278–279). As for Kant, there is no sovereign people or nation before and above its functions *within* the constitution (PR §279)—and in this framework no legal functions of the people as a whole, but only of its particular estates ('corporations') and state powers, exist. As a lasting institutional will, the state is the 'substance' and 'essence' of the self-conscious individual wills, even if legal actions are taken by individuals conforming to their rights, duties, and functions. Acting according to these functions realizes the 'substantial freedom' of the citizens. This freedom is, to put it in the terms of classical political philosophy, their 'political virtue', the 'feeling [*Empfindung*]' and willing of the state as "that thought end which has being in and for itself" (PR §257R). In his remark to this paragraph, Hegel explicitly compares the state as the "reality of the ethical idea" with the Greek conception of the deified 'people's spirit [*Volksgeist*]', that is, as the "divine knowing and willing itself."

Since his early Jena writings, Hegel combined Aristotle's politics and metaphysics. In this vein he uses the concepts of the divine 'unmoved mover' to which as an end every movement strives by 'love' or imitation, and the 'thinking of thinking' (*noesis noeseos*) for the rational state: according to PR §258 it is the "absolute unmoved end in itself" and the "in and for itself rational." This end has the "supreme right against the individual," and to be a member of such a state is the 'supreme duty' of the individual human being. However, since the fulfilling of this duty is, as we have seen, the highest degree of self-liberation, it is at the same time the supreme right of the individual. As in Kant and Aristotle, no human being can fulfill its rational nature without living in a state organized by reason. The sections preceding the 'ethical state' have proved that for this organization the protection of personal rights, well-being, group-interest, and so on, are essential. But as we will see, the highest manifestation of the state's sovereignty is just the 'annihilation' of all particular rights and interests.

Hegel defends this conception in PR §258 and the following paragraphs against two opposite theories of state, namely the contract theory and the theory of the right of the natural and traditional authorities, be they private (paternal), political, or religious. Contract theory, in his view, confuses the state with civil society whose members seek to realize their personal rights and private interests. In this view, to be a member of a state is just one among other possible means ('something optional', transl. Knox, 156). In transcending both Aristotle's thesis of the political nature of man and Kant's categorical duty to become a member of a state securing everybody's rights, Hegel claims that the individual gains "objectivity, truth, and ethical life" (PR §258 R) only within the state as objective spirit. Behind this conception of the state is not only the republican idea of identification with a free nation,[15] its autonomy and self-government, but also the 'ontological' thesis of the higher reality of the unification of individuals over their separate existence. As we will see, in participating in the objective spirit of the state, the

---

[15] In this respect, Hegel is a follower of Rousseau, whose idea of the social contract he mistakes as another version of the instrumental view of the state in contract theory (PR §258R). Regarding Hegel's critique of contract theory, cf. Moyar, "The Political Theory of Kant, Fichte and Hegel."

individual even gains a form of ethical immortality. To be sure, this is not a totalitarian form of nationalism since the protection of personal rights and well-being remains a necessary task of the state—as long as it is compatible with the latter's 'honor' as an independent entity among other states (PR §322).

If Hegel uses 'divine' attributes in his conception of the state, such as the Aristotelian unmoved mover and absolute end in itself, or neo-platonic concepts of unification,[16] this does not mean a simple deification of the state or its sources of authority. This he makes clear in his bitter irony against C. L. von Haller and his 'romantic' theory of 'natural authority' as the will of God. Against this theory he defends the rule of law, the 'national rights [*Nationalfreiheiten*]' and conventions like the Magna Carta, the bills and declarations of rights—American and French—and the 'Prussian general legal code [*Allgemeines Landrecht*]' with its Kantian basis. The architecture and 'organism' of the 'inner constitution' of the state which Hegel develops in PR §§260–320 seek to harmonize the personal and group rights, the division of powers,[17] and the rule of law with the independence of the state's will from particular interests and rights. Hegel's constitutionalism, however, is far from the republicanism of the American or the revolutionary French constitutions—leaving aside their differences for the moment—and even from a constitutional monarchy like the British or the French after 1815. In the years after 1821, Hegel became even more critical of all forms of parliamentarianism based on general elections. Instead of going into the details of his chapter on constitutional law (both in its 'inner' perspective and the institutions concerning external affairs), international law, and world history, I try to sketch Hegel's ideal of a constitutional monarchy.

(2) Many forms of constitutional monarchy developed in the eighteenth and nineteenth centuries in different parts of the world. Usually the British form, originating in the Glorious Revolution of 1688, and the French versions since 1815 come to the mind of the political philosopher. Germany, however, in the nineteenth century developed its own form of constitutional monarchy[18] to which Hegel seems much closer than to the 'West European' type. The conceptual difference lies mainly in the absence of the theory of 'people's sovereignty' as the ultimate principle of legislation und obligation. Instead, legislation is shared between the king and his administration on one side and the representatives of estates or classes of the people on the other. Historically, this goes back to contracts between the estates and the king regarding special rights and competencies. State sovereignty, however, remains with the monarchy as the representation or

---

[16] Regarding the influences of the neo-platonic and neo-spinozist 'philosophy of unification' (*Vereinigungsphilosophie*), see Henrich, *Hegel im Kontext*; Kotkavirtta, "Liebe und Vereinigung"; Jens Halfwassen, *Hegel und der spätantike Neuplatonismus*; cf. also Ilting (see note 3).

[17] However, in a form far from Locke, Montesquieu, and other conceptions of 'checks and balances'. See Siep, "Hegels Theorie der Gewaltenteilung." However, Hegel's concept of 'organism' is not the romantic one, but rather the Kantian of mutual support between the whole and its parts. It contains important elements of 'subsidiarity' (cf. for instance PR §§289, 297)—however, only during the 'peaceful state' of society and state (PR §278).

[18] Cf. Böckenförde, "Der deutsche Typ der konstitutionellen Monarchie im 19. Jahrhundert."

manifestation of the whole nation-state. And the administration (civil and military) is subordinated to the crown and not responsible to a parliament (PR §§289, 329).

There has been a long debate about Hegel's concept of the monarchy or 'power of the prince [*fürstliche Gewalt*]' in relation to the legislative power and the 'executive power [*Regierungsgewalt*]'. In Hegel's writings, especially between 1816 and 1820, there are subtle differences regarding this relation. Historically he seems to side with the 'Prussian Reformers' around Hardenberg, Stein, Altenstein, and others, who for some time demanded a national assembly and a constitution to be accepted by the assembly. In 1821 this policy failed and the reformers concentrated on the development of a civil society to overcome the dominance of the old Prussian aristocracy as a condition of any national representation. In addition, the result of the Vienna Conference in 1819 strengthened the 'monarchical principle' in all European countries.

Hegel's emphasis on the constitutional role of the princely power and the hereditary monarchy has been interpreted as a 'double writing' concealing his republican sympathies from Prussian censure. However, there is little evidence for this hypothesis.[19] The strength of the monarchy in Hegel's concept of constitution has both deeply philosophical—or as he calls it, 'speculative'—reasons as well as a historical affinity to the development of a 'German' type of constitutional monarchy. Both suggestions can only briefly be sketched here.

There are two main 'speculative' reasons for the strong positon of the monarchy in Hegel's thought. One is the concept of unfolding an undifferentiated whole in its internal determinations and reintegrating them in a simple, self-reflected unity. The latter process Hegel terms 'idealization', meaning the negation of any independence of these determinations from each other and from the whole. In terms of political philosophy, this idealization is the core of sovereignty. Since the structure of subjectivity central for Hegel's concept of 'spirit' is characterized by this 'idealized' unity of moments, sovereignty not limited by particular rights or guarantees is central for his political philosophy.

The second deeply philosophical reason for his conception of constitutional monarchy is the conception of an immediate, even natural individuality, in which the whole of the unfolded and idealized determinations is concentrated and made 'manifest'. In analogy with the ontological proof of God's existence and the Christian theology of God's incarnation in an individual human being, Hegel conceives of the 'natural' monarch and the hereditary monarchy as manifestations of the whole constitution. The 'personality' of a state has to be represented in the natural (not simply 'juridical') 'person' of the monarch (PR §279).

In opposition to theological voluntarism and legal absolutism, however, this is no justification of absolute monarchy in the sense of the monarch being completely beyond the law (*lege absolutus*).[20] Hegel calls any form of government 'despotism' which remains

---

[19] Cf. Lucas and Rameil, "Furcht vor der Zensur? Zur Entstehungs- und Druckgeschichte von Hegels Grundlinien der Philosophie des Rechts."

[20] This does not preclude, however, that the monarch in special questions—like the right of pardon or the decision on emergencies—acts independently from positive law according to the 'spirit of the

outside of "lawful and constitutional conditions" (PR §278R). Both the existence of such a state order and the "ideality of the particular spheres and functions" Hegel calls sovereignty. The sovereignty of the monarch is therefore the representation and manifestation of 'state sovereignty'—another concept from a special German tradition of constitutional law.[21]

In this representation of state sovereignty, however, the monarch is in most respects independent from any other representation—except from a joint legislation with the two legislative chambers, the first of the landed aristocracy and the second composed of delegations of the corporations from the commercial estates. In this legislation, which is restricted to the inner affairs of the state, the king and his administration have an equal share. Anything related to the external sovereignty, namely the decisions on war and peace, but also the diplomatic service and the military in peacetime, is reserved for the king (PR §329; compare Enz. 1830, PR §544). Since a great part of the budget in his time was related to the military, this limits the legislative control of the budget—which in Hegel's view is no exclusive right of the legislative chambers anyway (cf. PR § 299). And reserving the decision on war and peace, of course, runs counter to a key element of republican theory, even in Kant's sense.

It cannot be further discussed that Hegel's concept of constitutional monarchy lacks other aspects of the limited sovereignty of 'western' constitutions, namely regarding the control and check of administrative power and its possible abuse. The main instrument of such control, in his view, lies in the 'vertical' division of power, namely the self-administration of local and regional communities (PR §§287–289). The strengthening of these competences, which Hegel justifies against French centralism, was a result of the reforms initiated by one of the most important Prussian reformers, the Baron von Stein. The communal authorities and the corporations are the first to detect the abuse of power by the central administration (PR §295). They can appeal to the higher authorities up to the monarch and probably discuss them "when the Estates are in session" (PR §301). However, Hegel does not follow the tradition of a definite limitation of state sovereignty by human and civil rights. And this not for contingent historical reasons but on the basis of his fundamental conception of the 'idealized unity' of objective spirit.

(3) This becomes manifest in Hegel's view that the highest manifestation of sovereignty consists in the 'idealization' of all particular rights in states of emergency. There is a long discussion about Hegel's conception of war, and some myths are rightly criticized.[22] In my view, however, the differences between Hegel and the traditional and modern 'just war' theory are often mistakenly blurred. Although Hegel is no admirer of war for its own sake, he understands war as a necessary means and manifestation of the

constitution'. For Hegel, different from, say, John Locke, the power of the prerogative (or executive privilege) is not even in need of legislative approbation in hindsight.

[21] Grimm, *Souveränität. Herkunft und Zukunft eines Schlüsselbegriffs*, 52.

[22] Cf. part 3, "The Myth That Hegel Glorified War" in John Stewart (ed.), *The Hegel Myths and Legends*, 131–180.

'ethical' state and its sovereignty.[23] In this function, war is necessary for the ethical perfection of the citizens, the overcoming of their private 'idiocy' in the Greek sense, and even the transformation of their natural mortality. Since this is the significance of war, it cannot be restricted to defensive wars justified by the protection of the rights of present and future citizens.

It is in line with the previously discussed 'idealization' of all particular moments within a single and simple whole that Hegel affirms in PR §323:

> It is that aspect whereby the substance, as the state's absolute power over everything individual and particular, over life, property, and the latter's rights, and over the wider circles within it, gives the nullity of such things an existence [*Dasein*] and makes it present to the consciousness. (PR §323)[24]

In modern theory the justification of war would certainly not be the manifestation of state power, the demonstration of the ultimate 'nullity' of civil rights and the becoming aware of these spiritual and ethical truths. Rather, war in all its aspects would have to be justified as an ultimate and unavoidable means to protect and defend human and civil rights. It would have to manifest the limitation of sovereignty in light of the 'responsibility to protect'—either against an external intruder or against a state neglecting this responsibility. Any war that is not purely defensive can be justified only by 'humanitarian interventions' to defend a citizenry not able to protect itself by substitutional execution of its right to resistance. For Hegel, the opposite is true: war is necessary to manifest the sovereignty of a state to negate the particular rights of its citizens. This negation is not an unavoidable 'side effect' to maintain the state's monopoly of legitimate physical power. War has a necessary 'ethical moment' (PR §324), not only for creating the inner unity and integration of the citizens against their private egoism or particular convictions. For Hegel, the 'idealization' of the particular right is at the same time the realization of the citizens' highest right to be a member of an immortal ethical institution. This is a liberation from the natural necessity to die, which is transformed into a free ethical decision to offer one's life in a war that is voluntarily waged by the state (the 'ethical essence', cf. PR §324R)—however, through a decision made by the king alone.

To be sure, the conscious disposition to such an offer in cases of state-declared emergency is sufficient. For the 'normal' wars, for which states may find many reasons stemming from violations of their honor (PR §334), there is a particular professional estate, the military, which takes over this duty while normal civil life goes on (PR §§278, 325). However, the possibility of wars to become a danger for the existence of the state and therefore a duty for every citizen to participate must remain alive. Hegel explicitly refuses the Kantian idea of a perpetual peace, if only as a legal order for the regulation of

---

[23] It is important to keep in mind the reversal of the meaning of fighting in a war for the citizens by the French Revolution: "In den Revolutionskriegen kämpften auf französischer Seite zum ersten Male Bürger für ihr Vaterland und nicht mehr Untertanen für ihren König." Osterhammel, *Die Verwandlung der Welt. Eine Geschichte des 19. Jahrhunderts*, 883.

[24] Hegel seems to have families, corporations, and possibly the legal chambers in mind.

international conflicts, because it would endanger the "ethical health of the nations" (PR § 324).

(4) One of the reasons for such a strong theory of a state, a theory even justifying the sacrifice of one's life, may be the 'competition' in which the secular state is involved. Not only is the realm of the persecution of private interests in the market society, as we have seen, such a competitor. A power that traditionally has demanded the voluntary and even enthusiastic offer of one's goods and life is religion. Hegel's long remark regarding the relation between religion and state added to PR §270 of the *Philosophy of Right* proves how important he regards this competitor. The text cannot be explained in detail here. As is well known, Hegel places the churches[25] under the legal control of the state. He also confirms—and repeats in the last paragraph (PR §360) of the book—that the state is an equivalent manifestation of the same absolute which religion 'represents [*vorstellen*]' as God, the holy Spirit, and so on. But at the same time he adheres to the traditional view that the state needs the support of religion, in particular the religious convictions of his citizens, to be sure of a stable loyalty to its laws and requirements. For Hegel, however, it is not the fear of divine punishment after death—a view shared by philosophers from antiquity[26] up to Hobbes and Rousseau—which binds even those who despise the sanctions of the state. Neither does he share Kant's and Fichte's view of the necessity of a moral 'church' to improve the virtues and in consequence also the legal behavior of the citizens. Instead he regards the religious conscience, the 'innermost' theoretical and emotional convictions about absolute truth and unconditioned duty, to be the force that either supports or undermines the rational state.

It is the task of philosophy to demonstrate that the state and the religious ideas of God and his commandments are manifestations of the same absolute spirit. In Hegel's view of the history of religion and of constitutions, philosophy is supported in this task by the progress of reason in both fields. But it needs the philosophical proof—in the sense of the development of the system from objective to absolute spirit—to show[27] that the same idea unfolds and reflects itself not only in the state as objective spirit but also in art, religion, and philosophy as absolute spirit. The additional sense of 'absolute' in this latter form of spirit is that the self-reflection in this sphere is now completely independent of the needs and contingencies of human nature, whereas objective spirit is still bound to cope with these factors. But the ascension from objective to absolute spirit does not mean that religious norms are higher and can excuse the individual from the obedience to state laws. Regarding social norms, not only legal but also customary norms and those based on mutual expectations, there is nothing above or beyond the state.

---

[25] It is unclear whether Hegel has more than the traditional Christian confessions in view—which would correspond to the legal reality in most European states of his time (and in the final act of the Vienna Congress, 1819). Cf. Böckenförde, "Bemerkungen zum Verhältnis von Staat und Religion bei Hegel," 134. For a much wider understanding of 'church' in Hegel, see Vieweg, *Das Denken der Freiheit. Hegels Grundlinien der Philosophie des Rechts*, 465–471.

[26] Döring, "Antike Theorien über die staatspolitische Notwendigkeit der Götterfurcht," 43–56.

[27] In Hegel's methodology, the advancement to the telos as 'true ground' (cf., for instance, PR §256).

From the fact, however, that religion enlightened by philosophy and reconciled with state norms is a necessary support of state loyalty, Hegel in his *Philosophy of Right* even draws the consequence that the state 'fulfils a duty' to require from all its citizens to "belong to a church [*sich an eine Kirchengemeinde zu halten*]" (PR §270). This cast doubts on the full secularity or impartiality of the Hegelian state—for instance, regarding atheists or other non-believers. Even regarding such a limitation of secularity, however, Hegel scarcely diverges from a tradition of 'enlightened' political philosophy from Hobbes to Kant.[28]

23.4. Hegel's State: Within and Beyond the Categories of Modern Political Philosophy

To sum up the discussion of the liberal, social, and ethical meaning of Hegel's state, one might simply claim that his conception is not to be subsumed under the current categories of political philosophy. But this is an easy way out, which tells us nothing of interest for our dealing with such an impressive and influential work of our philosophical tradition. The preceding discussion was intended to shed some light on the sense of 'liberalism', of 'social welfare state', and of the secular 'ethical' state to be found in Hegel—and the limits of his conception in view of the post-Hegelian social and theoretical history.

Hegel's state is liberal in the sense that the protection of individual rights, including a great part of what belongs to modern human and civil rights, is a necessary task of any legitimate state. These rights are in need of material and institutional conditions for which the state, together with professional organizations and the family, has to provide. In this latter sense and in view of a range of measures and institutions needed for this task, Hegel's state can be called 'social', or social welfare state. But from a contemporary point of view, both attributes have their limits. The state is not liberal in the sense that its sovereignty is restricted in view of human or civil rights. These rights have no basis beyond the states' legislation, neither on an international level nor as constitutional rights that citizens could refer to before a constitutional court. State sovereignty is not dependent on fulfilling the "responsibility to protect" those rights. The 'active rights' of participating in the legislation are only weakly developed in Hegel's constitutional theory. He criticizes the concept of people's sovereignty, as well as the contract justification of the state. In the Hobbesian and Kantian tradition—against Locke or Hume—he does not allow for a right of resistance. These and other traces of his political philosophy separate him from the liberal tradition.

As to the 'social' elements of his conception of civil society and the state functions supporting it, he is certainly aware of the dangers of a market society for individual

---

[28] Cf. Siep, *Der Staat als irdischer Gott. Genese und Relevanz einer Hegelschen Idee.*

needs, liberties, and social harmony. However, against early socialist conceptions—as for instance in Fichte—he defends the market as a necessary means for the development of individual life-plans and a self-determined 'pursuit of happiness'. Instead of a 'dialectical'[29] or revolutionary overcoming of the crises of the market society, which culminate in the separation of classes and the decrease of loyalty to the legal order, he conceives—or rather justifies—an open system of absorbing or cushioning measures and institutions. This includes the state's interference in private property but not its abolition. In the end, the sense and aims of the 'bourgeois', the private market participant, are superseded—or sublated—by the 'ethos [*Gesinnung*]' of the citizen.

For the citizen of the 'ethical' state, the belonging to a system of rational institutions and to the 'unified' people acting for them—in different degrees of consciousness and intentionality—is the highest 'destiny' and form of freedom. This belonging to a community that transcends any private interest is the ultimate realization of the rational as political being. In normal everyday life, this consciousness is in accordance with private aims and interests that are better served within a state than without it. But this sort of utilitarian patriotism (PR §268) must be complemented, or rather grounded, by the consciousness that in extraordinary situations the state can claim any offer from its citizens, including their rights, goods, and life. By fulfilling this duty, at least by being constantly disposed to it, the citizens realize their highest freedom as liberation from mortality forced on them by nature.

These traits of the ethical state belong to another conception of the state than the one that prevails in our times. It has its roots in the classical republicanism renewed in Hegel's time by the pupils of Rousseau and by some of the protagonists of the American and French Revolution. It was alive in other countries as well, even in their religious traditions.[30] Different from these currents, however, Hegel's mature philosophy of right is neither republican, nor does he conceive of a state cult or political religion in the sense of the French revolution or other forms of civil religion. Since the end of his Jena period, he considers enlightened Protestantism and the rational—regarding its justification and the content of its norms—'secular' state as supporting each other. In this conception, as in his view of the constitutional monarchy, he may belong to a special German tradition.

This ethical or in some sense 'quasi-divine' character of the state—which Karl Marx and other Left-Hegelians rightly identified—separates his conception from the tradition of liberalism and socialism or the 'social-liberal' welfare state. Its 'communitarianism' is much stronger than in most contemporary forms. But this does not eliminate the liberal character of the state, especially in normal times (cf. PR § 268, 278).

---

[29] The 'dialectic' of the civil society which Hegel mentions in PR §246 is not a historical process (as in dialectical historical materialism). It leads to a transition "first" (*zunächst*) beyond the limits of a particular national economy into international exchange (in modern terms: globalization). Second, and more important for Hegel's philosophy of spirit, it requires an "ethical" transition on the level of institutions, habits and mentalities (*Gesinnungen*). But the most 'modern' and rational state still requires a market society (see earlier discussion in this chapter).

[30] For German Protestantism, cf. Kaiser, *Pietismus und Patriotismus im literarischen Deutschland. Ein Beitrag zum Problem der Säkularisation.*

Nevertheless, his conception of the state is still important for modern political philosophy in several respects. One aspect is his conception of rational right as standing between natural law and historicist traditions;[31] another is his view of the relation between a secular state and its dominant religious traditions. Also still relevant are Hegel's analyses of the pros and cons of market societies—although the contemporary national state has an even weaker position in relation to the globalized economy and companies as 'global players'. Even if the strengthening of state sovereignty and its ethical elevation does not seem plausible any more, the problems of transferring sovereignty to international institutions without producing 'failed' states are as urgent as the strengthening of solidarity without eliminating individual freedom. But the fruitfulness of dealing with these problems informed by Hegelian insights presupposes that we not 'modernize' his premises and consequences by neglecting the historical and theoretical divide. Hegel was aware of the historical limits of a philosophical system. Hegel interpreters should stick to this insight as well.

Works Cited

Primary Texts

Hegel, G. W. F. *Elements of the Philosophy of Right* [PR], edited by Allen Wood, translated by H. B. Nisbet. Cambridge: Cambridge University Press, 1991.

Hegel, G. W. F. "Ueber die wissenschaftlichen Behandlungsarten des Naturrechts, seine Stelle in der praktischen Philosophie, und sein Verhältniß zu den positiven Rechtswissenschaften [NL]" (1803), in *Gesammelte Werke*, Bd. 4: *Jenaer Kritische Schriften*, edited by Hartmut Buchner and Otto Pöggeler. Hamburg/Düsseldorf: Meiner, 1968, 417–485.

Hegel, G. W. F. *Vorlesungen über Naturrecht und Staatswissenschaft* [VNS]. Heidelberg 1817/18 mit Nachträgen aus der Vorlesung 1818/19. Nachgeschrieben von P. Wannenmann, in G. W. F. Hegel, *Vorlesungen. Ausgewählte Nachschriften und Manuskripte*, Bd. 1, edited by Claudia Becker et al. Hamburg: Meiner, 1983.

Kant, Immanuel. *The Metaphysics of Morals* [MM]. Translated and edited by Mary Gregor. Cambridge: Cambridge University Press, 1996.

Secondary Literature

Böckenförde, Ernst-Wolfgang. "Bemerkungen zum Verhältnis von Staat und Religion bei Hegel," in *Recht, Staat, Freiheit. Studien zu Rechtsphilosophie, Staatstheorie und Verfassungsgeschichte*, by E.-W. Böckenförde. Frankfurt am Main: Suhrkamp, 1991, 115–142.

Böckenförde, Ernst-Wolfgang. "Der deutsche Typ der konstitutionellen Monarchie im 19. Jahrhundert," in *Staat, Gesellschaft, Freiheit. Studien zur Staatstheorie und zum Verfassungsrecht*, by E.-W. Böckenförde. Frankfurt am Main: Suhrkamp, 1976, 112–145.

Brauer, Susanne. *Natur und Sittlichkeit, Die Familie in Hegels Rechtsphilosophie*. Freiburg: Alber, 2007.

Döring, Klaus. "Antike Theorien über die staatspolitische Notwendigkeit der Götterfurcht." *Antike und Abendland* 24 (1978): 43–56.

---

[31] Regarding this problem, cf. Pippin, *Hegel's Practical Philosophy*, especially chapters 8 and 9. Pinkard, "Reason, Recognition, and Historicity."

Grimm, Dieter. *Souveränität. Herkunft und Zukunft eines Schlüsselbegriffs*. Berlin: Berlin University Press, 2009.

Halfwassen, Jens. *Hegel und der spätantike Neuplatonismus*. Hamburg: Meiner, 2005, Hegel-Studien Beiheft 40.

Henrich, Dieter. *Hegel im Kontext. Mit einem Nachwort zur Neuauflage*. Frankfurt am Main: Suhrkamp, 2010.

Herzog, Lisa. *Inventing the Market: Smith, Hegel, and Political Theory*. Oxford: Oxford University Press, 2013.

Ilting, Karl-Heinz. "Hegels Auseinandersetzung mit der aristotelischen Politik." *Philosophisches Jahrbuch* 71 (1963/64): 38–58.

Jaeschke, Walter. *Hegel-Handbuch*. Stuttgart: Metzler, 2003.

Kaiser, Gerhard. *Pietismus und Patriotismus im literarischen Deutschland. Ein Beitrag zum Problem der Säkularisation*. Frankfurt am Main: Athenäum, 1973.

Kotkavirtta, Jussi. "Liebe und Vereinigung," in *Subjektivität und Anerkennung*, edited by Barbara Merker, Georg Mohr, and Michael Quante. Paderborn: mentis, 2004, 15–31.

Lucas, Hans-Christian, and Udo Rameil. "Furcht vor der Zensur? Zur Entstehungs- und Druckgeschichte von Hegels Grundlinien der Philosophie des Rechts." *Hegel-Studien* 15 (1980): 63–93.

Mohr, Georg. "Unrecht und Strafe (PR §§ 82–104)," in *G.W. F. Hegel, Grundlinien der Philosophie des Rechts*, 4th edition, edited by Ludwig Siep. Berlin: De Gruyter, 2014, 95–124.

Mohseni, Amir. *Abstrakte Freiheit. Zum Begriff des Eigentums bei Hegel*. Hamburg: Meiner, 2015, Hegel-Studien Beiheft 62.

Moyar, Dean. "The Political Theory of Kant, Fichte and Hegel," in *The Routledge Companion to 19th Century Philosophy*, edited by D. Moyar. New York: Routledge, 2010, 131–164.

Neschen, Albena. *Ethik und Ökonomie in Hegels Philosophie und in modernen wirtschaftsethischen Entwürfen*. Hamburg: Meiner, 2008, Hegel-Studien Beiheft 49.

Osterhammel, Jürgen. *Die Verwandlung der Welt. Eine Geschichte des 19. Jahrhunderts*. München: Beck, 2009.

Pinkard, Terry. "Reason, Recognition, and Historicity," in *Subjektivität und Anerkennung*, edited by Barbara Merker, Georg Mohr, and Michael Quante. Paderborn: mentis, 2004, 47–66.

Pippin, Robert. *Hegel's Practical Philosophy*. Cambridge: Cambridge University Press, 2008.

Primoratz, Igor. *Banquos Geist. Hegels Theorie der Strafe*. Bonn: Bouvier, 1986.

Reinhard, Wolfgang. *Geschichte der Staatsgewalt. Eine vergleichende Verfassungsgeschichte Europas von den Anfängen bis zur Gegenwart*. München: Beck, 2002.

Ritter, Joachim. "Person und Eigentum," in *G.W. F. Hegel, Grundlinien der Philosophie des Rechts*, 3rd Edition, edited by Ludwig Siep. Berlin: De Gruyter, 2014, 55–72.

Siep, Ludwig. "Constitution, Fundamental Rights, and Social Welfare in Hegel's *Philosophy of Right*," translated by N. Walker, in *Hegel on Ethics and Politics*, edited by Robert B. Pippin, Ottfried Höffe. Cambridge: Cambridge University Press, 2004, 268–290.

Siep, Ludwig. *Der Staat als irdischer Gott. Genese und Relevanz einer Hegelschen Idee*. Tübingen: Mohr Siebeck, 2015.

Siep, Ludwig. "*Hegels praktische Philosophie und das 'Projekt der Moderne.*" Baden-Baden: Nomos, 2011.

Siep, Ludwig. "Hegels Rezeption der aristotelischen Politik," in *Aktualität und Grenzen der praktischen Philosophie Hegels*, by Ludwig Siep. München: Fink, 2010, 59–76.

Siep, Ludwig. "Hegels Theorie der Gewaltenteilung," in *Praktische Philosophie im Deutschen Idealismus*, by Ludwig Siep. Frankfurt am Main: Suhrkamp, 1992, 240–269.

Stewart, John (ed.). *The Hegel Myths and Legends* Evanston, IL: Northwestern University Press, 1996.

Vieweg, Klaus. *Das Denken der Freiheit. Hegels Grundlinien der Philosophie des Rechts.* München: Fink, 2012, 465–471.

Waldron, Jeremy. *The Right to Private Property.* New York: Oxford University Press, 1988.

CHAPTER 24

HEGEL'S PHILOSOPHY OF HISTORY AS THE METAPHYSICS OF AGENCY

TERRY PINKARD

THE broad outline of Hegel's philosophy of history is well known. From a philosophical point of view, world history begins in the East and moves to the West, and in the movement of history Hegel claims to discern necessary progress. Influential as this conception might have been, almost nobody thinks that there is any prospect for it nowadays. Is there anything left of Hegel's argument for such progress other than, say, weak comparisons of contemporary affirmations of rights against past oppressive practices? Or is Hegel's view merely a celebration of the present against the past?

24.1. SELF-CONSCIOUS LIFE IN HISTORICAL FORM

As with all of his philosophy, Hegel's philosophy of history involves a story about *Geist*, rendered as 'spirit' or 'mind' (depending on the translator). For the purposes here, I shall be taking *Geist* to be Hegel's name for the species of self-conscious rational animals that make up humanity.[1] *Geist* denotes, as Hegel calls it in some places, a shape of life. That is

---

[1] This requires more explication than can be given here. However, here are two citations from Hegel to put the general idea into relief: "In short, life must be grasped as an end in itself as an end which possesses its means within itself, as a totality in which each distinct moment is alike end and means. It is, therefore, in the consciousness of this *dialectical*, this *living* unity of distinct moments that self-consciousness is ignited, the consciousness of the simple, ideal existence that is its own object and therefore differentiated within itself, in other words, the knowledge of the *truth* of natural existence, of the 'I'" (E §423A). This takes Hegel's way of speaking of '*der Geist*' as a species term in the way that 'whale' or 'wolf' is a species term, and it does not imply that '*Geist*' therefore names some kind of entity, anymore than 'whale' names

the concept 'in itself [*an sich*]', as Hegel would put it, and its development in history—its being 'posited [*gesetzt*]', as Hegel would also put it—develops the tensions inherent but not at first apparent in the concept as it initially is 'in itself'.

From a philosophical point of view, history is the series of events in which men and women attempt to make sense of what it is to be the strange creatures we are, namely, those for whom the meaning of what it is to be that kind of creature is a problem.[2] Such creatures have a history, and to know if that history has a sense, we need to know in the most general way what it is to make sense in general.

In his *Science of Logic*, Hegel argued that we make sense of things in two very general ways. We point things out, classify them, describe them, generalize about them, and count them. We also ask questions that are not those of pointing out and counting but of explaining why things manifest themselves as they do (Why does the tie look green in the shop but blue in the sunlight?), and why things happen as they do (Why did the pipes burst?). Beyond that, we are also pushed into making sense of making sense.[3] When we do that, we ask, for example, whether conclusions follow from premises, or whether assertions cohere with other ways of viewing how things hang together. When pushed further, we are also led to ask whether this or that way of making sense of making sense itself makes any sense. We typically do that in philosophy, although the practices of art and religion also do something similar.

When we think about the senses in which, for example, conclusions follow from premises, we also think about our own agency. The concept of agency that emerges from such reflections is not merely that of an entity that causes itself to act in light of its reasons or passions, but also that of an entity whose being has to do with its moving within a logical space of reasons. Unlike counting, classifying, pointing out, explaining by underlying conditions, and the like (what Hegel calls the logics of 'being' and 'essence') where truths about the world are at issue, speaking of agency involves a space of reasons in which such truths also have to do with agency going well or badly ("Your inferences are way off"), or artifacts performing well or badly ("Your clock is running far too fast"), of living things being defective or non-defective, and even of people who are being or

an entity. This is also why Hegel says things such as "[t]he individual exists as a determinate being, unlike man in general, who has no existence as such" (VPW, 85; LPH, 72). I discuss this in its application to a more Hegelian conception in Pinkard, *Does History Make Sense?* (2017).

[2]   "Freedom is that which is the 'in itself' of spirit. Spirit must know what it is in itself. We know it, but at the outset [of history] spirit does not know it. World history begins with this self-knowledge, and it has taken 3,000 years of work on the part of spirit in order to know itself." This is a not fully literal translation of: "Die Freiheit ist das An sich des Geistes; er muß wissen, was er an sich ist; wir wissen es; aber zunächst weiß es der Geist nicht von Anfang; die Weltgeschichte fängt mit diesem Wissen von sich an; es ist eine Arbeit von 3000 Jahren, die der Geist gemacht hat, um sich zu wissen" (Hegel, PG, 37).

[3]   This distinction between "making sense of things" and "making sense of making sense" is lifted from A. W. Moore, *The Evolution of Modern Metaphysics*, xxi. Robert Pippin has picked up on Moore's use in his explications of Hegel's thought, although his and Moore's conceptions of making sense of making sense do differ in important ways. Pippin, "The Significance of Self-Consciousness in Idealist Theories of Logic," 145–166; "Die Logik der Negation bei Hegel"; and "Hegel on Logic as Metaphysics," Chapter 9 in this volume.

acting well or badly in terms of meeting or failing to meet ethical requirements ("You are at heart an outlaw"). Hegel's *Logic* culminates in the 'absolute Idea', which expresses the 'true infinity' of concepts inasmuch as it expresses the self-bounding nature of reason itself, the more or less Kantian idea that reason has no standard outside of itself, which includes setting limits to itself. The 'absolute Idea' is the developed concept of the intelligibility of all that is to thought, just as 'Being' (the first concept of the *Logic*) is the same concept, only as not fully developed. The very general thought of thought's development is the structure of self-consciousness itself. Thinking is always a thinking about thinking, even when it is not explicitly so reflective. In thinking of 'Being', we are already, necessarily thinking of it as distinct from and excluding nothing.[4] In following that thought to its conclusion, we end up with a conception of thought's self-relation and thus ultimately of self-consciousness itself. Agents are self-relating entities from the ground up.

The logical concept of a subject as an entity both theoretically and practically moving within the space of reasons, taking them as reasons, is the underlying conception behind the philosophy of history. However, if left at that level of generality, the initial concept of the subject rules a few things in, but rules little else out. It does, however, set up the problem of how different conceptions of what the space of reasons requires of us, when put into concrete detail, in order to come to terms with what those reasons mean vis-à-vis each other. Hegel's rather audacious thesis about this has two parts: first, that different shapes of spirit (*Geist*) in history display different metaphysical embodiments of agency, such that the very metaphysics of agency itself develops over time; and, second, that history shows us that these different shapes of agency appear in a particular temporal order (which is accidental), an order that has a deeper intelligibility to it when seen from the vantage point of something like the *Logic*, such that we can confidently assert that there has been progress in the conceptions of agency that have developed in history and that there is a kind of conceptual necessity to that progress.[5]

[4] This has to be hedged more than a bit. In thinking of 'being', we are simply thinking of what is in the most general sense. However, that thought is itself indeterminate, which makes it an impossible thought. Yet in thinking of that indeterminate thought, we also realize that we are not thinking of it as an indeterminate thought at all but as, at the least, different from nothing, although that difference cannot, framed in the terms of such a pure thought, be articulated. (One simply finds oneself asserting that being is different from nothing and having no way to state the difference.) The thought of 'pure being' thus turns out not really to be a thought at all, but only something that seems like a genuine thought.

[5] "That which exists only in itself is a possibility or potentiality [*Vermögen*] which has not yet emerged from being an inner into existence. A second moment is necessary before it can attain actuality—that of actuation or actualization; and its principle is the will, the activity of mankind in the world at large. It is only by means of this activity that the original concepts or determinations existing in themselves are realized and actualized" (VPW, 81; LPH, 69). Hegel also speaks of the *Logic*'s relation to his philosophy of history in his lectures when he says, "Our presupposition only asserts that reason rules the world. . . . Furthermore, reason is immanent in historical existence and brings itself to completion in and through it. The unification of the universal that exists in and for itself with the singular, that is, the subjective, is the sole truth, is speculative in nature, and in this general form is treated in the 'Logic.' But in the course of world history itself, conceived as still in progress, the pure and final purpose of history is not yet the content of [the subject's] needs and interests, and since [the subjects with] those needs and interests are not yet aware of this end, the universal is nonetheless present in their particular purposes and completes itself through them. The former question also takes on the form of freedom and necessity, since we note

To see how that goes, we need to look at some of Hegel's more audacious assertions about agency and the 'absolute'. Agents act in terms of finite and infinite ends. An 'infinite end' has no internal limit at which it has finally been accomplished.[6] It is instead manifested in a series of actions as the principle behind them, that which makes them into manifestations of the end they are. A 'finite' end, on the other hand, can be achieved and fully exhausted. A finite end has its limit within itself. To give an example, soon to be extinct: walking to the mailbox to mail a letter is a finite end. For such a finite end, one exhausts the various elements of achieving it in putting the stamped, sealed letter into the box. Justice, or, for example, Aristotle's conception of *Eudaimonia*, are examples of infinite ends. Finite ends simply add up, but infinite ends must be continually manifested in order for them to count as guiding an action, an institution, or a practice. Likewise, an infinite end can inform a series of actions without it being the explanation of many actions that occur in the series it informs. One can, for example, be acting in light of *Eudaimonia* without having each action occurring because one was seeking that single end. One comprehends such an infinite end not when one has merely added up all the actions that manifest it, but when one has comprehended the principle that is at work in the way those actions manifest it.[7] One comprehends an infinite end when one comprehends its individual manifestations, but its individual manifestations never exhaust the principle itself—for example, the various actions and practices that are carried out in light of justice do not exhaust the concept of justice. (The same is true for all the activities of 'absolute spirit', such as art, religion, and philosophy: all those practices are what artists, religious people, and philosophers do, but neither art, religion, nor philosophy is exhausted by adding all those doings up.)

24.2. Hegel's Inadequate Account of "stalled" Shapes of Self-Conscious Life

Hegel thinks that by attending to the facts of history in light of his *Logic* he can show that agency has taken different shapes over time, and that there is a kind of progress to be found in the way it has taken shape. He also realizes that he cannot simply enumerate these various changes with only a promissory note that he will fill in the decisive details later. (That is more or less the tactic he takes in both the *Encyclopedia* and at the end of

---

the inner course of spirit, a course existing in and for itself, as what is necessary, and, on the other hand, we ascribe freedom to the conscious will of people as their interests. Since the metaphysical coherence (that is, the coherence in the concept) of these determinations belongs within the 'Logic', we cannot give an explication of those coherencies here" (VPG, 40–41; PH, 25).

[6] On the idea that infinite ends have no internal limit, see Rödl, "The Form of the Will."

[7] Dean Moyar explains this in terms of a nesting of purposes within other purposes within Hegel's system. See the summary given by Moyar, *Hegel's Conscience*, 75.

the *Philosophy of Right* toward the philosophy of history.) Nonetheless, for the purposes of this chapter, we have to take the shortcut Hegel advises against.

For Hegel's thesis about agency in history to be shown to be correct, it must look at world history on a global scale, and not just attend only to parts of it or selective time slices of it. For that reason, Hegel at first spent his semesters lecturing on the philosophy of history by looking more specifically at Africa and what he and those in his own time summed up as the 'Orientals' (China, India, Persia, Egypt). There were many people in his day that were arguing, for example, that China and India presented equally good or perhaps better alternatives to European ways of life. He more or less set out to show that they were not alternatives at all, and in doing so, he ended up with an account of them that was condescending and even racist. More than almost anything else, for many people later on, his so-called findings played a large role in discrediting his entire philosophy of history. It is true that in talking about Africa, China, and India, he more or less ends up talking about his own fantasies about Africa, China, and India. Nonetheless, what he has to say about them casts a light on some of the more interesting aspects of his theory of socially and historically embedded agency. (To say this is not to let Hegel off the hook for his damaging characterizations. It is, however, to be far more generous to him than he was to Africa, China, and India.)

What Hegel thinks is at work in those civilizations is a type of agency and a collective enterprise that cannot fully proceed to a certain kind of reflective self-consciousness. It cannot, that is, make things problematic for itself in ways that open up the possibility for progress. He starts with Africa, and in unfortunately but predictably typical nineteenth-century European fashion, he thinks that Africans barely distinguish themselves from nature. Their idea of collective agency is thus that of unreflective rule-following. They simply do what they take their ancestors to have done, and this gives them little room to establish any kind of distance from their own immediate concerns and lives so that they could develop properly critical evaluative stances toward them. For them, the world and their lives just are the way they are, and if unjust domination and irrationality are part of the rules, they follow them. Not surprisingly, he concludes that there is therefore nothing for Europeans to learn from Africa, although (of course) there is much Africans need to learn from Europeans. There is no reason to excuse Hegel on this point, but it is easy to point out how wrong Hegel was about this since he was so obviously wrong about it.[8]

This idea that non-European civilizations are inherently rule-following civilizations or unhelpfully negative reactions to rule-following informs the rest of Hegel's discussions of non-European alternatives. On Hegel's reconstruction, the Chinese have a civilization that embodies the conception that all obligation comes from rules issued by a sovereign emperor backed up by a credible threat of force. This means that although they are efficient, perhaps happy, and capable of great craftsmanship in the arts, they are also unimaginative and prone to domination by one or a few over the many. Where

---

[8] See Appiah, "Africa: The Hidden History." On the dreadful consequences of Hegel's views, see Taiwo, "Exorcising Hegel's Ghost: Africa's Challenge to Philosophy."

all obligation is modeled after that of legal obligation taken on the model of sovereign commands, there is no basic need to be able to put the whole into a more rational form. There are simply authoritative rules to follow, and where they conflict, a certain pragmatism is called for to work around the conflicts. Thus, in such a system, the Chinese citizenry has to remain infantilized when it comes to such rules. Such rules have the force that a parent's commands have over children: they are simply authoritative, and if they make no sense, then that is just the way the world goes. Having no higher principles by which to criticize the sovereign's rules, China is essentially a land of 'political atheism'.[9] Nor can the ethical life holding it together supply such principles from within. Its morality is only that of traditional rules and principles, and thus "there can be nothing more ethical [*sittlicher*] than the Chinese empire."[10] (The less than implicit contrast here is supposed to be with European life which brings universal moral standards to bear on such ethical and political life; the contrast is complicated by the fact that for Hegel European 'ethical life' is necessary to make up for the practical failings that would otherwise be experienced in a purely moral life.) Such a political psychology is welcoming to despotism, and, so Hegel thought, the history of China is a history of one despotism supplanting another with no progress to be found in the series. China is essentially a stalled civilization, spinning its wheels in historical time, unable to move forward. It is therefore not an alternative to European life. That Hegel's description of China does not in fact match up with the reality of China is, to say the least, a major drawback in Hegel's characterization of China, but the point is in line with his views on the way a shape of agency can be embodied in practices that fall short of progress.

If 'China' is locked into rule-following and is therefore unimaginative, Hegel's 'India' rejects all such rules and is governed only by the imagination. To all those of his day who looked to India for an example of spiritual regeneration in contrast to what they took to be the exhaustion of European spirituality, Hegel's retort was that India only reflected back to them their own emptiness, which in their daydreams about India they mistook for fullness. In Hegel's account, India rejects the rigid Chinese adherence to rules, but its dreamy rejection of such rigidity leads to the same result: despotism. Although 'China' cannot adequately distinguish the 'is' from the 'ought', the Indian adherence to constant change and difference means that there is also no way for them to adequately draw that distinction.

Hegel's charge against his contemporaries that they were reading their own dreaminess into India to make up for the emptiness of their own dreaminess is, alas, mirrored by Hegel's own reading of his critique of his contemporaries writing on India. His writing on China and India is less about them than it is a kind of warning to his fellow Europeans: if you think that European problems are to be solved by becoming more oriental-spiritual, look at where that will lead you—to Indian emptiness.

Persians and Egyptians display more of the same. They try to go beyond legalistic rigidity and ineffectual dreaminess by constructing religions that provide a kind of

---

[9] Hegel, PG, 84.
[10] Ibid., 72.

external standard by which to measure their own ethical life. However, since their religions are for the most part indeterminate (the divinity as 'light', the various man-animal deities of Egypt, etc.), the kinds of standards they bring from the outside to the otherwise dreamy or rule-governed shapes of life in which they arise are not really capable of providing much in the way of critical distance. On Hegel's reconstruction, these too remain stalled social and political orders.

Hegel's treatment of what he bundles together under the idea of 'the East' is not really enlightening about any of the civilizations he describes, although it is enlightening about the deeper issues he is pursuing. One cannot help believing that he set out to discover that the 'East' was no alternative, and, no surprise, he found it. What he found, though, was himself staring back at himself, rather than confronting the 'other' he took himself to be confronting. How serious a failure is this for Hegel's project? To answer that, we need first to look at the rest of the project.

24.3. GREECE: SLAVERY AS THE CONDITION OF EQUALITY

Hegel's philosophy of history really gains its focus when it moves from the 'Orient' to ancient Greece (that is, from the 'East' to 'Europe'). Here, he thinks, is where progress in history begins because it is first in ancient Greece that humanity becomes problematic to itself in the right way. The Greek world had a conception of the world as an organic whole, in which all the major elements of that world functioned together to produce a beautiful whole, and the divinities in that world were key elements of it. Their interventions in nature and in human life were part of that organic structure, such that an imbalance in one part could set off an imbalance in another part. Human life was supposed to be intelligible as part of this cosmic order. When each member of a community acted in the terms required of him or her by virtue of his or her place in the overall human and cosmic order, the result was a spontaneous harmony among all the elements that produced a thing of beauty. That is, if men did what was required of men, women what was required of women, and statesmen, parents, children, artisans, warriors, and all others did what was required of them in their status, the result would be spontaneously harmonious. Moreover, this harmony did not require any member to aim self-consciously at such a harmony. Agents needed only to aim at what was required of them in their particular status. As such, the Greeks did not move much beyond the rule-bound or imaginative world of the 'East'.

What set them apart was the construction of a new status at which nobody aimed: the 'individual'. This arose as the contradiction that lurks at the bottom of all such rule-governed shapes of life begins to make itself felt. If all obligation is a matter of rules, and if that culminates in a situation where rules have binding force only when issued by a sovereign emperor (who orders all below him and answers to nobody else), then it is a matter of pure contingency as to whether all these rules do not clash with each other. Likewise, if all is in flux and change, then there can be no contradiction, only difference among the myriad changing things of the world. (This corresponded, as Hegel thought, respectively to China and India.)

Instead, as Hegel put it, "the Greeks in their immediate actuality lived in the happy middle between both self-conscious subjective freedom and the ethical substance."[11] That is, they lived in an ethical world that was paradigmatically dyadic: to wrong a person or do right by them depended on the relation one had with the person. Even the relation among the individually self-sufficient men of the polis was that of justice (or "complete virtue", as Aristotle called it, "in relation to one's neighbor"). This dyadic 'ethical relation' is different from the modern and more monadically conceived 'moral relation' in which individuals relate to each other via an established set of rules. (Thus, the 'moral' relation resembles somewhat that of players in a game in which certain acts are declared fouls or offsides.)[12]

Greek tragedy brought the contradictions always latent in that conception into full view and made their force felt, most emphatically in Sophocles' *Antigone*. In the play, there is a fight for rulership among the children of Oedipus, and the two brothers end up fighting against each other and both dying in the struggle. Their uncle, Creon, steps into the rulership to bring the city to order and commands that the brother who initiated the attack be denied all the traditional burial rites. His sister, Antigone, knowing that she has an unconditional requirement to perform those rites for her brother, fanatically sets out to do so in defiance of Creon's order. However, she also realizes that as a Greek and especially as a woman, she also is unconditionally required to obey Creon in these matters. What is required of her makes it impossible for her to satisfy what she is required to do. Worse, also as a Greek and a woman, she is also unconditionally required not to make up her own mind about what she is required to do. What kind of spontaneous harmony can result from each doing what is required of him or her in such cases? The answer, of course, is tragic. Antigone must be punished for her transgressions even though they were unavoidable. So too must the others.

---

[11] Hegel, VA, 24; A, 436; Hegel goes on to say on page 437 (page 25 in VA), "Nor, on the other hand, did the Greeks make the advance to that deepening of subjective life in which the individual subject separates himself from the whole and the universal in order to be independent in his own inner being; and only through a higher return into the inner totality of a purely spiritual world does he attain a reunification with the substantial and essential. On the contrary, in Greek ethical life the individual was independent and free in himself, though without cutting himself adrift from the universal interests present in the actual state and from the affirmative immanence of spiritual freedom in the temporal present. The universal element in ethical life, and the abstract freedom of the person in his inner and outer life, remain, in conformity with the principle of Greek life, in undisturbed harmony with one another, and at the time when this principle asserted itself in the actual present in still undamaged purity there was no question of an independence of the political sphere contrasted with a subjective morality distinct from it; the substance of political life was merged in individuals just as much as they sought this their own freedom only in pursuing the universal aims of the whole."

[12] See the discussion in Thompson, "What Is It to Wrong Someone?"; and Pinkard, *Does History Make Sense?*

In the play, Antigone is driven to the point where whatever she does, she is making up her own mind about where her requirements lay. She becomes something non-Greek, the individual with something resembling a moral point of view, standing above the social rules and deciding what is right for herself. However, she can have no standard by which to evaluate that issue. In the play, only her own fanatical desire to stake a claim to greatness seems to emerge as filling that gap. The character, Antigone, becomes a reflective individual, and the deeper contradiction at work in Greek life became more and more evident to the Greeks themselves. In the figure of Antigone, the contradictory demands of dyadic, 'ethical', Greek life made themselves felt without a full move to a more modern and 'monadic' commitment becoming fully present.

Such tragedies made Greek life problematic to itself in a way that provoked it into moving in a more reflective direction. Although such tragic plays did not on their own challenge the Greek conception of the absolute, they did make manifest the irrationalities to which a conception of the gods moving on one plane and humans on another led. It did not cause, but it did provoke, the Greeks to become more philosophical about that matter and to look for a way to put the picture back together in a more rational form.

Greek life also made itself problematic in yet another way. It organized itself into a democratic form of government after the ruling families of its distant past undid themselves in battles and collapsed in the face of their inability to hold on to any kind of normative allegiance on the part of their subjects. In their place stepped a group of men in which each was now an equal to the other since there was then no overarching sovereign (no king, no emperor) under which they would serve. In such a situation without a sovereign, either there is a struggle to assert supremacy (to bring the other men under one's heel), or there is an acceptance that the political order can only be that of equal citizens of a city-state meeting together to work out their differences and set policy without resorting to violence. The Greeks ended up with the latter, and this created a new form of authority that operated in a different fashion from that of an order based on social rules. The public disputes and debates that go on in the polis involve a kind of spontaneity that is not formulable in social rules.

For this to be possible, there had to be no natural authority of one person over another, so that each citizen of the polis had to encounter the others as equals. To be such an equal also required that each citizen be self-sufficient, such that his life was not dependent on the arbitrary wills of others. Self-sufficiency itself was thus a condition of participation in the polis and a virtue. For that to be real, these self-sufficient citizens had to have others do the dirty work of daily life for them, and for that, in the ancient world, they needed slaves. In fact, one of the striking facts of the ancient world was the fact that with almost no exceptions, it accepted the institution of slavery, problematic as it was. It was for them simply a fact of the world that the economy could not work without the compelled labor of some for the advantage of others.

However, the development of the self-reflectivity that makes its appearance in tragic drama and the spontaneity that is built into the debates among equals in the polis also made slavery problematic for the Greeks in a way that, so Hegel thought the historical record showed, it could not have been for others. Even though slavery was a clearly established social institution, and even though the justification for it was also well established—those vanquished in a war could expect enslavement as the cost of defeat—for the newly reflective Greeks, it was nonetheless problematic although (so they thought) necessary and established. If the more subtle use of reason distinguished the noble from the base, what then could justify enslaving a well-reasoning person? Aristotle drew the conclusion that there could be no justification. If it was wrong to enslave somebody equal to a citizen's own status, how could it be justified to do that to anybody else of equal status? Yet Aristotle also concluded that slavery was necessary, and he endorsed, or at least entertained, the idea that some people were natural slaves who could exercise reason but only in terms of following the rules. Aristotle's own conflicted ideas about the justifiability of slavery only highlighted the increasingly problematic status of slavery in Greek life. Nonetheless, however contradictory the attitudes to slavery were, they did not lead the Greeks in any significant way to question the institution.

The self-reflectivity of the Greeks, which developed without anyone aiming at such reflectivity, made the contradictions of slavery more salient than it was for the more rule-governed civilizations of its own time. Other societies were no less contradictory than Greek society. However, those contradictions, while making them unintelligible to themselves, did not interfere with their daily life. The Greeks, on the other hand, pushed themselves, at first unwittingly, into becoming intelligible to themselves, and that put a new strain on their life as committed to their version of the 'absolute'. That required a view of agency as a natural status within a world that functioned as an organic whole and that naturally righted itself when it was pushed into disequilibrium as a whole or when it was wronged by human action. Human action had a natural and final end, *Eudaimonia*, which required rational thought and proper training to be actual in life. Human law was different from divine law, but it took on the same kind of structure, aiming at an equilibrium among the various passions and inclinations in human life. To achieve that end, agents had to become self-sufficient, and in order to do that, they had to have others (women, slaves) who were dependent on their wills. Self-sufficient men were political equals, and, more important, they were free. As noble natures, they were, as Aristotle himself put it, not "at the beck and call of another," but that could be real only if others were at their beck and call. A world of flourishing, noble men equal to each other in political authority and thereby free, who were supported by the unfree, was in that shape of life a just order. Agency, in its paradigmatic form, was male and was committed to equality among the male citizens of the polis.

The Greek polis was ultimately too small to defend itself, and it was also in the process of becoming unintelligible to itself. It might have stumbled along this path for longer, but it came into contact and then conflict with another power it could not have anticipated, nor could it resist: Rome.

24.4. ROME: FROM OFFICE-HOLDERS TO CHRISTIAN INWARDNESS

Although Hegel's philosophy of history is often taken to describe history as a dialectically necessary succession, this seems far-fetched as a description of what he actually says (and it is even more far-fetched as a description of historical development as a whole). Rome did not proceed 'dialectically' out of Greece. Rome developed on its own, and in its Mediterranean area of operation, it eventually came into contact and conflict with Greece, emerging as triumphant over it. When the two eventually did come into a kind of open struggle with each other, Greek life was already decaying in its vitality as it struggled to come to terms with its own ways of making sense of its senselessness, and it was in Rome that the remaining elements of Greek life were incorporated into a new shape of life. The Romans took the elements of Greek life that still worked and used them to fashion a new way of being an agent. Hegel used the German term *Aufhebung*, in its double meaning of canceling and preserving, to describe this process of incorporation.

As Rome emerged as a power in its region, it did so first as a conquest state, one whose fortunes depended on extracting wealth from its conquered lands. It became an empire by incorporating non-Romans under its rule, and it eventually became a tributary state. Unlike Greece, it had no claim to being a natural unity since it was so obviously a political unity forged out of one people forcing various other peoples of different linguistic, religious, and ethnic groups together under one political administration. The Greek polis was equally a 'constructed' unity of citizens, but it still laid claim to echoing a cosmic order in its practices.

Romans invented a story for themselves as one 'people' in the past rising in revolt against foreign rule (by Etruscan kings) and founding an order which their descendants were to respect and to which they were required to keep faith. In that narrative, the 'founders' were thus the key building blocks of the Roman self-conception. That founding moment, Hegel argued, was therefore that of a form of revolt, and its founding ethic, he sarcastically noted, was more like that of a band of thieves. (They even invented a story about how they originally had to steal their wives from the Sabines.) This idea of a Roman founding thus brought with it a conception of various virtues such as courage, fidelity, devotion to the good of the Roman collective, and so forth. Hegel takes Herodotus's claim that Homer and Hesiod gave the Greeks their myths (and their gods) as an adequate shorthand for the Greek conception of the founding moment as having to do with beauty. For the Romans, the founding moment was more down to earth and human in its outlook.

This was not the equality of the Greek polis. It instead rested on a kind of struggle for recognition as to who was in possession of more power and all the virtues and wealth that were necessary to sustain such power. If the Greeks had concluded that the consequences of the dissolution of royal power was the absence of any natural authority of one citizen over another and thus a polis based on equality, the Romans concluded that it meant that authority had to do with establishing some way of exercising a power to get other people to do what the person of authority thought they should be doing. This authority could be claimed in various ways (property, family history, military standing, prestige, etc.), but it all rested on a struggle for recognition that was continually shifting. It also required a sharp pragmatism on how to maintain such authority, and it rested on what had to be taken as self-evident that women and slaves were naturally subject to the authority of those men in power.

In such a system, there was always an undercurrent of those seeking to upend the authority of those who claimed to exercise such power. This manifested itself in various ways, such as that between plebs and aristocrats over power (with the plebs finally winning a place for themselves) and over various groups within the system that Roman thinkers could only comprehend as a struggle between those who kept faith with the founders and were thus virtuous, and those who lacked such virtue. Rome quite necessarily became transfixed by what it had to take as its golden age, when authority was supposedly distributed justly and those who ruled had the interests of Rome, and not just themselves and their own families, as their highest interest.

Agency thus took the shape not of a kind of development that when it unfolded along its proper lines went well and which could go wrong in very natural ways, but instead as a place in a social, legally organized system of recognition. It was in effect a conception of agency as that of an 'officeholder' and the power to carry out the specific requirements of that 'office'. An agent failed if he could not realize the aims of his office. There could of course be other aims in life, but one did not fail as a Roman if one failed to realize those aims, nor did one succeed as a Roman if one realized those aims but not those of a recognized 'office'.

This provoked the development within Roman life of a different type of agency that could succeed independently of its offices. Such a conception of agency involved a deeper sense of inwardness than had been the case with either the Greeks or the early Romans themselves, and it manifested itself in the Greco-Roman philosophies of Stoicism, Skepticism, and Epicureanism. As the Roman Empire itself began to unravel, it also became clear that success at being a Roman agent had either become impossible or was a matter of sheer luck, and that a successful life required a conception of inwardness that did not depend on such social-legal recognition. (The Stoic-Skeptical-Epicurean self was in effect the Roman self as a loci of commitments and responsibilities detached from the Roman legal principles that made such an idea intelligible.)

Christianity stepped in to fill that conceptual space. In it, the nature of the world as a divine order claimed a spot for the individual to succeed in her status as an agent, and this success in fact transcended all the elements of this life itself. The freedom that existed in the Greek polis among citizens now seemed to take shape as a freedom not so much from the actual chains of slavery, but from the sins of this life that stood in the way of success as an agent. In becoming Christian, one was freed from one's 'slavery' to sin.

After the initial success of the Roman conception of agency, a different one emerged out of its failure and breakdown.

Christianity thus seemed to displace the idea that freedom could only be obtained negatively, by having others dependent on you but oneself being free of such dependence on others. It substituted instead an idea that none of us was free in relation to each other since all of us were slaves to a heavenly master, who, like a Roman father, had powers of life and death over us, but who, unlike a Roman father, loved us all. It was a short step from that to the idea that none of us therefore possessed natural authority over anybody else, which was also a short step to the conclusion that in the human world, each of us was free since none of us was naturally a slave to anybody else. It did not, however, determine what could be meant by that freedom. The heavenly kingdom was a just order, and in that system of justice all of us, by accepting Christian faith, were now freed from slavery of a certain type. But what was this freedom? It certainly did not at first exclude mundane subordination, slavery, or serfdom.

24.5. FROM ROME TO EUROPE: THE MYTH OF THE *GERMANEN*

In Greek and Roman life, Hegel says that spirit takes its leave of nature. The justice of any human order is now seen not to depend on a basic 'cosmic natural' order of things but instead on the will of a benevolent, loving, all-knowing, and all-powerful deity. Justice in the human order was no longer a plaything of different gods (and thus perhaps contradictory at its heart) but something that in principle was available to reason and to rational reshaping. More important, the Christian principle supposed that agency was not merely an office in social space but something having to do with the individual's own inwardness and self-direction. The agent could be his or her own person—could be, in Hegel's terms, *bei sich*—in the Christian world-order provided he or she was willing to repent of sin and thus to shed the slavery to those passions and inclinations that were at odds with the subjective core of agency, which was to be found in religious faith. If even the masters of Rome had turned out to be slaves to such passions, then the 'truth' that was embodied in the Christian message would set all free.

Although Rome was the incubator of such a sense of freedom, it could not make that principle a reality in people's lives and stay truly Roman. The true standing that individual agents had could not come from each other but only from the one king of kings, the Christian God himself. Paul formulated this Christian idea in his well-known pronouncement in Galatians 3:28 that in Christ there was neither master nor slave, male nor female, Jew nor Gentile. All now occupied not so much an office as a metaphorical place in the divine family. Each was a beloved son or daughter of God.

If the original sense of freedom had been negative—that of not being a slave, of being owned by another—the new sense of freedom was not in not being owned but in being obligated to carry out the principles of the 'Father'. This added a positive, subjective sense of self-direction. Each was now called to figure out what really was required of them as individuals to make those principles real, at work (*wirklich*), in their lives. As such, the statement of the faith still had little institutional import until it became the established Roman church. However, the established Roman church remained in its heart Roman.

Christianity achieved a more practical and institutional import by being taken up, or so Hegel thought, by the barbarian *Germanen* who lived on the borders of Rome and who had always resisted Roman rule. Here Hegel, like generations of Germans and non-Germans alike since the Renaissance, took the treatise by the Roman historian, Tacitus, on the Germans as an account of who these ancient barbarians were. Those *Germanen*—as distinct from the modern *Deutsche*—supposedly were racially pure, had always lived in their native lands, had always spoken their own language, loved freedom, were brave fighters, and were supremely loyal. They were also simple, unsophisticated, and virtuous. Their native love of freedom, rooted in their ethnic makeup itself, made them the ideal vessel for the reception of the Christian message and for making it a principle for changing the world.

Unfortunately, Tacitus's account was for the most part a completely concocted document. It was more or less a political tract on the corruption of his own contemporary fellow Romans and an unfavorable comparison of them to the crude barbarians living just beyond the Roman borders.[13] Tacitus's account of those crude barbarians was for the most part freely imagined in order to make the invidious comparison with the Rome of his own times. Now, although Hegel was not taken in by the more extreme forms of the myth of the noble, freedom-loving *Germanen* (as were unfortunately some of his contemporaries, and, in an insanely poisonous way, even many more of those who followed him in time), he did nonetheless think that they existed. But there were no such *Germanen*, at least not in the sense that Hegel and others thought there had been.

Just as his accounts of the 'East' failed to live up to the facts, Hegel's account of the transition from Rome to 'Europe' as a transition from the Mediterranean world to the northern European world of 'Germanic' peoples thus failed to live up to some other facts. The *Germanen* played a key part in Hegel's narration, since the supposed 'love of freedom' to be found in the Germanic tribes explained how the Christian conception of subjectivity could take such firm affective root in a people in such a way that justice as an order of freedom, and not merely justice as conforming to an unequal cosmic order, could develop itself. The 'Idea' of freedom—the unity of its concept and its reality, or objectivity, in the life of a people—supposedly found its place in the *Germanen* taking over the Christianized Roman Empire. That there were no real *Germanen* in that sense puts a spanner into Hegel's narration of that 'Idea'.

---

[13] See Krebs, *A Most Dangerous Book*, 303.

24.6. Feudalism's Failures

Hegel's point in linking the development of modern Europe to the *Germanen* had to do with how it was that a transition of such magnitude could have been made and what it meant for the structure of agency itself. Nobody in the ancient world significantly questioned the institutional reality of slavery, but by Hegel's own times, slavery had come to be seen not merely as a problematic practice but as a moral evil. This modern Christian world, he argued, had at its heart a different principle. It was not the guiding principle of the ancient world, that "some (that is, male aristocrats) are free," but the new "all are free" principle of the Christian world. That did not end the practice of slavery, but it made it problematic in a different way. If the world was no longer to be conceived as a theater in which arbitrary clashes among the gods were played out, but instead as an order ruled by one God who brought everything together in a comprehensible system, then the necessity of enforced servitude had to be given more of a justification than the shrug and the quip that such was the way of the world. Christianity did not end such enforced servitude, but it made it problematic to itself in a way that had first appeared in Greek philosophy. It gave it a monotheistic underpinning that ultimately made such forms of servitude unintelligible.

The new Christendom that gradually built itself out of the ruins of the Roman breakdown not only did not end such servitude, but on Hegel's account, it actually made it worse. The failure of Christian princes such as Charlemagne to turn their military conquests into a stable set of enduring institutions led to the feudal order, to a system of complete dependence. The Roman system of dependence and the struggle for recognition gave way to a more systematic struggle as people sought protection from violence from more powerful lords. This feudal system, however, was informed by the Christian principle of subjectivity giving itself its own direction. Thus, although each was dependent on some other (and ultimately, only the 'sovereign', the political creation of modernity, was ultimately free, although even he was subject to divine judgment), each was nonetheless free as a 'son' or 'daughter' of God. The idea that some 'sons' are by nature bound to be ruled by other 'sons' was now obviously more problematic.

In the light of the failure of the post-Roman world to make good on that, the *Aufhebung* performed by the European world in that time (its picking up the pieces from the rubble and making something work with them) led to the creation of a new order of things and a different conception of agency.

The feudal order arose because there was no basis yet in practice for the actualization of the Christian ideal. It created a vast system of dependencies, which also turned into a system of inheritable possessions. Might became the basis of right, but that raw power masquerading as right was also given a justification as an expression of the divine order of things. The church embodied all kinds of contradictions in its practices, and the whole system of justice was on its face a system of injustice.

In its reality, it was a system of dependencies on the more powerful, with the powerful always on the lookout for ways to seize even more power for themselves. However, in its art, it thought of itself in terms of a code of chivalry and honor. Whatever the realities of chivalry were—and they were certainly distinct from the ideal, since the reality involved a fair amount of thuggishness to itself—the ideal was based on the new conception of a person committing himself to another (such as pledging eternal fealty to a lord), not his being committed by some kind of natural order of things. Likewise, honor, rather than conceived as a virtue belonging to a member of a determinate social order as committed to the common good of that order, becomes conceived in the art of late medieval Europe as a personal commitment, a code imposed on oneself by oneself. Love, a theme of the ancients as well as the moderns, assumed a more privileged place in the aesthetic reflection on the part of what these new kinds of agent took to be the underlying reality of their lives. The very meaning of tragedy itself changed for such people. Less a clash between the plane of the gods and the plane of the mortals, it became a clash of hearts (love versus the cold reality of social life, honor versus love, etc.) and sometimes a tension among humans seeking to make something of themselves but finding the contingent facts of life too overwhelming. Other times such aesthetic reflection involved the absurdities resulting from a collapsing ethos confronting a new way of living (as in Cervantes' *Don Quixote*). In their Shakespearean form, such figures became recognizable moderns, "consistent within themselves. They remain true to themselves and their passion, and in what they are and in what confronts them they beat about according only to their own fixed determinateness of who they are."[14] They keep the faith of their equal standing in the world, and they reveal themselves simply as who they are, not as moving embodiments of some more abstract pathos. They are the secularized, free Christians who are equals to each other.

In its art, feudal society pictured the agent as an independent source of authority. In its reality, no individual was independent, since everybody was involved in a web of obligations to others, and there was no rational system regulating these obligations. Yet there was also the idea that such a system was not the arbitrary result of different gods feuding or playing with each other, but of one God who was rational and who ensured that there were no contradictions in the system. The long rule of feudalism in Europe proved that a manifestly contradictory political reality could sustain itself for a long time.

24.7. MODERNITY AS FREEDOM

For Hegel, the conception of the modern agent as being at one with himself while being at odds with himself, and of being his own person in and through his relations to

---

[14] " . . . denn Shakespeares Charakters sind in sich selbst konsequent, bleiben sich und ihrer Leidenschaft treu, und was sie sind und was ihnen begegnet, darin schlagen sie sich nur ihrer festen Bestimmtheit nach herum" (Hegel, VA, 202; A, 579).

others—*bei sich im anderen*[15]—goes through a variety of permutations in modern history, with each permutation yielding a different shape for this very general modern conception of agency. In Hegel's philosophy of history, this is not an a priori study of all the possible forms in which this shape of agency can take. It is rather the path-dependent account of the forms it did in fact take. ('Path dependency' here means that the specific conclusion reached depended upon the specific past that led up to it.) Its shapes manifested themselves in a variety of ways: for example, the ways in which we are bound to each other within structures of authority (in political life, the overall focus of the lectures on the philosophy of history); in art, religion, and philosophy; in the difference of very basic types of characters who inhabit certain permutations of the modern world (what Hegel calls 'shapes of consciousness' in his 1807 *Phenomenology*) and in the different shapes of collective-mindedness in various periods and countries (what in the 1807 *Phenomenology* is called a 'shape of spirit'). In each of these ways of looking at historical development, there is an overall story that emerges, but the way the story works is different in each case, even though Hegel is aiming at showing the logic of the whole development.

Overall the story is not that of unrelenting progress, as Hegel's philosophy of history is often (and usually negatively) portrayed. On Hegel's actual conception, failure of agency is failure in achieving the absolute commitments of a 'shape of spirit' or failure in making those commitments stick. In the new 'Christian' order of things, failure in agency would have to be an unconditional, 'infinite' failure, not merely a lapse on the part of a few. Failure in agency means a failure in meaning, such that such failure seems to disclose the very senselessness not of just this or that life, but of the whole of life itself. Thus, in the development of modern Europe, there are wild outbreaks of irrationality, such as the Crusades, culminating, as Hegel memorably described it, as the Crusaders, having begun "with the slaughter and plundering of many thousands of Jews," reaching Jerusalem, where "still dripping with the blood of the slaughtered inhabitants, the Christians fell down on their faces at the tomb of the Redeemer, and directed their impassioned prayers to him."[16] The Crusades themselves were provoked when, in Hegel's words, "as it were, a universal feeling of the nothingness of their conditions coursed through the world."[17] Later, this kind of underlying skepticism (bordering on nihilism) in European life manifested itself in the burning of witches, in which thousands of women were judicially murdered, and in similar outbreaks of mass insanity. The manifest injustice of the feudal system did not count as progress at all, even though it fashioned the conditions for genuine progress to be made later.

The collapse of feudalism was not contingently related to its no longer making sense. That itself was also path-dependent. The ruling nobility and aristocracy claimed their privilege to rule as a result of their military standing. By fighting and protecting the others, and in their willingness to sacrifice their fortunes and even life itself, they

---

[15] Hegel, PR §7.
[16] Hegel, VPG, 449.
[17] Ibid., 449.

supposedly proved their right to rule. However, new technologies, such as the adoption of gunpowder, altered the conditions of battle such that professional armies, and not glory-seeking aristocrats, became the backbone of military matters. With that, the aristocrats lost a good portion of their claim to legitimacy.[18] As it became clear that they had become merely the powdered wig version of bourgeois real estate developers, their own claim to privilege further rotted away.

The Dutch creation of a bourgeois merchant-world based on toleration and a lively civil society brought feudalism almost to its end, and feudalism's decisive end was then sealed by the French Revolution. Most explosively, the French drew the conclusions from the emerging sense of modern agency as based not on this or that tradition but on universal human rights, and this raised the ante for a conception of justice. Securing the conditions of an 'eternal justice' had been the aim of all peoples. With justice now conceived as a system of freedom in which no person exercises natural authority over another, the conditions for legitimate rule and the conditions under which free agency is developed take on a new shape. Individuality becomes the watchword, having one's 'own voice' begins to highlight itself, and political life seems to hang on respecting the various claims that such individuality makes on itself and on others.

The practical and institutional materials to assemble the new order of 'justice as freedom' have, so Hegel argues, been worked out and prepared such that the business of philosophy and practical life itself is to take these materials and put them to work in the right order of things.[19] These consist in a set of general rights that individuals are said to have (life, liberty, property), a set of moral duties they owe to all rational beings (the modern universalistic conception of morality as a 'monadic' order), and a set of institutions with purposes that enable finite humans to realize basic social goods in a non-self-undermining way. He called this the 'ethical' order, indicating that he took it to be a modernized version of a dyadic order of life. (It included the bourgeois family, civil society, and citizenship within a modern, representative, constitutional, although monarchical and not democratic, state, thus setting up a kind of dyadic order of family, followed by a somewhat monadic order of civil society, and capped by the dyadic relation of citizens to each other in the state.) His 1820 *Philosophy of Right* was his argument that his way of assembling them in theory—and not a utilitarian or Kantian or traditionally Aristotelian theory—was the only real way to make that assembly intelligible. In it, modern individuals could be their own person in relation to others and thus be free.

This is not the 'end of history', as if there were no more to be said or no further progress to be made. It is, however, as far as we have come. Hegel concluded his 1831 lectures,

---

[18] "Another technical means was then found to deprive [the nobility] of their superior strength in weaponry—that of *gunpowder*. Humanity needed it, and it immediately appeared. It was one of the chief instruments in liberating the world from the dominion of physical force, and equalizing the various orders of society. As the distinction between the weapons [of the nobility and non-nobility] vanished, that between lords and serfs also vanished" (ibid., 481).

[19] On the relations between Hegel's theory of freedom and recognition with more contemporary literature on oppression, see Anderson, *Hegel's Theory of Recognition*.

as his son, Karl, transcribed it: "It is this far that spirit's consciousness about its freedom has come, it is this far that the concept of spirit has been developed in world history."[20]

24.8. NECESSITY IN HISTORY?

Hegel claimed to have shown a necessity at work in history. This has most often been taken at face value as claiming that the temporal development in history follows a set of laws, or that it non-accidentally fits into some kind of pattern. The most popular way of taking this has been to see it as modeled on something like human action: a human-like entity, *Geist*, has a developmental end, and it proceeds by fits and starts to bring about that end. This has the advantage of ease of interpretation, but it fails as an interpretation of Hegel's overall system in general and his particular working out of the philosophy of history.

The necessity at work in history is a kind of conceptual necessity that depends on Hegel's claim in his *Logic* that metaphysics in its older sense has been supplanted (or *aufgehoben*) in the new post-Kantian Hegelian philosophy. It rests on the claim that the modern conception of agency is intelligible and marks a kind of conceptual progress when measured against earlier conceptions. It is, by implication, an argument that 'declinist' conceptions of modern agency are wrong.[21] It is also the claim that the path-dependent course of modern history has also been shown on philosophical grounds to have a better philosophical conception of agency. The necessity that philosophy claims to find in history is not that of a causal chain (even a non-empirical chain of some kind of cosmic *Geist* pursuing its own end) such that once the Egyptians had built the pyramids, the occurrence of the French Revolution was only a matter of time. Nor is it a thesis about convergence such that once certain elements are in place, a certain type of social order and political system will arrive (as many so-called 'modernization' theories in the social sciences claim). Although it is contingent that history makes sense, the conditions of its making sense are not themselves contingent. Those latter conditions are explicated in the *Logic* and the *Encyclopedia*.

Since the entire account depends on there being no legitimate alternative conception of agency to be found in Hegel's mythical 'East', and he has not given an adequate account at all of Africa and the 'East', then he has not shown that the course of history moves from failed 'Eastern' agencies to more successful European ones—even if his treatment of European history is judged to be more or less correct. Moreover, if in fact China, India, and Africa have developed genuinely alternative structures of agency—which no a priori analysis is going to show—then the failure of Hegel's 'China', 'India',

---

[20] Hegel, PG, 241.

[21] The best-known contemporary version is that found in MacIntyre, *After Virtue: A Study in Moral Theory*. MacIntyre, it is well known, argues that the rise of individualism as a core belief in ethical theory was in fact not progress but a step in the wrong direction.

and 'Africa' does not show that there are no alternative structures of agency at work in the world. If the philosophy of history depends on the facts, and Hegel got the facts wrong, then on his own terms, he would have to start again. This means that on its own self-defined terms, Hegel's philosophy of history fails to make its case. In the broader terms he set for himself, he may have come closer to success. Whereas justice is rarely on the front pages of history's story, it is in fact a good part of what the story is all about.[22]

WORKS CITED

Primary Texts

Hegel, G. W. F. *Die Philosophie der Geschichte: Vorlesungsmitschrift Heimann (Winter 1830/1831)* [PG]. Munich: Wilhelm Fink, 2005.

Hegel, G. W. F. *Elements of the Philosophy of Right* [PR], translated by H. B. Nisbett, edited by Allen Wood. Cambridge: Cambridge University Press, 1991.

Hegel, G. W. F. *Hegel's Philosophy of Mind* [E], translated by W. Wallace and A.V. Miller, with revisions and commentary by M. J. Inwood. Oxford: Oxford University Press, 2007.

Hegel, G. W. F. *Hegel's Aesthetics: Lectures on Fine Art* [A], translated by T. M. Knox. Oxford: Oxford University Press, 1975.

Hegel, G. W. F. *Lectures on the Philosophy of World History. Introduction: Reason in History* [LPH], translated by H. B. Nisbet. Cambridge: Cambridge University Press, 1975.

Hegel, G. W. F. *The Philosophy of History* [PH], translated by J. Sibree. New York: Dover, 1956.

Hegel, G. W. F. *Vorlesungen über die Ästhetik II* [VA]. Frankfurt am Main: Suhrkamp, 1969.

Hegel, G. W. F. *Vorlesungen über die Philosophie der Geschichte* [VPG], Frankfurt am Main: Suhrkamp, 1969.

Hegel, G. W. F., and J. Hoffmeister. *Vorlesungen über die Philosophie der Weltgeschichte: Band I: Die Vernunft in der Geschichte* [VPW]. Hamburg: 1994.

Secondary Literature

Anderson, S. C. *Hegel's Theory of Recognition: From Oppression to Ethical Liberal Modernity*. London; New York, 2009.

Appiah, K. A. "Africa: The Hidden History." *New York Review of Books*. New York, December 17, 1998.

Krebs, C. B. *A Most Dangerous Book: Tacitus's Germania from the Roman Empire to the Third Reich*. New York: W. W. Norton, 2011.

MacIntyre, A. C. *After Virtue: A Study in Moral Theory*. Notre Dame, IN: Nortre Dame University Press, 1981.

Moore, A. W. *The Evolution of Modern Metaphysics: Making Sense of Things* Cambridge; New York: Cambridge University Press, 2012.

Moyar, D. *Hegel's Conscience*. Oxford; New York: Oxford University Press, 2011.

Pinkard, T. *Does History Make Sense?* Cambridge, MA: Harvard University Press, 2017.

Pippin, R. "Die Logik der Negation bei Hegel," in *Hegel: 200 Jahre Wissenschaft der Logik*, edited by C. Wirsing, K. A. F. Koch, F. Schick, and K. Vieweg. Hamburg: Felix Meiner, 2014, 87–110.

---

[22] I give a more full account of this in Pinkard, *Does History Make Sense?*

Pippin, R. "The Significance of Self-Consciousness in Idealist Theories of Logic." *Proceedings of the Aristotelian Society* CXIV, part 2 (2014): 145–166.

Rödl, S. "The Form of the Will," in *Desire, Practical Reason, and the Good*, edited by S. Tenenbaum. New York: Oxford University Press, 2010, 138–160.

Taiwo, O. "Exorcising Hegel's Ghost: Africa's Challenge to Philosophy." *African Studies Quarterly* 1 (1998): 1–16.

Thompson, M. "What Is It to Wrong Someone? A Puzzle about Justice," in *Reason and Value: Themes from the Moral Philosophy of Joseph Raz*, edited by R. J. Wallace et al. Oxford; New York: Clarendon Press, 2004, 333–384.

PART VI

ABSOLUTE SPIRIT

CHAPTER 25

....

HEGEL'S
PHILOSOPHY OF ART

....

LYDIA L. MOLAND

AMONG the philosophers of Hegel's generation, art achieved unprecedented status. Kant's *Critique of Judgment* suggested that aesthetic experience was key to the achievement of human freedom. Schiller's letters on aesthetic education claimed that art could heal the modern world's alienation and inspire political enlightenment. Friedrich Schlegel and the poet Novalis launched German Romanticism with the assertion that art provided humans' only access to truth. The young Hegel himself, together with his fellow students Friedrich Schelling and Friedrich Hölderlin, concluded that "the highest act of reason is an aesthetic act" and that the philosopher "must possess as much aesthetic power as the poet."[1] These more romantic views did not survive into Hegel's adulthood, but art continued to figure prominently in his philosophy. The *Phenomenology of Spirit* (1806) includes frequent and systematically pivotal references to art; art's importance in Hegel's mature philosophy is clear from its status in the *Encyclopedia of the Philosophical Sciences* as a form of absolute spirit. Hegel's wide-ranging knowledge of art and its history is evidenced by his regular university lectures on the topic, given at the height of his career. His interest in art was also personal. Students reported him to be an assiduous opera-goer; his letters to his wife recount how deeply great works of art, which he sought out on his travels, affected him.[2]

Given this background, it is not surprising that art's significance, according to Hegel, far exceeds its ability to please, amuse, or edify. Art, instead, is nothing less than "one way of bringing to our minds and expressing the *Divine*, the deepest interests of mankind, and the most comprehensive truths of the spirit" (*Ä:I*, 21/7).[3] Not only this: it is partly through art that we become fully human in the first place. In art, Hegel says,

---

[1] Anonymous, "The Oldest Systematic Program of German Idealism," 4.

[2] See James, *Art, Myth and Society in Hegel's Aesthetics*, 79; Kolb, "Hegel's Architecture," 40; Sallis, "Carnation and the Eccentricity of Painting," 107.

[3] G. W. F. Hegel, *Vorlesungen über die Ästhetik I*, ed. Eva Moldenhauer and Karl Markus Michel, vol. 13–15, *Werke in 20 Bänden* (Frankfurt am Main: Suhrkamp, 1970). The English translation is *Hegel's*

man brings himself before himself by *practical* activity, since he has the impulse, in whatever is directly given to him, in what is present to him externally, to produce himself and therein equally to recognize himself. This aim he achieves by altering external things whereon he impresses the seal of his inner being and in which he now finds again his own characteristics. Man does this in order, as a free subject, to strip the external world of its inflexible foreignness and to enjoy in the shape of things only an external realization of himself. (*Ä:I*, 51/31)

This pronouncement has two components, both of which are central to Hegel's idealism. The first is that freedom for Hegel means recognizing that the world is not inflexibly foreign: we do not confront an independently existing world that awaits our passive understanding. Instead, reality is formed by humans, together with each other and input from the world. The second is that being human is not a matter of belonging to a predetermined natural kind, but instead involves a process of collective self-determination and mutual recognition of that self-determination. Art merges these two insights by being an activity in which humans explicitly do what they otherwise implicitly do: they alter the external world's otherness—by forming marble into sculptures or combining pigments to create paintings—and, in the process, both impress their 'inner being' on the world and are in turn formed by that world. In the object that results, humans discover the 'deepest interests' that characterize them and their societies: their conceptions of the divine, their understanding of their humanness, their attitude toward nature. In doing so, it has the potential to embody the unification of subject and object at the heart of Hegel's idealism.[4] Art's importance for Hegel, in short, can hardly be exaggerated.

Given art's clear significance for Hegel's philosophy, it is all the more surprising to find him describing art's potential as decidedly limited. Despite its ability to manifest philosophical truth as Hegel understands it, art's sensuous essence limits its ability to articulate these claims *as* claims about truth; somewhat ironically, the closer a work comes to articulating these claims, the less likely it is to be art. This limitation puts art in a particularly difficult position in the modern world, which, in Hegel's view, has achieved the most self-consciously articulated understanding of truth. Despite the 'universal need for art', *modern* humans will never be able to express their deepest truths sensuously. "Art," Hegel writes, "no longer affords that satisfaction of spiritual needs which earlier ages and nations sought in it, and found in it alone" (*Ä:I*, 24/10).

Aesthetics: Lectures on Fine Art, trans. T. M. Knox (Oxford: Oxford University Press, 1975). Abbreviated Ä, followed by the volume and page number of the Suhrkamp edition, then by the page number of the English translation.

[4] Even this brief synopsis of his views makes Hegel's path-breaking approach to art evident. He rejects imitation as art's basis, denies that beauty is a necessary characteristic for art, repudiates the ancient quarrel between poetry and philosophy, and virtually ignores art's pedagogical or political potential. Most strikingly, Hegel essentially neglects to discuss aesthetic experience, a topic that had dominated philosophical conversations about art in the eighteenth century (Ä: I, 13/1).

These two claims—that art's sensuous status limits its ability to make philosophical claims explicit and that art's power in the modern world is diminished—together contribute to Hegel's so-called 'end of art' thesis. This thesis, controversial already in Hegel's lifetime, has precipitated no end of confusion, resulting perhaps most notoriously in the suggestion that Hegel predicted the 'death' of art and believed that no new art would be produced after his lifetime. Although this particular myth has been debunked by decades of scholarship, Hegel's pronouncements about art's limitations remain opaque, admitting, as do many of Hegel's central claims, of multiple interpretations.[5] For the purposes of this chapter, I will interpret Hegel's thesis about art's end as referencing his concern that the emergence of modern subjectivity—a positive development in itself—exposes art to trends that threaten its status *as art*. This becomes evident if we follow Hegel's intricately constructed, two-part story about art: the first illustrating how subjectivity's historical unfolding shapes the development of art; the second assessing how subjectivity is embodied in individual arts from architecture to poetry. At several points in both accounts, art risks disintegrating: it risks, for instance, developing into religion, collapsing into incoherence, or dissipating into prose. Focusing on these points of possible dissolution allows us to address two central questions. The first concerns what future art must be like in order to continue fulfilling the ambitious mission Hegel assigns to it. The second regards what the value of art, not just as an articulation of humans' deepest truths but as a *sensuous* articulation of those truths, might be.

25.1. SOURCES

The difficulty of parsing claims such as the 'end of art' thesis is much exacerbated by the fact that Hegel's published references to art after the *Phenomenology* are minimal. The *Encyclopedia* contains only eight sections on art and references no particular artworks or even aesthetic genres. Although Hegel lectured on the philosophy of art several times (1818 in Heidelberg and then 1820/1821, 1823, 1826, and 1828/1829 in Berlin), his sudden death in 1831 prevented him from carrying out his plan to publish a student handbook to accompany his lectures.[6] Soon after his death, Hegel's student Heinrich Gustav Hotho gathered the two notebooks Hegel had used in his lectures and expanded them, with the help of several students' lecture notes (*Nachschriften*), into a work he entitled *Vorlesungen über die Ästhetik* (Lectures on Aesthetics).[7] This text, first published in

---

[5] Donougho lists several possible interpretations in "Art and History: Hegel on the End, the Beginning, and the Future of Art." See also Gethmann-Siefert, *Ist die Kunst tot und zu Ende?*

[6] Gethmann-Siefert details this history in *Einführung in Hegels Ästhetik*, 17–18. Gethmann-Siefert's extensive scholarship generally is essential reading on the topic of Hegel's philosophy of art.

[7] See Gethmann-Siefert's discussion of this issue in her introduction to G. W. F. Hegel, *Vorlesungen über die Philosophie der Kunst (Mitschrift Hotho 1823)*, xxii.

1835, became the standard reference for scholarship on Hegel's philosophy of art. Its 1975 translation into English by T. M. Knox, entitled *Hegel's Aesthetics: Lectures on Fine Art*, further solidified this status.

In the past decades, German scholar Annemarie Gethmann-Siefert has led a group of researchers who, referencing surviving student notes from individual lecture cycles, have cast disquieting doubt on the integrity of Hotho's text. Hotho, this research suggests, revised and displaced examples, substituted in some cases his own aesthetic philosophy for Hegel's, and—perhaps most seriously—altered the dialectical structure of Hegel's argument. Gethmann-Siefert also claims that enduring controversies about Hegel's position on art—his purported 'classicism', his description of art as the "sensible shining of the idea," and the status of his claim about art's end—are a result of Hotho's tendentious editing. In an effort to establish what of the 1835 edition is actually attributable to Hegel, Gethmann-Siefert and others have published student *Nachschriften* from three of the years Hegel lectured on art.[8] These publications unquestionably bear out some of Gethmann-Siefert's concerns. Philosophical issues aside, the fact that Hotho's 1835 text runs to over 1,200 pages, while none of the student transcripts totals more than 400, suggests significant editorial license. The individual lecture notes also confirm that Hegel's thoughts about art evolved, sometimes dramatically, between lecture cycles. Given the lack of a verifiably Hegelian text, no definitive account of Hegel's mature reflections on art is likely to be forthcoming. Interpreting Hegel's philosophy of art is for these reasons particularly difficult, even by the standards of Hegel scholarship.

Reactions to these difficulties have varied widely. Some scholars, convinced by Gethmann-Siefert's concerns, now base their research only on the *Encyclopedia* or on the student transcripts. Others argue that Hotho's text is as close as we can come to Hegel's thought; moreover, Hotho's text itself now has an almost 200-year history in the scholarship that deserves consideration. Still others attempt to strike a balance by using both Hotho's text and the student transcripts. Given the richness of Hotho's text—possibly based in sources now lost to us—and its history in the scholarship, this balanced approach seems to me warranted. I have relied on Hegel's published comments in the *Encyclopedia* for systematic outlines but have used the lectures—both Hotho's amalgamation and the more recently published student transcripts—in the hope of giving a sense of the depth and breadth of Hegel's interest in art.

---

[8] *Vorlesung über Ästhetik: Berlin 1820/21: eine Nachschrift; Vorlesung über die Philosophie der Kunst* (Mitschrift Hotho 1823); *Philosophie der Kunst oder Ästhetik* (Mitschrift von Kehler 1826); *Philosophie der Kunst* (Mitschrift von der Pfordten 1826). The edition of Hotho's 1823 lecture notes (not to be confused with his 1835 compendium) has recently been translated into English: see *Lectures on the Philosophy of Art: The Hotho Transcript of the 1823 Berlin Lectures*. The 1828/1829 student lecture notes are still in preparation.

25.2. Preliminaries: Art, the Idea, the Ideal, and the Beautiful

One thing we can be sure of, given both the *Encyclopedia*'s account and the lecture sources, is the position of art in Hegel's system. The true, as Hegel famously says, is the whole; everything that exists is part of a self-producing totality. This totality dialectically generates the entirety of Hegel's system from logic to chemistry to the family to politics. It also generates the opposition between the un-self-conscious (nature) and the self-conscious (humans). The aspects of this totality that have to do specifically with humans as self-conscious beings—their psychology, their moral status, their institutions, their modes of reflection—Hegel classifies as 'spirit'. Self-consciousness implies reflectivity, or the capacity to understand why we do what we do. For this reason, the realm of spirit is normative. We ask for and give reasons for our decisions; together we create roles and their corresponding norms; we negotiate with each other for recognition of our actions within those roles. Ultimately, Hegel hopes, mutual recognition among self-determining subjects will generate institutions, such as civil society and the state, that support the further development of freedom and so are what he calls *rational*.

The fact that these institutions (ideally) derive from mutual recognition means that ethical life—the sphere of the family, civil society, and the state—is itself a form of self-legislation and so of freedom. It is also an expression of our *unity with* the world rather than our separation from it. The norms of ethical life do not originate in an otherworldly divine sphere, nor do they position us in opposition to nature. They are instead an outgrowth of our own activities. An important consequence of this view is Hegel's claim that humans should not seek external sources of authority. We should not look to our senses for 'real' knowledge of the external world; neither should we look to nature or gods for the source of our laws. We, as the self-conscious part of the self-generating totality, are the creators of the world's normative structure. Hegel calls this normative sphere the Idea.

The nature of the Idea, however, is such that it is not enough for humans to create the normative sphere and then cooperate within it. As the part of the whole that is self-conscious and so reflective, we must also reflect on the normative sphere itself. Genuine totality in Hegel's scheme requires *understanding* of the totality; otherwise the totality would be not total but limited by its understanding. *Absolute spirit* is the term Hegel uses to describe the struggle to reflect on and articulate the Idea. Absolute spirit consists of art, religion, and philosophy, all of which have the same subject matter, namely, apprehension of the absolute Idea.[9] The three components of absolute spirit are, in other words, forms of humans' attempts to articulate their status as co-authors of the normative sphere and so as free.

---

[9] *Hegel's Science of Logic*, trans. A. V. Miller, 824. Quoted in Pippin, *After the Beautiful*, 6.

Art, as Hegel explains in Part I of the *Aesthetics*, differs from religion and philosophy in being sensuously embodied. Whereas religion is pictorial thinking and philosophy is free thinking (*Ä:I*, 139/101), art "has no other mission but to bring before sensuous contemplation the truth as it is in the spirit" (*Ä:II*, 257/623). Hegel calls art's attempts to put the Idea in 'determinate form'—in other words, to give sensuous embodiment to the fundamental unity underlying the normative sphere—'the Ideal' (*Ä:I*, 145/106).[10] Art's sensuous embodiment explains its position as the first, least explicit stage of absolute spirit. Although art is a vehicle for understanding truth, it does not present itself *as such*. Since the Idea requires that humans *know* the truth about their place in the world (as opposed only to sensing it), art falls below religion and philosophy, both of which depict their knowledge of the totality more explicitly *as* knowledge.

Humans throughout history, Hegel claims, have always endeavored to articulate the Idea. In other words, evaluation of the normative sphere has always been the *content* of art, religion, and philosophy as *forms* of reflection. But humans' understanding of the normative sphere has frequently been inaccurate, attributing normative authority to nature or the gods instead of acknowledging the normative sphere as their own achievement. The modern age, Hegel thinks, had begun to remedy this inaccuracy by asserting that all humans (as opposed to only some) are free and so sources of normative authority. This positive development in terms of content, as we will see, generates the strange consequence that art—as an incomplete form of absolute spirit—can only *adequately* represent conceptions of the Idea that are themselves *inadequate*. Once a more adequate understanding of the Idea is achieved as absolute spirit's content, religion and philosophy supplant art as the most fitting forms of reflection on that content.

Hegel extends the requirement for the appropriate balance of form and content to his definition of art itself. All art, he claims, seeks to represent the Idea in sensuous form. Art should then be judged by how well its sensuous form expresses the conception of the Idea in question, however inadequate that conception is. The two should interpenetrate each other such that "the external, the particular, appears exclusively as a presentation of the inner" (*Ä:I*, 132/95). Bad art results not necessarily from the artist's lack of skill but from an inadequate pairing of form and content. But even good art is not necessarily in Hegel's conception *beautiful* art. Beautiful art, by contrast, is achieved only if the worldview in question is perfectly expressible *in art* such that "the figure shows [the Idea] and it alone" (E §556). The beautiful, in other words, leaves nothing left over; there is no part of the worldview's content that it does not express, and it includes nothing that does not express the worldview in question. Beautiful art is, Hegel says, thus a "penetration of the vision or image by the spiritual principle" (E §559), "the pure appearance of the Idea to sense" (*Ä:I*, 151/111). As we will see in what follows, Hegel thinks such beauty was achieved in only one of the three historical worldviews into which, he claims, history is divided.

---

[10] Pinkard gives a more detailed summary of this range of terms in "Symbolic, Classical, and Romantic Art," 8–13.

25.3. The Symbolic, Classical, and Romantic Forms of Art

To repeat, the content of art has, in one sense, always remained constant. Like religion and philosophy, art chronicles humans' attempts to articulate the Idea, to make sense of their place in the world's normative structure. But in another sense, that content changes as the accuracy of their understanding of the Idea (from Hegel's point of view) improves or worsens.[11] In Part II of his lectures, entitled "The Development of the Ideal into the Particular Forms of Art," Hegel describes how the two elements of art—the Idea and its sensuous expression—yield three *forms* of art (which he also calls worldviews): an *inadequate* conception of the Idea can be given *inadequate* expression (symbolic art); an *inadequate* conception of the Idea can also be given *adequate* expression (classical art); and, finally, an *adequate* conception of the Idea can be given *inadequate* expression (romantic art). Tracing this development clarifies the role Hegel thinks art is capable of playing; it also reveals points at which art threatens to dissolve.

The symbolic worldview is inadequate in Hegel's estimation because it depicts gods as independent sources of authority who hide meaning that humans are left to decipher. Symbolic art emerges, in other words, in religions "where the Idea has not yet been revealed and known in its free character" and "figuration suitable to the Idea is not yet found" (E §562). The divine is abstract and inscrutable; the artist can engage only in "a restless and unappeased effort which throws itself into shape after shape as it vainly tries to find its goal" (E §561). The result is often "hideous idols regarded as wonder-working talismans" produced in an attempt to interpret the gods' commands (E §562). In the symbolic worldview, humans are 'superficial' (E §561), mere supplicants seeking to wrest meaning from an indecipherable universe.

Egyptian art is Hegel's example of 'symbolism proper'. Pyramids are an "external environment in which an inner meaning rests concealed" (*Ä:I*, 460/356); the story of Isis and Osiris is "a symbol for the sun's yearly course"; the Sphinx is the "objective riddle par excellence," "the symbol of the symbolic itself" (*Ä:I*, 465/360). Hindu epics, Islamic poetry, and Jewish psalms loosen the identification of the divine with the natural, a development that for Hegel counts as progress *within* the symbolic worldview toward better articulation of the Idea. But these religious views maintain a separation between an incomprehensible, sublime deity and the human, meaning that their art continues to embody what Hegel believes to be an inadequate understanding of humans' place in the world. Because it gestures at content that cannot be contained in its form, symbolic art also cannot, according to Hegel, be beautiful.

---

[11] Hegel's use of art to isolate and explain a culture's commitments has led some to call him the 'father of art history'. Pippin discusses this claim in *After the Beautiful*, 17–18. *After the Beautiful* is itself an extended argument for using Hegel's claims about art's historical nature and normative essence to explore an art form Hegel could not have foreseen, namely modernist painting.

This radical separation is resolved with the advent of the classical worldview in which gods begin appearing in human form. The human body—as opposed to grotesque talismans or towering pyramids—is of all natural forms "the highest and the true, because only in it can the spirit have its corporeity and thus its visible expression" (E §558). Everything from the position of humans' mouths to the transparency of our veins indicates, according to Hegel, that the human body is as harmonious an expression of the spiritual as is physically possible (Ä:I, 194/146, Ä:II, 21/433). In addition to giving gods human form, Greek mythology attributes human passions to the gods and divine motivation to humans. This interpenetration of human and divine increases within the evolution of Greek mythology itself, Hegel claims: Greeks first anthropomorphized the gods of nature (Poseidon as god of the sea), then deified human emotion (Aphrodite as goddess of love) and ultimately human institutions (Athena as guardian of Athens).

Unlike the symbolic world's restless struggle to discover and interpret the normative, ancient Greeks (in Hegel's oversimplified assessment) existed entirely in harmony with the community's ethical life (Ä:II, 25/437). There was, in other words, no interiority in the Greek worldview, no subjective perspective at odds with traditional mores. Art could therefore depict it fully: there was no content in the Greek worldview that art could not embody, and Greek art included nothing that did not express its worldview. Subject and substance, human and divine existed in complete accord, allowing the Greeks, uniquely among civilizations, to achieve pure beauty. "[T]he perfection of art reached its peak" in the cheerful peace of the classical world, Hegel says (Ä:II, 127/517); classical art was "a conceptually adequate representation of the Ideal." Nothing, Hegel wistfully concludes, "can be or become more beautiful" (Ä:II, 128/517).

Ultimately, however, the classical world's depiction of gods in human form was its undoing. Interpreting their motivations as divine suggested to humans that the divine was *within* them, a discovery that in turn produced a sense of individual moral agency independent of divine law or community practice. A new sense of interiority grew from this independence, prompting citizens to assess and dispute traditional laws, awakening "thought's discontent with the reality which is given to it and which no longer corresponds with it" (Ä:II, 107/501). Hegel describes this development as a clash between substance—understood here as the ethical order—and subjectivity—the individual's assessment of that order. The resulting discontentment is most famously articulated in Socrates' defiance of the government of Athens, but it also takes artistic form. In lampooning Athens' sophists or its wars, Aristophanes' comedies depict his protagonists' subjectivity—their assertion of themselves as sources of moral authority—undermining substance, or the ethical life around them. In portraying this conflict, Aristophanes acknowledges a point of view that did not exist at the high point of classical culture.

Individuals' insistence that their moral assessments be recognized represents a significant advance for humans' understanding of themselves as free. But it also signals the end of art as an adequate expression of human self-understanding for the simple reason that interiority, Hegel claims, cannot successfully be given sensuous form. This, then, is one way that art threatens to dissolve. Interiority is better captured by religion's narratives (specifically, in Hegel's undoubtedly narrow view, by Christianity's claim that

God, in the form of the Holy Spirit, inhabits every believer) and by philosophy's self-articulation in thought. Nevertheless, the development of interiority means not that art will not continue, but instead that humans will use art *imperfectly* to embody their new sense of interiority and their status as sources of authority.

In the romantic worldview—by which Hegel means any art after the appearance of Christianity—content and form again diverge. The topic of art is still the divine, but Christianity claims that the divine exists "in the spiritual world alone," so any sensuous embodiment will by definition be inadequate (E §562). Painting depicting the suffering of martyrs is, for instance, unable to express the fullness of Christian piety. Tales of the Crusades only accentuate the incongruity between Christians' territorial aims and Jesus' spiritual kingdom. In medieval chivalric legends, the subjective drive for honor becomes so detached from any objective ethical assessment that knights ride to the aid even of "a gang of rascals" to prove their courage (*Ä:II*, 215/589). Such contrast between subjective goals and objective reality forms the basis of comic writings by Ariosto, Cervantes, and Shakespeare in which "we find marvelous ramifications and conflicts introduced, begun, broken off, re-entangled, cross-cut, and finally resolved in a surprising way" (*Ä:II*, 217/ 591). The romantic age's characteristic subjectivity ultimately produces the romantic fiction of Hegel's generation in which young, usually bourgeois protagonists, despairing at the world's refusal to understand them, throw themselves against "the will of a father or an aunt" (*Ä:II*, 219/593). Such novels, in Hegel's laconic description, generally end when subjective idiosyncrasy capitulates to the prosaic: when the protagonist "gets his girl and some sort of position, marries her, and becomes as good a Philistine as others" (*Ä:II*, 220/593).

After the domestication of romance in fiction, the separation of subjectivity and objectivity, implicit from the beginning of romantic art, becomes explicit. Art goes in two directions, both of which threaten its status *as art*. On the one hand, the artist, finding it impossible to give her interiority sensuous expression, abandons her subjectivity and resorts to imitating the object. Hegel's example is the hyper-realism and domesticity of Dutch genre painting, in which anything, even tooth extraction, can be the subject of art (*Ä:II*, 226/598). Although Hegel deeply admired the work of Vermeer and Rembrandt, he concludes that only their sheer talent and 'subjective vivacity' save their works from collapsing into mere imitation and ceasing to be art altogether. On the other hand, the artist abandons all pretentions to objectivity and loses herself in subjective whim. This results in what Hegel calls 'subjective humor', a novelistic genre (with disconcertingly little resemblance to contemporary definitions of humor) in which authors such as Jean Paul seek no objectivity or even coherence, instead stringing together whatever occurs to them into loose, fantastical plots (*Ä:II*, 229/601). For most of his career, this development prompted Hegel to conclude that subjective humor marks the disintegration of art.[12]

---

[12] In 1826, for instance, Hegel concludes that "[w]ith humor art runs out [*Beim Humoristischen also geht es mit der Kunst aus*] . . . . This is the disintegration [*Zerfallen*] of art" (*Philosophie der Kunst oder Ästhetik (Mitschrift von Kehler 1826)*, 153).

Art's complex status in Hegel's philosophy is evident again in the fact that precisely in its dissolution, art tracks the *positive* development of humans' understanding of their place in the normative sphere: their understanding, in short, of the Idea. Because it could not tolerate subjectivity's critique of the normative structure, the unity of the Greek worldview, however beautiful, reflected an inadequate understanding of the Idea. We can mourn its loss, but returning to Greek harmony would mean abandoning our ability to make moral judgments independently of our communities. We would then be denying that we are co-authors of our norms and so self-determining. Like it or not, art's attempts to articulate the Idea will now concern "the depths and heights of the human heart as such, mankind in its joys and sorrows, its strivings, deeds, and fates" (*Ä:II*, 238/ 607). *Humanus*, Hegel says in an echo of Goethe's gentle irony, is art's new 'holy of holies' (*Ä:II*, 237/607).[13] This humanistic reorientation explains Hegel's contention that modern humans can no longer 'bend the knee' to art: art can no longer celebrate the epoch-forming deeds of gods or heroes but must instead depict a reality all too human (*Ä:I*, 142/103). In the deepest Hegelian sense, this radical secularization tracks the truth: the divine is the human, and human concerns are divine concerns. Only with this realization can we begin to understand the fully articulated Idea, which is to say the fundamental totality and our place in it. The fact that this truth is not adequately presentable in art does not make it any less true.

But art's new human focus need not signal its demise. Art that resists spiritless imitation of objectivity, on the one hand, and subjective self-indulgence, on the other, could still fulfill art's role in the modern world. In his last lectures, Hegel seems to have given more thought to this possibility, concluding that with the right effort, the modern artist can successfully depict the Idea.[14] The artist must (unlike the subjective humorist) take his work seriously (*Ä:II*, 233/604); the content of the artwork must be "imbued with living and contemporary interest," not a rehashing of old or sentimental themes (*Ä:II*, 239/ 608). Finally, the artist must choose the right form for this inmost, contemporary truth. If these criteria are met, Hegel concedes that a kind of 'spiritual beauty' can be achieved in romantic art, even if the most perfect form of sensual beauty cannot (*Ä:II*, 129/518). He concludes by suggesting that an art form he calls *objective humor* might reunite the two extremes of romantic art. In objective humor—a genre also not to be confused with the comical or the funny—the artist focuses her creative talents on the object, describing and enlivening it through her subjective associations. As a modern example of such synthesis, Hegel somewhat surprisingly lauds Goethe's *West-östlicher Divan,* a lyrical cycle in which Goethe's poetic imagination is employed not to parade or indulge his subjectivity (as in the case of Jean Paul's fantastical plots) but to imbue everyday objects with beauty and meaning. In the process, both Goethe and the object are transformed and so embody the mutual formation of self and world that is at the heart of Hegel's idealism.

We will likely never know what prompted Hegel's more optimistic assessment of art's potential in his 1828 lectures. But objective humor as a redemption of art's potential

---

[13] See Donougho, "Remarks on 'Humanus heißt der Heilige.'"
[14] See Rutter, *Hegel on the Modern Arts,* 49.

aligns with another of Hegel's philosophical claims. Art that includes objective humor's acknowledgment of the mutual formation between subject and object is positioned to address yet another misunderstanding of the Idea, namely, the claim that any given subject *alone* can determine normativity. Aesthetically, we see this claim play out in chivalry's haphazard definition of honor and the subjective humorist's refusal to construct plots comprehensible to anyone but herself. In both cases, the subject refuses to negotiate with the world around her. We can understand Hegel's objection to such art by considering a correlate mistake in ethical life: namely, an individual's belief that her conscience alone can determine right and wrong. The ultimate truth—both in aesthetics and in ethics—is for Hegel otherwise: only in communities founded on mutual recognition can negotiation about normativity yield true freedom. Objective humor will never express this truth completely: no matter how skillfully the artist enlivens the object through her subjectivity, there will still be interiority left unexpressed. But in modeling the mutual determination between subject and object, objective humor provides a prototype, however limited, for the sensuous embodiment of the Idea in the romantic world.[15]

25.4. The System of the Individual Arts

This mixed assessment of art's potential within historical worldviews concludes Part II of the lectures. In Part III, entitled "The System of the Individual Arts," Hegel leaves worldviews generally behind and instead explores the *external* aspect of art: the kinds of sensuous embodiment (visual, tactile, audial) that individual arts employ (*Ä:II*, 245/613). In this second trajectory, which allows him to analyze art not as a historical phenomenon but on its own terms, Hegel has two principal aims that are distinct from his aims in Part II. One is to show the extent to which each art helps humans understand their relation to the totality—in other words, to what extent each art *in itself* expresses the Idea. The second is to develop the claim that art enables us to produce ourselves both individually and collectively. Also in tracing Hegel's assessment of art's external aspect, we find that the closer art comes to articulating the Idea, the more its status as art is undermined. Hegel considers five individual arts in an order that begins with architecture, which he considers barely an art, and ends with poetry, which in its furthest development risks no longer being art.

Architecture from Hegel's standpoint is limited since it "has not found for the presentation of its spiritual content either the adequate material or the corresponding forms" (*Ä:II*, 258/624). Architecture barely lifts itself above the sensuous: its material is heavy, natural, and raw, and so is 'non-spiritual'. Its form must explicitly obey the laws of gravity and so is also not free (*Ä:II*, 259/624). Nevertheless, each of the worldviews discussed in Part II expresses its 'spiritual convictions' through architecture. Paradigmatically

---

[15] Pillow suggests that some modern art fits this description as well: see *Sublime Understanding*, 228.

symbolic architecture emerges when a developing nation seeks to express itself and, because its self-understanding is indefinite and abstract, "catches at what is equally abstract, i.e. matter as such, as what has mass and weight" (*Ä:II*, 273/635). As examples, Hegel cites colossal structures in Babylon, India, and Egypt that serve as a 'unifying point' for a nation's religious ideas, despite those ideas being vague and mutable. By contrast, the harmony of the classical worldview expresses itself architecturally through its embodiment of laws of proportion and gravity and by Greek temples' perfect unity of form and function. Through their breadth rather than height, exposure to open air, and lack of a central gathering place, Greek temples embody the "cheerfulness, openness, and comfort" of the worldview that produced them (*Ä:II*, 321/676). Romantic architecture, by contrast, "struggles upwards immeasurably and lifts itself to the sky," inspiring its viewers to raise their spiritual gaze above the earthly (*Ä:II*, 319/674). Gothic cathedrals, for instance, embody Christianity's interiority by allowing no intrusion by nature—even natural light, Hegel points out, is filtered through stained glass windows. This contrast indicates that Christianity's "spiritual meaning does not reside exclusively in the building" but in the hearts of its adherents (*Ä:II*, 303–304/661). In allowing humans to express their spiritual understanding materially, architecture indeed contributes to humans' ability to impress themselves on the world and see themselves in it. But architecture's unspiritual matter and its trend toward functionality limit its potential to express the Idea.

Sculpture, like architecture, uses "heavy matter in its spatial entirety," transforming inorganic material into an expression of spirit. Unlike architecture, however, sculpture's form is not dictated by symmetry and functionality. In Hegel's somewhat idiosyncratic view, only sculpture depicting the human body is *true* sculpture. Again because humans' unique physiognomy (our upright posture, our recessed eyes) so perfectly captures spirituality, sculpture "comprises the miracle of spirit's giving itself an image of itself in something purely material" (*Ä:II*, 362/710). In achieving this unity of form and content, sculpture "more than any other art always points particularly to the Ideal" (*Ä:II*, 372/ 718).

Sculpture proper is impossible in the symbolic worldview, given that it did not recognize the divine in the human and so could not portray their unity. The classical world, as we have already seen, by contrast depicted the human in divine form and so was the first to produce, in Hegel's sense, sculpture as such. The height of classical sculpture, Hegel suggests, is found in fifth-century BC images of deities such as the *Athena Parthenos* and the *Olympian Zeus*, statues whose stillness and equipoise embodied the harmony of Greek life (*Ä:II*, 439/773). Such sculptures give no indication of interior struggle or deliberation; their stillness is enhanced by their vacant eyes and impassive expressions. Paradigmatic sculptures also do not depict action since action suggests desire, restlessness, and a tension between the subject and the external world that is absent from classical Greek sensibility. Hegel acknowledges that even classical sculpture sometimes depicted gods undertaking simple actions and so does not fit this paradigm. But sculpture in its purest form depicts abstract, peaceful harmony and so achieves "beauty at once free and necessary" (*Ä:II*, 373/718).

Once this harmony begins to disintegrate, however, sculpture's essential three-dimensionality prevents it from being able to depict the range of emotions unleashed by romantic interiority (*Ä:II*, 458/788). This task is assumed by 'the romantic arts'—painting, music, and poetry—"whose mission it is to give shape to the inner side of personal life" (*Ä:II*, 239/625). We recall Hegel's claim that through art, humans also produce ourselves: in having the kinds of experiences made possible by the three romantic arts, we not only discover the form we give the external world; we also come to understand how our sense of ourselves as spatial, temporal creatures is achieved through interaction with the world.

Painting is an interior art, first of all, because the forms it depicts exist only in the mind of the viewer. Whereas a sculpture's perceived shape *is* its physical shape (Athena's sculpted head looks, and is, spherical), the figures in a painting are not actually the shape they appear to be (the painted apple looks, but is not, spherical). The mind is instead led, through conventions and techniques of painting, to infer the painted object's shape through the contrast of colors. Painting's ability to make us see three dimensions when there are only two means that painting is not concerned simply with making things visible, but with visibility as a phenomenon that occurs within an individual.[16] Painting does not reproduce the natural object, but "becomes a reflection of the spirit in which the spirit only reveals its spiritual quality by cancelling the real existent and transforming it into a pure appearance in the domain of spirit for apprehension by spirit" (*Ä:III*, 27/805). In other words, painting prompts us to recognize how our reflective capacities 'cancel' the real object and convert it into something purely reflected, which can then itself become an object of reflection. On this account, painting is "the inner life of the spirit which undertakes to express itself as *inner* in the mirror of externality." Because painting showcases interiority, the 'real heart of painting' is in the romantic world, rather than in oriental or classical painting (*Ä:III*, 23–24/801–802).

Since painting's images exist in full only through the viewer's perception, it should be no surprise that painting is capable of depicting subjective interiority with fullness and vivacity. More completely than sculpture or certainly architecture, painting can depict "willing, feeling, . . . suffering, grief, and death, in the whole range of passions and satisfactions" (*Ä:II*, 259/625). It can also express the complexity of action better than architecture or sculpture, thus coming closer to explicit reflection on the normative sphere's assessment of motivations, intentions, and outcomes. Both because of this proliferation of factors and because context is necessary to make sense of them, painting's subject matter varies much more widely than sculpture's. Painting is called on to depict "great historical events, the most pre-eminent individuals," but also, as again in Dutch genre painting, the "shimmering and glittering of wine in a glass, a flash of the eye, a momentary look or smile" (*Ä:III*, 36/812). Painting additionally highlights subjectivity in that the particular artist's take on any given subject matter becomes central in a way it was not in architecture or sculpture: whether thematizing scenes from the life of Christ, depicting landscapes, or portraying the struggles of the lower classes, in painting

---

[16] See also Sallis, "Carnation and the Eccentricity of Painting," 104–107.

"something new is added," namely, the "love, the mind and spirit, the soul, with which the artist seizes on them, makes them his own, and so breathes his own inspiration of production as a new life into what he creates" (*Ä:III*, 37/837).

Music intensifies the interiority initiated in painting. Whereas a painting's juxtaposition of color persists whether or not it is being viewed, a series of notes becomes a melody only through memory: the melody does not even come into existence without a listener (*Ä:III*, 135/891–892).[17] In a clear case of mutual formation of self and world, music correspondingly gives the listener a sense of her temporal self (*Ä:III*, 156/907–908). Music eliminates not only one dimension, as painting does, but "the whole of space"; it "keeps firmly to the inner life without giving it an outward shape or figure." Purely instrumental music (which Hegel seems to consider music's paradigmatic form), in having no recourse to images, is sound treated "as an end in itself" (*Ä:III*, 133/899). Music is thus "manifested as a *subjective* inwardness" and occupies the most interior point of art.

While painting captured emotion better than sculpture or architecture, music embodies purified, ephemeral emotion: its "proper element is the inner life as such, explicitly shapeless feeling which cannot manifest itself in the outer world and its reality but only through an external medium which quickly vanishes and is cancelled at the very moment of expression" (*Ä:II*, 261/626). Music's shapeless and transitory nature, in other words, comes closest to capturing emotion's essence. Music thus makes, as Hegel puts it, our "inner life intelligible" (*Ä:III*, 149/902) and, for that reason, it has an extraordinary effect on us—to the point, Hegel comments, that we sometimes cannot help moving in time to music we hear. Through meter, intervals, and key, music makes laws of harmony audible the way architecture makes laws of gravity visible. By thus embodying the symbiotic relation between the world and human expression, music represents the Idea in sensuous form.

Music and poetry make use of the same sensible material, namely sound. But unlike music's paradigmatic lack of language, poetry is the 'art of speech' (*Ä:III*, 224/960). Poetry takes art's embodiment of humans' self-production a step further: instead of taking sensuous materials and forming them into art, in poetry humans take speech, and through speech their own ideas, as art's material. In poetry, humans learn about their own concepts through the words they themselves use to signify those concepts. Poetry, as Hegel puts it, presents "to *spiritual* imagination and contemplation the spiritual meanings which it has shaped within its own soul" (*Ä:II*, 261/626). As such, poetry is "the absolute and true art of the spirit and its expression as spirit," meaning that more explicitly than any other art, poetry enables humans to reflect on their place in the world.

But again this high achievement poses a challenge for art. Poetry "works neither for contemplation, by the *senses*, as the visual arts do, nor for purely ideal *feeling*, as music does" (*Ä:II*, 261/626). It is instead "a withdrawal from the real world of sense-perception and a subordination of that world." What poetry wins, in other words, "on the spiritual side it all the same loses again on the sensuous." Poetry risks no longer doing what

---

[17] See Eldridge, "Hegel on Music," 133.

art is meant to do: while sculpture, painting, and music make spiritual content "intelligible alike to sense and spirit," poetry risks being unintelligible to sense. The further poetry moves from sense, the more it begins to "dissolve and acquire in the eyes of philosophy its point of transition to religious pictorial thinking as such, as well as to the prose of scientific thought" (*Ä:III*, 234–235/968). Again we see art's almost paradoxical dilemma: the closer it gets to explicitly depicting adequate human self-understanding, the more it risks ceasing to be art altogether.

To avoid this fate, poetry must explicitly undertake the project of remaining art, striking a mean "between the abstract universality of thought and sensuously concrete corporeal objects." Poetry must do this, above all, by distancing itself from humans' quotidian use of speech, namely prose. Through "choice, placing, and sound of words," through rhyme schemes and meter, poetry must lift its language above the prosaic. Poetry must also distinguish itself from religion and philosophy by making its content an end in itself, as opposed to serving moralistic or pedagogical ends. It must weave its parts into an organic-seeming whole, giving "appearance of a close connection and coherence." In these ways, poetry contrasts with the rambling contingency of everyday life and can exist "for its own sake and free on its own account" (*Ä:III*, 231/965).

As long as poetry retains these artistic characteristics and resists the transition into religion or philosophy, it can take three forms that Hegel lists again in dialectical order: epic, lyric, and dramatic. Epic poetry is best suited to the understanding of a heroic age in which the individual does not distinguish between himself and his nation and creates an ethical order through his actions. Hegel's disdain for attempts to revive 'Germanic' epics makes clear that such poetry is no longer appropriate for the modern world (*Ä:III*, 347/1057). In lyric poetry, by contrast, the poet turns inward to express her emotions and longings; all is filtered through her experience and given meaning by her attitudes (*Ä:III*, 415/1111).

Dramatic poetry—plays written not in prose but in a particular poetic meter and rhyme scheme—synthesizes the broad historical themes of epic poetry and the interiority of lyric poetry. It thus "is more capable than any other art of completely unfolding the totality of an event," but can also display the ways modern subjects' interiority plays out: in deliberation, resolution, and in the ways a dramatic character "picks the fruit of his own deeds" (*Ä:III*, 479/1161). Dramatic poetry is consequently particularly well situated to consider questions of action and of responsibility, concepts that are central to humans' understanding of themselves within the normative sphere. For these reasons, dramatic poetry ranks as the "highest stage of poetry and of art generally" (*Ä:III*, 474/1158): it most explicitly thematizes the normative sphere that art, as a part of absolute spirit, is meant to address.

The protagonists' actions and their relations to them determine three genres within dramatic poetry. If, through their actions, "individuals destroy themselves through their one-sidedness" in collision with the ethical order, tragedy results. Hegel's standard example from the ancient world is Sophocles' *Antigone*, in which Antigone and Creon, as instantiations of opposing sides of the ethical order, clash and are destroyed in the process. But if poetry is to depict a *modern* conception of the Idea, it must depict modern agents' critical assessment of norms. Accordingly, modern tragic heroes, such as Shakespeare's Hamlet or Schiller's Wallenstein, deliberate, often excessively, about their options with little clarity about what duty requires (*Ä:III*, 562/1228).[18] The increased importance of the protagonists' attitude toward norms poses another challenge to artistic expression, this time to tragedy as a genre. If individuals are acting not as instantiations of eternal law but on their own preferences, it is all too easy to imagine that they could act otherwise. The inevitability necessary for tragic conflict is weakened, suggesting that the plays in question might as well have happy endings.[19] This fact, according to Hegel, explains the proliferation of modern tragicomedies in which the scoundrel—who in more restricted situations would have precipitated a tragedy—is converted to the good and, however implausibly, pledges to reform (*Ä:III*, 568/1233). Comedy, by contrast, depicts collisions in which the comic protagonist, regardless of disasters that befall him, "remains undisturbed in himself and at ease" (*Ä:III*, 531/1202). Here Hegel's favorite example is again Aristophanes, whose characters employ ridiculous means in the pursuit of foolish ends, yet endure their resulting failures cheerfully.

Hegel's high praise for Aristophanes seems to suggest that ancient comedy, at least, has the potential to express the truth of humans' self-legislating capacities. Aristophanes' protagonists make themselves "completely master of everything" (*Ä:III*, 527/1199); they do not look to nature or tradition for their norms and retain light-hearted self-control, regardless of what happens. Although Aristophanes' comedies sometimes end with the restoration of the old order, they nevertheless depict norms not as immutable laws against which characters throw themselves in tragic conflict, but as human creations open to criticism, mockery, and change. Unlike the ironic standpoint that was the target of Hegel's lifelong scorn, comedy does not suggest that critiquing a given norm undermines normativity altogether. Instead it suggests that humans are collectively responsible for normativity. In this sense, it has the potential to fulfill art's potential: if poetry consists of humans taking up their ideas as their subject matter and recognizing their ownership of those ideas, comedy is, among poetic genres, powerfully positioned to prevent us from reifying our norms and losing sight of our authority over them.

Hegel is, however, pessimistic about instances of comedy in his own age. Unlike Aristophanes' merry arsonists, for instance, modern protagonists such as Moliere's Tartuffe fully endorse their desires. This intensified subjectivity, typical again of the modern age, means that they are "deadly serious" in their degenerate aims. When those aims fail, they are bitter, and the audience's laughter is at them, not with them. Such plays fall into the prosaic and become moralistic. Here once again, as in romantic art's dissolution in subjective humor, art risks losing its status as art (*Ä:III*, 570/1234).

The reflective nature of modern subjectivity means we will never have as easy a relation to ourselves and our aims as did Aristophanes' characters. But by his own description, comedy need not fail in the way Hegel fears. Hotho's edition includes the enticing suggestion that Hegel mentioned Shakespeare as a modern example of "comedy which is

---

[18] See Moland, "An Unrelieved Heart: Hegel, Tragedy, and Schiller's *Wallenstein*," 9.
[19] See Moland, "'And Why Not?' Hegel, Comedy, and the End of Art."

truly comical and truly poetic," boasting a "deeper wealth and inwardness of humor" that can rival Aristophanes' triumphs in ancient Greece.[20] Certainly some of Shakespeare's comedies resist moralizing in favor of cheerfully exposing the complex negotiations involved in modern love or politics. Protagonists in comedies such as *A Midsummer Night's Dream* call irrational norms into question through their antic undertakings, then cooperate with others to secure reform.[21] All of this is achieved in language that resists lapsing into prose through its intricate use of metaphor and simile, its carefully crafted soliloquies, and its neatly integrated plotlines (*Ä:I*, 523/408). So expressed, dramatic poetry has the potential to present the Idea in sensuous form, even in the late flowering of the romantic age.

25.5. THE END AND FUTURE OF ART

Both the trajectory of forms of art and the trajectory of individual arts illustrate ways art might end: by becoming entirely prosaic or entirely subjective, by transitioning into religion, or by becoming moralistic. I have suggested that even if art in the modern world *can*, logically as it were, run to these extremes, this does not imply that it *must*. There is some indication that Hegel acknowledged examples of successful art in his lifetime: in addition to his praise for Shakespeare, Hegel speaks favorably of Goethe's *Iphigenie auf Tauris* (*Ä:I*, 297/229–230), as well as of some aspects of Schiller's plays. For every Jean Paul and Molière, perhaps there is a more sincere artist (T. G. von Hippel and Friedrich Rückert are two of Hegel's admittedly obscure examples) who can further art's mission (*Ä:II*, 231/602, 242/610). Hegel also failed to anticipate how novelists—Proust, Woolf, or Joyce, for instance—would appropriate poetry's ability to bring our concepts to our spiritual attention through the creative use of speech.[22] It seems possible, then, that as long as the artist sincerely, in the terms of her time, grapples with humans' role in the world, she can still give the Idea sensuous form. She may, in order to embody modern agents' hyper-reflectivity, need to do so in a way that reflects more self-consciously on what art is or means. There may also always be a 'pastness' to art in the sense that we only recognize a truth about ourselves once an artist expresses it, thus closing it off conceptually and consigning it to history. But art's self-criticism or pastness need not negate its modified effectiveness.

Still, the question remains: even if art *can* resist these extremes and remain art, why should it? In tending toward prose—in, that is, stripping language of its poetic elements—modern art risks not failing to articulate the Idea so much as failing, in doing so, to be art. But what sort of risk is this? Perhaps we need not lament art's dissolution

---

[20] There is unfortunately no indication in the available lecture editions that Hegel mentions Shakespeare in this context.

[21] See MacDonald, *Finding Freedom*.

[22] See again Rutter, *Hegel on the Modern Arts*, for instance 265–266.

since, as Hegel suggests, the fundamental truths of the modern world are best expressed in philosophy's prose. But what would a world without art look like? What is, in short, the value of art?

Art's continued value for Hegel is rooted, first of all, in his claim that the truth is the whole. While philosophy ultimately articulates the fullest conception of the Idea, it cannot do so sensuously and so is itself incomplete. In order not to be limited by philosophy's lack of sensuousness, the Idea requires sensuous expression and so requires art. Despite the many differences between objective and absolute spirit, the position of the family in the state may provide a helpful analogy. The state is the fullest expression of objective spirit by virtue of the fact that it explicitly articulates the political principles on which it is built. The family's basis in blood ties and loyalty, being by definition unreflective, cannot be the basis of the state. This does not mean the family is not legitimate or should be done away with, but only that it must find an appropriate place within the state. Art's sensuality is no less relevant to the modern world than the family's immediacy is within the state, but the modern world cannot be fully articulated in art any more than the state can be governed like a family.

A second description of art's continued value may help us shift to thinking about art's future from a Hegelian point of view, applying his theory in ways he could not have anticipated. In the service of this shift, we might consider a way in which Hegel's 'end of art' thesis is reminiscent of his even more notorious 'end of history' thesis. History, Hegel says, is the history of *freedom*. Early civilizations, Hegel contends, knew that one person (the ruler) was free; classical civilizations knew that some humans (excepting slaves) were free; only in the modern world has the realization that *all* humans are free been articulated.[23] When history ends, it is not because nothing more will happen or people will no longer write history. It is because history has reached the last logical articulation of freedom (there is nowhere to go, conceptually, beyond 'all') and will now always be the story of humans working out the immense consequences implied by the claim that all humans are free. The case is similar with art. Art, Hegel claimed, is one way we explore our deepest interests, including freedom. If this is true, art's future will consist of artists working out, in new and revealing ways, what the modern assertion of universal human freedom actually commits us to. It will mean that artists will continue to hold our norms and self-understandings up to us and show us when those self-understandings are flawed, or when we are treating them as given (as natural or bestowed by a divinity) in a way we should not. Art will continue to articulate truths about us or our culture of which we are barely aware: it can continue to be an eye "whereby the inner soul and spirit is [*sic*] seen" (*Ä:I*, 204/154). Art can do this in part through its refusal to promote a single answer or definite message. The fact that it cannot express the fully realized Idea means that it *can* remind us of the ambiguity endemic in even our most cherished principles. A world without art might be a world in which we begin to take philosophical truths as given and so relinquish the possibility of critiquing or reforming them. Especially in times of social upheaval, as Hegel himself says, when our norms face challenge or

---

[23] G. W. F. Hegel, *Lectures on the Philosophy of World History*, 54.

collapse, art can help us feel our way forward (*Ä:II*, 234/605). Art may in fact be more relevant now than ever since its essential ambiguity aesthetically mirrors our postmodern uncertainty about our most fundamental principles.[24]

The idea that artists can productively challenge received norms certainly seems true of artists (e.g., Kara Walker, Ai Weiwei) who explicitly thematize ways in which our attitudes toward race, gender, globalization, and so forth might be in tension with our professed belief—expressed in the prose of political declarations and manifestos—in human freedom. But it is also true of architecture that encourages us to rethink our conceptions of gravity, visual art that allows us to see color and shape anew, music that challenges received understandings of sound's meaning and significance, and drama that unsettles our understandings of narrative or personhood. Artists such as Alexander Calder, Agnes Martin, and John Cage decenter and disrupt our perceptions; in so doing, they challenge perceptual norms and draw our attention to the ways in which we form and are formed by the sensuous world. Such art reminds us that if we assume that colors or sounds are simply in the world waiting to be perceived, we discount our own participation in the existence even of things that seem objectively independent of us. In Hegel's terms, such art offers a vision of our unity with the world and so is a sensuous embodiment of the Idea.

Art's continued value, then, derives from its inclusion of the sensuous in our perpetual quest for self-understanding and in its ability to disrupt our prosaic relationship to experience. Both aspects serve to remind us of our role in the world's normative structure. Hegel puts it this way:

> [T]he pure appearance of art has the advantage that it points through and beyond itself, and itself hints at something spiritual of which it is to give us an idea, whereas immediate appearance does not present itself as deceptive but rather as the real and the true . . . [T]he hard shell of nature and the ordinary world make it more difficult for the spirit to penetrate through them to the Idea than works of art do. (*Ä:I*, 23/9)

Art, then, breaks through the hard shell of the ordinary, making us alive to the unity and interdependence at the heart of reality. Art offers us this insight in a way no other medium can and therefore maintains its status as an expression of our deepest interests and highest truths.

Hegel's philosophy of art presupposes a metaphysics and a systematicity likely unpalatable to many contemporary readers. His jarring generalizations about civilizations and insistence on 'paradigmatic' instances of art forms cast doubt on his openness to the richness of art or the societies that produce it. Despite these limitations, Hegel seems to have been remarkably prescient regarding the revolutionary changes in art that took place after his lifetime. He was certainly correct about beauty's decreasing relevance in art. His prediction that art would become ever more intertwined with philosophy is borne out by theorists such as Arthur Danto, who, inspired by Hegel, argue for the

---

[24] See for instance Walker, "Art, Religion, and the Modernity of Hegel," 275.

inseparability of philosophical theory and contemporary art.[25] Although not even his acknowledgment of tooth extractions as a possible subject matter for art could have prepared him for urinals in museums or colossal balloon poodles, Hegel does seem correctly to have predicted contemporary art's inexhaustible subject matter. The cult of the contemporary artist would also not have surprised him: already Jean Paul's subjective humor risked suggesting that something is art only because a famous-enough artist claims it is. As to Hegel's description of romantic art's dissolution into either subjective humor or artless objectivity: television's too-frequent celebration of content-free nonsense, on the one hand, and ostensibly unreconstructed reality, on the other, gives long-term vindication of Hegel's fear that art, succumbing to the pressures of subjectivity, will someday disintegrate.

But in asserting art's ability to assist us in understanding the human condition, Hegel also correctly predicted its continued importance. The development of subjectivity means that art can never reflect our condition with the seamless beauty that characterized the sculptures of ancient Greece. But art that can express "imperishable humanity in its many-sided significance and endless all-round development" (*Ä:II*, 239/608) continues to move and inspire us. In so doing, art fulfills its role within absolute spirit of prompting reflection on the normative sphere and articulating, in sensuous form, the truth of the Idea.

WORKS CITED

Primary Texts

Anonymous. "The Oldest Systematic Program of German Idealism," in *The Early Political Writings of the German Romantics*, edited by Frederick C. Beiser. Cambridge: Cambridge University Press, 1996, 3–5.

Hegel, G. W. F. *Enzyklopädie der philosophischen Wissenschaften im Grundrisse (1830)* [E]. Hamburg: Meiner Verlag, 1959.

Hegel, G. W. F.. *Hegel's Aesthetics: Lectures on Fine Art* [Ä, followed by German volume and page number, then English page number], translated by T. M. Knox. Oxford: Oxford University Press, 1975.

Hegel, G. W. F.. *Hegel's Science of Logic* [SL], translated by A. V. Miller. London: George Allen and Unwin, 1969.

Hegel, G. W. F.. *Lectures on the Philosophy of Art: The Hotho Transcript of the 1823 Berlin Lectures*, translated by Robert F. Brown. Oxford: Oxford University Press, 2014.

Hegel, G. W. F.. *Lectures on the Philosophy of World History: Introduction: Reason in History*. Translated by H. B. Nisbet. Cambridge: Cambridge University Press, 1975.

Hegel, G. W. F.. *Philosophie der Kunst (Mitschrift von der Pfordten 1826)*, edited by Annemarie Gethmann-Siefert, Jeong-Im Kwon, and Karsten Berr. Frankfurt am Main: Suhrkamp, 2004.

---

[25] For an example of Danto's influential claims about Hegel, see Danto, *Unnatural Wonders*, 5–18.

Hegel, G. W. F.. *Philosophie der Kunst oder Ästhetik (Mitschrift von Kehler 1826)*, edited by Annemarie Gethmann-Siefert and Bernadette Collenberg-Plotnikov. Munich: Wilhelm Fink Verlag, 2004.

Hegel, G. W. F.. *Philosophy of Mind*, translated by A. V. Miller. and William Wallace. Oxford: Clarendon Press, 1971.

Hegel, G. W. F.. *Vorlesung über Ästhetik: Berlin 1820/21: eine Nachschrift*, edited by Helmut Schneider. New York: Lang, 1995.

Hegel, G. W. F.. *Vorlesungen über die Ästhetik I–III [Ä]*, edited by Eva Moldenhauer and Karl Markus Michel. Vol. 13–15, *Werke in 20 Bänden*. Frankfurt am Main: Suhrkamp, 1970.

Hegel, G. W. F.. *Vorlesungen über die Philosophie der Kunst (Mitschrift Hotho 1823)*, edited by Annemarie Gethmann-Siefert. Hamburg: Felix Meiner Verlag, 2003.

Secondary Literature

Danto, Arthur C. *Unnatural Wonders: Essays from the Gap between Art and Life*. New York: Columbia University Press, 2005.

Donougho, Martin. "Art and History: Hegel on the End, the Beginning, and the Future of Art," in *Hegel and the Arts*, edited by Stephen Houlgate. Chicago: Northwestern University Press, 2007, 179–215.

Donougho, Martin. "Remarks on 'Humanus heisst der Heilige.'" *Hegel-Studien* 17 (1982): 214–225.

Eldridge, Richard. "Hegel on Music," in *Hegel and the Arts*, edited by Stephen Houlgate. Chicago: Northwestern University Press, 2007, 119–145.

Gethmann-Siefert, Annemarie. *Einführung in Hegels Ästhetik*. Munich: Wilhelm Fink Verlag, 2005.

Gethmann-Siefert, Annemarie. *Ist die Kunst tot und zu Ende?: Überlegungen zu Hegels Ästhetik, Jenaer philosophische Vorträge und Studien 7*. Erlangen: Palm & Enke, 1994.

James, David. *Art, Myth and Society in Hegel's Aesthetics*. New York: Continuum, 2009.

Kolb, David. "Hegel's Architecture," in *Hegel and the Arts*, edited by Stephen Houlgate. Chicago: Northwestern University Press, 2007, 29–55.

MacDonald, Sara. *Finding Freedom: Hegel's Philosophy and the Emancipation of Women*. Montreal: McGill-Queen's University Press, 2008.

Moland, Lydia L. "An Unrelieved Heart: Hegel, Tragedy, and Schiller's *Wallenstein*." *New German Critique* 113, no. 38 (2011): 1–23.

Moland, Lydia L. "'And Why Not?' Hegel, Comedy, and the End of Art." *Verifiche: Rivista di scienze umane* (forthcoming).

Pillow, Kirk. *Sublime Understanding: Aesthetic Reflection in Kant and Hegel*. Cambridge, MA: MIT Press, 2000.

Pinkard, Terry. "Symbolic, Classical, and Romantic Art," in *Hegel and the Arts*, edited by Stephen Houlgate. Chicago: Northwestern University Press, 2007, 3–28.

Pippin, Robert. *After the Beautiful: Hegel and the Philosophy of Pictorial Modernism*. Chicago: University of Chicago Press, 2014.

Pippin, Robert. "The Absence of Aesthetics in Hegel's Aesthetics," in *Hegel and Nineteenth-Century Philosophy*, edited by Frederick C. Beiser. Cambridge Cambridge University Press, 2008, 394–418.

Rutter, Benjamin. *Hegel on the Modern Arts*. Cambridge: Cambridge University Press, 2010.

Sallis, John. "Carnation and the Eccentricity of Painting," in *Hegel and the Arts*, edited by Stephen Houlgate. Chicago: Northwestern University Press, 2007, 90–118.

Walker, John. "Art, Religion, and the Modernity of Hegel," in *Hegel and the Arts*, edited by Stephen Houlgate. Chicago: Northwestern University Press, 2007, 296–309.

Further Reading

Desmond, William. *Art and the Absolute*. Albany: State University of New York Press, 1986.

Gethmann-Siefert, Annemarie. *Die Funktion der Kunst in der Geschichte: Untersuchungen zu Hegels Ästhetik*. Bonn: Bouvier Verlag, 1984.

Gethmann-Siefert, Annemarie. *Phänomen versus system: zum Verhältnis von philosophischer Systematik und Kunsturteil in Hegels Berliner Vorlesungen über Ästhetik oder Philosophie der Kunst. Hegel-Studien*. Bonn: Bouvier, 1992.

Henrich, Dieter. "The Contemporary Relevance of Hegel's Aesthetics," in *Hegel*, edited by Michael Inwood. Oxford: Oxford University Press, 1985, 199–207.

Hilmer, Brigitte. "Being Hegelian after Danto." *History and Theory* 37, no. 4 (1998): 71–86.

Houlgate, Stephen. "Hegel and the 'End' of Art." *The Owl of Minerva* 29, no. 1 (1997): 1–21.

Maker, William, ed. *Hegel and Aesthetics*. Albany: State University of New York Press, 2000.

McCumber, John. *Poetic Interaction: Language, Freedom, Reason*. Chicago: University of Chicago Press, 1989.

Speight, Allen. *Hegel, Literature, and the Problem of Agency*. Cambridge: Cambridge University Press, 2001.

Winfield, Richard Dien. *Stylistics: Rethinking the Artforms after Hegel*. Albany: State University of New York Press, 1995.

CHAPTER 26

....

FEELING, REPRESENTATION, AND PRACTICE IN HEGEL'S *LECTURES ON THE PHILOSOPHY OF RELIGION*

....

THOMAS A. LEWIS

[Religion] is the loftiest object that can occupy human beings; it is the absolute object. It is the region of eternal truth and eternal virtue, the region where all the riddles of thought, all contradictions, and all the sorrows of the heart should show themselves to be resolved, and the region of the eternal peace through which the human being is truly human.

(LPR 1:61)

FROM their opening, Hegel's lectures on the philosophy of religion stress religion's importance in his larger intellectual project. Despite this importance—and Hegel's claims that the "riddles of thought" are resolved therein—its interpretation has been deeply contested from the beginning and continues to be so today. When David Friedrich Strauss first divided Hegel's followers into Left, Right, and Center Hegelians in 1837, competing interpretations of Hegel's philosophy of religion and its political implications were at the heart of the divisions.[1] In recent years, Hegel's philosophy of religion has again become a prominent point of contention between opposing strands of Hegel interpretation: critics of a family of 'non-traditional' interpretations of Hegel's project— those that see him as emphatically extending Kant's critical project—often appeal to

---

[1] For a now classic treatment of this period and the initial division of the Hegelian school, see Toews, *Hegelianism*.

Hegel's philosophy of religion as an insurmountable obstacle to such interpretations.[2] No less important, even among what are sometimes considered more traditional readings, there are dramatic differences between more rationalist and more mystical readings and between more and less theistic readings.

This degree of dissension, I suggest, tells us something crucial about Hegel's philosophy of religion. It is essential to his project that it speak in multiple registers: Hegel seeks to articulate the philosophical significance of religious representations, and doing so means that he must draw upon and engage both more traditional religious language itself and his own philosophical account of the content he takes to be expressed representationally in this religious language. Consequently, a central challenge will always be to discern where Hegel is conveying the representational form of a claim and where he is offering the philosophical version thereof. More fundamentally, this movement between registers reflects the vital thrust of Hegel's philosophy of religion as a whole: that the defining claims of the consummate religion, Christianity, are vindicated and justified by philosophy. Making this claim involves not only a distinctive conception of philosophy and reason, but also a specific understanding of Christianity. Hegel argues for—rather than simply assuming—this understanding of Christianity; but the resulting account, like any account of Christianity, is a contested one. Some—such as Kierkegaard and his descendants, from Karl Barth to William Desmond—will see Hegel's Christianity as an offense to what they present as authentic Christianity. Others see Hegel as providing valuable resources for a compelling and liberating vision of Christianity: he is taken up directly by contemporary thinkers such as Peter Hodgson, Anselm Min, and Andrew Shanks; and he has also had a broader yet less direct impact on a wide range of other Christian thought, both conservative and liberationist.[3] Grasping the distinctiveness of Hegel's philosophy of religion requires appreciating both the way that it subordinates the authority of religion to the authority of philosophy *and* that Hegel makes this claim not to delegitimize religion, but rather to defend what he takes to be the genuine content of Christianity.

26.1. HEGEL'S PHILOSOPHY OF RELIGION IN OVERVIEW

Seen broadly, Hegel takes religion to consist in arrays of social practices that express and cultivate, principally through feeling and representation, a consciousness of spirit. While Hegel's philosophical language for the object of this consciousness is spirit, or

---

[2] See, for instance, Beiser, "Introduction" and *Hegel*; and O'Regan, *The Heterodox Hegel*. On the language of 'non-traditional', rather than non-metaphysical, to designate this interpretive current, see Kreines, "Hegel's Metaphysics."

[3] See, for instance, Hodgson, *Hegel and Christian Theology*; Min, *Dialectic of Salvation*; and Shanks, *A Neo-Hegelian Theology*.

Geist, Hegel equates this with that toward which religions point with terms such as God. The consciousness of spirit transforms dramatically through the course of religion's history, such that humans achieve a more and more adequate grasp thereof. Religion shares with philosophy this common object, spirit or God; yet religion and philosophy are distinguished largely by the form of cognition dominant in each: representation and thought, respectively. As the higher form of cognition, philosophical thought ultimately provides a more adequate and authoritative account of this content than religious representation can. The resulting picture is one in which philosophy plays the defining role in interpreting religion. Philosophy, for Hegel, holds the key to distinguishing and comprehending religion's essential content.

While most treatments of the relation between religion and philosophy in Hegel's thought highlight this distinction in the forms of cognition, no less important is the crucial role that Hegel attributes to practice. For Hegel, participation in communal religious practices plays a central role in forming or educating individuals. Through this formation, the judgments and general consciousness of spirit of a community become second nature to its members. Both because representation is more widely grasped than philosophical thought and because religious practices form and educate the group as a whole, not simply a subset of intellectual elites, religion is the form in which most people are conscious of spirit.

Hegel developed his most extensive account of this philosophy of religion in his lectures as a professor in Berlin during the final stage of his career. He lectured on the philosophy of religion four different semesters: in 1821, 1824, 1827, and 1831. Hegel himself did not publish any of these lectures. After his sudden death in 1831, Hegel's friends, colleagues, and students published editions of many of his lectures. Both early editions of Hegel's *Lectures on the Philosophy of Religion* (1832 and 1840) drew from Hegel's notes as well as students' transcriptions from all four series of lectures to assemble a unified version of Hegel's philosophy of religion.[4] The result of these attempts to provide a single, unified account of Hegel's philosophy of religion is that these editions eclipsed crucial developments in Hegel's thinking during this period. Only with the publication of a critical edition between 1983 and 1985 have we had access to key differences between the lectures. This edition provides Hegel's lecture manuscript from 1821, as well as relatively complete student transcriptions from the 1824 and 1827 lectures. Unfortunately, no complete transcription of the 1831 lectures is known to survive, though David Friedrich Strauss's summary notes illuminate the larger structure of Hegel's final set of lectures on this topic.[5] I sketch this editorial history not simply for the sake of scholarly precision, but because attention to the changes in Hegel's philosophy of religion from one series of lectures to the next reveals important points about his views. Walter Jaeschke even suggests that the divergent readings of Hegel's philosophy of religion that were at the heart of the split into Left, Center, and Right Hegelians may have been partly due to the first

---

[4] On the history of these early editions, see Jaeschke, "Vorwort des Herausgebers," xli–xliv.

[5] On these sources for the critical edition, see Jaeschke "Vorwort des Herausgebers"; and Hodgson, "Editorial Introduction."

editor's (Philipp Marheineke's) efforts to synthesize these importantly different series of lectures into a single account.[6] Perhaps most significantly, the revisions—in many cases quite substantial—demonstrate Hegel to be far from the rigidly dogmatic thinker he is often accused of being: in response to new information and ideas, Hegel reconceived important aspects of the project, rather than simply inserting new material in the same framework. Thus, while most of this discussion will focus on the 1827 lectures, in which Hegel seems to have worked through what he came to see as important problems in earlier versions of the lectures and to have achieved a degree of satisfaction with at least the treatments of parts 1 and 3, I will make reference to other versions as well.[7]

Despite their differences, all four cycles of the lectures consist in an introduction and then three major sections: "The Concept of Religion," "Determinate Religion," and the "Consummate Religion." Hegel's structuring of the project does important work and provides essential cues for an adequate interpretation. If we fail to attend closely to this structure, as well as to situate his philosophy of religion in relation to his larger system, we risk launching our interpretive venture in a false direction that distorts our orientation throughout the project. We then too easily miss or misconstrue crucial distinctions between Hegel's deployment of the language of representation and his philosophical account of these representations. More broadly, if we neglect some of these elements and narrow our focus to one or two prominent themes, we lose sight of the nuance and richness of Hegel's thinking on religion. For this reason, the present treatment begins by situating the philosophy of religion in relation to Hegel's larger intellectual project and then traces Hegel's structuring of the philosophy of religion into three parts.

26.2. Hegel's Philosophy of Religion in His Philosophical System

Hegel opens part 1 of the 1827 lectures with a question, "The question with which we have to begin is: 'How are we to secure a beginning?'" (LPR 1:265). In responding to the question, Hegel offers an account of what can and cannot be presupposed at the beginning of this section of his system and consequently vital keys for the interpretation of these lectures as a whole. After brief reflections on the general challenge of determining where to begin, he states,

---

[6] Jaeschke, "Vorwort des Herausgebers," xlii.

[7] D. F. Strauss's summary notes of the 1831 lectures provide significant evidence that Hegel's treatments of parts 1 and 3 were largely consistent with that in 1827, while Hegel had continued to be unsatisfied with part 2 and had significantly reworked it again. For useful diagrams indicating some of the important shifts among the editions, see Hodgson, ed., *Lectures on the Philosophy of Religion: One-Volume Edition*, 492–501.

In the present case, however, we are not beginning philosophy afresh. The science of religion is one science within philosophy; indeed it is the *final* one. In that respect it presupposes the other philosophical disciplines and is therefore a result. In its philosophical aspect we are already dealing with a result of premises that lie behind us. We have only to begin from religion, and to make sure that this standpoint of religion has been proved and that we can advert from it to our own consciousness. . . . The original content, the foundation of the philosophy of religion, is a result, namely a lemma or subsidiary proposition to the effect that the content with which we begin is genuine content. (LPR 1:265–266, emphasis in original)

Hegel conceives his philosophy of religion as one element, in some sense the final element, of a larger philosophical system; and the presuppositions or premises of this part of the system consist in the results of the previous elements of the system. The developments of the system that have brought us to the standpoint of religion provide us with a starting point that is already justified. Hegel thereby indicates how much his philosophy of religion will draw on arguments that have been defended elsewhere in his system, arguments that he will briefly gesture toward rather than develop again in these lectures. Yet the inverse is also true: only those claims that have already been validated by these developments can be taken for granted. Most important, as we will see in the first subsection of part 1, the concept of God is at this point in the project a largely abstract conception of what is taken to be absolute. Thus, while it is certainly the case that the opening sections of Hegel's lectures on the philosophy of religion emphatically and repeatedly tell us that the object of both religion and philosophy is God, the passage just quoted cautions us that what that claim means—and what 'God' means—can only be authoritatively determined on the basis of previous developments in the philosophical system, as well as their further unfolding in the philosophy of religion itself. Hegel thereby warns against the often unacknowledged importation into readings of his work of just those assumptions about the nature of religion and God that he seeks to undermine. The implication is that general assumptions about the meaning of the term 'God' cannot be relied upon for the interpretation of Hegel's philosophy of religion.

The remainder of Hegel's paragraph might appear to substantially qualify this claim. Hegel continues, immediately following the passage quoted previously:

In regard to this initial content, however, we can also appeal to the general consciousness and in that way take hold of a starting point that is generally valid at least empirically. Whatever is to be valid in science must be something proved; something conceded is what is presupposed in a subjective way, so that the beginning can be made from it. (LPR 1:266)

The first of these sentences initially appears to challenge the claim that we cannot import any non-philosophical assumptions about the meaning of key concepts; the second sentence places that point in the proper frame. Hegel does invite his audience, who may not be familiar with the many aspects of his system to which he referred earlier, to draw upon general presuppositions about the concept of God; but he indicates explicitly that these function as nothing more than general orienting preconceptions. They are always subordinate to and must be interpreted by the philosophical conceptions. The latter, not the former, function as the authoritative criteria for the interpretation of the project. While Hegel seeks to demonstrate that the genuine content of Christianity accords with his own philosophical system, Christian doctrine itself requires interpretation; and the most adequate interpretation is that provided by the *philosophy* of religion. In accord with this introductory material, the body of part 1 of the lectures, The Concept of Religion, will take as its starting point the yield of these earlier developments in the system.

26.3. THE CONCEPT OF RELIGION

The first of the three parts of Hegel's philosophy of religion treats religion in the abstract. It introduces the essential elements of religion yet portrays them in abstraction from their actual existence in the world. The three subsections of this part, "The Concept of God," "Knowledge of God," and "The Cultus," examine the abstract concept of the absolute (i.e., of religion's object); our theoretical or cognitive relation to this object; and our practical relationship to this object in the religious community.[8]

The first subsection, "The Concept of God," has the task of articulating the fruit of those earlier developments in the system that were gestured to earlier. This yield is remarkably abstract: this result of the previous developments through the logic, philosophy of nature, and philosophies of subjective and objective spirit is "the proof that God is, or in other words that this universal, which is in and for itself, embracing and containing absolutely everything, is that through which alone everything is and has subsistence—that this universal is the truth. This One is the result of philosophy" (LPR 1:267). Though such language is by no means foreign to Christian traditions, these claims in themselves are a far cry from the specificity and determinacy of many theistic conceptions of God: "Scientifically regarded, the expression 'God' is, to begin with, a general, abstract name that has not yet received any genuine import" (LPR 1:266). What we have at this point is simply an abstract conception of an absolute that will ultimately be articulated in terms of Hegel's philosophical account of spirit. Even when Hegel sketches what he takes to be the less philosophical but more widespread forms of this point, the content is remarkably abstract. 'God' is here largely a placeholder, not a license to attribute to Hegel a more familiar conception of a theistic divine being.

---

[8] I focus here on the 1827 lectures. Part 1 of the lectures changes significantly from 1821 to 1824 and again in 1827; the 1831 lectures seem to have maintained the same basic structure as in 1827. I have argued elsewhere that the 1827 lectures offer a far more coherent handling of this material than the earlier versions and should therefore be taken as authoritative. See Lewis, *Religion, Modernity, and Politics in Hegel*, 136–137.

Having put in place this largely indeterminate conception of religion's object, God, Hegel turns to our relationship to this object. The second subsection, "Knowledge of God," traces developments in cognition of this object. Hegel begins with the most immediate form of this cognitive relationship, immediate knowledge, and moves through feeling and representation to thought—that mode of cognition that moves beyond religion as such and into philosophy. His handling of knowledge of God appears in many respects as his most prominent contribution to philosophy of religion. His account of representation and thought as two distinct forms of knowledge of God, for instance, has garnered much of the attention in secondary scholarship on his philosophy of religion. Not unrelatedly, Hegel's treatments of these moments of cognition are simultaneously his handling of prominent competing conceptions of religion—both from his day and ours. Hegel's relation to Immanuel Kant, Friedrich Jacobi, and Friedrich Schleiermacher arguably comes out more clearly here than anywhere else in these lectures. Thus, the account of distinct forms of cognition also enables Hegel to incorporate competing conceptions of religion within his own project, demonstrating both their partial validity and their shortcomings.

At the same time, the treatment of knowledge of God here is—despite important distinctions—closely connected to the treatments of intuition, representation, and thought in Hegel's account of theoretical spirit in subjective spirit. Both the *Encyclopedia* and his lectures on this material thus provide valuable material for the interpretation of this aspect of his philosophy of religion.[9] As there, Hegel here seeks to show how cognition moves of its own accord through these distinct forms; prior to the stage of thought, the limitations within each of these moments of cognition push cognition further. As it proceeds to the next moment, cognition retains the essential content of the earlier moments. Thus, Hegel's account of the moments of knowledge of God, if successful, illuminates the distinctiveness of the forms of cognition most closely associated with religion—particularly feeling and representation—while also demonstrating that thought (and thus philosophy) provides the most authoritative expression of this same content.

Immediate knowledge, for Hegel, provides a certainty that God is—but little more. In immediate certainty, God is virtually without content. Against efforts of thinkers such as Jacobi to ground religion in an immediate knowledge that is impervious to the challenge of critical reason, Hegel contends that such appeals to immediacy are empty. As soon as cognition seeks to determine any meaning of the purported object of this certainty, it moves past this immediate form and into the second moment of knowledge of God: feeling. Hegel treats feeling not simply as a form of knowledge but as a form with more content than mere immediate knowing. This content still has a rather indeterminate form; it is vague and imprecise. Yet it is powerful. Much of religion's impact, for Hegel, can be attributed to feeling's prominence in religion. Herein lies the

---

[9] See E §§445–468 and LPS 184–237. Note, however, that Hegel's account of knowledge of God contains two moments—immediate knowledge and feeling—prior to representation and thought; by contrast, theoretical spirit provides only intuition, which is itself closely connected to feeling.

contribution of conceptions of religion that link it to feeling rather than reason. Despite feeling's importance and power, however, it is not self-justifying. Schleiermacher is part of Hegel's target here, but the point concerns a broader family of ways of thinking about religion. Both good and evil content can exist in feelings, which is why "it is also said that one's feelings or one's heart must be purified and cultivated; natural feelings cannot be the proper impulses to action" (LPR 1:291). Feelings are not a given for Hegel but ought to be properly formed in accord with truth. Perhaps more fundamentally, in developing an account of feeling as carrying cognitive content and linking it to other forms of cognition, Hegel refutes non-cognitivist accounts of religion that seek to protect it from rationalist criticism by undermining the conceptions of feeling on which those accounts depend.

Feelings both inform and are informed by the next moment of cognition, representation (*Vorstellung*). Representation is the dominant form in which religion expresses its content and is therefore central to Hegel's conception of religion. Representation provides more determinate content than feeling, yet lacks the self-determining quality of thought. The most obvious instances of representations are those associated with images; Hegel's examples of these sensuous forms of intuition include God's begetting a son, God's wrath, Pandora's box, and the tree of knowledge (LPR 1:293). In such cases, "we have before us something twofold, first the immediate and then what is meant by it, its inner meaning [*das Innere*]. The latter is to be distinguished from the former, which is the external aspect" (LPR 1:293). This "inner meaning" constitutes the essential content—what will be preserved in philosophical thought—while the external aspect is merely an attribute of the representational form. Even in the case of the "story [*Geschichte*] of Jesus," Hegel distinguishes two levels of significance: one is an "outward history" that is the story of a human being; the other is a "divine happening, a divine deed, an absolutely divine action. This absolute divine action is the inward, the genuine, the substantial dimension of this story [*Geschichte*], and this is just what is the object of reason" (LPR 1: 294). Again, the authentic significance lies in what is inner. It does not depend on the external events, which are merely a representation of the genuine content. In telling us that the latter is an object of reason, Hegel indicates that its ultimate meaning cannot be derived from or determined by the external events; it is not determined by something particular or given. An authoritative account of the absolute can be *represented* in a story or a history, but it can only be *determined* by reason. Already here, Hegel's conception of representation has moved well beyond more classical claims that important passages in the Bible must be read metaphorically.

While these imagistic, metaphorical, and allegorical instances are perhaps the most straightforward forms of representation, appreciating the extensive work that the notion of representation does in Hegel's philosophy of religion requires attending to the non-sensuous, non-imagistic forms of representation as well. Creation, for instance, generates sensuous and imagist form, so it cannot be given a fully imagistic representation. God standing over and above the world is also a representation for Hegel (LPR 1:295–296). As these examples suggest, the defining feature of representation is not that it presents its objects in metaphorical or sensuous terms, but rather that it presents them as standing in external and contingent relations to each other. In representation, objects stand over against the subject as well as each other. The objects are thereby conceived as given in their particularity, rather than as constituted through their relations. They are therefore connected with other representations by terms such as 'and' or 'also,' which posit merely an external, not an intrinsic and necessary relation (LPR 1:296). In some sense, then, representation provides us with a relatively superficial account of the content it shares with philosophy; it does not penetrate the apparent contingency to reveal the internal relations.

Thought strips away this contingency. Hegel's accounts of thought and of its differentiation from representation are developed more extensively and systematically in the account of theoretical spirit in the *Encyclopedia* version of subjective spirit, as well as in the corresponding lectures.[10] Most important, those are the sections in which Hegel defends the conception in a way that he does not in the lectures on religion. In the present context, Hegel does not seek to fully rearticulate those arguments, but rather focuses on the implications for the relation of religion and philosophy.

Thought presents objects in their necessary relations, overcoming the externality and contingency of the relations as they are presented in representation. Religious representations present a story of Adam, Eve, and a serpent as independent agents interacting, a story in which other decisions could have been made and things could have turned out otherwise. The relations are external and the proceedings contingent. Thought, Hegel contends, demonstrates the essential content of the representation—which concerns the relations among knowledge, consciousness, and evil (LPR 3:224–225). Philosophy will show that the relations between consciousness, internal division or cleavage, and evil are necessary rather than contingent; the relationships are constitutive of consciousness itself.

Consequently, their truth is independent of the external forms in which representation presents them. The implications of this point are vast and pertain to the dramatic divisions in the interpretation of Hegel's philosophy of religion. If the essential truth does not depend upon the representational form, then it cannot depend on the historical aspect. Even in the case of Jesus, the truth of the content cannot depend upon any particular historical claim. The quest to determine the actual history of a man named Jesus is necessarily distinct from an investigation into the truth of the essential content of the teachings. The latter does not depend on the former: "Only by philosophy can this simply present content be justified, not by history. What spirit does is not history [*Historie*]" (LPR 3:163). The genuinely spiritual activity ("what spirit does") or content is not a matter of contingent, empirical historical events (mere *Historie*) and cannot be proven by the latter. Philosophy will provide the most authoritative justification of the content of religious representations.

The second section of the "Concept of Religion" thus establishes representation's relation to thought, and therewith religion's relation to philosophy, in a manner that both affirms the truth and significance of the former—when properly understood—and sets

[10]   See E §§465–468 and LPS 223–37.

up the latter as the ultimate authority for the interpretation of the former. In this affirmation of representation, Hegel simultaneously defends the importance of the determinate content of religious doctrine over against conceptualizations of religion that focus principally on purportedly immediate knowledge or experience. He thereby positions himself as the genuine defender of Christian doctrine, in response to critics such as Pietists like Friedrich A. G. Tholuck who were accusing Hegel of pantheism. More broadly, Hegel's account of representation and thought undergirds Hegel's defense of religion from a broad array of philosophical challenges frequently associated with the Enlightenment. For these reasons, it has often played the dominant, nearly exclusive, role in accounts of Hegel's philosophy of religion.

The third and final subsection of the "Concept of Religion," however, makes attention to practices an equally crucial feature of Hegel's account of religion. "The Cultus" turns from religion's cognitive to its practical aspect. Where the second section treated religion through the lens of the various ways in which we know the absolute, ultimately arriving in thought at the knowledge that this object is not other than us, the third section focuses on those activities through which this union becomes actual in the world: "I have not only to know the object, to be filled, but to know myself as filled by this object, to know it as within me and likewise myself as within this object that is the truth—and so to know myself in the truth. To bring forth this unity is action, or the aspect of the cultus" (LPR 1:330). Without this activity, this consciousness is not achieved. These activities consist, for instance, in forms of devotion, sacrament, sacrifice, and repentance. More concretely, they comprise the rich array of practices associated with religion, such as prayer, pilgrimage, and asceticism, to mention only a few possibilities. The treatment offered here in the first part of the *Lectures* is relatively schematic, but Hegel will develop the account of particular religious communities in significant detail later in the lectures. Collectively, these practices bring about a transformation of the subject that consists in more than a new cognition. Ultimately, in the most developed forms, the transformation will become so comprehensive that it becomes intertwined with a much broader range of practice: "If heart and will are earnestly and thoroughly cultivated to the universal and the true, then there is present what appears as ethical life. To that extent ethical life is the most genuine cultus" (LPR 1:334). This connection to broader forms of social and political life will become prominent in the account of the Christian cultus.[11] Even though this initial treatment of the cultus remains in certain respects schematic, it already demonstrates the prominence of religious practice in Hegel's conception of religion. In a challenge to portrayals of Protestant conceptions of religion as deeming practice marginal to religion, Hegel reveals the depth of Protestant contestation over just these issues.

---

[11] This is also one of the points on which Hegel's thought develops most significantly from the 1821 manuscript to the 1827 lectures. On this point, see Thomas A. Lewis, "Religion, Reconciliation, and Modern Society."

26.4. DETERMINATE RELIGION

The second part of the lectures on the philosophy of religion, "Determinate Religion," is composed of Hegel's astoundingly ambitious attempt to provide an account of the moments of the determinate manifestation of religion. It in some sense consists in Hegel's treatment of all religions of the world other than Christianity, though even this seemingly obvious point will require crucial qualification. Despite being the longest part of the *Lectures*, this section has been far less studied and discussed than the first and third parts. It often stands as an embarrassment within more recent scholarship, both because Hegel's accounts of religion in Africa, India, and China, for instance, appear so profoundly inadequate by contemporary standards of scholarship and because the larger conception of ordering all religions of the world in a hierarchy at whose apex stands (Lutheran) Christianity raises deep ethical concerns. Despite these very real concerns, to ignore this section of the *Lectures* is to ignore a central element of Hegel's account as well as the way that it may challenge one's own position, more than a hasty dismissal appreciates.

The present treatment focuses on Hegel's conception of this project, rather than on his treatment of the actual moments of determinate religion. Not only would analyzing the entirety of the body of this part of the *Lectures* require at least a book in itself; more important, concentrating on the conception of Determinate Religion highlights the ways in which much that initially appears so objectionable in the project may be something we cannot and should not give up.

"Determinate Religion" seeks to respond to the vast quantities of information about people in other parts of the world that were flowing into Europe in Hegel's day. Two of the most revealing aspects of the bibliography of Hegel's likely sources are the number of sources on which he drew for part 2 of the lectures and how recently published so many of these sources were. For Hegel, this material is an object of far more than curiosity; he holds that it needs to be integrated into a philosophical system in order for that system to be adequate. As a result, Hegel's extensive engagement with religion around the world and across time has no precedent or parallel in Kant or Schleiermacher. Yet Hegel himself views this project as both daunting and incomplete. He was never satisfied with his treatment of Determinate Religion and continued to make significant revisions in every iteration of the lectures—unlike his handling of other sections.[12]

Hegel conceives Determinate Religion as unfolding the moments of the actualization of the concept of religion that was set out in part 1. In the decisive formulations of the conception of Determinate Religion, Hegel contends that the concept of religion must take determinate forms in the world; it must be actualized (LPR 1:28, 1:84).[13] The

---

[12] On this constant revision and its significance, see Lewis, *Religion, Modernity, and Politics in Hegel*, 183–184.

[13] The most important statements regarding the project of Determinate Religion are found in the introductions to the lectures (in the section where Hegel sets out the structure of the topic) and in the opening pages of part 2 itself.

necessity of this manifestation or actualization derives from the concept of spirit itself, and Hegel implicitly refers us to other points in his system, rather than defending the point here. Spirit necessarily develops in history. The crucial implication in this context, however, is that the developments traced over the course of "Determinate Religion" are fundamentally moments in the actualization of the concept of religion. They manifest, in incomplete rather than consummate form, the moments traced earlier—the concept of God, knowledge of God, and the cultus. Insofar as we are dealing with Determinate Religion, we are dealing with the manifestation of these moments in history, in the world. Thus, we are dealing with actual, historically existing religions.

Yet the moments of Determinate Religion themselves are fundamentally moments of the actualization of the concept, rather than particular religions. To avoid subtle but profound distortions in the interpretation of "Determinate Religion," it is essential to distinguish the conceptual moments from their instantiations in specific historical phenomena. Although Hegel claims to show that particular religions exemplify these moments of manifestation, the particular religions do not constitute the moments themselves. The former cannot be identified with the latter.

This crucial distinction between the moments of Determinate Religion and the specific religious formations that exemplify these moments is perhaps most obvious in relation to the opening stages of the development. In his treatment of 'immediate or natural religion', Hegel begins with two days of lectures on the conception of this moment itself, without reference to historical instantiations.[14] Only then does he turn to the concrete forms in which it has appeared in history. The first form of this immediate religion Hegel labels the religion of magic, and in this class he includes the contemporary religion of the "Eskimo" and much of religion in Africa (LPR 2:439). In reading such material, we can and should be alarmed by the haste with which Hegel relegates great numbers of people to the lowest stages of religion; I in no sense want to dismiss these concerns and the political consequences. Nonetheless, if one stops the examination there, one easily fails to appreciate how close one may stand to Hegel's project. In order to be able to make that point, we have to attend to specific features of Hegel's treatment. In particular, note that Hegel here indicates that several different religious groups fall equally into the category. Moreover, Hegel's claim that "[w]e still find this form widely practiced in Africa" implies that it was previously practiced in other places as well. This first moment of Determinate Religion thus cannot be identified with any single historical religion or the religion of any single group of people.

Later sections of "Determinate Religion" may appear to collapse this distinction, but even here it is preserved. I suspect one reason the distinction becomes harder to notice is that for the more developed forms of religion, Hegel finds only one manifestation in history. As far as he knows, for instance, only Greek religion manifests the moment of Determinate Religion that he labels the religion of beauty. The same can almost be said for Judaism and the religion of sublimity, but even here he notes in brief, undeveloped comments that Islam, or at least what he sometimes calls "Mohammedanism," is also

---

[14] See the notes with the marginalia from 1827.

a religion of sublimity.[15] Even if it becomes more subtle, the distinction between the moments of the concept and their historical manifestations is preserved.[16]

The distinction matters so much because it enables us to see that the most essential element of Hegel's project consists not in the ranking of historically existing religions into a hierarchy, but rather in the articulation of the moments of religion itself. To deem a set of practices religious is, for Hegel, to view them as manifesting—however partially or completely—the concept of religion. Accordingly, they can be analyzed in terms of the way in which they manifest this concept—specifically, how fully and adequately they do so. Hegel's particular formulation of this point depends upon systematic claims that he makes about manifestation and determination.

Precisely what alarms so many people about Hegel's Determinate Religion is less the treatment of historical religions as manifestations of the concept of religion than the arrangement of competing conceptions into a hierarchy. Yet the arrangement of competing options into a hierarchy with one's own position at the top is far less unique to Hegel than it initially appears. To the contrary, in this respect Hegel's account of Determinate Religion simply places in the foreground what it means to hold a view of an issue: to hold a position is to take it to be superior to the alternatives of which one is aware. That judgment of superiority implicitly and/or explicitly makes the claim that one's position better accounts for the topic at hand. Strong versions of relativism may seek to escape these implications of holding a view, but very few of us actually adopt such radical forms of pluralism.[17] Brutal histories of religious persecution may make us think that judgments of the superiority of one's religion are different from other kinds of judgments of superiority, but Hegel both implicitly and explicitly distinguishes the judgment of the superiority of one's own position from the issue of how one responds— practically, ethically, and politically—to this purported judgment of superiority. Hegel defends religious toleration quite explicitly, for instance.[18] More important, by conceiving of religion in terms of the consciousness of spirit, Hegel situates it in the same realm

[15] See LPR 2:62, 64, 337, and 577 n.

[16] The distinction is even easier to miss in reading the English translations than the German editions of the lectures due to seemingly small changes in the tables of contents that are offered. The headings in the former tend to use more terms that are seen as referring to discrete religious traditions. In the 1827 lectures, for instance, "Die Religion des Insichseins [the religion being-in-itself]" becomes "The Religion of Being-Within-Self (Buddhism, Lamaism)"; "Die indische Religion [Indian religion]" becomes "The Hindu Religion"; and "Die Religion der Römer [the religion of the Romans]" becomes "Roman Religion." The translations thus tend to reify the categories and to obfuscate the distinction between moments of the concept and the religious practices of particular groups of people. I have also argued elsewhere that our tendency to identify moments of Determinate Religion with purportedly self-evident entities such as Buddhism, Islam, and Hinduism reflects the projection back on to Hegel of models of discrete 'world religions', models that were developing but were not fully in place in Hegel's own work. See Thomas A. Lewis, "Hegel's Determinate Religion Today."

[17] Peter Hodgson suggests a revision to Hegel's view of religions along such pluralistic lines, but my point is that this pluralism is far more of an outlier than the claim that holding a view involves judging it superior to known alternatives. Hodgson's view presents further difficulties on its own, but I do not enter into those here. See Hodgson, *Hegel and Christian Theology*, 205–243.

[18] See, for instance, PR §270A and Lewis, *Religion, Modernity, and Politics*, 232–247.

as judgments about art and philosophy, neither of which raise the same kinds of alarms about intolerance and persecution.

In this sense, precisely those aspects of Hegel's Determinate Religion that initially provoke such strong objections—the judgment of the superiority of his own view vis-à-vis others—is not a uniquely Hegelian claim, even if Hegel places it in relief. To the contrary, it is a claim that most of us hold and that we have good reasons not to give up. One can make this point while still criticizing much about Hegel's account: the strong conclusions he draws on the basis of so little evidence; the manner in which he employs the relatively little evidence that he does have;[19] and the way that he groups assemblages of practices into a relatively coherent and unified traditions. My point is not to simply defend Hegel on Determinate Religion. But we fail to grasp the challenge it poses to our own self-understanding if we dismiss it too quickly.

26.5. THE CONSUMMATE RELIGION

Hegel's treatment of the consummate religion provides his interpretation of Christianity. While it is explicitly concerned with Christianity, however, its most fundamental task is to articulate what it means for the concept of religion to be fully actualized. Where "Determinate Religion" treats the partial manifestations, the "Consummate Religion" treats the complete manifestation. Because this task coincides with the interpretation of Christianity, the section has a double task: to show this complete manifestation and to demonstrate that Christianity is this manifestation. Thus, the consummate religion is consummate not because it is Christianity but because it fully manifests the concept of religion; and Christianity is the consummate religion because it meets these criteria, not simply by virtue of being Christianity. Of course, there is much to be discussed regarding to what extent the project, including the concept of religion, is already shaped by assumptions coming out of Hegel's own Christian background; but if we treat Christianity's being the consummate religion as a *presupposition*, rather than as one of the points *to be demonstrated*, we easily overlook central aspects of the task of the "Consummate Religion" and will be hard pressed to understand the rationale for the distinctiveness of Hegel's formulation of Christianity.

This point entails that a central aspect of the project will be Hegel's argument for what he takes to be the genuine content of Christianity. He develops this account through interpretations of the philosophical content *represented* in Christian doctrines, together with arguments against a number of other ways one might interpret the tradition. Like any effort to determine what Christianity is 'really about', Hegel's version is controversial. It is quite different from many more common versions, and one reaction is to say that whatever this is, it is not Christianity. William Desmond makes a move of this sort when he contends that "some sense of transcendence as other to human self-transcendence

---

[19] On this point, see for instance Robert Bernasconi, "Hegel at the Court of Ashanti."

and nature as a totality of finite beings is essentially entailed by this monotheistic God."[20] Hegel's response to such a reaction lies in the substance of the argument he has been developing all along. He has systematically worked through alternative construals and has set out powerful arguments against them. While a reader can still say, "but I don't like it," to stop there is to fail to appreciate the challenges that Hegel poses to alternative manners of construing Christianity.

Hegel's most encompassing account of the consummate religion is that it is the religion that has religion itself for its object (LPR 3:177–179). In the consummate religion, the absolute is grasped as relating to itself in this religion. Religion as such concerns consciousness of God; through the developments traced so far, this object has been conceived as other than the relationship itself. Here, however, this consciousness, this relationship, is grasped as a moment of this absolute object—not simply as a relationship to it. As such, the object of religion, God, is—finally—grasped as spirit. Hegel's language on these points is abstract, but the implications are concrete and dramatic. The practices of the Christian community, for instance, are grasped not simply as relating to God but as moments of God. God, then, is not other to this community.

The first element of Hegel's treatment of the consummate religion consists in his account of the concept of God in itself. This section exemplifies Hegel's movement between the representational accounts provided in religious teachings and the more philosophical accounts that Hegel takes to be authoritative. With regard to the latter, Hegel tells us in the 1827 lectures that "God in his eternal idea is still within the abstract element of thinking in general—the abstract idea of thinking. . . . We already know this pure idea, and therefore we need only dwell on it briefly" (LPR 3:201). Hegel thereby refers back to the account of the idea offered in the final sections of his logic. This idea is what he takes religious language about the concept of God to be referring to, and in some sense he says little more about this object itself in this context. Rather, this section of the lectures on religion focuses on the way that religious accounts have represented this object. Most generally, "the eternal idea is expressed [*ausgesprochen*] as what is called the holy Trinity; it is God himself, eternally triune" (LPR 3:201). Hegel does not thereby subordinate the logic's account of the idea to Christian discussions of the Trinity; rather, the account of the idea offered in Hegel's logic is posited as the key to revealing the genuine content of Christian doctrines of the Trinity. Even the classic predicates attributed to God Hegel treats as examples of representation and understanding (*Verstand*), rather than as the more authoritative account of the absolute offered by philosophy (LPR 3:202). And accounts of God as a mystery, for Hegel, reflect the finitude not only of sensibility but also of the understanding. Modes of cognition that remain at the level of understanding, rather than rising to genuine thought, are unable to grasp the internal determinacy and complexity of God; God is consequently described with attributes that are juxtaposed with each other, such that God appears a mystery (LPR 3:205–209). Thus, what is ultimately most striking about Hegel's treatment of the first element of the consummate religion is how little it elaborates this element itself: it defines this element

[20] Desmond, *Hegel's God*, 6.

by referring back to the discussion of the idea in the logic and devotes itself largely to explaining how Christian representations relate to this philosophical account.

The next section of the "Consummate Religion" provides Hegel's treatment of perhaps the most prominent Christian narratives and doctrines. As in the first section, Hegel is centrally engaged with demonstrating the philosophical content and thus the validity of these teachings. Conceptually speaking, it moves beyond the abstract identity of the first moment, through differentiation, and toward a partial reconciliation. More concretely, it deals with the internal differentiation of humanity wrought by consciousness and the path toward reconciling this internal division. In terms of Christian representations, it deals with creation, the Fall, the incarnation of God in Christ, and his death and resurrection—though this final point is only completed in the third section.

Hegel initially deals with several different dimensions of division or cleavage. The most prominent among these concerns the division within the human subject, the division between how we are immediately and our consciousness of that immediacy. Consciousness, which makes us objects for ourselves, able to reflect on ourselves, thus generates this division. Hegel initially develops this point in relation to the seemingly contradictory claims that "humanity is by nature good" and "humanity . . . is by nature evil" (LPR 3:220). His tactic is to demonstrate the genuine insight as well as the limitation of both of these propositions. The first contains the crucial insight that human beings are "implicitly spirit and rationality, created in and after the image of God" (LPR 3:221). We are thus implicitly good. "The other side, however, is that human beings ought to be explicitly what they are implicitly. . . . 'Good by nature' means 'immediately good', and spirit is precisely something that is not natural and immediate" (LPR 3:221). Insofar as the realization of what we are requires moving beyond what we are immediately—to actualize what we are implicitly—we can also say that humanity is by nature evil. In this immediate, natural state, our will is determined by what is merely given, not by reason; we are selfish. Without consciousness, there would be no alternative to an immediate responsiveness to impulses and stimuli. With consciousness and the knowledge it brings, however, what would otherwise be morally neutral becomes evil, a failure of the will. Insofar as we are originally determined by this will, we are evil. Yet even this selfishness stands at odds with our implicit rationality, our being implicitly spirit.

Genesis expresses these points in the story of the Fall. Hegel's careful framing of the analysis of the story exemplifies one of the dominant ways that he handles religious representations. They are the "mode and manner of the shape" in which the content appears; they represent the content in an "intuitable, sensible manner"; and in this case, they present the content so that it is "*regarded* as something that happened" (LPR 3:224, my emphasis). What is crucial is not whether the portrayed event took place but that it is regarded as having happened. The truth of the content is independent of the history. The narrative tells us of human beings being tempted by a serpent to eat from the tree of knowledge of good and evil: "What it really means is that humanity has elevated itself to the knowledge of good and evil; and this cognition, this distinction, is the source of evil, is evil itself. Being evil is located in the act of cognition, in consciousness" (LPR 3:225). This bifurcation of the self—between what we are in our immediacy and what we ought to be, between our consciousness of our nature and that nature itself—is here represented powerfully, though not precisely. That is, the representations do not offer the conceptual precision about these points that is found in the philosophical accounts elsewhere in Hegel's own treatments.

This internal division is also reflected in a sense of alienation from the world, as well as from God. Humans are poised between them. This internal division, however, is not the end of the story, for the overcoming of this division, the reconciliation that neither remains bifurcated nor returns to an original, unmediated unity, is central to Hegel's reading of Christianity.

Christ represents the most powerful image of overcoming these divisions. This reconciliation is implicitly already present, but it only comes to the consciousness of human beings through its appearance in sensible form. In other words, this sense of internal division, as powerful as it is, can itself be overcome through developments in consciousness, through a consciousness of the internal unity of these two moments; but the confidence in this reconciliation does not first come in philosophical form. Rather, initially "this content—the unity of divine and human nature—achieves certainty, obtaining the form of immediate sensible intuition and external existence for humankind, so that it appears as something that has been seen in the world, something that has been experienced in the world" (LPR 3:237–238). Careful attention to Hegel's language is essential to avoiding misconstruals. Hegel carefully directs our attention to "appear[ing] as something that has been seen." What matters for Hegel is the certainty or belief that it was there—and in a sensible, not merely abstract, form—not some claims about actual historical events.

Because the need here concerns an immediate, sensible form, Hegel argues, this had to be conceived as occurring in a particular individual. As he puts it,

> At the same time there is this more precise specification to be added, namely, that the unity of divine and human nature must appear in a [*einem*] human being. Humanity in itself is the universal, or the thought of humanity. From the present standpoint, however, it is not a question of the thought of humanity but of sensible certainty; thus it is one [*ein*] human being in whom this unity is envisaged. (LPR 3:238)[21]

Here as well, Hegel's point is that in order for human beings to arrive at this consciousness of divine-human unity, it had to be represented as taking sensible form; and that could only happen in the conception of a particular individual as the God-man. Yet this unity that is presented as occurring uniquely in this individual is in fact a unity that is implicit in humanity as such. This particular individual had to be represented as unique as a step along a path toward developing a consciousness of all humanity possessing this reconciliation in an implicit form. The necessity at issue is that involved in saying that a particular development is needed in order to arrive at the next step.

---

[21] The Hodgson translation somewhat distorts this point by rendering an un-italicized 'einem', which could be 'a' or 'one', as an italicized 'just one'.

On its own, however, this sensible, particular representation of reconciliation is inadequate. Precisely the immediacy and particularity that made it concrete enough for humanity's advancement to this point also preclude its universality: insofar as this reconciliation is understood as occurring uniquely here, this reconciliation is posited as other to the rest of humanity. We are reconciled neither with the world nor with ourselves. In this moment, then, the rest of humanity remains alienated. A binitarian Christianity would leave us here.

The Christian account of the religious community, or cultus, for Hegel, will ultimately move us beyond this alienation by representing the Holy Spirit as present within this community. Hegel had conceived of the Christian cultus as playing some version of this role since much earlier in his corpus, yet it is one of the elements of his views on religion that continues to develop significantly even through the 1820s. In the treatment of religion in the 1807 *Phenomenology of Spirit*, Hegel portrays even the cultus as unable to fully overcome this alienation. Here, the form of representation projects this reconciliation into a "beyond" (PS 420/¶787). The overcoming of alienation is conceived as past (in Christ's appearance) and future (in the eschaton) but not present: "Its reconciliation, therefore, is in its heart, but its consciousness is still divided against itself and its actuality is still disrupted" (PS 421/¶787).

Over the course of the Berlin lectures on religion, Hegel's treatment of the possibilities for achieving this reconciliation in and with the present transforms substantially. The 1821 manuscript concludes with "The Passing Away of the Community" and what Hegel labels "a discordant note" (LPR 3:94). Here he judges the dominant religion of the day to offer no viable reconciliation with modern society—no way to overcome a profound alienation from the world. As a result, "[r]eligion [must] take refuge in philosophy"; but philosophy cannot replace religion because it is not for everyone (LPR 3:96). It is confined to "an isolated order of priests" who necessarily remain distant from the world (LPR 3:97). In the 1821 lectures, then, neither religion nor philosophy overcomes the projection of reconciliation elsewhere.[22]

By 1827, however, Hegel has developed a conclusion to the lectures in which the genuine cultus thoroughly overcomes the alienation that still seemed to plague these earlier versions. As becomes particularly apparent here, the reconciliation between the absolute and the individual is just as much a reconciliation between human beings and the world; it is a realization that the divisions that have characterized developments up to this point are—when we grasp our situation fully—already overcome here, not waiting to be resolved in some distant future. The conclusion to the 1827 lectures on the philosophy of religion thus represents the high-water mark of Hegel's fluctuating confidence in the possibilities of achieving reconciliation in this world, and specifically in the new, distinctly modern world he saw emerging.

Doctrinally, the third moment of the consummate religion originates from the account of the outpouring of the Holy Spirit in chapter 2 of the book of Acts (LPR 3:252).

---

[22] On these developments in the lectures, see Thomas A. Lewis, "Religion, Reconciliation, and Modern Society."

For Hegel, this representation teaches that the cultus is not simply a group that worships God; rather, God is present in, not other than, this community. This moment is thus "the identity of the divine and human. The third element then, is this consciousness—God as spirit. This spirit as existing and realizing itself in the community" (LPR 3:254).

Though the result is a new consciousness, this consciousness only comes about through a combination of theoretical and practical developments. While Christian teachings provide the theoretical (though representational) account of this content, this content only transforms the subject in tandem with the activities of the cultus. The practical activities of the religious community—most obviously rituals such as baptism and communion—are essential to the emergence of this consciousness and are central to Hegel's conception of the cultus. This section thus illuminates the deeply practical dimensions of Hegel's account of religion. He both emphasizes the vital role of practices in the conception of religion and connects the possibility of satisfactory reconciliation to the emergence of modern ethical life.

Hegel presents these practices in terms of a broad process of education or habituation, which is one of the principal tasks of the subsisting religious community. Through participation in the rituals and other practices of the religious community, individuals—particularly children—take in the content of the religion. Initially, this content appears as something external, imposed by authority, to which the individual must conform (LPR 3:258). Through a process of habituation, however, this initial externality or otherness is overcome. The corresponding intuitions, drives, and inclinations become second nature: "This is the concern of education, practice, cultivation. With such education and appropriation it is a question merely of becoming habituated to the good and the true" (LPR 3:259). While Hegel attends to practices such as baptism and the eucharist, he is no less attentive to the kind of consciousness ingrained by dressing and otherwise behaving 'appropriately'. Participation in the religious community thus molds the subject into an ethical being with the corresponding consciousness of spirit.

The final section of Hegel's 1827 treatment of the cultus, and thus of the lectures as a whole, provides a brief, rather schematic treatment of what he describes as "the realization [*Realisierung*] of the spirituality of the community." This treatment concerns the actualization or making real in the world of the religious community, and Hegel here first traces three different modes of the community's relation to the world. In the first, which appears to be Hegel's interpretation of the dominant form of Christianity from its origins until about the time of Constantine or Charlemagne, the community seeks to achieve reconciliation by renouncing the world and worldliness. In this stage of "monkish withdrawal," our own worldly desires are rejected through ascetic programs and retreat (LPR 3:263). For precisely these reasons, it is only an immediate, not a genuine, form of reconciliation. In the second stage, which would seem to map historically onto the period from Constantine or Charlemagne to Luther, the religious community and the world are brought into greater relation, but in such a form that the community dominates the world and seeks to control and transform it from above. The relation thus remains external; and, rather than overcoming the corruptions of the world, the church inadvertently takes these up into itself and thereby falls into corruption (LPR 3:263–264).

In the third mode, which seems to map historically onto the outworking of the Reformation as Hegel views it, this reconciliation achieves a satisfactory form as the principles of the religious community come to permeate the ethical life of the society as a whole: "The third way is that this contradiction is resolved in ethical life, that the principle of freedom has penetrated into the worldly realm itself, and that the worldly, because it has been thus conformed to the concept, reason, and eternal truth, is freedom that has become concrete and will that is rational" (LPR 3:264). In this most developed form of the cultus, the religious community does not stand over against the world at large. Rather, the social practices as well as the political institutions of the latter have been formed such that they manifest the consciousness of spirit that is represented in the teachings of the consummate religion. Whereas in the second moment the church stood over and ruled social and political life, in this stage ethical life manifests the same self-consciousness of spirit as the consummate religion. The latter therefore does not stand as an authority over the former; Hegel is not defending theocracy and in fact explicitly critiques it elsewhere. Hegel thus claims that "[t]he institutions of ethical life are divine [göttliche] institutions—not holy [heilige]" in the sense that the latter involves a juxtaposition with what are seen as the normal practices of the world: celibacy versus marriage, and voluntary poverty versus the pursuit of wealth (LPR 3:264). The full actualization of the consummate religion thus involves full participation in the everyday practices and institutions of a world whose practices themselves express the same consciousness of spirit as the consummate religion.

Hegel's account of the Christian cultus thus not only powerfully illustrates his larger conception of religion as pervasively practical and active—not just a matter of consciousness, beliefs, and teachings. It also, in the final form achieved in 1827, depicts a striking convergence of religion and politics—of the ethical aspirations of a religious tradition and the actual, existing state of the world.

In the remarkable final pages of the Lectures, Hegel pairs these practical developments in the cultus with three moments of theoretical consciousness—of cognition of religion. Providing brief characterizations that build on accounts given elsewhere, Hegel first describes a form of Enlightenment thinking that rejects all religious content; here God can be nothing more than an abstraction. For Hegel, this form of abstract thinking—which he identifies as understanding (Verstand)—is inadequate not because it rejects all religious content but because it is ruled by a principle of abstract identity. Hegel's elaborated critique of this standpoint is thus ultimately based in his logic. The second form of thought treated appears to be Enlightenment's opposite: Pietism. It too rejects all content and doctrine, but it seeks to preserve what it sees as the essential element of religion through a focus on "feeling and inner sensibility" (LPR 3:267). For Hegel, this Pietism destroys the content of religion no less than an Enlightenment stuck at the level of the understanding does.

The multiple inadequacies of these two moments are overcome in a form of cognition that is genuine thinking. This moment "knows and recognizes that a content is necessary and that this necessary content is objective, being in and for itself. This is the standpoint of philosophy, according to which the content takes refuge in the concept and attains its justification by thinking" (LPR 3:267). Philosophy here demonstrates the content of religion—specifically, of the consummate religion—to be rational content. Philosophical thought demonstrates this content in a manner that rises above contingency and the mere authority of tradition: "The content is justified by the witness of spirit, insofar as it is thinking spirit. The witness of spirit is thought" (LPR 3:268). In this final moment, philosophy—and philosophy alone—defends, justifies, and rescues religion from the open hostility of Enlightenment critiques of religion and the hidden undermining of religious content by its Pietistic defenders.

Hegel's closing defense of religion is compact; it sketches arguments rather than develops then, but it does so in part because the underlying claims about the nature of cognition have been developed at length elsewhere in his thought. What is important in these closing paragraphs is not a novel set of claims about the nature of cognition, but the way that he brings the previously elaborated account of cognition to bear in articulating what his *philosophy* of religion has been doing all along: providing what he sees as a defense of Christianity from a host of modern social and intellectual challenges (some of which are still being elaborated today)—but a defense that proceeds by substantially reinterpreting what many have taken Christianity to be.

Works Cited

Primary Texts

Hegel, G. W. F. *Elements of the Philosophy of Right* [PR], translated by H. B. Nisbet and edited by Allen W. Wood. Cambridge: Cambridge University Press, 1991.

Hegel, G. W. F. *Enzyklopädie der philosophischen Wissenschaften im Grundrisse (1830)* [E], edited by Eva Moldenhauer and Karl Markus Michel. Vol. 8–10. *Werke*. Frankfurt am Main: Suhrkamp, 1970.

Hegel, G. W. F. *Grundlinien der Philosophie des Rechts* [PR], edited by Eva Moldenhauer and Karl Markus Michel. Vol. 7. *Werke*. Frankfurt am Main: Suhrkamp, 1970.

Hegel, G. W. F. *Hegel's Philosophy of Mind* [E], translated by M. J. Inwood. Oxford; New York: Clarendon Press; Oxford University Press, 2007.

Hegel, G. W. F. *Lectures on the Philosophy of Religion* [LPR], translated by R. F. Brown, P. C. Hodgson, and J. M. Stewart, edited by Peter C. Hodgson. 3 vols. Berkeley; Los Angeles: University of California Press, 1984–1987 [Cited by the German pagination, which is included in the English translation].

Hegel, G. W. F. *Phänomenologie des Geistes* [PS], edited by Eva Moldenhauer and Karl Markus Michel. Vol. 3. *Werke*. Frankfurt am Main: Suhrkamp, 1986.

Hegel, G. W. F. *Phenomenology of Spirit* [PS], translated by A. V. Miller. Oxford: Oxford University Press, 1977.

Hegel, G. W. F. *Vorlesungen über die Philosophie des Geistes: Berlin 1827/1828* [LPS], edited by Franz Hespe and Burkhard Tuschling. Vol. 13. Vorlesungen. Hamburg: Felix Meiner, 1994.

Hegel, G. W. F. *Vorlesungen über die Philosophie der Religion* [LPR], edited by Walter Jaeschke. Vol. 3–5. Vorlesungen. Hamburg: Felix Meiner Verlag, 1983.

Secondary Literature

Barth, Karl. *Protestant Theology in the Nineteenth Century: Its Background and History*, translated by Brian Cozens and John Bowden. New ed. Grand Rapids, MI: William B. Eerdmans, 2002.

Beiser, Frederick C. *Hegel*. London: Routledge, 2005.

Beiser, Frederick C. "Introduction: The Puzzling Hegel Renaissance," in *The Cambridge Companion to Hegel and Nineteenth-Century Philosophy*, edited by Frederick C. Beiser. Cambridge: Cambridge University Press, 2008, 1–14.

Bernasconi, Robert. "Hegel at the Court of Ashanti," in *Hegel after Derrida*, edited by Stuart Barnett. London: Routledge, 1998, 41–63.

Desmond, William. *Hegel's God: A Counterfeit Double?* Aldershot, UK: Ashgate, 2003.

Hodgson, Peter C. "Editorial Introduction," in G. W. F. Hegel, *Lectures on the Philosophy of Religion*, 1:1–81. Berkeley; Los Angeles: University of California Press, 1984.

Hodgson, Peter C. *Hegel and Christian Theology: A Reading of the Lectures on the Philosophy of Religion*. Oxford: Oxford University Press, 2005.

Hodgson, Peter C., ed. *Lectures on the Philosophy of Religion: One-Volume Edition: The Lectures of 1827, by G. W. F. Hegel*. Berkeley; Los Angeles: University of California Press, 1988.

Jaeschke, Walter. *Reason in Religion: The Foundations of Hegel's Philosophy of Religion*, translated by J. Michael Stewart and Peter C. Hodgson. Berkeley; Los Angeles: University of California Press, 1990.

Jaeschke, Walter. "Vorwort des Herausgebers," in *Vorlesungen über die Philosophie der Religion: Teil 1*, 3:ix–lxxxvi. Vorlesungen. Hamburg: Felix Meiner Verlag, 1983.

Kreines, James. "Hegel's Metaphysics: Changing the Debate." *Philosophy Compass* 1, no. 5 (2006): 466–480.

Lewis, Thomas A. "Hegel's Determinate Religion Today: Foreign yet Not So Far Away," in *Religion und Religionen im Deutschen Idealismus: Schleiermacher—Hegel—Schelling*, edited by Friedrich Hermanni, Burkhard Nonnenmacher, and Friedrike Shick. Collegium Metaphysicum 13. Tübingen: Mohr Siebeck, 2015, 211–231.

Lewis, Thomas A. *Religion, Modernity, and Politics in Hegel*. Oxford: Oxford University Press, 2011.

Lewis, Thomas A. "Religion, Reconciliation, and Modern Society: The Shifting Conclusions of Hegel's Lectures on the Philosophy of Religion." *Harvard Theological Review* 106 (2013): 37–60.

Min, Anselm Kyongsuk. *Dialectic of Salvation: Issues in Theology of Liberation*. Albany: State University of New York Press, 1989.

O'Regan, Cyril. *The Heterodox Hegel*. Albany: State University of New York Press, 1994.

Shanks, Andrew. *A Neo-Hegelian Theology: The God of Greatest Hospitality*. Burlington, VT: Ashgate, 2014.

Toews, John Edward. *Hegelianism: The Path toward Dialectical Humanism, 1805–1841*. Cambridge: Cambridge University Press, 1980.

Wendte, Martin. *Gottmenschliche Einheit bei Hegel: Eine logische und theologische Untersuchung*. Berlin; New York: Walter de Gruyter, 2007.

CHAPTER 27

··

HEGEL'S LECTURES ON THE HISTORY OF ANCIENT AND MEDIEVAL PHILOSOPHY

··

PAUL REDDING

In his *Lectures on the History of Philosophy*, Hegel comments that while Europe had taken its religion and conception of the afterlife from the *East*, its attitude to *this world*, as in its approach to the arts, philosophy and science, had been taken from the Greeks.[1] What had struck modern Europeans about Greek life and culture was its '*Heimatlichkeit*', the capacity of the Greeks to feel 'at home'—at home *in the world* and *with themselves*. Moreover, the modern *renaissance* of ancient culture could occur only when Europeans themselves had come to be able to be, once more, 'at home [*zu Hause*]' with themselves and their own humanness (LHP 2: 10 [7:1]). Thus Hegel describes a "shared spirit of *Heimatlichkeit*" as what binds modern Europeans like himself to the Greeks (LHP 2: 10 [7:2]).

Hegel's treatment of the history of philosophy is, as might be grasped from this alone, decidedly Eurocentric. "Only with Greek philosophy do we make our beginning in the proper sense, for what went before [that is, oriental philosophy] was just a preliminary" (LHP 2: 9 [7: 1]). Because there is a direct link between "free, philosophical thought" and

---

[1] Hegel, *Lectures on the History of Philosophy 1825–6*, vol. 2, 9–10. This translation is based on volumes of 6–9 of Hegel, *Vorlesungen: Ausgewählte Nachschriften und Manuskripte*, and the page numbers to the latter are given in square brackets. While the edition of the 1825–1826 lectures is at present that closest to a critical edition of Hegel's lectures, a greater range of material is to be found in the editions originally compiled by Karl Ludwig Michelet, *Vorlesungen über die Geschichte der Philosophie*, the second edition of which was translated by Haldane and Simson as Hegel, *Lectures on the History of Philosophy*. I have in places supplemented material from the 1825–1826 lectures with material from this source, indicated by "Hegel, *Lectures on the History of Philosophy* (H&S)" followed by volume and page numbers with corresponding volume and page numbers to Michelet, 'M', in square brackets. The Michelet edition is, however, generally regarded as less reliable. On the history of these various editions and the materials on which they relied, as well as the background to Hegel's own lectures on the history of philosophy, see Karin de Boer, 'Hegel's Lectures on the History of Modern Philosophy', Chapter 28 in this volume.

practical freedom, philosophy only appears in history "where, and to the extent that, free political institutions are formed" (LHP 1: 91 [6: 266]). Therefore philosophy proper "first emerges in the West" (LHP 1: 91 [6: 269]). This freedom was, of course, only available to a few, but a shift from the oriental principle that only *one* (the despot) is free, to the principle that *some* are free[2] (LPWH 88, 404 [154], 362) was, for Hegel, important progress, nevertheless.

That in the strict sense philosophy has only existed in the West does not mean that the type of thought that is often associated with philosophy—*abstraction*—has not appeared elsewhere. Abstraction of thought into the realm of universality has so characterized Eastern religions as to confer on them a philosophical dimension *missing* in other religions, *including* Christianity (LHP 1: 103 [6: 366]). But the abstraction of Eastern thought is at the expense of the individual thinker such that it works to *dissolve* individual conscious subjectivity in a 'boundless' universal—the bliss of 'Oriental sublimity' (LHP 1: 105 [6: 308]). This is a type of thought characteristic of fear and unfreedom. In contrast, "the freedom of the subject is the principle of Greek philosophy—the I that knows itself to be infinite, in which the universal is specified as present" (LHP 2: 11 [7: 3]). Thus Hegel will only take the most cursory look the philosophy of the Indians and the Chinese, as he will do later with regard to the philosophy of the Jews and the Arabs. While this theme of the one-sided abstraction *from* concrete existence to an empty and abstract *infinite* will have a *role* within the history of Western philosophy itself, there it will mark one aspect of a complex movement that involves a contrary *return* of thought to the concrete, achieving a reconciliation between thought and existence. It is *this* that allows the thinking subject to feel at home in the actual world it inhabits, and to grasp the rationality within it.

The foregoing is likely to be sufficient to lead many a reader to think that as both philosopher and historian of philosophy Hegel is simply *beyond* redemption. Does not this attitude reveal that for him the history of philosophy can be no more than a mirror within which he, as a self-styled exemplary modern European, narcissistically contemplates the embryogenesis of his own thought? Many have indeed understood Hegel in this way, but perhaps this purported tight interpenetration between his philosophy and his account of the history of philosophy can be understood otherwise. Might it not also be claimed that *not* to acknowledge the history of philosophy as leading to one's own philosophical stance is to presume that one can, as philosopher, understand, judge, and evaluate philosophy's history from a rational standpoint informed by norms that are *not* historically given? Might not Hegel's position be the expression of an approach to rationality that refuses to take the mind as a magical ingredient added, from somewhere else, to the mix of physical, organic, sociocultural, and historical forces that have otherwise made one the being that one is?

Whatever answer we come up with here presupposes that we understand Hegel's project as clearly as possible. To this end I have adopted a basically expositional and

---

[2] The source for this translation is Hegel, *Vorlesungen: Ausgewälte Nachschriften und Manuskripte*, vol. 12. Page references to the latter are included in square brackets.

uncritical presentation. Hegel's own philosophy clearly bears many similarities to Greek 'speculative' thought, but it is also premised on the necessity that the Greek experiment in freedom would fail. To understand Hegel himself, it is therefore essential that we get into as clear a focus as possible his understanding of ancient philosophy and its fate.

27.1. GREEK 'AT-HOMENESS'

Hegel's *Lectures on the Philosophy of World History* allow us to obtain a fuller understanding of what it means for the Greeks to have been 'at home' in the world. What had been distinctive about Greek religious consciousness was that spirit represented itself as "something that is not exterior and natural but interior and human" (LPWH 387 [337–338]). This Greek intuition was close to the Oriental concerning "the substantial unity of spirit and nature," but in the Greek case, "the spiritual is encountered twice: as subjective being-for-self and in unity with the natural" (LPWH 388–389 [339–340]). Thus "the spiritual opposes itself to what is merely submerged in materiality" (LPWH 389 [340]), giving it a "power over nature, as what initially appears as other to it" (LPWH 392 [345]). Thus, while nature might first have been perceived as external and foreign, it was nevertheless conceived as "animated and ensouled," bearing within it something 'genial' to the human spirit and so receptive to its acts of transformation (LPWH 392–393 [345–347]). This meant that although the Greeks had taken cultural and religious material from elsewhere, they could transform this material into something bearing *their own* stamp and within which they could collectively recognize *themselves* as a people (LPWH 394 [347–348]).[3] It allowed a heterogeneous "conglomeration of tribes that came from elsewhere" to *become* the Greeks (LPWH 377 [322]).

This capacity to recognize one's own action *as one's own*, to "fully or truly stand behind it, own up to it, claim ownership of it," is, as Robert Pippin has argued,[4] at the core of Hegel's conception of freedom. Conceived in this way, freedom will be thought as equally necessary to *theoretical* life as it is to practical activity in that it allows one to have thoughts that are held to *one's own* normative standards, rather than merely caused by external considerations. In its Greek form, however, this freedom came with limitations. The exercise of Greek freedom was always "within the condition of naturalness" (LPWH 392 [345]), a condition reflected in the fact that Greek religion was "found in beauty—a spiritual quality burdened with sensuous elements" (LPWH 415–416 [379]), rather than in 'truth'. It was the 'contradiction' between this freedom and its limitation by an externally given content within which it could manifest itself that would underlie the dissolution of both the *polis* and the philosophy to which it gave rise.[5] And this was

---

[3] Robert Pippin summarizes Hegel's appreciation of Greek art in terms that echo the idea of the 'friendliness' of the materials of art to the expression of inner intention (Pippin, *After the Beautiful*, 22).

[4] Pippin, *Hegel's Practical Philosophy*, 5.

[5] While the "external political destruction of Greece" lies in the Peloponnesian Wars, these wars reflected the structural features of Greek society that had resulted in Athens and Sparta striving to

a limitation that Hegel confidently believed modern European society could overcome. This emerging society would thereby be able to recognize its own origins, childhood, and youth in the Greek world, and find in that world the origins of the renewed philosophy in which *it* expresses its own freedom.

In Rome and the Middle Ages, the earlier perceived 'genial' interchanges between intentional life and the external world would be replaced by a conception of thought and existence as two rigidly distinct realms—a distinction that would be brought to the level of explicit self-consciousness in the early modern period. But Hegel would not, like some contemporaries, simply lament the loss of Greek 'objectivity' and its replacement by the opposed realms underlying modern subjectivity. Rather, this abstract early-modern opposition between inner life and external existence that was largely foreign to the Greeks would, he thought, be reintegrated into a modern, complex and universalized version of Greek *Heimatlichkeit*, allowing a *subjective* dimension of freedom to coexist with *Heimatlichkeit* in a way that had been impossible for the Greeks.

Hegel devotes over half the space of the published lectures to the history of Greek philosophy, which he treats in three phases: an initial development stretching from Thales to Aristotle; a period in which it divides into antithetical outlooks such as those of Skepticism and Stoicism; and a final period of Neoplatonism. We cannot here afford the space for even-handedness and will concentrate on what, from Hegel's point of view, was the highest point of Greek philosophy and what makes it particularly relevant to the modern reader—the *scientifically* speculative philosophies of Plato and Aristotle,[6] together with the strictly pre-scientific philosophy of Plato's teacher, Socrates. As for the philosophies of Rome and the Middle Ages, while they properly fall within the history of philosophy as Hegel considers it, these respective societies had clearly not been marked by the free political institutions that formed the soil from which Greek philosophy had sprung. It will then not come as a surprise that Hegel was far from enthusiastic about the philosophy of these periods, and only the briefest account of his treatment of them will be given here. From Hegel's point of view, it will only be with the philosophy of the modern period that philosophy *proper* is re-commenced.

---

become the political center of Greece under conditions that made the establishment of any such center *impossible* (*Lectures on the Philosophy of World* History, 414–415 [378–379]).

[6] "The development of philosophic science as science [*philosophische Wissenschaft als Wissenschaft*], and, further, the progress from the Socratic point of view to the scientific, begins with Plato and is completed by Aristotle" (Hegel, *Lectures on the History of Philosophy* (H&S) 2: 1 [M 2: 147]). In the 1825–1826 lectures, Hegel seems to locate the point at which Greek philosophy became *science* specifically with Aristotle (Hegel, *Lectures on the History of Philosophy 1825–6*, 2: 13 [7: 5]). Hegel freely talks of pre-Platonic philosophy (that of Parmenides and the Parmenideans, for example) and post-Aristotelian philosophy (the Neoplatonism of Plotinus and Proclus) as 'speculative', an adjective meant to capture the dynamic relations among conceptual determinations to contrast with the more static approaches he associates with the operations of the 'understanding'. But speculative content can also be found in the form of *Vorstellungen* in non-philosophical traditions, such as Eastern religions, and in periods where philosophy is not *freely* pursued, as in medieval Catholicism. Speculative content treated in a *speculative manner* proper to conceptuality itself constitutes *scientific* philosophy.

|

27.2. Pre-Scientific Greek Philosophy

The history of Greek philosophy, and so the history of philosophy itself, begins with Thales and Ionian natural philosophy. This philosophy had devoted itself to finding something *natural* as the 'principle' or '*archi*' of all that is, and Thales took that to be *water* (LHP 2: 23–24 [7: 15–16]). Actually, what had been chosen *as* the principle, whether it be "water, air, or the infinite," is of little interest (LHP 2: 24 [7: 16]): it is the fact *that* such a principle was asserted at all that is important for Hegel. Ironically, despite the fact that the Ionians take the principles from the materials of the empirical world, this is "the beginning of a departure from what is in our sense perception, a stepping-back from this immediately existing being" (LHP 2: 26 [7: 17]). When Thales declares that *everything* is really water, his specifying *water* must involve the *thought or concept* of water as the purported explanans of everything: even if he had subjectively had in mind the sort of immediately perceivable stuff in the puddle before him, the water of *this* puddle cannot be identical to the abstraction *posited* as the principle of everything. On Hegel's understanding of the term, this makes Thales an 'idealist'.[7] No philosophical explanation in this sense, no matter how naturalistic, could avoid conceptualization, and so 'thought' is the real principle behind *any* type of philosophy. As Hegel puts it in *The Science of Logic*, "every philosophy is essentially idealism" (SL 21.142/124).

The Pythagoreans represent the transition from such Ionic *naturalism* to a more abstracted and intellectual philosophy. Pythagoras and the Pythagoreans consciously grasped what was only implicit in Thales: the absolute could *not* be understood as some particular sensuous matter. Becoming conscious of the fact that its determinations must be *posits* rather than sensuous givens, the Pythagoreans had taken *number* to represent the eternal and unchanging *explanans* of everything. Thus what we know as 'category theory', *qua* systematic account of the fundamental determinations of thought, begins with the Pythagoreans as modeled on the relations among *numbers*. Particular limitations, however, follow from this numerical model. Thus *counting* takes one (the monas) as its basic category, from which is generated duality (dyas), taken to represent multiplicity, otherness, and opposition. But while this introduces the important idea of opposition *as* an essential moment of the absolute, it does not allow any *determinate* conception of opposition or otherness, since the moments of the dyad are themselves simply different 'ones' considered in their most abstract self-identities (LHP 2: 39 [7: 31–32]). The limitations of modeling the components of thought on numbers soon become obvious, and later philosophers, including Aristotle and Plato, had "stolen its fruits and have passed them off as their own by a facile alteration, substituting categories of thought in place of number" (LHP 2: 39 [7: 31]). These formal and abstractive 'oriental'

---

[7] In *The Science of Logic* Hegel notes that "[n]ot even the "water" of Thales is that, for, although also empirical water, it is besides that the *in-itself* or *essence* of all other things, and these things do not stand on their own, self-grounded, but are *posited* on the basis of an other, of 'water', that is, they are idealized" (SL 21.142/124).

features of Pythagoras's thought are consonant with the fact of his having spent much time in Egypt in the company of the Egyptian priesthood (LHP 2: 32 [7: 23–24]).

With their numericism, the Pythagoreans had not found an adequate form of expression for the speculative *concept*—that is, for pure unencumbered *thought*—and it was only with the Eleatic school (essentially Xenophanes, Parmenides, Melissus, and Zeno) that a more adequate understanding of pure thought and its dynamics—its 'movement'—could be achieved. For Parmenides "only being *is*, and what is nothing *is not at all*," and the achievement of this *pure thought* represents "a tremendous advance" over the Ionians and Pythagoreans. Here, "thought, properly speaking, begins to be free for the first time on its own account, as essence, or as that which alone is true; now thought grasps its own self"(LHP 2: 57 [7: 53]). In particular, with the approach of *Zeno* the beginnings of *dialectical thought* is to be found. Reading this relation through Plato's *Parmenides*, Hegel says that "Parmenides proved that the One is, but Zeno showed that the many is not" (LHP 2: 65 [7:62]). But the truth here appears in a somewhat inverted form: while Zeno himself might have taken this to show the unreality of change (a claim that can be refuted *by walking*), for Hegel it shows the *reality* of change and thereby, "that the representation of motion inherently involves contradictory determinations" (LHP 2: 66 [7: 63]). As a *principle*, the dialectic implicit in Zeno would emerge in Heraclitus's "bold and more profound dictum that being no more is than is non-being" by which he "grasped the dialectic of the Eliatic school objectively and . . . treated this objective dialect as the principle, or as the absolute" (LHP 2: 73 [7: 71]). Such a concept of the absolute as unity of opposites would later come to fruition in Plato's dialogue, *Parmenides* (LHP 2: 205–207 [8: 33–36]). We cannot understand Plato, however, without understanding the most significant of the pre-scientific philosophers—Socrates—and we will pass over Hegel's discussion of intervening figures and go straight to him.

For Hegel, Socrates was more than a philosopher: the principle he introduced constitutes a "major turning-point [*einen grossen Wendepunkt*] in the world's consciousness" (LHP 2: 124 [7: 127]). Socrates had added a *subjective dimension* to the otherwise habitual moral lives of Athenian citizens: his challenge to his interlocutors being "to discover and learn from themselves what their vocation and final goal, and also what the world's purpose is, what is true in and for itself; they must attain truth by and through themselves" (LHP 2: 124–125 [7: 127]). In short, he challenged them to discover this within the resources of *their own individual consciousnesses*, and not to simply take on in an unquestioning way the duties that were assigned to them by custom.

Philosophy for Socrates did not entail any withdrawal from everyday existence into any realm of abstract thought. He could combine a questioning attitude with living the life of a citizen engaged in the political life of Athens, fighting in three campaigns in the Peloponnesian war and occupying various public offices. Moreover, *as a philosopher*, his occupation "properly consisted in associating with all and sundry, with people of different ages and of quite diverse vocations . . . getting individuals involved in thinking things over [*Nachdenken*]" (LHP 2: 130 [7: 134]). His unfortunate end, however, would signal the incompatibility of Socratic reflection with its "right of consciousness, the right of knowing, of subjective freedom" with "the divine right of unquestioned custom, the law of the fatherland, and religion" (LHP 2: 127 [7: 130]), the context within which Greek *Heimatlichkeit* had flourished. As we know most about the famous 'Socratic method' through the dialogues of Plato, we will discuss this later in the context of Plato's account of dialectic.

27.3. HEGEL'S *DEPLATONIZED* PLATO

It might be thought that Plato, along with the Pythagoreans who had influenced him, would present the greatest challenge for Hegel's general construal of Greek philosophy as a manifestation of the Greek spirit of 'being-at-home' in the world. The attitudes that we typically think as 'Platonic' seem marked by a yearning for the transcendent or 'otherworldly' typical of Eastern thinking, and to express anything but *Heimatlichkeit*. Hegel thus pursues a certain 'deep reading' of Plato's texts in an effort to separate the essential features from those obscuring superficial ones that, he claims, have led to the misunderstanding of his philosophy. To appreciate Hegel's argument here, we must invoke a distinction that is crucial for him between the German words '*Darstellung*' and '*Vorstellung*', often translated as 'presentation' and 'representation', respectively.

'*Vorstellung*' had been the term used in German philosophy to translate the subjective 'ideas' characteristic of philosophy in the seventeenth and eighteenth centuries, but in Hegel's usage, to think in *Vorstellungen* is to draw on images from everyday life and employ them to express some conceptual content in an indirect, metaphorical way. Such thought is ubiquitous and, importantly, is typical of how a more 'universal' content is expressed in *religion*. In contrast, *philosophy* demands that the true conceptual content be somehow extracted from this superficial, imagistic form. The term '*Darstellung*' had come to be used in a more realistic and *non-psychologistic* mode to refer to the way in which some *objective* content could be *presented* in thought and knowledge.[8]

Hegel acknowledges that Plato had freely used everyday *Vorstellungen*, especially from contemporary religious myth, to convey philosophical content. This may make them attractive, but it is the source of misunderstanding, as there is "the inevitable danger of taking what belongs only to representation [*was nur der Vorstellung angehört*], and not to thought, as the essential element" (LHP 2: 182–183 [8: 7]). Reading Plato without this distinction results in the popular picture of Plato as an otherworldly thinker—the 'Platonist' of tradition. Consider, for example, the slave boy in Plato's *Meno*, whose seemingly innate knowledge of geometry recovered by Socrates' questioning is explained by the doctrine of the soul's 'remembrance' of forms the soul, once unencumbered by corporeality, had been able to 'perceive' directly.[9] While Plato's texts speak of the incorporeal soul and the transcendent realm within which it originally moved, such an idea should not be taken as part of his philosophy (LHP 2: 183 [8: 8]). Such representations are

---

[8] On a history of this notion, see Martha B. Helfer, *The Retreat of Representation*.
[9] Plato, *Complete* Works, 871–897.

meant to convey that *thinking*, in the way involved in geometric proofs, grasps its content in a *universal*, that is, conceptually mediated, manner. Rather than expressing an ontological thesis about the mind *qua* soul having a timeless existence amid the 'Ideas' or 'Forms' in some Platonic realm—a decidedly *oriental idea*—these pictures are meant to refer to the way we know *the truth* about the *this-worldly* reality we *actually* inhabit.

We will also appreciate the *positive* sense in which Plato's philosophy manifests Greek *Heimatlichkeit* if we remember how this notion is to be understood in terms of a certain optimism and confidence concerning the receptiveness of nature and externality to human thought and purposeful activity. Thus when Plato in the *Republic* posits the rule of the state by *philosophers*, this signals the rule in human affairs of *philosophy*—reason—itself. That communal life is capable of being governed by universal principles in this way signals its congeniality to being shaped by rational thought. Ultimately, however, this will not be achievable in the ancient polis, the contradictions within which will be revealed in Plato's political thought.

Hegel discusses Plato's philosophy under the headings 'dialectic', 'philosophy of nature', and 'philosophy of spirit'. Clearly, he thinks that Plato's importance lies primarily in the first and last of these areas, and in both of these areas the profound influence of Socrates is apparent.

Plato's major significance lies in his development of a 'dialectic' that had first made its appearance in Zeno. Plato had grasped the 'movement' of pure categories of thought that had earlier been presented in 'static' ways in the approaches of the Pythagoreans and Eleatics. Zeno had, inadvertently, broken though this static Eleatic approach: attempting to show the *unreality* of motion, he had effectively showed the *reality of contradiction*. It is Socrates, however, who was the crucial forerunner to Plato in regard to the development of this dialectic, and Socrates must be understood in relation to the appearance of cultural figures who accompanied the rise of Greek democracy—the Sophists.

Influenced by both the Sophists and their critic, Socrates, Plato had linked the *dialectic* of thought to the *dialogical* use of language. Hegel notes the important development in Athens of an urbane *conversational* culture among the leisured Athenian males in which participation in conversations was governed by "the ongoing recognition of the rights of other persons" (LPWH 410 [371]). Conversation had been the medium employed by the Sophists to show how, on questioning, particular ideas could become transformed into their opposites. Here they relied on the fact of the perspectivity of many everyday claims: "Some of us freeze in the wind and others do not. So we cannot say that the wind is cold or warm, for it is warm and cold according to its relationship to a subject" (LHP 2: 122 [7: 125]). Socrates *too* had used these apparent contradictions to produce confusions or *aporiae* in which assumptions unreflectively held by the interlocutor were confounded (LHP 2: 134–135; 196 [7: 139–140; 8: 23] but whereas the Sophists used this confusion to *deny* the ultimate distinction between truth and falsity, Socrates used technique to free the interlocutor from the constraints of the immediate certitudes of empirical consciousness and to draw "something universal from the particular," from "experience or representation, whatever is in our consciousness in a naïve way" (LHP 2: 134 [7: 138]).[10]

However, this goal was by no means always achieved in Plato, especially in his early dialogues, which often ended with only the confusion of opinion and the awakening (rather than the satisfaction) of a need for knowledge. However, in the later dialogues, such as the *Sophist, Philebus*, and, especially, *Parmenides*, Plato had achieved more positive results, unraveling the categorical structure of the universal 'Idea' in more concrete ways. Thus, in his *Parmenides*, the absolute is grasped as *being*, but, in a departure from Parmenides himself, as no longer understood in abstract opposition to *non*-being. Rather, it is *becoming*.[11] This means that *being* is to be understood as having *non-being* as internal to it: "In the One, being is non-being and non-being is being; the unity of the two is in becoming" (LHP 2: 206 [8: 35]).[12] The Neoplatonist Proclus had taken this doctrine from Plato's *Parmenides* as "the authentic theology, the authentic unveiling of all the mysteries of the divine essence," but Plato's dialectic is "not complete in every respect," as it starts from what are themselves *fixed* categories such 'the One' and 'being' and cannot ultimately capture their authentically *dialectical* relation (LHP 2: 207 [8: 36]).

Hegel is largely dismissive of Plato's philosophy of nature, but for different reasons to those commonly encountered. Rather than *criticizing* Plato for ignoring the sensory world, Hegel sees this refusal of 'the given' as central to his achievements. The problem with Plato's approach is that it doesn't use contradictions *within* the empirical to guide reason's way beyond it. It was Plato's *practical* philosophy that was of greater significance. In particular, Plato's achievement had consisted in his understanding of the links between man's moral nature, the nature of justice, and the state, as developed in *The Republic*. This, however, must be understood within the context of the limitations on the realization of the Greek capacity for freedom. To remind us of Plato's historical context, Hegel employs a saying familiar from his *Philosophy of Right*: "one cannot overleap one's own time; the spirit of one's age is one's own spirit too" (LHP 2: 219 [8: 51]),[13] and appeals to this nexus between the spirit of Plato's philosophy and the historically specific spirit of the Greeks to explain the grounds of what is commonly taken to be the 'totalitarian' dimension of Plato's political philosophy—Hegel's explicitly *critical* explication of this dimension seemingly being lost on many of Hegel's political critics.[14]

For Hegel, we moderns are attracted to the life and culture of the ancient Greeks because of the expression of freedom found there, but that freedom was not what we

---

[10] For a more recent reading of Plato that stresses the role of the dialogue, see Hans-Georg Gadamer, *Plato's Dialectical Ethics*.

[11] That is, Plato has here worked his way through the initial set of 'thought-determinations' as Hegel himself sets them out in the first book of *The Science of Logic*, the "Logic of Being," advancing thought's grasp of itself beyond the earlier efforts of the likes of Parmenides and Heraclitus.

[12] Gadamer has argued that the conception of the dialectic attributed to Plato by Hegel rests on some clear *misreadings* of Plato's approach to contradiction (Gadamer, "Hegel and the Dialectic of the Ancient Philosophers").

[13] C.f., Hegel, *Philosophy of Right*, 21.

[14] E.g., Popper, *The Open Society*.

moderns typically think of as freedom, with our stress on its *subjective* and *individual* dimensions. The principle of subjective freedom had entered into Greek life with Socrates' individual questioning approach to morality, but was "the principle that destroyed the Greek states and Greek life generally" (LHP 2: 220 [8: 52]) and was in tension with the collective 'at homeness' of Greeks in their world. Plato had recognized this disparity between the principle of subjectivity represented by Socrates and the unquestioning adherence to its customs that life in the polis required, and for that reason had sought "to exclude and banish this new principle, to preclude all possibility of it" (LHP 2: 220 [8: 53]). This suppression of subjective freedom can be seen reflected in various features of life as set out there: in the denial to individuals of a *choice* as to which class they belong; in the abolition of all private property; and in the abolition of marriage and the family. From the perspective of the present and in the light of the Christian idea that "the soul of the individual is the absolute end . . . we can see that the Platonic constitution is of a lower order; it cannot fulfill the higher requirements of an ethical organization" (LHP 2: 225 [8: 58]). However, no one, Plato included, can overleap their own time, and while it matters for the *modern* state whether or not individuals have freedom of conscience or are able to pursue their particular interests in their own way, such considerations are "excluded from the Platonic idea" (LHP 2: 220 [8: 53]). That he fully expressed the limitations of the spirit of his time in thought is not a sign of the failure of Plato as a philosopher, but rather a sign of his greatness.

27.4. Hegel's *De-Empiricized* Aristotle

As we have seen, Hegel's Plato is not really the Plato with whom we are familiar, and the same might be said of Hegel's Aristotle.[15] Hegel rejects the commonplace contrasting of Plato and Aristotle as representatives of antithetical extremes such as idealism and realism, or rationalism and empiricism (LHP 2: 226 [8: 59–60]). Aristotle was a *developer* of Plato's speculative philosophy, a follower who took dialectic beyond the limitations found there and who, like the later Neoplatonists, made the divine 'noesis noeseos noesis[16] [thought thinking itself]', the pinnacle to his metaphysics (LHP 2: 254 [8: 91]). While the unity of being and non-being had been implicit but somewhat hidden in Plato, who had focused on the 'affirmative principle' concerning the idea's abstract self-identity, Aristotle had made explicit this hidden moment of negativity (LHP 2: 236 [8: 70]).

The priority of change and movement over the static that had first emerged in Zeno is expressed in Aristotle's metaphysics in terms of the conception of *energia*. Like Heraclitus, Aristotle treated *change* as fundamental, but in contrast to Heraclitus, for Aristotle change was not mere alteration but "self-preservation within identity with self" or "within the universal" (LHP 2: 235 [8: 69]). While Heraclitus captured the way "a

---

[15] For a careful and critical evaluation of Hegel's reading of Aristotle, see Ferrarin, *Hegel and Aristotle*.

[16] Aristotle, *Metaphysics*, bk. 12, ch. 9.

stream is ever-changing," Aristotle captures the fact that it is "also ever the same" (LHP 2: 235 [8: 68–69]). This dynamic and concrete equivalent to the abstract 'Idea' of Platonic philosophy is found in Aristotle in various forms: as the separable *form* of sensuous per-ceptible substances; as the 'higher kind of substance' that we think of as the souls of plants, animals and humans; and as *absolute* substance which, in contrast to Plato and the Pythagoreans, is conceived as *pure activity*, thought thinking itself. Nevertheless, the commonplace construal of the essentially speculative Aristotle as a type of empir-icist, interested primarily in 'natural history', is not entirely wrong. His procedure of "bringing into thought the determinations from the ordinary representation [*gewöhn-lichen Vorstellung*] of an object and then combining them in unity, in the concept" had an empirical dimension which works counter to the *necessity* required for the "passage of one determination [*Bestimmung*] to another." This approach of *at first* considering objects in the way they are apprehended in *Vorstellungen* leads him to treat the whole universe in its spiritual and sensible dimensions as an 'aggregate', a 'series of objects' (LHP 2: 233 [8: 66]). His divine conception of substance seems thus overlaid and ulti-mately compromised by a static conception of individual substantial forms underlying appearances and devoid of self-negation. But there were nevertheless clearly *positive* benefits of Aristotle's 'empiricism' for the development of Greek philosophy. To appreci-ate these, we need to return to the limits of Plato's quasi-sophistical linguistic or '*dialogi-cal*' form of presentation of the essentially *dialectical* content of his thought.

Michelet's edition of the *Lectures on the History of Philosophy* has Hegel summing up Plato's standpoint as that of, first, "the contingent form of speech, in which men of noble and unfettered nature converse without other interest than that of theory which is being worked out" (H&S 2: 116 [M, 2: 226]), a conversational form of life that, as Hegel was aware, was dependent on the existence of slaves to free the few for the leisure time to devote to such conversations (LPWH 404 [362–363]).[17] For Aristotle, by contrast, phi-losophy was more to be identified with the thoughtful response to being struck by the world in sensuous experience: "Aristotle appears as a thoughtful observer of the world who attends to all aspects of the universe" (LHP 2: 232 [8: 65]). This 'empirical' dimen-sion allowed Aristotle to make distinctions among the relations of 'negation' between predicates of judgments that had *not* been apparent within Plato's more 'conversation-ally' based analyses.

The first phase of the Socratic method was, as we have seen, intended to dissolve the force of particular claims by showing how a claim could be turned into its opposite so as to allow the 'universal' to emerge out of this confusion and so replace the sensuous givens *as* the true object of knowledge (LHP 2: 196 [7: 22–23]). But Plato's Socrates did this by transiting from sensuous existence directly to that which *could not* be sensibly perceived: "An action, viewed empirically, can be said to be just, whereas from another aspect it can be shown to have quite the opposite character. The good or the true, how-ever, is to be apprehended by itself, devoid of individuality or empirical concretion of this sort; it alone is what *is*" (LHP 2: 200–201 [8: 28]). The element that is 'universal and

[17] Thus, while freedom is seen as an essential element of Greek life, there only *some* are free.

true' that emerges out of this dissolution, however, remains "very general and abstract" (LHP 2: 201 [8: 28]), and while Plato had endeavored to go *beyond* the abstract idea of 'the good' and to give it concrete determination, his problem was that of unifying the opposing determinations of universality and determinateness. But this is just where Aristotle "surpassed Plato in speculative depth" by bringing the determination supplied by the *empirical world* to the 'idealist tradition' initiated by Plato (LHP 2: 226 [8: 20]).

Plato had resisted the skeptical conclusions that the Sophists had drawn from the relativity of perceptual judgments by shifting the focus of philosophical investigation away from sensuous experience to the *ideas themselves*, but in so doing he had effectively *conceded* the Sophists' skepticism about the empirical world, and had tacitly accepted their conception of the objects of perception as the unity of different subject-relative qualities that were 'indifferent' to each other and thus *indifferently* applied in claims about the sensible world.[18] But, as Hegel points out in the *Phenomenology of Spirit*, "if the many determinate properties were strictly indifferent to one another, if they were simply and solely self-related, they would not be determinate; for they are only determinate in so far as they *differentiate* themselves from one another, and *relate* themselves *to others* as their opposites" (PS 9.73/¶114). It had been Aristotle's explicit focus on the *empirical world* that allowed him to discover the operations of the dialectic *in empirical experience itself* and so to grasp the universal as generated *from* this starting point. But Aristotle's limits are revealed in the fact that, for him, thinking could not reflect on itself *directly*, but only in the form of the thinkable forms of objects taken from the empirical world.

Hegel considers Aristotle's corpus in terms of the classification: *Metaphysics, Philosophy of Nature* (*physics*), *Philosophy of Spirit* (*psychology* and *practical philosophy* (*ethics* and *politics*) and, finally, *Logic*. We have noted the central features of Aristotle's *metaphysics* in the preceding, and as for his *physics*, it is clear that this concept meant something much more general to Aristotle than the name suggests today. Aristotle's fascination with every facet of the empirical world will ensure that the study of movement is not limited to *physical* movement narrowly understood: it will extend to the movements of particular types of things, and, importantly, *animals* and *ourselves, qua* spiritual beings. Thus this fascination with the empirical will be continued into his *Philosophy of Spirit*, which divides into theoretical (*De Anima* and other psychological treatises) and practical parts, the latter dividing into ethics (*Nichomachean Ethics, Magna Moralia*, and the *Eudemean Ethics*) and politics (*Politics*). As his speculative *logic* is at the core of all these areas of his philosophy, however, we will concentrate on this to try to appreciate what for Hegel represented Aristotle's surpassing of Plato in the realm of dialectic.

We might learn something of the complex relation between the *logics* governing the respective dialectics of Plato and Aristotle from a passage in the Michelet edition of

---

[18] This conception of sensuous qualities Hegel discusses in the *Phenomenology of Spirit* as simple positivities related only to themselves and so "indifferent to one another, each . . . on its own and free from the others" (PS 9.72/¶113) (Hegel, *Phenomenology of Spirit*, §113). Allan Silverman argues for a conception of sensuous objects in Plato as constituted by bundles of mutually indifferent *trope-like* proto-properties (Silverman, *The Dialectic of Essence*, 21).

the *Lectures* where Hegel quotes from Aristotle's *Categories* when discussing his logical *Organon*. Here Aristotle, discussing "things that are said," effectively distinguishes two different underlying conceptions of predication—the distinction between predicates that are 'in' the subject and those that can be 'said of' the subject.[19] Hegel renders the 'said of' relation thus: "There are determinations (*onta*), that are said of a subject (*kath hypokeimenou legetai*), but are in no subject, as 'man' [said of] a determinate man, but is not in a determinate man" (H&S 2: 212 [M 2: 358]).[20] A suggestion by E. J. Lowe as to the general point may help here: while, say, the existence of the universal *doghood* relies on the existence of *particular dogs*, it will not rely upon *any specific* dog, say, Fido or Rover, that one could point to as *this* dog.[21]

Following Socrates, Plato, we might say, had been too quick to pass from such imperfect empirical instances as Fido or Rover to the idea of *doghood* itself, while in contrast the 'thinking empiricist' Aristotle had assigned a more positive place to the consideration of such specific instances. This was reflected in their different logics. Plato had proposed the process of 'division' or '*diaresis*' by which a genus concept is divided into different species concepts by adding differentiating features, as when humans, say, are distinguished from other animals by the feature of their *rationality*. As Plato thinks of 'the idea' as what is ultimately real, this descent from the idea to its particular instantiations will be understood as a type of gradual *privation* of reality. Moreover, the process of division shies away from empirical reality in another sense: the divider passes from, say, *generic* doghood to more particular *species* of doghood, but not to *specific actual dogs*, which are not arrived at by division. Aristotle's 'said of'/'is in' distinction, however, signals a distinction between things and their statuses *as* instances of species. While the universal *doghood* can be *said of* Rover, it is equally said of Fido. It should not be thought of as 'in' Rover *as* Rover himself, in the way that, say, Rover's particular color is 'in' Rover. What are properly 'in' Rover are akin to what Plato had treated as particular property instances 'bundled' together in objects,[22] but for Aristotle such properties are conceived as 'in' something that they cannot exist without—the *substantial form* of the individual that the Medievals later spoke of as its '*thisness*' ('*haecceity*', as opposed to its '*whatness*' or '*quiddity*'). And reflection upon empirically given objects makes it apparent that a thisness's possession of one determinate quality *excludes* its simultaneous possession of that property's *contrary*. (The *redness* of an object can coexist with its roundness but not its *blueness*, just as its *roundness* cannot coexist with its *squareness*.) With this, those property instances no longer are 'indifferent' to each other, as they seem to be in Plato's 'bundles'. Aristotle thus affirms a peculiar logical form that applies to these individual empirical substances—a claim effectively repeated a century ago by the logician W. E. Johnson, who wanted to separate the genus-species relation, derived from Platonic

[19] Aristotle, *Categories*, ch. v, 3b18–22.
[20] This dualism of 'is in' and 'is said of' conceptions of predication reappears in Hegel's own dialectical logic in his *Science of Logic* as the difference between 'inherence' and 'subsumption' (Hegel, *Science of Logic*, Volume 2, Section 1, Chapter 2, "Judgment").
[21] E. J. Lowe, *Four-Category Ontology*, 36.
[22] See note 18.

diaresis, from what he described as the 'determinable-determinate' structure of a thing's *qualitative* properties.[23] In this way, Aristotle's logic instantiates a capacity to grasp the relations of negation that exist *among* empirical properties, allowing what Hegel took to be a dialectical progression at the level of empirical phenomena that was missing in Plato. Nevertheless, the underlying substantial form itself will be *without* negation—a limiting consequence of Aristotle's methodological 'empiricism'.

Underneath the quasi-empiricist appearance of Aristotle's *formal* logic, Hegel thus sees a properly speculative content that is continuous with the *concrete* conceptions of logical structure developed later by the Neoplatonists.[24] But the limitations of Aristotle's dialectic will only become obvious with the emergence of a type of thought giving a more explicit role to the category of 'singularity [*Einzelnheit*]', which Hegel sees emerging with the Stoics.

27.5. POST-SCIENTIFIC PHILOSOPHY AND THE DECLINE OF THE POLIS: STOICISM, SKEPTICISM, NEOPLATONISM, AND CHRISTIANITY

From a contemporary perspective, aspects of Aristotle's treatment of empirical judgments can look unreflectively egocentric. While the propositional content of a judgment, if true, now tends to be thought of as *eternally* or *timelessly* true, this was not Aristotle's view: "'He sits' may, for instance, be true," says Aristotle, but "if he rises, it then becomes false."[25] While now the bare assertion "this man is sitting" is likely to be understood as short for "this man is sitting *at such and such a time*"—*that* proposition remaining true when the man later stands, for Aristotle, the belief is complete as it is, and *changes truth value* with time.[26] This 'presentist' approach to time in fact seems to reflect the generally ego- and geo-centric worldview expressed in Aristotelian thought overall—a type of thought that seems irreducibly 'terrestrial' in contrast to the 'celestial' dimensions of Plato's thought as it is commonly understood. This was the dimension

---

[23] W. E. Johnson, *Logic*, vol. I, 9–17, and Ch. XI. For Johnson "several colours are put in the same group and given the same name colour, *not* on the ground of any partial agreement, but on the ground of the special kind of difference which distinguishes one colour from another; whereas no such difference exists between a colour and a shape" (ibid., vol I, 176).

[24] Martin, *Themes*. Hegel's own logic, with its 'concrete universals', was to owe much to this implicit dynamic logic he saw running below the surface of the *merely* formal logic that is commonly taken from Aristotle's *Organon*.

[25] Aristotle, *Categories*, 4a17–23. See also Aristotle, *Metaphysics*, 1051b8–18.

[26] As A. N. Prior expresses it, "Instead of statements being true and false *at* different times, we have predicates being timeless true or false *of* different times" (Prior, *Time and Modality*, 25).

of Aristotelian thought that would come to be seen as incompatible with science in the early modern period.[27]

In *this* sense, Aristotle's theoretical philosophy seems to reflect the collective 'at-homeness' that Hegel purports characterizes Greek thought in general, in contrast to thought of the East. Thought is *at home* in the midst of the givens of empirical existence, and conceives of its objects in the way they are given in perception.[28] Just as with *practical reason*, this attitude will turn out to be incompatible with the 'subjective' and 'reflective' turn introduced by Socrates, a reflective turn developed within *logic* by the Stoics.[29]

For Hegel, the eclipse of Greek 'speculative' philosophy and the move to more formal and abstract, and therefore 'Eastern', philosophies like Stoicism and Skepticism was bound up with the historical decline of the democratic life of the Greek polis itself and the loss of Greek *Heimatlichkeit* (LHP 2: 265 [7: 102–103]). Socrates had already represented the emergence of a type of individual, reflective point of view that would ultimately prove incompatible with the form of life found in the Greek polis, and the speculative form of thought articulating it. Stoicism, and later Christianity, would come to give expression to an alienated subjective point of view characteristic of the unfree Roman form of life that replaced that of the polis. But for Hegel, prior to the modern world there would be no *actual* place in either everyday life or in philosophical culture for *non*-alienated versions of the reflective or subjective position that had first emerged with Socrates. One problem was the level of abstraction at which the free individual came to be conceived. In Michelet's edition of the *Lectures*, Hegel, describing the Stoics' abstract conception of the reflective individual subject—the Stoic sage—repeats a saying from Cicero to the effect that nobody can say *who this sage is* (H&S 2: 250–251, 256 [M 2: 395, 401]). The idea of the sage was that of an abstract ideal with no identifiable concrete instantiations, like the idea of perfect *doghood* without a Rover or a Fido. But Hegel's comments clearly signal the later appearance of a *specific concrete* figure who would be the analogue of the otherwise abstract 'sage' and who would bring about a historical change in human consciousness. For the *Christians, Jesus Christ*, or more properly, Jesus *the Christ*,[30] would replace the Stoics' sage—God becoming an actual and identifiable "*this* and (taking) the character of the *this* into the character of the divine concept." Such an event would be necessary for the development of an idea of which the Greeks were incapable, that "*this* person, each and every person, should be redeemed and eternally blessed" (LPWH 396 [351]).

[27] See, for example, Alexandre Koyré, *From the Closed World*.

[28] As Hegel points out in the *Phenomenology of Spirit*, chapter 2, this type of thinking treats perception (*Wahrnehmung*) as the taking (*nehmen*) of the truth (*Wahrheit*) of things.

[29] Thus the Stoics, more in line with Plato's principle of division, held to the principle of bivalence that every judgment must be 'eternally' either true or false and held decidedly more 'modern' conceptions of the logical structure of judgment.

[30] 'Christos' was the ancient Greek equivalent of 'messiah' and was literally 'the anointed one'. But as with Greek proper names, *Christos* comes with a definite article, *O Christos*. In Hegel's category theory, the name itself conflates the 'particularity' of a description and the 'singularity' (*thisness*) of a proper name. It needs, however, to be integrated with universality, and this would mark the later transition to *Protestant* Christianity; *all* humans become *this person* recognized by God.

The stories about Christ as 'son of God' would form the *content* of Christian philosophy in the Middle Ages, but *qua philosophical content* this would only be thought at the level of *Vorstellungen* representing the historical person, *Jesus*. Overcoming these limitations would require the reconciliation of the categories that could never be reconciled in ancient thought: singular *thisness*, particular *whatness*, and universality. Such a reconciliation would be predicated on the religious radicalism of Luther and other Reformers.

27.6. WAITING FOR PHILOSOPHY'S RETURN: ROME AND THE MIDDLE AGES

As with Greek philosophy, we must understand the philosophy of Rome and the Middle Ages in terms of the historical conditions that had given rise to those forms of thought. The collapse of the Greek polis had broken that nexus between individual and the community in which that individual could recognize him- or herself as a member, and an individualistic but alienated self-conception, in which one's identity was now bound up more with the contents of an 'inner' life, had emerged. Hegel sees this as increasingly reflected in the post-scientific philosophical movements of Stoicism, Skepticism, and Epicureanism and, finally medieval Catholicism. In Catholicism in particular, this gave rise to a type of anti-naturalism that ran contrary to the earlier Greek attitude to the actual world. Hegel lists consequences of the rise of this form of Christianity that would further undermine the basis of the type of social life found in ancient Greece. Christianity ruled out slavery—clearly a plus for freedom, but at the same time destroying the cultured life of the Athenians on which philosophy had depended (LPWH, 396 [432–433]). Among the casualties here was the type of 'beautiful ethical life' found in those particular 'plastic' Greek individuals like Socrates, Pericles, and Thucydides—individuals who had worked on themselves, *producing* themselves like great works of art, by shaping themselves into characters whose features expressed some underlying 'idea' (LHP 2: 129 [7: 133]). Most dramatically, however, Greek at-homeness in the world was replaced by "the establishment of two worlds"—Christianity's imagined *other world* stepping in to fill the void as the source of an individual's self-conception, consolidating the break initiated by Socrates between "the unconscious unity of my will with the state" that had been essential for Greek democracy. In Rome, political domination by a single person, the emperor— "the god of the world" (LPWH, 451 [424]) —now characterized the temporal realm, motivating a fearful oriental 'flight' to the imagined *other* world. All this, however, provided a type of worldly, if alienated, support for the *idea* of the reflective subjectivity first introduced by Socrates.

Hegel portrays Rome and, in particular, Alexandria as places where "the principles of East and West coalesce in virtue of conquest" (LPWH, 452 [426]), the abstract singularity that we have seen in Pythagorean numericism and the Stoic philosophy that bloomed in Rome becoming combined with the speculative philosophy of Plato and Aristotle to produce the Neoplatonism of Plotinus and Proclus. For its philosophical foundations, the early Christians would look to Neoplatonism, from which they would forge a framework for their doctrines, especially that of the Holy Trinity, but this philosophy was now pressed into the service of an 'external' content, the freedom of the earlier philosophy shackled by its being limited to providing *justification* for this content. This would result in neither the Church Fathers nor the later Scholastics making any real progress in philosophy *as philosophy*, giving to philosophy in the Middle Ages the type of monotonous *lack* of dialectical development that, Hegel thinks, characterizes all philosophical culture between Greek speculative philosophy and the philosophy of modernity.

Rome had come to an end with an "onrush of foreign people" making up the great migrations of the early Middle Ages, and central to Hegel's narrative are those Nordic and Eastern barbarians called '*Germanen*' (LPWH, 460 [438]).[31] The situation resulting from the ways in which these Germanic tribes assimilated what was left of the crumbling Greek and Roman cultures can be starkly contrasted with the ways in which the *earlier* Greeks had transformed foreign religious and cultural material to create something new. Rather than recognizing themselves in something newly created from materials derived from elsewhere, the new nations found themselves burdened by this richly developed foreign material (H&S 3: 47 [M 3: 130–131]). While the imposition of Christian spirituality on the barbarian people was necessary to discipline them out of their barbarous state, the price to be paid for this would be the shackling of free thought that had emerged in the polis. For its part, the new Christian church, which had been founded on other-worldly principles, soon became dragged into the power-plays of 'worldly existence', effectively imposing the 'rule of passion' onto the church's *supposedly* spiritual rule, leaving these spiritual and worldly realms 'mutually estranged'. This period thus witnesses a split between 'two kingdoms' operative on a number of levels. First, the rules of emperor and pope are estranged, but there also arises an *internal split* within the life of the Church itself between its external practices and the inner subjective life of its followers—a split that would burst the Church asunder in the Reformation. Philosophically, this was to be expressed in the 'Cartesian' split between body and mind that would seem so natural in the early modern period.

In line with these splits, Hegel portrays medieval Catholicism as dominated by the performance of 'external acts' directed against one's own sinning external nature, such as in fasting, making pilgrimages, and so on. The great contribution of Catholic dogma to philosophy had been that of the Holy Trinity resulting from an amalgam of Christian and Neoplatonic thought, but the figure of the Trinity itself provides Hegel with a way

---

[31] For a critical discussion of Hegel's view of the 'Germanen' see Pinkard, "Hegel's Philosophy of History as the Metaphysics of Agency," Chapter 24 in this volume.

of periodizing the history of philosophy from a theological point of view. Thus he notes that the medieval period is marked by the "lordship of the Son, not of the Spirit" (LHP 3: 39 [9: 28]): "the Son, the mediator, is known as *this man*; this is the identity of spirit with God for the heart as such" (H&S 3: 57–58 [M 3: 141]). Clearly, we are to think of the 'Oriental' religion of the Old Testament as the 'dominion of the Father', with God conceived as a type of other-worldly Patriarch-King. The conception of Jesus of Nazareth as divine, of course, signals that the gap between the Patriarch and his creations has been somehow bridged. From a philosophical point of view, Jesus conceived as the Christ represents a further step in the change in the world-spirit that had started with Socrates' internalization of morality. "The reflection of consciousness into itself begins here [with Socrates], the knowledge of the consciousness of self as such, that it is real existence—or that God is a Spirit, or again, in a cruder and more sensuous form, that God takes human form" (H&S 1: 407408 [M 2: 63]).

But the period of the 'dominion of the Son' would contrast with the later period of the *domination of the Spirit*, a period that will only properly commence with the Reformation. Prior to that, the fact that 'the Christ' was exclusively identified with a particular historical being—*this* man, Jesus—would reflect the limitations of the excessively concrete and 'external' nature of medieval Catholicism along with the (still Greek) categorial nature of scholastic thought, in which 'thisness' was not extended universally. Such fixation on the external would be reflected in the medieval search for traces of the historical Christ in the Crusades, as well as the honoring of the Host—the consecrated bread and wine as body and blood of Christ—"as an external thing." For Luther, however, "all externality with reference to me is banished, including the externality that was present in the sacramental host. Only in communion and in faith am I connected with something divine" (LHP 3: 76–77 [8: 63]). In this new form of Christianity, "the person must himself or herself feel penitence and remorse; the heart must be filled with a genuinely holy spirit.... Within the inmost aspect of the human being, therefore, a place was posited that is all that matters and where a person is present only with self and with God. I must be at home in my conscience [*Im Gewissen muss ich zu Hause sein*]" (LHP 3: 76--7 [8: 63]). Effectively, the Protestant move to finding the *truth* of religion within consciousness would repeat, but now within a *universalized* Christian culture, the world-historical event first introduced within the Athenian polis by Socrates, and the changes brought about would be just as great. Ultimately the outcome of this would be the re-emergence of scientific speculative philosophy, but now shed of the restricting relation to an external sensuousness, as well as the failure to mediate the universal and the singular that had compromised its classical form.[32]

[32] I am grateful to Dean Moyar and Karin de Boer for helpful comments on an earlier draft of this chapter.

WORKS CITED

Primary Texts

Aristotle. *Metaphysics*, in *Loeb Classical Library, Aristotle XVIII*, translated by Hugh Tredennick. Cambridge, MA: Harvard University Press, 1996.

Aristotle. *Categories*, in *Loeb Classical Library, Aristotle I*, edited and translated by H. B. Cooke. Cambridge, MA: Harvard University Press, 1996.

Hegel, G. W. F. *Elements of the Philosophy of Right* [PR], edited by Allen W. Wood and translated by H. B. Nisbet. Cambridge: Cambridge University Press, 1991.

Hegel, G. W. F. *Gesammelte Werke*. Deutsche Forschungsgemainschaft. Hamburg: Meiner, 1968–.

Hegel, G. W. F. *Lectures on the History of Philosophy 1825–6* [LHP], in 3 volumes, edited by Robert F. Brown, translated by R. F. Brown and J. M. Stewart with the assistance of H. S. Harris. Oxford: Clarendon Press, 2006.

Hegel, G. W. F. *Lectures on the History of Philosophy* [H&S], in 3 volumes, translated by E. S. Haldane and F. H. Simson, with introduction by F. C. Beiser. Lincoln: University of Nebraska Press, 1995.

Hegel, G. W. F. *Lectures on the Philosophy of World History* [LPWH], Vol. 1: *Manuscripts of the Introduction and the Lectures of 1822–3*, edited and translated by R. F. Brown and P. C. Hodgson. Oxford: Clarendon Press, 2011.

Hegel, G. W. F. *Phenomenology of Spirit* [PS], translated by A. V. Miller. Oxford: Clarendon Press, 1975.

Hegel, G. W. F. *The Science of Logic* [SL], translated and edited by George di Giovanni. Cambridge: Cambridge University Press, 2010.

Hegel, G. W. F. *Vorlesungen: Ausgewählte Nachschriften und Manuskripte*. Hamburg: Felix Meiner Verlag, 1983–.

Hegel, G. W. F. *Vorlesungen über die Geschichte der Philosophie* [M], in 3 volumes, edited by Karl Ludwig Michelet. Berlin: Duncker und Humblot, 1840–1844.

Plato. *Complete Works*. Edited by John M. Cooper, D. S. Hutchinson, associate editor. Indianapolis: Hackett, 1997.

Secondary Literature

Ferrarin, Alfredo. *Hegel and Aristotle*. Cambridge: Cambridge University Press, 2001.

Gadamer, Hans-Georg. "Hegel and the Dialectic of the Ancient Philosophers," in *Hegel's Dialectic: Five Hermeneutical Studies*, translated and with an Introduction by P. Christopher Smith. New Haven, CT: Yale University Press, 1976.

Gadamer, Hans-Georg. *Plato's Dialectical Ethics: Phenomenological Interpretations Relating to the Philebus*. Translated and with an introduction by Robert M. Wallace. New Haven, CT: Yale University Press, 1991.

Helfer, Martha B. *The Retreat of Representation: The Concept of Darstellung in German Critical Discourse*. Albany: State University of New York Press, 1996.

Johnson, W. E. *Logic*. 3 volumes. Cambridge: Cambridge University Press, 1921–1924.

Koyré, Alexandre. *From the Closed World to the Infinite Universe*. Baltimore, MD: Johns Hopkins Press, 1957.

Lowe, E. J. *The Four-Category Ontology: A Metaphysical Foundation for Natural Science*. Oxford: Oxford University Press, 2006.

Martin, John N. *Themes in Neoplatonic and Aristotelian Logic*. Aldershot, UK: Ashgate, 2004.

Pippin, Robert B. *After the Beautiful: Hegel and the Philosophy of Pictorial Modernism*. Chicago: University of Chicago Press, 2014.

Popper, Karl. *The Open Society and Its Enemies, New One-Volume Edition*. Princeton, NJ: Princeton University Press, 2013.

Prior, Arthur N. *Time and Modality: Being the John Locke Lectures for 1955–6 Delivered in the University of Oxford*. Oxford: Clarendon Press, 1957.

Silverman, Allan. *The Dialectic of Essence: A Study of Plato's Metaphysics*. Princeton, NJ: Princeton University Press, 2002.

CHAPTER 28

HEGEL'S LECTURES ON THE HISTORY OF MODERN PHILOSOPHY

KARIN DE BOER

28.1. INTRODUCTION

THE young Hegel began lecturing on the history of philosophy in 1805, that is, while working on the *Phenomenology of Spirit* in Jena. He later taught on the subject in Heidelberg (1816–1817 and 1817–1818) as well as in Berlin (six times between 1819 and 1830). Hegel's lectures on the history of philosophy stand out because of their ambition to conceive of every past philosophical system as an element of an encompassing whole—a whole, moreover, that testifies to a development that is necessary rather than contingent. What is at stake in the lectures, therefore, is philosophy's effort to grasp its proper past in a truly philosophical way. We have to take into account, however, that the texts we possess were not intended for publication. Their primary aim was to introduce students to the history of philosophy, or even to philosophy as such. It is no wonder, therefore, that the lectures, largely handed down through student transcripts, exhibit a tension between Hegel's philosophical aim and the less lofty requirements of the classroom. Apart from these, the lectures can also be considered to expose a tension between Hegel's basic philosophical convictions and, on the other hand, the need to discuss a wide range of philosophers who appear to pursue a variety of particular and often diverging aims. In this contribution I will examine the lectures on the history of modern philosophy in view of this tension.

Before turning to the lectures, a few words about their various editions are needed. The first edition was published by Michelet between 1833 and 1836.[1] Michelet could

---

[1] The Suhrkamp edition of the lectures by Moldenhauer and Michel (LHPM, vols. 18–20) is based on this edition. The translation published by Haldane and Simson is based on Michelet's second, abridged, edition of the lectures, published 1840–1844.

make use of a number of manuscripts and transcripts, part of which have since been lost. Michelet's edition is valuable because it contains materials that are not found elsewhere. Yet it is impossible, given his editorial principles, to know to what extent the text corresponds to what Hegel has actually said or in which stage of his career he has done so.[2] At the time Hoffmeister prepared his own edition of the lectures, published in 1940, he could draw on fewer sources than Michelet. His one-volume edition, which contains only the Introduction and the section on Oriental philosophy, will be ignored here. This chapter primarily draws on the critical edition of the various manuscripts of Hegel's introduction to the lectures on the history of philosophy, especially the one from 1820 (IHP), and on the critical edition of the lecture series of 1825–1826, which is based on five student transcripts (LHP).[3] The editors of this edition consider this lecture series to be representative of Hegel's Berlin lectures as a whole.[4]

Since Hegel's view on the history of philosophy did not come from nowhere, I begin by contextualizing his endeavor (section 28.2). In order to put his work in relief, I compare it, both here and later, to Tennemann's *History of Philosophy*, the eleven volumes of which were published between 1789 and 1819.[5] Section 28.3 examines the Introduction to Hegel's lectures. After discussing his conception of modern philosophy as a whole (section 28.4), I turn to his readings of Locke and Leibniz (section 28.5) and Kant (section 28.6).[6] The latter part of the lectures is singled out because both Tennemann and Hegel assign an important—though quite different—role to Kant's philosophy. I conclude by a brief analysis of Hegel's account of the final moment of the history of philosophy (section 28.7). Even though this account is largely devoted to Schelling, it allows us to infer what Hegel thought about his own contribution to the history of philosophy.

---

[2] As he writes in his introduction, Michelet took his task to consist "in the art of interweaving not only larger pieces of different lecture series, but also, where necessary, individual sentences." Cited in Brown, "Editorial Introduction," LHP 6.27.

[3] The text from which Hegel lectured in Jena has not survived. The Introduction to the 1820 lecture series is the oldest manuscript on this subject that has been preserved. The lectures edited by Garniron and Jaeschke (LHP 6–9) contain transcripts of a number of introductions, as well as an edition of the complete lecture series of 1825–1826. In Brown's translation of these texts, the part on modern philosophy covers not more than 117 pages. The same part takes up 390 pages in the Suhrkamp edition of Michelet's edition.

[4] Brown, "Editorial Introduction," LHP 6.36.

[5] Because Volume VIII was a double volume, the series might also be considered to consist of twelve volumes, as is sometimes done. I will also draw on Tennemann's one-volume *Grundriß der Geschichte der Philosophie für den akademischen Unterricht*, which was published in 1812.

[6] While Hegel's lectures include discussions of texts on political philosophy (Grotius, Hobbes) and ethics (Kant, Fichte), I will limit myself to Hegel's discussion of theoretical philosophy, which clearly constituted his primary interest.

28.2. Thoughts on the History of Philosophy at the Turn of the Nineteenth Century

At the time Hegel offered his first lectures on the history of philosophy, this was not an evident choice: philosophers such as Tiedemann (1748–1803) and Buhle (1763–1821) had published multiple-volume histories of philosophy but never taught courses on this subject. Tennemann (1761–1819) seems to have been the only philosopher who both published a history of philosophy and lectured on the history of philosophy, as he did between 1794 and 1804 at the university of Jena and from then onward at the university of Marburg.[7] Hegel started to lecture on the history of philosophy in Jena in 1805, which means that he took over the course of a scholar whose influential work he would come to challenge.[8] No more than a few others had preceded Tennemann and Hegel: only during the first decades of the nineteenth century did the German academic curriculum begin to reflect the historical perspective on human culture that distinguishes nineteenth-century thought as a whole from the preceding centuries, and that today is largely identified with Hegel.[9]

Because the histories of philosophy published by Hegel's immediate predecessors were primarily intended as handbooks, their aim and methodology differed substantially from that of a lecture series. Yet Hegel was not the first to maintain that the history of philosophy should not be treated as a succession of more or less independent

---

[7] Tennemann did so eleven times, as is shown in Neuper (ed.), *Das Vorlesungsangebot an der Universität Jena* (with thanks to Klaus Vieweg and Johannes Korngiebel for their help). See also Schneider, *Philosophie und Universität*, 104, 162 n; Braun, *Histoire de l'histoire de la philosophie*, 240. However, both Schneider and Braun only mention the time Tennemann spent in Marburg, as a professor, between 1804 and 1819. In the absence of lecture transcripts, we cannot compare Tennemann's published work to the lectures. Prior to Hegel and Tennemann, only a few German philosophers had actually lectured on the history of philosophy. On this, see Köhler, "Hegels Vorlesungen über Geschichte der Philosophie," 53–54; Schneider, *Philosophie und Universität*, 104. Among them was Johann August Eberhard, who published *Allgemeine Geschichte der Philosophie zum Gebrauch akademischer Vorlesungen* in 1787 (Halle), a work that he presents as a guide to support the lectures on the history of philosophy he had given since an unspecified number of years. Schneider mentions Eberhard's work without commenting on it (217). Christian Weiss taught on the history of philosophy in Leipzig at least from 1799 onward, when he published *Über die Behandlungsart der Geschichte der Philosophie auf Universitäten. Zur Ankündigung der Vorlesungen über Geschichte der Philosophie* (Leipzig: Kramer, 1799); see Geldsetzer, *Philosophie der Philosophiegeschichte*, 43.

[8] I am not aware of works that point out this connection between Tennemann and Hegel. Like Tennemann, Hegel started out in Jena as an unsalaried *Privatdozent*. In 1805 he was promoted to the position of extraordinary professor, a position that did not come with a salary either. See Pinkard, *Hegel: A Biography*, 221–223. The fact that Hegel followed in Tennemann's footsteps puts into perspective Köhler's claim that Hegel, "deviating from the then common curriculum," must have started teaching on the history of philosophy *because* of his particular interest in the subject. See Köhler, "Hegels Vorlesungen über Geschichte der Philosophie," 53.

[9] See Schneider, *Philosophie und Universität*, 103–119.

positions and systems: Tennemann thought so as well, and he was not alone. At the turn of the century, German philosophers, mostly Kantians, were engaged in a lively debate on the relationship between philosophy and its history. This debate had been initiated by Kant's own suggestion, in the final chapter of the *Critique of Pure Reason* (1781/1787), that the history of philosophy expresses the nature of pure reason and can therefore be grasped independently of the temporal order of the actual philosophical systems (CPR A852–853/B880–881).[10] Reinhold (1757–1823), one of the first to elaborate on Kant's idea of a history of pure reason, argued in 1791 that a philosophical account of the history of philosophy requires the assessment of each philosophical system in view of the idea of a truly scientific philosophy.[11] After Reinhold, various other Kantians discussed the extent to which an a priori history of philosophy is possible.[12]

Tennemann contributed to this debate in the first, methodological, part of his *History of Philosophy*. Rejecting the mere compilations of his predecessors, Tennemann argues that a history of philosophy should attempt to order its material organically (GP iv). Following Kant, he writes that any philosophy is concerned with the ultimate grounds and laws of both nature and freedom, as well as with their relationship. Moreover, he takes any philosopher, however vaguely, to possess the idea of a science that achieves the most encompassing and most perfect knowledge of these grounds and laws (GP §13) and aims to actualize this ideal (GP §14). Tennemann accordingly defines the history of philosophy as "the exposition of . . . the efforts of reason to actualize the idea of the science of the ultimate grounds and laws of nature and freedom" (GP §15). This exposition assesses each philosophical system in view of the extent to which it approaches this ideal science (GP §14). The one-volume *Grundriß* that Tennemann published in 1812 makes it clear that he considered this science to be represented preeminently by Kant's critical philosophy: the latter not only lays bare the principles of human cognition and action, but also confines the domain of pure reason to that which can be thought.[13] Mentioning Hegel only in passing, he notes with reference to Fichte and Schelling that Kant had not succeeded "in thwarting the bold flight of the spirit of speculation" (GGP §393). He is convinced, nevertheless, that the modesty advocated by Kant will ultimately prevail over the speculation he attributes to Schelling and his followers (GGP §370).

We have seen, however, that Tennemann's own propaedeutic reflections of 1798 testify to a conception of the historiography of philosophy that is all but modest. He clearly shares the ambition of the Kantians—and of Kant himself—to treat the history

---

[10] For illuminating accounts of this debate, see Geldsetzer, *Philosophie der Philosophiegeschichte*, 19–80; Braun, *Histoire de l'histoire de la philosophie*, 206–259.

[11] See Geldsetzer, *Philosophie der Philosophiegeschichte*, 20.

[12] Christian Weiss, mentioned earlier, was one of them. See ibid., 28–30; Braun, *Histoire de l'histoire de la philosophie*, 206–224. Thus, the debate on the historiography of the history of philosophy and the introduction of the history of philosophy into the academic curriculum took place simultaneously. Regardless of whether there is a causal relation between the two developments, the beginning of the nineteenth century clearly saw the emancipation of the history of philosophy from its merely historical treatment in reference works.

[13] Tennemann died before he had written the final volume of his *Geschichte der Philosophie*.

of philosophy in view of the effort of reason as such to establish a science of the ultimate principles of nature and human spirit. In this regard, his reflections can be said to anticipate those of Hegel. Yet in Tennemann's actual history of philosophy the 'inorganic' presentation of facts and outlines typical of the reference works of his predecessors takes the upper hand. His writings thus exemplify the tension between the two paradigms at stake in the debate that spans the years between Kant and Hegel: the idea of a truly philosophical history of the history of pure reason versus the idea of a detailed and fact-based account of the successive philosophical positions and systems. Without ever referring to Tennemann or Kant in this regard, Hegel took it upon himself to elaborate the philosophical history of pure reason, which until then had been a mere ideal. This is not to say, however, that he succeeded in resolving the tension between the two paradigms at stake.

28.3. PHILOSOPHY AND THE HISTORY OF PHILOSOPHY

In order to determine to what extent Hegel's account of the history of philosophy differs from that of his contemporaries, it might be useful to consider his own view of the matter in the introductory part of his Berlin lectures. In most histories of philosophy, he writes, "the idea-less eye is merely presented with a disorderly heap of opinions" (IHP 18.50). Ignoring Tennemann's methodological reflections, he admits that the latter's discussion of modern philosophy is an improvement (LHP 6.362).[14] Yet Hegel takes issue with Tennemann because he purports to be impartial while actually taking sides with Kant. According to Hegel, Kant's philosophy implies the view that the truth cannot be known (LHP 6.232). He attributes to Tennemann the position that philosophies which have not reached this Kantian insight are nothing but 'failed attempts' (LHP 6.232) or opinions that falsely purport to be true (LHP 6.212).[15] If one assumes that the truth about the history of philosophy itself cannot be known either, as Hegel suggests Tennemann does, then one's account of this history comes down to a mere "narration and enumeration" of such false opinions (LHP 6.221).[16] In Hegel's view, a philosophical account of the history of philosophy should not attempt to be impartial, but should rather take sides with

---

[14] References in the main text to Hegel's 1820 Introduction (GW 18) and the lecture series of 1825–26 (LHP, vols. 6 and 9) are by volume number and page number alone.

[15] Tennemann writes in this regard that "[t]he inner ground of its striving, connected to its partial failures, guides reason through . . . conflicts and cases of censorship to the attempt at determining the domain of reason and the capacity to achieve knowledge as such" (GGP §3).

[16] On the various versions of Hegel's Introduction, see Nuzzo, "Hegel's Method for a History of Philosophy"; Thompson, "Systematicity and Experience"; De Laurentiis, "Metaphysical Foundations of the History of Philosophy"; Fulda, "Hegels These". In "Hegel on the History of Philosophy", Walsh assesses the principles Hegel discusses in the Introduction in view of the lectures on the history of philosophy that follow it, observing that Hegel regularly relies on the handbooks of his predecessors (70).

"thinking spirit, with thought" (LHP 6.233), something which he takes to imply that philosophy should assert, against Kant, that the truth can be known (cf. IHP 18.45–46).

But what does it mean to contend that the history of philosophy testifies to the view that the truth can be known? Clearly, Hegel is not referring to the truth about a particular matter of fact. He considers any particular philosophy, whatever its immediate content, to produce, and rely on, a specific determination of the ultimate principle of both thought and reality, that is, of the idea. What can be known, and what philosophy has always sought to know, is the 'truth' of apparently opposite determinations such as thought and being, spirit and nature, or subject and object. Whereas most philosophers, especially in the modern era, tend to affirm these oppositions, speculative philosophy conceives of them in view of the unity that encompasses both contraries. Thus, Hegel writes that within modern philosophy, thought emerges as something subjective that appears to be opposed to being as such. As he sees it, the sole interest of philosophy consists in overcoming every single guise of this opposition (LHP 9.71).[17]

As noted earlier, one of these guises consists in the opposition between subject and object. By grasping self-consciousness as a mode of thought in which subject and object are one, modern philosophy can be said to testify to the ability to grasp pure thought as that which actualizes itself by positing and annulling the opposition between itself and its contrary. At the same time, most particular philosophical systems are unable, according to Hegel, to grasp this unity in an absolute manner. Hegel's lectures on the history of philosophy pursue the efforts of philosophy to adequately conceive of this unity, which is nothing but what he means by 'idea'. In line with his Kantian predecessors, Hegel maintains that a truly philosophical account of the history of philosophy is one that takes thought as such to be the ultimate subject of the history of philosophy. Hegel distinguishes his own approach from theirs, however, by using the term 'idea', rather than 'reason', to refer to this subject (LHP 6.211).[18]

Hegel asserts repeatedly that a particular philosophy is bound up with the assumptions that define a particular historical context (LHP 6.237). Yet to the extent that a philosophy determines the idea in a certain manner, it at the same time becomes part of a history that transcends the confines of a particular cultural epoch:

> With respect to its form, however, philosophy does stand above its age, in that it consists of thinking the substantial spirit of the age—insofar as it takes this spirit as its object. (LHP 6.237)

Focusing on the latter aspect of the history of philosophy, Hegel's lectures aim to discover in each particular philosophical system a core that constitutes a moment of the self-actualization of thought as such and therefore cannot be destroyed by time. The

---

[17] Cf. LHP 6.275.

[18] In this context, Hegel does not refer to Kant's conception of the idea as the unconditioned that constitutes the proper object of reason (cf. Kant, CPR A308–311/B364–367). He does mention this point during his discussion of Kant (LHP 9.162).

essential, true thought at stake in each particular philosophy, Hegel tells his students, is "not capable of changing, is eternal, not merely something that is gone and belongs to the past, but is" (206, cf. 231). What remains to be done, in his view, is to comprehend the 'system of philosophy' that constitutes the intransient core of the history of philosophy in a scientific manner. In his own work, he suggests, philosophy as such achieves its final self-comprehension:

> Philosophy as such, the contemporary or latest philosophy, contains the very fruit of the labor of millennia; this philosophy is the result of all that has gone before. . . . The history of philosophy is this same development, for there is but *one* reason, although in its case this development is presented historically, in the way that these moments or stages have ensued in time. . . . It follows that the history of philosophy is the same as the system of philosophy. (LHP 6.220)[19]

For Hegel, his lectures on the history of philosophy are but one way of grasping the system of philosophy as such. In the Introduction to the lectures of 1820/1821 he suggests that *The Science of Logic* likewise treats the various determinations of the idea. Contrary to the lectures, however, it does so by completely abstracting from the temporal mode of appearance of successive philosophical systems:

> I assert that by completely stripping the basic concepts of the systems that have appeared in the history of philosophy of that which concerns their external shape, their application to the particular, and so on, one obtains the various stages of the determination of the idea itself insofar as the latter is conceived logically. (IHP 18.49–50)[20]

Thus, Hegel considers both *The Science of Logic* and the lectures on the history of philosophy to be concerned with the various determinations of the idea. In both cases, philosophy abstracts from elements that may seem to determine a particular philosophical system from the outside, such as economical or cultural developments (cf. LHP 6.236–237). In both cases, this is done in order to conceive of a particular determination of the idea as developing necessarily—or organically—from the preceding one.[21]

The lectures differ from *The Science of Logic*, however, to the extent that they do not, and cannot, completely abstract from the temporal order in which philosophical systems actually appeared:

---

[19] Cf. IHP 18.50, E §§12–13.

[20] Cf. E §14. I agree with Fulda that Hegel never defended a full-fledged parallel between the *Logic* and the history of philosophy ('Hegel's These', 6). Contrary to Fulda, I hold that all determinations treated in *The Science of Logic* occur in the history of philosophy as well simply because that is where Hegel took them from. The order in which these determinations are treated in the *Logic* differs from their historical order, however, if only because the work is divided into a Doctrine of Being, a Doctrine of Essence, and a Doctrine of the Concept. On this, see De Boer, *On Hegel: The Sway of the Negative*, 54–68.

[21] Seen in this way, Hegel writes, the idea itself is "an organic system, a totality that contains a wealth of stages and moments" (IHP 18.47, cf. 49; LHP 6.221).

> Because these lectures are to be historical in nature, we have to conduct ourselves historically, by taking up the shapes as they follow upon another in time.... But we must also notice the necessity of their issuing from one another. (LHP 6.221, cf. 224)

Whereas, according to Hegel, a truly philosophical history of philosophy must pay heed to the actual sequence of philosophical systems, it is imperative that it recognize the necessary development of the idea *in* this sequence (IHP 18.50). This requires that philosophy from the outset "bring along the cognition of the idea" (IHP 18.50).[22] Evidently, Hegel takes himself to be doing just this.

Even though he himself does not quite put it this way, it might be argued that Hegel's lectures on the history of philosophy face a twofold challenge. First, they must conceive of every single philosophical system as an element of an overarching meta-system. Second, they must consider the historical order of these systems to exhibit a necessity that cannot be completely explained in terms of the influence that one philosopher exerts on another. But do the actual lectures meet these challenges? Do they differ from contemporaneous accounts of the history of modern philosophy to the extent Hegel suggests they do? Does he really resolve the tension between reason and fact that his immediate predecessors struggled with?

28.4. HEGEL'S DIVISION
OF MODERN PHILOSOPHY

In line with the tradition, Hegel distinguishes between ancient, medieval and modern philosophy. Considering medieval philosophy as a mere "period of fermentation" (LHP 6.275), he regards modern philosophy to be defined by the idea of the free, self-knowing subject, as well as by the attempt to overcome its initial opposition to being (LHP 9.71, cf. 6.274–275). Because of the emancipatory role of the Reformation (cf. LHP 9.69), Hegel does not hesitate to equate modern philosophy with German philosophy, asserting that "Italy, Spain, France, England, etc. received a new form through the German nations" (LHP 6.269).

Yet his actual discussion of modern philosophy begins with someone who responded to Italian developments in physics and astronomy rather than to the Reformation, namely, Bacon. Hegel presents Bacon as someone who advanced a merely external way of doing philosophy (LHP 9.78). He admits, however, that Bacon's fostering of empirical knowledge paved the way for the development of modern philosophy proper and, more profoundly, for the development of the unity of contraries that he calls 'idea' (LHP 9.76). Bacon is juxtaposed with Boehme, who is likewise presented as a transitional figure. On

---

[22] Cf. LHP 6: 224, 226. Here, as elsewhere, Hegel opposes his own perspective to that of his predecessors, not mentioning their efforts to move beyond the mere narration of past philosophical positions.

Hegel's account, Boehme stands out for his restless struggle to conceive of God as the unity of contraries such as the positive and the negative (LHP 9.80, 86–87). However, he denounces Boehme's barbarous exposition of his speculative insights (LHP 9.85).

Hegel's subsequent fourfold division of modern philosophy proper is not strictly chronological. Descartes, Spinoza, and Malebranche are considered the main representatives of the first form of modern philosophy. This form coincides with the first phase of metaphysics, which Hegel takes to be defined by the understanding, that is, the finite, discursive mode of thought that operates by means of conceptual oppositions and ignores their underlying unity (LHP 9.89).

The second form of modern philosophy he distinguishes is that of skeptical and critical attacks on the first (LHP 9.89). In this regard, he mentions the criticisms of religion, as well as the materialism and naturalism typical of the Enlightenment (LHP 9.143–144). Hume is also treated as a representative of this form (LHP 9.146). While the philosophers belonging to this second form of modern philosophy turn against the assumptions of the first, their thought is no less than the first defined by the understanding (LHP 9.142–143).

Hegel identifies the third form of modern philosophy with the second phase of metaphysics, a phase he takes to be represented by Leibniz, Locke, and Wolff (LHP 9.90). This phase is said to differ from the first in that both Locke and Leibniz, despite their differences, adopt "the particular, finite determinateness and the singular" as their principle (LHP 9.116). Hegel regards Locke's investigations of the human mind as a 'metaphysicizing empiricism' (LHP 9.117) and Leibniz's system as a metaphysics that proceeds from a limited determination of absolute plurality (LHP 9.136).

The fourth form of modern philosophy, finally, is said to be represented by Kant, Fichte, and Schelling, while Jacobi is also treated in this context. This is to say that Hegel, at least in his lectures, did not want to include his own philosophy in this category. He neither refers to the fourth form of modern philosophy as a form of metaphysics nor tells us whether it is dominated by the understanding. Only with regard to Schelling's philosophy does he remark that here "speculation proper has re-emerged" (LHP 9.182), which means that in his view only Schelling was able to grasp the unity of oppositions such as finite and infinite, cause and effect, the positive and the negative (LHP 9.181–182).[23]

Contemporary readers might find it surprising that Locke and Leibniz are treated together, and that Spinoza and Leibniz, as well as Locke and Hume, are assigned to different forms of modern philosophy. Hegel indeed considers the opposition between rationalism and empiricism to be subordinate, because, as he sees it, rationalists no less

---

[23] In Michelet's edition, Hegel considers Kant's philosophy, contrary to Schelling's, to be dominated by the understanding and to renounce reason (LHPM III, 385/476). Elsewhere he notes that while Kant points to the way in which oppositions can be resolved, he failed to attain the speculative standpoint in that he attributed this resolution to subjective thought alone (LHPM III, 381/472). Hegel's fourfold distinction in the 1825–1826 lectures does not correspond to the division of modern philosophy in Michelet's edition. In the latter, modern philosophy proper is divided into a part devoted to philosophies dominated by the understanding (itself divided into metaphysics and a transitional period) and, on the other hand, the most recent German philosophy (Kant to Schelling).

than empiricists take the content of their reflections from either inner or outer experience (LHP 9.89). He opposes this procedure to a method that actually achieves what
rationalism failed to achieve, namely, a form of philosophy that grants validity to immanent thought alone. This method is said to consist in a rigorous development of all determinations of thought from the principle of thought itself (LHP 9.89).

It emerges from the discussion so far that Hegel basically distinguishes between metaphysics, skepticism, and a form of philosophy that culminates in the re-emergence
of speculation. As we have seen, he singles out Schelling's philosophy for its capacity
to grasp the unity of apparently contrary determinations, that is, to actualize the idea.
At one point, Hegel states that the two phases of metaphysics are characterized by the
awareness of oppositions such as that between thought and being, or God and the world,
as well as by the effort to resolve them (LHP 9.140).[24] In his view, metaphysics from
Descartes to Wolff basically posited God as the resolution of these oppositions. Hegel
does not consider this positing to be satisfactory, for in this case "the nullity of these
oppositions and their presuppositions has not been exhibited in the domain of these
oppositions themselves" (LHP 9.140). Accordingly, "God remains the beyond, and all
the contradictions remain on this side, unresolved according to their content" (LHP
9.141). According to Hegel, Descartes also posited the unity of thought and being by
conceiving of the cogito as that which necessarily exists. By doing so, he was the first to
put forward "the most interesting idea of modern philosophy as such" (LHP 9.95).[25] Yet
on Hegel's account, Descartes did not offer a satisfactory proof of the unity of thought
and being. Moreover, his position exemplifies that of metaphysics as such, in the sense
that he did not overcome the distinction between the finite human mind, on the one
hand, and the infinite mind of God, on the other.

In sum, Hegel seems to define modern philosophy as a whole in terms of its effort
to overcome the oppositions established by the discursive tendency of metaphysics. He
seems to hold, moreover, that both Skepticism and Kantianism were necessary to achieve
this end in the highest possible manner.[26] Yet in his actual discussion of particular

[24] This overall paradigm, if it can be called that, also constitutes the content of the second part of *The
Science of Logic*, the Doctrine of Essence. This part, Hegel notes in the *Encyclopedia*, "mainly contains
the categories of metaphysics and of the sciences as such,—as the products of reflective understanding,
which *at once* assumes the *independence* of the distinctions and affirms their relativity. [It] connects
both [thoughts] by means of an 'also', as occurring simultaneously or subsequently, without bringing
these thoughts together, without unifying them into the concept" (E §114, R, cf. L I, 109–110/122). Hegel's
remark offers an example, albeit a not very specific one, of his claim that the history of philosophy and
The Science of Logic deal with the same content in two different ways.

[25] On Hegel's reading of Descartes, see Andrews, "Hegel's Presentation of the Cartesian Philosophy,"
22–42. On Hegel's account of specific modern philosophers—both in the *Lectures* and in his
published works—see Düsing, *Hegel und die Geschichte der Philosophie*, as well as three collections of
essays: O'Malley, Algozin, and Weiss (eds.), *Hegel and the History of Philosophy*; Arndt, Bal, and Ottmann
(eds.), *Hegel und die Geschichte der Philosophie*; Heidemann and Krijnen (eds.), *Hegel und die Geschichte
der Philosophie*.

[26] In the 1825–1826 lectures Hegel does not maintain this explicitly. In Michelet's edition he writes
that, because of Kant, "thinking had become once and for all an absolute requisite that could no longer
be set aside" (LHPM 386/478). He notes in the Introduction to *The Science of Logic* that it was necessary
"that the interest of thought should be drawn to a consideration of . . . the abstract relation of a subjective

philosophical systems he rarely refers to the view, presented in the Introduction, that the various forms of philosophy constitute various determinations of the idea. Providing his students with an overview of the most important texts and developments, his lectures differ rather less radically from Tennemann's works than he purports.

However, Hegel's fourfold division of modern philosophy differs considerably from the approach of his predecessors. Tennemann's *Grundriß* divides modern philosophy into three periods. The first period is characterized by a large number of philosophers, including Boehme and Montaigne, who one way or another departed from the Scholastic tradition. As regards modern philosophy proper, Tennemann distinguishes the period between Bacon and Kant from that between Kant and Schulze. While he uses common distinctions, such as that between rationalism and empiricism, they do not affect the structure of the text. There is no doubt that Hegel's lectures embody the idea of a truly philosophical account of the history of philosophy to a larger extent than the works of his predecessors. Yet this is not to say that his speculative approach does full justice to the subject matter of these lectures.

28.5. LOCKE AND LEIBNIZ

Apart from a number of critical remarks, Hegel's discussion of empiricism does not essentially differ from the handbooks available to him. The 1825/1826 lectures devote seven pages to Locke and only two to Hume. As regards his assessment of Locke, Hegel considers the latter to have rightly argued that consciousness proceeds by distinguishing the universal from the particular (LHP 9.118). Echoing Kant, he notes, however, that Locke only dealt with the empirical origin of concepts (LHP 9.118).[27] Yet Kant's transcendental deduction is deemed insufficient as well: according to Hegel, philosophy ought to investigate whether concepts such as infinity or substance are true in and for themselves, that is, whether they are conceived as the unity of contrary determinations (LHP 9.118–119, cf. 122). Clearly, this is done by neither Locke nor Kant.

As said, Hegel treats Locke and Leibniz in the same section because they represent two forms of metaphysics. While turning his attention from Locke to Leibniz, he does not try to present Leibniz's position as developing out of Locke's, let alone as a necessary development (cf. LHP 9.128). For Hegel, the most interesting element of Leibniz's system is its idealism, that is, the view that every single monad represents the world in a specific way (LHP 9.132). This idealism is said to entail that a monad, which is simple, "is differentiated in itself and, regardless of its implicit differentiation, . . . is and remains only one" (LHP 9.132–133). Clearly, this thought matters to Hegel because it testifies to

knowing to an object, so that in this way the cognition of the *infinite form*, that is, of the concept, would be introduced. But in order to reach this cognition, that form had still to be stripped of the finite determinateness in which it is ego, or consciousness" (L I, 48/63).

[27] Cf. Kant, CPR A86/B118.

the speculative insight into the idea that he takes to be at stake in the history of philosophy as a whole. As he sees it, however, this insight remains buried below an 'artificial system' that is based on an abstract conception of absolute plurality (LHP 9.136).

28.6. KANT

Using Tennemann's account as a foil, this section focuses on Hegel's reading of Kant. As we have seen, Tennemann assesses the history of philosophy from the standpoint of Kant's philosophy, which he regards as the highest possible one. In his *Grundriß*, he describes Kant as a second Socrates who let reason achieve knowledge of itself so as to put it on the path to science (GGP §370). Kant is said to preclude dogmatism, speculation, and the vain striving for rational knowledge of that which cannot be known (GGP §371) and, on the other hand, to provide philosophy with the basic outline of its system. Critical philosophy, he notes,

> reveals the architectonic outline of the system of philosophy that is contained in reason, shows the principles that serve to distinguish its various parts, assigns to each of these parts the principle and domain that belongs to it, and reunites the separated parts into a harmonious whole. (GGP §371)

Tennemann deplores the dogmatization of critical philosophy that, in his view, set in after Kant (GGP §379). While he does not ignore the merits of Schelling's philosophy, he dismisses the latter's ambition to annul the limits Kant had imposed on cognition. What Schelling took to be a scientific system is said to lack a proper ground and to be a "poetry of the human spirit" rather than a contribution to philosophy proper (GGP §386).

Tennemann's assessment of post-Kantian philosophy follows from the twofold criterion he derives from Kant, in particular from its second, negative, element: ideally, philosophy (1) treats the principles of human cognition and action in a systematic and exhaustive manner, and (2) respects the inherent limits of philosophical cognition. By contrast, Hegel, as noted, assesses the history of modern philosophy (3) in terms of its capacity to grasp the unity of contrary conceptual determinations, that is, to actualize the idea. As his comments make clear, he also holds (4) that philosophy ought to derive all determinations of thought from the principle of thought itself (cf. LHP 9.89). Arguably, the 'system of philosophy' Hegel himself elaborated in *The Science of Logic* and the *Encyclopedia* meets both of these criteria. While these criteria need not conflict with (1), they might be considered to conflict with (2).

Since Hegel's assessment of the history of modern philosophy relies on different criteria, it is not surprising that his account of Kant also differs from Tennemann's. As regards its content, Hegel's and Tennemann's presentations of Kant's philosophy have much in common: on behalf of their students, both summarize the main ideas of Kant's most important texts in a relatively condensed and accessible manner. Hegel's evaluation of Kant, which is partly positive and partly critical, is based on a reading that can hardly be called original: it draws not only on earlier texts such as the *Differenzschrift* (1801), *Faith and Knowledge* (1802), and the *Science of Logic* (1812/1816), but also, as in these texts themselves, on the interpretations of Kant put forward by Fichte, Jacobi, and others.[28]

A first positive feature that Hegel discusses is Kant's insight that, "before we can get to the truth itself, we must first investigate the nature or type of the instrument in order to see whether it is capable of accomplishing what is required of it" (LHP 9.149, cf. 182), as is done in the *Critique of Pure Reason*. Though he clearly disagrees with the outcome of Kant's investigation, Hegel calls this insight "a great and important step" (LHP 9.149). This judgment is remarkable, because many readers will be familiar with Hegel's criticism of this very procedure in the *Phenomenology of Spirit* and the *Encyclopedia*. What Hegel dismisses in these works is the conception of reason as an instrument by means of which the mind acquires knowledge of something, but which differs from the mode of reason that is carrying out the preliminary investigation.[29] For Hegel, moreover, the 'absolute' or the 'absolute idea'—considered as the purported object of reason—refers not to a mode of knowing assigned to a transcendent being, but to a mode of knowing that speculative reason itself enacts.

However, it is not quite clear whether Hegel's criticism is directed at Kant himself or rather at someone like Jacobi. Whereas both deny that God can be known, Kant can hardly be said to have conceived of reason as an "instrument for getting hold of the absolute," as Hegel puts it in the *Phenomenology of Spirit* (54/48). Hegel writes of Jacobi, by contrast, that "God—being in-and-for itself, the absolute as such, the unconditioned, and so forth—cannot be demonstrated," because this means "deriving it from conditions" (LHP 9.172). At any rate, Hegel's criticism of the view that reason is an instrument covers over his basic agreement with Kant's conception of philosophy as an investigation into the determinations of thought constitutive of any cognition of material objects (nature) as well as immaterial objects (spirit).

---

[28] Hegel never questions the accuracy of these interpretations. Evidently, it cannot be excluded that his account of Kant in the *Science of Logic* is indebted to his early Jena lectures. For nuanced assessments of Hegel's reading of Kant that take into account the *Lectures on the History of Philosophy* as well as Hegel's published works, see Düsing, *Hegel und die Geschichte der Philosophie*; and Engelhard, "Hegel über Kant." I largely agree with Düsing that Hegel's reading of Kant is often at odds with Kant's texts and that he criticizes Kant's philosophy in terms that are foreign to it. As Düsing points out, Hegel pays almost no attention to Kant's effort to establish a scientific metaphysics (231–232). More generally, Düsing is skeptical about the teleological outlook of Hegel's conception of the history of philosophy (1–2, 244–245).

[29] E §10, R, cf. §41, A. It might be argued, against Hegel, that Kant does consider the activity carried out by former metaphysics (its attempt to achieve a priori knowledge of purported objects) and, on the other hand, the reflection on this activity carried out in the *Critique of Pure Reason* to be two modes of pure reason. However, it must be admitted that Kant does not make this explicit.

In line with his immediate predecessors, Hegel also offers qualified praise for Kant's effort to conceive of unity in a concrete manner, that is, as something that results from a process of unification. According to Kant, he writes, thought establishes the unity of a manifold of representations and, by doing so, establishes itself as a unity:

> This unity of the manifold is posited by my spontaneity; thinking is in general this synthesizing of the manifold. This is an important awareness, a momentous knowledge. But the fact that I am *one*—as thinking, active, positing unity—Kant does not explain so precisely. What thinking produces is thus the unity, and so it produces only itself, for it is what is one. (LHP 9.153)

What Hegel does not mention, however, is that what Kant calls the 'unity of transcendental apperception' can only be established if the purely intellectual mode of synthesis—to which Hegel refers in the passage just quoted—cooperates with the pure imagination and pure intuition.[30] Kant thus argues that pure thought cannot achieve knowledge of objects all by itself. Fichte and Hegel, by contrast, highlight Kant's account of the spontaneity of thought because that is a strand of critical philosophy that they value and further develop in their own philosophical projects.

A similar point concerns Kant's account of synthetic a priori judgments in the Introduction to the *Critique of Pure Reason*. Hegel's explanation, which is extremely brief at this point, comes down to the view that, for Kant, synthetic a priori judgments are synthetic in that they connect categories such as subject and predicate, or cause and effect, prior to experience (LHP 9.150–151). In Michelet's edition of the lectures, Hegel praises the idea that "synthetic judgments a priori are nothing but a connection of that which is opposed," but blames Kant's unscientific elaboration of it (LHPM III, 337/430). Clearly, Hegel held that Kant's account testified to the speculative insight into the unity of contrary conceptual determinations, but that he was not yet ready to develop this insight in a truly systematic manner (cf. LHP 9.181).

Yet I do not think that Hegel's interpretation of Kant is correct in this regard. For Kant, synthetic a priori judgments are a priori because they connect a subject and a predicate prior to experience. They are synthetic, on the other hand, because in this case the predicate cannot be derived from the subject (CPR, A7/B11). In the case of synthetic a priori judgments, categories such as causality or substance function as predicates that are attributed to any possible object of experience. Thus, the concept of a cause, Kant writes,

> indicates something different from the concept of something that happens and is not contained in the latter representation at all. How then do I come to say something about that which happens as such [*von dem, was überhaupt geschieht*] that is completely different from it and to cognize the concept of cause as belonging to everything that happens even though it is not contained in it? (CPR, A9, translation modified)[31]

---

[30] Kant, CPR, A116–119, cf. B150–152, A158/B197.
[31] Cf. CPR, B13, A155/B194.

In Kant's example, the category of causality is connected to "that which happens as such," which means that the human mind, in order to make objective judgments about actual matters of fact, must conceive of all possible objects of experience as causally related. On Kant's account, the synthesis at stake in synthetic a priori judgments has nothing to do with the connection of contrary conceptual determinations such as cause and effect or substance and accident: his point is rather that these judgments 'connect' categories (qua predicates) and possible objects of experience (qua subject). Ignoring the text, Hegel here attributes to Kant an insight that is foreign to Kant's own purposes.

Hegel's straightforward criticism of Kant's philosophy concerns the lack of a proper deduction of both the categories and the faculties of the human mind. As far as the categories are concerned, this criticism is widespread: Kant is said to adopt the categories "empirically, just in the way they have been ordered in logic" instead of conceiving of them as particular ways of producing unity and deriving them from this unity itself (LHP 9.153). Hegel makes the same point with regard to the faculties that are involved in the production of (a priori and a posteriori) cognition:

> Kant proceeds only psychologically, that is, historically. Sensibility, understanding, and reason are present in human beings; he just tells us about this, taking it up wholly empirically, without developing it from the concept. (LHP 9.151)

In Michelet's edition, Hegel's judgment is even harsher. Kant, he notes, moves from the understanding to reason in a merely psychological manner:

> The soul's bag [Seelensack] is being searched to see what faculties are still to be found there; by chance, reason is also found there—it might as well not have been there. (LHPM III, 351/443, translation modified)

Whether or not this criticism is fair I leave to the reader to decide. In any case, Hegel does not dismiss Kant's distinction between the various faculties as such. He even refers to Kant's distinction between the understanding and reason as a necessary one (LHP 9.161). The understanding, he explains,

> is thinking within finite relationships, whereas reason—according to Kant—is thinking that has the unconditioned or the infinite as its object, and this unconditioned he calls 'idea'. (LHP 9.162)[32]

---

[32] In his own work, Hegel draws on Kant's distinction between the understanding and reason to refer to the distinction between the discursive and speculative strand of philosophy as he understands it. Thus, he writes in the 1820 Introduction that the task of philosophy, considered as knowledge obtained by reason, consists in showing, "against the understanding, that the true, the idea . . . is something universal that in itself is the particular or the determined" (IHP 18.45). Hegel does not point out that his distinction is borrowed from Kant's.

Hegel suggests that Kant was right in arguing that reason not only consists in *thinking* the unconditioned, but also aims to achieve *knowledge* of the latter (LHP 9.162–163). He briefly discusses Kant's reasons for denying that reason can achieve this aim. The first reason Hegel attributes to Kant is that the infinite is not given in experience (LHP 9.163). This suggests that for Kant only empirical cognition is warranted, which is definitely not Kant's position. The *Critique of Pure Reason* merely denies the possibility of a specific kind of synthetic a priori judgments, namely, judgments that purport to determine particular objects of thought—the soul, the world as such, and God—independently of experience.[33]

The second reason Hegel mentions concerns Kant's view that reason, in its attempts to determine the unconditioned, produces antinomies, that is, a priori judgments that are equally well founded but have contrary contents (LHP 9.163–164). Whereas Hegel praises Kant's insight into "the necessary occurrence of contradictions of this kind" (LHP 9.164), he clearly does not consider these two reasons to warrant the claim that the unconditioned cannot be known.[34] Reason, he writes, "needs to know the infinite or the unconditioned, that is, to determine it, to discover and derive its determinations" (LHP 9.162).

This raises the question as to how Hegel thinks the unconditioned can be known. Even though he does not put it this way, I hold that he accepts Kant's criticism of former metaphysics: Hegel nowhere maintains that reason ought to make judgments such as "God is the cause of all things" or "the soul is an indivisible substance" (cf. LHP 9.149–150).[35] He would agree with Kant that in this case reason is dominated by the understanding.

But what about the mode of reason that has liberated itself from the understanding? As is well known, Kant distinguishes three ideas of reason: the soul, the world as such, and God (CPR, A334/B391). Since Kant considers the latter to encompass the other two, Hegel's reference to the unconditioned as the idea as such is not really at odds with Kant's position. Hegel's conception of the idea as the object of reason can therefore be said to be indebted to Kant. However, he rejects Kant's account of the idea as something that is merely subjective. The idea, he writes,

> is only subjective, only a concept, and the being of what is existing, namely, the objective, is forever distinct from it. Therefore what reason retains of the idea is nothing but the form of its unity or identity, and all that this suffices for is the systematizing of the manifold laws and relations of the understanding. (LHP 9.164)

Hegel here draws on the Appendix to the Transcendental Dialectic, in which Kant argues that the various sciences must necessarily assume that the cognitions they produce are

---

[33] Cf. Kant, CPR, A147/B187, A246/B303.

[34] On this, see De Boer, "The Dissolving Force of the Concept," 787–822.

[35] Former metaphysics, Hegel writes in the *Science of Logic*, "incurred the justified reproach of having employed these forms [i.e., pure concepts] *uncritically*, without a preliminary investigation as to whether and how they were capable of being determinations of the thing-in-itself, to use the Kantian expression, or rather of the rational (*das Vernünftige*)" (L I, 49/64).

elements of an encompassing whole.[36] However, Hegel does not refer, here or elsewhere in the lectures, to Kant's stated ambition to erect a philosophical system of all a priori elements of cognition.[37] There is no indication in the *Critique of Pure Reason* or else-where that Kant wanted to curb the ambition of pure reason in this regard. By ignoring this, Hegel arguably exaggerates the difference between Kant's philosophy and his own.

Yet what Kant does not seem to hold, unlike Hegel, is the view that reason, by inves-tigating the totality of determinations of thought, takes thought itself as its object and, by doing so, resolves the opposition between subject and object that characterizes non-speculative thought to the highest possible extent.[38] This is what Hegel regards as knowledge of the unconditioned or the truth as such. What is likewise absent from Kant's critical philosophy is the view that each of the determinations of thought can be derived from a single principle—the concept—that itself is nothing but the activity of positing and overcoming oppositions.[39]

As was noted earlier, Tennemann approaches actual philosophical systems in view of their capacity to abstain from vain speculations and to treat the principles of human cognition and action in a systematic way. It is doubtful whether these criteria possess the force he attributes to them. But do the criteria that Hegel brings into play fare much bet-ter? Do they allow him, for instance, to determine the difference between Descartes and Kant in a satisfactory way?

We can gather from Hegel's lectures that he considered both Descartes and Kant to have conceived of self-consciousness in a speculative manner. Whereas Descartes did so by positing the subject as that which necessarily exists (LHP 9.95), Kant did so by positing the subject as that which produces itself by producing unity among its repre-sentations (LHP 9.153). Moreover, Hegel takes Kant to have taken the first steps toward a speculative understanding of the unity of contrary conceptual determinations as such. But apart from this he does not try to explain the difference between Descartes and Kant by referring to the determinations of the idea their philosophies presuppose. More gen-erally, he does not tell his students which determinations of the idea are constitutive of the history between Descartes and Kant, or why the succession of these determinations testifies to logical necessity. Does the 'truth' about Kant's philosophy consist in the as yet 'unscientific' effort to grasp the unity of conceptual oppositions that Hegel attributes to him? Is Kant's philosophy to be assessed exclusively in terms of the extent to which

---

[36] Cf. CPR, B673, B679–680.

[37] Kant discusses this in the Preface, the Introduction, and the Doctrine of Method. See CPR, Axx–xxi, BA12–13/B26, A707–708/B735–736, A841/B869. See De Boer, "Kant, Hegel, and the System of Pure Reason," 77–87.

[38] One might object to this by referring to the passage in the *Critique of Pure Reason* which posits the identity between the conditions of possibility of experience and those of the objects of experience (A158/B197). To my knowledge, Hegel never refers to this passage.

[39] Hegel clarifies what he means by the concept in various ways. One of these clarifications draws on the language of classical logic. In this regard, Hegel considers the concept to contain the moments of universality, particularity, and individuality. The concept is said to enact these moments by, respectively, abstracting from determination, positing determination, and resolving the opposition between these contary moments (cf. E §163).

it paves the way for Fichte and Schelling? If not, is this one-sidedness perhaps the price that any philosophical account of the history of philosophy has to pay?

28.7. THE END OF THE HISTORY OF PHILOSOPHY

As was already mentioned, Tennemann expressed the hope that Kantian philosophy would prevail despite Fichte's and Schelling's regressive denial of the inherent limits of reason. For Hegel, conversely, his own age testifies to the ever increasing force of speculative thought.

Schelling, adopting the principle of intellectual intuition, Hegel writes, took the object of philosophy to consist in "the absolute or God," and this in such a way that "this content is expressed as concrete and internally self-mediating, as the absolute unity of the subjective and the objective" (LHP 9.180). Accordingly, Schelling is said to have moved beyond the view—defended most notably by Kant—that philosophy consists in the investigation of subjective cognition alone (LHP 9.182). He did so by treating the realm of nature (the objective) and that of intelligence (the subjective) as poles that mutually presuppose one another (LHP 9.183), which means, according to Hegel, the resolution of the Cartesian opposition between the subjective and objective (LHP 9.188).

While Hegel praises Schelling for "having introduced the concept and the form of the concept into the consideration of nature" (LHP 9.186), he also points to the formalism to which his treatment of nature sometimes falls prey (LHP 9.185, 187). More important, what Hegel finds lacking in Schelling's thought is a demonstration of the identity of subject and object in purely logical terms (LHP 9.184). What it lacks is "the form of development" or "the necessity of the progression" (LHP 9.188) that he considers to require a logical treatment.[40]

Hegel remains silent about his own contribution to the history of philosophy. Yet we can infer from his criticism of Schelling that he considered *The Science of Logic* to remedy the defect of his former friend's system. Since the *Encyclopedia*, which contains a logic, a philosophy of nature, and a philosophy of spirit, replaces Schelling's twofold system, it seems likely that he regarded this work as a major achievement as well. We know from the Introduction, moreover, that Hegel considered *The Science of Logic* and his lectures on the history of philosophy to possess the same content, namely, the determinations of thought constitutive of any cognition of objects. If this is the case, then he must have valued these lectures as an important contribution to the unconditioned self-knowledge of pure reason that, according to Hegel, had been achieved in his time. This can also be gathered from his concluding words:

---

[40] On this point, see De Boer, *On Hegel: The Sway of the Negative*, 105–109.

This then is the standpoint of the current age, and for now [*für jetzt*] the series of spiritual forms has thereby been concluded. I have tried to exhibit their necessary procession out of one another, so that each philosophy necessarily presupposes the one preceding it. Our standpoint is the cognition of spirit, the knowledge of the idea as spirit, as absolute spirit, which as absolute opposes itself to another spirit, to the finite spirit. To recognize that absolute spirit is for it [*für ihn sei*] is this finite spirit's principle and vocation [*Bestimmung*]. (LHP 9.212, translation modified)[41]

Contrary to what might be expected, Hegel, using the expression 'for now', does not tell his students that his standpoint represents the highest possible one. Nor does he state that his lectures have as yet completely succeeded in showing how each philosophy necessarily follows from the preceding one. Likewise, the final sentence refers to the vocation, or end, of philosophy rather than to its actual achievement. On the other hand, Hegel leaves no doubt that he considers his own philosophy to have made absolute thought—or all possible modes of thought—the object of thought itself. Given Hegel's remarks in the Introduction, this means that he took himself to have demonstrated—at least in principle—that Kant's criticism of former metaphysics need not prevent philosophy from completely attaining the truth.

28.8. Conclusion

Hegel's lectures certainly approach the idea of a truly philosophical account of the history of philosophy to a larger extent than Tennemann's published works. Yet I hope to have shown that the difference between Tennemann and Hegel, despite the latter's own judgment, is gradual rather than absolute. Just as Tennemann, Hegel tells his students about the main ideas of the main texts in the history of modern philosophy and provides them with the necessary information about their authors. Both philosophers, we have seen, hold that a philosophical approach to the history of philosophy requires that one rely on certain criteria, in other words, on a certain conception of the most perfect mode of philosophy. Whereas Tennemann tends to regard philosophical systems as failed efforts to achieve Kant's position, Hegel considers them to fail to conceive of the absolute idea in an adequate way.

To be sure, Hegel's approach is more sophisticated than Tennemann's, if only because he does not base his account of ancient and medieval philosophy on the same criteria as his account of modern philosophy. Nevertheless, his standpoint with regard to the history of philosophy as a whole—the actualization of the 'idea'—implies that every single philosophy is conceived as an element of an ahistorical meta-system. As regards the modern age, each philosophy is treated in view of its capacity to overcome the oppositions produced by the discursive strand of modern philosophy as such. This means that

---

[41] Brown's translation omits the 'for now'.

Hegel, "taking sides with thought," disregards the various aims that motivated particular philosophies, as well as the criteria they put forward themselves. His account of Kant seems to be a clear case in point.

As was suggested earlier, this may well be a price that any philosophical account of the history of philosophy would have to pay. However, the actual lectures do not seem to meet the requirements Hegel imposes on such an account either. They do not really demonstrate that one philosophy necessarily ensues from the preceding one—other than by showing, for example, that Fichte's philosophy presupposes Kant's. Contrary to *The Science of Logic*, the lectures cannot completely abstract from the temporal dimension of philosophy. But can they therefore annul the contingency that this dimension seems to imply? It might be argued, of course, that Hegel does not foreground the 'logic' he takes to be at work in the history of philosophy because of the introductory nature of his classes or the provisional character of any lecture. Yet it could also be that the medium of the lectures makes it more difficult to see that a philosophical history of philosophy such as Hegel envisioned meets with a resistance that no speculation can overcome: the texts themselves.

Works Cited

Primary Texts

Hegel, G. W. F. *Enzyklopädie der philosophischen Wissenschaften im Grundrisse I* [E], Werke, Vol. 8, edited by Eva Moldenhauer and Karl Markus Michel. Frankfurt am Main: Suhrkamp, 1986. Translated by William Wallace as *Hegel's Logic*. Oxford: Clarendon Press, 1975.

Hegel, G. W. F. *Phänomenologie des Geistes* [Phen], Gesammelte Werke IX, edited by Wolfgang Bonsiepen and Reinhard Heede. Hamburg: Felix Meiner Verlag. Translated by A. V. Miller as *Phenomenology of Spirit*. Oxford: Oxford University Press, 1977.

Hegel, G. W. F. *Vorlesungen über die Geschichte der Philosophie* [LHP]. In Vorlesungen. Ausgewählte Nachschriften und Manuskripte, Vols. 6 and 9, edited by Pierre Garniron and Walter Jaeschke. Hamburg: Felix Meiner Verlag, 1986–1994. Translated by Robert F. Brown and Jon M. Stewart as *Lectures on the History of Philosophy 1825-6*, edited by Robert. F. Brown, Vols. I and III. Oxford: Clarendon Press, 2009.

Hegel, G. W. F. *Vorlesungen über die Geschichte der Philosophie* [LHPM], Werke, Vols. 18 and 20, edited by Eva Moldenhauer and Karl Markus Michel (based on Michelet's edition). Frankfurt am Main: Suhrkamp, 1969–1972. Translated by E. S. Haldane and Frances H. Simson as *Lectures on the History of Philosophy*, Vols. I and III. Lincoln; London: University of Nebraska Press, 1995.

Hegel, G. W. F. *Vorlesungsmanuskripte II* (1816–1831) [IHP], Gesammelte Werke XVIII, edited by Walter Jaeschke. Hamburg: Felix Meiner Verlag, 1995.

Hegel, G. W. F. *Wissenschaft der Logik I* [L1], Gesammelte Werke XI, edited by Friedrich Hogemann and Walter Jaeschke. Hamburg: Felix Meiner Verlag, 1978. Translated by A. V. Miller as *Hegel's Science of Logic*. London: George Allen & Unwin, 1969.

Kant, Immanuel. *Critique of Pure Reason* [CPR], edited and translated by Paul Guyer and Allen W. Wood. Cambridge: Cambridge University Press 1998.

Tennemann, Wilhelm Gottlieb. *Grundriß der Geschichte der Philosophie für den akademischen Unterricht* [Manual of the History of Philosophy] [GGP]. Leipzig: Barth, 1812.

Tennemann, Wilhelm Gottlieb. *Geschichte der Philosophie* [History of Philosophy] [GP], 11 vols. Leipzig: Barth, 1798–1819.

Secondary Literature

Andrews, Floy E. "Hegel's Presentation of the Cartesian Philosophy in the Lectures On The History of Philosophy." *Animus* 5 (2000): 22–42.

Arndt, Andreas, Karol Bal, and Henning Ottmann (eds.). *Hegel und die Geschichte der Philosophie. Erster Teil*. Hegel-Jahrbuch 1997. Berlin: Oldenbourg Akademieverlag, 1998.

Braun, Lucien. *Histoire de l'histoire de la philosophie*. Paris: Editions Ophrys, 1973.

De Boer, Karin. "Kant, Hegel, and the System of Pure Reason," in *Die Begründung der Philosophie im Deutschen Idealismus*, edited by Elena Ficara. Würzburg: Königshausen und Neumann, 2011, 77–87.

De Boer, Karin. *On Hegel: The Sway of the Negative*. Basingstoke, UK: Palgrave Macmillan, 2010.

De Boer, Karin. "The Dissolving Force of the Concept: Hegel's Ontological Logic." *Review of Metaphysics* 57, no. 4 (2004): 787–822.

De Laurentiis, Allegra. "Metaphysical Foundations of the History of Philosophy: Hegel's 1820 Introduction to the Lectures on the History of Philosophy." *Review of Metaphysics* 59, no. 1 (2005): 3–31.

Duquette, David A. (ed.). *Hegel's History of Philosophy: New Interpretations*. Albany: State University of New York Press, 2003.

Düsing, Klaus. *Hegel und die Geschichte der Philosophie. Ontologie und Dialektik in Antike und Neuzeit*. Darmstadt: Wissenschaftliche Buchgesellschaft, 1983.

Engelhard, Kristina. "Hegel über Kant. Die Einwände gegen den transzendentalen Idealismus," in *Hegel und die Geschichte der Philosophie*, edited by Dietmar H. Heidemann and Christian Krijnen. Darmstadt: Wissenschaftliche Buchgesellschaft, 2007, 150–170.

Fulda, Hans Friedrich. "Hegels These, dass die Aufeinanderfolge von philosophischen Systemen dieselbe sei wie die von Stufen logischer Gedankenentwicklung," in *Hegel und die Geschichte der Philosophie*, edited by Dietmar H. Heidemann and Christian Krijnen. Darmstadt: Wissenschaftliche Buchgesellschaft, 2007, 4–14.

Geldsetzer, Lutz. *Die Philosophie der Philosophiegeschichte im 19. Jahrhundert*. Meisenheim am Glan: Hain, 1968.

Gérard, Gilbert. *Le concept hégélien de l'histoire de la philosophie*. Paris: Vrin, 2008.

Heidemann, Dietmar H., and Christian Krijnen (eds.). *Hegel und die Geschichte der Philosophie*. Darmstadt: Wissenschaftliche Buchgesellschaft, 2007.

Köhler, Dietmar. "Hegels Vorlesungen über Geschichte der Philosophie. Anmerkungen zur Editionsproblematik." *Hegel-Studien* 33 (1998): 53–83.

Neuper, Horst (ed.). *Das Vorlesungsangebot an der Universität Jena von 1749 bis 1854*, Vols. 1 and 2. Weimar: Verlag und Datenbank für Geisteswissenschaften, 2003.

Nuzzo, Angelica: "Hegel's Method for a History of Philosophy: The Berlin Introductions to the Lectures on the History of Philosophy (1819–1831)," in *Hegel's History of Philosophy: New Interpretations*, edited by David A. Duquette. Albany: State University of New York Press, 2003, 19–34.

O'Malley, Joseph J., Keith W. Algozin, and Frederick G. Weiss (eds.). *Hegel and the History of Philosophy: Proceedings of the 1972 Hegel Society of America Conference.* The Hague: Martinus Nijhoff, 1974.

Pinkard, Terry. *Hegel: A Biography.* Cambridge: Cambridge University Press, 2000.

Schneider, Ulrich J. *Philosophie und Universität. Historisierung der Vernunft im 19. Jahrhundert.* Hamburg: Felix Meiner Verlag, 1998.

Thompson, Kevin. "Systematicity and Experience: Hegel and the Function of the History of Philosophy," in *Hegel's History of Philosophy: New Interpretations*, edited by David A. Duquette. Albany: State University of New York Press, 2003, 167–183.

Walsh, W. H. "Hegel on the History of Philosophy." *History and Theory. Studies in the Philosophy of History*, Beiheft 5 (1965): 67–82.

PART VII

HEGEL'S LEGACY

CHAPTER 29

MARX AND HEGEL

SHUANGLI ZHANG

29.1. MARX'S CRITICAL ENGAGEMENT
WITH HEGEL

THE relationship between Karl Marx and Hegel is one of the most important threads guiding Marx's entire intellectual journey.[1] As pointed out clearly by Marx himself,[2] this relationship is mainly of two intertwined aspects: his inheritance of Hegel's dialectic, and his criticism of Hegel's idealism. But if dialectic and idealism are always integrated together in Hegel's philosophy, how could Marx arrive at this separation, and why is this separation of such extreme importance to his own project? Reflecting on the important moments within Marx's own intellectual journey, we may find that it is only through his critical engagement with Hegel that Marx was able to accomplish his project of the critique of political economy. Through the investigation into the process of his critical discourse with Hegel, we will find the clues to an understanding of how Marx inherited Hegel's philosophical legacy.

Marx's independent thinking started from his direct critique of Hegel's philosophy of right. It is through this critique that Marx put forward the critique of civil society (through the critique of political economy) as the main task of inquiry. Then, through the comparative interpretation of Hegel's philosophy and of political economy, Marx came upon two main perspectives to carry out this project: the critique of power and the analysis of the historical character[3] of civil society (or bourgeois society). As for the

---

[1] As the letter to his father written from Berlin University in 1837 (see *Marx and Engels Collected Works*, Vol. 1:19) shows, Marx became seriously interested in Hegel's philosophy from November of that year. Ever since that point, his engagement with Hegel's philosophy never stopped, except during the time of his active involvement in the 1848 revolution (the years of 1848 and 1849).

[2] See Karl Marx, *Capital*, Volume I ("Afterword to the Second German Edition"), MECW, Vol. 35:19–20.

[3] Marx did not use the term 'historical character' in *Economic and Philosophic Manuscripts of 1844*. This is the term he used in *Capital* to explain the contrast between the standpoint of political economy and that of dialectic (see MECW, Vol. 35:86). However, in *Economic and Philosophic Manuscripts of*

project itself, it also contained two moments. Before 1850, the focus of Marx's critique had been class domination. Within that context, although his analysis of the historical character of the modern bourgeois society was directly inspired by Hegel, Hegel's philosophy was criticized by Marx as being at root an ideology. After 1850, Marx resumed his serious study of political economy and thus deepened his critique of political economy. In *Capital* and the manuscripts for it, the focus of his critique shifted to the structure of the power relationship within the capitalist mode of production. It is within this context that he finally realized that he and Hegel have been concerned with the same problem with modern society—that is, the intertwinement of reification[4] and the standpoint of

1844, Marx already started his self-conscious efforts to critically inherit Hegel's dialectic. Marx points out clearly there that Hegel has in his dialectic understood the essence of human labor and has found a speculative expression of the movement of history. Based on this, he claims that the task is then to explain why this dialectic still remains in the abstract form in Hegel and to figure out the critical form of it (see MECW, Vol. 3:329). As it is manifested in his following works (for example, *The German Ideology* and *Capital*), the primary feature of Marx's dialectic is to analyze the historical character of civil society (or, to use Marx's later term, capitalist society). To analyze the historical character of civil society does not mean only to grasp its transitory nature. In correspondence to Hegel's dialectic, there are at least three dimensions of it. First, it is to grasp the essence of human labor (or human action) as the self-affirmation and self-creation of humanity by way of the critique of real alienation. Second, it is to concretely analyze the historical characteristics of capitalist society from the perspective of the development of division of labor, which in turn consists in the analysis of its historical origin, its main determinations, and its self-contradictory nature. Finally, it is to grasp the totality of history through the concrete analysis of the historical character of capitalist society. It includes not only the insights of the qualitative differences between the earlier forms of life and the present capitalist one, but also the prediction of the necessary transition from the present capitalist society to the future stage of history through the proletarian revolution, which would be the actualization of human freedom. As for the totality of history grasped in thought in this way, Marx emphasizes that it never concerns concrete predictions about the next stage of history (that is, communist society), since we can only think about the real world and can never prophesy the future. It is the totality of history that has not yet been fully actualized. Connected with this, what we have grasped in this concept of the totality of history is only the historical necessity of the proletarian revolution, rather than the ultimate guarantee for the revolution to finally succeed.

    [4] Reification is the term that Georg Lukács used to articulate Karl Marx's criticism of commodity fetishism in *Capital*. It mainly refers to the two interconnected aspects of the relationship among people in the capitalist society. On the one hand, this relation among people has taken on the character of a thing; on the other hand, this 'objective' relation is taken as itself rational (see Lukács, *History and Class Consciousness*, 83). Since Marx himself disclosed the same thing in both his *Economic Manuscripts of 1857–58* and in *Capital*, I directly use this concept to explain Marx's analysis of the defining characteristics of the human connections in capitalist society. In the *Economic Manuscripts of 1857–58*, Marx points out that the universal social relationship among individuals, which is actualized as the general exchange of activities and products, has become an alien thing to the individuals. Necessarily connected with this, the domination of this universal social relationship over the individuals appears to them as the 'rule of abstractions'. That is, it is taken by them as the rule by the abstract laws, which are believed to be inherent in the relationship itself (see MECW, Vol. 28:94, 101). In *Capital*, Marx develops this analysis further through the criticism of the secret of commodity fetishism. As for why the social connections among people has become 'objective', he points out that it is because the social character of human labor can only be actualized as value and the quantity of value of the commodities. As for how this 'objective' relationship is taken by us as inherently rational, he discloses that political economy is a typical example of the so-called scientific analysis of the inherent laws within it (see MECW, Vol. 35:82, 86).

the understanding (*Verstand*)[5]. With this insight, Marx realized that it is only through the Hegelian speculative dialectic that we could grasp the totality of capitalist society. In this sense, Marx avowed clearly that he himself was the pupil of Hegel.[6]

Although Marx and Hegel were concerned with the same problem having to do with civil society, their judgments about the modern world were entirely different. Hegel's philosophy is preconditioned by his belief in the modern ethical world as the realm of the actualization of freedom. Just as the reification of the social relations and the standpoint of the understanding are intertwined with each other, the emergence of the modern ethical world and the grasp of the truth of it in philosophy were for Hegel two aspects of the same process. In contrast, Marx emphasized that the intertwinement of reification and the standpoint of the understanding had been only one mediating moment within the structure of the domination of capital over labor. In this sense, he claimed that his own dialectic was just the opposite of Hegel's. While Hegel's dialectic resulted in the mystification (vindication and glorification) of the existing state, Marx's own dialectic was only about the tendency of self-negation within the development of capitalist society. To further explain the reason for this opposition, he then attributed it to the opposition between Hegel's idealism and his own materialism.

29.2. Marx's Critique of Hegel's Philosophy of Right

As Marx clearly stated in the preface to *A Contribution to the Critique of Political Economy* (1859), there were mainly two reasons for him to start the critical re-examination of Hegel's philosophy of right.[7] One was the difficult problem about 'material interests', and the other was the influence of French socialism and communism. Since both of them

---

[5] The term 'understanding' is here used in the Hegelian sense. As is well known, Hegel clearly contrasts the standpoint of understanding to that of reason or the dialectic. Whereas the former could only arrive at the knowledge of abstract laws of objects, the latter could enable us to grasp the concrete concepts of them. In the preface to *Elements of the Philosophy of Right*, he particularly emphasizes that the understanding can only help us to arrive at the laws of nature, but never at the laws of right. In the sphere of human actions, what is really important is not to arrive at the cognition of the abstract laws of the existent, but rather to grasp why they are rational. Thus, it is only dialectic that could help us to arrive at the laws of right (see Hegel, PR, 13–34). With this as the background, we can see clearly that in his analysis of the structure of power relationships in capitalist society, Marx is just talking about the dominance of the standpoint of the understanding in the sphere of human actions. He discloses that the reification of the social relationship in the capitalist society has resulted in the dominance of the standpoint of the understanding. Political economy, which is usually taken as the science of the capitalist mode of production, is actually the typical example of this standpoint. In contrast to it, Marx claims that only the critique of political economy, whose method is the speculative dialectic, could help us to grasp the truth of the capitalist society.

[6] See Marx, *Capital*, Vol. I ("Afterword to the Second German Edition"), MECW, Vol. 35:19.

[7] See Marx, *A Contribution to the Critique of Political Economy. Part One* (Preface), MECW, Vol. 29:261–262.

were essentially related to the relationship between civil society and the state, this relationship had been the central question in his critique of Hegel's philosophy of right. In his *Critique*, he frankly admitted that Hegel, as the philosopher of the French Revolution, had attained deep insights about the defining feature of the modern world, which is the separation and opposition between civil society and the political state. Preconditioned by this, he read Hegel's philosophy of right as the effort to figure out the resolution of this opposition.

However, he argued at the same time that Hegel has only put forward a false solution to this real problem. This argument was developed through two steps. First, in *Critique of Hegel's Philosophy of Right* (1843) (see MECW, Vol. 3:3–129), Marx directly contradicted Hegel's model of the relationship between civil society and the political state by pointing out that the Hegelian solution was, in the final analysis, only a kind of mysticism. With this, we were thus brought back to the opposition between civil society and the state. Second, in "On the Jewish Question" (1843–1844) (see MECW, Vol. 3:146–174), he provided his own interpretation of the necessary tendency of the development of the relationship between civil society and the state through the analysis of the complicated relationship between religion and the state. Through this reinterpretation, he concluded that the state would necessarily be degraded into being only the instrument of the development of civil society. Thus, the real task before us would be the critique of civil society itself.

The relation between family, civil society, and the state was been the core question for Marx's entire *Critique of Hegel's Philosophy of Right* (1843). The main target of his critique in this book was the Hegelian interpretation of this relationship among these three spheres. Marx believed that while Hegel was faced with the separation and opposition between civil society and the state, he had moved a step backward in his concept of the state. Hegel took family and civil society as being only the finite spheres of the concept of the state, such that they could then be conceived as necessarily resolving their opposition within the idea. Thus, in the picture provided by Hegel, the relationship between civil society and the state is not static but is a movement. The state is taken as the agent of this movement, which gives civil society the freedom to develop itself and then necessarily brings it back within its, the state's, sphere.

As we noted, Marx immediately claimed that this kind of understanding was only "the logical, pantheistic mysticism,"[8]. He argued that there were actually movements along two directions within this relationship, and that both of them were only the movement of the Idea. The movement in the first direction is that from the Idea to the finite spheres of the family and civil society. Here, the actual existence of civil society is only taken as the appearance, not the actuality, of the state. It is considered as the result brought about by the activity of the Idea that operates behind the scenes. In this way, the Idea is taken as the subject, and family and civil society are only taken as the objective moments of the Idea.[9]

---

[8] Marx, *Contribution to the Critique of Hegel's Philosophy of Law*, MECW, Vol. 3:7.
[9] See Marx, *Contribution to the Critique of Hegel's Philosophy of Law*, MECW, Vol. 3:7–8.

The movement in the second direction is the transition from the family and civil society to the political state. Here, the transition is derived neither from the specific essence of the family and civil society, nor from the specific essence of the political state. On the contrary, the transition is derived from the universal relation of necessity and freedom.[10] It means that in the spheres of the family and civil society, the relation between spirit as objective universality and its moments (singularity and particularity) is that of necessity. In the sphere of the political state, with the self-awareness of universality as the end, the relation between spirit and its moments had supposedly been developed into that of freedom. Marx emphasized that Hegel did not touch on the real transition from the family and civil society to the political state. He only resorted to the logical transition (the transition from necessity to freedom) to make the real transition necessary.

Through this critique of Hegel's "logical and pantheistic mysticism," Marx has brought us back to the starting point again, that is, the separation and opposition between civil society and the state. If we just stopped at this kind of separation and opposition, then what would be the real relation between state and civil society? In "On the Jewish Question" (1843–1844), Marx clearly claimed that the state would be necessarily degraded into being only the instrument of civil society. Corresponding to Hegel's conception, Marx also took the relationship between civil society and the state as a movement, and he particularly highlighted three aspects. First, political revolution has brought about the de-politicization of traditional society, which has resulted in the separation and opposition between civil society and the political state. Marx emphasized that although the political state is abstract, it is also real, because its citizens take it to be the end of civil society in their political consciousness.[11] Second, the political state will necessarily bring about the full development of civil society, because it takes the development of the rights of the individuals living in civil society (mistaken by it as human rights) as its end.[12] Third, with the full development of civil society, the political state will necessarily be degraded into only the precondition and the instrument of civil society, instead of its end. The reason for this is the decline of its citizens' political consciousness, which will be necessarily brought about by the dominance of "Judaism"[13] (by which Marx means money fetishism) in civil society.[14]

If so, then what would be the condition of civil society? In the years of 1843 and 1844, Marx entirely agreed with Hegel that if the development of civil society were not limited by the state, which was its inherent end, then civil society itself would be overwhelmed by its two tendencies toward universal alienation and the radical difference of wealth. While in "On the Jewish Question" he emphasized the former tendency, in "Contribution to the Critique of Hegel's Philosophy of Law: Introduction" (1844) (see MECW, Vol.3:175–187) he emphasized the latter. Marx has his own terms to characterize

[10] See Marx, *Contribution to the Critique of Hegel's Philosophy of Law*, MECW, Vol. 3:10.
[11] See Marx, "On the Jewish Question," MECW, Vol. 3:159.
[12] See Marx, "On the Jewish Question," MECW, Vol. 3:164.
[13] Marx, "On the Jewish Question," MECW, Vol. 3:170.
[14] See Marx, "On the Jewish Question," MECW, Vol. 3:173.

these two necessary tendencies. He used the dominance of "Judaism" in civil society to characterize universal self-alienation and the emergence of "the proletariat"[15] to characterize the radical difference of wealth. Concerning these two necessary tendencies, his judgment about their meaning in the modern world is very different from Hegel's. Noticing these two tendencies, Hegel took them as strong proof that civil society is not self-sustainable and must be sublated by the state. In contrast to Hegel, Marx took them as strong proof that the modern political state had been totally impotent to limit the development of civil society and that there was actually no "modern ethical world" at all.

Once Marx has arrived at these conclusions, it is clear that the real task before us will be the critique of civil society. The critique will include both concrete inquiries into the real reasons for these two tendencies and the search for the practical solutions to them. When Marx arrived in Paris in 1844, he became intensively engaged in the study and critique of political economy. It needs to be pointed out, however, that his critical dialogue with political economy at this time was actually carried out through the comparative reading of Hegel's philosophy and political economy. Through this comparative reading, he determined two main perspectives to carry out the critique of civil society: the critique of domination, and the analysis of the historical character of civil society.

29.3. MARX'S COMPARATIVE READING OF POLITICAL ECONOMY AND HEGEL'S PHILOSOPHY

The *Economic and Philosophic Manuscripts of 1844* is clearly a comparative reading of Hegel's philosophy and of political economy. Roughly speaking, this comparative reading includes two interrelated aspects. First, it contains a move from Hegelian philosophy to political economy. Marx started from Hegel's diagnosis of the two necessary tendencies of the development of civil society and tried to figure out the concrete reasons for them through the critical reading of political economy. His efforts along this direction resulted in his creative analysis of the relationship between private property and alienated labor. Based on this analysis, Marx touched on the structure of domination within civil society. Second, it is a move from political economy back to Hegelian philosophy. With his working out what he took to be the relationship between private property and alienated labor, Marx also realized that Hegel himself had been well aware of the reality of universal alienation in modern bourgeois society, whereas political economy had been totally ignorant of it. He then started to reconsider Hegel's dialectic and tried to explicate how Hegel's dialectic could help us to grasp the essence of human labor and the historical character of modern bourgeois society.

---

[15] Marx, *Contribution to Critique of Hegel's Philosophy of Law. Introduction*, MECW, Vol. 3:186.

Let us first look at the way Marx moves from Hegelian philosophy to political econ-omy. We will start from Marx's explanation of the reasons for the tendency of univer-sal self-alienation.[16] According to political economy, civil society is characterized by the division of labor and universal exchange among private individuals. Political economy holds that although individuals' exchange activities are motivated only by self-interested needs, those activities have at the same time brought about the universal social rela-tions among people. In contrast to this, Marx argues that this kind of production for the sake of exchange, which is motivated by self-interested desires, had only brought about the general domination of 'the thing' over the person. First, in the relationship of universal exchanges among the private owners, what is involved is the alienation of private property. Private property becomes alienated private property and has lost its inherent relations to the former private owner. It is then brought into relation with a different kind of private property and becomes the equivalent of the other. Its mode of existence thus becomes that of an equivalent. That is, it becomes value. Second, this rela-tionship of universal exchanges among the individuals is preconditioned by alienated labor ("labor to earn a living"). This kind of alienated labor is characterized by the dis-connection between labor and the laborer, labor and the object, as well as the laborer's subjection to the social need only out of his own selfish need, and his taking the laboring activity as only the instrument to gain the means to maintain his life.[17] As the result of this "labor to make a living," private property becomes only an equivalent for the pro-ducer. Thus, what is involved here is not only the alienation of private property, but also the domination of the thing (the estranged private property) over the person. What was the domination of person over person has now been actualized as the domination of the thing over the person, which is expressed as the domination of money (as the medium of exchange) over individuals.

Marx's explanation for the reason for workers' poverty is necessarily connected with this first explanation. Marx begins his argument by pointing out that political economy presupposed the existence of private property. However, private property means not only the separation of the private owners, the relationship of labor division, and uni-versal exchanges among them. With the development of competition and monopoly, private property has taken the form of the separation of capital and labor. The whole society has been divided into the class of property owners and that of propertyless work-ers.[18] Under this condition, alienated labor means not only the domination of the thing, the estranged private property over the person, but also the domination of the capitalist over the worker. The worker's labor belongs to the capitalist and is subject to the capital-ist's orders. Necessarily connected with this, the products of workers' labor also become the capitalist's private property. Thus, private property is both the precondition for and

[16] This part is mainly developed in Marx's "Comments on James Mill," which is believed to be the preparatory work for *Second Manuscript*. Though it was written after *First Manuscript*, in which Marx has given direct explanation of the reasons for workers' absolute poverty, logically this part (the explanation of the reasons for universal alienation) should have been developed first.

[17] Marx, *Comments on James Mill*, MECW, Vol. 3:220.

[18] Marx, *Economic and Philosophic Manuscripts of 1844*, MECW, Vol. 3:270.

the necessary result of alienated labor. Combining these two explanations, Marx arrived at the conclusion that the two problems with civil society were actually two kinds of domination brought about by alienated labor. While the universal self-alienation is explained as the domination of the thing over the person, the absolute poverty of the workers is explained as the result of the domination of property owners over the propertyless workers. In this way, he has figured out an important perspective to carry out his critique of civil society—that is, the critique of power relationship within civil society.

Second, let us look at the way he moves from political economy back to Hegelian philosophy. It is just through this critical dialogue with political economy that Marx has also grasped the important contribution of Hegel's dialectic. Following Feuerbach, he summarizes Hegel's dialectic as the principle of negation of negation. But his understanding of the exact meaning of this principle is quite different from Feuerbach's.[19] Marx noticed that Hegel's dialectic was closely connected with the conception of labor developed by political economy. Political economy holds that human labor and universal exchange have brought about universal human social relations. In other words, the "labor in general" has produced not only the "wealth in general," but also human society itself. Marx points out that Hegel has gone further than this and has grasped the essence of labor. There are two interconnected aspects included in this insight. First, it means that Hegel has realized that labor (objectification, alienation, and the transcendence of alienation) is the process of man's self-creation.

> The outstanding achievement of Hegel's *Phenomenology* and of its final outcome, the dialectic of negativity as the moving and generating principle, is thus first that Hegel conceives the self-creation of man as a process, conceives objectification as loss of the object, as alienation and as transcendence of this alienation; that he thus grasps the essence of labour and comprehends objective man—true, because real man—as the outcome of man's own labour. (MECW03, 332–333)[20]

By referring to the historical development articulated in *Phenomenology of Spirit*, Marx wants to stress that for Hegel the self-creation of man (self-affirmation of man [or woman] in his or her objective labor) would be the result of a whole historical development. Second, it means that Hegel has realized that human labor in modern bourgeois society would necessarily bring about the universal alienation of individuals.

> The real, active orientation of man to himself as a species-being, or his manifestation as a real species-being (i.e., as a human being), is only possible if he really brings out all his species-powers—something which in turn is only possible through the co-operative action of all of mankind, only as the result of history—and treats

---

[19] See Marx, *Economic and Philosophic Manuscripts of 1844*, MECW, Vol. 3:329. According to Marx's interpretation, Feuerbach opposes the Hegelian dialectic (the negation of the negation) to "the position of sense-certainty based on itself." Based on this opposition, Feuerbach has criticized Hegel's philosophy as the restoration of religion and theology.

[20] Marx, *Economic and Philosophic Manuscripts of 1844*, MECW, Vol. 3:332–333.

these powers as objects: and this, to begin with, is again only possible in the form of estrangement.[21]

Here Marx is referring to the difference between Hegel's dialectic and political economy in their judgments about the condition of civil society. Whereas political economy was totally ignorant of alienated labor, Hegel had already noticed the necessary tendency toward universal alienation in civil society. Combining these two aspects together, it could be said that Hegel's dialectic of negativity has already included a strong critique of civil society. The strength of this critique lies not only in its disclosure of the necessary tendency of universal alienation, but also its grasp of the historical character of modern bourgeois society. In other words, Hegel in his dialectic of negativity has grasped the totality of history (the history of human's self-creation), as well as the necessary tendency for civil society to be transcended in the future stage of history.

In spite of this affirmative reading of Hegel's dialectic, Marx also points out that the relationship between Hegel's philosophy and the existing state is not critical. Just like political economy, Hegel's dialectic is only the uncritical positivism of the existing state. Marx attributes this to Hegel's idealism. Based on his reading of Hegel's *Phenomenology of Spirit*, especially the last chapter on "Absolute Knowledge," Marx points out three aspects of Hegel's idealism. First, it is a mistaken understanding of alienation, which goes with Hegel's phenomenological viewpoint. Marx believes that although Hegel had been talking about real alienation in our relationship to religion, state power, and wealth, he considered the essence of alienation as the alienation of abstract thought and took all of these real contradictions to be only the phenomena, or the cloak of the real opposition within thought between self-consciousness and consciousness. Second, it is a mistaken understanding of the sublation of alienation. Marx argues that since Hegel has taken the essence of alienation to be the alienation of abstract thought, he necessarily has misunderstood the real meaning of the positive sublation of these real alienations. To Marx, the positive sublation means the positive appropriation of man's essential capacities, which have become alien things. But to Hegel, it only means the appropriation of these objects as thoughts and thought processes. According to Marx, sublation in this sense means only "that philosophic dissolution and restoration of the existing empirical world."[22] Third, it is the reversal of the relationship between the subject and the predicate. Basing on the critique of these two aspects, Marx concludes that the history of human self-creation was finally taken by Hegel to be only the process of the self-creation of the absolute spirit. While the self-knowing absolute spirit, as the result of the whole process, is taken as the subject of it, the actual individuals and nature in history are taken as only the predicates of the historical process.

From the preceding analysis of Marx's comparative reading of Hegel's philosophy and political economy, we can see that Marx has roughly figured out the right way to carry out the critique of civil society. Based on his move from Hegelian philosophy to political

---

[21] Marx, *Economic and Philosophic Manuscripts of 1844*, MECW, Vol. 3:333.
[22] Marx, *Economic and Philosophic Manuscripts of 1844*, MECW, Vol. 3:332.

economy, Marx has realized that the substantial content of the critique of civil society would be the critique of power relationships within civil society. We should start from the actual condition of the division of labor and private property to analyze the structure of domination within civil society. Based on his move from political economy back to Hegelian philosophy, Marx has realized that the critique of civil society would necessarily be the concrete analysis of its historical character. It is not only the concrete analysis of the historical characteristics of modern bourgeois society, but also the effort to grasp the totality of history in thought through this analysis.

29.4. CLASS DOMINATION AND IDEOLOGY

Marx's project of the critique of civil society developed in two steps. While the focus of the critique in the first step (from 1844 to 1848) is class domination, it shifted into the intertwinement of reification of social relations and the standpoint of the understanding in capitalist society in the second step (1850–1883). Necessarily connected with this change, his judgment about the nature of Hegel's philosophy also seriously changed. In the first step, especially in *The German Ideology* (1845), he announced clearly that Hegel's philosophy was only a kind of ideology and that the opposition between his and Engel's own philosophy and Hegel's was that between science (*Wissenschaft*) and ideology. In contrast to this, in the second step, especially in his statements about the method of the critique of political economy,[23] Marx claimed directly that Hegel's dialectic was just the method for us to develop the science (in the broad sense of a *Wissenschaft*) of capitalist society. However, if the whole project of the critique of civil society has been characterized by the critique of domination, as well as by the analysis of the historical character of civil society, why has this change in his judgment about Hegel's philosophy occurred? To answer this question, we need to know concretely how his critique of class domination is inherently connected with the critique of German philosophy in *The German Ideology*, as well as how his critique of the domination of capital over labor is then necessarily connected with the critique of the standpoint of the understanding in *Economic Manuscripts of 1857–58* and *Capital*.

Let us first discuss *The German Ideology*, which is a representative book in the first step and is characterized by their simultaneous critique of civil society and German philosophy. When Marx and Engels decided to write *The German Ideology* together in 1845, their aim was twofold: first, they wished to set forth their new conception of history, which is the direct result of their critique of civil society; second, they wished to criticize the ideological conception lying behind German philosophy.[24] The latter is a constituent

---

[23] See Marx, *Capital*, Vol. I ("Afterword to the Second German Edition"), MECW, Vol. 35:19–20.
[24] See Marx, *A Contribution to the Critique of Political Economy* (Preface), MECW, Vol. 29:264: "when in the spring of 1845 he too came to live in Brussels, we decided to set forth together our conception as opposed to the ideological one of German philosophy, in fact to set accounts with our former

part of their critique of civil society. So, the critique of civil society was the basis of their argument about the direct opposition between their own conception and the ideological conceptions underlying German philosophy. Compared with *Economic and Philosophic Manuscripts of 1844*, there were two important developments in their critique of civil society in *The German Ideology*. One is the concrete analysis of the historical character of modern bourgeois society, and the other is the reinterpretation of the relationship between civil society and the state from the perspective of class domination. Through the concrete analysis of the historical character of modern bourgeois society, they arrived at their new conception of history. Through the critique of the structure of class domination in the modern world, they grasped the relationship between philosophy (German philosophy) and reality (the social reality of class domination). Combining these two aspects together, they concluded that the opposition between their new conception and the conception of German philosophy was the opposition between *Wissenschaft* and ideology.

As for the historical character of modern bourgeois society, Marx and Engels have particularly highlighted three aspects of it in *The German Ideology*. First, they clearly differentiate civil society in the general sense from "civil society as such" (or modern bourgeois society), admitting that "civil society as such" only developed with the bourgeois.[25] Marx and Engels were well aware that the term 'civil society' emerged in the eighteenth century and that it refers to all the social organizations that go together with modern property relations (that is, the relations of private ownership, which has totally eliminated the form of communal ownership). Starting from this, they argue further that we could also use this same term to refer to "the whole material intercourse of individuals"[26] in any of the earlier stages in history. They particularly made this extension of the term, 'civil society', because they believed that it could help us to find the right perspective to understand human history. Starting from civil society, we could then grasp the totality of social life (civil society, the state, and different forms of consciousness) in each of the different stages in history and thus understand the historical development from the earlier forms of life to later ones. In this sense, it could be said that the differentiation of "civil society as such" from civil society in the general sense is the precondition for Marx and Engels to arrive at a concrete analysis of the historical character of the modern bourgeois society.

Second, they tried to figure out the qualitative difference between modern bourgeois society and civil society in the early stages of human history. As is common in many of

philosophical conscience. The intention was carried out in the form of a critique of post-Hegelian philosophy."

[25] See Karl Marx and Frederick Engels, *The German Ideology*, MECW, Vol. 5:89. "The term 'civil society' emerged in the eighteenth century when property relations had already extricated themselves from the ancient and medieval community. Civil society as such only develops with the bourgeoisie. The social organization evolving directly from production and intercourse, which in all stages forms the basis of the state and the rest of the idealistic superstructure, has, however, always been designated by the same name."

[26] Marx and Engels, *The German Ideology*, MECW, Vol. 5:89.

their works about capitalism, their theoretical analysis of the particular determination of the modern bourgeois society is always accompanied by their empirical investigations into the historical process of the origin and the development of capitalist society. In *The German Ideology*, they briefly describe both the historical process of the emergence of the capitalist mode of production and that of the origin of the bourgeoisie as a class. In the history of the emergence of the capitalist mode of production, they mention the moments of the emergence of manufacturing, the rapid development of commerce, and finally the development of machinery industry.[27] Corresponding to this development is the emergence of the bourgeoisie as the ruling class in modern society. In the process of the formation of the bourgeoisie as the ruling class, they mention the moments of the emergence of the burgher estate, its becoming the burgher class, its development into the ruling class of the bourgeoisie, and the simultaneous formation of the proletariat as the class of the propertyless people.[28] With this as the background, they then develop the critique of both the property relations within civil society and the relationship between civil society and the modern state. It is through this critique that they disclose the secret

[27] See Marx and Engels, *The German Ideology*, MECW, Vol. 5:66–74. In these pages, Marx and Engels particularly mention three moments in the process of the formation of the capitalist mode of production. The first moment is the emergence of manufacturing. It is preconditioned by three elements: the dissolution of traditional social relationships, which had brought about huge number of vagabonds in the cities who were impossible to be absorbed into the medieval guilds; the accumulation of capital (especially in the hands of merchants); and the concentration of people. The second one is the rapid development of commerce and navigation, which starts from the mid-seventeenth century and lasts until the end of the eighteenth century. Within this period, the development of manufacturing in each country was heavily dependent upon the development of commerce. The third moment is the development of large-scale industry in England. It is again preconditioned by three important facts: the concentration of trade and manufacture in one country, which has brought about the conflict between the demand of the world market and the supply of the manufactured products; the great development of natural science, especially Newton's mechanics, which has made the application of elemental forces to industrial ends possible; and the social relationship of free competition among the individual citizens, which is the result of the bourgeois political revolution. As the result of this whole process of development, the capitalist form of private property has taken the place of the medieval one.

[28] See Marx and Engels, *The German Ideology*, MECW, Vol. 5:76–77 and 78–80. In these pages, Marx and Engels explain how the burgher estate had become the ruling class (the modern bourgeois class) in modern society. The explanation is divided into two parts. First, they explain the process of the emergence of the burgher class and its development into the bourgeois class. They point out that the burghers in those towns had become a class (the middle class) because all of them were defined by the common living condition, which was at that time particularly manifested in their having a common antagonist (the landed nobility). With their common struggle against the feudal system, they then finally changed the whole structure of the private property system. When all property had been changed into industrial and commercial capital, they became the bourgeois class, which was actually the ruling class of the whole society. Necessarily connected with this, this radical change also simultaneously brought about a new class (the proletariat) as the propertyless class. Second, they made the additional remark that when the burghers first emerged in late medieval society, it was the burgher estate. It was only an estate because their condition of existence (for example, the movable property and craft labor) was formed in feudal society. It appeared as something positive, which was asserted by them against landed property. Thus, just like the landed property, it was still in the feudal form. Combining these two parts together, Marx and Engels tried to argue that the process of the burghers' liberation from the feudal system is just to free the newly formed elements from the fetters of the old system and to bring about a new system.

of class domination in modern bourgeois society, that is, the rule of the bourgeois will necessarily appear as the rule of universal ideas. Based on this insight, they then analyze the relation between German philosophy and the social reality of class domination and criticize the limitation of German philosophy's ideological conceptions (we will come back to this later when we are discussing their critique of ideology).

Third, through the investigation into the contradictions within the modern mode of production, they argue for the historical necessity of the proletarian revolution. In his earlier works, Marx has only analyzed the two tendencies of the developments of civil society (universal self-alienation and radical difference in wealth). In *The German Ideology*, he and Engels develop this into the criticism of the contradiction within the capitalist mode of production and the argument for the historical necessity of the proletarian revolution. Through the comparison of the capitalist mode of production with the traditional mode of production, Marx and Engels realized that the capitalist mode of production is characterized by the contradiction between the universal intercourse among individuals and the capitalist form of private ownership.[29] Seen from this perspective, it could be said that the universal alienation of individuals is actually one of the results of this contradiction. Basing their views on the analysis of this contradiction, they conclude that the capitalist mode of production will necessarily bring about crises. Because of the separation of private property and labor, it is always those propertyless workers who will be the victims during these disasters. Thus, crisis and the emergence of the proletariat will be always connected with each other. Since the capitalist mode of production is actually the condition for the rule of the bourgeoisie, the proletarian revolution will necessarily be a revolution against the bourgeoisie. The meaning of this revolution is not only the abolition of the domination of the bourgeoisie over the workers, but also the abolition of the opposition between the objective social conditions and individuals. Instead of the opposition between our self-activity and the objective

[29] See Marx and Engels, *The German Ideology*, MECW, Vol. 5:86–87. In *The German Ideology*, Marx and Engels often use the phrase "the contradiction between the productive forces and the form of intercourse" to characterize the basic contradiction to drive the development of history from the earlier form of ownership to the later one. They also use the same phrase to articulate the basic contradiction in capitalist society under the condition of the full development of large-scale industry. However, in their concrete explanations of the exact meaning of this contradiction in capitalist society, what is really important is its qualitative difference from all of those in the earlier stages of history. As for the new characteristic of the productive forces in modern bourgeois society under the condition of the development of large-scale industry, they particularly emphasize that it is the result of the universal intercourse among the individuals, which has been conditioned by the full development of division of labor and private ownership of the means of production. As the result of this particular kind of universal intercourse, the productive forces appear as something totally independent of and separated from the individuals. The relation between it and the individuals is that of opposition. To the capitalists, it is expressed as their being dominated by the 'laws' of the world market. To the workers, it is expressed as their labor being reduced to only the means to continue their material life. As for the new characteristic of the form of intercourse in capitalist society, they point out clearly that it is the pure form of private ownership, which has totally replaced the form of communal ownership. Thus the exact meaning of the contradiction between productive forces and the form of intercourse in capitalist society is just the contradiction between the universal intercourse among individuals and the capitalist form of private property, which has been its given precondition in capitalist society.

condition brought about by the universal intercourse among separated individuals, it aims toward the unity of our self-activity with the objective living condition.

In this way, Marx and Engels have not only arrived at the cognition of the concrete historical characteristics of modern bourgeois society, but also have grasped the totality of history in thought through these analyses. In comparison to this new conception of history, they argue that German philosophy has never arrived at this and has stopped at the appearance of "the rule of certain ideas."[30] This judgment is based upon their concrete analysis of the structure of class domination in modern bourgeois society. They started the critique from the analysis of the property relations in civil society. Basing their views on the achievements Marx has made in the *Economic and Philosophic Manuscripts of 1844*, they argue that the relationship of private property has two dimensions. On the one hand, it means the separation of individuals from each other as private owners. Necessarily connected with this, there is also the relationship of mutual interdependence among all these separated individuals. To give further explanations for this dimension of the modern property relationship, Marx and Engels also investigate the differences among the different forms of ownership in history. They argue that the capitalist form of private ownership differs from all the earlier forms of private ownership because it has totally eliminated the ancient form of communal ownership. On the other hand, the relationship of private property also means the separation of private property and labor, that is, of people with private property from the propertyless people. Since private property is "the power of disposing of the labor-power of others,"[31] this is actually the true power relationship among individuals in civil society.

Basing itself on these observations, the critique is then developed further as the analysis of the relationship between civil society and the state. Compared with Marx's earlier thoughts about the nature of the modern state, their judgments about both the nature of the state and the relationship between civil society and the state have changed in *The German Ideology*. In his earlier texts, Marx has only stressed the abstract nature of the modern state, but in *The German Ideology* Marx and Engels point out that class domination is the main content of the relationship between civil society and the state. This means that only when the social power of the bourgeoisie (the class with private property) was expressed in the form of the state was the rule of the bourgeoisie established and justified. Necessarily related to this is the famous judgment that the state is an illusory community. They mention two reasons for the state to be believed by its members to be a genuine community. First, because of the conflicts among the particular interests in the sphere of civil society, the common interest has to take the form of the independent state. Second, the state is always based on the real ties existing in the society, such as language, the division of labor, and so on. But what is really important for them is that the state is only an illusory community because it is only the actualization of the domination of a particular class over the entire society. In modern bourgeois society, through the form of state, the power of the bourgeoisie over the propertyless class is actualized as

---

[30] Marx and Engels, *The German Ideology*, MECW, Vol. 5:61.
[31] Marx and Engels, *The German Ideology*, MECW, Vol. 5:46.

the power of the state over the particular interests in civil society. Or, to put it in another way, it is actualized as the domination of the illusory general interest over particular interests.

Following this direction, they argue further that class domination will necessarily be manifested as "the rule of certain ideas." This means that once the power of a certain class over all the other classes has been expressed as the power of the state over civil society, the latter will necessarily be understood as the rule of certain ideas. As for the origin and content of those ruling ideas in a determinate society, Marx and Engels point out that they are only the ideas of the ruling class about the dominant material relations, which are the relations that make it the ruling class in the society.[32] However, in those societies that are organized in the form of class domination, these ideas will not appear as the ideas of the ruling class. Once the social power of the ruling class has been expressed as the power of the state, these ideas will appear as only the independent universal ideas. The power of the ruling class over the entire society will appear as the power of these universal ideas over real life.

With all of these analyses as the background, Marx and Engels conclude that German philosophy (including both Hegel's philosophy and that of the young Hegelians) stopped at this appearance of "the rule of certain ideas." It is totally ignorant of both the relationship between the ruling ideas and the ruling class and that between these ruling ideas and the material relations that make this class the ruling class in that society. In other words, it is totally ignorant of the structure of class domination in modern bourgeois society. German philosophy is therefore, in essence, German ideology. The various German philosophies are ideologies mainly in two senses. Theoretically, they insist that the ideas are the reasons for the real life-processes. This means that they have totally accepted the appearance of the "rule of certain ideas" and have taken it as the whole truth of our life. Because of this, they have thus turned the relationship between consciousness and being totally upside-down. Consciousness is not taken as 'the conscious being' (that is, a human's material life-process), but the being (a human's material life-process) is taken to be the result of consciousness.[33] Consciousness, conceptions, or ideas have thus acquired the semblance of independence. History is also grasped as the history of the independent development of these ideas. Practically, they stop at the vindication of existing reality. Marx and Engels claim that both Hegel and all the young Hegelians (Feuerbach included) are only theorists and philosophers. Facing the problematic conditions of modern bourgeois society, the Hegelians believe that the solution is to grasp the essence of being in thought and by that means to arrive at the unity of being and essence.[34] This kind of purely theoretical solution has thus negated any possibility of a practical revolution within the existing reality.

---

[32] Marx and Engels, *The German Ideology*, MECW, Vol. 5:59. "The ruling ideas are nothing more than the ideal expression of the dominant material relations, the dominant material relations grasped as ideas; hence of the relations which make the one class the ruling one, therefore, the ideas of its dominance."

[33] See Marx and Engels, *The German Ideology*, MECW, Vol. 5:36.

[34] See Marx and Engels, *The German Ideology*, MECW, Vol. 5:58.

From the preceding analysis, we can see very clearly that the relationship between Marx and Hegel at this stage is twofold: on the one hand, Marx has actually been following the lead of Hegel's dialectic in his critique of civil society, for the focus of his critique has just been the analysis of the historical character of civil society; on the other hand, with his disclosure of the structure of class domination in modern bourgeois society, Marx claims that German philosophy (with Hegel as its main representative) is totally unaware of class domination and has stopped at the appearance of the rule of ideas. He characterizes the opposition between his own conception and that of German philosophy as the opposition between science (*Wissenschaft*) and ideology. While *Wissenschaft* involves the grasp of the totality of history through the analysis of the historical character of modern bourgeois society, ideology involves the vindication and glorification of the existing state.

29.5. REIFICATION AND DIALECTIC

As mentioned earlier, when Marx resumed his study of political economy in the 1850s, he claimed that Hegel's dialectic was the method for him to carry out the critique of political economy. But why did he change his attitude toward Hegel's philosophy at this time? The reason lies in the development of his critique of class domination in capitalist society. Compared with the analysis in *The German Ideology*, the phenomenon of "the rule of abstractions" has now become the focus of his critique. This means that he has gone deeper into the structure of power relationship within civil society. Marx had stopped at the disclosure of the domination of capital over labor, but he now develops concrete analyses about how the domination of capital over labor is mediated by the domination of universal social relations over individuals and how the latter is necessarily intertwined with the dominance of the standpoint of the understanding (that is, the standpoint of political economy). Based on these analyses, he is now more concerned with the opposition between his own standpoint (embodied in his critique of political economy) and that of the understanding (embodied in political economy). He emphasizes that the essential difference between political economy and the critique of political economy lies in that the latter is about the antagonistic nature of the capitalist mode of production.[35] It is actually the grasp of the totality of history in thought, through the analysis of the historical character of the capitalist mode of production. Within this context, he has realized that his own standpoint was actually the direct continuation of Hegel's standpoint of dialectical reason. In other words, he and Hegel have

---

[35] See Marx, *Capital*, Vol. I ("Afterword to the Second German Edition"), MECW, Vol. 35:12–22. Marx points out that political economy, as the 'neutral' science about capitalist society, is possible only when the class struggle within it is still latent. Since it takes the capitalist regime as the final form of production, it necessarily loses its scientific feature once the class struggle has become the outstanding reality in capitalist society. What is taking its place is the critique of political economy, which is the science of the antagonistic nature of the capitalist society.

been concerned with the same problem, that is, the dominance of the standpoint of the understanding in modern bourgeois society. Both of them realized that they could only transcend the limited standpoint of the understanding through the speculative dialectic.

Let us first look at his analysis of the phenomenon of "the rule of abstractions," which is mainly developed in *Economic Manuscripts of 1857–58* (the *Grundrisse*, the first draft of *Capital*) and the first chapter of the first volume of *Capital*. In the former text, he directly mentions the phenomenon of 'rule of abstractions' through the critique of reification. The critique of this phenomenon is then developed further through the critique of commodity fetishism in the latter one. In *Economic Manuscripts of 1857–58*, as in his earlier works, his analysis starts from property relations in modern bourgeois society. However, his analysis of the first dimension of property relations has gone deeper. Marx points out that under the condition of commodity production, private ownership means not only the separation of the individuals, but also the absolute dependence of individuals on each other. Through the analysis of the phenomenon of the dominance of exchange value in the capitalist mode of production, Marx has pointed out four main determinations of this universal relationship of mutual dependence.

First, it has necessarily become an independent, alien 'thing' to the individuals. The relationship of mutual dependence of separated individuals is made possible through exchange value as the universal mediator. Only through the exchange of labor and products could these separated individuals get connected with others and acquire what they need from others. This means that the laborer must produce exchange value if he or she were to be really connected with others and to acquire their products. This also necessarily means that in this relationship both the individuality of the labor and the particularity of the product have been totally negated. They are both reduced to the general thing, that is, the exchange value. Because of these, this universal connection of separated individuals, which is actualized as the universal exchange of their labor and their products, appears as an alien 'thing' to the individuals.

Second, the reification of this relationship means the domination of individuals by it. Marx points out that, though the dominance of exchange value has brought about the dissolution of all the established relationships of human dependence, it does not mean the abolition of human dependence (or limitation and domination). With the reification of social relations, human dependence has been developed from the personal one to the objective one. The individuals are now not limited directly by other individuals, but are now limited by the universal social relations, which are independent and self-sufficient. It is still a relationship of dependence, but with the change that it is now in a general form. Individuals are not depending on particular persons, but on the inherent universal law of this external relationship.

Third, the domination of this 'objective' social relationship over individuals necessarily appears as a 'rule of abstractions': "These *objective* relations of dependence, in contrast to the *personal* ones, also appear in such a way that the individuals are now ruled by *abstractions* whereas previously they were dependent on one another."[36] Marx points

---

[36] Marx, *Economic Manuscripts of 1857–58*, MECW, Vol. 28:101.

out here that in consciousness this 'objective' social relationship will be necessarily grasped as ideas or abstract reason. The domination of this relationship over individuals will then be necessarily taken as the 'rule of ideas' or 'rule of abstractions'. According to Marx, this standpoint of consciousness (or the standpoint of the understanding) is the ideological standpoint necessarily accompanying the reification of social relations. With this ideological standpoint, the reification of the social relations is mistakenly believed to be a natural condition. Connected with this, the dominance of this universal relationship over individuals is then taken to be the rule of ideas or abstractions. With this false belief, individuals have thereby totally lost the ability to investigate either the reasons for their reification or the power relationship behind this phenomenon of reification. Marx believes that even those philosophers who try to find the solution to this condition of social un-freedom have been locked into this ideological standpoint. They insist that the peculiarity of modern times is the domination of individuals by ideas (or their being limited by the standpoint of the understanding). Because of this, they necessarily argued that the solution to this problematic condition is to get rid of the domination of ideas (or to get rid of the limited standpoint of the understanding).

Finally, behind this phenomenon of the 'rule of abstractions' lies the reality of the domination of capitalists over laborers. "From the ideological standpoint, this mistake was the easier to make because that domination of relationships (that objective dependence, which, incidentally is in its turn transformed into certain personal relationships of dependence, only divested of all illusion) appears in the consciousness of individuals themselves to be the rule of ideas."[37] Compared to his critique of the structure of class domination in *The German Ideology*, as we can see, Marx's analysis of the structure of social domination in the capitalist society has gone deeper here. In *The German Ideology*, he argued that the domination of capitalists over the propertyless workers was actualized as the domination of the state over civil society, which then appeared as 'the rule of ideas'. Here, however, he points out that there is another important aspect within this structure, that is, the domination of the universal social relationship over the individuals. The domination of capitalists over workers is actualized through the domination of the universal social relationship over the individuals, which is then understood as 'rule of abstractions'. Combining these four determinations together, Marx has thus disclosed two main aspects of the modern form of domination in bourgeois society. On the one hand, it is a dual domination, which means that the domination of capital over labor is mediated by the domination of the objective social conditions over individuals; on the other hand, it is the intertwinement of social domination and rationality (the limited standpoint of the understanding).

The critique of the phenomenon of the 'rule of abstractions' was then developed further in *Capital* through the critique of commodity fetishism. It is developed mainly along two directions: on the one hand, with the help of the term 'commodity fetishism', Marx has found a way to explain clearly how individuals are dominated by the universal social relationship; on the other hand, through the analysis of the relationship between

---

[37] Marx, *Economic Manuscripts of 1857–58*, MECW, Vol. 28:101.

political economy and commodity fetishism, Marx points out clearly that the scientific analysis, as represented by political economy, has been both a necessary result of and then an important mediating force for the reification of social relations. In other words, this scientific analysis has been an important element to construct the illusion of the 'rule of abstractions'. Since the latter is more closely related to his critique of the dominance of the standpoint of the understanding, we will look at it a little more concretely.

> Man's reflections on the forms of social life, and consequently, also, his scientific analysis of those forms, take a course directly opposite to that of their actual historical development. He begins, *post festum* with the results of the process of development ready to hand before him. The characters that stamp products as commodities, and whose establishment is a necessary preliminary to the circulation of commodities, have already acquired the stability of natural, self-understood forms of social life, before man seeks to decipher, not their historical character, for in his eyes they are immutable, but their meaning.[38]

Marx points out clearly here that the scientific analysis of political economy is preconditioned by the belief in the dominant commodity forms as natural. In other words, it takes the sphere of social actions as 'nature'. According to Marx, this attitude itself is the necessary result of the reification of social relations. With this false belief, political economy then tries to figure out the laws governing the movement within this 'nature'. According to Marx's further analysis, this scientific analysis of the objective laws in this sphere will also necessarily bring about individuals' self-conscious submission to the rule of these laws. In this way, this 'scientific' standpoint has been disclosed to be an important moment within the structure of reification.

Up to now, we can see clearly how Marx has come back to the problem that Hegel had been concerned with. When Hegel tried to grasp the truth of the social sphere in thought through the speculative dialectic, he was very well aware that the limited standpoint of the understanding (*Verstand*) had been the dominating one in this sphere of 'second nature'.[39] This standpoint is inherently limited, for it could not understand the historical genesis of the social forms and thus could never know the inherent relations between them and us. Marx is now dealing with the same problem, that is, the intertwinement of the reification of social relations and the limited standpoint of understanding. As for the reason for this intertwinement, Marx has gone a step further than Hegel. Based on his critique of the phenomenon of 'rule of abstractions', he points out that the dominance of the standpoint of understanding is both the necessary result of reification and an important element to strengthen the dual domination in civil society. Thus, to transcend this limited standpoint is the precondition for us to carry out the critique of social domination in capitalist society. In this context, Marx has begun to take Hegel's contrast between speculative dialectic and the understanding more seriously. While arguing that

[38] Marx, *Capital*, Vol. I, MECW, Vol. 35:86.
[39] Hegel, PR, §4.

political economy has stopped at the standpoint of the understanding, he has also clearly announced that Hegel's dialectic is the method for the critique of political economy.

In his own explanations about the method of the critique of political economy, Marx has particularly highlighted two aspects of dialectic, both of which could help us to understand the contrast between dialectic and the standpoint of the understanding. One is that it could enable us to think about 'the matter itself'[40] (to borrow Hegel's term), while political economy could only talk about some abstractions of it. The other is that it could help us to grasp the whole (the totality of history) in thought, while political economy can never understand the historical character of the capitalist mode of production. Based on these, Marx then tries to articulate the differentiations between Hegel's dialectic and his own. He insists that his own dialectic is necessarily revolutionary in relation to the existing state (the capitalist form of social domination), whereas the dialectic in Hegel's hands had only resulted in the vindication and glorification of the existing state. He believes that the reason for this direct opposition lay in the opposition between his materialism and Hegel's idealism.

First, how could the dialectical method enable us to think about 'the matter itself'? In his Introduction to *A Contribution to the Critique of Political Economy* (1859), Marx explains that the dialectical method is to help us to reproduce the concrete situation in thought. It necessarily contains two procedures: the move from the concrete situation to the abstract definitions, and then the move from these abstract definitions to the concrete concept of the totality of the situation. While political economy has only achieved the first move, the critique of political economy needs both of these two procedures to think about the concrete situation itself. In the "Afterword to the Second German Edition" of *Capital*, Marx then gives further explanations for this. He emphasizes that the dialectical method is both realistic and speculative. It is realistic because it starts from an inquiry into the material. This inquiry is actually "to appropriate the material in detail, to analyze its different forms of development, to trace out their inner connection."[41] It is also speculative because it is then to represent the actual movement of the subject matter in thought. "Only after this work is done, can the actual movement be adequately described. If this is done successfully, if the life of the subject matter is ideally reflected as in a mirror, then it may appear as if we had before us only a mere a priori construction."[42] Here Marx explains why some people think that his work (*Capital*) is purely speculative. Since the representation of the movement of the subject matter is done through the self-development of the concept (its movement from the abstract definitions to the concrete concept of totality), the whole movement would appear as only a priori construction if we do not know how the representation of it is based upon the realistic inquiry into the material.

Second, how could the dialectical method help us to grasp the totality of history in thought? Marx's famous statement that "[t]he anatomy of man is a key to the anatomy

---

[40] Hegel, PR, 10.

[41] Karl Marx, *Capital*, Vol. I ("Afterword to the Second German Edition"), MECW, Vol. 35:19.

[42] Marx, *Capital*, Vol. I ("Afterword to the Second German Edition"), MECW, Vol. 35:19.

of the ape"[43] is just the direct answer to this question. It means that the analysis of the structure of the capitalist society is of key importance for us to grasp the structure of the earlier forms of life. The key point here is not the so-called historical evolution from the earlier forms of life to the present one, but to grasp the historical difference between these earlier forms and the present capitalist one. It means that the analysis of the structure of the capitalist society is at the same time also the understanding of the qualitative difference between the pre-capitalist modes of production and the capitalist one, as well as the historical necessity of the transition from the former to the latter. Furthermore, Marx insists that this is possible only when we have adopted the critical attitude toward the present society itself. When we have not yet self-consciously adopted this critical attitude toward the existing state, we would necessarily either take the existing state as natural, or take the 'historical evolution' from the earlier forms of life to the present one as the 'one-sided' development. And that is just the standpoint of political economy, which has been transcended by dialectic. In this sense, it could be said that the dialectical method is the means to help us grasp the totality of history in thought, through the analysis of the historical character of capitalist society.

Then, what is the difference between Marx's dialectic and Hegel's? And what are the essential reasons for this difference? Based on the previously mentioned explanations of the dialectical method, Marx concludes that dialectic is by its nature revolutionary:

> In its rational form it is a scandal and abomination to bourgeoisdom and its doctrinaire professors, because it includes in its comprehension and affirmative recognition of the existing state of things, at the same time also, the recognition of the negation of that state, of its inevitable breaking up; because it regards every historically developed social form as in fluid movement, and therefore takes into account its transient nature not less than its momentary existence; because it lets nothing impose upon it, and is in its essence critical and revolutionary.[44]

Marx announces here that dialectic is in its essence about the tendency of self-negation within the existing state. This has constituted the essential difference between the dialectical standpoint and the standpoint of the understanding. While the latter takes the bourgeois society as a kind of natural and permanent condition, dialectic is just about the historical necessity for it to be transcended. Compared to dialectic in the rational form, Marx concludes that Hegel's dialectic is dialectic in the mystified form (See Marx, *Capital*, Vol.1 ["Afterword to the Second German Edition"], MECW, Vol. 35:19–20). As the method for us to grasp the totality of history in thought, it has mysteriously identified 'the Idea' (the totality of history grasped in thought) with the existing state of things. Thus, it has resulted in the glorification of the present bourgeois society.

But, what is the reason for the mystification of dialectic in Hegel's hands? Marx believes that it was because of his idealism.

---

[43] Marx, *Economic Manuscripts of 1857–58*, MECW, Vol. 28:42.
[44] Marx, *Capital*, Vol. I ("Afterword to the Second German Edition"), MECW, Vol. 35:20.

To Hegel, the life process of the human brain, i.e., the process of thinking, which, under the name of 'the Idea', he even transforms into an independent subject, is the demiurge of the real world, and the real world is only the external, phenomenal form of 'the Idea'. With me, on the contrary, the ideal is nothing else than the material world reflected by the human mind, and translated into forms of thought.[45]

This is Marx's typical articulation of Hegel's idealism: it takes 'the Idea', which is according to Marx only the result of the process of thinking (the whole we grasp in thought), as the subject, whereas the real world is on the contrary taken as only the phenomenal form of it. For example, Marx believes that Hegel takes the reality of reification of social relations to be only a phenomenal moment within the process of the development toward 'the Idea'. Marx argues further that once Hegel took the relationship between the real world and 'the Idea' in this way, the critical nature of his dialectic has been canceled, because it has in this way reconciled the existing state of things with 'the Idea'. In opposition to this Hegelian standpoint, Marx argues that 'the Idea' as the whole grasped by us in thought is only the result of the process of thinking. The process starts from our critical attitude toward the existing state. This process can be spelled out along three dimensions. As the critique of the real alienation, it first includes the understanding of the essence of human labor (humanity's self-affirmation and self-creation). With this as the precondition, it is then developed as the concrete analysis of the historical characteristics of the existing state. This consists in the analysis of its historical origin, its main determinations, and the self-contradictory nature of the existing state. As the result of this concrete analysis, it is finally developed as the concrete concept of the totality of history. However, this concept of the totality of history is not one that has already been actualized in the real world. Besides the analysis of the qualitative difference between the former modes of production and the present one, it also includes the prediction of the necessary transition from the capitalist mode of production to the future one, which would be the actualization of human freedom. In this way, Marx believes that his understanding of the relationship between 'the Idea' and the real world is just the opposite of Hegel's. While Hegel takes 'the Idea' as the demiurge of the real world and thus has it reconciled with the existing state, Marx insists that 'the Idea' is only the real world we have grasped in thought and that it is always in tension with the existing state.

Reflecting on the entire process of Marx's critical discourses with Hegel, it could be said that Marx has self-consciously inherited Hegel's philosophical legacy from three aspects: through the direct critique of Hegel's philosophy of right, Marx has put forward the critique of civil society as the topic of his own thinking; through the comparative reading of Hegel's philosophy and political economy, Marx has figured out the main perspective to carry out the critique of civil society, that is, to analyze the historical character of modern bourgeois society through investigating the relations of labor division;

---

[45] Marx, *Capital*, Vol. I ("Afterword to the Second German Edition"), MECW, Vol. 35:19.

through the critique of social domination in capitalist society, especially the intertwinement of the reification of social relationships and the standpoint of the understanding, Marx has realized that Hegel's speculative dialectic was just the method for him to carry out the project of the critique of political economy. As the result of this threefold inheritance, Marx has actually been self-consciously practicing the motto Hegel set for all the philosophers: to grasp his own time in thought.

However, Marx's diagnosis of modern times was totally different from Hegel's. When Hegel was lecturing about the philosophy of right, he was quite sure that he had witnessed the emergence of the modern ethical world and that he was only reconstructing it in philosophy. But when Marx started his independent thinking, he noticed that the antagonistic nature of the modern world had become the outstanding reality. In his early writings, he was primarily concerned with the separation and opposition between civil society and the modern state. In his later writings, when his critique of civil society has deepened, the structure of social domination has become the main concern. It could be said that throughout his whole lifetime, his main effort was to grasp the antagonistic nature of the modern capitalist world. This difference has necessarily led to Marx's criticism of Hegel. Putting Hegel's philosophy back into this capitalist world, Marx claimed that Hegel's philosophy (the philosophy about how the modern world is the actualization of freedom) was only a kind of ideology. So, the real issue is not that Hegel's idealism has made his dialectic uncritical toward the existing state of 'things'. It is rather that Hegel's philosophy of the actualization of freedom in the modern ethical world appears as totally uncritical when it is believed that the real world is only the world of modern forms of social domination. We are now faced with the second-round Hegelian reconstruction of the modern ethical world.[46] But with Marx's critique of Hegel's reconstruction and his diagnosis of the self-contradictory nature of capitalist society, it could be said that this second-round reconstruction can never be effective without the effective response to Marx.

Works Cited

Hegel, G. W. F. *Elements of the Philosophy of Right* [PR], edited by Allen W. Wood, translated by H. B. Nisbet. Cambridge: Cambridge University Press, 1991.

Honneth, Axel. *Das Recht Der Freiheit*. Berlin: Suhrkamp Verlag, 2011.

Lukács, Georg. *History and Class Consciousness*, translated by Rodney Livingstone. Cambridge, MA: MIT Press, 1971,

Marx, Karl, and Frederick Engels. *Marx and Engels Collected Works* [MECW]. New York: International Publishers, 1975–2005.

---

[46] See Honneth, *Das Recht Der Freiheit*. If we take Hegel's philosophy of right as the first-round reconstruction of the modern ethical world in thought, and then take into consideration the critique of this reconstruction in the hands of Marx, Lukács, and then Adorno, it could be said that Axel Honneth's book represents the self-conscious second-round efforts to reconstruct the modern ethical world in thought.

CHAPTER 30

THE AMERICAN RECEPTION OF HEGEL (1830–1930)

JOHN KAAG AND KIPTON E. JENSEN

30.1. HEGEL'S REACH AND THE ANXIETY OF INFLUENCE

IN his "Pragmatist Account of Truth and its Misunderstanders," William James suggested that German philosophers had spent the better part of three decades egregiously misunderstanding pragmatism.[1] Ninety years later, Hans Joas suggests that "the German, French, and Italian reception of pragmatism is a concatenation of misunderstandings"; in a subsequent effort to explain why American pragmatism has remained probably the least known of the major modern philosophical currents, in *Pragmatism and Social Thought*, Joas provides "a *history* of misunderstandings, deliberate distortions, and well-meaning incomprehension—and to show that these misunderstandings were compounded over generations."[2] A similar history could—and should—be told about the appropriation of German thought, especially Hegelian thought, by American philosophers from Emerson to Dewey. What follows is in large part an attempt to tell that story. Many contemporary scholars have told parts of this story, but it is so varied and so rich that it is quite difficult to manage in a single volume, much less an article or chapter.

As Europeans made their way across the North American continent in the first half of the nineteenth century, they took Hegel with them—to New England, Pennsylvania, Ohio, Missouri, and California—and did so for particular purposes. The legacy of Hegel, therefore, meant different things in these American locales, a thesis that is developed at great length in William Goetzmann's edited collection, *The American Hegelians: An*

---

[1] James. "Pragmatist Account of Truth and Its Misunderstanders."
[2] See Joas, "The Inspiration of Pragmatism," 191; also see his *Pragmatism and Social Theory*, 94.

Intellectual Episode in Western America.[3] We attempt, very briefly in the opening sections of this chapter, to describe the early currents of Hegelian thought in the United States, but then turn most of our attention to a unique relationship between Hegelian thought and the growing philosophical mainstream in America in the aftermath of the Civil War.

The relationship between the philosophy of Hegel and classical American philosophy, especially pragmatism, is defined by deep-seated misreadings that can be traced to what Harold Bloom called "the anxiety of influence."[4] American philosophers writing in the nineteenth and twentieth centuries had to contend with the powerful legacy of post-Kantian thought and spent no small amount of energy attempting to minimize its influence so as to create an intellectual space for themselves. This attempt resulted in what might be fruitfully construed as representative misreadings of Hegel by American philosophers; we have coined these various misreadings, in deference to William James, 'Hegelisms'. These misreadings, which Bloom assures us are "involuntary if not inevitable" for strong readers, teach us something about Hegel, but they can teach us a great deal more about American philosophy: reading misreadings teaches us more about those misreading than those misread. The history of how certain 'Hegelisms' worked their way into the American grain is instructive; the history of how Hegel was misread, in Bloom's sense of misreading, discloses what American philosophers considered to be "worth fighting for."

In 1822, Hegel declared that America was "the land of the future."[5] The Hegelian philosophy, as a system and a watchword, achieved mythological status in many parts of America, usually at the farthest frontier of westward expansion, landing in New England and then migrating to St. Louis and Cincinnati as well as Chicago, and eventually to California (whence came the premier American Hegelian, Josiah Royce). Indeed, by the late 1870s, even Walt Whitman thought that "only Hegel is fit for America—is large enough and free enough."[6] While Hegelianism was waning in Germany, either collapsing altogether, or splitting into left- and right-wing Hegelianism, the central teachings of Hegel were rapidly gaining ground in the United States.

The reception of Hegelianism in America was but part of the broader reception of all things German toward the beginning of the nineteenth century. Surely Emerson is

---

[3] Goetzmann, *The American Hegelians.*

[4] This interpretive thesis is inspired by Harold Bloom's provocative examination of influence in *The Anxiety of Influence*; Bloom develops this theory of influence in *A Map of Misreading; Agon: Towards a Theory of Revisionism; Kabbalah and Criticism; How to Read and Why*; and *The Anatomy of Influence.*

[5] Goetzmann cites this passage from Hegel's *Lectures on the Philosophy of History* in his Prologue to *The American Hegelians.* The context of the quote runs as follows: "America is therefore the land of the future, where, in the ages that lie before us, the burden of the World's History shall review itself— perhaps in a contest between North and South America. It is a land of desire for all those who are weary of the historical lumber-room of old Europe." In *Walking*, Thoreau quips: "We go eastward to realize history and study the works of art and literature, retracing the steps of the race; we go westward as into the future, with a spirit of enterprise and adventure. The Atlantic is a Lethean stream . . ." (*The Atlantic Monthly*, 9, 1862), 662.

[6] Whitman, *Notebooks and Unpublished Prose Manuscripts.*

correct that "'tis not easy to date these eras of activity with any precision, but in this region one made itself remarked, say in 1820 and the twenty years following."[7] Emerson is referring here, in his *Historic Notes of Life and Letters in New England*, to a movement initiated by Edward Everett, who—after several years of study in Göttingen—introduced his Harvard audiences to German scholarship and criticism, an event that Emerson treated as a milestone in the intellectual life of a generation. According to Goetzmann, "in nineteenth century America, German culture was so pervasive as to be virtually dominant."[8] By 1840 the *North American Review* could report that "translations from all the distinguished authors, and imitations of every sort, already abound. A German mania prevails ... manifest[ing] itself not only in poetry, but in various departments of literature and philosophy."[9] Despite this early mania for all things German, there is no denying that—as Thoreau put it—"the Mississippi is a Rhine stream of a different kind."[10]

Although it might be uniquely useful to retrace the history of various misunderstandings or misreadings of Hegel in classical American philosophy, the tradition of misreading Hegel is by no means unique to American philosophers. Stewart claims,

> [t]he oeuvre of Hegel, like that of many thinkers of the post-Kantian tradition in European philosophy, has been subject to a number of misreadings and misrepresentations by both specialists and non-specialists alike that have until fairly recently rendered Hegel's reception in the Anglo-American philosophical world extremely problematic. These often willful misrepresentations, variously referred to by scholars as Hegel myths or legends, have given rise to a number of prejudices against Hegel's philosophy, primarily, although by no means exclusively, in the English-speaking world.[11]

Even before his death in 1831 and the so-called Hegelian aftermath, Hegel bemoaned and cursed—perhaps as James did—what he considered to be the egregious misunderstandings of his philosophical theories.[12] And while some Hegel experts are still eager to "set the historical record straight and clear Hegel's name of unjust charges," as Stewart puts it, or disabusing us of these "rooted misconceptions," which Croce called "half comical and half disgusting," that is certainly not the task of the present chapter, which is limited to an examination of the Hegelian influence on various representative classical American philosophers. Although it is fairly common for Hegelians to read Hegel as the decisive, if not sole, progenitor of "virtually all of the major schools of contemporary thought," writes Stewart, including pragmatism, this chapter is concerned far less with "building

---

[7] Emerson, *The Complete Works*, vol. X, 324.

[8] Goetzmann, *The American Hegelians*, 10.

[9] See the "Quarterly List of New Publications," as quoted by van Cromphout in *Emerson's Modernity and the Example of Goethe*, 524.

[10] Thoreau, "Walking," in *H. D. Thoreau: Essays*, 259.

[11] Stewart, *The Hegel Myths and Legends*, 306.

[12] Even within Germany, "Hegels Nachleben ist auch eine Kette von Missverstaendnissen in den Interpretation, zu denen Hegel wie jeder bedeutende Mann verdammt hat" (Fulda, *Hegel*, 18).

sepulchers to [Hegel]" than with exploring the question of what these Hegelisms can teach us about classical American philosophy and the trans-Atlantic community of philosophical discourse.

Before turning our attention to the particular reading and misreadings of Hegel in the American philosophical canon, a final word is warranted concerning the anxiety of influence. Applying Bloom's interpretative paradigm to the philosophical enterprise will strike some readers as scandalous. After all, Bloom was describing the history of poetry, not the history of philosophy. But we see meaningful similarities between these histories that shed light on the appropriation of Hegel in America. According to Bloom, and substituting philosophy for poetry, the history of philosophy is "indistinguishable from [philosophical] influence, since strong [philosophers] make that history by misreading one another, so as to clear imaginative space for themselves." On Bloom's account, the phenomenon of misreading is inevitable because (a) every strong reading insists upon itself, which is to say that it involuntarily assumes its own superiority or denies its own partiality, (b) we read in ways that chiefly reveal the shape of our own countenance, (c) texts are not substances but intertextual events, (d) all readings overload certain features of the precursor text with meaning, and (e) all readings arise from ambivalent psycho-linguistic defense strategies against influence and belatedness. All of these factors emerge in a careful study of the relationship between Hegelian philosophy and nineteenth-century American thought.

Applying Bloom's thesis to the American pragmatists in particular presupposes that the philosophers in question—from Peirce, to Royce, to James, to Dewey—were, in fact, 'strong readers' of Hegel. In *A Map of Misreading*, Bloom suggests that "the strong reader, whose readings will matter to others as well as to himself, is thus placed in the dilemmas of the revisionist, who wishes to find his own original relation to truth, whether in texts or in reality . . . but also wishes to open received texts to his own sufferings, or what he wants to call the suffering of history."[13] Because philosophers in America were considered (and often considered themselves) latecomers to philosophy, they were interested not only in transplanting, as it were, Hegelianism into the American intellectual soil, they were also—*at least* equally—interested in liberating themselves from what Emerson, in his 1836 *Nature*, described as the drudgery of "building sepulchers to our fathers."[14] This ambivalent relation to the philosophical tradition is fertile ground for Bloom's celebrated revisionist thesis. American philosophers were often unabashed in their appropriation of Hegel for their own purposes. And American philosophers, far more than German philosophers, have—argues Bloom apropos of American poets—"rebelled overtly against ancestral voices, partly because of temperament, but also because of Emerson's polemic against the very idea of influence," his insistence in the *American Scholar* that "one must be an inventor to read well."[15]

[13] Bloom, *A Map of Misreading*, 4.
[14] Emerson, *Nature*, 1.
[15] Quoted in Bloom, *Figures of Capable Imagination*, iv.

30.2. HEGELIAN WELLSPRINGS
IN AMERICA (1830–1867)

Emerson may have been set against accepting intellectual influence from European philosophers, and in this case from Hegel, but many of his contemporaries in the 1840s were not nearly as averse. These early American Hegelians came to represent separate 'Hegelian streams' in the New World: New England (with centers in Concord, Cambridge, and Burlington), St. Louis, and Ohio. "The diffusion of Hegel's ideas through America," wrote Goetzmann, "is a symbolic component of the much larger history of a pluralistic [and] cosmopolitan America." Although specialists vaguely recognize that the American Hegelians constituted an important episode in the social history of the United States, again Goetzmann, "it has been largely neglected and forgotten." Goetzmann's anthology, *The American Hegelians* (1973), was intended "to remedy that neglect." As if inspired by Goetzmann's valiant effort "to bring out of the dusty book depository into the sober light of day where their ideas can be considered in more convenience and in an atmosphere of genuine excitement," James A. Good and Michael H. DeArmey have co-edited and introduced multivolume collections of the pertinent materials in the *St. Louis Hegelians* (2001) and *The Ohio Hegelians* (2005); Good has also edited a reprint edition of the *Journal of Speculative Philosophy, 1867–1893* (22 volumes, 2002), which was crucial in the dissemination of Hegelian ideas in America, and has written on Dewey's "permanent Hegelian deposit." Our present description of these streams of Hegelianism in America, especially the St. Louis Hegelians, is beholden to Goetzmann and Good.[16]

As active interlocutors of the American transcendentalists, Friedrich Hedge and James Marsh were largely responsible for bringing German idealism to New England in the first quarter of the nineteenth century. Both of them assumed formal philosophical positions at established universities—Hedge at Harvard and Marsh at the University of Vermont—and maintained that a proper understanding of Hegel and post-Kantian philosophy was the only way for American philosophers to ground themselves in the canon and not succumb to the force of philosophical materialism. Their use of Hegel was pointedly disciplinary. The St. Louis and Ohio Hegelians, in contrast, took Hegel to the frontier of the United States, eschewed most of the trappings of professional philosophy, and insisted that Hegel was the only way to understand the science, culture, and politics of the expanding nation of the nineteenth century. Their use of Hegel was pointedly practical in nature.

As Gura notes, American scholars' fascination with German Higher Criticism in the early nineteenth century led them to idealize the German educational system and for those "who chafed under the rationalism and materialism of Locke's empiricism, an

---

[16] See DeArmey and Good, *The Ohio Hegelians*; DeArmey and Good, *The St. Louis Hegelians*; Good (ed.), *Journal of Speculative Philosophy, 1867–1893*; and Good, *A Search for Unity in Diversity*.

introduction to German Idealism and its ethical implications was both liberating and exhilarating."[17] In this sprit, a twelve-year-old by the name of Henry Hedge, son of the Harvard logic professor Levi Hedge, embarked on an educational tour of Germany, eventually being installed first at the gymnasium at Göttingen and then at Ilfeld. Hedge excelled in Germany and would never, through a lengthy academic career, leave German idealism behind. As described by Good, Hedge befriended Emerson while still a student at Harvard Divinity School and made sustained efforts to unite Hegelian thought to the budding transcendentalism of the time.[18] Hedge would publish on Coleridge (in the *Christian Examiner* of 1833) and then focus more specifically on German philosophy and culture in his *Prose Writers of Germany* (1848), which translated portions of Hegel's *Philosophy of History*. This book was one of the most influential texts in introducing Hegel to American transcendentalists such as Emerson and Theodore Parker; indeed Walt Whitman's seemingly extensive use of Hegel in *Leaves of Grass* really only extended to the selections that Hedge had translated in *Prose Writers*. Working in Cambridge and Concord in the 1830s, Hedge advanced a liberal interpretation of Hegel, one shot through by his simultaneous study of Schelling that dovetailed nicely with the type of natural pantheism that appealed to many transcendentalists of the time. Similarly, his interest in Hegel's notion of history resonated with liberal ministers, such as Theodore Parker, who endorsed and then extended the findings of German Higher Criticism, arguing against the divine inspiration of the Bible. Theirs was a pointedly liberal and romantic reading of Hegel.

James Marsh, the president of the University of Vermont from 1826 to 1833, joined Hedge in helping to found American transcendentalism. His rejection of Lockean empiricism and Scottish realism was motivated by his study of German idealism and by a deep devotion to the work of Samuel Taylor Coleridge, whose *Aids to Reflection* (published with Marsh's introduction in 1833) became the standard guide for New Englanders who wanted to learn about Kantian and post-Kantian philosophy. Marsh was Coleridge's principal advocate in the New World, but also undertook a detailed study of Hegel and his intellectual disciples such as the biblical scholar F. A. G. Tholuck.[19] As Naoko Saito explains in her analysis of Marsh and John Dewey (who would extend the tenets of Marsh's Burlington School of Philosophy), Marsh followed German idealists, including Hegel, by emphasizing the

> ... mind's growing process, the regenerative power of the human will in its continual striving, and the capacity for individual self-realization and affirmation. ... Additionally [Marsh] shared the organic metaphor of German idealism which asserted the ultimate unity of both mind and the world, and of the individual and the universal in a dynamic and creative process of growth.[20]

[17] Gura, *American Transcendentalism*, 25.
[18] Good, *A Search for Unity in Diversity*, 60.
[19] Conser, *God and the Natural World*, 89.
[20] Saito, *The Gleam of Light*, 37.

The vast majority of Classical American philosophers—from Emerson, to Margaret Fuller, to C. S. Peirce and John Dewey—would come to hold a similar view that would, despite their various misgivings about Hegelian thought, draw them repeatedly into Hegel's wake.

Of all the early scholars of Hegel in America, Henry Brokmeyer was arguably the most influential. But his was a very odd sort of influence—both powerful and extremely indirect. Brokmeyer, born in 1828 into a traditional German family on the outskirts of Minden, Prussia, ran away from home—to the United States—at the age of sixteen when his mother, a Pietist, burned his copies of Goethe's lyrics.[21] He arrived in New York City with the knowledge of the rudiments of nineteenth-century German idealism, three words of English, and twenty-five cents in his pocket. His lack of means initially led Brokmeyer into work at a tannery in New York and then to operate his own in Mississippi, before beginning courses of study, first at Georgetown College in Kentucky, and then at Brown University. At Brown, Brokmeyer disputed the nature of the 'Higher Laws' with Francis Wayland, the president of the University and another of Hegel's early advocates in the United States. Brokmeyer, unsurprisingly, did not find a permanent place at Brown, but rather headed west again, arriving in Warren County, Missouri, in 1854. The St. Louis Hegelians were about to get their start.

Brokmeyer had encountered Friedrich Hedge during his stay in Providence—reading *The German Poets and Prose Writers* in detail—and had formed close friendships with New England transcendentalists such as Sarah Whitman. These biographical tidbits had philosophical significance for Brokmeyer. In his move to an abandoned cabin in the wilderness of Warren County, Brokmeyer transplanted the transcendentalist ideals of freedom, individuality, self-reliance, and reverence of nature. In the words of Henry Pochmann, "Thoreau's famed flight to his shanty on Walden Pond was an inconsequential lark compared with Brokmeyer's life in the primeval forest...."[22] Unlike Thoreau, Brokmeyer's was not an *experiment* in simple living. It was simply life. And the harsh realism of frontier life led Brokmeyer to philosophers who would temper the Romantic individualism of the transcendentalists with a superstructure that made sense of the reversals, contradictions, and apparent tragedies of life. In short, he was led to an interpretation of Hegel. In 1855, he undertook the first English translation of Hegel's *Logik* and continued this work for the next thirty years. A copy of this translation was supposedly never formally published, but served as the basis for many pivotal discussions at the Concord School of Philosophy in the late 1870s and early 1880s.[23] Brokmeyer's tale might come across as the story of an intellectual recluse who holed up in a frontier cabin with a famously inaccessible book if it were not for the fact that Brokmeyer became the linchpin in Hegel scholarship in America. While Stallo and the other Ohio Hegelians

---

[21] Whiting, "A Group of St. Louis Idealists," 359.

[22] Pochman, *German Culture in America*, 9.

[23] To the authors' knowledge, two extant copies of this translation remain: one in the archives of the Missouri Historical Society and one (partial, Book II) in the general stacks of Widener Library at Harvard University.

were relatively marginalized in American academe, and Hedge and Marsh served to incubate an interest in Hegel in the centers of the Northeast, it was Brokmeyer and his followers who cultivated the study of Hegel in America and who would return Hegel to a place of prominence in New England universities in the 1880s.

In 1858, Brokmeyer met a young William Torrey Harris at the Mercantile Library in St. Louis. Harris was immediately fascinated by Brokmeyer's idealism, particularly the developmental teleology modified from Hegel, and convinced Brokmeyer to conduct a series of readings groups on Hegel's philosophy, especially his logic. Harris, who would become superintendent of schools in St. Louis, and later the head of the US Department of Education, translated Hegelian notions of growth and development into practical educational reforms (for example, it is Harris who instituted the idea that schools be divided by aged-based grades). Thanks to Harris and Denton Snider, the American Hegelians were responsible for transforming education—including the Kindergarten Movement and the Hull House—in the United States. Reading Hegel as a political liberal and neo-humanist, the St. Louis Hegelians applied the Hegelian dialectic in support of the abolitionist cause and viewed the Civil War as a concrete expression of the world historical process. So while it is true that there is a "surprisingly long tradition" of Hegelianism in America, as well as a Hegelian deposit to be found within American pragmatism, Hegel exercised a broader influence also—perhaps even a greater influence—on nineteenth-century theological, educational, and political movements.

The St. Louis reading groups on Hegel also resulted in the Brokmeyer translation of the *Logik* and in Harris's thoroughgoing commitment to Hegelian idealism when he assumed the editorship of the *Journal of Speculative Philosophy*, the first philosophical periodical in the United States, in 1867. Harris would force classical American pragmatists—particularly Peirce, James, Royce, and Dewey—to tarry with Hegel as they began to submit their first manuscripts to this up-and-coming journal in the 1870s. This point will be developed further in the subsequent section of this chapter on the pragmatic response to Hegel in the New World.

Before turning our attention to the ways in which these pragmatists received Hegelian thought, it is necessary to address a final stream of American thinkers that predate the birth of pragmatism at the end of the 1860s. Hegelian thought came to America by diverse routes, often indirectly, usually inconspicuously, but the more fascinating phenomenon is the wide array of ways that it has been appropriated, applied, and put to good work. The St. Louis Hegelians are perhaps illustrative of a broader pattern in the Midwest during the second half of the nineteenth century. The Ohio Hegelians constituted a rather small but terribly ambitious coterie of public intellectuals who promoted Hegelian or post-Hegelian thought in and around Cincinnati: Peter Kaufmann (1800–1869), August Willich (1810–1878), John Bernhardt Stallo (1823–1900), and Moncure Daniel Conway (1832–1907); Kaufmann emigrated to the United States in 1820, Stallo in 1839, Willich in 1851.

Although the term 'Ohio Hegelians' is somewhat tendentious, perhaps even a misnomer, a quick comparison to the St. Louis Hegelians seems instructive: compared to the organizational infrastructure and the sustained philosophical focus of the St. Louis

Hegelians, the Ohio Hegelians were largely unorganized and unfocused: even Easton, who coined the designation in 1962, conceded that the 'Ohio Hegelians' were only loosely affiliated and probably did not constitute an American school of Hegelian philosophy. Perhaps it is fair to say that, in the main, the Ohioans were more interested in how Hegel helped them understand and respond to concrete socio-ethical or geopolitical problems than in his solution to the philosophical problem of the one and the many. Similar to the St. Louis Hegelians, the Ohio Hegelians tended to view the sectional crisis as Hegel's dialectical march of freedom and construed history, which Hegel likened to the slaughter bench, as a struggle for recognition. Whereas Brokmeyer once wrote that the most pressing concern was to teach Hegel to speak English, a conviction demonstrated in his Sisyphean effort to translate Hegel's *Logik*, the Ohioans seemed relatively successful in Americanizing Hegel and, as Good terms it, Hegelianizing utopian socialism. Whereas the St. Louis Hegelians had the *Journal of Speculative Philosophy*, the Ohio Hegelians promoted left Hegelian Christian socialism in newspapers, almanacs, and periodicals.

Similar to W. T. Harris in St. Louis, but earlier, Kaufmann was an educational reformer: Kaufmann's 1838 *Treatise on American Popular Education* espoused lifelong learning as essential to the success of representative government. Easton suggests that Kaufmann's thought constitutes a form of philosophy mysticism, one beholden especially to Johannes Tauler; Good claims that Kaufmann was "developing a pantheistic, Christian perfectionism that necessitated action in this world as man aligned himself with the aims of the cosmos."[24] Although trained Hegelians would located Kaufmann's *Temple of Truth* (1858) closer to Schelling's *Naturphilosophie* (1797) or *System der transcendentalen Idealismus* (1800) than Hegel, the central theme and general conclusions were at that time those typically associated with Hegelianism. Before coming to the United States, August Willich fought alongside Marx in the Rhineland campaigns and with Engels in Baden in 1849. Stallo invited Willich to edit the German newspaper in Cincinnati, the *Republikaner*, in 1856. When the Civil War broke out, Willich commanded a regiment of German volunteers; Goetzmann claims that Willich, who was "one of four Marxists who rose to the rank of general in the Union Army," represents "the way in which Hegel's thought did so much to inspire abolitionist and workingmen's causes in nineteenth-century America."

John Bernhardt Stallo confessed that his earliest manuscript, *The Philosophy of Nature* (1848), published when he was twenty-five, was composed while "under the spell of Hegel's ontological reveries' and in the throes of 'metaphysical malady.'" (Dewey will say something similar about his early Hegelianism.) In this case, 'Hegel' stands also—rightly or wrongly—for Schelling. Not unlike Kaufmann, the working assumption of Stallo's 'evolutionary idealism'—as Easton calls it—"was that mind or thought is fundamentally identical with the forces which activate the whole natural world." And while some suggest that Stallo eventually became the most un-Hegelian of the Ohio Hegelians, in letter

---

[24] See Good, *The Ohio Hegelians*. For more on the Ohio Hegelians, see Easton's "Hegelianism in Nineteenth-Century Ohio"; also see Easton's *Hegel's First American Followers*.

if not also in spirit, since he explicitly renounced his early Hegelianism, it seems that Stallo, similar again to Dewey, retained a "permanent Hegelian deposit." In his *Concepts and Theories of Modern Physics* (1881), which he "designed as a contribution not to physics nor, certainly, to metaphysics but to a theory of cognition," Stallo strove to disclose and refute the "latent metaphysical elements in the [then] prevailing atomo-mechanical theory."[25] At about the same time that Peirce was writing his anti-Cartesian essays (e.g., his "Some Consequences of Four Incapacities"), Stallo was attacking—from separate but parallel trenches—similar fallacies of cognition in science and physics.

Although he was the only Ohio Hegelian born in the States, Conway had a long row to hoe before arriving in Cincinnati: while at Harvard, Conway fell under the spell of Emerson and Theodore Parker. At least initially, Hegelianism stood in for the new theology and historical criticism of Strauss. After he was dismissed from his first church in Washington, D.C., because of his zeal for the abolitionist cause, Conway moved to Cincinnati.

In 1856, Conway worked with Willich and Stallo in support of the "free-soil" candidate for president, John C. Fremont. Conway was influential, mostly as a social critic: he was critical of industrial capitalism and institutionalized Christianity, as well as segregation and imperialism in America, often for the same reason, namely, that it exploited and disenfranchised as well as alienated the most vulnerable. In 1864, Conway traveled to Germany where, writes Pochmann, he began "making special efforts to consult Strauss at Heilbronn and Gervinus at Heidelberg."[26] For many, Conway's *Earthward Pilgrimage* served as an introduction in all but name to the religious criticism of Feuerbach as well as political economy in Marx. Although he did not deal directly with Hegel's philosophical doctrines and did not reflect the religious skepticism of some of Hegel's followers, Conway's work displays a historical method that is distinctly Hegelian.

The Ohio Hegelians are worth remembering for what they reveal about the origins of utopianism in America, about the manner in which idealism took root in the practical affairs of the American public. Perhaps the Ohio Hegelians represent the 'Left Hegelian' if not early Marxist sociopolitical position during the second half of the nineteenth century.

30.3. The Widening Stream (1867–1890)

As Hegelianism gained momentum in the late 1860s, the cast of philosophical characters who promoted idealism in the New World widened. In the coming sections, we try to give a reader a mere sense of the philosophical landscape before diving into the specific ways Hegelian thought effected the philosophy of four American thinkers: William James, C. S. Peirce, Josiah Royce, and John Dewey.

[25] Stallo, *The Concepts and Theories of Modern Physics.*
[26] Pochman, *German Culture in America*, 253.

The American Civil War did absolutely nothing to diminish the popularity of Hegel's philosophy in the United States. Thinkers, especially the St. Louis Hegelians, turned to Hegel to explain the way that conflict might beget new political and social growth and undertook their studies of the *Logic* with increased vigor in the years that followed the conflict. Brokmeyer maintained his near-prophetic status and attracted not only Harris and Denton Snider but also the educational reformers, Susan Blow and Anna Brackett (Rogers).[27] As mentioned earlier, Hegelian theories of development and growth found a practical use, first in the primary and secondary school systems of the Midwest and then across the country. But it was during the years between 1870 and 1880, in the years when modern professional philosophy was born in the United States, that the specter of Hegel loomed especially large over American academic life.

Harris and Brokmeyer founded the St. Louis Philosophical Society in 1866 and launched the *Journal of Speculative Philosophy* in the subsequent year. This became the first and only philosophy periodical in the United States and the mouthpiece for Classical American pragmatism as it gathered steam in the early 1870s. Harris, as editor of the journal, was the gatekeeper of professional philosophy in the United States and demanded that contributing authors come to terms with Hegel. Pragmatism, in effect, had to go through a Hegelian filter before it was exposed to the public. As we describe shortly, this is most pointed in the case of C. S. Peirce, widely considered the founder of American pragmatism, who received—and took to heart—extensive Hegelian pointers when he submitted his three foundational papers to the *Journal*: "Questions Concerning Certain Faculties Claimed for Man" (1868), "Some Consequences of Four Incapacities" (1868), and "Grounds of Validity of the Laws of Logic" (1869). When a young John Dewey submitted his first paper to the *Journal*, it was Harris's encouragement that led Dewey to further his studies of philosophy. And when William James submitted his first essays in the mid-1870s, it was Harris's initial refusal to publish them that caused James to bristle against the idealism that took New England universities by storm in the 1880s.

As Robert Richardson has explained in great detail, readers of Hegel initially based in St. Louis, like Harris and Snider, along with George Howison and Thomas Davidson, who joined the St. Louis Hegelians and served as philosophical tutor to both William James and Josiah Royce, migrated to New England in the 1870s. During this time, Brokmeyer's translation of the *Logic* spread to academic locales beyond St. Louis. In 1872, according to William James, two Illinois businessmen carried the three-volume set of the Brokmeyer *Logic* to Boston, where they, along with James and James Eliot Cabot (Emerson's literary executor), undertook an extensive study of this work.[28] One of these Illinois businessmen was Samuel Emery, a close friend to the transcendentalist Bronson Alcott. Emery, Alcott, and William Torrey Harris would be the leaders of what in 1879 became the Concord School of Philosophy.[29] The Concord School, the last bastion of American transcendentalism, was a series of summer lectures, open to academics and

---

[27]   See Rogers, "Before Care."
[28]   Cited in Good, *A Search for Unity in Diversity*, 94.
[29]   Ibid.

the general public, on a wide array of philosophical and literary themes that were loosely held together by their idealist and transcendentalist character. Emery and Harris made sure that Hegel was front and center at these lectures. Harris, for example, led a full course on Hegel's logic, psychology, and dialectic in 1882.

As Hegel was being disseminated to a general audience in Concord, Hegelian philosophy became an active force in shaping the fledgling philosophy graduate programs in Cambridge. George Howison, who had moved from Washington University in St. Louis to the Massachusetts Institute of Technology in the early 1870s, began teaching Hegel regularly to his students. James Eliot Cabot was elected as an overseer at Harvard and, as Richardson writes, turned to Howison's class for a benchmark to measure the offerings at Harvard.[30] In the following years, Howison was also elected to the Harvard Board of Overseers and ensured that Hegel would have a serious hearing at the University throughout the 1870s and into the early 1880s. Transplanting and reviving Brokmeyer's reading group on the *Logic*, Harris convened an informal group to study the Brokmeyer translation in Boston; this group included James Eliot Cabot, C. C. Everett (the head of Harvard Divinity School), A. C. Andrews, George Palmer, Thomas Davidson, and an up-and coming William James. Palmer would go on to carry the Hegelian banner at Harvard, and James would endeavor, for the most part, to tear it down.

30.4. PRAGMATIC CROSSCURRENTS (1890–1930)

Before turning to the relationship between Hegel and classical pragmatic thought, a comment concerning secondary literature is warranted. A growing number of scholars have explored this relationship, led by Richard Bernstein and James Good. More recently the 'Pittsburgh Hegelians'—most notably Robert Brandom and John McDowell—have articulated the way in which analytic philosophy of the Sellarsian tradition, which focused on the criticism of the Myth of the Given, resonates both with segments of Hegel's *Phenomenology* but also the philosophy of Peirce and James. The scope of this chapter, however, does not allow us to address these important philosophical turns in detail since our charge is to investigate and explain Hegel's reception in America. At various points, however, we cite neo-pragmatic literature that bears on this reception.

30.4.1. James on Hegel

James is often caricatured in his persistent and deep dissatisfaction with Hegel. This isn't quite right. James grew up in an intellectual atmosphere that was Hegelian through

---

[30] Richardson, *William James*, 213.

and through. And in order to cut his own path, it was necessary, at least for James, to run counter to the mainstream, counter to the many senior academics of his time who seemed to accept Hegel's system as a matter of course. There are undoubtedly many points of divergence between James and Hegel, most significantly James's worry that what he took to be Hegel's absolutism would severely compromise the individualism that James was beginning to articulate, but we suspect that this worry was at least as personal as it was philosophical. James was worried that the groups at Concord and Cambridge, led by venerable American Hegelians, would compromise his own sense of philosophical particularity by cowing him into the Hegelian fold.

It is in this spirit that we can fully understand James's "On Some Hegelisms," a contentious essay written in 1888 that would form the boundaries between James's pragmatism and the idealism of American Hegelians like Harris, Howison, and Palmer.[31] The essay was explicitly aimed at Palmer, his colleague in the philosophy department at Harvard, whose reading of Hegel was heavily influenced by Caird. James wrote,

> We are just now witnessing a singular phenomenon in British and American philosophy. Hegelism, so defunct on its native soil that I believe but a single youthful disciple of the school is to be counted among the privat-docenten and younger professors of Germany, and whose older champions are all passing off the stage, has found among us so zealous and able a set of propagandists that to-day it may really be reckoned one of the most powerful influences of the time in the higher walks of thought. And there is no doubt that, as a movement of reaction against the traditional British empiricism, the Hegelian influence represents expansion and freedom, and is doing service of a certain kind. Such service, however, ought not to make us blindly indulgent. Hegel's philosophy mingles mountain-loads of corruption with its scanty merits, and must, now that it has become quasi-official, make ready to defend itself as well as to attack others. It is with no hope of converting independent thinkers, but rather with the sole aspiration of showing some chance youthful disciple that there is another point of view in philosophy that I fire this skirmisher's shot, which may, I hope, soon be followed by somebody else's heavier musketry.[32]

A few points need to be emphasized in light of this blatantly critical comment. James was probably better-versed in German Hegelianism—and his German better—than most American Hegelians. This stands in marked contrast to Menand's questionable claim that "James had actually not read very much Hegel."[33] What is considerably more certain is that James was wholly unwilling to concede ground to those he took to be Hegelian ideologues like Harris and Palmer. James objected to their lockstep adoration of the Hegelian system and their adamant belief that Hegel's teleology and philosophy of history could fully explain the political developments of the current age.

---

[31] In a letter written to Royce in February 1880, James conceded that his "ignorant prejudice against all Hegelians except Hegel himself grows wusser and wusser. Their Sacerdotal airs! And their sterility"; also see Richardson, *William James*, 214 ff.

[32] James, "On Some Hegelisms," 263.

[33] Menand, *The Metaphysical Club*, 358.

These professional and personal considerations aside, there were substantive differences between the philosophy of Hegel and the American pragmatism that James developed in his early and mid-career. James Pawelski articulates these differences quite nicely by making a distinction between James's partial endorsement of what Pawelski calls "Hegel's vision" and James's wholesale dismissal of what he terms "Hegel's technical apparatus."[34] James could almost endorse "Hegel's vision," the idea that reason is developmental and that this development can transcend irrational appearances by subsuming them into itself. This vision promises a certain intimacy with the empirical flux of experience, an intimacy that James would build into his radical empiricism. Hegel's prioritization of the concept of experience (in terms of *Erfahrung* rather than *Erlebnis*) might have suited James, but Hegel seemed to overlook something that James simply could not, namely the frequent *discontinuity* of experience. James suggested that Hegel's rationalism implied that all experience, no matter how seemingly jarring or shocking, could ultimately be subsumed in the continuous unfolding of mind. In this, James writes that, Hegel ignores "the jolt, jolt, jolt we get when we pass over the facts of the world."[35] Instead of facing the facts of experience, James suspects that Hegelian idealism commits what pragmatists tend to call the 'philosopher's fallacy' in which a thinker substitutes static and general conceptions for the flux of immediate experience. This fallacy, according to James, results in a toothless intellectualism that does little to clarify, negotiate, or enrich actual experience.

In James's later life, as he developed his radical empiricism and his focus on religious matters intensified, there is a gradual shift in his thinking on Hegel. If Royce is a reliable critic of James, James was more heavily indebted to Hegelianism than he realized or otherwise admitted to himself.[36] Indeed, Wilshire argues that late in life, "James evolved what he called a 'comminuted'—pulverized—'*Identitätsphilosophie*.' Without grasping this world-view, there is no way to know what James was up to, for example, [in] his pragmatic theory of truth."[37] But quite apart from his own reading of Hegel, which was intermittent but serious, James is particularly useful in terms of his description of how 'Hegelisms' functioned as a trope within the community of philosophical inquiry in America and abroad. James's association by disassociation with Hegelianism serves a pedagogical function in James: Hegel is a foil against which James explained his own philosophical views. So while James may have been more or less ambivalent about Hegel's own philosophical insights, he was quite convinced that tenacious and authoritarian philosophical formulae of all sorts were ultimately detrimental to the progressive

---

[34] Pawelski, *The Dynamic Individualism of William James*, 86.

[35] Ibid.

[36] Bruce Wilshire suggests that, "early on, James has little or nothing to say about Schelling, as if even acknowledging his existence were to give him too much credit. With regard to Hegel, he bristles with contempt. We will see how he inched over the decades toward the views he ridiculed. He tried to retain a vision of the individual's intimate inclusion in a whole, but a whole construed pluralistically. His method was phenomenology divested of rationalistic presuppositions" (Wilshire, "The Breathtaking Intimacy of the Material World," 103).

[37] Ibid.

spirit of scientific inquiry in general, as well as radical empiricism and pluralism in particular.

30.4.2. Royce on Hegel

Royce scholarship over the past fifty years in America has certainly swerved away from what John Smith considered to be a national proclivity for reading Royce as though he were "merely repeating Hegel and the classical German idealists" (1953, 126). The situation is complicated in the case of Royce, to be sure, but it does seem that at least Royce believed that it was possible to be both a Hegelian and a pragmatist; indeed, his 'absolute pragmatism' might best be viewed as an attempt to show how Hegelianism and pragmatism were allies who were advancing as if in "parallel trenches."

Royce began his studies of German idealism in 1875 and extended them when he moved to Johns Hopkins University for graduate study the subsequent year. As John McDermott notes, Royce came as close as any American to being a neo-Hegelian and continued to maintain a Hegelian project, "to provide a *strengwissenschaftliche Geistesgeschichte*," until the middle of his career. Kaag has elaborated on this point, arguing that "Royce did not simply have a 'Hegel period' in the 1890s, as John Clendenning suggests, but that his entire philosophy was shot through by a particular reading of Hegel.... This is not to say that Royce was a Hegelian, but the development of this intellectual lineage gives us a better sense of the origins of Royce's philosophy and also exposes the Hegelian legacy of American philosophy more broadly construed."[38] These factors led Walter Kaufman to claim in 1965 that Royce was in fact "Hegel's unauthorized deputy in America for a generation."[39]

One can understand Royce's role in the American reception of Hegel in two ways. First, it is clear that Royce employs Hegel's *Phenomenology* and *Logic* in particular ways in the development of his own form of Absolute Idealism from the early 1880s until his death in 1916. This is particularly clear in Royce's use of the *Phenomenology of Spirit* in his own ethical and political writings after 1890 and most pointedly in his *Philosophy of Loyalty*, published in 1908. Second, Royce's *Lectures on Modern Idealism* (1906) reflected a valuable and unique meta-theoretical understanding of Hegel's intellectual destiny in

---

[38] John Kaag, "American Interpretations of Hegel," 83; also "[t]his is the point where the problem of evil makes its entrance in Royce's *Phenomenology*. Royce understands Hegel as developing Absolute Knowledge [*Wissen*] as a response to this problem, to the danger of dislocation and disintegration that conscious selfhood continually faces. In this sense Hegel, according to Royce, envisions the fulfilled self of Absolute *Wissen* as 'a self that on principle appears to itself as an interrelated community of selves without being the less one Self (Geist).' As the 'special embodiment' of Absolute *Wissen*, finite consciousness forever seeks a home in an interrelated community of selves, yet seeks this ideal largely in vain. In an especially candid interpretation of ¶238 of the *Phenomenology*, Royce writes, 'In just this position of endless search, conscious of the contradiction of purpose and of fact, driven by the contradiction to work for unity that we cannot hope to attain, are we all today, Hegelians however much they may protest. The only alternative is indolence." (Kaag, "American Interpretations of Hegel," 90).

[39] Kaufman, *Hegel, A Reinterpretation*, 121.

the New World. Royce, more than any scholar at the turn of the century, understood and articulated the two interpretive readings by which Hegel came to be evaluated in the nineteenth and early twentieth centuries, which might today be called the 'traditional' and the 'post-critical' readings of Hegel.

The first of these frames, which Royce articulated, delimits the 'traditional' understanding of Hegel and presents his writing as advancing a particular metaphysical system. Scholars who maintained this position gave priority to a particular interpretation of Hegel's later works, particularly the *Logic*, as reflected in Brokmeyer's near obsession with the book that he aptly called "The Book of Fate." American scholars such as Harris and Palmer, who followed Brokmeyer's lead, found out that this interpretation was vulnerable to criticism. F. H. Bradley and Bernard Bosanquet, on the other side of the Atlantic, assumed similar metaphysical interpretations and confronted similar criticism from the likes of James and Peirce. On the ground of this traditional view, Hegel was in fact a *pre*-Kantian philosopher who embraced the same form of dogmatism and metaphysical monism that Kant sought to abolish in his critical project. Critics of this traditional view claim that it was defined by Neoplatonic ideals and did little to transcend the Christian mysticism of the modern period. In this light, Hegel did nothing to extend or revise Kant's transcendental deduction of the categories, but rather established a 'transcendental logic' that affirmed the theologically rooted metaphysics of Leibniz or other early moderns. It was on these grounds that pragmatists, along with analytic philosophers such as G. E. Moore and Bertrand Russell, thoroughly rejected the writings of Hegel and his acolytes in Europe and in the United States. Royce did not support this metaphysical interpretation of Hegel. But that would scarcely matter. He too would be largely dismissed in this pragmatic/analytic-idealist controversy.

In truth, Royce supported an alternative vision of the Hegelian project, a fact that was placed in stark relief in 1902 in his famed exchange with Bradley over Royce's *World and the Individual*. Royce's was a 'post-critical' interpretation of Hegel's corpus that downplayed the absolutist metaphysics and attempted to declaw the critics of Hegelian thought. As Kaag has argued elsewhere in more detail, Royce

> highlighted the way in which Hegel successfully negotiated the reflective and historical aspects of critical philosophy. In effect, these interpretations suggest that Hegel is best understood as a post-critical philosopher who investigates not only the form but also the social and historical content of transcendental philosophy.[40]

The gloss that Royce provides in *Lectures on Modern Idealism* anticipates Klaus Hartmann's work in the 1960s; both of them foreground the *Phenomenology of Spirit* instead of emphasizing some of Hegel's later works.[41] Royce rightly notes that Hegel's later writings had a distinctively 'bureaucratic' flavor, one that reflected Hegel's tenure at Berlin. And like bureaucracy, these writings failed to take account of the aspects of

---

[40] Kaag, "American Interpretations of Hegel," 83.
[41] See, e.g., Klaus Hartmann, *Grundzüge der Ontologie Sartres*.

human life and thought that thinkers like James found so important: pluralism, individuality, creativity, and spontaneity. Writing in 1906, without the advantage of interpretative distance, Royce is still able to understand why Hegel was dismissed so perfunctorily and prematurely: he was roundly criticized on the grounds of these later metaphysical works and dismissed as dogmatically absolutist for this reason. Royce's own use of Hegel avoided this problem by principally employing the early and middle sections of the *Phenomenology* (those sections that lead up to the Ethical Order). This interpretative work—supported by the marginal notes in Royce's copy of the *Phenomenology*—led Kaag to echo John Smith, J. C. Cotton, and Gabriel Marcel in their belief that Royce believed "the Hegel of the *Phenomenology* is superior to the Hegel of the *Logic*."[42] Royce seems to believe that the phenomenological method employed by Hegel ought to serve as the foundation for a study of human nature. Indeed, even his readings of the *Logic* are marked by a willingness to read Hegel's systematic work phenomenologically and analogically, as the unfolding of conscious personhood. Additionally, Royce's concern for the human self, as described by Cotton and others, coincides with the *Phenomenology's* abiding question concerning the self and the dialectic of human experience.

So how exactly did Royce use Hegel's *Phenomenology of Spirit* in the development of his Absolute Idealism after his return from Australia in 1888? This was the time in which Royce was explicitly wrestling with his own version of Unhappy Consciousness and turned his full attention on the problem of evil. Royce, with the help of Hegel, explores these philosophical issues, without an eye to static final solution, but to a solution in the making. Specifically, Royce employs Hegel's notion of the ethical order as he begins to develop his own ideas concerning loyalty, interpretation, community formation, and immortality. Royce conceives of the *Phenomenology* as primarily a description of the unfolding and development of selfhood, not ostensibly as the final coming to consciousness of God or Spirit. The *Phenomenology* focuses on the 'phenomenal or imperfect' transformations of forms or images (*Bilder*) and the ongoing metamorphosis of these images (*Bildung*).[43] This gallery of images, composed by the stages of conscious selfhood, is defined by either a practical or a theoretical attitude. In either case, as Royce observes, the stage of consciousness remains an imperfect one: the practical stages are blind and the theoretical stages are empty. Obviously, these are not Royce's words, but rather those of Kant when he states that "'[t]houghts without content are empty, intuitions without concepts are blind [*Gedanken ohne Inhalt sind leer, Anschauungen ohne Begriffe sind blind.*"[44] This is important since it shows Royce as explicitly interpreting Hegel's philosophical project as a post-Kantian one. Kant continually confronts the problem of how sensation and understanding are related such that conception might have empirical content. It is significant that Royce understands Hegel as dealing explicitly with the epistemic tangle of Kant's first critique, one of the primary obstacles to transcendental idealism on the whole. Royce also notes that this knot can only be untangled

---

[42]   Kaag, "American Interpretations of Hegel," 84.
[43]   Ibid., 86.
[44]   Cited in Ibid., 87.

by the union of the practical and theoretical knowledge, in the dynamic of *Bildung* as presented in Hegel's *Phenomenology.*

30.4.3. Peirce on Hegel

The spleen that James so readily vented on American Hegelians such as Palmer was not in short supply in Peirce. Peirce spent much of his philosophical youth railing against the metaphysical and teleological position that Hegel's followers advanced. Most pointedly, he, like James, rejected the cartooned version of Hegel that absorbed all contradiction and negation into a totalizing whole. In this view, Hegel recognized only Thirdness (continuity), maintaining that "Firstness (spontaneity) and Secondness (concrete reaction or conflict) must somehow be *aufgehoben*" (5.77 n., 5.91).[45] Along these lines, Douglas Anderson writes,

> Peirce, like James, argued that the universe of concreteness was continuous and shot through with relations. A Peircean self or personality, therefore, was never a matter of 'immediate limits' but was an ongoing developmental history. Generality, as he sometimes put it, has a life or career. In this much, Peirce was a standard idealist—he was in agreement with Harris [and Hegel]. However, as Harris seemed to suggest . . . the concrete, in achieving its perpetuity in the Form of Eternity, seems to leave behind its concreteness.[46]

And concreteness was precisely what James and Peirce were unwilling to leave behind in the development of American pragmatic thought. Peirce was also unwilling to affirm what he took to be Hegel's insistence that the universe was reasonable in a strictly deductive sense. Peirce, unlike Hegel, took the universe to be fundamentally hypothetical rather than deductive in nature. These criticisms led Peirce to regularly suggest that the Hegelian-Schellingian mansion, a *Gedankengebäude* constructed according to the German taste, was "pronounced uninhabitable" in America.[47] The uninhabitable mansion is elsewhere described by Peirce as "a pasteboard model of a philosophy that in reality does not exist."[48]

This being said, Peirce, who sharply and repeatedly denied Hegelian influence, found it necessary both to import Hegel into the seminal moments of American pragmatism and later to amend his philosophical views such that they were far more amenable to German idealism (that, of course, included Hegel). Even as he said that Hegel had ignored fundamental aspects of the universe, like spontaneity and concrete reaction, he conceded that "[m]y three categories [i.e., Firstness, Secondness, and Thirdness] are

---

[45] See Shapiro's "Peirce's Critique of Hegel's Phenomenology and Dialectic." Also see Jensen, "Peirce as Educator."

[46] Anderson, "Peirce: Pragmatism and Nature after Hegel," 224.

[47] Peirce, CP 1.1.

[48] CP 6.305.

nothing but Hegel's three grades of thinking."[49] In fact, at the end of his life, he admitted that his own thought was "Hegelianism in a strange costume."[50] Some might think that this ultimate agreement with Hegel stemmed from Peirce's extensive interaction with Royce in the first years of the twentieth century (Royce after all suggested to Peirce that he had to read more Hegel in 1902), but Douglas Anderson has effectively argued that the Hegelian influence was much deeper and ultimately stems from his interaction with W. T. Harris.

The first formative contact Peirce had with Hegel—which should be distinguished from his first reading—came early in 1868 as Peirce prepared to send his first manuscripts to W. T. Harris for the *Journal of Speculative Philosophy*. Anderson's work is the first and most detailed analysis of the correspondence between the one of the primary members of the St. Louis Hegelians and Peirce, an interaction that Anderson persuasively argues altered the trajectory of Peirce's thinking. Harris's reading of Hegel had led him to believe that the whole gist of philosophy is to figure out where one stands in the nominalist-realist debate. Anderson argues that Peirce would come to embrace this position. He, echoing many St. Louis Hegelians, claimed that "all modern philosophy, of every sect, has been nominalistic."[51] With the rise of post-Kantian philosophy, Peirce believed that something had changed. And he was happy to be part of the transition toward a certain sort of realism—that harkens back to Duns Scotus—that took ideas to have real efficacy. Indeed, in his correspondence with Harris, Peirce is happy to recognize the way that realism might resonate closely with the idealism to which Harris was wed. Therefore, as Anderson has argued in detail,

> Amidst Peirce's criticisms, we find his deep respect and admiration for Hegel. [Peirce] appreciated the historical and evolutionary dimension of Hegel's objective logic and argued that 'Hegel's system of Nature represents tolerably the science of his day....' (CP 5:385) We can hear here the implicit suggestion that it will be up to Peirce, the pragmatists, and others to take the Hegelian method and bring it into alliance with the evolutionary science of the late nineteenth century. And, finally, Peirce, like James, appreciated the down-to-earthness of the *Phenomenology*.[52]

An additional word regarding this "down-to-earthness" is warranted. While Peirce admitted to Harris in May of 1868 that "I should come on the same side as Hegel, because I am idealistic," both Hegel and his transcendentalist and pragmatic followers held that this idealism should take 'experience' as its philosophical touchstone.[53] Following Hegel, Americans like Emerson, Peirce, and James maintained that "experience" shared little in common with its development by modern philosophers of the past (particularly Descartes or the British empiricists). Indeed, much of contemporary

---

[49] CP 8.213.
[50] CP 1.42.
[51] CP 1.19.
[52] Anderson, "Peirce: Pragmatism and Nature after Hegel," 224.
[53] Cited in Elton, "Peirce's Marginalia in W.T. Harris' Hegel's Logic."

pragmatism—from John J. McDermott's attention to the philosophical possibilities of mundane experience to Anderson's philosophical exploration of popular culture—has attempted to extend this focus on, and enrichment of, experience.[54] Robert Brandom makes explicit the Hegelian roots of this pragmatic reconstruction of experience by noting that, for thinkers like Peirce, experience "is something *done* rather than something that merely *happens*—a process, engaging in a practice, the exercise of abilities, rather than an episode. It is experience, not in the sense of *Erlebnis* (or *Empfindung*), but of Hegel's *Erfahrung*."[55] This notion of experience as a form of transaction that is both done and undergone is highlighted in Dewey's "Having an Experience" and *Art as Experience*, but it is present also in Peirce and James, a sediment of their Hegelian inheritance. In Brandom's words, "For the pragmatists, experience is not an input to the learning process. It just *is* learning: the process of perception and performance, followed by perception and assessment of the results of the performance, and then further performance. . . ."[56]

30.3.4. Dewey on Hegel

Although John Dewey was grateful to Hegel for liberating him from "the shackles of Cartesian dualisms," he eventually "drifted away" from Hegel and came to consider the dialectical form to be mechanical and the schematism of Hegel's system to have been "artificial to the last degree." Dewey acknowledged a subsequent debt to James for a similar liberation "out of bondage in the land of Hegel and into the wonderful land of naturalism." Though Dewey conceded that "Hegel ha[d] left a permanent deposit in his thinking" he continued—following White's *The Origin of Dewey's Instrumentalism*—"to hammer away at his [Hegelian] chains" even after he had liberated himself from his need for transcendental realities."[57] Contemporary scholars have contested White's account of Dewey's relationship to Hegel. Following James Good, Dewey rejected the 'metaphysical' reading of Hegel by the British Hegelians, yet retained the valuable insights that he discovered in his own—'historicist'—reading of Hegel. John E. Smith makes a similar point: "There is no point in the attempt to keep Dewey's Hegelian background a secret; not only has the secret long been revealed, but much of what is sound in Dewey's thought can be traced to the tradition stemming from Aristotle and Plato which Hegel represented."[58] Richard Rorty claims not only that Dewey's best insights emerge from his insipient Hegelianism, he also suggests that Dewey's ultimate undoing was that he wasn't "Hegelian all the way."[59]

54 McDermott, *The Drama of Possibility*; Anderson, *Philosophy Americana*.
55 Brandom, "From German Idealism to American Pragmatism—and Back."
56 Ibid. np.
57 Dewey, *The Later Works*, 5, 154. Also see White, *The Origin of Dewey's Instrumentalism*.
58 Smith, *Themes in American Philosophy*, 117.
59 Rorty, *Consequences of Pragmatism*, 85. Elsewhere, Rorty claimed that "Hegelians are those people who say that 'humanity' is a biological rather than a moral notion, that there is no human dignity that

While most Dewey scholars concede, some reluctantly, that Dewey was a Hegelian at some point in his career, they tend to disagree on when and whether Dewey broke with Hegelianism. Between 1884 and 1894, roughly, Dewey seems to have been a "committed idealist influenced by Hegel, the American Hegelian George S. Morris, and the British absolute idealists particularly T. H. Green and Edward Caird."[60] Although it is often suggested that Dewey was introduced to Hegel at Johns Hopkins (1882–1884), where he worked with Morris, who had studied with Trendelenburg in Berlin, Dewey was surely exposed to at least the theological aspects of Hegelianism in Vermont, where he was introduced to German philosophy by James Marsh and subsequently tutored by H. A. P. Torrey. (Perhaps the exposure was much earlier: in 1878, e.g., Dewey delivered a commencement oration at the University of Vermont on "the limits of political economy.") That said, Dewey himself claims that when he sent his initial philosophical essays to W. T. Harris, the Hegelian in St. Louis who edited the *Speculative Journal of Philosophy*, he was "ignorant of Hegel." Dewey claims that Hegel appealed to him for subjective as well as objective reasons: Hegel's thought, wrote Dewey,

> supplied a demand for unification that was doubtless an intensive emotional craving, and yet was a hunger that only an intellectualized subject-matter could satisfy.... Hegel's synthesis of subject and object, matter and spirit, the divine and the human, was, however, no mere intellectual formula; it operated as an immense release, a liberation. Hegel's treatment of human culture, of institutions and the arts, involved the same dissolution of hard-and-fast dividing walls, and had a special attraction to me.[61]

Dewey claimed that he "drifted away from Hegelianism": the word 'drifting,' he says, "expresses the slow and, for a long time, imperceptible character of the movement, though it does not convey the impression that there was an adequate cause for the change."[62] On other occasions, however, for example, between 1910 and 1915, the cause for distancing himself from Hegel was both clear and abrupt. Some scholars say that Dewey's break with Hegel was more or less complete by 1893, others as late as 1903, though some claim that even his later work was noticeably Hegelian in spirit if not also the letter; all admit a permanent deposit, and all agree that Dewey was adamantly opposed to Hegel, as if it were a matter of patriotism, by 1915. Whereas Dykhuizen claims that the first published indication of Dewey's break with Hegel and 'experimental idealism,' or what Morton White called 'instrumental Hegelianism,' was in 1900, other scholars claim that this "places the change in Dewey's thought ten years too late."[63] Dewey himself claimed that "[t]here was a period extending into my earlier years at

is not derivative from the dignity of some specific community, and no appeal beyond the relative merits of various actual or proposed communities to impartial criteria which will help us weigh those merits" (*Objectivity, Relativism, and Truth*, 197 ff.).

[60]   See Buxton, "The Influence of William James on John Dewey's Early Work," 456 ff.

[61]   John Dewey, *The Later Works*, 153. Also see Bernstein, *The Pragmatic Turn*, 91 ff.

[62]   Dewey, *The Essential Dewey - Volume 1, Pragmatism, Education, Democracy*, 18.

[63]   See Dykhuizen, *The Life and Mind of John Dewey*; also see Morton White and Michael Buxton.

Chicago, when in connection with a seminar in Hegel's *Logic*, I tried reinterpreting his categories in terms of 'readjustment' and 'reconstruction'—but gradually came to realize that what the principles actually stood for could be better understood and stated when completely emancipated from Hegelian garb."[64] Whereas some suggest that the decisive shift occurred as the result of Dewey's encounter with James's psychological and logical writings, others claim that Dewey came to 'naturalize Hegel' under the influence of Darwin.[65] And there are also scholars who believe that Dewey remained a Hegelian, more or less, to the very end; even Dewey's mature philosophy, they say, displays rather a gradual and naturalist modification of his Hegelianism.[66]

What, ultimately, if anything at all, was the "permanent Hegelian deposit" in Dewey? Without trying to suggest a consensus within the secondary literature, it would seem that Hegel's notion of spirit translates fairly naturally into Dewey's conception of individuality. Perhaps Dewey's democratic community is designed as an answer to Hegel's quest for freedom (i.e., that democracy is the implicit conclusion of Hegel's dialectic of the state). For Dewey and Hegel, ideals are never fixed and permanent, but instead evolve within communities. Dewey, like Hegel, opposed materialism because it was inadequate to deal with consciousness or moral conduct. Like Hegel, Dewey rejected transcendental conceptions of divinity. It seems plausible to say that Dewey's expansive conception of God as the unity of coordinated ideals, or as the active relation between the ideal and the actual, is noticeably beholden to Hegel's socio-religious construal of the 'absolute spirit'. Similar to Hegel, Dewey's overarching philosophical project aimed at reconciling morality, religion, and politics. In broad strokes, one might even draw a comparison between the religious or philosophical environment to which Hegel and Dewey were responding; interestingly, Dewey suggests that Hegel's philosophy emerged from a cultural milieu not altogether unlike the one that fostered pragmatism in America, namely, American transcendentalism. Dewey, like Hegel, quite possibly, came to believe that an increase of moral responsibility required an increase in the freedoms exercised by the people. Hegel's dialectical 'categories of being' are pragmatically translated or otherwise transformed by Dewey into the 'sphere of the event' and the 'category of happening'. Dewey was not solely or even primarily interested in "getting Hegel right";[67] instead,

[64] Dewey, "The Biography of John Dewey," 18.

[65] The thesis of a naturalization of Hegel can be called into question, writes Bellmann, in "Re-Interpretation in Historiography," 474. Indeed, in 1891, in the context of justifying Hegel's dialectic, Dewey uses a functional analysis; just as a human organism sustains any one organ, so the organ "in turn, contributes to and thus helps constitute the organism"; also see Buxton, "The Influence of William James on John Dewey's Early Work," 456.

[66] Jim Garrison, "Dewey's Philosophy and the Experience of Working"; also see Good, *A Search for Unity in Diversity* and "John Dewey's 'Permanent Hegelian Deposit' and the Exigencies of War." For more on Dewey's philosophy of spirit, see Shook and Good, *John Dewey's Philosophy of Spirit*.

[67] Johannas Bellman makes a point with respect to Dewey that we are trying to make about the American philosophers in general: "In any case we have to describe reception as a creative process. The question of whether Dewey understood the tradition correctly or whether he misunderstood it [over-]simplifies this process. It is not a pointless question, but it would probably be better to ask why Dewey understood the tradition [e.g., Hegel, who Bellman claims was the most influential among the great philosophers of the tradition on Dewey's pragmatism] exactly as he did or which alternative

Dewey is offering an interpretation and dialectical appropriation of Hegelian themes with an eye turned toward a unifying yet diverse set of pragmatic and democratic ideals.

The remaining task for the Deweyian pragmatist, writes Shook and Good, "is to explain how the religious devotion to ideals, still useful (and perhaps necessary) in any democracy, can be aroused and maintained without trespassing the boundaries set by naturalism."[68] Dewey's lectures on Hegel, in 1891 in Michigan and 1897 in Chicago, display a sophisticated interpretation if not an ambivalent appropriation of Hegel; there is also Dewey's fascinating comment to his wife, Alice, in a letter dated 1894, that he "had always been interpreting the Hegelian dialectic the wrong end up." Dewey tended to read Hegel as someone who took a "generally pragmatic approach to religion" and who was "ultimately concerned with individuality and the social conditions requisite for the growth of individuality"; scholars are just now beginning to explore the consequences of Dewey's alleged Hegelianism for his mature formulations of 'social psychology' and 'deliberative democracy' as well as his 'idealism of action' and 'religious humanism' or 'spiritual naturalism'. Dewey's mature philosophy, suggests Shook, can be seen to be "a non-Marxist and non-metaphysical type of left Hegelian." Good speculates that "Dewey embraced the moderately left of center reading of Hegel that Rosenkranz defended" (i.e., Hegel construed as "a liberal reformer concerned with theoretical issues only to the extent that they illuminate momentous concrete issues").[69] Shook and Good argue that when we revise or otherwise recalibrate our reading of Hegel, as well as our reading of Dewey's reading of Hegel, we discover a far more significant Hegelian deposit than previously acknowledged.

The question of Dewey's indebtedness to Hegel was complicated by the exigencies of war. Perhaps too little attention has been paid to Dewey's most abrupt break from Hegel between 1911 and 1915. Consider Dewey's audacious suggestion in his 1911 "Truth and Consequences" in which he says that "to *be* a truth means to have been verified by use under test condition," to be 'tried and true', that even Hegel can be sublated or otherwise *aufgehoben* by the pragmatic account of truth:

> The pragmatist may even accept the verbal statement of Hegel that truth is complete identification of existence with meaning; but he will recall that such equivalence is not born, nor thrust upon an existence by accident, but is achieved. Blood will tell, but the blood that surely tells right is the blood of the strain that embodies the selective influence of long testings through struggle.[70]

By the time that Dewey wrote his 1915 *German Philosophy and Politics*, which explored the philosophical roots of German militarism and Prussian authoritarianism,

---

understanding he ignored for which reasons. To answer these questions one has to identify the contexts of the recipient and at the same time achieve a multi-layered understanding of the tradition without leveling its inner controversies" (2004, xxx).

[68]   Shook and Good, *John Dewey's Philosophy of Spirit*, 44.
[69]   Ibid., 63.
[70]   Dewey, "The Problem of Truth," in *The Essential Dewey*, Vol. 2, 118.

the trans-Atlantic or at least the German-America philosophical dialogue was frozen, or worse, and the "permanent enemy of human bellicosity"—as James describes it in his 1910 "Moral Equivalent of War"—was granted free reign. Dewey suggests that Kant's 'two-world thesis', together with Hegel's identification of the actual with the rational, served as a philosophical justification of warfare and subordination in historical conflicts.

By 1928, however, Dewey was again able to—or perhaps he considered it politically prudent to—show continuity between "institutional idealism, Hegel being selected as its representative,"[71] and his own philosophy of freedom, which is intended to explain how "freedom defined in terms of choice and freedom defined in terms of power in action." Hegel's construal of freedom, which is "a deliberately reflective and reactionary one," claims Dewey in 1928, consists in the doctrine that "freedom is a growth, an attainment, not an original possession, and it is attained by idealization of institutions and law and the active participation of individuals in their loyal maintenance, not by their abolition or reduction in the interest of personal judgments and wants."[72] In his 1930 "From Absolutism to Experimentalism," which includes his recollection of the influence of Hegel on his thought, Dewey claimed that despite his disenchantment with the 'form' of Hegel's system as well as the 'dialectic method', which eventually struck Dewey as 'artificial' and 'mechanical', he claimed that in "the content of [Hegel's] ideas there is often extraordinary depth" and that he would "never think of ignoring, much less denying, what an astute critic occasionally refers to as a novel discovery." Indeed, Dewey goes so far as to suggest—again in 1930—that "were it possible for me to be a devotee of any system, I still should believe that there is greater richness and greater variety of insight in Hegel than in any single systematic philosopher."[73]

WORKS CITED

Anderson, Douglas. "Peirce: Pragmatism and Nature after Hegel," in *Nineteenth Century Philosophy: Revolutionary Responses to the Existing Order*, edited by D. Conway and A. Schrift. New York: Routledge, 2014, 217–238.

Anderson, Douglas. *Philosophy Americana*. New York: Fordham University Press, 2006.

Bellmann, Johannes. "Re-Interpretation in Historiography: John Dewey and the Neo-Humanist Tradition." *Studies in Philosophy and Education* 23 (2004): 467–488.

[71] Dewey offers his most succinct description of Hegel's position as follows: "Hegel substituted a single substance, called Spirit, for the two-faced substance of Spinoza, and restated the order and law of the whole in terms of an evolutionary or unfolding development instead of in terms of relations conceived upon a geometrical pattern. This development is intrinsically timeless or logical, after the manner of dialectic as conceived by Hegel. But externally this inner logic development of the whole is manifested serially or temporally in history. Absolute spirit embodies itself, by a series of piecemeal steps, in law and institutions; they are objective reason, and an individual becomes rational and free by virtue of participation in the life of these institutions, since in that participation he [or she] absorbs their spirit and meaning" ("Philosophies of Freedom," 308).

[72] Dewey, ibid.

[73] Dewey, *Essential Writings*, vol. 1, 18.

Bernstein, Richard. *The Pragmatic Turn*. Cambridge: Polity Press, 2010.

Bloom, Harold. *Agon: Towards a Theory of Revisionism*. New York: Oxford University Press, 1982.

Bloom, Harold. *A map of misreading*. New York: Oxford University Press, 1975.

Bloom, Harold. *Figures of Capable Imagination*. New York: Seabury Press, 1976.

Bloom, Harold. *How to Read and Why*. New York: Scribner, 2000.

Bloom, Harold. *Kabbalah and Criticism*. New York: Continuum, 1983.

Bloom, Harold. *The Anatomy of Influence: Literature as a Way of Life*. New Haven, CT: Yale University Press, 2011.

Bloom, Harold. *The Anxiety of Influence: A Theory of Poetry*. New York: Oxford University Press, 1973.

Brandom, Robert. "From German Idealism to American Pragmatism—and Back." Conference Presentation. Center for the Study of Language, Mind and Society. http://lms.ff.uhk.cz/pool/download_14.pdf.np.

Buxton, Michael. "The Influence of William James on John Dewey's Early Work." *Journal of the History of Ideas* 45, no. 3 (1984): 456 ff.

Conser, Walter. *God and the Natural World*. Columbia: University of South Carolina Press, 1993.

DeArmey, Michael H., and Good, James A. *The Ohio Hegelians: Peter Kaufmann, Moncure Daniel Conway, and J. B. Stallo*. Bristol: Thoemmes Continuum, 3 vols., 2005.

DeArmey, Michael H., and Good, James A. *The St. Louis Hegelians*. Bristol: Thoemmes Continuum, 2001.

Dewey, John. "The Biography of John Dewey," in *The Philosophy of John Dewey*, edited by Paul Schilpp. Evanston: Northwestern University Press, 1939, 18.

Dewey, John. *The Essential Dewey, Volume 1, Pragmatism, Education, Democracy*. Edited by Larry A. Hickman and Thomas M. Alexander. Bloomington and Indianapolis: Indiana University Press, 1998.

Dewey, John. *The Essential Dewey, Volume 2, Ethics, Logic, Psychology*. Edited by Larry A. Hickman and Thomas M. Alexander. Bloomington and Indianapolis: Indiana University Press, 2009.

Dewey, John. "Philosophies of Freedom," in *The Essential Dewey*, Vol. 2: *Ethics, Logic, Psychology*, edited by Larry A. Hickman and Thomas M. Alexander. Bloomington: Indiana University Press, 1998.

Dewey, John. *The Later Works, 1925–1953*. Carbondale: Southern Illinois Press.

Dykhuizen, George. *The Life and Mind of John Dewey*. Carbondale: Southern Illinois University Press, 1975.

Easton, Loyd D. "Hegelianism in Nineteenth-Century Ohio." *Journal of the History of Ideas*. 23 no. 3 (1962): 355–378.

Easton, Loyd D. *Hegel's First American Followers: The Ohio Hegelians: John B. Stallo, Peter Kaufmann, Moncure Conway, and August Willich, with key writings*. Athens: Ohio University Press, 1966.

Elton, William. "Peirce's Marginalia in W.T. Harris' Hegel's Logic." *Journal of the History of Philosophy* 2, no. 1 (1964): 82–84.

Emerson, Ralph Waldo. *Nature*. Boston: James Munroe, 1849.

Emerson, Ralph Waldo. *The Complete Works of Ralph Waldo Emerson*. Boston and New York: Houghton and Mifflin, 1904.

Fulda, Hans Friedrich. *Hegel*. Munchen: Verlag C. H. Beck, 2003.

Garrison, Jim. "Dewey's Philosophy and the Experience of Working: Labor, Tools and Language." *Synthese* 105, no. 1 (1995): 87–114

Goetzmann, William. *The American Hegelians: An Intellectual Episode in the History of Western America*. New York: A. A. Knopf, 1973.

Good, James A. (ed.). *Journal of Speculative Philosophy, 1867–1893*, 22 volumes, 2002.

Good, James A. *A Search for Unity in Diversity: The 'Permanent Hegelian Deposit' in the Philosophy of John Dewey*. Lanham, MD: Lexington Books, 2006.

Good, James A. "John Dewey's 'Permanent Hegelian Deposit' and the Exigencies of War." *Journal of the History of Philosophy*, 44, no. 2 (2006): 293–313.

Gura, Philip. *American Transcendentalism: A History*. New York: Hill and Wang, 2008.

Hartmann, Klaus. *Grundzüge der Ontologie Sartres. in ihrem Verhältnis zu Hegels Logik: Eine Untersuchung zu "L'être et le néant"*. Berlin: Walter de Gruyter, 1963.

James, William. "On Some Hegelisms," in *The Will to Believe, Human Immortality, and Other Essays in Popular Philosophy*. New York: Dover Publications, 1956, 127–142.

James, William. "Pragmatist Account of Truth and Its Misunderstanders." *The Philosophical Review* 17, no. 1 (1908): 1–17.

Joas, Hans. *Pragmatism and Social Theory*. Chicago: University of Chicago Press, 1993.

Joas, Hans. "The Inspiration of Pragmatism," in *The Revival of Pragmatism: New Essays on Social Thought, Law, and Culture*, edited by Morris Dickstein. Durham, NC: Duke University Press, 1998.

Jensen, Kipton E. "Peirce as Educator: On Some Hegelisms." *Transactions of the C. S. Peirce Society* 40 (2004): 271–288.

Kaag, John. "American Interpretations of Hegel: Josiah Royce's Philosophy of Loyalty." *History of Philosophy Quarterly* 26, no. 1 (January 2009): 83–101.

Kaufman, Walter. *Hegel, A Reinterpretation*. South Bend, IN: University of Notre Dame, 1966.

McDermott, John J. *The Drama of Possibility: Experience as Philosophy of Culture*. New York: Fordham University Press, 2007.

Menand, Louis. *The Metaphysical Club*. New York: Harper Collins, 2001.

Pawelski, James. *The Dynamic Individualism of William James*. Albany: State University of New York Press, 2012.

Peirce, Charles Sanders. *Collected Papers of Charles Sanders Peirce*, 8 vols., edited by Charles Hartshorne, Paul Weiss, and Arthur W. Burks. Cambridge, MA: Harvard University Press, 1931–1958; vols. 1–6 edited by Charles Harteshorne and Paul Weiss, 1931–1935; vols. 7–8 edited by Arthur W. Burks, 1958.

Pochman, Henry. *German Culture in America: Philosophical and Literary Influences*. Madison: University of Wisconsin Press, 1957.

Richardson, Robert. *William James: In the Maelstrom of American Modernism*. New York: Houghton Mifflin, 2007.

Rogers, Dorothy. "Before Care: Marietta Kies, Lucia Ames Mead, and Feminist Political Theory." *Hypatia* 19, no. 2 (2004): 105–117.

Rorty, Richard. *Consequences of Pragmatism: Essays, 1972–1980*. Minneapolis: University of Minnesota Press, 1982.

Rorty, Richard. *Objectivity, Relativism, and Truth*, Cambridge: Cambridge University Press, 1991.

Saito, Naoko. *The Gleam of Light: Moral Perfectionism and Education in Emerson and Dewey*. New York: Fordham University Press, 2005.

Shapiro, Gary. "Peirce's Critique of Hegel's Phenomenology and Dialectic." *Transactions of the C. S. Peirce Society* 17 (1981): 269–275.

Shook, John R., and James A. Good. *John Dewey's Philosophy of Spirit: With the 1897 Lecture on Hegel*. New York: Fordham University Press, 2010.

Smith, John E. *Themes in American Philosophy: Purpose, Experience, and Community*. New York: Harper & Row, 1970.

Stallo, J. B. *The Concepts and Theories of Modern Physics*. New York: Appleton, 1885.

Stewart, Jon. *The Hegel Myths and Legends*. Evanston, IL: Northwestern University Press, 1996.

Thoreau, Henry David. "Walking," in *H. D. Thoreau: Essays*. New Haven, CT: Yale University Press, 2013, 243–280.

van Cromphout, Gustaaf. *Emerson's Modernity and the Example of Goethe*. Columbia: University of Missouri Press, 1990.

White, Morton Gabriel. *The Origin of Dewey's Instrumentalism*. New York: Columbia University Press, 1943.

Whiting, Lilian. "A Group of St. Louis Idealists," in *Theosophical Path*. Vol. VII. Point Loma: New Century, 1914, 356–362.

Whitman, Walt. *Notebooks and Unpublished Prose Manuscripts*, edited by E. F. Greier. 6 vol. New York: New York University Press, 1984.

Wilshire, Bruce. "The Breathtaking Intimacy of the Material World: William James's Last Thoughts," in *Cambridge Companion to William James*, edited by Ruth Anna Putnam. Cambridge: Cambridge University Press, 1997, 103–124.

CHAPTER 31

....

HEGEL AND TWENTIETH-CENTURY FRENCH PHILOSOPHY

....

ALISON STONE

31.1. INTRODUCTION

....

HEGEL's thought has had immense influence on twentieth-century French philosophy and intellectual life. Having held little significance for French philosophers in the early 1900s, Hegel's thought burst onto the intellectual scene in the 1930s through, above all, the lectures on Hegel given from 1933 to 1939 by the Russian émigré Alexandre Kojève. Kojève placed the master/slave dialectic at the heart of Hegel's philosophy, along with exciting ideas about labor, recognition, and the end of history. Kojève's lectures were attended by, among others, Raymond Aron, Georges Bataille, the surrealist André Breton, Jacques Lacan, and Maurice Merleau-Ponty, all of whom engaged with aspects of Kojève's ideas. Those ideas also became widely known through Kojève's 1939 commentary on the master/slave dialectic in the journal *Mesures* and the subsequent publication of selections from his lectures in 1947 as *Introduction to the Reading of Hegel*.[1] Becoming important to Simone de Beauvoir and Sartre, Kojève's ideas fed into their key formulations of existentialism. Overall, Kojève's ideas decisively stamped virtually every area of twentieth-century French thought: psychoanalysis; religious thought; international relations theory; phenomenology and existentialism; and postcolonial thought, by way of its founding father Frantz Fanon.

---

[1] *Introduction to the Reading of Hegel* was compiled by Kojève's student Raymond Queneau, using lecture notes, transcripts, and other materials; Kojève reviewed the text and added footnotes. Queneau made the 1939 *Mesures* article into the opening chapter, "In Place of an Introduction." See Kojève, *Introduction to the Reading of Hegel*, xiii.

In the 1960s the ascendancy that Kojève had given to Hegelian ideas began to wane with the rise of post-structuralism. Its key representatives, Foucault and Derrida, sought to escape what they saw as the all-pervasive power of Hegelian thought. Derrida addresses the difficulty of departing from Hegel—any critique of Hegel being liable to fall into a standpoint that Hegel has already surpassed and incorporated into his system. As Foucault puts it, "our anti-Hegelianism is possibly one of his tricks directed against us, at the end of which he stands, motionless, waiting for us."[2] This post-1960s preoccupation with the dual necessity and difficulty of overcoming Hegel shows how far French thought had become permeated by Hegelianism. Even Gilles Deleuze, who detested Hegel, could not ignore his thought, but set out to craft a non-Hegelian philosophy that revolves around difference rather than the identity that Deleuze saw Hegel as championing.

Cutting across these major intellectual shifts, French Hegel scholars were active throughout the century, some of them exerting considerable influence. Jean Hyppolite's 1939–1941 French translation of the *Phenomenology of Spirit* consolidated Hegel's burgeoning popularity, to which Jean Wahl's 1929 study of Hegel's unhappy consciousness also contributed. But in France, Hegel's ideas gained a much wider reception than they have had in the English-speaking world, reaching well beyond Hegel scholars and being regarded as ideas with which any serious philosopher must engage. Among recent French philosophers, for instance, Alain Badiou criticizes Hegel for reducing the pure, proliferating multiplicity of number to the unity of thought.[3] Others continue to read Hegel more favorably: Catherine Malabou takes Hegel's idea of 'plasticity' as a starting-point for reconsidering neuroscience and proposing an intrinsic, 'plastic' creativity and freedom within our brains.[4]

An overview of the countless elements in Hegel's French reception would inevitably become superficial.[5] Instead I will concentrate on one strand in this reception that I consider especially fruitful. This strand proceeds, through Kojève and Sartre, to the rethinkings of the 'struggle for recognition' developed by Beauvoir and Fanon, who conceive of sexual and racial hierarchies as deformations in human relations of recognition. The struggle for recognition should be open to all, but women (for Beauvoir) and black people (for Fanon) have unjustly been excluded from this struggle. Thus Hegel's ideas, filtered through Kojève and Sartre, gave Beauvoir and Fanon theoretical resources for conceptualizing sexual and racial hierarchies.

Beauvoir and Fanon distinguish these hierarchies from biological differences—for these hierarchies obtain within our relations to one another as conscious subjects, not mere biological organisms—and also from the economic class relations that Marxists had long insisted have moral and explanatory priority. Beauvoir and Fanon establish

---

[2] Foucault, "The Discourse on Language," 235.
[3] Badiou, *Being and Event*, 161–170.
[4] Malabou, *What Should We Do with Our Brain?*.
[5] Other accounts of Hegel-in-France include Baugh, *French Hegel*; Judith Butler, *Subjects of Desire*; Tom Rockmore, "Hegel in France"; Roth, *Knowing and History*; and Russon, "Dialectic, Difference, and the Other: The Hegelianizing of French Phenomenology."

that racial and sexual hierarchies, unlike economic inequalities, are primarily problems of recognition, not redistribution.[6] Even so, these hierarchies are no less damaging than economic injustice, since—in Beauvoir's and Fanon's existential-Hegelian framework—it is fundamental to human existence for us to affirm ourselves as free subjects and demand that others recognize us as such. To be prevented from doing so is to be unjustly excluded from full human existence. Thanks to the French reception of Hegel, then, racial and sexual hierarchies could be conceived as distinct forms of oppression that need to be understood and challenged in their own right. Besides being innovative philosophically, this position provided theoretical support for the movements for women's liberation, anti-racism, and decolonization that became driving political forces in the 1960s.

But has the politics of existential-Hegelianism been superseded by the anti-Hegelianism of post-1960s French thought? To address this concern, I will consider how the 'French feminist' Luce Irigaray, an important member of the post-structuralist generation, takes up and transforms Hegel's notion of mutual recognition, urging that differently sexed individuals should learn to accept and recognize one another in their irreducible difference. Thus, positive engagement with Hegel as a thinker of recognition (following Kojève) informs Irigaray's ethics of sexual difference, which is one instance of recent French thinking about difference and otherness. This indicates that Hegel, specifically as read in light of Kojève, remains important for contemporary French philosophy—not merely as an irritant but also as a positive interlocutor.

It may be objected that all this has little to do with the 'actual Hegel'. Kojève has been accused of distorting Hegel; Sartre, Beauvoir, Fanon, and Irigaray seek to take Hegel's ideas in new directions, rather than provide faithful exegesis of his texts. Still, their ideas have *some* relation to those expressed by Hegel, not least because the difficulty of his texts opens them to widely varying interpretations. Moreover, it is precisely by recasting Hegel's ideas that Beauvoir, Fanon, and Irigaray have forged from them the critical accounts of gender and race relations that are a lasting achievement of the French reception of Hegel.

31.2. KOJÈVE

The essentials of Kojève's interpretation of Hegel are these. Kojève translates the lord/bondsman (*Herr/Knecht*) relation as that between *maître* and *esclave*—master and slave. Seeing this relation as the pivot on which Hegel's thought turns, Kojève begins his reading of Hegel with 'desire [*Begierde*]' in Chapter IV of *Phenomenology*. For Kojève, we have here a human being submerged in mere biological life: still essentially an animal, with merely animal desires to consume and eat living beings. The transition to truly

---

[6] On the recognition/redistribution distinction, see Fraser, "From Redistribution to Recognition? Dilemmas of Justice in a 'Post-Socialist' Age."

human existence begins as, in consuming and thus destroying living objects, we are negating mere life. We start to establish that we are not at life's mercy, as animals are, but 'go beyond' life in the name of values that we prioritize over self-preservation.[7] Thus we begin to stand out from life as free agents who transcend the given (*transcender le donné*).

Already we see a major departure from Hegel: Kojève wrests life and desire out of the epistemological and metaphysical context in which Hegel addresses them. For Hegel, life arises from the preceding shape of consciousness, 'understanding'. The understanding comes to conceive of its object—laws of nature and the phenomena that they generate—as 'infinity', an unceasing process whereby laws endlessly unfold into manifold appearances (PS 9.99/¶161). This generative process is "the simple essence of life" (PS 9.99/¶162). The understanding now sees this real movement as being essentially the same as the intellectual movement that *it* is making in explaining phenomena from the laws underlying them. Consciousness thereby becomes *self*-consciousness (PS 9.101/¶164), for in relating to the outer world as life, it is relating to something that it sees as having the same essential character as itself. This brings us to desire, in which self-consciousness consumes and destroys living beings in the effort to realize their essential identity with it and thus confirm the truth of its metaphysical standpoint (PS 9.104/¶167).

By extracting life and desire from this epistemological and metaphysical setting, Kojève frees these concepts from Hegel's absolute idealism and from the manifold interpretive difficulties that surround the *Phenomenology*.[8] In this way, Kojève makes Hegel's concepts more accessible—as Kojève does, too, by resituating those concepts as elements of an account of human existence. *Introduction to the Reading of Hegel* begins: "Man is Self-Consciousness [*Conscience de soi*]. He is conscious of himself, conscious of his human reality and dignity; and it is in this that he is essentially different from animals."[9] Our vocation, for Kojève, is to be human and *not* merely animal, natural beings. Whereas for Hegel the desiring subject seeks to prove its *identity* with life, for Kojève that subject seeks to prove that it *transcends* nature. In place of the metaphysical complexities of absolute idealism, then, we get immediate, practical concerns with freedom and human agency.

Kojève continues by following the broad steps of Hegel's narrative in Chapters IV and IVA of *Phenomenology*, within which desire gives way to the struggle for recognition. However, Kojève fills in the logic connecting these steps in his own way, which often

---

[7]   Kojève, *Introduction to the Reading of Hegel*, 5. Throughout this chapter translations from French or German are sometimes amended without special notice.

[8]   Kojève does provide a reading of the entire sweep of the *Phenomenology*, but he takes Chapter IV as its starting point. His justification is that absolute knowledge depends on universal human history, the building-blocks of which are human agents; and their fundamental character is set out in Chapter IV and IVA (*Introduction*, 33).

[9]   Kojeve, *Introduction*, 3. For exegetical accuracy when discussing Kojève, Hegel, Sartre, and Fanon, I follow their use of masculine language, which reflects their equation of the masculine with the universal.

differs from Hegel's. For Kojève, desire is unsatisfactory because even in negating living beings, I remain absorbed with them and dependent upon them.[10] To realize my humanity I must obtain recognition of it from other human beings who, being human, are uniquely qualified to give this recognition. But to obtain recognition of my humanity as it differs from my animality, I must risk my life. "The supreme value for an animal is its animal life. . . . Human Desire, therefore, must win out over this desire for preservation. In other words, man 'proves' himself human only if he risks his (animal) life for the sake of his human Desire."[11] By risking my life, I try to prove to the other that I value prestige and recognition over life. But the other, desiring recognition from me in turn, takes the same risks. Thus provoking one another, we find ourselves embroiled in a fight to the death.

Unless this fight ends with either or both parties dead, eventually one subject concedes that it puts life first. That loser becomes slave, while the victor becomes master. The master, having proven his status as a free agent, decides on the slave's actions, which are all forms of labor performed on material objects to adapt them to the master's desires. The master will not deign to do this work but only to enjoy, consume, and destroy its products. The slave, conversely, has shown that he is suited to work, for "by the refusal of risk, [he] ties himself to the things on which he depends."[12] He thus has to labor on material objects in their intractable reality.

Overarching Kojève's differences from Hegel on the details of the master/slave dialectic, Kojève also departs from Hegel by giving that dialectic direct social and political significance. Hegel leaves us uncertain as to how the master/servant dialectic is to be related to the actual social world, but for Kojève matters are clear: master/slave relations really obtain throughout human history. Marx saw human history as the history of class struggles and relations of class exploitation. Kojève, under Marx's influence, interprets those class relations, in which one group labors on behalf of a ruling group, as master/slave relations in his sense: "history [is] the history of the interaction between Mastery and Servitude: the historical 'dialectic' is the 'dialectic of Master and slave'."[13] By giving the master/slave dialectic this direct historical application, Kojève has made it seem bold, radical, and relevant to the cause of revolution.

Just as Marx saw the progression to socialism taking place by the revolutionary agency of the working class, Kojève sees the slaves as the collective agent of historical progress. "If idle Mastery is an impasse, laborious Slavery . . . is the source of all human, social, historical progress. History is the history of the working Slave."[14] The goal of this historical progression is reciprocal recognition. Slaves must become recognized as the agents into which they have already made themselves by their labor; and masters cannot be adequately recognized by those—the slaves—to whom they deny human status.

[10] Ibid., 4–5.
[11] Ibid., 7.
[12] Ibid., 17.
[13] Ibid., 9.
[14] Ibid., 20.

History advances, then, as slaves progressively do 'impose themselves' on the masters. The French Revolution was a crucial milestone, initiating the modern era in which universal recognition of each by all is becoming a reality. When this process is completed, history will end—for history is nothing more than the history of master/slave relations and their overcoming.[15]

Kojève no doubt found inspiration for these claims in elements of Hegel's work, such as his view that Christian Europe is the third and last main historical stage in which, at last, all are becoming recognized as free. But Kojève's claims add up to a position sufficiently removed from Hegel's idealism that some have accused Kojève of simply foisting his own views onto Hegel.[16] In particular, what distinguishes Kojève's views is that he regards self-consciousness, negativity, and the desire and struggle for recognition as essential and universal features of human existence, consequently elevating master/slave relations, too, into a historical constant. In contrast, for Hegel, these are only *stages* in the much broader progression of consciousness that the *Phenomenology* narrates. Desire, recognition, and master/servant relations become superseded by later shapes of consciousness, into which they are partially incorporated (for example, private property owners reciprocally recognize one another, according to Hegel in the *Philosophy of Right*). Thus Hegel does not give desire, recognition, or the master/servant relation the organizing centrality that they have in Kojève's thought. Nonetheless, those concepts do have their place in Hegel's *Phenomenology*, and as such Kojève's account of free human existence remains a form of Hegelianism. Moreover, this form of Hegelianism not only allies Hegel with the cause of human emancipation, but also challenges the economistic bias of conventional Marxism by reframing relations of economic exploitation as resting on a prior distortion in relations of recognition. This move would make it possible for Beauvoir and Fanon to pay theoretical attention to forms of sexual and racial oppression that are not primarily or exclusively economic. They did so, though, by way of Sartre.

31.3. SARTRE

How far Sartre's 1943 *magnum opus, Being and Nothingness*, bears Kojève's influence is disputed. Sartre did not attend Kojève's lectures but may have read his *Mesures* article. Certainly Sartre informed himself about Kojève, for as Nancy Bauer remarks, "No one thinking about Hegel during those years [1930s–1950s] could possibly avoid having to take account of his [Kojève's] interpretations."[17] Kojève's impact shows in the simple fact that Sartre substantially discusses Hegel's *Phenomenology* IVA in *Being and Nothingness*,

---

[15]   Ibid., 57, 70, 135, 148.

[16]   See, e.g., Rockmore, "Hegel in France," 325.

[17]   Bauer, *Simone de Beauvoir, Philosophy and Feminism*, 86. Later Sartre read the 1947 edition of Kojève's lectures, which may in turn be influenced by Sartre—see Fry, *Sartre and Hegel*, 6. Surprisingly, and clearly falsely given the extensive discussion of Hegel in *Being and Nothingness*, Sartre subsequently claimed to have seriously studied Hegel only in the late 1940s.

having previously paid Hegel little mind. *Being and Nothingness* includes both an assessment of *Phenomenology* IVA and—our focus here—a critical reworking of the struggle for recognition.[18] Hegelian recognition thus became a central theme of existentialism.

In *Being and Nothingness*, Sartre maintains that reality is fundamentally divided. Reality contains, first, beings-for-self: conscious human existents who are freely self-creating and always exist toward possibilities of action. Second, reality contains being-in-itself: the brute givenness of non-conscious material stuff, which through human action and projection becomes divided into discrete objects located in causal chains. Sartre treats being-for-others as a modification of being-for-self, which arises because we always exist among other existents. The fundamental way that we encounter other existents, Sartre insists, is *not* to perceive them as objects. That mistaken thesis generates the problem of other minds as we try to establish that the bodies of my neighbors, passersby, and so on, contain minds like my own.[19] Actually, I fundamentally encounter the other as an other *subject*; any perception of the other as an object is derivative. Sartre supports this claim with two imaginative examples.

In the first, I am sitting in a park. The space around me and the objects in it—benches, grass, signs, litter bins—are organized around my possible actions and interests. Then a man walks past. I do not apprehend him simply as an object toward which I may undertake various actions, as I do with the benches. Instead, my experience is that my space and objects rearrange themselves around his possible actions: "there is a total space which is grouped around the other, and this space is made *with my space*; it is a regrouping—in which I assist and which escapes me—of all the objects that people my universe." My world 'hemorrhages' toward the other, as Sartre strikingly puts it.[20] Even so, Sartre says, I *am* still aware of this other as an object of a peculiar kind, one that is also a subject who effects the rearrangement of space. Things change, though, if the other turns and looks at me: I become an object within his frame of reference, toward which he may act in various ways and to which he assigns a meaning within the ensemble of his projects and interests. 'The look [*le regard*]', then, is central to intersubjective relations.

This brings Sartre to his second example: a man spying through a keyhole. "Let us imagine that moved by jealousy, curiosity, or vice, I have come to glue my ear to a door and look through the keyhole." I am completely taken up in spying—but then I hear footsteps. "I am suddenly affected in my being and . . . essential modifications appear in my structures."[21] I undergo a 'radical metamorphosis': I am now directly aware of myself as looked at. Crucially, it is not that I first perceive the footsteps (as an audible object) then infer that I am looked at; my awareness of being looked at is primary. I can be aware of being looked at by the other through his footsteps, just as I would be were his eyes trained on me.

[18] Sartre, *Being and Nothingness*, 235–244, 252–303.
[19] Ibid., 253.
[20] Ibid., 255, 257.
[21] Ibid., 259, 260.

In being aware of being looked at, I apprehend how I look from the other's perspective, in an immediate "*recognition* [*reconnaissance*] of the fact that I *am* indeed that object that the other is looking at and judging."[22] I view myself, as the other does, from the outside, thus as an object. My future projects and possibilities are not visible to the other, who merely sees me as what I have already visibly become. In this case, in the other's eyes I am merely this individual spying through the keyhole, nothing more. Transfixed, like a butterfly pinned to a board, I am reduced to how I appear from the third-person perspective.

There appears to have been a shift in Sartre's analysis. In his park example, I saw the other as a kind of object that was also a subject. But in the keyhole example, this qualification has disappeared: the other simply sees me as a thing seen, just as a park bench can be seen. "For the other, I *am leant* over the keyhole as this tree *is bent* by the wind."[23] Apparently, I am reduced to an object that bears the properties that the other assigns me, rather than giving myself qualities in undertaking my free projects and actions. This experience of objectification is the most basic way that I encounter the other, Sartre asserts:

> He is the one who looks at me and at whom I am not yet looking, the one who delivers me to myself . . . without revealing himself, the one who is present to me in that he looks at me [*me vise*] and not in that he is looked at; he is the pole, concrete and out of reach, . . . of the flow of the world toward another world. . . .[24]

Far from being primarily perceived as an object (even one infused with subjectivity), the other is primarily the one to whom *I* appear as an object and who therefore strips me of my freedom.

These claims underpin Sartre's reworking of the struggle for recognition. Under the other's look, I become a kind of slave. I am not literally forced to work for the other, but now "I am a slave to the degree that I am dependent in my being . . . [on] a freedom that is not mine and that is the very condition of my being."[25] I was a free agent absorbed in my projects, for example when spying through the keyhole—roughly as, for Hegel, self-consciousness was initially focused on "supersession of the independent object" (PS 9.109/¶180). But then, for Sartre, I encounter the other, and my freedom is taken away. For Hegel, though, that is true only of those who become enslaved after defeat in the life-and-death struggle. In contrast for Sartre, my transformation into an object occurs immediately when I encounter another subject.

However, Sartre reintroduces a version of the life-and-death struggle by claiming that each of us resists our objectification and fights back against the other. After all, I acquire objective status not only for the other, but also for myself insofar as I adopt the other's

---

[22] Ibid., 261.
[23] Ibid., 262.
[24] Ibid., 269.
[25] Ibid., 267.

perspective on myself. But in doing so I remain *aware* of myself, self-consciously. Thus even in experiencing myself as object, I necessarily remain a subject.[26] So I become provoked to reassert the subjective freedom that I always retain. I look back at the other, reasserting that I am an agent engaged in projects by placing the other in my frame of reference and spatial field. I thereby affirm that I am no mere thing, but rather one who exercises negativity (language reminiscent of Hegel and Kojève). Yet the other in turn reasserts himself against me, and we become locked into an endless struggle between competing looks, each endeavoring to establish his agency at the other's expense.

From this perspective, Sartre can explain why my perception of the other as a subjective object, as in the park example, is always derivative. In regarding the other as object, I was *already* trying to master him in reaction against his looking at me or having the threatening possibility of doing so. In sum,

> ... my own *look* ... is stripped [*dépouillé*] of its transcendence by the very fact that it is a *look-looked-at*. The people that I *see*, I am fixing them into objects; ... in looking at them I measure my power. But if the other ... sees me, then my look loses its power.[27]

In this reworking of the recognition struggle, Sartre has changed the order in which events unfolded in Hegel's narrative. For Hegel, the life-and-death struggle preceded the reduction of the defeated party to a servant. Conversely, for Sartre, the reduction of each subject to a slave *prompts* a version of the life-and-death struggle as each subject resists this reduction. Moreover, the struggle for Sartre need not literally be to the death, just as the slavery in question need not be literal slavery. Sartre has transposed Hegel's narrative away from social structures and onto everyday intersubjective relations.

Sartre's other key difference from Hegel, and from Kojève, is to insist that the struggle is endless and irresolvable. Sartre sees no possibility of each subject reciprocally recognizing the other, because in the fundamental structure of human existence the other primarily steals my freedom. This is reflected in the order of events in Sartre's narrative. I primarily encounter the other as the one who objectifies me, thus straightaway recognizing the other *as* an agent—but the agent of my objectification. I then move *from* recognizing the other's agency to reasserting my own agency. Thus Sartre's narrative closes off the space in which mutual recognition might come in to resolve the conflict. Sartre is pessimistic about human relations as Hegel and Kojève are not, seeing no prospect of a harmonious post-historical society. This pessimism informs Sartre's well-known remark "Hell is other people," actually voiced by his character Garcin in the 1944 play *No Exit*, initially titled *The Others*.[28]

---

[26] Consequently, for Sartre, I necessarily feel ashamed of how I appear to the other. My shame embodies my tacit judgement that I am more than my appearance, to which I therefore ought not to be reduced as I have been (ibid., 261–262).

[27] Ibid., 266.

[28] Sartre, *No Exit and Three Other Plays*, 47.

Yet there are respects in which Sartre might be considered more optimistic than Hegel or Kojève. First, for Sartre, a fundamental reciprocity structures relations between subjects: each objectifies the other, each resists. Reciprocal recognition may be ruled out, but reciprocal struggling and continual reversals of power are ruled in. Second, although Sartre says that the other's look strips me of my transcendence, ultimately his ontology entails that the other cannot ever deprive me of my freedom, for that freedom remains necessary for my (self-)objectification and for my whole way of existing. Has Sartre thus jettisoned Hegel's insight that human agents can only fully achieve freedom by receiving recognition from other agents? Not entirely: Sartre does hold that my lack of recognition from others who objectify me deprives me of my freedom, which I seek to regain by reasserting myself. To make Sartre's position consistent, we may take it that the other temporarily diminishes my freedom by inflicting quasi-objective status on me and by so affecting me that I regard myself as an object. By the other's presence, my freedom becomes turned back against itself to stymie its own exercise. But by the same token, no other can ever eradicate my freedom. This has a parallel in Hegel, for whom the other's recognition of my agency enables me to realize more fully an agency that I already possess *in nuce* just in being self-conscious.[29]

For Sartre, then, when the other objectifies me, I can and always do fight back. My freedom may be diminished; not so my capacity to resist this diminution. Consequently, even a literal slave always remains free to decide what attitude to take to his master, for "man cannot be sometimes slave and sometimes free; he is wholly and forever free or he is not free at all."[30] This leaves unclear how, for Sartre, any individual or group can ever be oppressed. Whatever situation I am in, whatever constraints others impose on me, my basic freedom remains intact. If I bow down to the constraints, the fault is mine—I have lapsed into 'bad faith'. Yet Sartre wanted to acknowledge and theorize oppression. Applying his account of competing looks to anti-Semitism, he claimed that anti-Semites strive to fix Jews permanently in the position of those looked at, never allowing Jews to look back.[31] This is a promising approach to oppression as consisting in the fixation of a group's members in the position of those who are looked at and objectified. But, given Sartre's ontology of freedom, it is unclear how any individual or group ever can be fixed in that position. This problem gives Beauvoir the task of taking forward Sartre's account of the master/slave dialectic of everyday lived relationships, while transforming this account to recognize group oppression.[32]

[29] Hegel says, "A self-consciousness is *for a self-consciousness*. Only so is it first self-consciousness in fact; for only in this way does the unity of itself in its otherness first come to be for it" (PS 3.108/¶177). Unity-with-self-in-the-other is one of Hegel's formulae for freedom or self-determination. Thus, for Hegel, self-consciousness already has freedom (unity-with-itself-in-otherness) but this only becomes so *for* it, i.e. becomes fully real and developed, through recognition.

[30] Sartre, *Being and Nothingness*, 550, 441. Prefiguring Sartre, Hegel claims that "if a people does not merely imagine that it wants to be free but actually has the energetic will to freedom, then no human power can hold it back in . . . servitude" (E §435A). I thank Dean Moyar for pointing this out to me.

[31] Sartre, *Anti-Semite and Jew*.

[32] For further argument that Beauvoir undertook this task, see Kruks, "Simone de Beauvoir: Teaching Sartre About Freedom."

31.4. Beauvoir

One of Beauvoir's achievements in *The Second Sex* is to provide a theoretical account of women's oppression. She rejects the Marxist explanation that women's oppression is a side effect of class inequalities, which fails to grasp that oppression in its own right. She also rejects the psychoanalytic explanation with reference to penis envy, which neglects the ways that subjects confer meaning on anatomical facts. And she rejects the biological explanation that women's reproductive function determines their subordinate status, which again neglects subjectivity. To construct her own explanation, as I shall reconstruct, Beauvoir employs Hegel's master/slave dialectic—which, following Kojève, she locates at the heart of Hegel's thought. Her entire reading of Hegel is informed by Kojève; she did not attend his lectures, but read his work with great interest.[33]

For Beauvoir, women have been defined as men's 'other' across history, as they still are today.

> Masculine and feminine appear symmetrical only as a matter of form, as on . . . legal papers. . . . [But actually] man represents both the positive and the neutral, to the point where in French we speak of *men* to designate human beings in general . . . [while] woman appears as the negative.[34]

Necessarily, to be the negative or other (*autre*) is to be other *from* something else that counts as the norm, point of reference, or comparison. Thus women are always understood in negative relation to men—as men's inferior counterpart, opposite, shadowy underside, and so on.

For Beauvoir, this status took root during the early period of hunter-gatherer societies. Without birth control, Beauvoir says, women in this period had to spend nearly all their time on childbearing, childbirth, breastfeeding, and infant care, while men hunted. By hunting, men were able to lay claim to transcendence. Following Kojève and Sartre, by 'transcendence' Beauvoir means going beyond the circumstances already given to us by creating and positing new values. In doing so, we establish our status as free existents who steer our own lives. By risking their lives in hunting, men established that they were free to overcome (to 'transcend') the goal of individual self-preservation that is given to us in our biology. Men instead privileged new, self-created values—conquering nature, securing the clan's future, winning glory and prowess, and so on. Men *decided* what to value and that they valued these values more than mere life. Meanwhile, being exhaustively occupied in gestation and child care, women could only maintain life—a goal supplied to women by their reproductive bodies without their having any choice about it. In Beauvoir's terms, women were confined to *immanence*—the status of merely

---

[33] See Lundgren-Gothlin, *Sex and Existence: Simone de Beauvoir's 'The Second Sex'*, 273. Beauvoir began to read Hegel in 1940, under Kojève's impact; see Bauer, *Simone de Beauvoir*, 86–87.

[34] Beauvoir, *The Second Sex*, 15.

reproducing and not surpassing life. Beauvoir thus takes up Kojève's contrast between risking life and merely preserving life, and aligns it with the division of labor between men and women in nomadic times.

In these conditions men began to position women as the other—inevitably so, because no individual or group can assert its free agency without opposing another individual or group.

> No group ever defines itself as One without immediately positing the Other that opposes it. If three travelers are by chance united in the same train compartment, that is enough to make all the other travelers become vaguely hostile 'others'. For the villager, all those not belonging to his village are 'strangers' and suspect; to the native of a country, the inhabitants of countries not his own appear as 'foreigners'. . . . Things become clear . . . if, following Hegel, we find in consciousness itself a fundamental hostility towards any other consciousness; the subject can only posit himself by opposing himself—he claims to affirm himself as the essential and to constitute the other as inessential, as object.[35]

Although Beauvoir imputes to Hegel the thesis that subjectivity requires antagonism, for Hegel that is true only of subjectivity at the developmental stage of self-consciousness; it is Sartre who maintains that subjectivity generally requires antagonism. Sartre's influence is also visible in Beauvoir's claim that ordinarily the other fights back, reasserting its agency: "The other consciousness . . . opposes to the first a reciprocal claim."

In hunter-gatherer times, women could not do that. Absorbed in immanence, they could not convincingly oppose men's othering of them by reciprocating with claims to free agency. In sum, women could not struggle for recognition. Beauvoir contrasts their position with that of Hegelian slaves as she understands it.[36] Slaves have lost the struggle for recognition, conceding that they favor life, and so they have been assigned their position as laborers, their proven attachment to mere life qualifying them only to work for the satisfaction of our material needs as living beings. Women do not lose the struggle in that way because they never even participate in it.[37] Consequently women can only submit, unresisting, to being positioned as 'other' to men.

Beauvoir, then, does not simply apply Hegel's master/slave dialectic to man/woman relations. Rather, she uses Hegel's narrative (as Kojève reconstructed it) to identify an alternative pathway along which recognition relations can become structured, not into master/slave relations but into a form where one group—women—becomes othered by failing ever to resist objectification. By returning to Hegel and Kojève, Beauvoir can thus explain, as Sartre could not, how a group can become fixed in the position of 'other' despite everyone's fundamental existential freedom. To claim freedom, one must be in a

---

[35] Ibid., 17.
[36] Ibid., 96.
[37] As Lundgren-Gothlin puts it, "Female human beings do not seek recognition; . . . man, in the relationship to woman, nurtures the hope of achieving confirmation without engaging in this kind of dialectics. . . . Woman has not raised a reciprocal demand for recognition" (*Sex and Existence*, 98).

position to perform the actions that support this claim, which in early conditions meant risking life (as per Kojève). But the nomadic division of labor prevented women from doing that. This is "how it is, then, that . . . reciprocity has not been established between the sexes, that one of the terms has affirmed itself as the only essential one . . . [and] that women have not contested male sovereignty."[38]

Once women had become 'other', a whole culture gradually accumulated that portrays women from men's perspectives—across myth, religion, art, science, and so on. Positioned in contrast to men, women have been cast as beings of nature not culture, puppets of biology not agents of their own existence, and thus suited neither for the public sphere nor the life of the mind. These accreted ideas keep women in the place of 'other' today, although the industrial and technological advances of modernity mean that risking life is no longer necessary for demonstrating free agency. Instead, one proves agency today by laboring—broadly following Kojève's vision of modernity in which labor and recognition are becoming universalized. For Beauvoir, this change from risk to labor potentially allows women to assert their agency at last, given the parallel development of abortion and contraception, which can free women to participate fully in paid work. However, entrenched ideas and myths about women's nature often continue to keep women in the private sphere. Thus even today, Beauvoir concludes, women are often in no position to lay claim to the free agency that they do in fact possess. This is no moral fault on their part. Rather, women's exclusion from the struggle for recognition is "inflicted upon" them and as such "it takes the shape of frustration and oppression."[39]

31.5. Fanon

At the same time as Beauvoir was theorizing women's oppression, but independently of her, Fanon likewise took up Hegel's master/slave dialectic, which he too read by way of Kojève and Sartre, to analyze racial oppression.[40] Fanon did so in *Black Skin, White Masks*, published in 1952 and written while he was studying medicine and psychiatry in Lyon (he had come to France from his native Martinique to fight with the Free French in World War II). The book ranges widely, covering language, inter-racial relationships, the psychology of colonialism—and including an essay "The Black Man and Hegel

---

[38] Beauvoir, *The Second Sex*, 18.

[39] Ibid., 29.

[40] It is not clear whether Fanon read Kojève directly or read Hegel through Kojèvian eyes only due to the influence of Sartre, especially his *Anti-Semite and Jew*. Ethan Kleinberg, though, shows that Fanon's view of recognition is so close to Kojève's that perhaps Fanon did read Kojève's *Mesures* piece; see Kleinberg, "Kojève and Fanon: The Desire for Recognition and the Fact of Blackness." Fanon did not read *The Second Sex*, but he read Beauvoir's account of her travels in America; see Macey, *Frantz Fanon: A Biography*, 124–126, 367. Beauvoir read Fanon's work only later, before meeting him in 1961. Thus the two did not influence one another; their affinities instead reflect their shared influences in Hegel, Kojève, and Sartre.

[*Le Nègre et Hegel*]"—on how far Hegel's master/slave dialectic applies to white/black relations.

Sartre's and Kojève's influences are apparent in how Fanon construes Hegel's conception of recognition:

> Man is human only to the extent to which he tries to impose himself on another man in order to be recognized by him ... [First] self-consciousness reaches the experience of *desire*, ... It agrees to risk life, and consequently threatens the other in his bodily being.... This risk implies that I surpass life [*dépasse la vie*] towards a supreme good ... I demand that I be taken into consideration on account of my desire. I am not merely here-now, locked in thinghood, I am for elsewhere and for something else.... I pursue something other than life....[41]

For Fanon, the human condition is for individuals to struggle for recognition adversarially. To be truly recognized, one must win recognition from the other through struggle rather than being granted recognition without having fought for it.[42] I fight for recognition by risking my life and threatening the other person. Unless I undertake this risk, I cannot possibly be recognized as one who freely *negates* life in favor of 'something else'.

Despite the antagonism of the struggle, Fanon regards it as an ideal human condition insofar as its two parties are in positions of reciprocity. "There is at the base of the Hegelian dialectic an absolute reciprocity that must be demonstrated."[43] *Each* tries to impose his own existence on the other, and when the other reciprocally tries to impose his existence, the first subject struggles to reverse the imposition. This struggle continues endlessly, for Fanon as for Sartre, with each party wishing to be 'absolute', to be the only one recognized as free. So, for Fanon, the reciprocity between the two strugglers is not that they reach equilibrium and recognize one another mutually. Rather, reciprocity obtains just when each party can keep struggling to be absolute, when I impose myself upon the other yet he fights back against me, incessantly.

Fanon deems this condition ideal, in contrast to the situation under colonialism, thus using Hegel's and Sartre's ideas to criticize the colonial system. Under colonialism, reciprocity is blocked: by being constructed *as* black, black people are prevented from ever asserting their freedom. Thus "[o]ntology is made unrealisable in a colonised ... society."[44] Colonial society prevents people from living in accordance with their ontological condition, which is to struggle for recognition reciprocally. Black people are prevented from exercising negation and so from ever claiming or winning freedom. White people cannot truly exercise negation either, for they never encounter any resistance against which to prove themselves—they are never 'othered', at least not by black people. Still,

---

[41] Fanon, *Black Skin, White Masks*, 191–193.

[42] Ibid., 194. This view that recognition must be wrested from the other, not passively received, is the germ of Fanon's later defense of anti-colonial violence in *The Wretched of the Earth*.

[43] Fanon, *Black Skin*, 191.

[44] Ibid., 89.

if colonialism distorts human existence universally, it distorts that of black people most deeply.

As Beauvoir held that women across history have been unable to participate in the struggle for recognition, then, Fanon's related claim is that under colonialism black people are precluded from struggling for recognition. Fanon explores this in his chapter "The Lived Experience of the Black Man [*l'expérience vécue du Noir*]", much of it written in the first person, and opening dramatically:

> "Dirty nigger!" or simply "Look! A Negro!" I came into this world anxious to uncover the meaning of things, my soul desirous to be at the origin of the world, and here I found myself an object among other objects. Locked into this crushing objectivity, I appealed to the other.... But ... the other fixes me, through his gestures, attitudes and looks [*regards*], in the way that one fixes a preparation with a dye.[45]

Like Sartre's man spying through the keyhole, Fanon is engaged in projects, anxious to disclose meanings in things in view of these projects (as a mountain might be disclosed as resistant in light of my project of climbing it). But Fanon finds himself looked at by the other, judged and classified as physical objects are. He appeals back for recognition. His appeal is not met; instead he finds himself fixed by the other's gaze—fixed in the race that the other attributes to him, as when a chemical mixture has a dye added to it. Fanon finds that he is seen as black, thus *not* as an agent. The racial attribution is what gives the other's look its fixity: Fanon is prevented from challenging the other's perception of him because he cannot escape from the racial category under which the (white) other views him.

It is not that Fanon is perceived as having a race that he already biologically has. Some of his perceptible physical properties—primarily his skin but perhaps his hair and facial features as well—are taken to mark him out as black. But it is not that these properties reveal the race that Fanon has already: Fanon denies that race categories have a biological basis. Rather, Fanon is *made* black—in the way that the chemical mixture has a dye *added* to it—by being inescapably perceived in terms of certain of his visible properties and above all his skin color. Fanon adds that to become black is to acquire an 'epidermal racial schema'. Ontologically, we each have a 'body schema': as embodied agents, we act in view of a tacit, practical model of the spatial field around us.[46] But, superimposed upon that schema, Fanon acquires a further schema that consists in his constant inhibiting awareness of being viewed in terms of his skin color, from the outside.

Whatever actions Fanon makes in appealing for recognition, those actions are referred back to his physical appearance, to which he finds himself unavoidably tied. His actions are seen in a particular light in view of the race to which he is assigned: these actions are differently evaluated, or differently interpreted; they may even literally be perceived differently. Take, for example, the little girl Pecola Breedlove in Toni Morrison's harrowing

[45] Ibid.
[46] Ibid., 92, 90.

novel *The Bluest Eye*, set in 1930s Ohio. In one of the many distressing episodes that Pecola suffers, she is visiting the household where her mother works as a servant and she reaches out tentatively toward a berry cobbler, only to knock it over, hurting herself with the hot juice but prompting her mother to slap her to the floor and shout at her ferociously. Pecola is not seen as having hurt herself and deserving sympathy but as being incorrigible, 'crazy', incapable of keeping to her place.[47]

Here there is a revealing difference from the predicament of Sartre's man spying through the keyhole. He was seen and judged in terms of the activity, spying, in which he was caught. The net of judgment in which he was caught centered on his *activity*, with reference to which he was classified as a voyeur or peeping Tom. He was a *transcendence*-transcended, in Sartre's language. In contrast, Fanon argues that black people are seen, judged, and classified in terms not simply of their activities but specifically of those activities as always referred back to, qualified with reference to, the visible physical appearance of their skin. But the latter is a merely objective property. It is not the objective side of an intentional activity, but is a property that *only* exists inasmuch as one is seen from the outside. Just in constantly having his activities referred back to his epidermal appearance from the outside, Fanon is made black. Meanwhile those whose activities are not so referred are made white—acquiring a racial identity that is characteristically *un*marked, *in*visible.

For Fanon, this process renders black people powerless to resist objectification. To claim recognition, I must prove that I exercise *transcendence* or *negation*. I must show that *I* decide the meaning of my existence, rather than its meaning being bestowed by the other. Since others are invariably looking at me, establishing my agency thus requires that I negate the meanings that others have already bestowed on me. To prove my agency is to show, in action, that I always surpass others' perceptions of me. This the black person cannot do, Fanon reasons, because he is "locked in his body":[48] his acts are always perceived with reference to and in light of his perceptible epidermal appearance, as acts by white people are not. In that way, black people are never permitted to escape from their visibility to the other's perspective. The possibility of their actions negating that perspective is cut off at the outset.

Racial hierarchy has a different structure from sexual hierarchy as Beauvoir understands it. For Beauvoir, across history the division of labor has prevented women from performing the kinds of action—risk, labor—that demonstrate agency at a given time. For Fanon, whatever actions black people perform, they are still fundamentally perceived in terms of their visible appearance from the outside, and thus are prevented from making convincing counter-claims to define themselves from the inside. Further indicating the difference between Beauvoir's and Fanon's analyses, Fanon denies that it is ideas about race that exclude black people from the struggle for recognition: "I am a slave not to the 'idea' others have of me, but to my appearance" (Fanon's concern here is to distinguish colonial racism from anti-Semitism).[49] For Beauvoir, in contrast,

---

[47] Morrison, *The Bluest Eye*, 84–85.
[48] Fanon, *Black Skin*, 200.
[49] Ibid., 95.

accumulated myths and ideas about women have led them to be more or less restricted to the private sphere and so unable to participate fully in labor and claim agency through it. To be sure, Fanon does identify accumulated meanings that the colonial nations attach to being black: backwardness, cannibalism, evil, ugliness, closeness to animals, dangerous savagery, brute strength. Overall, "in Europe the black man has one function: to represent lower feelings, base urges, the dark side of the soul."[50] But for Fanon, these meanings only attach to being black on the basis of this identity first being constituted by the look.

Although Beauvoir and Fanon give different accounts of the mechanisms by which women and black people are oppressed, they both conceive these forms of oppression as having distinctive structures in their own right.[51] Refusing to reduce these oppressions to biology or economics, they turn to Hegel as filtered via Kojève to grasp these oppressions as consisting of distortions in the relations of recognition that are fundamental to human existence. Gender and racial oppression, then, are ultimately forms of recognition injustice—but they are no less real for that. However, they are particular forms of recognition injustice, different from the master/slave relation. Neither group has lost the struggle and become subjugated on that basis, as Hegelian slaves did. Instead, both groups have been debarred from participating in the struggle in the first place. So the ideal human condition from which women and black people have unjustly been excluded is, ironically, that of the struggle between looks as Sartre theorized it—ideal because of its reciprocity. Beauvoir and Fanon thus give this struggle a more optimistic, Hegelian cast than Sartre gave it. The struggle against others is not hell: much better to take part in this struggle and share in full humanity than to be stuck outside the struggle in second-class status.[52]

31.6. IRIGARAY

For the post-structuralist generation, Hegel is the philosopher of identity, in particular the identity-with-itself that the self-conscious subject achieves by satisfying its desires.

---

[50] Ibid., 167.

[51] The phrase "women and black people" is unsatisfactory: as many black feminists have pointed out, some women are black and some black people are women. I use this phrase nonetheless to reflect a limitation of Beauvoir's and Fanon's views: Beauvoir takes white women as the norm, Fanon takes black men as the norm.

[52] Actually, in Beauvoir's ideal condition each subject asserts its agency *and* admits its being-for-other, which together make up its ambiguity. In this way each subject opens itself to the look while looking back as well. Fanon stresses more how central agency is to the human condition. However, he vacillates over the merits of *Négritude*, the literary and political movement to revalue black culture and identity. Fanon fears that *Négritude* may further trap black people in their race. But he also wonders whether, since this racial status is inescapable anyway, *Négritude* might be the only way for black people to reclaim subjectivity by making their race itself something whose meaning they freely define (Fanon, *Black Skin*, 101–119).

Again following Kojève's lead, the account of self-consciousness in *Phenomenology* IV and IVA is construed as being centrally revealing about Hegel's overarching orientation toward identity. Against identity, post-structuralists value difference: as Deleuze puts it, in a "generalised anti-Hegelianism ... difference and repetition have taken the place of the identical and the negative, of identity and contradiction."[53] For Hegel, difference seems to exist as part of or on the way toward identity—be it the difference between life and self-consciousness which the subject negates in desire, or the difference between master and servant which must cede way to reciprocal recognition. In contrast specifically to Hegel, post-structuralists set out to think of difference as ontologically prior to identity and, ethically, to avoid subordinating difference to identity. This difference assumes various more concrete guises: the differential play of power relations (Foucault), of language (Derrida) or language-games (Lyotard), pure becoming (Deleuze), multiplicity (Badiou), or sexual difference (Irigaray). It might be objected that, far from privileging identity, the characteristic movement of Hegel's dialectic is to incorporate *both* what initially claims self-identity (e.g., 'I', self-consciousness) and what differs from it (e.g., the other) into broader, unifying structures (e.g., the 'We'). But for post-structuralists that 'We' remains a '*We* that is *I*' (PS 9.108/¶177), an 'I' that has only become 'We' by expanding to take in the other. This exemplifies the overall movement of Hegel's thought: to absorb difference into the self-same.

This critique of Hegel's conception of the self-conscious subject may seem to leave the basis of Beauvoir's and Fanon's theories undermined and their work discredited. But that conclusion would be too hasty. To see why, let's consider Irigaray's philosophy of sexual difference, an instance of positive post-structuralist engagement with Hegel. Moreover, Irigaray also engages positively with Beauvoir's view of sexual hierarchy as a deformation in recognition relations. Thus Irigaray's work testifies to Hegel's continuing positive importance for French thought.

Irigaray shares Beauvoir's conviction that women have been positioned as 'other' throughout Western cultural history and remain so today. The "'feminine' is always described as lack, atrophy, reverse of the sex that alone holds a monopoly on value."[54] By way of Beauvoir, Irigaray's overall conception of women's subordination thus comes out of the French tradition of reading Hegel. But Irigaray differs from Beauvoir on what makes women's othering unjust. For Irigaray, its injustice is—paradoxical as it might sound—that women have been positioned as *the same* as men but in reverse, or 'less so', an inferior version of the same. Women's status has been that of the other-of-the-same: an other constantly referred or adversely compared to the 'same' (i.e., the masculine position taken as norm and standard). While Beauvoir had already effectively recognized this, unlike Beauvoir, Irigaray concludes that women need to assume a new subjective position as the other-of-the-other—to cease to be men's inferior correlate (the other-of-the-same) and assume a *sui generis* identity as women. That identity would be different from—other to—women's traditional position as men's other. Irigaray aspires

---

[53] Deleuze, *Difference and Repetition*, xix.
[54] Irigaray, *This Sex Which Is Not One*, 69.

for women to belong to a sex/gender or kind that genuinely differs from the male kind: what is needed is recognition of genuine sexual difference.

This vision clearly diverges from Beauvoir's. Beauvoir aspires for women to join in the struggle for recognition and share with men in the continual movement between the two poles of the subject/object, self/other ambiguity. This positive valuation of reciprocity descends to Beauvoir from Hegel, via Sartre's insistence on irresolvable antagonism. Irigaray rejects that valuation of reciprocity, as we see from her alternative vision of ideal relationships between sexed individuals in *I Love to You*, one of the books where she engages with Hegel most extensively.[55]

Here Irigaray claims that each sex should accomplish the 'labor of the negative' toward itself.[56] To do so is to depart from our inherent tendency to negate the other: to refuse to let the other exist as other and instead try to absorb the other into the self, to declare "I am the whole." To negate oneself is to negate that tendency and so allow the other to be other. Irigaray is indebted to a broadly Sartrean-Kojèvian-Hegelian view that each consciousness finds the other threatening to its own agency and so seeks to make that other into its mere vehicle or appendage, resulting in master/slave relations. For Hegel, though, we ultimately must recognize one another as agents and, instead of partitioning body and agency unequally between us, we must recognize that we are all embodied agents. Irigaray agrees. But she asks: must we not, then, all accept that we are *sexually* embodied? We do not have bodies in the neuter—we have male or female bodies (a minority of people are intersexed, but let's bracket this). Moreover, as subjects, we *are* our bodies. My sexed embodiment does not sit idly by while I act, feel, think, and so on; my embodiment inevitably qualifies and affects the mode of my subjectivity.

On these grounds, Irigaray contests Hegel's view that the two parties to the struggle for recognition are in symmetrical positions, whereby the action of each is "indivisibly the action of one as well as of the other" (PS 3.148/112). If I, a woman, am relating in some way to a man (not necessarily romantically—we might, say, be in intellectual or political dialogue), I cannot rightly assume that he will make toward me the same subjective movements that I make toward him. Yet, Irigaray thinks, I *do* tend to assume that the sexed other will relate to me as I do to him: I project my own form of subjectivity upon everyone else. Instead, I should cultivate my ability to be open to the other however he or she may manifest him- or herself—an attitude of wonder, as Irigaray sometimes puts it.[57]

Overall, for Irigaray, each sexed individual should perform upon him- or herself a negating movement—negating his or his propensity to assimilate the other sex. I do not try to transcend the other; instead I acknowledge that he or she transcends *me*.[58] For Beauvoir and Fanon, the solution to the othering of women and black people was

[55] On Irigaray's engagement with Hegel, see Stone, *Luce Irigaray and the Philosophy of Sexual Difference*, ch. 5.

[56] Irigaray, *I Love to You*, 36.

[57] Ibid., 39.

[58] Ibid., 105.

to open up the recognition struggle to reciprocal participation by all. Irigaray departs further from Hegel's ideal of reciprocity by aspiring for sexed individuals to accept one another in their irreducible difference.

Nevertheless, Irigaray does not wholly reject Hegel's ideal of reciprocal recognition. First, she envisages *each* sex exercising negativity upon itself. To be sure, she anticipates that each sex will carry out that exercise differently.[59] Moreover, she maintains that the urge to assimilate the other arises for each sex along different routes (threatened by being born of mothers, young boys become accustomed to negate what is other, whereas girls never properly extricate themselves from their mothers to appreciate that others are other). But second, Irigaray explicitly states that each sex is to *recognize* the other as irreducibly different. This is necessary, she agrees with Hegel, to overcome master/slave relations.[60] Yet this is a recognition of difference, of what is irreducibly other to the self and beyond its ken. Recognition is the way for us to value difference in its own right and as irreducibly real. If this ideal sounds non- or anti-Hegelian in that it ranks difference above identity, on the other hand Irigaray's ideal is for sexed differences to be held together within a broader structure of reciprocal recognition—a distinctly Hegelian vision.

Thus, Irigaray's ethics of sexual difference descends from Hegel's vision of reciprocal recognition. This is indicative that existential-Hegelianism remains important for French thought after post-structuralism—not only as a foil against which post-structuralists define themselves, but also positively, as a source of ideas that continue to inform. To be sure, post-structuralist insights into the value and ontological reality of difference pose problems for anyone who would endorse existential-Hegelian ideas wholesale. But we should not reject those ideas wholesale either. Existential-Hegelian ideas about the human need for recognition, and how distortions in recognition are constitutive of harmful sexual and racial hierarchies, remain an inescapable starting point for thinking critically about these hierarchies and how we might overcome them.

Works Cited

Badiou, Alain. *Being and Event*, translated by Oliver Feltham. London: Continuum, 2005.

Bauer, Nancy. *Simone de Beauvoir, Philosophy and Feminism*. New York: Columbia University Press, 2001.

Baugh, Bruce. *French Hegel: From Surrealism to Postmodernism*. New York: Routledge, 2003.

Beauvoir, Simone de. *The Second Sex*, translated by H. M. Parshley. London: Picador, 1953.

Butler, Judith. *Subjects of Desire: Hegelian Reflections in Twentieth-Century France*. New York: Columbia University Press, 1987.

Deleuze, Gilles. *Difference and Repetition*, translated by Paul Patton. New York: Columbia University Press, 1994.

Fanon, Frantz. *Black Skin, White Masks*, translated by Richard Philcox. New York: Grove, 2008.

---

[59] Ibid., 27.
[60] Ibid., 105.

Fanon, Frantz. *The Wretched of the Earth*, translated by Constance Farringdon. New York: Grove Press, 1963.

Foucault, Michel. "The Discourse on Language," in *The Archaeology of Knowledge and the Discourse on Language*, translated by A. M. Sheridan Smith. New York: Pantheon, 1972, 215–238.

Fraser, Nancy. "From Redistribution to Recognition? Dilemmas of Justice in a 'Post-Socialist' Age." *New Left Review* I, no. 212 (1995): 68–93.

Fry, Christopher M. *Sartre and Hegel*. Bonn: Bouvier, 1988.

Hegel, G. W. F. *Phenomenology of Spirit* [PS]. Translated by A. V. Miller. Oxford: Oxford University Press, 1977.

Irigaray, Luce. 1996. *I Love to You*, translated by Alison Martin. London: Athlone.

Irigaray, Luce. *This Sex Which Is Not One*, translated by Catherine Porter. Ithaca, NY: Cornell University Press, 1985.

Kleinberg, Ethan. "Kojève and Fanon: The Desire for Recognition and the Fact of Blackness," in *French Civilization and Its Discontents*, edited by Tyler Stovall et al. Lanham, MD: Lexington Books, 2003, 115–128.

Kojève, Alexandre. *Introduction to the Reading of Hegel*, translated by James H. Nichols. New York: Basic Books, 1969.

Kruks, Sonia. "Simone de Beauvoir: Teaching Sartre About Freedom," in *Feminist Interpretations of Simone de Beauvoir*, edited by Margaret A. Simons. University Park: Penn State Press, 1995, 79–96.

Lundgren-Gothlin, Eva. *Sex and Existence: Simone de Beauvoir's 'The Second Sex'*, translated by Linda Schenck. London: Athlone, 1996.

Macey, David. *Frantz Fanon: A Biography*. London: Verso, 2000.

Malabou, Catherine. *What Should We Do with Our Brain?* Translated by Sebastian Rand. New York: Fordham University Press, 2008.

Morrison, Toni. *The Bluest Eye*. New York: Vintage, 1970.

Rockmore, Tom. "Hegel in France," in *The Bloomsbury Companion to Hegel*, edited by Allegra de Laurentiis and Jeffrey Edwards. New York: Bloomsbury, 2013, 321–328.

Roth, Michael S. *Knowing and History: Appropriations of Hegel in Twentieth-Century France*. Ithaca, NY: Cornell University Press, 1988.

Russon, John. "Dialectic, Difference, and the Other: The Hegelianizing of French Phenomenology," in *Phenomenology: Responses and Developments*, edited by Leonard Lawlor. Durham, UK: Acumen, 2010, 17–42.

Sartre, Jean-Paul. *Anti-Semite and Jew*, translated by George J. Becker. New York: Schocken, 1965.

Sartre, Jean-Paul. *Being and Nothingness*, translated by Hazel E. Barnes. London: Routledge, 1958.

Sartre, Jean-Paul. *No Exit and Three Other Plays*. New York: Vintage, 1989.

Stone, Alison. *Luce Irigaray and the Philosophy of Sexual Difference*. Cambridge: Cambridge University Press, 2006.

CHAPTER 32

···

HEGEL AND THE FRANKFURT SCHOOL

···

JAMES GORDON FINLAYSON

32.1. INTRODUCTION

THERE are two sets of important issues underlying the topic "Hegel and the Frankfurt School." The first concerns the way in which the various Frankfurt School thinkers interpret and evaluate Hegel's philosophy. For they were among a minority of philosophers in Germany who were interested in and engaged with Hegel's philosophy at a time when it had fallen out of favor. This was in part due to the rise of empiricism, positivism, and the natural sciences, but also to the erroneous accusation that Hegel's philosophy had influenced Nazi ideology, which cast a shadow over Hegel's philosophy, so that in England and the United States it was roundly denounced as illiberal and proto-totalitarian.[1] In this period, three members of the so-called inner circle of the Institute for Social Research—Max Horkheimer, Herbert Marcuse, and Theodor Adorno—wrote studies on Hegel, and made important contributions to Hegel scholarship. More recently, 'second-generation' and 'third-generation' Frankfurt School theorists such as Jürgen Habermas and Axel Honneth have continued the tradition of writing about Hegel.[2]

---

[1] See K. R. Popper, *The Open Society and Its Enemies*, Vol II; Isaiah Berlin's, "Two Concepts of Liberty" (1958). In the original inaugural lecture as Chichele Professor of Social and Political Theory at Oxford, Berlin claims, "A socialised form of this belief (in positive liberty GF) has taken many contemporary forms: nationalism, Marxism, Hegelianism, authoritarianism of various types, as well as what has been called totalitarian democracy (Isaiah Berlin, "Two Concepts of Liberty' Original Dictation," The Isaiah Berlin virtual Library, http://berlin.wolf.ox.ac.uk/published_works/tcl/).

[2] Jürgen Habermas's *Theory and Practice* contains three important essays on Hegel which he wrote in the 1960s. Axel Honneth's work on Hegel includes *The Struggle for Recognition* (1995); *The Pathologies of Individual Freedom: Hegel's Social Theory* (2010); and *Freedom's Right* (2014). I use the terms 'second' and 'third' generation here as a now accepted shorthand, but this nomenclature homogenizes and hides the all-important discontinuities between the earlier and later thinkers.

The second set of issues concerns Hegel's influence on the theoretical work of the Frankfurt School thinkers that came to be known as 'critical theory', as the philosophies of the Frankfurt School thinkers were inspired and shaped by their respective interpretations of Hegel. It is worth considering why the first-generation Frankfurt theorists held Hegel's philosophy to be so important. What was it about Hegel's philosophy, and the Frankfurt School critical theorists, that gave rise to the magnetic attraction between them? One reason is that, as Habermas noted, these thinkers were at bottom Marxists, who rejected the supposedly 'scientific' conception of Marxism of Karl Kautsky and Eduard Bernstein, and were enthused by the pioneering works by Georg Lukács and Karl Korsch, *History and Class-Consciousness*, and *Marxism and Philosophy*, respectively, both of which were published in 1923, and put a renewed focus on the dialectic and its origins in Hegel.[3] The second reason is the resurgence of interest in the young Marx's relation to Hegel, prompted by the publication in 1932 of Marx's *Economic and Philosophical Manuscripts of 1844*, a text that Marcuse was one of the first to review (HM 86–122). A third, equally decisive factor, was that, in the first half of the twentieth century neo-Kantianism in one tradition or other was the dominant philosophical paradigm in Europe. Against the backdrop of neo-Kantianism, Hegel, who had developed the most nuanced and powerful criticisms of Kant, looked like a natural ally for anyone trying to break away from the predominant neo-Kantian paradigms.[4]

32.2. HORKHEIMER AND HEGEL

32.2.1. Horkheimer's Interpretation of Hegel

In his lectures of the mid-1920s, Horkheimer construes Hegel's philosophy from three perspectives: as the culmination of German Idealism and the development of its underlying metaphysics of the identity between subject and object (MHGS 10, 154–155); as the critique of Kantian critical philosophy, its overcoming and ultimate betrayal (of its task of limiting the claims of metaphysics); and as the simultaneous completion and exhaustion of the paradigm of rationalist metaphysics.

---

[3] Marcuse explicitly attacks Bernstein in *Reason and Revolution*, 398–399.

[4] As Gillian Rose puts it in *Hegel contra Sociology*, "the Marxism of the Frankfurt School . . . [is] . . . motivated by the desire to break out of the constrictions of the neo-Kantian paradigm" (Rose, *Hegel contra Sociology*, 1). Rose, in my view, mistakenly thinks that even the Frankfurt School Marxist thinkers were fundamentally neo-Kantians. In *Hegel contra Sociology*, she proposes to revivify Hegel's absolute idealism as a tonic against the latent neo-Kantianism of all sociology, including the critical theory of the Frankfurt School. By comparison, as we will see, Horkheimer, Marcuse, and Adorno are all far more critical and more cautious in their embrace of Hegel's philosophy than is Rose. Indeed, she might be guilty of the error for which Horkheimer criticizes Wilhelm Windelband, who maintained that the then contemporary debate between neo-Kantians and neo-Hegelians merely rehearses the development of philosophy from Kant through German Idealism to Hegel, an argument which Horkheimer rightly claims "abstracts from the historically decisive context" (Horkheimer, MHGS 10, 106).

In his first lecture as a Privatdozent at the University of Frankfurt, Horkheimer reads Hegel's critique of Kant in the light of a contemporary philosophical problem.[5] The problem, as he sees it, consists in Kant's renouncing metaphysics in favor of epistemology. What this does, he maintains, is to buy epistemological certainties at the price of emptying philosophy of positive metaphysical content. We cannot go into the details of Horkheimer's Kant interpretation, nor can we investigate his assessment of the relation of neo-Kantianism to Kant. Suffice it to say that Horkheimer was schooled in neo-Kantianism, and wrote his D Phil and Habilitation thesis on Kant, and the problem he outlines applies to the whole area of Kantian and neo-Kantian thought. According to Horkheimer, Hegel responds to Kant's reduction of metaphysics to epistemology by turning criticism against the critical philosophy itself, by biting the bullet and proclaiming consciousness "as the final, itself unconditioned reality, . . . as the sole true and actual being" in such a way that epistemology becomes metaphysics once more (MHGS 11, 112). "Had Kant," argues Horkheimer, "not only criticized natural experience, but also reflected on critical thought itself, he would have been forced to understand that critical thought itself is not bound by any limitations, and thus metaphysics is born of critique: it has become knowledge of the absolutely unconditioned" (MHGS 11, 113).

Although in these lectures Horkheimer sides with Hegel's criticisms of Kant, we know that he was far from enthused by Hegel's own conclusions, and was no advocate of a return to metaphysics. His overall position is certainly not a Hegelian one, nor even some kind of interim position between Kant and Hegel. Rather, he advocates a neither/nor: neither a Kantian reduction of metaphysics to epistemology, nor Hegel's rebirth of metaphysics out of the spirit of critical philosophy; neither the formal but empty certainties of Kant's philosophy of consciousness, nor Hegel's absolute idealism. As Gunzelin Schmid Noerr puts it, "From this point forth the problem for Horkheimer consists in the attempt to break out from the restriction of philosophy to epistemology in the aftermath of Kant without however regressing to metaphysics in the aftermath of Hegel. For Horkheimer's basic conviction is that after Hegel metaphysics as a discrete philosophical terrain becomes obsolete" (MHGS 11, 411).

32.2.1.1. *Horkheimer and Lukács's Critique of the Antinomies of Bourgeois Philosophy*

Horkheimer's early lectures were composed just after the publication of Lukács's *History and Class-Consciousness*, which was a work of tremendous significance in its time, and one with which Horkheimer was familiar. It seems likely that Horkheimer's talk of "a presently emerging problem" and of the current oscillation between Hegelianism and Kantianism is a reference to Lukács's essay on "Reification and the Consciousness of the Proletariat", for Lukács was the highest profile thinker of the era to attempt to find

---

[5] Abromeit, in what is the most comprehensive account in English of Horkheimer's early work, persuasively argues that Horkheimer attempts to break away from the philosophy of consciousness, and work toward a 'materialist interpretation' of the history modern philosophy. Abromeit, *Max Horkheimer and the Foundations of the Frankfurt School*, 85–92.

neo-Hegelian solutions to problems with the then dominant neo-Kantianism, without merely returning to Hegel (HCC 120/GK 224).

In the second part of the "Reification" essay, Lukács asserts that all modern German philosophy from Kant to Hegel, arose out of "the reified structure of consciousness" and was faced with two basic problems:

> There is, firstly, the problem of matter (in the logical, technical sense), the problem of the content of those forms with the aid of which 'we' know and are able to know the world because we have created it ourselves. And, secondly, there is the problem of the whole and of the ultimate substance of knowledge, the problem of those 'ultimate' objects of knowledge which are needed to round off the partial systems into a totality, a system of the perfectly understood world. (HC115/GK 215)

Lukács contends that the resolution of these twin problems called for the formulation of a system, a project which itself falls prey to what he understands as the *antinomy of form and content*. Either the content is deduced from the form—in which case the world is rational but contentless; or the irrational content is given to form, in which case the 'system' dissolves into a passive 'register' of external content. In the former case, there is a system, but it remains empty and formalistic; in the latter case there is no system at all, but a mere register of an aggregate of antecedently constituted facts (HC 115/GK 215).

Lukács's discussion of this antinomy, which he sees as the fundamental problem of bourgeois philosophy, has a very wide sweep. In brief, he sees the four major developments from Kant to Hegel as failed solutions to the antimony: (1) Kant's Copernican revolution in epistemology; (2) Kant's (and Fichte's) thesis of the primacy of practical reason; (3) the Romantic turn to the ideal of organic wholeness in the philosophy of nature and art; and finally (4) Hegel's turn to history and the dialectic. It is Hegel, argues Lukács, who comes closest to resolving the problem (of how to conceive the unity of form and content without reducing the one to another) by means of the dialectical method, and by means of a historical analysis of "the underlying order and the connections between things." However, he claims, Hegel believed wrongly that spirit had already accomplished its work via "the cunning of reason" and had come to an end in the Prussian state. He also failed to make clear the relation in which history (and the historical dialectic) stands to absolute spirit. So, although he gave the antinomies of bourgeois thought "the highest possible intellectual expression," he ultimately fell back into the reified and contemplative attitude of bourgeois consciousness, providing merely an 'intellectual copy' and 'a priori deduction' of bourgeois society (HC 148/GK 266).

Lukács's account of the antinomy of form and content bears interesting comparison with the 'current problem' Horkheimer sets out in his "Kant and Hegel" lecture. What is required on Horkheimer's view is an account of the world as a mediated relation of form and content. However, according to Kant, the world consists in the unity of 'heterogeneous factors': the forms of the understanding and reason on the one hand, and a 'meaningless and chaotic' material on the other, and he fails, Horkheimer contends, to explain how this unity is achieved. By contrast, Hegel offers a substantial, historical explanation of why the relation of form to content "is not a contingent one." He does this by demonstrating that "the abstract Kantian forms of understanding are the product of an analysis of the concrete material world" (MHGS 11, 115). Like Lukács, Horkheimer sees this as the achievement of the dialectical method, which develops from abstraction toward concretion in the form a system of actuality manifest in nature and history (MHGS 11, 116). Horkheimer also follows Lukács closely in bringing Hegel's Kant criticism to bear on contemporary neo-Kantian paradigms of philosophy.

However, he parts company decisively from the Hungarian in his conclusion. For Lukács goes on to argue that the antinomy of bourgeois consciousness can only be solved once the proletariat constitutes itself as a class, and grasps itself as the subject-object of history and as the revolutionary agent. Horkheimer counters that this neo-Hegelian 'solution' suffers from the exactly same flaws as the Hegelian metaphysics that inspired it. It remains within the framework of the philosophy of history, and the philosophy of consciousness. Not only does it hypostatize history as a unitary process, it falsely personifies the proletariat. It is, in the final analysis, a re-application of the monistic metaphysics of identity to the Marxist theory of class struggle.[6]

32.2.1.2. *Horkheimer and the Criticism of Hegel's Metaphysics*

By the 1930s, Horkheimer's own criticisms of Hegel had crystallized. In "Hegel and the Problem of Metaphysics," he levels objections to what he holds to be the keystone of the metaphysics of German Idealism, still present in Hegel, the identity of subject and object. The identity thesis, maintains Horkheimer, grounds the knowledge of individual objects in the knowledge of the totality. It supports (1) the idea that knowledge is a systemic unity; (2) the idea of philosophy as an ascending order of stages; (3) the idea of the development of history of spirit, as a totality governed by necessity; and (4) the organic composition of all its domains. Once the ultimate ground—the identity of subject and object—falls away, so does everything it supports. Along with the identity thesis, Horkheimer rejects Hegel's monism: there is no such thing as Being as such; the notion of Being is a hypostatization, no more than a construct out of plurality of individual beings. Moreover, there is no such thing as Thought as such. Thought as such "is only ever the determinate thought of a determinate individual person" (HPM, 89). In the same vein, Horkheimer denies there is anything such as History as such, or Nature as such. All these totalities, by virtue of which the great totality—the subject-object—is determined, Horkheimer contends, are meaningless abstractions (HPM, 90).

Furthermore, Horkheimer rejects the methodological 'transfiguration' of the empirical contributions of the individual specialized sciences into absolute knowledge. Empirical theory, he maintains, is of a completely different kind of metaphysical

---

[6] "Lukács too . . . connects the knowledge of the totality to a subject-object, albeit in contrast to absolute spirit, to the practical manifestation of the class-consciousness of the proletariat; thus he too cleaves to the identity as the condition of the possibility of truth, and thus makes a supra-individual unity into the bearer of both knowledge and history" (Horkheimer, cited by Gunzelin Schmid Noerr, MHGS 11, 223).

knowledge, namely the divine self-knowledge of the all-encompassing absolute spirit, into which Hegel attempts to transfigure it by means of the dialectic. "The opposition between empiricism and metaphysics, between the epitome of the most manifold experiential knowledge, that is theoretically mediated and ordered according to a whole variety of perspectives, and the supposed insight into an independent order of being, cannot be 'overcome'" (HPM 94). The empirically won insights of a plurality of distinct disciplines, the natural and the social and historical sciences, are indeed partial and defeasible, but do not stand in need of being elevated into the a priori truths of metaphysics. After the fall of metaphysics, the natural and social sciences must stand on their own ground.

The notion of 'transfiguration [*Verklärung*]' is central to Horkheimer's critique of metaphysics.[7] The idea is multidimensional, but its core meaning is the projection of an illusory realm in which real and persisting contradictions appear to be overcome. It has both theoretical and practical dimensions. Theoretically speaking, Horkheimer contends, Hegel sets out to 'transfigure' the empirical and natural sciences, by shaping them into the systematic and logical forms of absolute spirit conceived as the 'completion of truth'. Although Hegel develops his categories dynamically, the final end of this development is an order of categories, and a "constant relation between concept and reality" that is immutable, like that of all previous rationalist metaphysics (TRD 218). The dialectic, as well as the real history that subtends it, is supposed to culminate in the final end of the absolute idea. So although Hegel rightly claims that neither experience nor history can be transcended, in claiming that they have already been completed, he traduces them nonetheless. As Horkheimer puts it, Hegel's "dialectic is closed" (TRD 239; HP 115). Hegel thus seals off knowledge (and history) from further experience, and generates an illusion in the form of a "conceptual eternalization of the earthly relationships on which it was based" (OPT 187). Practically speaking, the projection of an illusory realm in which suffering is ended, and final meaning and satisfaction granted, provides a justification of the present suffering of real individuals. The subject-object identity, and the concept of absolute knowing, is the criterion by means of which Hegel distinguishes between existence and actuality, and grounds the rationality of the actual. Note that Horkheimer interprets Hegel's *Doppelsatz* in the Preface to the Philosophy of Right—"What is rational is actual: and what is actual is rational"—as a theodicy of existing society (i.e., as a blanket justification of the status quo).[8] Hegel's idealist metaphysics of identity, Horkheimer argues, supports his apologetic social theory: philosophical extravagance leads to political conservatism.

---

[7] See Rush, "The Conceptual Foundations of Early Critical Theory," 13; and Abromeit, *Max Horkheimer and the Foundations of the Frankfurt School*, 319.

[8] Hegel, PR, 14,1.14/20. Horkheimer modulates his interpretation by construing the second sentence as one that, were it not for the subject-object identity thesis, would contradict the first. Hegel's idea of a rational actuality is an ideal that is betrayed by the false claim that it already obtains. Nevertheless, the upshot, he claims, is that Hegel "sanctions the way of the world by means of pure thought; for the claim that everything actual is rational implies that it is in order" (Horkheimer, "Hegel und Das Problem der Metaphysik," 84).

32.2.2. Hegel's Influence on Horkheimer

32.2.2.1. *Materialist History of Philosophy*

The first place in Horkheimer's work where Hegel's influence is to be found is his project in the mid-1920s for a materialist history of philosophy. Horkheimer claims that the resources for understanding German Idealism lie just as much "in the disciplines of history, philology and sociology" as they do in philosophy (MHGS 11, 105). His approach to modern philosophy in general (and the philosophy of history in particular) is to show how it emerged in the context of the emancipation of the bourgeoisie from the twin yokes of feudalism and the established Church (BPSS 314). Hegel famously wrote in the Introduction to the *History of Philosophy*, that just like a nation's manners or science, philosophy is a matter of tradition, which itself is not like a 'statue' diligently tended by a housekeeper, but rather a "material which is to be transformed by spirit."[9] The lesson Horkheimer draws from Hegel is the following:

> The intellectual life of individuals is bound up with the life process of the social body of which they are a part, and which determines their activity.... This is why it is impossible to understand the content or nature of people's intellectual make up, without knowledge of the epoch in which they live . . . or indeed . . . the specific position they occupy in the social production process. (BPSS 360–361)

To be sure the influence of Marx is also present, in particular his view in *The German Ideology* that the "class which has the means of material production at its disposal, has control at the same time over the means of mental production, so that thereby, generally speaking, the ideas of those who lack the means of mental production are subject to it."[10] But Marx is nowhere mentioned by name, and Hegel is the chief source from which Horkheimer draws.

32.2.2.2. *Dialectical Logic*

Another place where the influence of Hegel on Horkheimer is significant is the dialectical and materialist 'logic' he attempted to develop in the 1930s. Materialism, Horkheimer claims—and by this he has in mind both Marx's dialectic and his own—"is schooled in Hegel's Logic" (BPSS 234). By this remark, Horkheimer means that philosophy should not proceed by fixing the meaning of singular terms, and then subjecting them to a scheme of invariable and repeatable procedures. This is because, as he puts it, "abstraction and analysis are transformative activities" (BPSS 234). As with the sentences of ordinary language, the meaning of individual terms is modified by those around it.

---

[9] "This tradition is not merely like a housekeeper who diligently looks after what she has received and hence preserves and hands it down to her descendants like statues . . . rather the tradition of what the spiritual world has brought forth swells like a mighty stream and grows larger the further away from its source it advances" (Hegel W 18, 36–37).

[10] *Marx—Engels—Werke*, vol. 3, 16.

Horkheimer's dialectical logic remained unfinished, but the lineaments are of Hegelian provenance. Horkheimer proposes to proceed, like Hegel and Marx, by developing concepts from their most abstract form into determinate representation of a concrete, individual whole (BPSS 236–237). This development takes the form of a presentation (*Darstellung*) of a material that has already been empirically researched (*Forschung*). Negatively, this presentation involves the "continuous critique of abstract determinations," a theme common to Hegel's and Marx's procedures (BPSS, 236, 239). Positively, it is harder to say what this *Darstellung* involves. Horkheimer denies that the philosophical presentation of the material constitutes a system, as it did in Hegel. And he denies that philosophy is the final arbiter of truth, but sees it as ancillary to the social and historical sciences (BPSS, 240). Already in his lecture on German Idealism, he observed that "the most important successor of this philosophical process (i.e. Marx's dialectic) no longer belongs to the history of philosophy" (MHGS 10, 103). In other words, Horkheimer's conception of dialectical materialist logic looks like a modified Hegelianism continued by other—non-philosophical—means.[11]

32.2.2.3. *Critical Theory of Society*

Some of the main ideas of Horkheimer's dialectal logic find their way into his seminal essay "Traditional and Critical Theory," now seen as the founding text of Frankfurt School critical theory. One basic theme of the essay is that knowledge is socially constituted and has a social function. Traditional science and forms of knowledge, Horkheimer claims, are—unbeknownst to the knowers—"moments in the social process of production" (TCT 197). Like Hegel, Horkheimer holds that both knowledge and the known world are "shaped by human activity" and that they are properly understood as moments in an unfolding social whole (TCT 195). Even the naturalness of nature, he claims, is "determined by contrast with the social world, and to that extent, depends on the latter" (TCT 201–202).[12] Equally Hegelian is the claim that a rational society would be one constituted by the intellectual and manual labor of free rational subjects that would manifest the freedom and rationality that produced it. However, Horkheimer denies that existing society, characterized by monopoly capitalism and ruling elites, is in fact rational. There are certain immanent tendencies within it that express free rational human subjectivity, but these do not impinge on its blind and chaotic organization. In other words, his view is that the existing social order is only potentially rational.

The fact that society, though made by human beings, is not yet rational is due to the fact that the "social process of production," which is also man made, is not rationally organized, but is organized along the chaotic and irrational lines of capitalism. This has

---

[11] Note the contrast with Marcuse, who, as we will see later, argues that what look like merely social economic concepts in Marx have deeper, philosophical foundations. This difference is at the heart of the contrast I am drawing between Horkheimer's attenuated Hegelianism and Marcuse's committed Hegelian-Marxism.

[12] That said, Horkheimer stops short of claiming that spirit is superordinate to nature, as Hegel often does: "For everything spiritual is better than anything natural" (Hegel, W 28,1: *Introductory Lectures on Fine Art*, 34).

epistemological consequences. Much as Lukács had attacked the contemplative attitude as a 'reification' of consciousness, Horkheimer attacks the conceptual scheme-content dualism he thinks pervades both the empiricist and rationalist traditions, and which he sees as still operative in most contemporary philosophical approaches. Knowers, particularly natural scientists and positivists influenced by the natural sciences, are captivated, he argues, by a picture of knowledge according to which knowers merely register and order the facts of a given and apparently independent external world. By contrast, critical theory—Horkheimer maintains—overcomes this dualism by demonstrating in Hegelian fashion that both the object of cognition and the subject are parts of an ongoing historical process of social production (TCT 200). However, as we have seen, Horkheimer conceives the process of social constitution as the blind self-reproduction and renewal of existing society, unlike Hegel, who conceives it as the progressive work of spirit toward freedom. In gaining and transmitting empirical and scientific knowledge (practicing 'traditional theory'), knowers thus participate unwittingly in "the continuous renewal of the existing state of affairs" (TCT 195). The chief task of critical theory— as the expression of free rational subjectivity—is to be not just "a moment in the renewal of the present" society, but a moment in the constitution of "a more just . . . more harmoniously ordered one as well" (TCT 205).

According to Horkheimer, critical theory is a practical activity, guided by the interests of rational subjects in creating and living in a rationally ordered society that serves their interests, both material and spiritual. But Horkheimer follows Marx in the claim that the current social world "is not their own, but the world of capital" (TCT 208). The existing social world is not the rational actuality it could (and should) be, and hence not intelligible, transparent, and good, as Hegel believed, but opaque, impenetrable, and bad. And insofar as it can be understood, it shows itself to be the product of blind, chaotic, human activities, coordinated by the irrational force of capital. Critical theorists, he claims, who are able to break through the limitations of disciplinary research, and to reflect on the social and historical conditions of their cognitive activity, are also able to see through the illusion of the fixed appearance of the external world of facts, and to understand that this world "in principle should be under human control and in the future at least, will in fact come under it" (TCT 209). The Marxist features of Horkheimer's critical theory are his diagnosis of existing society, and his conception of criticism as an incipient practice, but its aim, the creation of a rational and organic society by free rational subjects, is inspired by Hegel: "Reason cannot become transparent to itself so long as men act as members of an organism which lacks reason" (TCT 208, 213).

Indeed, it is noticeable that Horkheimer's essay "Traditional and Critical Theory" is in some respects closer to Hegel's idealism (which he rejects) than he likes to admit. He attempts to construct a theory that suffers neither from the perceived abstractions of methodological individualism, nor from the ontological extravagance of monism.[13]

---

[13] "Critical theory . . . is the function neither of the isolated individual nor of a sum-total of individuals. Its subject is rather a definite individual in his relation so other individuals and groups, in his conflict with a particular class, and finally in the resultant web of relationships with the social totality and with nature" (TCT 211).

Ultimately, however, Horkheimer's conceptual palette is not refined enough to capture the position he is aiming at. He rejects pragmatism out of hand, even though G. H. Mead's notion of the social subject might have given him a model, as it later did Habermas, with which to conceive society as an intersubjective construct. Instead, he follows in Lukács's footsteps, when he construes society as a " 'community of free men' as an 'active' albeit 'non-conscious subject' . . . and to that extent a subject only in an improper sense" (TCT 199). This presupposes that society is a blind, irrational organism presently lacking self-awareness and self-transparency, which will come to full self-consciousness in the future. These latent Lukácsian elements sit at odds with Horkheimer's rejection of Hegel's monistic conception of spirit as a unitary subject capable of becoming self-conscious, and also with his objections to Lukács's neo-Hegelianism.

32.2.3. Horkheimer and Hegel: A Reassessment

Horkheimer's development has been portrayed by Martin Jay as a "retreat from Hegelian Marxism."[14] Jay makes this evaluation on the basis of Horkheimer's disillusionment with the revolutionary hopes of Western Marxism and his growing despair at the prospects of a socialist transformation, which developments also reflect, Jay contends, "the growing influence of Adorno on his thinking" during and after the war.[15]

I think this assessment is partly right, but misleading in two respects. First, one might think that if Adorno had an increasing influence on Horkheimer, he would have become more Hegelian, not less, for Adorno remained a far more committed Hegelian, albeit a critical one, than the latter ever was. Second, it is true that Horkheimer was a Marxist who retreated from Marxism, in that he abandoned the view that the potential for social transformation—not gradual reform but 'revolution' in the sense of radical and sweeping social change—is immanent in existing society.[16] And it may have been Adorno who convinced him of this, though Adorno was certainly not the only person who came to this view. But as for his Hegelianism, Horkheimer was only ever Hegelian in an attenuated sense. And the truth is that, despite his growing skepticism about the immanent potential for social change, and the related idea that the relation to a transformed praxis can be thought of as an essentially maieutic project, Horkheimer remained as Hegelian as ever he had been: for the Hegelian notions that repelled him, he rejected from the beginning; while those that attracted him, and shaped his own thought, he never abandoned.

---

[14] Jay, *Marxism and Totality*, 196–219.

[15] Jay, *Marxism and Totality*, 215.

[16] This is the view he espouses in "Traditional and Critical Theory," where he claims that "the idea of a reasonable organization of society . . . is immanent in human labour," and that it is "possible through technical means already at hand" (TCT 211, 217).

32.3. ADORNO AND HEGEL

Adorno and Horkheimer became close friends and embarked on an intensive period of collaboration from about 1941, which resulted in their quirky and inspirational co-authored book *Dialectic of Enlightenment* in 1944. Writing of his own *Eclipse of Reason* in 1946, Horkheimer says, "It would be difficult to say which of the ideas originated in his mind and which in my own; our philosophy is one" (ER vii). Certainly in the fertile period, when they were thrown together by historical circumstance, the basic ideas of their respective projects come into alignment. As we will see, however, Adorno's interpretation and assessment of Hegel is in important respects quite different from those of Horkheimer, and the influence of Hegel on his own work is more pronounced.

32.3.1. Adorno's Interpretation of Hegel

Caution is called for in a discussion of Adorno's interpretation of Hegel. Horkheimer works in two more or less distinct genres; his lectures are mainly expository and interpretative, whereas his essays advance his own views. Adorno's work is quite different. Even where he purports to be expounding Hegel, as in *Hegel: Three Studies*, he is at the same time propounding his own philosophy; and conversely, where he is propounding his own philosophy, he is always commenting on Hegel.

Another significant factor is that, while Horkheimer wrote on Hegel before the war, most of Adorno's important work on Hegel was written after the war. Horkheimer objects that Hegel's metaphysics were obsolete, that his politics were quiescent and conservative, and that he was guilty of a 'transfiguration' of a not yet rational world. For Adorno the stakes are much higher. After Auschwitz, Adorno writes in *Negative Dialectics*, "our metaphysical faculty is paralyzed because actual events have shattered the basis on which speculative metaphysical thought could be reconciled with reality" (ND 361/GS 6 354). Hegel described his philosophy as a 'true theodicy', because he believed the work of spirit had begun to shape the world in a fundamentally rational way. Hitler and the Third Reich had, however, in Adorno's eyes, shown the world to be 'radically evil' and had destroyed any pretensions, metaphysical or otherwise, of reason to justify it. At the same time, the radically evil social world that Adorno inhabited was, he thought, more than ever in need of redemption. Metaphysics, in its task as theodicy, is thus at once impossible and also necessary (ND 408/GS6 400).

32.3.1.1. *Similarities between Horkheimer's and Adorno's Interpretations of Hegel*

Although I want to draw attention to the distinctiveness of Adorno's interpretation of Hegel, it would be wrong not to point out some base-line similarities between

Horkheimer's Hegel and Adorno's.[17] Like Horkheimer, Adorno rejects Hegel's idealist metaphysics—particularly the subject-object identity thesis—as untrue. Like Horkheimer, he sees Hegel's idealist metaphysics as the ground of his conservatism, his apologetic stance toward the existing world, his alleged cult of the state, and "deification of . . . what is" (HTS 80–81). Like Horkheimer, Adorno values the dialectic, its component notions such as 'determinate negation', and its mode of operation 'immanent criticism', as ways of thinking that he endorsed and appropriated in spite of his rejection of Hegel's systematic metaphysics. Like Horkheimer, Adorno interprets spirit as social labor. They both endorse Hegel's criticism of Kant, and argue that by retranslating the work of synthetic apperception as a social achievement of spirit in history, Hegel overcomes the fundamental arbitrariness of Kant's account of the relation of cognitive form to sensible content. As a consequence, Adorno, like Horkheimer, sees an affinity between these aspects of Hegel's idealism and the guiding ideas of historical materialism (HTS 68).

That said, Adorno understands the connection between idealism and materialism differently from the young Horkheimer. It is not that the social and historical aspects of Hegel's philosophy are henceforth to be continued by other means, namely by social and historical sciences informed by philosophical reflection. Shorn of idealism, argues Adorno, nothing is left of Hegel's philosophy but "positivism . . . and superficial intellectual history" (HTS 3). Rather, Hegel's legacy for materialism has to be wrested from the ongoing immanent criticism of Hegel's idealism. Indeed, characteristic of Adorno's peculiar relation to Hegel is the importance of understanding Hegel's philosophy as a whole, including his absolute idealism, and objective spirit, which he holds to be not just conservative, but implicitly totalitarian aspects of his philosophy.

32.3.1.2. *Adorno on Interpretation and Criticism*

To understand Adorno's Hegel, one has to appreciate his technique of interpretation. Horkheimer's materialist history of philosophy is Marxist in orientation. He recommends a historical approach whereby scholars approach figures by "diligently immersing themselves in the concrete spiritual [*geistige*] situation" in which their work originated (MHGS 11,105). He has no compunction about adopting a macro-conceptual approach. The meaning of an individual work of philosophy is vouchsafed by the social and historical conditions of its production, and that is the primary context, in which light it should be interpreted.

---

[17] These similarities may stem in part from the influence that Horkheimer's work of the 1930s had on Adorno. For this period in his life is marked by a discernible shift away from the Benjaminian approach of esoteric interpretation he had adopted in his Kierkegaard book, toward a more philosophical approach of "immanent critique" that was born from "a renewed and extremely fruitful study of Hegel" undertaken while at Oxford (A-BC 147). It was also coeval with a thawing of relations between Adorno and Horkheimer that had become decidedly frosty. The Hegelianization of Adorno's work at this point appears to have been a crucial factor not only in his gaining Horkheimer's approval, but also in gaining his own distinctive philosophical voice (see Abromeit, *Max Horkheimer and the Foundations of the Frankfurt School*, 362–375).

Adorno occasionally adopts that approach, but for the most part proceeds quite differently.[18] Though his stance toward works of philosophy and works of art is not the same (because, unlike in the case of artworks, the *meaning* of philosophical theories is not inscribed primarily in their form), nonetheless what Adorno says *à propos* of the meaning and interpretation of artworks is revealing of his approach to philosophy. For one thing, Adorno's approach is one of immersion in and attention to particular works, which he subjects to a micrological analysis. He works from the particular toward the universal. Second, he digs beneath the surface content of the work, to its hidden recesses. "Art works become language-like in the becoming of the combination of their elements, a syntax without words in linguistic figures. What these works say is not what their words say" (AT 252/GS6 274). (In both respects, Benjamin's lingering influence is still at work.)

Adorno looks beneath the surface meaning of particular works of philosophy to their social 'substratum'. In itself there is nothing new in that. All Marxists, who interpret Hegel's works in the light of the socioeconomic and cultural conditions of their production, do that. However, where for example Lukács and Horkheimer interpret Hegel's work in the light of the social and conditions of its production (early nineteenth-century Germany), Adorno does not. He interprets Hegel in the light of the actual historical, social, and cultural conditions in which he—Adorno—is reading, and writing on, Hegel, namely those of late capitalist, liberal democratic society, in the United States and the *Bundesrepublik*, in the aftermath of World War II.[19] Thus in the beginning of *Hegel: Three Studies*, Adorno replaces the "loathsome question . . . of what in Hegel . . . has any meaning for the present" with the rather more controversial and oblique question of "what the present means in the face of Hegel" (HTS 1). What Adorno has in mind is that Hegel's system—not in the promise of reconciliation inscribed in the organicist absolute idea, which it ultimately fails to live up to, but in the mechanisms it actually relies on to ensure its integrity, namely the "principle of violence . . . the principle of division" and the subordination of the universal by the particular—expresses the actuality of late capitalist, postwar social democracy (HTS 79).

> Satanically, the world as grasped by the Hegelian system has only now, a hundred and fifty years later, proved itself to be a system in the literal sense, namely that of a radically societalized society. One of the most remarkable aspects of Hegel's accomplishment is that he inferred that systematic character of society from the concept long before it could gain ascendancy in the sphere of Hegel's own experience, that of a

[18] For example, "In the early idealist period, when bourgeois society had not yet really taken shape as a totality in underdeveloped Germany, the critique of the particular had a different kind of dignity" (Adorno, HTS, 62; see also MM 16–17).

[19] This technique was probably one Adorno borrowed and adapted from Walter Benjamin. "Denn es handelt sich ja nicht darum, die Werke des Schrifttums im Zusammenhang ihrer Zeit darzustellen, sondern in der Zeit, da sie entstanden, die Zeit, die sie erkennt—das ist die unsere—zur Darstellung zu bringen. Damit wird die Literatur ein Organon der Geschichte und sie dazu—nicht das Schrifttum zum Stoffgebiet der Historie zu machen, ist die Aufgabe der Literaturgeschichte" (Benjamin, GS III, 290). Thanks to Sami Khatib for drawing my attention to this passage in Benjamin.

Germany far behind in its bourgeois development. A world integrated through 'production', through the exchange relationship, depends in all its moments on the social conditions of its production, and in that sense actually realizes the primacy of the whole over its parts; in this regard the desperate impotence of every single individual now verifies Hegel's extravagant conception of the system. (HTS 27)

This is a very peculiar way of interpreting the 'meaning' of Hegel's system for a Marxist who claims that works have to be understood historically. When Adorno contends, for example, that the "insatiable and destructive expansive principle of the exchange society is reflected [*spiegelt sich*] in Hegelian metaphysics," just what kind of relation of 'reflection' is supposed to be at issue? (HTS 28/GS5 274). Adorno is definitely not talking about the possessive individualism that characterized civil society as Hegel observed it in the early nineteenth century being 'reflected in' the structure of Hegel's Logic. He is talking about the 'totally administered society' that came into being 130 years or so after Hegel's death. This approach sits uncomfortably with historical materialism, for the social 'substratum' which Adorno takes to constitute the meaning of Hegel's philosophy is temporally and historically non-congruent with the social, economic, and cultural conditions of its production (HTS 32). It lies in the distant future. To put it starkly, Adorno's approach looks textually cavalier, and historically anachronistic: a somewhat arbitrary attempt to press the philosophy he was most familiar with into the service of the criticism of the society he lived in.

On Adorno's behalf, one might respond that reading a work primarily or exclusively in the light of its proximate social, economic, intellectual, and cultural context is to restrict a work's meaning to its present, which, since the work of interpretation occurs in the aftermath of its production, is to confine it to the past. Maybe that is why Adorno warns against reducing Hegel's philosophy to 'superficial intellectual history' (HTS 3 GS5 252). By contrast, Adorno maintains, the meaning of a work of philosophy, like that of a work of music, is reconstituted and renewed by the tradition of its reception and interpretation, which is ongoing and open-ended. Adorno shares with Hegel, the early Romantics, and later Dilthey and Gadamer a dynamic conception of meaning and interpretation that includes the work's *Wirkungsgeschichte*.[20]

Adorno calls his peculiar technique a 'rescuing' or 'saving' interpretation (and critique) of Hegel. What is salvatory about it is that it manages to find a moment of truth, even in its untruth. "Rescuing Hegel, and only rescue not renewal is appropriate—means facing up to his philosophy where it is most painful, and wresting truth from it where its untruth is obvious" (HTS 83/GS5 320).[21] Still, though Adorno runs the risk of

---

[20] H.-G. Gadamer, *Truth and Method*, 299ff.

[21] Lukács had attempted something similar in section II of his Reification essay. Lukács argued that the contradictions on which Hegel's philosophy ultimately founders express (or 'reflect') the real contradictions (class-antagonisms) of bourgeois society. Real social contradictions, though they can be expressed intellectually, cannot be resolved intellectually. The attempt to do so leads to what he calls a 'reification of consciousness' and what Horkheimer later calls 'transfiguration'. Here Lukács identifies a truth moment—namely that real social contradictions receive "the most complete profound and magnificent theoretical expression" (HCC 148/GK 266) in the untruth of Hegel's philosophy—namely

anachronism, he avoids what he presumably considers the greater sin of confining Hegel to the heritage park of intellectual history.[22] His approach may be considered preferable to two other interpretative ways of 'saving' Hegel: namely, either separating out what is living from what is dead in Hegel's philosophy, which he castigates Benedetto Croce for doing (HTS 1/GS5 251); or distinguishing between the critical, progressive republican Young Hegel, and the later conservative, quietist Old Hegel, as did Lukács and also Habermas (albeit differently and for different reasons). [23]

Finally, Adorno mostly refuses to water down or to mitigate what he thinks of as the 'painful' aspects of Hegel, namely his complacent justifications of the inner rationality of the existing social order, although there are moments where Adorno relents. For example, after noting that Hegel's "tendency to resignation is undeniable," he notes that even the most questionable of his doctrines—that what is actual is rational—was not 'merely apologetic' because rationality is constellated with freedom, the ideal of which shines through actuality (HTS 44/GS 5 288). In the main, however, Adorno, like Horkheimer, accepts the rudiments of a long-standing interpretation of Hegel's *Philosophy of Right* dating from contemporary reviewers, and leading through Rudolf Haym, the Young Hegelians, Marx and Engels, right up to Hobhouse and Popper, which interprets Hegel's famous Doppelsatz in the Preface—"What is rational is actual; and what is actual is rational"—and indeed the work as a whole, as a justification of the existing Prussian state or, as Haym puts it, "the absolute formula of political conservatism, quietism and optimism." [24]

In truth, the evidence against the view that Hegel was an apologist for the Prussian state, and for the existing social order, which both Horkheimer and Adorno take as read, is compelling. Such a view ignores, for example, Hegel's rejoinder to those criticisms, namely that on his view of actuality, not everything that exists is actual. In the revised version of the *Encyclopedia Logic*, Hegel points out that "a contingent existence does not deserve to be called something actual in the emphatic sense of the word."[25] It also

---

its inability to resolve the antinomies of bourgeois consciousness. Note that the relation of reflection identified by Lukács holds between temporally and historically congruent domains, thus the charge of anachronism cannot be leveled at him.

[22] The point of Benjamin's approach is to distinguish literary criticism from literary history, and presupposes his critique of the historicist and value-theoretical presuppositions of traditional cultural criticism.

[23] Lukács, *Der Junge Hegel*; Habermas, *Theory and Praxis*, 142ff. One assumes Adorno believes he can, by means of his rescuing approach, avoid severing the aspects of Hegel he welcomes and endorses—the dialectic, the idea of determinate negation, and the concept of experience—from those he rejects—Hegel's absolute idealism and the subject-object identity thesis—since he explicitly criticizes Benedetto Croce for doing just that. I have argued elsewhere that Adorno fails in this aim (Finlayson, "Hegel, Adorno and the Origins of Immanent Criticism").

[24] Rudolf Haym's critique in „Preussen und die Rechtsphilosophie" in Manfred Riedel ed., *Materialien zu Hegels Rechtsphilosophie*, vol. 1, 372. Adorno frequently refers to Hegel's "apology for the status quo" and "legitimation of what exists," and so forth (HTS 28, 47, 81, 82, 85). In England, L. T Hobhouse roundly criticized Hegel's illiberal conception of the state in his *The Metaphysical Theory of the State: A Criticism*, a reading that Marcuse counter-criticizes in *Reason and Revolution*, 390–392.

[25] See for example, Hegel, E §6.

neglects to take into consideration the political climate of Draconian censorship following the Carlsbad Decrees under which Hegel wrote the 1820 version of his *Philosophy of Right*, which helps explain Hegel's ambiguous phrasing of the *Doppelsatz* in the Preface to that version.[26] Finally, it seems that Adorno was either unaware of, or neglects to consider, the scholarship that existed in his own time, questioning and overturning the view that Hegel was a reactionary apologist for the Prussian state, and which rather demonstrates that he was an advocate of gradual progressive political reform.[27] Such evidence would have allowed Adorno to be fairer to Hegel and his actual political views. It would also have fitted with the broad lines of Adorno's own interpretation of Hegel, which claims that "Hegel's philosophy is eminently critical philosophy" (HTS 77: see also 65, 75, 8081), and that "immanent criticism is the centerpiece of his method" (HTS 56: see also 14, 19, 76 146.) That said, what such evidence shows is that Hegel's philosophy is (and that he intended it to be) compatible with social criticism that is conservative about what is good in the existing institutions and ideals (i.e., rational actuality) and critical of what is bad, nugatory, or merely existent, and that it leans in the direction of gradual piecemeal reform. So such a reading, though textually supported and historically accurate, would not sit well with Adorno's primary purpose of recruiting Hegel's philosophy to the radical task of critical theory, namely to disclose the pervasively evil nature of the 'totally administered society' and to bring about sweeping social transformation.

32.3.2. Hegel's Influence on Adorno

The question of what Hegel's influence on Adorno's philosophy was appears to be an open and shut one: Adorno is a self-proclaimed Hegelian. "I think of myself as a Hegelian," he tells his students, in his *Lectures on Negative Dialectics* (LND 10). Earlier, in the dedication to *Minima Moralia*, he claims that its method was "schooled in Hegel" (MM 4/ GS 4 14) (something Horkheimer also says of his own work). The essays in *Hegel: Three Studies* were intended, he writes, as the preparation for a "revised conception of the dialectic," a project which came to fruit four years later in his major theoretical work, *Negative Dialectics* (HTS xv/GS5 250). So Adorno presents his own philosophical method, and also his negative dialectic, as a revised version of the Hegelian dialectic. Moreover, he claims for his own dialectic an essential component of the Hegelian

---

[26] Hegel's *Doppelsatz*, "What is rational is actual: and what is actual is rational," calls to mind the line from Alexander Pope's "Essay on Man": "One truth is clear, Whatever is, is right." In earlier versions of his lectures, for example in 1817/1818, when censorship was not such a pressing factor, Hegel had written, "what is rational, must happen" (G. W. F. Hegel, *Die Philosophie des Rechts*, ed. K.-H. Ilting, vol. 1, 157). The Griesheim transcription of 1824/1825 has Hegel saying "The form is, that law exists, the content can be a rational, in and for itself lawful one or it can be a very irrational, unlawful and quite arbitrary one, that is merely imposed by external authority: it can be a content given by being, whose validity however says nothing about its value" (ibid., vol. 4, 82).

[27] T. M. Knox, "Hegel and Prussianism"; Walther A. Kaufman, "The Hegel Myth and Its Method."

dialectic, namely the notion of 'determinate negation'. The places where Adorno claims that his own dialectic proceeds by way of determinate negation are too many to enumerate.[28] For Adorno argues that Hegel's dialectic is essentially critical. "Hegel's philosophy is essentially negative: critique" (HTS 30/GS5 276). And the kind of negation by way of which his own immanent criticism works, he argues, is Hegelian determinate negation: "If the whole is . . . the negative, a negation of particularities . . . remains negative: Its only positive would be criticism, determinate negation . . ." (ND 159/GS6 161).

Most critics and commentators accept these claims by Adorno at face value.[29] On closer inspection, however, his position here, and the questions concerning Hegel's influence on Adorno's approach, are less clear cut. Can Adorno really welcome Hegel's dialectic, and in particular, Hegel's notion of 'determinate negation' as his own, while rejecting outright Hegel's Logic and systematic metaphysics? I believe not, for the following reasons. Hegel contrasts determinate negation with abstract negation. Abstract negation is indifferent to and destroys its object, like a board eraser wipes off whatever is written on the board. [30] Determinate negation, by contrast, adapts and responds to its object, like a refutation to an argument. Furthermore, in so doing, determinate negation not only annuls its object, it produces something new and better: it is thus positive and productive. As Hegel writes, "The dialectic has a positive result, because it has a determinate content, or because its result is in truth not the empty, abstract nothing, but the negation of certain determinations, which are contained in the result . . ." (E §82).

The crucial question is, what grounds the determinacy of negation? For Hegel, the answer to this question is that each negation is a step in a self-completing system that culminates in the absolute idea. The dialectic is not just moving away from error, it is moving onward and upward toward absolute truth. This is what makes the dialectic an ascent, in the sense that it is not just a sequence, but that it is a progressive cognitive (and ontological) gain—in refinement, concretion, and coherence.[31] Now, Adorno, since he lays claim to determinate negation, needs to answer the same question. His answer, however, cannot be Hegel's, since Adorno repudiates absolute idealism and the subject-object identity thesis as an ideological imposition of the subject (HTS 13/GS 5 261). Adorno's rescuing critique, which exposes Hegel's system as a prefiguration of the totally administered society, and condemns it as totalitarian, will not help him. As I see it, nothing in Adorno's philosophy explains why his criticism is responsive and also productive, and thus counts as a *determinate negation in Hegel's sense*. At certain junctures, for example in the *Lectures on Negative Dialectics*, Adorno realizes this, and tries to find a way out of the problem, but ultimately he does not succeed in developing an alternative

---

[28] E.g. Adorno, DE 205/GS 3, HTS 87/GS 5, 324–325; ND 174/GS6 177.

[29] See Habermas, *Philosophical Discourse of Modernity*, 128; Zuidervaart, Lambert, "Theodor W. Adorno," *The Stanford Encyclopedia of Philosophy*; J. M. Bernstein, "Negative Dialectics as Fate: Adorno and Hegel," in *The Cambridge Companion to Adorno*; and Brian O'Connor, *Adorno*, 46, 63.

[30] For this example, and a discussion of the relevant issue, see Michael Rosen, *Hegel's Dialectic and Its Criticism*, 30–35.

[31] For a more detailed discussion of this issue, see my "Hegel, Adorno and the Origins of Immanent Criticism."

account of the determinacy of determinate negation (LND, 12–32). Consequently, he cannot coherently endorse, and base his conception of immanent criticism on, Hegel's dialectic, and its most important component notion, Hegelian 'determinate negation'. [32]

None of this shows that Adorno is wrong to claim that he is a Hegelian, or that his negative dialectic is a revision of Hegel's dialectic. It shows only that Hegel's influence on Adorno is not what he says, and that Adorno's negative dialectic and his conception of immanent criticism are further removed from Hegel's thinking than Adorno claims. Insofar as it is true to say that Hegel's method "schooled that of *Minima Moralia*," this cannot mean that his approach is an application of Hegelian dialectic, and his criticisms proceed by way of Hegelian 'determinate negation'. It can only mean that the aphoristic presentation of the material in *Minima Moralia*, like the anti-systematic Models and Concepts of *Negative Dialectics*, exemplify Adorno's magnetic repulsion to Hegel's system.[33] At best Adorno can (and occasionally does) claim that the power of the whole system is somehow reflected in the fragments that are deliberately designed to resist being assimilated to it (QF 258).[34]

32.3.3. Adorno and Hegel: An Assessment

Though both Horkheimer and Adorno claim that their own approaches to philosophy are 'schooled in' Hegel, they drew different lessons. The young Horkheimer was an Hegelian Marxist who, as he matured, grew more disillusioned with Marxism's claims about the immanent potential for social transformation, but never abandoned his always highly qualified Hegelianism. He acknowledged to what extent Hegel's dialectic philosophy rested on an outdated monistic metaphysics. In place of Hegel's system and absolute idealism, he embraced what he considered to be a continuation of Hegelianism by other—non-philosophical—means, namely the historically ongoing task of piecing together and managing the partial and defeasible results of the natural, social, and historical sciences, and reflecting on their social function. By contrast, Adorno was a Marxist Hegelian, whose commitment to Hegel, and to the continuing relevance of his philosophy, which was renewed in the mid-1930s, never wavered thereafter. Through his creative and imaginative interpretation of Hegel, he developed not only a negative

---

[32] This does not mean that there is not a coherent position available to Adorno, but it would have to meet the constraint of being compatible with his austere negativism, and that is a very demanding constraint for a conception of determinate negation to meet. A similar problem faces Horkheimer, if he is to help himself to determinate negation, à la Hegel, but reject Hegel's system and metaphysics, then he needs to offer an alternative ground of the determinacy of negation. However, it is not so acute, as in Adorno, since, as I have argued, Horkheimer does not identify his own philosophical so closely with Hegel's.

[33] This reading is supported by a passage in the dedication where directly after saying that *Minima Moralia*'s method was "schooled in Hegel," Adorno notes that "Dialectical Theory, abhorring anything isolated, cannot admit aphorisms as such" (MM 16/GS, 4, 14). See also MM 70–71.

[34] Adorno does not share Benjamin's admiration for the early German Romantics. Nevertheless, it is evident that such claims have their origins in thinkers such as Friedrich Schlegel and Novalis.

dialectic, but attempted to make the ongoing critical engagement with Hegel relevant for the social sciences, for the philosophy of art, and for critical social theory.

32.4. MARCUSE AND HEGEL

Herbert Marcuse was first and foremost a Marxist. He was a Marxist even before he was a philosopher. A crude way of summing up his intellectual career would be to say that he began as a Heideggerian-Marxist and then shifted to Hegelian-Marxism.[35]

In *Hegel's Ontology and the Theory of Historicity*, written as a Habilitation thesis under Heidegger's direction, he attempted to establish the concept of 'Leben' in Hegel's early writings up to the *Phenomenology* and the *Logic*, as the basis of his ontology. In other essays of this period, in which he is more open about his Marxist commitments, he attempts to develop a 'concrete philosophy' out of a synthesis between existentialism and Marxism (HM 34). Around 1932–1933, Marcuse turned toward Hegelian-Marxism and what was to become critical theory.[36] A singular combination of factors provoked this turn. Heidegger, his supervisor, 'blocked' his Habilitation thesis, and then joined the Nazi party, just after Hitler's ascent to power. Marcuse realized he had no prospect of an academic career in Germany, and eventually secured a post at the Institute for Social Research.[37] The most significant intellectual factor in this development was Marcuse's reception of Marx's *Economic and Philosophical Manuscripts* in 1932, which inspired him to pay renewed attention to the ideas of labor, the dialectic, and to the young Marx's relation to Hegel. While at the Institute in Geneva and the United States, Marcuse begins to distance himself from phenomenology and existentialism, and under the influence of Horkheimer, to gravitate toward critical social theory, the development of which came to fruit in his 1941 monograph, *Reason and Revolution: Hegel and the Rise of Social Theory*.

32.4.1. Marcuse's Reading of Hegel

Marcuse's chief concern in his earlier work is to uncover the philosophical foundations of political economy. Reading the 1844 *Manuscripts* for the first time convinced him of

---

[35] The term "Heideggerian-Marxism" is an apposite description of Marcuse's early work. Marx remained a central concern of his until the end of his life.

[36] I use the term "Hegelian-Marxism" as distinct from "Marxist-Hegelianism." This is a useful distinction I owe to Andrew Chitty and Joe McCarney. I consider Adorno a Marxist-Hegelian, namely a Hegelian of a broadly Marxist kind, and Lukács (after 1917) and Marcuse from about 1932 onward Hegelian-Marxists, for they were Marxists of a Hegelian kind.

[37] Wiggershaus, *The Frankfurt School*, 113–114; Kellner, *Herbert Marcuse and the Crisis of Marxism*, 13–18.

the centrality and philosophical significance of the concept of labor, both in Marx and in Hegel (HM xxiv).

32.4.1.1. *Labor*

For Marx, Marcuse maintains, the notion of labor is not just an economic concept but a "philosophical critique and foundation of political economy as a theory of revolution" (HM 86). This philosophical critique arose, he argues, out of a philosophical dispute with Hegel about the human essence and the conditions of its possible realization. In itself, Marcuse thinks this shows the naïveté of the orthodox Marxist claim that in his mature work Marx's theory shifted from a philosophical to a scientific economic basis. But the real issue now becomes that of expounding the philosophical concept of labor in order to identify the lines of that dispute.

The 1844 *Manuscripts* show, Marcuse claims, that "Marx adopts the Hegelian concept of labour in all its aspects, namely as a theory of the realization of the human essence" (HM 87). Labor, he maintains, is an ontological category, "a happening of human Dasein" which must take place "because the world, as it is, can never satisfy his 'needs.'" (HM 132). He emphasizes that labor is essentially burdensome, for in labor human effort encounters, and has to overcome, the resistance of things, in contrast to play, which is an expression of freedom (HM 130–139). This is not to say that nature is essentially recalcitrant to human needs and interests, but rather, that the realization of the human essence requires strenuous human effort.[38] That said, unlike Horkheimer and Adorno, Marcuse nowhere sees labor either merely as an instrumental activity or as an implicit form of domination, as Horkheimer and Adorno did in the *Dialectic of Enlightenment* and afterward.

32.4.1.2. *Historicity*

For Marcuse, the fact that the human being only exists, and only becomes what she is through labor—that is, through the formation of the external world and of herself—is the fundamental mark of her historicity. Marcuse's initial thesis, which he believed was confirmed by Marx in the 1844 *Manuscripts*, is that Hegel holds that the essence of human beings is their 'ontological historicity'. Marx's contribution was not to rescue the dialectical method from Hegel's system, as had been claimed, but to rediscover "the dialectical motility of historical life that Hegel had discovered but covered up once again" (HM 84).

It is primarily in Hegel's early writings and in Chapter IV of the *Phenomenology* that Hegel's ontology is to be found, according to Marcuse. Thus, he argues it is a mistake to try to winkle out Hegel's concept of history from the Lectures on the Philosophy of History, or from the *Philosophy of Right*, which offer only "a curtailment and transformation of the original concept of history" (HM, 84). Furthermore, Marcuse contends, it

---

[38] C.f. "In the form that it assumed as authentic Being in modern philosophy, reason has to produce itself and its reality continuously in recalcitrant material" (*Negations*, 138). But Marcuse's point here is that recalcitrant reality is eventually shaped by rational activity.

is this notion of the fundamental historicality of human being, and not Hegel's systematic metaphysics, that gives the key to understanding the Hegelian dialectic.

32.4.1.3. *Dialectic*

Hegel shows, Marcuse avers, that "only human Dasein" and the object it forms "are ontologically historical." It follows, he argues, that "the foundation of the dialectic lies in the ontological historicity of being itself" (HM 61). Now this implies first that the dialectic is not so much a method, a way of reasoning and a route to knowledge, as the way of being itself. But second, and more crucial, it follows that "not all beings are dialectical . . . only those whose being is historicity are," namely only human beings and the world of human affairs (HM 65). There is an implicit criticism of Hegel here. Dialectic, properly understood, is not, as Hegel (and Engels later) conceived it, a general epistemology or metaphysics; it is a more restricted social epistemology and ontology. Nor is it "a moribund residue of Hegelianism in Marx," as the scientific Marxists would have it, something that can be sloughed off along with Hegel's systematic metaphysics. To the contrary, Marcuse maintains, the dialectic is essential to understanding the significance of Marx, and Marxism, and to the criticism of the contemporary social world.

32.4.2. Marcuse's Critique of Hegel

In Marcuse's eyes, the philosophical concept of labor and the related ideas of the historicity of human *Dasein* and the dialectic are at the root of Marx's dispute with Hegel. The point that Hegel covers over, and Marx brings to light again, he argues, is that capitalism is "not just a political crisis but . . . a catastrophe of the human essence" (HM 106). What causes the crisis are two economic facts: the fact of alienated labor and the fact of private property, which thwart the realization of human essence, and hence call for an equally "cataclysmic sublation of the actual situation through total revolution" (HM 106).

The emphasis in Marcuse's "Philosophy and Critical Theory" (1937) and *Reason and Revolution* (1941), works that represent Marcuse's apprenticeship in critical theory, is somewhat different, and their central categories—reason, subjectivity, freedom, language, and mind (Geist)—open different avenues of inquiry, yet the overall trajectory is similar. "Man has set out to organize reality according to the demands of his free rational thinking. . . . Consequently the unreasonable reality has to be altered until it comes into conformity with reason" (RR 5). These are the 'critical tendencies' of Hegel's philosophy, which, Marcuse claims "went over to Marxian theory" (RR 257).

While Marcuse is generally eager to defend the actuality of Hegel and his relevance for social theory, he does criticize Hegel's work and his person. He saves his harshest words for Hegel's opportunistic and self-serving repudiation of J. F. Fries and the democratic critics of the Carlsbad Decrees, and he frequently levies the lesser charge of resignation at Hegel's political philosophy (RR, 176, 195, 260). Note, though, that, in contrast to Adorno and Horkheimer, he never convicts Hegel of conservatism or apologetics. After all, 'resignation' to the way the world is does not imply approval of it. Marcuse observes that Hegel thought the dynamics of civil society, the anarchic interactions of possessive individuals, calls for the discipline of an authoritarian state to make it subserve the common interest and bring it back in conformity with reason (RR 56, 174, 214). But he mitigates the force of the criticism, and virtually exonerates Hegel, by pointing out (rather like Lukács) that Hegel's philosophy is—in Hegel's own phrase—"its time comprehended in thoughts" (Hegel W 7, 26/EPR 21). "The Objective Mind, with which the *Philosophy of Right* deals, unfolds itself in time, and the dialectical analysis of its content has to be guided by the forms that this content has taken in history" (RR 214).[39] Unlike both Horkheimer and Adorno, then, Marcuse does not blame Hegel's 'resignation' on the metaphysics and the system, nor does he even convict them along with it. Indeed, in his eyes, absolute spirit—the complete realization of freedom proper—takes on a utopian significance (malgré Hegel and Marx). While the philosophy of objective spirit, Marcuse claims, is marked by the limitations of Hegel's realism, this is not the case with absolute spirit, for "the ideas and values that pointed beyond this social system were stowed away in the realm of the absolute mind" (RR 257).

Moreover, unlike his two colleagues at the Institute, Marcuse observes perceptiently that Hegel's state, though authoritarian, is anything but fascist (RR 216). Even the authoritarian state, he claims, is necessary in order to make civil society serve the common interest, where its own dynamic strays from the ideals of freedom and reason (RR 214). Indeed, Marcuse points out, the Romantic anti-rationalist nationalism of Fries and the *Burschenschaften* (student fraternities) that Hegel castigated is far more akin to national socialism than anything in Hegel's philosophy. Marcuse's attitude on this point should not be surprising; one of the motivations for writing *Reason and Revolution* at that time was, as Jay points out, "to rescue Hegel from his association . . . with Nazism."[40] What is perhaps surprising is not that Marcuse sides with scholars such T. M. Knox (and later Walter Kaufmann) against Hegel's critics from the liberal left, Haym, Hobhouse, Popper, and Berlin, but that Adorno, in convicting Hegel's system of totalitarianism, sides with Hegel's critics.

In sum, Marcuse's interpretation is more charitable to Hegel than either Adorno's or Horkheimer's. His approach, which is both scholarly and academic, is quite different from Adorno's. Marcuse has a greater knowledge of, and respect for, the relevant secondary literature than Adorno, and is a more cautious interpreter and a more careful intellectual historian. And while Adorno's writings are a more exciting read, Marcuse offers a more thorough and reliable exposition of Hegel's ideas.

---

[39] Hegel's ideas, Marcuse claims, "absorb and consciously retain the contradictions of this society and follow them to their bitter end. The work is reactionary insofar as the social order it reflects is so, and progressive in so far as it is progressive" (RR 178) C.f. Lukács HC 148/GK 266.

[40] Martin Jay, *The Dialectical Imagination*, 71.

32.4.3. Hegel's Influence on Marcuse

Unlike Horkheimer and Adorno, Marcuse never abandoned the conviction that capitalist society contained immanent possibilities for its revolutionary transformation, even despite the fact that, in his later work, he acknowledges that advanced industrial societies are able effectively to contain and repress the forces of qualitative social change. As one perceptive commentator puts it, Marcuse's later critical theory is riven with equivocation so deep, it is "an intellectual equivalent of trauma."[41] Trauma aside, Marcuse continued all his life to locate, identify, and show solidarity with whatever forces of opposition and radical social change were to hand. In this sense, he remained a Hegelian-Marxist. He maintained a firm belief in the actuality of Hegel's philosophy, and in the critical animus "continued in, the Marxian social theory."[42] And the critical point he held fast to was this: "the given state of affairs is negative and can be rendered positive only by liberating possibilities immanent to it. This last, the negation of the negation, is accomplished by establishing a new order of things" (RR 315).[43]

WORKS CITED

Horkheimer, Max

Between Philosophy and Social Science [BPSS]. Cambridge, MA: MIT Press, 1993.
Dialectic of Enlightenment [DE], translated by John Cumming. London: Verso, 1997.
Eclipse of Reason [ER]. New York: Oxford University Press, 1947.
Hegel und Das Problem der Metaphysik [HPM]. Frankfurt am Main: Fischer Verlag, 1971.
Max Horkheimer, Gesammelte Schriften [MHGS], vols. 10 & 11. Frankfurt am Main: Fischer Verlag, 1990.
Max Horkheimer Critical Theory: Selected Essays. New York: Herder and Herder, 1972.
"The Rationalist Debate in Contemporary Philosophy [TRD]," in *Max Horkheimer between Philosophy and Social Science.* Cambridge, MA: MIT Press, 1993.
"Traditional and Critical Theory," in *Max Horkheimer Critical Theory: Selected Essays* [TCT]. New York: Herder and Herder, 1972.

Adorno, Theodor.

Aesthetic Theory [AT], translated by R. Hullot-Kentor. London: Athlone Press, 1999.
Hegel: Three Studies [HTS], translated by S. Weber-Nicholson. Cambridge, MA: MIT Press, 1993.

---

[41] McCarney, *Social Theory and the Crisis of Marxism*, 34.

[42] Frederick Olafson asked Marcuse whether it is still possible to build living philosophies on the great classical authors Hegel and Kant. He replied "definitely . . . yes. And I would definitely say that one of the proofs is the continued existence and development of Marxist theory" (HM 174).

[43] Thanks to Dean Moyar, Asger Sorensen, and especially to John Abromeit for comments on draft versions.

Lectures on Negative Dialectics: Fragments of Lecture Course 1965/1966 [LND], translated by Rodney Livingstone. Cambridge: Polity, 2008.

Minima Moralia [MM], translated by E. B. Ashton. London: Verso, 1974.

Negative Dialectics [ND], translated by E. B. Ashton. London: Routledge, 1973.

Quasi una Fantasia [QF], translated by Rodney Livingstone. London: Verso, 1992.

T. W. Adorno, Gesammelte Schriften [GS], edited by R. Tiedemann. Frankfurt am Main: Suhrkamp, 1970.

Theodor Adorno and Walter Benjamin: The Complete Correspondence 1928–1940 [A-BC]. Cambridge: Polity, 1999.

Marcuse, Herbert

Hegel's Ontology and the Theory of Historicity [HO], translated by Seyla Benhabib. Cambridge, MA: MIT Press, 1987.

Heideggerian Marxism [HM], edited by R. Wolin and J. Abromeit. Lincoln: University of Nebraska Press, 2005.

Reason and Revolution: Hegel and the Rise of Social Theory [RR]. Oxford: Oxford University Press, 1941.

Other Works Cited

Abromeit, John. *Max Horkheimer and the Foundations of the Frankfurt School.* Cambridge: Cambridge University Press, 2013.

Benjamin, W. *Gesammelte Schriften, vol. 3: Kritiken und Rezensionen*, edited by Hella Tiedemann-Bartels. Frankfurt am Main: Suhrkamp, 1991.

Berlin, Isaiah. "Two Concepts of Liberty" (1958) in *Four Essays on Liberty*, edited by Isaiah Berlin. Oxford: Oxford University Press, 1969.

Bernstein, J. M. "Negative Dialectics as Fate: Adorno and Hegel," in *The Cambridge Companion to Adorno*, edited by Tom Huhn. Cambridge: Cambridge University Press, 2004, 19–51.

Finlayson, J. G. "Hegel, Adorno and the Origins of Immanent Criticism." *British Journal of the History of Philosophy* 22, no. 6 (2014): 1142–1166.

Gadamer, H.-G. *Truth and Method.* London: Continuum, 2004.

Haym, Rudolf. "Preussen und die Rechtsphilosophie," in *Materialien zu Hegels Rechtsphilosophie*, vol. 1, edited by Manfred Riedel. Frankfurt am Main: Suhrkamp, 1975.

Hegel, G. W. F. *Introductory Lectures on Fine Art*, translated by Bernard Bosanquet. London: Penguin, 1993.

Habermas, J. *Philosophical Discourse of Modernity*, translated by Frederick Lawrence. Cambridge: Polity Press, 1988.

Habermas, J. *Theory and Praxis.* Cambridge: Polity Press, 1986.

Hobhouse, L. T. *The Metaphysical Theory of the State: A Criticism.* London: G. Allen and Unwin, 1918.

Honneth, Axel. *Freedom's Right: The Social Foundations of Democratic Life*, translated by Joseph Ganahl. New York: Columbia University Press, 2014.

Honneth, Axel. *The Pathologies of Individual Freedom: Hegel's Social Theory.* Princeton, NJ: Princeton University Press, 2010.

Honneth, Axel. *The Struggle for Recognition: The Moral Grammar of Social Conflicts.* Cambridge: Polity Press, 1995.

Ilting, K.-H., ed. *G. W. F. Hegel, Die Philosophie des Rechts*, 4 vols. Stuttgart: Klett-Cotta, 1973.

Jay, Martin. *Marxism and Totality*. Berkeley: University of California Press, 1984.

Jay, Martin, *The Dialectical Imagination*. Berkeley: University of California Press, 1973.

Kaufman, Walter A. "The Hegel Myth and Its Method." *Philosophical Review* 60, no. 4 (1951): 459–486.

Kellner, Douglas. *Herbert Marcuse and the Crisis of Marxism*. Berkeley: University of California Press, 1984.

Korsch, Karl, *Marxism and Philosophy*. London: New Left Books, 1972 [1923].

Knox, T. M. "Hegel and Prussianism." *Philosophy* 15, no. 57 (1940): 51–63.

Lukács, György. *Geschichte und Klassenbewusstsein*. Darmstadt: Hermann Luchterhand, 1986 [1923].

Lukács, György. *The Young Hegel: Studies in the Relations Between Dialectics and Economics*. Cambridge, MA: MIT Press, 1976 [1948].

Marx, Karl. *Marx—Engels—Werke*, vol. 3. Berlin/DDR: Dietz Verlag, 1969.

McCarney, Joseph. *Social Theory and the Crisis of Marxism*. London: Verso, 1990.

O'Connor, Brian. *Adorno*. Abingdon; Oxford: Routledge, 2013.

Popper, K. R. *The Open Society and Its Enemies*, Vol. II: *The High Tide of Prophecy: Hegel and Marx*. London: George Routledge & Sons, 1945.

Rose, Gillian. *Hegel contra Sociology*. London: Athlone Press, 1981.

Rosen, Michael. *Hegel's Dialectic and Its Criticism*. Cambridge: Cambridge University Press, 1985.

Rush, Fred. "The Conceptual Foundations of Early Critical Theory," in *The Cambridge Companion to Critical Theory*, edited by Fred Rush. Cambridge: Cambridge University Press, 2008, 6–40.

Wiggershaus, Rolf. *The Frankfurt School*. Cambridge: Polity, 2010.

Zuidervaart, Lambert. "Theodor W. Adorno," *The Stanford Encyclopedia of Philosophy* (Fall 2008 Edition), Edward N. Zalta (ed.), http://plato.stanford.edu/archives/fall2008/entries/adorno/.

....

CHAPTER 33

HEGEL'S REVIVAL IN ANALYTIC PHILOSOPHY

....

WILLEM A. DEVRIES

33.1. INTRODUCTION: ANALYTIC PHILOSOPHY CONTRA HEGEL

....

THE analytic tradition dominant in Anglo-American philosophy was born in part in a revolt against the neo-Hegelianism that was fairly dominant in English-speaking lands at the end of the nineteenth century. Throughout much of the twentieth century, Hegel was not merely shunned, but also scorned and derided as the exemplar of all that analytic philosophy abjured. However, a significant revival of interest in Hegel's philosophy among analytically oriented philosophers has recently emerged and continues to grow.

Opposition to nineteenth-century (neo-)Hegelian idealism took several forms. One was a revival of realism. 'Realism', however, is a protean word; in this case the focus is on the contrast to idealism. Realists hold that there is at least some non-mentalistic component in the vocabulary that most fundamentally describes the world; mentalistic vocabulary applies only to a limited set of entities and not to the world-whole. A second form of opposition to Hegelianism was the reassertion of atomism, not only in nature, but also in semantics and the analysis of the mental. Atomism, in turn, tends to associate with foundationalist, hierarchical structures; once the fundamental elements are decided upon, everything else must be composed of them.

The tremendous growth in the sciences during the nineteenth century surely contributed to the rise of realism and atomism. By the turn of the century, the idea that the fundamental nature of the world is to be explicated in terms of a universal self-consciousness or spirit seemed less and less compelling. With analytic methodologies proving increasingly fruitful time and again in both science and philosophy, their influence made itself felt in the development of modern logic in the work of Frege, Peano, and Russell and Whitehead; in the popularity of positivism (the doctrines of Comte and then Mach, not yet those of the Vienna Circle); in the revival of the British Empiricist tradition (J. S. Mill was Russell's godfather); in the careful attention to scientific methodology paid by C. S. Peirce; and in the rise of the philosophy of science as a significant subdiscipline. In Germany, Hermann von Helmholtz and the neo-Kantians paid much greater attention to the empirical sciences, substituting philosophy of science for Hegelian philosophy of nature.[1]

The general secularization of Western society, and especially the universities, also seemed incompatible with Hegel, who (rightly or wrongly) was widely associated with a heavily theological and metaphysical philosophy. Similarly, the Hegelianism of the schools (as opposed to left-wing or Marxist Hegelianism) was associated with political conservatism.

This catalog is far from complete, and these forces did not always push in the same direction. The empiricism of the early twentieth century, for instance, was often phenomenalistic, not realistic. Philosophy of science, especially in the first few decades following the tremendous blossoming of physics early in the century, seemed to take theoretical physics, with its increasing panoply of unobservable entities, as the exemplar of everything scientific, and this put pressure on the shape any realism could take. The interpretation Russell gave the new symbolic logic was highly atomistic, foundationalistic, individualistic, and phenomenalistic, which, again, was in tension with the urge to realism and, at least arguably, the actual procedures of the empirical sciences.

This brief overview helps explain why Hegel was anathema to the analysts: he stood in direct opposition to the atomism, foundationalism, individualism, reductionism, and materialist realism that operated in the newfound analytic tradition as regulative ideals. Each of these 'ideals' has since come under attack, not just from outside the analytic tradition, but by the development of arguments within the tradition (in good Hegelian dialectical fashion). The rest of this chapter will follow perhaps the most significant rapprochement with Hegelian philosophy attempted from within the analytic tradition: the efforts of the so-called Pittsburgh school.

The Pittsburgh school originated in the work of Wilfrid S. Sellars (1912–1989). Sellars's training in philosophy was cosmopolitan, with schooling in both the United States and England. In particular, he had strong ties to the realist traditions in both American and British thought through his father, Roy Wood Sellars—himself a significant American philosopher, a founder of critical realism and professor at the University of Michigan for the first half of the twentieth century—and his teachers at Oxford, H. A. Prichard and H. H. Price.

Sellars wrote in the analytic tradition; arguably, he became one of its pillars. *Readings in Philosophical Analysis* (1949), edited with Herbert Feigl, became the industry standard reader for a generation of analysts, and *Philosophical Studies*, the journal Sellars and Feigl founded in 1950, was the first journal solely devoted to "philosophy in the analytic tradition." Still, Sellars distinguished himself from most analysts by his broad knowledge

---

[1] A caveat: Hegel himself was very interested and well informed about the sciences of his day. His followers, particularly those ensconced in academia, not so much.

and sensitive interpretations of the history of philosophy, particularly of Aristotle and early modern philosophy through Kant. He was an empirically minded philosopher who was nonetheless fascinated by rationalist philosophy. His hope was to move analytic philosophy from its empiricist beginnings into a more adequate and sophisticated Kantian phase. Arguably, though, Sellars's own awareness of the shortcomings of Kant prompted him to develop a far more Hegelian philosophy than would have been politic at the time to admit. His younger colleagues at Pittsburgh, John McDowell (1942–) and Robert B. Brandom (1950–), further developed some of Sellars's insights in their own work, while also departing from Sellars in various ways.

33.2. Sociality and Historicity

Some of Sellars's references to Hegel are either indirect or subtly critical when read closely, but some declare his clear allegiance to a Hegelian position. The clearest of these is in "Philosophy and the Scientific Image of Man," when Sellars rejects the "Robinson Crusoe conception of the world as generating conceptual thinking directly in the individual":[2]

> It was not until the time of Hegel that the essential role of the group as a mediating factor in this causation [of the presence in the individual of the framework of conceptual thinking] was recognized, and while it is easy for us to see that the immanence and transcendence of conceptual frameworks with respect to the individual thinker is a social phenomenon, and to find a recognition of this fact implicit in the very form of our image of man in the world, it was not until the nineteenth century that this feature of the manifest image was, however inadequately, taken into account.[3]

The social nature of thought and conceptuality remains an invariant commitment of the Pittsburgh school, reinforced by the influence of Wittgenstein's later works.

Sellars quickly hedges his endorsement of this Hegelian insight with criticism:

> The manifest image must, therefore, be construed as containing a conception of itself as a group phenomenon, the group mediating between the individual and the intelligible order. But any attempt to explain this mediation within the framework of the manifest image was bound to fail, for the manifest image contains the resources for such an attempt only in the sense that it provides the foundation on which scientific theory can build an explanatory framework; and while conceptual structures of this

---

[2] Wilfrid Sellars, "Philosophy and the Scientific Image of Man" [PSIM] ¶44, in *Science, Perception and Reality* [SPR]: 16; in *In the Space of Reasons: Selected Essays of Wilfrid Sellars*, eds. Kevin Scharp and Robert B. Brandom [ISR]: 384. Available online at http://www.ditext.com/sellars/psim.html.

[3] Sellars, PSIM ¶44.

framework are built on the manifest image, they are not definable within it. Thus, the Hegelian, like the Platonist of whom he is the heir, was limited to the attempt to understand the relation between intelligible order and individual minds in analogical terms.[4]

There are several different issues at play here, and we need to keep them separate. One issue concerns the general status of the conceptual or intelligible order, while another concerns the particular status of our currently dominant conceptual framework and its major features. The relations between these two are complex for both Hegel and Sellars. Both philosophers are, in one sense of the term, epistemic realists about the conceptual order. That is, they both think that (descriptive) concepts aim at delimiting the very nature of things; they see no sense in the Kantian notion of a thing-in-itself that is in principle beyond the reach of the conceptual or the knowable. But at the same time, they are hardly naïve realists: though concepts *aim* at delimiting the nature of things, they also tend to fall short of their target. Indeed, both of them acknowledge that it takes significant effort to develop successively better and better concepts. For both Hegel and Sellars, the *sociality* of thought entails also its *historicity*. We always operate with a less than ultimately satisfactory conceptual framework that is fated to be replaced by something more satisfactory, whether on the basis of conceptual or empirical considerations.

Hegel sketches a complex sequence of ever more sophisticated conceptual schemes in the *Phenomenology*. Sellars boils this down to a clash between what he calls the 'manifest image [MI]'—the rich common-sense scheme in terms of which we ordinarily make sense of the world—and the 'scientific image [SI]'—the incipient and (potentially) radically different scheme that is starting to be constructed by the empirical sciences.[5] For both Hegel and Sellars, grasp of the Truth lies at the end of a long process.

Although Hegel and Sellars think along related lines with regard to the status of conceptual frameworks vis-à-vis reality, they differ significantly concerning the content of the ultimate framework. For any complex conceptual framework, there will be some architecture of explanatory priorities that makes some concepts more fundamental than others that are to be explained in terms of more basic concepts. For Hegel, the most general and explanatorily most basic concepts are those of spirit: reason, concept, subjectivity and objectivity, and so on. Ultimately, we understand nature in terms of its relation to spirit, and the process by which we come to be able to grasp the truth is a process by which spirit comes to know itself. Things are quite otherwise with Sellars, who thinks the explanatorily prior concepts in the scientific image will be the concepts of materiality:

---

[4]   Sellars, PSIM ¶ 48, in SPR: 17; in ISR: 385.

[5]   The 'manifest image' is the more-or-less refined 'common-sense' conceptual framework in terms of which humans have come to understand and cope with themselves in their world. It is a Strawsonian/Aristotelian framework in which persons and things are the basic objects. In Sellars's view, it is currently being challenged by the growth of a new and categorially distinct framework that is being developed by the empirical sciences, the "scientific image of humanity in the world."

The concepts of ideal matter-of-factual truth and of what there really is are as fraught with subjectives pertaining to conceptualization as the idealists have ever claimed. But *no* picture[6] of the world contains *as such* mentalistic expressions functioning *as such*. The indispensibility and logical irreducibility of mentalistic discourse is compatible with the idea that in *this* sense *there are no mental acts*. Though full of important insights, Idealism is, therefore, radically false.[7]

This is a complex claim, but it comes down to the idea that even though mentalistic (or spiritual) discourse is both indispensible for creatures like us and irreducible to material-object discourse, in the scientific image the mental will be seen to depend on the material ontologically.[8] One's ontology is determined by the explanatorily most basic kinds recognized in one's conceptual framework. Hegel is undoubtedly an idealist; we can let others worry about how weighty a *metaphysical* idealism it is. Sellars is a decided materialist: "the solution of the puzzle lay in correctly locating the conceptual order in the causal order and correctly interpreting the causality involved."[9]

According to Sellars, the manifest image generates questions it cannot answer on its own. Even augmented with the Hegelian insight that the community is an essential intermediary between the individual and the intelligible order, Sellars claims that the manifest framework is not in a position to explain *how* the community serves this role. This is a complex thought. First, what Sellars calls the 'intelligible order' is the network of rational connections among the concepts of a conceptual framework.[10] For example, our confidence that brothers are male siblings and that water turns to ice when cooled sufficiently are both expressions of connections that have come to be built into the intelligible order made available to us by our conceptual framework/language.

---

[6] Sellars uses 'picture' here in a technical sense that is *not* equivalent to *proposition* or *statement*. Mentalistic expressions, Sellars is telling us, do not participate in the basic, naturalistically unproblematic, pre-semantic picturing relations that hold between objects in the world and the occurrence of particular sign-design types. Mentalistic expressions relate to real-world objects and events in much more complex ways.

[7] Wilfrid Sellars, *Science and Metaphysics*, chap. 5, ¶78: 142–143.

[8] A full interpretation of this passage would require an explication of Sellars's obscure notion of *picturing*, which he thinks is a key to realism. But that goes beyond the scope of this chapter. See W. A. deVries, "Getting Beyond Idealisms."

[9] Wilfrid Sellars, "Autobiographical Reflections: (February, 1973)," 285. Available online at http://www.ditext.com/sellars/ar.html.

[10] It is also worth noting that Sellars would not think that rational connections among concepts are always *analytic* or *a priori*. Sellars makes room for *material* connections that are nonetheless rational. In general, Sellars thinks of rational connections, not on the containment model that Kant employed, but as inference tickets, and then recognizes both formally and materially valid inferences.

It is also worth remarking here that Sellars's phrase 'the intelligible order' implies a unique referent. But if the intelligible order is the set of rational connections among concepts, then there will be, of course, many possible intelligible orders, since there are multiple possible conceptual frameworks. Sellars does seem to assume that we can sensibly posit a Peircean ideal framework that, given world enough and time, we would be fated to accept.

As noted earlier, until the nineteenth century, philosophers believed that these rational connections are learned by means of some action of the world (broadly construed) upon our individual minds. Furthermore, according to Sellars, "[i]n the Platonic tradition this mode of causation is attributed to a being which is analogous, to a greater or lesser degree, to a person."[11] In Sellars's view, Hegel, as a member in good standing of the Platonic tradition, also sought to understand the relation between intelligible order and individual mind in terms of something person-like that accounts for how individuals come to possess a (normatively constituted) conceptual framework in terms of which the world in which they live can be understood. This is spirit informing the activity and pervading the being of the human individual. Spirit is not like an individual person, localized in space and time, nor is it outside of space and time, but its fundamental structure is still that of a *synthetic, rational unity*, a mind. It makes sense to attribute 'cunning' to spirit, for instance.

Sellars's view is that the manifest image *cannot* explain how it is that the community (or spirit) mediates the individual's acquisition of a conceptual framework. Sellars gives us no argument in PSIM for this negative claim. He needs a positive argument to establish that the manifest image cannot develop such an explanation and that we must turn to a radically novel scientific framework to do so. The manifest image has shown itself in the past to be a flexible tool for coping with reality, capable of growth and development in order to accommodate an ever richer understanding of the structure of reality and our relation to it.

Sellars does say that with the resources of the MI, we could generate an understanding of the relation between the individual and the intelligible order 'in analogical terms'. That is, their relationship is understood by construing it as analogous to something else understood fairly well independently, such as a form of *perception*, which we have some grasp of, aimed at a special object (e.g., Platonic forms). Calling it an analogical understanding sounds fairly dismissive, as if such an understanding is something to be transcended. In a sense, that's what Sellars thinks, but even if we manage to *transcend* this analogy-based understanding, it does not follow that it should or even can be *discarded*. According to Sellars, conceptions of psychological states are developed in analogical terms, and even though Sellars believes that, in the final wash, there are no mental acts, he never intimates that we can or should abandon the language of psychology (although some of Sellars's students have drawn that conclusion). Sellars insists that the language of "individual and community intentions"—the very heart of the manifest image— must be joined to, or better, preserved within the future scientific image.[12] Refining the language of intentions—the language of sociology, social psychology, family life, and

---

[11] Sellars, PSIM ¶44, in SPR: 16; in ISR: 384.
[12] I have argued that *preservation* of the "language of individual and community intentions" in the scientific image (as opposed to mere 'joining') is the proper conception in several places; see deVries, "Ontology and the Completeness of Sellars's Two Images," and "Images, Descriptions, and Pictures: Personhood and the Clash."

politics—has been on the agenda since the time of Hegel, but Sellars thinks there is a limit to the progress that can be made in these directions with armchair methodologies.

A split has developed among the followers of Sellars, often described (with obvious reference to the history of Hegel reception) as a split between 'right-wing' and 'left-wing' Sellarsians. Not everyone agrees on just what the divide is, but it seems to center on the weight one gives the natural sciences in ontology. Right-wing Sellarsians retain Sellars's declared scientific realism: the empirical ontology of the world is strictly a matter for science to settle, and that means displacing the everyday ontology of common sense. Left-wing Sellarsians endorse Sellars's rejection of the given and his analysis of the intentional (by and large), but reject the strident scientific realism that declares that "in the dimension of describing and explaining the world, science is the measure of all things, of what is that it is, and of what is not that it is not."[13] (Interestingly, it is the right-wing Sellarsians who are more radical and the left more conservative.) Brandom and McDowell are left-wing Sellarsians; both reject the notion that science will cast significant light on the norm-constituted concepts that articulate human intentionality.

Sellars himself was a right-wing Sellarsian, and he thinks we are now able "to see this [problem of the acquisition of a conceptual scheme] as a matter of evolutionary development as a group phenomenon."[14] The point is that evolution can generate categorially new objects, even something like a conceptual scheme.[15] Ruth Millikan, for instance, has shown how such processes can be accommodated within a generally Sellarsian view.[16] Yet one of the great lacks in Sellars's philosophy is a treatment of the biological and social sciences. This is not sheer accident, for accommodating teleologically constituted biological or normatively constituted social phenomena within the causal structures central to science's concerns is a daunting challenge.

How are we to construe the relations among irreducibly distinct groups of concepts, all of which seem to be necessary for a full comprehension of our multifarious world? Arguably, both Sellars and Hegel believe that there is some privileged set of concepts, some privileged layer of discourse, that provides the most universal and encompassing viewpoint on the world, its history, and our place in it. This then determines our ultimate ontology: materialistic for Sellars, idealistic for Hegel. Neither seems to take seriously that the irreducibility of these different sets of concepts is itself indicative of the ultimate furniture of the world.

---

[13] Wilfrid Sellars, EPM. This passage, often called the '*scientia mensura*', occurs in §41; in SPR: 173; in KMG: 253. Also available online at http://www.ditext.com/sellars/epm.html.

[14] Sellars, PSIM ¶49; in SPR: 17; in ISR: 385.

[15] I take it, e.g., that plants are categorially different from animals in the manifest image.

[16] Ruth Millikan, *Language, Thought, and Other Biological Categories*. Millikan is a right-wing Sellarsian who would agree with Sellars that we need to turn to natural science for the *ultimate* story about language, thought, and other biological categories. For an interesting review of her differences with the left-wing Brandom, see Ruth Millikan, "The Father, the Son, and the Daughter." For further discussion of their differences, see Willem A. deVries, "All in the Family."

33.3. THE MYTH OF THE ATOMIC

Sellars is most commonly identified with the critique of the *myth of the given* first articulated in his classic essay "Empiricism and the Philosophy of Mind." This critique can be
construed along fairly narrow epistemological lines, but it really reaches across the full
range of the cognitive as a critique of any atomistic, foundationalistic construal of the
structure of meaningful human activity, both theoretical and practical. That is, Sellars
denies that the epistemic, semantic, or intentional properties of any episodes or states
accrue to them either in *isolation* or as simply *descriptive* properties:

> The essential point is that in characterizing an episode or a state as that of knowing,
> we are not giving an empirical description of that episode or state; we are placing it
> in the logical space of reasons, of justifying and being able to justify what one says.[17]

'Empirical' is used here as G. E. Moore used 'natural', to stand for the purely matter-of-
factual, in contrast to anything normative or evaluative. The "logical space of reasons"
is, first, an abstract *space*, that is, an array of potential positions, the identity of which is
determined (holistically) by their relations to the other potential positions, and, second,
an essentially *normative* realm, structured by the oughts and ought-nots of good inference (both formal and material).[18] Epistemic givens would be states that possess their
epistemic status independently of their (epistemic) relations to any other states (e.g., a
self-justifying belief or a belief that is warranted simply because it is caused in a certain
way). Semantic givens would be states that possess a certain meaning independently of
their (semantic) relations to any other states, for example, because they are intrinsically
intelligible or derive meaning from some (non-normative) 'ostensive tie' to some object.

Thus, Sellars denies both that there are 'atoms' of knowledge or meaning independent
of their relation to other 'pieces' of knowledge or meaning, and that they are structured
in a neat hierarchy rather than an interlocking (social) network. The determinate content of a thought or utterance is fixed by its position in the space of implications and
employments available to the community in its language or conceptual framework. This
kind of holism is congenial to Hegelian modes of thinking. It is important to see, however, that Sellars also rejects standard forms of coherentism.

> *Above all*, the [standard] picture is misleading because of its static character. One
> seems forced to choose between the picture of an elephant which rests on a tor-
> toise (What supports the tortoise?) and the picture of a great Hegelian serpent of

---

[17] Sellars, EPM §36, in SPR: 169; in KMG: 248.

[18] *Formally* valid inferences are so in virtue of the syntactic structures of the sentences involved,
without regard to their content. *Modus ponens* or a valid syllogism are classic examples. *Materially*
good inferences are not formally valid, but are such that it is part of the language that the truth of the
premise(s) entails the truth of the conclusion. For example, "A is red" materially implies "A is colored."
Sellars thinks of scientific laws as proposed and corroborated material inference tickets.

|

knowledge with its tail in its mouth (Where does it begin?). Neither will do. For empirical knowledge, like its sophisticated extension, science, is rational, not because it has a foundation but because it is a self-correcting enterprise which can put any claim in jeopardy, though not all at once.[19]

This seems like a rejection of Hegel, but it is, of course, a rejection of the cartoon version of Hegel that was all too dominant in Anglo-American philosophy. Recognition of the dynamics, of the dialectics of thought, is precisely what is needed to fix the imagery.

33.4. THE RETURN TO EXPERIENCE

Sellars's attempt to escape the apparently forced choice between foundationalism and coherentism was picked up to great notice in John McDowell's 1994 book *Mind and World*, wherein he wants to help us escape the 'intolerable oscillation' that has characterized modern philosophy between coherentism, a theory that gives us only a "frictionless spinning in the void" which "cannot make sense of the bearing of thought on objective reality," and foundationalism, "an appeal to the given, which turns out to be useless."[20] For both Sellars and McDowell, resolving this tension means developing a more adequate conception of experience itself, one that embodies the Kantian insight that experience is both sensory and conceptual, aetiologically non-inferential yet justificationally embedded in an inferentially structured matrix. But Sellars and McDowell do not agree on the proper conception of experience. Sellars retains a significant, though non-epistemic role for the sensory, non-conceptual content of experience.

> [B]y denying that sense impressions, however indispensable to cognition, were themselves cognitive, Kant made a radical break with all his predecessors, empiricists and rationalists alike. The 'of-ness' of sensation simply isn't the 'of-ness' of even the most rudimentary thought. . . . But his own question haunted me. How is it possible that knowledge has this structure? . . . It wasn't until much later that I came to see that the solution of the puzzle lay in correctly locating the conceptual order in the causal order and correctly interpreting the causality involved.[21]

For Sellars, then, experience is a double-sided coin. The sensory aspect of experience is part of the causal story of the impact of the world upon us, but its conceptual aspect locates it within the logical space of reasons, the space of reasons for belief and for action.[22] Early on, McDowell rejected the idea that "receptivity makes an even

---

[19] Sellars, EPM §38: in SPR: 170; in KMG: 250.
[20] John McDowell, *Mind and World*, 23.
[21] Sellars, "Autobiographical Reflections," 285.
[22] For an intelligible, thorough examination of Sellars's two-component analysis of perceptual experience, see Paul Coates, *The Metaphysics of Perception: Wilfrid Sellars, Perceptual Consciousness and Critical Realism*.

notionally separable contribution to its co-operation with spontaneity,"[23] though in later works he backs away from this fairly extreme position.

33.4.1. Realism, the Phenomenal, and Transcendental Idealism

The differences between Sellars and McDowell are significant, and we can see them as differing responses to Kant's transcendental idealism, which neither Sellars nor McDowell finds attractive. Both Sellars and McDowell want to be realists, not merely *empirical* realists à la Kant, but realists for whom the distinction between things as we know them and things as they are evaporates. But they take very different routes to this desired goal. McDowell proclaims that

> [i]n a particular experience in which one is not misled, what one takes in is that things are thus and so. That things are thus and so is the content of the experience, and it can also be the content of a judgement: it becomes the content of a judgement if the subject decides to take the experience at face value. So it is conceptual content. But that things are thus and so is also, if one is not misled, an aspect of the layout of the world: it is how things are. Thus the idea of conceptually structured operations of receptivity puts us in a position to speak of experience as openness to the layout of reality.[24]

Sellars's and McDowell's different responses to Kantian transcendental idealism reveal their relations to Hegel. Like Sellars and McDowell, Hegel is an epistemological realist: he rejects the idea that we do not (or are not even able to) know things as they are in themselves. Yet neither Hegel nor Sellars wants to reject altogether the distinction between phenomenal reality and things as they are in themselves. Sellars calls the distinction between the phenomenal and the real the distinction between the manifest and the scientific images of man in the world. Hegel provides for numerous phenomenal realities related in ways that require a phenomenology to understand. It is not the distinction between phenomenon and reality itself that Hegel and Sellars attack, but the notion that it is *absolute*, establishing an unbridgeable divide.[25] McDowell, however, is concerned to defend our "openness to the layout of reality" and seems not to take seriously the idea that we might have systematically false beliefs about the nature of things.[26] On this score, Sellars is more Hegelian than McDowell.

---

[23] John McDowell, *Mind and World*, 51.

[24] McDowell, *Mind and World*, 26.

[25] It is notable that attacking the absoluteness of familiar philosophical distinctions is a standard move for pragmatists. This connection to pragmatism is particularly important for Brandom.

[26] This is probably the influence of Donald Davidson on McDowell.

33.4.2. Space, Time, and a Full-Fledged Epistemological Realism

Kant's arguments for transcendental idealism turn crucially on the status of space and time. Hegel, Sellars, and McDowell, however, all reject Kant's notion that space and time can be only subjective conditions of human receptivity.

Despite the many differences between Hegel and Sellars in their development of a full-fledged epistemological realism, there is a fundamental similarity in their strategy.[27] The strategy, boiled down, is this: Kant's critical philosophy is formulated in terms of basic dualisms, *a priori/a posteriori*, analytic/synthetic, receptivity/spontaneity, even empirical science/philosophy. Hegel insists that, trapped in these dualisms, Kant cannot satisfactorily explain human cognition or action. The gaps imposed by the assumed dualisms never get properly bridged. Hegel therefore reconceives the critical project. Hegel abandons rigid dualisms and recognizes that human life is a dynamic, fallible enterprise that begins from relative ignorance (even of ourselves), is fraught with contradictions to be overcome, and works itself slowly via constant revision toward an ever more adequate grasp of and fittedness to the reality *within* which (as opposed to *over against* which) we live. Any distinctions that arise must be explained, not assumed, including categorial distinctions. If we do not begin with starkly dualistic assumptions, the reasonableness of a belief in unknowable things in themselves never forces itself upon us.

Sellars's response to Kant is strikingly similar, for Sellars also recognizes that there is no Archimedean point outside of common reality from which the critic can operate. He also rejects absolute, hard and fast dualisms in favor of limited and pragmatically justified distinctions. As Paul Redding argues, Hegel and Sellars reject both an exogenous and an endogenous given.[28] That is, neither empirical content nor conceptual scheme is given to us independently of the other. But if conceptual form is not given independently of the real world, there is little reason to think that it is related only contingently to that world and affords us a mode of access to it unrelated to what that world is in itself. In Sellars's view, as well as Hegel's, human life is a dynamic, fallible enterprise that begins from relative ignorance (even of ourselves), is fraught with contradictions to be overcome, and works itself slowly via constant revision toward an ever more adequate grasp of and fittedness to the reality *within* which (as opposed to *over against* which) we live.

McDowell expresses his concern with Kant's transcendental idealism as a worry that it reduces experience and knowledge to 'facts about us'. He agrees that neither empirical content nor conceptual scheme is given to us independently of the other. But rather than trying to accord sensation, as something non-conceptual, a distinguishable place in experience, like Sellars and Hegel, McDowell denies that there is *anything* non-conceptual in experience. Space and time should not be seen as forms of a distinct,

---

[27] Sally Sedgewick's analysis in *Hegel's Critique of Kant: From Dichotomy to Identity* is very helpful.

[28] See Paul Redding, *Analytic Philosophy and the Return of Hegelian Thought*.

non-conceptual element in experience, but, as McDowell claims Hegel also thought, as further categorial forms of the conceptual content in experience. The sensory is, thus, not an intermediary between understanding and the world, but a way in which we are open to the world, a shaping of our consciousness of the world.

> When Kant makes it look as if the forms of our sensibility are brute-fact features of our subjectivity, it becomes difficult to see how they could also be forms of the manifestness to us of what is genuinely objective. But when, in the move Hegel applauds, Kant puts the forms of our sensibility on a level with the categories, he takes a step towards making it possible to see the forms of our sensibility, no less than the categories, as genuinely forms of cognition—at once forms of subjective activity and forms of genuine objectivity with which that activity engages.[29]

Assimilating space and time to the other categories of conceptuality and essentially ignoring them as forms intrinsic to the self-external is not at all clearly Hegelian.[30] Furthermore, McDowell's deconstruction of the intuition/concept distinction undercuts the Kantianism that he claims to be defending. What, after all, is left once Kant's claim that there are two independent sources of knowledge that combine in experience is rejected?[31] In this light, McDowell's move seems less a radicalization of Kant than a retreat to Leibniz.

33.4.3. A Form of Idealism

Still, there is a clear sense in which McDowell espouses idealism. For McDowell endorses Wittgenstein's dictum that "[t]he world is everything that is the case."[32]

> And if we do say that and mean it, we conceive the world, not . . . as a totality of the describable things—zebras and so forth—that there are (as we say) in it, but as precisely, everything that can be truly thought or said: not everything we would think about if we thought truly, but everything we would think.[33]

---

[29] John McDowell, "Having the World in View: Sellars, Kant, and Intentionality," 102–103.

[30] The problematic explananda here are the facts that (1) space and time receive dialectical treatment in Hegel's system at two very different locations: once early on in the *Philosophy of Nature* and once in the last third of the *Philosophy of Subjective Spirit*; and (2) animals, who operate at the level of sensation and not thought, must nonetheless be able to track and in some sense represent space and time. The obvious answer seems to be that, as Hegel himself says, space and time are forms embodied in different substrata, one of which is non-conceptual.

[31] This point is elaborated and defended more fully in Paul Redding, "McDowell's Radicalization of Kant's Account of Concepts and Intuitions."

[32] Ludwig Wittgenstein, *Tractatus Logico-Philosophicus*, Proposition 1.

[33] McDowell, "Having the World in View," 143.

McDowell goes on to say, "This is an idealism in an obvious sense. On this conception, the world itself is indeed structured by the form of judgment."[34]

These claims reveal McDowell's idealism as a form of logical realism. The fundamental structure of McDowell's world is logical or conceptual structure, and the primary force of that claim is that it (1) denies that either spatiotemporal or causal structure is fundamental except insofar as space, time, and causation are themselves logical categories; and (2) explains the sense in which we are 'open to the world'. Said differently, for McDowell, the logical space of reasons includes the entirety of the world and subsumes the nominally distinct spaces of objects, causes, and laws. McDowell's normative realism, the doctrine that normative demands and prohibitions are not just believed-in, but actually are out there in the world for us to respond to, is essential to his view here. It is a Hegelian position to see a deep identity between the fundamental structures of world and the fundamental structure of good thought. Here McDowell is clearly more Hegelian than Sellars.

Sellars rejects the idea that the world is the totality of facts, for, according to Sellars, fact-talk is material-mode truth-talk. That is why facts have logical structure. Sellars thinks the world itself is a totality of *objects*, and objects do not have logical structure. Empirical objects have causal and spatiotemporal structure; logical analysis and empirical science are different enterprises, however much cross-fertilization is desirable. Whereas McDowell (and Hegel) unifies the causal and the conceptual realms by subsuming the causal under the conceptual, Sellars unifies them, as we saw earlier (cf. "Autobiographical Reflections," 285), by incorporating the conceptual within the causal order. This does not mean *reducing* the conceptual to the causal, but only, as he says, "locating the conceptual order in the causal order."

McDowell's quietism departs from Hegel, however. McDowell abjures grand philosophical or metaphysical constructions and insists that the point of good philosophy is to make it possible to stop doing philosophy, to remove any spur or urge to engage in such abstruse speculations. Also missing from McDowell's position is a Hegelian sense of philosophical development or growth. Since McDowell holds (like Wittgenstein) that in ordinary language and common sense everything is in order, there is and could be no grand narrative of the development of philosophy, only a contingent series of corrections when thinking goes awry. Deep metaphysical modesty combined with a static conception of the philosophical realm seems, however, un-Hegelian. Hegel argues for the *need* for philosophy, and he does not intend that his efforts will leave everything in place. And who has a deeper commitment to the dynamism of philosophical theory than Hegel? Whether metaphysical or not, Hegel is a philosophical theoretician on a grand scale, and Sellars, with his metaphysical courage and dynamic understanding of the development of human understanding, is closer to Hegel's spirit in this regard, however much his philosophical materialism opposes Hegel's absolute idealism.

---

[34] McDowell, "Having the World in View," 143.

33.5. Semantic Dynamism

33.5.1. Sellars, Functional Classification, and Inferentialism

In different ways, Sellars and McDowell resemble Hegel in their attempts to avoid Kant's transcendental idealism while still maintaining an anti-foundationalist epistemological realism. This concerns relatively large-scale structural features of the mind's relation to the world. If that were the only way in which the Pittsburgh school 'revived' Hegel, it would be pretty thin beer. But the school also has a lot to say about the nature of conceptuality itself, and what it says resonates with Hegelian overtones. It is here that Brandom's work comes to the fore, elaborating a base established by Sellars.

Coherence can be invoked in a theory of truth, a theory of meaning (or of concepts), and a theory of justification or knowledge.[35] Sellars exploits all three forms. As mentioned, epistemologically there are no stand-alone justifiers for Sellars, and semantically, meaning and intentionality concern the functional role of symbolic states in complex systems of behavioral modulation.

According to Sellars, semantics is a matter of *functional classification*. To say what an utterance or a thought means is to say what role it plays in the linguistic/conceptual economy of the community. We do not usually do this by giving a detailed and complex description of that role, but by giving an equivalent phrase, hopefully intelligible to one's interlocutor, that plays a similar role. So, when we say things like

'Brother' means *male sibling*

'*Geschwindigkeitsbegrenzung*' in German means *speed limit*

we use the phrase to the right of 'means' to delimit the role of the phrase on the left-hand side by providing a phrase in our background language with a relevantly similar role. Sellars points to three dimensions of the functional role of an expression: its role in (1) language-entry transitions; (2) language-exit transitions; and (3) intralinguistic transitions. Thus, this is a *use* theory of semantics. Language-entry transitions include observation statements, in which interaction with one's environment evokes a linguistic response; language-exit transitions include statements of intention that evolve into actions. Most interesting for our purposes are the intralinguistic transitions, in which one moves from one utterance or thought to another. When purporting to adhere to conceptual proprieties, such transitions are known as inferences. In "Inference and Meaning," Sellars argues that the meaning of an expression is crucially determined by its contribution to good inferences, both formal

---

[35] This is a point made also by Roderick Firth in an article Sellars referred to often: "Coherence, Certainty, and Epistemic Priority."

and material.[36] Formally good inferences (e.g., *modus ponens*) are good in virtue of their syntactic form. Materially good inferences do not rely on syntax. The inferences

The cube is red	It is raining
So, the cube is colored	So, it will be wet outside

are not *formally* valid, but they are good material inferences. Sellars denies that we ought to think of them as essentially enthymematic: not all inference licenses can be made into explicit premises.[37] For Sellars, such facts about inferential proprieties determine both the *form* and the *content* of our judgings and the concepts used in them.

> 23. To say of a judging that it has a certain logical form is to classify it and its constitu- ents with respect to their epistemic powers.
> 24. If judgings qua conceptual acts have "form," they also have "content." . . . The temptation is to think of the "content" of an act as an entity that is "contained" by it. But if the "form" of a judging is the structure by virtue of which it is possessed of certain generic logical or epistemic powers, surely the content must be the character by virtue of which the act has specific modes of these generic logical or epistemic powers.[38]

One consequence of this view is that linguistic/semantic form and content are not rad- ically different. If, for example, physical object judgments have their own 'form' (per- haps, e.g., suppressible default inferences concerning spatiotemporal location, causal connectivity, or appropriate forms of evidence), then judgments about rocks fill in or specify this form in determinate ways.

In Sellars's view, *all* semantic predicates are ultimately meta-linguistic functional clas- sifiers. It is not just *meaning statements* that classify expressions functionally; so do *ref- erence statements* and even *truth attributions*. Sellars thus denies that *meaning, reference,* or *truth* denote relations between words or thoughts and objects in the world.[39] This is sometimes described as a rejection of representationalism, though Sellars talks reg- ularly about representations, both linguistic and mental. He certainly rejects the idea that there is some set of specific, fundamental semantic 'relations' between language or concept and the world (say, the meaning, reference, or satisfaction relations) that deter- mines our ontology.

Sellars's doctrine relates fairly clearly to Hegel. One of Kant's revisions to the 'new way of ideas' that dominated the thought of his predecessors was his insistence on the

---

[36] Wilfrid Sellars, "Inference and Meaning." Note the order of explication here: meaning is determined by inferential proprieties, not the other way around.

[37] Lewis Carroll, "What the Tortoise said to Achilles."

[38] Wilfrid Sellars, "Some Remarks on Kant's Theory of Experience."

[39] There is a trivial sense of 'relation' in which any statement the surface grammar of which contains a relational (that is, n-place for n > 1) predicate describes a relation. But surface grammar is not decisive here. After all, sentences of the form "X is related to Y" are not all true for every substituend X and Y.

priority of *judgment* over *concepts*; a concept, for Kant, is basically a predicate of a possible judgment (CPR A69/B94). Hegel takes this move one step further: judgments are
elements of possible inferences. Hegel's Concept self-elaborates into a syllogism, showing itself as a synthesizer or unifier of other concepts. The Hegelian view that concepts
are determined by their place in an inferentially articulated system is highly compatible
with Sellars's overall view of semantics and intentionality.

33.5.2. Brandom's Hegelianism: Intentionality, Normativity, and the Structure of Authority

Brandom spells out more fully how this is supposed to work, taking up the inferentialist
conception of semantics that Sellars really only sketched in outline and elaborating it
significantly. In this regard, Brandom is the most explicitly Hegelian of the Pittsburgh
school. He has also written more on Hegel than his colleagues, and has been working
for years on a commentary on the *Phenomenology of Spirit*, successive drafts of which
are available on his website. Here I draw mainly on his Woodbridge Lectures, a broad
overview of his interpretation of German idealism and Hegel's particular position in
that movement.[40] These lectures are more relevant to our purposes here than the details
of the *Phenomenology*.

Brandom sees Hegel as modifying several central themes in Kant's transcendental
idealism. The first of these Kantian themes is the realization that intentionality, the fundamental defining trait of the mental, is, at root, a normative affair:

> What distinguishes judging and intentional doing from the activities of non-sapient
> creatures is not that they involve some special sort of mental processes, but that they
> are things knowers and agents are in a distinctive way responsible for. Judging and
> acting involve commitments. They are endorsements, exercises of authority.[41]

This is Sellars's idea that intentional state attributions locate the subject in 'the logical
space of reasons'. Sapience (conceptual thought) involves *responsibility*, and the fundamental responsibility, according to Brandom, is to integrate one's intentional states
(both one's past states and one's growing accumulation of new intentional states) into
a total *unity of apperception*. This involves elaborating and adopting the material and
formal consequences of one's intentional states and eliminating conflicts that may arise
among them. One is, thus, responsible *for* one's thoughts and actions, the contents of
which are determined by their relations (again, both formal and material) to other
intentional states (echoing Sellars's coherence theory of meaning and intentionality);
and one is responsible *to* the objects of one's judgments insofar as they (the objects)
set the standard of correctness for the commitments one undertakes in judging. It is

---

[40] Robert B. Brandom, "Animating Ideas," 27–110.
[41] Brandom, "Animating Ideas," 32.

the synthetic activity of "integrating judgments with one another, by critical exclusion and ampliative inclusion or extension [that] makes the concepts both of subject and of object intelligible."[42]

The second Kantian theme in Hegel concerns the nature of normativity itself. Kant's Enlightenment twist is the attitude-dependence of norms, which come to exist only when humans start taking and treating each other *as* authoritative, responsible, committed, and so on. Kant's understanding of the attitude-dependence of normativity puts the notion of *autonomy*, self-governance, center stage: "we, as subjects, are genuinely *normatively* constrained only by rules we constrain *ourselves* by, those that we adopt and acknowledge *as* binding on us."[43] If normativity is grounded in the autonomy of individuals, however, there is a potential problem. If it were up to us both *whether* we are bound by or responsible to a particular conceptual norm, which is a matter of the normative *force* of our judgmental act, and *what it is* we are bound to, the *content* of the judgmental act, then whatever *seems* right to one would *be* right. In that case, normativity collapses, because there is no sense to getting things right or wrong. The norms of force and content must be relatively independent of each other.

> Hegel's principal innovation is his idea that in order to follow through on Kant's fundamental insight into the essentially *normative* character of mind, meaning, and rationality, we need to recognize that normative statuses such as authority and responsibility are at base *social* statuses.[44]

It is not just *within* an individual that the synthetic activity of rational integration occurs. Such activity is meaningful only when individuals rationally integrate themselves into a *community*. We could put it this way: the older obedience model of authority takes the status of the commander to be the relevant independent variable in the normative; Kant's autonomy model takes the status of commandee to be the relevant independent variable; Hegel insists that both are relevant and importantly but not absolutely independent.

> What institutes normative statuses is *reciprocal* recognition. Someone becomes responsible only when others *hold* him responsible, and exercises authority only when others *acknowledge* that authority. One has the authority to *petition* others for recognition, in an attempt to become responsible or authoritative. To do that, one must recognize others as able to *hold* one responsible or *acknowledge* one's authority. This is according those others a certain kind of authority. To achieve such statuses, one must be recognized by them in turn. That is to make oneself in a certain sense responsible to them. But they have that authority only insofar as one grants it to them by recognizing them as authoritative.[45]

---

[42] Brandom, "Animating Ideas," 49.
[43] Brandom, "Animating Ideas," 62.
[44] Brandom, "Animating Ideas," 66.
[45] Brandom, "Animating Ideas," 70.

It is up to me whether I assert, doubt, imagine, and so on, that the wire in my hand is copper; it is not up to me what the formal and material consequences connected with that particular content are. By subjecting myself to the constraints of linguistic rules that are not 'up to me' (a surrender of a certain negative freedom), I in fact gain access to the expressive power of a natural language and the radical semantic novelty it makes available. This enables a massive expansion of my positive expressive freedom. Language is not the only social practice in which reciprocally recognitive structures yield huge gains in positive freedom.

How do these two stories, the synthesis of the self and the social model of normativity, fit together into an overall Hegelian view? According to Brandom, they must both be placed in a larger *historical* developmental structure. Brandom employs the common law tradition of jurisprudence as a partial model of the kind of historical developmental structure he has in mind here. In common law, judges have a fair amount of discretion in deciding whether and how a law applies to a given situation, but they are under an obligation to say how their application of the law is consistent with, extends, or even corrects the precedents at hand. And no one decision settles such matters; each is a petition to future judges to see their cases in the same light. Ongoing social practices of integrating old and new commitments *institute* the normative statuses of authority and responsibility—that is, they are *sufficient* to create and sustain the normative statuses that constitute the logical space of reasons.

It is this historical process that determines (by progressive refinement) the contents of our concepts. In order to understand how that could be, however, Brandom argues that we need a different notion of determinateness from the one generally assumed by mainstream analytic philosophy. Brandom describes what he calls 'Fregean determinateness' as involving "sharp, complete boundaries."[46] For each such concept, it is a settled matter, semantically speaking, whether it applies to any object, definitively and in advance of any actual application. Hegel disparages such a vision of the conceptual realm as the attitude of 'Verstand' (understanding). In its place, Hegel proposes a vision of the conceptual realm he calls 'Vernunft' (reason). The rational knower realizes that her concepts (her commitments and entitlements) are rarely finally fixed, they are almost always open-ended, susceptible to refinement, correction, even relocation in the overall scheme, and these adjustments are moments in an ongoing story of the justification and integration of our commitments. (Recall here the de-absolutization of the *a priori/a posteriori* distinction mentioned earlier.) The rational unity we strive for among our representations is not a merely synchronic unity, but also a diachronic narrative of growth and elaboration. This view of conceptual determinateness is temporally perspectival: concepts exist in time with both forward- and backward-looking components.[47]

---

[46] Brandom, "Animating Ideas," 88.
[47] Cf. Sellars's remark, "[S]cientific terms have, as part of their logic a 'line of retreat' as well as a 'plan of advance," CDCM, 288. This is a point that, given Sellars's treatment of meanings, applies to *all* terms, not just scientific terms.

Such a sequence reconstructs the history of one's current view as gradually making explicit what was previously only implicit; it reveals one's present view as the result of progress in the epistemic and/or practical realms from an earlier, less refined position.

> In taking one's current commitments as the standard to judge what counts as expressive progress, one *is* taking them as the *reality* of which previous constellations of endorsements were ever more complete and accurate *appearances.*[48]

Hegel is working out the idea that conceptual content is

> articulated by non-monotonic, seriously multipremise material inferential and incompatibility relations, in the context of the realization (which we latecomers to the point associate with Quine, and he associated with Duhem) that those relations depend on the whole context of collateral discursive commitments.[49]

The conceptual contents of thoughts are articulated by the material consequential and incompatibility relations that hold among them. Brandom then makes his own move toward a conceptual realism:

> The principled parallel between the *deontic* modal relations of inclusion and exclusion that articulate our thought on the subjective side, and the *alethic* modal relations of inclusion and exclusion that articulate the world on the objective side . . . define a structural conception of the <u>conceptual</u> according to which thought and the world thought about can both be seen to be *conceptually* structured. This *conceptual realism* about objective reality is, in the context of the other metatheoretic commitments we have been considering, just a consequence of *modal realism*: taking it that objective states of affairs really do necessitate and rule out one another.[50]

Thus, while Sellars would shudder at the thought that the (quasi-)logical relations that connect the contents of our thoughts are "of the *same* generic kind" as the causal and compositional relations among the objects, events, and facts of nature, Brandom makes common cause with McDowell's logico-conceptual realism. This is the truth in Hegel's absolute idealism. As Brandom argues, the claim is not that natural objects are mind-dependent, particularly not on the peculiarities of human subjectivity nor in any causal sense of 'dependent'. Rather, the activities pragmatically constitutive of the objectivity of thinking about a modally structured world are connected intrinsically with the activities pragmatically constitutive of normatively well-structured thought. Being an object and being a fact are themselves also normative statuses.

Brandom's Hegel ends up, then, preparing the way for Brandom himself. While Brandom shows us a way to read Hegel that puts logic and semantics properly at the

---

[48] Brandom, "Animating Ideas," 100.
[49] Brandom, "Animating Ideas," 102.
[50] Brandom, "Animating Ideas," 97–98.

heart of his concerns and ties those to modern approaches to such issues, it is far from clear how smoothly Brandom's view maps onto Hegel's. Brandom's own cavalier attitude toward the notion of 'experience' seems quite foreign to Hegel. Brandom has not delved far into social or political philosophy, though its foundations play a large role in his philosophy. He has mostly borrowed his social/political philosophy eclectically from the German idealists. He faces, at bottom, the task of reconciling three doctrines:

1. Concepts are constituted by norms.
2. Norms are attitude-dependent.
3. Conceptual realism: the world (not just our thinking about it) is conceptually structured.

Brandom's non-metaphysical reading of Hegel convinces him he can claim to be Hegelian without incurring the metaphysical commitments traditionally attributed to Hegel. Thus, Brandom's reconstruction of the Hegelian system does not seem to constitute an ontological proof of God's existence, but we can pose the question to Brandom: Does his conceptual realism ultimately commit him as well to the Idea?

33.6. Conclusion: Reality and Concept in Dynamic Interaction

Their conceptual realism is the most significant tie to Hegelian doctrine shared by McDowell and Brandom. But there are distinctions to be drawn between them, despite this common element. McDowell rejects the Sellarsian functionalistic analysis of meaning (and reference) in favor of a Davidsonian view that, he thinks, still entitles him to think of intentionality as a relation.[51] However, this generates some tension with McDowell's Sellarsian commitments. The notion that intentionality is a mind-world relation runs into difficulties in either a Sellarsian or Hegelian context. First, it makes it difficult to make sense out of conceptual change: if our concept of, say, water changes, wouldn't it either have to relate to a different object or relate in a different way to the same object? It thus is not clear how a concept can be the *same* concept through conceptual change. Second, if intentionality is a matter of normative status—one of the founding insights of the Pittsburgh school—then the relation between word (or mind) and world is, well, what? A normative relation? But what is that? A relation that *ought to be* or *is supposed to be* is not therefore a relation that *is*.

In contrast to McDowell, Brandom retains and elaborates Sellars's functionalist semantics, fitting much more smoothly with both the phenomena of conceptual change

---

[51] See the last of McDowell's Woodbridge Lectures, "Intentionality as a Relation," in McDowell, *Having the World in View*, 44–65.

and the commitment to the normativity of intentionality. Sellars attempts to fit the structural insights of German idealism into a naturalistic framework that assigns to natural science authority over the ontology of the empirical world. This, however, in Sellars's view, requires denying that *normative* features of the world are part of its *empirical* furniture; they are solely features of our social relationships and practices. Both McDowell and Brandom seek to give the normative realm a deeper tie to empirical reality, either by virtue of a relation that unites the intentional and the material realms or a structural parallelism that plays that role.

This review has skimmed a number of surfaces; it has not plumbed the depths or the details of these sophisticated thinkers to any great degree. Yet the Pittsburgh school acknowledges and accommodates significant Hegelian insights. Foremost among these are Hegel's recognition of the dynamic, inferential, social, and historical realization of rational and normative structures in human thought. The ontology of the normative remains in dispute, but there is every reason for analytic philosophers to recognize Hegel as one of the most significant and profound contributors to the canon of Western philosophy, someone whom we can with profit study and learn from.[52]

Works Cited

Brandom, Robert B. "Animating Ideas of Idealism: A Semantic Sonata in Kant and Hegel," in *Reason in Philosophy: Animating Ideas*. Cambridge, MA: Harvard University Press, 2009, 27–110.

Carroll, Lewis. "What the Tortoise Said to Achilles." *Mind*, New Series, 4, no. 14 (April 1895): 278–280.

Coates, Paul. *The Metaphysics of Perception: Wilfrid Sellars, Perceptual Consciousness and Critical Realism*. London: Routledge, 2007.

deVries, Willem A. "All in the Family," in *Millikan and Her Critics*, edited by Dan Ryder, Justine Kingsbury, and Kenneth Williford. Malden, MA: John Wiley & Sons, 2013, 259–275.

deVries, Willem A. "Getting Beyond Idealisms," in *Empiricism, Perceptual Knowledge, Normativity and Realism: Essays on the Anniversary of "Empiricism and the Philosophy of Mind,"* edited by W. A. deVries. Oxford: Oxford University Press, 2009, 211–245.

deVries, Willem A. "Images, Descriptions, and Pictures: Personhood and the Clash," in *Sellars and His Legacy*, edited by James O'Shea. Oxford: Oxford University Press, 2016, 47–59.

deVries, Willem A. "Ontology and the Completeness of Sellars's Two Images." *Humana. Mente: Journal of Philosophical Studies* 21 (2012): 1–18. http://www.humanamente.eu/PDF/Issue_21_Paper_deVries.pdf.

Firth, Roderick. "Coherence, Certainty, and Epistemic Priority." *The Journal of Philosophy* 66 (October 1964): 545–557.

[52] I would like to thank Paul Redding, Carl Sachs, and Dean Moyar for helpful comments on an earlier draft of this chapter. Parts of this chapter have also been the target of feedback from audiences at Kent State University and the University of Sheffield. Thanks to them as well.

McDowell, John. "Having the World in View: Sellars, Kant, and Intentionality," in *Having the World in View: Essays on Kant, Hegel, and Sellars*, by John McDowell. Cambridge, MA: Harvard University Press, 2009.

McDowell, John. "Hegel's Idealism as Radicalization of Kant," in *Having the World in View: Essays on Kant, Hegel, and Sellars*, by John McDowell. Cambridge MA: Harvard University Press, 2009, 69–89.

McDowell, John. *Mind and World*. Cambridge, MA: Harvard University Press, 1994.

Millikan, Ruth. *Language, Thought, and Other Biological Categories: New Foundations for Realism*. Cambridge, MA: MIT Press, 1984.

Millikan, Ruth. "The Father, the Son, and the Daughter: Sellars, Brandom, and Millikan." *Pragmatics & Cognition* 13, no. 1 (2005): 59–71.

Redding, Paul. *Analytic Philosophy and the Return of Hegelian Thought*. Cambridge: Cambridge University Press, 2007.

Redding, Paul. "McDowell's Radicalization of Kant's Account of Concepts and Intuitions: A Sellarsian Critique." *Verifiche: Rivista di scienze umane* 41, no. 1–3 (2012): 9–37.

Sedgewick, Sally. *Hegel's Critique of Kant: From Dichotomy to Identity*. Oxford: Oxford University Press, 2012.

Sellars, Wilfrid S. "Autobiographical Reflections: (February, 1973)," in *Action, Knowledge and Reality: Studies in Honor of Wilfrid Sellars*, edited by H.-N. Castañeda. New York: Bobbs-Merrill, 1975, 277–293.

Sellars, Wilfrid. "Inference and Meaning," *Mind* 62 (1953): 313–338.

Sellars, Wilfrid S. "Philosophy and the Scientific Image of Man" [PSIM], in *Frontiers of Science and Philosophy*, edited by Robert Colodny. Pittsburgh: University of Pittsburgh Press, 1962, 35–78. Reprinted in W. S. Sellars, *Science, Perception and Reality*. London: Routledge and Kegan Paul, 1963, 1–40; and in *In the Space of Reasons: Selected Essays of Wilfrid Sellars* [ISR], edited by K. Scharp and R. B. Brandom. Cambridge, MA: Harvard University Press, 2007, 369–408.

Sellars, Wilfrid S. *Science and Metaphysics: Variations on Kantian Themes* [SM]. London: Routledge and Kegan Paul, 1967.

Wittgenstein, Ludwig. *Tractatus Logico-Philosophicus*, translated by David Pears and Brian McGuinness. London: Routledge & Kegan Paul, 1961.

FURTHER READING

Bernstein, Richard J. "McDowell's Domesticated Hegelianism," in *Reading McDowell: On Mind and World*, edited by Nicholas Smith. New York: Routledge, 2002, 9–24.

Brandom, Robert B. "A Hegelian Model of Legal Concept Determination: The Normative Fine Structure of the Judges' Chain Novel," in *Pragmatism, Law, and Language*, edited by Graham Hubbs and Douglas Lind. London: Routledge, 2014, 19–39.

Brandom, Robert. B. "Holism and Idealism in Hegel's Phenomenology," in *Tales of the Mighty Dead: Historical Essays in the Metaphysics of Intentionality*. Cambridge, MA: Harvard University Press, 2002, 178–209.

Brandom, Robert B. "Some Hegelian Ideas of Note for Contemporary Analytic Philosophy." *Hegel Bulletin* 35 (2014): 1–15.

Brandom, Robert B. "Some Pragmatist Themes in Hegel's Idealism," in *Tales of the Mighty Dead: Historical Essays in the Metaphysics of Intentionality*. Cambridge, MA: Harvard University Press, 2002, 210–234.

Brandom, Robert B. "Untimely Review of Georg Hegel's Phenomenology of Spirit." *Topoi: An International Review of Philosophy* 27 (2008): 161–164.

deVries, Willem A. "Brandom and the Spirit of Hegel," in *Robert Brandoms expressive Vernunft,* edited by Holger Sturm and Christian Barth. Paderborn: Mentis, 2011, 159–174.

deVries, Willem A. "Sense-Certainty and the 'This-Such'," in *Hegel's Phenomenology of Spirit: A Critical Guide*, edited by Dean Moyar and Michael Quante. Cambridge Critical Guides. Cambridge: Cambridge University Press, 2008, 63–75.

Habermas, Jürgen. "From Kant to Hegel: On Robert Brandom's Pragmatic Philosophy of Language." *European Journal of Philosophy* 8, no. 3 (2000): 322–355.

Halbig, Christoph. "Varieties of Nature in Hegel and McDowell." *European Journal of Philosophy* 14, no. 2 (2006): 222–241.

Houlgate, Stephen. "McDowell, Hegel and the Phenomenology of Spirit." *The Owl of Minerva* 41 (2009): 13–26.

Houlgate, Stephen. "Phenomenology and de re Interpretation: A Critique of Brandom's Reading of Hegel." *International Journal of Philosophical Studies* 17, no. 1 (2009): 29–47.

Houlgate, Stephen. "Response to John McDowell." *Owl of Minerva* 41 (2009): 39–51.

Houlgate, Stephen. "Thought and Experience in Hegel and McDowell." *European Journal of Philosophy* 14, no. 2 (2006): 242–261.

Hylton, Peter. "Hegel and Analytic Philosophy," in *The Cambridge Companion to Hegel*, edited by Frederick Beiser. Cambridge: Cambridge University Press, 1993, 445–486.

Landy, David. "Hegel's Account of Rule-Following." *Inquiry* 51 (April 2008): 169–192.

McDowell, John. "Response to Stephen Houlgate." *Owl of Minerva* 41 (2009): 27–38.

McDowell, John. "Response to Stephen Houlgate's Response." *Owl of Minerva* 41 (2009): 53–60.

McDowell, John. "The Apperceptive I and the Empirical Self: Towards a Heterodox Reading of 'Lordship and Bondage' in Hegel's *Phenomenology*," in *Having the World in View: Essays on Kant, Hegel, and Sellars*, by John McDowell. Cambridge MA: Harvard University Press, 2009, 147–165.

McDowell, John. "Towards a Reading of Hegel on Action in the 'Reason' Chapter of the *Phenomenology*," in *Having the World in View: Essays on Kant, Hegel, and Sellars,* by John McDowell. Cambridge MA: Harvard University Press, 2009, 166–184.

Nuzzo, Angelica. *Hegel and the Analytic Tradition*. Continuum Studies in Philosophy. London: Continuum/Bloomsbury, 2010.

Pinkard, Terry. "Hegelianism in the Twentieth Century," in *Routledge Encyclopedia of Twentieth Century Philosophy*, edited by Dermot Moran. London: Routledge, 2008, 118–137.

Pinkard, Terry. "Sellars the Post-Kantian?" In *The Self-Correcting Enterprise: Essays on Wilfrid Sellars*, edited by Michael P. Wolf and Mark Norris Lance. Poznan Studies in the Philosophy of Science and the Humanities 93. Amsterdam; New York: Rodopi, 2006, 21–52.

Pippin, Robert B. "Brandom's Hegel." *European Journal of Philosophy* 13, no. 3 (2005): 381–408.

Quante, Michael. *Hegel's Concept of Action*. Cambridge: Cambridge University Press, 2004.

Quante, Michael. "Reconciling Mind and World: Some Initial Considerations for Opening a Dialogue between Hegel and McDowell." *Southern Journal of Philosophy* 40, no. 1 (2002): 75–96.

Redding, Paul. "Hegel and Analytic Philosophy," in *The Bloomsbury Companion to Hegel*, edited by Allegra de Lauentiis and Jeffrey Edwards. London: Continuum Press, 2013, 313–319.

Redding, Paul. "Hegel's Anticipation of the Early History of Analytic Philosophy." *The Owl of Minerva* 42 (2010–2011): 18–40.

Redding, Paul. "The Analytic Neo-Hegelianism of John McDowell and Robert Brandom," in *The Blackwell Companion to Hegel*, edited by Stephen Houlgate and Michael Baur. Oxford: Blackwell, 2011, 576–593.

Redding, Paul. "The Possibility of German Idealism after Analytic Philosophy: McDowell, Brandom and Beyond," in *On the Futures of Philosophy: Post-Analytic and Meta-Continental Thinking*, edited by James Chase, Edwin Mares, Jack Reynolds, and James Williams. London: Continuum, 2010, 191–202.

Rockmore, Tom. "Analytic Philosophy and the Hegelian Turn." *The Review of Metaphysics* 55 (2001): 339–370.

Rockmore, Tom. "Brandom, Hegel and Inferentialism." *International Journal of Philosophical Studies* 10, no. 4 (2002): 429–447.

Rockmore, Tom. *Hegel, Idealism and Analytic Philosophy*. New Haven, CT: Yale University Press, 2005.

Sellars, Wilfrid S. "Counterfactuals, Dispositions, and the Causal Modalities" [CDCM], in *Minnesota Studies in The Philosophy of Science*, Vol. II, edited by Herbert Feigl, Michael Scriven, and Grover Maxwell. Minneapolis: University of Minnesota Press, 1957, 288.

Sellars, Wilfrid S. "Empiricism and the Philosophy of Mind" [EPM], in *Minnesota Studies in the Philosophy of Science*, Vol. I, edited by H. Feigl and M. Scriven. Minneapolis: University of Minnesota Press, 1956, 253–329. Reprinted in Wilfrid Sellars, *Science, Perception and Reality* [SPR]. London: Routledge and Kegan Paul, 1963, 127–196, with additional footnotes. Published separately as *Empiricism and the Philosophy of Mind: With an Introduction by Richard Rorty and a Study Guide by Robert Brandom*, edited by R. Brandom. Cambridge, MA: Harvard University Press, 1997. Also reprinted in W. deVries and T. Triplett, *Knowledge, Mind, and the Given: A Reading of Sellars' "Empiricism and the Philosophy of Mind."* Indianapolis, IN: Hackett, 2000.

Sellars, Wilfrid S. "Some Remarks on Kant's Theory of Experience." *The Journal of Philosophy* 64 (1967): 633–647. Reprinted in *Kant's Transcendental Metaphysics Sellars' Cassirer Lectures Notes and Other Essays*, edited by Jeffrey F. Sicha. Atascadero, CA: Ridgeview, 2002, 295–296.

Westphal, Kenneth R. "Analytic Philosophy and the Long Tail of Scientia: Hegel and the Historicity of Philosophy." *The Owl of Minerva* 42, no. 1–2 (2010–2011): 1–18.

Westphal, Kenneth R. "Contemporary Epistemology: Kant, Hegel, McDowell." *European Journal of Philosophy* 14 (2006): 274–301. Reprinted in *John McDowell: Experience, Norm and Nature*, edited by J. Lindgaard. Oxford: Blackwell, 2008, 124–151.

Westphal, Kenneth R. "Hegel, Russell, and the Foundations of Philosophy," in *Hegel and the Analytical Tradition*, edited by A. Nuzzo. New York: Continuum, 2010, 174–194.

Westphal, Kenneth R. *Hegel's Epistemological Realism: A Study of the Aim and Method of Hegel's* Phenomenology of Spirit. Philosophical Studies Series in Philosophy, 43. Dordrecht; Boston: Kluwer, 1989.

Westphal, Kenneth R. *Hegel's Epistemology: A Philosophical Introduction to the* Phenomenology of Spirit. Cambridge, MA: Hackett, 2003.

Westphal, Kenneth R. "Self-Consciousness, Anti-Cartesianism and Cognitive Semantics in Hegel's 1807 Phenomenology," in *The Blackwell Companion to Hegel*, edited by S. Houlgate and M. Baur. Oxford: Wiley-Blackwell, 2011, 68–90.

Wretzel, Joshua I. "Despair and the Determinate Negation of Brandom's Hegel." *Continental Philosophy Review* 47, no. 2 (2014): 195–216.

CHAPTER 34

···

LIBERALISM AND RECOGNITION

···

SYBOL COOK ANDERSON

34.1. INTRODUCTION

TOLERATION is a fundamental liberal principle, yet liberal democracies remain remarkably challenged by difference. This is unsurprising given the numbers of groups pressing for recognition in today's 'politics of difference': religious groups, indigenous and other colonized peoples, the descendants of former slaves, immigrants, women, LGBT (lesbian, gay, bisexual, transgendered) people, the poor and working classes, people with disabilities, and more. Their numbers may account for their being characterized as "clamouring for special accommodation," but clearly it is the content of their demands that has prompted some critics to dismiss them as "claim[ants] to honor and position" on the basis of "victimization."[1] On the other hand, several theorists have grasped that what these groups seek is recognition of their rights as full and equal citizens.[2] This egalitarian demand for recognition is crucial to comprehend and is the focus of this chapter.

The demands of groups for recognition of their equality would seem simple enough for liberal theory to answer, given liberalism's core concern with equal liberty, a commitment grounded classically in the 'self-evident' thesis that all persons are natural equals and equally entitled to freedom as their natural, inalienable right. In truth, the persistence in liberal democracies of pervasive social inequality belies liberal faith in natural equality and in the natural right of freedom.[3] A more adequate response to group demands is suggested by Hegel's conception of liberal freedom as the intersubjective

[1] Barclay, "Liberalism and Diversity," 155; Ceaser, "Multiculturalism," 155.
[2] Taylor, "The Politics of Recognition"; Honneth, *The Struggle for Recognition*; Kymlicka, *Multicultural Citizenship*; Barry, *Culture and Equality*; Fraser, "Rethinking Recognition"; Seglow, "Theorizing Recognition"; and Darby, *Rights, Race, and Recognition*.
[3] Harvey, *Civilized Oppression*; Barry, *Culture and Equality*; and S. Anderson, *Hegel's Theory of Recognition*.

achievement of modern citizens, the product of historical *struggles* for recognition. Hegel is best known for his metaphorical depiction, in the *Phenomenology of Spirit*, of subjects' original struggle in the state of nature for 'independent self-consciousness'— their quest for freedom fueled by desire for recognition of their mastery (PS 9.127–132/ ¶¶178–189). Less well known is that Hegel refined and elaborated his theory of recognition throughout his corpus, from his early Jena writings ([1802/1803] 1979), through his *Phenomenology* account of subjects' achievement of mutual recognition (PS 9.415–442/ ¶¶632–671), to his analysis of the actualization of social relationships of recognition in the *Philosophy of Right*. His persistence attests to the depth of his conviction that achieving liberal freedom—the freedom of self-actualizing citizens to find themselves at home (*zu Hause*) in the world (VPR 4: 102)—is a historical *project*, with struggles for recognition as its core mechanism.

Of present concern for this chapter are the contemporary struggles for recognition identified with the 'politics of difference' and the efforts of liberal theorists to address them. If the number and complexity of demands were not challenging enough—bids for self-government rights, exemptions from burdensome laws and policies, protection from discrimination and hate crimes, and reparations for past injustices—they sometimes involve claims for group rights that are in tension with individual rights, and group claims that conflict with each other, as, for example, when illiberal minority cultures seek autonomy that would threaten the rights of women.[4] The challenge is more daunting if we consider the need for recognition to originate in the very structure of liberal institutions, arranged in ways that benefit dominant groups at the expense of subordinated groups.[5] From this perspective, the demands of women and minority groups for recognition are pitted against the (ostensibly) stable edifices of liberal-capitalist states. Does the demand for group recognition, even for egalitarian ends, justify potentially destabilizing reforms of liberal doctrines, policies, and institutions?

A flurry of liberal theorizing about the meaning and justification of group recognition followed the 1992 publication of two works credited with bringing Hegelian recognition to the fore in discussions of multiculturalism and social justice. Charles Taylor, in "The Politics of Recognition," and Axel Honneth, in *The Struggle for Recognition*, advance versions of Hegel's thesis that intersubjective recognition is a requirement of identity and freedom inasmuch as the formation and actualization of practical identity depend upon it. Taylor reframes the liberal-communitarian debates of the 1980s to address the emerging 'politics of recognition', the pursuit of minority cultural groups for what Taylor characterizes as recognition of their dignity and distinctness, a 'vital human need' suppressed by Enlightenment universalism.[6] Honneth argues, similarly, for a conception of recognition as the legitimate demand of emancipatory social movements for the restoration of normative social relationships, which have been violated

---

[4] Okin, "Multiculturalism Bad for Women"; Maddox, "Durkheim beyond Liberalism."

[5] Pateman, *The Sexual Contract*; Young, *Justice and the Politics of Difference*; Mills, *The Racial Contract*.

[6] Taylor, "Politics of Recognition," 26.

by various forms of social and political disrespect.[7] The response by liberal theorists to Taylor's and Honneth's arguments has been swift and vibrant. One aim of this chapter is to survey key responses to each that endeavor to justify recognition for groups given its tensions: political theoretical debates over multiculturalism spurred by Taylor, and investigations of emancipatory justice inspired by Honneth.

In both strands of discussion, critics of recognition have been formidable, such that one may wonder if (to borrow Brian Barry's suggestion) the idea of liberal recognition is in truth a dead end. But if groups fundamentally seek recognition of their status and rights as equals, then liberalism, to be true to itself, must answer: Is the egalitarian demand for recognition justified, in light of its tensions? A second aim of this chapter is to suggest a way forward by appeal to Derrick Darby's rights recognition thesis,[8] which illuminates the responsibility of liberal citizens to pursue rights-granting relationships of mutual recognition. That discussion makes evident that liberalism contains resources with which to recognize groups appropriately and with potentially stabilizing results. I call attention to the political liberalism of John Rawls, his theory of justice as fairness revised to acknowledge the 'fact of reasonable pluralism', and which prescribes culturally and morally inclusive deliberation on the basic structures of liberal institutions as a means of actualizing the liberal conception of citizens as free and equal while securing social justice and social stability.[9]

34.2. Recognition and the Politics of Multiculturalism

The politics of difference is to be credited, at least partly, for the nearly concurrent revival of interest in Hegel by neo-Marxists and communitarians, the resuscitation of liberal theory by John Rawls, and the rise of multiculturalism in the 1970s. Contemporary liberal discussions of equal liberty, particularly for marginalized groups, might be said to have begun with Rawls's 1971 publication of *A Theory of Justice*, in which, in addition to defending the primacy of equal liberty, he argues that to secure for citizens 'the social bases of self-respect', political arrangements must always benefit the least advantaged in society, and citizens must embrace a duty of mutual respect.[10] Rawls's theory of justice as fairness was monumental in its influence, but among its early and equally influential critics was Charles Taylor, communitarian theorist and author of two important works on Hegel in the 1970s, who challenged Rawls's universalist and atomistic-individualist presuppositions on the basis of his own conviction of the epistemological and political salience of the social constitution and cultural situatedness of subjects.[11]

---

[7] Honneth, *Struggle*, 92–93.
[8] Darby, *Race, Rights, and Recognition.*
[9] Rawls, *Political Liberalism*, xix.
[10] Rawls, *A Theory of Justice*, 266, 386.
[11] Taylor, *Hegel* and *Hegel and Modern Society*. Taylor, *Philosophical Papers*, 274 ff.

Increasing interest in the political significance of cultural differences and multiculturalism set a challenging agenda for liberal theory. Demands of social groups for recognition, interpreted as demands for special group rights and for recognition of group
identities, prompted reconsideration of the primacy that liberalism accords to individual
rights, as well as liberalism's relationship to non-liberal cultures. This, in turn, inspired
new dialogues among liberal theorists and both proponents and critics of Hegelian theories of recognition about the justification of group recognition, its compatibility with
liberal principles, and what might count as legitimate liberal policies and practices of
recognition. The contributions of liberal theorists to these discussions are impressive,
encompassing considerations of culture and equality,[12] of group-differentiated rights,[13]
and alternative liberal theories of recognition.[14] In this section, I highlight Taylor's land-
mark essay and two responses to it that illuminate key critical arguments in the 'politics
of recognition'.

Taylor cites as justification for extending recognition to cultural minorities the
Hegelian thesis that "our identity is partly shaped by recognition or its absence," such
that "due recognition is not just a courtesy we owe people . . . [but] a vital human need."[15]
Taylor regards the rise of multiculturalism as an act of resistance to the suppression
of particularity by Enlightenment universalism, culminating in a politics of difference emerging in the wake of the politics of equal dignity. He sees minority cultures as
demanding recognition of their distinctness, which has been repressed and sometimes
demeaned as groups are pressured to recognize and assimilate into a dominant cultural identity. Deeming this form of misrecognition "the cardinal sin against the ideal
of authenticity," the capacity of individuals to live in accordance with values determined
inwardly, Taylor makes this more challenging demand the focal point of his analysis.[16]

Taylor endorses special rights for national minorities, such as the Québècois who seek
institutional immunities to secure their cultural survival, provided individual rights are
secured invariantly. He also supports demands by minority groups for the equal valuation of their cultures in public—for instance, the inclusion of non-Western texts in
the Western canon. However, the conception of recognition that Taylor understands

[12] Taylor, "Politics of Recognition"; Raz, "Multiculturalism: A Liberal Perspective"; Forst, "Theory of
Multicultural Justice"; Kukathas, "Multiculturalism as Fairness," "Liberalism and Multiculturalism," and
Liberal Archipelago; Barry, *Culture and Equality* and "Second Thoughts"; Galston, *Liberal Pluralism*; and
Kelly, *Multiculturalism Reconsidered*.

[13] Waldron, "Minority Cultures"; Margalit and Halbertal, "Right to Culture"; Kymlicka, *Multicultural
Citizenship*; Tully, *Strange Multiplicity*; Parekh, "Dilemmas" and *Rethinking Multiculturalism*; and
Spinner-Halev, *Surviving Diversity*.

[14] Galeotti, *Toleration as Recognition*; Seglow, "Theorizing Recognition"; and Laegaard, "Liberal
Theory of Recognition."

[15] Taylor, "Politics," 26.

[16] Taylor, "Politics," 38. Taylor's concern with authenticity, the focus of *The Ethics of Authenticity*,
resembles that of the Romantics, a position of which Hegel was deeply critical. The Romantics' extreme
valorization of subjectivity was at odds with Hegel's conviction of the equal salience of objectivity, of the
significance and legitimacy of community norms. In truth, Taylor shares Hegel's belief that while free
subjectivity requires the cultivation of inwardness and self-determination, it must also be reconciled
with the community, with 'horizons of significance'. Taylor, *Ethics of Authenticity*, 38.

these latter groups as demanding, the according of equal value unreflectively to their cultures, is, he claims, misguided. A more reasonable object of recognition is the 'universal human *potential*' present in all cultures.[17] That is, Taylor reasons that two forms of cultural recognition are possible, corresponding to two dimensions of personhood acknowledged by post-Enlightenment modernity: recognition of the equal *dignity* of cultures, and recognition of their *distinctness*. Recognizing the dignity of cultures amounts to acknowledging their equal human potential as sources of identity and agency. But Taylor rejects a strong conception of equal valuation, understood as the a priori acknowledgement of cultural value, for although it might lead to greater inclusion and mitigate the 'demeaning picture' minority groups are given of themselves by their exclusion, it ultimately entails an ill-advised 'act of faith'.[18] Instead, Taylor supports a weak conception of equal valuation, understood as acknowledging the universal potential inherent in cultures that have been influential in shaping whole societies, and which might therefore be capable of speaking to all humanity, and investigating them on that basis to comprehend and appreciate their value more fully over time. For such a project, he recommends engaging in intercultural dialogue aimed at a Gadamerian 'fusion of horizons', in which we acquire 'new vocabularies of comparison' that inform our judgments of other cultures.[19]

The idea of fusing cultural horizons is attractive, but not without problems. For example, it is not clear that it amounts to more than an assimilation of otherness to sameness, that is, persistent misrecognition. One of the dangers of trying to comprehend another culture is that we may apprehend otherness solely through our own categories and overlook the irreducible otherness, the true distinctness, of the other. Critics have pointed out, in fact, that the 'politicization of culture' threatens to reify identities.[20] Moreover, it is unreasonable to assign value to cultures on the basis of their ability to speak to all humanity. Outsiders may never comprehend what makes a given culture valuable to its members—and yet it remains valuable to its members. Other critics point out that any effort to 'enforce' or 'institutionalize' cultural appreciation is illiberal insofar as it places a coercive demand upon individuals to affirm and value cultures, "replac[ing] one kind of tyranny with another."[21] Still others consider cultural recognition incoherent insofar as it requires according equal value to cultures whose values conflict.[22] The latter two criticisms appear not to stick, however, since Taylor endorses only a weak conception of cultural recognition as acknowledgment of the dignity of cultures—a conception consistent with the doctrine of equal human dignity—and argues only that we *may* build upon that foundation in order to understand and appreciate cultures more fully over time.

---

[17] Taylor, "Politics," 42; my emphasis.
[18] Ibid., 36, 66.
[19] Ibid., 66, 67; cf. Gadamer, *Truth and Method*, 305 ff.
[20] Seglow, *Theorizing Recognition*, 80; Fraser, "Rethinking Recognition," 108.
[21] Appiah, "Identity, Authenticity, Survival," 163.
[22] Jones, "Cultural Diversity," 45; Seglow, *Theorizing Recognition*, 81.

Will Kymlicka, like Taylor, advocates strongly for cultural recognition, citing, as its justification, his belief that "justice requires removing or compensating for undeserved or 'morally arbitrary' disadvantages, particularly if they are, for cultural members, 'profound and pervasive and present from birth.' "[23] To reconcile multiculturalism's concern for groups with liberalism's commitment to individuals, Kymlicka conceives the problem of liberal multiculturalism as that of specifying the political measures needed to protect individuals against the injustices they suffer because of their group membership. Accordingly, in *Multicultural Citizenship*, he advocates for group-differentiated rights to benefit individuals identified with disadvantaged cultures, not to benefit cultures per se.

Kymlicka's 'equality-based arguments' cite the necessity of cultural membership, and in some cases political autonomy, for minority cultures, for achieving the effective equal status of citizens.[24] He sees autonomy bound up with cultural membership because a culture, understood as an "intergenerational community, more or less institutionally complete," provides a choice context in which individuals both form beliefs and acquire a sense of their value as sources of agency.[25] Preserving cultures is therefore essential to citizens' flourishing as autonomous agents, whereas neglecting their cultures, even by means of insufficiently determinate societal norms, may undermine it. For example, the language of law may be too abstract to *secure* rights: "The right to free speech does not tell us what an appropriate language policy is."[26] Because majority groups may establish policies that are unduly burdensome to minority groups and that fail to secure their ability to exercise rights, guaranteeing equal autonomy for members of minority groups may require extending them special group-differentiated rights.[27]

Kymlicka's analysis of minority group claims for rights centers on his distinction between 'national minorities' and 'ethnic groups', whose claims for special rights have different bases of legitimacy.[28] Equality for members of national minorities, that is, societal cultures that have at one time been autonomous, may require according them some measure of political autonomy as a protection against policies that threaten their cultural survival. Ethnic groups, or immigrant cultures formed by the voluntary migration of individuals into a new societal culture, are not entitled to autonomy but do require "equal access to the mainstream culture," which entails that the dominant culture mitigate discrimination.[29] Both ethnic groups and national minorities legitimately pursue legal immunities (e.g., exemption from 'blue laws'), rights to engage in cultural practices in public, public support for programs that promote cultural appreciation, and special representation rights within the central institutions of the state.[30] In all cases, group-differentiated rights must aim at providing 'external protections' to minority

---

[23]   Kymlicka, *Multicultural Citizenship*, 126; quoting Rawls, *Theory of Justice*, 82.
[24]   Kymlicka, *Multicultural Citizenship*, 6, 8, 108–115.
[25]   Ibid., 18, 82.
[26]   Ibid., 5.
[27]   Ibid., 83, 101, 107 ff.
[28]   Ibid., 6.
[29]   Ibid., 109 ff., 114.
[30]   Ibid., 30–33.

cultures against harmful political and economic policies; they may not place autonomy-undermining 'internal restrictions' upon individuals in the name of cultural preservation. Liberalism "requires *freedom within* the minority group, and *equality between* minority and majority groups."[31]

Kymlicka's critics have charged him with intolerance toward non-liberal cultures, for instance in suggesting that non-liberal minority groups be 'liberalized' to embrace values such as autonomy.[32] But Kymlicka acknowledges that this is a complex issue and distinguishes two questions: that concerning a liberal state's right to affirm or deny the legitimacy of claims to special rights, and that concerning the authority of a liberal government to impose its values on non-liberal minorities. It is appropriate for liberal states to deny the legitimacy of 'illiberal' claims to rights, but whether or not states are authorized to impose liberal values depends upon the type of minority. Kymlicka contends that liberal governments may 'compel respect' for liberal values from members of ethnic groups, since they have entered the societal culture voluntarily.[33] But they must practice toleration toward non-liberal national minorities, refraining from imposition here, as with any sovereign nation. Still, Kymlicka's insistence that liberal democracies should promote liberalization has led to the charge that he fails to appreciate the 'authentic otherness' of non-liberal cultures[34]—what Hegel might call their 'absolute difference' (PS 9.441/ ¶671).[35] However, this criticism does not seem entirely fair; although Kymlicka rejects practices that compromise individual autonomy, he concedes the authority of national minorities to retain their 'authentically other', non-liberal practices.[36]

Upon assessing multiculturalist arguments such as Taylor's and Kymlicka's, Brian Barry finds them on the whole untenable. In *Culture and Equality*, Barry undertakes the largely negative project of demonstrating how multiculturalist arguments are incompatible with egalitarian principles or are superfluous in the sense of not accomplishing any more than a commitment to universalist liberal egalitarianism does. He questions both the prudence and the necessity of special exemptions for groups and stands by the equal application of the law. If a law or policy disadvantages a group, then we should assess the legitimacy of that law, rather than grant exemptions from it. In assessing the law, we ask whether or not there is a compelling public interest protected by it. If there is, the law should be upheld, even if doing so is burdensome to some groups. If there is

---

[31] Ibid., 35, 152.

[32] E.g., Parekh, in *Dilemmas*. See Kymlicka, *Multicultural Citizenship*, 172.

[33] Kymlicka, *Multicultural Citizenship*, 164, 170.

[34] Parekh, *Dilemmas*, 59.

[35] In the *Phenomenology*, Hegel describes the difference between the penultimate shapes of moral spirit, 'conscience', and the 'beautiful soul' as 'absolute', even in their moment of reconciliation: "Each of these two self-certain Spirits has no other purpose than its own pure self, and no other reality and existence than just this pure self. But yet they are different; and the difference is absolute because it is set in this element of the pure Notion" (PS 9.441/ ¶671). Thus, Hegel grants the compatibility of absolute difference—genuine particularity—with stable political community. Subjects are reconciled in their differences when they can acknowledge their mutual legitimacy in virtue of the ineradicable particularity of all subjects and shapes of spirit.

[36] Kymlicka, *Multicultural Citizenship*, 65.

no compelling public interest involved, the law should perhaps be repealed rather than differentially applied.

Thus, on the question of whether Sikhs should be exempt from British laws requiring motorcyclists to wear crash helmets, Barry is clear. Because helmet laws protect a compelling public interest—safety and the reduction of healthcare costs—*and* because turbans do not provide adequate protection, he opposes exemptions to helmet laws for Sikhs. Circumstances are different, however, for a Sikh boy seeking exemption from a school's uniform cap policy. First, there is no compelling public interest protected by the equal application of a rule concerning school uniforms, but, second, there *is* a public interest in securing equality of opportunity for all citizens. Exemption, in this case, secures equality of opportunity for Sikh boys. Very importantly, however, Barry insists that policies from which citizens would legitimately be exempt ought not to be policies in the first place.[37]

Barry's main point is that, for a wide range of injustices, including but not limited to ethnic and racial discrimination, "culture is not the problem, and it is not the solution."[38] The 'culturalization' of groups—the presumption that their core concern is the protection of their cultural identities and cultural products—is not only inaccurate, but also deflects attention from what really is their core concern: equality. For instance, we obviously must regard the concerns of the poor to be about something other than the devaluing of 'their culture', because there is no poor culture. Barry sees women and minority groups as fundamentally concerned with social and economic inequality; the solution has to be the pursuit of equality.

Yet if universalist liberal egalitarianism can be said to adjudicate justly claims of unjust treatment and the pursuit of equality, we may well ask why it has not yet succeeded. We cannot deny (nor does Barry deny) that inequities persist in the determination and application of laws. For instance, it is hard to square, on the one hand, the Supreme Court's ruling against protecting the Native American Church's sacramental use of peyote with, on the other hand, the legal exemption granted to the Catholic Church that permitted its sacramental use of wine during Prohibition. In the former case, the Court ruled on the basis of there not being an exemption built into anti-drug laws and its sense that 'free exercise' of religion does not protect sacramental use of illegal substances. Nevertheless, the result is that one (particularly marginalized) group has been prohibited from administering a central religious sacrament, whereas another group has not, only because the former did not secure an exemption from the law. Of course, as Barry points out, winning exemption from legislation comes down to the ability of groups to lobby successfully for their interests, and that requires not only that groups be 'well-organized' but also that governments take groups seriously.[39] And so it remains an open question whether what the majority deems a compelling public interest really is one. Even when minority groups contest laws that are harmful or discriminatory, they

---

[37] Barry, "Second Thoughts," 213, 216–217.
[38] Barry, *Culture and Equality*, 306; quoting Appiah, "Multicultural Misunderstanding," 36.
[39] Barry, *Culture and Equality*, 39.

remain at the mercy of the majority, who assess the legitimacy of claims through the lens of their own conceptions of the good. Barry is right to spotlight inequality as the fundamental concern of groups, but the misrecognition of groups *and* their cultures remains a problem.

34.3. Recognition and Critical Theory

Of course, group demands for recognition extend well beyond concerns with culture. A long tradition within critical theory has, since the early twentieth century, attended to the wider scope of struggles by social movements for economic, political, and social justice consistent with its concern with human emancipation from all forms of social domination. Accordingly, critical theorists of recognition, influenced largely by the French reading of Hegel that followed Alexandre Kojève's 1930s lectures on the *Phenomenology*[40] have applied descriptive and normative lenses to the analysis of modern societies to assess not only how and why struggles for recognition emerge, but also how relationships of recognition ought to be structured in societies to secure the conditions of human flourishing. Liberal theorists have been less vocal in that discussion but attentive, as evidenced by their references to Axel Honneth's analysis of contemporary struggles for recognition and Nancy Fraser's important criticism of it—that is, Honneth and Fraser's influential debate concerning recognition and redistribution.

In *The Struggle for Recognition*, Honneth develops an account of emancipatory social movements as struggles for recognition that not only discloses their fundamentally moral nature, but also grounds Hegel's early Jena theory of recognition empirically. He appropriates from Hegel the idea that the formation and continued actualization of practical identity occurs through an agonistic developmental process that begins in private experiences of mutual recognition (love) and progresses logically, hence normatively, into and through a series of public recognitive relationships (law and ethical life). Because mutual recognition is normative, individuals react to failures of recognition with feelings of moral indignation. Contemporary struggles for recognition are therefore attempts to restore three modes of mutual recognition—'love, law, and solidarity'—through which individuals can cultivate, in private and in public life, 'practical relations-to-self' required for full autonomy: 'basic self-confidence, self-respect, and self-esteem'.[41] Because the corresponding forms of misrecognition—violence, the denial of rights, and the denigration of ways of life—are moral harms, recognition is a moral obligation and a requirement of justice.

Honneth observes that Hegel's characterization of love, 'being of oneself in another', as the first form of mutual recognition highlights a salient feature of normative recognition: that interaction partners strike a balance between dependence and independence

---

[40] Kojève, *Introduction.*
[41] Honneth, *Struggle*, 76, 92 ff., 128–131, 136 ff.

(SEL, 110). For example, as parents meet the needs of dependent children, they also cultivate their independence. Children's ability to balance dependence and independence in love forms the foundation of their basic self-confidence as autonomous agents and of their ability to cultivate recognitive relationships with wider circles of interaction partners. In competitive, rule-governed play, they learn to integrate the norms and expectations of a 'generalized other'. As they develop, their willingness to let rules of interaction govern their behavior heightens their awareness of both their own efficacy and their sensitivity to others.[42] Honneth considers this openness to the perspective of a generalized other to be a ground of the capacity for mutual legal recognition.

Being accorded legal status means that one is recognized as a morally responsible person, capable of embracing community norms. The extension of legal rights is therefore a basis of self-respect, evidence of a community's recognition of an individual's moral accountability and suitability for political participation. Conversely, being denied rights is an injury to self-respect, inasmuch as it not only denies one's moral responsibility, but also "deprives one of . . . the cognitive regard for the status of moral responsibility that *had to be so painstakingly acquired* in the interactive processes of socialization."[43]

Because legal recognition acknowledges only an individual's status as a 'person' like all others, Honneth maintains that this leaves an important dimension of selfhood unrecognized in the public sphere. Individuals, in order to experience their whole selves as free, must enjoy not only love and legal status, but also public recognition of their particularity, their distinctness. They must win social esteem by means of "a social medium that . . . express[es] the characteristic *differences* among human subjects in a universal and, more specifically, intersubjectively obligatory way."[44] That is, social esteem presupposes some normative standard whereby differences are acknowledged not only as worthy, but also as in some sense necessary for the community's success and flourishing. Individuals therefore require 'solidarity', a shared evaluative framework that inspires them to make distinctive social contributions that merit community recognition.[45]

Honneth claims that in *The Struggle for Recognition* he presented only his 'vague intuitions' about recognition. He pursues a more precise and general conception in "Grounding Recognition" by isolating the fundamental concept underlying the three modes of recognition specified in the earlier work. Honneth concludes that recognition is "a behavioural reaction in which we respond rationally to evaluative qualities that we have learned to perceive, to the extent to which we are integrated into the second nature of our lifeworld."[46] Evaluative qualities are the attributes of individuals that are the object of valuation by others, and which compel recognition insofar as they reflect normative traits, abilities, behaviors, and so on. Honneth maintains that it is rational for modern democracies to acknowledge attributes that further freedom: *singularity*, the

[42] Mead, *Mind, Self, and Society*, 77, 106–107.
[43] Honneth, *Struggle*, 134.
[44] Ibid., 122.
[45] Ibid.
[46] Honneth, "Grounding Recognition," 499, 513.

individual's physical integrity and well-being that are the objects of love; *autonomy*, the individual's rational and moral agency that is the object of rights and respect; and *particularity*, the individual's capability and ingenuity, the object of solidarity.[47] These evaluative qualities and the modes of recognition accorded them constitute the core normative content of Honneth's critical theory of recognition.

Nancy Fraser acknowledges the demand for recognition, but denies that all group struggles are for recognition and, moreover, that those that are for recognition aim for the recognition of identity. For these and other reasons, the politics of recognition is fraught with problems: it threatens to displace discussions of distribution when what subordinated groups truly seek is 'participatory parity' through both recognition and redistribution; it reifies cultural identities by promoting the dubious concept of authentic group identity; and it excessively psychologizes recognition, obscuring the role of institutions in inculcating cultural values that inform the structure of social relationships.[48]

Fraser's initial framing of the problem as that of determining the conditions under which a politics of recognition supports or undermines a politics of redistribution[49] provoked criticisms that she accordingly subordinated recognition to redistribution. She therefore elaborated her position more fully in "Rethinking Recognition," where she endorses a 'perspectival dualism' that posits misrecognition and maldistribution as irreducible and 'mutually imbricated' dimensions of the more fundamental problem of social subordination.[50] That is, sociopolitical recognition and economic redistribution are alternative lenses through which to interpret social relationships, such that one may understand a given social movement now as seeking recognition, and now as concerned with redistribution. For example, the feminist movement aims simultaneously to 'valorize gender specificity' through recognition and to 'abolish gender differentiation' in the economic sphere through redistribution.[51] Similarly, racial minorities resist both cultural misrepresentations of their identities (for instance, in the media) and racialized income inequality.

Far from subordinating the politics of recognition, then, Fraser acknowledges its equal significance with redistribution as a requirement of justice. However, she jettisons the 'identity model' of recognition in favor of a 'status model', shifting the focus of recognition from group identity to participatory parity. Such a shift avoids the problem of reifying identities and directs attention to the ultimate injustice of misrecognition: that

---

[47] Ibid., 511–513.

[48] Fraser, "Rethinking Recognition," 108 ff., 113.

[49] Fraser, "From Redistribution to Recognition," 69.

[50] Fraser, "Rethinking Recognition," 109, 113, 114. For instance, groups may be exploited economically in virtue of their cultural identity, or the lower economic status of a group may lead to its becoming perceived as culturally inferior—but cultural identity is not the only basis of economic exploitation, any more than lower economic status is the basis of some groups being labeled inferior. Moreover, not all members of subordinated cultural groups experience economic exploitation, and not all members of lower economic groups are viewed as inferior.

[51] Fraser, *Justice Interruptus*, 21.

"some individuals and groups are denied the status of full partners in social interaction simply as a consequence of institutionalized patterns of cultural value in whose construction they have not equally participated."[52] To be sure, these patterns of value have had, as their means and consequence, the denigration of group identities, but Fraser considers the social subordination at which identity constructions have aimed to be the more fundamental problem of misrecognition.

For this reason, too, Fraser is critical of Taylor's and Honneth's efforts to justify political recognition by appeal to individuals' subjective needs for normative identity formation, affirmation, and actualization. The salient mechanisms of social subordination that motivate the need for recognition and redistribution are distinctively *institutional*. To be misrecognized is not merely to be demeaned or denigrated, nor is it to be the target of 'free-floating' cultural values and representations. Rather, it is to be subjected to institutionalized cultural values and representations that not only demean one's cultural group, but, more important, relegate one's group to a subordinated social position that undermines participatory parity—for example, laws that prohibit same-sex marriage, gendered and racialized income disparities, and racial profiling.[53] Fraser therefore endorses 'transformative' remedies against injustice that target the 'underlying generative framework' of societal norms and structures.[54] While there is also a role for 'affirmative' remedies that address specific unjust outcomes (e.g., legal exemptions for cultural groups), justice requires more thoroughgoing, transformative solutions.

Honneth and other critics challenge Fraser's denial that redistribution is reducible to recognition, insisting that demands for redistribution are always, in some sense, grounded in the recognition or misrecognition of the status of persons. Honneth maintains that the motive force for socioeconomic struggles under capitalism, as in all forms of social and political resistance, is the *moral* conviction of subjects that "recognition principles considered legitimate are incorrectly or inadequately applied."[55] In this case, struggles for redistribution can be understood specifically as resistance to societal valuations of individual achievement recognized under modern capitalism—valuations by which they have been disrespected; accordingly, we can interpret the redistributive endeavor of feminists to valorize 'female' labor (e.g., housework) as a struggle for recognition.[56] Fraser responds, in part, by throwing doubt on the possibility of reducing any society to a 'recognition order': "To analyze any society exclusively as a recognition order is illegitimately to totalize one mode of integration, truncating the full range of social processes," in particular those that "produce relations of subordination" and which therefore require most careful illumination and analysis.[57] In keeping with this insight, Fraser has expanded her own account of barriers to participatory parity by including a third dimension of justice—the political—which concerns the inclusiveness

---

[52] Fraser, "Rethinking Recognition," 109, 113. Fraser and Honneth, *Redistribution or Recognition*, 29.
[53] Fraser, "Rethinking Recognition," 113–114.
[54] Fraser and Honneth, *Redistribution or Recognition*, 23.
[55] Ibid., 157.
[56] Ibid., 140, 154.
[57] Ibid., 214.

of democratic decision-making: "The corresponding injustice would be 'political marginalization' or 'exclusion', the corresponding remedy, 'democratization.'"[58]

34.4. RECOGNITION, RIGHTS, AND LIBERAL EQUALITY: A WAY FORWARD

The foregoing analysis makes clear that, notwithstanding their differences, several liberal, communitarian, and critical theorists agree that subordinated social groups seek recognition in order to secure their status and rights as equal citizens. From this perspective, what they are 'clamoring' for are not 'special' accommodations and privileges *simpliciter*, but rights and entitlements that are required to bring them into participatory parity, given their unjust subordination under current social and political arrangements. And so the question is, how can liberalism *secure* the equal status and equal rights said to accrue to all liberal democratic citizens? Brian Barry seems right to suggest that we defend liberal egalitarianism, in part because according special, group-differentiated rights may not ultimately solve problems of injustice so much as entrench them. As Fraser argues, what are needed are transformative remedies, not only affirmative ones. Barry also grants that liberalism requires a more adequate account of what equal treatment entails given the fact of diversity.[59]

But defending liberal universalist egalitarianism should not be understood in vague terms as simply the mandate to live up to traditional liberal egalitarian ideals. The pressing issue is how we *come*, in truth, to actualize liberal egalitarian ideals required by justice. I contend that success requires, in the first instance, regarding all social members—not only members of marginalized groups—as bearers of multiple particular identities, and hence as members of multiple groups standing in various social, political, and economic relations to one another within the political community. With Charles Taylor, "we give due acknowledgement ... to what is universally present— everyone has an identity,"[60] and acknowledge that these group identities are implicated in systems of social domination and subordination in complex ways. Accordingly, with Taylor, Honneth, and others, we spotlight the problems of the traditional liberal conception of persons as 'universal humans'—a conception that has enabled a privileged set of identities to stand in for universal, and to fade, as Marion Maddox observes, into the 'liberal background' into which they disappear as unmarked by a problematic particularity.[61] Rendering *all* identities visible is essential for disclosing the full range, character, and magnitude of contemporary social and economic inequalities.

---

[58] Ibid., 68.
[59] Barry, "Second Thoughts," 205.
[60] Taylor, "Politics," 39.
[61] Maddox, "Durkheim beyond Liberalism," 2.

A second requirement is that we shoulder, collectively as political communities, responsibility for the persistence of social inequality, including denials of equal rights. I find compelling Derrick Darby's argument, in *Rights, Race, and Recognition*, that if citizens do not in fact enjoy equal rights, it is because the political community refuses to recognize their entitlement to them. Darby insists that we are only taken seriously as citizens when we in fact possess our rights, and the conferral in practice of social recognition of those rights—by means of the treatment and protection of social members—is a necessary condition of their possession: "To determine whether a subject actually has rights we must consider not only what people think but also, and more importantly, what they do."[62] We are collectively responsible for securing citizens' rights.

Accordingly, Darby challenges the prevailing liberal doctrine of natural human rights, for he finds no compelling reason to believe that such rights exist. He endorses instead Thomas Hill Green's Hegel-inspired rights recognition thesis, which defines a right as "a power claimed and recognised as contributory to a common good."[63] Darby particularly emphasizes Green's distinction between a subject's *claim* to rights and social members' *recognition* of that claim in advancing his thesis that "there are no rights that exist prior to and independent of social recognition of ways of acting and being treated."[64] He considers Green's view of rights to accord more with history, most notably the withholding of rights from African Americans during and after the era of chattel slavery. That natural rights arguments could be deployed successfully by slavery apologists as well as by abolitionists reveals their mercurial quality as a ground of moral and political rights. More attractive, and better for liberalism, is an externalist theory of rights that places responsibility for the extension and denial of rights where they in fact reside: in the recognition practices of a community.

Proponents of the prevailing, presocial view of natural rights, or rights internalists, advance two basic arguments in support of their claim that all humans possess some inalienable moral rights independently of their social recognition: moral rights are grounded either in (1) subjects' natures or some property of their natures (such as rationality or sentience), or (2) subjects' 'morally valid claims' to the rights in question.[65] With regard to the ontological arguments, Darby contends that theories about which properties constitute subjects as rights-bearers seem more to reflect the moral or political commitments of their proponents than to indicate, in any convincing manner, identifiable right-endowing properties. The result has been the proliferation of criteria for bearing rights, and lack of a consensus regarding them, rendering the ontological approach a dead end. Meanwhile, proponents of the 'morally valid claim' argument, who maintain that subjects are moral rights-bearers on the basis of claims justified by substantive moral theories, presuppose some theory about the properties in virtue of

---

[62] Darby, *Rights*, 143.
[63] Green, *Lectures*, 79.
[64] Darby, *Rights*, 1.
[65] Ibid., 16.

which subjects can make moral claims, hence fare no better than the defenders of onto-logical arguments.[66] Darby therefore rejects rights internalism.

For rights internalists, natural, presocial rights that are "beyond the power of human authority to change" are indispensable to justice, but Darby immediately dispatches worries that abandoning the prevailing view of natural rights leaves us 'morally impov-erished'.[67] Three potential outcomes are of particular concern: that jettisoning the pre-vailing view (1) leaves us without a basis for complaining when wronged, (2) leaves no basis for human respect (including self-respect), and (3) leaves us without resources to protest severe injustices, such as slavery. Darby observes, first, that the converse claim, that the prevailing view of natural rights provides bases for these, is question begging, since the existence of presocial rights must first be established. Second, the claim that rejecting the prevailing view leaves us without resources for complaining of wrongs, for respecting others, and for protesting severe injustices is false. To say that it is impossi-ble to complain of wrongs if we deny presocial natural rights amounts to saying that we are only morally justified in complaining when presocial rights are violated. But Darby observes that we can of course complain of wrongs if we can appeal to other moral con-cepts, such as the duty not to harm others. Similarly, there are bases other than rights upon which we can ground respect for other humans, self-respect, and even respect for non-humans, such as sentience, qualities of character, or social status. That is, there is "no necessary conceptual connection" between being a rights-bearer and respect.[68]

Darby's treatment of the third worry, that rejecting the prevailing view of natural rights leaves us without resources to protest severe injustices, such as slavery, becomes the linchpin by which he proceeds from a critique of presocial natural rights to his pos-itive argument for the dependence of rights upon recognition. The problem of appeal-ing to presocial natural rights is most evident in the case of antebellum slavery in the United States, wherein both abolitionists and slavery apologists appealed to natural human rights to advance their causes. Slavery apologists supplied a striking variety of arguments to deny the humanity of African-descended people or, failing that, to deny Africans' possession of ostensibly relevant properties, such as rationality, intelligence, and morality. Given that natural rights arguments can be deployed to *legitimate* severe injustices (and that there remain today adherents of the 'black inferiority thesis'[69], which could come into the service of such arguments), Darby insists both upon the unreliabil-ity of traditional natural rights arguments as a resource for resisting oppression and the urgent need for an alternative theory of moral rights more adequate to the task.

Accordingly, Darby sets out to demonstrate how a rights externalist theory, according to which all rights are recognition-dependent, is efficacious as an argument against slav-ery and other severe injustices. He begins with a 'crucial' observation: "a natural right need not be a presocial right, though it may certainly be a prepolitical one."[70] Thus, even

---

[66] Ibid., 57.
[67] Ibid., 62, 79.
[68] Ibid. 67, 72.
[69] Ibid., 115. See, e.g., Herrnstein and Murray, *Bell Curve*.
[70] Darby, *Rights*, 142, 144.

if every society were to fail to recognize the moral rights of slaves, we could, he observes, still defend the proposition "a slave has a 'right' to be free," without appealing to presocial natural rights. Extending moral and political rights to slaves is justified morally by the prepolitical social recognition accorded them by one or more communities to which they belong: the family, the slave community, even in some cases the slaveholding family. Darby derives this important insight from Green:

> The claim of the slave to be free, his right *implicit* to have rights *explicit*, i.e., to membership of a society of which each member is treated by the rest as entitled to seek his own good in his own way on supposition that he so seeks it as not to interfere with the like freedom of quest on the part of others, rests . . . on the fact that the slave is determined by conceptions of a good common to himself with others, as shown by the actual social relations in which he lives.[71]

For Green, an implicit right amounts to a valid but unrecognized moral claim, which only becomes an explicit right when its validity is recognized, not only in thought but in practice. But we must not assume that an implicit right must be a presocial natural right. Again, for Darby, the crucial insight is that we can conceive of a class of natural rights that are not presocial.

Darby elaborates by citing Green's paradigm example of the right 'to free life'.[72] For Green, the ability of individuals to pursue conceptions of the good depends in part upon their ability to move freely in the pursuit of their ends, which depends, in turn, upon the will of others not to inhibit individuals' pursuits and sometimes to provide assistance. Because their willingness to do so depends upon the individual's willingness to reciprocate, the right of freedom is secured only under conditions of mutual recognition exchanged by social members who understand free life-making for each as 'being for a common good'.[73] And so, very importantly, the right of freedom is a justified moral right. We accordingly establish that slavery is wrong by observing that when any community recognizes an individual's claim (her implicit right) to move freely in pursuit of her ends by actually allowing her that liberty, she has in fact acquired the explicit moral right of freedom. But if any community recognizes this moral right, considering its extension to serve the good of that community, the larger political community ought also to recognize the individual's right as consistent with its common good (barring evidence to the contrary). The argument against slavery, then, is that the explicit right of slaves to free agency, recognized by their social communities, justifies the recognition of their right of free agency by the larger political community. Furthermore, because recognizing the moral right of slaves to freedom is acknowledged as serving a common

---

[71] Green, *Lectures*, 115; qtd. in Darby, *Rights*, 153.

[72] Darby, *Rights*, 156.

[73] Green, *Lectures*, 90. Cf. Hegel's " 'Conscience'. The 'beautiful soul', evil and its forgiveness" in the *Phenomenology* (PS 9.415–442/ ¶¶ 632–671). See also PR §§112, 112A, and 132.

good, "to withhold it would be morally inconsistent, unfair, and would undermine the pursuit of a complete political society."[74]

Of course, conceptions of the common good vary across communities, including between communities and the state, as we have seen in discussions of multicultural-ism. Darby's analysis is attractive in that it makes explicit that the legitimacy of subjects' claims ought to be entertained and deliberated and the question asked: Is extending the rights they seek in the interest of the common good? The all-important question, of course, is, who determines the common good? I shall return to this question.

But first, I wish to emphasize again the strength of the rights recognition thesis in explicitly assigning responsibility for the extension and withholding of rights where it in truth resides: in the will and actions of the political community. It is vital to acknowl-edge our responsibility, for the prevailing view can mislead us into thinking a subject's possession or lack of rights is ultimately determined by his or her nature—which is to blame the victim. To say that a citizen lacks the right to marry because he is homosexual is, strictly speaking, false. He lacks the right to marry because his political community denies him that right. This is evidenced by the fact that some communities recognize his right to marry.

And so who determines the common good, including the compelling public inter-ests, of a political community? John Rawls has provided a persuasive answer in *Political Liberalism*, by means of his conception of a purely 'political' form of liberalism that is neutral among reasonable comprehensive moral views, including comprehensive liber-alism, understood as one particular conception of the good among many. This concep-tion is crucial, given that an insistence upon determining the basic structure of political institutions by appeal to comprehensive liberalism is potentially coercive and ultimately illiberal. Rawls accordingly grounds his 'political' liberalism in a thin theory of the good that specifies the ends thought to be pursued by all reasonable citizens insofar as they are all presumed to endorse ideas implicit in the conception of liberal democracy: "society as a fair system of cooperation . . ."; "citizens . . . as free and equal persons"; and "a well-ordered society as a society effectively regulated by a political conception of justice."[75] On Rawls's view, a political conception of the common good, articulated as principles of justice, is best determined by achieving an 'overlapping consensus' concerning it by 'symmetrically situated' representative citizens endorsing a plurality of reasonable com-prehensive views. Their principles of justice, assented to by each for different substan-tive reasons, constitute justice as fairness as both a 'freestanding' liberal politics (not grounded in any single comprehensive worldview) and as legitimate.[76] Political liberal-ism is also importantly 'public', in that its procedures and principles are to be transpar-ent, accessible, and recognized by all if it is to accord with their freedom.[77]

---

[74] Darby, *Rights,* 163.
[75] Rawls, *Political Liberalism,* 13–14.
[76] Ibid., 10; 133 ff.
[77] Ibid., 66–67.

Rawls's political liberalism would seem indeed to optimize the ability of citizens to live as free and equal, for they are liberated equally to live in accordance with their own values, within political structures they co-create.[78] The mutual respect presupposed by and embodied in this 'freestanding' political framework appears equally effective for securing citizens' self-respect and for promoting social stability. Rawls's conception of political liberalism thus resembles Hegel's *Phenomenology* account of the mutual recognition of shapes of moral spirit ('conscience' and the 'beautiful soul') who, in their reconciliation, retain their difference as 'absolute' (PS 9.441/ ¶671).

Political liberalism also bears some resemblance to Hegel's vision of *Sittlichkeit* (ethical life), in which citizens acknowledge the legitimacy of moral commitments and forms of life that differ from their own.[79] There are important disanalogies: in political liberalism, citizens come procedurally to the collective deliberations of the 'original situation', whereas in *Sittlichkeit* the collective spirit is part of citizens' lifelong *Bildung* (education); hence is their way of life. Perhaps the reciprocity of mutual respect is accordingly less robust or less deep than that of mutual recognition. Or perhaps Rawls's original situation is, like liberalism's doctrine of natural equality, too facile a 'device' to be useful politically, since it obscures the agonistic processes of struggle through which social members historically have come to recognize the legitimacy of the claims of others. Nonetheless, perhaps what Hegel says of reconciled, mutually recognizing shapes of spirit can be said of some future 'politically liberal' community that liberates its citizens equally through collective deliberation and mutual respect: that the "wounds of the Spirit heal, and leave no scars behind" (PS 9.440, 441/ ¶¶669, 671).

WORKS CITED

Anderson, Sybol S. C. *Hegel's Theory of Recognition: From Oppression to Ethical Liberal Modernity*. New York: Continuum International, 2009.

Appiah, K. A. "Identity, Authenticity, and Survival," in C. Taylor, *Multiculturalism: Examining the Politics of Recognition*, edited by A. Gutmann. Princeton, NJ: Princeton University Press, 1994, 149–163.

Appiah, K. A. "Multicultural Misunderstanding." *New York Review of Books* 44 (1997): 36.

Barclay, L. "Liberalism and Diversity," in *The Oxford Handbook of Contemporary Philosophy*, edited by F. Jackson and M. Smith. New York: Oxford University Press, 2007, 155–180.

Barry, B. M. *Culture and Equality: An Egalitarian Critique of Multiculturalism*. Cambridge, MA: Harvard University Press, 2001.

Barry, B. M. "Second Thoughts—and Some First Thoughts Revived," in *Multiculturalism Reconsidered*, edited by P. Kelly. Malden, MA: Polity Press, 2002, 204–238.

Ceaser, J. "Multiculturalism and American Liberal Democracy," in *Multiculturalism and American Democracy*, edited by A. Melzer, J. Weinberger, and R. Zinman. Lawrence: University Press of Kansas, 1998, 139–156.

Darby, D. *Rights, Race, and Recognition*. New York: Cambridge University Press, 2009.

---

[78] Ibid., 15.

[79] S. Anderson, *Hegel's Theory of Recognition*, 185.

Forst, R. "Foundations of a Theory of Multicultural Justice." *Constellations* 4 (1997): 63–71.

Fraser, N. "From Redistribution to Recognition? Dilemmas of Justice in a 'Post-Socialist' Age." *New Left Review* 212 (1995): 68–93.

Fraser, N. *Justice Interruptus: Critical Reflections on the 'Postsocialist' Condition.* New York: Routledge, 1997.

Fraser, N. "Rethinking Recognition." *New Left Review* 3 (2000): 107–120.

Fraser, N., and A. Honneth. *Redistribution or Recognition? A Political-Philosophical Exchange.* New York: Verso, 2003.

Gadamer, H.-G. *Truth and Method* (2nd revised ed.), translated by J. Weinsheimer and D. G. Marshall. New York: Continuum, 1989.

Galeotti, A. E. *Toleration as Recognition.* New York: Cambridge University Press, 2002.

Galston, W. A. *Liberal Pluralism: The Implications of Value Pluralism for Political Theory and Practice.* Cambridge: Cambridge University Press, 2002.

Green, T. H. *Lectures on the Principles of Political Obligation*, edited by P. Harris and J. Morrow. New York: Cambridge University Press, 1986.

Harvey, J. *Civilized Oppression.* Lanham, MD: Rowman & Littlefield, 1999.

Hegel, G. W. F. *Elements of the Philosophy of Right* [PR], edited by A. Wood, translated by H. B. Nisbet. New York: Cambridge University Press, 2000.

Hegel, G. W. F.. *Phenomenology of Spirit* [PS], translated by A. V. Miller. New York: Oxford University Press, 1977.

Hegel, G. W. F.. *System of Ethical Life* [SEL], in *System of Ethical Life and First Philosophy of Spirit*, edited and translated by H. S. Harris and T. M. Knox. Albany: State University of New York Press, 1979.

Hegel, G. W. F.. *Vorlesungen über Rechtsphilosophie* [VR], 4 vols., edited by Karl-Heinz Ilting. Stuttgart: Frommann Verlag, 1974.

Herrnstein, R. J., and C. Murray. *The Bell Curve: Intelligence and Class Structure.* New York: Free Press Paperbacks, 1994.

Honneth, A. 'Grounding Recognition: A Rejoinder to Critical Questions." *Inquiry* 45 (2002): 499–520.

Honneth, A. *The Struggle for Recognition: The Moral Grammar of Social Conflicts*, translated by J. Anderson. Cambridge, MA: MIT Press, 1996.

Jones, P. "Political Theory and Cultural Diversity." *Critical Review of Social Philosophy and Policy* 1 (1998): 28–62.

Kelly, P. (ed.). *Multiculturalism Reconsidered.* Malden, MA: Polity Press, 2002.

Kojève, A. *Introduction to the Reading of Hegel*, edited by A. Bloom, translated by J. H. Nichols, Jr. Ithaca, NY: Cornell University Press, 1980.

Kukathas, C. "Liberalism and Multiculturalism: The Politics of Difference." *Political Theory* 26 (1998): 686–699.

Kukathas, C. "Multiculturalism as Fairness: Will Kymlicka's Multicultural Citizenship." *The Journal of Political Philosophy* 5 (1997): 406–427.

Kukathas, C. *The Liberal Archipelago: A Theory of Diversity and Freedom.* Oxford: Oxford University Press, 2003.

Kymlicka, W. *Multicultural Citizenship.* New York: Oxford University Press, 1995.

Laegaard, S. "On the Prospects for a Liberal Theory of Recognition." *Res Publica* 11 (2005): 325–348.

Maddox, M. "Durkheim beyond Liberalism: Liberal Accommodations of Group Rights." *Human Rights Research* 1 (2003): 1–32.

Margalit, A., and M. Halbertal. "Liberalism and the Right to Culture." *Social Research* 61 (1994): 491–510.

Mead, G. H. *Mind, Self, and Society*, edited by C. W. Morris. Chicago: University of Chicago Press, 1962.

Mills, C. *The Racial Contract*. Ithaca, NY: Cornell University Press, 1997.

Okin, S. M. "Is Multiculturalism Bad for Women?" in *Is Multiculturalism Bad for Women?* edited by J. Cohen, M. Howard, and M. Nussbaum. Princeton, NJ: Princeton University Press, 1999, 9–24.

Parekh, B. "Dilemmas of a Multicultural Theory of Citizenship." *Constellations* 4 (1997): 54–62.

Parekh, B. *Rethinking Multiculturalism: Cultural Diversity and Political Theory*. Cambridge, MA: Harvard University Press, 2000.

Pateman, C. *The Sexual Contract*. Palo Alto, CA: Stanford University Press, 1998.

Rawls, J. *Political Liberalism*. New York: Columbia University Press, 1993.

Rawls, J. *A Theory of Justice*, revised ed. Cambridge, MA: Harvard University Press, 1999.

Raz, J. "Multiculturalism: A Liberal Perspective," in J. Raz, *Ethics in the Public Domain: Essays in the Morality of Law and Politics*. New York: Oxford University Press, 1994, 170–191.

Seglow, J. 'Theorizing Recognition," in *Multiculturalism, Identity and Rights*, edited by B. Haddock and P. Sutch. London: Routledge, 2003, 78–110.

Spinner-Halev, J. *Surviving Diversity: Religion and Democratic Citizenship*. Baltimore, MD: Johns Hopkins University Press, 2000.

Taylor, C. *Hegel*. New York: Cambridge University Press, 1975.

Taylor, C. *Hegel and Modern Society*. New York: Cambridge University Press, 1979.

Taylor, C. *Philosophical Papers*, Vol. 2: *Philosophy and the Human Sciences*. New York: Cambridge University Press, 1985.

Taylor, C. *The Ethics of Authenticity*. Cambridge, MA: Harvard University Press, 1991.

Taylor, C. "The Politics of Recognition," in *Multiculturalism: Examining the Politics of Recognition*, edited by Amy Gutmann. Princeton, NJ: Princeton University Press, 1994, 25–73.

Tully, J. *Strange Multiplicity: Constitutionalism in an Age of Diversity*. Cambridge: Cambridge University Press, 1995.

Waldron, J. "Minority Cultures and the Cosmopolitan Alternative," in *The Rights of Minority Cultures*, edited by W. Kymlicka. New York: Oxford University Press, 1992.

Young, I. M. *Justice and the Politics of Difference*. Princeton, NJ: Princeton University Press, 1990.

INDEX

Page numbers followed by *t* indicate tables.